Fodors92

USA

FODOR'S TRAVEL PUBLICATIONS, INC.
New York & London

ISBN 0-679-02108-6

Fodor's USA

Editor: Andrew E. Beresky
Contributors: Stephen Allen, Karen Lingo Allord, Barry and Hilda Anderson, Moira Bailey, Carol Barrington, Jodi Belknap, Curtis W. Casewit, Rita Chabot, Edgar and Patricia Cheatham, Don Davenport, Joyce Eisenberg, Alma Eshenfelder, Lee Foster, Marael Johnson, Bob Karolevitz, Jerome Klein, Carolyn R. Langdon, J. P. MacBean, Tom Mason, Rathe Miller, Jerry Minnich, Lyle E. Nelson, Barbara Pepe, Francis X. Rocca, Archie Satterfield, William G. Scheller, William Schemmel, Norma Spring, Robert Taylor, Jake Thompson, Deborah Williams, Ed Wojtas, Jane E. Zarem
Illustrations: Ted Burwell, Amy Harold, Michael Kaplan, Sandra Lang
Maps: Jaye Zimet Design, Jon Bauch Design, Mark Stein Studios, Pictograph
Cover Photograph: Nicholas Devore/Photographers/Aspen

Cover Design: Vignelli Associates

Special Sales

Fodor's Travel Publications are available at special discounts for bulk purchases (100 copies or more) for sales promotions or premiums. Special editions, including personalized covers, excerpts of existing guides, and corporate imprints, can be created in large quantities for special needs. For more information, write to Special Marketing, Fodor's Travel Publications, 201 East 50th Street, New York, NY 10022; or call 800/800-3246. Inquiries from the United Kingdom should be sent to Fodor's Travel Publications, 20 Vauxhall Bridge Road, London SW1V 25A.

MANUFACTURED IN THE UNITED STATES OF AMERICA
10 9 8 7 6 5 4 3 2 1

CONTENTS

FOREWORD

The immensity of the United States and the great variety of its natural and cultural attractions can overwhelm both the first-time visitor and the seasoned traveler.

To help you structure your trip and organize your time, *Fodor's USA* divides the country into 26 principal tourist destinations: the major cities, the most popular states, and those regions where vacationers will want to explore widely over large areas.

While every care has been taken to assure the accuracy of the information in this guide, the passage of time will always bring change, and consequently the publisher cannot accept responsibility for errors that may occur.

All prices and opening times quoted here are based on information available to us at press time. Hours and admission fees may change, however, and the prudent traveler will avoid inconvenience by calling ahead.

Fodor's wants to hear about your travel experiences, both pleasant and unpleasant. When a hotel or restaurant fails to live up to its billing, let us know and we will investigate the complaint and revise our entries where the facts warrant it.

Send your letters to the editors of Fodor's Travel Publications, 201 E. 50th Street, New York, NY 10022.

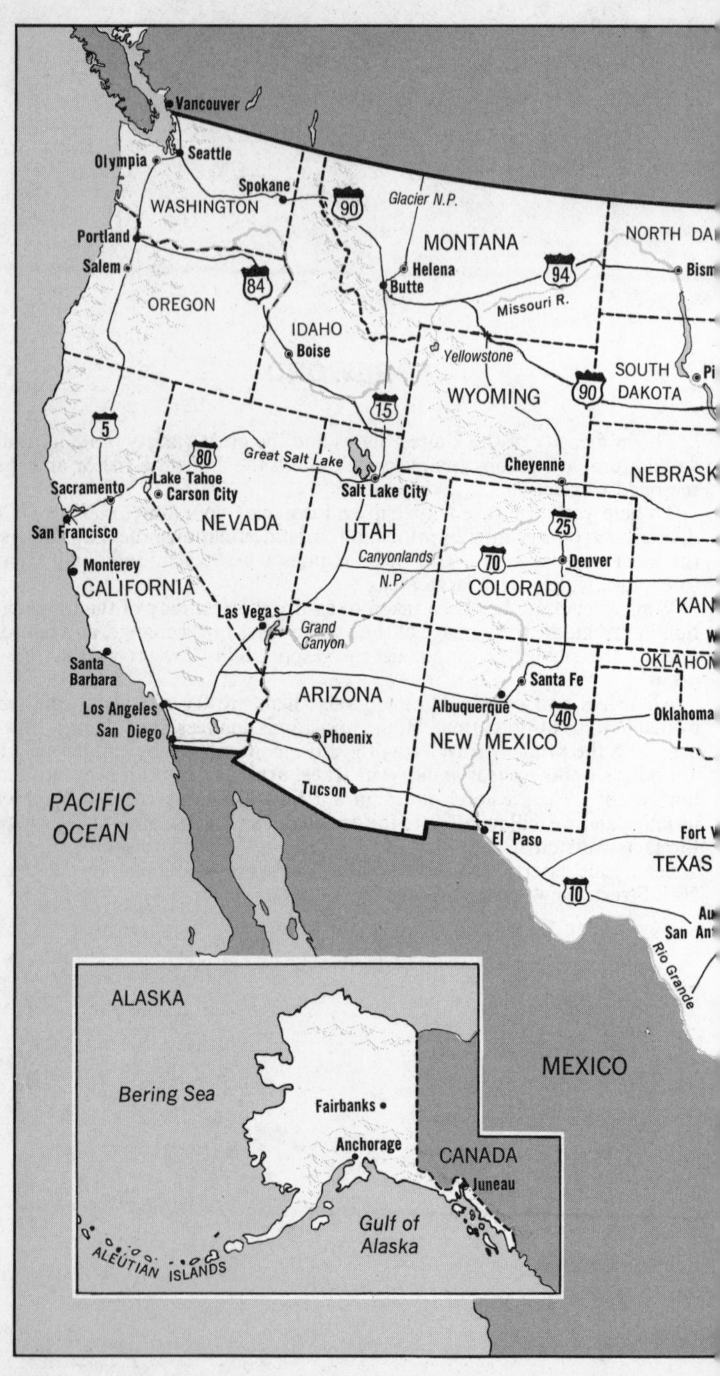

Vancouver
Seattle
Olympia
Spokane
WASHINGTON
90
Glacier N.P.
Portland
MONTANA
Salem
84
Helena
Butte
94
OREGON
Missouri R.
IDAHO
Boise
Yellowstone
SOUTH DAKOTA
90
WYOMING
15
5
80
Great Salt Lake
Cheyenne
Lake Tahoe
Sacramento
Carson City
Salt Lake City
San Francisco
NEVADA
UTAH
25
Canyonlands N.P.
70
Denver
Monterey
CALIFORNIA
COLORADO
Las Vegas
Grand Canyon
Santa Barbara
ARIZONA
Santa Fe
Los Angeles
Albuquerque
40
San Diego
Phoenix
NEW MEXICO
Tucson
PACIFIC OCEAN
El Paso
TEXAS
10
Rio Grande
ALASKA
MEXICO
Bering Sea
Fairbanks
Anchorage
CANADA
Juneau
Gulf of Alaska
ALEUTIAN ISLANDS

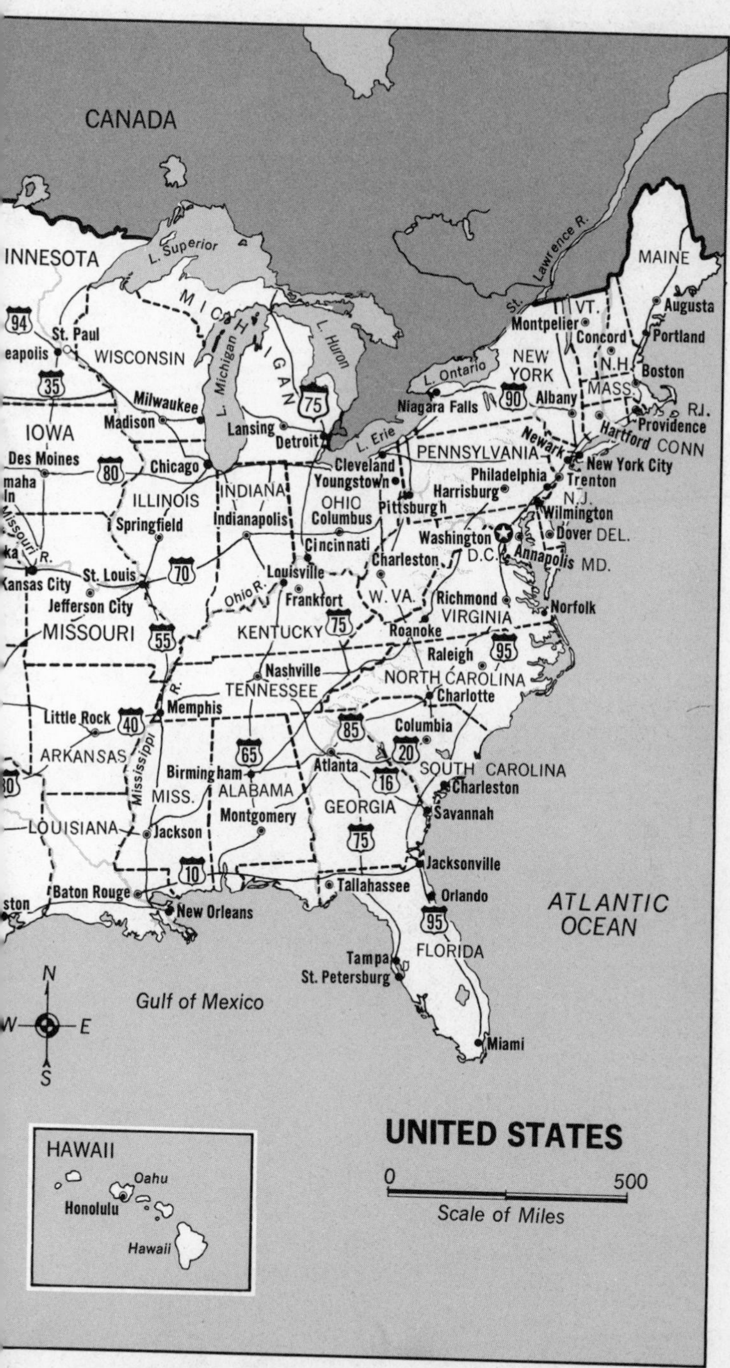
CANADA
UNITED STATES
ATLANTIC OCEAN
Gulf of Mexico
HAWAII
Oahu
Honolulu
Hawaii
0
500
Scale of Miles
MAINE
Augusta
Portland
VT.
Montpelier
Concord
N.H.
Boston
MASS.
R.I.
Providence
Hartford
CONN
NEW YORK
Albany
Niagara Falls
New York City
Newark
PENNSYLVANIA
Philadelphia
Harrisburg
Pittsburgh
Trenton
N.J.
Wilmington
Dover
DEL.
Washington
D.C.
Annapolis
MD.
Richmond
VIRGINIA
Norfolk
W. VA.
Charleston
Roanoke
Raleigh
NORTH CAROLINA
Charlotte
Columbia
SOUTH CAROLINA
Charleston
Savannah
GEORGIA
Atlanta
Jacksonville
Tallahassee
Orlando
FLORIDA
Tampa
St. Petersburg
Miami
OHIO
Cleveland
Youngstown
Columbus
Cincinnati
INDIANA
Indianapolis
ILLINOIS
Chicago
Springfield
MICHIGAN
Lansing
Detroit
L. Superior
L. Michigan
L. Huron
L. Erie
L. Ontario
St. Lawrence R.
WISCONSIN
Milwaukee
Madison
INNESOTA
St. Paul
eapolis
IOWA
Des Moines
maha
Missouri R.
Kansas City
Jefferson City
St. Louis
MISSOURI
KENTUCKY
Louisville
Frankfort
Ohio R.
TENNESSEE
Nashville
Memphis
Mississippi R.
ARKANSAS
Little Rock
MISS.
Jackson
ALABAMA
Birmingham
Montgomery
LOUISIANA
Baton Rouge
New Orleans
ston
N
S
E
W
94
35
80
70
55
40
65
75
85
20
16
10
95
90

FACTS AT YOUR FINGERTIPS

PLANNING YOUR TRIP. Careful planning will enhance your trip and help keep expenses down. This introductory chapter provides general information for planning a trip in the United States. Particular facts are included in the individual chapters.

WHAT IT WILL COST. Your major expenses will probably be transportation, accommodations, and food. Count the cost of transportation to and from your destination first and then work out a daily budget for accommodations and food. The price categories in the accommodation and dining out sections in each chapter should serve as useful guidelines. (Necessarily, they vary from chapter to chapter.) Remember to budget money for all the meals you usually eat in an active day. If you require a substantial breakfast before a day of sightseeing, take that into account. We have supplied as many prices as possible for attractions and activities, so that you can estimate how much money you are likely to spend on the things you want to do in a particular city—and how much you can afford to do. Many of the events and attractions listed in this guide are free, so if you budget your accommodation and food expenses carefully—even without settling for the cheapest possibilities—you should be able to keep the cost of your vacation within reason.

TRAVEL AGENTS. The best feature of the travel agents' role is that they do all your arranging, leaving you free to use your precious time elsewhere. But what should not be overlooked is their value in suggesting tailor-made vacations. Experienced agents have seen many tourist attractions firsthand and can suggest the best places for you—your purse, your age, your needs, and your desires. It is in the agents' best interest to help you avoid the problems or complexities of traveling.

For all this service, the travel agents do not charge you a fee. Their fee is collected from the transportation carriers and hotels as a commission for promoting and making the sale. Your only charge might be for extra phone calls, cables, or other special services. On package tours and groups, the agents' and organizers' services are included in the total price. If an agency has to arrange a complex itinerary and perform myriad services, it may charge you, and you should discuss its charges in advance.

The *American Society of Travel Agents, Inc. (ASTA)* is the world's largest professional travel trade association, composed of all elements of the travel business. ASTA was established in New York in 1931 to promote travel, to prevent unethical practices, and to provide a public forum for travel agents. It is the duty of every ASTA member agency to protect the public against any fraud, misrepresentation, or unethical practices. To avoid being victimized by fly-by-night operators who might claim better bargains, look for the ASTA member shield—the hallmark of dependable travel service. You'll find the shield on entrance doors, windows, and all office forms of the member agency you select.

ASTA membership indicates that the agent has been in business for at least three years and is officially approved by the Society to sell tickets on behalf of airlines and cruise ships. ASTA agents also will arrange bookings for trains, buses, or car rentals. For further information write ASTA, 1101 King St., Alexandria, VA 22314, or phone (703) 739–2782.

The volatility of the travel field in the last several years has led to the failure of some tour operators and to losses on the part of their clients. To avoid this, a number of leading tour operators have formed a bonding association. For a list of these agencies whose stability is protected, write to: *United States Tour Operators Association,* 211 E. 51st St., Suite 12B, New York, NY 10022, or phone (212) 944–5727.

TOURIST INFORMATION. The Travel Industry Association of America publishes *Discover America,* a comprehensive listing of U.S. state and territorial tourist offices. To obtain a copy, send a self-addressed, stamped envelope to: *Discover America,* c/o Travel Industry Association of America, Two Lafayette Centre, 1133 21st St. N.W., Washington, DC 20036.

For more information on individual state tourist offices, see the Practical Information sections in each chapter.

PACKAGE TOURS. Time, convenience, cost, and the type of travel that most interests you are the factors to consider when it comes to choosing an all-inclusive, fully escorted tour, a loose plan-your-own-itinerary package tour, or totally independent travel. In between are fly-drive deals that might include a few nights lodging; hotel-only packages; and hotel packages with certain added services. Package tours are the easiest to arrange and probably the most economical and efficient way for a first-time traveler to get an overview of the most famous sights. Even a simple two-hour orientation bus tour on a first visit to a city can be enormously helpful in getting your bearings. Among the general terms to check when considering any package are:

- Does the price quoted cover air as well as land arrangements? If air fare is not included, does the tour operator have a special rate available?
- How many meals are included?
- Does the rate for an automobile included in the package carry an additional fee per mile or is mileage unlimited? Is the car in the base rate exactly what you need? For example, is air conditioning included?
- What "extras"—usually hotel services such as a bottle of wine, first night cocktail, transportation to another part of town—are thrown in that you don't need? A package for similar accommodations but without these unwanted extras might help keep the price even more within reason.

DISCOUNT TRAVEL. If you have the flexibility, you can sometimes benefit from last-minute sales tour operators have in order to fill a plane or prebooked hotels. A number of brokers specializing in such discount sales have sprung up. All charge an annual membership fee, usually about $40 to $50. Among these are the following: *Traveler's Advantage, CUC Travel Services,* 40 Oakview Dr., Trumball, CT 06611 (800–835–8747); *Moments Notice,* 425 Madison Ave., New York, NY 10017 (212–486–0503); *Discount Travel International,* 114 Forrest Ave., The Ives Building, Suite 205, Narberth, PA 19072 (215–668–2182); and *Worldwide Discount Travel Club,* 1674 Meridian Ave., Suite 300, Miami Beach, FL 33139 (305–534–2082).

INSURANCE. In planning your trip, think about three kinds of insurance: *property, medical,* and *automobile.* The best person to consult about insuring your household furnishings and personal property while you are away is your insurance agent. For Americans, he is also the person to consult about whatever special adjustments might be advisable in your medical coverage while traveling. Foreigners visiting the United States should bear in mind that medical expenses in this country may seem astronomical by comparison with those they are accustomed to at home, and that the kind of protection that some countries (Britain, for example) extend to their own nationals and foreigners alike does not exist here.

Every state has some sort of financial responsibility law establishing the minimum and maximum amounts for which you can be held liable in auto accidents. Most states require insurance to be offered, and 17 states require you to have it in order to register a car or get a license within their jurisdictions. In any case, it is almost essential to have at least third party coverage, or "liability insurance," as claims can run very high both for car repairs and medical treatment. Insurance premiums vary according to place and person; they are generally highest for males under 25, and for drivers who live in large urban areas.

One possibility is the *American Automobile Association* (AAA), which offers both group personal accident insurance ($3,000) and bail bond protection up to $5,000 as part of its annual membership (fee $39). The AAA can also arrange the validation of foreign driving permits for use in the United States. Foreigners should consider getting their insurance before leaving their own countries since short-term tourists will find it difficult and expensive to buy here. For the AAA, write to *AAA,* 12600 Fair Lakes Circle, Fairfax, VA 22033, or phone (703) 222–2000 or (800) 763–2100. Persons over 50 who are members of NRTA/AARP (annual fee $5) may join that organization's motoring plan (annual fee $33.95) which offers, among other things, reimbursement for legal fees, hospital emergency room bonding, arrest bonding, and emergency breakdown service. Write to: *AARP Motoring Plan,* Box 9048, Des Moines, IA 50369, or phone (800) 334–3300.

Trip cancellation insurance is also available (usually from travel agents) to protect you against losing any advance payments should you have to cancel your trip at the last moment.

TIPS FOR BRITISH VISITORS. Passports and Visas. You will need a valid passport (cost £15 for a standard 32-page passport, £30 for a 94-page passport). Application forms are available from most travel agents and major post offices and from the Passport Office (Clive House, 70 Petty France, London SW1H 9HD; tel. 071–279–3434 for recorded information, or 071–279–4000). You do not need a visa if you are visiting either on business or pleasure, are staying less than 90 days, have a return ticket or onward ticket, are traveling with a major airline (in effect, any airline that flies from the United Kingdom to the United States), and complete visa waiver 1791, which is supplied either at the airport of departure or on the plane. If you fail to comply with any one of these requirements or are entering the United States by land, you will need a visa. Apply to a travel agent or the United States Visa and Immigration Department (5 Upper Grosvenor St., London W1A 2JB; tel. 071–499–3443 for recorded information or 071–499–7010). Visa applications to the U.S. Embassy must be made by mail, not in person. Visas can be given only to holders of 10-year passports, although visas in expired passports remain valid. If you think you might stay longer than three months, you must apply for a visa before you travel. No vaccinations are required.

Customs. If you are 21 or over, you can take in 200 cigarettes or 50 cigars or 2 kilograms of tobacco; 1 U.S. liter of alcohol; duty-free gifts to a value of $100. Be careful not to try to take in meat or meat products, seeds, plants, fruits, etc. Avoid narcotics like the plague.

Returning to Britain, if you are 17 or over, you may bring home: (1) 200 cigarettes or 100 cigarillos or 50 cigars or 250 grams of tobacco; (2) two liters of table wine with additional allowances for (a) one liter of alcohol over 22% by volume (38.8° proof, most spirits), (b) two liters of alcohol under 22% by volume, or (c) two liters of fortified or sparkling wine; (3) 60 cc of perfume and 250 mililiters of toilet water; (4) no more than 50 liters of beer or 25 mechanical lighters; and (5) other goods up to a value of £32.

Insurance. We heartily recommend that to cover health and motoring mishaps you insure yourself with Europ Assistance, 252 High St., Croydon, Surrey CRO

INF. Tel. 081–680–1234. Their excellent service is all the more valuable when you consider the possible cost of health care.

It is also wise to take out insurance to cover loss of luggage (though check that this isn't already covered in any existing homeowner's policies you may have). Trip cancellation insurance is another wise buy. The Association of British Insurers (Aldermary House, 10–15 Queen St., London EC4N 1TT, tel. 071–248–4477) will give comprehensive advice on all aspects of vacation insurance.

Tour Operators. The price battle that has raged over transatlantic fares has meant that most tour operators now offer excellent budget packages to the U.S. Among those you might consider as you plan your trip are:

American Airplan, Airplan House, Churchfield Rd., Walton-on-Thames, Surrey KT12 2TZ (0932–246347).

Intasun Holidays, Intasun House, 2 Cromwell Ave., Bromley, Kent BR2 9AQ (081–290–0511).

Kuoni Travel, Kuoni House, Dorking, Surrey RH5 4AZ (0306–740500).

Speedbird Holidays, Pacific House, Hazelwick Ave., Three Bridges, Crawley, West Sussex RH10 1NP (0293–611611).

Thomas Cook Faraway Holidays, Box 36, Thorpe Wood, Peterborough PE3 6SB (0733–63200).

Trekamerica, Trek House, The Bullring, Deddington, Banbury, Oxfordshire OX15 0TT (0869–38777).

Airfares. We suggest that you explore the current scene for budget flight possibilities, including *Virgin Atlantic Airways.*

Some of these cut-rate fares can be extremely difficult to come by, so be sure to book well in advance. Be sure to check on APEX and other money-saving fares, as, quite frankly, only business travelers who don't have to watch the price of their tickets fly full-price these days—and find themselves sitting right beside an APEX passenger! Also check out the small ads in Sun. newspapers and magazines, such as *Time Out,* as cheap, seat-only tickets can often be found here. If you're flexible about when you travel you can pick up a bargain. Also check up on the vacations which offer free car rental as part of the package, as these can often work out as very competitive prices.

HINTS TO THE DISABLED. One of the newest, and largest, groups to enter the travel scene is the handicapped, literally millions of people who are in fact physically able to travel and who do so enthusiastically when they know that they can move about in safety and comfort. Generally their tours parallel those of the non-handicapped traveler, but at a more leisurely pace, and with all the logistics carefully checked out in advance. Three important sources of information in this field are: 1) the book, *Access to the World: A Travel Guide for the Handicapped,* by Louise Weiss, available from Facts on File, 460 Park Ave. S., New York, NY 10016 (212–683–2244); 2) the *Travel Information Center,* Moss Rehabilitation Hospital, 1200 W. Tabor Rd., Philadelphia, PA 19141 (215–456–9600); 3) *Information Center for Individuals with Disabilities,* Fort Point Pl., 1st fl., 27–43 Wormwood St., Boston, MA 02210 (617–727–5540). In Britain, there are *Mobility International,* 228 Borough High St., London SE1 1JX (071–403–5688); and *The Royal Association for Disability and Rehabilitation,* 25 Mortimer St., London W1N 8AB (071–637–5400).

The Itinerary, which bills itself as "the magazine for travelers with physical disabilities," is published bimonthly by Whole Person Tours. Useful articles describe accessible destinations and devices that aid travel. Subscriptions cost $10 per year. For information, write the magazine at Box 2012, Bayonne, NJ 07002, or phone (201) 858–3400.

Lists of commercial tour operators who arrange or conduct tours for the handicapped are available from the *Society for the Advancement of Travel for the Handicapped,* International Office, 26 Court St., Penthouse Suite, Brooklyn, NY 11242 (718–858–5483). The Greyhound Bus system has special assistance for handicapped travelers. International Air Transport Association (IATA) publishes a free pamphlet entitled *Incapacitated Passengers' Air Travel Guide.* Write IATA, 2000 Peel St., Montreal, Quebec H3A 2R4 (514–844–6311). The Air Transport Association of America (ATA) also publishes a free pamphlet, *Air Travel for the Handicapped.* Write the ATA, 1709 New York Ave., N.W., Washington, DC 20006 (202–626–4000). At press time, the pamphlet was being rewritten; call or write ahead to see if it is again available.

STUDENT AND YOUTH TRAVEL. The *International Student Identity Card* is not as universally recognized in the U.S. as it is abroad, though it can sometimes be used in place of a high-school or college identification card. Apply to *Council On International Educational Exchange (CIEE),* 205 E. 42 St., New York, NY 10017 (212–661–1414) or 312 Sutter St., Suite 407, San Francisco, CA 94108 (415–421–3473). Their *Whole World Handbook* ($10.95 plus state sales tax and $1 postage) is the best listing of both work and study possibilities. Canadian students should apply to the *Association of Student Councils,* 187 College St., Toronto, Ontario M5T 1P7 (416–979–2406).

Students might also find it worthwhile to contact *Educational Travel Center,* 438 N. Frances, Madison, WI 53703 (608–256–5551), and *American Youth Hostels* (AYH), Box 37613, Washington, DC 20013–7613 (202–783–6161). AYH members are eligible for entree to the worldwide network of youth hostels, which isn't as extensive in the U.S. as in Europe but is a substantial resource nonetheless. Despite its name, AYH is also open to travelers of all ages. The organization publishes an extensive directory.

Among the leading specialists in the field of youth travel are the following:

Bailey Travel Service Inc., 123 E. Market St., York, PA 17401 (717–854–5511). School-group, escorted, and independent tours.

Campus Holidays, 242 Bellevue Ave., Upper Montclair, NJ 07043 (800–526–2915).

In Canada: *AOSC (Association of Student Councils),* 187 College St., Toronto, Ontario M5T 1P7 (416–979–2406) is a nonprofit student-service cooperative owned and operated by over 50 college and university student unions. Its travel bureau provides transportation, tours, and work camps worldwide. Try also *Tourbec,* 3419 St-Denis, Montreal, Quebec H2X 3L2 (514–288–4455).

AMERICA BY PLANE. A network of thousands of airline flights a day means that even with the limited time most vacations allow, you can see a lot of this country by flying from place to place. Seven airlines link the major U.S. cities. These are called *trunk lines.* They are *American, Continental, Delta, Northwest Orient, Trans World (TWA), United,* and *Western* (mainly west of Minnesota, but now flying out of some East Coast cities). However, deregulation has opened the airways to literally dozens of other lines, many of which had formerly been limited to regional runs. (Deregulation has also prompted several of the larger airlines to buy up the smaller airlines.) Among the latter are *USAir,* in the Northeast; *Frontier,* Midwest and West except the West Coast. Information on connecting flights between trunk and regional airlines is available from any of the airlines or your travel agent.

Smoking Regulations. As of Feb. 1990, smoking has been banned on all routes within the 48 contiguous states, within the states of Hawaii and Alaska, to and from the U.S. Virgin Islands and Puerto Rico, and on flights of under six hours to and from Hawaii and Alaska. The rule applies to both domestic and foreign carriers.

On a flight where smoking is permitted, you can request a seat in the nonsmoking section during check-in or when you book your ticket. If the airline tells you there are no seats available in the nonsmoking section, insist on one. Department of Transportation regulations require carriers to find seats for all nonsmokers, provided they meet check-in restrictions. These regulations apply to all international flights on domestic carriers; however, the Department of Transportation does not have jurisdiction over foreign carriers traveling out of, or into, the United States.

FLY-DRIVE VACATIONS. Among the many ways you can travel, the fly-drive package can be an economical way to visit American cities. Most airlines, in conjunction with car rental companies, offer these combination opportunities to most parts of the country all year round. Fly-drive package rates and flexibilities vary considerably from one to another. Generally, they cover one or more cities plus the use of a rented car for the specified number of days.

Car usage also varies from one to another. For example, with some you can drive an unlimited number of miles, free. On others you get a specified amount of mileage free, and then must pay an additional charge per mile for the overage. Gas, generally, is not included.

Some packages offer plans for small groups and a choice of hotel accommodations. Some even offer motor homes, if you're interested in roughing it. Check into special children's rates.

Before booking, though, you should check with your agent about where you pick up the car (whether at the airport or some other station), and about the time it will take you to arrive at your hotel to meet your reservation. If you are not going to pick up the car at the airport, you should check ahead on airport limousines and bus and taxi service to your hotel. These are important details that should be included in or provided for by any good package-tour combination.

AMERICA BY TRAIN. *Amtrak* is the semi-governmental corporation that has taken over passenger service on most of the nation's railroads. At present the system has some 26,000 miles of track linking over 500 cities and towns in 44 states (except Maine, New Hampshire, Oklahoma, South Dakota, Alaska, and Hawaii) and since mid-1979, under the pressure of soaring gasoline prices the number of passengers carried has risen sharply. Amtrak's equipment, at best, is among the most modern and comfortable anywhere in the world; not all of the equipment is up to this standard, however; and the condition of the tracks and the adequacy of the auxiliary services (stations, meals, punctuality, etc.) is highly uneven. In general, the system seems to work best in the "Northeast Corridor," the Boston-New York-Philadelphia-Baltimore-Washington megalopolis, and in southern California, where distances are short and getting to and from airports is inconvenient and expensive. On medium and longer runs the advantages of rail travel are in the spaciousness of the cars (against the cramped immobility of bus and plane) and the chance to enjoy the changing American landscape.

The simplest train accommodation is the day coach. There you ride in reclining seats, which may be reserved, with ample leg room, never more than two abreast. Next up is the leg-rest coach with (of course) leg rests, head rests, and deeper cushioning for the simplest kind of long distance nighttime accommodation. Slumbercoaches have lounge seats that convert into either a single bed or upper berths at night. For more space and privacy, a roomette gives a sitting room by day and at night a sleeping room with a full-length bed, and private toilet facilities. Bedrooms have two separate sleeping berths and private washing and toilet facilities. Superliner cars, operating between Chicago and the West Coast, also have family bedrooms that can sleep up to two adults and two children. Other types of special cars include dining cars, of course, and tavern lounges—an informal setting for a quiet drink, a game of cards, or just conversation. Some trains, especially where the scenery is best, have dome lounge cars, which give a great view of the countryside through high glass domes.

The reservation system is computerized and operates nationwide. Call 800–USA–RAIL. Amtrak has about 75 different travel packages in addition to its regularly scheduled service. The packages may include hotels, meals, sightseeing, even Broadway shows. Write to *Amtrak,* Distribution Center, Box 7717, Itasca, IL 60143, for free timetables and brochures on the package tours available in the part of the country to which you are traveling.

Senior citizens, disabled travelers, and families should inquire about discounts.

AMERICA BY BUS. The most extensive and one of the less expensive means of travel in America is the motor coach—the bus; 1,050 intercity and suburban bus companies operate to about 15,000 cities, towns, and villages in the United States, 14,000 of which have no other kind of intercity public transportation. The network totals over 277,000 miles of routes, carrying 10,000 buses. The major national bus company is *Greyhound.* It operates 6,700 buses and covers the entire country with regularly scheduled routes. America's intercity buses carry over 350,000,000 passengers a year, more than Amtrak and all the airlines combined.

With more than 8,000 coaches on the road daily, you can go almost anywhere with little delay at connecting points. Reservations can be made for only a few trips. "Open date" tickets, good for travel any day, any time, are the rule. So, you just get your ticket, choose the time you want to travel, and show up early enough to get your bags checked in (15 minutes ahead in small towns, 45 minutes in cities).

Bargain-rate passes for unlimited travel on any regularly scheduled route in the United States and Canada are available. These passes are available to both residents and visitors, so there are no restrictions about when and where you can buy them. If they are bought abroad, the period of validity begins on the first day of use in this country; if they are bought here, it begins on the day of purchase.

Long-distance buses carry about 45 passengers. They are air-conditioned in summer, heated in winter. Baggage goes underneath, so the passenger compartment is up high, providing a better view through the big, tinted windows. Seats are the lounge chair type, with reclining backs and adjustable head rests. Reading lamps are individually controlled. Almost all long-distance buses have rest rooms.

HINTS TO THE MOTORIST. If you plan to take your own car on your trip, the first precaution you should take is to have your car thoroughly checked by your regular dealer or service station to make sure that everything is in good shape. The *National Institute for Automotive Service Excellence,* 13505 Dulles Technology Dr., Herndon, VA 22071 (703–742–3800), tests and certifies the competence of auto mechanics.

Each chapter, in the Hints to Motorists section, provides information about traffic laws and driving and parking conditions.

RENTAL CARS. Perhaps you would prefer to rent a car at your destination. If so, keep in mind that most companies require that you be at least 25; some, under special conditions, will rent to those who are only 21. Most companies accept major credit cards for deposit and payment. Cash transactions will require an advance cash deposit upon rental, and usually an application must be filled out and verified—which may be difficult after regular business hours or on weekends.

The rent-it-here-leave-it-there option allows you to rent the car in one place and drop it off at any other company location in the United States for a substantial drop-off charge. Check into special rates offered for different categories of cars and for weekends, holidays, and extended trips. Rates and conditions can vary enormously; this is one area in which comparison shopping will pay off.

Car rental companies generally charge substantial per-day fees for insurance coverage. You should check the company of your choice for specifics. Here again, the services of a travel agent can save you time, money, and trouble, as he will have on file the relevant data for the major rental firms so that you will not have to check them all one by one yourself.

Most companies now charge between $9 and $12 *per day* for a collision damage waiver. Without this coverage you are fully responsible for any damage to the car, including theft. There is a less costly alternative: at least one insurance firm, *Travel Guard International,* 1145 Clark St., Stevens Point, WI 54481 (715–345–0505 or 800–826–1300), offers residents of the United States or Canada a policy for about $50 for up to 45 days of your vacation that will pay for repairs up to $25,000. It can be obtained before you start your trip, from your travel agent or directory from Travel Guard. The policy can be used at any car rental agency.

In most cases, a valid driver's license issued by any state or possession of the United States, by any province of Canada, or by any country which ratified the 1949 Geneva Motoring Convention, is valid and is required to rent a car.

Some of the nationwide rental agencies that provide 24-hour toll-free information and rental service are *Hertz* (800–654–3131), *Avis* (800–331–1212), *National* (800–227–7368), *Dollar* (800–4000), *Thrifty* (800–331–4200), and *Budget* (800–527–0700). In many chapters we have listed the names and numbers of local agencies that rent older or smaller cars at rates considerably less than those of the national companies.

AUTO CLUBS. If you don't belong to an auto club, now is the time to join one, even if you don't plan to drive to your destination. The maps, suggested routes, and emergency road service they offer can be helpful to those who rent a car as well as to those who drive from home. The *American Automobile Association* (AAA), in addition to its information services, has a nationwide network of some 14,000 contractors which provide emergency repair service. Its offices are at 12600 Fair Lakes Circle, Fairfax, VA 22033 (703–222–6000 or 800–763–6600). If you plan the route yourself, make certain the map you get is dated for the current year. Some of the major oil companies will send maps and mark preferred routes on them if you tell them what you have in mind. Try: *AMOCO Motor Club,* Box 9014, Des Moines, IA 50306 (800–334–3300).

MAPS. The tradition of free road maps at gasoline stations has almost totally disappeared in the United States today. However, many of the local tourist bureaus listed in each chapter will send maps of cities, and state travel departments provide excellent road maps. The auto clubs offer members many maps to help them get around U.S. metropolitan areas. Another alternative is, of course, a road atlas, purchased at a bookstore, and costing anywhere from $1.50 to $6. There are three major ones published in this country now: by Rand McNally, by Grossett, and by Hammond. Rand McNally also publishes a "Standard Reference Map and Guide" for each state individually. The Hagstrom Company is the country's leading publisher of city street maps.

NATIONAL PARKS AND FORESTS. A vacation unequaled elsewhere in the world is a week or two in one of the 40 national parks in the United States. These parks preserve in beauty and naturalness the variety of landscapes that makes the country so fascinating both to lovers of free space, clear air, and the great outdoors. With some 26½ million acres, the National Park Service has within the last half century managed to preserve about one percent of the total American land as it was before the coming of civilization. Future generations will forever—it is hoped—have access to some parts of their country that are unfenced, unworked, unsullied by man's incessant urges to profit from his ground, change it, force his will upon it.

The system of national forests is another fine source of recreational opportunities for vacationers. These are multiuse areas, catering to the needs of industry as well as individuals. They are often less crowded and less rule-bound than the national parks. You may, for instance, camp with your dog in many national forest campgrounds.

For information on national parks, battlefields, and recreation areas, write to National Parks Service, Dept. of the Interior, Washington, DC 20240. For information on national forests and recreation areas, write to National Forest Service, Public Affairs Office, Box 96090, U.S. Dept. of Agriculture, Washington, DC 20090.

ACCOMMODATIONS. In this guide we have organized lists of accommodations in two basic ways. If the section deals with one or only a few cities with many hotels and motels, we have listed them according to price categories. If there are only a few establishments in each of many towns, we have listed them alphabetically under their towns, which are also arranged alphabetically. The categories we have used are *Super Deluxe, Deluxe, Expensive, Moderate,* and *Inexpensive.* The actual prices vary from chapter to chapter, as they do from city to city; they are given at the beginning of each accommodation section. All hotel rates are for two people in a room and, unless otherwise noted, for European plan—no meals included.

Don't take potluck for lodgings. You'll waste a lot of time hunting for a place and often you won't be happy with what you finally find. The hotels we've listed give good value for your money, and they represent the range of standard prices for reasonable and economical accommodations in a particular city. If you don't have reservations, start looking in the afternoon. Each chapter provides information about when reservations are necessary in the city you plan to visit, but it's probably a good idea to make reservations whenever your plans are firm enough to allow it.

If you do have reservations (but expect to arrive later than 5 or 6 P.M.), advise the hotel or motel in advance. Some places will not otherwise hold reservations after 6 P.M. A hotel or motel will also usually guarantee a room regardless of your arrival time if you book using a major credit card. Of course, if you don't end up using the room in such instances, you are still charged the full rate (unless you cancel by a specified time). And if you hope to get a room at the hotel's *minimum* rates, be sure to reserve ahead or arrive early.

Hotel and motel chains. Although these establishments may not offer much local charm, they do offer two important conveniences: nationwide, toll-free reservation services (in most cases) and fairly dependable standards of quality. If you've stayed in one hotel in a chain, you've stayed in them all. Also, there are a number of budget motel chains that can be a good way to keep expenses down—if luxurious accommodations are not high on your list of vacation necessities. The following are some national chains and their toll-free numbers:

Comfort Inns Quality Hotels (800–228–5150 or 800–228–3323 for hearing impaired), *Days Inns* (800–325–2525), *Econo Lodges* (800–446–6900 or 800–624–7687 for hearing impaired), *Holiday Inns* (800–HOLIDAY or 800–238–5544 for hearing impaired), *Howard Johnson* (800–654–2000 or 800–654–8442 for hearing impaired), *La Quinta* (800–531–5900 or 800–426–3101 for hearing impaired), *Quality International* (800–228–5151 or 800–228–3323 for hearing impaired), *Ramada* (800–2RAMADA or 800–228–3232 for hearing impaired), *Super 8 Motels* (800–843–1991 or 800–533–6634 for hearing impaired), and *TraveLodge* (800–255–3050).

RESTAURANTS. Restaurants are listed in this guide according to the same principals explained above for accommodations. Although many of the less expensive restaurants do not require or accept reservations, it is probably a good idea to call and ask about dinner reservations—and even lunch reservations in the larger cities. It's a good idea to call anyway, because, although we've made every effort to ensure that the restaurant lists are up to date, restaurants come and go very suddenly.

TIPPING. There is no law in the United States that says you must leave a tip for service. The unwritten laws of custom, however, make tipping necessary more often than not. Tipping is an accepted way of expressing appreciation for service that is attentive and efficient. You can make the amount of the tip reflect the quality of the service you receive, and you need not leave any tip for service that is very poor.

In a restaurant, it is common to leave 15% of the charge *before* taxes. At counters, many people leave 50 cents, or 10%, whichever is greater. For bellboys, 50 cents per bag is usual. Taxi drivers in cities expect 15%; car-rental agencies, nothing. Bus porters are tipped 50 cents per bag; drivers, nothing. On charter and package tours, conductors and drivers usually get $10 per day from the group, but be sure to ask if this has already been figured into the package cost. On short, local sightseeing runs, the driver-guide may get 50 cents–$1 per person, more if he has been especially helpful or informative. At airports and train stations, porters get $1 for a bag or two, and another 50 cents for each additional bag.

TRAVELER'S CHECKS. We urge you to use traveler's checks rather than cash when on the road. Many banks offer traveler's checks free as a service to their customers, but even if you have to pay one percent of the amount purchased, this is a small expense for the assurance that the checks will be replaced if stolen or otherwise lost. Don't forget to record the check numbers and carry them separately from the checks themselves.

CREDIT CARDS. Credit cards are widely accepted at hotels and motels and at many restaurants. However, many restaurants and shops have a minimum amount below which they do not accept the cards. Also, some establishments listed in this book manage to stay in the budget category in part because they don't contend with the extra fees involved in processing credit-card purchases. We have done our best to indicate establishments that don't accept credit cards, but if you're short on cash, double check before sitting down for a meal.

TIME ZONES. There are four time zones as you cross the continental United States. From east to west they are: Eastern, Central, Mountain, and Pacific. Daylight saving time, whereby clocks are set back an hour in the fall and forward again in the spring, keeps the maximum of sunshine available during summer days. Alaska is one hour earlier than California, and Hawaii is one hour earlier than Alaska.

HOLIDAYS. Five major holidays are marked uniformly every year throughout the nation: New Year's Day, Jan. 1; Independence Day, July 4; Labor Day, the first Mon. in Sept.; Thanksgiving Day, the fourth Thurs. in Nov.; and Christmas Day, Dec. 25. Banks and stock exchanges are closed on all of these days and selectively on other national and state holidays; many stores and restaurants are closed on some of them. It is best to check local papers. Most other holidays, such as Washington's Birthday and Memorial Day, are celebrated on Mon. in order to provide three-day weekends.

COLUMBUS QUINCENTENARY. Throughout 1992, events and celebrations are scheduled in many parts of the country to commemorate the 500th anniversary of Christopher Columbus's journey to the New World. Included are arts, music, and museum programs; conventions and conferences; festivals, parades, and fairs; sports production and competitions; tall ship flotillas and regattas; and travel and tour programs. Hosts of activities are slated at two namesake cities—Columbus GA, and Columbus, OH. Among celebrations scheduled in New York City is the opening of a second section of the American Immigrants Wall of Honor on Ellis Island. For a listing of events in the area you plan to visit, consult the state's tourist office or a local chamber of commerce. Many events are also registered with the Christopher Columbus Quincentenary Jubilee Commission, 1801 F St., N.W., Washington, DC 20006, tel. 202–632–1992.

BANK HOURS. Banks are usually open Mon.–Fri., 9 A.M.–3 or 4 P.M., though these times vary somewhat. Most are open at least one evening a week, and some have Sat. hours. Increasingly popular are the automated-teller machines that dispense cash 24 hours a day. Certain bank cards are good nationally; you may wish to find out if the one you use at home will be honored in the cities you will be visiting.

MAIL. Stamps can be purchased at any post office in the United States, often from your hotel desk, or from coin-operated vending machines located in transportation terminals, banks, and some shops (stationers and drugstores, for example). They cost more if you get them from a machine—you pay for packaging and convenience—so for the sake of economy you may wish to buy as many as you think you will need when you find a handy post office.

There is no separate air mail rate for letters or postcards posted in the United States for delivery within the country or to Canada. Mail for distant points is automatically airlifted. The following are the postal rates in effect as of Feb., 1991.

	Letters		*Postcards*
United States, Mexico	29¢	oz.	19¢
Canada	40¢		30¢
Overseas			
Air to Europe	50¢	½ oz.	40¢
Air to Central America and Caribbean	50¢	½ oz.	40¢
Air to most other countries	50¢	½ oz.	40¢
Surface to most foreign countries	70¢	oz.	30¢
Air Letter Forms to all countries	45¢		

TELEPHONES. Coin-operated public telephones are available almost everywhere: in hotel lobbies, transportation terminals, drugstores, department stores, restaurants, gasoline filling stations, in sidewalk booths, and along the highway. To use the coin telephone, just follow the instructions on the phone box. Local calls usually cost 25 cents and can be dialed directly. If you don't reach your party, your money is refunded to you automatically when you hang up.

For long-distance calls, dial 0 (zero) and have plenty of coins available, or ask to have the call charged to your home telephone (USA only; someone must be home to accept the charges). The operator may ask for enough change to cover the initial time period before he or she connects you. Often a 1 must be dialed before the area code; check the directions on the phone. To place a call outside the United States, dial 0 and ask for the overseas operator. If your telephone company provides direct dialing service, you can place an overseas call yourself by dialing, in order, the country code, the area code, and the local number.

In hotels, your switchboard operator will either place your outside call for you, or tell you how to dial directly from your room. The telephone charges will be added to your hotel bill (although many times local calls are free) and you will pay for them when you check out.

TELEGRAPH. To send a telegram to a destination anywhere within the United States, ask for assistance at your hotel, or go to the nearest *Western Union* telegraph office. You'll find it listed in the classified section (yellow pages) of the telephone directory under "Telegraph." Overseas cablegrams can also be dispatched by Western Union, or by any cable company (also listed under "Telegraph"). You can phone Western Union and have a telegram charged to your home telephone (USA only). Mailgrams are similar to telegrams only they are delivered with the following day's mail and cost less than half what is charged for regular telegrams.

LIQUOR LAWS. All 50 states now require that you be at least 21 years of age to buy or drink alcohol. The laws establishing the times and places for the sale of alcohol vary from state to state (and sometimes from county to county within a state). Hard liquor and wines are generally not sold in package stores on Sundays, holidays, or late at night.

NORTHERN NEW ENGLAND

by
JANE E. ZAREM

A born-and-bred New Englander, Jane Zarem is a freelance writer and editor who has traveled extensively throughout the New England states. She is a member of the New York Travel Writers Association.

Maine, New Hampshire, and Vermont, northern New England's ruggedly scenic states, owe their dramatic beauty to eons of geologic action. Some 11,000 years ago the continental ice sheet melted, and a bedrock of sandstone, limestone, and shale remained. The soft rock eroded over time into valleys and lowlands, which stand in relief to the more ancient rock of the majestic Appalachian mountains, rolling hills, and natural gorges.

The receding glaciers produced several mighty rivers and thousands of lakes, ponds, and streams as the ocean seeped inland. The resulting shoreline consists of long stretches of sandy beach, tidal pools, quiet coves, and marshy lowlands along 18 miles in New Hampshire and as far north as the Kennebec River in Maine. From Maine's Kennebec River "Down East," the coast is rugged and rocky, with scores of craggy peninsulas jutting into the ocean, along with numerous offshore islands.

The three northern New England states were the great outback in Colonial days—the northern reaches were a virtual no-man's-land. They are still sparsely populated states today compared with their three southern New England neighbors. Bitter battles with the native Indians and the remote wilderness confined early 17th-century settlements to the coast.

Early settlers soon discovered the tremendous natural resources available in this territory: excellent harbors and offshore banks teeming with fish; tall trees for ship hulls and masts; wildlife for food and fur; granite, marble, sand, and stone for building materials. The network of navigable rivers enabled lumbermen and trappers to transport their harvests through the remote wilderness of the great north woods to the population centers along the coast. The land rush was on! Logging camps and sawmills sprouted along the streams. Sharing the land and its wealth with the native Americans, however, usually resulted in bitter and bloody battles.

As time passed and battles for territorial control and independence were won, the Industrial Revolution took hold and manufacturing became predominant. The same rivers used so successfully for transportation now provided a power supply for hundreds of mills. The production of textiles, leather goods, lumber, and wood products attracted workers and their families to these new sources of employment, and mill towns were created all along the major rivers.

Despite poor, stony soil, New England farmers managed limited commercial farming to supply the increased nonfarming population. As the American West opened up, many New Englanders were among the pioneers who resettled the vast new territory, and commercial farming moved west with them. Agriculture was streamlined to more appropriate dairying, poultry, hay, apples, and potatoes in the farming areas along the Connecticut River Valley and in Maine's enormous Aroostook County.

Some early mills are still in operation, still producing shoes, clothing, and wood products. In Maine, for example, 87 percent of the land is still vast timber and woodlots, most owned by private corporations that operate pulp and paper mills. Since World War II, however, many mills have seen hard economic times as production has moved elsewhere. Recognizing their historic significance in the early growth of northern New England, some of these mills have been restored and refurbished to a new luster. They now serve as shopping centers, offices, or residential properties, but the architecture remains: a three- or four-story red-brick factory along the riverfront, often near a waterfall, with a clock tower.

The northern New England states have attempted to keep up with the fickle economy. Shipbuilding in Maine and New Hampshire, important since 1800, remains relatively healthy, with production ranging from tankers and naval ships to private fishing and sailing boats. Southern New Hampshire is burgeoning as a virtual suburb of Boston. Its heavy growth in high-tech electronics in the 1980s has made New Hampshire one of the most economically healthy states in the country.

To stem the tide of economic fluctuations, the region's greatest resource—the natural beauty of the land itself—has been put to work. Tourism is a leading industry, and all three states encourage and heavily promote themselves as four-season vacationlands. And it's true!

Excellent interstate road systems allow easy access from the northeastern United States and southeastern Canada—winter and summer—to and through Maine, New Hampshire, and Vermont. Local roads through scenic villages, across covered bridges, and through mountain passes captivate visitors. The climate is invigorating; healthful, clean air prevails because of the abundance of public and private forest land. Hundreds of thousands of acres of protected land are open for public recreation: national and state parks and forests, wildlife preserves, mountain trails, lakes, and waterfront.

Alpine and cross-country skiing reigns supreme in winter. Modern resorts and traditional inns abound. Ski conditions and facilities at mountain peaks throughout the area are excellent, and trails are varied to accommodate the beginner or challenge the expert. Skating, sledding, snowmobiling, and ice fishing add to winter enjoyment.

Sportsmen are lured to the wilderness areas and the thousands of streams for hunting and fishing. The fall foliage season is world-renowned.

Family vacations in summer are ideal: boating, swimming, amusements, bicycling, special-interest museums, golf, tennis, and horseback riding await. Hiking and mountain climbing can be approached as family fun or as an exhausting challenge.

Each of the three northern New England states is unique in atmosphere and topography, but the New England spirit is unmistakably present. Whether among the rolling hills and farmland of Vermont, the mountain peaks and woodland—and bustling towns—of New Hampshire, or the seacoast and vast wilderness of Maine, the regional pride is evident. These Yankees are congenial, yet reserved; freedom-loving and patriotic; thrifty, yet generous for a worthy cause; independent and resourceful. There is a feeling of continuity and stability due to a history that dates back more than 350 years. The reticence toward strangers that visitors may notice is often misunderstood; privacy is cherished. Drawn by the solitude necessary for concentration and the beauty and serenity of the mountains and seacoast, the region has inspired literary and artistic geniuses from the early 19th century to the present.

The presence of many fine educational institutions, as in all of New England, ensures a strong cultural involvement by residents. The art, music, and literary programs and exhibits in colleges and universities, museums, and local halls are available to visitors as well. Cultural experiences may range from a symphony orchestra or an exhibit of paintings by local artists to a square dance or a chain-saw contest.

MAINE

There is a part of the marvelous state of Maine that will appeal to nearly everyone at one time of the year or another. For a vacation by the sea, waves smashing on the rocky shore, views of fishing boats bringing home the day's catch, lighthouses blinking at passing gulls, islands dotting the horizon—or fishing and canoeing on crystal-clear mountain lakes, roaring rivers, and rushing streams—or hiking, camping, skiing and snowmobiling, and north woods hunting—Maine is the perfect place. You can even find a little cottage on a quiet cove where you can read, write, or paint.

Irregularly diamond-shaped, Maine is 320 miles from north to south and 210 miles from east to west at its widest point. The total land area is 33,215 square miles, which comprises just under half of all New England.

Maine is famous for the rugged beauty of its rocky, indented coastline, dotted with over 2,000 small islands and dozens of popular waterfront resort areas. Although the coast is just 230 miles long, if you were to follow the shoreline around all the bays and harbors, capes and peninsulas, it would be some 3,500 miles—much of it spectacular.

Parts of the Pine Tree State are mountainous, and the vast majority of the land is heavily wooded with broad vistas of open wilderness between populated areas. Timber and wood lots comprise 87 percent of the state. There are more than 6,000 lakes and ponds and 5,100 rivers and streams.

Burial mounds and shell heaps found along the coast indicate Indians inhabited the area well over 2,000 years ago. These early residents were the ancestors of the Abnaki Indians, descendents of whom are represented now on the Penobscot and Passamaquoddy Reservations.

Norse, British, French, and Spanish explorers all visited what is now known as Maine, but Samuel de Champlain and Pierre du Guast established the first French colony at the mouth of the St. Croix River in 1604. English settlements were attempted over the next few years and ultimately

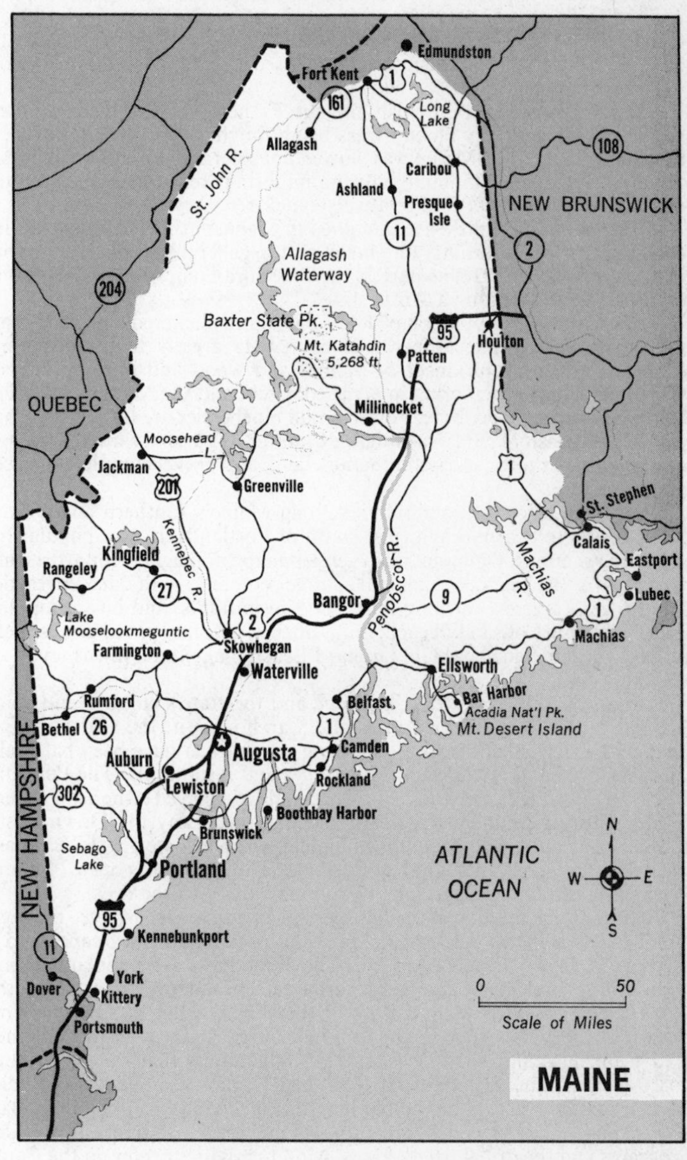
Edmundston
Fort Kent
1
161
Long Lake
Allagash
108
St. John R.
Caribou
Ashland
Presque Isle
NEW BRUNSWICK
11
2
Allagash Waterway
204
Baxter State Pk.
95
Houlton
Mt. Katahdin 5,268 ft.
Patten
Millinocket
QUEBEC
Moosehead L.
Jackman
201
1
Greenville
St. Stephen
Kennebec R.
Penobscot R.
Calais
Kingfield
Machias R.
Eastport
Rangeley
27
Bangor
9
Lubec
Lake Mooselookmeguntic
2
1
Machias
Skowhegan
Farmington
Waterville
Ellsworth
Bar Harbor
Rumford
Belfast
Acadia Nat'l Pk.
Bethel
26
1
Mt. Desert Island
Augusta
Camden
Auburn
NEW HAMPSHIRE
Lewiston
Rockland
302
Boothbay Harbor
Brunswick
N
Sebago Lake
ATLANTIC OCEAN
W
E
Portland
95
S
Kennebunkport
11
York
Dover
Kittery
0
50
Portsmouth
Scale of Miles
MAINE

abandoned by the few settlers who endured the harsh weather and disease. Territorial disagreements between France and England continued until 1642, when York became the first city chartered by England in the New World and the capital of the Province of Maine. Title to the territory remained in dispute between Englishman Ferdinando Gorges, who held a charter from Charles I, and the Massachusetts Bay Colony, which also claimed title, until Massachusetts purchased the rights to the land from Gorges' grandson in 1677.

Struggles between the British and the French and Indians continued, with half a dozen very bloody wars being fought. The British prevailed, but the settlement of Maine was slowed considerably by this strife. Fishing, lumbering, and shipbuilding were important resources which led the devastated settlements to a relatively quick recovery.

A British military presence remained in Maine until 1814, due to political polarization regarding statehood and a general dissatisfaction with Massachusetts. In 1820, as part of the Missouri Compromise, Maine was admitted to the Union as a free state.

Today, Maine's population of 1,177,550 is still clustered along the coast and major rivers. The timberlands contribute greatly to the economy; Maine is a leading producer of lumber and wood and paper products. Commercial fishermen bring in a varied catch, and the Maine lobster has achieved international fame. Potatoes and blueberries are large cash crops grown in Aroostook and Washington Counties. Tourism, sardines, apples, corn, poultry, shoes, textiles, minerals, sand, and gravel complete the economic picture.

The string of resort communities along Maine's southern coast, from York Beach to Scarborough (just south of Portland), is very popular for summer vacations. Ogunquit and Kennebunkport, magnets for artists and writers over the years, are colorful summer colonies, with quiet coves, delightful resorts and charming inns, good restaurants, and busy shopping areas. The miles of sandy beach, amusements, and fast-paced atmosphere at York Beach, Saco, and Old Orchard Beach make these towns favorites of youngsters.

Portland is the largest city in Maine and the state's cultural and commercial center. The old buildings and warehouses in the Old Port Exchange district (adjacent to the bustling waterfront) have been painstakingly restored and revitalized as boutiques and restaurants. The Portland Museum of Art is fascinating, with beautifully displayed American art exhibits featuring Maine artists. Portland is the gateway to "Down East" Maine. And no trip to Maine is complete without a stop at L. L. Bean, located in Freeport, just north of Portland. The outfitter is open 24 hours every day, attracting thousands of shoppers daily to the area.

Poking along the untrammeled byways of mid-coast Maine, through small towns and tiny settlements, provides breathtaking seascapes and a glimpse of Down East village life. The Boothbays are popular boating communities and a busy summer resort area. The narrow streets of Boothbay Harbor are filled with visitors to the shops, galleries, marinas, and restaurants. Several excursion boats cruise the coastal waters around pine-clad peninsulas and offshore islands. Windjammers that sail the Maine coast each summer depart from Rockland Harbor, Camden, and Rockport. Camden, with its incredible long-distance views of Penobscot Bay and its many islands, is delightful. In summer there are frequent musical programs and theatrical productions; winter activities center on the Camden Snow Bowl, Maine's oldest ski area.

Mount Desert Island has always been the destination of many travelers to the Maine coast. From the mid-1800s until the great fire of 1947, when dozens of estate homes were reduced to rubble, Bar Harbor was a society resort. It is again a busy resort community, but the 4 million annual visitors attracted to Mt. Desert Island are primarily visitors to Acadia National Park. Along miles of scenic drives, bicycle trails, and footpaths, travelers can stop to poke about the great ragged cliffs and coves and to see Thunder Hole, the fjord at Somes Sound, and peaceful Jordan Pond. Glaciers, winds, and sea have worked marvels here. Cadillac Mountain rises 1,530 feet. and commands an unmatched view of both coastal and inland Maine. The summit is easily reached by car from Bar Harbor.

Washington County, way down east, has a definite frontier feeling about it—blueberry barrens and a rugged coast which marks the highest tides in the country (20–28 feet). It is the easternmost point in the United States.

And in enormous Aroostook County, the eastern portion is home to the Maine potato. The far northern and western regions make up a vast unspoiled wilderness, a sportsman's paradise for hunting, fishing, canoeing, and snowmobiling, and they are the center of Maine's logging industry.

Maine's western lakes and mountains create a virtual playground for lovers of the great outdoors: boating, swimming, camping, flyfishing, and backpacking along the Appalachian Trail in warmer months; downhill or cross-country skiing at several excellent ski areas in winter.

The hundreds of square miles around the Sebago-Long Lakes chain, just 25 miles northwest of Portland, annually attract thousands of families for summer vacations. A little farther north, the White Mountain National Forest spreads over the New Hampshire border into Maine. The hills become mountains, the towns are farther apart, and lumber trucks barrel along the highways going from forest to sawmill.

Rangeley, a frontier town on the edge of the northern wilderness, is the centerpiece of a chain of lakes and connecting streams that create a 450-square-mile mecca for sportsmen. Fly fishing is fabulous. Winter skiing is excellent and not crowded. Snowmobile trails are everywhere. For the most serious fishermen and hunters—or to really leave civilization behind—the remote north country around Moosehead Lake is ideal. Float planes are available for flights to sporting camps, and guide service is available and recommended. Wilderness canoeing and rafting on the upper Kennebec and Penobscot Rivers is a thrilling adventure. Baxter State Park, a 2,000-acre wildlife sanctuary that surrounds mile-high Mt. Katahdin, the northern terminus of the Appalachian Trail, has marked hiking trails, campsites, and shelters available for mountain climbers and nature lovers.

PRACTICAL INFORMATION FOR MAINE

WHEN TO GO. Maine's busiest tourist season is summer, especially at the beach resorts and boating communities along the coast. Visitors can be assured of a cool summer holiday anywhere in Maine. An occasional day in mid-July can be hot and sticky, but average summer temperatures in the 70s make it more likely that you'll want a sweater, particularly in the evening.

Winters are long and cold, with temperatures averaging in the low 20s in the coldest months of Jan. and Feb. Winter days are usually sunny and crystal clear. The almost guaranteed availability of excellent snow conditions is the payoff for skiers who make the trek to Maine.

Fall is hunting season. Autumn foliage is magnificent; the color "peaks" in late September. The least desirable time to head to Maine is in May and early June, when the black flies become a very unpleasant distraction—unless, of course, you're a fisherman and come prepared!

HOW TO GET THERE. By plane. National airlines have scheduled flights between major cities in the northeast and Portland and/or Bangor—with connecting service to Augusta, Rockland, Presque Isle, Frenchville, and Bar Harbor. For information: *Business Express* (800–345–3400), *Delta Connection* (800–221–1212), *Continental* (800–525–0280), *Northwest Airlink* (800–322–1008), *United* (800–241–

6522), *Trans World Express* (800–221–2000), and *USAir* (800–428–4322). General aviation is accommodated at many airfields throughout the state.

By bus. Daily service is available from Boston to major points in Maine via *Greyhound.* Canadian service is available from Montreal, Quebec, and the Maritime Provinces.

By car. I-95 enters at Kittery, Maine's southern tip, and continues northeasterly across the state to New Brunswick, Canada. From northern New Hampshire, Rte. 16 is a scenic entry to Maine's western mountains and northern wilderness areas. Primary access from Quebec is Canadian Rte. 173, which connects with U. S. Rte. 201 near Jackman. From New Brunswick, an exit at Woodstock on the Trans Canada Hwy. is just a few miles by connecting road from Houlton, Maine, and the northern terminus of I-95. Also from New Brunswick, coastal Rte. 1 continues along Maine's "Down East" coast.

By boat. Passenger/auto ferry service is available (May–Oct.) on *Scotia Prince* between Portland and Yarmouth, Nova Scotia, a 10-hr. trip. For information: *Prince of Fundy Cruises, Ltd.,* Box 4216, Station A, Portland, ME 04101 (800–341–7540). The *M. V. Bluenose Ferry* provides service (year-round) between Bar Harbor and Yarmouth, Nova Scotia, a 6-hr. trip. For information: *Marine Atlantic,* 121 Eden St., Rte. 3, Bar Harbor, ME 04609 (800–341–7981).

TOURIST INFORMATION. Colorful and informative folders and booklets are provided by the *Maine Publicity Bureau,* 97 Winthrop St., Hallowell, ME 04347 (207–289–2423); *New England Vacation Center,* Shop #2, Concourse Level, 630 Fifth Avenue, New York, NY 10111 (212–307–5780); and *New England USA,* 76 Summer St., Boston MA 02110 (617–423–6967). For seasonal information and a free Maine vacation guide, call 800–533–9595.

The state operates year-round Tourist Information Centers just off I-95 and U.S. Rte. 1 at Kittery; 7 Union St., Calais; I-95 in Hampden; Ludlow Rd., near Jct. I-95 & U.S. 1, Houlton; and I-95 in Yarmouth. Seasonal information centers are operated by Maine Publicity Bureau in Bangor, Bethel, and Fryeburg.

Local chambers of commerce will provide information upon request.

TELEPHONES. The area code for the entire state of Maine is 207. To direct dial a long-distance or toll-free (800) number, dial 1 before the area code. For operator assistance on person-to-person, credit card, or collect calls, dial 0 before the area code. For directory assistance, dial 1–555–1212 for all Maine numbers. Local calls from a pay phone cost 20 cents for 3 minutes.

EMERGENCY TELEPHONE NUMBERS. The emergency number in Portland and other major cities and towns is 911; elsewhere, consult the local telephone directory or call 0 for emergency assistance. To contact the *Maine State Police* in an emergency: 800–452–4664 in Augusta, Skowhegan, and Bath areas; 800–432–7384 in Houlton; 800–432–7381 in Orono; 800–482–0730 in Gray; or 800–432–7381 in Washington County.

Other helpful emergency numbers: *Poison Control* (800–442–6305); *Coast Guard Search & Rescue,* S. Portland (207–799–1680); and *Maine Medical Center,* 22 Bramhall St., Portland (207–871–0111).

HOW TO GET AROUND. By plane. Intrastate flights are available on scheduled airlines via *Business Express* (800–345–3400), *Delta Connection* (800–221–1212), or *Northwest Airlink* (800–322–1008). Float planes from Greenville, Jackman, Brewer, Millinocket, Patten, Rangeley, and Portage carry fishermen and hunters to remote areas.

By car. Maine has about 22,000 miles of public highway, over 300 miles included in the U.S. Interstate System. I-95 cuts the state nearly in half diagonally from Kittery, on the New Hampshire border, to Houlton, on Maine's eastern border with New Brunswick, Canada. (The Maine Turnpike is that portion of I-95 from York to Augusta-Hallowell.) U.S. Rte. 1 meanders along the coast and then turns northward, following the Canadian border, to its terminus at Fort Kent. Rte. 2 cuts through central Maine from Bethel and the White Mountains in the west through Bangor to Houlton on Maine's eastern border. U.S. Rte. 201 is the major route from Canada through the wilderness and Jackman to Portland.

By rental car. Car rental companies are represented at major airports and in large cities and towns frequented by tourists.

By boat. Car ferry service to Maine's coastal islands is available at Rockland, Lincolnville, and Bass Harbor; passengers only between Boothbay or New Harbor and Monhegan and on the mailboats between Stonington and Isle au Haut and between Port Clyde and Monhegan. For information: *Maine State Ferry Service,* Box 645, 517A Main St., Rockland, ME 04841 (207–596–2202 or 800–521–3939).

HINTS TO MOTORISTS. Maine's maximum speed limit on interstate highways in nonurban areas is 65 mph. On interstate highways in urban areas (Portland, Lewiston/Auburn, and Bangor), the maximum is 55 mph. Unless otherwise posted, maximum speed is 45 mph in rural areas; 25 mph in urban areas. Travel is not usually limited on public roads by winter snows; roads are kept cleared and sanded.

There are very few public roads in the northern wilderness areas. Logging roads are privately owned, but many are available for public use (weather permitting). Some require permits; some have road access fees. For information: *North Maine Woods,* Box 421, Ashland, ME 04732 (207–435–6213).

Tourist attractions are well marked by small roadside directional signs. The *Official Maine State Map* is an excellent, up-to-date resource. A copy may be obtained by mail from the Maine Publicity Bureau (see Tourist Information); but a quick stop at the Bureau's Information Center in Kittery, accessible from both I-95 and U.S. Rte. 1, is worth your while.

Maine has instituted very strict drunk-driving laws, with stiff fines and penalties. Do not drink and drive.

TOURS AND SPECIAL-INTEREST SIGHTSEEING. Boat tours. The *Maine Windjammer Association,* Box 317, Rockport, ME 04856 (800–MAINE–80), will send a list of week-long windjammer cruises departing from Rockport, Rockland, and Camden. *Longfellow Cruise Line,* Long Wharf, Portland, ME 04101 (207–774–3578), operates several daily cruises around Portland Harbor and Casco Bay. Excursion boats depart from Kennebunkport, Boothbay Harbor, Bar Harbor, Northeast Harbor, Machias, and Jonesport for ocean cruises and whale/seal watching; from Naples for cruises around Sebago Lake; from Greenville for trips around Moosehead Lake. On *Lobsta' Boat Rides,* out of Bass Harbor (207–244–5667), you can tag along as lobstermen check their traps.

Bus tours. Guided tours of popular touring areas can be arranged through: *Maine Experience Guided Tours,* Waldoboro (207–832–4596); *Greater Portland Landmarks,* Portland (207–774–5561); *Northstar Escorted Tours,* Boothbay (207–633–6336); *Bar Harbor Limousine Service,* Bar Harbor (207–288–5398); and *National Park Tours,* Bar Harbor (207–288–3327).

Walking tours. Self-conducted tours have been outlined for the capital city of Augusta, the Old Port section of Portland, the Marginal Way in Ogunquit, the Cliff and River Walk in York Village, and the historic districts of Bangor, Bethel, Bath, Wiscasset, and Camden. Information is available at local hotels or tourist information centers.

Fall foliage. The sweeping views one gets in the mountains of western Maine offer the most striking panorama of brilliant fall color, beginning in mid-Sept. through early Oct.

Wildlife. *Maine Audubon Society,* 118 U.S. Rte. 1, Falmouth, ME 04105 (207–781–2330), and *The Nature Conservancy,* 122 Main St., Topsham, ME 04086 (207–729–5181), organize field trips to offshore islands to view native vegetation and wildlife. *Rachel Carson National Wildlife Refuge* (Wells), *Birdsacre Sanctuary* (Ellsworth), *Moosehorn National Wildlife Refuge* (Calais), *Hunter Cove Wildlife Sanctuary* (Rangeley), *Acadia National Park* (Mt. Desert Island), and *Baxter State Park* (Millinocket area) have guided nature walks and/or walking trails for viewing the region's wildlife and natural history.

Quarries. Rockhounds can pan for gold in the Swift River along Rte. 17 in Byron or can search for semiprecious stones in quarries operated by Perham's Mineral Store, Rtes. 26 and 219, W. Paris (674–2341).

Factory outlets. Outlets are situated at mills throughout Maine; Freeport, Kittery, and Wells have a concentration of outlet stores.

By plane. Sightseeing flights can be arranged at local airports, at Bar Harbor Airport for a tour over Acadia National Park, at Rangeley for a seaplane tour around Rangeley Lake, and at Greenville Junction for a wilderness ride over the Great North Woods.

NATIONAL PARKS. Acadia National Park, Box 177, Hulls Cove, Rte. 3, Bar Harbor, ME 04609 (207–288–3338), encompasses more than 30,000 acres on Mt. Desert Island. Glaciers, wind, and sea have worked marvels; along spectacular scenic drives past great ragged cliffs and coves, travelers can stop at Thunder Hole, the fjord at Somes Sound, and peaceful Jordan Pond. A drive to the summit of 1,530-ft. Cadillac Mt. offers a 360° view of coastal and inland Maine. Camping, trailer sites, and picnic areas are plentiful. Nature guide service offers varied daily programs. There are miles of hiking trails, bicycle and bridle paths; carriage and haywagon rides can be arranged at *Wildwood Stable,* Park Loop Rd. (207–276–3622). Additional sections of Acadia National Park are on Isle au Haut and on Schoodic Peninsula. (The park is open 24 hours a day throughout the year.)

White Mountain National Forest, Bethel, ME 04217 (207–824–2134), is partly in Maine, southwest of Bethel. There are campsites, hiking trails, picnic grounds, and magnificent mountain scenery.

STATE PARKS. Maine's 30 state parks provide excellent facilities and a variety of outdoor experiences: wilderness hiking, ocean or lake swimming, boating, fishing, camping, picnicking, or snowmobiling. Leashed pets are allowed, but not on beaches nor at Sebago Lake State Park and Baxter State Park. Baxter State Park, a 200,000-acre wilderness preserve, requires special permits to use or to travel through the park. For information: Baxter Park Authority, 64 Balsam Dr., Millinocket, ME 04462 (207–723–5140). Most state parks are open by May 15; the season usually extends to mid-Oct. For further information: *Maine Bureau of Parks and Recreation,* Station #22, Augusta, ME 04333 (207–289–3821).

CAMPING. About half the state parks in Maine, as well as Acadia National Park, allow camping. Three-fourths of the state-park campsites may be reserved at least 14 days in advance; 25 percent are available on a first-come, first-served basis. Fees vary, but are modest. (See National Parks and State Parks above for further information.)

There are about 90 wilderness campsites maintained by the Maine Forest Service and available at no charge. For information on these campsites and on fire permits: Maine Forest Service, State House Station #22, Augusta, ME 04333 (207–289–2791).

More than 300 backcountry campsites on private commercial forest land may be reserved at least one month in advance through North Maine Woods, Box 421, Ashland, ME 04732 (207–435–6213).

Facilities in privately owned campsites range from simple basics in the wilderness to deluxe cabins and cottages for rent—sometimes including tennis and shuffleboard courts, canoe and boat rentals, automatic laundry equipment, restaurants and snack bars, swimming pools, or recreation halls.

Sporting camps for hunters and fishermen abound from Greenville north throughout Aroostook County. Lodgings may consist of housekeeping cabins or a central lodge with sleeping cabins. Meals are often included. Float-plane service is frequently necessary and guide service is available.

In their Maine Guide to Camping, the Maine Publicity Bureau (see Tourist Information) provides a current listing of trailer parks, campsites, and conveniences available. Or contact Maine Campground Owners Association, 655 Main St., Lewiston, ME 04240 (207–782–5874).

FISHING AND HUNTING. Saltwater anglers bring in striped bass, tuna, cod, and other ocean fish year-round. Boat rentals are widely available; a list of charter and head boats for deep-sea fishing is available from Maine Publicity Bureau (see Tourist Information). No license is required for saltwater fishing, although there are some bag limits and equipment restrictions. Freshwater fishermen catch trout and bass in the lakes and streams; a fishing license is required for nonresidents 12 years old or over. Special licenses are required for Atlantic salmon and ice fishing.

Hunting regulations are strictly enforced when sportsmen take to the wilderness after deer, bear, and game birds. Moose hunting is limited by lottery. Licenses are required for all hunters 10 years old or over. Hunting on certain Indian territories is regulated by the tribes, and special permission must be obtained.

Fishing and hunting licenses and information on regulations may be obtained from agents in local towns or by writing: Dept. of Inland Fisheries & Wildlife, State House Station #41, Augusta, ME 04333 (207–289–2043). License fees vary by class, purpose, and residence.

For a first trip to the north woods, the assistance of a guide can be invaluable. Contact: Maine Professional Guides Assn., Box 159, Orono, ME 04473.

PARTICIPANT SPORTS. Boating. In towns along Maine's endless coastline, sail and power boats are available for hire, excursion boats embark, and charter fishing trips are available. On inland lakes, canoes, rowboats, and speedboats are generally available for rent.

Canoeing and rafting. Canoeists can choose between placid ponds and lakes or rivers that present a more challenging run. Enthusiasts head for the Allagash Wilderness Waterway or the St. John, St. Croix, and Machias rivers. Premier locations for rafting are the upper reaches of the Kennebec and the west branch of the Penobscot Rivers. Flat-water and white-water day trips may be made from ice-out in May through Oct.; a Maine guide is suggested for wilderness expeditions.

Swimming. Swimming and waterskiing are available in lakes all over Maine. Many state parks offer saltwater or lake swimming. Maine's southern coast, from York Beach to Old Orchard Beach, has miles of white, sandy beach and ocean bathing. Farther down east, ocean swimming can be bone-chilling.

Horseback riding. Acadia National Park has a 40-mile system of bridle paths. Horses can be hired in the park. Some state parks have riding trails. The Maine Publicity Bureau (see Tourist Information) publishes a list of riding stables.

Golf. There are 27 18-hole courses open to the public throughout the state, about 60 9-hole courses, a 27-hole course in Portland, and a 15-hole course in Northeast Harbor.

Mountain climbing. Maine boasts 10 peaks of 4,000 feet or more. Mt. Katahdin, in Baxter State Park, is a favorite destination; state parks and forests in the western mountains have marked trails.

Hiking. Trails in the White Mountain National Forest, near Bethel, connect with the 280-mile stretch of the Appalachian Trail that traverses Maine northeast to its terminus at Mt. Katahdin in Baxter State Park. (For information: *Maine Appalachian Trail Club,* Box 283, Augusta, ME 04330.) Acadia National Park and most state parks have marked hiking trails.

Bicycling. Bicycles are readily available for hire at bike shops all over Maine. There are few designated bikeways, but Acadia National Park has 50 miles of car-free carriage paths. *Maine Coast Cyclers,* Camden (207–236–8608), offers coastal or mountain tours, with overnight stays at B&Bs.

Skiing. "Winter" begins in mid-Nov. and lasts until May at ski areas in western Maine. Slopes are less crowded and lift lines shorter than in neighboring states, and snow conditions and facilities easily can compete. Cross-country skiing is also booming in Maine. Major ski areas are: Sugarloaf USA (Kingfield, ME 04947, 207–237–2000), Saddleback (Box 490, Rangeley, ME 04970, 207–864–5671), Sunday River (Box 450, Bethel, ME 04217, 207–824–3000), Shawnee Peak (Rte. 302, Bridgton, ME 04009, 207–647–8444), Moosehead Resort and Ski Area (Greenville, ME 04441, 207–695–2272), and Camden Snow Bowl (Ragged Mt., Camden, ME 04843, 207–236–3438).

Snowmobiling. Thousands of miles of marked and groomed trails interconnect throughout northern and western Maine and into Canada and New Hampshire. For trail maps and snowmobile registration information: Maine Snowmobile Assn., Box 77, Augusta, ME 04330 (207–622–6983); or Bureau of Parks & Recreation, Snowmobile Division (207–289–3821) year-round, (800–462–1019) in winter.

HISTORIC SITES AND HOUSES. Maine has designated many historic sites and districts to preserve its long history for future generations; private interests have restored many historic houses. For example: *Col. Black Mansion,* W. Main St., Ellsworth (207–667–8671); *Fort Western* (1754), Bowman St., Augusta (207–626–2385); *Fort William Henry* (1692), Rte. 130, Pemaquid Pt., Bristol; *Katahdin Iron Works* (1843), off Rte. 11, Brownville Jct.; *Wadsworth-Longfellow House* (1785),

487 Congress St., Portland (207–772–1807); and *York Historic District,* on Lindsay Rd. and York St., York Village (includes Old Gaol, Emerson-Wilcox House, Elizabeth Perkins House, Jefferds Tavern, George Marshall Store, and John Hancock Warehouse). Information on historic sites and homes is available in a booklet published by the Maine Publicity Bureau (see Tourist Information).

MUSEUMS AND GALLERIES. Maine's colorful and romantic history is carefully preserved in museums operated by local historical societies and private interests throughout the state. Specialized museums document Maine's lumbering, shipbuilding, and fishing industries; historic homes contain collections of local artifacts and often have original furnishings; galleries proudly display the works of Maine artists and craftsmen. Some suggestions: *The Lumberman's Museum,* Rte. 159, Patten (207–528–2650); *Maine Maritime Museum,* 243 Washington St., Bath (207–443–1316); *Portland Museum of Art,* Congress Sq., Portland (207–775–6148); *Seashore Trolley Museum,* Log Cabin Rd., Kennebunkport (207–967–2712); *Wm. A. Farnsworth Homestead and Art Museum,* 19–21 Elm St., Rockland (207–596–6457); *Willowbrook at Newfield,* Main St., Newfield (207–793–2784); *Mt. Desert Oceanarium,* Clark Pt. Rd., Southwest Harbor (207–244–7330); and *Maine State Museum,* State St., Augusta (207–289–2301). Most museums charge admission or request a donation. The descriptive booklet, Maine Guide to Museums and Historic Houses, is available from the Maine Publicity Bureau (see Tourist Information).

ARTS AND ENTERTAINMENT. In mid-Aug., the annual *Maine Festival* is held in Portland. Several hundred artists, musicians, dancers, and craftspeople participate, making it the most comprehensive artistic event in the state each year.

Music. Portland and Bangor each have a symphony orchestra. Classical music concerts are presented in summer at Blue Hill, Hancock, Rockport, Machias, Bridgton, and Cornish. Concert series and festivals are held in July at Bowdoin College (Brunswick), Colby College (Waterville), and the University of Maine (Orono); folk festivals in July in Rangeley, Bar Harbor, and Rockport.

Stage. The Portland Performing Arts Center presents theater and dance programs year-round. Summer theaters in Berwick, Ogunquit, Portland, Bath, Brunswick, Camden, Bar Harbor, Monmouth, Skowhegan, S. Casco, and Waterville present productions of Broadway hits, contemporary drama, and comedy. Penobscot Theatre Co. performs in Bangor (winter) and as Acadia Repertory Theatre in Somesville (summer).

ACCOMMODATIONS. Lodgings range from spectacular resorts on Maine's historic coast to charming inns and guest houses, hotels, and simple motels. Many hotels and inns along the coast are closed from Oct. to May; some remain open year-round with considerably lower rates. Rates are based on double occupancy, in season: *Deluxe,* $125 and up; *Expensive,* $100–$125; *Moderate,* $75–$100; *Inexpensive,* $75 and under. There is a Maine room tax of 5%.

Bangor. The Phenix Inn. *Moderate.* 20 West Market Sq., Bangor, ME 04401 (207–947–3850). Restored downtown hotel with modern facilities and "Old World" ambience. Convenient to business district.

Bar Harbor. Bar Harbor Inn. *Deluxe.* Newport Dr., Bar Harbor, ME 04609 (207–288–3351 or 800–248–3351). Luxurious full-service hotel, built in 1887, on the shore of Frenchman's Bay. Pool and sundeck. Restaurant and lounge. Open May–Nov.

Cleftstone Manor Inn. *Expensive–Deluxe.* 92 Eden St., Bar Harbor, ME 04609 (207–288–4951). Historic Victorian mansion at foot of Cadillac Mountain. Gracious rooms, a well-stocked library, and a game room. Continental breakfast and afternoon tea included. No children under 12; no smoking. Open May–Oct.

Manor House Inn. *Expensive–Deluxe.* 16 West St., Bar Harbor, ME 04609 (207–288–3759). Turn-of-the-century decor in restored Bar Harbor "cottage." Quiet, comfortable, convenient to town. Pool and tennis privileges across the street. Open May–Oct.

Park Entrance Motel. *Expensive.* Rte. 3, Box 180, Bar Harbor, ME 04609 (207–288–9703). Pleasant motel rooms with patios or balconies overlooking the ocean. Pool, beach, putting green, boats. Picnic area. Open May–Oct.

Bethel. Bethel Inn & Country Club. *Expensive.* Broad St., Bethel, ME 04217 (207–824–2175 or 800–654–0125). On the Common. Classic country inn with lovely grounds. Modern comforts, personal service, excellent cuisine, friendly atmosphere. Winter skiing, golf, pool or lake swimming.

Boothbay Harbor. Spruce Point Inn. *Expensive–Deluxe.* Spruce Pt. Rd., Boothbay Harbor, ME 04538 (207–633–4152). Picturesquely situated on a wooded peninsula. Pools, putting green, tennis, beach, boats, fishing. Formal dining (MAP available). Open June–Sept.

Tugboat Inn. *Expensive.* 100 Commercial St., Boothbay Harbor, ME 04538 (207–633–4434). The original tugboat *Maine* is the centerpiece of the inn's guestrooms, efficiency units, and apartments—all with a water view. Restaurant and marina.

Ocean Point Inn. *Moderate–Expensive.* Shore Rd., East Boothbay, ME 04544 (207–633–4200). Charming seacoast motor inn and cottages. Down East hospitality; home-cooked food. Boat trips leave from wharf. Pool. Open May–Oct.

Camden. Whitehall Inn. *Deluxe.* 52 High St., Camden, ME 04843 (207–236–3391). Historic Colonial inn. Tennis, boat trips, concerts, entertainment, gracious dining, cocktails. Open May–Oct.

The Belmont. *Expensive.* 6 Belmont Ave., Camden, ME 04843 (207–236–8053). Cozy rooms are available in this restored inn, which is Camden's oldest! It's a small, quiet, and classy place with an excellent dining room.

Center Lovell. Westways on Kezar Lake. *Expensive.* Rte. 5, Center Lovell, ME 04016 (207–928–2663). At White Mt. Natl. Forest. Rustic main lodge and surrounding cottages offer woodsy seclusion and magnificent lake views. Dining, sports activities. Weekly rates. Closed Apr. and Nov.

Deer Isle. Goose Cove Lodge. *Expensive.* Sunset, ME 04683 (4 mi. from Deer Isle village) (207–348–2508). Lodge and rustic cottages. Miles of nature trails on grounds overlooking cove. Private beach, boating. Weekly rates; MAP. Open May–Oct.

Greenville. Greenville Inn. *Inexpensive.* Norris St., Greenville, ME 04441 (207–695–2206). Former lumber baron's home (1895). Ten cozy guest rooms, two with fireplaces. Snowmobile trails, skiing nearby; boating and watersports at Moosehead Lake.

Kennebunkport. The Colony. *Deluxe.* Ocean Ave., Kennebunkport, ME 04046 (207–967–3331). Grand white clapboard resort hotel, with spectacular ocean setting. Pool, putting green, shuffleboard. Fine dining. Open June–Sept.

Village Cove Inn. *Deluxe.* S. Maine St., Kennebunkport, ME 04046 (207–967–3993). Rustic elegance, peaceful and quiet, overlooks private cove. Restaurant, bar. Indoor and outdoor pools. Open May–Oct.

The Captain Lord Mansion. *Expensive.* Green and Pleasant Sts., Kennebunkport, ME 04046 (207–967–3141). This intimate Maine coast inn, vintage 1812, offers quiet elegance, with fireplaces in most rooms; breakfast included. Walk to shops and restaurants.

Ogunquit. The Cliff House. *Deluxe.* Bald Head Cliff, Ogunquit, ME 03907 (207–361–1000). Original family inn and several motel units on 9 acres. Panoramic ocean views. Near beach, shops, and theater. Tennis, water sports, pool, dining room. Open Mar.–Dec.

The Colonial Inn. *Moderate–Expensive.* 71 Shore Rd., Ogunquit, ME 03907 (207–646–5191). Large Victorian inn in the heart of town; modern efficiencies and studios in adjacent buildings. Pool and picnic area; coffee shop. Open May–Oct.

Portland. Portland Regency Inn. *Deluxe.* 20 Milk St., Portland ME 04101 (207–774–4200 or 800–727–3436). Luxury and style are the results of the renovation of what had been a 19th-century armory in the heart of the Old Port Exchange. Add to the perfect location comfortable rooms, a pleasant atmosphere, a good restaurant, and a great health club—and you can't miss.

The Inn at Park Spring. *Expensive.* 135 Spring St., Portland, ME 04101 (207–774–1059). Very small hotel in a three-story town house. Personal attention in the grand style. Help yourself to breakfast; traditional tea at 4 P.M.

Rangeley. Country Club Inn. *Expensive.* Country Club Rd. (off Rtes. 4 and 16), Rangeley, ME 04970 (207–864–3831). A delightful resort perched high on a hill overlooking Rangeley Lake. Good restaurant, golf course adjacent, pool, fishing, water sports, winter skiing. Closed Apr. and Nov.

Rangeley Inn. *Moderate.* Main St., Rangeley, ME 04970 (207–864–3341). Pleasant turn-of-the-century lakeside inn with modern motel wing. Old-fashioned comfort and hospitality. Good restaurant; bar.

Town & Lake Motel. *Moderate.* 47 Main St., Rangeley, ME 04970 (207–864–3755). On Rangeley Lake. Pleasant family motel and housekeeping cottages. Beach area, boating, canoeing, play area. Winter skiing and snowmobiling.

Scarborough. Black Point Inn. *Deluxe.* Black Point Rd., Prouts Neck, ME 04074 (207–883–4126). A secluded oceanfront inn, this is one of Maine's oldtime classics. Elegant and impressive; fine service. Full American Plan. PGA golf course, tennis, heated pool, sailing, beaches. Open May–Oct.

York Harbor. Stage Neck Inn. *Deluxe.* Stage Neck Rd., Rte. 1A, York Harbor, ME 03911 (207–363–3850 or 800–222–3238). An inviting resort on a rocky point of land jutting into the ocean. Modern, attractive rooms with balconies. Saltwater pool and beach, golf, tennis, and fishing.

Dockside Guest Quarters. *Moderate.* Harris Island, off Rte. 103, York Harbor, ME 03911 (207–363–2868). Early Maine homestead with comfortable rooms.

BED AND BREAKFASTS. Guest houses, delightful tourist homes, and bed-and-breakfast inns abound in Maine and are often a most charming alternative. The Maine Publicity Bureau (see Tourist Information) or the chamber of commerce in the town or area you will be visiting will send names and addresses of these small inns. Or contact the following: *Bed & Breakfast Down East Ltd.,* Box 547, Eastbrook, ME 04634 (207–565–3517); *Maine Farm Vacation and B&B Assn.,* Box 2350, Kents Hill, ME 04349.

YS AND HOSTELS. American Youth Hostels are located in Bar Harbor (207–288–5587), Carmel (207–848–2262), Greenville (207–695–2278), and Monson (207–997–3691).

RESTAURANTS. Travelers to Maine are guaranteed of finding fresh Maine lobster featured in most restaurants. Just as consistently, diners will find warm home-baked breads and desserts. The restaurants suggested below are open year-round, serve lunch and dinner, and accept major credit cards, unless noted. Price per person for a complete dinner is: *Deluxe,* $35 and up; *Expensive,* $25–$35; *Moderate,* $15–$25; *Inexpensive,* $15 and under.

Bailey Island. Cook's Lobster House. *Moderate-Expensive.* Garrison Cove Rd., off Rte. 24 (207–833–6641). Boiled lobster and shore dinners a specialty. Open May–Sept.

Bangor. Seguino's. *Expensive.* 735 Main St. (207–942–1240). Comfortable, yet stylish, this restaurant serves Italian food—gnocchi, pasta, veal specialties, and homemade desserts. Pizza, too.

Bar Harbor. Brick Oven. *Moderate-Expensive.* 21 Cottage St. (207–288–3708). American traditional specialties, grilled over an open fire, are served in several dining rooms filled with 1960s memorabilia. Summer only.

Jordan Pond House. *Moderate–Expensive.* Loop Rd. (in Acadia Natl. Park) (207–276–3316). Enjoy a lovely luncheon, or popovers and homemade ice cream on the lawn for tea. Dinners served before a crackling fire. View is magnificent during the day; mood memorable in the evening. Open June–Oct.

Testa's. *Moderate-Expensive.* 53 Main St. (207–288–3327). Grill Room and Garden Room. Steaks, shellfish, Italian specialties; fresh fruit pies. Breakfast also served. Open Jun.–Oct.

Bethel. Bethel Inn. *Moderate–Expensive.* On the Common (207–824–2175). Pleasant dining in elegant dining room, on the veranda, or in the tavern. Traditional New England fare. Sun. brunch.

Boothbay Harbor. Brown Bros. Wharf. *Expensive.* Atlantic Ave. (207–633–5440). Complete menu includes lobster from the tank, native seafood. Breakfast also served. Open June–Oct.

Andrew's Harborside. *Moderate.* At Foot Bridge (207–633–4074). Chef-owned and operated. Seafood, steak, sandwiches, and chowder. Homemade breads and pastries. Wonderful cinnamon buns for breakfast. Open May–Oct.

Robinson's Wharf. *Inexpensive.* At the drawbridge, Rte. 27, Southport (207–633–3830). Lobster, clams, and sandwiches to eat on the wharf or take out. Ice cream shop. Beer and wine. Open June–Sept.

Bridgton. Switzer Stubli Restaurant. *Moderate–Expensive.* Ridge Rd. (at Tarry-a-While Resort) (207–647–2522). Swiss specialties: wiener schnitzel, raclette, fondue. Homebaked breads and pastries. Open June–Sept.

Brunswick. 22 Lincoln. *Expensive.* 22 Lincoln St. (207–725–5893). The atmosphere here is casual and friendly, the rich gourmet cuisine artfully prepared, and the elegant service is attentive yet unobtrusive. Light, less expensive suppers at the Side Door Cafe.

Camden. The Belmont. *Deluxe.* 6 Belmont Ave. (207–236–8053). Intimate dining is enjoyed in this lovely inn (Camden's oldest!). New American cuisine with seasonal local ingredients. Closed Mon. Open May–Oct.

Lobster Pound. *Moderate–Expensive.* Rte. 1, Lincolnville (207–789–5550). Pick your lobster from the pool, then eat it on the deck. Shore dinners; landlubber specials also. Open May–Oct.

Greenville. Lake View Manor. *Moderate.* Lily Bay Rd. (207–695–3810). Seafood and steaks served in cozy dining room with view of Moosehead Lake and Squaw Mt. Dinner only. Closed Sun.

Hancock. Le Domaine. *Expensive.* Rte. 1, Hancock Pt. (207–422–3395). Classic French country cuisine is served in a French country atmosphere here. Superbly prepared entrees and pastries. Open May–Oct.

Kennebunkport. Olde Grist Mill. *Deluxe.* Mill Lane (207–967–4781). Traditional Maine dishes from chowder to Indian pudding. Open Apr.–Dec. Closed Mon.

Mabel's Lobster Claw. *Moderate.* 425 Ocean Ave. (207–967–2562). Delicious home cooking; informal atmosphere. Seafood, homemade soups and chowders, breads and pastries. Sidewalk café in summer. President and Mrs. Bush have been patrons for years. Open Apr.–Oct.

Kingfield. One Stanley Avenue. *Expensive.* 1 Stanley Ave. (207–265–5541). Billed as the "classic cuisine of Maine," the menu offered in this Victorian inn includes ambitious preparations of veal, chicken, pork, and beef as well as stylized Maine seafood dishes. Closed Mon., Nov., and May.

Ogunquit. Barnacle Billy's. *Inexpensive–Moderate.* Shore Rd., Perkins Cove (207–646–5575). Dine outside here on the deck or inside by the hearth. Offered are sandwiches, salads, seafood, chicken, and lobster (boiled or stewed). Scenic cruises from the wharf. Open May–Oct.

Portland. Raphael's. *Expensive–Deluxe.* 36 Market St. (207–773–4500). Fine northern Italian cuisine served in elegantly austere surroundings. Extensive wine list. Reservations suggested.

DiMillo's Floating Restaurant. *Expensive.* 121 Commercial St. (207–772–2216). A former car ferry docked at Long Wharf. Fresh fish, lobster, shore dinners, steamers. Very popular.

Alberta's. *Moderate–Expensive.* 21 Pleasant St. (207–774–5408). The eclectic menu at this popular Portland café features mesquite-grilled and pan-blackened specialties. Beer and wine only. No reservations.

Rangeley. Rangeley Inn. *Moderate–Expensive.* Main St. (207–864–3341). Breakfast and dinner are served in dining room of turn-of-the-century inn. American cooking is punctuated with international specialties. Casual. Live entertainment; dancing. Closed Apr.–May.

Oquossoc House. *Moderate.* Rtes. 17 and 4, Oquossoc (207–864–3881). Family restaurant, rustic decor. Char-broiled steaks, seafood, daily specials. Reservations necessary. Closed Sun.

York Harbor. Bill Foster's Down East Lobster & Clambake. *Moderate.* Rte. 1A (208–363–3255). Clams, lobster, and all the fixin's (or steak or chicken). Features an old-fashioned sing-along! Reserve ahead. Summer only.

LIQUOR LAWS. In Maine, minimum age for the purchase or consumption of alcohol is 21. Bottled liquor is sold only at state liquor stores and agencies. Beer and wine are sold at grocery stores. Alcoholic beverages may be sold by the bottle Mon.-Sat., and on Sun. where approved. By local option, alcoholic drinks may be sold in hotels, restaurants, and bars Mon.–Sat., 6 A.M.–1 A.M.; Sun. and Memorial Day, noon–1 A.M.

Maine has instituted a deposit on beer and soft drink bottles and cans. Deposits are refunded when empties are returned to stores or redemption centers.

NEW HAMPSHIRE

Vacationers have been attracted to New Hampshire since early in the 19th century. Travelers first ventured north by horse-drawn coach, lured by the beautiful lakes, the snow-covered peaks of New England's highest mountains, and the ocean beaches along the seacoast. Through the era of the steam-powered railroad they—especially the affluent—came to the charming villages that dot the landscape—and especially to the White Mountains. Some of the magnificent hotels and resorts of the last century have continued in operation through the years, offering today's travelers a taste of past luxury.

For the most part, present-day visitors to New Hampshire come by automobile. With over 200 miles of expressways, New Hampshire is easily accessible from all major cities in the northeast. Travel through the state to a mountain, lake, or coastal destination can be accomplished swiftly along the interstates or on well-maintained "shunpikes" and secondary roads through scenic villages.

The Granite State is shaped like a right angle, wedged in between Vermont and Maine. Only an 18-mile-long section along its southeast border is exposed to the Atlantic Ocean; the rest of the state is landlocked. New Hampshire measures 180 miles from north to south. At its widest, in the south, it is nearly 100 miles wide (if you include the offshore Isles of Shoals), tapering to only about 20 miles in width where its northern tip projects into Quebec. The winding Connecticut River forms the western border with Vermont. Orchards and dairy farms are scattered picturesquely along the fertile lowlands of the Connecticut River Valley. In the cities and towns along the southern border with Massachusetts, the high-tech belt, business is booming. Tourism and industry have made New Hampshire the fastest-growing state in New England.

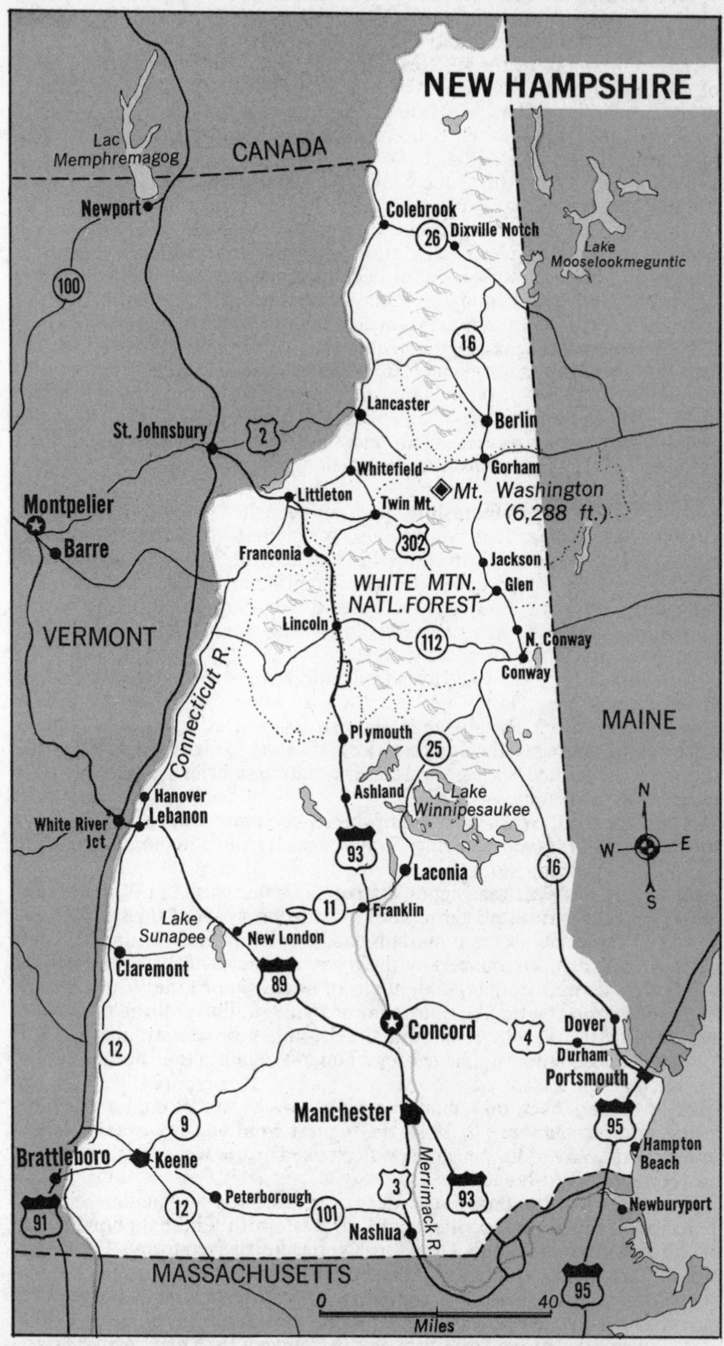
NEW HAMPSHIRE
CANADA
Lac Memphremagog
Newport
100
Colebrook
26
Dixville Notch
Lake Mooselookmeguntic
16
Lancaster
Berlin
St. Johnsbury
2
Whitefield
Gorham
Mt. Washington (6,288 ft.)
Littleton
Twin Mt.
Montpelier
Barre
302
Franconia
Jackson
Glen
WHITE MTN. NATL. FOREST
VERMONT
Lincoln
112
N. Conway
Conway
Connecticut R.
MAINE
Plymouth
25
Ashland
Lake Winnipesaukee
N
W
E
S
Hanover
Lebanon
White River Jct
93
Laconia
16
11
Franklin
Lake Sunapee
New London
Claremont
89
Concord
4
Dover
Durham
Portsmouth
12
Manchester
95
9
Hampton Beach
Brattleboro
Keene
Merrimack R.
3
93
Peterborough
Newburyport
91
12
101
Nashua
MASSACHUSETTS
0
40
95
Miles

New Hampshire's total land area is a compact 9,300 square miles, which includes 1,100 square miles of the White Mountain National Forest (with massive Mt. Washington) and 310 square miles of water surface. It is the most mountainous of the six New England states, with more than a third of the land above 2,000 feet. About 85 percent of the state, particularly in the northern reaches, is forested. The forests were heavily and rapidly exploited until 1911, when conservation measures were enacted to preserve large tracts of woodland.

One of the original thirteen colonies, New Hampshire has a long American history. It was first explored by Martin Pring in 1603 and Samuel de Champlain in 1605. In 1620, the Council for New England (Plymouth Colony) received a royal land grant. English councilmen Ferdinando Gorges and Capt. John Mason formed a partnership to share the land between the Merrimack and the Kennebec rivers. By agreement, Gorges took the area now known as Maine; Mason kept New Hampshire.

New Hampshire's first permanent colony was established at Dover before 1628. Soon after, Anglican farmers and fishermen settled Portsmouth, on the coast. In 1641, New Hampshire was annexed by Massachusetts.

The French and Indian Wars stifled colonization of inland areas; but as the French were pushed north and the Indians were defeated, a land rush began. Lumber camps were set up along rivers and streams; and sawmills were built.

Residents of New Hampshire, then as now, had strong opinions and were fiercely independent. Massachusetts's claim to the land was not recognized by New Hampshire until 1741, when the eastern and southern boundaries were agreed upon. Because of conflicting claims by Massachusetts and New York, however, the western boundary continued to be disputed throughout the American Revolution and was not settled until 1791, when Vermont finally became a state.

Inhabitants tired early of British rule and were eager to be independent of the crown. New Hampshire was the first American colony to declare independence from Britain and establish its own government (January 1776). In 1788, it was the ninth and deciding state to ratify the new Constitution of the United States, the action which bound the original 13 states together as a republic.

After the Civil War, New Hampshire's economy turned primarily to textile and shoe manufacturing. Today, tourism and manufacturing are the most important industries.

At any time of year, the biggest attraction by far is still the White Mountains region, a natural playground in the northern part of the state. Sightseers can travel on scenic mountain roads, twisting and turning through notches and gaps, surrounded by the rocky pinnacles of the 86 mountains in the Presidential Range. A highlight of a vacation to the White Mountains includes a trip on the auto road or by cog railway to the 6,288-foot summit of Mt. Washington. Both the 3½-mile cog railway line and the 8-mile carriage/auto road have been in operation since the 1860s, weather permitting! On a clear day the view is superb. Be prepared, though, for tricky weather. Even on a sunny summer day, it can be cool and windy at the summit. On April 2, 1934, the highest wind velocity ever recorded in the world, 231 miles per hour, was clocked at the weather observatory on top of Mt. Washington.

Between the mountain peaks, deep notches offer spectacular scenery. The most famous are: Dixville Notch, farthest north; Pinkham Notch, east of the Presidential Range; Crawford Notch, to the west; and Franconia Notch, farthest west. At Franconia Notch State Park, visitors can see the "Old Man of the Mountain," the stone profile overlooking a steep precipice that nature carved some 200 million years ago. The Flume, an 800-foot natural chasm, and the first aerial tramway in North America are also located here.

Throughout the White Mountains National Forest, there are opportunities to hike along an extensive network of foot trails, to camp at designated areas, or to have a roadside picnic. In autumn, the foliage along the mountain roads, especially the Kancamagus Highway, is breathtaking. And in snow season, skiers flock to several major ski areas to be challenged by the mountain peaks or to tour along forest trails.

New Hampshire's lakes are as attractive to tourists as its mountains, though mostly in summertime. Lake Winnipesaukee, at 72 square miles, is the largest lake in the state. Swimming, boating, and lake cruises are the attractions, of course; but nearby towns offer amusements, shopping, theaters, and museums. Hundreds of comfortable lakeshore rental cottages and other attractive lodgings, including a variety of bed-and-breakfast inns, are available. The Lakes region is interrupted by isolated mountain peaks—"monadnocks"—which offer skiing in winter, hiking and camping in milder weather.

Although New Hampshire's seacoast is only 18 miles long, the bays and rivers give the state a 131-mile saltwater shoreline. In summer, the area bustles with action. Just north of the Massachusetts border, Seabrook Beach, Hampton Beach, and Great Boars Head are summer resorts with wide, sandy beaches and superb swimming; but they can become very crowded.

Portsmouth, the commercial center of the area, is the largest town along the seacoast. The Portsmouth Navy Yard, which has been making ships since 1800, is the major employer in the area. The town's history dates back to New Hampshire's earliest days, and several carefully preserved 18th-century homes, including the John Paul Jones House, are open to visitors. Strawbery Banke Restoration depicts the settlement of Old Portsmouth. Visitors can see reconstructed 17th–19th century homes, many on original foundations, and maritime craftsmen at work on early Colonial crafts.

PRACTICAL INFORMATION FOR NEW HAMPSHIRE

WHEN TO GO. Summer vacationers head to New Hampshire's heavily developed 18-mi. seacoast on the Atlantic Ocean for saltwater swimming. Inland, cool summer temperatures in the 70s, accompanied by low humidity, lure many travelers to the Lakes region, around Lake Winnipesaukee, for freshwater swimming and boating, and to the White Mountains farther north.

The highest mountains in the northeastern U.S. attract skiers to New Hampshire from mid-Nov. to Apr. Even if it must be augmented artificially, snow is ensured by the constant cold weather of the winter months, which averages in the high teens.

Autumn is a spectacular but crowded time. Weekends are jam-packed with leaflookers. The panorama of colors begins after Labor Day in the far north, inching south as the days grow colder, and usually peaking by mid-Oct. Try to travel midweek, and be sure to make advance reservations.

The invigorating spring weather and the blossoms on the fruit trees make minivacations a delight in Mar. and Apr.

HOW TO GET THERE. By plane. Air service is provided between major cities and Manchester on: *Continental Express* (800–525–0280), *American* (800–433–7300), *Delta* (800–221–1212), *Northwest* (800–225–2525), *United* (800–241–6522), and *USAir* (800–428–4322). Private air service (including helicopter) is available at small airports throughout the state. Limousine service is available from Boston's Logan Int. Airport to seacoast locations: *C & J Limo,* Box 190, Dover, NH 03820 (603–692–5111, 800–258–7111 elsewhere).

By train. The only rail service in New Hampshire is on *Amtrak,* with two stops daily in Claremont Jct.—one before dawn and one before midnight. For information, call (800) USA–RAIL.

By bus. *Concord Trailways* (800–258–3722, 800–852–3317 in NH) and *Vermont Transit* (800–451–3292) serve New Hampshire towns from major cities.

By car. From Boston or Maine, I-95 (N.H. Tpk.) passes along the 18-mi. coast. I-93 enters New Hampshire at Salem and continues north to Littleton. I-91 north from Connecticut and Massachusetts continues along the Vermont side of the Connecticut River (New Hampshire's western border), offering access to western New Hampshire towns at key locations. Rte. 2 from Bangor and northeast Maine heads west to the White Mountains. Canadian Rtes. 10 and 55 from Montreal and Quebec connect with I-91 in Vermont; at St. Johnsbury, VT, pick up I-93 to Littleton, NH.

TOURIST INFORMATION. Maps and *The Official New Hampshire Guidebook* can be obtained by contacting *New Hampshire Office of Vacation Travel,* Box 856, Concord, NH 03301 (603–271–2666); and *New England Vacation Center,* Shop #2, Concourse Level, 630 Fifth Avenue, New York, NY 10111 (212–307–5780).

Regional promotion organizations: *Lake Sunapee Business Assn.,* Box 400, Sunapee, NH 03782 (603–763–2495); *Lakes Region Assn.,* Box 300, Wolfeboro, NH 03894 (603–569–1117); *Merrimack Valley Regional Assn.,* Sheraton Tara Hotel, Nashua, NH 03061 (603–888–9970); *Monadnock Travel Council,* The Benjamin Prescott Inn, Rte. 124 E., Jaffrey, NH 03452 (603–532–6637); *Seacoast Council on Tourism,* 1000 Market St., Portsmouth, NH 03802 (603–436–7678); *White Mountains Attractions Assn.,* Box 176, N. Woodstock, NH 03262 (603–745–8720).

Visitor information centers are open daily year-round at several locations on I-89, I-93, I-95, and Everett Tpke. (Rte. 3).

For recorded information on seasonal events, call 800–258–3608; 603–224–2525 in New Hampshire.

TELEPHONES. The area code for all of New Hampshire is 603. To direct dial a long-distance or toll-free (800) number, dial 1 before the area code. For operator assistance on person-to-person, credit card, or collect calls, dial 0 before the area code. For directory assistance, dial 1–555–1212 for all New Hampshire numbers. Local calls from a pay phone in New Hampshire cost 10 cents for 3 minutes.

EMERGENCY TELEPHONE NUMBERS. In an emergency, dial 0 and the operator will connect you with the proper assistance. Or dial 800–852–3411 for the New Hampshire State Police. The Poison Control Center can be reached at 800–562–8236. For boating emergencies, call Marine Services, 603–293–2037, or USCG and Rescue Service, 603–436–4414. Highway Emergency Communication Center, 603–485–5767.

HOW TO GET AROUND. By plane. There are 24 airports available to general aviation. Pilots may request information from New Hampshire Aeronautics Division, Concord Municipal Airport, Concord, NH 03302 (603–271–2551).

By bus. Intercity bus service is available between major towns via Concord Trailways. Local bus service is available in Keene, Manchester, Nashua, Portsmouth, and Rochester.

By car. I-93 cuts New Hampshire virtually in half, providing a direct route to the Lakes Region and the White Mountains. Everett Tpke. (U.S. Rte. 3) connects Nashua with Manchester and I-93. I-89 begins in Concord (at I-93) and shoots northwest to Lebanon and White River Jct., VT. Spaulding Tpke. (U.S. Rte. 4) hugs the eastern border from Portsmouth north through Farmington. New Hampshire Tpke. (I-95) skirts the coast and is heavily traveled in summer. Well-maintained secondary roads provide miles of scenic "shunpike." Most spectacular is the Kancamagus Highway (Rte. 112), which passes through White Mountains National Forest.

HINTS TO MOTORISTS. Unless otherwise posted, speed limits on interstates are maximum 65 mph, minimum 45 mph. All other roads, including turnpikes, require a reasonable and prudent speed, with posted limits. Open rural highway limit is 55 mph, or as posted; rural residential districts, 35 mph; urban areas, 30 mph; school zones, 20 mph. Roadside and mobile radar speed checks are used; state police use some unmarked vehicles and aircraft. Local roadblocks may be used to enforce strict drunk-driving laws.

New Hampshire Child Passenger Safety Law requires children under 5 years of age to be restrained by a seat belt or a car seat while riding in a motor vehicle.

In winter, driving may be difficult on secondary roads in mountain areas unless you have a 4-wheel-drive vehicle. Weather and driving conditions are posted at all turnpike toll plazas; or contact: *Hooksett Division Five Highway Office,* Hooksett, NH 03106 (603–485–9526).

HINTS TO DISABLED TRAVELERS. In *The Official New Hampshire Guidebook,* available from the Office of Vacation Travel (see Tourist Information), many listings are coded as to relative accessibility for physically disabled visitors and whether special assistance can be requested.

TOURS AND SPECIAL-INTEREST SIGHTSEEING. Covered bridges. Locations of New Hampshire's 51 covered bridges, mostly in the White Mountains, Monadnock, and the Lake Sunapee areas, are pinpointed on the New Hampshire Tourist Map, available from the N.H. Office of Vacation Travel (see Tourist Information).

Natural wonders. *Old Man of the Mountain,* above Rte. 3, Franconia Notch, is the state symbol—the natural granite profile of a man's face jutting out of a sheer 1,200-ft. cliff. *The Flume,* Rte. 3, Franconia Notch, is a ½-mi. scenic walk through an 800-ft. long geologic chasm, open daily from Memorial Day–mid-Oct. *Polar Caves,* on Rte. 25 west of Plymouth, and *Lost River Reservation,* Rte. 112, N. Woodstock, are both glacial gorges with daily guided tours from May–mid-Oct.

Summer boat tours. On *Lake Winnipesaukee: M/S Mt. Washington* departs Weirs Beach and other lake towns for 3¼-hr. cruises twice daily. Smaller vessels depart Weirs Beach for shorter cruises. For information: 603–366–5531. On *Lake Sunapee: M/V Kearsarge* is a restaurant ship departing Steamboat Landing twice each evening. For reservations: 603–763–5488; *M/V Mt. Sunapee II* departs Sunapee Harbor twice daily for 1½-hr. cruises (603–763–4030). *Ocean cruises:* New Hampshire Seacoast Cruises (603–964–5545) leave Rye Harbor twice daily for 2-hr. narrated tours of the nine islands of the Isles of Shoals. *Portsmouth Harbor Cruises,* Portsmouth, has daily narrated tours through the Isles of Shoals (603–436–8084). Whale and seabird expeditions are offered by *Oceanic Whale Watch Expeditions* (603–431–5500), out of Portsmouth.

Train rides. *Conway Scenic Railroad,* Rtes. 16 and 302, N. Conway (603–356–5251), offers a delightful 11-mi. ride through the countryside several times daily. *Winnipesaukee Railroad,* Weirs Beach and Meredith (603–528–2330), travels 36 mi. along the shores of Lake Winnipesaukee, May–Oct. *Hobo Railroad,* Lincoln (603–745–2135), travels 15 mi. round-trip through the White Mountains.

Mountain rides. *Mt. Washington Auto Road,* off Rte. 16, Pinkham Notch (603–466–3988), is an 8-mi. toll road to the alpine summit of the highest peak in the northeast. Chauffered vans are available for those who prefer not to drive. On the western slope, the *Mt. Washington Cog Railway,* off U.S. 302 north of Crawford Notch (603–922–8825), takes passengers on a 3-mi. climb to the top of Mt. Washington behind a quaint steam engine. Both attractions are open mid-May–mid-Oct. The 34-mi. *Kancamagus Highway,* between Lincoln and N. Conway, affords spectacular mountain views as it winds its way through the White Mountain National Forest.

Several ski areas open their lifts to sightseers in the off-season. The *Cannon Mt. Aerial Tramway,* Rte. 3, Franconia Notch (603–823–5563), is an 80-passenger cable car that ascends to the 4,200-ft. summit. Four-passenger gondolas are available for sky-rides at *Loon Mt.* in Lincoln, *Mt. Sunapee* in Newbury, and *Wildcat Mt.* at Pinkham Notch in Jackson.

NATIONAL FORESTS. *White Mountain National Forest,* Box 638, Laconia, NH 03247 (603–524–6450), the largest area of public land in New England, is a 763,000-acre outdoor playground of dense, pine-scented forest. The bulk of the WMNF is in New Hampshire, with a small portion in adjacent Maine. Mt. Washington, at 6,288 ft. the highest mountain in the northeast, is one of 86 mountain peaks in the area. The entire forest is open for fishing and hunting during open season, and there are 20 federal campgrounds. A 1,200-mi. network of foot trails, including the Appalachian Trail, is maintained for hiking.

STATE PARKS. New Hampshire has 37 state parks and beaches, offering opportunities for ocean or lake swimming, fishing, hiking, camping, skiing, mountain-climbing, and picnicking. Franconia Notch State Park, with its towering mountain peaks, many natural wonders, and attractions, is the leading tourist attraction in New Hampshire. Most state parks are open to visitors year-round. Because of bitter winter weather at the summit, however, Mt. Washington State Park is open only from mid-May–mid-Oct. For further information: *N.H. Division of Parks & Recreation,* Box 856, Concord, NH 03301 (603–271–3556). For up-to-date recorded information on state parks, call 603–224–2525 or 800–258–3608 elsewhere in New England.

CAMPING. Campsites are available in 6 state parks, at 20 campgrounds in the White Mountain National Forest, and in more than 125 privately owned campgrounds. For a comprehensive state-wide camping guide, contact New Hampshire Campground Owners Assn., Box 320, Twin Mountain, NH 03595 (800–822–6764 or 800–3–CAMPNH).

Anyone camping in a state park must have a tent or camping unit; camping with only a sleeping bag is not permitted. Each campsite in a state park or at the WMNF includes a fireplace or grate, a picnic table, and a car park. Running water and toilets are available nearby. Camping is permitted May–Oct., slightly longer at some campsites. Reservations are not accepted at state parks—first come, first served—and there is a modest charge ($8–$17 per night). Some WMNF campsites are on a reservation system; for information, call 800–283–CAMP. The Forest Service charges $7–9 per night.

FISHING AND HUNTING. From ice-out in Apr. until Autumn, New Hampshire's lakes, ponds, and streams provide fishing for beginner or expert: trout, landlocked salmon, bass, and many other varieties. All persons 16 years of age and over and nonresident minors 12 and over must be licensed to fish in inland waters.

Saltwater anglers go after tuna, striped bass, mackerel, cod, and other ocean fish. Charter and party boats are available for deep-sea fishing. No license is required for saltwater fishing, except for taking smelt, shellfish, and Coho salmon.

In hunting season, deer, bear, and game birds are most commonly sought by hunters. All persons 16 years of age and over and all nonresident minors are required to be licensed to hunt and to have completed a hunter's safety course. (Special licenses are required for hunting with bow and arrow or muzzle loaders.)

Fishing and hunting licenses are sold by town clerks and at some sporting-goods stores. There are precisely stated, strictly enforced seasons and limits for most game, furbearers, freshwater fish, and some saltwater fish. For complete information on licensing and regulations, write: *New Hampshire Fish & Game Dept.,* 2 Hazen Dr., Concord, NH 03301 (603–271–3421).

PARTICIPANT SPORTS. Water sports. The major lakes in the central part of New Hampshire, including Lake Winnipesaukee and Lake Sunapee, have public beaches and boating facilities. The seacoast offers excellent public beaches for saltwater bathing. Sailboat rental and speedboat rides are available at Lake Winnipesaukee, Lake Sunapee, and Newfound Lake. To be used in inland waters, sailboats over 12 feet and all power boats must carry New Hampshire registration. For information: *N.H. Dept. of Safety,* Hazen Drive, Concord, NH 03305 (603–271–3336).

Hiking. An extensive network of marked trails is maintained throughout the state. In the White Mountain National Forest, there is a system of shelters (huts), each a day's hike apart. For general hiking information: Appalachian Mountain Club, Box 298, Gorham, NH 03581 (603–466–2725); or WMNF, Box 638, Laconia, NH 03246 (603–524–6450). The Audubon Society owns or maintains more than 3,000 acres of land in New Hampshire with marked trails and footpaths open to the public. For a free map and brochure: Audubon Society of N.H., 3 Silk Farm Rd., Concord, NH 03301 (603–224–9909).

Golf. Nearly half the 66 golf courses open to the public have 18 holes or more. Information is included in *The Official New Hampshire Guidebook* (see Tourist Information).

Skiing. The ski season begins around Thanksgiving in the higher elevations (reinforced by extensive snowmaking systems), and usually runs through Apr. in the nearly 60 Alpine and cross-country ski areas. For information on skiing in New Hampshire, contact N.H. Office of Vacation Travel or Ski-93, Box 517, Lincoln,

NH 03251 (603–745–8101). For recorded downhill ski reports, call 800–258–3608. For cross-country ski reports, call 800–262–6660.

Snowmobiling (off-highway vehicles). New Hampshire maintains some 4,500 mi. of snowmobile trails. All off-highway recreational vehicles must be registered, for a small fee. These vehicles are not allowed on state park lands, the Appalachian Trail, or the Mt. Washington Auto Road. For further information and trail maps: *Bureau of Off-Highway Vehicles,* Box 856, Concord, NH 03301 (603–271–3254). For recorded snowmobile conditions, call 603–224–4666 or 800–258–3609.

HISTORIC SITES AND HOUSES. The State of New Hampshire maintains several historic sites, including: *Daniel Webster Birthplace,* Rte. 127, Franklin; *Fort Constitution,* Rte. 1B (at U.S. Coast Guard Station), and *Fort Stark,* in New Castle; *Franklin Pierce Homestead* (1804), Rte. 31 at Rte. 9, Hillsborough (603–478–3204); *Robert Frost Farm,* Rte. 28, Derry; *Wentworth-Coolidge Mansion,* Little Harbor Rd., Portsmouth (home of Benning Wentworth, Royal Governor 1741–1767); and *John Wingate Weeks Estate,* off Rte. 3, Lancaster (home of U.S. senator who introduced legislation establishing White Mtn. Natl. Forest).

ARTS AND ENTERTAINMENT. Professional programs in theater, music, and dance are held year-round at the following major performing arts centers: *Arts Center at Brickyard Pond,* Keene State College, Keene, NH 03431 (603–357–4041); *Paul Creative Arts Center,* Univ. of New Hampshire, Durham, NH 03824 (603–862–3712); *Hopkins Center,* Dartmouth College, Hanover, NH 03755 (603–646–2422); and *Palace Theatre,* N.H. Performing Arts Center, 80 Hanover St., Manchester, NH 03105 (603–668–5588). UNH's Paul Center and Dartmouth's Hopkins Center also house marvelous art galleries. For information on upcoming arts, entertainment, and cultural events, call *NH Council on the Arts* (603–271–2789). For a guide to art galleries, museums, craft shops, and studios, call *League of NH Craftsmen* (603–224–1471).

Music. Summer concerts are given in various towns in southwestern New Hampshire by *Monadnock Music,* Box 255, Peterborough, NH 03458 (603–924–7610). Summer concerts in Plymouth and Gilford are sponsored by *New Hampshire Music Festival,* Box 147, Center Harbor, NH 03226 (603–253–4331).

Stage. Summer performances are held at *American Stage Festival,* Milford; *Andy's Summer Playhouse,* Wilton; *Barn Playhouse,* New London; *Eastern Slope Playhouse,* N. Conway; *Hampton Playhouse,* Hampton; *Dartmouth College,* Hanover; *The Old Homestead,* Swanzey Center; *Peterborough Players,* Peterborough; and *Pontine Movement Theater,* Portsmouth.

Film. *Keene State College Film Center* presents classic, foreign, restored, and uncut films. For schedules: KSC Film Center, Drenan Auditorium, Main St., Keene, NH 03431 (603–352–1909).

ACCOMMODATIONS. Travelers to New Hampshire will find rustic lodges, grand resorts, cozy guest houses, and slopeside condos. The establishments listed below are open year-round unless noted otherwise. Room rates do not vary a great deal from season to season, except along the seacoast. Major ski areas have toll-free numbers for lodging reservations. Rates are based on double occupancy: *Deluxe,* $125 and up; *Expensive,* $100–$125; *Moderate,* $75–$100; *Inexpensive,* $75 and under.

Bartlett. Attitash Mountain Village. *Deluxe.* Rte. 302, Bartlett, NH 03812 (603–374–6501 or 800–862–1600). Condominiums and trailside units in a mountain setting. Saunas, fireplaces, indoor pool, laundry, dining room. Beach and tennis in summer, skiing in winter.

Bretton Woods. Mt. Washington Hotel. *Deluxe.* Rte. 302, Bretton Woods, NH 03575 (603–278–1000 or 800–258–0330). Expected to reopen in May 1991 after a $20-million renovation, this grand resort hotel is at the foot of Mt. Washington. Gracious dining (MAP) with nightly entertainment. Tennis, golf, horseback riding, fishing, indoor and outdoor pools. Open May–Oct.

The Lodge at Bretton Woods. *Expensive.* Rte. 302, Bretton Woods, NH 03575 (603–278–1000 or 800–258–0330). Contemporary inn with 50 rooms, indoor pool, spa, and restaurant. Summer guests may use facilities at Mt. Washington Hotel.

Colebrook. Sportsman's Lodge & Cottages. *Expensive.* Big Diamond Lake, Colebrook, NH 03576 (603–237–5211). A quiet, secluded family sporting resort, with lodge rooms or stove-heated cottages. Swimming and boating in summer; hunting, cross-country skiing, and snowmobiling in winter; fresh mountain air year-round.

Dixville Notch. The Balsams. *Deluxe.* Rte. 26, Dixville Notch, NH 03576 (603–255–3400 or 800–255–0600). Spectacular, secluded setting on 15,000 acres high in the White Mountains. Grand resort (American Plan) offers all amenities, a variety of entertainment, and sports activities (including a 27-hole golf course). Superb cuisine at family-style sit-down dinners. Closed Apr. and Nov.

Durham. New England Center. *Expensive.* 15 Strafford Ave., Durham, NH 03824 (603–862–2800). Modern hotel in attractive natural setting at UNH campus. Art gallery on site. Excellent restaurant. Non-smoking rooms available.

Exeter. Exeter Inn. *Moderate–Expensive.* 90 Front St., Exeter, NH 03833 (603–772–5901 or 800–782–8444). Cordial, relaxing atmosphere in Georgian Inn at Phillips Exeter Academy. Traditional dining. A landmark for over 50 years.

Fitzwilliam. Fitzwilliam Inn. *Inexpensive.* Jct. Rtes. 12 & 119, Fitzwilliam, NH 03447 (603–585–9000). Dating back to 1796 as a stagecoach stop, this inn on the Village Green exudes Early American atmosphere. Pool and sauna are 20th-century additions. Award-winning restaurant.

Franconia. Lovett's Inn by Lafayette Brook. *Expensive–Deluxe.* Profile Rd., Rte. 18, Franconia, NH 03580 (603–823–7761 or 800–356–3802). This historic inn dates from 1784. Variety of rooms in inn and cottages, some with fireplaces or kitchenettes. Gourmet dining, game room, swimming pool. Spectacular views of Cannon Mt. Summer package plans. MAP available. Closed Apr.

Franconia Inn. *Moderate–Expensive.* Easton Rd., Rte. 116, Franconia, NH 03580 (603–823–5542). Rustic New England inn. Complete resort facilities include tennis courts, riding stable, pool, soaring, six golf courses nearby, cross-country skiing center in winter. Continental cuisine in dining room. Family suites available. Closed Apr., May, and Nov.

Hampton Beach. Ashworth by the Sea. *Expensive.* 295 Ocean Blvd., Rtes. 1A & 51, Hampton Beach, NH 03842 (603–926–6762). Oceanfront resort with superb accommodations, heated pool, and sandy beach. Good seafood restaurant.

Hanover. Hanover Inn. *Deluxe.* Main and Wheelock Sts., Hanover, NH 03755 (603–643–4300 or 800–443–7024). Dartmouth-run, 200-year-old inn perfectly located on the Green. Comfortable rooms with Colonial decor; first-rate dining. Golf and skiing packages available.

Holderness. The Manor on Golden Pond. *Expensive–Deluxe.* Rte. 3, Holderness, NH 03245 (603–968–3348 or 800–545–2141). This is an elegant country estate on Squam Lake. English manor house and cottages. Tennis, pool, lake swimming, and boating.

Jackson. Christmas Farm Inn. *Expensive–Deluxe.* Rte. 16B, Jackson, NH 03846 (603–383–4313). Resort village, surrounded by national forest, with rooms in historic (1786) main inn, salt box, barn, log cabin, and cottages. Fireplaces, a cozy lounge, reading and living rooms, and a full-menu dining room. Family atmosphere.

Wentworth Resort Hotel. *Expensive.* Rte. 16A, Jackson, NH 03846 (603–383–9700) or 800–637–0013). Gracious, restored hotel. Tastefully furnished guest rooms overlook Jackson Falls and the White Mtns. Dining room, 18-hole PGA golf course, pool, and tennis.

Jaffrey. The Monadnock Inn. *Moderate.* Main St., Jaffrey Ctr., NH 03452 (603–532–7001). This is a typically attractive New England inn, with rocking chairs on the wide front porch, in a beautiful village at the foot of Mt. Monadnock. Fine dining, too.

Laconia. The Margate Resort at Winnipesaukee. *Expensive–Deluxe.* 76 Lake St., Laconia, NH 03246 (603–524–5210 or 800–258–0304). Luxurious accommodations at lakeside full-service hotel. Sandy beach, indoor and outdoor pools, tennis, health club. Pleasant restaurant.

Lincoln. The Mountain Club on Loon. *Expensive–Deluxe.* Kancamagus Hwy., Lincoln, NH 03251 (603–745–8111 or 800–433–3413). Modern hotel rooms located at the foot of Loon Mt. Skiing at the door; tennis, swimming, andplay area in summer. Good restaurant and lounge; health club. Package plans available.

Lyme. Loch Lyme Lodge & Cottages. *Moderate.* Rte. 10, Lyme, NH 03768 (603–795–2141). 18th-century farmhouse and 26 cottages on unspoiled Post Pond. Cabins with fireplaces in spring and summer; lodge accommodations in fall and winter. Pond swimming, boating and fishing, tennis and lawn sports; cross-country skiing, skating, and ice fishing. Weekly rates available.

New London. New London Inn. *Expensive.* Main St., New London, NH 03257 (603–526–2791). Attractive Colonial inn (1792) in center of town. Warm New England hospitality. Near skiing, lakes, golf. Restaurant; full breakfast included.

North Conway. Fox Ridge Resort. *Deluxe.* Rte. 16, N. Conway, NH 03860 (603–356–3151 or 800–343–1804). This is a full-service resort on 300 acres at the forest's edge. Excellent for family vacations: close to White Mt. attractions and about a mile from Mt. Cranmore. Indoor pool, spa, game room, restaurant and lounge. Package plans.

Stonehurst Manor. *Expensive–Deluxe.* Rte. 16, N. Conway, NH 03860 (603–356–3271 or 800–525–9100). Converted turn-of-the-century mansion, this 25-room English-style country inn is full of old oak and stained glass. Gourmet dining; swimming pool, tennis, and some kitchenettes. No credit cards.

North Woodstock. The Woodstock Inn. *Inexpensive–Moderate.* Box 118, Rte. 3, N. Woodstock, NH 03262 (603–745–3951). A lovely, 100-year-old Victorian home restored and attractively decorated with antiques. Porch dining. Ski package plans; free shuttle service to Loon Mt. Full breakfast included.

Portsmouth. Sise Inn. *Expensive–Deluxe.* 40 Court St., Portsmouth, NH 03801 (603–433–1200). In the historic district this Queen Anne house (1881) turned country inn, the luxurious rooms and suites are decorated in Victorian style, but with up-to-date amenities. Short walk to shops, dining, and waterfront. Complimentary breakfast.

Inn at Christian Shore. *Moderate.* 335 Maplewood Ave., Portsmouth, NH 03801 (603–431–6770). Federal period (1800) home with period furnishings. Full-course breakfast included. Walk to town. No children under 12. No credit cards.

Whitefield. Spalding Inn Club. *Deluxe.* Mt. View Rd., off Rte. 3, Whitefield, NH 03598 (603–837–2572). A handsome 20th-century inn and deluxe cottages with golf, tennis, lawn games, and heated pool on 500 acres in the White Mountains. Superb dining, wine cellar. (AP) Open June–mid-Oct.

Wolfeboro. Pick Point Lodge & Cottages. *Expensive–Deluxe.* Box 220, Mirror Lake, NH 03853 (603–569–1338). On a knoll 150 feet from Lake Winnipesaukee, the lodge and housekeeping cottages are set in a 70-acre pine forest. Small and informal, private and secluded. Half-mile beach, boating and fishing, tennis, nature walks. Weekly rates. Open late May–late Oct.

BED AND BREAKFASTS. For listings of bed-and-breakfast inns in New Hampshire: *Traditional Bed & Breakfast Assn. of New Hampshire,* Box 575, RFD 5, 83 Old Lake Shore Rd., Gilford, NH 03246 (603–528–1172).

HOSTELS. American Youth Hostels are located in Peterborough (603–924–9832) and Randolph (603–466–5130).

RESTAURANTS. The restaurants suggested below offer settings and dining experiences from rustic to cozy to quite grand. All are open year-round, serve both lunch and dinner, and accept major credit cards unless noted. The average price per person for a complete dinner: *Deluxe:* $35 and up; *Expensive:* $25–$35; *Moderate:* $15–$25; *Inexpensive:* $15 and under.

Bretton Woods. Darby's Tavern. *Expensive.* Rte. 302 (603–278–1500). In Lodge at Bretton Woods; fireplaces and mountain vistas. Fine Continental dining. B also.

Concord. B. Mae Denny's (City Edition). *Moderate–Expensive.* Depot Sq. (603–225–3536). Attractive and informal. Greenhouse dining. Steaks, seafood, homemade breads and pastries. Sun. brunch.

Conway/N. Conway. Stonehurst Manor. *Deluxe.* Rte. 16, N. Conway (603–356–3271). Elegant, turn-of-the-century mansion; superb gourmet dining. D only.

Darby Field Inn. *Expensive.* Bald Hill Rd., off Rte. 16, Conway (603–447–2181). Secluded country inn with spectacular view and superb meals. Daily specials.

Dover. Newick's Lobster House. *Inexpensive–Moderate.* 431 Dover Pt. Rd. (603–742–3205). On the New England seacoast, lobster and other fresh seafood are always a best bet. Informal outdoor dining in summer. Closed Mon.

Exeter. Exeter Inn. *Expensive.* 90 Front St. (603–772–5901). The restaurant of this inn on the Phillips Exeter Academy campus has maintained a cordial atmosphere for over 50 years. Specialties are steak and seafood. Breakfast also served.

Franconia. Lovett's Inn. *Deluxe.* Rte. 18 at Rte. 141 (603–823–7761). Gracious dining in an attractive country inn. Excellent Continental cuisine; veal, lamb, broiled seafood. Reservations requested. B, D only. Closed Apr.

Gilford. Gunstock Inn. *Moderate–Expensive.* Rte. 11A (603–293–2021). Candlelight dining in an attractive inn overlooking Lake Winnipesaukee and the mountains. Traditional American and Continental fare.

Glen. The Bernerhof Inn. *Expensive.* Rte. 302 (603–383–4414). Superb Central European cuisine and contemporary menu offerings blend well at this chef-owned turn-of-the-century inn with Alpine styling. A Taste of the Mountains Cooking School courses are offered seasonally for both novices and serious cooks.

Hampton Beach. Ashworth by the Sea. *Expensive.* 295 Ocean Blvd. (603–926–6762). Premier seacoast restaurant; seafood, lobster, steaks. Superb service. B also.

Hanover. Daniel Webster Room. *Expensive.* Main and Wheelock sts. (603–643–4300). The dining room of the Hanover Inn, owned and operated by Dartmouth College and located on the College Green, serves classic New England favorites with a dash of contemporary flavorings. Reservations advised.

Peter Christian's. *Moderate.* 39 S. Main St. (603–643–2345). Handcarved booths and rugged stoneware set the mood for steaming stews and soups, cheese boards, hefty sandwiches, and homemade desserts. No smoking.

Jackson. The Plum Room. *Deluxe.* At Wentworth Resort Hotel, Rte. 16A (603–383–9700). Innovative menu includes superb Continental cuisine and traditional American selections. D only. Reservations required.

Keene. Henry David's. *Inexpensive–Moderate.* 81 Main St. (603–352–0608). Lots of greenery and inspired fare are the best links to this bistro's namesake. Thoreau might have approved the savory soups and meal-size salads—even the exciting entrees—but he would have definitely drawn the line at the "decadent desserts."

Laconia. Hickory Stick Farm. *Moderate.* 2 mi. from Jct. Rtes. 3 & 11 (603–524–3333). Colonial farm building furnished with antiques. Delicious New England fare; roast duckling the specialty. Children's menu. D only. Reservations required. Closed Mon. Open May–Oct.

Lincoln. Woodward's Open Hearth Steak House. *Moderate.* Rte. 3 (603–745–8141). Char-broiled steaks, chops, prime rib, lobster, seafood. Family breakfast menu. Closed Apr.–May and Nov.–Dec.

Lyme. D'Artagnan. *Expensive.* Rte. 10, north of Hanover (603–795–2137). French country cuisine accompanied by a crisp air of elegance. Prix fixe menu; flawless service; chef-owned. Reservations required. L Sun. only; D Wed.–Sun.

Meredith. Hart's Turkey Farm. *Moderate.* Jct. Rtes. 3 & 104 (603–279–6212). Family-style dinners; turkey, prime rib, steaks, and seafood. Home baking. Closed Tues., Wed. in winter.

Moultonborough. Sweetwater Inn. *Moderate.* Rte. 25 (603–476–5079). For a change of pace in this land of clapboard and chowder, tempt the palate with "nouvelle" treatments of homemade pasta, Spanish paella, and other flavorful dishes. Reservations advised.

Nashua. Levi Lowell's. *Expensive.* 585 Daniel Webster Hwy. (603–429–0885). Fireplaces, quiet music, and antiques set the tone here for superb Continental dining. Beef Wellington is a specialty. Jackets required at dinner.

North Woodstock. Truants Taverne. *Inexpensive–Moderate.* Main St., Jct. Rtes. 3 & 12. (603–745–2239). Rustic schoolhouse decor. Outstanding sandwiches and various dinner entrees.

Portsmouth. Blue Strawbery. *Deluxe.* 29 Ceres St. (603–431–6420). Look forward to a delectable American gourmet dining experience in Portsmouth's harbor area—a six-course, *prix fixe* dinner, by reservation only.

Strawbery Court Restaurant Francais. *Deluxe.* 20 Atkinson St. (603–431–7722). Two small dining rooms in a 19th-century Federal-style townhouse are the settings for classic French cuisine. Prix fixe menu. Closed Sun., Mon.

Waterville Valley. Carnevale's Ristorante. *Moderate.* Rte. 49, Waterville Valley Rd., Thornton (603–726–3618). Pretend you're in the Italian Alps while enjoying Northern Italian cuisine and regional American selections here in the White Mountains. Home-baked breads and desserts; outdoor dining in season. Closed Mon., Apr.–May, Nov.

LIQUOR LAWS. In New Hampshire, minimum age for the purchase or consumption of alcohol is 21. Bottled liquor is sold only at stores operated by the State Liquor Commission. All stores are open Mon.–Sat.; some remain open Sun. and some holidays. By local option, beer, ale, and wine may be sold in drugstores and grocery stores. Alcoholic beverages are sold by the drink at licensed hotels, restaurants, and clubs.

VERMONT

The rolling hills and mountains of Vermont set the stage for a particular way of life. Time has not exactly stopped here, but the naturally unhurried pace, strong rural tradition, and independent ways of Vermonters augment the pastoral landscape, making Vermont quite different from most other parts of the country.

Lacking a coast, and with boundary disputes on all sides, Vermont was settled later than its New England neighbors. It also lacked a wealthy aris-

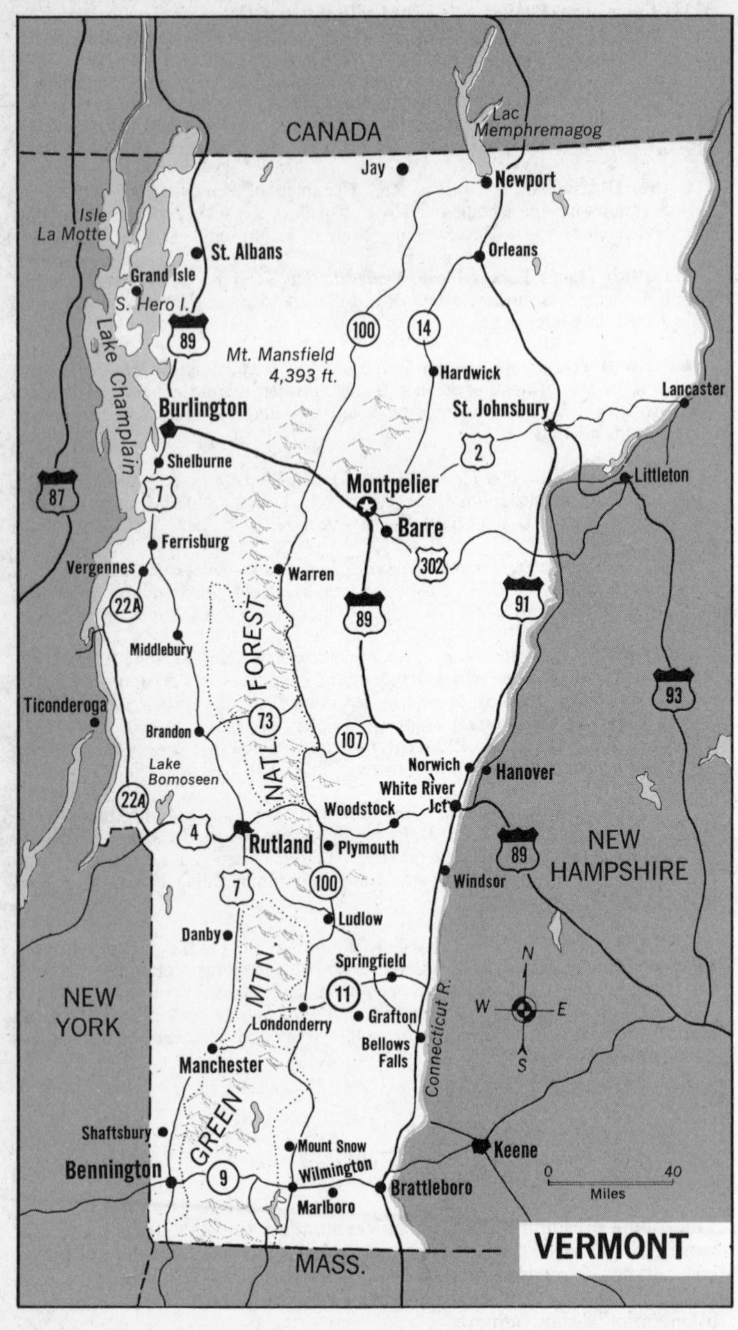

CANADA
Lac Memphremagog
Jay
Newport
Isle La Motte
St. Albans
Orleans
Grand Isle
S. Hero I.
Lake Champlain
89
100
14
Mt. Mansfield 4,393 ft.
Hardwick
Burlington
St. Johnsbury
Lancaster
2
Shelburne
Littleton
87
7
Montpelier
Barre
Ferrisburg
Vergennes
302
Warren
22A
89
91
Middlebury
NATL. FOREST
93
Ticonderoga
Brandon
73
107
Lake Bomoseen
Norwich
Hanover
White River Jct
22A
Woodstock
4
Rutland
Plymouth
NEW HAMPSHIRE
89
Windsor
7
100
Ludlow
Danby
GREEN MTN.
Springfield
N
NEW YORK
11
W
E
S
Grafton
Connecticut R.
Londonderry
Bellows Falls
Manchester
Shaftsbury
Mount Snow
Keene
Bennington
9
Wilmington
Brattleboro
0
40
Miles
Marlboro
VERMONT
MASS.

tocracy, enabling the settlements to be formed in a purely democratic way. Universal manhood suffrage was adopted from the earliest days, and pure democracy continues to this day in towns and villages throughout Vermont. The population is still small enough to permit the town-meeting form of government, where each tax-paying citizen is entitled to a voice and a vote. Conservative in nature, Vermonters have been traditionally opposed to any form of federal intervention in their affairs or any constraints on their individual voices.

Wedge-shaped, not quite the observe of neighboring New Hampshire, Vermont is about 157 miles long, north to south. It is about 90 miles wide along its northern border with Canada, tapering to only 42 miles in width along its southern border with Massachusetts. Though Vermont is the only New England state with no relation to the sea, 490-square-mile Lake Champlain forms almost 120 miles of Vermont's western border with New York; in the east, the peaceful Connecticut River forms a common border with New Hampshire.

The Green Mountains are the dominant physical feature of the state, forming its north–south spine. Much of the terrain is rugged and heavily wooded, and there are limited areas of arable land. The foothills and river valleys have proven suitable for grazing, making dairy farming and horse breeding important occupations. (The hardy Morgan horse was developed in Vermont.) Over the years, the resourceful Vermonters have put the abundant supply of native maples to use, tapping the trees at "sugaring time" in early spring and boiling down the sap to the maple syrup and maple sugar products for which Vermont has become famous.

With a population of only about 548,000 in its 9,600 square miles, Vermont is the least densely populated of the New England states, with half the number of people in equal-sized New Hampshire or in tiny Rhode Island. Burlington, home of the University of Vermont, is the only town with a population over 25,000.

Samuel de Champlain, in 1609, was the first European to reach the remote wilderness of Vermont, then an Indian hunting ground. The first French settlement, Fort St. Anne, was established in 1666 on Isle La Motte in Lake Champlain. Constant bloody battles between the French and the Iroquois Indians caused the abandonment of this French military outpost. The region remained a virtual no-man's-land until well into the 18th century. By 1724, English settlers began to push north from Massachusetts. Fort Dummer, the first permanent settlement in Vermont, was established in what is now Brattleboro to protect the settlers from Indian raids.

Boundary disputes persisted for the next 50 years between New York and New Hampshire, both colonies claiming the Vermont territory as their own. Interest in settling the dispute waned as the French and Indian War began (1754). When finally referred to the British Crown for settlement, in 1764, New York's claim was upheld. Land speculators holding New Hampshire land grants were up in arms, literally, over their now worthless claims. Under the leadership of Ethan Allen, a group of Vermonters called the "Green Mountain Boys" resisted New York's authority by creating local havoc.

When the American Revolution began in 1775, Allen and the "Boys" captured Fort Ticonderoga, proclaiming the Vermont territory an independent state. The Continental Congress refused to recognize Vermont as a state because of New York's opposition. Vermont, in turn, reaffirmed its independence and adopted a constitution (the first to specifically outlaw slavery). It remained a sovereign government until 1791. Settling the New York claim with a payment of $30,000, Vermont entered the union as the fourteenth state.

Population began to increase with statehood. But with the opening of the western United States, Vermont's grain farming and cattle ranching all but disappeared. Sheep replaced the cattle, supplying wool for New

England's textile mills; yet the rural population declined after the Civil War.

Present-day Vermont still has 3,285 active farms; and the manufacturing of textiles, electronic equipment, and wood products contributes to the economy. But Vermonters have turned to their mountains for renewed prosperity. Quarrying marble and Vermont granite from the rocky ledges continues, and "Vermont" and "skiing" have become almost synonymous. In the 1920s, Stowe was the first ski resort in the eastern United States. Today there are 24 alpine ski areas, nearly 50 ski touring centers, and 1,500 miles of snowmobile trails in the Green Mountain State. Modern condominium villages at many of Vermont's famous ski resorts present an interesting dichotomy of past and future when contrasted with the historic greens of adjacent 19th-century hamlets.

Tourism has become vitally important, the state's second-largest industry after manufacturing. Traveling by car, bicycle, canoe, or even by foot is a pleasure in this beautiful state. The major highway networks, running north–south along the river valleys, are crisscrossed by secondary byways. These backroads wind through mountain villages every few miles, where travelers can stop for lunch or browse in local craft or antique shops. Highway billboards have been outlawed to protect the pastoral landscape.

Vermont's countryside is visually intoxicating. Pastures are lush and green in summer, the hills dotted with hayfields, dairy farms, and grazing horses. The air is clean and crisp, scented only by an occasional whiff of new-mown hay.

The brilliant autumn foliage in New England is world renowned, but Vermont is special. Calendar-print villages with white church spires pointing skyward seem to lie around every turn. Add a covered bridge or two, and all that's needed is a crisp apple, some sweet cider, or a perfect pumpkin.

Heavy snows generally cover the ground three full months of the year, when those hundreds of thousands of skiers flock to the mountains. Roads are kept well plowed and sanded, allowing access even to remote areas.

As winter turns to spring, the sap begins to run in the maple trees—and it's "sugaring time." Millions of trees are tapped for the annual harvest, for it requires the output of about four trees to produce one gallon of maple syrup. Many sugarhouses are open to visitors.

The Green Mountain National Forest, 293,376 wooded acres in central and southern Vermont, offers an extensive variety of outdoor recreation experiences. Twelve of Vermont's leading ski areas are within the Forest, including Mt. Snow, Bromley, Sugarbush, and Stratton. Summer camping, hunting, hiking on the 263-mile Long Trail, fishing in countless ponds and streams, and scenic drives add to the enjoyment of communing with nature. Vermont's state parks and forests, wildlife sanctuaries, beaches, and recreation areas offer opportunities for public swimming and boating, camping, hiking, skiing and snowmobiling, or mountain climbing on 4,393-foot Mt. Mansfield (highest mountain in the state).

Man-made attractions exist as well: aerial rides up mountains or alpine slides down during the off-season, a cruise or a ferry crossing Lake Champlain, or a ride on a vintage train provide family fun. There are museums of all kinds, historic sites and battlefields, homes of two U.S. presidents to visit, and country fairs, harvest festivals, and auctions to attend. Vermont's fine educational institutions make a cultural contribution by presenting musical and theatrical productions, art and craft exhibits, all open to the public.

Visitors won't find much glitter in Vermont—other than a neon light or two in Burlington. Vermonters like it that way. Strict state statutes preceded federal legislation to protect the land and the environment for the health of the residents, to inhibit overdevelopment, and to preserve the natural beauty of the Green Mountain State.

PRACTICAL INFORMATION FOR VERMONT

WHEN TO GO. Hundreds of thousands of tourists descend on Vermont each fall to view the spectacular work of Mother Nature. The exploding colors of the foliage begin to peak in the far north in mid-Sept., moving gradually through the state as the days grow shorter. The phenomenon is usually over by mid-Oct. The state gets mobbed with throngs of people, so try to travel mid-week and be sure to make advance reservations.

Skiing brings many winter vacationers to Vermont. The season can begin as early as Oct. in the higher elevations (Killington and Sugarbush), but generally is underway by Thanksgiving and continues through Apr. Vermont winters are cold and snowy, with temperatures in mid-winter hovering in the single digits and teens.

Summers are comfortably warm in Vermont; hot, humid days are rare. Summer visitors are attracted by Vermont's unhurried pace and opportunities for hiking and camping.

Spring is maple sugaring time. Tourists are welcome to visit sugarhouses to watch maple syrup being made. But beware of early spring, when mud season plays havoc with country dirt roads.

HOW TO GET THERE. By plane. Burlington International Airport is served by *Business Express/Delta Connection* (800–221–1212), *Continental* (800–525–0280), *Northwest* (800–225–2525), *Trans-World Express* (800–221–2000), *United* (800–241–6522), and *USAir* (800–428–4322). Other gateways to Vermont for air travelers include Albany, Boston, Hartford, and Montreal. Commuter service is available to Montpelier, Rutland, and Springfield (at Hartness).

By bus. *Vermont Transit* (800–451–3292) has daily service connecting with *Greyhound* from New York City, Boston, and Montreal to points throughout Vermont.

By train. *Amtrak's "Montrealer"* stops at Brattleboro, Bellows Falls, White River Jct., Montpelier, Waterbury, Essex Jct., and St. Albans on its daily round-trip between Washington, D.C., and Montreal (via New York City). For information, contact Amtrak (800–872–7245).

By car. I-91 from Connecticut and Massachusetts goes directly north to Vermont and continues along the eastern border of the state to Canada. Exits off I-87 in New York lead to Rte. 7 and east to Bennington; to Rte. 4 and Rutland; to Rte. 4, then north on Rtes. 22A and 7 to Burlington. From Boston, I-93 connects with I-89 in Concord NH; I-89 continues to White River Jct. From Canada, Rtes. 10 and 133 from Montreal to the Vermont border connect with I-89 north of Burlington; from Quebec City, Rtes. 20 and 55 bring you to Vermont's northeast border and I-91.

By boat. Passenger/auto ferries operate across Lake Champlain: *Lake Champlain Transportation Co.,* King St. Dock, Burlington, VT 05401 (802–864–9804), operates between Cumberland Head, NY and Grand Isle, VT (year-round); between Port Kent, NY and Burlington (mid-May–Oct.); and between Essex, NY and Charlotte, VT (Apr. ice-out–Nov.). *Shorewell Ferry* (802–897–7999) operates between Ticonderoga, NY and Larrabee's Point, VT (year-round).

TOURIST INFORMATION. Travelers to Vermont may request vacation information from: *Vermont Travel Division,* 134 State St., Montpelier, VT 05602 (802–828–3236); and *New England Vacation Center,* Shop #2, Concourse Level, 630 Fifth Ave., New York, NY 10111 (212–307–5780).

The *Vermont Chamber of Commerce,* (Exit 7, I-89), Box 37, Montpelier, VT 05601 (802–223–3443), will provide a complete listing of member lodgings, restaurants, and attractions. In addition, the local chamber of commerce in the town or area in which you are interested will provide information upon request.

Vermont maps and vacation guides are available daily at highway Welcome Centers situated on I-91 at the Massachusetts border, on I-89 at the Canadian border, on I-93 at the New Hampshire border, and on Rte. 4A at the New York border.

TELEPHONES. The area code for all of Vermont is 802. To direct dial a long-distance or toll-free (800) number, dial 1 before the area code. For operator assistance on person-to-person, credit card, or collect calls, dial 0 before the area code.

For directory assistance, dial 1–555–1212 for all Vermont numbers. Local calls from a pay phone in Vermont generally cost 10 cents for 3 minutes.

EMERGENCY TELEPHONE NUMBERS. Consult a local directory or dial 0 for emergency assistance. For 24-hr. medical and emergency health information: *Burlington Medical Center* (802–864–0454); for 24-hr. poison control information: 802–658–3456; for weather: National Weather Service (802–862–2475).

HOW TO GET AROUND. By plane. General aviation facilities and air-taxi service are available at airports throught Vermont.

By bus. *Vermont Transit* has bus routes throughout the state. For information: 802–862–9671, 800–322–0428 in VT, or 800–451–3292 in New England and NY.

By car. I-91 extends the length of the state, following the Connecticut River along most of the state's eastern border to Canada. I-89 divides the state roughly in half, from White River Jct. northwest through Montpelier and Burlington to the Canadian border. U.S. Rte. 7 in western Vermont, and Rte. 100 in central Vermont, are scenic north–south routes.

By rental car. Car rental firms are located at airports and in the larger towns in Vermont.

HINTS TO MOTORISTS. An extensive travel information system is in place in Vermont for motorists. Official business directional signs are located just before appropriate road junctions. Travel information listings, including sightseeing, recreation, and services, are posted at rest plazas on major Vermont highways and at other key locations.

Unless otherwise posted, speed limits on Interstate highways in Vermont are: maximum 65 mph, minimum 40 mph; on all other highways, maximum 50 mph. Safety restraints are required for children under four years of age.

For information on highway conditions, especially in winter, call Vermont Transportation Agency, 802–828–2648.

The Official Vermont State Map, available at Welcome Centers and from the Vermont Travel Division (see Tourist Information), is kept up-to-date and includes a variety of helpful touring information.

HINTS TO DISABLED TRAVELERS. The Vermont Travelers Guidebook, available from Vermont Chamber of Commerce (see Tourist Information), lists lodgings, restaurants, shops, and attractions and indicates many that have facilities for the handicapped. All campgrounds and day-use areas in state parks have been retrofitted to accommodate handicapped visitors.

TOURS AND SPECIAL-INTEREST SIGHTSEEING. Fall foliage. Vermont's countryside is spectacular when the colors turn. The Vermont Travel Division operates a 24-hour hotline (802–828–3239) Sept.–Oct. that suggests the most colorful scenic routes.

Covered bridges. More than 100 of Vermont's covered bridges are indicated on the Official Vermont Map (available from the VT Travel Division). The largest groupings are in Lamoille County, east of Burlington, and in Orange County, crossing central Vermont's White River.

Bicycle touring. Several professional bicycle touring organizations operate trips from May–Oct. for all abilities. Bicycles are available for rent. Arrangements may include accommodations at a country inn, with daily guided tours, or may include inn-to-inn cross-country touring. The Vermont Travelers' Guidebook (available from VT Travel Division and Vermont Chamber of Commerce) provides a listing of bicycle touring organizations. Or contact: *Vermont Bicycle Touring,* Box 711, Bristol, VT 05443 (802–453–4811); or *Bike VT,* Box 207, Woodstock, VT 05091 (802–457–3553).

Farms and sugarhouses. The world-famous *UVM Morgan Horse Farm,* in Middlebury (802–388–2011) is open to visitors May–Oct. Several farms (mostly dairy farms) welcome visitors to see the animals and watch the daily operations. Some farms operate maple sugarhouses, which are open to visitors to observe sugaring operations and to purchase maple products. "Farm Vacations," a list of participating farms, and "Maple Sugarhouses Open to Visitors," a list of farms with sugaring operations, are available from Vermont Travel Division (see Tourist Information).

Mountain rides. In summer, gondola rides at Killington and Stowe and the tram ride at Jay Peak operate for sightseers. Alpine slides, especially thrilling for kids, are at Bromley, Stowe's Spruce Peak, and Pico near Rutland. Or take the auto road to the top of Mt. Mansfield, in Stowe, or the Mt. Equinox Skyline Drive, in Sunderland.

Balloons, boats, and trains. *Stowe Aviation,* Morrisville (802–888–7845) offers thrilling glider or balloon rides high above Vermont. Three ferries (see How To Get There above) and the sternwheeler *Spirit of Ethan Allen* (802–862–8300) out of Burlington ply the waters of Lake Champlain. *Lamoille Valley Railroad,* Morrisville (802–888–4255) and *Green Mountain Railroad,* Bellows Falls (802–463–3069), have scenic train rides on restored vintage coaches (special fall foliage trips).

Quarries. *Rock of Ages Quarry,* off Exit 6 of I-89, Barre (802–476–3115), is the world's largest monumental granite quarry. *Vermont Marble Co.,* Main St., Proctor (802–459–3311), is a production center for marble. Both have tours, exhibits, and a chance to watch artisans at work. Open daily May–Oct.

Factory outlets. Vermont has several, with products ranging from woodenware and name-brand clothing to maple sugar and Vermont cheddar. For a listing of outlets, contact Vermont Chamber of Commerce (see Tourist Information).

Antiquing. A popular pastime for visitors to Vermont is browsing through antique stores. A member directory, including a coded map, is available from: *Vermont Antiques Dealers' Assn.,* 55 Allen St., Rutland, VT 05701.

NATIONAL FOREST. In central and southern Vermont, the U.S. Forest Service (Federal Building, 151 West St., Rutland, VT 05701, 802–773–0300), manages the **Green Mountain National Forest,** nearly 300,000 acres of wilderness and recreation area that includes 130 mi. of the Appalachian Trail and Long Trail. Campsites are available at 7 areas in the Forest. Hunting and fishing are permitted in season. Ranger stations are located in Manchester Center, Middlebury, and Rochester.

STATE PARKS. The *Vermont Dept. of Forests, Parks and Recreation,* Waterbury, VT 05676 (802–244–8711), manages about 200,000 acres of public land, including 45 state parks and forest recreation areas. Campgrounds are available at 34 locations, and many parks have nature walks and programs organized by a resident naturalist. Day-use areas generally have hiking trails, beaches with lifeguards, boat launches and boat rentals, toilet and changing facilities, picnic sites, and snack bars. Cross-country skiing, snowmobiling, hunting, and fishing are permitted in Vermont state forests (hunting is prohibited near developed recreation areas, however). State parks are generally open from Memorial Day to Labor Day, with some open earlier and some later depending on weather conditions.

CAMPING. The State of Vermont operates 34 campgrounds with 2,200 campsites. Most campgrounds open Memorial Day weekend and close after Labor Day weekend, although some open earlier and close later as weather permits. Reservations will be honored if accompanied by advance payment of the nominal camping fee ($7.50 and up). All campgrounds have a resident ranger, water, and sanitary facilities. Campsites include a fireplace and picnic table; some have lean-tos. The State also operates year-round (except Nov.) camping areas for supervised groups and designates certain lands for primitive camping. For information: Vermont Dept. of Forests, Parks and Recreation, Waterbury, VT 05676 (802–244–8711).

The U.S. Forest Service allows camping at seven designated sites in the Green Mountain National Forest. Wilderness camping is also allowed, but a permit is required. For specific information on these areas: Forest Supervisor, Green Mountain National Forest, Federal Building, 151 West St., Rutland, VT 05701 (802–773–0300).

Vermont Association of Private Campground Owners and Operators (VAPCOO) publishes a free annual listing of its members and the facilities and services offered at each campground. Advance reservations are recommended and should be made directly to the campground. Write: VAPCOO, Silver Lake Family Campground, Barnard, VT 05031.

FISHING AND HUNTING. In Vermont's lakes, ponds, and streams, bass, northern pike, walleyes, and panfish lure warmwater anglers; coldwater fishermen go for landlocked salmon and trophy-sized trout. Fishing season runs mid-Apr.–Oct., although fishing for some varieties is permitted year-round. Licenses are required for all persons 16 years of age and over; they are available from all town or city clerks, at many general stores, and at sporting goods stores.

Tracts of open land for public hunting have been set aside by the State. Strict limits and seasonal regulations apply to hunting deer, other game animals, and game birds. Licenses are available from town or city clerks, or by writing the Fish & Wildlife Dept. Nonresident hunters must present a previous or current license from another state or province or a certificate showing completion of an approved hunter safety course.

For a copy of *The Vermont Guide to Fishing* and *The Vermont Guide to Hunting* (which detail species available and public areas open to sportsmen) and the *Digest of Fish & Wildlife Regulations* (which outlines seasons, bag limits, and exceptions), write: Vermont Fish & Wildlife Dept., 103 S. Main St., Waterbury, VT 05676.

PARTICIPANT SPORTS. Skiing. Vermont is renowned for its downhill skiing. Some 24 alpine ski areas are concentrated in this small state. Snowmaking systems and careful trail grooming provide consistent skiing conditions from Thanksgiving until June in some areas. Cross-country ski touring is increasingly appealing, with nearly 50 centers offering groomed trails and machine-set tracks. Inn-to-inn ski touring provides a memorable vacation experience. Ski touring is permitted in state and national parks and forests, but trails are not groomed or patrolled. For more information on skiing in Vermont: Vermont Ski Areas Assoc., 26 State St., Montpelier, VT 05602 (802–223–2439). For snow conditions, call 24-hr. Vermont Snowline Report (Nov.–June): alpine (802–229–0531); cross-country (802–828–3236).

Snowmobiling. The Vermont Association of Snow Travelers (VAST), an association of community snowmobiling clubs, maintain more than 3,700 mi. of marked, groomed snowmobile trails. Nonresidents must register their machines in Vermont and join a local club to operate on the VAST trail system. For information: VAST, Box 839, Montpelier, VT 05602 (802–229–0005).

Hiking. The Appalachian Trail and the Long Trail follow the same route north through the Green Mountains from Vermont's southwestern border to the Sherburne Pass, east of Rutland. There the Appalachian Trail turns east to New Hampshire and Maine; Long Trail heads north to Canada. Access to both trails is available at frequent intervals, and shelters are available for hikers' convenience. Marked trails can also be found at most state parks and national forest areas. For hiking information: *Green Mountain Club, Inc.,* Box 889, Montpelier, VT 05602 (802–223–3463). *Vermont Hiking Holidays,* Box 750, Bristol, VT 05443 (802–453–4816) arranges inn-to-inn hiking tours.

Boating. Lake Champlain, with 120 mi. of Vermont shoreline, is the favorite boating area. There are also over 400 smaller lakes and ponds and miles of rivers for boating of all kinds. Stretches of major rivers are ideal for canoeing, white-water kayaking, and rafting. Rental canoes and rowboats are available at most state parks. Public launch areas are available to boaters; however, recreational boaters are warned that "Fishing Access Areas" are to be used by licensed fishermen only. Information on laws and regulations governing the use and registration of motorboats is available from: Vermont Dept. of Public Safety, Marine Division, Waterbury, VT 05676.

Bicycling. Lush vistas, picturesque towns, and relatively low traffic volume make bicycling very popular on Vermont's scenic roads, for individual day trips and as part of a bicycle tour. Extra caution should be taken on mountainous or narrow, winding routes. Bicyclists should wear highly visible clothing and travel single file.

Golf. The rolling terrain and the temperate summer climate make golfing in Vermont challenging and enjoyable. There are 38 golf courses open to the public: 13 are 18-hole courses, the rest are 9 holes, except Stratton, with 27 holes. Locations are listed on the Official Vermont Map. There are additional private courses available to guests at certain resorts and lodges.

HISTORIC SITES AND HOUSES. Eager to preserve Vermont's heritage, the state owns and maintains the following historic sites: *Hyde Log Cabin* (1783), U.S. 2, Grand Isle; *Bennington Battle Monument,* Rte. 9, Old Bennington; *President Chester A. Arthur's Birthplace,* off Rte. 36 or 108, Fairfield; *President Calvin Coo-*

lidge's Homestead, Rte. 100A, Plymouth Union (802–672–3773). For further information on state-owned or privately operated historic sites, consult: Vermont Travel Division (see Tourist Information) or Division for Historic Preservation, Montpelier, VT 05602 (802–828–3226).

MUSEUMS. There are nearly 30 major museums in Vermont which display art, wildlife, scientific, or historical exhibits for the entertainment and education of Vermont's residents and visitors. For example: *The Bennington Museum,* Rte. 9, Bennington (802–447–1571) (early Americana, American glass, Bennington pottery); *Billings Farm & Museum,* Rte. 12, Woodstock (802–457–2355) (19th-century working farm, exhibits); *Fairbanks Museum & Planetarium,* 83 Main St., St. Johnsbury (802–748–2372) (natural history and astronomy); *Robert Hull Fleming Museum,* Univ. of Vermont, Colchester Ave., Burlington (802–656–0750) (changing exhibits); *New England Maple Museum,* Rte. 7, Rutland (802–483–9414) (complete story of maple sugaring); *Norman Rockwell Exhibition,* Rte. 7A, Arlington (802–375–6423); *Shelburne Museum,* Rte. 7, Shelburne (802–985–3346) (restoration of early Americana); *Southern Vermont Art Center,* off West Rd., Manchester (802–362–1405); and *Vermont Museum,* Pavilion Bldg., 109 State St., Montpelier (802–828–2291) (Vermont in a nutshell).

ARTS AND ENTERTAINMENT. Music. The *Marlboro Music Festival* (802–257–4333) is held in July and Aug. on the Marlboro College campus. Musical concerts are given frequently during the year at college auditoriums: *Bennington College* (802–442–5401); *Middlebury College* (802–388–3711); *Univ. of Vermont,* Burlington (802–656–3040); *Johnson State College,* Johnson (802–635–2356); and *Castleton State College,* Castleton (802–468–5611). Summer evening open-air band concerts are held in Burlington, Bristol, Lyndonville, S. Royalton, and Rutland. The *Vermont Symphony Orchestra* (802–864–5741) is located in Burlington; the *Vermont Philharmonic Orchestra* (802–233–8728) is in Montpelier.

Stage. With summer theaters in some 35 Vermont towns, visitors anywhere in the state can generally find live theater nearby in July and Aug.

Dance. *Vermont Dance Festival* is held at the historic art deco Flynn Theatre for the Performing Arts, 153 Main St., Burlington, VT 05401 (802–863–5966).

ACCOMMODATIONS. Travelers to Vermont can stay in full-service resorts, country inns, motels, condominiums, or chalets. *Vermont Travel Information Service* (802–276–3120) operates a statewide lodging bureau. Major ski areas have central lodging reservation services. (Call 800–555–1212 or 802–555–1212 for individual listings.) Most hotels and inns are open year-round; some require a minimum stay in season. Rates are based on double occupancy: *Deluxe,* \$125 and up; *Expensive,* \$100–\$125; *Moderate,* \$75–\$100; *Inexpensive,* \$75 and under. There is a Vermont room tax of 6%.

Bolton Valley. Black Bear Inn. *Moderate–Expensive.* Mountain Rd., off I-89, Bolton Valley, VT 05477 (802–434–2126). Contemporary mountaintop inn, steps away from ski area. Comfortable rooms; home-cooked meals. Privileges at nearby sports center. Package plans. Closed Apr. and Nov.

Burlington. Radisson Hotel. *Expensive–Deluxe.* 60 Battery Pl., Burlington, VT 05401 (802–658–6500 or 800–333–3333). Large modern downtown hotel, offering all amenities. Restaurants, indoor pool. Special family and weekend rates.

Chittenden. Mountain Top Inn. *Deluxe.* Mountain Top Rd. (off U.S. 4), Chittenden, VT 05737 (802–483–2311 or 800–445–2100). Lovely 40-room inn on 1,000 mountaintop acres. Summer watersports, tennis, golf, riding; winter skiing, sleighriding. Sauna. MAP.

Coventry. Heermansmith Farm Inn. *Inexpensive.* Heermansmith Farm Rd., Coventry, VT 05825 (802–754–8866). "Strawberry fields forever" is the view from the six cozy guest rooms in this century-old farmhouse. River swimming just beyond the fields, dirt roads, a covered bridge, hiking trails in summer, cross-country skiing in winter—pure Vermont. Dining room, breakfast included. A general treat.

Dorset. Dorset Inn. *Expensive.* Church and Main Sts., Dorset, VT 05251 (802–867–5500). Vermont's oldest inn in continuous operation is located smack in the center of one of the state's most picturesque towns. Fine dining in the café. Short drive to Bromley and Stratton for skiing.

Grafton. The Old Tavern. *Moderate–Expensive.* Rte. 121, Grafton, VT 05146 (802–843–2231). An 1801 stagecoach stop now a lovely inn. Individually decorated guest rooms, all with antiques. Excellent restaurant. Pool, tennis. Closed Apr.

Killington. The Inn at Long Trail. *Moderate.* Rte. 4, Box 267, Killington, VT 05751 (802–775–7181 or 800–325–2540). Historic country inn, rustic and cozy; fireplace suites. Convenient for skiing and hiking (Appalachian & Long Trails). Hot tub; Irish pub.

Londonderry. Dostal's. *Expensive–Deluxe.* Magic Mt. Ski Area, Londonderry, VT 05148 (802–824–6700). This is an Austrian-inspired inn with complete resort facilities. Spa; indoor and outdoor pools. Walk to slopes. Package plans available.

Londonderry Inn. *Inexpensive–Moderate.* Rte. 100, S. Londonderry, VT 05155 (802–824–5226). An 1826 homestead with comfortable rooms. Some shared bathrooms. Skiing nearby, swimming pool, billiards.

Lower Waterford. Rabbit Hill Inn. *Expensive.* Rte. 18, Lower Waterford, VT 05848 (802–748–5168). In this tiny community midway between St. Johnsbury and Littleton, NH, a 1795 tavern and general store and an 1825 house and workshop have been combined into a classic Vermont country inn, a romantic hideaway. All 18 bedrooms have private baths and all but two have mountain views. Walk in the woods, canoe on the Connecticut river, climb a mountain trail, or ski nearby. Breakfast and dinner included in rates.

Manchester. The Equinox. *Expensive–Deluxe.* Rte. 7A, Manchester Village, VT 05254 (802–362–4700). Grand hotel restored to its 19th-century splendor. All amenities; heated pool, tennis. Fine dining. Free transportation to ski areas.

Reluctant Panther Inn. *Expensive–Deluxe.* West Rd., off Rte. 7A, Manchester Village, VT 05254 (802–362–2568). This sophisticated country inn is painted deep purple to catch your eye. Fifteen lovely rooms, several with fireplaces; all with private bath. Three suites in adjacent building with Jacuzzis. Health club, pool, and sports privileges at Equinox Hotel. Superb dining.

Middlebury. The Middlebury Inn. *Moderate–Expensive.* 14 Courthouse Sq., Rte. 7, Middlebury, VT 05753 (802–388–4961 or 800–842–4666). Handsomely decorated rooms in large, red-brick Georgian inn (1827), on the green, or contemporary annex. Complimentary Continental breakfast. Dining room.

Newfane. Old Newfane Inn. *Expensive.* Court St., on the Green, Newfane, VT 05345 (802–365–4427). A 1787 inn furnished with antiques. Beamed dining room; delightful dining.

Quechee. Quechee Inn at Marshland Farm. *Expensive–Deluxe.* Club House Rd., Quechee, VT 05059 (802–295–3133). An 18th-century farmstead with attractive guest rooms. Club privileges for golf and tennis. Cross-country skiing at the door. No room phones.

Stowe. Topnotch at Stowe. *Deluxe.* Mt. Mansfield Rd., Rte. 108, Stowe, VT 05672 (802–253–8585 or 800–451–8686). Unique resort, with spa, heated pool, tennis, riding, and full amenities. Inn, town houses, or chalet accommodations. Fine dining. Top notch!

Trapp Family Lodge. *Deluxe.* Luce Hill Rd., off Rte. 108, Stowe, VT 05672 (802–253–8511 or 800–826–7000). Rebuilt after 1980 fire, it still maintains Trapp Family mystique. Cross-country skiing the magnet in winter. MAP; Austrian hospitality.

Stratton. Birkenhaus. *Moderate.* Stratton Rd., Stratton, VT 05155 (802–297–2000). Small chalet at base of Stratton Mt. Bunk rooms available; perfect for families. Good restaurant. Pool. Golf and tennis privileges.

Vergennes. Basin Harbor Club. *Deluxe.* Basin Harbor Rd. off Rte. 22A, Vergennes, VT 05491 (802–475–2311). Distinguished family resort on Lake Champlain, run by the same family since 1886. The lodge is grand and nearly 80 cottages are scattered over 700 lakefront acres. Golf, tennis, pool, all water sports. Excellent dining included in rates. Weekly rates available. Open June–mid-Oct.

Warren. Sugarbush Inn. *Expensive–Deluxe.* Mountain Rd., off Rte. 100, Warren, VT 05674 (802–583–2301 or 800–451–4320). Fine mountain resort. Chalets and condominiums or rooms in cozy Colonial inn. Golf, tennis, pool, and skiing—of course! Restaurants.

West Dover. Inn at Sawmill Farm. *Deluxe.* Rte. 100, W. Dover, VT 05356 (802–464–8131). Small, quiet, 200-yr.-old barn, now an antique-filled inn. Rooms with fireplaces; magnificent dining. Winter skiing at Mt. Snow; summer golf, tennis.

Woodstock. Woodstock Inn & Resort. *Deluxe.* 14 The Green, Woodstock, VT 05091 (802–457–1100 or 800–223–7637). Picturesque New England country resort; deluxe accommodations and all amenities. Elegant dining. Pool, golf, tennis.

Kedron Valley Inn. *Expensive.* Rte. 106, S. Woodstock, VT 05071 (802–457–1473). One of Vermont's oldest country inns. Rooms are beautifully decorated—canopy beds, antique quilts, wood stoves. Fine nouvelle Vermont cuisine in dining room. Pond swimming, horseback riding, and skiing available in season, Families welcome. MAP. Closed Apr.

BED AND BREAKFASTS. *Vermont Chamber of Commerce* (see Tourist Information) publishes a list of B&B lodgings. *Vermont Bed & Breakfast,* Box 1, E. Fairfield, VT 05448 (802–827–3827) is a reservation service.

YS AND HOSTELS. Scenic, rural Vermont is ideal for cycling and hosteling. Vermont has had youth hostels since after World War II. Some require membership in American Youth Hostels in order to stay, but others allow nonmember guests. In Vermont, hostels are located in: Burlington (802–865–3730); Craftsbury Common (802–586–7767); Ludlow (802–228–5244); Montpelier (802–223–2104); Rochester (802–767–9384); Stowe (802–253–4010); Underhill Center (802–899–2375); and Woodford (802–442–2547). For more information, contact *American Youth Hostels,* Box 37613, Washington, DC 20013 (202–783–6161).

RESTAURANTS. Vermont restaurants tend to serve traditional New England fare. At the same time, new and interesting methods of preparation are influencing Vermont's kitchens, reflecting the sophistication that comes with increased tourism and the continuing migration of cityfolk to rural Vermont. The restaurants suggested below are open year-round, serve lunch and dinner, and accept major credit cards unless noted. Price per person for a complete dinner is: *Deluxe:* $35 and up; *Expensive:* $25–$35; *Moderate:* $15–$25; *Inexpensive:* $15 and under.

Barnard. Barnard Inn. *Deluxe.* Rte. 12 (802–234–9961). Magnificent Continental cuisine prepared by Swiss owner-chef. Tempting desserts. Reservations recommended. Closed Apr.

Bennington. Four Chimneys. *Expensive.* 21 West St. (802–447–3500). This chef-owned Georgian Revival inn serves classic French cuisine, deftly prepared. Closed Apr., Nov., and Mon.

Burlington. Ice House Restaurant. *Moderate–Expensive.* 171 Battery St. (802–864–1800). Seafood restaurant and oyster bar on Lake Champlain waterfront. Sun. brunch.

Inn at Essex. *Moderate–Expensive.* 70 Essex Way, off Rte. 15, Essex Jct. (802–878–1100). A branch of the New England Culinary Institute has been installed in the inn's two restaurants. At **The Birch Tree Cafe** *(Moderate),* first-year students prepare informal meals. At **Butler's Restaurant** *(Expensive),* upper-classmen show their stuff. Expect traditional New England fare, prepared with fresh Vermont products and a nouvelle French twist.

Dorset. Barrows House. *Deluxe.* Rte. 30 (802–867–4455). Terrific food is served in this historic (1776) inn. Table d'hote menu. Traditional American selections with a Continental flair. Patio dining in summer. Jackets required at dinner.

Village Auberge. *Expensive.* Rte. 30 (802–867–5715). Gourmet dining in a country inn. Superb French cuisine. D only. Reservations necessary.

Grafton. The Old Tavern. *Moderate–Expensive.* Rte. 121 (802–843–2231). Delightful 1801 homestead, now an inn serving New England specialties. Reservations necessary; jackets for gentlemen at dinner. Reservations necessary.

Killington. Hemingway's. *Deluxe.* Rte. 4 (802–422–3886). Classic French menu served in several dining rooms, each with a separate setting, in a restored Vermont home. Reservations necessary; jackets for gentlemen. Closed May.

Londonderry. Three Clock Inn. *Expensive.* Off Rte. 100, S. Londonderry (802–824–6327). European-style cuisine served in a charming inn. Cozy and intimate. Reservations necessary. Closed Apr., May, Oct., and Mon.

Manchester. Wildflowers at the Reluctant Panther. *Expensive.* West Rd. (802–362–2568). First-class dining is offered in this sophisticated country inn right in the heart of the village. Intimate dining room with adjacent greenhouse. Continental cuisine. Reservations recommended. D only. Closed Wed.

Mulligan's Pub. *Moderate.* Rte. 7A (802–362–3663). This attractive pub serves burgers, snacks, and full meals. Abundant portions. Dancing weekends.

Middlebury. Middlebury Inn. *Expensive.* Rte. 7 (802–388–4961). On the Green, a favorite for Middlebury College families. Traditional New England fare; buffets and porch dining in summer. B also.

Newfane. Four Columns Inn. *Deluxe.* 230 West St. (802–365–7713). French and American cuisine served in attractive 1830 country inn. Fresh trout from the pond. Reservations requested. Closed Apr. and Nov.

Old Newfane Inn. *Expensive.* Rte. 30 (802–365–4427). Distinguished 1787 inn with superb Continental cuisine. Fireside dining. No young children. D only. Reservations suggested.

Quechee. Inn at Marshland Farm. *Expensive.* Club House Rd. (802–295–3133). Elegant country dining in historic 18th-century farmstead. Continental cuisine enhanced by innovative combinations of ingredients. D only; Sun. brunch. Reservations requested.

Rutland. Ernie's Grill at Royal's Hearthside. *Moderate–Expensive.* 37 N. Main St. (802–775–0856). Offered here is open-hearth American cooking: ribs, chops, steaks, seafood. Market next door for gourmet take-out.

Stowe. Topnotch Resort. *Expensive.* Rte. 108 (802–253–8585). Delicious dining experience in a "top-notch" ski resort. French cuisine marvelously prepared.

Austrian Tea Room. *Moderate–Expensive.* At Trapp Family Lodge, off Rte. 108 (802–253–8511). Viennese cuisine served in original coffeehouse (untouched by 1980 fire). Don't miss dessert!

West Dover. Inn at Sawmill Farm. *Expensive.* Rte. 100 (802–464–8131). Chef-owned converted sawmill. Continental–French cuisine of highest caliber. Table d'hote menu available.

Weston. The Inn at Weston. *Moderate.* Rte. 100 (802–824–5804). Well-prepared meals using fresh ingredients; everything homemade. Small inn with old-fashioned hospitality.

Woodstock. Kedron Valley Inn. *Expensive.* Rte. 106, S. Woodstock (802–457–1473). Classic French cuisine, prepared by a chef trained at La Varenne in Paris, will please the palate. The antique quilts displayed throughout the inn, one of Vermont's oldest, will please the eye. Closed Apr.

LIQUOR LAWS. In Vermont, minimum age for the purchase or consumption of alcohol is 21. Local option forbids the sale of alcoholic beverages in some towns. Bottled liquor is available only at state liquor stores and agencies. Beer, ale, and wine are available at grocery stores. Alcoholic beverages may be sold by the bottle Mon.–Sat., 6 A.M.–midnight; Sun., 8 A.M.–10 P.M. Drinks may be sold in licensed hotels, restaurants, and clubs Mon.–Fri., 8 A.M.–2 A.M.; Sat., 8 A.M.–1 A.M.; Sun., noon–1 A.M.

To discourage roadside littering, Vermont requires a minimum 5¢ deposit on each beer, wine cooler, and soda can or bottle sold in the state, as well as a 15¢ deposit on all liquor and fortified wine bottles (except the 50 ml. size). Deposits are refunded when empties are returned to stores or redemption centers.

SOUTHERN NEW ENGLAND

by
WILLIAM G. SCHELLER and ALMA ESHENFELDER

Mr. Scheller is the author of More Country Walks near Boston *and* Train Trips: Exploring America by Rail *as well as numerous articles on travel, conservation, and New England subjects. A member of the Society of American Travel Writers and the New York Travel Writers Association, Alma Eshenfelder has had many travel articles published. Her radio program "Travel Time" has been broadcast weekly since 1971.*

The three states that make up southern New England—Massachusetts, Connecticut, and Rhode Island—offer a rich, vibrant, yet remarkably compact sampling of just what most visitors expect of the region. While the three states lack the mountain scenery of New Hampshire and Vermont, and the wave-whipped rocky coasts of Maine, they contain an ample share of the steepled villages, ancient seaports, tree-lined country roads, rolling dunelands, and historic places that everyone thinks of when they hear the words New England. The area, in fact, is a lot like old England in that it encompasses tremendous variety in an extremely small space. You can drive from Hartford to Providence to Boston within a few hours; yet you might easily spend a month or more exploring the coast of Massachusetts north of Boston, the beaches and lively resort towns of Cape Cod, the hills, valleys, and seacoast villages of Connecticut, or the backwaters of Narragansett Bay. And it all comes complete with three and a half centuries of history.

MASSACHUSETTS

Massachusetts is the oldest, largest, and most populous of the trio of states that make up southern New England, and its capital city of Boston serves as the region's unofficial capital as well. Boston is the logical place to begin a tour of Massachusetts, a tour which—regardless of how you plan to continue your exploration of the state and its neighbors—should begin with a walk through the streets that once echoed with the footsteps of Benjamin Franklin, John Hancock, and Paul Revere. The many layers of Boston's colonial past translate here into a simple lesson in urban geography called the Freedom Trail, which you can begin at the Information Center on Tremont Street, a few yards down from the Park Street subway station.

Boston

The park that you are facing as you begin the Freedom Trail walk (self-guiding brochures to the sixteen sites along the way are available at the Information Center) is Boston Common, the oldest public park in the United States and really nothing more than a larger and slightly more famous version of the village commons that lie at the center of so many old New England settlements. It started out in the 17th century as just that—common land, where the townspeople grazed their animals and drilled with the militia. Now more than ever, it is a welcome oasis in the midst of a city whose vigorous construction program and economic growth belies the old image of a staid, unchanging Boston.

Just opposite the subway station (the tracks below are the oldest urban underground line in the country) stands the Park Street Church, built in 1809. Here the abolitionist William Lloyd Garrison began his heroic anti-slavery campaign with a fiery speech on the Fourth of July in 1829; three years later to the day, the hymn *America* was first sung in the church. Architecturally, the building is of interest as the last major church structure to be built in the Georgian style in Boston.

As you head up Park Street from the church, you are beginning an ascent of Beacon Hill, named for the tallow pot that was set on its summit in the 1600s as a warning device to be lit in times of danger. The summit was much steeper and craggier in those days; it was substantially leveled at the end of the 18th century so that the magnificent "new" State House could be built and the adjoining blocks developed with the fine brick rowhouses that still stand as the epitome of proper Bostonian residences. The State House was designed by Charles Bulfinch, America's first important native architect, and completed in 1798. The building and its newer wings still house the government of the Commonwealth of Massachusetts; the legislative chambers, and the Hall of Flags are open to visitors. The chamber of the State Senate contains the famous "Sacred Cod," a tribute to the fish that supported the state's economy long before computers took up the job.

The State House stands on Beacon Street, which Oliver Wendell Holmes once called "the sunny street that holds the sifted few." Take time for a walk down Beacon Street and a look at the Federalist-era bowfront mansions with which it fronts the Common, then turn into the narrower streets that lead off Beacon to explore Beacon Hill. At the foot of the Hill, stroll along Charles Street where you can be distracted by fine antiques as well as the latest flavors of *gelato.*

Returning to the Park Street station, turn left on Tremont Street to reach King's Chapel (corner of School Street), a simple stone structure

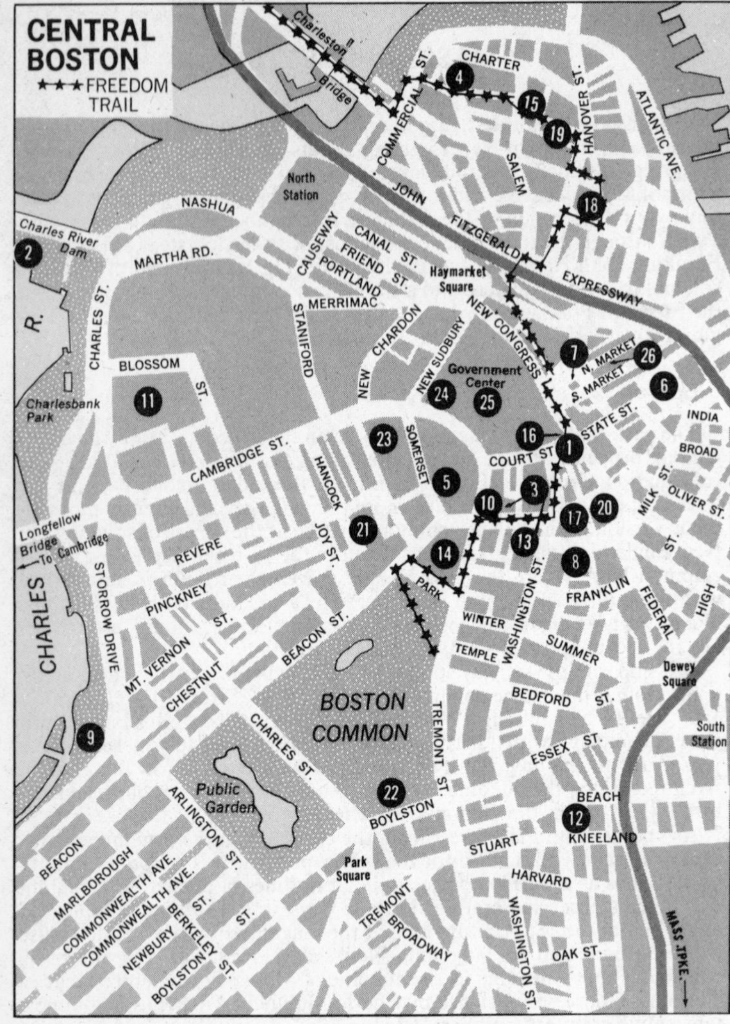

Points of Interest

1) Boston Massacre Site
2) Boston Museum of Science
3) Old City Hall
4) Copp's Hill Burying Ground
5) Court House
6) Custom House
7) Faneuil Hall
8) Franklin's Birthplace Site
9) Hatch Memorial Concert Shell
10) King's Chapel
11) Massachusetts General Hospital
12) Tufts New England Medical Center
13) Old Corner Book Store
14) Park Street Church and Old Granary Burying Ground
15) Old North Church (originally Christ Church)
16) Old State House
17) Old South Meeting House
18) Paul Revere's House
19) Paul Revere's Statue
20) Post Office
21) State House
22) Central Burying Ground
23) State Office Building
24) John F. Kennedy Federal Building
25) New City Hall
26) Faneuil Hall Marketplace

built in 1754 to house the city's first Episcopal congregation; its current denomination is Unitarian. The interior is a fine example of Georgian grace and elegance and should not be missed. Across the street is a secular institution of no small repute, the Parker House Hotel. Yes, this is where the rolls of the same name were first introduced. They're still served here at dinner.

On the left as you walk down School Street is the old City Hall. The statue before it is of Benjamin Franklin; the ghosts inside belong to the likes of Mayor James Michael Curley, the quintessential urban politician and the model for Frank Skeffington in Edwin O'Connor's novel *The Last Hurrah.* Curley lived before the era of "rehabbing"—he'd be surprised to see that the old place now houses a restaurant. Today the city's business is conducted in a starkly modern building in nearby Government Center, across from a federal office tower named for another famous Boston politician, John F. Kennedy.

School Street meets Washington Street at the Old Corner Bookstore. A century ago this little brick building housed the famous publishing house of Ticknor and Fields; today it houses a bookstore with an excellent collection of local authors and books about the area. Just across the street is the Old South Meeting House, where colonists gathered to protest British injustices. On December 16, 1773, Samuel Adams whipped his Old South audience into a seditious frenzy that resulted, later that night, in the Boston Tea Party. The site where the colonists threw the tea into the harbor (near present-day South Station) has long since been covered over in one of the city's many landfill operations, but a replica of *Beaver,* one of the ships involved, is anchored near the Congress Street Bridge (also near South Station) and is open to visitors.

At the corner of Washington and State streets stands the Old State House, built in 1713 as the seat of the British colonial government. In front of the restored building is the spot where British soldiers responded to the taunts and snowballs of an angry mob with musket shots, killing five Bostonians in what became known as the Boston Massacre. This was in 1770; within little more than a half decade the British lion and unicorn had been pulled down from the Old State House and what modern news broadcasts would call a "revolutionary government" had been installed.

In those days, the heart of Boston, in fact very nearly the entirety of Boston, was located in what is now known as the North End. The North End lies on the other side of the restored complex of buildings that collectively make up the Faneuil Hall Marketplace. The complex includes Faneuil Hall itself, the "cradle of liberty" where Colonial protest groups met and where civic meetings and debates still take place, along with the three early 19th-century arcades of Quincy Market, now chock full of upscale shops—and the elevated Southeast Expressway. Since about 1900, the North End has been an Italian neighborhood, and visitors come here for the markets, bakeries, and restaurants that line narrow streets where the dialects of the Old Country are still spoken. Among the Italian groceries and *trattorias* are some of the most famous shrines of Revolutionary Boston: the Paul Revere House and the Old North Church. Paul Revere lived in the now-restored wooden house on North Square, built in the 1670s and generally regarded to be the oldest frame structure in Boston. The Old North Church on Salem Street, built in 1723, was called Christ Church in Revere's day. On the night of April 18, 1775, his friend Robert Newman hung the famous signal lanterns in the church steeple, launching Revere on his ride from Charlestown "to every Middlesex village and farm," in the poet Longfellow's words. Here they both stand: the house Paul Revere left on that fateful night and the church in which the lanterns were hung. What more could be said about Boston as a mecca for students of American history?

Of course there is more to Boston than downtown and the North End. Across the Mystic River (which Revere crossed that night in a rowboat with muffled oarlocks) is Charlestown, where the USS *Constitution,* "Old Ironsides," is docked at a decommissioned shipyard reborn as a complex of museums, restaurants, and apartments. Nearby is the Bunker Hill Monument, a handsome and climbable granite obelisk located on Breed's Hill where the 1775 battle was actually fought. On the other side of the Common and its lovely companion, the Public Garden (the Garden lagoon, with its pedal-powered swanboats, was the setting for the Robert McCloskey children's classic, *Make Way for Ducklings*), is the Victorian gem of a neighborhood called the Back Bay. The Back Bay was a colossal mid-19th-century landfill project; when it was complete, it was *the* place for well-to-do Bostonians to build the elegant brownstone row houses that would later supply condominiums for generations yet unborn. Fortunately, the facades haven't changed, and a walk down Commonwealth Avenue is still an architectural delight. The neighborhood's public buildings include the two masterpieces of Copley Square, H. H. Richardson's Romanesque Trinity Church, with its interior decorations by John La Farge and Edward Burne-Jones; and McKim, Mead, and White's Boston Public Library, a magnificent Renaissance palazzo with an interior courtyard and garden.

Beyond the Back Bay lie the city's cultural treasures (not to mention Fenway Park, home of the Red Sox). Chief among them are the Boston Symphony Orchestra's acoustically exquisite Symphony Hall, at the corner of Massachusetts and Huntington Avenues; the Museum of Fine Arts (Huntington Avenue), with its world-renowned collections of Impressionist paintings, Egyptian antiquities, and American paintings and furniture; and the Isabella Stewart Gardner Museum, the private palace of a wealthy Boston matron, endowed with her savvy yet highly idiosyncratic collection of works of the European masters.

The greater Boston area boasts no fewer than ten major institutions of higher learning, yet when most people think of higher education in Boston what first comes to mind is a pair of schools on the other side of the Charles River in Cambridge: Harvard and the Massachusetts Institute of Technology (MIT). Positioned at either end of Massachusetts Avenue, the two schools tend to dominate this mid-size city in a way not all residents are completely comfortable with. Nevertheless, both are giants in their fields (which have come to include just about all fields) and both are well worth a visit. At MIT, see Eero Saarinen's Kresge Auditorium and Interdenominational Chapel; at Harvard, tour the Fogg, Busch-Reisinger, and Sackler art museums, the Peabody Museum of archaeology and ethnology; and the rotating exhibits of the Harvard Theater Collection and the Widener Library. Nor are the campuses all there is to see in Cambridge: Harvard Square is a polyglot of shops and restaurants, with more bookstores than several small states, and Brattle Street is a showcase of the colonial mansions that once formed "Tory Row." One of them, the home of the poet and Harvard professor Henry Wadsworth Longfellow, is now a National Historic Site open to the public.

North Shore

The coast north of Boston offers as fine a combination of scenery and history as any area of comparable size in New England. From the hard-working fishermen of Gloucester to the proud barons of the Salem China trade, its people have created one of those landscapes in which the natural and the artificial environments seem to clash a little less harshly than they do in so many places. This is most evident along the shoreline and north of the urban concentrations of Revere and Lynn; incidentally, you'll miss a good deal of the North Shore's charm if you dash to your destination

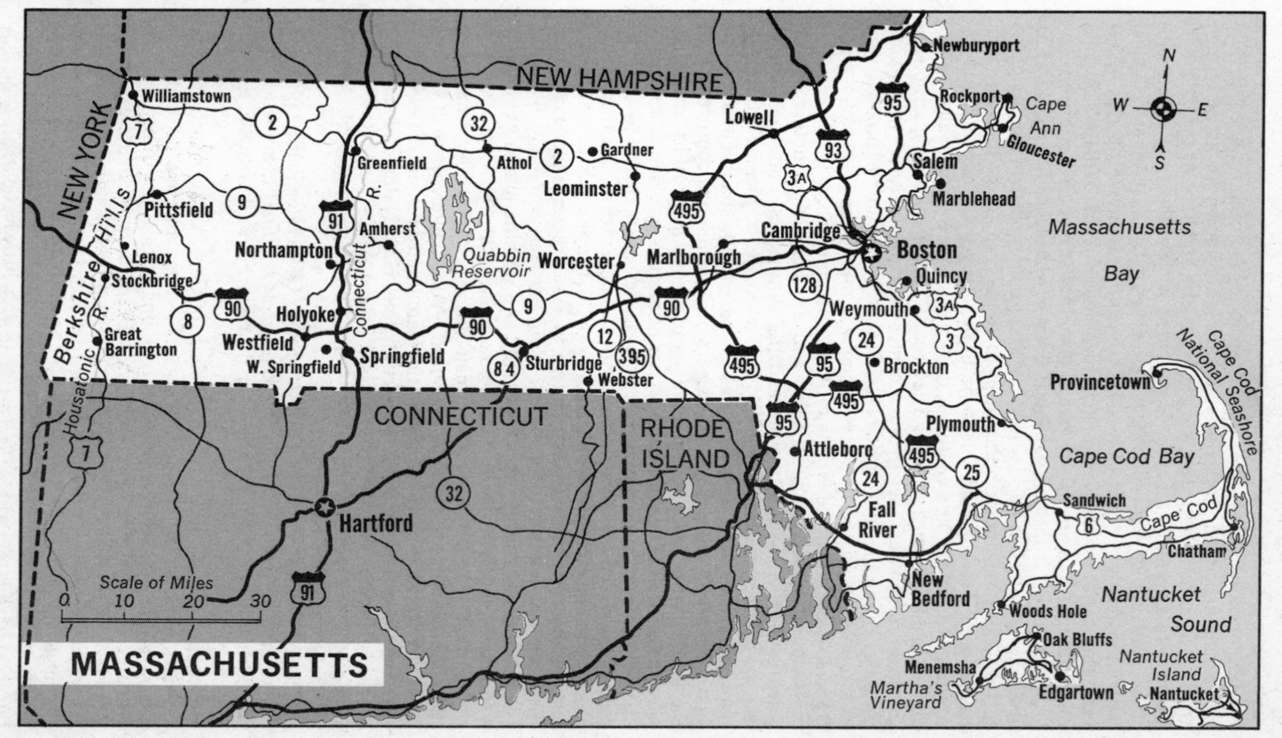
MASSACHUSETTS
NEW HAMPSHIRE
NEW YORK
CONNECTICUT
RHODE ISLAND
Massachusetts Bay
Cape Cod Bay
Nantucket Sound
Cape Cod National Seashore
Cape Cod
Cape Ann
Nantucket Island
Martha's Vineyard
Quabbin Reservoir
Berkshire Hills
Connecticut R.
Housatonic R.
Newburyport
Rockport
Gloucester
Salem
Marblehead
Boston
Quincy
Cambridge
Lowell
Weymouth
Brockton
Plymouth
Provincetown
Sandwich
Chatham
Woods Hole
Oak Bluffs
Edgartown
Menemsha
Nantucket
New Bedford
Fall River
Attleboro
Marlborough
Worcester
Leominster
Gardner
Athol
Webster
Sturbridge
Greenfield
Amherst
Northampton
Holyoke
Springfield
W. Springfield
Westfield
Hartford
Williamstown
Pittsfield
Lenox
Stockbridge
Great Barrington
Scale of Miles
0 10 20 30
N E S W

along the inland thoroughfares of Routes 1 and I–95. It's best to meander up the coast on Route 1A, taking side trips to Marblehead, Gloucester, and Rockport.

Marblehead is a year older than Boston, having been founded in 1629 by English fishermen. Today it is perhaps more known for its yachtsmen than its fishermen, with July's Race Week the highlight of the calendar. From spring to fall the harbor is peppered with sailboats of all descriptions. Any time of year is fine for walking the ancient, narrow streets lined with handsomely restored 17th- and 18th-century homes. Stop in at Abbot Hall, the seat of town government, which houses A. M. Willard's original oil painting *The Spirit of '76,* one of America's great patriotic icons.

Salem, which is located right next door to Marblehead, is as old as its sister community but was destined for a far grander place in New England history—and for commemoration in the darker annals of the American past as well. Trading built this town; in the last years of the 18th and the opening years of the 19th centuries, it seemed that everything Salem's merchants touched turned to gold. The proof is in the splendid mansions in the possession of the Essex Institute, which are open to visitors throughout the year, and in the collections of the Peabody Museum, originally begun as a repository for the treasures brought home by the seafaring Yankee traders who opened the Orient to American commerce.

The most dismal episode in Salem's history belongs to another period, a century earlier than the era of the merchant princes. This was the infamous witchcraft hysteria of 1692–1693, when the suspicions aroused by impressionable young girls who had listened to too many fireside ghost stories led to otherwise blameless citizens being accused of consorting with the devil. By the time the community's psychosis had run its course, 19 people had been put to death, their executions the outcome of a series of "trials" modeled on similar European travesties and managed by the local representatives of the colony's theocratic political order. Visit the "Witch House" (the home of Judge Jonathan Corwin), the Salem Witch Museum, and the museum of the Essex Institute to gain a closer understanding of the story.

Gloucester is a fishermen's town still, and nothing makes as eloquent a statement about this city's three and a half centuries of dependence on the sea than the Gloucester Fisherman Statue, a harborside memorial to those who go "down to the sea in ships." You should approach the city by way of Route 127, with a stop at the Hammond Museum, a fascinating reproduction of a castle, built by inventor John Hays Hammond and offering dramatic views of the rocky coast of Cape Ann. The Massachusetts Office of Travel and Tourism says Cape Ann claims to be "the whale-watching capital of the world."

Sharing the eastern tip of Cape Ann with Gloucester is Rockport, another seafaring town of ancient crooked streets and fine old homes. Principal attractions here are the shops of Bearskin Neck, downtown, and the picturesque drive along Pigeon Cove.

Heading west along the northern shore of Cape Ann, you will come to Ipswich, home of the famous clams of the same name and distinguished for having more surviving 17th-century homes than any other town in America. Take Argilla Road to Crane's Beach, a spotless and expansive stretch of dunes and surf maintained by the private Trustees of Reservations. Twelve miles to the north there are more beautiful beaches at the Parker River Wildlife Refuge on Plum Island, a federally protected salt marsh, dune, and beach environment accessible from Newburyport. Newburyport itself is remarkable as a textbook example of how a fading seaport can come back to life as a magnet not only for sightseers but for new residents seeking the pace of life in a very small city. Downtown's Market Square and environs are a redbrick, 1811 set piece; High Street is lined with dozens of Federalist mansions built by shipowners and captains in the city's pre-1810 heyday.

Lowell

North of Boston but farther inland, along Route I-93, is the old industrial city of Lowell. Lowell was once one of the textile-producing capitals of the world, but it fell on hard times after the cotton mills moved south. Today, thanks to the high-tech boom and the creation of a National Historical Park and a Heritage State Park based around the old mills of downtown Lowell, the city again thrives. The attractions include mill exhibits that interpret the growth of the Industrial Revolution in America, barge tours of the historic canals, and a trolley line. There's also a lively program of concerts and ethnic festivals each summer.

Lexington and Concord

Just west of Boston, via Cambridge and Arlington, are two suburban towns which, back when they were small farming communities, were etched indelibly into the annals of American history as the smell of black powder drifted through a spring morning. Just after dawn on April 19, 1775, a knot of Lexington farmers stood on the town green and faced a column of British regulars in the first battle of the American Revolution. The poignant Minuteman Statue stands there today, while the nearby Buckman Tavern (where the town's defenders gathered that morning) and Hancock-Clarke House, where Samuel Adams and John Hancock heard from Paul Revere of the British advance, are both open to visitors.

The next destination along the British line of march on that fateful day was Concord, where the Redcoats hoped to capture a cache of arms and ammunition. They were met at the North Bridge by the men of Concord, who gave them their second fight of the day. The bridge and surrounding territory are now part of a national historical park; there are frequent battle reenactments in summer, black powder and all. Concord achieved a different sort of fame a generation and more later, when the likes of Ralph Waldo Emerson, Henry David Thoreau, and Nathaniel Hawthorne gave the town a permanent place on the American intellectual map. Emerson's house and the Old Manse where Hawthorne lived and worked still stand and are open to visitors.

Plymouth and Cape Cod

Cape Cod is bright wild roses against the silvered cedar shingles of a lobsterman's shack; it's mile after mile of grassy dunes and white sand beaches strictly protected by federal law; it's the strip development of Hyannis and the jumbled, toylike streets of Provincetown; it is, after all, the only place in America to lend its name to a book by Henry David Thoreau and a song by Patti Page. It begins south of Plymouth, where the pine trees get scrubbier and the soil more sandy, and encompasses a frame of mind as old as the desire to listen to the waves at night. Cape Cod is at its most popular in high summer; it is at its most real on quiet days in gray November.

By all means stop at Plymouth on your approach to the Cape. This is where the Pilgrims landed in 1620, and even if they didn't step right onto Plymouth Rock as they got off the boat, the story is nevertheless the stuff of our national myth. Plymouth Rock is still there, covered by an elaborate stone canopy, but far more interesting is nearby Plimoth Plantation, where authentically costumed staff members relive the day-to-day routines of the hardy first settlers amid a reproduction of the thatched-roof village they built on the shores of the new land. Also near at hand is the *Mayflower II,* a replica of the original that was built in England and sailed to Plymouth in 1957. A visit below decks will reveal much about the hardships the religious refugees faced, hardships equalled by the rigors of the first winters on shore. On Cole's Hill the Pilgrims buried those of their number who did not survive.

The Cape Cod Canal, dug early in this century by the Army Corps of Engineers (Pilgrim Myles Standish suggested it first, according to legend), marks the beginning of the real Cape. Once across the canal, the visitor has several choices as to which route to follow on the trip "Down Cape." Yes, *down.* The part of the Cape nearest the mainland is "Up Cape," and traveling toward Provincetown takes you "Down Cape." It all has to do with sailing days and the direction of the winds. Your modern mainland alternatives are Route 6, an expressway through the relatively unpopulated midsection of the Upper Cape; Route 6A, which meanders through the quiet villages along the Upper Cape's north shore; and Route 28, which follows the south shore and heads straight through the busier parts of Falmouth, Dennis, and Hyannis. Once past the "elbow" of the Cape at Chatham, Route 6 is the only highway to the tip at Provincetown.

The first of the settlements along Route 6A is Sandwich, the oldest town on the Cape. It was once known far and wide for its manufacture of colored glass; the Sandwich Glass Museum contains an outstanding collection. Here also is Heritage Plantation, a complex of museums and exhibits of early American crafts. Barnstable, Yarmouth, and Brewster, which you will pass through as you continue east on 6A, are notable for their many surviving sea captains' mansions and more modest examples of the "Cape Cod" style of domestic architecture that later spread to suburbs throughout America. The comfortable country inns along this part of the Cape contrast with the resort and motel-oriented development on the Nantucket Sound side.

The coast along the Sound, however, is not without its attractions. Woods Hole, ferry gateway to Martha's Vineyard and Nantucket, is also the home of the famous Woods Hole Oceanographic Institute and the aquarium of the U.S. Bureau of Commercial Fisheries. Nearby Falmouth dates to a Quaker settlement of 1660; it retains its village character, especially in the off season. Paul Revere cast the bell that still hangs in the Falmouth Congregational Church. Perhaps the most heavily developed area on the Cape lies a few miles east around Hyannis, which has become the area's tourist hub. A good deal of publicity derives from the late President Kennedy's association with Hyannisport, a satellite resort town (tour boats still point out the Kennedy compound). If the president thus inadvertently created an increase in tourism and development in this part of the Cape, he was also directly responsible for the protection of much of the Cape's fragile "forearm" between Chatham and Provincetown in the form of the Cape Cod National Seashore.

Chatham, which occupies the outer elbow of the armlike landmass of the Cape, is a village deliberately frozen in pre-1900 time by means of rigid zoning restrictions. It is still a major scalloping capital; you can watch the boats unloading their catches of scallops and fish around noon at the fish pier. Needless to say, Cape Cod restaurants carry some of the freshest seafood you'll ever find.

The trip north from Chatham brings you into the heart of the Cape Cod National Seashore—over 40 miles of protected beach and dunelands. The headquarters and principal visitor center is at Eastham, where there are guidebooks, brochures, interpretive displays, and the beginning of a network of foot trails leading through the dunes, marshes, and moors of the National Seashore. If you feel up to the trudge, you can follow Thoreau's footsteps and walk the beach beneath the beetling (and relentlessly eroding) sand cliffs that stretch from here to Provincetown. For sunbathing and a bracing dip, the best place along the way is at Nauset Beach in Orleans.

Wellfleet, just off Route 6, is a pretty village still known for its oysters; Truro, farther along, has barely any village to speak of but encompasses hundreds of acres of moorland covered with vegetation that turns a beautiful deep crimson in September. It was here that the artist Edward Hopper lived and painted many of his Cape Cod landscapes. Finally, the wrist of the Cape narrows to a point where any high dune will offer close views of both the ocean and the bay, and Provincetown is at hand.

Provincetown is many things to many people. Look deeper than the gaudy summertime trappings of Commercial Street (is there a more aptly named street in the world?) and you find that it remains an 18th-century fishing village in layout, architecture, and scale. Here Portuguese fishermen still ply their trade in a fleet of small boats. By the beginning of the 20th century, though, Provincetown had begun to attract outsiders, many of them artists and writers and those who enjoy the atmosphere given off by creativity even if they aren't creating much themselves. Around the time of the First World War, Eugene O'Neill and his coterie set up in Provincetown and began their now-legendary work with the Provincetown Playhouse, which is still active today. In the years between the wars bohemians drifted in and out, and by the 1950s Provincetown was a minor beatnik capital. Today the town is the home of a considerable gay population, especially in the summer. At that time of year, though, the description that best fits the majority of the people in the street is "tourist." If you like crowds, shops, and galleries, come during the warm weather. If you like nearly as many shops and galleries but far fewer crowds, head to Provincetown in the off season. The place even has its January aficionados, for that's when a bowl of Portuguese kale soup or clam chowder really hits the spot.

The Islands: Martha's Vineyard and Nantucket

Martha's Vineyard lies seven miles out to sea by way of the ferries that leave Woods Hole; Nantucket is some 30 miles offshore. The respective characters of the two islands reflect their distances from the mainland—the Vineyard has bigger towns and more people, and its countryside possesses a horsey, genteel quality; Nantucket is a place of rolling moors with only one year-round settlement. Each has its partisans who are sometimes a little silly about the other's shortcomings.

Vineyard ferries land at the towns of Vineyard Haven and Oak Bluffs, on the north side of the island. Oak Bluffs, which dates from the late 1600s, acquired its whimsical gingerbread houses when the town became a popular site for Methodist camp meetings in the 19th century. Clustered on narrow streets about the central tabernacle where the meetings still take place, the houses make the place look like a surrealistic movie set built to a two-thirds scale. In addition to its Methodist connections, Oak Bluffs has the distinction of being one of the oldest black resorts in the United States.

Edgartown, the Vineyard's easternmost sizable town, is an old whaling port rich in white mansions of the Georgian and Federalist eras. In the summer, it looks like the Ellis Island of the preppies, with the alligator-shirt set out in full force. When you see a pair of boat shoes here, chances are they're worn on the deck of a real boat. Look for the best of the sea captains' houses on North and South Water Streets, and visit the Dukes County Historical Society Museum in the Thomas Cooke House.

The best of the Vineyard's beaches and views are to be found at the western side of the island, specifically toward the small towns of Menemsha and Gay Head. At Gay Head, home to this day of the Wampanoag Indians who were living here when the first Englishmen arrived, be sure to see a sunset bring out the reds, yellows, and rich brown hues of the famous cliffs. Turning inland, you'll find plenty of country lanes to bicycle (this is by far the best way of getting around both Martha's Vineyard and Nantucket) and even a real working vineyard to visit.

Nantucket was a whaling center too—but that's like saying that Detroit builds cars. Nantucket was the whaling capital of all the world in the early 19th century, as Herman Melville brought out so powerfully in *Moby-Dick:* "The Nantucketer, he alone resides and riots on the sea . . . to and fro ploughing it as his own special plantation." Although the silting of the harbor and the advent of petroleum finished Nantucket's whaling economy by the mid-1800s, the town is splendidly haunted by its past. There are magnificent mansions built with the fortunes harpooned and hauled from the deep on voyages that took three years and more, stout dockside counting houses where cagey Quaker shipmasters tallied their profits, and a fine Whaling Museum. Around these reminders of past glory stands a town in which zoning demands that everything new look like everything old, so there is no mistaking Nantucket for anyplace else.

You needn't travel far out of Nantucket town—a ten-minute bike ride will do—to be surrounded by an even more timeless landscape, a misty world of heathery moors and scrub pine where it seems as if the ocean is never far away. It isn't. Go east to Madaket, where the sea is wildest, or north to Great Point (you'll have to make this trip on foot) to where the waves crash together at the end of a spit of land no wider than the prow of a rowboat, and you'll know why the Gray Lady, as Nantucket is called, will never be just another tame summer resort.

The Berkshires

The Berkshire Hills rise near Massachusetts's border with New York State. Like the Hudson River Valley across that border, they are a rolling, pastoral terrain more closely related to the northern Appalachian environment than to coastal New England. Taken together with the towns and villages that dot their valleys, the Berkshires have the look and feel of an old English shire.

If you're starting out in eastern Massachusetts, you can approach the Berkshires from the south, in which case a stopover at Springfield is a good idea. Springfield is a Connecticut River town, once famous for its machine shops and for the Springfield Armory, where small arms for every American conflict from the Mexican War to Vietnam were turned out by the millions. Closed now, the Armory is maintained as a National Historical Site, where examples of its manufactures are on display. Springfield is also the home of the Basketball Hall of Fame (the game was invented here) and the institutions which make up its "museum quadrangle"—the Museum of Fine Arts, Science Museum, Connecticut Valley Historical Museum, and George Walter Vincent Smith Art Museum.

For a more northerly approach to the Berkshires, take Route 2, popularly known as the Mohawk Trail. The best time to drive along the trail is in early autumn, when the hardwoods of the foothills are blazing with color.

U.S. Route 7 is the main north–south artery of the Berkshires. Route 2 meets it up in the corner formed by the New York and Vermont borders, at Williamstown. Williamstown is the home of Williams College, with its picture-book campus and gracious Georgian architecture, and of the fine Sterling and Francine Clark Art Institute. The Clark possesses an important collection of Renoirs as well as silver, furniture, and porcelain.

The drive south along Route 7 takes you to the Berkshire County seat of Pittsfield, with a few interesting side trips along the way. One is the Hancock Shaker Village, in Hancock, where the lifestyle and handicrafts of this early 19th-century sect are commemorated within a group of restored farm buildings and Shaker residences. Another is the headquarters of the Crane Paper Company in Dalton, where there is a museum of paper-making.

In Pittsfield, visit the Berkshire Atheneum with its collection of artifacts related to the life of Herman Melville. Nearby is Arrowhead, where Melville lived for several years and wrote much of *Moby-Dick.* The home has been restored and is open to visitors. Back around 1850, when Melville smoked cigars on his piazza with his friend Nathaniel Hawthorne, this part of the Berkshires was acquiring a reputation as something of a literary capital; today its cachet as a cultural mecca is no less pronounced. The Berkshires bustle with culture in the summer, and in the winter skiing attracts many visitors. At Pittsfield there are the South Mountain Concerts, and at Becket, the Jacob's Pillow Dance Festival. The Williamstown Theatre Festival is a leading exponent of summer stock. But the most famous of all the Berkshire summer cultural attractions is Tanglewood, the July and August home of the Boston Symphony Orchestra. Seats in the spacious Music Shed are better for hearing the music. Shakespeare & Co. at The Mount, Lenox, and the Berkshire Theatre Festival in Stockbridge add further dimensions to a summer vacation.

South of Lenox is Stockbridge, with its broad main street made famous in the paintings of one-time resident Norman Rockwell. Over 50 of the artist's works are on display at the Rockwell Museum in town. Not far from Stockbridge is Chesterwood, the 150-acre estate of sculptor Daniel Chester French (Concord's Minuteman Statue; the Lincoln Memorial Statue in Washington), now owned by the National Trust for Historic Preservation and open to the public.

All this concentration on the arts need not obscure the natural beauty of the Berkshires. North of Pittsfield and just south of North Adams is 3,491-foot Mt. Greylock. From Greylock, Massachusetts's highest peak, you can look to the Hudson Valley of New York and the Green Mountains of Vermont. In the southwest corner of the state, below South Egremont, visit the Bash Bish Falls Reservation, where a 50-foot waterfall courses over a gash in the solid rock. Nearby Sheffield has two covered bridges and five scenic waterfalls. If Massachusetts begins with the crash of the Atlantic and the drama of a long social history, it finishes gently among these rolling green Berkshire Hills.

CONNECTICUT

Connecticut's four seasons offer year-round pleasure. Spells of rain, fog, or snow are usually short-lived, and the climate is never extreme.

The state is home to a cosmopolitan population. All branches of the military are represented here. Industrial employment is varied and includes shipbuilding, aeronautics, electronics, pharmaceuticals, toolmaking, and diverse manufacturing. The insurance business, centered in Hartford, employs many of the state's residents. Farming, both poultry and dairy, as well as truck gardening, continues to be important here, even as an avocation, perhaps because of the greater emphasis on good nutrition programs and home-grown products. Numerous colleges and universities attract students from around the world.

Connecticut has an area of 5,000 square miles, 75 percent of which is forest or woodland. There are picturesque villages and towns throughout the state, both on Long Island Sound and in the hills to the north.

With 96 state-maintained boat or canoe launching sites (10 with access to salt water), bow and arrow as well as muzzle-loader and shotgun hunting seasons, six downhill and four cross-country ski areas, more than 100 recreational areas (state parks and forests), and with more than 1,500 campsites in 20 of the 100 state-operated recreational areas and 57 private campgrounds, Connecticut not only welcomes visitors, it caters to them.

Hartford

The state capital is one of Connecticut's largest cities and perhaps its most interesting. The first building one passes approaching the city from the south on I-91 is easily identified by its onion-shaped dome topped by a gilded horse. The building is owned by the Colt Patent Firearms Company, which manufactured the famous Colt revolvers that "won the West."

Proceeding north along the Connecticut River, the highway turns into a maze of intersections. Urban renewal projects have resulted in tall buildings that have changed the skyline of downtown.

Entering the city via State Street, Constitution Plaza—a complex of office buildings, a TV studio, and a tree-dotted mall lined with shops and investment offices—is on the right. Across the street is the Phoenix Mutual Insurance Company's headquarters, which resembles a green glass boat.

Directly facing you as you proceed on State Street is the lovely Old State House (1796), a Federal red brick masterpiece with a white dome designed by Charles Bulfinch. It is now open to the public as a museum. Of special interest in the building is the beautiful Senate Chamber and a graceful unsupported spiral staircase.

South on Main Street is the Travelers Insurance Company building. The 527-foot-high tower may be visited on weekdays, by advance reservation. Free tours are offered June–August 8:30 A.M.–3:30 P.M. every half hour. Reservations are required April, May, September, and October. A plaque on the front of the tower building marks the spot of the old Zachary Sanford Tavern.

Past the Travelers on Main Street is the Wadsworth Atheneum (America's oldest continuously operating public art museum), with early paintings and contemporary art, an excellent collection of Middle Eastern and Oriental archaeological relics, and one of the largest exhibits anywhere of Meissen china. The gun room displays muskets, rifles, and Colt revolvers. The Avery Art Memorial boasts paintings by Rembrandt, Wyeth, Daumier, Gilbert Stuart, Picasso, Goya, Giordano, Cézanne, Whistler, and Sargent. The statue on the lawn in front of the Morgan Memorial honors the young Connecticut schoolteacher, Nathan Hale, who was caught by the British while spying on Long Island for Washington's forces and was hanged in New York City.

Capitol Hill

The present state capitol sits dramatically atop the highest point in Bushnell Park, the central park of Hartford. While the governor and top officials have their offices in the gold-domed capitol, most state workers are housed in the State Office Building at the edge of the park.

Across the street, The Connecticut State Museum is in the imposing building shared by the State Library. On display are Connecticut's Royal Charter, the Colt Collection of early rifles and revolvers, and the table upon which President Abraham Lincoln signed the Emancipation Proclamation that freed all slaves during the Civil War.

Two other buildings of note stand in the Capitol complex: the State Armory and the Bushnell Memorial. The Armory, to the west of the Capitol, is headquarters for the Connecticut National Guard and the military Reserve units. The Bushnell Memorial, on the east flank of the Capitol, is a beautiful auditorium that serves as the cultural heart of a community that places a high premium on theater and music.

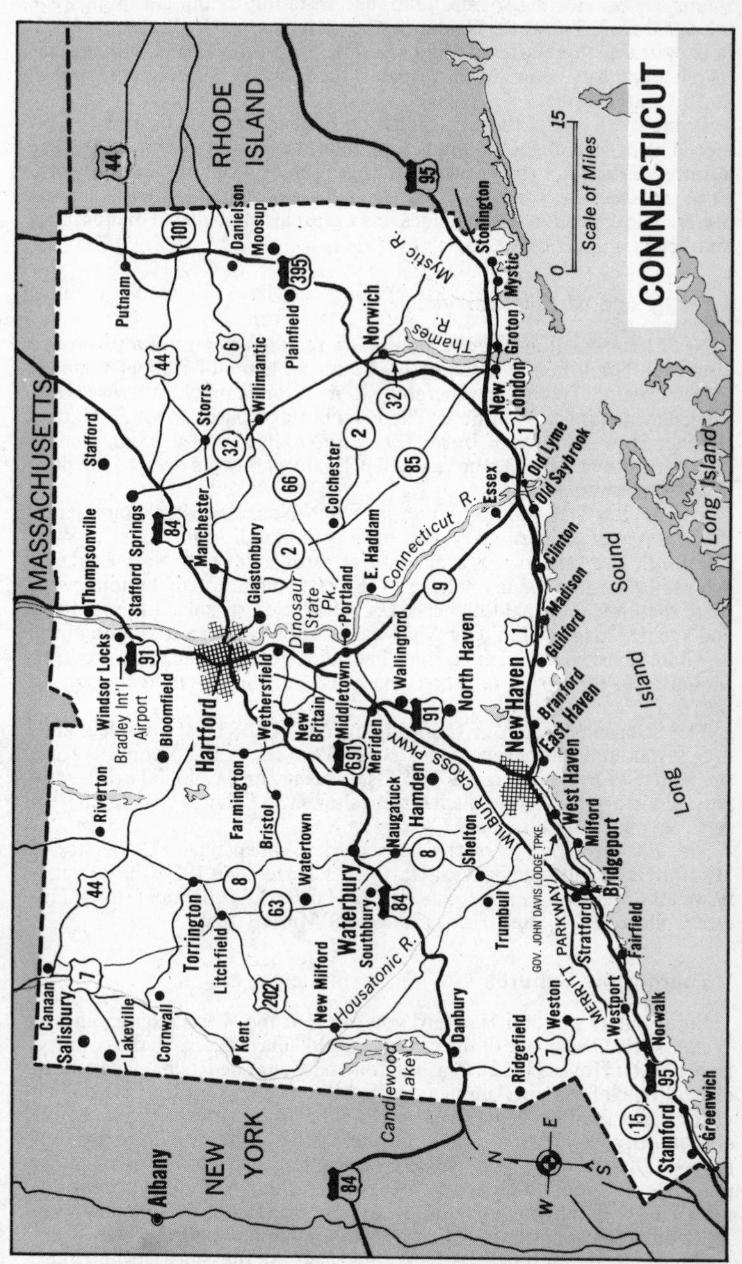
CONNECTICUT
MASSACHUSETTS
RHODE ISLAND
NEW YORK
Albany
Long Island Sound
Long Island
Scale of Miles
0
15
Hartford
New Haven
Bridgeport
Waterbury
Danbury
Stamford
Greenwich
Norwalk
Westport
Fairfield
Stratford
Milford
West Haven
East Haven
Branford
Guilford
Madison
Clinton
Old Saybrook
Old Lyme
Essex
New London
Groton
Mystic
Stonington
Norwich
Plainfield
Moosup
Danielson
Putnam
Willimantic
Storrs
Stafford
Stafford Springs
Thompsonville
Windsor Locks
Bradley Int'l Airport
Bloomfield
Manchester
Glastonbury
Wethersfield
New Britain
Middletown
Meriden
Wallingford
North Haven
Hamden
Portland
E. Haddam
Colchester
Dinosaur State Pk.
Farmington
Bristol
Riverton
Torrington
Litchfield
Watertown
Naugatuck
Southbury
Shelton
Trumbull
New Milford
Kent
Cornwall
Canaan
Salisbury
Lakeville
Ridgefield
Weston
Candlewood Lake
Housatonic R.
Connecticut R.
Thames R.
Mystic R.
WILBUR CROSS PKWY
MERRITT PARKWAY
GOV. JOHN DAVIS LODGE TPKE.
N
S
E
W
44
101
395
6
32
66
2
85
84
91
691
9
1
95
8
63
202
7
15

Hartford's Civic Center offers major shows, entertainments, and sports events, shops, meeting rooms, boutiques, restaurants, and parking garage for 4,000 cars. The Civic Center is headquarters for Connecticut's NHL hockey team, the Hartford Whalers. The Hartford Stage Company has its own repertory company and theater, the John W. Huntington Theater, at 50 Church Street.

In the south end of the city, high on a ridge of traprock, is Trinity College. The college chapel is a masterpiece of neo-Gothic architecture. The Trinity Watkinson Library owns a folio edition of Audubon's masterwork, *Birds of America,* considered the second most valuable in the United States. The collection also includes fine examples of medieval manuscripts and books.

Birthplace of Tom Sawyer

At 351 Farmington Avenue, on the few remaining acres of a tract once known as Nook Farm, is the grand Victorian home of Samuel Clemens (Mark Twain). Today the venerable old mansion is much as it was when the Clemens family lived here. The neighboring house, in which Harriet Beecher Stowe, author of *Uncle Tom's Cabin,* lived and worked, is filled with Mrs. Stowe's furnishings and, like Twain's house, is open to the public as a museum.

The modest little saltbox house in which Noah Webster, compiler of the first American dictionary, was born is on South Main Street in West Hartford. The saltbox, an architectural form unique to New England, evolved because of the tax policies of the first colonies. Any building with more than one floor paid higher taxes. The Colonists solved the problem and avoided taxes by building what was essentially a lean-to on top of the first floor, masked by a slanted roof. The name derived from the structure's similarity to the design of a box housewives of the day used for storing salt.

The Science Museum of Connecticut, one of the most complete children's museums in the country, is in West Hartford. Youngsters are fascinated with the numerous exhibits, ranging from Colonial artifacts to natural history displays to planetarium shows to a "Hands On" room with signs saying "Please touch."

The 200-acre campus of the nonsectarian, independent University of Hartford is also located in West Hartford. Chartered in 1957, the university was the result of a merger among the Hartford Art School (1877), Hillyer College (1879), and Hartt College of Music (1920).

Touring the Suburbs

Immediately south of Hartford you can tour the Webb House, close to Wethersfield Green, one of the most beautiful village greens in the country. In the Webb House (1752), Washington and Count de Rochambeau, head of the French forces in America, plotted the strategy that led to the allied victory over the British at Yorktown. As the Webb House reflects the life of a wealthy Connecticut family during the Revolution, the nearby Buttolph-Williams House, built in 1692, shows how the Colonists lived under much sterner conditions nearly a century earlier. Additions were made in keeping with the original building, a common practice in Colonial times. The numerous artifacts in the large kitchen are fascinating.

Other interesting buildings in Wethersfield are the Silas Deane House (1766), home of one of the special envoys sent to Europe by the Continental Congress, and the Old Academy Museum (1801), where household tools, utensils, and a loom are on display. North of Hartford is Windsor, a town which probably has more well-preserved pre-Revolutionary War houses than any other in the state. Only a few buildings are open to the public, but in them you can see examples of early architecture and early furnishings. The New England Air Museum at Bradley International Airport has one of the largest collections of aeronautical memorabilia in the world; it is open from 10 A.M. to 6 P.M. daily.

Farmington, on State 4 west of Hartford, is a lovely old community with many Colonial homes set on quiet, tree-lined streets. It's the home of Miss Porter's School, an exclusive preparatory school for girls. The Stanley-Whitman House (1720), now a museum, is one of the oldest frame houses in Connecticut. The Hill-Stead Museum was built in 1901 for Alfred Atmore Pope, whose daughter, Mrs. John Wallace Riddle, willed the property in 1946 to be a museum. The magnificent furnishings and extensive collection of French Impressionist paintings are in place as they were when the house was occupied by the Riddles.

New Haven

New Haven has a treasure trove of things to see, many of them connected with Yale University. A guided tour or an individual walking tour provides an overall view of the university. Next, visit the Art Gallery, the Peabody Museum of Natural History, or perhaps the Yale Center for British Art, the Beinecke Rare Book and Manuscript Library, and the Yale University Library, which stages regular exhibits. The Long Wharf Theatre, which offers one of the finest theatrical series in the East, and the Yale Repertory Theatre have outstanding winter seasons.

The historic Shubert Theatre, now the Shubert Performing Arts Center, in downtown New Haven, where many Broadway hit shows were first presented, has been completely renovated and refurbished. The Palace, formerly the Roger Sherman Theater, has been refurbished and reopened.

Northwestern Connecticut

Northwest of Hartford, via Route 44, lies Riverton on State 20 at the far side of the People's State Forest. Here the Hitchcock Chair Factory, founded in 1818, is still making chairs modeled after the original design. Visitors can watch the "rushing" operation on chair seats through glass windows or visit the John T. Kenney Hitchcock Museum specializing in 19th-century furnishings and artifacts. State 8 south through Winsted and Torrington is picturesque as it winds through state forest areas on the way to the city of Waterbury, an industrial city known for its brass factories.

The historic town of Litchfield should not be passed by. State 118 will lead from State 8 right to the village green, which is dominated by a beautiful (reconstructed) white-steepled Congregational Church. The area has been declared an historic district, so the white clapboard homes with their black or green shutters must remain unchanged. Harriet Beecher Stowe, Henry Ward Beecher, and Ethan Allen were born on North Street.

Nearby Litchfield is Bantam Lake, largest natural lake in the state and a popular summer playground. While there is much private property on the lakeside, there's public swimming at Sandy Beach; and at least half the lake is bordered by the 4,000-acre White Memorial Foundation, a bird and animal sanctuary. Lake Waramaug, in the town of New Preston, has several country inns on or overlooking the lakefront. Year-round activities include cross-country skiing, swimming, boating, tennis, and golf. Washington, a short distance from Litchfield, is a remarkable example of a colonial village—exquisite white houses around a small green. The American Indian Archaeological Institute and Museum, just off Route 199 displays Indian artifacts and offers a natural habitat trail and a weekend film series.

Sharon, Kent, Cornwall (with its one-lane covered bridge), and Canaan are lovely towns to explore in the northwest corner of the state; and farther south (toward Danbury) Roxbury, Bridgewater, Brookfield, and New Milford are charming as well. Candlewood Lake and Squantz Pond State Park are popular public swimming and boating areas.

One aspect of the more technical side of Connecticut history is reflected in the area of Thomaston, Terryville, and Bristol. This is clock country, with two of the towns taking their names from pioneer clockmakers. Seth Thomas started his clock works in Thomaston in 1812, after learning the trade with Eli Terry, who patented a clock with wooden works that became hugely successful. In Bristol, more than 1,600 clocks, some dating back to 1680, are on display at the American Clock and Watch Museum. Terryville has a Lock Museum of America where over 18,000 locks and keys manufactured in Connecticut over a century ago are housed.

Cutting east across the middle of the state on I-84 from the Danbury-Waterbury area, Route 66 from Bristol leads through Meriden back to Middletown. The space-age oriented may want to make a pilgrimage to the Wesleyan Olin Library, where the original manuscripts of Albert Einstein's theory of relativity are kept. The Davidson Art Center exhibits excellent examples of European and American art.

Across the Connecticut River through Portland and East Hampton is the Salmon River State Forest, providing a scenic drive along the river with a view of the Comstock Covered Bridge, one of the few remaining in Connecticut, but closed to traffic.

Connecticut's Southeastern Corner

Continuing on Route 66 and then on Route 32, you arrive in Norwich, "the rose of New England" and one of the earliest settlements in the state. The Leffingwell Inn (1675), where Washington and his officers were frequent guests, is now a museum of Colonial times. The Slater Memorial Museum, particularly noted for its Indian and Japanese collections and for its full-size replicas of Greek and Roman sculptures, is located on the grounds of the Norwich Free Academy, a coeducational secondary school. The Rose Arts Festival in June is a week-long celebration in Norwich, attracting thousands of visitors to its variety of programs.

Those who follow American Indian lore will want to stop in Montville, rich in the history of Uncas, chief of the Mohegans but born a Pequot. Reminders of Uncas are everywhere. Near the Mohegan Congregational Church is a small museum of Indian relics, the Tantaquidgeon Indian Museum. The frames of both a long house and a round house, types of dwelling common to eastern Indians, who didn't live in teepees as did their western counterparts, are on display in the yard.

South on State 32, lies New London, one of Connecticut's earliest towns and one integrally connected with the sea. Like Nantucket and New Bedford in Massachusetts, New London in the 19th century was home for whaling ships. Whaling provided the fortunes that built the mansions of Yankee sea captains and ship owners, some of which still stand today. New London is the site of the U.S. Coast Guard Academy. Visitors may tour the grounds, stopping first at the fine Visitors' Center, then visiting some buildings and the beautiful sailing vessel used in cadet training, *Eagle,* when she's in port. The Shaw Mansion (1756), now the New London County Historical Society, the Joshua and Nathaniel Hempsted Houses (17th and 18th centuries), the Old Town Mill (1650, rebuilt in 1712), and the Lyman Allen Museum are only a handful of the places to see here. Charter fishing and pleasure boating out of New London marinas attract sports fishermen from considerable distances.

Just across the Thames River in Groton is the headquarters of the North Atlantic submarine fleet. The vast U.S. Naval Submarine Base is open to visitors by appointment only. The USS *Nautilus,* world's first nuclear-powered submarine, and a Submarine Museum are located on the banks of the Thames River in Groton near the entrance to the base. Both the *Nautilus* and the museum are open to the public without charge.

Just east of Groton, in Mystic, the Age of Sail is recalled at Mystic Seaport Museum. The Seaport is a re-creation of an early 19th-century New England coastal village. The featured exhibit is the *Charles W. Morgan,* a venerable old whaleship which spent an incredible 80 years in pursuit of whales. The *Joseph Conrad,* a former Danish merchant marine training ship, is also permanently berthed at the Seaport and is headquarters for the Seaport Youth Training program. *Sabino,* one of the last passenger-carrying steamboats, operates seasonal daily tours on the Mystic River. A planetarium is an interesting compliment to the tiny village scene, and several galleries house seafaring treasures. A research library of maritime books and manuscripts is part of the complex.

The Mystic MarineLife Aquarium lies just north of the Seaport at Exit 90, I-95 (on the edge of Old Mystick Village, a unique shopping center). An hourly dolphin, whale, and seal show in the 1,400-seat marine theater is held daily for visitors.

The Borough of Stonington, east of Mystic, is reached via Route 1. There are interesting landmarks, elegantly restored homes once owned by sea captains, and the less pretentious cottages of the fishermen. A visit to this elm-shaded community leaves lasting memories.

RHODE ISLAND

Providence

Rhode Island's political, financial, commercial, and cultural center is Providence, the capital city.

Providence was founded in 1636 by Roger Williams (a Providence park memorializes his name), who was banished from Massachusetts for his nonconformist views on religion. It was here in 1638 that he founded the First Baptist Meeting House. The oldest church of any denomination in the state, it has been preserved in its Colonial form.

The largest concentration of original Colonial homes may be seen on College Hill, along Benefit Street's "Mile of History." This is the neighborhood of Brown University, the Rhode Island School of Design and its Museum of Art, and numerous Colonial homes, buildings, and churches. Serious attention is given to accurate renovation of these buildings, which feature architectural examples from many American eras.

There have been numerous renewal projects completed in Providence during the past few years, including the complete renovation of the area between the State Capitol and downtown.

Newport

Colonial Newport, founded in 1639, is one of New England's most fascinating towns. America's first Quakers settled here in 1657. Sephardic Jews arrived the following year and established a center of Jewish culture that has endured for three centuries.

Newport became the first American resort when wealthy merchants came here for the summer as early as 1720. The resort reached its apogee at the end of the 19th century in the extravagant and tax-free Gilded Age. Wealthy families such as the Vanderbilts, Astors, Belmonts, Berwinds, and Fishes built a series of "cottages" along Bellevue Avenue.

Many of these opulent residences are now open to the public as museum mansions, and they attract thousands of visitors each year.

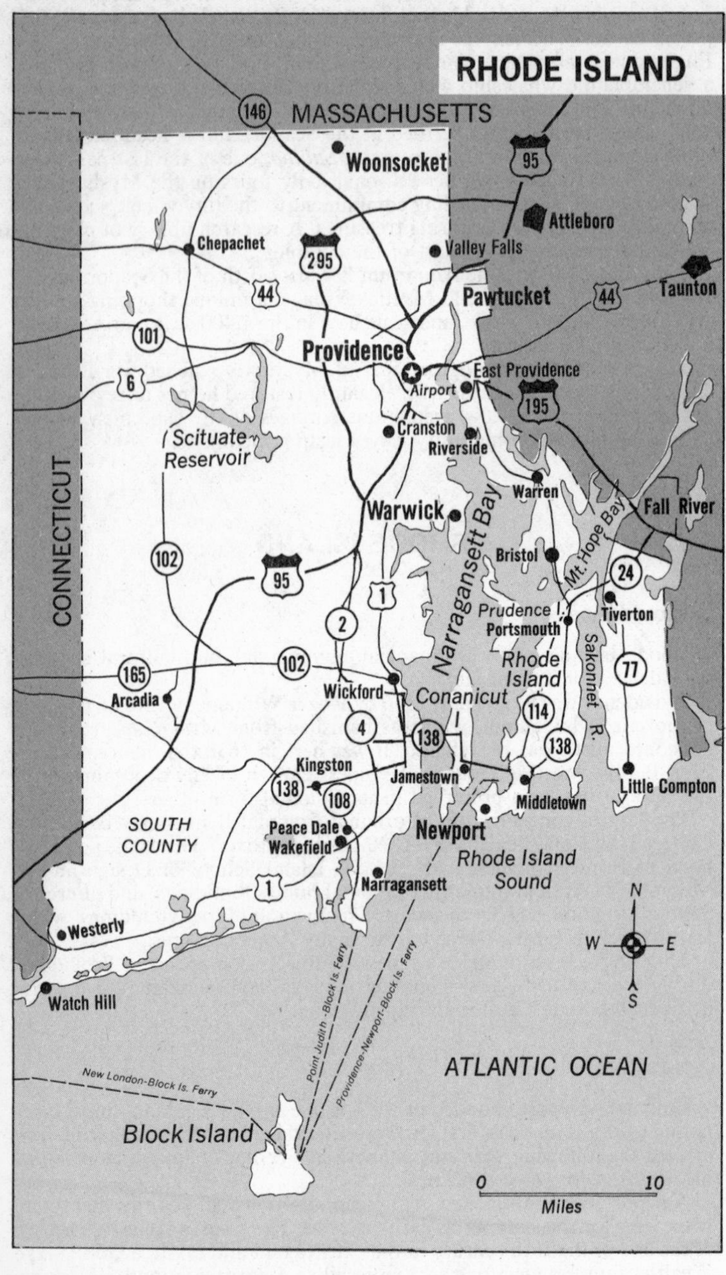
RHODE ISLAND
MASSACHUSETTS
CONNECTICUT
Woonsocket
Attleboro
Chepachet
Valley Falls
Pawtucket
Taunton
Providence
East Providence
Airport
Cranston
Riverside
Scituate Reservoir
Warren
Warwick
Narragansett Bay
Fall River
Mt. Hope Bay
Bristol
Prudence I.
Portsmouth
Tiverton
Rhode Island
Sakonnet R.
Conanicut I.
Wickford
Arcadia
Kingston
Jamestown
Middletown
Little Compton
Peace Dale
Wakefield
Newport
SOUTH COUNTY
Rhode Island Sound
Narragansett
Westerly
Watch Hill
Point Judith-Block Is. Ferry
Providence-Newport-Block Is. Ferry
New London-Block Is. Ferry
ATLANTIC OCEAN
Block Island
0 10
Miles
N
W
E
S
146
95
295
44
101
6
195
102
24
2
1
165
77
114
4
138
108

Even with the seeming worship of opulence, the town is not without religious landmarks. Trinity Church, buit in 1726, with its three-tier wine glass pulpit and well-preserved wood structure, has been called a supreme and matchless wonder of Colonial America. Touro Synagogue, designed by Peter Harrison and constructed in 1763 in Georgian style, is America's oldest synagogue.

The waterfront, made popular by America's Cup races, has become a mecca for yachtsmen, and the shops and fine restaurants along the waterfront attract tourists year-round.

Block Island

About 10 miles south of the mainland, Block Island is a summer beach resort and fishing center. Visitors spend many pleasant hours on Block Island State Beach or at the resorts where privately owned beaches are at the disposal of guests. Some deep-sea fishing for tuna, bluefish, cod, swordfish, striped bass, and flounder is another interest. At the southeastern corner of the island you can see Mohegan Bluffs, spectacular cliffs of clay which bear a strong resemblance to the chalk cliffs of Dover, England, rising to about 180 feet above sea level and stretching along the coast for about five miles.

Whittier's poem "The Palatine Light" commemorates the Palatine Graves area near Dickens Point, where the crew of an ill-fated Dutch ship lies buried. A man-made harbor, New Harbor, graces the western shore of the island. It was constructed by connecting the Atlantic with the Great Salt Pond by means of a channel dug across the separating narrow barrier of land. Old Harbor, on the other side of the island, is where a small fishing fleet and pleasure boats dock.

PRACTICAL INFORMATION FOR SOUTHERN NEW ENGLAND

WHEN TO GO. Southern New England comes as close as any region to living up to the old "four-season vacationland" cliché. It all comes down to what you want to do, and how many people you want to be doing it with. The seacoasts of Connecticut, Rhode Island, and Massachusetts are, naturally, at their most popular in the summer, with the largest crowds on some of the Long Island Sound and Cape Cod beaches. The farther north you go, the colder the water is, so beach crowds tend to thin out. The fine weather during spring and autumn is increasing the popularity for getaways during these seasons; it's easier to get reservations, and the peace and solitude of long beach walks in sweaters and windbreakers makes up for frolicking in the surf. This applies to winter as well, but only the hardy need apply: locations along the coast seldom experience the bitter temperatures common to inland New England, but the wind and dampness will reach the marrow of your bones.

If there is any place to avoid spending too much time during summer in the three-state area, it is probably the cities. Like other urban areas in the U.S. northeast, places like Boston, Providence, and Hartford can be awfully hot and sticky come July and Aug. The best time for a city vacation in southern New England is spring and fall.

Autumn throughout all New England is legendary for its display of color, and the region's southern states have no shortage of country roads ideal for foliage watching. Travelers used to leaf-peeking trips in Vermont and New Hampshire should note, however, that the peak season comes a little later in Massachusetts, and later still in Connecticut and Rhode Island. The situation varies from year to year, but expect the colors to start peaking around the end of Sept. in northern

Massachusetts and the higher elevations of the Berkshires, and the show to last into the third week of Oct. in the southern reaches of Connecticut and Rhode Island.

As for winter visits to southern New England, downhill skiers will generally find their opportunities clustered in the Berkshires, with the season somewhat shorter than in prime New England ski territory farther north. Cross-country skiers have a far wider array of places to choose from—just remember that there's usually a lot more snow inland than near the coast.

HOW TO GET THERE. By plane. The principal southern New England airports are *Logan International,* in Boston; *Bradley International,* Windsor Locks, CT (serving Hartford, CT and Springfield, MA); and *Theodore Francis Green State Airport* in Warwick, RI, south of Providence. In addition, there are smaller airports in places such as Bridgeport, Groton, New Haven, CT, and Hyannis on Cape Cod, MA. The larger airports are served by the major east coast air carriers, including *Delta, Piedmont, Pan American, Continental, TWA, United, American, USAir,* and *Northwest.* Several commuter airlines also schedule flights from these airports.

By bus. The national carrier *Greyhound* and regional affiliates connect terminals in larger southern New England cities with major destinations throughout the United States and Canada. Here are the main telephone numbers for schedules and information. In Boston: *Greyhound,* 617–423–5810. In Hartford: *Greyhound,* 203–547–1500 or 800–237–8211. In Providence: *Bonanza,* 401–751–8800 or 800–556–3815.

By train. *Amtrak*'s Northeast Corridor trains serve New Haven and New London, CT, and other shore points in that state; Providence, RI; and Boston, MA. Connecticut Valley and *Montrealer* trains serve New Haven and New London, CT. From the west, the *Lake Shore Limited,* Amtrak's Chicago-Boston connector, passes through Massachusetts points such as Pittsfield, Springfield, and Worcester. For Amtrak information in Boston, call 617–482–3660; in Hartford, 203–525–4580; in Providence, 401–751–5416. Or, call 800–USA–RAIL for Amtrak information from anywhere in the United States.

By car. The principal highways leading into southern New England are Interstate 95, which heads out of New York City and hugs the Long Island Sound coast of Connecticut before heading north through Providence, RI, and Boston on its way to New Hampshire and Maine. The Massachusetts Turnpike (I-90), which connects with a branch of the New York State Thruway at the New York-Massachusetts border just west of Albany, New York, has its eastern terminus in Boston. Hartford, CT, Springfield, MA, and other Connecticut River Valley communities are served by Interstate 91, which branches north from I-95 at New Haven, CT, and follows the river north towards Vermont. The most direct route from points south and west to Cape Cod is I-95 to Providence, then Route 195 to Route 25.

TOURIST INFORMATION. Massachusetts. Contact the *Massachusetts Department of Commerce,* Office of Travel and Tourism, 100 Cambridge St., Boston, MA 02202 (617–727–3201). The Division will supply free maps and brochures, as well as the addresses and telephone numbers of regional tourist bureaus throughout the state.

Connecticut. Contact the *Connecticut Division of Tourism,* 865 Brook St., Rocky Hill, CT 06067 (203–258–4290 or 800–282–6863). The Division can supply a free vacation guide, containing information on the state's points of interest, outdoor recreation, and lodgings.

Rhode Island. Contact the Tourism Division of the *Rhode Island Department of Economic Development,* 7 Jackson Walkway, Providence, RI 02903 (401–277–2601 or 800–556–2484; Fax 401–277–2102). Ask for the Department's comprehensive *Guide to Rhode Island.*

Finally, don't overlook the area's excellent newspapers. For up-to-date information on what's going on in southern New England once you arrive, check the arts and leisure sections of the *Boston Globe,* Hartford *Courant,* and Providence *Journal-Bulletin.* The *Boston Globe* and *Hartford Courant* both publish "Calendar" sections each Thurs. with comprehensive listings of interesting places and events.

TIME ZONES. All of southern New England is on Eastern Time.

TELEPHONES. Massachusetts has three area codes: 508 and 617 in the eastern part of the state, 413 in the west. The Connecticut area code is 203. Rhode Island is 401. In Massachusetts and Connecticut local pay telephone calls cost 10 cents for the first 3 minutes. In Rhode Island the charge is 15 cents. Throughout the area, it is necessary to dial 1 before the area code on all long-distance calls, and 1 before the seven-digit number when making calls outside specific calling areas within an area code. A recording will inform you if this procedure is necessary when you dial. Credit card and collect calls may be made by dialing 0 before the number to be dialed. For information in your immediate area, dial 411; for all other areas, 1, then the area code and 555–1212.

EMERGENCY TELEPHONE NUMBERS. In larger urban areas, the universal *emergency* number for police, fire department, ambulances, and paramedics is 911. In many smaller municipalities and rural areas, it will be necessary to dial the full telephone number of the department needed. Telephone directories contain crucial emergency numbers in their inside front covers throughout southern New England; or, you may dial 0 for the telephone operator, who will put you in contact with assistance.

HOW TO GET AROUND. By intercity bus. *Greyhound* and *Bonanza,* the major carriers, connect many large southern New England cities and suburban locations (*see* "How To Get There," above, for telephone numbers). The big city bus terminals are also the points of arrival and departure for smaller, regional intercity lines, many of which are subsidiaries of the big two. Call the main information numbers regarding secondary lines operating out of these terminals.

By rail. In addition to *Amtrak* services listed above (*see* How To Get There), Boston and its suburbs have commuter rail lines operated by *Amtrak,* under contract to the Massachusetts Bay Transportation Authority. For South Shore commuter rail information call 800–392–6099. The *Cape Cod Railway* runs in summer from Buzzards Bay to Falmouth and Hyannis; for information, call 508–771–3788.

Public transit. Metropolitan Boston bus and subway service, as well as trolley lines, are operated by the *Massachusetts Bay Transportation Authority (MBTA).* Maps are available at Park Street Station, Boston; for schedule information, call 617–722–3200 (722–5000 nights and weekends). Most of Rhode Island is served by the buses of the *Rhode Island Public Transit Authority* (401–781–9400). In the greater Hartford area, the buses are operated by *Connecticut Transit.* Call 203–525–9181 for information.

By taxi. With the exception of rural areas, virtually all of southern New England is accessible by taxi. Many taxi companies operate only in the immediate areas surrounding their headquarters; inquire regarding flat-rate service to popular destinations such as airports. Generally, this service is cheaper when it is provided by an airport limousine service; see the New England Telephone *Yellow Pages* for taxi and limousine service listings.

By rental car. The major nationwide car rental companies, including *Hertz, Avis, Dollar, Budget,* and *National,* are represented at airports and in the larger cities. For *Hertz,* call 800–654–3131; for *Avis,* call 800–331–1212. The following numbers apply to Logan Airport, Boston: *Budget,* 617–569–4000; *Dollar,* 617–569–5300; *National,* 617–569–6700. Remember to make reservations as far in advance as possible to assure availability of the model you prefer.

By ferry. Martha's Vineyard and Nantucket are accessible by air from Boston and New York, but if you want to take a car to the islands, you'll be using the services of the Woods Hole, Martha's Vineyard, and Nantucket Steamship Authority, serving Vineyard Haven and Nantucket from Woods Hole. Call 508–540–2022 for information. Block Island is accessible by ferry from Point Judith, RI, and New London, CT, and by air from Westerly, RI.

HINTS TO MOTORISTS. Southern New England has an excellent road system. The concentration of settlements in the area means that you'll seldom be far from services, with the possible exception of a few lonely stretches in northern Connecticut, central Massachusetts, and the Berkshires. Even these places are hardly what you'd call remote, especially if you're used to the expanses of the Midwest and western United States.

The very closeness of things in southern New England argues against spending too much time on the superhighways or trying to cover a great deal of distance in a day unless you are in a genuine hurry to get from one place to another. For instance, you can shoot from Boston to the New Hampshire border in an hour, but you will miss some of the most beautiful scenery in America along the coastal side roads.

The speed limit throughout the three-state area is the federally mandated 55 mph, except along secondary roads in settled areas where lower limits will be enforced. In and around places like Boston and Providence, however, there are times when you'll be more concerned with whether it's possible to move at all. This brings us to the cardinal rule of visiting old New England cities: if it's at all possible, leave your car in the hotel garage or on the outskirts when you go into town for sightseeing. These cities were laid out long before the automobile was invented, and negotiating narrow downtown streets—not to mention parking—can often be exasperating. Besides, you can't enjoy the charms of places like Boston's Beacon Hill or Providence's Benefit Street while keeping a wary eye on traffic. These are walker's cities, unless you know just where you're going and have a reasonable idea of where you're going to park. If you must drive, avoid rush hours—*especially* on the expressways in and out of Boston, Providence, and Hartford.

One more caveat for the motorist: southern New England roads go everywhere, but so will you if you don't pay *very* careful attention to the signs. The extra measure of alertness on your part is required because of the lackadaisical approach to signs on the part of whoever's in charge. This is especially true around the cities. One of the area's more annoying quirks, by the way, is the assumption that you know the name of the main drag you're on, and are only interested in the names of the side streets. You can go for miles without a clue from the street signs, so don't hesitate to ask questions as soon as you begin to be puzzled by your whereabouts.

HINTS TO DISABLED TRAVELERS. Nearly all modern facilities in southern New England—places such as airports, civic buildings, and newer museums—have been designed with handicapped access in mind. However, there is a problem connected with the fact that much of the built environment in this part of the United States dates back to a time well before there was any national consciousness-raising on subjects such as wheelchair access. If you are a handicapped traveler and have in mind experiences such as a visit to a quaint country inn, be sure to state your specific needs when inquiring about reservations. Many such establishments have first-floor rooms available—but since they are not as numerous as upper-floor accommodations, advance notice is strongly recommended.

SEASONAL EVENTS. Massachusetts. From federal holidays to anything made with strawberries, Massachusetts seasonal events are very diversified. Here is a sampling: JANUARY. *Boston Boat Show,* World Trade Center, Commonwealth Pier, Boston (617–536–8152). FEBRUARY. *Valentine Festival,* Boston (617–536–4100). MARCH. *Boston Spring Flower Show,* Bayside Expo Center, 200 Mt. Vernon St., Dorchester (617–536–9280). APRIL. *Boston Marathon,* one of world's greatest foot races, Hopkinton to Boston (508–435–4303 or 617–536–4100). *Paul Revere's Ride to Lexington,* a reenactment; for schedule, call 617–536–4100. JULY. Outdoor *Boston Pops Concerts,* Hatch Shell on the Esplanade (617–266–1492). Country fairs and festivals, including strawberry, are prolific throughout the state during summer and early autumn. NOVEMBER and DECEMBER. Traditional Thanksgiving and Christmas celebrations are on every town's schedule. For a complete Calendar of Annual Events, contact: Massachusetts Office of Travel and Tourism, 13th Floor, 100 Cambridge St., Boston, MA 02202; 617–727–3201.

Connecticut. The Tourism Division of the Connecticut Department of Economic Development keeps track of the listed events; for information, contact them at 865 Brook St., Rocky Hill, CT 06067 (800–CT–BOUND). MARCH. *Spring Antiques Show,* Hartford. APRIL. *Spring Blossom Season in Connecticut* begins. MAY. *New England Painting, Sculpture, and Drawing Exhibition,* Silvermine Guild Gallery, New Canaan. JUNE. *Yale-Harvard Rowing Regatta,* Thames River, New London. JULY. *Open House Tour* of colonial homes, Litchfield. AUGUST. *Volvo International Tournament,* Yale Bowl, New Haven. SEPTEMBER. *Oyster Festival,* Norwalk. OCTOBER. *Fall Foliage Trolley Trips* at Shore Line Trolley Museum, East Haven. DECEMBER. *Christmas at Mystic Seaport Museum,* Mystic.

Rhode Island. This is a small state with a big calendar; for particulars, contact the Rhode Island Department of Economic Development Tourism Promotion Division, 7 Jackson Walkway, Providence, RI 02903 (401–277–2601). MARCH. *Irish Heritage Month,* Newport (401–847–1600). JUNE. *Festival of Historic Houses,* Providence, Providence Preservation Society (401–831–7440). JULY. *Fourth of July Parade* Bristol (401–253–7739). *Newport Music Festival* (401–846–1133), and *Newport Jazz Festival* (401–847–3700). AUGUST. *Ben & Jerry's Folk Festival,* Newport (401–847–3709). SEPTEMBER. *Providence Waterfront Festival* (401–941–6790). DECEMBER. *Christmas in Newport* (401–849–6454).

TOURS. Massachusetts. A good way to see Boston and its historic suburbs is to sign on for one of the *Gray Line* tours which leave from the Park Plaza, Sheraton Boston, and Copley Plaza hotels. There are tours of Boston proper and of Lexington/Concord, each lasting 3 hours, as well as a combination tour taking in all of the above areas, plus a lunch stop, lasting 7 hours. Contact Gray Line, 275 Tremont St., Boston, 02116; in the Tremont House (617–426–8805). The same company offers a 4-hour *Plymouth Pilgrimage,* and excursions to Salem. *Peter Pan Lines,* 1776 Main St., Springfield, MA 01103 (413–781–3320) offers bus trips with stops in Old Sturbridge Village and Springfield as well as the Eastern States Exposition in September.

Connecticut. General tours in Hartford are offered by *DATTCO Tours* (800–382–0023 or in Hartford, 249–4458). *Heritage Trails,* Box 138, Farmington, CT 06034 (203–677–8867) has an appealing schedule of tours to scenic Connecticut areas limited to 10 persons per tour.

Rhode Island. For a comprehensive, 22-mi. guided tour of Newport, including access to one of three of the fabulous summer "cottages" built by turn-of-the-century millionaires, contact *Viking Tours,* 101 Swinburne Row (Brick Marketplace), Newport, RI (401–847–6921). The same company also offers harbor tours of Newport in summer. To get a good look at the historic neighborhoods of Providence, *Providence Preservation Society* offers tours (401–831–7440); *Executive Circle* offers full-service tours (401–944–2040).

SPECIAL-INTEREST SIGHTSEEING. Massachusetts. For a look at one of the state's oldest institutions, take a tour of *Harvard.* Tours depart daily from the Harvard University Information Office on the ground floor of Holyoke Center, Harvard Square, Cambridge; call 617–495–1573 for details. *Bay State Cruises,* 20 Long Wharf, Boston, offers trips around Boston Harbor with stops at several of the islands that make up a state park. Call 617–723–7800 for information. Another maritime adventure that has caught on big in Massachusetts is the *whale-watch cruise,* now offered at a number of places along the coast. Reservations should be made in advance: New England Aquarium, Central Wharf off Atlantic Ave., Boston (617–973–5277); Gloucester Whale Watch, Cape Ann Marina on Rte. 133, Exit 14 from Rte. 128 (508–283–6089 or 800–WHALING); Dolphin Whale Watch, MacMillan Wharf, Provincetown (508–255–3857 or 800–826–9300 in MA). For a pleasant cruise along the North Shore, try *AC Cruise Line,* 28 Northern Ave., Boston, MA (617–426–8419). Their summertime cruise itinerary is Boston to Gloucester. History buffs will enjoy a tour of the *Massachusetts State House* (617–727–3676) or a guided walk with *Boston By Foot,* 77 N. Washington St., Boston, MA (617–367–2345). Itineraries include the Freedom Trail, Copley Square, Beacon Hill, and the North End. Wrap it all up with a newspaper tour: the *Boston Globe* will take you through its giant plant by appointment on weekdays; call 617–929–2000 for details.

Connecticut. In New Haven, you can choose from a number of tours at *Yale University;* call 203–436–8330 for information. At Essex, the *Valley Railroad* offers an old-fashioned train and boat trip along the Connecticut River (203–767–0103). The U.S. Naval Submarine Base in Groton is off-limits, but tours of areas accessible to visitors can be arranged by calling 203–443–1831. There are also a dozen Connecticut wineries to tour. For a complete list see Connecticut *Vacation Guide* (see Tourist Information).

Rhode Island. Providence is rich in Early American architecture, and you can learn more about it by taking one of the walking tours sponsored by the *Providence Preservation Society,* 21 Meeting St., Providence (401–831–7440). For Newport sightseeing, try *Viking Tours* (401–847–6921), offering bus excursions and boat tours, as well as combination land-sea tours. The Newport Chamber of Commerce offers taped walking tours; call 401–847–1600 for information.

PARKS AND GARDENS. Massachusetts. Boston is rich in horticultural delights, starting right in town with the *Public Garden* with its lush seasonal plantings and stately trees. In the city's Jamaica Plain section, visit the famous *Arnold Arboretum,* Harvard's incomparable 265-acre preserve containing hundreds of temperate-zone trees, shrubs, and flowering plants. Call 617–524–1718 for special events information. In Lowell National Historical Park, 246 Market St. (508–459–1000) there are a local history museum, walking tours, and seasonal barge and trolley rides. In the Berkshires, visit *Naumkeag Gardens,* Prospect Hill, Stockbridge (413–298–3239), an early 20th-century estate. The mansion and several formal gardens are open to the public.

Connecticut. One of the nation's most beautiful municipal rose gardens is at *Elizabeth Park,* 915 Prospect Ave., Hartford (203–722–6490). The *White Flower Farm,* Rte. 63, Litchfield (203–567–0801) is a commercial enterprise with 10 acres of display gardens. In Waterford, visit *Harkness Memorial Park,* Rte. 213 (203–443–5725) for fine displays of roses and other flowers. *Caprilands Herb Farm,* Silver St., Coventry (203–742–7244) incorporates 28 herb gardens.

Rhode Island. Some of the state's more spectacular gardens are on the grounds of Newport's extravagant mansions. These include plantings at *The Elms, The Breakers,* and *Rosecliff.* In Bristol, visit *Blithewold Gardens and Arboretum,* Ferry Rd. (401–785–9450). *Roger Williams Park,* Providence, is a welcome bit of verdure on the outskirts of town.

ZOOS. Massachusetts. In Boston's Franklin Park, the *Franklin Park Zoo,* Blue Hill Ave. (617–442–0991) offers 50 acres of outdoor animal habitats, a petting zoo, a tropical rain forest, and an outstanding aviary. At press time there were reports that this zoo may be closing due to budget cuts.North of the city in Stoneham, the *Stone Memorial Zoo* (617–438–8420), an affiliate of the Boston Zoological Society which manages Franklin Park, also has a good aviary as well as Siberian tigers. In Springfield, visit the zoo and picnic grounds at *Forest Park* (413–733–2251).

Connecticut. The largest zoo in the state is the *Beardsley Zoological Gardens,* Noble Ave., Bridgeport (203–576–8082). Animals native to Connecticut are featured at *West Rock Nature Center,* Wintergreen Ave., New Haven (203–787–8016); trails wind through 40 acres of the center's property.

Rhode Island. In Providence, *Roger Williams Park* has the region's best zoo. There are also small zoos at the *Enchanted Forest,* Hopkinton, and at *Slater Memorial Park* in Pawtucket (401–728–0500, ext. 257).

NATIONAL AND STATE PARKS. Massachusetts. The gem of Massachusetts's national parks is the *Cape Cod National Seashore,* established 25 years ago through the initiative of President John Kennedy. Comprising over 20,000 acres of spectacular dunes and beaches, the Seashore assures that development will never come to this fragile environment. There are visitors' centers at the main entrance, off Rte. 6 near the Orleans–Eastham town line, and (in summer) at Provincetown. For information on facilities, which include trails, interpretive programs, and guided walks, contact the Superintendent, Cape Cod National Seashore, Race Pt. Rd., S. Wellfleet, MA 02663. (Other federal parks in the state are historical in nature; *see* Historic Sites and Houses below.)

Massachusetts has some 50 state parks and forests, all suitable for walks and picnicking and some equipped with campsites. For information on facilities, contact the Massachusetts Department of Environmental Management, 100 Cambridge St., Boston, MA 02202 (617–727–3180). Outstanding state parks include the *Boston Harbor Islands State Park,* made up of the small but fascinating archipelago that begins less than a mile from downtown; *Mount Greylock State Reservation,* with trails leading to the top of the state's highest mountain in the Berkshires; *Willard Brook State Forest,* on Rte. 119 near Fitchburg; *Walden Pond State Reservation,* containing the very same Walden Pond where Thoreau lived, today popular with swimmers; and *Salisbury Beach State Reservation,* Salisbury, on the Atlantic at the mouth of the Merrimack River.

Connecticut. *Weir National Site* in Ridgefield was authorized in 1990 and is Connecticut's only national park. There are 88 state parks and 30 state forests in this small state, providing over 150,000 acres of recreation land. For information on facilities, contact the State Department of Environmental Protection Parks and Recreation Division, 165 Capitol Ave., Hartford, CT 06106. Some standout Connecticut parks are: *Macedonia Brook Park,* Litchfield County, with views, trout fishing, and good hiking trails; *Mohawk Mountain State Park and Forest,* good for skiing and hiking; *Hammonassett Beach,* on Long Island Sound at Madison, with its popular sandy beach and temperate waters; and *Gillette Castle Park,* Hadlyme, where you can visit the mock-medieval castle built by the the first great Sherlock Holmes actor William Gillette 70 years ago.

Rhode Island. The state maintains over 12,000 acres of state parks and forests, many of them—as you might expect—on or near the ocean. Two of the most picturesque are *Fort Adams State Park,* Newport, a harborside facility surrounding the second largest seacoast fortification in the U.S.; and *Colt State Park,* Bristol, once a private estate along the shores of upper Naragansett Bay. Also recommended are *Goddard Memorial State Park,* Warwick; *Beach Pond State Park,* a large tract in Exeter; the *George Washington Camping Area,* Gloucester; *and Bay Island Park* on Prudence Island, Portsmouth. For information on these and other state park properties, write the Rhode Island Division of Parks and Recreation, 2321 Hartford Ave., Johnston, RI 02919.

CAMPING. Massachusetts. Camping in Boston, the state's largest city? Yes—on Lovells, Great Brewster, Grape, Bumpkin, and Peddocks Islands, in Boston Harbor Islands State Park. For information on campsites and water taxi service, contact the Massachusetts Department of Environmental Management, 100 Cambridge St., Boston, MA 02202 (617–727–3180). The same agency can provide information on other state parks with camping facilities. Among these are *Beartown State Forest,* near Great Barrington in the Berkshires; *Mohawk Trail State Forest,* near Charlemont; the 15,000-acre *October Mountain State Forest,* near Lee; and *Erving State Forest,* near West Orange.

Connecticut. Many of the state's state parks and forests are open to campers in late spring and during the summer. These include the abovementioned *Macedonia Brook State Park,* Kent; *Housatonic Meadows State Park,* Sharon; *Pachaug State Forest,* Voluntown; *Rocky Neck State Park,* Niantic; and *Cockaponset State Park,* Haddam. For information on fees and regulations, contact the Connecticut Department of Environmental Protection, State Office Building, Hartford, CT 06106 (203–566–2304). Private campgrounds are listed in the *Vacation Guide* (see Tourist Information).

Rhode Island. The best-equipped state park for camping in Rhode Island is *Burlingame,* in Charlestown. *Dyer Woods Nudist Campground,* on Johnson Rd., Foster 02825; 401–397–9927 (3 mi. south of Rte. 6). Cabins and recreational facilities are available as well as annual leases and memberships. Rhode Island statutes prohibit camping on Block Island. For "Camping" brochure with listings, contact Rhode Island Tourism Division, 7 Jackson Walkway, Providence, RI 02903 (401–556–2484).

FISHING AND HUNTING. Massachusetts. Massachusetts has outstanding saltwater fishing, whether you go out in a boat or cast from the surf. Principal species include cod, flounder, bluefish, mackerel, and the sadly depleted striped bass. Major coastal towns have "party boat" operators, who will take you out for a half day or day of fishing, often with tackle included. Surfcasting is at its best after late Apr., when the voracious bluefish start turning up at the state's beaches. Among the best spots are the ocean and bay beaches of Cape Cod; Great Point, on Nantucket; and the beaches of Cape Ann and Plum Island along the North Shore. For real excitement, go out in a charter boat after several hundred pounds of fighting tuna. No license is necessary for saltwater fishing. The state's rivers and streams offer an assortment of sport fish, including stocked supplies of trout. Opening day for trout is in mid-Apr. As for hunting, Massachusetts does not offer the abundance of deer found in northern New England, although the western parts of the state do offer some opportunities. The state's best hunting is for small game (rabbit, pheasant, grouse) on overgrown fields and the edges of marshlands. Out-of-state hunters and freshwater fishermen require special picenses; for information on fees and seasons, send self-addressed stamped No. 10 envelope to Division of Fisheries & Wildlife Headquarters, Westborough, MA 01581.

Connecticut and Rhode Island. Because the coastal and inland ecosystems of these two states are by and large similar to those of Massachusetts, the same information regarding game species applies. Both Connecticut and Rhode Island, of course, require visitors engaged in hunting or freshwater fishing to hold nonresident licenses. For fees, seasons, and regulations, contact the *Connecticut Department of Environmental Protection,* State Office Building, 165 Capitol Ave., Hartford, CT 06106 (203–566–2304), or the *Rhode Island Department of Environmental Management,* 83 Park St., Providence, RI 02903 (401–277–3075).

PARTICIPANT SPORTS. Massachusetts. If you're staying in the Boston area, you can take advantage of an excellent network of pools, tennis courts, and golf courses operated by the Metropolitan District Commission (MDC). For information, contact the MDC at 20 Somerset St., Boston (617–727–5215). Elsewhere in the state, you'll find good **golfing** at the Kittansett Club, Marion; Trull Brook Golf Club, Tewksbury; Taconic Golf Club, Williamstown; Bass River Golf Course, S. Yarmouth (Cape Cod); and Salem Country Club, Peabody. **Canoeing** is popular on the upper reaches of the Charles River, and on the Ipswich River between Middleton and Ipswich. Larger lakes and ponds throughout the state have launching ramps for **boating;** rowboats and outboards can often be rented. Massachusetts offers some fine roads for **bicycling,** and some towns have even set aside bike paths to keep two-wheeled and four-wheeled traffic separate. In Boston, the Dr. Paul Dudley White Bike Path follows the Charles River into Cambridge. For the winter visitor, Massachusetts **ski** areas include *Brodie Mtn.,* New Ashford (413–443–4752); *Jiminy Peak,* Hancock (413–738–5500); *Catamount,* S. Egremont (413–528–1262); and *Mt. Tom,* S. Holyoke (413–536–0416). **Cross-country skiing** is popular throughout the state; the largest area is *Northfield Mtn.,* Northfield (413–659–3713).

Connecticut. Golfing is popular in the state; at last count there were 75 public and 9 semi-public courses. Lists are available from the Tourism Division, Connecticut Economic Development Commission, 865 Brook St., Rocky Hill, CT 06067. **Tennis** courts are located in communities throughout the state. There are plenty of **boat launching** sites along Long Island Sound, most notably at Bridgeport, New Haven, Waterford, Groton, and Stonington. Others are at various freshwater sites inland and are designated on the official state map. Winter sports enthusiasts will find that the state has a fledgling **downhill ski** industry; write the Tourism Division (see address above) for a complete list of facilities. The largest ski area, with 24 trails, is Mohawk Mtn., Cornwall. State parks and forests are ideal for **cross-country skiing.**

Rhode Island. Even tiny Rhode Island finds room for 45 **golf courses,** about half of which are open to the public. Among them are: Triggs Memorial, 1533 Chalkstone Ave., Providence (401–272–4653); Montaup Country Club, Anthony Rd., Portsmouth (401–683–9882); Country View Golf Club, Colwell St., Burrillville (401–508–7157). Obtain information from the state's Tourism Promotion Division, 7 Jackson Walkway, Providence, RI 02903. The Division also provides **bicycling** maps for the greater Providence area. Rhode Island doesn't have much in the way of vertical drop, but nevertheless there is one **downhill ski** area. Ski Valley is in Yawgoo Valley, Cumberland (401–295–5366). Cross-country skiing is a bit more suited to the local landscape; see "State Parks," above, for ideas.

SPECTATOR SPORTS. Massachusetts. Boston is one of the most sports-minded cities in the nation, and its pro teams have loyal followers throughout New England. In summer, the *Red Sox* play **baseball** at the city's Fenway Park (617–267–8661). The *New England Patriots,* the region's pro **football** team, play at Sullivan Stadium in Foxborough (508–543–1776). In fall, winter, and early spring, the *Boston Celtics* (617–523–3030) carry on their winning ways in **basketball** at Boston Garden, which they share with **hockey's** *Boston Bruins* (617–227–3200). *College sports* are also a big draw; area teams include hockey, basketball, and football squads fielded by Harvard, Boston University, Boston College, and Northeastern University. There's **greyhound racing** at Wonderland, Revere (617–284–1300).

Connecticut. The *Hartford Whalers* of the National **Hockey** League play in the Civic Center; call 203–728–3366 for ticket information. College sports fans follow *Yale's* teams, particularly its **football** rivalry with other Ivy League schools. Lime Rock is one of the nation's most famous **sports car racing** tracks. There is **greyhound racing** in Plainfield, and another spectator sport with state-supervised betting is **jai-alai,** a fast-paced ball game played on indoor courts called *frontons.* There are jai-alai frontons at Bridgeport (203–333–2866); Milford (203–877–4211); and Hartford (203–525–8611).

Rhode Island. There are plenty of college sports in Rhode Island as well as the other southern New England states, with Brown (Ivy League), Providence College, and the University of Rhode Island. **Greyhounds** race at Lincoln Greyhound Park, Lincoln (401–723–3200). And Rhode Island has joined Connecticut in the **jai-alai** craze; the fronton is in Newport (401–849–5000). Newport is also a focus of major attention for **yacht racing** buffs: the Block Island Race takes place in late June, and the Newport to Bermuda and Annapolis to Newport races take place in alternate years. Newport is home to the International **Tennis** Hall of Fame and hosts the only tournament played on grass courts.

BEACHES. Massachusetts. The warmest ocean water (and the gentlest waves) in Massachusetts are found on the Atlantic side of Cape Cod, and along those parts of Martha's Vineyard and Nantucket that face Nantucket Sound. The Atlantic, north of Cape Ann, seldom gets far above 60°F before Aug. This doesn't seem to bother a good many of the natives, who come out in force even if it's just to sun and relax. There are fine beaches at the Cape Cod National Seashore (Nauset Beach; Province Lands), at Chappaquiddick on Martha's Vineyard, and just about anywhere on Nantucket. The best North Shore beaches are Crane's Beach (meticulously maintained by a private organization, and supported by hefty parking fees), and at the Parker River Wildlife Refuge, Newburyport.

Connecticut. The waters of Long Island Sound are warmer than those of the open Atlantic farther north; some good beaches include Ocean Beach Park, New London; Rocky Neck State Park, East Lyme: Hammonasset Beach State Park, between Madison and Clinton; and Sherwood Island State Park, a 233-acre island on Long Island Sound at Westport, for fishing and swimming.

Rhode Island. This state is mostly shoreline, and good beaches are easy to come by. They include the Narragansett Town Beach and Scarborough State Beach, Narragansett; Misquamicut State Beach, Westerly; East Matunuck State Beach, South Kingstown; and the beaches at Watch Hill, most southerly point on the state's mainland. Or, head out to Block Island, and Block Island State Beach.

CHILDREN'S ACTIVITIES. Massachusetts. Boston has its own *Children's Museum,* 300 Congress St. (617–426–8855). "Hands on" is the guiding spirit here; kids can even experiment with computers and video cameras. Each season brings new exhibits and special programs. At *Old Sturbridge Village,* Rtes. 20 and 15, Sturbridge (508–347–3362) children—and their parents—can learn volumes about the early American past by means of faithful re-creations of houses, farms, and workshops, complete with costumed staffers practicing crafts ranging from blacksmithing to weaving. Moving away from education into the realm of pure fun, there are amusement parks at *Salisbury Beach* (508–462–6631) near the New Hampshire border, Rte. 1A; and *Riverside Park,* Agawam (413–786–9300). On the way to the Cape, stop at the *Edaville Railroad,* Carver (508–866–4526) for a narrow-gauge train ride through working cranberry bogs and an interesting railroad museum. And, of course, kids always get enthusiastic about the *whale-watch cruises* listed above under "Special Interest Sightseeing."

Connecticut. One of the region's outstanding carousels is at *Bushnell Park,* Hartford; call 203–728–3089 for information. The *Science Museum of Connecticut,* W. Hartford, has a good planetarium; call 203–236–2961 for show times. Manchester, New Britain, and New Haven all have children's museums. The state's two best amusement parks are at Lake Quassapaug, Middlebury (203–758–9974); and at Lake Compounce, Bristol (203–566–4693). Perhaps the state's most fascinating attraction for children is the *Mystic Marinelife Aquarium.*

Rhode Island. The state's biggest amusement park is *Rocky Point Park,* Warwick (401–737–8000), which offers a huge shore dinner hall that accommodates hundreds of diners at a time. Other parks with rides and amusements include *Easton's Beach,* Newport; *Watch Hill Beach,* Watch Hill; *Lake Mishnock,* West Greenwich; and *The Enchanted Forest,* Hopkinton, a fairyland theme amusement park. There are a merry-go-round, paddle-boat rides, and a zoo in *Roger Williams Park,* Providence, and *Slater Memorial Park,* Pawtucket. *The Children's Museum,* 58 Walcott St., Pawtucket (401–726–2590) is located in a charming 1840 Victorian house.

HISTORIC SITES AND HOUSES. Massachusetts. *Paul Revere House.* 19 North Sq., Boston (617–523–2338). The oldest frame structure in Boston (circa 1670) was the home of silversmith and patriot Paul Revere at the time of his famous ride. Restored at the beginning of this century to an approximation of its 17th-century appearance, it contains period furniture and a few of Revere's own personal possessions. Open 9:30 A.M.–5:30 P.M. in summer; 9:30 A.M.–5:15 P.M., the rest of the year. Adults, $2; over 65 and college students, $1.50; under 17, 50 cents.

Old North Church. 193 Salem St., Boston (617–523–6676). This is the oldest church in Boston (1723) and one of the most beautiful. The lanterns that signaled Paul Revere were hung here on Apr. 18, 1775. Try to visit when the bells are to be rung; they were the first to be cast for an American church and have a lovely sound. A museum is adjacent. Open 9 A.M.–5 P.M. daily; Sun. worship (no casual visitors) at 9:30 A.M., 11 A.M., and 4 P.M. Free; donation accepted at museum.

Old South Meeting House. 310 Washington St., Boston (617–482–6439). Built as a church in 1729, the Old South was a favorite meeting place for colonial dissenters. Samuel Adams spoke here the night of the Boston Tea Party. The interior has been largely renovated to its colonial appearance. Tours on the half-hour. Open 9:30 A.M.–5 P.M., spring and fall; to 5:45 P.M., summer; to 4 P.M., winter. Adults, $1.75; seniors and students, $1.25; children 6–16, 50 cents.

Faneuil Hall. Faneuil Hall Sq., Boston (617–523–3886). Donated to the town in 1742 by Peter Faneuil and later enlarged by Charles Bulfinch, Faneuil Hall was another favorite meeting spot of disgruntled colonists. Shops below; upstairs is a public gallery and historic paintings, and the historical museum of the Ancient and Honorable Artillery Company. Interpretive talks by rangers; frequent weekend costumed presentations. Closed for renovations through Spring 1992.

State House. Beacon and Park Streets, Boston (617–727–3676; Archives 727–2816). Facing Boston Common, this is arguably the finest work of classical architecture in America. In addition to the legislative and executive branches of the Massachusetts government, the State House contains a hall of historic flags, and the State Archives, including the original royal charter for the Bay Colony and the state's original 1780 constitution, oldest such document still functioning in the world. Tours. Open Mon.–Fri., 10 A.M.–4 P.M.; Archives, 9 A.M.–5 P.M. Free.

Old State House. Washington and State sts., (617–720–1713). Once seat of colonial government; now restored, it houses the Bostonian Society's museum of local historical artifacts and nautical memorabilia. Closed for renovations through Spring 1992.

Old Ironsides (USS *Constitution*). Charlestown Navy Yard, Charlestown (617–242–5670, ship; 426–1812, museum). Her keel was laid in Boston in 1797, and she never lost an encounter. Still a commissioned ship, the *Constitution* has been carefully restored to show how officers and men lived in the navy of nearly 200 years ago. Open daily 9:30 A.M.–3:50 P.M.; museum open 9 A.M.–5 P.M. Ship free; museum admission. Adults, $2.50; seniors, $2; children, $1.50.

Longfellow National Historic Site. 105 Brattle St., Cambridge (617–876–4491). A handsome colonial-era home later lived in by poet and Harvard professor Henry Wadsworth Longfellow. House contains many of the poet's personal effects; also artifacts of the local literary scene in Longfellow's day. Open daily 10 A.M.–4:30 P.M. Adults, $2; seniors and children under 12, free.

Minute Man National Historical Park. Liberty St., Concord (508–369–6944). Park comprises the area surrounding the first battlefield of the Revolution, including the North Bridge made famous in Emerson's poem. Also on the grounds is the Old Manse, where Hawthorne once lived and worked. Grounds open daily dawn–dusk; Old Manse open weekends late Apr.–early June and Labor Day–mid-Oct.; daily in summer. Parking free. Adults, $3; reduced rates for seniors and children.

Lowell National Historical Park. Downtown Lowell; headquarters at Market Mills, Market St. (508–459–1000). Park commemorates industrial revolution in

U.S., through interpretive exhibits in restored mill buildings. Canal and trolley tours are an interesting sidelight, during summer months, to a visit to this one-time "spindle city" of textile manufacturers. Free.

John F. Kennedy National Historic Site. 83 Beals St., Brookline (617–566–7937). JFK was born here, in 1917; the house has been restored to reflect that era, with furnishings contributed by the president's mother. Open daily 10 A.M.–4:30 P.M. Adults, $1; children, free.

Connecticut. *Mark Twain House.* 351 Farmington Ave., Hartford (203–525–9317). The author began building this extravagant house in 1874 and spent some of the happiest and most productive years of his life here. Open Tues.–Sat., 9:30 A.M.–4 P.M. Call for rates, which include admission to the Harriet Beecher Stowe House next door.

Butler-McCook Homestead. 396 Main St., Hartford (203–522–1806). With its oldest section built in 1782, this is one of the few surviving colonial buildings in downtown Hartford. Open May 15–Oct. 15, noon–4 P.M. Tues., Thurs., and Sun. Adults, $2; seniors, $1; children, 50 cents.

Louis' Lunch. 263 Crown St., New Haven. This tiny inexpensive restaurant lays a good claim to being the spot where the hamburger was invented in 1898—and not a golden arch in sight.

Nathan Hale Homestead. South St., Coventry (203–742–6917). Built by the hero's father in 1776, it is furnished in period style.

Joshua Hempsted House, 11 Hempstead St., New London (203–443–7949). Built in 1678, this is one of the oldest houses in the state. Period furnishings. Open May 15–Oct. 15, 1–5 P.M. daily except Mon. Adults, $2; seniors, $1; children, 50 cents.

Monte Cristo Cottage. 325 Pequot Ave., New London (203–443–0051). Built around the turn of the century and once owned by the family of playwright Eugene O'Neill, the house today contains a theater library. Open Apr.–mid-Dec. weekdays, 1–4 P.M. Adults, $3; students and children, $1.

Rhode Island. Probably the most frequently visited of all Rhode Island attractions are the Newport summer "cottages" built during the late 19th century by people who had tens of millions of non-inflated dollars. Among the most famous: *The Breakers.* Ochre Point Ave. Designed for Cornelius Vanderbilt II by Richard Morris Hunt and finished in 1892, this is the largest and most opulent of them all. *The Elms.* Built in 1901 by Edward J. Berwind and modeled after a Parisian chateau. *Marble House.* Bellevue Ave. R.M. Hunt designed this one for another Vanderbilt, William K.; it was built in 1895. Original furnishings and Mr. Harold S. Vanderbilt's yachting trophies are on display; the restored Chinese Teahouse is really spectacular. For information on tours of these and other Newport mansions, including single and combination tour tickets, contact the Newport Preservation Society, 118 Mill St., Newport, RI 02840 (401–847–1000).

Elsewhere in the state: *First Baptist Church in America (1775),* 75 North Main St., Providence (401–751–2266). Though not in its original building, this church was founded by Roger Williams in 1638. Call to inquire concerning open hours. Free.

Roger Williams National Memorial. North Main and Smith sts., Providence (401–528–5385). Here is where Williams, a Massachusetts religious dissenter, founded the colony which later became Rhode Island. He lived nearby, circa 1636.

State House. Smith St., Providence (401–277–2357). There are only four unsupported marble domes in the world—the largest is that of St. Peter's in Rome—and this is the second largest. Archives contain original colonial charter of 1663; Gilbert Stuart full-length portrait of Washington.

MUSEUMS AND GALLERIES. Massachusetts. *Museum of Fine Arts.* 465 Huntington Ave., Boston (617–267–9300). The MFA, one of the great art museums of the United States, is particularly strong in Impressionists, antiquities, and early American silver, furniture, and paintings. Striking new West Wing contains changing exhibits. Open Tues.–Sun., 10 A.M.–5 P.M.; Wed. until 10 P.M.; West Wing hours vary. Adults, $6; seniors and students, $5; youth 6–17, $3; free to all members and their children under 17 and to all on Wed. 4–6 P.M.

Isabella Stewart Gardner Museum. 280 The Fenway, Boston (617–566–1401). Built as a private home by the imperious, eccentric Mrs. Gardner in 1902, the Gardner is filled with her carefully acquired collections of Old Masters, sculpture, and furniture. The atrium garden is delightful. Call for schedule of free concerts. Open Wed.–Sun., noon–5 P.M.; Tues., to 6:30 P.M. Closed Mon. Adults, $5; seniors and students with ID, $2.50.

Museum at the John F. Kennedy Library. Columbia Point, Dorchester, adjacent to University of Massachusetts campus (617–929–4523). In addition to the presidential papers, the museum contains memorabilia on exhibit, including a recreation of the JFK-era oval office, and several film presentations on John and Robert Kennedy. Open daily 9 A.M.–5 P.M.; last film showings at 3:50 P.M. Adults, $3.50; seniors, $2; under 16, free.

Museum of Science and Hayden Planetarium. Science Park, Charles River Dam, Boston (617–523–6664). Over 300 exhibits covering astronomy and astrophysics, anthropology, earth sciences, medicine, computers, and much more. Many hands-on exhibits. Check local papers for special temporary shows. Planetarium offers daily "Stars Tonight" show, special presentations. Hours vary; call for information. Adults, $6; seniors and children 4–14, $4.

Harvard Art Museums. The Fogg Art Museum, 32 Quincy St., Cambridge (617–495–9400) contains the bulk of the university's collections of American and European art. The Busch-Reisinger Museum, 29 Kirkland St., Cambridge (617–495–2317) is devoted to German and northern European art of all eras; sculpture gardens. The new Sackler Museum, opposite the Fogg (617–495–9400) houses a fine collection of Asian and Islamic art. Hours vary at the three institutions; call for information. Adults, $4; students $2.50; free to anyone with Harvard affiliation.

Other Harvard Museums. The Peabody Museum of Archaeology and Ethnology, 24 Oxford St., has fine anthropological collections. The Botanical Museum, same address (617–495–1910), contains, among other exhibits, the famous Glass Flowers. Both museums open Mon.–Sat., 9 A.M.–4:30 P.M.; Sun., 1 P.M.–4:30 P.M. Glass flowers: adults, $3; students, $2.50; children 5–15, $1; free. Sat. 9–11 A.M.

Museum of Our National Heritage. 33 Marrett Rd., Lexington (617–861–6559). Built and supported by Scottish-rite Masons, the museum focuses on the personalities and artifacts that make up America's political and cultural heritage. Hours vary with season; call for information. Free.

Plimoth Plantation. Rte. 3A, Plymouth (508–746–1622). Re-created Pilgrim Village circa 1627. See how the earliest English settlers lived; costumed staff members demonstrate farming, crafts, homemaking skills. Well-researched and painstakingly accurate portrayal. Open Apr. 1–Nov. 30, daily 9 A.M.–5 P.M. Adults, $15; children, $10.

Old Sturbridge Village. Sturbridge, off Rte. 20 (508–347–3362). 200-acre property contains 36 old houses surrounding a typical small-town green of the early 19th century. A staff of working artisans show how everyday life was lived in America before the industrial revolution took hold. Open all year; hours vary with season. Adults, $14; children 6–15, $6; under 6, free.

Heritage Plantation. Grove and Pine Sts., Sandwich (508–888–3300). Arts and crafts galleries; military museum; round stone barn displaying historic autos. Working grist mill. Gardens are especially fine. Open mid-May–mid-Oct., daily 10 A.M.–5 P.M. Adults, $7; children 6–12, $3; under 5 free.

Peabody Museum. 161 Essex St., Salem (508–745–9500). Exhibits show Salem's wealth of maritime history; also cultural and ethnographic artifacts brought back from the corners of the globe by Salem's seafarers. Local natural history exhibit. Open Mon.–Sat., 10 A.M.–5 P.M.; Sun. noon–5 P.M. Adults, $5; seniors and students, $4; children 6–16, $2.50.

Connecticut. *Wadsworth Atheneum.* 600 Main St., Hartford (203–278–2670). The state's most comprehensive museum; pre-Columbian art; American painting and sculpture; silver, glass, and furniture as well as oriental art and Colt firearms. Open Tues.–Sun., 11 A.M.–5 P.M.; Adults, $3; seniors and students, $1.50; under 13, free.

Connecticut Historical Society. 1 Elizabeth St., Hartford (203–236–5621). Fine collection of colonial furniture; changing historical exhibits. Open Tues.–Sun., 12–5 P.M. Adults, $2; children 3–12, $1. Free first Sun. of each month.

Hill-Stead Museum. Off Mountain Rd., Farmington (203–677–4787). 1901 country retreat designed by famed architect Stanford White contains Impressionist paintings, Chinese porcelains, other artworks in gracious home environment. Open Wed.–Fri., 2–5 P.M.; Sat.–Sun, 1–5 P.M. Rates on request.

USS Nautilus. Rte. 12, Groton (203–449–3174 or 203–449–3558). The first nuclear-powered submarine, permanently berthed here near the U.S. Navy submarine base, may be boarded by visitors. Museum with displays of submarine history from past two centuries. Seasonal schedules. Free.

Mystic Seaport Museum. Rte. 27, Mystic (203–572–0711). Outstanding re-creation of a 19th-century New England coastal village; tours of tall ships, museum of nautical arts and artifacts; crafts demonstrations; children's museum; working preservation shipyard. Excursions on 1908 steamboat. Open daily except Christmas and New Year's Day. Call for current rates.

Rhode Island. *Rhode Island School of Design Museum of Art.* 224 Benefit St., Providence (401–331–3511). Art from all periods, classical through contemporary; strong collections of 19th-century French art; 18th-century European porcelain. Pendleton Collection of American furniture and decorative arts in American wing. Call for information concerning open hours and rates.

Museum of Rhode Island History. 110 Benevolent St., Providence (401–331–8575). Operated by RI Historical Society; housed in 1822 Federalist mansion. Concentration is on history and native decorative arts of the state. Call for information concerning open hours and rates.

Slater Mill Historic Site. Roosevelt Ave., downtown, Pawtucket (401–725–8638). The Slater Mill, 1793, is where the mechanized production of textiles began in America; adjacent attractions include working water-powered mills and demonstrations of hand and mechanized weaving. Hours vary with the season; call for information. Adults, $4; seniors, $3; children 6–14, $2.

Touro Synagogue National Historic Site. 85 Touro St., Newport (401–847–4794). This is the oldest synagogue in the United States, and a building of considerable architectural distinction. Open Mon.–Fri. and Sun., 10 A.M.–5 P.M., summer. Open only for Jewish services Sat. and holy days. Free.

MUSIC. Massachusetts. One of the world's great orchestras, the *Boston Symphony,* makes its home in Symphony Hall, corner of Massachusetts and Huntington Avenues (617–266–1492). The BSO season runs from Oct. through Apr., with summer concerts given at Tanglewood in Lenox, MA. BSO members also perform in the *Boston Pops,* both in Symphony Hall, late spring, and outdoors in July at the Hatch Shell on the city's Charles River Esplanade. The *Opera Company of Boston* under Sarah Caldwell has established itself as an important regional company; performances are at 539 Washington St., Boston (617–426–2786). The *Handel and Haydn Society* is the oldest musical organization in the U.S., dating to 1815. Located at 295 Huntington Ave., Boston (617–266–3605), it performs its concert season at Symphony Hall and other area locations.

Connecticut. The *Bushnell Symphony Series,* at the Bushnell Memorial, Lafayette Circle, Hartford (203–246–6807), presents distinguished orchestras Oct.–Mar. and seasonal concerts by the *Hartford Symphony.* The *Hartford Ballet,* 308 Farmington Ave. (203–525–9396), performs at the Bushnell and tours throughout Connecticut. *Garde Center for the Arts,* 325 Captain's Walk, New London (203–444–7373), offers a vast variety of music, dance, and theater throughout the year.

Rhode Island. The *Rhode Island Philharmonic* performs at the Providence Performing Arts Center, 220 Weybosset St., Providence (401–831–3123).

THEATER. Massachusetts. Boston has three major legitimate theaters, the *Colonial,* 106 Boylston St. (617–426–9366); *Shubert,* 265 Tremont St. (617–426–4520); and *Wilbur,* 246 Tremont St. (617–423–4008). Across the Charles is Harvard's Loeb Drama Center, 64 Brattle St. (617–547–8300), home of the *American Repertory Theater.* In addition, there are many local theaters that are the Boston equivalent of "Off Broadway." Summer stock theaters elsewhere in the state include the *Falmouth Playhouse,* Falmouth (508–563–5922); *Provincetown Playhouse,* Provincetown, (508–487–0955); *North Shore Music Theater,* Beverly (508–922–8500); and *Williamstown Theater Festival,* Williams College, Williamstown (413–597–3400).

Connecticut. *The Long Wharf Theatre,* Sargent Dr., New Haven (203–787–4282), offers strong productions of new plays and revivals; *Hartford Stage Company,* Huntington Theater, 50 Church St. (203–527–5151), is a professional repertory company; *Goodspeed Opera House,* East Haddam (203–873–8668), is a restored Victorian gem offering a varied dramatic program; *Eugene O'Neill Memorial Theater*

Center, Rte. 213, Waterford (203–443–5378), dedicated to education in the theater arts, has readings of new plays at the Playwrights' Conference during the summer; *Yale Repertory Theater,* Chapel and York sts., New Haven (203–432–1234), is a university affiliate offering outstanding performances. There are numerous summer theaters and dinner theaters throughout the state.

Rhode Island. Brown University's three theaters in Providence offer a full winter season of performances (401–863–2838). The *Blackfriars Theatre,* Providence College, presents a variety of productions (401–865–2218). *Trinity Repertory Company* performs classics and contemporary drama at the Lederer Theater, 201 Washington St., Providence (401–351–4242). Providence, Newport, and smaller communities host a variety of summer stock companies, dinner theaters, and repertory outfits.

ACCOMMODATIONS—Massachusetts. Massachusetts offers just about any type of accommodation, from world-class urban hotels to quiet country inns. Since Boston differs in price structure from the rest of the state, we'll follow two sets of guidelines in these listings. In Boston, it's *Super Deluxe,* $300 and up; *Deluxe,* $200–$300; *Expensive,* $150–$200; *Moderate,* $100–$150; *Inexpensive,* under $100. For the rest of Massachusetts, use this scale: *Super Deluxe,* $175 and up; *Deluxe,* $100–$175; *Expensive–Moderate,* under $100. *Inexpensive,* under $40. Remember that prices will vary considerably between summer and off-season in resort areas such as the Berkshires and the Cape and in the neighborhood of Tanglewood during the concert season. For Boston and vicinity, accommodations under $100 may be found in bed and breakfasts. For a listing, contact the Massachusetts Office of Travel and Tourism, 13th Floor, 100 Cambridge St., Boston, MA 02202 (617–727–3493).

Boston and Vicinity

Super Deluxe

Charles. Eliot and Bennett Sts., Cambridge, MA 02138 (617–864–1200). Posh new hotel one block from Harvard Sq. Heated indoor pool and health spa; restaurants; bar features top-notch jazz.

Four Seasons. 200 Boylston St., Park Sq., Boston, MA 02116 (617–338–4400). Splendid new downtown hotel; beautiful suites face Public Garden. Heated indoor pool, health club. Fine restaurant, gracious public areas.

Ritz-Carlton. Arlington and Newbury Sts., Boston, MA 02117 (617–536–5700 or 800–241–3338). The *Grande Dame* of Boston hotels, traditionally understated and elegant. Some suites have fireplaces. Restaurant, café, famous Ritz Bar.

Westin. Copley Place, Boston, MA 02116 (617–262–9600). A sleek high rise with terrific views. Heated indoor pool, health club; several restaurants and indoor access to Copley Place shops.

Expensive

Sheraton-Boston Hotel. Prudential Center, Boston, MA 02116 (617–236–2000). Senior discounts. Heated indoor pool, fitness center, two restaurants and coffee shop. Parking garage.

Moderate

Copley Square. 47 Huntington Ave., Boston, MA 02116 (617–536–9000). Next to posh Copley Place, but worlds away in price. Very good value. Coffee shop, lounge.

Fenway Howard Johnson's. 1271 Boylston St., Boston, MA 02215 (617–267–8300). Convenient to Kenmore Sq., Fenway Park, art museums. Pool, restaurant, lounge. Free parking.

Harvard Manor House. 110 Mt. Auburn St., Cambridge, MA 02138 (617–864–5200). Small motor hotel right next to Harvard Sq. Parking right below; public transit near. Free coffee and donuts.

Rest of Massachusetts

Deluxe

Charlotte Inn. S. Summer St., Edgartown, Martha's Vineyard, MA 02539 (508–627–4751). Elegant decor and superior restaurant.

Harborview Hotel. N. Main St., Edgartown, Martha's Vineyard, MA 02539 (508–627–4333). Seasonal. Suites and housekeeping units. Water sports and tennis.

The Inn at Fernbrook. 481 Main St., Centerville, MA 02632 (800–775–4334). Individually decorated suites and guest rooms. Turn-of-the-century Victorian manse. Gourmet breakfast included. 3 mi. from Hyannis.

Expensive

Colonial Inn. 48 Monument Sq., Concord, MA 01742 (508–369–9200). Traditional inn on village green; main wing dates to 1716. Restaurant, lounge.

Jared Coffin House. Broad and Center Sts., Nantucket, MA 02554 (508–228–2405). Restored mansion filled with antiques. Restaurant. Renowned for Christmas celebration.

Lowell Hilton. 50 Warren St., Lowell, MA 01852 (508–452–1200). Brand new hotel. Indoor lap pool, health club. Two restaurants. Limo service to Boston; car rentals.

Red Lion Inn. Main St. (Rte. 7), Stockbridge, MA 01262 (413–298–5545). Antique-filled inn made famous in Norman Rockwell painting. Good restaurant, lounge.

Williams Inn. On the green, Williamstown, MA 01267 (413–458–9371). Near the campus of Williams College—a traditional New England inn. Pool, sauna.

Moderate

Bradford House. 41 Bradford St., Provincetown, MA 02657 (508–487–0173). Small inn and cottages convenient to town. Private patios. Seasonal.

Bramble Inn. 2019 Main St., Brewster, MA 02631 (508–896–7644). In the village; quiet setting ½ mi. from beach. Free Continental breakfast. Restaurant; art gallery.

Earl of Sandwich Motor Manor. Rte. 6A, E. Sandwich, MA 02537 (508–888–1415). Interesting decor. Continental breakfast. Restaurants nearby.

Heart of the Berkshires. 970 W. Housatonic St., Pittsfield, MA 01201 (413–443–1255). Pleasant motel; pool, play area. Free in-room coffee.

Seafarer. Route 28 and Ridgevale Rd., Chatham, MA 02633 (508–432–1739). Good location ½ mi. from beach. Several efficiency units.

Seven Hills Country Inn. 100 Plunkett St., Lenox, MA 01240 (413–637–0060). Restored Victorian country home. Tennis courts and ski trails.

ACCOMMODATIONS—Connecticut. There's plenty of Yankee hospitality in the Nutmeg State, from the high-rise hotels of Hartford and Stamford to inns on the byways. *Deluxe,* $150 and up; *Expensive,* $100–$150; *Moderate,* $60–$100; *Inexpensive,* under $60.

Deluxe

Inn at Mystic. U.S. I and Rte. 27, Mystic, CT 06355 (203–536–9604). Refurbished Victorian mansion overlooks the harbor. Restaurant.

Sheraton Stamford Hotel & Towers. One First Stamford Place, Stamford, CT 06902 (203–967–2222). This is a sumptuous urban hotel with spacious rooms, nice lobby, lounge, and restaurants. Special weekend rates.

Expensive

Bridgeport Hilton. 1070 Main St., Bridgeport, CT 06604. (800–HILTONS or 203–334–1234). In the heart of downtown and convenient to local transportation center. Senior-citizen rates.

Moderate

Days Inn. Rte. 27, Mystic, CT 06355 (800–325–2525). Near I–95; very close to Mystic Seaport, aquarium. Restaurant, pool. Senior citizen rates.

Holiday Inn at Yale. 30 Whalley Ave., New Haven, CT 06511 (203–777–6221). Across the street from Yale University. Pool. Restaurant; lounge.

Ramada Inn–Capitol Hill. 440 Asylum St., Hartford, CT 06103 (203–246–6591). Close to downtown. Sauna; restaurant. Family package rates available.

Inexpensive

Motel 6 (formerly Susse Chalet Motor Inn). 269 Flanders Rd., Niantic, CT 06351 (203–739–6991.Overlooking I-95 at Exit 74. Continental breakfast included in rate. Restaurant adjacent.

ACCOMMODATIONS—Rhode Island. This state is so small that you don't have to stay in an expensive, high-density area to be near attractions—remember this when you shop for lodgings at reasonable prices. *Expensive,* $90 and up; *Moderate,* $40–$90; *Inexpensive,* under $40.

Expensive

Biltmore Omni. Dorrance St., Kennedy Plaza, Providence, RI 02903 (401–421–0700). A fine restoration job brought this downtown hotel back to local prominence. Near business district, train station. Restaurants; lounge.

Hotel Manisses. Block Island, RI 02807, and **The 1661 Inn and Guest House** nearby (401–466–2421 or 401–466–2063). Both handsomely renovated and furnished with authentic antiques. Buffet breakfast at the Inn, and lunch and dinner at Manisses.

Hotel Viking and Motor Inn. 1 Bellevue Ave., Newport, RI 02840 (401–847–3300). One of Newport's more reasonable deals. Heated indoor pool, sauna. Restaurant; lounge.

Ocean House. Bluff Ave., Westerly, RI 02891 (401–348–8161). Beautiful hostelry overlooking the sea atop Watch Hill. Private ocean beach. Fine food. Modified American plan.

Moderate

Atlantic Motor Inn. 85 Ocean Rd., Narragansett Pier, RI 02882 (401–783–5534). This place is convenient to beaches and charter fishing boats.

Surf Hotel. Old Harbor, Block Island, RI 02807 (401–466–2241). A nice family hotel with a private beach. Home-style cooking. Centrally located.

BED AND BREAKFASTS. The B&B approach to lodgings has been spreading throughout southern New England. Arrangements are almost always made through organizations representing the householders who open their doors to the B&B clientele. Here are a few of the larger such outfits: *New England Bed and Breakfast,* 1045 Center St., Newton, MA (617–498–9819); *Berkshire Bed and Breakfast Connection,* 141 Newton Rd., Springfield, MA (413–268–2040); *B&B Agency of Boston and Boston Harbor,* 47 Commercial Wharf, Boston, MA 02110 (800–CITY–BNB); *B&B Associates-Bay Colony,* Box 57-166 Babson Park, Boston, MA 02157 (617–449–5302); and *Pineapple Hospitality, Bed and Breakfast Reservation Service,* 47 N. Second St., Suite 3A, New Bedford, MA 02740 (508–990–1696). In Connecticut: *Nutmeg Bed and Breakfast,* Box 1117, Hartford, CT 06105 (203–236–6698). In Rhode Island: *Bed and Breakfast of R.I.,* Box 3291, Newport, RI 02840 (401–849–1298; in Providence, 401–246–0142). Don't forget to call well in advance if you are planning a summer stay.

RESTAURANTS. Some old saws hold true, and one is that you can get good seafood in New England. The people who live here simply won't put up with fish and shellfish that aren't fresh, and the restaurants know it. Your best bets, of course, are right along the shore—little places that serve boiled-to-order lobsters, fried clams, and fish just off the boat that morning. The better city restaurants send their buyers to the fish piers at the crack of dawn.

You can get your fill of anything, though, and when it's time to switch from seafood you'll find plenty of alternatives. Ethnic restaurants abound, thanks to the influx of Italians, Portuguese, and more recently Asians into the area. And, at base, there is still the old Yankee cuisine founded on pot roast, turkey, blueberry pie, and apple cobbler. And even a baked bean or two.

Restaurants are listed according to the price of a complete dinner (drinks, tax, and tip not included): *Super Deluxe,* $35 and up; *Deluxe,* $25–$35; *Expensive,* $18–$25; *Moderate,* $12–$18; *Inexpensive,* under $12. Remember that as a rule, restaurants are more expensive in all categories in big cities and resort areas.

Massachusetts

Super Deluxe

Ritz Carlton Hotel Restaurant. 15 Arlington St., Boston 02117 (617–536–5700). The elegance that pervades this hotel extends into its dining room where the cuisine is French-inspired.

Deluxe

Bramble Inn Dining Room. 2019 Main St., Brewster 02631 (508–896–7644). This is a restored mid-19th-century house. Seafood is a specialty here.

Expensive

Candleworks Restaurant. 72 N. Water St., New Bedford 02740 (508–992–1635). Interesting ambience is experienced in this restored candle factory that features international cuisine.

Harvest. 44 Brattle St., Cambridge (617–492–1115). Cheerful and informal, with a nice international menu and good soups and sandwiches at lunch. Outdoor dining in season; lively bar. L, D, daily. AE, MC, V.

Locke-Ober. 3–4 Winter St., Boston 02117 (617–542–1340). Known for over a century for its traditional menus, this is truly a local historic site.

Publick House. Main St. (Rte. 131), Sturbridge, MA (508–347–3313). Seafood specialties at this early Colonial inn include lobster pie along with local farm produce.

Scandia. 25 State St., Newburyport (508–462–6271). An intimate little spot with a superb menu; rack of lamb, seafood chowder, pasta dishes are standouts. L, D, Mon.–Sat.; Sun. brunch. AE, MC, V.

Wiggins Tavern. 36 King St., Northampton, MA (413–584–3100). Traditional New England ambience here reflects a historical atmosphere. Variety of New England specialties on this menu.

Moderate

A. G. Pollard's. 98 Middle St., Lowell (508–934–9933). Excellent value—good steaks, rack of lamb, seafood, and a lunchtime salad bar that includes soup and cheese. L, D, daily. AE, MC, V.

Durgin Park. 340 N. Market St., Faneuil Hall Marketplace, Boston (617–227–2038). A famous local establishment, where you are seated family style by kibitzing waitresses and served mountains of Yankee favorites like roast prime rib, baked beans, and Indian pudding. L, D, daily. No credit cards.

Inexpensive

Imperial Tea House. 70 Beach St., Boston (617–426–8439). This Chinatown establishment is the place to go for *dim sum,* the two-bite lunchtime dainties filled with all sorts of surprises. Regular menu too (dim sum L only). Open till 2 A.M.; L, D, daily. All major credit cards.

Connecticut

Deluxe

Cobbs Mill. Old Mill Rd., Weston, CT 06883 (203–227–7221). Situated beside a waterfall and pond, this restored early 18th-century mill has kept its rustic ambience. Regional and seasonal menus are featured.

Expensive

L'Américain. 2 Hartford Sq. W., Hartford (203–522–6500). Acclaimed by food critics. French and American cuisine.

Moderate

Carbone's Ristorante. 588 Franklin St., Hartford (203–249–9646). Family-owned restaurant doing a good job on southern Italian standard fare. Nice atmosphere. L, D, Mon.–Fri.; Sat. D only; closed Sun. All major cards.

Leon's. 321 Washington Ave., New Haven (203–777–5366). Italian restaurant with a local following; good seafood. L, D, daily, except Mon.

Lighthouse Inn. Guthrie Pl., New London (203–443–8411). A restaurant with an enviable local reputation. Traditional American menu featuring seafood and beef. Live music for dancing Sat. nights. L, D.

Inexpensive

Goldy's. 566 Colman St. (Colman St. Exit off I-95), New London (203–442–7146). Open from 7 A.M. for breakfast; Lunch and dinner also served; salad bar. Children's menus. Cocktails. Orders to go.

Rhode Island

Expensive

Christie's. Christie's Landing, Newport (401–847–5400). Overlooks the marina; American-Continental menu. Popular with the yachting crowd; bar decorated with yacht pictures. L, D, daily. All major cards.

Moderate

Larchwood Inn. 176 Main St., Wakefield, RI 02874 (401–782–5454). This restored mid-19th-century mansion offers lunch and dinner in several dining rooms. There are traditional New England menus.

The Lobster Pot. 119 Hope St., Bristol (401–253–9100). Lobsters boiled to your order—good chowder too. The motif is yachts and more yachts. L, D, daily.

Pot au Feu. 44 Custom House St., Providence (401–273–8953). In downtown business district, this restaurant attracts a local clientele that appreciates the superior menu.

Inexpensive

Commons Restaurant. Little Compton Common, Little Compton (401–635–4388). For real Rhode Island cooking, this village restaurant serves jonnycakes, quahog pie, and local specialties seldom available elsewhere.

LIQUOR LAWS. Massachusetts. Legal age is 21. Liquor, wine, and beer sold in package stores only; Sun. sales not permitted. Bars fully licensed; restaurants may be licensed to sell all drinks, or wine and beer only. A few towns are dry.

Connecticut. Legal age is 21. Liquor and wine sold in package stores; grocery stores are permitted to sell beer. Sun. sales are not permitted.

Rhode Island. Legal age is 21. Liquor, wine, and beer for off-premises consumption sold in package stores only; Sun. sales not permitted.

Laws for bars and restaurants vary in the three states for selling hours on Sun. and holidays.

NIAGARA FALLS

by
DEBORAH WILLIAMS

Deborah Williams is a former reporter and editor for the late Buffalo Courier Express. *Her travel articles have appeared in a number of magazines and newspapers.*

The first recorded "tourist" to visit Niagara Falls was Father Louis Hennepin in 1678. Since that cold December day, it has been a world-class attraction.

It is an awesome spectacle: a sprawling 184-foot-high cataract of thundering water surrounded by towering clouds of mist and spray. For generations, Niagara Falls has been the stuff of romance. Millions of visitors pause here each year to witness one of the world's most impressive natural phenomena. They line the promenade opposite, gape from the deck of a boat below, peer out from the caves behind, ogle from a helicopter above—drinking in the vista from every conceivable angle.

Writers have long struggled to capture the immensity of the falls. Thomas Moore, the Irish poet, wrote: "It is impossible by pen or pencil to convey even a faint idea of their magnificence. . . . We must have new combinations of language to describe the Falls of Niagara."

The falls border the United States and Canada as part of the longest unprotected border in the world. The American and Bridal Veil Falls are in New York, and the Horseshoe Falls are on the Canadian side in Ontario. There is an impressive 3,175 feet of waterfall. Bridges make access across the border easy. The falls were the birthplace of alternating electric current and drive the largest hydroelectric development in the western world.

The first honeymooners arrived in 1803. They were rich newlyweds from Baltimore—Jerome Bonaparte, kin to the French emperor, and his bride, the daughter of a wealthy merchant—on a grand tour of the Northeast. They stayed for a week. By the mid-1800s, honeymoons at Niagara had become the rage. They were a definite status symbol for young couples, and the tradition continues today.

With the arrival of steamships in 1820, the Erie Canal in 1825, and the railroad in 1840, the town became accessible to millions of tourists. Since 1860, the falls have been lit at night. The spectacle of lights playing on the waters and mist has a special attraction for visitors.

The waters also lured a special breed of daredevil. The first stuntster, Sam Patch, survived two dives from Goat Island into the turbulent waters below the falls. Then, in 1859 and 1860, tightrope walker Jean Francois Gravelet, the great Blondin, thrilled onlookers as he walked, danced, rode a bike, and even carried his terrified manager on a high wire across the falls. The first person to go over in a barrel was a schoolteacher, Mrs. Annie Edson Taylor, in 1901. Such stunts are now illegal, but the law does not stop the determined stunter. During 1985 two more daredevils survived a plunge over the falls in a barrel.

Unrestricted viewing of Niagara Falls did not begin until 1885. "Free Niagara!" was the rallying cry in the 1870s as a group of dedicated Americans led by landscape architect Frederick Law Olmsted and artist Frederic E. Church set out to extricate the falls from the clutches of profit-hungry land owners.

The lands around the falls had become a vulgar tourist trap, with visitors having to pay to see the cataracts through peepholes in the fence. The campaign resulted in the establishment on July 15, 1885, of the nation's first state park, embracing 435 acres of land along the American falls. The Canadians followed with similar action around their portion of the cataract, and the protection of the falls was assured. The park's creation affirmed the premise that the nation's natural treasures belong to everyone.

Of course, the commercialism did not disappear. On the contrary, even a casual visitor today can see an abundance of souvenir shops, T-shirt emporia, chain motels, oddity museums, and fast-food eateries.

At Clifton Hill on the Canadian side, where the carnival atmosphere is strongest, there are museums dedicated to Houdini, sports heroes, Ripley's Believe It or Not, and the *Guinness Book of World Records,* not to mention a Louis Tussaud wax museum.

Several sightseeing towers stand as sentries over the Falls, and a cable car carries visitors across the Niagara rapids. On the American side, the city has been undergoing a massive urban renewal program designed to change the face of downtown.

The water that flows over the falls drains four Great Lakes—Superior, Michigan, Huron, and Erie—into the fifth, Ontario, at a rate of 700,000 gallons a second during the summer. It fluctuates with the seasons; although the river never completely freezes in winter, an ice bridge does form below the falls—a bridge that can grow to a thickness of 150 feet and a length of two miles.

On March 29, 1848, a strange silence fell in the city. The roar of the falls had stopped. Huge chunks of ice formed a dam in the river, stopping the flow of water and leaving the falls dry. This lasted for two days until the dam broke and water began to flow again.

But on June 12, 1969, man turned off the falls—actually just the American falls. Water was rerouted to Horseshoe Falls to enable engineers to survey the American falls and the rocks below in order to prevent further erosion. Some 185,000 tons of rock had fallen from Prospect Point. By December 1969, the falls were turned back on, and they have been flowing since without interruption.

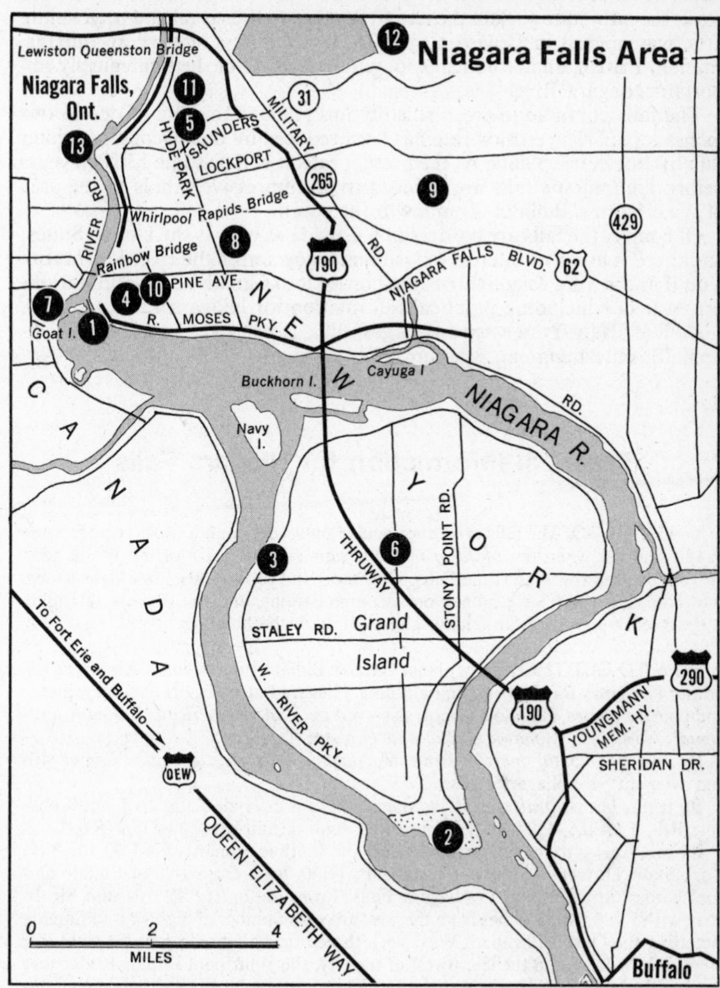

Points of Interest (Niagara Falls)

1) American Falls
2) Beaver Island State Park
3) Big Six Mile Creek Marine State Park
4) Convention Center
5) Devils Hole State Park
6) Fantasy Island
7) Horseshoe Falls
8) Hyde Park Stadium
9) Niagara Falls International Airport
10) Niagara Splash Water Park
11) Niagara University
12) Tuscarora Indian Reservation
13) Whirlpool State Park

Geologists say that Niagara Falls began 12,000 years ago, seven miles north of its present location in what is now the village of Lewiston. Artpark, the only state park in the nation devoted to the visual and performing arts, was opened in Lewiston in 1974. It occupies a site where Indians, French, British, and Americans fought for control of the strategically important Niagara River.

The falls continue to creep steadily upstream at the rate of one to two inches a year. The erosion rate has been reduced by the diversion of water into hydroelectric plants. At the present rate, it will be some 130,000 years before the majestic falls are reduced to an impressive rapids in the area of what is now Buffalo, 20 miles to the south.

Of course, the falls are bordered by Canada as well as the United States, and there is much of interest to visit and enjoy across the river in Ontario. You'll find it very easy to cross the border into Canada. Space limitations preclude our including practical information for Niagara Falls, Ontario.

Buffalo, New York's second largest city, is nearby, increasing the options for entertainment, museums, and dining.

Practical Information for Niagara Falls

WHEN TO GO. The falls are a spectacular sight year-round. Most visitors come in the summer when the *Maid of the Mist* sails and the Cave of the Winds tour is available, but the wintertime Falls, with snow and ice crystals, are a sight to see. It is cold, but you'll save money on accommodations, and the Festival of Lights is deservedly popular from Thanksgiving through the holidays.

HOW TO GET THERE. By plane. Greater Buffalo International Airport is the primary air entry for the Niagara Falls area. Niagara Falls Airport handles military and charter planes. Buffalo's airport is served by *USAir, American, United, Continental, Northwest, Mohawk, Delta, and Pan Am Express.*

By bus. *Greyhound* operates from the *Niagara Falls Transportation Center,* 4th and Niagara Sts., Niagara Falls.

By train. The *Amtrak* station in Niagara Falls is at Hyde Park Blvd. and Lockport Rd., 716–285–4224. Call the toll-free Amtrak number: 800–USA–RAIL.

By car. Access to the falls from the east and south is primarily via I-90, the New York State Thruway. An expressway spur, I-190, leads from I-90 at Buffalo and goes across Grand Island to Niagara Falls. From the north, SR 104 and SR 18 tie in with I-190. Approaches from the west are via a number of highways in Canada including the Queen Elizabeth Way, with three bridges funneling traffic stateside; the Rainbow Bridge in the southwest of the city; the Whirlpool Rapids Bridge just below Whirlpool State Park; and the Lewiston–Queenston Bridge, Lewiston, connecting the northern terminus of I-190 with Canada's Hwy. 405. Entering the Buffalo area from the south are U.S. 219 from Springville and SR 400 from South Wales. Both join I-90.

TOURIST INFORMATION. The *Niagara Falls Official Tourism Information Center,* 4th and Niagara Sts., is open 7 days a week, 9 A.M.–5 P.M.; during the Festival of Lights, hours are 4–10 P.M. (716–284–2000). The *Niagara Falls Convention & Visitors Bureau,* 345 Third St., Niagara Falls (716–278–8010), has guides, maps, and brochures. Their 24-hour telephone information service at 716–285–8711 provides a recorded message summarizing the day's events plus suggestions on what to do and see in the city. There is an information center in both terminals at the Buffalo Airport. During off hours a telephone number is provided for anyone needing information or assistance. The *Travelers Aid Society,* 295 Main St., Room 828, Buffalo (854–8661), provides emergency assistance to travelers. The *Buffalo Area Chamber of Commerce,* 107 Delaware Ave., Buffalo, NY (852–0511), provides maps, guides, and brochures on the Buffalo and Niagara Falls area. For information on the entire area, call *New York State Tourism Information* toll-free (800–342–3810).

TELEPHONES. The area code for Niagara Falls and western New York is 716. Dial 555–1212 for information (directory assistance). An operator will assist you on person-to-person, credit-card, and collect calls if you dial 0 first. From outside the area, directory information can be obtained by dialing 716–555–1212. Dial 800–555–1212, directory information for toll-free 800 numbers, to see if there is an 800 number for the business you want to reach. A call from a pay phone is 25 cents. Long-distance rates apply between Niagara Falls and Buffalo.

HOW TO GET AROUND. From the airport. Shuttle buses between the Buffalo airport and major hotels in Niagara Falls are operated by *Niagara Scenic Bus Lines, Inc.* (716–648–1500 or 282–7755). The shuttle runs 7 A.M.–5:30 P.M. and takes about an hour; the fare is $8 one way. Taxi service to Niagara Falls is also available for $26.

By bus. The *Niagara Frontier Transportation Authority (NFTA)* provides bus service in the Buffalo area, including the suburbs and Niagara Falls. The fare is $1.10 within both cities. The cost between Buffalo and Niagara Falls is $1.70; the fare for children under 12 is 50 cents. Transfers are 20 cents from bus to bus. Exact change is required. Buses generally operate 5 A.M.–12:30 A.M. For information, phone 716–855–7211 or 285–9319 in Niagara Falls.

By taxi. Taxi rates in Niagara Falls are $1.50 for the first tenth of a mi. and 20 cents for each sixth of a mi. thereafter. Call *United Cab Co.* (716–285–9331) or *LaSalle Cab* (716–284–8833).

By rental car. *Budget Rent-A-Car,* airport pickup (716–632–4662); *Avis,* airport pickup (716–632–1808); *Agency Rent-A-Car,* free pickup (716–836–4847); *Hertz,* airport pickup (716–632–4772). There are a number of limousine services for sightseeing in style: *Buffalo Limousine Service* (835–4997), *Niagara Scenic* (648–1500), *Arthur's Limousine Service* (683–4530).

HINTS TO MOTORISTS. Niagara Falls is an early town, and rush hours are generally 7–9 A.M. and 3–5 P.M. Parking is $3 in the state parking lots. Otherwise, parking meters have been removed from the street and parking is free. The ramp at the Rainbow Center is also free. There are designated handicapped spots in all lots, but the auto must have a special handicapped license plate.

HINTS TO DISABLED TRAVELERS. The parks on both sides of the falls, including Prospect Point and Goat Island, are accessible to wheelchairs. The *Maid of the Mist* is accessible. There is a newly installed ramp leading to the elevator which takes visitors down to the boat on the American side, and a van which takes handicapped visitors to the boat on the Canadian side.

SEASONAL EVENTS. January. The *Niagara Falls Festival of Lights* continues through the Sun. after New Year's Day. There are hundreds of thousands of colored lights, decorations, animated displays, entertainment, free events, and shows combined with the special beauty of the freezing mist crystallizing the surroundings.

May. At the end of the month on Sun. of Memorial Day weekend, Niagara Falls sponsors the *Concert in the Sky* with synchronized fireworks and music above Prospect Point and Goat Island at the falls.

June. The first weekend in June the *King's Birthday* is celebrated at Old Fort Niagara with 18th-century military ceremonies, drills, music, and cannon and musket firings. During the second weekend all of Allentown in Buffalo is turned into an outdoor art gallery as thousands flock to the area for the *Allentown Art Festival,* one of the largest outdoor art shows in the country.

July kicks off a series of outdoor festivals and concerts throughout the area. On the *Fourth of July* there is a celebration and fireworks at the E. Dent Lackey Plaza, in front of the Niagara Falls International Convention Center. This day begins the *Niagara Summer Experience,* a series of weekend ethnic entertainments outside at Lackey Plaza. The Niagara Falls airport hosts the Western New York International Air Show. The Waterfront Festival also begins at the Waterfront Pavilion, LaSalle Park.

August. The *Niagara Summer Experience* continues every weekend in Niagara Falls. For 10 days in mid-Aug., Hamburg, 10 mi. south of Buffalo, is home to the largest county fair in the country, the *Erie County Fair & Expo.* It features animals, food, amusement rides, tractor pulls, and national entertainers. It was here in 1885 that the hamburger was born.

October. A *Revolutionary War Encampment* is held the third weekend of the month at Old Fort Niagara. The troops are garrisoned as they would have been during the Revolutionary War, with period clothing and living conditions.

November–December. The *Niagara Falls Festival of Lights* begins the Sat. after Thanksgiving Day with nightly entertainment and thousands of lights, 5 P.M.–11 P.M.

TOURS. Sightseeing is what Niagara Falls is all about. Some of the providers: *Bedore Tours,* 454 Main St. (285–5261). *Bridal Veil Tours,* 9470 Niagara Falls Blvd. (297–0329). *Gray Line,* 3466 Niagara Falls Blvd. (694–3600). *International Honeymoon Tours,* 9393 Niagara Falls Blvd. (297–3797). *Niagara Scenic Tours,* S-5700 Maelou Dr., Hamburg (648–1500 or 800–N–SCENIC). *Two Nation Tours,* 1260 95th St. (297–5038).

Rainbow Helicopter, 454 Main St. (284–2800), provides year-round helicopter tours of the falls and area. *International Carriage Rides & Livery,* 6764 Walmore Rd. (731–3389), has horse-drawn carriage tours of the area.

Niagara Viewmobiles (278–1730), sightseeing trains, may be boarded at several locations on Goat Island and at Prospect Point near the Observation Tower. Stopovers are permitted at five sites. Daily Apr. 24–Nov. 15. Adults, $2.50; children, $1.50.

The *Cave of the Winds Trip* (278–1730) takes groups on wooden walkways to within 25 ft. of the base of the falls. Rainbows abound here, and in 1984 a Korean visitor was hit by a 15-pound chinook salmon trying to swim up the great cataract. Rain slickers and foot coverings are provided. Mid-May–mid-Oct. Adults, $3.50; children, $2.50.

By boat. The most famous boat ride of all is the *Maid of the Mist,* which has operated since 1843. The diesel boats may be boarded on either the American or the Canadian side. To get to the boats, there is a charge of 50 cents on the American side for the elevator and $1 for use of the incline railway on the Canadian side. The season opens mid-May and continues daily through Oct. 24. Adults, $6.75; children, $3.40; information, 284–8897.

Just about every celebrity and head of state who has ever visited the falls takes a ride on the *Maid of the Mist,* which travels to the very base of the falls, where the waters roar and the mist swirls upward in an ascending cloud. Theodore Roosevelt said that a ride on the *Maid* was "the only way to fully realize the Grandeur of the Great Falls of Niagara." The tour lasts approximately a half hour, with departures every 15 minutes. Rain slickers are provided.

PARKS. No individual has had a greater influence on the landscape and parks in Niagara Falls than Frederick Law Olmsted, architect of New York City's Central Park. He was the leader in the fight to free Niagara Falls for public viewing, and he designed the Niagara Falls Reservation, the first state park in the nation. He resisted all pressure to surround the falls with then-fashionable ornamental gardens and sought to preserve the character of the falls' natural environment. The 139 land acres and 296 water acres of the reservation include Prospect Park, Upper Rapids Park, and Goat Island and provide the closest viewing of the falls. Goat Island is in the middle of the river on the brink of the falls and has spectacular viewing areas.

In the center of the city is 600-acre *Hyde Park,* the largest of the city parks, with an 18-hole public golf course and swimming pool. Along the lower Niagara River are the 42-acre *Devil's Hole* and 109-acre *Whirlpool State parks. Artpark* is a 200-acre state park along the Niagara River gorge in the village of Lewiston; it is a theater and arts complex. Recreational facilities include nature trails, picnic areas, and fishing docks for trout and salmon. Summer theater season offers concerts, ballet, opera, and drama; call 716–694–8191 for schedule and ticket information. All activities free except theater events, which average $5–$8. Vehicle use fee, $2.50. Open Memorial Day–Labor Day. The 952-acre Beaver Island Park, Grand Island, has beaches, golf, tennis, fishing, boating, a restaurant, and skiing. *Niagara Splash*

Water Park (716–284–3555), 700 Rainbow Blvd., next to Convention Center. A private water park with wave pool, speed slides, water rides. Wave pool open year-round. Other rides open May–Labor Day. Adults, $11.95; children, $9.95. Nights, $7.95.

FISHING AND HUNTING. After years of negative publicity about pollution in area lakes and rivers, conditions have improved enough so that lake trout and other clean-water fish have returned to Lake Erie, the Niagara River, and Lake Ontario. There is still a health advisory regarding eating fish from Lake Ontario. Consult the State Department of Environmental Conservation (DEC) (716–847–4600) for health and license information.

Write or call DEC, 50 Wolf Rd., Albany, NY 12233 (518–457–5400), for booklets on Great Lakes fishing, trout and salmon fishing, and state boat launching sites. Bass, trout, muskie, salmon, and northern pike are caught in large numbers. There are a number of charter fishing operators in the Buffalo, Lake Erie, and Niagara River area and at Lake Ontario in Niagara County. They include Great Lakes Fishing Charters, 8255 West Point Dr., Amherst (716–741–3453); and Olcott Charter Service, Newfane (716–434–9902).

Excellent hunting opportunities for whitetail deer, wild turkey, upland birds, waterfowl, and small game exist within a 90-minute drive from Buffalo. For information on licenses, seasons, bag limits, permissible weapons, public hunting grounds, and private preserves, write the Department of Environmental Conservation (DEC), 50 Wolf Rd., Albany, NY 12233, or call 518–457–5400.

PARTICIPANT SPORTS. Water sports. With the ample supply of lakes and rivers and plenty of wind, water sports of all kinds are popular, including sailing, boating, wind surfing, and waterskiing. *Seven Seas Sailing School,* Erie Basin Marina (716–856–4109), and *Serendipity Sailing Services,* 2493 Garrison Rd., Ridgeway, Ontario (416–894–3061), provide sailboat rental and instruction. *Bouquard's Boat Livery,* 1581 Fuhrmann Blvd. (716–826–6189), and *Wolf's Boat House,* 327 S. Ellicott Creek Rd., Tonawanda (716–691–8740), have motor boat rentals. *Niagara Scuba Sports,* 2048 Niagara St. (716–875–6528), provides scuba diving instruction, equipment rentals, and dive trips year-round. The nearly 8-mi.-an-hour current in the Niagara River provides a particularly exciting dive for experienced divers.

Skiing. There are 20 skiing areas within a 90-mi. radius of Buffalo, with the nearest only a 45-minute drive from downtown. Kissing Bridge, Rte. 240, Glenwood (716–592–4963), is the closest to Buffalo and is one of the largest area ski centers. Holiday Valley, Rte. 219, Ellicottville (716–699–2345), has been called the Aspen of the East and is the most extensive ski center in the area. There is cross-country skiing in the city's parks. For ski conditions, call 800–CALL–NYS.

There are more than 100 **tennis** courts in the area and a number of public **golf courses** as well as jogging trails in the major parks. Contact the Buffalo Parks Department (716–851–5806) or the Erie County Department of Parks & Recreation (716–858–8355).

HISTORIC SITES AND HOUSES. Since 1726 **Old Fort Niagara,** Youngstown, 14 miles from Niagara Falls, has commanded a view of the Niagara River and Lake Ontario. The flags of Britain, France, and America have flown over this fort, which was an active military post well into the 20th century. During the summer, authentically clad militiamen give hourly cannon and musketry demonstrations and explain the fort's history. Closed Jan. 1, Thanksgiving, and Christmas. Adults, $5.25; over 65, $4.25; 6–12, $3. Call 716–745–7611.

Theodore Roosevelt Inaugural National Historic Site (Wilcox Mansion), 641 Delaware Ave., Buffalo, is a Greek Revival structure dating from 1838, when it served as military officers' headquarters. Restored and containing late Victorian furniture are the library, where Theodore Roosevelt was sworn in as the 26th President, a morning room, a dining room, and a bedroom. Items related to the inauguration of Roosevelt and the assassination of President McKinley in Buffalo in 1901 are displayed. Art gallery on second floor. Open daily. Closed Sat., Jan.–Mar. Adults, $2; under 12, $1. Call 716–884–0095.

MUSEUMS. Albright-Knox Art Gallery. 1285 Elmwood Ave., Buffalo (882–8700). A handsome Greek revival building with a modern addition. Painting and sculpture dating from 3000 B.C. to the present. The collection of 20th art is internationally known. It was the first U.S. museum to buy works by Picasso and Matisse. Included in the collection is the Mirrored Room, a life-size room, table, and chair made completely of mirrors. Museum shop and restaurant. Tues.–Sun. Donations.

Amherst Museum. 3755 Tonawanda Creek Rd., East Amherst (689–1440). Niagara Frontier Aviation Hall of Fame and aviation history exhibits of technology and building plus St. John Neumann log chapel reconstruction. 11:30 A.M.–4:30 P.M. Mon–Sat; 1–4 P.M. Sun. Gift shop. Free.

Buffalo Museum of Science. Humboldt Pkwy. at Northampton St., Buffalo (896–5200). Exhibits on anthropology, archaeology, astronomy, botany, geology, zoology, including gigantic insect models and a children's discovery room. Daily, 10–5, Fri., 10–10; Kellogg Observatory open Fri., dusk–9:30 P.M., Sept. 1–May 31. Museum shop. Adults, $2.50; senior citizens and children 4–17, $1; family, $5.

Buffalo and Erie County Historical Society. 25 Nottingham Ct., Buffalo (873–9644). The only remaining building from the Pan American Exposition of 1901, with an emphasis on history of area, including Indian culture. Former President Millard Fillmore was first president of society. Period rooms and shops. Tues.–Sat., 10 A.M.–5 P.M., Sun., noon–5 P.M. Closed Jan. 1, Thanksgiving, and Christmas. Museum shop. Adults, $2.50; seniors, $1.25; children 7–14, $1; family, $5.

Niagara Reservation Visitor Center. Niagara Reservation State Park. New center. Information, exhibits, gardens, theater, Free, daily. *Niagara Wonders,* a spectacular film. Adults, $2; senior citizens, $1.50; children, $1.

Schoellkopf Geological Museum. Niagara Reservation State Park (278–1780). Multimedia museum explains 500-million-year geologic history of the falls. A geological garden and nature trail on grounds. Daily; Nov.–Memorial Day, closed, Mon., Tues. Adults, 50 cents; children under 6, free.

The Turtle: Native American Center for the Living Arts. 25 Rainbow Mall (284–2427). Houses a museum and art gallery focusing on American Indian heritage, culture, symbols, and art. Iroquois dance performances held daily during summer season. Restaurant, gift shop. Daily, Nov. 1–May 1, closed Mon. Adults, $3; senior citizens, $2.50; ages 6–12, $1.50.

Power Vista. Rte. 104, 4 miles north of the falls (285–3211). Observation and information center and museum of Niagara Power Project with spectacular views of the river and gorge. Movies, working models, and dioramas explain how generators at the project operate. Mural by Thomas Hart Benton showing Father Hennepin viewing Niagara Falls for first time. Closed Thanksgiving, Christmas, Jan. 1. Free.

ARTS AND ENTERTAINMENT. The Niagara visitor may want to sample the arts in nearby Buffalo. Music, both classical and popular, has a long tradition here. The Arts Council in Buffalo and Erie County, 700 Main St. (856–7520), provides information about all area arts and music events on ARTSline, a 24-hour hotline (847–1444).

The 87-member **Buffalo Philharmonic Orchestra** (885–5000) begins its 56th season during 1991–92. Music directors have included Joseph Krips, Lukas Foss, Michael Tilson Thomas, and Julius Rudel. The orchestra plays symphony concerts in Kleinhans Music Hall, Symphony Circle, acclaimed as an acoustically perfect concert hall. The orchestra plays virtually year-round, holding concerts in area parks, including Artpark, during the summer.

Pops concerts are played by the Buffalo Philharmonic Orchestra, Fri., Oct.–Apr. Call 885–5000.

Buffalo has long been known as a good **theater** town. Actress Katharine Cornell was born and played here. The theater district on Main St. between Virginia and Chippewa Sts. has undergone a renaissance. The showpiece of the district is **Shea's Buffalo Theater,** 646 Main St. (847–0050), an ornate crystal palace refurbished to its original grandeur. It boasts one of the largest Wurlitzer organs ever built. Theater, dance, opera, and music performed by national touring companies.

Studio Arena Theater, 710 Main St. (856–5650), is the city's resident theater, with live performances Sept.–May. World premieres and pre-Broadway productions are staged here. This is the largest regional theater in the state. **The Pfeifer**

Theater, 681 Main St. (847–6461), across the street, is home to the State University of New York at Buffalo's Department of Theater and Dance, with performances Oct.–Dec. and Feb.–May. The Theater of Youth (TOY) Company (856–4410) performs at 282 Franklin St.

ACCOMMODATIONS. Hotels and motels in the Niagara Falls area primarily fall into the category of major hotel chains and lower-priced motels. High-season prices apply from Memorial Day through Labor Day. Off-season rates are at least $10 less per room. Elsewhere, prices remain the same throughout the year. The occupancy tax in Niagara Falls is 3%, plus 7% sales tax.

Hotel rates are based on double occupancy. Categories determined by price during high season are: *Deluxe,* $100 and above; *Expensive,* $80–$100; *Moderate,* $60–$80; *Inexpensive,* under $60.

Deluxe

Holiday Inn Downtown at the Falls. 114 Buffalo St., Niagara Falls, NY 14303 (716–285–2521 or 800–HOLIDAY). 194 units. Family plan, indoor pool, saunas, exercise room, dining room, cocktail lounge; pets allowed.

Inn at the Falls. 240 Rainbow Blvd., Niagara Falls, NY 14203 (716–282–1212). 217 units. Indoor pool, lobby overlooks Wintergarden, cocktail lounge, two restaurants.

Niagara Hilton. Third St. and Mall, Niagara Falls, NY 14304 (716–285–3361 or 800–HILTONS). 396 units. Adjoins Wintergarden. Indoor pool, health club, dining room, coffee shop, cocktail lounge, tropical indoor garden; some rooms have views of the falls.

Ramada Inn Niagara. 401 Buffalo Ave., Niagara Falls, NY 14303 (716–285–2541 or 800–2RAMADA). 193 units. Family plan, pool, dining room, cocktail lounge, pets.

Expensive

Best Western Red Jacket Inn. 7001 Buffalo Ave., Niagara Falls, NY 14304 (716–283–7612 or 800–528–1234). 150 units. Family plan, pool, dock, fishing, dining room, cocktail lounge.

Days Inn Falls View. 201 Rainbow Blvd., Niagara Falls, NY 14303 (716–285–9321 or 800–325–2325). 200 units downtown. Family plan, dining room, cocktail lounge.

Holiday Inn Resort & Conference Center. 100 Whitehaven Rd., Grand Island, NY 14072 (716–773–1111 or 800–HOLIDAY). 265 units. Family plan, indoor and outdoor pools, saunas, exercise room, dock, fishing, ski trails, ice skating, rental bikes, golf, dining room, coffee shop, cocktail lounge; pets allowed.

Howard Johnson's Downtown by the Falls. 454 Main St., Niagara Falls, NY 14301 (716–285–5261 or 800–654–2000). 75 units downtown. Family plan, indoor pool, sauna, restaurant, cocktail lounge.

Howard Johnson's Motor Lodge–East. 6505 Niagara Falls Blvd., Niagara Falls, NY 14304 (716–283–8791 or 800–654–2000). 84 units. Family plan, pool, restaurant, cocktail lounge; pets allowed.

Quality Inn Rainbow Bridge. 443 Main St., Niagara Falls, NY 14302 (716–284–8801 or 800–228–5151). 166 units. Family plan, pool, restaurant.

Moderate

Beacon Motel. 9900 Niagara Falls Blvd., Niagara Falls, NY 14304 (716–297–3647). 10 units. Restaurant adjacent.

Bit-O-Paris Motel. 9890 Niagara Falls Blvd., Niagara Falls, NY 14304 (716–297–1710). 28 units. Pool.

TraveLodge. 200 Rainbow Blvd., Niagara Falls, NY 14303 (716–285–7316 or 800–255–3050). 49 units. Family plan.

Inexpensive

Anchor Motel. 2332 River Rd., Niagara Falls, NY 14304 (716–693–0850). 21 units. Pool; grounds located on the Niagara River.

Bel Aire Motel. 9470 Niagara Falls Blvd., Niagara Falls, NY 14304 (716–297–2250). 23 units. Pool.

Coachman Motel. 523 Third St., Niagara Falls, NY 14301 (716–285–2295). 18 units. Refrigerators.

Driftwood Motel. 2754 Niagara Falls Blvd., Niagara Falls, NY 14304 (716–692–6650). 20 units. Pool.

Henwood's Motel. 9401 Niagara Falls Blvd., Niagara Falls, NY 14304 (716–297–2660). 30 units. Pool.

Pelican Motel. 6817 Niagara Falls Blvd., Niagara Falls, NY 14304 (716–283–9818). 14 units. Refrigerators, two efficiencies.

Sands Motel. 9393 Niagara Falls Blvd., Niagara Falls, NY 14304 (716–297–3797). 17 units. Pool.

Sharon Motel. 7560 Niagara Falls Blvd., Niagara Falls, NY 14304 (716–283–5646). 22 units. Pool.

BED AND BREAKFASTS. B&Bs in the Niagara Falls–Buffalo area are organized under *Rainbow Hospitality,* 9348 Hennepin Ave., Niagara Falls, NY 14304 (716–283–4794 or 716–283–0228). They include historic homes close to Niagara Falls, an elegant Victorian home on the banks of the lower Niagara River, a working farm about 10 miles from Niagara Falls, and a private ski chalet about 30 miles south of Buffalo. Prices vary but average $40–$60 for a double. Some welcome children, and one even offers a nursery and baby-sitting services. Others do not accept children. Inquire in advance.

RESTAURANTS. The price classifications of the following restaurants are based on the cost of an average three-course dinner for one person for food alone; beverages, tax (7%), and tip are extra. The categories are: *Expensive,* $15–$30; and *Moderate,* $8–$15. Unless otherwise noted, all the restaurants accept some or all major credit cards.

We have included a couple of restaurants across the river in Canada because of their spectacular views; otherwise we have limited the list to establishments in Niagara Falls. Buffalo also has a wide range of restaurants. There is currently a favorable exchange rate on American dollars in Canada, averaging 15%.

Expensive

Fortuna's. 827 19th St., Niagara Falls, NY (716–282–2252). Since 1945, a popular dining room with local residents. Italian home cooking. D, closed Mon.–Tues. AE, MC, V.

John's Flaming Hearth. 1965 Military Rd., Niagara Falls, NY (716–297–1414). Some of the finest steak in the country is served in ornate dining rooms. John's attracts area residents and tourists from all over the world, including visiting celebrities. Seafood, chicken, and veal are featured. Pumpkin ice cream pie a dessert specialty. L, D, daily. AE, CB, DC, MC, V.

Red Coach Inn Restaurant. 2 Buffalo Ave., Niagara Falls, NY (716–282–1459). A falls tradition since 1923, overlooking the spectacular upper rapids. Fireplaces, outside patio dining, prime rib a specialty. L, D, daily. AE, MC, DC.

The Rib Cage. 1124 Main St., Niagara Falls, NY (716–282–1004). Home of the gourmet lovers for two feast; prime rib is featured. Flaming desserts and coffee prepared tableside. L, Tues.–Fri.; D, Tues.–Sun.; closed Mon. Major credit cards.

Rolf's. 3840 Main St., Niagara Falls, Ontario (416–295–3472). Renovated old house is the setting for fine food prepared by European-trained chef-owner Rolf. Dinner daily, closed Mon.

Skylon Tower. 5200 Robinson Rd., Niagara Falls, Ontario (416–856–5788). Take an outside elevator high up to the tower with some of the best views of the falls anywhere. Dine in the revolving dining room with fine (Continental) food and service. L, D, daily. Major credit cards.

Table Rock Restaurant. Queen Victoria Park, Niagara Falls, Ontario (416–354–3631). Although Canadians sometimes object to being labeled American, this restaurant serves Canadian/American fare. It is at the brink of the Horseshoe Falls, and from your table you can view the falls on both sides of the border without the spray. B, L, D, daily. Major credit cards.

Top of the Falls Restaurant. Goat Island, Niagara Falls, NY (716–285–3311). The location is the big drawing card here (the food is American). Each table gives the feeling of being on top of the falls. Cafeteria style. L, daily. MC, V.

Wintergarden Restaurant. 240 Rainbow Blvd., Niagara Falls, NY (716–282–1215). Dine on pasta primavera, Cornish hen, chicken florentine, and other special dishes in a tropical park. L, D, daily. AE, MC, V.

LIQUOR LAWS. The drinking age in New York State is 21. Alcohol may be purchased at licensed liquor stores, beer and wine-coolers at supermarkets. If you are caught driving under the influence of alcohol, you can lose your license and possibly face a jail sentence and fine.

NIGHTLIFE. *Hello Vegas* is a Las Vegas–style revenue offered Wed.–Sun. at the Ramada Inn Niagara, 401 Buffalow Ave., Niagara Falls (716–285–2541). There are show-only and dinner show packages. *Club Exit,* 512 Third St., Niagara Falls (716–282–0108), has a high-tech lighting and sound system for disco dancing.

NEW YORK CITY

by
BARBARA PEPE

New Yorker Barbara Pepe's writing has appeared in the New York Daily News *and the* Los Angeles Times *as well as in the* Village Voice, Rolling Stone, American Way, Diversion, *and* Playboy.

Every New Yorker—born, bred, or transplanted—believes the Big Apple is the greatest city in the world. In fact, it is the world's leading tourism destination, attracting over 25 million visitors last year. Because most of the city's over 100 hotels are located in midtown Manhattan (a few are found near the airports in Queens), many visitors remain within a small rectangular section roughly bounded by 59th Street on the north, 34th Street on the south, Third Avenue on the east and Ninth Avenue on the west. This tight little area, less than a square mile, is known as Midtown. Contained therein are two major railroad stations, all the airline offices, the bus terminal, most of the major department stores, all of the Broadway area's legitimate theaters, many of the city's finest nightclubs and restaurants, plus such attractions as the Empire State Building, Madison Square Garden, Times Square, Rockefeller Center, the Fifth Avenue shopping area, the Museum of Modern Art, and the New York Public Library. Just outside its peripheries are Lincoln Center, Central Park, the United Nations, Jacob K. Javits Convention Center, and the most expensive and elegant residential areas.

The following is meant to take you outside midtown, to give you a taste of all the Big Apple has to offer. So let's begin at the beginning, the southern tip of the island—the Battery.

New York Harbor

Walking along the esplanade of Battery Park will give you an appreciation of the city's strategic geographic situation, one of the reasons for its rise as a commercial empire. The Victorian-cupolaed gray building with the red window frames and green roof is home to the city's fireboats. Look out over the water to a point called The Narrows, where the Lower Bay funnels into the Upper Bay. There you'll see the 4,260-foot main span of the Verrazano-Narrows Bridge, connecting Brooklyn and Staten Island. Here, in 1524, the Florentine navigator Giovanni da Verrazano, seeking a route to Asia at the behest of King Francis I of France, discovered what he described as "this very agreeable situation located within two small prominent hills, in the midst of which flowed to the sea a very giant river." The river bears the name of another explorer, Englishman Henry Hudson, who arrived 85 years later while searching out a northerly passage to India for his Dutch East India Company employers.

The Statue of Liberty

Three hundred years after Verrazano and Hudson made their initial forays, New York's most symbolic structure (if not a symbol for the entire United States) took her place in the harbor, on Liberty Island.

The idea for the Statue of Liberty was first discussed shortly after the American Civil War at a small dinner party in the Versailles home of French historian Edouard de Laboulaye. It was to be a gift from the people of France to the people of the United States to commemorate the long friendship between the two nations. One of the dinner guests was a young Alsatian sculptor, Frederic Auguste Bartholdi, who journeyed to America some years later to discuss the project with prominent philanthropists. As he sailed into New York's harbor, he conceived the idea of a "mighty woman with a torch," lighting the way to freedom in the New World.

Public fetes and lotteries were held in France to raise the $250,000 necessary for the statue's construction. In the United States, which had agreed to build the monument's pedestal, the public was unenthusiastic about contributing to what they considered a "New York lighthouse" until publisher Joseph Pulitzer used his *New York World* to "nationalize" the campaign. Then it became a crusade. Eventually, completion of the pedestal was assured and the statue shipped piecemeal, in 214 separate cases, to be assembled and mounted in New York. The Statue of Liberty Enlightening the World was dedicated October 28, 1886.

One hundred years of natural elements took its toll on Lady Liberty's iron and copper exterior, and a $230-million restoration project closed the Statue to visitors. It was reopened July 4, 1986, with a giant Harbor Festival celebration.

Another historical site in the Upper Bay is Ellis Island, whose buildings served as the entry point for over 17 million immigrants from 1892 to 1954. The island, now preparing for its centennial in 1992, has reopened its restored portions to the public.

Lower Manhattan

Disastrous fires in the latter part of the 18th and early 19th centuries destroyed many of New York's landmark buildings, and an ambitious building program during the city's rise to metropolitan heights demolished many remaining fine old structures. Nevertheless, a number of historic sites remain.

One of those still standing is found in Battery Park: Castle Clinton, built as a fort in 1811 to defend New York against British attacks during the

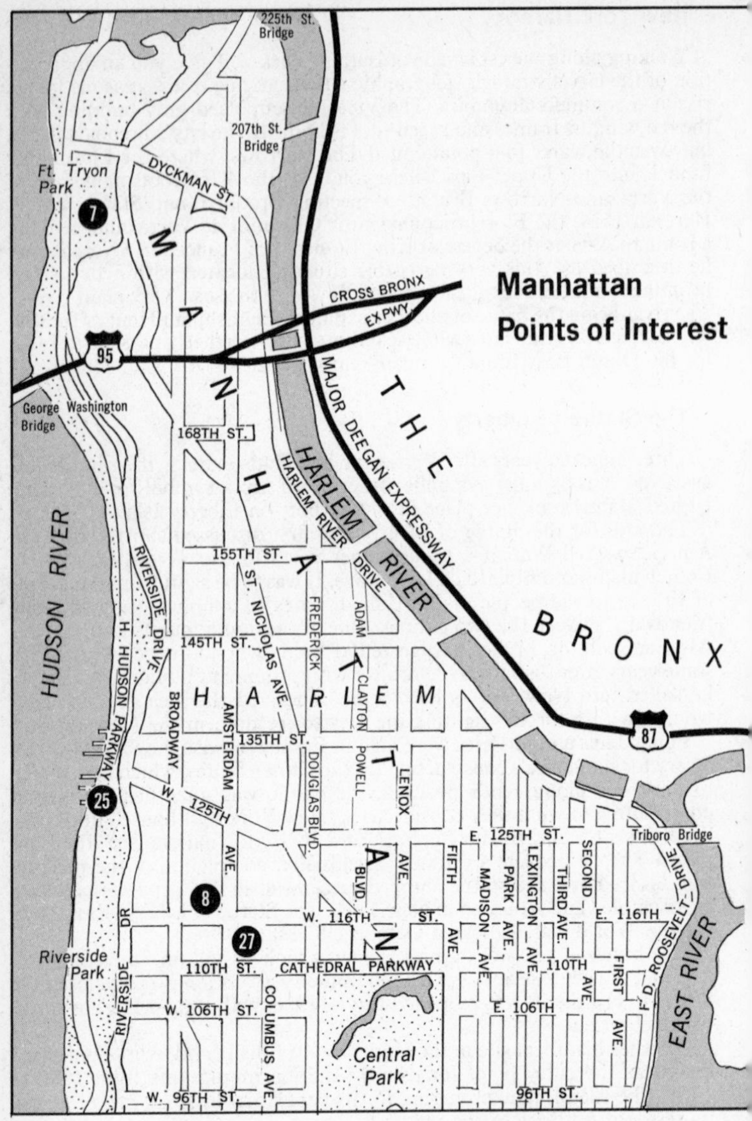

Points of Interest

1) American Museum of Natural History
2) Carnegie Hall
3) Central Park Zoo
4) Chinatown
5) Citicorp Center
6) City Hall
7) Cloisters
8) Columbia University
9) Empire State Building
10) Frick Museum
11) Gracie Mansion
12) Gramercy Park
13) Grand Central Station
14) Guggenheim Museum
15) Hayden Planetarium

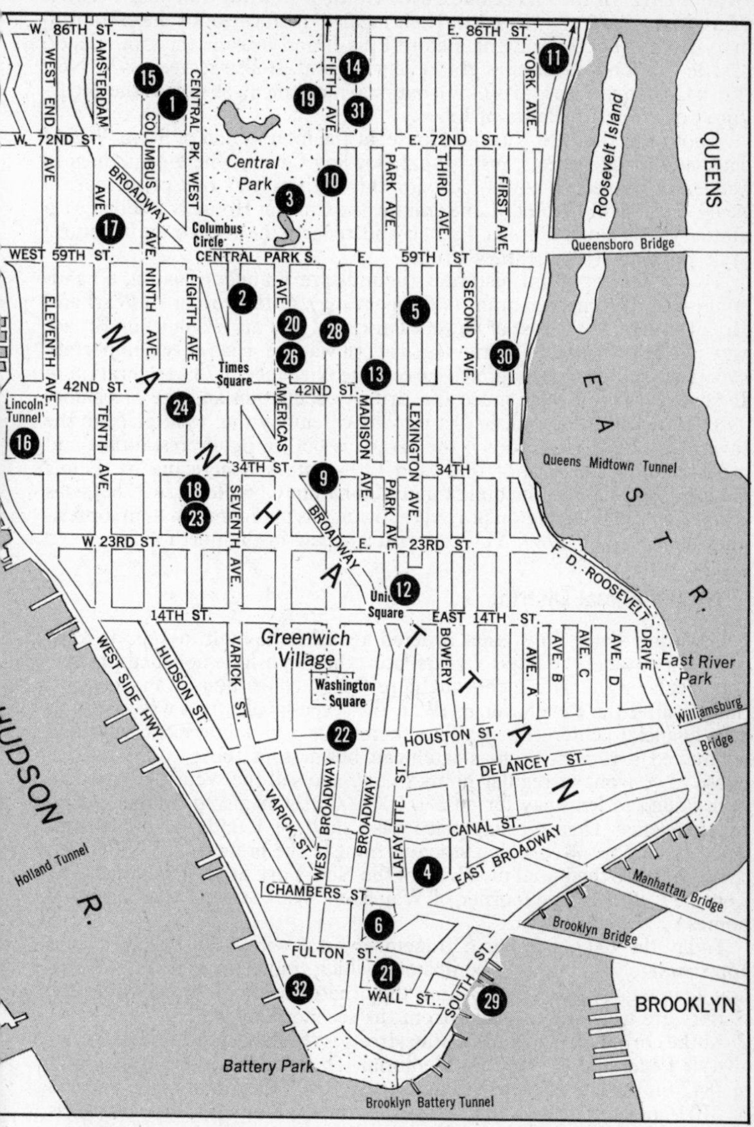

16) Jacob K. Javits Convention Center
17) Lincoln Center
18) Madison Square Garden
19) Metropolitan Museum of Art
20) Museum of Modern Art
21) N.Y. Stock Exchange
22) New York University
23) Pennsylvania Station
24) Port Authority Bus Terminal
25) Riverside Church
26) Rockefeller Center
27) St. John's Episcopal Cathedral
28) St. Patrick's Cathedral
29) South Street Seaport
30) United Nations
31) Whitney Museum
32) World Trade Center

War of 1812. In 1823 it became Castle Garden, a theater and public center. Here Jenny Lind, the "Swedish Nightingale," performed for the extraordinary fee of $1,000 per night. Before Ellis Island became the main depot, Castle Clinton was an immigration entry point. It also served as the New York City aquarium and is now a national monument, as well as the departure point for the Statue of Liberty.

Another is the U.S. Custom House, at the intersection of State, Whitehall, and Bridge streets, just behind Bowling Green, where gentlemen in the 1700s played at bowls (cost for this activity was one peppercorn a year). Erected in 1907 of Maine granite, the Custom House is studded with statuary by Daniel Chester French and reflects the rococo architectural style popular at the century's turn.

Two other important historic structures are Fraunces Tavern, a handsome 1719 tavern/restaurant (still operating), at the corner of Pearl and Broad streets (to the east of Battery Park) and St. Paul's Chapel on Broadway just below City Hall. Fraunces Tavern was the scene of two important events in George Washington's career: the November 1783 celebration of Evacuation Day which ended the British occupation and the December 1783 "farewell to his officers," a moving ceremony that took place in the tavern's Long Room. Today, the tavern is both a public restaurant and a five-building museum of 18th- and 19th-century Americana. St. Paul's Chapel, the oldest public building in Manhattan (completed in 1766), was where George Washington prayed following his inauguration as first president on April 30, 1789. You can visit his pew in the north aisle.

The Financial District

Governor Peter Stuyvesant ordered a wall to be built in 1653 to keep out Indian raiders. Forty-six years later, the English demolished the eyesore, replacing it with a thoroughfare full of coffee houses and taverns. Shortly after the Revolutionary War, the seven-block street was first used as a financial center. Twenty-four merchants and auctioneers, who had conducted a rather catch-as-catch-can business in those coffee houses, chose to convene at regular hours to buy and sell the securities that had been issued to help pay for an $80,000,000 debt incurred by the War of Independence. Their meeting place was a shady spot under an old buttonwood (sycamore) tree which stood in front of the present 68 Wall Street. These 24 were the initial members of the New York Stock Exchange. The Tontine Coffee House (corner of Water and Wall Streets) was their first home.

Today the Exchange has 630 member firms with 1,366 members and approximately 1,700 listed companies, which traded an average 165 million shares daily last year. Behind the ornate facade at 20 Broad Street, visitors are welcome to watch from the second floor gallery.

At the corner of Wall and Nassau streets is the handsome, Greek Revival-style Federal Hall National Memorial. The current structure was built in 1842 on the site of New York's first City Hall (begun in 1699, finished in 1703, and remodeled in 1788). In its time the building has served as a courthouse (John Peter Zenger was tried and acquitted here in the famous trial that upheld freedom of the press and freedom of speech), debtor's prison, customs house, subtreasury, and—as America's first capitol—meeting house for the First Congress. A pillory, where minor offenders were publicly derided, stood in front of the original City Hall, as did a stake. More serious criminals were tied and flogged there.

At Broadway and Wall Street stands Trinity Church, reputed to be the world's wealthiest parish and certainly one of New York's richest landlords with its extensive real estate holdings. A 1705 land grant from Queen Anne of England deeded the Episcopal church property along the Hudson River from St. Paul's Chapel on Fulton Street all the way up to Christopher Street in Greenwich Village. The oldest stone in its graveyard dates from 1681; Alexander Hamilton, Robert Fulton, publisher William Bradford, Jr., and other citizens integral in the history of New York are buried in this graveyard.

Directly behind St. Paul's Chapel at Broadway and Fulton Street loom the gigantic "twin towers" of the World Trade Center. From top to bottom, they measure 110 stories and offer a view of New York that extends nearly 50 miles, over rivers, harbor, bridges, ships, skyscrapers, out to the Atlantic Ocean. You can take in these sights from the Observation Deck of Two World Trade Center or while sipping a cocktail at Windows on the World, the restaurant atop One World Trade Center.

The enormous excavations for the World Trade Center's twin towers produced enough material to create a 92-acre landfill (along the Hudson River) running from the tip of Lower Manhattan to Chambers Street on the north. On this new land, a magnificent "city built onto a city" has risen. Battery Park City contains residential housing, office space, public parks, spacious plazas, promenades along the waterfront, outdoor sculptures, two small harbors (North and South Cove) and the World Financial Center. Within the four main buildings of the center—which is entered by the North Bridge from World Trade Center Tower One—are two floors of shops, designer boutiques, fine restaurants (both casual and ambitious), and a dazzling crystal palace called the Winter Garden, where you can dine, shop, relax, attend free performances, and marvel at the river views, all under 16 tall and stately palm trees. Notable restaurants beyond the Winter Garden area include the gracious Hudson River Club overlooking both the river and harbor and Donald Sacks, a more informal dining spot in The Courtyard, popular spot for lunch and Sunday brunch.

South Street Seaport

Continue east and backtrack slightly to Fulton Street where you will find the South Street Seaport at Water Street. New York City gained much of its prominence and wealth as a major seaport. A 12-block area around the Fulton Fish Market was renovated and opened to the public in mid-1983 as the South Street Seaport Museum. Schermerhorn Row, on the south side of Fulton Street, is a collection of shops and restaurants, and the Visitor's Center is found at 207 Water Street. The Museum Block, west side of Front Street, houses the Seaport Museum proper, as well as another collection of restaurants and shops, some on an interior courtyard called Cannon's Walk. The old Fulton Fish Market (still the center of the city's wholesale fish business) is a marvelously gutsy, frantically alive area along the waterfront, and the height of its activity comes during the wee hours of the morning. (Tours of the Seaport and its exhibits can be arranged by calling Seaport Tours: 212–669–9405.) Other area attractions include "New York Unearthed," a new archaeological museum facility; Piers 15 and 16, where the Museum's historic ships are moored; and the reconstructed Fulton Market Building and Pier 17, each of which offers several floors of shops, food stalls and restaurants (some offering stunning views of the East River and the Brooklyn Bridge, which dates from 1883).

Colorful Neighborhoods

Chinatown is only a short walk away—just north of the Brooklyn Bridge and behind the City Hall/Municipal Court area. Gone are the opium dens and notorious "tong wars" of yesterday. Today the tiny, dozen or so blocks that form Chinatown are a bright patchwork of Oriental shops and restaurants next to pseudo pagodas on tenement roofs, bright banners that garland the streets, temple bells, and the Cantonese dialect of venerable elders. There is a faint aura of China's 4,000-year-old civilization all around, from the apothecary shops where herbal medicines are compounded to the exotic condiments—shark fins, dried fungi, squid, duck eggs—displayed in grocery stalls. Even the sidewalk telephone booths look like tiny pagodas.

Leading north out of Chinatown is the Bowery, once an Indian trail used by Peter Stuyvesant to ride to his "bouwerie" or farm. This once-fashionable amusement and theater center has, for nearly a century, been the "street of forgotten men."

To the east of the Bowery is, what some observers feel, the most dramatic blending of races, religions, and cultures in the world. On the Lower East Side, crammed with immigrants, English was, for all practical purposes, a foreign language. From its ghettos have risen politicians, entertainers, businessmen, and not a few gangsters.

These days the street stalls bustle with bargain hunters seeking clothes, kitchen wares, linen, lamps, wholesale ties, bridal gowns, and more. Only on Saturday, when the mostly Jewish shopkeepers observe the Sabbath, does the activity cease.

West of the Bowery, centering around Grand Street, is Little Italy, still peopled by a few sons and daughters of the Mediterranean. In early September, the neighborhood's charms are on display during the Feast of San Gennaro. All of Mulberry Street turns into a carnival, with food stands hawking calzone, sausage-and-pepper heroes, zeppole, and other southern Italian favorites. Dozens of restaurants and coffee houses happily cook up equally hearty fare 365 days of the year.

As you head towards the Hudson River, past West Broadway, the ambience begins to change. This is TriBeCa (TRIangle BElow CAnal street), where former SoHo (South of Houston street) dwellers fled when rents went through the proverbial roof. Artists have turned empty factory floors into residential lofts and crumbling storefronts into trendy bars, restaurants, and night spots. SoHo, however, remains Lower Manhattan's leading shopping district for art and up-to-the-minute fashions.

SoHo is roughly bounded by Houston Street on the north, Broadway on the east, Canal Street to the south, and Avenue of the Americas to the west. In the last 20 years or so, artists and writers used their creative imaginations to transform dilapidated warehouses here into spacious lofts and showcases for their paintings. Unfortunately, they did such a good job of gentrification that rents became affordable only by young professionals and jet setters. The trendy eating spots were never within financial reach of the artists whose works they displayed. When they fled to the less expensive East Village and/or TriBeCa, they left behind an enchanting and unusual legacy of galleries, shops, bars, and boutiques for visitors and art patrons to enjoy today.

Greenwich Village

When you talk about "the Village," you must specify *which* part of Manhattan between 14th and Houston streets, from the East River to the Hudson River, you mean. Are you talking about the upscale brownstone apartments from the Hudson River to Seventh Avenue, where successful executives, lawyers, doctors, actors, and writers tend backyard gardens? Or do you mean the overwhelming variety of theaters, restaurants, bars, boutiques, and nightspots crunched between Seventh Avenue and Washington Square Park? Maybe you're speaking of the New York University community that ripples in all directions from its Washington Square nucleus? Perhaps you're referring to the remaining vestiges of bohemia and the ethnic culture that color the latticework of streets from Broadway to the East River? No matter which Village you seek, though, you'll find this part of town one of the friendliest and homiest sections of New York.

British colonists renamed the verdant little Indian settlement of Sapokanican for their town of Greenwich around the beginning of the 18th century. A stream of residents flooded the fairly sleepy, wooded countryside when smallpox and yellow fever plagued the lower tip of the island in the 1700s. They settled hastily on an old tobacco plantation and their byways spread haphazardly. Visitors find this crazy-quilt street pattern sweet and charming, but it frustrates uninitiated taxi drivers to no end. When immigrants overflowed the boundaries of Little Italy, they planted roots on the northerly side of Houston Street, which blossomed into a fairly sizeable Italian population. By the turn of the century, the area was attracting painters and sculptors who discovered cheap loft space for rent. Poets and playwrights, intellectuals and radicals followed, turning the Village into a bawdy little Montmartre in the midst of Manhattan by the time the 1920s roared around.

Washington Square

Perhaps the best way to experience the Village is to begin at its heart—Washington Square, located at the foot of Fifth Avenue. You'll find it marked by Washington Arch, designed by the famous architect, Stanford White. The Square served as a potter's field for victims of the plague, and also as a public execution ground. By the early 19th century, disease and the gallows had claimed over 10,000 souls. In 1823, the potter's field was closed, and in 1827, Washington Square Park was laid out and the handsome mansions of "The Row" (along Washington Square North) were built. In warm weather the park explodes with street entertainment—jugglers, impromptu jam sessions, poetry readings, roller skaters—but you'll have to thread your way through the runners jogging their laps on the sidewalk that surrounds the four-square-block area.

New York University was established in the 1830s; its original building, at 100 Washington Square East, was where Professor Samuel F. B. Morse developed the telegraph and Samuel Colt invented the single-shot pistol. Students, professors, classrooms, libraries—all the university's activities—are headquartered here. The tall, brick-and-glass Loeb Student Center covers the site of Madame Blanchard's boardinghouse, whose dwellers included Theodore Dreiser, Eugene O'Neill, O. Henry, and many other literary notables.

Exploring the West Village

From here it's a few short steps to MacDougal Street, and a few more to MacDougal Alley, beneath which Minetta Stream still flows. On MacDougal, amid long-established coffee houses and restaurants like Minetta's, Monte's, and The Derby, you'll find the rebuilt Provincetown Playhouse, made famous by the early works of Eugene O'Neill. Circle-in-the-Square Theater (Downtown), to the left on Bleecker Street, is the successor to the original, which once stood in Sheridan Square. Along Bleecker Street, and across Avenue of the Americas, is the beginning of the Italian shopping mart, which stretches to Seventh Avenue. Produce stands, meat and cheese shops, fish stores, and pastry emporiums give a unique character and flavor to the street.

No matter which street you choose to explore at this point, you'll find Village color: interesting and historic buildings—the homes of past New York celebrities—small shady gardens, quaint little antique shops and bookstores, and at Hudson and 11th streets, the White Horse Tavern, where Dylan Thomas hoisted many a glass. Look for the red-brick, Italian-Gothic clock tower of the Jefferson Market Courthouse (corner of Sixth Avenue and 10th Street), which once served as the neighborhood fire lookout. The structure is now a branch of the New York Public Library.

East Village Bohemia

East of Broadway, the surroundings assume a more vivid hue; do-it-yourself decorating and repairs mark the presence of painters and poets without pennies to spare. Squalor co-exists side by side with esthetically pleasing graffiti art; unconventional clothes are created from available patches. The wild informality, born of economic necessity, has become chic, and the adventurous styles are packaged as fashion in trendy boutiques and "alternative" galleries. Before the counterculture invaded the East Village, it was a quiet confluence of mixed cultures: Ukrainian, Czech, Polish, German, Russian, Italian, Jewish, and Puerto Rican. Now the avant-garde rubs shoulders with the strong ethnic personality. "Head" shops sit next door to sushi bars, which neighbor Polish and Ukrainian restaurants on First and Second avenues. A stroll through the neighborhood will prove contradictory, explosive, colorful, and anything but boring.

Moving Uptown

Parade grounds scattered across the city broke up the forward march of square block upon square block of brownstone houses. A few imaginative builders also individualized the city's face as its population expanded north. One was Samuel Ruggles, who purchased a large land tract between 20th and 21st streets, east of Park Avenue South and west of Third Avenue. This is Gramercy Park, one of the city's most exclusive residential areas. The elite of New York were attracted by the promise that only those who built houses around the square could use its park. Two golden keys to unlock the gate of the fenced-in park were given to each homeowner and socialites followed the lead of Mrs. Stuyvesant Fish, leader of the "400," to the square. The Social Register tenants are gone, replaced by writers, business executives, and wealthy widows, but on sunny days, lucky key-holders still amuse themselves in the park. Theodore Roosevelt's birthplace (28 East 20th Street) is now a National Historic Site; the home and adjacent museum are open to the public.

Across town from Gramercy Park is Chelsea. Though many historic landmarks have slipped away, the Chelsea Hotel (222 West 23rd Street) remains. Celebrated authors like Thomas Wolfe and Dylan Thomas lived here; Janis Joplin reveled in its halls during her extended trips to New York; and Sid Vicious (of Sex Pistol fame) died here. Though few vestiges of elegance are evident inside, the Victorian Gothic edifice with wrought iron balconies, turrets, and chimney stacks has been designated an architectural landmark.

Midtown

Once you reach midtown Manhattan you're in another world. Ranging roughly from 14th Street to 59th Street, and from river to river, this is a center of superlatives—the biggest buildings; best restaurants; brightest lights; greatest concentration of big business; largest complex of theater, concert, and opera houses; most exclusive couture houses and specialized services. The meandering mood of the lower island gives way to individual explorations. Shopping is concentrated from 34th to 59th streets between Sixth and Madison avenues. (See Shopping section for specific recommendations.) Museums of folklore, modern art, contemporary crafts, and more can be visited in the midtown area. There are awesome views to be seen from atop midtown's tallest buildings, an underground world to discover, and a thousand personal memories to treasure. Some of the city's greatest attractions are here: Times Square, Rockefeller Center, the United Nations, and the Empire State and Chrysler buildings.

The Great White Way starts at Times Square, in reality a triangle where Broadway and Seventh Avenue intersect 42nd Street. It is a monument to the vision and gambling spirit of three men. In 1894, impresario Oscar Hammerstein I sank his $2-million-dollar fortune (and then some) into building two theaters. August Belmont more than matched this gamble by extending the subway uptown into this new theater district. Adolph S. Ochs constructed the Times Tower in 1904 as headquarters for his newspaper, *The New York Times.*

The entire Times Square area is currently undergoing a renaissance. There is hardly a block between 42nd and 59th streets that does not contain a major new construction project, and the long-awaited, hotly debated redevelopment program for the sleazy stretch of 42nd Street between Seventh and Eighth avenues is proceeding, after going through some 30 separate lawsuits (proving that nothing is simple in the worlds of business and politics anymore). One huge piece of the overall Times Square project is already in place: the new Marriott Marquis Hotel with its Marquis Theatre, which opened with a hit musical, *Me and My Girl.* Other important new hotels in the area include the Novotel New York, Embassy Suites–Times Square, Holiday Inn Crowne Plaza, Macklowe, and the Rihga Royal.

Empire State Building

One of the first sights on any New York visitor's top-10 list is at Fifth Avenue and 34th Street—the Empire State Building. A few statistics are in order. It is 1,454 feet tall, including a television antenna on top that measures 204 feet. There are 1,860 steps to climb. It took less than two years to build (construction began in October, 1929, and finished in May, 1931) at a cost of $40 million. It weighs 365,000 tons, has 73 elevators, and five *acres* of windows in its 102 stories. About 15,000 people work there and 36,000 visit it each day. After they've left, it takes 150 people to vacuum. From the observation deck on the 102nd floor (there's also one on the 86th), the view extends out more than 50 miles. Now you know why over two million people travel to the third tallest building in the world annually.

Fifth Avenue

This, the world's most famous shopping street, was once millionaire's row. The Astors, Vanderbilts, and numerous others erected fine mansions here after the Civil War. The dividing line between the East and West sides of Manhattan, Fifth Avenue is still the most fashionable street in the city. High quality shops line both sides from 39th to 59th streets. At 51st Street is the Gothic-styled St. Patrick's Cathedral, next to Olympic Towers. Just up the avenue is the new Trump Tower, and at 59th Street and Central Park South you'll see Grand Army Plaza and F. Scott Fitzgerald's old haunt, the venerable Plaza Hotel. If you're feeling romantically inclined, you might take a ride in one of the horse-drawn carriages lined up across the street.

Rockefeller Center

Rockefeller Center is a city-within-a-city. You could easily spend a whole day within its complex of 21 buildings. Many of its 240,000 daytime residents do, never leaving the complex from their arrival in the morning until they go home at night. There's no need to, with restaurants, shops, a post office, a passport office, a movie theater, and subway transportation to all points of the metropolis.

Six formal flower beds, the Channel Gardens, run from Fifth Avenue to the Lower Plaza, and change with the seasons. Probably the best known annual floral draw is the giant Christmas tree, erected each December. The Lower Plaza, where you can skate from September to April and dine alfresco the rest of the year, is the site of two new restaurants, the elegant Sea Grill and more reasonably priced American Festival Cafe. The 70-story GE building at 30 Rockefeller Plaza, which contains the NBC network's headquarters (there are tours of the TV studios, Monday–Saturday), is crowned with the spectacular Rainbow Room, now reopened after a $20-million restoration.

The Avenue of the Americas

The midtown segment of this long, broad thoroughfare, still known to most New Yorkers as Sixth Avenue, begins at Herald Square outside the largest department store in the world—Macy's—and continues past a litter of jam-packed shop fronts to Bryant Park, at the rear side of New York Public Library's main branch at 42nd Street. Named for poet and journalist William Cullen Bryant, the green and relaxing spot contains a booth where half-price, day-of-performance tickets to music and dance events may be purchased.

At 47th Street, you could be tempted to take an eastern detour down the block known as the city's diamond center. It's obvious why when you see the countless glittering shop windows.

At 48th Street you begin to encounter some of the giant members of the Rockefeller Center community: the 45-story Celanese Building; the 51-story McGraw Hill Building (in its lower plaza is the "Sun Triangle" sculpture); 48 stories housing *Time* and *Life;* and Exxon's 54-story headquarters. Radio City Music Hall, on the avenue's east side at 50th Street, is a wondrous Art Deco attraction. With a seating capacity of 6,000, it is the world's largest indoor theater. A couple of blocks farther on are the main offices of two major television and radio networks—the "black rock" of CBS between 52nd and 53rd streets, and ABC at 54th Street.

The United Nations

The United Nations moved into the elegant quarters which overlook the East River between 42nd and 48th streets in 1952. Acres of parkland make the U.N. grounds a pleasant place to stroll and watch the busy river traffic ply the East River.

Visitors enter the United Nations Headquarters through the north end of the marble and limestone General Assembly Building at 45th Street and First Avenue. The lobby has a museum-like quality, with its free-form multiple galleries, soaring ceiling, and collection of art treasures donated by member nations. Guests may attend most official meetings free; tickets are issued in the lobby 15 minutes before the meetings start, on a first-come, first-served basis, since the schedules are not set in advance. At most meetings, speeches are simultaneously interpreted in Chinese, English, French, Russian, and Spanish. There are earphones at each visitor's seat with a dial system to tune in the language of your choice.

Lincoln Center

An elegant four-block cultural world, Lincoln Center for the Performing Arts is located between 62nd and 66th streets west of Broadway. Get acquainted with the buildings by taking one of the guided tours or wander around the open plazas and parks on your own. Standing on Broadway, the building you see to the left of the large central fountain plaza is the New York State Theater, home of the New York City Opera and New York City Ballet. On the right is Avery Fisher Hall, home of the New York Philharmonic. Between the two stands the Metropolitan Opera House, with its pair of colorful Marc Chagall murals depicting motifs and themes relating to music. Tucked behind Avery Fisher Hall are two charming legitimate theaters, the Vivian Beaumont and the Mitzi E. Newhouse, homes of the vibrant Lincoln Center Theater.

Central Park

This 843-acre oasis of rural beauty in the midst of a concrete jungle runs from 59th to 110th Street and from Fifth Avenue to Central Park West (an extension of Eighth Avenue). Frederick Law Olmsted and Calvert Vaux masterfully designed the park, which was designated a National Historic Landmark in 1965. The park is a many-splendored melange of fountains and ponds, statues and monuments, and promenades and wooded paths.

On warm weekdays, office workers spread out their lunches on a favorite rock by the pond. Weekends, families come to picnic, play softball, jog, pitch horseshoes, ride the merry-go-round, fly kites, row boats, roller skate, or ride bicycles on the curling, car-free drives and absorb enough sun and fresh air to last them through another week of molelike living.

East Side Museums and Galleries

On the Fifth Avenue side of Central Park, as well as the side streets jutting off Madison Avenue, is the city's greatest concentration of galleries and museums: the Frick Collection, in what was once the home of coke-and-steel industrialist Henry Clay Frick; The Metropolitan Museum of Art, which houses one of the most comprehensive collections in the world, more than a million art treasures representing the work of 50 centuries; the Solomon R. Guggenheim Museum, displaying 20th-century art in an extraordinary building designed by Frank Lloyd Wright; the Cooper-Hewitt Museum of Design, housed in the former home of another steel tycoon, Andrew Carnegie; the Jewish Museum, one of the three most important repositories of Jewish ceremonial objects in the world; the International Center for Photography; El Museo del Barrio; and the Museum of the City of New York, where the town's past and present are reflected.

One block east, on Madison Avenue, is yet another great museum, the Whitney Museum of American Art, which specializes in 20th-century American works. The building itself is startling. Given slightly less than one-third of an acre for the structure, architect Marcel Breuer elected to turn the traditional ziggurat ("wedding cake") design upside down, so that the second, third, and fourth floors each project 14 feet farther out over the street than the one below.

A bit farther downtown is the center of New York's art gallery district. Here you will find the Christie Galleries, the Kennedy Galleries, Perls Galleries, and the elegant Wildenstein Gallery, as well as dozens of smaller, more intimate institutions.

West Side Style

Once you cross Central Park, the Upper East Side's rich, tradition-bound feel gives way to the trendy preppiness prevalent in the Upper West Side. Shops and restaurants on Columbus Avenue spill out onto the sidewalk on sunny summer days. Year-round, there is a hive of activity stretching from Central Park West to Broadway, Lincoln Center up into the 80s.

The rocky ridge that begins in Central Park rises gradually as it travels uptown through Harlem and Morningside Heights to the precipitous lookout at Washington Heights. One of New York's most scenic rides is along Riverside Drive, following the Hudson River shoreline from 72nd Street to Inwood, at Manhattan's northern tip. Look to the left as you pass 79th Street, where large yachts anchor at the boat basin. Next, the Soldiers and Sailors Monument comes into view, a handsome Italian Carrara marble "silo" circled by 12 Corinthian columns. The 392-foot Gothic Tower of Riverside Church can be seen, a mile to the north. Its 72-bell carillon is the largest in the U.S.; the *Bourdon,* its biggest bell, weighs over 20 tons. In contrast, the smallest is just 10 pounds.

The cathedral Church of St. John the Divine is just a short detour east to Amsterdam Avenue and 112th Street. When it is finally completed (construction has been going on since 1892, mind you), this will be the largest Gothic cathedral in the world. Columbia University fills the center of Morningside Heights here while just to the north are the Union Theological Seminary and the Jewish Theological Seminary.

Past General Grant's tomb at 123rd Street, Riverside Drive begins to skirt Fort Washington Park.

Farther north still is Fort Tryon Park, site of the Cloisters, an outpost of the Metropolitan Museum that houses medieval art, including the famous "Hunt of the Unicorn" tapestries, considered to be among the greatest in the world. From this vantage point at the brow of Manhattan, you have an uninterrupted view of the magnificent sweep of the Hudson, all the way up to the Tappan Zee. New Jersey's Palisades shoreline, the graceful arc of the George Washington Bridge, and the far reaches of the Bronx all fall within your gaze.

PRACTICAL INFORMATION FOR NEW YORK CITY

WHEN TO GO. Anytime is the right time. New York is a 365-day-a-year town, and there's something happening every hour of the day. Seasonally speaking, spring and fall are optimum, with the months of Apr., May, Sept., and Oct. especially temperate and beautiful. Winter can be a tad frigid, allowing temperatures to hover in the 20-degree Fahrenheit range too long for taste. In summer, heat and humidity sometimes team to make July and Aug. steamy and uncomfortable. None of the discomforts are extreme, though, making New York a terrific year-round destination.

HOW TO GET THERE. By plane. New York City is served by virtually every major (and most minor) airlines at the following airports: *John F. Kennedy* in southeastern Queens; *LaGuardia* in northern Queens; and *Newark* in northern New Jersey. Newark, which has recently undergone an ambitious expansion program, is less hectic than either LaGuardia or JFK and just as easily accessible. Budget-minded tourists heading to New York should check travel agencies or newspaper travel pages for the latest on airfares.

By bus. The Port Authority Building (Eighth Ave. and 41st St., Manhattan) has over 200 platforms where commuter and transcontinental buses alike unload. This is the central terminal for buses serving parts of New Jersey, the Hudson Valley area, Putnam and Dutchess Counties, the Berkshires and the Poconos, as well as *Greyhound,* which serves the entire U.S. Central number for passenger information is 564–8484.

By train. Long distance *Amtrak* routes reach New York from Chicago and the West, Florida and the South, plus Boston, Montreal, and Toronto. All terminate in the city at either Grand Central Terminal (42nd to 46th Sts. on Park Ave.) or Penn Station (31st to 33rd Sts., Seventh to Eighth Aves.).

TOURIST INFORMATION. The *New York Convention and Visitors Bureau* on the south side of Columbus Circle, 59th St. and Broadway (212–397–8222), has multilingual aides to assist in making sightseeing plans. Subway and bus maps, hotel, motel, and restaurant information are free, as well as seasonal listings of the city's special entertainment attractions. The Information Center is open 9 A.M.–6 weekdays, 10–6 on weekends and holidays.

For wider ranging information on the Empire State, contact the *New York State Division of Tourism,* 1 Commerce Plaza, Albany, NY 12245. They also have a New York City office at 1515 Broadway, New York, NY 10036 (212–827–6255). The state's toll-free vacation information telephone number is 800–225–5697, and all the contiguous 48 states, from other areas and Canada, call 518–474–4116, Mon. through Fri., 9 A.M.–5 P.M.

Pick up *New York,* the *Village Voice,* or *The New Yorker,* weekly publications with extensive entertainment and cultural listings, or daily papers—*The New York Times, Newsday,* and the *Post*—for the most up-to-date information. The weighty Sunday *Times* is the best place to find out about forthcoming attractions. For more esoteric pastimes, *Details* magazine has up-to-date news on which clubs are "in" and which are not; and the new *Paper* is the best journal for discovering those exciting, just-opened restaurants, bars, shows, concerts, and galleries where the chic may come to meet.

TIME ZONES AND HOLIDAYS. New York lies in the Eastern Time Zone and observes Daylight Savings from the last Sun. in Apr. to the last Sun. in Oct. In addition to the standard national holidays, many banks and businesses are closed on Martin Luther King, Jr.'s birthday in Jan., Presidents Day in Feb., Good Friday, Columbus Day, Veterans' Day, and the important Jewish holidays: Passover, Rosh Hashanah, Yom Kippur, and Hanukkah.

TELEPHONES. The area code for Manhattan and the Bronx is 212; for Brooklyn, Queens, and Staten Island, it's 718. Parts of the Bronx was also scheduled to begin converting to the 718 area code in 1992. To get directory assistance when you're in Manhattan, dial 411. Otherwise, dial the appropriate area code, plus 555–1212. Pay telephones cost 25 cents for the first 3 minutes of a local call, although not all calls within the five boroughs are considered local. If this is the case, the operator will ask you for an additional deposit.

EMERGENCY PHONE NUMBERS. For *emergency* police, fire, or ambulance, dial 911. The Manhattan *fire department* may also be reached at 628–2900. The fire department also posesses medical emergency equipment.

HOW TO GET AROUND. From the airports. When you consider taxi prices, limo fares don't seem all that outrageous. A cab from JFK to Rockefeller Center, for example, is about $30, plus tip; from LaGuardia it's around $20. Some hotels serve the airport terminals with their own limousines, so check when you make reservations. Subway-bus service connecting points in Manhattan and Brooklyn with JFK, is available but can be slow and/or complicated and is impractical if you have more than carry-on luggage.

The *Carey Bus Company* (718–632–0500) will bring you into Manhattan for $7.50 from LaGuardia or $9.50 from JFK. Buses stop at five midtown Manhattan Carey coach locations: 125 Park Ave., opposite Grand Central Terminal; the Port Authority Bus Terminal's Air Trans Center, 42nd St. between 8th and 9th Aves.; the N. Y. Hilton Hotel, Sixth Ave. and W. 53rd St.; Sheraton City Squire Hotel, 7th Ave. between 51st and 52nd Sts.; and the Marriott Marquis Hotel, Broadway at 45th St.

Olympia Trails (212–964–6233) buses will also bring you to the 125 Park Ave. stop as well as the World Trade Center for $7 from Newark Airport.

The cheapest and most convenient way to and from Newark Airport is via the *New Jersey Transit* bus (201–460–8444). Every 15 minutes, from 5 A.M. to midnight, you can get to Newark from the Port Authority Terminal in Manhattan for $7. There is also *Air-Link,* a combination bus-train ride, which you can catch at any of the Path Train stations (201–963–2557). Before getting into a taxi at Newark, ascertain the proper flat rate (between $25 and $30) and any additional tolls or charges. A cab to the airport will run approximately $40 on the meter plus a $10 surcharge, tolls, and tip. To reserve a cab in advance, call the *Allstate Car & Limo* service, (212–741–7440 or 800–453–4099) if out of the city.

By subway. For all the verbal abuse this 24-hour system of mass transportation takes from New Yorkers as well as from visitors, it is the fastest way to get around 4 of the 5 boroughs. A $1.15 fare (you must purchase a token from a booth at any of the stations) will take you quickly, cheaply, and conveniently uptown, crosstown, all around town. Navigation is simply a matter of reading a map of the system, obtainable at any token booth or from the New York Visitors Bureau, (59th St. and Columbus Circle.

Trains are identified by number (1, 4) or letter (F, RR), which are displayed on the front and sides of the cars. Some are local and some express, which means they skip certain stations, so be sure the train you board stops where you need to get off. Read the signs above eye level on the platforms, which will determine where you wait for your train. And don't hesitate to ask the passengers hurrying along beside you for the proper platform. The system can seem complicated until you use it a few times. For information on subways and buses, call 718–330–1234. Have plenty of quarters ready if you're calling from a pay phone, as the operators are often busy and will keep you holding.

Please Note: If you travel after 10 P.M., wait for the train in the areas marked for off-peak hours. Usually located close to a manned token booth, they tend to be more highly lit than remote sections of the platform. Never get into an empty car or a car with only a few passengers you don't like the looks of.

By bus. Slower than the subway, and especially crowded during rush hours, the advantage of bus travel is that the routes are more varied and the stops more frequent, usually every two blocks. You must have the exact $1.15 fare—in coins or subway tokens, no bills—but transfers between a crosstown (east–west) and a north–south (uptown, downtown) route are free. Look on the bus front for its route number (M4, M27) and written destination. A bus map, available at the New York Visitors Bureau (59th St. and Columbus Circle) or from some bus drivers, will ferret out which route will take you where you want to go.

By taxi. The fare is $1.50 for the first one fifth of a mi. and 25 cents for each additional fifth. You also pay for waiting time (which is why the meter ticks over an additional 25 cents when you're stopped at lights or in a traffic jam), all bridge and tunnel tolls; some cabs are entitled to an extra 50 cents (per ride) between 8 P.M. and 6 A.M. There is no additional charge for two or more (up to four) sharing the same cab. Note that the driver expects (because he usually gets) a 15–20 percent tip. It is appropriate to tip more if you're heading to a destination far from where he can reasonably expect to find a return-trip passenger. Be sure the meter is running during your ride. Off-the-meter "bargains" do not exist, and the driver is subject to a fine if caught. Receipts are available for all taxi rides. Complaints can be made with the Taxi and Limousine Commission (840–4577).

Hailing a cab is simple; available cabs have their roof lights on, though if the words "Off Duty" surrounding the medallion numbers are also lit up, the cab does not have to stop. (Medallion numbers, sort of a social security number for cabbies, are displayed on their "hack" license, along with photo, inside the passenger door. They are an accurate source of identification if you leave something in the car or encounter trouble.) The driver, by law, may not refuse to take any "orderly" passenger anywhere in the 5 boroughs, Nassau, and Westchester counties, or to Newark Airport. The last three destinations entitle him or her to a fare beyond that on the meter—$10 extra to Newark, double to Nassau and Westchester.

Note: Beware the unofficial taxi "dispatchers" outside the Port Authority Bus Terminal and Madison Square Garden. You do not need them to get a cab, and they have no authority to negotiate rates—or to demand tips. Authorized dispatchers in uniform can be spotted at booths outside the bus terminal, at Grand Central Terminal, and at Pennsylvania Station. Doormen in hotels or apartments buildings are authorized and do expect a small gratuity.

By limousine. If you really want to do it up right, there's only one way—in a chauffeur-driven limousine. Fees are calculated by the hour, with tax, tolls, and gratuity extra. However, *Carey Cadillacs* (599–1122) will take you to New York's airports for a fixed fee, $50–$60 (depending on the car you choose) to JFK and Newark, $40–$50 to LaGuardia. Rates at *Fugazy Continental* (661–0100) are a little cheaper: $38 to JFK and Newark, $33 to LaGuardia. The aforementioned *Allstate Car & Limo* (741–7440) also provides reasonable limo service.

By car. If you can possibly avoid it, do not bring your car into Manhattan. Traffic crawls along, potholes will throw your wheels out of alignment, free parking space is next to impossible to find, and parking garages will empty your pocket at the rate of $15 an hour in some places. Signs that say "Don't Even Think of Parking Here" are for your benefit. Tow trucks will hook your illegally parked car in a matter of minutes, and it will cost you $100 *plus* the $25–$35 parking ticket—and possibly other charges—to get it back. As if those deterrents weren't enough, anything valuable left in the car will disappear rapidly, especially radios and tape players. Be sure to lock all doors.

When driving, you'll find the regular, gridlike street pattern easy to navigate. Greenwich Village, SoHo, TriBeCa, the Financial District, and the Lower East Side—some of the town's more interesting neighborhoods—are exceptions. Almost all the east–west streets and most of the north–south avenues are one way. All north–south avenues are parallel except Broadway, whose traffic winds from northwest (the 225th St. bridge to the Bronx) to southeast (South Ferry.) Traffic on Broadway becomes one-way, southbound, below 59th St. Parkways that run alongside the Hudson River on the west (the West Side Hwy., which turns into the Henry Hudson Pkwy north of 72nd St.; it is officially non-existent south of 57th St., though there is a patchwork street-level substitute) and the East River (FDR Dr., known as Harlem River Dr. from 125th St. until it reaches the George Washington Bridge) run fairly smoothly except in rush hour. They also eliminate the necessity of stopping for traffic lights at every block.

HINTS TO DISABLED TRAVELERS. Some buses have hydraulic lifts for the wheelchair bound and crosswalks generally have ramps. Subways are difficult to navigate in wheelchairs, as there are few stations with elevators. Many museums offer sign language interpretation of tours, and theaters are often outfitted with infrared systems to aid the hearing impaired.

The most comprehensive access guide to New York, *Access New York,* is available for a $2 charge from the *Institute of Rehabilitation,* Publications Office, NYU Medical Center, 530 First Ave., New York, NY 10016 (212–340–7204). Unfortunately, the Junior League no longer publishes *Access New York City;* however, the Information Line at the Mayor's Office for the Handicapped has a copy, and will read you specific listings if you dial 212–566–3913.

SEASONAL EVENTS. Under normal conditions, New York City overflows with exhibits, shows, and galleries, but the events listed here annually widen the choices for leisure-time activities. Many of the happenings are free.

January. Fireworks herald the *Chinese New Year,* which arrives the first full moon after Jan. 21. Call 397–8222. *National Boat Show* at Javits Center.

February. Dog fanciers view the best of breed at Madison Square Garden's prestigious *Westminster Dog Show* (682–6852). The American Museum of Natural History (Central Park West and 77th St.) marks *Black History Month* with films, exhibits, and discussions (769–5315).

March. Fifth Ave. turns Irish for the *St. Patrick's Day Parade* on the 17th.

Easter. *Macy's Flower Show,* spectacular display the week before Easter, at the department store. *The Easter Parade* (actually a promenade) takes place on Fifth Ave. from late morning to late afternoon.

April. *Baseball season* begins with the Yankees at Yankee Stadium in the Bronx and the Mets at Shea Stadium in Queens.

May. This is the month for *parades*—Armed Forces Day, Norwegian Constitution Day, and, of course, Memorial Day. Dates and route information are available at 397–8222. May also opens the street fair season when the *Ninth Avenue International Festival* stretches a global variety of ethnic foods and entertainment from 37th to 59th St. *Thoroughbred horse racing* starts its summer season at Belmont Park. Artists take over lower Fifth Ave. at Washington Square Park, displaying their wares at the *Washington Square Outdoor Art Exhibit.* New York's *beaches* open Memorial Day weekend.

June. The *Feast of St. Anthony of Padua* brings sizzling calzone (oversize cheese-filled dumplings fried in deep fat), grilled sausages, rides, raffles, and games of chance to Sullivan St. in SoHo. Call 777–2755. George Wein's annual *jazz festival* is world renowned. *Shakespeare in the Park,* produced by Joseph Papp's New York Shakespeare Festival Public Theater, brings the Bard—free—to the Delacorte Theater in Central Park (861–7277). More *parades:* Puerto Rican Day, Salute to Israel, and *Gay Pride Day. International Festival of the Arts* held every other year.

July. The *Fourth of July* is America's Independence Day. The fireworks literally begin at 9:15 P.M., sponsored by Macy's department store and emanate from barges on either the Hudson or East rivers. The *Hispanic World's Fair* is on display at the Javits Center (216–2000). Avery Fisher Hall (874–2424) hosts *Mostly Mozart* for six weeks. The Italian festivities continue at the *Lady of Pompeii Feast* on Carmine St., near Bleecker St., in Greenwich Village.

August. *Harlem Week* (actually a *two*-week festival of events) is held throughout the Capital of Black America. *Greenwich Village Jazz Festival* ends the month. All month long *Lincoln Center Out-of-Doors* (877–1800) fills Lincoln Center's parks and plazas with free music, dance, and theater. The *N.Y. Philharmonic* plays free in the parks.

September. *Parades* galore, marking Labor Day, West Indian-American Day, African-American Day, and Steuben Day. . . . Fifth Ave. from 47th to 57th St. is a literary connoisseur's delight during *New York Is Book Country.* Movie buffs preview soon-to-be-released blockbusters and art films during the *New York Film Festival* at Alice Tully Hall in Lincoln Center (362–1911).

October. Columbus Day, Pulaski Day, and Hispanic Day are all noted with *parades.* Call 397–8222 for routes and dates. *Halloween Parade* fills Greenwich Village with wild costumed revelers, beginning around 5:30 P.M.

November. Runners test their skill over the 26-mile route of the *New York City Marathon* (860–4455). *Macy's Thanksgiving Day Parade* (397–8222) is a thrill to see live as it wends its way down Central Park West (from 77th St.) and Broadway. Thanksgiving is usually the signal for the windows at Lord and Taylor, Saks, Tiffany, and F.A.O. Schwarz to light up with their spectacular, mechanical Christmas displays.

December. The annual *Christmas tree lighting* ceremony at Rockefeller Center between Fifth and Sixth aves. is always an event. Call 397–8222. Ringing in the new year in New York is an experience at Times Square on New Year's Eve, even if you hate crowds. Central Park is also the scene of celebrations.

TOURS AND SPECIAL-INTEREST SIGHTSEEING. Before taking on the city as a whole, a bus tour can help you get your bearings. *Gray Line,* 900 Eighth Ave. (397–2600), *Crossroads Sightseeing,* 701 Seventh Ave. (581–2828), and *Short Line Tours,* 166 West 46th St. (354–5122) cover many well known Manhattan sights. Scores of sightseeing companies offer special or personalized tours (check the Visitors Bureau's quarterly calendar for a complete list). Two of the firms are *Red Carpet Associates* (deluxe: 212–832–7297) and Personal Transit (budget: 718–238–0133).

While you're in the neighborhood, you might want to take a self-guided walking tour of *Rockefeller Center.* Pick up an attractive free folder (listing the high points of the 21-building, 22-acre business and entertainment complex) at the Visitors Bureau, 2 Columbus Circle, or at the GE Building, 30 Rockefeller Plaza. Just around the corner is *Radio City Music Hall,* 1260 Avenue of the Americas (246–4600). There is a guided tour to take you backstage for a look at theater magic behind the footlights.

You can skim New York by air—*Island Helicopter* is found in the heliport at 34th St. and East River Dr. (683–4575)—or by water, on a *Circle Line* cruise, which leaves Pier 83 at the intersection of West 42nd St. and 12th Ave. (563–3200). For a relaxing, old-fashioned tour, climb into the back of a hansom cab, one of those horse drawn carriages that line up at 59th St. and Fifth Ave., just outside the Plaza Hotel. For an elegant, romantic, and even delicious view of the city, take a luncheon, dinner, or brunch cruise aboard one of World Yacht's sleek vessels (212–929–7090 for details and reservations).

Two other guided tours that shouldn't be missed: the *New York Stock Exchange,* Visitor's Center, 20 Broad St., 3rd Floor, (656–5167); and the *United Nations,* First

Ave. at 45th St. (963–7713). And for a taste of something different, you might want to take in the soul food and nightlife, spirituals and gospel offered by *Harlem Spirituals,* whose offices are at 1457 Broadway, Suite 1008, 10036 (302–2594). On Sun. mornings, for $25, they'll take you to the mansions and town houses of Sugar Hill, Hamilton Terrace, and Striver's Row, then to a Baptist church service for an authentic gospel experience. Or spend Sat. night savoring a soul food dinner, then escorted on a crawl through Harlem's cabarets for $60. The Gray Line's *Harlem Renaissance Tours* (722–9534) also takes visitors on a variety of jaunts, plus Sun. morning gospel services. Prices range from $25 to $60 per person.

PARKS AND GARDENS. Nearly a sixth of the city's land has been set aside for parks, which have gradually evolved into recreational and cultural centers. Largest and most famous is **Central Park,** with 843 acres. Lakes, stables, baseball diamonds, and a stunning new zoo are among its delights. The New York Shakespeare Festival makes use of the Delacorte Theater near the 81st St. entrances (from either Central Park West or Fifth Ave.) for free performances of the classics. Belvedere Castle hosts exhibits while free concerts are often held in the Goldman Band Shell, in the Mall midway between East and West 72nd Sts. On nearby Conservatory Pond, people maneuver their battery-operated, remote-controlled model sailboats in good weather. A jogger's track and bridle path circle the Reservoir in the 80's. Strawberry Fields, a memorial to the late John Lennon, is located due north of the 72nd St. and Central Park West entrance. For general Park information, call 360–1333, 397–3156, or 860–1353 for tours.

It's true, there *is* more greenery to be found in New York than just the lush acreage of Central Park. The **New York Botanical Garden,** directly north of the Bronx Zoo, features 11 greenhouses and 12,000 different species of plants on its 250 rolling acres. Spectacular is the 40-acre Hemlock Forest, virgin land untouched since the Indians camped out there. Displays in the Museum explain the evolution of plants and their use to man. Call 9–GARDEN for general information.

Brooklyn offers the **Brooklyn Botanic Garden,** 50 acres directly behind the Brooklyn Museum. Its unique features include two Japanese Gardens, one of which replicates the 15th-century Ryoanji (Buddhist) Temple in Kyoto; the Fragrance Garden for the Blind; and the Shakespeare Garden, filled with various plants and flowers mentioned in the Bard's works. Especially beautiful is the early-May cherry blossom time. Recently opened: a dazzling new Conservatory. Open daily, the hours vary with the seasons. Phone 718–622–4433 for exact days and times.

ZOOS. The **Bronx Zoo,** Fordham Rd. and Southern Blvd., Bronx (367–1010), is one of the largest zoos in the world. Over 3,600 animals roam in their natural habitats whenever possible in this recently modernized facility; the Bengali Express monorail, Skyfari cable car, and the Safari Train make getting around its 265 acres quick, easy, and fun. Open 10 A.M.–4:30 P.M.; 4 P.M. Nov.–Jan. Admission to the Bronx Zoo is free Tues., Wed., and Thurs. Parking is $3; admission is $1.75 for adults, 75 cents for children. Some of the rides may require an extra $1 fee; adults will pay an additional $1, kids 75 cents to see the new children's zoo opposite the elephant house.

The **New York Aquarium,** Surf Ave. and West 8th St., Coney Island in Brooklyn (718–262–FISH), is filled with mammals, fish, and birds from the world's water environments. Hours are 10 A.M.–4:45 P.M. weekdays (5:45 P.M. weekends and holidays between Memorial Day and Labor Day). General admission is $3.75 for adults, $1.50 for children; senior citizens are admitted free after 2 P.M. Mon.–Fri.

PARTICIPANT SPORTS. New York isn't precisely a sporting paradise, but visitors and residents alike do find a large variety of methods for exercising in the sun and fresh air. **Jogging** and **bicycling** are the two most popular activities, practiced most often in Central Park, the huge patch of green between 59th and 110th St., Fifth Ave. and Central Park West, which contains over 6 miles of roadway plus a mile and a half running track around the Reservoir near 90th St. On weekends and from 10 A.M.–3 P.M. in the summer, the roads are closed to all motor traffic, freeing the pavement for individual exercise enthusiasts or entrants in one of the many running races sponsored by the New York Road Runners Club (860–4455) or cycling competitions.

Bridle paths ribbon Central Park. Claremont Stable, 175 West 89th St. (724–5100), will rent you the horses, but you must call to reserve your animal. Or you can take to the water in a rowboat on Central Park Lake, just north of 72nd St. Boats (and meals) are available from the Loeb Boathouse (288–7281 or 517–CAFE) for a $5 per hour fee. Most rentals will require a deposit.

In winter **ice skaters** flock to the 122 × 59 foot rink in Rockefeller Center (49th and 50th Sts. between Fifth and Sixth Aves.), as well as the Loula E. Lasker Memorial Rink (Central Park North and Lenox Ave.) and the city's newest facility, Rivergate (34th St. and First Ave.). Wollman Rink in Central Park recently reopened after a multimillion-dollar renovation; call 517–4800 for information.

SPECTATOR SPORTS. Major league **baseball,** Apr.–Oct., features the *Yankees* and the *Mets.* Each team schedules about 80 home dates, of which more than half are night games. The Mets' ballpark is Shea Stadium in Flushing, Queens (718–507–8499) while the Yankees play at their famous stadium in the Bronx (293–6000). New York's two National **Football** League teams, the *Jets* and the *Giants,* now call the Meadowlands Sports Complex in East Rutherford, NJ, their home. For ticket and game information call Giants Stadium, 201–935–8222 (Giants) or 212–421–6600 (Jets). The Meadowlands are also the base from which **basketball**'s *New Jersey Nets* (201–935–8888) and **hockey**'s *New Jersey Devils* (201–935–6050) operate. The *New York Islanders'* home ice is at Nassau Coliseum in Hempstead, Long Island (516–587–9222).

To see the *Knicks* play **basketball** or the *Rangers* compete in the National **Hockey** League, you'll have to become familiar with Madison Square Garden, above Penn Station at 32nd St. and Seventh Ave. (212–563–8300). **Tennis** events, like the Nabisco Masters and Virginia Slims tournaments, also take place here, as do some championship **boxing** matches and prestigious **track and field** competitions like the Millrose Games.

The *U.S. Open Tennis Championships* are played in late Aug. at the USTA National Tennis Center in Flushing Meadows, Queens (718–592–8000), while top **golf** pros vie at the annual *Westchester Classic,* held each June at the Westchester Country Club in Rye, NY (914–967–6000).

The final leg of horse racing's "Triple Crown," the *Belmont Stakes,* takes place at Belmont Park in Elmont, Long Island, each summer. The New York Racing Association (718–641–4700) provides post times for Belmont and the area's other thoroughbred track, Aqueduct Racetrack in Ozone Park, Queens. Harness racing is held at Yonkers in Westchester County (914–968–4200); and the Meadowlands Sports Complex (201–935–8500).

BEACHES. Coney Island, 3½ mi. of Brooklyn facing the Atlantic Ocean, is probably more famous these days for its hot dogs and the nearby Astroland Amusement Park than as a desirable place to swim and sun. Still, upwards of a million and a half people spread blankets on its shores on a bright summer day. **Jones Beach** is infinitely more pleasant. Just beyond the city limits on Long Island, it is more parklike than Coney Island and usually clean, despite the millions who bathe and swim in its waters from June to Sept.

Named for the turn of the century photographer and philanthropist, **Jacob Riis Park** in Queens is rated one of the cleanest of the city's beaches. Within the park's borders are an 18-hole, pitch-and-putt golf course, numerous playgrounds for children, free tennis, shuffleboard, handball, and squash courts, as well as grassy, shaded picnic areas.

HISTORIC SITES AND HOUSES. The following is a very selected list of some of New York's sites and buildings of historic, cultural, or architectural interest, arranged by neighborhood, starting all the way downtown with the Statue of Liberty and the financial district.

Lower Manhattan. This area encompasses the earliest settlements of the city and includes roughly everything south of Canal St. The section is, however, much larger than ever before. Many of the newer skyscrapers crowding the neighborhood sit on landfill, accounting for the current placement of, say, Water St., which is quite inland. Across the East River lies the borough of Brooklyn, connected to Manhattan by the Brooklyn, Manhattan, and Williamsburg Bridges.

The southern tip of Manhattan is known as the financial district because it houses the American Stock Exchange and the New York Stock Exchange as well as numerous trading, insurance, and banking firms. Few of these companies are actually located on Wall Street, which is in fact only a few narrow blocks along which once ran the northernmost wall of the city. This part of Manhattan is also the center of much of the city's official business, including City Hall and the courts.

Fraunces Tavern. 54 Pearl St. (212–269–0144). The restaurant where George Washington bade farewell to his troops before retiring as general. The current building is a rough estimate of the original. Interesting for its upstairs museum.

New York Stock Exchange. 20 Broad St. (212–623–5167). Look down as hundreds of brokers bandy shouts and papers and run around at incredible speed. The third-floor gallery is open during trading hours, 9:20 A.M.–4 P.M. Free. (A tip: Go early because the NYSE is *very* popular these days.)

South Street Seaport. Fulton St. The newly renovated seaport area centers on the three-story Fulton Market Building, which is replete with restaurants (sit-down and fast food), take-out shops, and food boutiques, and Pier Pavilion on Pier 17. Walking around the seaport is a treat in itself, but visitors wanting a sense of the area's history should also stop by the Visitors Center, 207 Water St. (212–SEA–PORT); and the historic ships docked in the harbor at Pier 16.

Statue of Liberty. This gift from the French marked its hundredth anniversary in New York Harbor in 1986. Catch the ferry in Battery Park at the booth in Castle Clinton. Admission to the statue is free. Round-trip charges, with stops made at both the statue and Ellis Island, are: adults, $6, ages 3–17, $3; under 3, free.

Trinity Church. Broadway and Wall Sts. (212–602–0800). The Gothic Revival structure, designed by Richard Upjohn, that currently occupies the site is the third Trinity Church. The small cemetery is the final resting place of Alexander Hamilton and Robert Fulton.

World Trade Center. Cortlandt and Church Sts. Best known for its gigantic twin towers, the complex in fact consists of seven buildings. The 107th floor of Building 2 is an enclosed observation deck (212–466–7397) with the highest such vantage point in the world, though the building is second to Chicago's Sears Roebuck Tower in height. Adults, $3.50; children, $1.75.

Little Italy and Chinatown. These areas border each other and play host to two of the city's major ethnic groups. Little Italy is quieter, and more Chinese signs appear every day. Chinatown is always streaming with people and features touches such as pagodalike phone booths. The major attraction of each is its food, but beware: Dessert in Little Italy can easily cost more than dinner in Chinatown.

SoHo. Roughly, the blocks between Canal and Houston Sts. (hence, SoHo, or *So*uth of *Ho*uston; but pronounced So Ho). A once-bleak neighborhood of warehouses, it has become the premier center for new art and to some extent high (avant garde) fashion. The marvelous cast-iron structures are of great historical significance, and the area has been designated a landmark district. West Broadway and the side streets (especially Prince and Spring) are better suited for walking and browsing, with lots of galleries and shops ready for the viewing. Sunday is an especially popular day for shopping (although a number of galleries are closed).

Greenwich Village. Whatever preconceived notions you have of the Village, as it is familiarly known, you will find verification in your travels. Two of the city's bigger universities are here: New York University and Cooper Union, in the East Village. The Village is constantly subdividing. The East Village is a mecca for punk-rock clubs and boutiques; it's easternmost part (called "alphabet city," because of Avenues A, B, C, and D) is the city's *newest* art spot. The West Village is much more placid and is where the *old* Bohemians congregated. This neighborhood is highlighted by twisting, tree-lined streets with 19th-century brownstones. Literary giants such as Edgar Allan Poe, Eugene O'Neill, Edna St. Vincent Millay, James Baldwin, Willa Cather, and Mark Twain have all made the West Village their home.

The twain meet, so to speak, at **Washington Square Park,** whose arch marks the beginning of Fifth Ave., Manhattan's dividing line between east and west. The park has been used as a burial place for plague victims and for unfortunates who were forced to pay a visit to the gallows. The Greek Revival row houses that stand guard over the park's north side are landmarks. There is more literary history here, with the former dwellings of Edith Wharton, Henry James, William Dean Howells, and John Dos Passos all a part of the "row."

On the Avenue of the Americas, one of the area's main thoroughfares, is the former **Jefferson Market Courthouse,** 475 Ave. of Americas. Built in 1877 and designed in part by Calvert Vaux, the coarchitect of Central Park, the building is an odd assemblage of architectural styles, with the result being a mock-castle. Now used as one of the Village branches of the New York Public Library.

Midtown. Midtown is the city's other major heart of business, with publishing, advertising, and multinational corporations based here. The area is designated as 14th to 59th Sts., with most interests centered between Second and Eighth Aves. Within those boundaries rest many pockets and neighborhoods: the Flatiron district, centered on the landmark triangular 1902 building of the same name on the corner of Broadway and 23 St.; the flower district, Ave. of the Americas from 22d to 27th streets; the fur and garment districts, in the West 20s and 30s; the warehouse-art district, Chelsea, in the West 20s; Gramercy Park, one of the city's most untouched areas, in the East 20s; the Kips Bay and Murray Hill residential neighborhoods in the East 30s; Hell's Kitchen (now called Clinton) and Herald Square in the West 30s and 40s; the Grand Central area in the East 40s, featuring the stately Grand Central Terminal and the always lovely Chrysler Building; Rockefeller Center in the West 50s; and the Tudor City-Turtle Bay area in the East 40s.

Some of these are more interesting than others, and you'll probably want to breeze through those areas replete with the spoils of industry, whether they be the crowds of suited folks milling around Grand Central or the legions of blue-collar workers pulling dress racks down Seventh Ave. in the 30s. Other areas, such as Gramercy Park, Tudor City, and some of the "parks" shoehorned between office buildings, can give the welcome gifts of quiet and breathing room. Among the specifics worth visiting:

Empire State Building. 350 Fifth Ave. (212–736–3100). This 1931 art deco skyscraper was once the tallest building in the world and a self-proclaimed Eighth Wonder of the World (its onetime visitor King Kong notwithstanding). The lobby is just as beautiful as the celebrated view from the 86th and 102nd floors. The observation deck is open 9:30 A.M. to midnight. Adults, $3.50; children, $1.75. The crystal-clear wintertime views can be breathtaking.

Grand Central Terminal. 42d St. and Park Ave. Now being restored in honor of its 75th anniversary, Grand Central is one of the city's great public spaces. Free tours meet in the main waiting room on Wed. at 12:30 P.M. The Oyster Bar—a vast restaurant on the lower level, with both counters and table service—is also a major attraction.

Madison Square Garden. 33rd St. and Seventh Ave. (212–563–8300). Third location for this complex; now used for sports and rock concerts. Connects to Penn Station.

New York Public Library. 42d St. and Fifth Ave. (212–221–7676). Gorgeous Beaux Arts structure, now the central research library, on the site of a former city reservoir. The library is noted for free exhibitions. Free tours meet Mon.–Sat. at 11 A.M. and 2 P.M. in the main lobby.

United Nations. First Ave. and 45th St. (212–963–7713). The world's diplomatic focal point; consists of the skyscraper Secretariat Building and the low-domed General Assembly. The outside gardens are graciously inviting, and inside the Assembly building works of art from all nations are displayed. Guided tours: adults, $5.50; children, $3.50. Free tickets to sessions are distributed for those who choose to go it alone.

Fifth Avenue. The 10 or so blocks of Fifth Ave. leading up to Central Park are home to some of the world's most exclusive shops. Inside the Trump Tower on 56th St. you'll find dozens of deluxe palaces where only the richest dare do more than window shop. On Fifth itself lie Saks, Gucci, Tiffany's, Mark Cross, F.A.O. Schwarz, and Cartier. None are generally for the budget-minded, though there are occasional sales.

Fifth Ave. also plays host to two of New York's greatest sights, Saint Patrick's Cathedral and Rockefeller Center. Even on Fifth Ave., separate districts are delineated, mainly in the one-block cross streets of 47th St. (diamond retailers) and 57th St. (art galleries).

AT&T and IBM Buildings. Two of the area's newest (and most striking) skyscrapers are located across from each other on Madison Ave. at 55th and 56th Sts. IBM has a marvelous art gallery in its lower level, and AT&T has the fascinating AT&T Infoquest Center of Science and Technology. Both facilities are free.

Rockefeller Center. Fifth Ave. at 48th St. The center links 47th through 50th Sts. and Fifth and Sixth Aves. through underground passages. The Art Deco GE Building, enhanced at night by floodlighting, is topped by the restored Rainbow Room restaurant and nightclub. An hour-long Radio City tour (no reservations necessary) is another option at $6. TV fans might be interested in a tour of NBC studios (212–664–7174) at $7.25.

Saint Patrick's Cathedral. Fifth Ave. and 50th St. This is a soaring French Gothic structure designed by James Renwick, who is also responsible for Grace Church in Greenwich Village. Church fanciers should also pay a visit to the more austere but in many ways lovelier Saint Thomas Church down the avenue at 53rd St.

Times Square. The theatrical and film center of the city, Times Square is literally the patch of ground at 42nd St. and Seventh Ave. where Broadway crosses. But New Yorkers generally mean the streets between 42nd and 49th from Broadway to Eighth Ave. It is within these blocks that most "Broadway" theaters are located, as well as numerous movie houses (some of them X-rated). Be sure to get a nighttime view with all the lights aglow.

Uptown. Away from the noise and confusion of midtown, both the Upper East Side and the Upper West Side, divided by Central Park, are fine places for strolling. Each side retains distinctive characteristics, and those who can afford to live on either end choose to do so for their opposing personalities. The stereotype has it that East Siders are traditional and old rich. That is borne out by the profusion of fashion showrooms, antique stores, and art galleries lining Madison Ave. Westsiders are supposed to be funky but chic, riche but nouveau. The proof is in the boutiques, novelty stores, and nouvelle-cuisine restaurants on Columbus Ave. Museum lovers should be on both ends of the park: The American Museum of Natural History straddles the West Side; the East Side is famous for its Museum Mile, including the Metropolitan Museum of Art, the Guggenheim, and eight others.

The Abigail Adams Smith Museum. 421 East 61st St. (212–838–6878). One of Manhattan's last 18th-century buildings. Originally the carriage house for the home the then Vice-President John Adams had built for his daughter Abigail. A gem kept in perfect condition by the Colonial Dames of America. Guide on duty. Mon.–Fri., 10 A.M.–4 P.M.; Sun., 1–5 P.M. Adults, $2; senior citizens, $1.

The Dyckman House. 204th St. and Broadway (212–304–9422). Built in 1783, this was the farm residence of the wealthy Dyckman family, which once owned most of northern Manhattan. The only remaining Dutch farmhouse in New York City. *To get there:* IND (Eighth Ave.) subway (A) to 207th St. Tues.–Sun., 11 A.M.–4 P.M. $1.

General Grant National Memorial. Riverside Dr. and 122nd St. (212–666–1640). The Civil War general and two-term president is buried in the crypt with his wife Julia. Photo and other exhibits also housed in the tomb. Open daily, 9 A.M.–4:30 P.M.; closed Mon.–Tues., Oct.–May.

Morris-Jumel Mansion. West 161st St. and Edgecombe Ave. (212–923–8008). This Georgian colonial hilltop house was built in 1765. A year later, George Washington slept here for a night; his camp bed may still be seen. Here too Aaron Burr married the wealthy Mme. Jumel, then in her sixties, and soon divorced her. *To get there:* Fifth Ave. bus 2 or 3 to 162nd St.; or IND (Eighth Ave.) subway to 163rd St. (AA local). Tues.–Sun., 10 A.M.–4 P.M. Adults, $2; students and senior citizens, $1.

MUSEUMS AND GALLERIES. New York has perhaps the largest concentration of museums anywhere in the world. Although most are art museums, others specialize in fashion, children, performing arts, dolls, fire engines, coins, architecture, and ethnic cultures. Two of the city's newest museums, both opened in 1989, are the *Museum of American Folk Art* opposite Lincoln Center (212–977–7298) and the *Children's Museum of Manhattan,* 212 West 83rd St. (212–721–1223). What follows is more than a dozen of the most popular museums. Make particular note of those offering free or pay-as-you-wish evening admissions (usually on Tues. evening). Also, most make available substantially discounted student rates; inquire before paying.

American Craft Museum. 40 West 53rd St. (212–956–3535). Changing exhibitions center on contemporary works of glass, tapestry, metal, and others. Wed.–Sun., 10 A.M.–5 P.M.; Tues., 10 A.M.–8 P.M. Adults, $3.50; children, $1.50.

American Museum of Natural History. Central Park West at 79th St. (212–769–5100). The granddaddy of New York museums, the one every school kid loves to visit. As its name implies, the museum is filled with artifacts of the earth's past and present. You'll find representations of every animal species, culture, and life form here. Naturemax Theater shows spectacular films on a giant screen. Open daily 10 A.M.–5:45 P.M.; to 9 P.M. on Wed., Fri., and Sat. Suggested contribution: adults, $4; children, $2. Free Fri. and Sat. evenings. An accompanying attraction is the Hayden Planetarium (212–769–5920), which extends the study to the skies. Separate admission is $4 for adults, $2 for children. Fri. and Sat. evenings feature the spectacular rock music-based Laser Concert (212–769–5921) at $6.

Brooklyn Museum. Eastern Parkway and Washington Ave., Brooklyn (718–638–5000). Some of the city's most exciting special and permanent exhibits can be seen at this massive museum, one of the nation's largest. The Egyptian, primitive art, and American painting collections are world-renowned, and the new Rodin Wing is a must. The sculpture garden of New York City building ornaments is charming. Daily 10 A.M.–5 P.M.; Sat. 11 A.M.–6 P.M.; Sun. 1 P.M.–6 P.M.; closed Tues. Adults, $3; students, $1.50; children under 12, free with adult.

The Cloisters. Fort Tryon Park (212–923–3700). A branch of the Metropolitan Museum of Art, this medieval art complex is perched on a hill overlooking the George Washington Bridge and the Hudson River. Constructed from the ruins of five French cloisters, some of the highlights include: 12th- and 13th-century Spanish frescoes; the extraordinary Unicorn tapestries; a complete 12th-century architectural ensemble from a ruined abbey of Gascony; the Bury Saint Edmunds Cross; stained-glass lancets from the Carmelite Church of Boppardam-Rhein; and an arcade from a Benedictine prior of Froville in eastern France. It's well worth the trip uptown to this very peaceful retreat. Can be reached on the M4 bus, which goes up Madison Ave. in midtown. Open Tues.–Sun., 9:30 A.M.–4:45 P.M. Suggested contribution: adults, $5; senior citizens and students, $2.50; children under 12, free.

Cooper-Hewitt Museum. 2 East 91st St. (212–860–6868). Again, the setting is almost as important as the work. The building is the former mansion of millionaire Andrew Carnegie, and both its small rooms and its landscaped garden are lovely. The museum houses the decorative arts collection of the Smithsonian Institution. Tues., 10 A.M.–9 P.M.; Wed.–Sat., 10 A.M.–5 P.M.; Sun. noon–5 P.M. Closed Mon. and holidays. Admission, $3. Free Tues. evenings.

Solomon R. Guggenheim Museum. 1071 Fifth Ave. at 88th St. (212–360–3500). The spiraling architecture of Frank Lloyd Wright's handiwork raised eyebrows in 1959 and still does today. Emphasis on 20th-century art, including Kandinsky, Ernst, and de Kooning. Tues., 11 A.M.–8 P.M.; Wed.–Sun. to 5 P.M. Closed Mon. Adults, $4.50; children under 7, free. Free Tues. evening.

International Center for Photography. 1130 Fifth Ave. at 94th St. (212–860–1777). Changing exhibits geared exclusively to the big-time best (Cartier-Bresson, et al.). Tues., noon–8 P.M.; Wed.–Fri. to 5 P.M.; Sat.–Sun., 11 A.M.–6 P.M. Admission, $3; students and seniors, $1; free Tues. evening.

Intrepid Sea-Air-Space Museum. Pier 86, Hudson River at 46th St. (212–245–0072). A U.S. Naval aircraft carrier transformed into a museum detailing U.S. military history and technology. Wed.–Sun., 10 A.M.–5 P.M. Adults, $6; seniors, $5; children, $3.25.

Lower East Side Tenement Museum. 97 Orchard St. (212–431–0233). An only-in-New York experience, this unique museum is dedicated to the millions of immigrants who gave New York its strength and vitality. Call for details of special exhibits and tours of the area. Tues.–Fri., 11 A.M.–4 P.M. Donations accepted.

Metropolitan Museum of Art. Fifth Ave. at 82nd St. (212–535–7710). The emphasis is on pre-20th-century painting, though a considerable cache of modern fare is also to be found. The recently added American Wing features an intact reconstruction of the living room from Frank Lloyd Wright's "Little House." Other highlights throughout the museum include the fabulous collection of antique musical instruments, the ever-changing costume gallery downstairs, and the assemblage of Tiffany and other glassworks behind the Egyptian Galleries. Tues., Wed., Thurs., Sun., 9:30 A.M.–5:15 P.M.; Fri. and Sat. till 8:45 P.M.; closed Mon. Suggested contribution, $5; children, $2.50.

Museum of Broadcasting. 1 East 53 St. (212–752–7684). More like a library than anything else. Features an enormous collection of tapes and videos covering the history of radio and television. Be forewarned that what you're most interested in is often the same thing everybody else wants to see (for example, a bored staffer will tell you the exact position of the Beatles performances on an old Ed Sullivan tape), so you may have a long wait ahead of you. Tues., noon–8 P.M.; Wed.–Sat. to 5 P.M. Adults, $4; students, $3; children and seniors, $2.

Museum of Modern Art. 11 West 53d St. (212–708–9480). Recently expanded, the museum now includes new architecture and photography galleries. MOMA's strength still lies in its collection of modern art, stemming from a few representations of late Impressionist works (particularly the huge panels of Monet's *Water Lilies*) to the present. Open daily 11 A.M.–6 P.M., to 9 P.M. on Thurs. Closed Wed. Adults, $7; students and seniors, $4; under 16, with adult, free. Pay what you wish Thurs. evening.

Museum of the City of New York. Fifth Ave. at 103rd St. (212–534–1034). Everything you always wanted to know about the city. Highlights include dioramas depicting historical scenes, a trolley car, and furnished rooms. Tues.–Sat., 10 A.M.–5 P.M.; Sun. and holidays opens at 1 P.M. Suggested contribution $3.

Whitney Museum of American Art. 945 Madison Ave. at 75th St. (212–570–3676). One of the best places for seeing the newest alternative art forms around. It was here that Nam Jun Paik foresaw the current video "revolution" with his (literally) video-as-art displays. Tues., 1 P.M.–8 P.M.; Wed.–Sat., 11 A.M.–5 P.M.; Sun., noon to 5 P.M. Closed Mon. Adults, $4.50; seniors, $2.50. Free Tues. evening.

FILM. Hundreds of movie houses can be found in Manhattan, but generally speaking, most are congregated around three areas: Times Square, the East 50s and 60s, and Greenwich Village. Movie tickets are higher in Manhattan than in other areas of the country, with prices for first-runs ranging between $7 and $7.50. Reservations are generally not taken, and you should get to the movie house *at least* half an hour early, more if the film is a major hit. You'll be expected to wait on a line to purchase tickets and then to get on a "ticket holders" line. You can avoid all of this by going in the afternoon, when prices are often cheaper as well.

The Upper East Side is especially known for movies that have not opened widely and foreign movies. You'll also find foreign films at the Lincoln Plaza Cinemas (Broadway and 63rd St., 757–2280). The Times Square movies are more populist and populated. The Village sports houses for about a dozen first-runs as well as several "revival houses," such as the Film Forum 1 & 2 (209 West Houston St.; 212–727–8110), Theatre 80 St. Marks (80 St. Marks Place; 212–254–7400), and the Cinema Village (Third Ave. at 12th St.; 212–505–7320). Other theaters devoted to old and cult films include the Biograph (the former New Carnegie on 57th St. near Broadway; 582–4582), the Anthology Film Archives (32–34 Second Ave. at 2nd St.; 212–477–2714), the American Museum of the Moving Image in Queens (35th Ave. at 36th St., Astoria; 718–784–0077), and the Museum of Modern Art (212–708–9490).

MUSIC. Called "Music Capital of the World" by *The New York Times,* New York boasts the largest population of professional musicians.

Lincoln Center, Broadway and 64th St., is the heart of this musical town. Located within the complex are *Avery Fisher Hall,* home of the New York Philharmonic, American Philharmonic, the Mostly Mozart Festival, and many other orchestral performances (874–2424); the *New York State Theater,* which houses the New York City Opera and the New York City Ballet (870–5570); *Alice Tully Hall,* renowned for its near perfect acoustics which makes it a proper site for numerous chamber music recitals (362–1911); the prestigious *Juilliard School of Music* (874–7515); and the *Guggenheim Bandshell* (877–1800) outdoors in Damrosch Park. The most beautiful building of the complex is the *Metropolitan Opera House* (362–6000) where that august company makes its home base. Dozens of free concerts are held outside in the plaza at Lincoln Center during the summer months. Outstanding young concert artists sometimes perform in the *Library and Museum of the Performing Arts* at Lincoln Center (870–1630).

Within *Carnegie Hall,* 57th St. and Seventh Ave. (247–7800), New Yorkers find their musical soul. Pop appearances by musicians from Frank Sinatra to Pia Zadora, orchestral performances by Solti's Chicago and Ozawa's Boston, individual recitals by Rudolf Serkin and Andre Watts have taken place under this roof since Tchaikovsky conducted its first concert in 1891.

Paying full price for events at either music mecca can be quite extravagant, but cheaper seats go for as little as $6. Standing room tickets are distributed just before performances at substantial discounts. In Bryant Park, 42nd St. between Fifth and Sixth Aves., the *TKTS* booth sells half-price, day-of-performance admissions to music and dance events. Also of interest is the *92nd St. Y,* 1395 Lexington Ave. (996–1100), which offers major chamber music and orchestral series as well as performances by artists of international stature. The *Brooklyn Academy of Music* (colloquially referred to as BAM), 30 Lafayette St., Brooklyn (718–636–4100) is the nation's oldest performing arts center and features a very popular avant-garde festival each winter.

Rock and pop's main venues are, in descending order of size: Madison Square Garden, 32nd St. and Seventh Ave. (563–8300); Radio City Music Hall, 1250 Sixth Ave. at 50th St. (757–3100); the Ritz, 254 West 54th St. (541–8900); and the Bottom Line, 15 West 4th St. (228–7880). In summertime, the South Street Seaport's Pier 16 and the Miller Time Pier 84 (43rd St. on the Hudson River) offer ongoing series.

Let us not forget that the biggest non-classical event in the city is George Wein's Jazz Festival, where jazz musicians jam all over town for ten days in June and July.

STAGE. Almost 10 million people will attend Broadway shows at legitimate theaters in New York this year. That doesn't even count tickets sold at some 20 Off-Broadway houses uptown and down or the more than 250 Off-Off-Broadway showcases strewn all over town, from SoHo to the Upper West Side, from Chelsea to the Bowery.

An orchestra seat to a Broadway musical runs in the vicinity of $60 these days, dramas slightly less. Seeing an Off-Broadway show costs around $30, a bargain considering these are the works that often move onto the "Great White Way." If this is still out of pocketbook range, try the *TKTS* booth in Times Square or the World Trade Center for half-price, day-of-performance tickets. (TKTS in Bryant Park is solely for music and dance events.) The lines tend to be long, so arrive early. The Times Square TKTS booth opens at 10 A.M. for matinee tickets (performances on Wed. and Sat. at 2 P.M., Sun. at 3 P.M.) and at 3 P.M. for evening tickets (generally performances at 8 P.M.). Many Broadway houses—but not all—are dark Mondays. The downtown World Trade Center TKTS booth opens at 11 A.M. for evening tickets, and some next-day matinee tickets are available. Look also for "twofers" (at hotels, restaurants, and the Visitors Bureau offices at 2 Columbus Circle); these, when presented at box offices, offer discounts on specific performances both current or advance.

Outstanding theater companies in residence are *Joseph Papp's Public Theater,* 425 Lafayette St. (598–7150) and *Circle Repertory Theater,* 99 Seventh Ave. S., at Sheridan Sq. (924–7100). At these small, yet prestigious theaters, playwrights like Sam Shepard and Lanford Wilson shape new works. Also worth attention are some of the newer theaters offering non-commercial alternatives on "Theater Row," West 42nd St. between Ninth and Tenth Aves. where such companies as the Intar and Playwrights Horizons mount their plays.

DANCE. New York is now the world's international dance capital, and Lincoln Center perhaps the largest and most important impresario of ballet. The late George Balanchine built the *New York City Ballet* into one of the world's great ballet companies, and his dancers whirl through abstract geometrical patterns at the New York State Theater. Across the plaza at the Metropolitan Opera House is the *American Ballet Theater.*

Beyond the classical greats, *Alvin Ailey, Martha Graham,* the *Paul Taylor* company, the *Harlem Dance Theater,* and the *Joffrey Ballet* (partially based in Los Angeles) dance to a spectrum of beats in the renovated Moorish-style City Center Theater, 131 West 55th St. (581–7907), as well as at several Broadway theaters. Rather new is the *Joyce Theater,* 175 Eighth Ave. at 19th St. (242–0800), where the *Eliot Feld* company and other small companies dance.

SHOPPING. New Yorkers love to boast that you can get anything here, and it's true, provided you know where to look. Good places to start searching for everything from a mahogany bedroom set to far-out make-up are the two major department stores—**Macy's** (which takes up the entire block between 34th and 35th Sts. and Sixth and Seventh Aves.) and **Bloomingdale's** (59th and 60th Sts. between Lexington and Third Aves.). Should your shopping time be limited, consolidate your browsing in the Macy's area. Great buys in women's wear are found at **National Ladies Specialty Corp.** (second floor, 470 Seventh Ave.) and **S&W Ladies Wear** (Seventh Ave. at 26th St.). **A&S Plaza Manhattan** is at Herald Square, or stroll up Fifth Ave. to **Lord and Taylor** at 39th St. In between, you'll encounter numerous specialty stores for sporting gear and men's and women's wear, among other treasures.

Surely not to be missed is the "Golden Mile" of **Fifth Avenue,** from 39th to 59th St., where some of the world's best known shops make their homes.

Those on a more leisurely schedule will enjoy poking into the fancy boutiques on the Upper West Side (concentrate on **Amsterdam** and **Columbus** Aves. between 72nd and 86th Sts.) or the Upper East Side. **Madison Avenue,** from 60th St. to the upper 80s, houses designer clothing for men, women, and children, gourmet shops, art galleries, and several pivotal antique houses. Bargains you'll find on the **Lower East Side.** Begin at the corner of Delancey and Houston Sts., wander south and east until the storefronts cease, but don't go on a Sat., as most of the shopkeepers are observing their sabbath. **SoHo** (south of Houston St., centering around West Broadway) is chock full of trendy (read "expensive") boutiques and the clothes, particularly, tend towards the outrageous.

ACCOMMODATIONS. Not only is the range of accommodations in Manhattan staggering, but the nearly 70,000 hotel rooms in more than 100 hotels offer prices to fit any budget. But you must plan carefully to catch the bargains. Obtain the free copies of the New York Convention and Visitors Bureau's Hotel Guide and Tour Package Directory; the first lists daily prices and the second gives "package plans" at reduced rates because they are built around weekends and other "soft" periods. Packages also throw in a host of extras, from museum and sightseeing tours to Broadway tickets and champagne brunches. Travel agents and the ads listed in such outlets as the travel section of the Sunday *New York Times* are also excellent ways to find special rates.

Although New York hotels are seldom totally booked, it is *not recommended* that you arrive without reservations. But if you do, immediately seek help at the Visitors Bureau Information Center, 2 Columbus Circle, New York, NY 10019; open Mon.–Fri., 9 A.M.–6 P.M.; weekends and holidays, 10–6.

We've categorized accommodations according to the cost of a double room (not including tax): *Super Deluxe,* $250 and up; *Deluxe,* $200–$250; *Expensive,* $150–$200; *Moderate,* $100–$150; *Inexpensive,* under $100. It may be that not every room in a hotel falls within the category we've put it in.

Super Deluxe

Berkshire Place. 21 East 52nd St., New York, NY 10019 (753–5800). Refurnished in 1979, the rooms are comfortable and the midtown location is prime for business appointments or Fifth Ave. browsing. 415 rooms and suites.

Carlyle. 35 East 76th St., New York, NY 10021 (744–1600). Posh, air-conditioned rooms and suites with private terraces and/or wood burning fireplaces. Elegant dining in the Cafe Carlyle, accompanied by singer/pianist Bobby Short. 175 rooms, many occupied by permanent residents.

Drake Swissotel. 440 Park Ave. at 56th St., New York, NY 10022 (421–0900). This beautifully renovated hotel is in the heart of the smart East Side. Four-star Lafayette restaurant; complimentary limo to Wall St. in the morning. 640 rooms.

Essex House. 160 Central Park South, New York, NY 10019 (247–0300). Like most of the establishments along "hotel row," the Essex has an incredible view of Central Park. Currently being renovated. 700 rooms.

Helmsley Palace. 455 Madison Ave., New York, NY 10022 (888–7000). Extravagantly rich-looking, central to most everything. 1050 rooms and suites.

Mayfair Regent. 610 Park Ave. at 65th St., New York, NY 10021 (288–0800). This elegant, European-style hotel features concierge, multilingual staff, and 24-hour room service. Le Cirque restaurant is one of the city's finest; it's packed with celebrities and power brokers every day. 119 suites; 80 rooms.

Park 51. 152 West 51st St., New York, NY 10019 (765–1900). This plush new beauty is convenient to Broadway theaters, the finest restaurants and midtown shopping. 178 rooms, including 52 elegant suites. Bellini by Cipriani restaurant.

Park Lane. 36 Central Park South, New York, NY 10019 (371–4000). Although one of the newer hotels here, the Park Lane ranks high in dignity and service. Staff is conversant in several languages and there is a park-view dining room. 640 rooms.

Parker Meridien. 118 West 57th St., New York, NY 10019 (245–5000). Owned by the Paris-based Meridien chain, this luxurious, 42-story building not only offers fine nouvelle cuisine in the Maurice dining room but has an indoor pool and well-equipped health club to boot. 700 rooms.

Peninsula New York. 700 Fifth Ave. at 55th St., New York, NY 10022 (247–2200). Formerly the Gotham, then Maxim's de Paris; now the new Hong Kong owners have moved in, and it's more lavish and posh than ever. 250 rooms and suites. Top-rated Adrienne restaurant and bistro.

Pierre. 2 East 61st St., New York, NY 10021 (838–8000). Open since 1930, more than half of this residential institution's fine rooms are permanently occupied, leaving just 196 available for visitors. European ambience, a multilingual staff, and 24-hour room service.

Plaza. 768 Fifth Ave., New York, NY 10019 (759–3000). New York's enclave of tradition and elegance in the European manner overlooks Central Park on one side and the graceful fountain in front of its entrance on another. Rooms are decorated in French Provincial style, restaurants like the Oak Room, Oyster Bar, and Edwardian Room have created traditions on their own. Now owned by Donald Trump, who has polished this gem top to bottom. 800 rooms.

Regency. 540 Park Ave., New York, NY 10021 (759–4100). Louis XVI decor, French tapestries, and Italian marble floors raise the level of elegance here to new heights. Kitchenettes are in many of the suites and, if you've brought your Rolls along, the garage has space for 140. 395 rooms and suites.

Ritz Carlton. 112 Central Park South, New York, NY 10019 (757–1900). Understated opulence and an emphasis on service took over when this chain transformed the Navarro in 1982. A night butler, as well as 24-hour room service, and a view of the Park, naturally. Superb Jockey Club restaurant. 235 rooms and suites.

Stanhope. 995 Fifth Ave., New York, NY 10028 (288–5800). Particularly gracious atmosphere and classic services. Antique furniture and paintings from the American Empire period. 275 rooms. Across from Metropolitan Museum of Art.

Waldorf-Astoria and Waldorf Towers. 301 Park Ave., New York, NY 10022 (355–3000). Another name that's synonymous with grandeur and elegance. Through the imposing art deco entrance on Park Ave. pass countless distinguished guests. Staff speaks Spanish, Japanese, French, and German. 1,753 rooms.

Westbury. 15 East 69th St., New York, NY 10023 (535–2000). In many ways, one of the city's better hotels. Dignified, European tone, furnishings in a grand, tasteful style. 24-hour room service, too. 240 rooms and suites.

Deluxe

Doral Park Avenue. 70 Park Ave., New York, NY 10016 (687–7050). Plush, luxurious interiors in this combination hotel renovation and new building. 203 rooms.

Doral Tuscany. 120 East 39th St., New York, NY 10016 (686–1600). All the rooms have pantries in this small luxury hotel. 136 rooms and suites.

Dorset. 30 West 54th St., New York, NY 10019 (247–7300). One of New York's top stop-overs, though not well known. Quiet, traditional, and located close to the Museum of Modern Art. 210 rooms.

Grand Hyatt of New York. 42nd St. between Lexington and Park Aves., New York, NY 10017 (883–1234). Glittery and lavish, this newly renovated chrome and brass tower is right next to Grand Central Terminal. 2 restaurants, several cocktail lounges, and 1,407 rooms.

Marriott Marquis. 1535 Broadway, New York, NY 10036 (398–1900 or 800–228–9290). One of the city's newest hotels, this imposing skyscraper boasts 5 restaurants, including one in the revolving rooftop, 4 lounges, a Broadway theater, the world's tallest atrium, 24-hour room service, and a lobby on the 8th floor. 1,800 rooms, some suites.

Morgans. 237 Madison Ave., New York, NY 10016 (686–0300). Palladium operator Ian Schrager has an interest in this small but chic downtown establishment. He also owns the newly renovated Paramount, Royalton, and the Barbizon (see below). 140 rooms.

New York Hilton and Towers. 1335 Ave. of the Americas, New York, NY 10019 (586–7000 or 800–HILTONS). This glittering, modern hotel has just had its main entrance renovated as part of an $80 million redesign. You might want to take advantage of the Video or Zipout checkout service from your well-appointed room. 1797 rooms and suites in the hotel and 237 in the Executive Tower. Excellent Grill 53 restaurant. Fitness and business centers; nonsmoking floors; 24-hour room service.

Novotel. 226 West 52nd St., New York, NY 10019 (315–0100). This French chain's glittering entree to New York is in the heart of the Broadway district. Brasserie restaurant serves regional French dishes. 478 rooms and suites. Fine wine bar.

Sheraton Centre. 811 Seventh Ave. at 52nd St., New York, NY 10019 (581–1000 or 800–325–3535). The former Americana is 50 stories of modern luxury, proffering all the necessary facilities and services, including plush Rainier's Restaurant. 1,850 rooms, 73 suites. At press time, being completely renovated.

Sheraton Park Avenue. 45 Park Ave., New York, NY 10016 (685–7676 or 800–325–3535). Beautifully renovated, top to bottom, this is one of the brightest stars below 42nd St. 150 rooms and suites.

UN Plaza. 1 UN Plaza, 44th St. at First Ave., New York, NY 10017 (355–3400). A splendid building, inside and out. Chic Ambassador grill room but watch out for the many mirrored walls, which many (waiters included) run into. Indoor tennis courts and a 27th-floor health club. 442 rooms and 115 rental apartments.

Vista International. 3 World Trade Center, New York, NY 10048 (938–9100). A place to stay if you're doing business in the financial district. The fitness center, pool, and racquetball courts alone are worth the trip downtown, and the cuisine in the American Harvest restaurant is exquisite too. 821 rooms.

Warwick. 65 West 54th St., New York, NY 10019 (247–2700). Members of the communications, advertising, and fashion industries lay their heads in these handsomely furnished accommodations. 575 rooms and suites.

Expensive

Algonquin. 59 West 44th St., New York, NY 10036 (840–6800). The ghost of Dorothy Parker et al. hangs over the "Round Table" and the richly paneled lobby. Perfect for theatergoers and the literary minded, and the 200 rooms are cozy/comfortable.

The Barbizon. 140 East 63rd St., New York, NY 10021 (838–5700). Hotelier Ian Schrager recently bought this fine property, and he plans to operate it as "New York's first urban spa." 467 rooms.

Beverly. 125 East 50th St., New York, NY 10022 (753–2700). Recently renovated, this convenient address is justly proud of its 300 small suites.

Elysee. 60 East 54th St., New York, NY 10022 (753–1066). Your room has a name, as well as a number, and each decor varies. The Monkey Bar has its home here. 110 rooms.

Kitano. 66 Park Ave., New York, NY 10016 (685–0022). New York's only Japanese-style hotel offers a peaceful retreat with all the niceties of Oriental attention. Some of the 94 rooms and suites feature Japanese decor.

Loews Summit. 569 Lexington Ave., New York, NY 10022 (752–7000 or 800–223–0888). Completely redone in recent years, the Summit's guest rooms now boast color televisions, refrigerators, and phones in the bathrooms. 766 rooms.

New York Penta. 401 Seventh Ave., New York, NY 10036 (736–5000). Located across from Madison Square Garden, this huge, busy hotel contains over 1,700 comfortable, though unspectacular rooms.

Omni Park Central. 870 Seventh Ave., New York, NY 10019 (247–8000 or 800–THE–OMNI). Rooms are attractive, sometimes even luxurious, but the noise level is often distracting. 1,450 rooms.

Paramount Hotel 235 West 46th St., New York, NY 10036 (764–5500). This long-established hotel in the heart of the theater district has been brilliantly restored and renovated for owner Ian Schrager by noted designer Philippe Starck as a "luxury hotel at reasonable prices." The lobby is a modern marvel, and the rooms are both sleek and comfortable. Stop by after the theater for dessert and coffee and watch the attractive young international set congregate. 610 rooms.

St. Moritz. 50 Central Park South, New York, NY 10019 (755–5800). Rooms small but tastefully done and service is not sacrificed for price. 773 rooms and suites.

Moderate

Day's Inn. 440 West 57th St., New York, NY 10019 (581–8100 or 800–633–1414). Plenty of groups and conventions lodge in this slightly out-of-the-mainstream location. 600 rooms and suites.

Howard Johnson's Motor Lodge. 851 Eighth Ave., New York, NY 10036 (581–4100 or 800–654–2000). Color television, radio, and in-room movies, all in the midst of the theater district. 300 rooms. Many new restaurants have opened nearby.

Mayflower. Central Park West and 61st St., New York, NY 10023 (265–0060). Lincoln Center performers favor the old-fashioned comfort and European ambience here. Service, however, is somewhat geriatric and extremely slow at times. 376 rooms and suites.

Milford Plaza. 700 Eighth Ave. at 45th St., New York, NY 10036 (869–3600). Very popular with tourist groups and offers many package deals. 1,323 rooms. In theater district.

Ramada Inn of New York. 790 Eighth Ave. at 48th St., New York, NY 10036 (581–7000 or 800–2–RAMADA). Rooftop outdoor pool (seasonally), color TV, radio, and parking, also in the center of the theater district. 366 rooms.

Sheraton City Squire. 790 Seventh Ave., New York, NY 10036 (581–3300 or 800–325–3535). Modern and attractive, the City Squire also has an indoor pool and Universal gym. 730 rooms and suites.

Shoreham. 33 West 55th St., New York, NY 10019 (247–6700). Dignified appearance and modest, clean rooms, each with pantry, perfectly located for shopping or museum hopping. 75 rooms and suites.

Wellington. 871 Seventh Ave., at 55th St., New York, NY 10019 (247–3900). Contemporary rooms and many of the services provided by more expensive establishments, but the hotel is a little run down. 700 rooms.

Wyndham. 42 West 58th St., New York, NY 10019 (753–3500). A top address for stage and film stars, this gem is almost always solidly booked, so plan ahead. 200 rooms.

Inexpensive

American Youth Hostel. 891 Amsterdam Ave. at 103rd St., New York, NY 10025 (932–2300). Located in a completely renovated landmark 1883 Richard Morris Hunt building, this handsome—and long-overdue—facility is a find for all budget travelers. 480 beds in 90 large, 2- to 8-person dormitory rooms. Cafeteria, restaurant, laundromat on premises.

Carlton Arms Hotel. 160 East 25th St. at Third Ave., New York, NY 10010 (679–0680). Uniquely and eccentrically decorated by local and visiting artists, this small hotel (49 rooms) is nevertheless extremely well run and quite popular with the younger generations.

Chelsea Inn. 46 West 17th St. (645–8989). Two charming adjacent town houses have been renovated and joined to create this small (13 units) find located a bit south of Midtown. The place is favored by international travelers. Available are single rooms and one- and two-room suites; all units have kitchen facilities, but some share baths.

Journey's End. 3 East 40th St. at Fifth Ave., New York, NY 10016 (447–1500 or 800–668–4200). Brand new and sparkling, this 189-room hotel could not be more centrally located. The views from the upper floors are spectacular.

Malibu Studios Hotel. 2688 Broadway (near Columbia University), New York, NY 10025 (633–0275). The beach decor reflects the name, the 100 rooms and suites are small but spotless and comfortable, and the management is both friendly and efficient. A bargain for all, from students to families.

Mansfield. 12 West 44th St., New York, NY 10036 (944–6050). Virtually next door to the Harvard and Princeton clubs, the quarters are unpretentious and not for the fussy. Multilingual staff is particularly good for a hotel in this price range. 200 rooms.

Washington Square Hotel. Washington Sq. Park North, 103 Waverly Place, New York, NY 10011 (777–9515). The rather shabby old Earle Hotel has been renovated into a charming, well-appointed, 160-room neighborhood hotel. The perfect spot for lovers of Greenwich Village.

Wentworth. 59 West 46th St., New York, NY 10036 (719–2300). An older hotel close to Fifth Ave. with undistinguished rooms and a multilingual staff. 245 rooms.

RESTAURANTS. Probably the favorite leisure-time activity in New York is eating out. Natives take their dining seriously, frivolously, enjoyably, and critically, depending on the individual, but they *do* pay close attention to their restaurants. Quality is sometimes indicated by the price, but not in every case. Expensive establishments don't always fulfill the promise of their prices; conversely, there are terrific bargains to be digested.

Price categories listed below are based on the approximate cost of an average three-course meal (appetizer, main course, and dessert) per person. It does not include wine, drinks, the 8.25% tax, or 15–20% tip. The categories are: *Super Deluxe,* $50 and up; *Deluxe,* $30–$50; *Expensive,* $20–$30; *Moderate,* $10–$20; and *Inexpensive* under $10. Unless otherwise noted, major credit cards are accepted. Remember that New Yorkers eat late; 8 P.M. is the usual dining hour, and an 11 P.M. meal isn't out of the ordinary. If you are trying to get to the theater on time, mention that when you sit down.

Midtown (42nd St.–65th St.)

American International

Arcadia. *Super Deluxe.* 21 East 62nd St. (223–2900). One of the city's trendiest restaurants, this place specializes in what they term "inventive American" cuisine. Specialties include chimney smoked lobster and an incredible chocolate bread pudding.

"21" Club. *Super Deluxe.* 21 West 52nd St. (582–7200). Several old New York brownstone houses, beautifully preserved, make up what is probably the Big Apple's most venerable restaurant. The cuisine was recently upgraded but old favorites like chicken hash and the "21" burger remain.

Sea Grill. *Expensive.* 19 West 49th St., Rockefeller Center (246–9201). This plush and comfortable seafood restaurant overlooks the Center's Lower Plaza. Try the crab cakes, grilled pompano, or red snapper.

American Festival Cafe. *Moderate.* Lower Plaza at Rockefeller Center (246–6699). Regional specialties (corn and crab chowder, Maryland crab cakes, Key lime pie) are served in a bright, airy setting overlooking Prometheus fountain.

The Ginger Man. *Moderate.* 51 West 64th St. (399–2358). This favorite lunch and dinner pub near Lincoln Center is noted for its simple but succulent cuisine.

Brazilian

Cabana Carioca. *Moderate.* 123 West 45th St. (581–8088). Pleasant, friendly, and anything but elegant, the food is relatively good, and cheap by today's standards. Standouts: the caldo verde (vegetable and potato soup) and shrimp dishes. No CB, DC. **Cabana Carioca II** is at 133 West 45th St. (730–8375).

Burgers

Hard Rock Cafe. *Moderate.* 221 West 57th St. (489–6565). Rock and roll memorabilia decorates the walls and a normal conversational tone is inhibited by the loud music. Terrific for celebrity watching and the burgers are midtown's best. Check ahead, though, as it's a favorite locale for private parties and closes to the public at those times.

Chinese

Dish of Salt. *Expensive.* 133 West 47th St. (921–4242). 2 exquisitely decorated floors and a wide variety of dishes to match. MC, V.

Pearl's. *Expensive.* 38 West 48th St. (221–6677). Cantonese nuances flavor the dishes in this fairly small establishment. The soups—all 12 of them—are almost a meal in themselves, but try the braised fish in sweet and sour sauce and sample the dim sum, too. MC, V.

Shun Lee Palace. *Expensive.* 155 East 55th St. (371–8844). Its Lincoln Center branch, Shun Lee West, is at 43 West 65th St. (595–8895). The menu is an amalgam of Mandarin, Szechuan, Hunan, and Shanghai dishes and the chef will even prepare Cantonese favorites on request. V, MC.

Continental

The Four Seasons. *Super Deluxe.* 99 East 52nd St. (754–9494). Decor and menus change with the seasons in this, one of New York's most beautiful, ambitious, and interesting restaurants. Entrée choices are staggering, the wine cellar is one of America's most complete, and the chocolate velvet for dessert is a once-in-a-lifetime experience. So is dining here.

Delicatessen

Carnegie Deli. *Inexpensive.* 854 Seventh Ave. (757–2245). By far the best deli in the city. Corned beef hash is a minor miracle, sandwiches are beyond overflowing, and every dish is tasty. An excellent choice for a very full breakfast. Cash and traveler's checks only.

Stage. *Inexpensive.* 834 Seventh Ave. (245–7850). Sandwiches are named for famous patrons in this bustling, noisy, and excellent deli. Try the Reuben, anything with rye bread, and don't pass up the pickles! Cash only.

French

La Caravelle. *Super Deluxe.* 33 West 55th St. (586–4252). Cognoscenti claim this is one of the top 2 or 3 French restaurants in Manhattan. A fashionable clientele dines amidst the elegant decor and sips from the top-notch wine cellar. Service is attentive, too, especially if you're well-known.

La Cote Basque. *Super Deluxe.* 5 East 55th St. (688–6525). Stunning Bernard Lamotte murals enhance this dining room, whose cuisine was made famous by the late founder, Henri Soulé. Classic French, which can be superb.

La Grenouille. *Super Deluxe.* 3 East 52nd St. (752–1495). The "in" place for expense account lunches and dinners. Often crowded, since it offers just about as good a French meal as can be found in the city.

Lutèce. *Super Deluxe.* 249 East 50th St. (752–2225). This town house-turned-*intime* restaurant serves perhaps the most ambitious and elaborate food in the U.S. If you have only the time (or budget) for one fine gastronomic adventure, we urge you to do it here. No CB.

Mondrian. *Deluxe–Super Deluxe.* 7 East 59th St. (935–3434). This handsome place is a gourmand's delight, with well-spaced tables and a low noise level. Try the braised red snapper in lemon vinaigrette or the squab with a gratin of parsnips and huckleberries. The chocolate *ganache* cake, which must be ordered with the entrée, oozes warm chocolate from its center.

Crepe Suzette. *Moderate.* 363 West 46th St. (581–9717). Simple, unpretentious hearty French country fare brought to you by a friendly staff.

Greek

Avgerinos. *Moderate.* In Citicorp Center, 153 East 53rd St. (688–8828). Intimate and cheerful setting where Greek specialties are prepared in an open kitchen.

Indian

Nirvana. *Expensive.* 30 Central Park South (486–5700). English rock stars eat their Indian nowhere else. The view of Central Park is romantic, especially when served under shamianas (multicolored tents), and the food is spicier than the decor. Unfortunately, it isn't always up to the surroundings.

Raga. *Expensive.* 57 West 48th St. (757–3450). One of the prettiest settings for top-notch Indian cuisine. The assortment of breads is mouthwatering, and if you fancy a kir, they do a superb one here.

Darbar. *Moderate.* 44 West 56th St. (432–7227). Highly praised by the city's leading restaurant critics as well as by *Gourmet* magazine, this place specializes in Tandoori dishes, *murgh Jalfrazie, saag gosht, bayngan bhurti, kulfi,* and *crab malabar.*

Italian

Il Gattopardo. *Expensive.* 49 West 56th St. (586–3978). Terrific northern Italian eating in midtown Manhattan. The angel hair pasta is divine (pun intended); prices are equally sky-high, but worth it.

Isle of Capri. *Expensive.* 1028 Third Ave. at 61st St. (223–9430). This trattoria-style operation is generally acknowledged as one of the best Italian restaurants in the city, though it can be uneven.

Prego. *Inexpensive.* 1365 Sixth Ave. (307–5775). Sub-named "Pasta d'Italia," this small, appealing storefront offers a wide variety of excellent pasta dishes, plus speedy, efficient service. No CB, DC, MC, V.

Japanese

Hatsuhana. *Deluxe.* 17 East 48th St. (355–3345). Impress friends and run up your expense account here. The sushi and sashimi are good, but what you really pay for is celebrity watching.

Nippon. *Expensive.* 155 East 52nd St. (758–0226). Unusual Japanese dishes are featured, along with the familiar sukiyaki, tempura, and sushi in a setting similar to a Japanese garden, complete with stream.

Takesushi. *Moderate.* 71 Vanderbilt Ave. (867–5120). For any money, the best Japanese in midtown. Private rooms for small parties of 4 to 8, a comfortable dining area for the rest where tables are not so close that you feel as if you're dining from the plate next door. Tasty sushi and sashimi, but other cuisine styles are equally well done.

Mexican

Rosa Mexicano. *Expensive.* 1063 First Ave. (753–7407). Considered by many one of the best (if not *the* best) Mexican restaurants in the city.

Caramba! *Moderate.* 918 Eighth Ave. (245–7910). Even with reservations there's usually a wait, but worth it. Beware the killer margaritas!

Rosa's Place. *Inexpensive.* 303 West 48th St. (586–4853). This warm, inviting, extremely friendly theater-district place serves superb guacamole, nachos, enchilladas suisas, tacos, and birdbath-size frozen margaritas. Open late; perfect for after the show.

Russian

Russian Tea Room. *Deluxe.* 150 West 57th St. (265–0947). Film deals are made, books are published, TV shows are given the go-ahead over "power" lunches of borscht, blinis (pancakes with caviar), and chicken Kiev. "Cossack" bartenders brew a bevy of lethal concoctions, so be forewarned.

Seafood

Oyster Bar. *Expensive.* 42nd St. between Lexington and Vanderbilt Aves., in the lower level of Grand Central Station (490–6650). This city landmark serves great stews and chowders, regular fish dishes too. Inexpensive if you stick to chowders and appetizers.

Paradis Barcelona. *Expensive.* 145 East 50th St. (754–3333). Catalan cuisine comes to the Big Apple in a chic, sophisticated East Side setting. Try the sliced salmon appetizer with garlic and white beans, followed by sweet peppers stuffed with creamed salt cod (and more garlic!), accompanied by a fine Spanish wine.

Steak

Christ Cella. *Deluxe.* 160 East 46th St. (697–2479). Perhaps the biggest slice of roast beef around (ditto the steaks) are served among simple decor. You'll get an argument, though, from fans of this next restaurant.

The Palm. *Deluxe.* 837 Second Ave. (687–2953). A branch, the Palm Too, is located across the street at 840 Second Ave. It can be a madhouse during prime dining hours, but the sirloins, cottage-fried potatoes, and crisp onion rings are a total delight.

Frankie and Johnnie's. *Expensive.* 269 West 45th St. (997–9494). It's in the heart of the theater district, so if you're starving for a steak after the show, stop here. The filet mignon is definitely worth the short climb to the second floor.

Downtown (Below 42nd St.)

American International

The Water Club. *Deluxe.* East River at 30th St. (683–3333). This 700-seat converted barge has added a cabaret to its changing menu of American dishes.

Capsouto Freres. *Expensive.* 451 Washington St. at Watts St. (966–4900). A feeling of grandiose spaciousness imbues this former factory that boasts one of the town's best chefs. Every mouthful tells you why the trip to this remote corner of TriBeCa, near Canal St., is worth it. No MC, V.

Windows on the World. *Expensive.* 107th floor, One World Trade Center (938–1111). This very famous, very elegant skytop restaurant overlooks glittering nighttime New York. Also open Sat. and Sun. for a lavish brunch. Jacket and tie required; no jeans.

Barrow Street Bistro. *Moderate.* 48 Barrow St., between 7th Ave. and Bedford St. (691–6800). Superb "California cuisine" served here in the lower level of a lovely West Village town house. Have the tender, curried scallops, the lightly flavored pasta, the mouth-watering raspberry-lemon tart.

Blue Mill Tavern. *Moderate.* 50 Commerce St. (243–7114). Tucked away on this quiet Village street is a good bargain in steaks. Vegetables, unfortunately, tend to be overcooked, but forgo minor errors for the lamb chops.

The Derby. *Moderate.* 109 MacDougal St., just below Washington Sq. (475–0520). This may be everyone's dream of the perfect Greenwich Village restaurant/bar. Cozy and warm, and the steaks and seafood (grilled before your eyes) are above reproach.

Elephant and Castle. *Inexpensive.* 68 Greenwich Ave. (243–1400). Also in SoHo at 183 Prince St. (260–3600). Omelets and burgers are the specialties of these houses, but if you're looking for the best Caesar salad around, you'll find it here.

Chinese

Say Eng Look. *Moderate.* 5 East Broadway (732–0796). The name means "Four, Five, Six," in Mandarin Chinese and refers to a particularly fine Mah Jong hand. Bring your own beer—perhaps a fine brand imported from the mainland—to wash down the mu-shoo pork, tai-chi chicken, or deep-fried fish wrapped in bean curd or seaweed.

Most **Chinatown** restaurants serve excellent food at bargain prices. Check the menu posted in the window before you enter, but if you're a Chinese food fan, just about anyplace is a fun adventure.

French

Black Sheep. *Moderate.* 344 West 11th St. (242–1010). One of the real "finds" in Village dining. From the crudités with aioli to the rich and tempting desserts, each bite is a treat. The wine list is unusually extensive, with owner's weekly suggestions an excellent value. (You get a discount if you pay cash.)

La Ripaille. *Moderate.* 605 Hudson St. at Abingdon Sq. (255–4406). Two cousins from Provence provide the ambience in this tiny jewel of a place while their wives cook up delicious escargots in cream sauce or vegetable pâté—and that's just for openers. Don't miss a meal here.

Italian

Chelsea Trattoria Italiana. *Expensive.* 108 8th Ave. at 16th St. (924–7786). Superb Northern Italian dishes in a most attractive setting.

Grotto Azzurra. *Expensive.* 387 Broome St. (925–8775). Probably the finest Little Italy has to offer. Cash only.

Grand Ticino. *Moderate.* 228 Thompson St., just below Washington Sq. (777–5922). The first floor of a Greenwich Village town house, where the movie *Moonstruck* was filmed, has served hearty Italian specialties like gnocchi al pesto and saltimbocca alla Romano since 1919.

Minetta Tavern. *Moderate.* 113 MacDougal St. (475–3850). A sister establishment to the Chelsea Trattoria.

Manganaro Hero Boy. *Inexpensive.* 592 Ninth Ave. (947–7325). Search no further for the finest hero sandwich in New York. Cash only.

Monte's. *Inexpensive.* 97 MacDougal St., below Washington Sq. (674–9456). A short flight of steps leads down to this long-established Greenwich Village basement restaurant serving excellent (and copious) Italian dishes like pasta al pesto, mussels in white wine, scampi and scallops, veal parmigiana, and a gigantic veal chop. Your friendly and gracious host will suggest other specialties.

Jewish

Ratner's. *Inexpensive.* 138 Delancey St. (677–5588). Visit this strictly Kosher dairy on Sun. for breakfast. Cash only.

Mexican

Viva Pancho. *Moderate.* 86 University Place (255–9378). Don't let the tattered awning put you off, for inside is one of the most surprisingly good—and cheap—downtown Mexican restaurants. Tacos are superb, so is the "mole verde," chicken in green pumpkin seed sauce.

Seafood

John Clancy's. *Expensive.* 181 West 10th St. at Sheridan Sq. (242–7350). This place is considered by many the finest seafood house in Greenwich Village; try the catch-of-the-day mesquite-grilled.

Marylou's. *Expensive.* 21 West Ninth St. (533–0012). The fish dishes are almost uniformly excellent and you'll recognize the faces of the fashion/photography/music business clientele.

Gulf Coast. *Moderate.* West 12th St. and West Side Hwy. (206–8790). Tasty delicacies flown up from the Gulf coast, well worth a venture into this formica-table-topped, out-of-the-way spot in the West Village. Cash only.

Jane Street Seafood Cafe. *Moderate.* 31 Eighth Ave. at Jane St. (243–9237). New England in Greenwich Village is evident in this comfortable and cozy place for chowders, shellfish, swordfish, lobsters, and other daily fresh catches.

Spanish

El Faro. *Moderate.* 823 Greenwich St. (929–8210). NYC's finest Spanish kitchen is hidden behind the unappetizing exterior and small, dark interior. The paellas are obligatory, but try the other shellfish dishes called mariscadas, as well. DC.

Uptown (Above 65th St.)

American-International:

Sign of the Dove. *Deluxe.* 1110 Third Ave. at 65th St. (861–8080). This elegant, romantic town house bar/restaurant has several beautiful rooms and an enclosed garden. The fine food matches the stunning decor.

Cafe Des Artistes. *Expensive.* 1 West 67th St. (877–3500). Elegant dining in a beautiful room. The Howard Chandler Christy nude murals are eye opening!

Tavern On The Green. *Expensive.* 67th St. and Central Park West (873–3200). A glittering wonderland set amid the greenery of Central Park. Several beautiful rooms, including the dazzling Crystal Room. Perfect for lunch, dinner or weekend brunch.

Cafe Luxembourg. *Moderate to Expensive.* 200 West 70th St. (873–7411). Universally acknowledged to be the finest restaurant on the Upper West Side—near Lincoln Center—this French-style bistro is jammed nightly before and after the theater, so plan ahead. Charming, lively, sophisticated in both decor and clientele.

Chinese

Hunan Balcony. *Inexpensive.* 2596 Broadway (865–0400). Excellent spicy sauces from one of the city's best Hunan restaurants.

French

Terrace. *Expensive.* 400 West 119th St. in the Columbia University area (666–9490). This is a very special place with splendid contemporary French cuisine (seafood and fresh game are the specialties) and spectacular views of the Upper West Side.

Mexican

Lucy's California Mexican. *Moderate.* 503 Columbus Ave. (787–3009). Lines form down the block on Fri. nights to dine at this friendly neighborhood bar and restaurant. Always a party-like atmosphere.

LIQUOR LAWS. You must be at least 21 to consume alcoholic beverages in New York. Bars in New York City can legally serve until 4 A.M. on weekends but must close at 3 A.M. on weekdays. Officially designated "social clubs" circumvent these restrictions and may serve "members" at any time. Beer can be purchased at supermarkets anytime except Sun. mornings (until noon). Liquor stores are the only legal vendors of wine and liquor and are closed on Sun.

NIGHTLIFE. Whatever your fancy in evening entertainment, you'll be able to indulge it in New York. Those old-fashioned nightclubs of the 1930s and 40s musicals have vanished, by and large, but if you insist on a floor show, you'll find a Paris style revue at *Cafe Versailles,* 151 East 50th St. (753–3471). *Asti,* 13 East 12th St. in the Village (741–9105), offers one too, in the form of live opera.

The big news is the triumphant return of the glittering Art Deco *Rainbow Room* atop 30 Rockefeller Plaza (632–5000); it's a glorious spot for dancing to a name band and catching the dazzling night lights, while dining on superb cuisine. Next door, along the 65th floor's north side, the *Rainbow and Stars* cabaret has opened, featuring top entertainers like Tony Bennett, Hildegarde, and Liliane Montevecchi.

Hotel rooms and piano bars offer a quiet, civilized antidote to the noise and hustle of Manhattan. Bobby Short, considered the piano man's piano man for his mastery of the 88s, holds forth at *Cafe Carlyle* in the Carlyle Hotel, 35 East 76th St. at Madison Ave. (744–1600). Piano expertise in a soothing setting is also to be found at *Chelsea Place,* 147 Eighth Ave. (924–8413); in the Grand Hyatt Hotel's *Trumpet's* restaurant, Park Avenue and 42nd St. (883–1234); and in *Harry's New York Bar,* the Helmsley Palace Hotel, 455 Madison Ave. and 50th St. (888–7000). A warm and delightful Greenwich Village experience awaits at *Five Oaks,* 49 Grove St. (243–8885), where the customers heartily sing along with Marie Blake's keyboard flourishes.

Dancing is generally a matter of choosing your music. 2 live orchestras provide the sounds for ballroom dancing at *Roseland,* 239 West 52nd St. (247–0200). Rock-and-roll reigns at the *Ritz,* now located in the old Studio 54 disco at 254 West 54th St. (541–8900). New and name acts are also showcased here. Though these matters change faster than you can slap down your admission charge, other "hot" clubs are *Laura Belle,* 120 West 43rd St. (819–1000); *The Grolier Club,* 29 East 32nd St. (679–2932); *Tatou,* 151 East 50th St. (753–1144); *M.K.,* 204 Fifth Ave. at 25th St. (779–1340); *Cafe Iguana,* 235 Park Ave. South (529–4770); the *Limelight,* a converted church at 47 West 20th St. (807–7850); the *Copacabana,* without chorus girls these days but still located at 10 East 60th St. (755–6010); and *Hot Rod Dance Club,* 270 11th Ave. at 28th St. (268–0182), a garagelike place filled with 50s rock 'n' roll memorabilia.

If you just want to listen—not dance—to music, you still must specify your favorite. Jazz buffs will find it hard to choose from over 25 name clubs in all sections of town, but you might consider *Michael's Pub,* 211 East 55th St. (758–2272), where Woody Allen tootles with a Dixieland group on Mon.; *Sweet Basil,* 88 Seventh Ave. South (242–1785), for mainstream and contemporary sounds; or the *Angry Squire,* 216 Seventh Ave. (242–9066), for duos and trios with a modern edge. Then, of course, there's the dean of jazz clubs, the *Village Vanguard,* 178 Seventh Ave.

South, just below Greenwich Avenue in the Village (255–4037). Smoky, with a lousy sound system and cramped quarters, it still draws the major names and crowds that have loved it for the past 40 years.

Besides the above-mentioned Ritz, pop and rollers perform at the *Bottom Line,* 15 East 4th St. (228–7880), a huge room in Greenwich Village. For a folksier feel, head to the *Bitter End,* 147 Bleecker St. (673–7030); or *Kenny's Castaways,* just a few doorways down the road at 157 Bleecker St. (473–9870). Brazilian musicians are at *S.O.B's,* 204 Varick St. (243–4940), which is only natural since the initials stand for Sounds Of Brazil. Cabaret has returned to the Big Apple in full plumage, and top spots include *The Ballroom,* 253 West 28th St. (244–3005); the Algonquin Hotel's *Oak Room* (840–6800); the Marriott Marquis Hotel's *J.W.'s* (398–1900); *The Duplex,* 61 Christopher St. at Sheridan Sq. (255–5438); and *Sweetwater's,* 170 Amsterdam Ave. near 68th St. (873–4100).

Let us not forget comedy. Two of the more popular laugh emporiums are *Catch A Rising Star,* 1487 First Ave. near 78th St. (794–1906); and the *Improvisation,* 358 West 44th St. (765–8268).

A brand-new comedy club, in a most unusual setting, is *Caroline's at the Seaport,* 89 South St. (233–4900). Here you can both eat and laugh yourself to death! Other new comedy/cabaret choices include *5 & 10 No Exaggeration,* in SoHo at 77 Greene St. (925–7414); *Stand-Up NY,* 236 West 78th St. at Broadway (595–0850); and *The Comic Strip,* 1568 Second Ave. at 81st St. (861–9386).

THE MID-ATLANTIC COAST

by
MIKE SCHWANZ

Mike Schwanz, a writer based in New York City, specializes in travel, sports, outdoor recreation, and entertainment. He has contributed to magazines and newspapers as well as to several books. The Maryland section was written by Jim Louttit.

THE JERSEY SHORE

In 1609, Dutch explorer Henry Hudson visited what is now Barnegat Inlet and wrote in his log, "This is a very good land to fall in with and a pleasant land to see." Hudson's words still ring true today, for now the New Jersey Shore is one of the most valuable pieces of real estate in the world. It remains a pleasant land to see.

Bordering the Atlantic Ocean on the eastern coast of the state, the Jersey Shore is composed of a nearly continuous chain of barrier-island beaches. Several major bays (Barnegat, Little Egg, Great, Lakes, and Absecon) separate these islands from the mainland.

The Shore encompasses a 127-mile stretch of land, from Sandy Hook in the north to Cape May in the south. More than 60 towns abut the sea; each one has a separate character of its own.

Atlantic City

The "queen" of shore towns is, of course, Atlantic City—about 85 miles south of Sandy Hook and 40 miles north of Cape May. In the early half of this century, this was the great seaside resort of the East Coast, made world-famous by its Boardwalk, saltwater taffy, and Miss America pageant. The town experienced a decline in the 1950s and 1960s. Then, in 1978, gambling casinos opened here, and Atlantic City became more popular than ever. In 1989, nearly 33 million people came here to experience its gambling casinos and world-class entertainment. In fact, 1989 was an important turning point for Atlantic City. A new train station, which opened in May of that year, provided service to both New York and Philadelphia. USAir airlines started to offer nonstop jet service from Pittsburgh and Louisville.

Most of the activities are centered around the Boardwalk. The best ones (swimming, people watching, kite flying, jogging) are free. During the summer, there are also many free concerts and craft fairs.

Even if you prefer not to gamble, you should at least walk through some of the casinos. You can feel the energy and excitement of those challenging lady luck. Watch their faces and the rituals some of them perform. A person must be twenty-one or older to enter a casino, and this is strictly enforced. Casinos are open from 10 A.M. to 4 A.M. on weekdays and stay open until 6 A.M. on weekends.

Fishing, boating, sailing, wind surfing, swimming, and water skiing can all be done right outside the big casino-hotels. Many of the casino-hotels also have their own tennis courts. Many public tennis courts, as well as public golf courses, are within five minutes of the casinos.

The nightlife is outstanding. Besides presenting the most famous names in show business, all the casino-hotels have lounges, piano bars, and cabarets. Several nightclubs in town stay open until 6 A.M. to accommodate local and visiting night owls.

More Shore Towns

Other Shore towns, of course, have personalities far different from Atlantic City.

Ocean Grove, for example, originally founded as a Methodist retreat, is ultraconservative and probably has the most restrictive blue laws on the Shore. Liquor is banned, and until recently, you couldn't even drive your car in town on Sundays!

Deal is the summer retreat of millionaires. It features huge mansions, many of which encompass several acres of beachfront property.

Although somewhat rundown these days, Asbury Park is still a lively, throbbing, pulsating town filled with young people who congregate around its boardwalk. Here, one can find amusement arcades, rides, and concessions. This town is also famed as one of the first hangouts of rock superstar Bruce Springsteen, who played at the Stone Pony early in his career, and still makes surprise appearances at this club.

Spring Lake is quiet, stately, and clean; it's filled with neat white Victorian houses. The boardwalk is nice (with very few concession stands) and there's a very pleasant beach.

Manasquan is a yuppie singles town—very crowded.

Point Pleasant and Seaside Heights have a sort of honky-tonk feel. Several amusement parks dot their boardwalks, which teem with teenagers.

Long Beach Island is a 12-mile-long strip of several small seaside communities. It's not as crowded as many other areas, probably because there isn't a boardwalk or an amusement pier. It's comprised of a lot of summer houses rented to New Yorkers and Philadelphians, as well as many motels.

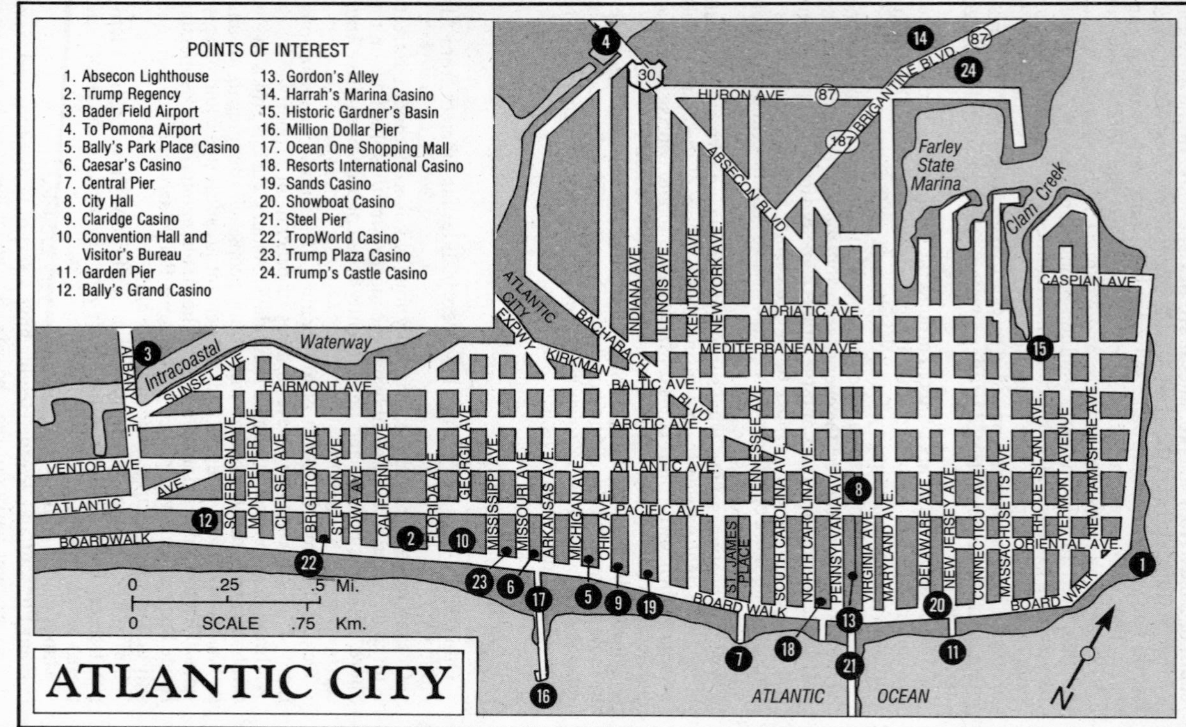
POINTS OF INTEREST
1. Absecon Lighthouse
2. Trump Regency
3. Bader Field Airport
4. To Pomona Airport
5. Bally's Park Place Casino
6. Caesar's Casino
7. Central Pier
8. City Hall
9. Claridge Casino
10. Convention Hall and Visitor's Bureau
11. Garden Pier
12. Bally's Grand Casino
13. Gordon's Alley
14. Harrah's Marina Casino
15. Historic Gardner's Basin
16. Million Dollar Pier
17. Ocean One Shopping Mall
18. Resorts International Casino
19. Sands Casino
20. Showboat Casino
21. Steel Pier
22. TropWorld Casino
23. Trump Plaza Casino
24. Trump's Castle Casino
HURON AVE.
BRIGANTINE BLVD.
ABSECON BLVD.
Farley State Marina
Clam Creek
CASPIAN AVE.
ADRIATIC AVE.
MEDITERRANEAN AVE.
BALTIC AVE.
ARCTIC AVE.
ATLANTIC AVE.
PACIFIC AVE.
ORIENTAL AVE.
ATLANTIC CITY EXPWY.
BACHARACH BLVD.
KIRKMAN BLVD.
Intracoastal Waterway
SUNSET AVE.
ALBANY AVE.
FAIRMONT AVE.
VENTOR AVE.
ATLANTIC AVE.
BOARDWALK
BOARD WALK
INDIANA AVE.
ILLINOIS AVE.
KENTUCKY AVE.
NEW YORK AVE.
SOVEREIGN AVE.
MONTPELIER AVE.
CHELSEA AVE.
BRIGHTON AVE.
STENTON AVE.
IOWA AVE.
CALIFORNIA AVE.
FLORIDA AVE.
GEORGIA AVE.
MISSISSIPPI AVE.
MISSOURI AVE.
ARKANSAS AVE.
MICHIGAN AVE.
OHIO AVE.
ST. JAMES PLACE
TENNESSEE AVE.
SOUTH CAROLINA AVE.
NORTH CAROLINA AVE.
PENNSYLVANIA AVE.
VIRGINIA AVE.
MARYLAND AVE.
DELAWARE AVE.
NEW JERSEY AVE.
CONNECTICUT AVE.
MASSACHUSETTS AVE.
RHODE ISLAND AVE.
VERMONT AVENUE
NEW HAMPSHIRE AVE.
30
87
187
0 .25 .5 Mi.
0 SCALE .75 Km.
ATLANTIC OCEAN
N
ATLANTIC CITY

Ocean City is ideal for families; it's very clean, with a lot of fun activities on the boardwalk there. No liquor is sold.

Stone Harbor is filled with scores of harbors and lagoons, and as a result, it has become the yachting and sailing center of the southern Shore. A small bird sanctuary attracts birdwatchers.

The Wildwoods (consisting of North Wildwood, West Wildwood, Wildwood, and Wildwood Crest) have beautiful wide beaches, countless boardwalk amusements and entertainment. The French-Canadians find Wildwood to be one of their favorite spots.

Last, but certainly not least, is one of the most charming towns on the entire East Coast: Cape May, the nation's oldest seaside resort. This pleasant, tree-lined village is a haven for enthusiasts of Victorian architecture. In fact, it is one of the few cities in the United States to be designated a national historic landmark. It has an excellent beach and many charming bed-and-breakfast inns.

History

For several centuries, the only humans who lived on the Jersey Shore were the Lenni Lenape (Delaware) Indians, who thrived here because of the land's rich variety of shellfish, waterfowl, and game. In the early 1600s, the Dutch settlers were the first whites to set up posts here. In 1664, England wrested control of the land from the Dutch and gave the area its present name, New Jersey. (It was named after nobleman George Carteret, who successfully defended the Isle of Jersey from invaders; he in turn received part of the new colony for his heroic action.)

In the late 1600s and early 1700s, the whaling industry flourished here, especially on Long Beach Island. During the Revolutionary War, the northern section of the shore (particularly the Tuckerton area) was a center for privateers, who often attacked British trading vessels. Pirates would use lanterns to lure ships onto dangerous shoals. The ships would run aground, break up, and spill their cargoes for pirates to seize. Captain Kidd and his band roamed here, escaping the British time after time in the maze of bays and coves. In fact, some people believe Captain Kidd's famous treasure is still entombed somewhere along Long Beach Island. A few gold coins have washed ashore over the years to support the myth.

Though the development of railroad lines had a profound effect on the Shore in the mid-19th century, when the automobile became a fixture in each American family in the early 1900s, the Shore area exploded in growth. It became perhaps the most popular vacation spot in America. Families bought second homes and then passed them on from generation to generation—a tradition that is very much alive today.

After World War II, the Jet Age expanded the horizons of travel for many visitors. As a result, many areas, including Atlantic City, suffered from a drop in tourism. But the introduction of gambling in the late 1970s brought a second surge of interest to the Shore, and it is booming once again.

The Unique Shore

Several things make the New Jersey Shore distinct from other seashore areas. Its wide, smooth, sandy, rock-free beaches are among the best anywhere. The ocean waters are fairly calm, and in summer they often warm up to over 70 degrees Fahrenheit. The gentle slope of the sea bottom and the gentle waves make it an ideal spot for people who like to wade.

Gambling also makes the Shore special, since the next-nearest major U.S. gambling area (Nevada) is 2,500 miles away. No matter where you are staying on the Shore, you are less than a 1½-hour drive from Atlantic City (in most cases, it's less than 45 minutes).

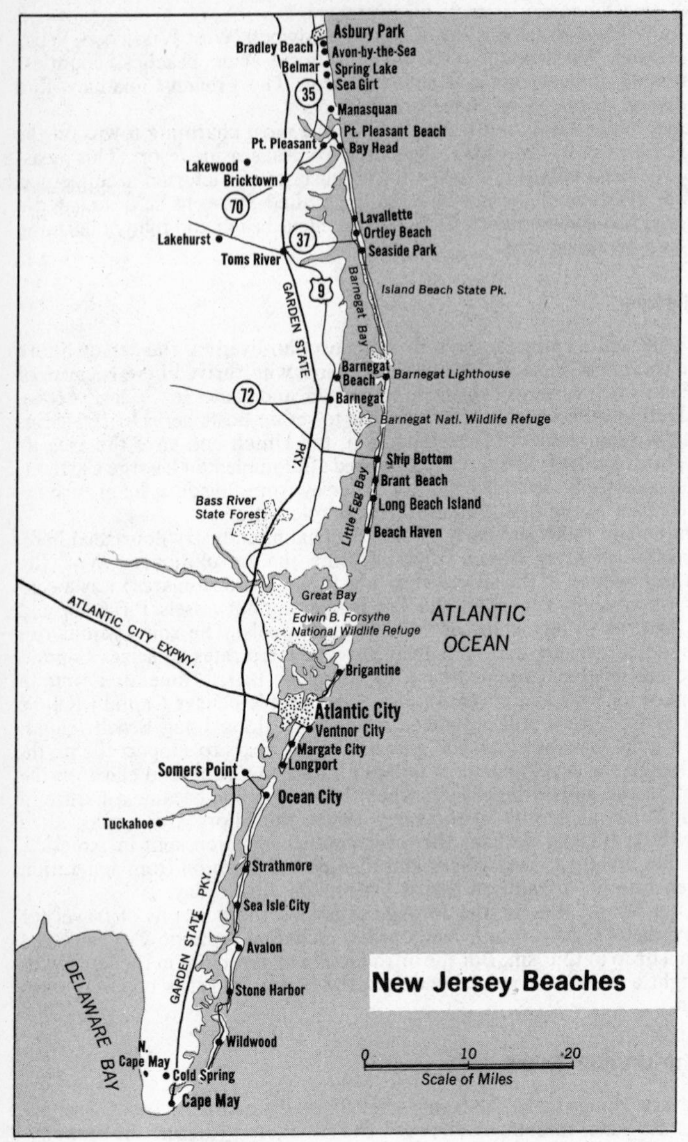
Asbury Park
Bradley Beach
Avon-by-the-Sea
Belmar
Spring Lake
Sea Girt
35
Manasquan
Pt. Pleasant Beach
Pt. Pleasant
Bay Head
Lakewood
Bricktown
70
Lavallette
Ortley Beach
Lakehurst
37
Seaside Park
Toms River
9
GARDEN STATE
Barnegat Bay
Island Beach State Pk.
Barnegat Beach
Barnegat Lighthouse
72
Barnegat
Barnegat Natl. Wildlife Refuge
PKY.
Ship Bottom
Brant Beach
Little Egg Bay
Long Beach Island
Bass River State Forest
Beach Haven
Great Bay
ATLANTIC CITY EXPWY.
Edwin B. Forsythe National Wildlife Refuge
ATLANTIC OCEAN
Brigantine
Atlantic City
Ventnor City
Margate City
Somers Point
Longport
Ocean City
Tuckahoe
Strathmore
GARDEN STATE PKY.
Sea Isle City
Avalon
DELAWARE BAY
New Jersey Beaches
Stone Harbor
Wildwood
N. Cape May
Cold Spring
Cape May
0
10
20
Scale of Miles

Many of the seaside communities have a boardwalk—a uniquely New Jersey feature. Atlantic City built the first boardwalk in 1870; other towns eventually followed suit. Today, much of the action in Shore communities is centered around their boardwalks. These wooden structures are a conglomeration of fast-food places, ice-cream parlors, souvenir stands, amusement parks, saltwater-taffy stands, and video arcades. They are filled with roller skaters, bikers, joggers, cyclists (in early mornings), mothers with strollers, and hand-holding lovers young and old. In many towns, free concerts are performed on boardwalks in the evenings.

Of course, the Atlantic Ocean has other attractions too. Sports enthusiasts love it because it is one of the best spots for saltwater fishing; more than thirty species are caught. Divers love it because there are literally thousands of shipwrecks, some still filled with treasure, just offshore. Many diving operators lead excursions to these sites. There are also many marinas, where one can launch a boat or rent one. In fact, in June, 1988, developer Donald Trump completed a $17-million renovation of Farley State Marina, to accommodate guests staying at his Trump's Castle casino-hotel. Jet skis, wind surfers, and sailboats can also be rented. Evening cocktail cruises are offered from a few boat basins.

Bicycles can be rented at many shore locations; an early morning ride along a boardwalk is particularly invigorating. (In some towns, bike riding on boardwalks is allowed only in early mornings.) Golf and tennis facilities are usually fairly near the beach.

More than Sand and Sun

Those who want to get away from the sand and sun for a few hours can enjoy a wide variety of other attractions in the Shore areas. History buffs will enjoy strolling through several fascinating sites. Victorian Wheaton Village is a 68-acre complex housing the Museum of American Glass and a working glass factory. The Ocean County Historical Museum in Toms River features nine rooms furnished in 1820- to 1890-era decor. The historic Village of Allaire has been restored to duplicate a community that made iron before the turn of the century. Historic Gardner's Basin is an early-1900s fishing village, with an aquarium museum and a tall ship that can be toured. The Towne of Historic Smithville is an authentic 1800s village with restored colonial buildings.

Many top-notch museums and art galleries capture the flavor of the Shore's rich culture. Most are within a 30-minute drive of the ocean. The Cape May Court House Historical Museum presents a fine collection of local Native American artifacts, decoys, whaling implements, glass and china, costumes, and genealogical material. The Ocean City Historical Museum has rooms of antique furniture, and mannequins wearing turn-of-the-century clothes. Somers Mansion, the oldest house (1725) in Atlantic County, features exhibits that show original furnishings from 260 years ago.

Of course, not all the shore is built up. Many areas still retain the natural beauty originally appreciated by Henry Hudson nearly 400 years ago. The Gateway National Recreation Area in Sandy Hook has dunes, a holly forest, many Revolutionary War historical sites, and the nation's oldest operating lighthouse. Island Beach State Park, just north of Long Beach Island, is a 10-mile stretch of beach that is seldom crowded, since just a limited number of cars a day are allowed in. Holgate, a state park at the southern end of Long Beach Island, is popular with surfers. It's one of the few spots along the coast that has some rough waves. The Edwin B. Forsythe (formerly called Brigantine) National Wildlife Refuge has 20,000 acres of marshland for birdwatching and nature photography. The Stone Harbor Bird Sanctuary in Stone Harbor has lots of herons, which can be seen at dawn and dusk. At Higbee Beach near Cape May, one can watch the sun set over Delaware Bay. This is one of the few beaches where fires are allowed.

Nightlife

The Shore is a lively place at night, especially in the summer. The epicenter of the action, of course, is Atlantic City. All 12 major casino-hotels have major showrooms, and they compete fiercely for the hottest names in show business. Bill Cosby, Frank Sinatra, Eddie Murphy, Liza Minnelli, Jackie Mason, and Don Rickles all appear regularly. In addition, each casino-hotel has at least one other lounge or cabaret with a piano bar or other form of entertainment; these smaller lounges can give you the chance to see some up-and-coming stars.

Most of the local towns have a pretty good selection of night spots, ranging from informal pubs to fancy, dress-to-kill discos. There's lots of live music, and many local bands consider themselves in the vanguard of the Jersey Shore music sound. Many local towns sponsor concerts along the beach in summer evenings.

Practical Information for the Jersey Shore

WHEN TO GO. The New Jersey Shore bustles in the summer. That is when the weather is best and also when most special events are held. In addition, this is the only season when all motels and restaurants are open; many close down during the winter.

Temperatures are generally in the high 70s or low 80s during the day, dropping to the 60s at night. By mid-July, the ocean temperature is at least 70° in most spots.

The big disadvantage of visiting the Shore in summer is that it can get very crowded. It's harder to get reservations at motels; traffic is congested; and there are often waits at night at restaurants. Lodging rates, of course, are most expensive in summer.

The best time to visit the Shore may be the two weeks after Labor Day. The weather is still warm then, and this is also the time when the ocean water is at its warmest (75° in some spots). Better yet, most of the crowds are gone. Many shore communities successfully attract visitors off season. They set up exciting events and in places like Cape May you have to make reservations well in advance for Thanksgiving, Christmas, and New Year's.

Sept. and Oct. are great months for fishing. Many species migrate past the area on their way south.

HOW TO GET THERE. The best way to get here, by far, is to drive.

By plane. The closest *major* airports to the Shore are those in Philadelphia, Newark, and New York. Atlantic City's large airport, the Atlantic City International Airport, is at Pomona. From there, one can rent a car for a 1- to 2-hour drive to most Shore points. The major local carrier is *USAir,* which offers nonstop jet service from Pittsburgh and Louisville, and prop plane service via its commuter line: *USAir Express,* which services most major East Coast cities. Call 412–922–7500 or 800–428–4322. Other carriers linking major Eastern cities to Atlantic City are *Continental Express* (800–525–0280) and *Trans World Express* (800–221–2000).

By bus. Getting to this region is fairly easy via bus. Several major carriers go to nearly all points along the coast, from such major cities as Trenton, Philadelphia, Newark, and New York. Major carriers include: *Asbury Park–New York Transit Company* (908–774–2727); *Atlantic City Transportation Company* (609–345–3201); *Domenico Bus Company* (908–339–6000); *Greyhound* (908–642–8205 or 212–971–6363); *New Jersey Transit* (908–762–5100 or 800–772–2222 in 908 area code and 800–582–5946 in 609 area code); *Ocean City Transportation Center* (609–398–9030); *Short Line* (908–529–3666); and *Transport of New Jersey* (800–772–2222).

Some bus lines take visitors directly to Atlantic City casinos for the day, and even throw in $10 worth of quarters.

By train. *New Jersey Transit Company* operates a rail line that goes to a few towns on the far northern shore. Bay Head is the last stop. Call 800–772–2222 in north Jersey; 908–762–5100 from out of state; and 800–582–5946 from south Jersey. In May, 1989, a new $14-million train station opened. *Amtrak* (212–736–4545 or 800–872–7245) started service to Atlantic City, Washington, and Baltimore. Round-trip rates range from $50 to $75.

By car. The Garden State Parkway is the main north-south route leading to the Shore. Virtually every exit leads into an east-bound route to a Shore town. (Most cities are 10–15 mi. from the Parkway.) From Philadelphia, the Atlantic City Expressway leads directly to Atlantic City and other Shore points. From Trenton, take I-195 to the Garden State Parkway. Try to avoid traveling on Fri. or Sun. afternoons. Bring change (35¢) for the tolls.

By helicopter. *Trump Air* helicopter service has several daily flights from Manhattan (West 30th St. and 12th Ave.). Cost is $250 Mon.–Thurs.; $290 Fri., Sat. (609–344–0833 or 800–448–4000).

By boat. From Washington and Baltimore, you might elect to take the *Cape May–Lewes Ferry,* which runs from Lewes, Delaware, to Cape May, New Jersey. It is a 70-minute ride over Delaware Bay. Cost is $4 for individuals; $6 for bicycle carriers; $16 per car. Call 609–886–2718 (Cape May Terminal) or 302–645–6313 (Lewes Terminal).

TOURIST INFORMATION. Potential visitors shouldn't have any trouble getting a ton of useful information from the state's very good, efficient tourism bureaus.

New Jersey Division of Travel and Tourism, CN 826, Trenton, NJ 08626 (800–JERSEY–7).

Monmouth County Department of Economic Development, Division of Tourism, Freehold, NJ 07728 (908–431–7476). *Ocean County Tourism Advisory Council,* CN 2191, Administration Bldg., Toms River, NJ 08753 (908–929–2163). *Atlantic City Visitors Bureau,* Department of Public Relations, Convention Center, 2310 Pacific Ave., Atlantic City, NJ 08401 (609–348–7044). *Mid-Atlantic Center for the Arts,* Box 164, Cape May, NJ 08204 (609–884–5404). *Long Beach–Southern Ocean Chamber of Commerce,* 265 W. 9th St., Ship Bottom, NJ 08008 (609–494–7211). *Cape May Convention and Visitors Bureau,* Box 403, Cape May, NJ 08204 (609–898–0280).

Once you arrive in your town, pick up a copy of the local paper. It will list ads for restaurants, special events, nightclubs, etc. There are three daily newspapers along the Shore: the *Asbury Park Press,* the *Ocean County Observer,* and the *Atlantic City Press.*

Atlantic City Magazine lists plenty of events in the southern-Shore region. Every June, *New Jersey Monthly,* widely available at Shore newsstands, publishes a special Shore issue that gives lots of useful information.

TIME ZONES. All of New Jersey is on eastern time.

TELEPHONES. In mid-1991, a new area code, 908, replaced 201 in the following counties: Monmouth, Ocean, Middlesex, Somerset, most of Union, Hunterdon, and Warren. Numbers given throughout this chapter reflect this change. From Barnegat south the area code still is 609. In most areas, the cost of a pay-phone call is 25 cents. For local information, call 411. If you are calling out of your area code for assistance, call 1 plus area code plus 555–1212. To dial long distance, dial 1 before the area code. Dial 0 before the area code for operator assistance on credit-card, collect, and person-to-person long-distance calls. Dial 911 for *emergencies.*

HOW TO GET AROUND. Nearly every town along the Shore is quite small. A few, in fact, can be walked from one end to another. But a car is the only practical way to get from one spot to another. In addition, the local routes that go from town to town often run right parallel to the Atlantic Ocean, offering beautiful vistas of the sea.

From the airport. If you fly into Newark and rent a car, you will have a 1½- to 3-hour drive to shore points. From Philadelphia, it is about 1½ hours to Atlantic City. Several shuttle limousines from Philadelphia International Airport go to Atlantic City. They are: *AA Limousine Service* (609–344–2444); *Airport Limousine Service* (609–345–3244); *Blue and White Airport Service* (609–848–0770); *Casino Limo* (800–452–1110 or 609–646–5555); *Maher Limousine Service* (609–398–7132); *May's Call-a-Cab* (609–646–7600); *Rapid Rover Airport Shuttle* (609–344–0100).

Taxis serving Bader Field in Atlantic City include *Airport Limousine Service* (609–345–3244); *Blue and White Airport Service* (609–228–3000); *Casino Limousine Service* (609–646–5555); *May's Call-a-Cab* (609–646–7600); and *Rapid Rover Airport Shuttle* (609–344–0100). From Bader, the cost is about $8.

By car. If you don't have your own car, you can rent one at major airports and Bader Field in Atlantic City. *Budget Rent-a-Car* (609–345–0600; 800–527–0700); *Avis* (609–345–3350; 800–331–1212); *Hertz* (609–646–1212; 800–654–3131); *National* (800–328–4567 or 609–344–0441); and *Dollar* (800–421–6868 or 609–344–4919). *Snappy* (800–321–7159) will deliver cars directly to all casino-hotels.

By taxi. Consult the local Yellow Pages. If your seaside town does not have its own taxi service, you may be able to take a casino bus to Atlantic City. Once in Atlantic City, simply go to a casino—taxis are usually lined up there. Or, call a cab. Among the most reliable Atlantic City companies are: *Ace Radio Cab* (347–1022); *City Cab Co.,* Pleasantville (641–0762); *Mutual Cab* (345–6111); *Ocean City Yellow Cab* (927–8471); *Radio Cab* (345–1105); *Red Top Cab* (344–4104); *Somers Point Cab,* Bargaintown (927–9665); *Stiles Taxi,* Cape May (884–5999); and *Yellow Cab* (344–1221). One of the most reliable companies in northern Jersey is *Shore Taxi* in Manasquan, based at the train station. Call 908–223–8294.

By trolley or jitney. A few shore towns have trolleys that go up and down their main drags in summer. A guided trolley tour of Cape May costs $3.50. The Golly Trolley in Long Beach Island goes from North Beach to Beach Haven Heights. It costs $1 and runs from late June to Labor Day, from 11 A.M. to 12:30 A.M. (609–597–4727). Atlantic City's jitneys run up and down Pacific Ave. continually, 24 hours a day, and also serve Farley State Marina. They cost $1. The hand-pushed Rolling Chairs on Atlantic City's Boardwalk (which can hold only two people) cost $25 per hour for two people, or $5 for two people for up to 1 mi. Call 347–7148. (Prices are negotiable for Rolling Chairs.) A motorized tram ($1) runs from North Wildwood to Wildwood Crest. Ocean City's trolley runs from 59th St. to Gardens Pkwy. Bridge; it costs 75 cents. This trolley runs every 30 minutes, in season, from 9 A.M. to midnight. The Spring Lake Trolley operates from 11 A.M. to 7 P.M. and goes to all main town points. It costs 75 cents. Call 908–449–1415.

HINTS TO MOTORISTS. The roads on the New Jersey Shore were not designed for heavy traffic. As a result, there are often traffic jams in the summer. Trying to get to the Shore on a Fri. afternoon or trying to leave on a Sun. afternoon can be extremely irritating.

Street parking can be very difficult near the ocean in summer in most Shore towns—especially Atlantic City. You may have to park a mile from the ocean on a Sun. afternoon! Most towns do have pay parking lots, as do many hotels and motels. Day (or night) visitors to the Atlantic City casinos can park for free at many casinos if they have their parking tickets validated.

HINTS TO DISABLED TRAVELERS. Most of the brochures published by the New Jersey Division of Tourism have extensive listings of the state's major tourist attractions. At the end of some listings, if applicable, is a wheelchair symbol that shows whether that tourist site has facilities for the handicapped. Contact Division of Tourism, CN 826, Trenton, NJ 08626. For additional information for the blind and handicapped call 800–582–5945.

As a general rule, the newer hotels in the state have better facilities for the handicapped. All the Atlantic City casino-hotels have excellent facilities.

For more specific information, contact: *Atlantic County Office for the Disabled,* 1333 Atlantic Ave., Atlantic City, NJ 08401 (609–345–6700, ext. 2831); *Monmouth County Office of the Handicapped,* 29 Main St., Freehold, NJ 07728 (908–431–7399); *Ocean County Office for the Disabled,* 34 Hadley Ave., CN 2191, Toms River, NJ 08754 (908–244–6804). Another source is the *Governor's Committee on the Disabled,* Labor & Industry Bldg., Room 200, Trenton, NJ 08625 (609–633–6959).

SEASONAL EVENTS. Many of the major special annual events on the New Jersey Shore are held in summer along boardwalks right on the sea. Consult local publications for specific listings. A few are worth mentioning here.

June. *Cape May Victorian Fair.* An annual, old-fashioned fair with crafts, food, and much more. Held on the Physick Estate in mid-June. Admission is free.

July. Ocean City's *Night in Venice Boat Parade* features about 100 decorated boats, of all shapes and sizes, which wind through the town's lagoons. People who live along the main bay decorate their homes; prizes are awarded.

August. In late Aug., Ocean City's annual *Sun Tanning Tournament* is open to all comers. Prizes are awarded in a number of categories, such as gold dome, driver's arm, and best bikini line. It's held at Music Pier. Call 609–399–6111 for information. *LPGA* golf tournament at Sands Country Club, Atlantic City.

September. The most famous Shore event of all—the *Miss America Pageant*—is held in mid-Sept. at Convention Hall in Atlantic City. A parade is also held on the boardwalk during Pageant Week.

October. *Victorian Week,* Cape May. Each year around Columbus Day, Cape May celebrates its Victorian heritage. Throughout 10 days there are tours of various buildings, a lawn party and fashion show, a concert, and an antique show. Contact Mid-Atlantic Center for the Arts, Box 164, Cape May, NJ 08204 (609–884–5404).

December. *Christmas in Cape May.* This town offers many holiday activities: candlelight walks amid Victorian shops; a citywide Christmas-lights competition; the annual Christmas Ball; and tours of several Victorian houses.

PARKS AND GARDENS. *Birch Grove Park.* Rte. 9 and Zion Rd., Northfield (609–641–3778). Open year-round for camping. Has 280 acres of woods, fields, and lakes and offers hiking, fishing, and birdwatching. Picnic and playground facilities are available.

Cape May County Park. Rte. 9, 2 mi. north of Cape May Courthouse (609–465–5271). There are nature trails, picnic areas, tennis courts, a zoo, and a pond. Forest includes such species as cherry, oak, dogwood, sassafras, and maple trees. Free.

Lenape Lake Park. Park Blvd. and 13th St., Mays Landing (609–625–2021). Excellent spot for watersports, such as canoeing (rentals available), swimming, water skiing. Picnic benches available. Open Wed.–Fri., 11 A.M.–5 P.M.; Sat.-Sun., 10 A.M.–8 P.M. Admission, $1.50.

Stone Harbor Bird Sanctuary. 111th to 116th Sts., on 3rd Ave., Stone Harbor (609–348–5102). A 21-acre nesting area for many bird species, including the American egret, Louisiana heron, green heron, black crowned night heron, yellow crowned night heron, cattle egret, and glossy ibis. A museum and observation tower are also here.

NATIONAL AND STATE PARKS. *Absecon Lighthouse.* Rhode Island and Pacific Avenues, Atlantic City. This 167-ft.-high lighthouse was built in 1857, to warn ships of tricky rocks and reefs. It is a New Jersey state park.

Allaire State Park, off Rte. I-95 in Farmingdale (908–938–2371). In 1822, James Allaire bought the existing bog-ore furnace and established an iron foundry—and a self-contained town. Today, this village is restored. A general store sells country trinkets and candy. The Pine Creek Railroad is the only live-steam, narrow-gauge train in New Jersey.

Barnegat Lighthouse State Park, Long Beach Island (609–494–2016). At the far northern tip of this island, this beach now offers swimming, fishing, and picnicking. Historic Barnegat Lighthouse is here, too.

Cape May Point State Park. About 3 mi. west of Cape May (609–884–2159). Park has 350 acres of freshwater marshland, woodland, and beaches. There are several self-guided nature walks offered, to see wildlife and fauna in the area. Fishing and hiking can be enjoyed. There is a visitor's center with marine museum open until 4:30 P.M. every day. Open March–Dec.

Edwin B. Forsythe National Wildlife Refuge (Brigantine Division). Great Creek Road, Oceanville (609–652–1665). This is a birdwatcher's heaven—more than 20,000 acres of wetlands, which attract huge flocks of migrating birds. There is a guided auto tour, plus hiking trails. There is a birding hotline (609–884–2626).

Gateway National Recreation Area. Off Rte. 36, Sandy Hook (908–872–0092). Features sand dunes, historic Fort Hancock, and a wonderful holly-tree grove. On clear days, New York's World Trade Center can be seen.

Island Beach State Park. South Seaside Park, Berkeley (908–793–0506). A wonderful undeveloped beach open for swimming, surfing, picnicking, and surf fishing. It is open 8 A.M.–8 P.M. Parking costs $4 on weekdays; $5 on weekends; it's free on Tues. Only a limited number of cars are allowed in, so get there early—by 9 A.M. on weekends.

CAMPING. The Shore is blessed with scores of outstanding campgrounds. Some are nothing more than bare stretches of beach; others offer swimming pools, video arcades, general stores, and just about every other convenience one could think of. The tourism bureau of each Shore county (listed earlier in this chapter) has brochures that list various camping facilities. Costs vary widely, from $5 to as much as $25 per site per night.

Some campgrounds take reservations; some don't. Since the Shore gets so crowded in summer, it's imperative that you call ahead for complete information, if you plan to camp.

A few of the largest campsite operators are listed below.

Avalon Campground, 492 Shore Rd. (Rte. 9), Clermont, NJ 08210 (609–624–0075). *Cape Island Campground,* 709 Rte. 9, Cape May Court House, 08210 (609–884–5777). *Cold Spring Campground,* 541 New England Rd., Cape May, NJ 08204 (609–884–8717). *Colonial Meadows Family Campgrounds,* 557 Somers Point Rd., Mays Landing, 08330 (609–653–8449). *Pine Haven Campground,* Rte. 9, Box 606, Ocean View; NJ 08230 (609–624–3437).

FISHING. Some of the best saltwater fishing in the country can be found right off the New Jersey Shore. There are a couple of reasons for this. First, the very deep Hudson Canyon (an underwater trench about 50 mi. offshore) is an underwater "highway" for tuna and marlin and other big-game fish. The shipwrecks (thousands of them) in the nearby Atlantic also attract lots of species. Finally, many species migrate from northern waters to southern waters (and vice versa), so there are always new species showing up.

Species often caught include bluefish, striped bass, mackerel, fluke, weakfish, bonito, and sometimes even sharks, tuna, and marlin. Surf fishers often catch bluefish, striped bass, and fluke from the surf off Manasquan, Belmar, Spring Lake, and Sea Girt.

Several piers in towns are open to the public. The ones at Long Branch, Brigantine, Seaside Heights, and Belmar are often productive.

Fishing licenses are needed only for freshwater fishing; contact the Division of Fish, Game, and Wildlife (609–292–2965).

Both charter boats and party boats (which accommodate up to 100 people) are available for rent at several marinas up and down the coast. Party boats cost from $25 to $35; charter boats cost from $250 to $600. See Boat Rentals under Sports, below.

All Shore-county tourism offices have brochures that list fishing-boat captains. Also, one excellent source is *New Jersey Fisherman,* 339 Herbertsville Rd., Bricktown, NJ 08724 (908–840–8600). It lists weekly news about saltwater and freshwater fishing. It costs $17.50 a year.

Or visit marinas to get more information: *South Jersey Marina,* Rte. 109, Cape May, NJ (609–884–2400). *Angler's Roost,* Pier IV, 9214 Amherst Ave., Margate, NJ (609–822–2272).

Farley State Marina, South Carolina Ave. and Brigantine Blvd., Atlantic City, NJ (609–441–3600).

Barnegat Light Yacht Basin, 18th St. and Bayview Ave., Barnegat Light, NJ 08006 (609–494–8956).

Black Whale, Beach Haven Fishing Centre, Centre St. and the Bay, Beach Haven, NJ 08008 (609–492–0333).

Brielle Yacht Club, 1 Ocean Ave. Brielle, NJ 08730 (908–528–6250).

South Jersey Fishing Center, Rte. 9, at the entrance to Cape May, NJ (609–884–4671). Three boats—*Sea Star II, Fiesta,* and *Miss Cape May*—offer deep-sea fishing charters of four, six, and eight hours. Rates are $14, $18, and $23, respectively.

Yachtsman's Anchorage Marina, 6th St. and Bay Blvd., Ortley Beach (908–793–9476).

Also write to: *Division of Fish, Game, and Wildlife,* CN 400, Trenton, NJ 08625 (609–292–2965).

PARTICIPANT SPORTS. Active people will really enjoy this region; it offers a plethora of activities, many of them water-oriented. **Swimming** and **jogging** can be done almost anywhere. Nearly all Shore towns have public **tennis** courts; many of the fancier motels and hotels have their own private courts. **Bike riding** can be done in most places, although some towns restrict bicycle riders on boardwalks to a few hours in the morning.

Check listings in *Atlantic City* magazine and *New Jersey Monthly* magazine; the locations for many sporting activities are listed there. Also, the tourism pamphlets of the county tourism offices (listed earlier) contain much useful information.

Bicycle rentals. *AAAA Bike Shop,* 5223 Ventnor Ave., Ventnor (609–487–0808). *Point Pleasant Bicycle,* 2701 Bridge Ave., Point Pleasant (908–899–9755). *Brielle Cyclery,* 205 Union Ave., Rte. 71, Brielle (908–528–9121). *Hawks Seashore Emporium,* 2306 S. Bay Ave., Beach Haven, (609–492–3298). *Margate Bike Shop,* 4 S. Douglas St., Margate (609–822–9415). *13th Street Bikes,* 13th St. and Boardwalk, Ocean City (609–399–7121). *Village Bike Shop,* Ocean St. at Washington Mall, Cape May (609–884–8500).

Boat rentals. *Inlet Basin Deep Sea Fishing,* 57 Inlet Dr., Point Pleasant (908–899–9755). *Bayside Boats,* Rte. 35 & Bay Blvd., Seaside Heights (908–793–8535). *Blue Water Marina,* 600 Whelk Dr., Ocean City (609–398–9090). *Charlie's Landing,* Main St., Bayville (908–681–6677). *Ed's Boat Rental,* 9th & Bayview aves., Barnegat Light (609–494–2447). *Frank's Boat Rentals,* Bayview and Whittier Rd., Strathmere (609–263–6913). *Harvey Cedars Marina & Sailing School,* 6318 Long Beach Blvd., Harvey Cedars (609–494–2884). *Anchor Reef Marina,* 3404 Rte. 37 E., Toms River, NJ (908–929–1585). *Gateway Marina,* Mays Landing Rd., Somers Point (609–927–3002). *Aqua Rentals,* 6th & New York Ave., North Wildwood (609–522–5778).

Golf. *Bel-Aire Golf Club,* Allaire Rd. and Rte. 34, Allenwood (908–449–6024). *Brigantine Country Club,* Roosevelt Blvd. and the Bay, Brigantine (609–266–1388). *Cedar Creek Golf Course,* Tilton Blvd., Berkeley Township, NJ 08721 (908–269–4460). *Ocean Acres Country Club,* 925 Buccaneer La., Manahawkin, NJ 08050 (609–597–9393). *Ocean City Municipal Golf Course,* Ocean City (609–399–1315). *Shark River Golf Course,* Old Corlies Ave., Neptune (908–922–4141). *Stone Harbor Golf Club,* Box 284, Cape May Court House, NJ 08210 (609–465–9270).

Horseback riding. *Windward Farm,* Bailey Corner Rd., Wall (908–449–6441). *Tall Oaks Farm,* Oak Glen Road, Howell (908–938–5445). *Lakewood Riding Center,* Cross St., Lakewood (908–367–6222). *Bill's Lazy B Riding Stables & Tack Shop,* 103 S. New York Rd., Oceanville (609–652–1973). *Hidden Valley Ranch,* 4070 Bay Shore Rd., Cold Springs (609–884–8205).

Jet-ski rentals and instruction. *Jet Ski Rentals,* Maryland Ave. & the Bay, Somers Point (609–927–3738). *Jet Ski of Sea Isle,* 88th St., Sea Isle City (609–263–7572). *Yacht Charters of Ocean City,* 227 Bay Shore Dr., Ocean City (609–399–2169). *Royal Flush Fleet,* 6100 Park Blvd., Wildwood Crest (609–522–1395). *Pier One Jet Ski Shop,* Rte. 37, Toms River (908–270–0914).

Sailing (Rentals and Instruction). *New Horizons Sailing School,* 1 First St., Rumson (908–530–3237). *C&C Sailing Charters,* 1 River Ave., Point Pleasant (908–295–3450). *Great Egg Bay Sailing Marina,* Woodlawn Ave., off Rte. 559, Somers Point (609–653–1198). *Teal Sailing School,* 668 Main Ave., Bay Head (908–295–8225). *Barnegat Bay Sailboat Rentals & School,* 1 Corrigan Ave., Pine Beach (908–244–2106). *Trixie's Landing,* 305 Brennan Concourse, Bayville (908–269–5838). *Todt Sailing Center,* 25th St. & Long Beach Blvd., Spray Beach (609–492–8550).

Scuba diving. *Divers Cove,* Rte. 35, Laurence Harbor (908–583–2717). *Dosil's Sports Center,* 261 Rte. 36, Keansburg (908–787–0508). *Four Divers Inc.,* 56 Broadway, Point Pleasant (908–899–7753). *Triton Divers,* 4404 Long Beach Blvd., Brant Beach, Long Beach Island (609–494–4400). *East Coast Diving Service, Inc.,* 340-F Spring Valley Rd., Morganville, (908–591–9374).

Surfing and board sailing. *Grog's Surf Palace,* 910 Central Ave., Seaside Park (908–793–0097). *Zodiac Water Sports,* 703 Belmar Plaza, Belmar (908–681–4502). *Bay Head Windsurfing,* 76 Bridge Ave., Bay Head (908–899–9394). *Heritage Surf Shop,* 3700 Landis Ave., Sea Isle City (609–263–3033). *Y-Knot Surf Shop,* 8 Long Beach Blvd., Surf City (609–494–4204). *Bayview Sailboats,* 312 Bay Ave., Ocean City (609–398–3049). *Brigantine Sailboards,* 406 West Shore Dr., Brigantine (609–226–2727). *Eastern Sailboards,* 202 Bay Ave., Ocean City (609–391–9650).

Water skiing. *Lawasaki Wheelhouse,* 501 Atlantic Ave., Point Pleasant (908–899–4050). *Maurita's The Skiers Place,* 2800 Rte. 37, Toms River (908–270–6404). *Shore Ski School,* 1154 17th Ave., Belmar (908–681–3838). *Bayside Boats,* Rte. 35 & Bay Blvd., Seaside Heights (908–793–8535). *Pelican Harbor,* Rte. 37, Pelican Island (908–793–1700). *Speed & Ski,* 916 Palen Ave., Ocean City (609–398–0424).

SPECTATOR SPORTS. The No. 1 spectator sport, by far, is boxing. Atlantic City casino-hotels compete fiercely to promote the best fight. Every July, the Ladies Professional Golf Association (LPGA) holds one of its tournaments at the Sands Country Club. Call 609–441–4000 for details.

Atlantic City Race Course. Rte. 322 and Rte. 40, McKee City, Hamilton Township (609–641–2190). Thoroughbred horse races are held from May to Sept., every day except Tues. and Sun. Post time: 7:15 P.M. Grandstand fee: $2.50.

Monmouth Park. Oceanport Ave., Oceanport (908–222–5100). Thoroughbred horse racing, early June through August, Mon.–Sat. Post time: 1:30 P.M. Admission to grandstand: $2.25.

New Jersey Horse Park, at Stone Tavern, Rte. 524, Allentown, 6 mi. east of Exit 7A of NJ Turnpike (609–259–0170). This new 140-acre park is the state's first major horse show grounds with 4 barns and 800 stalls, polo fields, a grand prix course, and a large hunt course.

Raceway Park. Rte. 527, Englishtown (908–446–6370). Home of National Hot Rod Association's Summer Nationals. Drag racing, motocross, bicycle motocross. Open: Mar.–Nov. Ticket prices range from $6–$12.

The Mattix Run Equestrian Center, Moss Mill Rd., Smithville. Features one of the best polo teams in New Jersey, sponsored by Resorts International. All matches are played at 1:30 P.M. Admission is $3. Call 609–344–6000 for information.

Wall Stadium, Rte. 34, Wall (908–681–6400). Call for information on events.

BEACHES. The wonderful beaches are the lifeblood of the Jersey Shore. Virtually the entire 127-mi.-long shoreline is covered with soft, rock-free, white sandy beaches. Better yet, you'll find that once you start wading into the water the bottom is also sandy. You don't have to worry about stubbing your toe on nasty, jagged underwater rocks.

Most towns have lifeguards on duty at public beaches (houses along the shore line will indicate a beach is private). And there is usually a marina within a few miles where one can rent a sailboat, board sail, jet ski, or fishing charter boat. There are usually places to change (sometimes these charge), though generally it's easier to wear your swimsuit to the beach.

Except for Atlantic City, Wildwood, and Cape May Point, every community requires some sort of a beach tag (seasonal, weekly, daily, or weekend). As a general rule, the small towns on Long Beach Island charge the least. The southern part of the coast, south of Bay Head, is somewhat cheaper than the northern half. Daily rates range from $2 to $8. In 1989, prices actually dropped!

CHILDREN'S ACTIVITIES. On the New Jersey Shore, you won't have to worry much about entertaining children. The beach will do it for you. And it's fun just to walk along the boardwalk, visit an arcade, and eat a hot dog. However, there are a few special sites worth seeing if you need a change of pace.

Fantasy Island Casino Arcade. Beach Haven beach, Long Beach Island (609–492–4000). Features many rides, ice cream parlor, miniature golf, video arcade.

Lucy the Elephant. 9200 Atlantic Ave., Margate (609–823–6473). This huge elephant, built as a real estate promotion a century ago, is six stories high and weighs 90 tons. Children can walk through it. It is open on weekends from May to Oct., 10 A.M.–5 P.M.; late June until Labor Day, daily, 10 A.M.–8:30 P.M. The fee is $1.50 for adults; $1 for children.

Wildwood Amusement Park. Situated right along the ocean, the 2-mi. stretch between 26th St. and Fun Pier in Wildwood has the largest concentration of amusement rides and arcade games in the state. Try Mariner's Landing, Nickel's Midway Pier, Morey's Pier, and Seaport Village; all have a plethora of games.

Storybook Land. Black Horse Pike, Cardiff (609–641–7847). This unique amusement park features characters and scenes from nursery rhymes and fairy tales. Included are rides, souvenir shop, playground, picnic areas. Seasonal hours. $6.50 admission fee.

HISTORIC SITES AND HOUSES. See also National and State Parks, above, and Museums, below. *Atlantic County Historical Society,* 907 Shore Rd., Somers Point (609–927–5218). The Victorian Museum features a short slide show of early Atlantic City. There are also a genealogical research library and a maritime museum. It is open year-round, Wed.–Sat., 10 A.M.–noon, 1–4 P.M. Free.

Cape May Point Lighthouse. At Cape May Point, at the far southern tip of the state, this lighthouse served as the guiding light of sailors centuries ago. Call 609–884–5404. Offers best view in region. Ground floor is free; tower charge (for view) is $3.

Gardner's Basin. 800 N. New Hampshire Ave., at the Inlet, Atlantic City (348–2880). A turn-of-the-century fishing village offers a lot, including a chance to board a tall ship, see special shows at the aquarium, visit the museum, sightsee, shop, and eat at a nice restaurant. Free. Open May–Sept., 11 A.M.–4 P.M..

Monmouth Battlefield State Park, Rte. 33, Freehold, just off Rte. 9 (908–462–9616). The place where Molly Pitcher became famous during a Revolutionary War battle. This is also the setting for the historic Craig House, visitors center, and playgrounds.

Ocean City Historical Museum, 409 Wesley Ave., Ocean City (609–399–1801). Contains several rooms filled with antique furniture. Mannequins wear turn-of-the-century clothes. A special room contains artifacts from the *Sindia,* a four-masted ship that sank off Ocean City in 1901. Hours: 1 P.M.–4 P.M., Tues.–Sat., Mar. through Nov. Free.

Physick Estate–Mid-Atlantic Center for the Arts, 1048 Washington St., Cape May (609–884–5405). The house, built in 1881, is classic Victorian. It holds an extensive museum of Victorian furniture, clothing, toys, and other artifacts. Open every day except Fri. in summer; on weekends in spring and fall. Free.

Somers Mansion, Shore Rd., Somers Point (609–927–2212). This is the oldest house in Atlantic County, built around 1725. It's partially furnished with original pieces from that era. It also has a great view of Great Egg Harbor Bay. Open year-round, Wed.–Fri., 9 A.M.–noon, 1–6 P.M.; Sat., 10 A.M.–noon, 1–6 P.M.; Sun., 1–6 P.M. Free.

Towne of Historic Smithville, Rte. 9, 12 mi. north of Atlantic City (609–652–7777). This beautiful little village is a replica of an 1800s Colonial village. It has cobblestoned paths, a little pond, and about 75 specialty shops. Open daily. Free. Thirty-five of these shops were recent additions with the opening of *The Village Greene at Smithville* with carousel, miniature railroad, and paddle boats on a lake. Free concerts and entertainment in season. Brand new is the *Smithville Antique Center* with 100 dealers in 30 shops. A few of them are very good.

Wheaton Village, Glasstown Rd., Millville (609–825–6800). This is a replica of a late-1800s glass-making town. You can watch glass-making and buy the finished product. Open 7 days a week, 10 A.M.–5 P.M. Admission: $3.50 adults; $2.50 students.

MUSEUMS AND GALLERIES. See also Historic Sites and Houses.

Atlantic City Historical Museum, Garden Pier, Atlantic City (609–347–5844). Features displays on theaters, nightlife, piers, the beach, and the Boardwalk. Other exhibits show contributions of various ethnic groups. Also houses Atlantic City Art Center, which has rotating special exhibits, plus photography, paintings, sculpture. Open 9 A.M.–4 P.M., seven days a week. Free.

Barnegat Light Museum. 5th and Central Aves., Barnegat Light (609–494–3407). Original one-room schoolhouse of Long Beach Island now houses original lens from the lighthouse. Also includes collection of historical items and memorabilia from the island's past. Open daily in summer; 2–5 P.M. No charge but donations accepted.

Long Beach Island Historical Association Museum, Engleside and Beach Aves., Beach Haven (609–492–0700). A series of exhibits portrays Long Beach Island life of long ago. Photos, books, and charts show the history of the commerce, leisure, and recreation of the area. Open 2–4 P.M., weekends; 7–9 P.M., weekdays, during summer. Charge: $1, adults; 25 cents for children. Formal programs Mon. at 7:45 P.M., during July and Aug.

Noyes Museum, Lily Lake Rd., Oceanville (609–652–8848). One of the better museums in the area. Has good rotating exhibits, plus collection of American art from Fred Noyes. There are working decoys and decoy-carving demonstrations.

Open 11 A.M.–4 P.M., Wed.–Sat.; noon–4 P.M., Sun. Admission: $1.50, adults; $1, senior citizens; 50 cents, children.

Ocean City Historical Museum. 18th St. and Simpson Ave. (609–399–1801). Shows 19th century furnishings, fashions, dolls, marine and wildlife exhibits, and Indian artifacts. Open June–Aug., Mon.–Sat. 10 A.M.–4 P.M.; Sept.–June, Tues.–Sat., 1–4 P.M. Donations requested.

ARTS AND ENTERTAINMENT. Music. The New Jersey Shore is much better suited for lovers of contemporary music than for classical or jazz enthusiasts. All the casinos, at one point or another throughout the year, bring in the top musical performers in the world for concerts. Contact the casinos directly for more information or pick up a copy of *Atlantic City Magazine.*

There are a few opportunities to see operas, symphonies, or string quartets at local Shore communities. Contact the following organizations for their complete schedules: *Ocean Grove Great Auditorium,* Auditorium Sq., Ocean Grove (908–775–0035). *Atlantic City Community Concerts Association* (609–822–7927). *Atlantic Community College,* Rte. 322, Mays Landing (609–625–1111). *Garden State Art Center,* Garden State Pkwy., Holmdel (908–442–9200). *Glassboro State College,* Rte. 322, Glassboro (609–863–5000). *Ocean City Music Pier,* Boardwalk at Moorlyn Terrace, between 8th and 9th Sts. Free concerts on Sun. nights. Call 609–399–6344 for information. *Pinelands Cultural Society Weekly Concert Series,* Rte. 9, Waretown Mall, Waretown (609–693–4188; 693–5491). *South Jersey Symphony Orchestra* (609–691–8572). *Ocean City Music Pier,* Boardwalk at Moorlyn Terrace Ocean City (609–399–2629).

Theater. A few local theaters in the Shore region put on well-known Broadway plays and musicals. Some of these are within casino-hotels in Atlantic City. *Atlantis Dinner Theatre,* Country Club Rd., Little Egg Harbor, NJ 08087 (609–296–2444). *Guggenheim Theatre,* Monmouth College (908–222–7241). *Jenkinson's Boardwalk Playhouse Dinner Theatre,* Boardwalk, Pt. Pleasant, NJ 08742 (908–892–0764). *Joseph P. Hayes Surflight Summer Theatre,* 211 Engleside Ave., Beach Haven, NJ 08008 (609–492–9477; 492–9710). *MidAtlantic Stage.* Operated by Mid-Atlantic Center for the Arts, 1048 Washington St., Cape May, NJ 08204 (609–884–5404). *South Jersey Regional Theater.* Gateway Playhouse, Bay and Higbee Aves., Somers Point (609–653–0553). *Spring Lake Theater Company.* Spring Lake Memorial Community House Theatre, 3rd and Madison Ave., Spring Lake (908–449–4530 or 908–449–1415). *Stockton State College.* Jimmie Leeds Rd., Pomona (609–652–1776).

ACCOMMODATIONS. There are literally thousands of motels, hotels, and country inns within a few blocks of the Atlantic Ocean along the New Jersey Shore. Many of these places are open six months a year, with summer being their primary season.

As a result, people planning a trip to the Shore should keep two things in mind: (1) Since the Shore is so accessible to the major East Coast population centers, it is necessary to make reservations as far ahead as possible, preferably at least a month; (2) due to this demand, the prices for accommodations are rather high.

Prices are highest from Memorial Day to Labor Day. In spring and fall, they can be 50% less than in summer. For places that stay open year-round, the prices also plummet as much as 50% from the summer rates, from $80 to $40, for example.

Atlantic City casino-hotels offer 2- and 3-day package deals. Prices are often lower at casinos if you stay from Mon. through Thurs. Many places on the sea charge much more for an ocean-view room. Also, many places impose a two- or three-night minimum for weekend stays during the summer.

The prices listed below pertain to the in-season (highest) rates for a standard double room. The price categories are as follows: *Super Deluxe,* $160 and higher; *Deluxe,* $110–$160; *Expensive,* $80–$110; *Moderate,* $60–$80; and *Inexpensive,* under $60.

Super Deluxe

(Casino-Hotels)

Bally's Grand. Boston and Pacific Aves. at Boardwalk, Atlantic City, NJ 08401 (800–257–8677 or 609–347–7111). Each of the 518 rooms faces the sea. Casino has a Victorian decor. Health club with pool, Opera House Theater, 8 restaurants, arcade, 2 lounges.

Bally's Park Place. Park Pl. and Boardwalk, Atlantic City, NJ 08401 (800–772–7777 or 609–340–2000). Has 1,300 guest rooms; 9 restaurants and 3 lounges. The Park Cabaret features a Las Vegas–style musical revue. Fresh flowers and greenery dominate the casino. The casino also has a 100-ft.-high escalator, surrounded by a waterfall.

Caesars. Arkansas Ave. at Boardwalk, Atlantic City, NJ 08401 (800–257–8555 or 609–348–4411). Offers 645 rooms, 15 shops, swimming pool, health club, tennis, platform tennis, and the Circus Maximus theater. Also has 5 dining rooms, 2 restaurants, 2 coffee shops, 3 cocktail lounges, indoor swimming pool, 3 tennis courts on roof.

Claridge. Indiana Ave. at Boardwalk, Atlantic City, NJ 08401 (800–257–8585 or 609–340–3400). The first "skyscraper" hotel in Atlantic City, the 500-room Claridge has been remodeled. It has split-level casino, cabaret theater, glass-enclosed swimming pool, health spa, indoor gardens, 2 dining rooms, 2 restaurants, a coffee shop, 3 lounges, and ice-cream parlor.

Harrah's Marina. 1725 Brigantine Blvd., Atlantic City, NJ 08401 (800–2–HARRAHS or 609–441–5000). Away from other casinos, on Absecon Inlet near the Inland Waterway and Farley State Marina. There are 8 shops, beauty salon, 5 dining rooms, 2 restaurants, a cafeteria, 2 cocktail lounges, Broadway-by-the-Bay Theater, 3 lighted tennis courts, paddle tennis, table tennis, shuffleboard courts, game room, exercise room, and a 107-slip marina.

Resorts International. North Carolina Ave. at Boardwalk, Atlantic City, NJ 08401 (800–GET–RICH or 609–344–6000). The first casino-hotel in Atlantic City. Has 681 rooms, 4 dining rooms, 3 restaurants, 2 cocktail lounges, musical revue show, Superstar Theatre for big-name stars, health club, sundeck, squash courts, 2 pools, 1 heated, 1 indoor/outdoor.

Sands. Indiana Ave. and Brighton Park, Atlantic City, NJ 08401 (609–441–4000 or 800–257–8580). Has 500 rooms, 3 dining rooms, a coffee shop, 3 cocktail lounges, Copa Room for big-name entertainment, indoor, glass-enclosed pool, health club, 2 gift shops, and a championship 18–hole golf course.

Showboat. Box 840, Delaware Ave. at the Boardwalk, Atlantic City, NJ 08404 (609–343–4000). Built to resemble a giant cruise ship, standing 24 stories high and containing 506 rooms and suites. Main recreational features include a 60-lane bowling center, plus a swimming pool, sundeck, a miniature golf course, and 2 whirlpools. Eleven restaurants, and 6 lounges. The 400-seat Mardi Gras Lounge is the main showroom.

TropWorld. Iowa Ave. at Boardwalk, Atlantic City, NJ 08401 (800–257–6227 or 609–340–4020). Now has 1,000 rooms with recently completed addition. 18 restaurants, 4 lounges, outdoor pool, 9 shops, 2 outdoor tennis courts, paddle tennis, health club; TropWorld Showroom has big stars. The new tower includes a health club and Tivoli Pier—a complete indoor amusement park.

Trump's Castle. Huron Ave. and Brigantine Blvd., Atlantic City, NJ 08401 (609–441–2000 or 800–441–5551). Contains 700 guest units, 3 dining rooms, restaurant, coffee shop, cafeteria, 3 lounges, pool, 3 tennis courts, jogging track, health spa, shuffleboard courts, miniature golf. The Castle recently completed a $17-million renovation of the adjoining marina, which added 640 new, floating slips. In the Clubhouse at the marina, Trump's Castle runs a delightful dining room with great views of Atlantic City.

Trump Plaza. Mississippi Ave. at Boardwalk, Atlantic City, NJ 08401 (609–441–6000). 566 rooms, 9 shops, tennis, swimming pool, health club, Trump Theatre, 4 dining rooms, 2 restaurants, coffee shop, cafeteria, 5 lounges (including one on the roof), 2 outdoor tennis courts, full health club with pool.

Trump's Taj Mahal. Virginia Ave. at Boardwalk, Atlantic City, NJ 08401 (609–348–2000). The newest and most exotic casino hotel opened Apr., 1990. The 42-

story building is the tallest in New Jersey. It has 1,250 rooms, 12 restaurants, spa, health club, indoor pool, tennis, 6,000-seat arena and a 1,500-seat theater.

Non-Casino Hotel

Marriott Seaview Golf Club. On U.S. 9 and Galloway Tpk., Absecon, NJ 08201 (609–652–1800). Started as a luxurious private club in 1912, this now luxury country golf resort hotel has 299 rooms, 2 championship golf courses, heated and indoor pool, wading pool, saunas, whirlpool, playground, exercise room, 4 lighted tennis courts, 2 dining rooms and a restaurant. Entertainment. About 7 mi. from Atlantic City.

Deluxe

Atlantic Palace. 1507 Boardwalk, Atlantic City, NJ 08401 (609–344–1200). A new, all-suite luxury hotel. All 202 units complete with kitchen, whirlpool bath, HBO, valet parking. Complete fitness center. Restaurant. Two blocks from Sands casino.

Breakers. 1507 Ocean Ave., Spring Lake, NJ 07762 (908–449–7700). Has 64 units. Serves breakfast, lunch, and dinner. Features color TV, swimming pool, private beach. Some rooms have own refrigerator.

Flanders. 11th St. at Boardwalk, Ocean City, NJ 08226 (609–399–1000 or 800–345–0211). Finest facility in Ocean City, with 220 rooms. Has heated pool, 2 tennis courts, shuffleboard, miniature golf, dinner music, and social programs in summer. The lobby is filled with magnificent antiques. Open year-round.

Golden Inn. Oceanfront at 78th St., Avalon, NJ 08202 (609–368–5155). 160 rooms, on beach, attractive pool, balconies, 90 efficiencies, heated and wading pools, 5 rooms with whirlpools, 2 dining rooms. In-season entertainment.

Hewitt Wellington Hotel. 200 Monmouth Ave., Spring Lake, NJ 07762. South side of lake. Grand Victorian style lakefront and oceanview suites. Near beach. Open year-round. Good dining room.

Trump Regency. Florida Ave. and the Boardwalk, Atlantic City, NJ 08401 (609–344–4000 or 800–257–8672). This was formerly the Atlantis casino-hotel. Although the casino has been closed, this facility—bought by Donald Trump in 1989—has recently been extensively renovated and is now one of the poshest hotels in town.

Expensive

Admiral's Quarters. 655 Absecon Blvd., Atlantic City, NJ 08401 (609–344–2201). Near marina and Trump's Castle and Harrah's Marina casino-hotels. Has 67 rooms and suites, each with full kitchen. Some have balconies. Complimentary Continental breakfast. Free parking.

Atlas Motor Inn. 1035 Beach Dr., Cape May, NJ 08204 (609–884–7000 or 800–257–8513). Efficiencies and deluxe units, all with ocean views. Olympic pool, saunas, barbecues, restaurant, lounge with entertainment.

Beachcomber Resort Motel. 79th St. and Dune Dr., Avalon, N.J. 08202 (609–368–5171). 55 units with 23 efficiencies. Very attractive 2-bedroom and suite units. Heated and wading pools. Nearby restaurant.

The Chateau. 500 Warren Ave., Spring Lake, NJ 07762 (908–974–2000). Award-wining Victorian Inn on 2 parks and lake. 40 rooms, balconies, porches. Deluxe parlors, suites with marble bathrooms. Continental breakfast.

Columns by the Sea. 1513 Beach Dr., Cape May, NJ 08204 (609–884–2228). 11 units. Italianette designed country inn filled with antiques. Open end of May to mid-Oct. No children under 12. No credit cards. Reserve well ahead.

Comfort Inn. Dover Place, Black Horse Pike (US 40), Atlantic City West, NJ 08232 (609–645–1818). 198 units with attractive rooms. Heated pool, exercise room, coffee shop. Casino shuttle.

Desert Sand Resort. 79th and Dune Dr., Avalon, NJ 08202 (609–368–5133). This place has 89 units, 15 with kitchens. Amenities include a heated and an indoor pool, room service, sun deck, art gallery, and gift shop. Coffee shop, restaurant, and bar. Open year-round.

Engleside Motel. 30 Engleside Ave., Beach Haven, NJ 08008 (609–492–1251). 69 units. Offers efficiencies with kitchens, as well as regular rooms. Health spa, pool, sauna, Jacuzzi. Restaurant.

Fleur de Lis. 6105 Ocean Ave., Wildwood Crest, NJ 08260 (609–522–0123). Open end of Apr. to mid-Oct. Has 44 rooms at beachfront. Large heated and kiddie pool. 21 efficiencies.

Historic Grenville Hotel. 345 Main Ave. (Rte. 35), Bay Head, NJ 08742 (908–892–3100). Built 100 years ago, this restored Queen Anne structure has 33 rooms, 14 with antique furniture, Victorian restaurant with excellent French and Italian cuisine.

The Mainstay. 635 Columbia Ave., Cape May, NJ 08204 (609–884–8690). 12 rooms, elegant Victorian inn by ocean. Open Apr. 1–end Nov.

Marquis de Lafayette. Between Ocean and Decatur, Beach Dr., Cape May, NJ 08204 (609–884–3431 or 800–257–0432). Located in heart of Cape May's Victorian section. 73 units, 43 efficiencies. Every room is oceanfront. Top of the Marc dining room, a restaurant, bar, and a pool.

Normandy Inn. 21 Tuttle Ave., Spring Lake, NJ 07762 (908–449–7172). An 1888 Victorian inn with 19 rooms, end of lake. Breakfast only in dining room. Charming and elegant.

Port-O-Call Hotel. 1510 Boardwalk, Ocean City, NJ 08226 (609–399–8812). 99 rooms overlooking ocean and beach. Attractive place with pool at Boardwalk, sauna. Dining room. Off-season rates.

Quality Inn. Pacific and South Carolina Aves., Atlantic City, NJ 08401 (609–345–7070). Attached to circa late-1800 Quaker school, this is the first non-casino-hotel built in Atlantic City since the 1960s. 206 rooms, coffee shop, cocktail lounge, game room, gift shop. Located near Resorts International. Open year-round.

Inexpensive–Moderate

Econo Lodge. 328 White Horse Pike, US 30, Absecon, NJ 08201 (609–652–3300). Free morning coffee. Hot tub. Seniors discount. Free HBO.

Isle of Capri Motel. 5th Ave., North Wildwood, NJ 08260 (609–522–1991). 20 rooms, 5 efficiencies. Heated and wading pools.

Mediterranean Motel. 5th and Ocean Aves., North Wildwood, NJ 08260 (609–522–0112). Open mid-May to mid-Sept. 33 rooms, 22 efficiencies. Heated and wading pools.

Monta Cello Motel. Seaview and Denver Aves., Wildwood Crest, NJ 08260 (609–522–4758). 22 rooms. Pool.

BED AND BREAKFASTS. For those who want a change of pace, there are scores of high-quality B&B inns up and down the New Jersey Shore. Many of them retain the charm of the Shore's Victorian heritage.

Bay Head. Bentley Inn. 649 Main Ave., Bay Head, NJ 08742 (908–892–9589). Newly renovated, with 20 rooms. All rooms have air conditioning; about half have private baths. Rooms are in the $60–$80 range.

Conover's Bay Head Inn. 646 Main St., Bay Head, NJ 08742 (908–892–4664). Has 12 rooms, many filled with antiques. Two rooms have private baths. Owners provide transportation to and from Bay Head train station. Rates $60–$100.

Cape May. Brass Bed. 719 Columbia Ave., Cape May, NJ 08204 (609–884–8075). Eight double rooms; all contain brass beds and other antique furniture. Some private baths. The formal parlor has 12-ft. French doors, an 1840 drop-leaf oak desk, and a beautiful Indian rug. Rates approximately $80–$100.

Captain Mey's Inn. 202 Ocean St., Cape May, NJ 08204 (609–884–7793). This is a restored Gothic Revival Victorian cottage. Guest rooms are decorated with antiques, Dutch artifacts, and handmade quilts. Three of the 8 rooms have private baths; others are shared. Full breakfast served every morning. A collection of Delft blue china highlights the Victorian sitting room. Open year-round. Fee range is $80–$115.

The Queen Victoria. 102 Ocean St., Cape May, NJ 08204 (609–884–8702). Has 11 guest rooms, plus two luxury suites. The innkeeper, Joan Wells, used to be executive director of the Victorian Society of America; her knowledge of the Victorian era is clearly evident in every room. The guest rooms are furnished with authentic Victorian pieces of walnut, wicker, oak, and pine. Fresh flowers are put in every room; beds are covered with handmade quilts. Rates range $75–$125. Open year-round.

The Victorian Rose. 715 Columbia Ave., Cape May, NJ 08204 (609–884–2497). The very romantic interior of this 110-year-old, 7-room guest house is done in a rose-colored decor. In the main public rooms downstairs, big-band music is often played. Especially beautiful at Christmas. Breakfast is included in the rates, $70–$100.

Long Beach Island. The Barque. 117 Centre St., Beach Haven, NJ 08008 (609–492–5216). A 19th-century Victorian inn, ½ block from the Atlantic. Has 9 comfortable rooms and a spacious porch. Continental breakfast. Rates $70–$95, in season.

Spring Lake. Ashling Cottage. 105 Sussex Ave., Spring Lake, NJ 07762 908–449–3553). Built in 1887, this 10-room rambling house is decorated with fine antiques. Homemade breakfast every morning. One block from sea. Double room (private bath) about $50–$115. Shared bath is cheaper.

Carriage House. 208 Jersey Ave., Spring Lake, NJ 07762 (908–449–1332). Eight spacious, airy rooms; most have private baths. Guests can use the living room with color TV and the big, shaded front porch, or sit at umbrella tables in beautiful backyard, which has flowers and trees. Complimentary coffee is served in morning. A double room (private bath) about $75–$95.

RESTAURANTS. Vacationers at the Jersey Shore will have an almost infinite variety of restaurants to choose from. Virtually every seaside town has a selection of fancy, moderate, or fast-food places. Although nearly every type of ethnic food is represented, the two specialties of the Shore seem to be Italian and seafood dishes.

As you might expect in a summer-vacation atmosphere, dress codes are very casual in most establishments. Only the poshest restaurants, such as those in Atlantic City casinos, require a jacket and tie for men, for example.

During the busy summer season, it is very wise to make a dinner reservation at the finer establishments, especially on weekends. Many restaurants close down for the winter. Always call ahead in the off season to verify that a place is open.

The price categories of Shore restaurants are: *Super Deluxe,* $35 and above; *Deluxe,* $20–$35; *Expensive,* $15–$20; *Moderate,* $10–$15; and *Inexpensive,* below $10. This covers the price of a typical 3-course meal for one person (drinks, tax, and tip not included).

Super Deluxe

Alexander's Inn. 653 Washington St., Cape May (609–884–2555). Offers a distinct Victorian elegance, with tuxedoed waiters. New American cuisine features sautéed sweetbreads served in puff pastry with brown sherry sauce, roast Cornish game hen with apple and wild rice stuffing, and broiled jumbo shrimp with garlic and lemon sauce. D, 6–10 P.M., daily except Tues.; Sun. brunch, 10 A.M.–1 P.M.; weekends only Dec.–Mar. Reservations recommended. No liquor license; BYOB. Entertainment Fri.–Sat. AE, MC, V.

By the Sea. Bally's Park Place Casino. Park Pl. and Boardwalk, Atlantic City (609–340–2000). Features terrific views and candlelight dining. Seafood entrees. D only, 6 P.M.–midnight. AE, DC, MC, V.

Delfino's. Trump's Castle Casino, Huron Ave. and Brigantine Blvd., Atlantic City (609–441–2000). Continental dining, Mediterranean decor. D, 6 P.M.–midnight. AE, DC, MC, V. Open Wed.–Sat.

Ivana's. Trump Plaza Casino, Mississippi Ave. and Boardwalk, Atlantic City (609–441–6000). Intimate, romantic atmosphere; French cuisine. D, 6 P.M.–midnight. AE, DC, MC, V. Closed Mon.

Mad Batter. 19 Jackson St., Cape May (609–884–5970). In a Victorian guest house, Carroll Villa. Specialties are from Mexico, Southeast Asia, and Indonesia. Cajun and Creole dishes also served. Fun and eclectic; even has its own pastry shop. During summer, open for breakfast and lunch (times vary). B, L: 8 A.M.–2:30 P.M. D, 5:30–10 P.M. Bring own wine. MC, V. Closed Nov.–March.

Meadows. Harrah's Marina, 1725 Brigantine Blvd., Atlantic City (609–441–5000). This hotel's flagship restaurant offers both spectacular French cuisine and great view of bay. Decorated in mahogany and brass. D only, 6 P.M.–midnight. AE, DC, MC, V.

Mes Amis. Sands Casino, Indiana Ave. and Brighton Park (609–441–4000). First-class French restaurant, with Cajun specialties of the house. D only, 6 P.M.–midnight. AE, DC, MC, V.

Mr. Kelley's. Showboat, Delaware Ave. at Boardwalk, Atlantic City (609–343–4000). Gourmet Continental cuisine, served in elegant, European-style dining room. D only, hours vary according to season. AE, DC, MC, V.

The Oaks. Bally's Grand Casino, Boston and Pacific Aves., Atlantic City (609–547–7111). One of the largest and best steak houses in town. Noted for its beautiful mural diorama on wall. Specialties of the house are Tomanian tenderloin, New York sirloin, or filet mignon. L, 11:30 A.M.–3:15 P.M.; D, 6–10 P.M. AE, DC, MC, V.

Ocean Gate Restaurant & Tavern. 401 Monmouth Ave., and E. Bayview, Ocean Gate, NJ 08740 (908–269–2888). Features American and Continental cuisine. Lovely tasteful setting. Fine service. Started 1986. L, Mon.–Sat. 11:30 A.M.–3 P.M.; D, Mon.–Sat. from 4:30 and Sun. from 4. Sun. brunch noon–5 P.M. AE, MC, V.

Pear Tree. 42 Ave. of the Two Rivers, Rumson (908–842–8747). In one of classier areas of the northern Shore (current home of Jersey's favorite son, Bruce Springsteen). Specializes in Northern Italian and French cuisine. L, Mon.–Fri., 11:30 A.M.–2:30 P.M.; D, Mon.–Thurs., 6–9 P.M.; Fri., 6–9:30 P.M.; Sat. 6–10 P.M.; Sun. 4–9 P.M. Sun Brunch 11:30 A.M.–2:30 P.M. AE, DC, MC, V.

Deluxe

The Bluffs. 575 East Ave., Bay Head (908–892–1710). One of the most popular restaurants on the northern shore. Continental fare specialties include quail, Peking duck, pheasant, grilled pork tenderloin; lighter fare includes lobster and many fish dishes. Reservations required. D, Tues.–Thurs., 5–10 P.M.; Fri.–Sat., 5–11 P.M.; Sun., 4:30–8:30 P.M. AE, MC, V.

Bookbinders Bay Club. Amherst and Monroe on the Bay, Margate (609–823–2121). A branch of the famous Philadelphia eatery of the same name, this place is just as good. Specialties include seafood, chops, steaks, pasta, and lobster. D, 5–10:30 P.M. AE, MC, V.

Chuckling Oyster. 280 Ocean Ave. (Rte. 36), Sea Bright (908–291–8880). Offers terrific view of Navesink River. Seafood specialties such as she-crab soup, smoked shark, and fresh shad row. Entertainment Fri.–Sat. L, Mon.–Fri., 11:30 A.M.–3 P.M.; D, Mon.–Thurs., 5–10:30 P.M.; Fri.–Sat., 5–11:30 P.M.; Sun. 3–9:30 P.M. Sun. brunch. AE.

Grenville Hotel Restaurant. 345 Main St., Bay Head, NJ 08742 (908–892–3100). Continental and American cuisine in Victorian dining room of old restored inn. Features grilled seafood, certified black Angus beef and veal. Only Renault wine. AE, MC, V.

Harry's Lobster House. Ocean Ave., Sea Bright (908–842–0205). A Shore institution since 1933. Offers many varieties of fresh seafood, and imaginative dishes. D, 5–10 P.M., daily; closed Tues. AE, DC, MC, V.

Knife and Fork. Atlantic and Pacific Aves., Atlantic City (609–344–1133). Known for excellence since 1927, with fine seafood, steaks, fresh vegetables. Huge wine list. D, 5:30–10:30 P.M. Reservations suggested. AE, MC, V.

Lobster House. Fisherman's Wharf, Cape May (609–884–8296). Seafood specialties include lobster, shrimp, scallops, lobsters. Great homemade desserts. Be prepared to wait; outdoor bar on the marina. L, Mon.–Sat., 11:30 A.M.–3 P.M.; D, Mon.–Sat., 5–10 P.M.; Sun., 2–9 P.M. AE, MC, V.

Periwinkle's. 1070 Ocean Ave., Sea Bright (908–741–0041). Cozy, intimate restaurant, Continental fare, with an assortment of sauce dishes. Excellent desserts. L, Wed.–Fri., 11:30 A.M.–2:30 P.M.; D, Mon.–Fri., 5:30–11 P.M.; Sun. 4–9:30 P.M. brunch, 10 A.M.–2 P.M. Sun. Closed Tues. AE, MC, V.

Ram's Head Inn. 9 W. White Horse Pike, Absecon (609–652–1700). Hangout of celebrities working at nearby Atlantic City. Superb all-around menu; 4-star rated. L, noon–3 P.M., Mon.–Fri.; D, 5–9:30 P.M.; Sat. 5–10 P.M.; Sun. 3:30–9 P.M. Reservations recommended. Jackets required. AE, DC, MC, V.

Expensive

A&J Blue Claw. Ocean Drive, Cape May (609–884–5878). Charming restaurant that overlooks the marina. Specializes in freshly prepared local seafood. Intimate cocktail lounge. D, 5 P.M.–midnight. MC, V.

Dock's Oyster House. 2405 Atlantic Ave., Atlantic City (609–345–0092). One of the best seafood places in town—it's been around since the turn of the century. Specializes in lobster and salmon. D, Tues.–Sun., 5–11 P.M. Closed Mon. Reservations advised. AE, MC, V.

Doris & Ed's. 348 Shore Dr., Highlands (908–872–1565). Excellent seafood appetizers and entrées. Great lobster bisque and crabmeat Virginia. Best place to be seated is the porchlike dining room. Look for specials listed on blackboard. Has fiercely loyal clientele. Closed Jan. and Feb. D, 5–10 P.M., Wed.–Fri.; 5–11 P.M., Sat.; 3–10 P.M., Sun. AE, DC, MC, V.

The Mooring Restaurant. 9th St. & Bay Ave., Beach Haven (609–492–2828). Overlooks Little Egg Harbor Bay. Several seafood specials and prime rib daily, served with salad bar. D, 5–10 P.M., May 25–Oct. 13. Late-night menu, 10 P.M.–2 A.M. Reservations needed for parties of 7 or more. Entertainment. AE, MC, V.

Orsatti's. 24 S. North Carolina Ave., Atlantic City (609–347–7667). Locals have come here for more than a half century. Specialties include filet mignon, crab Imperial, and other seafood. Regular menu is augmented by a large selection of fresh fish displayed on ice on a clear-domed cart rolled to your table. Favorites are wedding and snapper soups. Piano bar. Valet parking. D, 4–11:30 P.M., Tues.–Sat. AE, DC, MC, V.

Tuckahoe Inn. Rte. 9 and Beesley's Point Bridge, Beesley's Point (609–390–3322). Situated on Great Egg Harbor Bay; inns have been at site since 1736. Seafood, roast duck, and prime rib are specialties. L, noon–3 P.M. daily; D, 3–9 P.M. Sun.–Fri., 3–10 P.M. Sat. AE, MC, V.

Moderate

Angelo's Fairmount Tavern. 2300 Fairmount Ave., Atlantic City (609–344–2439). One of best Italian places on shore. Open 7 days. L, 11:30 A.M.–2 P.M.; D, 5–10:30 P.M. No credit cards.

Aubrey's. Arkansas and Pacific Aves., Atlantic City (609–344–1632). Features glass-enclosed sidewalk patio. Salads, croissants, pastries are specialties. D, 4–11 P.M.; late snack, 11 P.M.–7 A.M. AE, DC, MC, V.

Culinary Garden. 841 Central Ave., Ocean City (609–399–3713). Friendly, cozy place, serving seafood and Italian fare. Homemade desserts. No liquor license. Open daily. L, 11 A.M.–2 P.M.; D, 5–9 P.M. Closed Nov.–Apr. AE, DC, MC, V.

Dear's Place. 9400 Atlantic Ave., Margate (609–822–8830). Famous for homemade specialties, ranging from French toast to corned beef. Also known for excellent desserts. Open 7:30 A.M. to 9 P.M. every day, except Tues.

Ed Zaberer's Restaurant. 400 Spruce Ave., North Wildwood, NJ 08260 (609–522–1423). This friendly, old-style family restaurant specializes in steaks, seafood, and nosh items. Home baking. Open May 1–Sep. 30, 4 P.M.–10 P.M. AE, MC, V.

Golden Inn. Ocean front at 78th St., Avalon, (609–368–5155). American/European cuisine is featured here, and specialties include bouillabaisse, blackened redfish, roast duck, and steak au poivre. AE, MC, V.

Lagoon. 3700 Brigantine Blvd., Brigantine (609–266–7057). Nice place for intimate dining. General-interest menu, with seafood, steak, prime rib, and veal. D, 4–10 P.M. weekdays; till 11 P.M. Fri., Sat. AE, DC, MC, V.

Little Rock Cafe. 5214 Atlantic Ave., Ventnor (609–823–4411). Artsy-type café, featuring fresh fish, charbroiled foods, omelettes. L, 11 A.M.–3 P.M.; D, 5:30–9 P.M.; Sun. brunch, 10 A.M.–3 P.M. No credit cards.

Sabatini's. 2210–14 Pacific Ave., Atlantic City (609–345–4816). Offers several different pasta dishes, plus seafood, steaks, chops, and prime ribs. Hours: noon–8 A.M., daily. AE, MC, V.

Yvonne's. 525 Ocean Blvd., Long Branch (908–222–3456). Located in a Georgian colonial-style home, built in the 1800's. Specialties include French-style dishes such as duckling à l'orange, frog legs, chateaubriand, and coq au vin. Main dining room offers ocean views. Open daily, 11 A.M.–11:30 P.M.; open to 10 P.M. Sun. Closed from late Nov. to early spring. All major credit cards.

Inexpensive

Canal 42 Restaurant. Corner of 42nd Park Rd., Sea Isle City (609–263–2300). Good, cheap seafood is offered here, where specialties include mussels with creamy white garlic wine sauce or marinara sauce. Clams on half shell. Open daily 11:30 A.M.–10 P.M. No credit cards.

Casa Comida. 336 Branchport Ave., Long Branch (908–229–7774). Offers cheap but excellent Mexican fare. Specialties include fajitas and mesquite-grilled seafood. Daily lunch buffet. Open 11:30 A.M.–10 P.M., Tues.–Thurs.; 11 A.M.–11 P.M. Fri., Sat.; noon–10 P.M. Sun. Closed Mon. AE.

Cici's Pizza. 311 Boardwalk and Central Ave., Point Pleasant Beach (908–892–5005). Serves great pizza and sandwiches; small dining room. Open 11:30 A.M.–10 P.M., Sun.–Thurs.; 11 A.M.–midnight Fri., Sat.

Lou's. 5011 Ventnor Ave., Ventnor (609–823–2733). Hasn't changed in 40 years; same wooden booths . . . and same great food. Everything is homemade. Specialties are corned beef, fresh roast turkey, steaks, salads, and extra-thick milk shakes. Open 8 A.M.–10 P.M. daily in summer; to 9 P.M. in winter. No credit cards.

Seaport. 7801 Long Beach Blvd., Harvey Cedars (908–494–4389). Serves deli sandwiches year-round; B, L, D in summer; hours 8 A.M.–11 P.M.; jazz brunch on Sun. BYOB. Closed Tues., Wed. in winter. No credit cards.

White House Sub Shop. 2301 Arctic Ave., Atlantic City (609–345–1564). Currently performing show-business celebrities often dash in here; it's known as one of the best submarine sandwich shops in the East Coast. Open 10 A.M. to midnight. No credit cards.

LIQUOR LAWS. In New Jersey, a person must be 21 or older to buy or drink alcoholic beverages. This is enforced fairly strictly in Shore communities. Each town has its own closing deadline for taverns and bars.

NIGHTLIFE. As one might expect, the nightlife along the New Jersey Shore centers around Atlantic City, which is now arguably the second-most-exciting nighttime city on the East Coast, behind New York. The casino-hotels, which dominate Pacific Ave. along the Boardwalk, remain open until 4 A.M. on weekdays and 6 A.M. on weekends. In addition to the gambling—black jack, roulette, slot machines, baccarat, and so on—every casino has one big showroom theater where top entertainers perform. All the casinos have several piano bars and lounges. In addition to the casinos, many taverns and local nightclubs cater to both tourists and residents. Some of these local establishments stay open until 6 A.M., for the benefit of both local casino workers who work odd hours and night-owl tourists.

Nightlife on other shore points is much more sedate; most places close down by midnight. Live entertainment at these spots features local singers and musicians.

The Casinos

It is pretty easy, in most cases, to obtain tickets for various casino acts. Tickets for big, headline engagements can be purchased at individual casino box offices or local Ticketron outlets or charged on credit-card numbers through Teletron (North Jersey: 908–627–0532; New York: 212–947–5850; Pennsylvania: 215–627–0532). In all cases, try to reserve as early as possible.

Bally's Grand. Boston and Pacific Aves. (609–347–7111). Opera House Theatre showcases big-name stars. Gatsby's offers mellow music and piano bar.

Bally's Park Place. Park Pl. and Boardwalk (609–340–2000). The Park Place Cabaret features a musical revue. Billy's Pub offers nightly entertainment ("Top 40" lounge acts), as does Upstairs in the Park.

Caesars. Arkansas Ave. at Boardwalk (609–348–4411). Circus Maximus has continual headliners. Other performers at Forum lounge and Cleopatra's Barge, a night club.

Claridge. Indiana Ave. at Brighton Park (609–340–3400). Palace Theatre has old Broadway musicals, plus occasional headliners. The Celebrity Cabaret features live entertainment, usually two shows a night.

Harrah's Marina. 1725 Brigantine Blvd. (609–441–5165). Broadway-by-the-Bay Theatre offers first-rate performers during most of the year. The Atrium Lounge, a beautiful garden bar with waterfalls, trees, and skylights, is a good setting for late-night drinks. Bay Cabaret Theater has live music.

Resorts International. North Carolina Ave. at Boardwalk (609–344–6000). Top-name performers entertain in the Superstar Theatre. Carousel Cabaret offers musical revues, Las Vegas-style. Rendezvous Lounge is cozy, quiet. Coconut Bar Room with big band entertainment.

Sands. Indiana Ave. at Boardwalk (609–441–4000). Copa Room features nationally known stars. Punch Bowl and Players lounges offer continual music. Island Club admits Ambassador Club card holders.

Showboat. 800 Boardwalk, Box 840, Atlantic City, NJ 08406 (609–343–4000). Top show-biz performers and musical revues appear in the 400-seat Mardi Gras Showroom, whose decor simulates New Orleans' famed Bourbon St. The Hall of Fame Lounge is decorated with authentic sports memorabilia, and contains televisions showing sporting events. Bourbon Street Lounge. Mississippi Steak and Seafood Lounge, a popular bar.

TropWorld. Iowa Ave. at Boardwalk (609–340–4000). Tropicana Showroom features major show-business headliners. Top of the Trop lounge offers jazz and a great view of the ocean from the 21st floor. The Comedy Stop features top-notch comedians. The quiet, intimate Sandbar has four large aquariums filled with tropical fish. Sizzle's, a sports lounge, and the Red Lips Saloon at the Tivoli Pier.

Trump's Castle. Huron Ave. and Brigantine Blvd. (609–441–2000). King's Court Theatre is the center for a great variety of acts; recent show had dancing, singing, and ice skating. Nightly entertainment is provided at Viva's and the Casino Lounge. D.J.'s is fine piano bar. Boardwalker Bar.

Trump Plaza. Mississippi Ave. at Boardwalk (609–441–6000). Trump Theater has headliners. Jezebel's is nice piano bar. Swizzle's—a two-level bar—overlooks the casino.

Trump Taj Mahal. Virginia Ave. at Boardwalk (609–449–1000). Mark G. Etess Arena has 5,200 seats for major sports events and concerts. Oasis Lounge at the main lobby features light music, Paddy's Saloon is a 120-seat bar in the atrium. The Casbah Night Club Lounge is multileveled featuring live bands and reviews. Rain Forest is a 50-seat bar.

Other Shore Night Spots

The Bluffs. 575 East Ave., Bay Head (908–892–1114). The best-known bar in town, a local institution. Extremely informal; many people wear bathing suits in early afternoon. Can be hard to find; there's no sign. Hours vary: early afternoon to late evening.

Carney's. Beach Dr. and Decatur St., Cape May (609–884–4425). Lively rock club, located right on beach. Mostly younger crowd.

Le Club. Enclave condominiums, Lincoln Pl. and Boardwalk, Atlantic City (609–347–0400). Offers excellent jazz. Highlights include a great view of ocean and a nice clam bar.

Copa Club. Large disco in the Sands, Indiana Ave. and Brighton Park, Atlantic City (609–441–4000). In late evening during weekends, the main showroom of this casino-hotel becomes a dance club, open to 5 A.M.

Crazy Jane's. Bay Avenue, just north of Somers Point Circle, Somers Point (609–653–8999). One of several hot new clubs on the Southern Shore. A DJ spins records 9 P.M.–3 A.M. Open Wed.–Sun.

Gilhooley's. 9314 Amherst Ave., Margate (609–823–2800). An upscale club, filled with greenery. DJ every night. 4 P.M. to 4 A.M. (winter); 11 A.M.–4 A.M. (summer).

Green Parrot. Rte. 33, Neptune (908–775–1991). One of the leading rock clubs on the entire shore, featuring many up-and-coming groups. Live music is played Wed.–Sat. nights. Reggae on Thurs. nights.

The Owl Tree. 80th St. and Long Beach Blvd., Harvey Cedars, Long Beach Island (908–494–8191). Live performers specialize in folk-rock. Soloists appear during the week; duos on weekend. Hours vary depending on season; call ahead.

Pete's Bar and Grill. Hwy. 35 and Delaware Ave., Point Pleasant (908–892–3382). Good food and good live music. Very informal. One of the most popular clubs on the northern Shore. Visitors dance to the music played by a disc jockey every night during summer. Open 11 A.M.–11 P.M., Mon.–Sat.; 10:30 A.M.–11 P.M. Sun.

Playpen. 9900 Atlantic Ave., Wildwood (609–729–3566). One of the largest clubs on the entire Jersey Shore. Has four separate areas—the Rock Room, the Game Room, Club Malibu Dance Room, and Sir Winston's Pub and Deli. Live rock bands Wed.–Sat.; DJ other nights. Open to 5 A.M. in summer.

The Stadium. Plaza Blvd., Sea Girt (908–449–1444). Perhaps the best-known sports bar on northern Shore. Several sporting events at once are shown on the many television sets strategically placed throughout the bar.

Steamers. MacArthur Blvd., Somers Point (609–926–0505). One of newest and hottest discos in area. Live bands on Fri. and Sat. nights; DJ on other nights. Open 5 P.M.–3 A.M.

Summers Lounge. Maureen's Restaurant, Beach and Decatur, Cape May (609–884–3774). This tavern resembles an old-time Victorian pub. Local singers do saloon songs after 10 P.M., until 2 A.M. or later. Dressy attire preferred.

The Top of the Marq. Ocean St. and Beach Dr., Cape May (609–884–3431). Part of restaurant at top of Marquis de Lafayette Motel. Offers terrific view of sea. Dancing after 8:30 P.M., until 1 A.M. (sometimes later). Bar open 5 P.M.–1 A.M.; open May–Oct.

THE DELAWARE SHORE

The stretch of shore from Lewes, Delaware, south to Fenwick Island (at the Maryland border) is among the most beautiful seafront land in the East.

This area is accessible via the Cape May—Lewes Ferry, a pleasant 70-minute boat ride across Delaware Bay.

The major tourist areas, from north to south, are Lewes, Rehoboth Beach, Dewey Beach, Bethany Beach, and Fenwick Island.

Rehoboth Beach is Delaware's largest seaside summer resort is a favorite playground of residents up and down the Eastern Seaboard, especially humidity-weary residents of nearby Washington, D.C., giving it the name "Summer Capital." It's especially ideal for families, with a boardwalk, lots of daytime and nighttime activities, recreational opportunities, and great restaurants. The bandstand in the center of town has concerts on weekend evenings, and the convention hall has events scheduled throughout the summer.

About a mile south of Rehoboth Beach is Dewey Beach, which is much smaller but just as nice. It's only two blocks wide, so outdoor enthusiasts have a choice of sailboarding, water skiing, swimming, or fishing in either Rehoboth Bay (an inland bay two blocks to the west) or the Atlantic Ocean. Most swimmers, of course, choose to stay in the Atlantic.

The 10-mile stretch from Dewey Beach to Bethany Beach is composed mostly of Delaware Seashore State Park. Its fine public beaches are ideal for swimming, surfing, and fishing, as well as crabbing and clamming.

Bethany Beach and Fenwick Island are called the Quiet Resorts. Bethany's boardwalk appeals to many visitors because there are no arcades or other commercial ventures. The Bethany Beach Recreation Program provides daily summertime activities such as basketball and volleyball. Children's movies are shown in the evening twice a week. The Bethany Beach Bandstand features musical programs and other entertainment on weekends. Headquarters for this program are at Garfield Parkway and Pennsylvania Avenue, at the Christian Church Conference Grounds. For more information, call the Bethany Beach Town Hall (302–539–8011).

Fenwick Island, founded in 1677, has four miles of oceanfront and is laced with canals leading into Little Assawoman Bay.

Lewes, called the first town in the first state with over 350 years of history, was discovered by Henry Hudson in 1609 and in 1631 was selected by the Dutch as an ideal spot to build a whaling station. In 1682 it was named Lewes (loo-iss) in honor of a town in Sussex, England. It's an interesting town to explore, with museums and restored homes dating back to the 18th and 19th centuries. It is still a seafaring town and an East Coast port of call for a large fleet of charter fishing boats.

PRACTICAL INFORMATION FOR THE DELAWARE SHORE

HOW TO GET THERE. Lewes is about 85 mi. south of Wilmington, 120 mi. from Washington, and 108 mi. from Baltimore. It is not especially easy to get to; several two-lane highways must be taken to traverse the state from west to east. Eventually, you will want to end up on U.S. 9, which leads to downtown Lewes and Cape Henlopen State Park just east of Lewes, or Rte. 1, which runs north and south right along the shore and leads to all other shore points. The ferry from Cape May to Lewes leaves virtually every hour in summer during the day, every 2 hours in spring and fall, and about every 4 hours in winter. Rates are $4 for foot passengers and $16 per vehicle.

TOURIST INFORMATION. The main source of tourism information is the *Delaware Tourism Office,* 99 Kings Hwy., Box 1401, Dover, DE 19903 (800–441–8846; 302–739–4271). In Delaware, call 800–282–8667.

For specific information about lodging, restaurants, nightlife, and recreational opportunities in the Fenwick–Bethany Beach areas, contact: *Bethany-Fenwick Area Chamber of Commerce,* Rte. 1, Box 1450, Bethany Beach, DE 19930 (302–539–2100 or 800–962–7873).

For information about Rehoboth Beach and Dewey Beach, contact: *Rehoboth Beach-Dewey Beach Chamber of Commerce,* Box 216, Rehoboth Beach, DE 19971–0216 (800–441–1329; 302–227–2233).

For information about Lewes, contact: *Lewes Chamber of Commerce,* Box 1, Lewes, DE 19958 (302–645–8073).

STATE PARKS. *Cape Henlopen,* East of Lewes. Over 4 mi. and 300 acres of open shoreline where the Atlantic meets Delaware Bay. Here, the Great Dune rises 80 ft. above the shore, the highest sand dune between Cape Hatteras and Cape Cod. There are showers and facilities for **camping, hiking,** a nature trail, **bike** trails, **disc golf, tennis, swimming, fishing,** a **softball** field, and **basketball** courts. Cape Henlopen State Park, 42 Cape Henlopen Dr., Lewes, DE 19958 (302–645–8983).

Delaware Seashore., Rte. 1 between Rehoboth and Bethany beaches. Swimming, surfing, and fishing are major recreational activities along this sandy ocean beach. Campground on the Indian River Inlet has about 300 sites. Nearby is the *Indian River Marina,* 838 Inlet, Rehoboth Beach, DE 19971 (302–227–3071). This is the main **boating** and **fishing** center in beach area. There are launching ramps, a charter-boat fleet, and party boats. Main fish caught are flounder, sea bass, sea trout, bluefish, marlin, and tuna. There's a bait and tackle shop.

There are shower facilities, as well as areas for **sailing, dune-buggy driving, swimming, surfing,** and a special **fishing pier** designed for handicapped people.

The park is on Rte. 1, just south of Dewey Beach. Delaware Seashore State Park, Inlet 850, Rehoboth Beach, DE 19971 (302–227–2800).

Fenwick Island. A 1-mi. stretch encompasses the far southeastern corner of the state. It abuts the Maryland border. Nice beach; within the park.

ACCOMMODATIONS. When you stay on the Delaware coast, you can expect first-rate accommodations—and first-rate prices. This area is a classic example of "paying for location." Establishments on the beach can cost 50% more than places a few blocks away.

With very few exceptions, the hotels and motels in this area are open only for the summer season. As a rough rule of thumb, they open in early April and close down in October. Rates are cheaper before Memorial Day and after Labor Day.

Getting a reservation can be difficult, especially in July and Aug. Plan way ahead, if possible.

The price categories listed below are based on the cost of a double room during the high season (summer). *Deluxe,* above $100; *Expensive,* $80–$100; and *Moderate,* $60–$80.

Deluxe

Atlantic Sands. Boardwalk, between Maryland and Baltimore Aves., Rehoboth Beach, DE 19971 (302–227–2511 or 800–422–0600). One of the nicest facilities on whole Delaware Shore, right on boardwalk. Each room has private balcony and view of ocean. Swimming pool and all other luxuries. One of few places open year-round.

Henlopen Hotel. Lake Ave. and Boardwalk, Rehoboth Beach, DE 19971 (302–227–2551 or 800–441–8450 out of state; 800–282–8628 in state). Features 90 luxuriously appointed rooms—all have ocean views. Beautiful roof-top dining room. Open year-round.

Expensive

Admiral Motel. 2 Baltimore Ave., Rehoboth Beach, DE 19971 (302–227–2103 or 800–428–2424). 66 units. Right off beach, 60 ft. from Boardwalk. Pool, sundeck, in-room coffee, cable color TV, coffee shop. Open year-round.

The Bay Resort. Bellevue St. on the Bay, Box 461, Dewey Beach, DE 19971 (302–227–6400 or 800–922–9240). 68 units. Waterfront property on Rehoboth Bay. Built in 1984. All rooms face bay or pool; balconies, cable color TV, 3 stories, no elevator. Swimming pool. 1½ blocks from ocean. Open Easter to Oct.

The Inn at Canal Square. 122 Market St., Lewes, DE 19958 (302–645–8499). Furnished with 18th-century reproductions. Continental breakfast in lobby. On waterfront close to dining and shopping.

Oceanus Motel. 6 Second St., Box 324, Rehoboth Beach, DE 19971 (302–227–9436 or 800–852–5011). 38 units. 3 stories, no elevator. Great location near restaurants and shops. Free morning coffee, guarded swimming pool. Open mid-Apr.–mid-Oct.

Surf Club. 1 Read St., Box 509, Dewey Beach, DE 19971 (302–227–7059 or 800–441–8341). This, one of the newer, fancier shore facilities, recently underwent major remodeling program. Has private beach. Enclosed balconies turn rooms into efficiencies. Swimming pool and European sauna. Open late Apr. to late fall.

Sandcastle Motel. 123 Second St., Rehoboth Beach, DE 19971 (302–227–0400 or 800–372–2112). Centrally located to beach, Boardwalk, shops, restaurants, and night spots. The 60 rooms feature wet bar with refrigerators, color cable TV; many have private balconies. Indoor/outdoor pool. Open year-round.

Moderate

The Addy Sea. Ocean View Pkwy., Box 275, Bethany Beach, DE 19930 (302–539–3707). A wonderful bed-and-breakfast place, with 14 guest rooms. Building nominated for the National Register of Historic Places. Decorated with antiques. Open for general public July and Aug. No credit cards.

Beach View Motel. Boardwalk and 6 Wilmington Ave., Rehoboth Beach, DE 19930 (302–227–2999). 38 units. One of newest facilities on the beach, with pool, color TV, shops. Some rooms with balconies.

Fenwick Sea Charm. Lighthouse Rd. and Oceanfront, Fenwick Island, DE 19944 (302–539–9613). Comfortable, cozy, well-maintained motel right on the ocean.

The New Devon Inn. 2nd & Market, Lewes, DE 19958 (302–645–6466). 24 rooms, 2 suites, antique furnishings. Open year-round. Charming place at a convenient location.

The Sands. Ocean Hwy., Fenwick Island, DE 19944 (302–539–7745). Just off the main beach; many 2nd-floor rooms have view of either ocean or bay. Cable TV with HBO, large swimming pool.

RESTAURANTS. There's a respectable number of good restaurants on the southern Delaware shore, offering most seafood. Many are open only six months a year, approximately May to Oct. Attire is usually casual, although the more elegant ones prefer a slightly dressier clientele. During the summer season, reservations are recommended.

The price ranges can be roughly divided into three categories: *Expensive,* $13–$20; *Moderate,* $10–$13; and *Inexpensive,* $5–$10. Prices are based on a complete dinner (drinks, tax, and tip not included).

Expensive

Café on the Green. 247 Rehoboth Ave., Rehoboth Beach (302–227–0789). Features fresh seafood, sautéed veal dishes, hand-cut steaks; prime rib. Open 7 A.M.–10 P.M. B, L, D. AE, MC, V.

Chez la Mer. 2nd & Wilmington Ave., Rehoboth Beach (302–227–6494). Open mid-April to New Year's Eve, 5:30 P.M.–midnight. Extensive wine list. Elegant dining, in a cozy French atmosphere in a restored house. Provence and local seafood specialties are featured. Reservations suggested in summer. AE, DC, MC, V.

Sea Horse. Rehoboth Ave. & State Rd., Rehoboth Beach (227–7451). Fresh seafood daily, as well as lamb chops, pork chops, steaks, prime rib. Open for lunch and dinner, year-round, every day. Sun. brunch. AE, DC, MC, V.

Moderate

Ann Marie's Italian & Seafood Restaurant. 2nd & Wilmington Aves., Rehoboth Beach (227–9902). Specializing in fresh seafood, steaks, and Italian cuisine. Lasagna is homemade. D, 5 P.M.–midnight, summer only. MC, V.

Rusty Rudder. Dickinson St. on the Bay, Dewey Beach (227–3888). Large complex, with terrace overlooking Rehoboth Bay. Serves lunch and dinner. Open 11:30 A.M.–9 P.M. weekdays; 11:30 A.M.–10 P.M. weekends. AE, MC, V. Open year-round. Summer concert series. Sun.–Thurs. in season.

The Spinnaker. 110 Rehoboth Ave., Rehoboth Beach (227–2770). Recently redecorated by new owners (this was formerly The Avenue). The place now has separate bar split off from main dining room. Specializes in fresh fish, with the area's largest seafood selection. Open year-round. 11 A.M.–9 P.M., Fri. and Sat. to 10 P.M., Sun. 8 A.M.–9 P.M. MC, V. Closed Mon., Tues. in winter.

MARYLAND'S ATLANTIC COAST

Ocean City, Maryland's Atlantic Ocean resort, is sun, sand, surf, and sky—a salt-air mecca of sun-washed days and soft summer nights, soaring gulls and sauntering bikinis, sandcastles, beach cottages, highrise hotels and condominiums. Inland from Ocean City (and Assateague Island to the south), Worcester County is a haven of rural tranquility. Here, along deep rivers with unusual Indian names, lie villages, hamlets, and towns that have changed little over the last century. Berlin, Snow Hill, Pocomoke City, and Whitehaven have all maintained their Victorian elegance.

Built along a barrier island that is often only four blocks wide, Ocean City stretches south from the Delaware state line for more than 156 city blocks. Blessed with 10 miles of sandy ocean beach, the city looks eastward toward the Atlantic and westward toward the mainland over a series of picturesque and protected bays—Montego, Big Assawoman, Isle of Wight, and Sinepuxent. The bays and the city's commercial boat harbor are open to the ocean through the Inlet between Ocean City and Assateague Island to the south.

Assateague Island

Assateague Island, like Ocean City, is a barrier strip of seashore and a major touring destination—but the similarity between the two stops there. Each has more than a fair share of sun, sand, and surf, but if Ocean City is the epicenter of activities and boardwalk fun, Assateague is the lovely and natural home of the Assateague pony, the great blue heron, white-tailed deer, the tern, and the gull.

Berlin is a small gem of the Eastern Shore with shaded streets, old homes, browseable shops, and a pleasant historic setting. In 1677 it was a land grant called Burley and by 1800 became a hamlet called Berlin. A substantial part of the town is a designated National Historic District and many buildings are in the Register of Historic Places.

North Assateague is the Maryland section of the island. The National Park Service has a headquarters and maintains a Visitor's Center (on your right) shortly before you cross the bridge over Sinepuxent Bay to Assateague. North Assateague is divided into three parts: six sandy miles of "wild" beach, accessible only on foot, on your left as you drive onto the island; Assateague State Park in the mid-section; and, to the south, Assateague Island National Seashore, another natural expanse of surf and sandy dunes. There is a State Park Information Center (with campground registration) on your left near the park end of Sinepuxent Bay Bridge.

And now, a word about those free spirits of the seashore—Assateague's famous wild ponies: They may look gentle, and usually they are, but they're also unpredictable—they kick and sometimes they bite, especially if you've been feeding them and then stop. It's really hard to blame them, considering the fact that their forebearers swam ashore from a foundering Spanish galleon in the 16th century and they've been munching on marsh grass and bayberry leaves ever since.

There are two herds of Assateague ponies on the island, a larger group in the Virginia section to the south, and a smaller herd in Maryland. Virginia's Chincoteague Volunteer Fire Department owns the southern ponies and manages an annual July roundup and auction; the National Park Service manages Maryland's Assateague's wild pony herd.

PRACTICAL INFORMATION FOR MARYLAND'S ATLANTIC COAST

HOW TO GET THERE. Most visitors will enter Worcester County by car: U.S. 113 or Hwys. 528/1 south from Delaware; U.S. 50 east from Salisbury to Ocean City, and then Rte. 90 to N. Ocean City; State Rte. 12 between Salisbury and Snow Hill; or U.S. 13 south from Salisbury or north from Norfolk, Virginia. North Assateague is accessible by car from Ocean City. Take U.S. 50 west for about a mile, then turn left on Rte. 611 (south). Go approximately 6 mi. and watch for the left turn (a short distance past "Frontier Town") over the New Bridge to Assateague Island.

THE BEACH. First there is the beach, then the Boardwalk, then the city, and finally the Bay. But it all starts with the beach, where Atlantic surf meets the shore. Ocean City's clean, wide beaches, which fringe the ocean for 10 sandy mi., lie totally within the city's limits, stretching northward from the Inlet to the Maryland-Delaware line. Sunbathing, swimming, jogging, shelling, and people-watching are the main beach pursuits, but designated sections of the beach have been set aside for fishing and surfboarding. If you've never splashed in salt water, ridden a bike along the boardwalk in early morning, listened to the raucous cry of a gull, or helped a child build a sandcastle, don't worry—it's really easy; you'll catch on soon enough.

THE BOARDWALK. Ocean City is proud of its oceanfront boardwalk—and rightly so. About 3 mi. long (the Inlet to 28th St.), the Boardwalk is open every day for strolling, jogging, and ocean or people watching. Many shops, restaurants, and amusements are located there. Bicyclists may use the boardwalk between 6 and 10 in the morning. The Boardwalk Train runs the length of the boardwalk about every 20 minutes, Memorial Day through Labor Day. The train also runs weekends in May, and on weekends Sept.–Dec. The fare is $1 one way, $2 round-trip.

Ocean City Life Saving Station Museum. Located at the south end of the boardwalk, overlooking the Inlet, the Life Saving Station Museum traces Ocean City's history from its founding as a fishing village in the 1800s to the resort it is today. It also houses five saltwater aquariums, with sea horses and other native fish. Also included is sand from 100 beaches around the world, maps of shipwrecks off Ocean City's coast, and antique bathing costumes from the turn of the century. Housed in the former Life Saving Station, built in 1891, the museum is open daily from 11 A.M. to 10 P.M., June through Sept.; 11 A.M.–4 P.M. daily May and Oct.; and weekends the rest of the year, noon to 4 P.M. Call 301–289–4991. Adults, $1.25, children 12 and under, 50 cents.

Jolly Roger. 30th St. and Coastal Hwy. A full-scale family amusement complex, featuring a water slide, golf courses, parks, driving range, major roller coaster and kiddie rides, and mini-speed and bumper boats. Food is available. Free dolphin shows, high-wire acts, diving exhibitions, family theater, and a petting zoo are all available. One admission for all rides. Open May to Sept. daily, noon to midnight.

Trimper's Amusement Park. Inlet at the Boardwalk. A complete amusement park with a giant waterslide, a double reverse-gravity roller coaster, bumper cars, and one of the world's oldest operating wood carousels. Open daily June–Aug., 10 A.M.–1 A.M.; open weekends May and Sept., 10 A.M.–1 A.M.

Pier Amusements. Inlet at the Boardwalk. Giant waterslide park, thrilling rides, games and amusements, giant Ferris wheel.

OLD TOWN. "Downtown" Ocean City, bounded by South First St. on the Inlet to 15th St. and the ocean to the bay, features Inlet Village with fine restaurants and shops, "the widest beach in town" on the ocean side, docks and fishing boats on the bayside, interesting shops, hotels, and restaurants throughout Old Town, and live and lively entertainment from Commander Boardwalk Cabaret (14th St. and Boardwalk) and The Purple Moose Saloon (Boardwalk between Talbot and Caroline Sts.). Marty's Playland, Trimper Rides (featuring an antique merry-go-round), and Bamboo Mini Golf for the younger crowd. And, for everyone, two favorites are Rayne's Olde Fashioned Soda Fountain (7 Dorchester St., just off the Boardwalk) or Zip's Happy Kid's, "the Original Make-Your-Own-Sundae" (203 N. Baltimore Ave. or Boardwalk near Division St.).

WATER SPORTS. In Ocean City's calm bay waters, water-sports lovers can choose from a spectrum of activities, including sailing, jet-skiing, waterskiing, parasailing, and windsurfing. Call the Visitor's Information Center at 301–289–2800 for updated rental information on all water sports.

CRUISES. The following is a partial listing of evening, ocean, and bay cruises out of Ocean City. Times, number of daily cruises, and destinations are subject to change, so call before making your plans. Boats include *Angler,* evening scenic cruises, 7, and 9 P.M., Talbot St., 289–7424, *Bay Queen,* Assawoman Bay cruises, 10:30 A.M., 12:15 P.M., and 2 P.M., Shanty Town Pier, 289–0926; *Captain Bunting,* Dorchester St., 289–6720. Twilight cruises, leaving 7:30 P.M., *Mariner,* Atlantic cruises, 7:30 P.M., Talbot St., 289–9125, *Miss Ocean City,* 1st St., Ocean City, 289–8234. Evening scenic cruises in the Atlantic. Apr.–Oct., 6:25, 7:55, and 9:25 P.M. and *Misty,* cruise to Assateague Island; Bahia Marina, Bay between 21st and 22nd Sts., 10:30 A.M. and 12:30, 2, and 4 P.M., 289–7438. One can also take a half-day sail on *The Therapy*—a 34-foot yacht sailing out of Shanty Town Marina (289–8818). For updated cruise information, call 289–2800.

Tangier Island Cruises. Memorial Day through Oct., the *Steven Thomas* leaves from Crisfield, MD, at 12:30 P.M. to Tangier Island. Chartered by Capt. John Smith in 1607, Tangier is in Chesapeake Bay, 14 mi. from Crisfield. Little has changed since settled by John Crockett and his wife and four sons in 1686. Most local residents (850) still speak with Elizabethan accents and this quaint island has narrow streets for walking and cycling. Boat returns to Crisfield at 5:15 P.M.

Tillie the Tug. Docked at Snow Hills' Sturgis Park along the Pocomoke River. 1-hour narrated tours of river, daily at 11:30 A.M., 2, and 5 P.M., $3. Call 301–632–2240.

SPORTFISHING. Ocean City is the White Marlin Capital of the World, and the Ocean City Marlin Club is one of the oldest fishing clubs in the country. The

$50,000 White Marlin Open is held in mid-Aug., with the White Marlin Tournament following Labor Day Weekend. In addition to white marlin, deep-sea fishing includes blue marlin, tuna, wahoo, and dolphinfish. Outboard motor boats may be rented from marinas; private charterboats may also be hired. All headboats sail early each morning for ocean fishing, and boats may be chartered with captain and mate. Some boats available are: *Pursuer,* a 42-footer, docked at Talbot St. Pier (289–9125); *Canyon Lady,* Dorchester St. (289–2154); and *Wet Whiskers,* Talbot St. (289–9125). Another large fishing boat at Talbot is the *Baby Grand,* a 48-footer (289–6980). The *Tortuga,* 24 passengers, and *Taylor Maid,* 78 passengers, operate out of Bahia Marina, on the Bay between 21st and 22nd Sts. (289–7438). More fishing information is available from the Visitor Information Center (301–289–2800).

OPEN-AIR ANTIQUES & CRAFTS MARKET. Ocean City Convention Center (north parking lot), 40th St. and Coastal Hwy., 289–2800. Open Fri., Sat., and Sun., 9 A.M. to 5 P.M. (if it doesn't rain), early May through early Oct. Ocean City's giant outdoor market features antiques, second-hand items, and handmade crafts. The Convention Center in season presents top entertainers, big dance bands, trade shows, etc. In April there is a Vacation Travel Show and the World Championship Carving Competition.

CHILDREN'S ACTIVITIES. Frontier Town. Rte. 611, a short drive south of Ocean City (289–7877). Rte. 50, west one mi., then south a few mi. on Rte. 611. The Wild, Wild West on the Eastern Shore—a family theme park with bank holdups, Indian dancers, gunfights, and cancan girls, plus rides on a riverboat, steam train, stagecoach, and ponies. Open daily during the summer, 10 A.M. to 6 P.M. One admission for all shows and rides. Light lunches at Longhorn and Golden Nugget saloons. Adults, $7; over 65 and ages 4–13, $6.

OUTDOOR PARKS AND PICNIC AREAS. Shad Landing Park, boating and picnicking on the Pocomoke River, Rte. 113 south of Snow Hill; **Milburn Landing Park,** west bank of Pocomoke, Rte. 364, north of Pocomoke City; **Pocomoke River State Park,** Rte. 12, west of Snow Hill; **Byrd Park** in Snow Hill; **Stephen Decatur Park** in Berlin; **Pocomoke Cypress Swamps** (Pocomoke River State Park), accessible from Rte. 113, Pocomoke, and—of course—**Assateague Island State Park and National Seashore.**

HISTORIC SITES. Snow Hill. A charming and historic hamlet—and Worcester County seat—on the Pocomoke River, Rtes. 12 and 394. Founded in 1642, Snow Hill was once a busy river port. The Julia A. Purnell Museum, 208 West Market St., is Snow Hill's showcase of Worcester County lore. The museum is open weekdays, 9 A.M. to 5 P.M., and weekends, 1 P.M. to 5 P.M. (301–632–0515). The Nassawango (Iron) Furnace at Furnace Town, one of the oldest industrial sites in Maryland, has been registered as a National Historic Place, Rte. 12, Old Furnace Rd., near Snow Hill. Call 301–632–2032. Open daily 11–5, first weekend in Apr.–last weekend in Oct. Adults, $1.50; under 14, 75 cents.

ACCOMMODATIONS. Ocean City is a family seaside resort, filled with sun worshippers of all ages. It's also attracting an increasing number of visitors during the balmy days of spring, the crisp days of autumn, and even the quiet months of winter. Room rates in the following selection of accommodations will vary widely between summer and winter, and our categories are intended merely as a guide. When possible, call or write before you commit yourself. If this isn't possible, pin down the price before you sign in, perhaps even request to see the unit or room. Finally, keep in mind that this is a *selection* only, and we can't include all of the many excellent accommodations in the Ocean City resort area. The price categories are broken down as follows: *Deluxe,* $125 and up; *Expensive,* $80–$125; *Moderate,* $60–$80; and *Inexpensive,* under $60. These are peak season rates, discounts usually apply in winter.

Carousel Hotel. *Deluxe.* 118th St., on the Beach, 21842 (301–524–1000 or 800–641–0011). Efficiencies, 20 large suites, with June to Sept. rates higher. Dining room open 7:30 A.M.–10 P.M. (summer till 11.), two cocktail lounges, open year-round. Three lighted tennis courts, indoor ice-skating rink, heated indoor pool, health spa. Senior discount. AE, DC, MC, V.

Coconut Malorie Hotel. *Deluxe.* 60th St. and the Bay, 21842 (301–723–6100 or 800–767–6060. There are 86 opulent suites with a Caribbean flavor offered here. Marble baths, whirlpools in every room, pool, health and racquet club privileges; 2-day minimum stay in season. Next door to Fager's Island Restaurant. AE, DC, MC, V.

Dunes Manor Hotel. *Deluxe.* 28th St. and the Ocean, 21842 (301–289–1100 or 800–523–2888). 170 units, 10 efficiencies. All rooms have a view of the ocean. Decorated in Victorian elegance. Indoor/outdoor pool, exercise room. Victorian Room Restaurant, Zippy Lewis Lounge. Afternoon high tea. Senior discount. AE, DC, MC, V.

Lighthouse Club Hotel. *Deluxe.* 56th St. in the Bay (301–524–5400 or 800–767–6060). This is Ocean City's only hotel on a small island. There are 23 elegant sumptuous suites, each overlooking the bay. Marble baths, fireplaces, whirlpools in each suite. All major credit cards.

Sheraton Ocean City Resort & Conference Center. *Deluxe.* Oceanfront at 101st St., 21842 (301–524–3535 or 800–638–2100). 250 rooms, and 22 2-bedroom condos, most with an ocean view. Horizon Restaurant & Nightclub, casual Breakers Club, and Lenny's Beach Bar & Grill (in season). Large conference center. Heated indoor pool and fully equipped health spa. Open year-round. AE, DC, MC, V.

Quality Inn-Ocean Front. *Expensive–Deluxe.* On the Oceanfront & 54th St., 21842 (301–524–7200 or 800–228–5151). 130 rooms. Year-round inn with 5-story plant-filled atrium. Indoor/outdoor pool, tennis. Atrium Cafe & Bar. AE, DC, MC, V.

Quality Inn-Boardwalk. *Expensive.* Boardwalk at 17th St., 21842 (301–289–4401 or 800–228–5151). 172 rooms. All efficiencies, with honeymoon suites. Bike rentals, game room, indoor/outdoor pool, steam and exercise room, ocean front restaurant. Open year-round. AE, DC, MC, V.

Ramada Inn Ocean City. *Expensive.* 138th St., 21842 (301–250–1100 or 800–492–1873). 201 rooms in a year-round inn. Rooftop Lookout Restaurant & Lounge with nightly entertainment in summer. Indoor heated pool, game room. Senior discounts.

Best Western Flagship Ocean Front. *Moderate–Expensive.* 26th St. and Oceanfront, 21842 (301–289–3384 or 800–638–2106 out-of-state, or 800–492–3147 in-state). 93 rooms. Jonah and the Whale Seafood Buffet. Exercise room, lighted tennis, indoor/outdoor pool. The Flagship is on the ocean. Open year-round. AE, DC, MC, V.

Holiday Inn-Ocean Front. *Moderate–Expensive.* 67th St. and Ocean Front, 21842 (301–524–1600 or 800–HOLIDAY). 217 rooms, open year-round. Indoor/outdoor and children's pools. Tennis, exercise room. Restaurant and lounge. AE, DC, MC, V.

Phillips Beach Plaza Hotel. *Moderate–Expensive.* Oceanfront at 13th St., 21842 (301–289–9121). 86 rooms. Phillips-by-the-Sea Restaurant. Cocktail lounge and Beach Plaza Cafe. Open all year. AE, DC, MC, V.

Spinnaker Motel. *Moderate–Expensive.* 18th St. and Baltimore Ave., 21842 (301–289–5442 or 800–638–3244). 100 rooms, all units with kitchens. Private balconies with ocean views. Heated outdoor pool with sundeck. Coffee shop. Open mid-March to Mid-Oct. AE, MC, V.

Stowaway Americana Hotel. *Moderate–Expensive.* 22nd St. and Boardwalk, 21842 (301–289–6191). 132 rooms, open year-round. Pool and restaurant.

Surf and Sands Motel. *Moderate–Expensive.* 23rd St. and Boardwalk, 21842 (301–289–7161). 95 rooms, open Easter to Oct. Coffee shop, breakfast and lunch. Outdoor and heated kiddy pool.

Sahara Motel. *Moderate.* 19th St. and Oceanfront, 21842 (301–289–8101 or 800–638–1600). 113 rooms, mid-April through Sept. Poolside, oceanview, and oceanfront rooms. Pool.

Misty Harbor. *Inexpensive–Moderate.* 25th St. and Philadelphia Ave., 21842 (301–289–7284). 57 rooms, 26 apartments and efficiencies. Apartments $250 and up, July through Labor Day. Rowboats. Outdoor pool. Open Apr.–Sept.

Spanish Main Motel. *Inexpensive.* 305 14th St., 21842 (301–289–9155). 43 units. Boat slips available, tennis courts nearby. Within walking distance of beach and restaurants. Outdoor pool. Offers singles, doubles and efficiencies.

RESTAURANTS. As is true with any popular resort city, visitors to Ocean City are faced with a happy but bewildering selection of places to eat—fast food to fabulous food, hot dogs to chateaubriand. The following selection of restaurants is not meant to be all-inclusive. We have attempted to include eating places that will appeal to a wide variety of tastes and pocketbooks—family groups to swinging singles, the inexpensive to the wildly extravagant. Keep in mind that at least half of these restaurants are open only during the peak season. The price categories below are broken down as follows: *Expensive,* above $15; *Moderate,* $8–$15; *Inexpensive,* under $8.

Fager's Island. *Expensive.* 60th St. in the Bay (524–5500). In the Coconut Malorie Hotel. Fine dining 5:30–10 P.M. (Fri. and Sat. to 10:30) indoors or on 4 spacious outdoor decks. The Raw Bar is especially excellent. Spectacular sunsets on the quiet side of the beach. Entrees from traditional to exotic. Open year-round. Best wine list in the state. Live entertainment nightly in season, weekends off season. AE, DC, MC, V.

The Garden. *Expensive.* 45th St. Village (289–4592). Continental cuisine and fresh seafood. Extensive wine list. Reservations. Early-bird specials. Open year-round, 5 P.M.–11 P.M. (Oct.–May, till 9:30). Closed Sun., Mon., Tues., Nov–Apr. DC, MC, V.

BJ's on the Water. *Moderate–Expensive.* 75th St. and the Bay (524–7575). Soups, salads, sandwiches, steaks, seafood. Enclosed bayfront dining room and outside deck. Open every day, year-round. 11 A.M.–2 A.M. Major credit cards. A second BJ's recently opened on 1st Street and the Bay.

The Embers. *Moderate–Expensive.* 24th St. and Philadelphia Ave. (289–3322). Steaks, seafood, prime rib. Casual, friendly atmosphere. Open March through Nov., 4:30 P.M.–2 A.M. Reservations preferred. Major credit cards.

The Hobbitt Restaurant and Bar. *Moderate–Expensive.* 81st St. and the Bay (524–8100). Fish, fowl, and veal française—all entrees served with salad and fresh-baked bread. Fresh seafood daily. Overlooking Bay. Entertainment weekends. Open 5–10:30 P.M. (till 10 off season). MC, V.

Reflections. *Moderate–Expensive.* 67th St. and Coastal Hwy. (524–5252). In Holiday Inn Oceanfront. French-American cuisine in the European tradition. A respectable wine list, with local seafood, beef, and veal. Year round. Open 7 A.M.–2 P.M. and 5–10 P.M. AE, DC, D, MC, V.

The Wharf. *Moderate–Expensive.* 128th St. and Coastal Hwy. (524–1001). Seafood, veal, steaks, and chicken in a nautical atmosphere. Lounge with happy hour between 5 and 6 P.M. Adjacent to Wharf Seafood & Spirits Market. Open 11 A.M.–2 A.M. Feb.–Dec. AE, MC, V.

Angler. *Moderate.* Talbot St. and the Bay (289–7424). Sit on the dock and enjoy the Bay. Fresh seafood daily, breakfast, lunch, and dinner. Reservations suggested. Eat indoors or on huge outdoor deck. Open 5 A.M.–2 A.M.

Harpoon Hanna's. *Moderate.* Rte. 54 and the Bay. (723–1570). Open year-round. Soups, salads, steaks, fresh seafood, including lobster. Enclosed waterfront dining, with spacious outdoor deck. Live entertainment. AE, DC, MC, V.

JR's North. *Moderate.* 131st St. and Coastal Hwy. (723–2600). Ribs, steak, onion ring loaf. Open year-round, every day, 4 P.M.–midnight.

The Marina Deck. *Moderate.* 306 Dorchester St. (289–4411). Fresh seafood, with a raw bar. Domestic wine list, but there's always that strawberry shortcake or pecan pie. Famous for its coconut muffins. Live lobster tank. Open 11:30 A.M.–1 A.M., Easter to mid-Oct.

Paul Revere Smorgasboard. *Moderate.* Boardwalk at 2nd St. (524–1776). Roast beef, pork chops, chicken, and 100 other home-cooked entrees, including homemade bread and desserts. All-you-can-eat buffet. Children's prices. April through Oct., 4–10 P.M. MC, V.

Phillips by the Sea. *Moderate.* Boardwalk and 13th St. (289–9121). A "seafood adventure" in Phillips Beach Plaza Hotel, featuring crab cakes, crab claws, and steamed spiced shrimp. Open for breakfast and dinner only. Old World atmosphere. Open year-round. AE, DC, MC, V.

Philips Crab House. *Moderate.* Boardwalk at 21st St. Informal and popular family restaurant with casual, nautical atmosphere. Children's menu. Open noon–11 P.M. Apr. 1–Oct. 31. AE, MC, V.

Tony's. *Moderate.* 33rd St. and Coastal Hwy. (289–4588). A full Italian menu, with homemade pastas. Live entertainment in the Sandbar Lounge. Open 5 P.M.–midnight.

Harrison's Harbor Watch. *Inexpensive–Moderate.* Boardwalk South, overlooking the Inlet (289–5121). A spectacular view and overstuffed sandwiches; raw bar and fresh local seafood. Open May 15–Oct. 15, 5–10 P.M. (July 4–Sept. 3, 4:30–10:30 P.M.). AE.

Alaska Stand. *Inexpensive.* 50th St. and Coastal Hwy. (524–5050). This family standby serves great food in an informal atmosphere. Best hamburgers in Ocean City. Open Apr.–Dec., 11:30 A.M.–9 P.M.

Atrium Cafe & Bar. *Inexpensive.* 54th St. and the Oceanfront, at Quality Inn (723–1646). Serves sandwiches, light drinks and frozen drinks. Open atrium filled with tropical plants and trees. Open 9 A.M.–10 P.M., year-round. AE, MC, V.

Gold Dust Deli. *Inexpensive.* 115th St. and Coastal Hwy.—"Home of Mama Del Camp" in Gold Coast Mall (723–DELI). Dine in or carry out. Sandwiches, spaghetti, and bagels and lox, all in the $3 to $6 range. Beer and wine. Open year-round.

Weitzel's Restaurant. *Inexpensive.* 51st St. and Coastal Hwy. (524–6990). A family favorite, serving crab cakes and chicken, informal style. Also a carryout. Open April–Sept., 8 A.M.–11 P.M.

PHILADELPHIA

by
JOYCE EISENBERG

Joyce Eisenberg is a freelance writer and editor whose travel and feature articles have appeared in local and national publications. She is editor of the Delaware Valley edition of Travelhost Magazine *and a contributor to* Fodor's Philadelphia.

Philadelphia is a city of charming contradictions. It counts among its most beloved performers both the world-famous Philadelphia Orchestra, which plays at the opulent, dignified Academy of Music on Broad Street, and the sequined-and-feathered Mummers string bands, which on New Year's Day strut and prance along that same street. It's a city nationally known by gourmets for its sophisticated new cuisine and praised by locals for the quality of its "junk" food—cheese steaks, hoagies, and soft pretzels with mustard. The city's residents include descendants of the staid Quaker founding fathers, the self-possessed socialites of the Main Line, and the sports fans who have reportedly booed the Easter Bunny when their team failed them.

Although Philadelphia is the fifth-largest city in the nation with close to 1.7 million people, it has maintained the feel of a friendly small town. It's a cosmopolitan, exciting, but not overwhelming city, a town that's easy to explore on foot but big enough to keep surprising even those most familiar with it.

City planners have pegged Philadelphia as a very livable city. The same features that keep the native-born in residence—neighborhood spirit, nationally prominent cultural institutions, a respect for the city's history, excellent restaurants, scenic public parks, and a manageable cost of living—make a vacation here especially rewarding for the visitor. There are three aspects of the city that all tourists should sample: its history, its cultural attractions, and its neighborhoods. (There are 109 by one count, but we'll just pick a few.)

Philadelphia was the birthplace of the nation and the home of its first government. The spirit of the early days is palpable along the cobbled streets and in the red-brick Georgian buildings in the city's historic district, which runs from the Delaware River west to about 6th Street.

Most of the sites that played an important role in history are clustered in the 46-acre Independence National Historical Park, known as America's most historic square mile. Like most of the city, this area is best explored on foot. The place to orient yourself is at the *Visitor Center,* 3rd and Chestnut streets, where you can get a map of the park's important sites and some tips on what to see if your time is limited. Then, hurry over to *Independence Hall* to get a place at the head of the classes of schoolchildren who've come to tour one of our nation's most precious gems. The hall, built in 1732, is the place where Thomas Jefferson's eloquent Declaration of Independence was signed and later where the U.S. Constitution was written.

The *Liberty Bell,* which had hung in the belfry of Independence Hall since 1753, was moved to a glass pavilion on Independence Mall north of the Hall in 1976, during the Bicentennial celebration. The bell fulfilled the words of its inscription when it rang to "proclaim liberty throughout all the land unto all the inhabitants thereof," beckoning Philadelphians to the State House Yard to hear the first reading of the Declaration of Independence.

The underground museum at *Franklin Court,* once the site of Ben Franklin's home, is an imaginative tribute to that Renaissance man. You can dial-a-quote to hear his thoughts; pick up a telephone and call his contemporaries to find out what they really thought of him.

Old City, the neighborhood north of Market Street and Independence National Historical Park, was always "the other side of the tracks." Its earliest residents were a strict sect of William Penn's followers called "stiff Quakers." South of Market, in *Society Hill,* lived the "World's People," the wealthier Anglicans who arrived after Penn and who loved music and dancing—pursuits the Quakers shunned. Society Hill's southern neighbor, *Southwark,* contained the modest dwellings of artisans and craftsmen. Today, many homes in these three areas have been lovingly restored by pioneers who began moving in to the city 15 to 20 years ago and who stemmed the tide of urban decay. Inspired urban renewal efforts have transformed vast empty spaces into airy lofts; colonial houses have been rehabbed, and charming courtyards rediscovered. As a result, these areas are not just showcases for historic churches and mansions, but living, breathing neighborhoods.

A tour of Old City will complete your picture of colonial Philadelphia. *Christ Church,* an architectural gem, was the only Anglican church in the city for at least half a century; 15 signers of the Declaration of Independence worshiped there, and Ben Franklin lies in its burial ground. *Elfreth's Alley,* the oldest continuously occupied residential street in the country, offers a glimpse of what much of colonial Philadelphia looked like.

One of the most famous residents of this neighborhood was Betsy Ross, who is credited with sewing the first Stars and Stripes. Her authentically furnished home is a top tourist attraction. Nearby is the *Friend's Meeting House,* a Quaker building of simple lines, in keeping with their faith. Penn's life and achievements are depicted in exhibits within.

Society Hill was—and still is—Philadelphia's showplace. It is a fashionable residential district where beautifully preserved Colonial, Georgian, and Federal homes are interspersed with some historically relevant tourist attractions, like the *Powel* and *Hill-Physick-Keith* houses, and numerous old churches. The area is well-marked with signs for self-guided tours. On a leisurely stroll here, you'll stumble upon an occasional hitching post, or wrought-iron foot scraper, see exquisite ironwork on railings and balconies, and enjoy delightful gardens. At 2nd and Pine streets is *Head House Square,* a colonial marketplace that is the site of the *Head House Crafts Fair* on summer weekends.

Between 6th Street and the Delaware River are three other areas worth exploring. *Penn's Landing,* the six-block-long river-front promenade running from Market Street to South Street, is a popular spot for concerts, festivals, and sunning. Permanent attractions include the *Port of History Museum,* and several historic ships turned floating museums. The dramatic *Chart House* restaurant, "docked" at Lombard Street has fine views of the Delaware, one of the world's largest freshwater ports, and the city skyline.

South Street, the dividing line between Society Hill and Southwark, is where you'll see Philadelphia at its funkiest. This city's version of New York's Greenwich Village, it is an eclectic, artsy strip (from Front Street to about 8th Street) of antique shops, bookstores, galleries, trendy boutiques, café's, and many of the restaurants that began the city's recent restaurant renaissance. One of Philadelphia's liveliest late-night spots, South Street is great for people watching.

Across from Independence Mall is *The Bourse,* a magnificently restored Victorian commodities exchange housing a collection of moderately priced stores catering to tourists, a floor of ethnic eateries, and a supper club and popular disco. A five-screen movie theater opened in mid-1990.

The mile-long *Benjamin Franklin Parkway,* which stretches from City Hall to the Philadelphia Museum of Art, is the city's museum row. There may be more cultural attractions per square foot here than along any boulevard in the world. The parkway was designed by French architects to be the city's Champs Elysées, a broad street lined with fountains, trees, sculpture, and flags of many nations. To explore the parkway and Fairmount Park just beyond, your best bet is to head to the *Visitor Center* at 16th Street and John F. Kennedy Boulevard to board the Fairmount Park Trolley bus, which stops at all the museums and many sites in the park.

At Logan Circle are the *Academy of Natural Sciences,* the oldest institution of its kind in America and best known for its displays of stuffed animals in their natural habitats, dinosaurs, birds, and extinct and endangered species, and the *Franklin Institute Science Museum* and *Planetarium.* The Institute, the national memorial to Ben Franklin, is as stimulating and imaginative as was its namesake. A gigantic walk-though human heart and astronomy and aviation halls delight both children and adults. In 1990, the 200th anniversary of Franklin's death, Philadelphia staged a year-long celebration of his life and legacy with special exhibits and commemorative events. In the spring of 1990, the Franklin Institute's Futures Center and Omniverse Theater opened.

Nearby is the *Rodin Museum,* which houses a priceless collection of the sculptor's originals and castings and the largest exhibit of his works outside the Musée Rodin in Paris. Crowning the parkway atop a hill sits the Greco-Roman temple known as the *Philadelphia Museum of Art.* Ranked among the world's major art museums, it is Philadelphia's cultural highlight. Its collections include American crafts, furniture, and glass; Renaissance treasures; 20th-century art; and architectural acquisitions like a Hindu temple, a medieval cloister, and a Chinese Buddhist temple hall.

Beyond the museum is *Fairmount Park,* the largest landscaped city park in the world. The park offers something for everyone—historic mansions furnished with period pieces, an authentic Japanese house, Victorian boathouses strung along Kelly Drive, the Philadelphia Zoo, hiking and biking

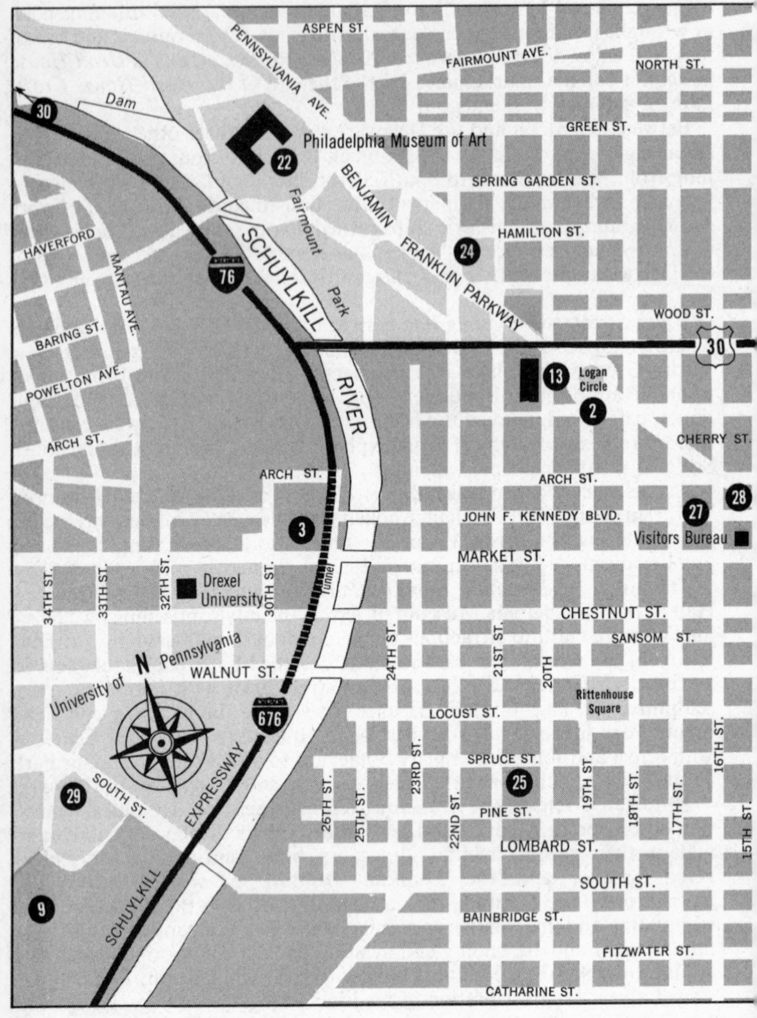

Points of Interest

1) Academy of Music
2) Academy of Natural Sciences
3) Amtrak 30th Street Station
4) Betsy Ross House
5) The Bourse
6) Chinatown
7) City Hall
8) Christ Church
9) Convention Hall/Civic Center
10) Edgar Allan Poe National Historic Site
11) Elfreth's Alley
12) Franklin Court
13) Franklin Institute Science Museum
14) Gallery at Market East/Market Street East Station
15) Greyhound-Trailways Station
16) Independence Hall
17) Independence National Historical Park Visitor Center

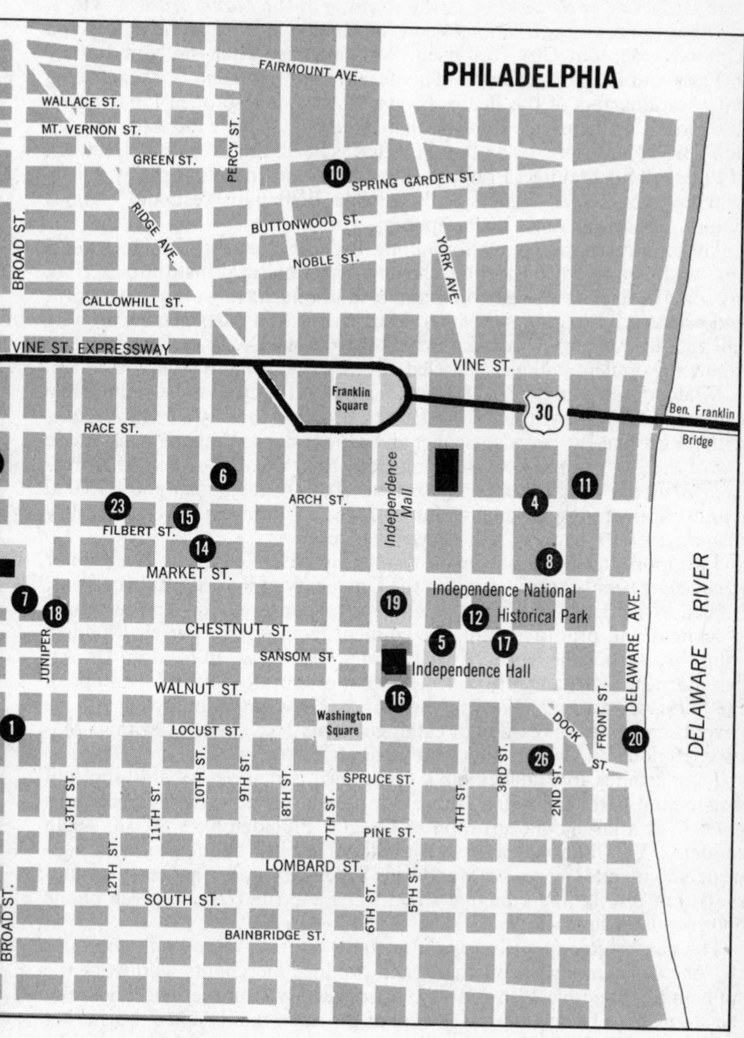

18) John Wanamaker
19) Liberty Bell
20) Penn's Landing
21) Pennsylvania Academy of the Fine Arts
22) Philadelphia Museum of Art
23) Reading Terminal Market
24) Rodin Museum
25) Rosenbach Museum and Library
26) Society Hill
27) Suburban Station
28) Convention and Visitors Bureau's Visitor Center
29) University Museum of Archeology and Anthropology
30) Zoo

trails, picnic areas, and amphitheaters for summer concerts. (The Philadelphia Orchestra performs free in the summer at the *Mann Music Center*).

Other important attractions sit in the shadow of *City Hall.* Before you explore these, tour City Hall itself; it is patterned after the New Louvre in Paris and is splendid inside. The nearby *Masonic Temple,* the very ornate headquarters of the Pennsylvania Masons, is also open for tours. A few blocks north is the *Pennsylvania Academy of the Fine Arts,* housed in a gingerbready Victorian building that is itself a masterpiece, the work of Philadelphia architect Frank Furness. Inside are masterworks by American painters such as Charles Willson Peale, Benjamin West, and Thomas Eakins, as well as more contemporary works.

The midtown area, stretching along Broad Street and the blocks east and west, is a mix of residential, business, and cultural institutions. Here are some of the city's finest hotels and restaurants, its most exclusive stores and private clubs, and its theaters. Many performing arts groups proudly call the *Academy of Music* (known as the Grand Dame of Broad Street) home; the opulent hall was modeled after La Scala Opera House in Milan.

Rittenhouse Square, near 18th and Walnut, is the city's most fashionable address, and Walnut Street, from 19th to Broad, is the city's Fifth Avenue, with shops like Burberry's, Cache, and Dimensions. You can peek inside one of the city's grand homes dating from 1860 when you visit the *Rosenbach Museum and Library.* Among its 30,000 rare books and 270,000 manuscripts are the original of James Joyce's *Ulysses* and a 15th-century manuscript of Chaucer's *Canterbury Tales.*

Two more museums on the don't-miss list: The *University Museum of Archaeology and Anthropology,* on the University of Pennsylvania campus, is filled with artifacts collected on university-sponsored digs. In their study of ancient and primitive man, the eminent faculty have dug up wonders from throughout the world. At the *Barnes Foundation* in Merion, Dr. Albert Barnes singlehandedly collected what art curators have called one of the finest private collections in the world. These are paintings that have never been loaned for exhibit or catalogued, masterpieces by Cézanne, Matisse, Renoir, and others that you've never seen.

The entrance to Philadelphia's *Chinatown* is marked by a 40-foot-tall ornamental gate that spans 10th Street north of Arch. In this neighborhood lives a large concentration of Greater Philadelphia's 80,000 Asian residents. You'll know you're in Chinatown not just by the groceries, souvenir shops, and scores of Mandarin, Szechuan, and Cantonese restaurants, but also by the bilingual street signs and the red and green phone booths with pagoda tops.

The nearby *Reading Terminal Market* is another close-knit community—one of fishmongers, butchers, and produce merchants who work the stalls in a still-active 19th-century, European-style marketplace. Some of the shops have been run by members of the same family since the market opened in 1893. More than 20 stalls serve ready-to-eat treats. Here, amidst the local color, you can sample Bassetts ice cream, down a cheese steak, or try a bowl of Philadelphia snapper soup.

John Wanamaker's is a Philadelphia institution. One of the first of the great department stores, it was dedicated by President Taft in 1911. The Eagle sculpture in the marble, pillared Grand Court has been a meeting place for generations. Here, daily concerts show off the world's largest pipe organ.

The *Gallery* at Market East, a skylit, four-level urban mall, spans three city blocks along Market Street. In addition to the ground floor international eateries and the Strawbridge & Clothier, Stern's, and J.C. Penney department stores, there are more than 220 assorted shops. At 8th and Market is *Market*Place*East,* a three-level mall of upscale shops and restaurants.

South Philadelphia, the city's "Little Italy," is an expanse of almost identical row homes with gleaming white marble steps. It may well be the city's most colorful neighborhood. At its heart is the five-block long *Italian Market,* an open-air marketplace jammed with sidewalk stalls and push-carts filled with caged chickens and crawling crabs, sides of beef, fresh produce, and even clothing. The shops behind are brimming with ricotta-cheese-filled cannolis, imported Parmesan, sweet sausages, and exotic olives. This is the neighborhood where "Rocky" grew up; where the restaurants display the gold records of neighborhood celebrities like Bobby Rydell, Frankie Avalon, and James Darren. This is where you sample what many would say is the best meal in South Philly—a cheese steak from Pat's—and eat it leaning against a car.

At Second Street and Washington Avenue is the *Mummers Museum.* If you aren't lucky enough to catch the January 1 extravaganza, you can see the costumes (some take a whole year to make) and other exhibits glorifying a century of Mummers folklore here.

Philadelphia is in the midst of a construction boom, creating new office towers, hotels, expressways, and meeting places. Financiers and developers have discovered what city residents already know: Philadelphia is a very pleasant place to live and visit, a city with an impressive past and a promising future.

PRACTICAL INFORMATION FOR PHILADELPHIA

WHEN TO GO. Summer is Philadelphia's busiest tourist season; the main attraction is the week-long July 4th Freedom Festival, when the nation's birth and Philadelphia's role in it are celebrated with spectacular fireworks, free concerts, and hot-air balloon races.

Philadelphia has four distinct seasons, with average temperatures ranging from the upper eighties in July and Aug. to the mid-20s in Jan. and Feb. In late summer, when Philadelphia tends to be uncomfortably humid, residents escape en masse to the seashore. Some recent winters have been mild with little snow, others have brought long periods of near-zero weather. The mild late spring (when Philadelphia's blooming cherry blossoms rival Washington, D.C.'s) and the crisp, early fall, when temperatures average 50 to 60 degrees, are ideal times to visit in terms of weather. But as William Penn noted 300 years ago, the city's weather "often changeth without notice, and is constant almost in its inconstancy."

HOW TO GET THERE. By plane. *Philadelphia International Airport,* located in the southwest section of Philadelphia eight mi. from Center City, has flights to more than 100 U.S. cities. It is served by most major airlines including *Air Jamaica, American, Continental, Delta, Lufthaansa, Mexicana, Midway, Northwest, Pan American, TWA, USAir,* and *United.*

By bus. *Greyhound/Trailways* now operates out of a sparkling new terminal at 10th and Filbert Sts., just north of the Gallery at Market East (215–931–4000). The terminal also serves N.J. Transit's Jersey shore buses.

By train. Philadelphia is served by *Amtrak,* which operates rail service along the busy Northeast Corridor stretching from Boston to Washington. Intercity service is also provided to many points south and west as well as to Montreal. By train, Philadelphia is less than 90 minutes from New York City and 2 hours from Washington, D.C.

Amtrak pulls into 30th Street Station at 30th and Market Sts. To reach Center City, show your Amtrak ticket stub and (for free) board a local train to Suburban Station at 16th St. and John F. Kennedy Blvd. (close to major hotels) or Market Street East Station at 10th and Market Sts. (closer to the historic area). Phone 215–824–1600 for Amtrak information.

By car. The major north-south highway passing through Philadelphia is I-95. Since there is no Center City exit northbound, motorists coming from the airport should follow 291 north to I-76 west to Vine St. From the west, the Pennsylvania Turnpike runs from Pittsburgh to Valley Forge and enters Philadelphia at the Schuylkill Expressway (I-76), which has several exits in the downtown area. From the east, the New Jersey Turnpike and I-295 provide ready access to either U.S. 30 or New Jersey S.R. 42, both of which lead to the city's downtown area. For additional information, call *Keystone AAA Automobile Club* at 215–569–4321. Their emergency road service number is 215–569–4411.

TOURIST INFORMATION. Before your visit, call or write the *Philadelphia Visitors Center,* 16th St. and John F. Kennedy Blvd., Phila., PA 19102 (215–636–1666 or 800–321–WKND) to request a copy of the Official Visitors Guide. When you arrive, stop in at their round building across the street from Suburban Station. The center provides free transit and city maps; hotel, restaurant, and sightseeing information; and seasonal listings of the city's special events. It also offers services to groups, foreign visitors, and the handicapped, and discount tickets to various events. Open daily 9 A.M. to 5 P.M. (until 6 P.M. in summer).

Information and maps for the most important historic sites are available from the Visitor Center at *Independence National Historical Park,* 3rd and Chestnut Sts. Open daily 9 A.M. to 5 P.M.; phone 597–8974, or 627–1776 for a recorded message.

The *Nationalities Service Center* of Philadelphia (893–8415) provides volunteer translators.

The Donnelley Directory *Philadelphia Events Hotline* (337–7777) offers a prerecorded listing of tours, displays, and special events.

For current calendar listings, refer to *Philadelphia* magazine, published monthly; the *Welcomat,* published Wed.; or the weekend pullout sections (available Friday) of Philadelphia's daily papers—the *Inquirer* and the *Daily News.* The latter three are available free at the Visitor Center.

TELEPHONES. The area code for Philadelphia and the surrounding counties is 215. You don't need to dial the area code if it is the same as the one from which you are calling. To dial long distance out of Philadelphia, dial 1 before the area code and seven-digit number. For a person-to-person or collect call, or to charge a call to a credit card, dial 0 plus the number (including the area code if it's outside the 215 area). To call Directory Assistance within the city, dial 1–555–1212; from elsewhere, dial 1–215–555–1212. A local call from a public telephone costs 25 cents.

EMERGENCY TELEPHONE NUMBERS. The emergency number for fire, police, ambulance and paramedics is 911. Or dial 0 and ask the operator for help in connecting you immediately with the appropriate agency. Other numbers: suicide and crisis prevention center, 686–4420; poison control, 386–2100; rape hotline, 922–3434.

HOW TO GET AROUND. From the airport. Allow at least 30 minutes travel time for the 8-mi. trip between Center City and Philadelphia International Airport. Cab fare averages $19, without tip. *Deluxe Transportation Company* (463–8787) travels between the airport and Center City hotels for a $6 fare; vans stop regularly outside baggage claim. The Airport High Speed Line connects the airport to 30th St., Suburban, and Market St. East stations. Trains run every half hour between 5:30 A.M. and midnight; the trip takes about 25 minutes. One-way fare is $4.75 if purchased at the ticket booth; $5.75 on the train. For exact times, call SEPTA (574–7800) or the airport information desk (492–3333).

By bus, trolley, subway. *SEPTA* (574–7800) operates an extensive system of buses, trolleys, subways, and commuter trains with convenient routes and frequent stops. Timetables, routes, and the official street and transit map are available at information centers in the underground concourse at 15th and Market Sts. or at the Market St. East Station, 10th and Market Sts. Fares are uniform: $1.50 for the base fare; 40 cents additional for a transfer. Exact change is required. Information centers sell tokens (10 for $10.50) and a weekly Transpass for $16, which entitles you to unlimited rides on most routes. The #76 bus, which runs on Chestnut St. between Independence Mall and 18th St., will drop you off close to shopping and historic attractions. SEPTA offers free rides to seniors during off-peak hours.

By commuter train. Philadelphia has a fine commuter rail network serving its suburban regions. These trains are your best bet for reaching attractions in Germantown, Chestnut Hill, and Merion. Trains leave from 30th St., Suburban, and Market St. East stations. Call SEPTA at 574–7800.

By taxi. Taxi fares are competitive and the cabs are metered: Rates average $2.90 for the first mile; $1.40 for each additional mile. Cabs are easiest to find outside major hotels. The primary cab companies are *Yellow Cab* (922–8400), *United Cab* (625–2881) and *Quaker City* (728–8000).

By foot. Most of the historic and cultural attractions are easy walks from the midtown area. Pick up a map at the Visitors Center at 16th St. and John F. Kennedy Blvd. AudioWalk & Tour of Historic Philadelphia, 6th and Sansom Sts. (925–1234), offers a taped walking tour. (See Tours.)

By rental car. The major car rental agencies have offices at the airport and at convenient downtown locations: *Avis* (492–0900 airport, 563–8980 downtown), *Budget* (492–9447 airport or 492–9400 downtown), *Hertz* (800–654–3131), and *National* (800–328–4567). Advance reservations are usually necessary. The best savings are on the weekends when rental rates are half as much as the weekday prices. For a super discount, try *Rent-a-Dent* (521–2300); the cars aren't wrecks and they are located 2½ mi. from the airport.

HINTS TO MOTORISTS. If your visit to Philadelphia will be focused in Center City, it's wise to leave your car at home and depend on public transportation, which services the nearby suburbs as well. Narrow streets and congestion, especially during rush hours (7–9:30 A.M., 4–6:30 P.M.), makes driving difficult. A right turn on red is permitted after a full stop unless prohibited by a sign. In Center City, streets generally alternate one way.

On-street parking is often forbidden during rush hours, but some metered parking is permitted at other times. Most parking meters are 25 cents for 15 minutes with a 2-hour time limit. Some meters don't need to be fed after 6:30 P.M. or on Sundays, but be sure to carefully read the signs as the regulations vary from street to street, and the meter maids are vigilant. Illegally parked cars will be ticketed or towed. Parking lots and garages average from about $2.50–$3.50 an hour and $7.50 to park from 9 A.M. to 5 P.M. Evening rates vary. Check prices before you enter, so you can avoid paying $8 when there's a $5 lot a block away.

If you do drive, avoid going into and out of the city during rush hours. During the morning rush, avoid the major arteries leading into the city, particularly I-95, U.S. 1 and the Schuylkill Expressway (I-76). The traffic pattern reverses during the outgoing rush period. For frequent traffic reports, tune into KYW news radio (1060 AM). The *Keystone Automobile Club* (AAA) offers auto travel information (569–4321) and emergency road service (569–4411) to all members (members of the American Automobile Association included).

Vine St., a busy east-west artery cutting through Center City, is being torn up so the Schuylkill Expressway can extend right to the Ben Franklin Bridge. Expect traffic jams. For routes, call Keystone's travel information number.

HINTS TO DISABLED TRAVELERS. Some newer SEPTA buses are equipped with lifts for passengers in wheelchairs. Call 574–7800 for details. Most downtown streets have been ramped for wheelchairs. When renting a car in Philadelphia, bring your own disabled sign. There are no on-street parking spaces specifically marked for use by handicapped drivers. However, drivers of cars with handicapped plates can park free for one hour in a metered space. Parking lots have spaces specifically marked for the handicapped with blue and white symbols.

A pertinent publication is the *Guide to Philadelphia for the Handicapped,* available free of charge from the *Mayor's Commission on People With Disabilities,* Room 143, City Hall, Philadelphia, PA 19107. To order it, call 215–MU6–2798. One of the best sources of information about handicapped travel (local and national) is *The Travel Information Service,* Moss Rehabilitation Hospital, 12th St. and Tabor Rd., Philadelphia, PA 19141 (215–329–5715). *Access Pennsylvania: A Guide for Travelers with Physical Disabilities* includes information about Philadelphia and surrounding areas and is available from the *Pennsylvania Bureau of Travel Development* (800–VISIT–PA).

SEASONAL EVENTS. Although the events listed below are annual happenings, the exact dates change from year to year. Before your visit, contact the Visitor Center (see *Tourist Information,* above) for their "Quarterly Calendar of Events."

January. Philadelphia's favorite tradition, the Mummers, celebrate on New Year's Day by strutting up Broad St. to City Hall for the annual Mummers Parade. More than 30,000 members of the string bands, fancies, and comic divisions don their feathers and glitter for a day-long performance.

February. *Black History Month* is marked with exhibitions, lectures and music at the *Afro-American Historical and Cultural Museum,* 7th and Arch Sts. From Feb. through Apr., the *Chinese Cultural Center,* 125 N. 10th St., celebrates the Chinese New Year with a 10-course festival banquet Tues.–Sun. nights at 6:30 P.M. Chefs come from mainland China to prepare the feast. Reservations required; call 215–923–6767. For one week in early Feb., the *Philadelphia Boat Show* displays more than 500 yachts, sailboats, and power boats at the Civic Center, 34th St. and Civic Center Blvd. The top-ranking men in the world of tennis meet head to head at the Spectrum for the *Ebel-U.S. Pro Indoor Tennis Championships* (947–2530) around the middle of the month.

March. The *Philadelphia Flower Show,* touted as the nation's largest indoor flower show, transforms the Civic Center the second week of Mar. Later in the month, *The Book and The Cook* teams the city's best chefs with the world's top cookbook authors for prix fixe meals at area restaurants. The *American Music Theater Festival* brings a repertory of opera, musical comedy, cabaret-style revues, and experimental works to theaters across the city from Mar. until May.

April. The *Easter Promenade* celebrates the holy day with a fashion contest, entertainment, and celebrity guests. Early in the month, The *Philadelphia Antiques Show* features museum-quality antiques, gallery tours, lectures, and appraisals at the 103rd Engineers Armory, 33rd St. north of Market St. High school and college athletes gather at the University of Pennsylvania the last weekend of Apr. for the *Penn Relays,* the world's oldest and largest track meet.

May. The first half of May, Philadelphians open their houses to visitors for Philadelphia Open House—foot, bus, trolley, and boat tours conducted by the Friends of Independence National Historical Park. Call 928–1188 or 597–7919. The *Devon Horse Show and Country Fair,* one of the nation's greatest outdoor horse shows, is a week-long attraction at the Devon Fairgrounds on the Main Line the last week of May. *Jambalaya Jam,* a New Orleans festival, enlivens Memorial Day weekend with New Orleans musicians and Creole and Cajun cooking.

June. In early June, America's oldest outdoor exhibit of fine art, the *Rittenhouse Square Fine Arts Annual,* displays works of over 100 local artists. *Elfreth's Alley,* America's oldest continuously occupied street, opens it homes to the public the first weekend of the month. In mid-June, Philadelphia hosts the *CoreStates Pro Cycling Championship,* the nation's only professional cycling competition. The open-air *Mann Music Center* in Fairmount Park is home to the Philadelphia Orchestra's free concerts through July. More than 40 artisans exhibit jewelry, stained glass, leathers and other items on summer weekends at 2nd and Pine Sts. for the *Head House Crafts Fair.*

July. The city goes all out in celebration of America's birth with a week-long *Freedom Festival.* Highlights include free concerts, parades (a summer Mummers procession), hot-air balloon races, special ceremonies and spectacular fireworks choreographed to music. If you can choose one week to visit Philadelphia, this should be it. *Riverblues,* in mid-July, is a weekend waterfront festival featuring top names in blues and the down-home taste of "blues cities" foods.

August. The last weekend of the month, folk music lovers camp out at the Olde Poole Farm in Schwenksville for the *Philadelphia Folk Festival,* a Woodstock-like gathering of the top names in folk music. Phone: 242–0150.

September. More than 300 sail and power boats tie up on the Delaware River at Penn's Landing for the annual *Penn's Landing In-Water Boat Show* in late September. Also scheduled is the *Harvest Show,* a fall flower and garden show at the Horticulture Center in Fairmount Park. Philadelphia designers spotlight their latest fashions in fashion and trade shows at the Civic Center, in the annual *Philadelphia Dresses the World* event.

October. *Super Sunday,* a giant-block party the Sun. before Columbus Day, draws thousands of people to the Benjamin Franklin Parkway for games, rides, food, and entertainment.

November. The *Philadelphia Craft Show* takes over the Civic Center the first or second weekend of the month. The annual *Thanksgiving Day Parade* includes thousands of marchers, plenty of floats, TV and radio personalities, and the real star—Santa Claus. The most traditional of football clashes, the *Army–Navy Game,* takes place at Veterans Stadium, usually the Sat. following Thanksgiving. The next day, the *Fairmount Park Marathon* has leading runners dashing through the city's streets.

December. *Philadelphia Loves Christmas* is a month-long feast of special events and holiday entertainment. The *Christmas Tours of Historic Houses* take visitors in Victorian trolley buses to Fairmount Park's holiday-adorned colonial mansions the first weekend of Dec. During the Christmas season, John Wanamaker stages its annual light show and pipe organ concert several times a day in the Grand Court of the department store at 13th and Market Sts.

TOURS. The best way to explore Philadelphia's historic and cultural attractions are on self-guided walking tours, which give you a chance to discover the city's charming nooks and crannies. An 80-minute taped narration about the city's historic sites, including a map, is available from *AudioWalk & Tour of Historic Philadelphia,* in the Norman Rockwell Museum, 6th and Sansom Sts. (925–1234). $8 per person to rent cassette and player; $16 for two or more people sharing the unit. Rent daily 10 A.M.–1 P.M. From May to Oct., *Centipede Tours* (735–3123) supplies guides in colonial dress who lead 1½-hour Candlelight Strolls through Colonial City (Fri.) and Society Hill (Thurs. and Sat.). Groups leave at 6:30 P.M. from City Tavern, 2nd and Walnut Sts., mid-May to mid-Oct. Adults, $5; seniors and children, $4.

If the weather is bleak or your feet are aching, try one of *Gray Line's* daily tours, which depart from the Philadelphia Visitors Center, 16th St. and John F. Kennedy Blvd. (569–3666). Tours include the 2½-hour Cultural Tour, $15; 3-hour Historic Tour, $13.50; day-long combination tour, $24.50. *Philadelphia Tours'* open-air, double-decker buses stop at about a half-dozen major attractions daily (271–2999). Charter only.

The creator of the AudioWalk & Tour, Nancy Gilboy, is one of the masterminds behind the new *American Trolley Tours* (925–4567), which takes visitors on a 3-hour tour of the city in a recreation of a Victorian trolley. The excursion, led by well-informed guides in 18th-century dress, focuses on Independence National Historical Park, Antique Row, and Society Hill. Departs four times a day from major hotels and the Visitors Center at 16th St. and Kennedy Blvd. Reservations required.

The *Philadelphia Carriage Company* has costumed drivers in antique horse-drawn carriages to guide you through Old City or Society Hill year-round. Rides leave from 6th and Chestnut Sts.; a 20-minute ride is $10 for up to four people. The *Spirit of Philadelphia* cruises along the Delaware River daily year-round. Lunch ($18), Sunday brunch ($20), dinner ($30–$38) and sightseeing cruises (one is under the moonlight), boarding at Pier 24, Delaware Ave. between Race and Spring Garden sts.; all with entertainment, are available. Phone 923–1419 for reservations; 923–4962 for recording of times and prices. *Liberty Belle Charters'* paddle-wheel boats ply the Delaware River from Apr. to Dec. They offer a one-hour narrated sightseeing cruise (about $8 per person) as well as lunch, dinner, and Sun. brunch excursions. Reservations required; 824–0889.

SPECIAL-INTEREST SIGHTSEEING. City Hall. Broad and Market Sts. (568–3351). Free one-hour tour of the seat of Philadelphia's municipal government. The observation deck at the foot of William Penn's statue was scheduled to reopen in mid-1991 after extensive repairs. Mon.–Fri., 12:30 P.M.; meet in Conversation Hall, Room 201, through North Broad St. entrance. Group tours at 10:30 A.M.; call to reserve.

Foundation for Architecture. (569–3187). Themed walking tours—the littlest streets, Art Deco, skyscrapers, etc.—from mid-April to mid-Nov. Informative, fun walks focus on history and architecture. (Call for schedule and departure points.)

The Free Library of Philadelphia. 19th and Vine Sts. (686–5322). Free half-hour tours of the Rare Books Department (from cuneiform tablets to Dickens' letters) at 11 A.M. weekdays.

Masonic Temple. One N. Broad St. (988–1917). Free tours of the very ornate headquarters of the Pennsylvania Masons, an architectural treasure. Weekdays at 10 and 11 A.M., 1, 2, and 3 P.M.; Sat., except July and Aug., 10 and 11 A.M.

Philadelphia Naval Base. South Broad St. (897–8775). This is where our moth-ball fleet docks. Free tour of the shipbuilding center and land facilities on their special tour bus. U.S. citizens only; children under eight not permitted. Reservations required: Fri. 10 A.M.

United States Mint. 5th and Arch Sts. (597–7350). An hour-long, free self-guided tour with audiovisual assistance to see how coins are made. Hours 9 A.M.–4:30 P.M. Open daily May–Sept., weekdays only Jan.–Mar., Mon.–Sat. Apr., Oct.–Dec.

PARKS AND GARDENS. Philadelphia is dotted by five public squares that were planned by William Penn himself: *Franklin Square,* at 7th and Race Sts.; the London-park-like *Washington Square,* which brightens the southeast section of the city at 6th and Walnut Sts; *Rittenhouse Square,* a well-manicured park by 18th and Walnut Sts. in the southwest; *Logan Circle,* enhanced by Alexander Stirling Calder's Swann Memorial Fountain at 18th and the Benjamin Franklin Pkwy.; and *Centre Square,* which is now occupied by City Hall. The first four squares are scenic spots where you can relax or eat a picnic lunch during your touring.

Bartram's Garden. 54th St. and Lindbergh Blvd. (729–5281). The historic home of colonial botanists John and William Bartram and the nation's first arboretum still blooms with exotic flora from all over the "New World." Gardens open daily, dawn–dusk. Free. House, filled with 18th-century period furnishings, open Wed.–Fri., noon–4 P.M. (Nov.–April); Wed.–Sun., noon–4 P.M. (May–Oct.). Adults, $2; children, $1.

Longwood Gardens. Rte. 1, Kennett Sq. (1–388–6741). About 30 mi. southwest of Philadelphia in the Brandywine Valley lies one of the world's great gardens—Longwood Gardens, once the country home of Pierre S. Du Pont. It's a dazzling combination of Old World pleasure gardens, like Versailles, and New World vigor. Don't miss it. *Summer Festival of Fountains,* with concerts and fireworks Tues., Thurs., Sat. nights, fall *Chrysanthemum Festival,* Christmas displays. Conservatories bloom year-round. Open daily, 9 A.M.–5 P.M. Adults $8, children 6–14, $2.

Fairmount Park, the largest landscaped city park in the world, has more than 8,900 acres containing historic and cultural treasures, woods, meadows, flowers, statues, sports facilities, and five particularly scenic acres along the banks of the Schuylkill River. Along Kelly Dr. are the Victorian houses of Boat House Row, home to the "Schuylkill Navy" rowing clubs. Tourists are particularly drawn to the park's seven historic, authentically furnished houses dating from the mid-1700s. Phone 787–5449 for hours. Other park attractions include the Japanese House (open May through Oct.), patterned after a 17th-century Japanese residence, and the Horticultural Center, a 28-acre arboretum and a working greenhouse with thousands of plants and trees used to beautify city properties. Phone 879–4062 for information on both.

Also in the park are the Philadelphia Museum of Art (see Museums section), the Philadelphia Zoological Gardens (see Zoo section below), and sports facilities (see Participant Sports section).

Tinicum National Environmental Center. 86th St. and Lindbergh Blvd., near the airport (365–3118). The largest remaining freshwater tidal marsh in Pennsylvania dates back to 1643. Foot trails, an observation platform, and a boardwalk afford a good view of the marshland's abundant birds and wildlife. Fishing, biking and photography permitted. Visitors center open daily, 8:30 A.M.–4 P.M. Free.

Schuylkill Center for Environmental Education. Hagy's Mill Rd., Roxborough (482–7300). 500 acres of nature trails, streams, ponds, forests, and wildlife habitats, plus a Discovery Room for the kids. Open Mon.–Sat. 8:30 A.M.–5 P.M.; Sun. 1–5 P.M. Admission: Adults, $5; children, $3.

ZOOS. When the *Philadelphia Zoological Gardens,* at 34th St. and Girard Ave. in West Philadelphia (243–1100), opened in 1874, people flocked there on foot, by horse and carriage, and even by steamboat. They've been showing up in herds ever since. Today, the country's oldest zoo has over 1,600 animals representing more than 540 species, plus more than 500 species of native and exotic plants, adding botanical garden to its list of credits. The Treehouse has larger-than-life habitats where children can hatch out of an egg, sit inside a frog, climb into a beehive and otherwise experience life as an animal. World of Primates shows off the apes and monkeys in an outdoor natural habitat; the Bird House exhibits 101 species from around the world, including some in a free-flight area. Bear Country, the five-acre

African Plain, Jungle Bird Walk, and Wolf Woods are highlights. You can touch and feed the animals at the Children's Zoo where there is an hourly animal show. Open weekdays 9:30 A.M.–5 P.M., till 6 P.M. weekends. Admission: Adults, $5.75, seniors, $4.75; children 2–11, $4; children under 2, free. Additional fee for Treehouse and Children's Zoo.

PARTICIPANT SPORTS. *Fairmount Park* is a sportsman's paradise for bikers, hikers, joggers, golfers and fisherman. No area is more popular for **jogging** than the scenic eight-mi. loop along the Schuylkill River behind the Art Museum (around the Kelly and West River Drs.). Or, try the run that Rocky made famous—from City Hall along the Benjamin Franklin Parkway and up the steps of the Philadelphia Museum of Art.

The park has 25 mi. of paved **bike paths.** Cyclists can rent "wheels" from *Fairmount Park Bike Rental,* 1 Boat House Row (236–4359). Rental rates are $6 an hour; a $10 deposit and picture ID are required on all bikes. Call ahead; bike rentals were not available at press time.

Boaters interested in testing the waters of the Schuylkill can head to the *Public Canoe House,* Kelly Dr., just south of the Strawberry Mansion Bridge (225–3560). Canoes and rowboats go for $10 an hour; $10 deposit and picture ID required.

Several public **golf courses** wind through Fairmount Park. They are open throughout the year and charge between $13 and $16 for 18 holes. *Cobbs Creek,* 7800 Lansdowne Ave. (877–8707); *Karakung,* 7800 Lansdowne Ave. (877–8707); *Juniata,* L and Cayuga Sts. (743–4060); *Walnut Lane,* Walnut Lane and Henry Ave. (482–3370); and *Franklin D. Roosevelt,* 20th St. and Pattison Ave. (462–8997).

Ice skaters can take to the rink at the University of Pennsylvania's *Class of 1923 Skating Rink,* 3130 Walnut St. (898–1923). Open daily Oct.–Mar. Admission, $4.50; rentals $1.50. Call for hours.

If the weather is contrary, you can jog **indoors**—as well as swim, work out, relax in a whirlpool, or sauna and play handball, racquetball, tennis, and squash at *Clark's Uptown,* a health club in the Wyndham Franklin Plaza Hotel, 17th and Race Sts. (864–0616). Check at your hotel desk about arrangements to use their facilities.

SPECTATOR SPORTS. Philadelphia has become known as a "City of Champions," thanks to winning efforts by its professional teams. The National League *Phillies* (463–1000) play **baseball** Apr.–Oct. at Veterans Stadium. Home games are played mostly at night; prices range from $4.50 for general admission to $10 for field boxes.

The *Philadelphia 76ers* (339–7676), the city's pro **basketball** team, shoot the hoops from Oct. to Apr. at the Spectrum. There are 41 home dates, mostly at night. Tickets are $6 to $35. Sharing the Spectrum, and the same time span, with the Sixers are the *Flyers* (755–9700), two-time Stanley Cup **hockey** champions. Tickets range from $12 to $28.

The *Eagles* (463–5500), the city's entry in the National **Football** League, kick off on Sunday afternoons at the Vet from Aug. to Dec. Tickets are about $25.

Tickets for all pro games are available at the ball parks and at Center City ticket agencies (expect a surcharge up to $5). Veterans Stadium and the Spectrum are located in the South Philadelphia sports complex at Broad St. and Pattison Ave. They can be reached by subway (the southern end of the Broad St. line), by the C bus, which runs south on Broad St., or by car. Parking is ample and costs about $4.

For information about professional **tennis** and **cycling** events and collegiate **track, rowing,** and **football** competitions (including the Army-Navy Game), see the *Seasonal Events* section.

CHILDREN'S ACTIVITIES. For children 7 and younger, the top attraction is the **Please Touch Museum,** 210 N. 21st St. (963–0666), where kids are invited to climb, explore, dress up and play with everything. There's a trolley to ride like the one in Mr. Rogers' Neighborhood, a Health Care Center with medical equipment, small animals, and children's films. 9 A.M.–4:30 P.M., daily. Admission $5 for ages 1 and up.

Within the **Academy of Natural Sciences** is Outside-In, a hands-on children's museum where youngsters can touch live animals and explore nature by using all five of their senses. Open 1–4 P.M., Mon.–Fri. during the school year, 10–4 on summer weekdays; 10 A.M.–5 P.M. Sat.–Sun. year-round. The Fels Planetarium of the Franklin Institute Science Museum features a special program for children ages 1–7 Sat. at 11 A.M. and the *University Museum of Archeology and Anthropology* (their mummies are especially popular) has a Children's Film Program on Sat. at 10:30 A.M. from Oct. to Mar. Films are chosen for children ages 5 and up. See the *Museums* section for locations and prices.

Philadelphia Marionette Theater & Museum, Playhouse in the Park, Belmont Mansion Dr. (879–1213) delights youngsters with performances 10:30 A.M. weekdays and some Sun. at 2 P.M. Reservations required; $4.50 per person. Museum features puppets from around the world. For children's theater events, check the weekend listings of the daily papers.

Sesame Place in Langhorne (752–4900), about an hour ride north of Center City, is a family play park that takes up where Sesame Street leaves off. Featured are a Sesame Neighborhood, a replica of the TV show's street; outdoor play and water activities (bring a swimsuit); a computer gallery; the Count's Gallery, filled with 180,000 balls to climb through; and a variety of live shows, including one featuring Bert and Ernie and Big Bird. Newly added in 1991 was Sesame Island, a Caribbean-theme attraction. Ideal for children 3–13. Open daily May–mid-Sept.; weekends only till mid-Oct.

HISTORIC SITES AND HOUSES. Independence National Historical Park. The most historic square mile in the U.S. incorporates many of the country's most important sites. More than 4.5 million people visit these attractions each year, all of which are free. Most of the buildings are open daily from 9 A.M.–5 P.M.; later hours in summer. Head first to the *Visitor Center,* 3rd and Chestnut Sts. (597–8974; 627–1776 for a taped message). The staff here will supply you with a map and outline a tour for you, dependent upon your interests and time. They also have brochures on historic sites outside the park. Information in 10 foreign languages, plus a 28-minute film, *Independence,* which dramatizes the events from 1774 to 1800.

Don't miss these three sites: **Independence Hall,** Chestnut between 5th and 6th Sts. America's most historic building, this is where the Declaration of Independence was adopted and the U.S. Constitution written. Guided tours leave every 15–20 minutes from the East Wing. Lines are long, so get in line early. **Liberty Bell Pavilion,** Market St. between 5th and 6th Sts. The nation's most hallowed symbol of liberty resides here. **Franklin Court,** Market St. between 3rd and 4th Sts. This museum serves as an imaginative tribute to Old Ben; the genius of the statesman, diplomat, scientist, printer, and author are revealed through hands-on exhibits.

Other important sites in the park include *Carpenters' Hall,* where the First Continental Congress met; *Second Bank of the United States,* with its portrait gallery; *Graff House,* the reconstructed house where Thomas Jefferson wrote the Declaration of Independence; the *Bishop White House,* home of the first bishop of the Episcopal Diocese of Pennsylvania; and the *Todd House,* home of Dolley Payne Todd, who later became Dolley Madison. Tour tickets for these last two must be picked up at the Visitor Center on the day of your tour.

Historic sites outside of the park include the following:

Betsy Ross House. 239 Arch St. (627–5343). The 13-star Old Glory waves from the second floor window of the restored 18th-century home of Betsy Ross, who is credited with sewing the first American flag. Furnished with period pieces. Open daily 10 A.M.–5 P.M. Free.

Christ Church. 2nd St. north of Market St. (922–1695). Many who were instrumental in America's independence worshiped here at the oldest Episcopal church in America—an architectural treasure. Open daily 9 A.M.–5 P.M. Donations welcome. At Christ Church Burial Ground, 5th and Arch Sts., five signers of the Declaration of Independence are buried. Its most famous "resident" is Benjamin Franklin. Open May–Sept. Call church for times.

Edgar Allan Poe National Historic Site. 532 N. 7th St. (597–8780). The author's only Philadelphia residence still standing is where he lived when "The Gold Bug" and "The Tell-Tale Heart" were published. Open Tues.–Sat. 9 A.M.–5 P.M. Free.

Elfreth's Alley. 2nd St. between Arch and Race Sts. (574–0560). The cobblestone lane and small houses on this, the oldest continuously occupied street in America, offer a glimpse of what much of colonial Philadelphia looked like. No. 126 is a museum, open to the public daily, 10 A.M.–4 P.M. Weekends only, Jan. and Feb. Free.

Friends Meeting House. 4th and Arch Sts. (627–2667). William Penn gave the land on which this meeting house sits to the Religious Society of Friends, called Quakers. Exhibits inside depict Penn's life and contributions. Open Mon.–Sat., 10 A.M.–4 P.M. Free. Meetings for Worship, to which visitors are welcome, are Thurs. 10 A.M. and Sun. 10:30 A.M.

Hill-Physick-Keith House. 321 S. 4th St. (925–7866). Only freestanding Federal mansion in Center City, this house has an outstanding collection of early Philadelphia silver and Empire and Federal pieces. Tours Tues.–Sat., at 11 A.M., 1:30 and 3 P.M., Sun. at 1:30 and 3 P.M. Adults, $3; children, $2.

Penn's Landing. Delaware River waterfront between Market and Lombard Sts. The Port of History Museum and several ships turned floating museum, including a World War II sub and Commodore Dewey's flagship, are among the permanent attractions along this promenade. Ships open daily for tours. 10 A.M.–4 P.M. Adults, $3; children under 12, $1.50. Call 922–1898.

Powel House. 244 S. 3rd St. (627–0364). Many colonial leaders dined at Mayor Samuel Powel's elegant table; furnishings reflect the mid-Georgian era. Tues.–Sat., 10 A.M.–4 P.M.; Sun., 1 P.M.–4 P.M. Adults, $3; children, $2.

MUSEUMS AND GALLERIES. Philadelphia is brimming with museums. Many house fine art collections, others specialize in science, ethnic cultures, fire engines, medicine, rare books, or shoes. What follows is a sampling of the most popular. For a complete listing, refer to the Visitor Center's Official Visitors Guide.

Academy of Natural Sciences. 19th St. and Benjamin Franklin Pkwy. (299–1000). America's first natural history museum has achieved international fame for its displays of stuffed animals in their natural habitats, extinct and endangered species, birds, and insects. Open Mon.–Fri., 10 A.M.–4:30 P.M., Sat.–Sun., 10 A.M.–5 P.M. "Discovering Dinosaurs" is a popular multimedia exhibit. Adults, $5.50; children 3–12; $4.50.

Barnes Foundation. 300 N. Latches Ln., Merion (667–0290). Call the Tourist Center (636–1666) for directions. One of the world's finest private art collections, it is never lent for exhibit. Impressionists, including Renoir, Cézanne and Matisse, are well-represented. Fri.–Sat, 9:30 A.M.–4:30 P.M.; Sun., 1 P.M.–4:30 P.M. Closed July and Aug. Admission $1; children under 12 not admitted.

Franklin Institute Science Museum. 20th St. and Benjamin Franklin Pkwy. (448–1200 for taped message). Imaginative, hands-on exhibits bring science and technology to life. Newest displays explore astronomy, electricity, and electronics. Aviation Hall and a giant walk-through human heart are favorites. Daily shows in Fels Planetarium. Open daily 9:30 A.M.–5 P.M. New Futures Center and Omniverse Theater open some evenings. Admission $5–$12.50.

Mummers Museum. 2nd St. and Washington Ave. (336–3050). The history, costumes, and folklore of the Mummers, one of the city's most colorful and unique traditions, are on display. Open Tues.–Sat., 9:30 A.M.–5 P.M.; Sun., noon–5 P.M. Adults, $2, children under 12 and seniors, $1. String Band concerts are held outside the museum on Tues. evenings, May through Sept., 8 P.M.

Pennsylvania Academy of the Fine Arts. Broad and Cherry Sts. (972–7600). The country's oldest museum and art school is a National Historic Landmark containing three centuries of American art. Tues.–Sat., 10 A.M.–5 P.M.; Sun., 11 A.M.–5 P.M. Adults, $5; seniors and students, $3. Free Sat., 10 A.M.–1 P.M. Tours Tues.–Fri., 11 A.M. and 2 P.M.; Sat.–Sun., 2 P.M.

Philadelphia Museum of Art. 26th St. and Benjamin Franklin Pkwy. (763–8100, 787–5488 for taped message). The city's cultural highlight, a Greco-Roman temple, holds dazzling collections of American crafts, furniture and glass; Renaissance treasures; 20th-century art; and a wing of original architectural wonders including a Hindu temple hall, Japanese teahouse, and Chinese reception hall. There are frequent special exhibits; recent ones have showcased the works of artists Auguste Renoir and Henry Tanner. Tues.–Sun., 10 A.M.–5 P.M. Adults, $5; students, seniors, children 5–18, $2.50. Free Sun. until 1 P.M. Tours leave every hour 11 A.M.–3 P.M.

Rodin Museum. 22nd St. and Benjamin Franklin Pkwy. (787–5476). A priceless collection of Auguste Rodin's originals and castings—the largest exhibit of his works outside the Musée Rodin in Paris—are on display. Tues.–Sun., 10 A.M.–5 P.M. Donations welcome.

Rosenbach Museum and Library. 2010 Delancey Pl. (732–1600). 18th- and 19th-century English and French prints; Chippendale, Hepplewhite, and Louis XV furniture; thousands of rare books and manuscripts including the original manuscript of James Joyce's *Ulysses;* Maurice Sendak drawings; the archive of poet Marianne Moore, and more in a 19th-century townhouse. Tues.–Sun., 11 A.M.–4 P.M. (closed in Aug.). Adults, $2.50 for guided tour; students and seniors, $1.50.

The University Museum of Archaeology and Anthropology. 33rd and Spruce Sts. (898–4000). A world-renowned collection of artifacts from ancient and primitive cultures. Galleries devoted to Southeast Asia, China, Africa, Mesopotamia, and the Americas. Tues.–Sat., 10 A.M.–4:30 P.M.; Sun., 1 P.M.–5 P.M. Closed Sun., July and Aug. Tours Sat.–Sun., 1:15 P.M., Oct.–May. Adults, $3; students and seniors $1.50; under 6, free.

MUSIC. If there is one art which shapes the cultural skyline of Philadelphia, it is music. From the world-famous Philadelphia Orchestra to chamber music groups, the city offers music for a myriad of moods and interests. The **Philadelphia Orchestra** performs its classical concerts from Sept. to May at the *Academy of Music,* Broad and Locust streets. For tickets, call the box office (893–1930). Also, 45 minutes before each Fri. and Sat. performance, a line forms for $2.50 tickets to the amphitheater. From mid-June through July, the orchestra gives free open-air concerts at the Mann Music Center in West Fairmount Park. Tickets are available the day of the concert at the Visitors Center at 16th St. and John F. Kennedy Blvd. Be there when they open at 9 A.M.

The Emmy Award-winning **Opera Company of Philadelphia** (732–5814) attracts the biggest names in the operatic field; they perform at the Academy of Music from Oct. to Apr. The **Concerto Soloists of Philadelphia** (574–3550) perform classical music under the batons of Marc Mostovoy and Max Rudolf, Sept. to June at the Academy of Music, the Walnut Street Theater, and the Church of the Holy Trinity.

Moe Septee's **All-Star Forum** showcases such classical artists as Itzhak Perlman and Isaac Stern. Septee also presents the **Philly Pops,** conducted by Peter Nero. Both seasons run from Oct. to May at the Academy of Music. Phone 735–7506. The innovative new **American Music Theater Festival** (567–0670) stages its shows at the Zellerbach Theater and other sites in the spring.

Popular artists like Billy Joel, Sting, and Madonna are in town often under the auspices of *Electric Factory Concerts.* For information about who'll be performing where and when and how to get tickets, call 976–HITS. In July and Aug., the **Robin Hood Dell East** (477–8810), on Strawberry Mansion Dr. near Ridge Ave. and Dauphin St., stages a mix of rhythm and blues and soul sounds.

During the summer, there are numerous **music festivals** and outdoor concerts at Penn's Landing, John F. Kennedy Plaza, and other sites. The **Philadelphia Folk Festival** takes root the last weekend in Aug. at the Old Poole Farm in Schwenksville (242–0150).

DANCE. In 1990 Christopher d'Amboise took the lead of the **Pennsylvania Ballet** (551–7014), which performs its repertory at the Academy of Music and the Shubert Theatre, Broad and Locust Sts., from Oct. to June. Its "Nutcracker" is a Christmastime favorite. The **Annenberg Center,** 3680 Walnut St. (898–6791), plays host annually to Dance Celebration, featuring modern dance talents like Twyla Tharp and Alvin Ailey. The shows run from Nov. to May.

STAGE. The **Forrest Theater,** 1114 Walnut St. (923–1515) is the top Broadway house in town, with such fare as *Cats* and *Les Miserables.* The **Walnut Street Theatre Company,** 9th and Walnut sts. (574–3550), offers a schedule of musicals, comedy, and drama in the oldest operating theater in the United States. Their season runs from Nov. to Mar. The **Philadelphia Drama Guild** (898–6791) favors 20th-century works; it performs at the **Annenberg Center,** 3680 Walnut St., from Oct. to May. The Annenberg Center (898–6791) also plays host to visiting theater companies, which present eclectic fare.

Both the **Wilma Theater,** 2030 Sansom St. (963–0345) and **Society Hill Playhouse,** 507 S. 8th St. (923–0210) contribute to the theater scene with offbeat, contemporary works. **The Shubert Theatre** (732–5446), 250 S. Broad, now part of the University of Arts, is a showcase for ballet, opera, and other entertainers.

The **Theater of the Living Arts,** 334 South St. (922–1010), features live performances of current productions, such as *Little Shop of Horrors,* in a small 400-seat theater. Live bands are scheduled in between theater runs.

FILM. The crown jewels of all local houses are the five-screen *Ritz Five,* 214 Walnut St., and the *Ritz at the Bourse,* 4th and Chestnut Sts. (215–925–7900), with the latest in foreign fare as well as small gems. The *Roxy Screening Rooms,* 2023 Sansom St. (215–561–0114), is an "art" house featuring intellectual and esoteric fare.

Independent- and art-film buffs choose the Temple *Cinematheque,* 1619 Walnut St. (215–787–1529); *International House,* 3701 Chestnut St. (215–387–5125); *University Museum,* 33rd and Spruce Sts. (215–898–4025) for their weekend revivals; and the *Art Museum,* 26th St. and the Parkway (215–763–8100), for the Sun. afternoon film series.

ACCOMMODATIONS. Philadelphia has over 11,000 rooms to satisfy a variety of tastes and budgets. Though the majority of hotels are in the expensive and deluxe categories, most offer significantly reduced weekend rates and appealing packages—often as much as 35% off—when the business travelers go home. Rates do not vary seasonally. Most of the hotels are concentrated in Center City, others are conveniently located near the airport, in University City (two mi. from downtown), or by the City Line exit of the Schuylkill Expressway (about five mi. west of Center City). Price categories are based on double occupancy on weeknights: *Super Deluxe,* $175 and up; *Deluxe,* $130–$175; *Expensive,* $100–$130; *Moderate,* $85–$100; *Inexpensive,* $40–$85; *Rock Bottom,* under $40. Most hotels offer weekend discounts and some mid-week packages. A six percent state sales tax and five percent occupancy tax will be added to your bill.

Super Deluxe

Four Seasons. One Logan Square, Phila., PA 19103 (215–963–1500 or 800–322–3442). Top-notch hotel with breathtaking lobby; rooms furnished in the Federal style. Extraordinary service and every imaginable amenity. Health spa with indoor pool, superb Fountain Restaurant which serves the city's best Sun. brunch.

Hotel Atop the Bellevue. Broad and Walnut Sts., Philadelphia, PA 19102 (215–893–1776 or 800–222–0939). The Cunard Line, known for its *Queen Elizabeth 2,* operates this 170-room, luxury European-style hotel on the top seven floors of a Philadelphia landmark, the old Bellevue Stratford Hotel. The hotel has been totally renovated; there are retail shops (Polo/Ralph Lauren), a private club for hotel guests, and a 70,000-square-foot Sporting Club on the premises.

The Rittenhouse. 210 W. Rittenhouse Sq., Philadelphia, PA 19103 (215–546–9000 or 800–635–1042). The city's newest addition to its classiest one-block-square park is a 98-room luxury property occupying five floors of a high-rise condo. Two restaurants, health club with indoor pool, 24-hour concierge service, and two lounges. Rooms decorated in traditional French style; armoire hides a VCR and minibar.

Sheraton Society Hill. 1 Dock St., Phila., PA 19106 (215–238–6000 or 800–325–3535). The hotel, which opened in Society Hill in 1986, is convenient to historical attractions. Gracious red-brick town house-style hotel with four-story atrium lobby. Indoor pool, health club, popular video nightclub.

Deluxe

Barclay. Rittenhouse Sq. East, Phila., PA 19103 (215–545–0300 or 800–421–6662). Old World elegance and a fashionable location distinguish this dignified, service-oriented hotel. Award-winning cuisine, piano bar.

Guest Quarters. 4101 Island Ave., Phila. PA 19153 (215–365–6600 or 800–424–2900). An all-suites hotel near airport. Refrigerator, wet bar in rooms, indoor pool, Jacuzzi, sauna.

Hershey Philadelphia Hotel. Broad and Locust Sts., Phila., PA 19107 (215–893–1600 or 800–HERSHEY). Handsome, glass-faced tower across from Academy of Music. Bustling with conventioneers; great family plans. Indoor pool, health club, live entertainment.

Latham. 17th and Walnut Sts., Phila., PA 19103 (215–563–7474 or 800–528–4261). Charming, intimate, European-style hostelry was totally renovated in Sept. '88. Personal attention and thoughtful extras make this home away from home for many corporate travelers. Casablanca inspired restaurant, popular lounge.

Marriott—Philadelphia Airport. 4509 Island Ave., Phila., PA 19153 (215–365–4150 or 800–228–9290). Fine airport hotel with many amenities. Attractive lobby built around indoor pool, dancing nightly.

Ritz-Carlton. 17th and Chestnut Sts., Phila., PA 19103 (215–563–1600 or 800–241–3333). The city's newest hotel, with 290 rooms, is part of the new Liberty Place shopping-office complex with more than 70 stores and restaurants.

Warwick. 17th and Locust Sts., Phila., PA 19103 (215–735–6000 or 800–523–4210). Elegant, stylish hotel popular with young business and leisure travelers. Attentive service. Polo Bay Club is one of the city's hottest nightspots. 1701 Café serves a fine Sun. brunch.

Wyndham Franklin Plaza. 17th and Race Sts., Phila., PA 19103 (215–448–2000 or 800–822–4200). Stunning, modern 758-room hotel popular with conventioneers. Highly rated. Indoor pool, health club, tennis, running track, comfortable, contemporary rooms.

Expensive

Adam's Mark. City Ave. and Monument Rd., Phila., PA 19131 (215–581–5000 or 800–444–2326). 10 minutes from downtown. 510 guest rooms in attractive highrise hotel; health club with indoor pool; jazz at Pierre's, Quincy's for dancing; beauty salon. Sun. buffet brunch. Car rental.

Airport Hilton Inn. 10th St. and Packer Ave., Phila., PA 19148 (215–755–9500 or 800–HILTONS). Across from the sports complex. Spacious rooms, nightclub with DJ, outdoor pool.

Holiday Inn—Center City. 1800 Market St., Phila., PA 19103 (215–561–7500 or 800–HOLIDAY). Popular for its central location and better-than-usual Holiday Inn amenities.

Holiday Inn—Independence Mall. 4th and Arch Sts., Phila., PA 19106 (215–923–8660 or 800–HOLIDAY). Comfortable highrise close to historic area; good choice for families on vacation. Outdoor pool.

Independence Park Inn. 235 Chestnut St., Phila., PA 19106 (215–922–4443). An 1856 warehouse near the city's historical attractions has been transformed into a cozy, elegant 36-room hostelry with a five-story atrium and glass-enclosed courtyard where a European breakfast is served. Afternoon tea.

Penn Tower. 34th St. and Civic Center Blvd., Phila., PA 19104 (215–387–8333 or 800–356–PENN). High rise owned by University of Pennsylvania, adjacent to the campus. Totally renovated. Concierge level offers extras at additional charge.

Moderate

Airport Tower Hotel. 20th St. and Penrose Ave., Phila., PA 19145 (215–755–6500 or 800–247–7676). Circular high rise with outdoor pool, restaurant, DJ in lounge. Seven blocks from sports complex.

Chestnut Hill Hotel. 8229 Germantown Ave., Phila., PA 19118 (215–242–5905). In the heart of Chestnut Hill, nine miles northwest of Center City. 28 cozy, well-appointed rooms in a restored colonial country inn. Charming and comfortable. 18th-century reproduction furniture. Two restaurants.

Holiday Inn—City Line. 4100 Presidential Blvd. at City Ave. exit of I-76 (215–477–0200 or 800–HOLIDAY). Recently refurbished hotel about 6 mi. from Center City. Restaurant, indoor/outdoor pool, whirlpool, game room.

Quality Inn-Downtown Suites. 1010 Race St., Chinatown (215–922–1730 or 800–221–2222). Old Bentwood rocker factory has been transformed into an eight-story hotel. Two or three-room suites with full kitchens. Nonsmokers' floor. Breakfast included in room rate.

Inexpensive

Comfort Inn at Penn's Landing. 100 N. Delaware Ave. at Race St. Phila., PA 19106 (215–627–7900 or 800–228–5150). Ten-story hotel, opened Nov. 1987, is convenient to waterfront and historical attractions. Complimentary Continental breakfast. No restaurant on premises. Request a river view.

Quality Inn—Center City. 501 N. 22nd St. (one block north of Benjamin Franklin Pkwy.), Phila., PA 19130 (215–568–8300 or 800–228–5151). Comfortable motel within walking distance of major museums. Excellent value and location. Entertainment, pool, restaurant, room service, free parking.

Rock Bottom

Apollo. 1918 Arch St., Phila., PA 19103 (215–567–8925). Budget hotel popular with young travelers. In a convenient, safe location. Rooms with private baths available. AC, HBO, elevator. No credit cards.

International House. 3701 Chestnut St., Phila., PA 19143 (215–387–5125). Must be academically affiliated. Not fancy, but fun. Single rooms only; only towels and linens provided. No children allowed. Gourmet cafeteria, AC.

BED AND BREAKFASTS. Society Hill Hotel. 301 Chestnut St., Phila., PA 19106 (215–925–1394). The city's oldest bed-and-breakfast establishment is an urban inn. 12 rooms with brass double beds, antiques, fresh flowers, chocolates, private baths. Continental breakfast in bed. Jazz piano bar/restaurant. Rooms from $79.

Thomas Bond House. 129 S. Second St., Phila., PA 19106 (215–923–8523). A 12-bedroom inn in a historically restored Georgian and Federal house which belongs to the National Park Service. Private baths; three rooms have whirlpool baths. Library with woodburning fireplace. Continental breakfast weekdays, full breakfast on weekends. Innkeeper: Jerry Dunn. Rooms $80–$150.

YOUTH HOTELS. Chamounix Mansion. Chamounix Dr., West Fairmount Park, Phila., PA 19131 (215–878–3676). Philadelphia's youth hostel is in a renovated Quaker farmhouse. American Youth Hostels members: $7 per night. Additional $3 guest fee for nonmembers. Dorm style; linen rental, $2. Check in from 4:30–8 P.M., lock up at 11 P.M. Kitchen facilities available; bring food with you. No credit cards. Closed Dec. 15–Jan. 15.

RESTAURANTS. Philadelphia has garnered national attention for its restaurant renaissance and the cuisine it engendered, an artful blend of American, French, and Oriental. The other local cuisine—Philadelphia junk food—doesn't get as much attention, but don't miss out on tasting hoagies, cheesesteaks, and soft pretzels with mustard. Ethnic cuisine is fairly well represented here, particularly French, Italian, and Chinese. For evening meals, it's best to make reservations in advance whenever possible. Some restaurants are fussy about the dress code, but a neatly dressed patron will usually experience no problem.

Restaurants are listed according to the price of a three-course dinner (drinks, 6% tax, and tip not included): *Deluxe,* over $35; *Expensive,* $25–$35; *Moderate,* $12–$25; *Inexpensive,* less than $12.

Super Deluxe

Le Bec-Fin. 1523 Walnut St. (567–1000). Philadelphia's premier French restaurant and one of the best French restaurants on the East Coast. Dazzling haute cuisine in a setting Louis XVI would feel right at home in. Master chef and proprietor Georges Perrier learned his skills in the kitchens of France's Pyramide and Baumanière. Invisible service. Lunch, prix fixe at $31, prix-fixe dinner at $89. Two seatings at lunch and dinner. L, D, Mon.–Fri.; D only, Sat. All major cards.

Deluxe

Bookbinder's. 125 Walnut St. (925–7027). Officially, "Old Original Bookbinder." Tourists and devotees of fresh, quality seafood frequent this Philadelphia landmark. Massive lobsters and excellent soups are specialties. L, D, daily (dinner menu all day Sat. and Sun.). AE, DC, MC, V.

DiLullo Centro. 1407 Locust St. (546–2000). The best Northern Italian cuisine in the city is served in a smashing, bilevel renovation of an old theater. Seasonal specialties like mushroom pasta with wild mushroom sauce, baked artichokes with pancetta and cheese, and grilled marinated pheasant. Don't miss the gelato. Impeccable service. L, D, Mon.–Fri.; D only, Sat. All major cards.

The Fountain. Four Seasons Hotel, 18th St. and the Benjamin Franklin Pkwy. (963–1500). Exceptional food in a magnificent flower-filled setting overlooking the Swann Fountain in Logan Circle. International menu deftly prepared by French chefs. Sun. brunch is outstanding. L, D, daily. All major cards.

Morton's of Chicago. One Logan Sq. (557–0724). Classic steakhouse fare in a chic, club-like atmosphere. Choose your own aged prime steak or chop, in its raw state, and have it cooked to perfection. Excellent lobsters as well. Reservations accepted only till 7 P.M. L, D, Mon.–Fri.; D only, Sat. and Sun. AE, DC, MC, V.

Expensive

Alouette. 4th and Bainbridge Sts. (629–1126). "New Asian" cuisine and superb French food is served in a charmingly romantic, candlelit atmosphere. L, Mon.–Fri.; D daily; Sun. brunch. AE, MC, V.

Apropos. 211 S. Broad St. (546–4424). The decor is high-tech modern with a California-style menu that features mesquite wood grilling and dishes with a Mediterranean accent. European bakery. Brazilian music some nights. Late supper served until midnight. B, L, D, daily. AE, DC, MC, V.

Friday, Saturday, Sunday. 261 S. 21st St. (546–4232). A blackboard menu and a casually romantic atmosphere make this a particularly popular dining spot. Specialties include cream of mushroom soup and poached salmon with sorrel sauce. Reservations only for parties of 5 or more. L, Mon.–Fri., D daily. All major cards.

Il Gallo Nero. 254 S. 15th St. (546–8065). The accent is Florentine and the ambience coolly elegant. Meals are leisurely but the food is worth the wait. Fresh white truffles in season, homemade pasta and gelati, game dishes. L, D, Tues.–Fri.; D only, Sat. All major cards.

Odeon. 114 S. 12th St. (922–5875). An elegant sophisticated bistro serving French regional specialties. Exceptional desserts. Wine bar with 16-spout cruvinet. L, D Mon.–Fri.; D only Sat. AE, MC, V.

Susanna Foo. 1512 Walnut St. (545–2666). Authentic upscale Chinese cuisine like sautéed quail with shitake mushrooms and filet mignon with pepper sauce. *Esquire* voted this one of the best Chinese restaurants in the country. L, D Mon.–Fri.; D only Sat. AE, MC, V.

Moderate

Carolina's. 261 S. 20th St. (545–1000). Something for everyone, from Chinese dumplings to chili chicken, but built on a down-home base. (Remember veal loaf and mashed potatoes?) Country bread and sinful desserts. L, Mon.–Fri.; D, nightly; Sun. brunch. Reservations required. AE, DC, MC, V.

The Commissary. 1710 Sansom St. (569–2240). Gourmet cafeteria with well-prepared soups, salads, omelets, pates, desserts, and daily entree specials. Wine by the glass. Open daily from breakfast to late supper. AE, DC, MC, V.

Marabella's. 1420 Locust St. (545–1845). This trendy trattoria offers everything from mesquite-grilled seafood to homemade pastas and pizza with goat cheese and sun-dried tomatoes. Fun, casual, and near the theaters; great for an after-show bite. Reservations taken for lunch only. L, D, daily. AE, MC, V.

Sansom Street Oyster House. 1516 Samson St. (567–7683). The best raw oysters and clams in town are found at this old-fashioned, informal oyster house. L, D, Mon.–Sat. AE, DC, MC, V.

Siam Cuisine. 925 Arch St. (922–7135). What many consider the city's best Thai cuisine is served in a very pretty pastel setting. Good service, good wine list. Try the *nua num tok* (spicy beef salad). L, D; Mon–Sat.; D only Sun. AE, MC, V.

White Dog Cafe. 3420 Sansom St., University City (386–9224). Regional American cuisine served with country-inn charm in antique-filled dining rooms. Grilled meats and fish, smoked duck, apple brown betty are specialties. B, L Mon.–Fri., D daily, Brunch, Sat.–Sun. All major cards.

Inexpensive

Eden. 1527 Chestnut St. (972–0400). A stylish cafeteria that features great hamburgers, gourmet stir-fry dishes, pasta, salads, quiche, delicious homemade soups, and desserts. Good and quick. B, L, D, Mon–Fri., L, D, Sat. Wine and beer served. No credit cards.

Pat's King of Steaks. 1237 E. Passyunk Ave., South Philadelphia (468–1546). The No. 1 place for a sidewalk steak sandwich with onions, cheese, and peppers. Open 24 hours daily.

Reading Terminal Market. 12th and Filbert Sts. (922–2317). A 19th-century European style marketplace lined with meat, fish, and produce stands, plus more than

25 stalls with ready-to-eat ethnic treats. Eat at least one lunch here, and don't miss Bassetts ice cream, the soft pretzels at Fisher's Ice Cream, and the Amish farm-fresh goodies on Wed.–Sat. Open Mon.–Sat., 8 A.M.–6 P.M.

Silveri's. 315 S. 13th St. (545–5115). A friendly neighborhood bar famous for its Buffalo chicken wings and great hamburgers. Other items include salads and homemade pasta. L, Mon.–Fri.; D, daily. MC, V.

Triangle Tavern. 10th and Reed Sts., South Philadelphia (467–8683). A casual neighborhood spot known for old-style Italian cooking—ravioli, manicotti, mussels in white or red sauce—just like Mama used to make. Live entertainment on weekends. D, daily. No credit cards.

Walt's King of Crabs. 804–6 S. 2nd St. (339–9124). Good fresh seafood in a casual atmosphere; crabs, mussels, and a $9.50 lobster are specialties. L, D, Mon.–Sat., D only, Sun. No credit cards.

LIQUOR LAWS. In Pennsylvania, the legal age for the purchase and consumption of alcoholic beverages is 21. In bars and restaurants, drinks may be ordered from 7 A.M. until 2 A.M. Mon.–Sat.; from 11 A.M.–2 A.M. Sun. (if the establishment has a special permit). Stores where liquor can be purchased are called State Stores and are operated by the Pennsylvania Liquor Control Board. Generally, store hours are 11 A.M. to 7 P.M., Mon.–Tues.; 9 A.M.–9 P.M., Wed.–Sat. Up to 144 fluid ounces of beer may be purchased over the counter in bars.

NIGHTLIFE. Reports that Philadelphia has no nightlife are greatly exaggerated—you just have to know where to look. Whether you like mellow piano music, jazz favorites, or the light show and pick-up scene, you can find it. Certain clubs are members-only, after-hours places that can stay open after the 2 A.M. legal closing time. Usually, anyone can join them on the spot by paying a guest fee. Many of these nightspots have strict ideas about proper dress; it's wise to call ahead to find out about dress, hours and who the night's entertainers will be.

Bars with Music

The Hershey Bar. Hershey Hotel, Broad and Locust Sts. (893–1600). Handsome lounge with combo from 9 P.M.–1:30 A.M. daily. You can even dance to contemporary and '40s music. Some of the city's best happy-hour munchies, weeknights 5–7 P.M.

Liberties. 705 N. 2nd St., above Fairmount (238–0660). A hot spot with a great old look. This handsome restored Victorian pub features live music—contemporary folk rock and jazz—Fri.–Sat. nights, at 9 P.M.

Not Quite Crickett. 17th and Walnut Sts. (563–9444). A dark, pleasing lounge with good sound: jazz and Top-40 hits, Tues.–Fri., 8:30 P.M.–1:30 A.M.

Top of Centre Square. First Pennsylvania Bank Tower, 15th and Market Sts. (563–9494). Hot and cold happy hour snacks weeknights, jazzy vocalist and pianist Fri.–Sat., from 9 P.M. The view from the bar (41 stories up) is spectacular.

Music and Dancing

Apropos. 211 S. Broad St. (546–4424). A Brazilian band delivers terrific sambas, bossa novas and slow tunes for dancing on a small dance floor in the middle of this chic eatery. Wed., Fri., Sat., from 10 P.M.

Aztec. 939 N. Delaware Ave. (574–5730). The city's newest and hottest club. Different music every night till 2 A.M. Weekend dress code. Cover about $5.

Babe's Steakhouse. 3400 Aramingo Ave., Port Richmond (423–6000). Dance to romantic tunes, show music, and Cole Porter gems nightly (except Mon.) from 6 P.M. in the balcony lounge of this dramatic new restaurant. The live bands glide through the balcony on a movable stage. Jackets required.

Bacchanal. 1320 South St. (545–6983). A hangout for poets, artists and South St. denizens. Live rock, blues, R&B, and reggae bands nightly. On Sat. night, Philly Gumbo packs in the crowds with its original mix of rock, reggae and be-bop. Open daily. Cover $4.

The Bank. 600 Spring Garden St. (351–9404). This disco, in a historic bank building designed by Frank Furness, draws a fashionable crowd to hear progressive dance sounds. Open Wed.–Sat., 9 P.M.–2 A.M. Free parking. Cover: about $6.

Chestnut Cabaret. 3801 Chestnut St. (382–1201). This concert hall cum dance club by the Penn campus features live music by top national and local rock and rhythm & blues musicians. Popular with college students. Casual, but men's shirts should have collars. Tues.–Sat., 8 P.M.–2 A.M. Cover charge varies.

Flanigan's. Abbotts Square, 2nd and South Sts. (928–9898). A lively mid-20s crowd enjoys happy hour here with a complimentary 18-foot buffet, Wed.–Fri. 4:30–8 P.M. A DJ spins Top 40 sounds Tues.–Sat., until 2:30 A.M. Weekend cover $5.

Monte Carlo Living Room. 2nd and South Sts. (925–2220). A sophisticated, romantic cocktail lounge with a DJ manning the turntable with Top 40 hits and slow music for touch dancing. Open Tues.–Sat., 6 P.M.–2 A.M. Jackets required. $10 cover charge.

Phoenix. 718 Arch St. (625–2446). This huge multilevel club with intimate spaces draws a 25–30-year-old crowd. Adult contemporary music; local radio stations broadcast live from here most nights. Wed.–Fri., 4 P.M.–2 A.M., Sat.–Sun., 7 P.M.–2 A.M. Cover about $5. Popular happy hour weeknights, 4–6:30 P.M.

Polo Bay Club. Warwick Hotel, 17th and Locust Sts. (546–8800). Sophisticated "in" spot for business people and professionals who stop by for the great happy-hour buffet and stay for dancing. A DJ programs the sounds Tues.–Sat., 5 P.M.–2 A.M. Cover: about $5.

Trocadero. 10th and Arch Sts. (592–TROC). A hot rock 'n' roll club in a former burlesque house. Nationally known concert acts on some weeknights (call for schedule and ticket information). Dance parties Thurs. (9 P.M.–2 A.M. with unlimited buffet), Fri. (4 P.M.–2 A.M.) and Sat. (7 P.M.–2 A.M.). $5 admission after 8 P.M. Fri., 9 P.M. Sat. Concert tickets available at Ticketron outlets, at the door, or by calling Telecharge (800–233–4050).

Jazz

Borgia Cafe. 406 S. 2nd St., downstairs at Lautrec restaurant (574–0414). Voted one of the best 100 bars in America by *Esquire* magazine. Live jazz nightly. Music begins at 9:30 P.M.

Magnolia Cafe. 1602 Locust St. (546–4180). This popular Cajun restaurant serves up Dixieland jazz Tues. 6–11 P.M. in their attractive bar. Fine food as well.

Morgan's. 17 E. Price St., Germantown (844–6067). A premier restaurant/lounge for jazz fans, Morgan's presents artists like Max Roach, Arthur Prysock, and Les McCann. Call for schedule. Prices vary.

Comedy Clubs

Comedy Factory Outlet. 31 Bank St., between Market and Chestnut, 2nd and 3rd (FUNNY–11). Local and national yuksters tickle your funny bone, Thurs.–Sat. Open stage night Wed., 8 P.M. (sign up at 7:30). Tickets $12.50. Reservations required.

Comedy Works. 126 Chestnut St., upstairs (phone: WACKY–97). The city's original full-time comedy club. Top young comics from both coasts perform nightly Thurs.–Sat. Wed. is open mike night for aspiring comics. Prices vary.

Hard to Categorize

Painted Bride Art Center. 230 Vine St. (925–9914). A contemporary art gallery by day, a club featuring folk, electronic and new music, jazz, dance, poetry readings, and theater at night. Call for schedule.

WASHINGTON, D.C.

by
FRANCIS X. ROCCA and RITA CHABOT

Mr. Rocca is a writer based in Alexandria, Virginia. Ms. Chabot is a writer and editor. Some material in this chapter is based on the work of Judy Liberson, Betty Ross, and Katherine Walker.

Washington embodies the nation's history in everything from the White House to the Vietnam Veterans Memorial to the National Archives, where the Declaration of Independence, the Constitution, and the Bill of Rights are displayed. Time has seeped into the fibers of a city woven out of compromise.

In 1790, when the First Congress was meeting in New York City, a hot debate exploded between northerners and southerners. Should the "Federal City" be in the North or the South? Alexander Hamilton, a New York Federalist, and Thomas Jefferson, a Virginia liberal, reached an agreement found acceptable by all: the new government would assume the war debts of the 13 states, especially the large Northern ones, if the capital would be built in the South. George Washington chose a site on the banks of the Potomac River near Mount Vernon, his estate. A French engineer, Pierre L'Enfant, volunteered to design a city that would be "magnificent enough to grace a nation."

L'Enfant decided to build the "Congress House" on a "pedestal awaiting a monument," Jenkins Hill (now Capitol Hill), and proceeded to plan the Capitol and the rest of the city. With the Capitol at the center, Washington is divided into four sections. Even though L'Enfant thought the city would grow eastward toward the Anacostia River, the Northwest sec-

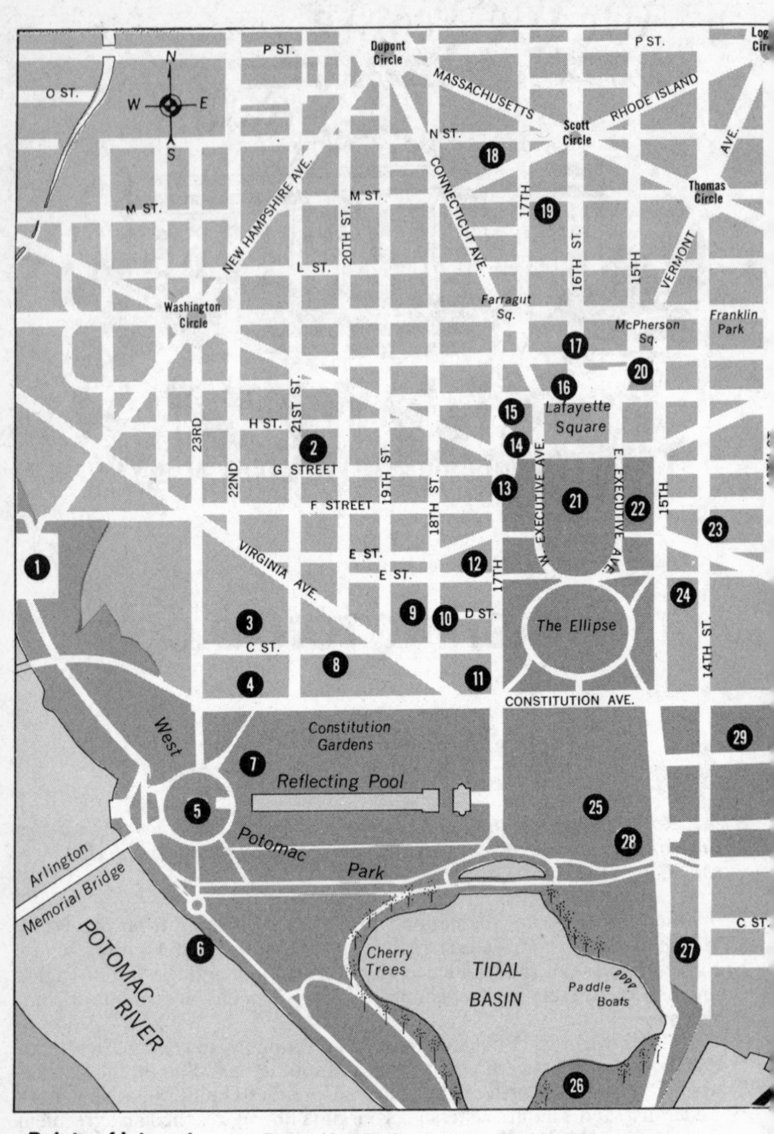

Points of Interest
Arthur M. Sackler Gallery **54**
Blair House **14**
Botanical Gardens **45**
Bureau of Printing and Engraving **27**
Capitol **47**
Constitution Hall **10**
Corcoran Art Gallery **12**
Commerce Dept. Building (Aquarium & Visitor's Center) **24**
Dept. of Energy **52**
Dept. of Interior **9**
Dept. of Justice **36**
Dept. of State **3**
Executive Office Building (former) **13**
FBI (J.E. Hoover Building) **35**
Federal Reserve Board **8**
Ford's Theater **34**
Freer Gallery of Art **40**
George Washington University **2**
Government Printing Office **53**
Hirshhorn Museum & Sculpture Garden **41**
House Office Buildings **46**
Jefferson Memorial **26**
John F. Kennedy Center **1**
Library of Congress **48**
Lincoln Memorial **5**
Metro Center **31**
National Academy of Sciences **4**
National Air & Space Museum **42**

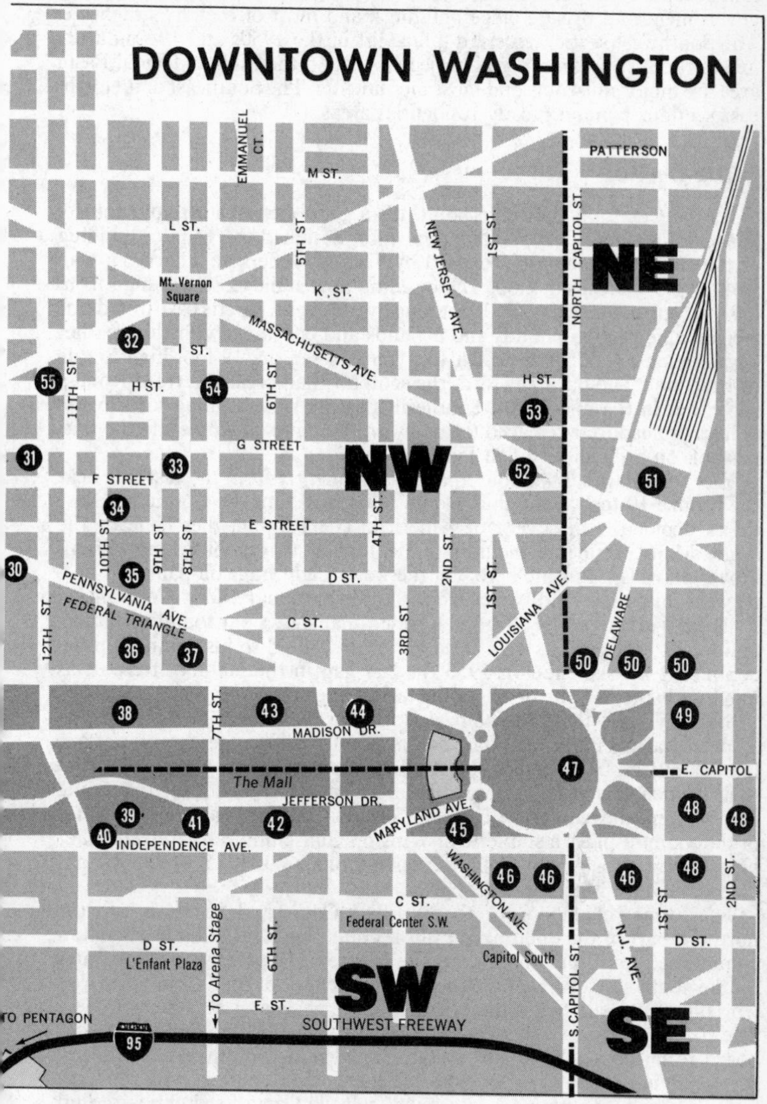

DOWNTOWN WASHINGTON

National Archives **37**
National Gallery of Art (East Building) **44**
National Gallery of Art (West Building) **43**
National Geographic Society **19**
National Museum of African Art **55**
National Museum of American Art & Portrait Gallery **33**
National Museum of American History **29**
National Natural History Museum **38**
National Theater **23**
Organization of American States **11**
The Pavilion at the Old Post Office **30**
Potomac Boat Tour Dock **6**
Renwick Gallery **15**
St. John's Church **16**
St. Matthew's Cathedral **18**
Senate Office Buildings **50**
Smithsonian Institution **39**
Supreme Court **49**
Sylvan Theater **28**
Treasury Dept. **22**
Union Station **51**
Veterans' Administration **20**
Vietnam Veterans Memorial **7**
Washington Convention & Visitors Assn. **17**
Washington D.C. Convention Center **32**
Washington Monument **25**
White House **21**

tion became the biggest. It contains Georgetown, Rock Creek Park, many government and private office buildings, and most of the city's nightlife. The Southwest section received a face-lift in the 1950s and 1960s during one of the first urban renewal projects. Around the Mall and Tidal Basin area are major museums and most monuments. The Southeast and Northeast sections contain mostly residential areas.

The Capitol

As the Capitol is the centerpoint, it's a good idea to start your tour of Washington there. Dr. William Thornton designed the Capitol building as the result of a contest proposed by Thomas Jefferson. Thornton, who won in 1793, received $500. The building now stands 287 feet high from base to top, and measures 751 feet long by 350 feet wide. Its cast-iron dome weighs nine million pounds and expands and contracts with the weather by as much as four inches. On top you can see the 19-foot-high Statue of Freedom. Thomas Crawford, the sculptor, had created a freed Roman slave, but in the mid-1850s, Southern senators were arguing for slavery. A feather headdress replaced the cap worn by slaves in Rome and the statue took on a distinct Indian look.

Free tours last half an hour and leave frequently from the east side near the bronze 10-ton "Columbus Doors" that lead into the Rotunda. These doors depict the discovery of America. The Rotunda lies beneath the dome. Many presidents, including Lincoln, Kennedy, Johnson, and Eisenhower, have lain in state here. On the walls, eight huge oil paintings portray colonial times and scenes from the Revolutionary War. Constantino Brumidi worked on the allegorical fresco that shows our founding fathers amid gods and goddesses until he fell off a scaffold to his death. A pupil completed his sketches. In 1953 the last gap in the 300-foot fresco was filled with the Wright brothers' historical flight at Kitty Hawk.

Statuary Hall, the next room, was used as a chamber of the House of Representatives until 1857. The hall now contains a representation of one famous citizen from each state. At first, each state had two statues, but their tremendous weight strained the floor beams. Many of the remaining statues were moved to the Hall of Columns. A glass case in the center of the room displays a statuette of Winston Churchill; Margaret Thatcher presented it as a gift to Congress on February 20, 1985, when she addressed a Joint Meeting of Congress.

The former chambers for the Supreme Court and Senate are in the northern part of the building. In this section, you'll also find the Senate's committee rooms and chambers. The House of Representatives operates on the south side. To watch either for any length of time (tours give you a brief look), a pass from your representative or senator must be obtained. The six congressional office buildings are nearby. Call the Capitol switchboard to find out where your congressional representatives have offices. A free miniature subway connects the Senate office buildings with the Capitol. To check if Congress is in session, call the Capitol switchboard, find the "Activities in Congress" column printed in the *Washington Post,* or look for the American flag over the House and Senate wings of the Capitol. The lantern in the dome is always lit when the Senate or House is in session.

The Supreme Court is across from the Capitol, on the corner of 1st and East Capitol streets. Designed by Cass Gilbert, the white marble building with gigantic columns was completed in 1935. From 1800 to 1935, the Court moved to seven different sites in Washington. Two statues, *The Contemplation of Justice* and *The Guardian (or Authority) of Law,* grace the main entrance. Before walking into the Great Hall, note the bronze doors. Each weighs over six tons. Sculpted on them are scenes from the development of law. Columns line the Great Hall and busts of past chief justices are on display. Beyond this lies the marbled Court Chamber.

Just south of the Supreme Court Building is the Library of Congress. It began in 1800 when Congress appropriated $5,000 to stock a room in the Capitol. The library has 532 miles of bookshelves containing about 80 million items in three buildings. Among its treasures are a Gutenberg Bible, a Stradivarius collection, the private library of Thomas Jefferson, and a folk-music collection. The library serves as a research center for Congress. More than 800 people in its Congressional Research Service gather information for senators, representatives, and their staffs. Another arm of the library, the National Library Services for the Blind and Physically Handicapped, provides recorded books and magazines as well as material in Braille. On the ground floor of the Thomas Jefferson Building (main building), you'll find an information desk and sales area. The library is open seven days a week.

Other places to see on Capitol Hill include the Botanic Garden at the foot of the Capitol's west front. Catch one of the four seasonal flower shows: azaleas (end of February), spring flowers (just before Easter), chrysanthemums (November), and poinsettias (mid-December). If you have children, the Capital Children's Museum on 3rd Street offers hands-on fun. Gonzaga College, at 19 Eye Street, NW, is the oldest high school in Washington (founded in 1821); on its campus, St. Aloysius' Church boasts work by Brumidi, the painter of the Capitol.

The White House

The design for the "President's Palace," as L'Enfant referred to it, resulted from a contest. James Hoban, an Irish architect living in Charleston, South Carolina, won. He drew his idea from Leinster Hall in Dublin. The work on the White House began in 1792 and was still uncompleted by 1829, when Andrew Jackson began his term as the seventh president. Not all first families were happy living here. Abigail Adams, who hung her laundry in the East Room, complained that "not a single apartment [was] finished." And Thomas Jefferson, who had anonymously submitted a plan to the contest, thought that the White House was "big enough for two emperors, one Pope, and the grand lama." In 1948 President Truman and his family moved to Blair House, across the street, while major renovations in the White House took place.

Two types of tours are available and both are free: a VIP tour that you must arrange for months in advance with your representative or senator, and an unguided "walk-through" tour for the general public. The VIP tour covers more than the regular tour, but all tourists see only the ground-floor rooms, not the presidential suite or offices on the second and third floors. Between Memorial Day and Labor Day, you'll have to line up on the Ellipse (a 54-acre lawn on the south side of the White House) for time-designated tickets. Sometimes the White House closes because of a special event, and notice may not be given until that day. At other times of the year, tourists line up at the East Gate on East Executive Avenue, and those there by noon are assured entrance.

On the tour you'll see five of the most famous rooms, starting with the East room. Several weddings and presidential funerals (including the funerals of Lincoln and Kennedy) have taken place here, as well as receptions and recitals. Familiar portraits of George and Martha Washington by Gilbert Stuart hang on the walls.

The Green Room is decked with moss-green wall coverings and decorated in American Federal style. Note the New England sofa that originally belonged to Daniel Webster and the paintings by Monet and Whistler.

In the elegant, oval-shaped Blue Room hang portraits of the first seven presidents. President Grover Cleveland married Frances Folsom in this French Empire-style room.

Cerise silk bordered with gold decorates the Red Room. Originally Hoban called this the President's Ante-Chamber. It is furnished in the Empire style of the early 1800s.

Abraham Lincoln's portrait hangs in the white and gold State Dining Room. This English Regency room is the second largest in the White House and the last on the tour.

Lafayette Square, an 8.2-acre park, sits directly north of the White House. Though named after Revolutionary War hero Marquis de Lafayette, a statue of Andrew Jackson marks the center of the square and dominates the park. This is said to be the first equestrian statue produced in the United States. In each of the park's four corners, you'll find a statue of a foreign Revolutionary War leader: Lafayette in the southeast corner, Comte Jean de Rochambeau in the southwest corner, Baron von Steuben in the northwest corner, and Thaddeus Kosciuszko in the northeast corner. You may find it interesting to read various organizations' protest signs, which sit on the outer edges of the park, which they call "Peace Park."

St. John's Church, just north of Lafayette Square at 16th and H Streets, NW, is known as the Church of the Presidents because each president since Madison has attended a service there.

It is not open to the public, but you may want to walk by the Executive Office Building on 17th Street. The Vice-President and President have offices here. Patterned after Paris's Louvre, this building was called the War, Navy, and State Building until the Pentagon was finished in 1943.

To the east of the White House lie the J. Edgar Hoover Building, Ford's Theater, the National Portrait Gallery, and the National Museum of American Art. The J. Edgar Hoover Building houses the FBI. Tourists watch marksmanship demonstrations and see crime labs and displays on aspects of modern criminology.

The National Museum of American Art and the National Portrait Gallery are housed on Eighth Street in the Old Patent Building, a stunning example of Greek Revival architecture designed by Robert Mills, the architect for the Washington Monument and Treasury Building. The National Museum of American Art contains over 23,000 items including works by Gilbert Stuart, Benjamin West, Helen Frankenthaler, Alexander Calder, and George Catlin (who gained fame for his Indian paintings). On the third floor is the Lincoln Gallery, where Lincoln's second inaugural ball took place on March 7, 1865. The National Portrait Gallery displays portraits of, among others, Pocahontas and Horace Greeley. Don't miss the Presidential Corridor, where each president's portrait is hung.

The Monuments of the Mall

Washington's major museums and monuments are set out in the area of the Mall and the Tidal Basin. The four famous monuments are the Washington Monument, Lincoln Memorial, Vietnam Veterans Memorial, and the Jefferson Memorial. The Washington Monument, the world's tallest masonry structure, rises a little over 555 feet into the air and dominates the district's skyline. (There is a law restricting the height of buildings in Washington.) Many of its blocks were contributed by foreign governments, organizations, or states. Inscriptions on the inside faces of the stones indicate donors. Take the elevator ride to the top and see a panoramic view of the city. You may no longer climb up the 897 stairs, but a special permit to walk down them is available. In the summer, free concerts are given, and on the 4th of July a spectacular fireworks show awes visitors and residents alike.

At the Lincoln Memorial, the 19-foot statue of Lincoln seems infused with life. Daniel Chester French sculpted the statue and seated Lincoln to look past the Mall toward the Capitol. Above the statue are inscribed the words: "In this temple, as in the hearts of the people for whom he saved the Union, the memory of Abraham Lincoln is enshrined forever." On the walls of the chamber the words of the Gettysburg Address and the Second Inaugural are carved. The views from the memorial are worth noting: on one side you can see the Mall, Washington Monument, and the Capitol; on the other side, across the Potomac, rises Robert E. Lee's home above the Arlington Cemetery. Near the Lincoln Memorial stands the new Vietnam Veterans Memorial.

The nearby Tidal Basin with its Japanese cherry trees adds a unique beauty to the city. The annual Cherry Blossom Festival lasts for a week in late March or early April; it should coincide with the blossoming of the trees, but more often than not nature has a mind of its own. The festival begins when a woman from the Japanese Embassy lights a stone lantern found among the cherry trees. For a relaxing respite from the crowds that gather for the festival, try to rent one of the paddle boats and enjoy navigating the basin's water. The Jefferson Memorial overlooks the basin from the south shore.

The Museums of the Mall

The branches of the Smithsonian Institution dot the Mall. Called "the nation's attic," the Smithsonian contains over 30 million items. It began with half a million dollars willed by James Smithson, an English scientist who had never seen the United States. Among its many museums, the most popular in this area are the main building, the National Air and Space Museum, the National Museum of Natural History, and the National Museum of American History.

The unique, red-brick "Castle" (Jefferson Dr.) houses the main offices of the Smithsonian Institution. Built in 1849 and designed by James Renwick, it houses a permanent exhibit on the city's past and present. Close to the entrance is James Smithson's tomb.

The National Air and Space Museum (Jefferson Dr. and Independence Ave.) is the most visited museum in the U.S., if not the world. The *Spirit of St. Louis* hangs from the ceiling. Lindbergh flew this plane across the Atlantic on May 20–21, 1927, in 33 1/3 hours—the first nonstop solo flight across the ocean. And you may walk through a full-size model of *Skylab* and see the first plane that broke the sound barrier.

The National Museum of American History houses many treasures from our past, such as the exhibit of First Ladies' gowns, a Conestoga freight wagon, a 1913 Model T Ford, George Washington's false teeth, Eli Whitney's cotton gin, and Thomas Edison's phonograph.

At the National Museum of Natural History (Constituiton Ave., NW), you'll be shocked as you walk into the octagonal rotunda: an enormous African bush elephant (13 feet and 2 inches high at the shoulder, weighing eight tons before he was shot in Angola in 1955) stands to greet you. Many think this is the largest elephant recorded. The cursed Hope Diamond, displayed in the Hall of Gems, has brought misfortune to the various people who have owned it since it was smuggled out of India in the 1600s. It is the largest blue diamond in the world, weighing 44.5 carats. Don't forget the Hall of Mammals, where you can see a 92-foot life-size model of a blue whale, and the Dinosaur Hall, where you can gaze at skeletal exhibits of extinct creatures.

If you happen to visit Washington in late June and early July, don't miss the Smithsonian's Festival of American Folklife on the Mall. Regional crafts, music, dance, and food show the variety of our culture and provide great fun for an afternoon.

Although not under the Smithsonian umbrella, the National Gallery of Art is another important museum on the Mall. Andrew Mellon donated $15 million for the construction of the West Building (which opened in 1941) and gave 126 paintings from his private collection. Italian painting and sculpture is well represented here. The East Building (1978), designed by I.M. Pei, is formed by two interlocking triangles. Inside, note the 920-pound mobile by Alexander Calder. Its rods and pods sway with air currents.

While in the Mall area, view the original copies of the Declaration of Independence, the Constitution, and the Bill of Rights at the National Archives (Constitution Ave., N.W.). Historical and genealogical research facilities are available. To listen to the Archives' Watergate tapes, you'll have to take a shuttle to Alexandria, Virginia.

Northwest Washington

If you'd like to say you've been to the Watergate Complex, travel northwest to an area of Washington called Foggy Bottom. The nearby John F. Kennedy Center for the Performing Arts on New Hampshire Avenue and Rock Creek Parkway is just south of that famous luxury complex where the Democratic National Committee headquarters was broken into and bugged in 1972. The Kennedy Center, host to international dance, theater, and music companies since 1971, measures 630 feet long and 300 feet wide. Tour guides will tell you that the Grand Foyer, which runs the length of the building, could fit into the Washington Monument laid on its side. The center holds five halls: an opera house, a concert hall, and three theaters. Flags decorate two long corridors: the Hall of States and the Hall of Nations.

From the Kennedy Center you'll be able to see Rock Creek Park, very popular with sports enthusiasts. The National Zoo, home of those famous Chinese pandas Hsing-Hsing and Ling-Ling, is in the park.

North of Foggy Bottom is the oldest section of the city, Georgetown. Founded in 1751, this area began as a tobacco port. Today it sports nightclubs and fine restaurants that tantalize passersby with a variety of ethnic cuisines. Specialty shops offer unusual items. Federal-period homes still line narrow streets; several historic houses are open to the public.

When you leave Georgetown, drive along Massachusetts Avenue, N.W., through Embassy Row. This stretch holds the biggest concentration of embassies in Washington. Turn north off the avenue onto 21st Street to find the Phillips Collection, a distinguished art museum that contains many paintings by French Impressionists and Post-Impressionists. Klee, Rothko, Bonnard, and John Marin were favorites of Mr. Phillips. Renoir's *Luncheon of the Boating Party* is probably the best known picture in the collection.

Whether you want to wind up your tour of Washington or just close the day in convivial surroundings, enjoy a taste of the city's nightlife around Dupont Circle. Many boutiques, specialty shops, bookstores, and restaurants have clustered in this area, especially along Connecticut Avenue.

PRACTICAL INFORMATION FOR WASHINGTON, D.C.

WHEN TO GO. Although the Japanese cherry trees do not bloom on a specific week each year, their colorful display in late Mar. or early Apr. along the banks of the Tidal Basin traditionally heralds the opening of tourist season and the beginning of spring. The city is at its most beautiful then, with the cherry blossoms and the thousands of tulips and daffodils that fill parks and line highways. However, for pure, natural beauty, fall rivals spring with leaf colors and optimal weather conditions for sightseeing. The weather is generally delightful and the heavy family vacation season is over. Expect high humidity in the summer and moderate weather in the winter.

HOW TO GET THERE. Washington exemplifies accessibility. You can travel here easily from almost anywhere, nationally or internationally. Fares are not necessarily competitive, due to the city's popularity.

By plane. *Washington National Airport* handles most of the city's domestic traffic and is accessible by the Metro subway. *American, Delta,* and *United* are among the long-distance carriers serving the airport, and the short hops are flown by *USAir. Dulles International Airport,* 25 mi. away in Virginia, serves the larger jets and most international traffic. The third area airport, the *Baltimore-Washington International Airport* (BWIA), is a 45-minute trip from the capital.

By train. *Amtrak* offers frequent rail travel along the Northeast corridor. (Metroliner trains that service this corridor are faster and more expensive.) Trains arrive at Union Station (Massachusetts Ave. and North Capitol St.), near the Capitol Building and adjacent to a Metro stop.

By bus. Washington is a major terminal for *Greyhound.* The terminal is at First and L Sts., N.E. (3 blocks north of Union Station, 202–565–2662).

By car. I–95 is the major access route from north or south; 270 enters the city from the northwest coming from Hagerstown and Frederick, Maryland. If you are on the eastern shore of the Chesapeake, take U.S. 50 over the toll bridge, through Annapolis and into Washington. The Beltway, Rte 495, encircles the city for 60 mi. Motorists unaccustomed to three-lane high-speed driving with exits and access roads at frequent intervals should use extreme care in negotiating this dangerous stretch of highway.

TOURIST INFORMATION. Contact the *Washington Convention and Visitors Association,* 1212 New York Ave., N.W., Sixth Floor, Washington, D.C. 20005, (202–789–7000), for pamphlets and brochures on hotels, motels, and sightseeing here and in the environs. Open Mon.–Fri., 9–5. For daily recorded event information call 202–737–8866. They also operate the *Washington Tourist Information Center* at 1455 Pennsylvania Ave., N.W., where visitors can stop by for maps, booklets, or general information. Hours are Mon.–Sat. 9 A.M.–5 P.M. from Apr. until the end of Sept.

During the summer the *National Park Service* maintains kiosks at several downtown locations such as the Lincoln Memorial, Lafayette Park, and the Washington Monument. At the *Smithsonian* museums free pamphlets are distributed. The *National Gallery of Art* offers excellent free guides to the East and West Buildings.

IVIS, the International Visitors Information Service, 733 15th St. N.W. (202–783–6540), stands ready to help foreign visitors with free maps in foreign languages and some multilingual pamphlets. The IVIS Language Bank helps visitors with a language problem.

The *Washington Post* carries information on movies, theater, sports, and cultural events in the Fri. supplement, *Weekend.* The rival *Washington Times* is also a good source.

Especially helpful to the tourist is the top-flight monthly *Washingtonian* magazine ($1.95) which details current happenings in its "Where and When" section.

The *Theatre Guide,* published semi-annually, provides theater schedules, seating plans, curtain times, and box office hours. On sale at newsstands for $2.

TELEPHONES. The area code for all of Washington, D.C., is 202. You do not need to dial the area code when calling from nearby Virginia (area code 703) or close-in Maryland (area code 301). When direct dialing a long-distance number from this area, it is necessary to dial the number 1 before the area code and the number itself. For assistance from the operator on person-to-person, credit-card, and collect calls dial 0 first. Pay telephones cost 20 cents. From pay telephones there is no charge for directory assistance, 411. Outside of Washington dial 202–555–1212 for information. Many hotels and businesses have toll-free 800 numbers (call 800–555–1212 for specific information).

EMERGENCY TELEPHONE NUMBERS. For *police, fire,* and *ambulance* emergencies in the city, dial 911. Or dial 0 for operator assistance and have that person place the call. The non-emergency *police* number is 727–4326; non-emergency *fire* is 462–1616. For the *Poison Control Center* dial 625–3333.

HOW TO GET AROUND. From the airport. The taxi fare from National Airport to the 16th and K Sts. downtown corridor should be about $15; additional passengers pay a hefty surcharge based on destination. To the Baltimore-Washington International Airport a taxi would cost around $40. The *Washington Flyer* (202–685–1400) serves all three airports from its Downtown Terminal at 16th and K Sts., next to the Capital Hilton. It serves both National and Dulles from three other city hotels: the Washington Hilton and Towers (1919 Connecticut Ave., N.W.), the Mayflower (1127 Connecticut Ave., N.W.), and the Sheraton-Washington (Woodley Rd. and Connecticut Ave., N.W.). *Metrorail* service is available from National Airport; fares range from 85 cents up, depending on the time of day and your destination.

By bus. *Metrobus* (637–7000) services all jurisdictions in the metropolitan areas. The basic non-rush hour fare is 85 cents in D.C., Maryland, and Virginia. Buses link to subway trains for a coordinated mass transit system, and passengers planning on a subway-to-bus trip can obtain a transfer at the entering subway station for a free connecting bus ride in D.C. and as partial payment in Maryland and Virginia.

By Tourmobile. We highly recommend sightseeing the Tourmobile way. (Leave your car at hotel or nearby parking lot and hop aboard at one of 18 stops at major attractions between the Capitol, Lincoln Memorial, and Arlington Cemetery. Locations with all-day parking are the Kennedy Center, West Potomac Park, and Ohio Drive, south of the Lincoln Memorial, all stops on the tour route.) You will enjoy a narrated tour of all the principal monuments and points of historical interest along the way, dispense with driving and parking worries, and go at your own pace, getting on and off as often as you like at no extra charge. The Washington-Arlington Cemetery tour costs under $7.50 for adults and under $3.75 for children (ages 3–11). Call 202–554–7950 for detailed information. The Tourmobile operates from 9:30 A.M. to 4:30 P.M. daily.

By subway. Getting around Washington and its nearby suburbs is easier than ever with Metrorail service (637–7000) available from downtown D.C. to numerous points in suburban Maryland and Virginia. Stations are easily recognized by the "M," a tall brown-colored column that has color stripes (red, orange, blue, or yellow) to indicate specific lines. Inside the station there are well-detailed direction maps and each subway car has an easy-to-follow destination guide. Already more than 70 mi. of Metro have been completed, with 61 stations in operation. It is far easier and more economical to travel by subway (fares range from 85 cents to $2.55) than to maneuver the streets and compete for limited parking meters. On almost every line, trains run every 12 minutes during off-peak periods and every 5–8 minutes during rush hour. Hours of operation: Mon–Fri., 5:30 A.M. to midnight; Sat., 8 A.M. to midnight Sun., and 10 A.M. to midnight. Holiday schedules are posted in the stations and listed in the daily newspapers.

By taxi. In the city itself, taxicab fares are based on the unmetered zone system with the minimum ride $2.70 and additional zones charged at 90 cents per zone. There is a dollar surcharge late at night, and fares double during snow emergencies.

There are no savings for sharing a cab; three people pay triple fare. Cabs are required to post the current basic rates and zone map. Inquire in advance how many zones your ride will be so you appear in-the-know and can tabulate the fare—and ask for a receipt. Complaints in writing (with the driver's number and name and receipts) should be reported to *D.C. Taxicab Commission,* 2141 Martin Luther King, Jr. Ave., S.E., 2nd Floor, Washington, D.C. 20020 (767–8380). Complaints about taxi fares from Virginia or Maryland into Washington (e.g., from the airports) should be addressed in writing with driver's name, cab number, and receipts to the *Washington Metropolitan Area Transit Commission* at 1828 L St., N.W., Suite 103, Washington, D.C. 20036 (202–331–1671).

By rental car. Every major car rental company has offices in the Washington area, most with branches at the airports. *Thrifty* (800–367–2277 or 703–548–1600) combines good service and low price at 35 locations around town. *National* (800–328–4567), *Hertz* (800–654–3131), and *Avis* (800–331–1212) have rental offices at all three airports and downtown D.C. A number of companies, such as *Rent-a-Wreck* (800–421–7253), rent older models for more moderate rates.

HINTS TO THE MOTORIST. Bear in mind that the city is laid out in four quadrants, with the Capitol as the center point. Every address in the District of Columbia is followed by N.W., S.W., S.E., or N.E. Remember that numbered streets run from north to south; lettered streets run from east to west; avenues named after the states run out from the Capitol at angles, like the spokes of a wheel. The Potomac River divides the District from Virginia; Maryland lies to the north, east, and south. AAA (the Washington chapter's number is 331–3000; emergency road service for members: 222–5000) advises its members and all visitors to take mass transit because of the city's confusing traffic patterns and the shortage of parking spaces. Parking lots frequently charge $7 to $8 for several hours.

Most major thoroughfares observe special rush-hour driving rules from 7 A.M.–9:30 A.M. and from 4 P.M.–6:30 P.M. with some jurisdictions having different starting and concluding times. No parking is allowed on rush-hour designated streets during posted times; those who ignore such signs are likely to have their vehicles towed to some far-off city lot. Most city meter spaces cost a quarter for 15 minutes, and meter enforcement crews speedily issue tickets for expired meters.

The highway speed limit is 55 mph, but most of the parkways that surround the city have a maximum 40 mph posted speed. Right turns on red are permitted only after a full stop and at intersections that do not have posted restrictive turn signs; many downtown intersections do not allow right turns on red. During snow emergencies, no parking is allowed on designated snow emergency routes.

HINTS TO DISABLED TRAVELERS. Many major restaurants and most hotels have ramps to make handicapped accessibility a reality. It is always a good idea to telephone ahead to make any advance reservations that may help eliminate last-minute concerns. Most sidewalks have curb ramps and most parking lots and street parking areas have well-marked reserved spaces for cars that are identified by license plate or special sticker as handicapped. If you are traveling to the city by train, plane, or bus, notify the carrier so that any needs can be accommodated prior to arrival. While in Washington, if your plans include a Tourmobile ride, telephone 202–554–5100 to make advance plans for their hydraulic-lift van. The Washington Convention and Visitors Association (*see* Tourist Information) publishes an "attractions" brochure that details facilities readily available for handicapped persons and those facilities that need advance arrangements to be utilized. Likewise, the *Information Center for Handicapped Individuals,* 300 Eye St., N.E., Washington, D.C. 20002 (202–547–8081) publishes a *Directory of Services for Handicapping Conditions* and a booklet *Access Washington.* Write for specific titles and price information.

TOURS. More than 50 sightseeing companies serve Washington visitors. The larger companies (see *Yellow Pages*) will pick you up at your hotel or motel 30 minutes before the scheduled time of your tour's departure and return you without extra charge. The Washington Convention and Visitors Association will also provide a list of sightseeing and guide services.

The National Fine Arts Associates, Inc. (NFAA) will arrange custom-made tours for individuals or groups. Museum-trained guides conduct general sightseeing tours and/or special tours highlighting museums, historic houses, gardens, and walking tours. Arrange for tours well in advance in order to give the NFAA time to design your tour. Contact NFAA, 4801 Massachusetts Ave., N.W., Washington, D.C. 20016 (202–966–3800).

Tailored Tours, 6211 Crathie Lane, Bethesda, MD 20816 (301–229–6221), will custom-design short or long tours for small or large groups. Arrange tours several weeks in advance.

Washington à la Carte calls itself "the premier custom tour service organization in the nation's capital." Write to them at 1706 Surrey La., N.W., Washington, D.C. 20007, or call 202–337–7300. Needs at least 24-hour notice to arrange a tour for a small groups; larger groups should call well in advance.

Information on the highly recommended **Tourmobiles** is presented under "How to Get Around."

There are two ways for the general public to see many of the major tourist attractions in Washington, by **Congressional Ticket** (VIP pass), or in a first-come, first-served line. Congressional tickets are available for the White House, the FBI, the State Department, the Capitol, and the John F. Kennedy Center for the Performing Arts. Contact your appropriate congressional office (House zip code is 20515; Senate zip is 20510) and ask for VIP tickets; specify the date and the number of people and if you prefer morning or afternoon—the FBI and State Department tours are the only ones offered both in the morning and the afternoon. These tickets are free, but each senator and representative has a monthly quota so visitors are advised to contact the congressional offices as soon as possible. When you arrive in town, go to your appropriate congressional office and get **Senate and House gallery passes,** required for Visitors' Gallery admission, and a congressional letter that lets you dine in the Senate dining room during specified luncheon hours. Call the general congressional information number (202–224–3121) and ask for your member's direct-dial number.

SPECIAL-INTEREST SIGHTSEEING. The Bureau of Engraving and Printing. 14th and C Sts., S.W. (447–9709), offers tours to observe how our money is printed. Open weekdays 9 A.M.–2 P.M. Come early; tickets issued on a first-come, first-served basis, and this is a popular tour. Admission free. Metro: Smithsonian.

FBI. 10th St. and Pennsylvania Ave., N.W. (324–3447). Free hour-long tours are available Mon.–Fri., 8:45 A.M.–4:15 P.M. Visitors see crime labs, photos of the 10 most-wanted criminals, and watch a firearms target demonstration. Metro: Metro Center.

The Folger Shakespeare Library. 201 East Capitol St., S.E. (544–7077), houses the world's largest collection of Shakespeareana and an extraordinary collection of material in English dealing with the 17th and 18th centuries. The *Exhibition Hall* reproduces the great hall of an Elizabethan palace. The *Shakespearean Theater* is a full-size replica of a public playhouse of Shakespeare's day, except that it does not open to the sky. Plays are presented throughout the year by the *Folger Theater Group.* (See *Theater.*) Metro: Capitol South.

The John F. Kennedy Center for the Performing Arts. New Hampshire Ave. at Rock Creek Pkwy. (416–8340). Free tours are conducted by the Friends of the Kennedy Center and held daily except Christmas and Thanksgiving. The first public tour begins at 10 A.M. with 60-minute tours continuing until 1 P.M. Participants will see each of the four theaters (subject to availability) and learn about the center's history. Metro: Foggy Bottom.

Library of Congress. The Thomas Jefferson Building (main building) on First and East Capitol Sts. (707–5000) has an information desk (707–5458) and sales area. The library is open Mon.–Fri., 8:30 A.M.–9:30 P.M.; Sat., until 5 P.M.; Sun., 1–5 P.M. (Exhibits open until 6 P.M. on weekends.) Admission free. Metro: Capitol South.

National Geographic Explorers Hall. 17th and M Sts., N.W. (857–7588, 857–7000 weekends). Exhibits on explorations conducted by the society. This tour is like walking into the pages of the magazine. Group tours: 857–7689. Open Mon.–Sat., 9 A.M.–5 P.M.; Sun., 10 A.M.–5 P.M. Closed Christmas. Free. Metro: Farragut North.

The Naval Observatory. Massachusetts Ave. at 34th St., N.W. (202–653–1543). Evening tours are given every Mon. at 7:30 P.M. during standard time, 8:30 P.M. during daylight time. They last two hours and 75 passes are given on a first-come, first-served basis. The elderly and the handicapped may park on the grounds with a special permit; call 653–1571; otherwise, there is ample parking nearby. Group tours can be arranged at least two months in advance; call 653–1541. Admission free.

The Organization of American States. Formerly known as Pan American Union, 17th St. and Constitution Ave., N.W. (458–3751). See the lush greenery maintained by a year-round tropical atmosphere in the interior patio. Busts of the founders of the American republics and other heroes are in the Hall of Flags and Heroes. A small art gallery features temporary exhibits. Conducted tours of building by reservation only. Hours are Mon.–Fri., 9:30 A.M.–3:30 P.M.; closed holidays. Admission free. Metro: Farragut West.

State Department Reception Rooms. 2201 C St., N.W. (647–3241). Tours, available by reservation, last approximately 45 minutes and include the diplomatic reception rooms on the 8th floor, with their detailed collection of 18th-century Americana. Young children are discouraged from taking this tour. Mon.–Fri., 9:30 A.M., 10:30 A.M., and 3 P.M. Admission free. Metro: Foggy Bottom.

The Supreme Court. 1st St. and Maryland Ave., N.E. (479–3211). Tours given from 9 A.M. to 4:30 P.M. when the Court is not in session, and courtroom lectures are given 9:30–3:30; tours are given at 10 A.M., 11 A.M., 1 P.M., and 2 P.M. when the Court is in session. When Court is in session, its hours are Mon.–Wed. from 10 A.M. to noon and from 1 to 3 P.M. Arrive at least a half hour early to watch. Seating is on a first-come basis. To find out if Court is in session or has recessed, call the number listed above. Newspapers publish court schedules. Admission free. Metro: Capitol South.

U.S. Capitol. National Mall, East End (225–6827); Capitol switchboard, (202–224–3121). Free half-hour tours depart almost continuously from the Capitol's east side near the ten-ton bronze doors. Visitors see the Rotunda, Statuary Hall, the House of Representatives, the Senate, the old Senate Chamber, the old Supreme Court Chambers, and the Crypt. To watch a session from the Visitors' Gallery, you need a special pass available directly from your senator or congressman's office. Tours are available daily except Thanksgiving, Christmas, and New Year's, from 9 A.M.–3:45 P.M. Metro: Capitol South or Union Station.

Voice of America. 330 Independence Ave., S.W. (485–6231). Visitors' entrance on C St., S.W., between 3d and 4th Sts. The VOA, which broadcasts in 42 languages, has tours daily that leave promptly at 8:40 A.M., 9:40 A.M., 10:40 A.M., 1:40 P.M., and 2:40 P.M. Reservations preferred. Tours last approximately 45 minutes and include visits to the master control room, the newsroom, and recording studios. Admission free. Metro: Federal Center S.W.

White House. 1600 Pennsylvania Ave., N.W. (456–1414; taped tour information, 456–7041). VIP visitors see a little more of the White House than those on the general tours. Basically, the five mansion rooms that all groups see are the celebrated East Room, the Green Room, the Blue Room, the Red Room, and the State Dining Room. The White House is open to the public free of charge, with entry through the East Gate, Tues.–Sat., 10 A.M.–noon. Normally no tickets are necessary, but from Memorial Day to Labor Day specific time-designated admission tickets are available at a booth on the Ellipse from 8 A.M. until none are left. Each person must pick up his own ticket. Arrive early; tickets run out quickly. Admission free. Metro: McPherson Square.

PARKS AND GARDENS. If you want to see some of the city's private gardens, there's the Georgetown Garden Tour in mid-Apr. (333–4953), the Old Town House and Garden Tour in late Apr., and Chevy Chase and Cleveland Park house and garden tours in late spring. The *Washington Post* Weekend section lists such events. Most of these have admission fees.

Dumbarton Oaks, R and 31st St., N.W. (338–8278), sits in the heart of Georgetown. The 19th-century mansion with ten acres of formal gardens houses a Byzantine and pre-Columbian art collection. The museum (entrance at 1703 32nd St., N.W.) is open Tues.–Sun. 2–5 P.M. (free). Guided garden tours are available (342–3212). The gardens are open daily, Nov.–Mar., 2–5 P.M. (free), and Apr.–Oct., 2–6 P.M. ($2 adults; children under 12 free with adult; seniors free on Wed).

Hillwood, 4155 Linnean Ave., N.W. (686–5807), sits almost squarely in the middle of the city. Visitors see the gardens (Japanese Gardens, French Gardens, Rhododendron Walk, and Rose Garden) and the well-furnished rooms of what was the

Marjorie Merriweather Post mansion. The house and gardens are closed Tues. and Sun., open the rest of the week, 11 A.M.–3 P.M. Two-hour tours of the mansion, advanced reservations required, start at 9 A.M., 10:30 A.M., noon, and 1:30 P.M. $7. Garden visit $2. No one under 12 admitted. Make reservation for cafe (686–8893).

Kenilworth Aquatic Gardens, Kenilworth Ave. and Douglas St., N.E. (426–6905) are home to water plants including lotuses and bamboo that grow in ponds along the Anacostia River. Flowers are in bloom from mid-June to early fall. Open daily 7 A.M.–dark. Free tours daily during the summer at 9 A.M., 11 A.M., and 1 P.M.

Rock Creek Park, one of the country's largest urban parks, with over 1,700 acres and miles of biking, hiking, and jogging trails, is a thing of beauty that almost everyone comments on after a visit to Washington. Some roads (Beach Dr. at Broad Branch Rd. up to the Maryland line) are closed from 7 A.M.–7 P.M. Sat. and Sun., so that recreational pursuits can continue without the annoyance of motorized vehicles. There are picnic tables and fields, exercise courses, a Nature Center with a planetarium (5200 Glover Rd. N.W., 426–6829), tennis courts, and a working mill. The National Zoological Park (3001 Connecticut Ave., N.W., 673–4717) sits inside its perimeter. Free.

U.S. Botanic Garden, Maryland Ave. at First St., S.W. (225–7099). When you're visiting Capitol Hill, you're a grassy area away from an in-town garden with Easter lily, azalea, cacti, and palm tree collections. Open daily 9 A.M.–5 P.M., until 9 P.M., June–Aug. Free. Metro: Federal Center S.W.

U.S. National Arboretum, 3501 New York Ave., N.E. (475–4815). For the city's largest azalea display, you'll have to join the springtime crowds lining up on the park's 444 acres complete with a bonsai collection (10–2:30 daily) and a National Herb Garden. Open Mon.–Fri. 8 A.M.–5 P.M. and weekends from 10 A.M. Free.

ZOOS. The National Zoological Park in the 3000 block of Connecticut Ave., N.W. (673–4800) is part of the Smithsonian Institution. Another entrance is on Adams Rd. and Beach Dr. An ongoing modernization program has provided a new home for the white Bengal tigers, a giant walk-through aviary area, and fun-filled Monkey Island. The giant pandas (a gift from China) are the zoo's most famous residents. The zoo can be quite a hilly outing for some, but there are plenty of benches and quick food stops to regain strength. Admission is free but parking, which can fill up quickly on a bright sunny day, is $3–$7, depending on length of visit. Or you can arrive by Connecticut Ave. bus or Metro: Woodley Park. The grounds are open daily, except Christmas, 8 A.M.–6 P.M.; buildings open 9 A.M.–4:30 P.M. From May 1–Sept. 15 the grounds are open until 8 P.M. and the buildings until 6 P.M.

CHILDREN'S ACTIVITIES. What better way for a child to unwind from the demands of sight-seeing than a romp on the grass of the **National Mall!** All the museums and monuments that surround the Mall are child-oriented as well as filled with adult pleasures; there's plenty for everyone. Some of the **Smithsonian** highlights include The Insect Zoo, a live collection with an actual beehive and the Discovery Room, a hands-on young person's science lab (need advance, free tickets from the information booth), in the National Museum of Natural History. *Discovery Theater,* Smithsonian Arts and Industries Bldg. (357–1500), gives children's music, dance, mime, and puppet presentations. Weekday morning schedule; weekend afternoons. Reservations needed.

The Capital Children's Museum, 800 Third St., at H St., N.E. (543–8600), is just as its name implies. A young person's hands-on museum with a working Mexican village, a metric room, a Future Center complete with computers, and additional city "touch and do" exhibits in every nook and cranny of the building. Admission $5, senior citizens $2, under 2 free. Open daily, 10 A.M.–5 P.M. Metro: Union Station.

For $2.50 ($3 adults), climb aboard "Uncle Beazley," a statue of a triceratops dinosaur on the Mall side of Natural History or a springtime ride (Apr.–Sept., weather permitting) aboard an old-fashioned beautifully maintained late 1940s carousel near the Arts and Industries Building.

Children won't want to miss the **Bureau of Engraving and Printing** at 14th and C Sts., S.W. (447–9709) where they'll be able to join a free self-guided tour and watch real money being made. The Gift Shop does a brisk business in selling souvenir sacks of shredded money! Mon.–Fri., 9 A.M.–2 P.M. Metro: Smithsonian.

The National Aquarium is the nation's oldest public aquarium (established 1873). Shark feeding on Mon., Wed., and Sat. at 2 P.M.; piranhas on Tues., Thurs., and

Sun. at 2 P.M. Dept. of Commerce Building, 14th St. and Constitution Ave., N.W. (377–2825). Open daily, 9 A.M.–5 P.M. Closed Christmas. Admission: adults, $1.50, for children under 12 and senior citizens 75 cents. Metro: Federal Triangle.

The Naval Yard and Navy Memorial Museum provide a great refuge after the hassle of downtown crowds and parking. Turn the youngsters loose to climb old tanks and cannons in the outdoor playground on the banks of the Anacostia River. Then go into the adjoining museum to see the model ships and Naval history exhibits, and best of all, to man the working periscopes and to operate the—unloaded—anti-aircraft guns. The Visitors Center has a slide show and a map of the Yard's Historic Precincts. Free. Abundant parking. Washington Navy Yard, 9th and M Sts., S.E. (433–2651). Open Mon.–Fri., 9 A.M.–5 P.M.; weekends and holidays, 10 A.M.–5 P.M. Free parking. Metro: Eastern Market.

Dolls' House and Toy Museum of Washington is a charmer. From an ornate Mexican mansion to an austere, antique German kitchen, all the exhibits are in miniature and displayed in subdued-lighting intimacy that allows imagination a free rein. Dolls, doll houses, and furniture tastefully fill two floors. Dolls and furniture on sale in the lobby, and a unique toyshop on the second floor, plus an "Edwardian tearoom" for birthday parties (arrange well in advance). 5236 44th St., N.W. Open Tues.–Sat. 10 A.M.–5 P.M., Sun., noon–5 P.M. Admission $3 for adults, $2 seniors, $1 for children under 14. Street parking and in nearby garages. Call 244–0024. Metro: Friendship Heights.

Daughters of the American Revolution New Hampshire Attic is full of toys from Revolutionary times, especially dolls, including hands-on exhibits. There is also a children's tour of the remaining museum. 1776 D St., N.W. (628–1776). Open Mon.–Fri., 10 A.M.–3 P.M., Sun., 1–5 P.M., closed holidays. Free. Closed Apr.

Or take the kids over to the **Tidal Basin Boat House** (484–3475) at 15th St. and Maine Ave., S.W., and exercise those legs with a paddleboat rental. Rentals ($5 an hour at press time) are available, depending on the weather, from 9 A.M.–dark and prove to be especially popular during Jefferson Memorial outdoor concert evenings. If you want someone else to do the work, then you can take a narrated **mule-drawn barge** ride along the C&O Canal aboard *The Georgetown* from 30th and Thomas Jefferson Sts., N.W., at $4 for adults, $2.50 for children, and $3 for senior citizens. Call (472–4376) for exact Wed.–Sun. schedule. Or grab a frisbee, pack a picnic, and enjoy the Mall grounds and Rock Creek Parkway.

Spirit of Washington Cruises runs boat trips on the Potomac from the end of Mar. until mid–Oct. The four-hour trip down the Potomac to Mount Vernon includes plenty of sightseeing time at George Washington's estate. The cruise itself takes a little over an hour each way. Departures from Pier 4 on 6th and Water Sts., S.W., at 9 A.M. and 2 P.M. daily. Fares for adults $13.25, children ages 6–11 $8.25. Call 554–8000 to check on departure times.

HISTORIC SITES AND HOUSES. It's hard to talk about historic sites in Washington as almost everything seems to qualify. We'll just list a couple of different ones not mentioned elsewhere in this chapter.

Decatur House, 748 Jackson Pl., N.W. (842–0920), is the 19th-century former home of Naval officer Stephen Decatur. Convenient to the White House, it was the first private residence at Lafayette Sq. Visitors see both Victorian-and Federal-styled period rooms in the designated National Historic Landmark. Open Tues.–Fri., 10 A.M.–2 P.M. and on weekends from noon–4 P.M. Entrance fee $3, students and senior citizens $2. Metro: McPherson Square.

Ford's Theater. 511 10th St., N.W. (638–2941). Ford's Theater reopened in Feb. 1968, almost 103 years after President Lincoln was shot while sitting in his box on the night of Apr. 14, 1865. Below the theater is a museum filled with Lincoln memorabilia and an exhibit containing John Wilkes Booth's diary as well as one of his boots. Performances (347–4833) of musicals, reviews, and presentations of Americana are given in the theater, which has been recently restored. Should you wish to see the Petersen House, 516 10th St., N.W. (426–6830), where Lincoln was carried after being shot by John Wilkes Booth, walk across the street. The small and simple house has been restored to the way it was when Lincoln died in the bedroom at the rear of the house on the morning of Apr. 15, 1865. Both Ford's Theater and the Petersen House are open daily, 9 A.M.–5 P.M. During matinees on Thurs. and Sun. afternoons, and during rehearsals, the theater is closed, but the museum and Petersen House remain open. It's a good idea to call before you visit. Tours of both the Petersen House and the Ford's Theater are free. Metro: Metro Center.

Jefferson Memorial. 14th St., S.W. On the south bank of the Tidal Basin, West Potomac Park (426–6822). John Russell Pope designed this memorial to Thomas Jefferson, which was dedicated in 1943, 200 years after his birth. The graceful, domed building features architectural motifs favored by Jefferson, an amateur architect, in buildings he designed—his home, Monticello, and the rotunda of the University of Virginia. The heroic 19-foot bronze statue of Jefferson by Rudolph Evans weighs five tons and stands on a black granite pedestal six feet high. The four interior walls set forth excerpts from Jefferson's writings. The site of the Memorial and the surrounding land have been entirely reclaimed from the Potomac. Jefferson died on July 4, 1826, aged 83. He is buried near his Virginia home. Always open. Very beautiful at night. If you are here during the summer, try to attend a Service band concert on the plaza in front of the Memorial.

Lincoln Memorial. Foot of 23rd St., N.W. West end of Mall, (426–6895). To most visitors the Lincoln Memorial is Washington's most impressive and inspiring building. Henry Bacon, the architect, chose a classic Greek temple of purest white marble for the Memorial; it was completed in 1922. Daniel Chester French was the sculptor of the seated Lincoln, which is 19 feet high and required 28 blocks of marble and four years of carving. Try to see the Memorial both by day and by night. Open daily 8 A.M.–midnight. For an added dimension enter the Memorial through the small door at the end of the sidewalk to the left of the Memorial's staircase. You will see the gigantic underpinnings which hold up the huge marble edifice. An elevator will take you up to view the seated Lincoln.

For a surprise, call 202–426–6841 (6 weeks in advance) to arrange a weekend tour of the stalactites and stalagmites in the caves beneath the Lincoln Memorial, Mar.–May, Sept.–Nov.

The Octagon House. 1799 New York Ave., N.W. (638–3105). Dr. William Thornton, architect of the Capitol, designed the house in 1800 for the Taylor family. Despite its name there are only six, not eight, sides. During the War of 1812 it served as temporary quarters for the French foreign minister. The French tricolor flying from its roof may have saved it when the British marched on Washington in August, 1814, setting fire to both the Capitol and the White House. Driven from the Presidential Palace by the burning, President and Dolley Madison moved into the Octagon for nine months while their residence was rebuilt. President Madison signed the Treaty of Ghent that ended the War of 1812 on a table in a second floor room on Feb. 17, 1815. Open Tues.–Fri., 10 A.M.–4 P.M.; Sat. and Sun. noon–4 P.M. Closed Mon. Admission $2, adults; $1.50, seniors. (Call in advance for group tours.) Metro: Farragut West.

Old Stone House. 3051 M St., N.W. (426–6851). The oldest surviving house in Washington, built in 1765. Its five rooms have been restored and furnished in colonial American decor. Open Wed.–Sun., 9:30 A.M.–5 P.M. except Thanksgiving, Christmas, and New Years. Free.

Vietnam Veterans Memorial. 23rd St. between Independence and Constitution Aves. (634–1568). The V-shaped black granite memorial, designed by Maya Lin and dedicated in November 1982. Listing the names of 58,156 Americans who died or were lost in Vietnam, the sobering monument has become one of Washington's most visited. Open daily 24 hours. Free.

Washington Monument. Center of Mall, Constitution Ave. at 16th St., N.W. (426–6839). The 555-foot high marble obelisk designed by Robert Mills as a memorial to our first president bears a tell-tale line about a third of the way up, marking the place where construction stopped for 26 years between 1854 and 1880. Lack of funds, political squabbling, and the Civil War were responsible for the long delay; the shaft was completed in 1888. The top may be reached only by elevator, and the view from the top will not disappoint (except on a foggy day). Open daily, 8 A.M.–midnight, Apr.–Labor Day; 9 A.M.–5 P.M., Sept.—Mar. Free. Metro: Smithsonian.

MUSEUMS AND GALLERIES. How can you miss learning about our nation in a city so totally devoted to the cultural enrichment of its residents and visitors? The Smithsonian Institution, founded in 1846, now has 14 local museums and the

National Zoo under its domain. There are over 78 million collected artifacts, with about 1 percent of that total on display at any one time. There's never an admission charge and visitors have no difficulty spending days within each building or touring some of the temporary special exhibits. The only word of caution for first-timers is that you probably can't see it all or do it all, so plan your time carefully and visit the special exhibit or museum that caters to your particular interests. For recorded information, call Dial-A-Museum (357–2020). Buildings are open daily except Christmas from 10 A.M.–5:30 P.M. with extended summer hours. 357–1300 is the information number for this and other museums, unless noted.

The best place for an orientation to museums is in the original 1846 "Castle" at 1000 Jefferson Dr., S.W. (357–2700). The **National Museum of American History** at 14th St. and Constitution Ave., N.W., is home to Americana collections, with everything from George Washington's teeth to the original "star spangled banner." At 10th St. and Constitution Ave., N.W., dinosaurs, giant meteorites, and living coral reef are at the **National Museum of Natural History.** The **Freer Gallery of Art** at 12th St. and Jefferson Dr., S.W., closed at press time for renovation, is home to late 19th- and early 20th-century American works and a large collection of Oriental art. Modern art followers will delight to the indoor and outdoor collections at the **Hirshhorn Museum and Sculpture Garden** at 7th St. and Independence Ave., S.W. In the summertime you can enjoy lunch at the outdoor terrace restaurant. Next door is the museum world's most popular attraction, the **National Air and Space Museum,** with its 23 galleries that trace the contributions of aviation. The **National Gallery of Art** at 6th St. and Constitution Ave., N.W. (737–4215), houses European and American paintings and sculpture from the 13th century to the present day in its East and West Wings. Open 10 A.M.–5 P.M. daily, Sun. hours are from noon to 9 P.M. The **Arts and Industries Building** at 900 Jefferson St., S.W., is the second oldest Smithsonian building on the Mall, and home of the "1876 Centennial Exhibition." Away from the Mall area is the **National Museum of American Art** at 9th and G Sts., N.W., home of the **National Portrait Gallery** and site of Abraham Lincoln's second inaugural reception. Across from the White House at 17th St. and Pennsylvania Ave., N.W., is the **Renwick Gallery,** which is devoted to contemporary and historic American crafts and decorative arts. New on the Mall are two underground museums: the **Museum of African Art** houses textiles, sculptures, and art exclusively from African cultures, the only such museum in the nation; next door, the **Arthur M. Sackler Gallery** is a showcase of Asian and Near Eastern art.

The **Corcoran Gallery of Art,** 17th St. and New York Ave., N.W. (638–3211), is the city's largest private gallery with a major emphasis on American paintings and sculpture from the 18th century to the present day. Photography exhibits are frequent and local Washington artists receive particular attention. Open Tues.–Sun. 10 A.M.–4:30 P.M.; Thurs., until 9 P.M. Free. Metro: Farragut West.

Around the corner, the **Museum of Modern Art of Latin America,** 201 18 St., N.W. (458–6301), houses a stunning collection of paintings and sculpture by artists from Mexico and farther south. Open Tues.–Sat., 10 A.M.–5 P.M. Metro: Farragut West.

Phillips Collection, 1600 21st St., N.W. (387–2151), one block north from Dupont Circle and just off Massachusetts Ave. Opened to the public in 1918, this collection was the first museum of modern art. The paintings of many French Impressionists and Post-Impressionists hang in this gallery. The large Goh Annex, opened in 1989, has provided the space for widely enlarged displays and many cultural events. Chamber music recitals are held each Sun. at 5 P.M. in the music room. Open Tues.–Sat., 10 A.M.–5 P.M.; Sun., 2–7 P.M. Closed Mon. Admission by contribution. Metro: Dupont Circle.

The National Archives, 8th St. and Constitution Ave., N.W. (523–3000), house the original documents upon which our nation is based—the Declaration of Independence, the Constitution, and the Bill of Rights. Open daily except Dec. 25, 10 A.M.–5:30 P.M. with longer summer hours. Those who want to trace family histories should enter through the 9th St. and Pennsylvania Ave. N.W., entrance for the upstairs Microfilm and Research Rooms open Mon.–Fri., 8:45 A.M.–10 P.M. and Sat. 9A.M. –5 P.M. The Nixon Presidential Materials Project, the well-known Watergate tapes, are available at 845 S. Pickett St. in Alexandria. A shuttle runs from the 7th and Pennsylvania Ave. Archive entrance. Call for schedule. Tours of the Archives building, by reservation (523–3183), 10:15 A.M. and 1:15 P.M., Mon.–Fri. Free. Metro: Archives.

ARTS AND ENTERTAINMENT. Even in this high-priced city, there are numerous opportunities to see a variety of cultural productions for reduced prices. *Ticketplace* on F Street Plaza, between 12th and 13th Sts., N.W. (842–5387), operates a same-day half-price ticket window and sells full-price (future performances) tickets for some events. Most events at the Kennedy Center are included under the Friends of the Kennedy Center format, which offers half-price tickets for senior citizens, students, handicapped individuals, those on fixed incomes, and certain members of the military (416–8340).

FILMS. There is no shortage of movie houses in the city and surrounding suburbs; many have three or four smaller screens under one roof. The only city theater with first-run features that has remained intact, complete with balcony, without being subdivided, is the *Circle Uptown* at 3426 Connecticut Ave. N.W. (966–5400). The **American Film Institute** (Kennedy Center Hall of States entrance) emphasizes theme-oriented festivals. The box office is open 5–9 P.M., with two shows daily. Nonmember tickets are $4.50 (785–4600). The major theater chains in the city that specialize in first-run productions are the *K-B* and the *Circle* chains. Two theaters, both in Georgetown, specialize in foreign and "art" movies, recent and vintage: the **Biograph,** 2819 M St., N.W. (333–2696), and the **Key,** 1222 Wisconsin Ave., N.W. (333–5100). Name your neighborhood and most likely you'll find a set of theaters.

MUSIC. The weekly music scene in Washington is discussed in detail in the local newspapers and specifically in Fri.'s *Washington Post* Weekend tabloid and in the Sunday Show section. Some highlights to plan for are free summer outdoor events by the military bands and orchestras and performances by the National Symphony Orchestra on major holidays.

The National Symphony performs at the John F. Kennedy Center for the Performing Arts (800–444–1324 or 416–8100) Sept.–June in the Concert Hall. Mstislav Rostropovich is the conductor.

The Washington Opera is the resident opera company of the John F. Kennedy Center for the Performing Arts. It has a full calendar from the end of Oct. until early Feb. Depending on production, they use both the 2,200-seat Opera House and the smaller, more intimate 475-seat Terrace Theater for their ensemble opera productions. Standing room available for all performances in the Opera House and Terrace Theater. Call 800–444–1324 or 416–7800; open for ticket information.

DANCE. Dance productions in Washington run the range from full-scale university performances to those sponsored by the Washington Performing Arts Society and held at the Kennedy Center.

Washington Ballet has a box office at George Washington University's Lisner Auditorium, 21st and H Sts., N.W. (362–3606). Metro: Foggy Bottom.

Arena Stage at the Old Vat Room, 6th St. and Maine Ave., S.W. (488–3300), has played host to Stephen Wade's *Banjo Dancing* for over eight years. He clogs and jigs and spins his yarns as he makes history come alive on the small stage.

STAGE. Theater in Washington begins at the **Kennedy Center** (New Hampshire Ave. at Rock Creek Pkwy.) with dramatic plays and musical productions in the Eisenhower Theater. Each year for two weeks in the spring the **American College Theater,** the best in college productions chosen from 12 regional festival competitions throughout the country, gives free performances in the Terrace Theater. Free productions are often available in spring at Imagination Celebration, in the summertime, and at the December Holiday Festival. For all information, call 800–444–1324 or 467–4600, daily, 10 A.M.–9 P.M. Metro: Foggy Bottom.

Arena Stage, 6th St. and Maine Ave., S.W. (488–3300), houses the Arena, the Kreeger, and the Old Vat Room theaters. Productions range from new works to foreign productions, including a number of revivals. Student and senior citizen discounts available.

Folger Theater Group, 201 East Capitol St., S.E. (546–4000). The works of Shakespeare and modern playwrights produced. Connected with the well-known Folger Shakespeare Library (544–4600). Metro: Capitol South.

Ford's Theater. Box office: 347–4833. See Historic Sites.

National Theater, 1321 Pennsylvania Ave., N.W. (628–6161), is the oldest cultural institution in Washington, dating back to 1835. It has undergone a major $6-million renovation and has been restored to its original prominence as the "theater of Presidents." There is a special patron ticket half-price program for senior citizens, full-time students, handicapped persons, the economically disadvantaged, and certain grades of the military. There are also free special Sat. and Mon. amateur theater programs. Metro: Metro Center.

The Woolly Mammoth Theatre Company, 14th and Church Sts., N.W. (393–3939), may be the best small theater in town. It offers an eclectic program, energetic performances, innovative staging, low prices, and free parking across the street.

As for university theater productions, the most elaborate ones are in the **Hartke Theater,** Harwood Rd., N.E. (529–3333) at Catholic University. There are discounts for senior citizens and students. Metro: Brookland-C.U.A.

Other productions of interest include those at the *Source Theater* (462–1073) and the *Olney Theater* (924–3400).

ACCOMMODATIONS. Tourism is big business in Washington—the second biggest employer, after the government. Nearly 18 million people visit the capital each year, so even with over 30,000 hotel and motel rooms in the metropolitan area, and new accommodations opening every month, it's hard to keep up with the demand at certain times of the year.

The best time to find a room in downtown hotels is on the weekend, because business travelers and conventioneers are generally out of the city by then. In fact, many hotels and motels offer especially low weekend rates—ask the clerk, as such information is rarely volunteered. Chances for securing lower rates are more easily available outside of the center of the city and in nearby Virginia (especially Alexandria and Arlington) and Maryland.

Although summer is traditionally the peak travel time for families, it is a slow season for business travelers in Washington. Hotels are busiest in the spring and fall, and reservations are especially heavy in Apr., when the cherry trees are in full blossom and the summer heat has not descended. At any time of the year phone ahead for reservations, or, outside of D.C., call the *Washington, D.C. Central Reservation Center* (800–554–2220).

Hotel rates are based on double occupancy. District hotel tax is 10%; add $1 per day occupancy charge. Categories, determined by price weekday rates, in peak season, are: *Super Deluxe,* over $255; *Deluxe,* $175–$255; *Expensive,* $125–$174; *Moderate,* $75–$124; *Inexpensive,* under $75.

Super Deluxe

Four Seasons Hotel. 2800 Pennsylvania Ave., N.W., Washington, D.C. 20007 (202–342–0444 or 800–332–3442). At the edge of Georgetown, with the C&O Canal on one side and Rock Creek Park on the other, it has the city's most idyllic location. A beautiful hotel, skillfully operated, with a concierge and 24-hour room service. Only 197 rooms and each of them a gem. Features include *Aux Beaux Champs Restaurant, Garden Terrace* (light meals, high tea), *Plaza Café,* and a disco called *Desirée.*

Deluxe

Capital Hilton. 16th and K Sts., N.W., Washington, D.C. 20036 (202–393–1000 or 800–445–8667). A bustling hotel right in the middle of things, two blocks from the White House. Popular for conventions and tour groups. Trader Vic's and Twigs restaurants. 539 rooms, health club, concierge, lounge. Metro: Farragut North.

The Embassy Row Hotel. 2015 Massachusetts Ave., N.W., Washington, D.C. 20036 (202–265–1600 or 800–424–2400). Off Dupont Circle and near an enclave of major embassies, this 196-unit hostelry is popular with foreign visitors. Restaurants include Lucie, serving French cuisine, and The Wintergarden. Metro: Dupont Circle.

Hay-Adams. 1 Lafayette Sq., Washington, D.C. 20006 (202–638–6600 or 800–424–5054). Overlooking both Lafayette Park and the White House, on the site of the former Henry Adams and John Hay mansions, this famous hotel occupies some truly upper-crust real estate. The paneled lobby, Tudor dining rooms, and grill room give it the look and feel of a fine old London hotel. A sunny restaurant, serving breakfast, lunch, weekend brunch, and high tea, overlooks the park. 134 units. Metro: McPherson Square.

The Mayflower. 1127 Connecticut Ave., N.W., Washington, D.C. 20036 (202–347–3000 or 800–468–3571). A Washington landmark with a block-long lobby, this Stouffer Hotel is close to Metro stops and shopping. Two restaurants. 685 rooms. Metro: Farragut North.

Ritz Carlton Hotel. 2100 Massachusetts Ave., N.W., Washington, D.C. 20008 (202–293–2100 or 800–241–3333). Refurbished, expanded, and refurnished with federal antiques, this elegant 240-room hotel, formerly the Fairfax, caters to chairmen-of-the-board types and their spouses. Home of the Jockey Club restaurant. Metro: Dupont Circle.

Expensive

The Capitol Hill. 200 C St., S.E., Washington, D.C. 20003 (202–543–6000 or 800–424–9165). A 153-unit all-suite hotel especially popular with G.O.P. politicos because of its location near the Capitol Hill (Republican) Club and the House of Representatives office buildings. Metro: Capitol South.

Hotel Washington. 515 15th St. at Pennsylvania Ave., N.W., Washington, D.C. 20004 (202–638–5900 or 800–424–9540). A fine older hotel with 350 rooms. Roof garden offers finest view in the city of July 4th fireworks and Pennsylvania Ave. parades. Two Continents Restaurant. Metro: McPherson Square.

Loew's L'Enfant Plaza. 480 L'Enfant Plaza, S.W., Washington, D.C. 20024 (202–484–1000 or 800–223–0888). One of the city's most dramatic locations, overlooking a plaza, just off the Mall. Close to museums, the Metro, and shopping. 372 units, often used for corporate meetings. Rooftop swimming pool. Metro: L'Enfant Plaza.

Quality Hotel Central. 1900 Connecticut Ave., N.W., Washington, D.C. 20009 (202–332–9300 or 800–228–5151). This recently renovated place with a pool is convenient to lively Dupont Circle. 149 units. Metro: Dupont Circle.

Sheraton Washington. 2660 Woodley Rd., N.W., Washington, D.C. 20008 (202–328–2000, or 800–325–3535). Formerly Sheraton Park Hotel. The city's biggest hotel (1,320 units). Near Rock Creek Park and the National Zoo, off one of the most pleasant stretches of Connecticut Ave. 4 restaurants, 2 outdoor swimming pools. Metro: Woodley Park.

Moderate

Carlyle Suites. 1731 New Hampshire Ave., N.W., Washington, D.C. 20009 (202–234–3200). Converted former apartment building with larger-than-normal-size rooms. Near Connecticut Ave. and Dupont Circle. Restaurant on premises. All suites with kitchenettes. Metro: Dupont Circle.

Connecticut Avenue Days Inn. 4400 Connecticut Ave., N.W., Washington, D.C. 20008 (202–244–5600 or 800–325–2525). Former independent hotel that has been completely renovated. 155 rooms. Complimentary Continental breakfast served daily in lobby. Parking available. On a bus line. Metro: Van Ness.

Envoy Best Western. 501 New York Ave., N.E., Washington, D.C. 20002 (202–543–7400 or 800–528–1234). On crowded throughfare with parking available and restaurant on property. 78 rooms.

Howard Johnson's at Kennedy Center. 2601 Virginia Ave., N.W., Washington, D.C. 20037 (202–965–2700 or 800–654–2000). Across the street from the Watergate Complex and the Kennedy Center. Near Rock Creek Park and the monuments. 192 rooms. Restaurant with take-out service and an underground garage.

Quality Hotel Capitol Hill. 415 New Jersey Ave., N.W., Washington, D.C. 20001 (202–638–1616 or 800–228–5151). Less than two blocks from the Capitol or Union Station, this 341-unit establishment offers restaurant, bar, and rooftop pool. Recently renovated. Metro: Union Station.

Inexpensive

Allen Lee Hotel. 2224 F St., N.W., Washington, D.C. 20037 (202–331–1224). Despite the redone lobby, the Allen Lee retains its rundown charm and a convenient downtown location. It seems quite clean. Metro: Foggy Bottom.

Harrington Hotel. 11th and E Sts., N.W., Washington, D.C. 20004 (202–628–8140 or 800–424–8532). Rooms refurbished in one of the city's largest older properties. 310 rooms. Within walking distance of the majority of sights. Full-service cafeteria, the Kitcheteria. Metro: Metro Center.

Master Host Inn. 1917 Bladensburg Rd., N.E., Washington, D.C. 20002 (202–832–8600 or 800–251–1962). This well-maintained inn has 150 spacious family rooms, a restaurant, and a pool. Conveniently located at New York Ave. and the Baltimore–Washington Pkwy. Sightseeing tours are available from the lobby.

Walter Reed Hospitality House. 6711 Georgia Ave., N.W., Washington, D.C. 20012 (202–722–1600). Near Walter Reed Hospital. Restaurant and off-street parking. 70 rooms. Military discounts. Metro: Silver Spring.

Windsor Park Hotel. 2116 Kalorama Rd., N.W., Washington, D.C. 20008 (202–483–7700). Right off Connecticut Ave., near major, more expensive convention hotels. 43 rooms. No restaurant on premises. Metro: Woodley or Dupont Circle.

BED AND BREAKFASTS. As the concept of bed-and-breakfast inns established itself across the nation, it was no wonder that the Washington area would offer quaint properties and reservation service organizations that list a variety of homes within the city's finer neighborhoods. Each property is quite different, and not all offer guests private-bath facilities. Many provide a quick cup of coffee or morning tea with a sweet roll while others get into more elaborate food arrangements. *Bed 'n' Breakfast Ltd. of Washington, D.C.,* Box 12011, Washington, D.C. 20005 (202–328–3510), is a reservation center that has homes in Capitol Hill, Georgetown, Logan Circle, and Dupont Circle. Singles run from $50, doubles from $60.

RESTAURANTS. Dining out in the Washington area can be an adventure. New restaurants open and close with such alarming frequency that it's hard even for residents to keep up with the changing scene. So no listing of restaurants can be complete.

The capital is rich in ethnic restaurants that offer interesting food at reasonable prices. The proliferation of Middle Eastern, Latin American, Afghan, Ethiopian, Thai, and Vietnamese restaurants run by people who have immigrated here immensely enriches the local culinary scene. However, prices in Washington restaurants vary as much as hotel rates do. Restaurants frequented by the expense account crowd are usually much more expensive than those in which the clientele reach into their jeans and pay cash.

Restaurant categories, based on a three-course dinner for one person, not including beverage, tax, and tip, are: *Super Deluxe,* over $35; *Deluxe,* $25–$35; *Expensive,* $15–$25; *Moderate,* $10–$15; *Inexpensive,* less than $10. The symbols AE, DC, MC, and V indicate that restaurants accept American Express, Diner's Club, MasterCard, and Visa. But we suggest you call to check each restaurant's credit card policy *before* you decide to dine there; these things have a way of changing.

Super Deluxe

Dominique's. 1900 Pennsylvania Ave., N.W. (452–1126). A bustling restaurant, famous for unusual game dishes (and infamous at one point for serving rattlesnake) and super-rich chocolate truffles. Take advantage of the fixed-price, pre- and post-theater dinners. All major credit cards.

Jean-Pierre. 1835 K St., N.W. (466–2022). A mixture of traditional and new French cuisine, in a distinguished downtown restaurant. All major credit cards.

Le Lion d'Or. 1150 Connecticut Ave., N.W. (296–7972). Long the undisputed champion of fine French restaurants in Washington. The dining room is large and elegant, the service attentive. But the restaurant's strength is the creative culinary skill of chef-owner Jean-Pierre Goyenvalle. Try his lamb with thyme, and finish with an exquisite orange soufflé. All major credit cards.

Occidental. 1475 Pennsylvania Ave., N.W. (783–1475). Regional delicacies amid all-American elegance. Perfect service in the original Washington "power restaurant." The Grill downstairs has lower prices and a more casual atmosphere. All major credit cards.

Le Pavillon. Washington Sq., 1050 Connecticut Ave., N.W. (833–3846). Chef Yannick Cam is back in business in a gorgeous new location, serving nouvelle cuisine legendary for its beauty, tastiness, high cost, and small portions. Tasting dinners offer small portions of several courses at lunch and dinner. All major credit cards.

1789. 1226 36th St., N.W. (965–1789). A most traditional Georgetown restaurant, located near the University campus. A variety of fine American dishes served in small dining rooms among elegant period furnishings. All major credit cards.

Deluxe

La Colline. 400 N. Capitol St., N.W. (737–0400). The wine bar in this pleasant Capitol Hill bistro offers daily specials of wine by the glass, and an outdoor café facing the courtyard fountains in good weather. Set-price dinner. AE, DC, MC, V.

F. Scott's. 1232 36th St., N.W. (342–0009). As the name suggests, the Jazz Age is evoked by music of the era in the background and vintage posters on the walls. A chef skilled in the New (Italian-) American cuisine lends prominence to the kitchen of a fine restaurant as well as a first-rate bar. All major credit cards.

Gary's. 1800 M St., N.W. (in the courtyard) (463–6470). This is an airy space with a well-stocked bar, catering to a high-wallet meat and potatoes crowd. AE, MC, V.

Germaine's. 2400 Wisconsin Ave., N.W. (965–1185). The flair and good taste Germaine Swanson brings to her pan-Asian culinary experiments have helped this chic and airy restaurant maintain its popularity with Washington's upper crust. Daily specials such as pine cone fish are generally excellent, and on the regular menu you'll want to try the house spring rolls, sate, and lemongrass BBQ spareribs. Vietnamese, Thai, Indonesian, Korean, and Chinese dishes, with Germaine's unique accent. All major credit cards.

Old Ebbitt Grill. 675 15th St., N.W. (347–4800). A venerable eatery has been restored to its antebellum finery. Tasty patriotic favorites are served a stone's throw from the White House. All major credit cards.

Vincenzo. 1606 20th St., N.W. (667–0047). Simplicity and authenticity are the keywords at this Italian seafood restaurant, so much so that when Vincenzo first opened, talk was evenly divided between how good the fish was and why he refused to serve butter with the bread. Fresh and uncommon fish dishes, served in a bright and airy setting. AE, MC, V.

Expensive

Cafe Berlin. 322 Massachusetts Ave., N.E. (543–7656). A block from the capital, this place boasts the most authentic central German cuisine in D.C. Any of the duck dishes on the menu can be recommended, as can the *dunkelbier* (in liter glasses), which flown in from Germany each *Oktoberfest.*

Clyde's. 3236 M St., N.W. (333–9180). Billed as "an exceptional American saloon." Nothing surprising on the menu, and everything is well made. A comfortable, popular spot in the middle of Georgetown; filled with diners and drinkers of all ages. Dependable and enjoyable. All major credit cards.

Japan Inn. 1715 Wisconsin Ave., N.W. (337–3400). In the Japanese Room you eat sukiyaki or shabu seated on the floor; in the Teppan-Yaki Room you eat grilled steak, shrimp, and chicken Benihana style; or you may opt for sushi at the new sushi bar. AE, DC, MC, V.

Moderate

Astor. 1813 M St., N.W. (331–7994). If it's a Greek dish you've never tried, then start with a salad and add a moussaka. Save room for baklava. Upstairs entertainment. AE, MC, V, Choice.

Bullfeathers. 410 First St., S.E. (543–5005). Beef and seafood in a popular hangout with a Teddy Roosevelt theme. The *New York Times* comes with the Louisiana-style brunch. AE, C, DC, MC, V.

Hamburger Hamlet. 3125 M St., N.W., Georgetown (965–6970). Stay with the hamburger portion of the menu and save room for the ultimate fudge cake. AE, DC, MC, V.

Omega. 1858 Columbia Rd., N.W. (745–9158). One of the original neighborhood restaurants in Adams-Morgan. Black beans and white rice accompany the generous Cuban and South American dishes. Good place to try paella. All major credit cards.

El Tamarindo. 1785 Florida Ave., N.W. (328–3660). The after-five Bohemians of Adams-Morgan pack tightly here around tiny tables for Salvadoran food piled high. Salvadoran beer is served cold, and Salvadoran music is played loud. Also at 4910 Wisconsin Ave., N.W. (244–8888).

Thai Room. 5037 Connecticut Ave., N.W. (244–5933). Lots of appetizers and your choice of spicy seasonings. Sample the satays. AE, MC, V.

Yenching Palace. 3524 Connecticut Ave., N.W. (362–8200). Well-known as the scene of important East-West visits and negotiations and the source of Peking duck ($18.95) that does not require 24 hours' advance notice. Sun. brunch. All major credit cards.

Inexpensive

Armand's Chicago Pizzeria. 4231 Wisconsin Ave., N.W. (686–9450). Popular with nearby college students for its deep-dish pies and six-foot subs. Long lines often, but it's open late and has take-out. Will deliver (363–5500). All major credit cards.

Hawk 'n' Dove. 329 Pennsylvania Ave., S.E. (543–3300). A long-time Hill favorite for burgers and deli-type sandwiches. Homemade soups and chili. AE, DC, MC, V.

Kramerbooks & Afterwords. 1517 Connecticut Ave., N.W. (387–1462). If you've always wanted to eat in a library, this is for you. Homemade soups, pastas, and desserts. Perfect for a leisurely cappuccino breakfast. AE, MC, V.

Sholl's Colonial Cafeteria. 1990 K St., N.W. (296–3065). Long regarded as Washington's premier cafeteria with homemade pies and fresh vegetables. Crowds line up early. Closed Sun. No credit cards.

El Torito. 700 Water St., S.W. (554–5302). Large number of dishes under $7 in this festive atmosphere. Popular for happy hour and frozen margaritas. AE, DC, MC, V.

Vie de France. 1725 K St., N.W. (775–9193), and three other locations in D.C. Bakery-turned-café. Indulge yourself with croissant or brioche dishes. Also, soups, quiches, burgers, and daily specials. Popular for weekend brunches. AE, MC, V.

The Zebra Room. 3238 Wisconsin Ave., N.W. (362–8307). This is a cult haunt-cum-pizza dive, complete with blue-plate specials, a vintage-70s crescent-shape bar, and a sidewalk café.

LIQUOR LAWS. Liquor is sold in package stores 9 A.M.–9 P.M. Mon.–Thurs., until 10 P.M. Fri., until midnight on Sat., never on Sun. In restaurants it is served 8 A.M.–2 A.M. Mon.–Thurs.; 8 A.M.–3 A.M., Fri. and Sat.; 10 A.M.–2 A.M., Sun. The legal drinking age is 21 for all alcoholic beverages. Proof of age in the form of a driver's license is usually required. Beer and wine may be bought daily in grocery stores and at some other places.

NIGHTLIFE AND BARS. There is no shortage of lively clubs and bars throughout town. The downtown professional corridor, Georgetown, Capitol Hill, and Dupont Circle house the most spots. Some partygoers get started with happy hour prices and stay until closing. All areas, even popular ones, can become a little suspect late at night. Security is a definite concern; after all, this is a big city and it's easy to have problems.

Hard liquor drinks top $3.50 in the majority of establishments, with wine and beer near $3. Picture identification is an acceptable form of proof of age.

Clubs are constantly changing. Call ahead to see who's in town or read the Friday Weekend section, of the *Washington Post.*

The Bayou. 3135 K St., N.W. (333–2897). Located under the Whitehurst Freeway at the foot of Georgetown, the Bayou attracts an 18- to 30-year-old clientele by booking such international acts as Terence Trent Darby and Laura Nyro. Cover charge: $5–$15.50. Arrive before 9 P.M. when the action picks up. There's dancing on weekends. The dress is casual, and sandwiches and pizza are served. Open Sun.–Thurs., 8 P.M.–2 A.M.; Fri.–Sat., 8 P.M.–3 A.M. No credit cards.

Blues Alley. Rear of 1073 Wisconsin Ave., N.W., Georgetown (337–4141). The city's oldest jazz supper club with a New Orleans Creole-style menu and big-name performers. Open evenings. Shows at 8 P.M. and 10 P.M., plus a midnight show on Fri. and Sat. Cover charge from $10–$30.

Childe Harold. 20th and Q Sts., N.W. (483–6700). A club where the Ramones once performed. No more live music, but a friendly, not-too-noisy neighborhood bar where the regulars make you feel at home. A solid menu, too, for lunch or dinner. AE, DC, MC, V.

Comedy Café. 1520 K St., N.W. (638–5653). Dinner specials are available. Thurs. is Open Mike Night: aspiring comedians try out their acts (8:30 P.M.). On Fri. comedians perform two shows, at 8:30 P.M. and 10:30 P.M. On Sat. shows are at 7:30, 9:30, and 11:30 P.M. Cover varies from night to night. Happy hour with reduced-priced drinks Mon. through Fri. Casually dressed young crowd. Open Mon.–Wed., 10:30 A.M.–2 A.M.; Thurs., 11:30 A.M.–show finishes; Fri.–Sat., 10 A.M.–2 A.M.; closed Sun.

One Step Down. 2517 Pennsylvania Ave., N.W. (331–8863). Live music Fri.–Mon. nights. Workshop jam sessions Sat. and Sun. afternoons. Cover charge for evening shows.

HISTORIC VIRGINIA

by
FRANCIS X. ROCCA and ED WOJTAS

Mr. Rocca is a writer formerly based in Alexandria, Virginia. Mr. Wojtas lives in Springfield, Virginia, and is a member of the Society of American Travel Writers.

Located midway between Maine and Florida on the Atlantic Coast, Virginia is shaped roughly like a triangle with each of its points aimed at a gateway to another world. The southwestern tip is at historic Cumberland Gap, which marked the way for early settlers to make their way into the interior of the country. The southeastern tip is at the mouth of Chesapeake Bay. And the northern point aims at Washington, D.C. and the megalopolis that stretches northeast from there to Philadelphia, New York, and Boston.

The state's topography ranges from mountains in the west, through a gently rolling Piedmont region to Tidewater and the isolated Eastern Shore. Its 40,817 square miles houses a population of nearly 5.7 million people. Highest point is Mount Rogers, at 5,729 feet, while the lowest point is the land abutting Chesapeake Bay and the Atlantic Ocean at sea level.

Virginia was the site of the first permanent English-speaking colony in the New World. Three tiny sailing ships—the *Susan Constant, Discovery,*

Please note that much of western Virginia is covered in the chapter "The Southern Appalachian Mountains."

and *Godspeed*—made history when they sailed up the James River on May 13, 1607, to deposit their band of resolute adventurers on the swampy river bank. After some hardships, including a virtual wipeout of the colony during the harsh winter of 1609–10, Jamestown ultimately prospered and the flood of settlers and visitors began.

Northern Virginia

The teeming Washington suburbs of northern Virginia lie directly across the Potomac River from the nation's capital. George Washington was largely responsible for the federal city being located so close to his home of Mount Vernon and his adopted home town of Alexandria.

Original plans called for inclusion into the District of Columbia of some 30 square miles of what is now Arlington County and the city of Alexandria. That land was ceded back to the Commonwealth of Virginia in 1845 as unneeded; today two sections of Arlington County—Rosslyn and Crystal City—house thousands of federal workers.

One stunning entrance to northern Virginia is via the Dulles Access Road, which connects Dulles International Airport, 25 miles west, to the metropolitan area. You arrive at the handsome Eero Saarinen terminal and from the airport are whisked through the green fields of Virginia and over a landscape that is rapidly developing into complexes of office buildings of all shapes, heights, and sizes. Enroute you pass the planned "new city" of Reston.

Arlington and the Pentagon

Arlington National Cemetery was carved out of the estate of Mary Anna Randolph Custis, wife of Robert E. Lee, who had inherited the property in 1857 from her father, George Washington Parke Custis, who in turn had obtained the land from his foster father, John Parke Custis. Lee, who was married here in 1831, after graduation from West Point, considered the estate his home for some 30 years prior to leaving to participate in the Civil War. Arlington House, the Robert E. Lee Memorial, is the mansion one sees as one approaches the cemetery over the Memorial Bridge from downtown Washington.

Among the famous buried in Arlington Cemetery are Generals John J. Pershing and George C. Marshall, Senator Robert F. Kennedy, and Presidents William Howard Taft and John F. Kennedy.

The most familiar feature of the cemetery is the Tomb of the Unknowns, which is guarded by elite sentinels of the "Old Guard" 3rd U.S. Infantry Regiment, whose precision—as they march exactly 21 steps, pause 21 seconds and march back—is as measured as if they were automatons. The tomb is guarded 24 hours a day with a change of guard every half-hour in daytime from April to September, every hour the rest of the year, and every two hours at night.

The tomb was originally constructed for the body of an unknown soldier from World War I. In 1958, the bodies of unknown American servicemen from World War II and the Korean War were interred here. And on Memorial Day 1984, an unidentified serviceman from the Vietnam War was laid to rest here.

Just outside the cemetery is the U.S. Marine Corps War Memorial, more familiarly known as the Iwo Jima statue. The 78-foot-high, 100-ton bronze casting recreates Joseph Rosenthal's Pulitzer Prize-winning World War II photo of Marines raising the flag on Iwo Jima's Mount Suribachi.

Not far from Arlington Cemetery is the world's largest office building, appropriately surrounded by the world's largest parking lots and one of the world's biggest arrays of access roads. It's the Pentagon, headquarters

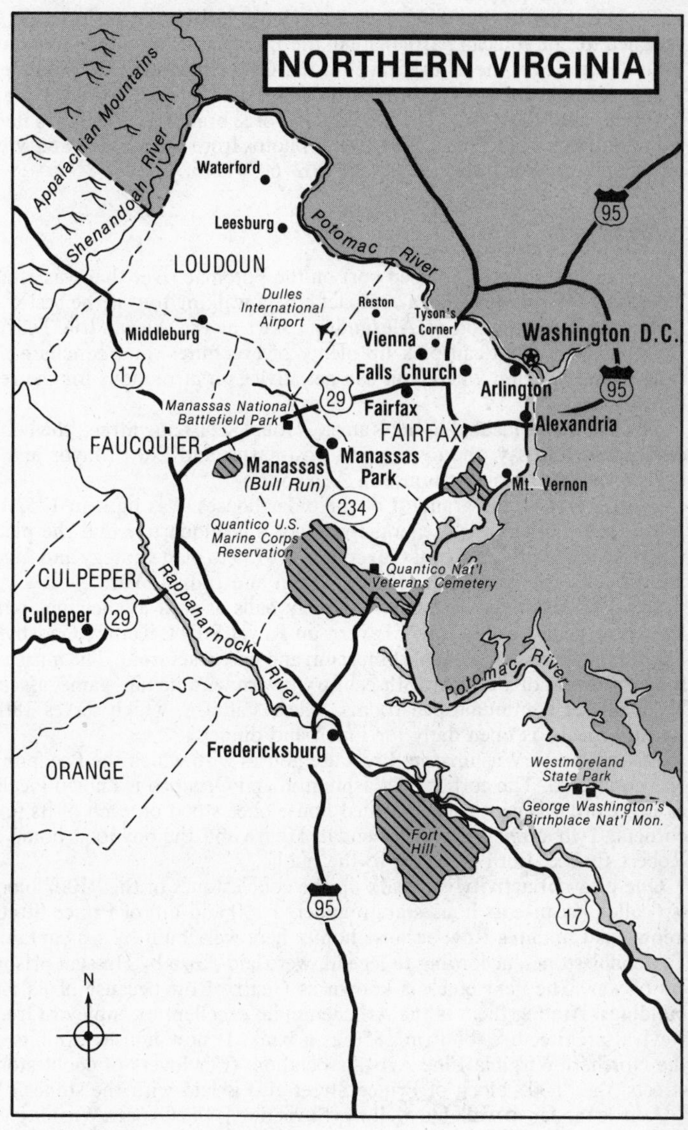
NORTHERN VIRGINIA
Appalachian Mountains
Shenandoah River
Waterford
Leesburg
Potomac River
LOUDOUN
Dulles International Airport
Reston
Tyson's Corner
Middleburg
Vienna
Washington D.C.
95
17
Falls Church
Arlington
29
Manassas National Battlefield Park
Fairfax
FAIRFAX
Alexandria
FAUCQUIER
Manassas (Bull Run)
Manassas Park
Mt. Vernon
234
Quantico U.S. Marine Corps Reservation
Quantico Nat'l Veterans Cemetery
CULPEPER
Rappahannock River
Culpeper
Potomac River
Fredericksburg
ORANGE
Westmoreland State Park
George Washington's Birthplace Nat'l Mon.
Fort Hill
N

and symbol of the U.S. Department of Defense. The five-sided—hence the name—building covers 29 acres, has 17½ miles of corridors, and houses some 26,000 employees.

To get into the building you must have legitimate business or be vouched for, or you can participate in the 1¼-hour, 1½ mile-long free tour. Tours begin from the Tour Office on the Concourse near the public entrance. Visitors see an orientation film and then are taken down the maze of corridors of the Army, Navy, and Air Force branches, which are lined with paintings from World War II and photos from the Korean and Vietnam conflicts. For information, call 202–695–1776.

Alexandria

Alexandria is an old tobacco port on the Potomac river that was established in 1749. Because it is a compact city, a walking tour is the best way to see the older section of Alexandria. Start at the Alexandria Tourist Council (where you can pick up plenty of brochures) and conclude the walk at the Lyceum where you can get advice on attractions for the rest of the area.

The Council is located in the Ramsay House, 221 King Street, the home of William Ramsay, the town's first postmaster and Lord Mayor and is believed to be the oldest house in Alexandria.

Carlyle House, the grandest of the older houses, was built in 1752 by John Carlyle. This was General Braddock's headquarters and the place where he met with five Royal Governors in 1755 to plan strategy and funding for the early campaigns of the French and Indian War.

George Washington attended birthday balls as well as meetings with his fellow gentry at Gadsby's Tavern on Royal Street. Today, Gadsby's, housed in two buildings, is part museum and part restaurant. The museum is a re-creation of a typical 18th-century tavern with its tap, game, assembly, ball and communal bed rooms. The restaurant, which serves 18th-century meals, is open daily for lunch and dinner.

Just off North Washington Street are houses with which the Lee family was connected. The corner of Washington and Oronoco is known locally as Lee Corner because a Lee-owned house once stood on each of its four corners. Two survive: the Lee-Fendall House and the boyhood home of Robert E. Lee. Both are open to the public.

One pleasant activity is a walk up the cobblestones of the "100" block (so called because its houses are numbered 100 and up) of Prince Street, known as Captain's Row because homes here were built by sea captains. The cobblestones, according to legend, were laid down by Hessian prisoners of war. The next block is known as Gentry Row because of its fine buildings. Among them is the Atheneum, an excellent example of Greek Revival architecture, built in 1850 as a bank. It now houses exhibits of the Northern Virginia Fine Arts Association. (For lovers of cobblestone streets, the "600" block of Prince Street also is laid with the stones.)

A little too far to walk but well worth visiting is the George Washington Masonic National Memorial at Callahan Drive and King Street, a mile west of the center of the city. There is a local bus service that can take you there from Old Town. The Memorial's spire, resembling the Pharos Lighthouse, one of the seven wonders of the ancient world, soars 333 feet into the sky and dominates its surroundings. It contains furnishing of the first Masonic Lodge in Alexandria in which George Washington was Worshipful Master while he served as President. There are free guided tours of the building and observation deck.

Mount Vernon

You can almost feel the presence of George Washington at Mount Vernon. His home with its stately pillared portico is far from spacious but reflects the quiet dignity of our first President. There's a wonderful view of the Potomac river over wide, sweeping lawns and the surrounding grounds are a delight. The towering trees surrounding the home include some planted by Washington himself. You can even buy a tiny boxwood, or other plant, nurtured at Mount Vernon as a memento of your visit.

This was Washington's home from 1754 until his death here in 1799, except for absences for Army and Presidential duties. The house and museum contain the bed in which he died and clothing and other articles belonging both to himself and his wife, Martha Custis Washington. A path leads to his and Martha's crypt.

Mount Vernon is one of the most visited of America's shrines, drawing a million visitors a year. Tours of the sprawling grounds are self-guided. Inside the home, small groups are ushered from room to room, each of which is staffed by a guide who describes the furnishings and answers questions. It's best to visit on weekdays, preferably not during summer months.

Two mansions in the Mount Vernon area are worth a visit. The Woodlawn Plantation was a gift from George Washington to his ward, Eleanor Parke Custis, and his nephew, Maj. Lawrence Lewis, after their wedding in 1799. Gunston Hall, completed in 1758, was the home of George Mason, author of the Virginia Declaration of Rights. On the grounds of Woodlawn is the Pope-Leighey House, designed by Frank Lloyd Wright in the 1940s and moved here in 1965. There are guided tours of Woodlawn Plantation and Gunston Hall.

Fredericksburg

Fifty miles south of Washington, D.C., on I-95, Fredericksburg is a city rich in Civil War nostalgia and Washington lore. Start your visit at the National Park Service Visitor Center, at Lafayette Boulevard (U.S.1) and Sunken Road. You'll enjoy an electric map program as well as the pictorial exhibits and displays of war relics. This is the starting point for a self-guided auto tour of the 5,644-acre Fredericksburg—Spotsylvania National Military Park which includes the Civil War battlefields of Fredericksburg, Chancellorsville, the Wilderness, and Spotsylvania Court House. In addition, it contains the Jackson Shrine, where the famed Confederate general died, the Fredericksburg National Cemetery with the graves of over 15,000 Union soldiers, and several sites associated with George Washington.

The Mary Washington House is the home Washington bought for his mother in 1772. Here he said goodbye to her before leaving for New York and his inauguration as President. She died in the house in 1789. Some of the boxwood on the grounds was planted by her. Mary Washington lies buried in a quiet cemetery at Washington Avenue and Pitt Street. The obelisk monument—a mini-Washington monument, if you please—above her grave was dedicated by President Grover Cleveland in 1894.

At 1201 Washington Avenue is Kenmore. Betty Washington, George's only sister, came here as the bride of Col. Fielding Lewis in 1752. The graceful Georgian Manor house once overlooked an 863-acre flax and tobacco plantation.

The Rising Sun Tavern was built about 1760 by George Washington's brother, Charles. Designated in 1964 a National Historic Landmark, it was a favorite meeting place of early patriots.

President James Monroe's law practice began in what is now the James Monroe Museum and Memorial Library. Today it houses a large collection of the personal possessions of the former President, including furniture, portraits, china, silver, jewelry, and porcelain used by the Monroes in the White House. A major piece of furniture is the Louis XVI desk, with its secret compartments, on which he signed the Monroe Doctrine.

Richmond

Start your tour of Richmond, the capital of Virginia, with a visit to the City Hall Sky Deck, for a striking view of modern skyscrapers and historic buildings. The State Capitol was designed by Thomas Jefferson in 1785. Set in a 12-acre park-like setting, the capitol was the first building in America constructed in the form of a classical temple. It is home to one of the oldest legislative bodies in the western hemisphere. Gracing the interior is the famous Houdin statue of George Washington.

The Edgar Allan Poe Museum is housed in the Old Stone House, built in 1737 and probably Richmond's oldest surviving stone structure. The Museum of the Confederacy has the world's largest collection of Confederate memorabilia. Next to it is the White House of the Confederacy, where Jefferson Davis lived during the Civil War.

The Valentine Museum, devoted to the history and lore of Richmond, is located in Heritage Square, a downtown city block that has been restored to its 19th-century elegance. St. John's Church, built in 1741, was the site of the 1775 Revolutionary Convention where Patrick Henry made his famous "Give me liberty or give me death" speech.

Richmond National Battlefield Park preserves the battlegrounds that were the setting of the 1861–65 defense of the city. Park headquarters, at 3215 East Broad Street, offers exhibits, an audio-visual program, and maps for the 97-mile auto tour of the battle sites in Hanover, Henrico, and Chesterfield counties.

Shockoe Slip, in downtown Richmond, was the cobblestoned tobacco warehouse district of the 18th and 19th centuries. Today, refurbished and sparkling clean, it is home to many of the city's fine restaurants, cafés, boutiques, and gourmet and specialty shops. Sixth Street Marketplace, a glass-enclosed promenade of over 100 shops, restaurants, landscaped plazas, and places of entertainment, stretches three blocks through the main retail and business district.

Charlottesville

Some 60 miles west of Richmond, on I-64, is Charlottesville, named for Queen Charlotte, wife of England's George III. The town might just as well be called Jeffersonville because the spirit of the man is so deeply imbued in the heritage of the countryside. This is where he lived and this is where his crowning achievement, the University of Virginia, is located.

Monticello, his domed mansion, is set in the countryside outside the city. It was his 41-year labor of love: "All my wishes end where I hope my days will end—at Monticello." Here he died, and here he is buried. The three-story building has 35 rooms but looks deceptively modest because 12 rooms are in the basement and in a series of outbuildings.

The mansion is crammed with Jeffersonian inventions. There's a tightly winding staircase, just 24 inches wide; a revolving door with shelves to serve dishes from the kitchen; a dumb-waiter built into the side of the dining room fireplace to hoist wines from the cellar, and a unique seven-day clock over the entry door that uses cannonballs for counterweights and registers hours as well as the day of the week.

The house commands a view of the rolling Virginia countryside that Jefferson so dearly loved. Through a telescope, he would watch construction of the University back in town. Calling it his "academical village," Jefferson referred to its building as the "last act of usefulness I can render."

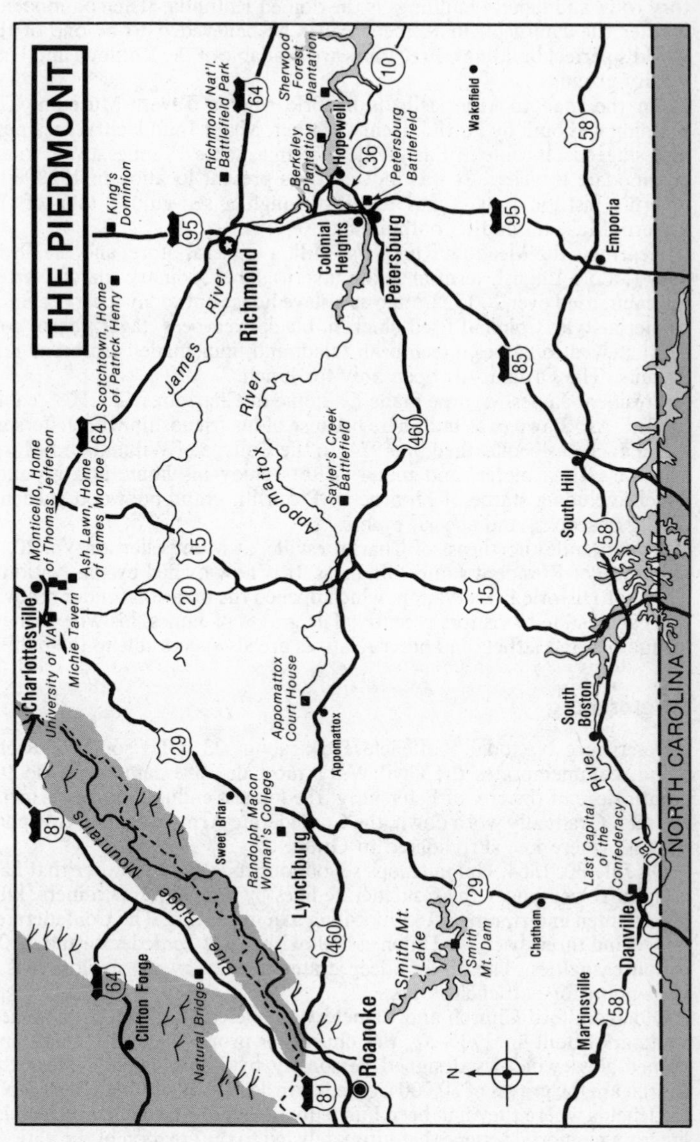
THE PIEDMONT
King's Dominion
Scotchtown, Home of Patrick Henry
Monticello, Home of Thomas Jefferson
Ash Lawn, Home of James Monroe
Charlottesville
University of VA
Michie Tavern
Richmond Nat'l. Battlefield Park
Sherwood Forest Plantation
Berkeley Plantation
Hopewell
Petersburg Battlefield
Colonial Heights
Petersburg
Richmond
James River
Appomattox River
Sayler's Creek Battlefield
Appomattox Court House
Appomattox
Wakefield
Emporia
South Hill
South Boston
Dan River
Last Capital of the Confederacy
Danville
Chatham
Martinsville
NORTH CAROLINA
Sweet Briar
Randolph Macon Woman's College
Lynchburg
Smith Mt. Lake
Smith Mt. Dam
Roanoke
Clifton Forge
Natural Bridge
Blue Ridge Mountains
N
95
64
10
36
58
85
460
15
20
29
81

The University, with its classical pavilions, sweeping lawns and 7ardens, and serpentine walls is one of the country's architectural treasures. Dominating the two-acre stretch of lawn that is bordered by colonnaded dormitory rows and faculty buildings is the domed Rotunda. Jefferson modeled it after the Pantheon in Rome because he believed it to be one of the world's perfect buildings. Free tours are available of the Rotunda and University grounds.

On the road to Monticello is historic Michie Tavern-Museum. The building was built by Patrick Henry's father, Major John Henry, on a popular stagecoach route in Earlysville, Virginia, some 17 miles away, to accommodate travelers. It was moved to its present location in 1928. The tavern's historic past comes to life through a self-guided tour of the Tavern–Museum and its outbuildings.

Nearby is the Meadow Run Grist Mill, a General Store, and the Ordinary (an old English term meaning tavern). The Ordinary is a converted log cabin used over 200 years ago as a slave house but today it serves lunch cafeteria-style: Colonial fried chicken, black-eyed peas, tavern corn, cole slaw, stewed tomatoes, green bean salad, and homemade corn bread and biscuits. The Ordinary is open only for lunch.

President James Monroe made his home in Charlottesville. His "cabin castle," Ash Lawn, was built here because of his friendship with Jefferson. Ash Lawn was bequeathed, in 1974, to the College of William and Mary, Monroe's alma mater, and today visitors enjoy his home and grounds which include a statue of Monroe by Piccirilli, grand boxwood gardens, roving peacocks, and special events.

Twenty miles northeast of Charlottesville, at Montpelier, on Va. 20, is the estate of President James Madison. It is now owned by the National Trust for Historic Preservation, which opened the mansion (under renovation) and estate to visitors recently. The graves of James, his wife Dolley, his mother and father, and other relatives are also accessible to the public.

Petersburg

Petersburg National Battlefield Park, about 23 miles south of Richmond, commemorates the Civil War's most decisive campaign, the 10-month siege of the city of Petersburg, the longest endured by any American city. Gradually worn down, the Confederate Army retreated to Appomattox, where Lee surrendered to Grant.

On July 30, 1864, Union troops set off four tons of gunpowder that had been burrowed under the Confederate lines by Pennsylvania miners, killing 278 men and ripping a 180-foot-long gap in the line. The Confederates rallied and threw back the Union assault with 1,500 Confederate and 4,000 Union casualties. The 30-foot-deep crater created by the explosion is a focal point for battlefield tours.

Old Blandford Church and Cemetery are Petersburg's most cherished landmark. Built in 1735–37, the church is proud of its 15 handsome stained-glass windows designed personally by Louis Tiffany. Near the church are the graves of 30,000 Confederate dead, brought here from other battlefields where they had been hurriedly interred. The cemetery was the site for a memorial service that ultimately led to the creation of the national Memorial Day.

The Quartermaster Museum, at nearby Fort Lee, is a tribute to the Corps that has fed, housed, clothed, and supplied American forces for almost 200 years.

There are life-size exhibits of the horse cavalry that won the west, the 37 different flags that have flown over America since 1753, uniforms that go back to the Revolution, and General George Patton's jeep.

Appomattox

Appomattox Court House National Historical Park, about 100 miles west of Petersburg on U.S. 460, covers some 1,318 acres. It was here on April 9, 1865, that Robert E. Lee's army surrendered to Ulysses S. Grant to end the long and difficult Civil War.

A village of 27 historic structures has been restored to its appearance on that fateful date. Included are the Meeks General Store, the Woodson Law Office, the county jail, Clover Hill Tavern, and the McLean House where the surrender actually took place. All of the buildings are within easy walking distance of the National Park Visitor Center, which is housed in the reconstructed court house building.

Northern Neck

The Northern Neck, lying between the Rappahannock and Potomac Rivers, is noted for producing presidents and statesmen. James Madison came from King George County and George Washington, James Monroe, and Robert E. Lee were from Westmoreland County.

Stratford Hall, home of the Lees, gave the nation a host of public servants, including twelve members of the House of Burgesses and four governors. Thomas Lee, who began building the house about 1725, was a Burgess who became president of His Majesty's Council. Two of his sons, Richard Henry and Francis Lightfoot, signed the Declaration of Independence, while two other sons, Arthur and William, represented the United States abroad as diplomats. Another Lee, Light Horse Harry, was Washington's cavalry leader and later, as a congressman, eulogized his commander as "first in war, first in peace, and first in the hearts of his countrymen."

Stratford Hall has massive proportions. Designed in the shape of a capital H, the house measures 90 by 60 feet. It has four huge chimneys at each end. The plantation's 1,600 acres are worked today as they were when Stratford was a showplace among Colonial plantations. The house is within sight of the Potomac River and only eight miles from Popes Creek Plantation, the birthplace of George Washington.

The building at Popes Creek is an approximate reproduction of the Washington birthplace. The National Park Service built it of old brick on the site of the original which burned on Christmas Day in 1799, the year Washington died. Many of the Washington family furnishings are among the early 18th-century antiques on display. Nearby is Monrovia, where President James Monroe was born. No buildings are there.

Williamsburg

Williamsburg, originally called Middle Plantation, was first settled in 1633 by colonists from Jamestown as an outpost against Indian attacks.

In 1698 the Statehouse at Jamestown was leveled by fire, and the following year the legislators decided to move the capital to Middle Plantation, which they promptly renamed Williamsburg in honor of William III, then King of England. The town remained the capital until 1780, when the capital of the new Commonwealth was moved to Richmond.

The restored historic area covers some 173 acres in the heart of contemporary Williamsburg. It is about one mile long with the Christopher Wren building of the College of William and Mary on the west end and the Capitol on the east end. There are nearly 500 preserved, restored, or rebuilt houses, shops, taverns, public, and out buildings in the historic area. Major structures are the Governor's Palace, the Capitol, the Magazine and

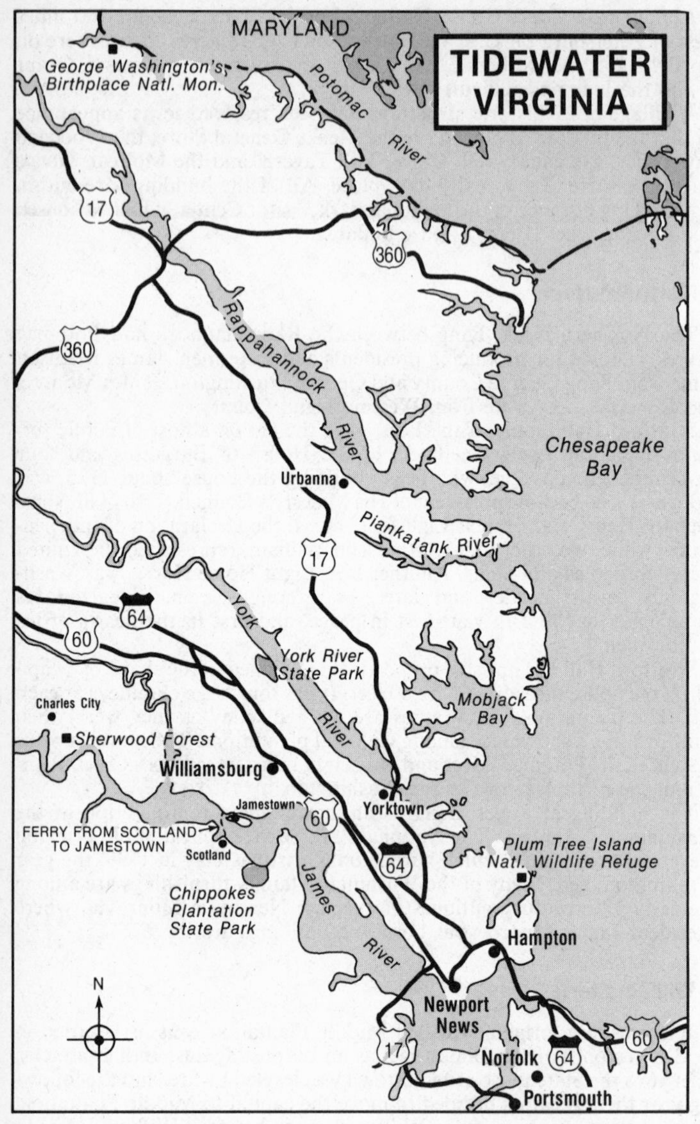

TIDEWATER VIRGINIA
MARYLAND
George Washington's Birthplace Natl. Mon.
Potomac River
Rappahannock River
Urbanna
Piankatank River
Chesapeake Bay
York River
York River State Park
Mobjack Bay
Charles City
Sherwood Forest
Williamsburg
Jamestown
FERRY FROM SCOTLAND TO JAMESTOWN
Scotland
Yorktown
Plum Tree Island Natl. Wildlife Refuge
Chippokes Plantation State Park
James River
Hampton
Newport News
Norfolk
Portsmouth
17
360
64
60
N

Guardhouse, Bruton Parish Church, the Courthouse of 1770, and the Wren Building. The major recent addition to Colonial Williamsburg is the reconstructed Public Hospital of 1773, the first institution in America that was devoted exclusively to treating the mentally ill.

One delight of a visit to Williamsburg are the craft shops. Interpreters and artisans explain trades and demonstrate 18th-century methods and skills. In the Tarplay, Greenhow, and Prentis stores, you can buy many of the products. You'll see spinning and weaving, corn meal being ground by wind power at the Windmill, furniture being created at the Cabinet-maker's Shop, wigs being shaped at the Wigshop, and wrought iron being molded on a hand anvil at the Blacksmith's. Sample fresh gingerbread and cookies at the Raleigh Bake Shop, watch a book being bound at the Printing Office and Bookbindery, and mail a letter from the reconstructed first Virginia post office.

Just five minutes east of Williamsburg is Busch Gardens, The Old Country, a modern theme park that pays tribute to England, Germany, Italy, and France. It offers a gaggle of thrill rides that include a double looping serpentine roller coaster dubbed the "Loch Ness Monster."

Seven miles east of Williamsburg on U.S. 60 is Carter's Grove Plantation, operated by Colonial Williamsburg. The mansion was built in 1750 by the wealthy Robert "King" Carter and is considered by many to be one of the most beautiful in America. Of special note is the magnificent carved stairway and paneled entrance hall. Deep scars in the stair railing are reputed to have been hacked there by a British cavalryman who rode his horse up the stairs, slashing away at the balustrade with his sabre.

Jamestown and Yorktown

Located on the James River, Jamestown was the first permanent English-speaking colony settled in the New World.

Start your visit with a stop at the National Park Visitor Center, then walk around the grounds. There's the 103-foot obelisk that was built in 1907 to commemorate the 300th anniversary of the English folks' arrival, statues of John Smith and Pocahontas, and the Memorial Cross that marks the graves of the 300 settlers who died during the severe winter of 1609–10. An old church tower, now only a shell, is the only 17th-century structure still standing.

At the Glasshouse of 1608—the first industry set up in America—costumed glassblowers demonstrate their craft. You can buy samples of their work.

Jamestown Settlement, formerly known as Jamestown Festival Park, not to be confused with the original settlement area, is an attraction run by the Commonwealth of Virginia. Inside the park are replicas of the three ships that arrived on that historic day, a re-created James Fort of 1607, a reproduction of Chief Powhatan's lodge, and a re-created typical Algonquin Indian village of the times. The Old World pavilion depicts the heritage from Great Britain in a series of displays. There is an admission charge to the Festival Park.

Running from Jamestown for 23 miles to Yorktown, via Williamsburg, is the Colonial Parkway. It's a pleasant drive with speeds restricted to 45 miles an hour. Trucks are banned. Jamestown, Yorktown and the Parkway collectively are the Colonial National Historic Park, operated by the National Park Service as a single unit.

Yorktown is where George Washington accepted the surrender of Lord Cornwallis to end the Revolutionary War. As at Jamestown, there's a National Park Service Visitor Center plus an attraction operated by the Commonwealth of Virginia, Yorktown Victory Center.

The National Park Visitor Center features a short orientation film, exhibits, and a special overlook of the battlefield. On a self-guided tour of the grounds, you'll see the site of Washington's headquarters, siege lines and redoubts, and the Moore House where American, French, and British officers met to draft the terms of surrender. The home of Thomas Nelson, a signer of the Declaration of Independence, has cannonballs wedged in its walls. Towering over the grounds is the 95-foot-high Victory Monument which salutes the centennial of the battle.

Hampton Roads

Hampton Roads, at the entry to Chesapeake Bay, is one of the great harbors of the world, and much of the activity in the cities that surround it is sea-oriented. The naval bases, shipyards, harbor tours, and old forts were designed to protect the seaport in years past.

History abounds. It was here, for example, that the famed battle between the two Civil War ironclads, the *Merrimac* and the *Monitor,* took place.

Four major cities ring Hampton Roads, two on the north—Hampton and Newport News—on the tip of the peninsula between the York and James Rivers, with the other two—Norfolk and Portsmouth—on the south side of the harbor. The two sides are connected by I-64 through the Hampton Roads Bridge-Tunnel.

Newport News

One of Newport News's prize attractions is the magnificent Mariner's Museum. Visitors are greeted in the Great Hall by a gilded eagle figurehead that once graced the prow of the frigate, U.S.S. *Lancaster.* The golden bird sports a wingspan of 18½ feet. The museum is crammed with nautical history, more figureheads, small boats, paintings, name boards, and ship models.

Over 60 years of aviation history mark the birthplace of NASA at Langley Air Force Base. It was here that the astronauts practiced their moon landings. At the Visitor Center are many exhibits reviewing the early history of flight, moon rocks, space suits, satellite photos, and the Apollo 12 spacecraft that journeyed to the moon.

One of the largest shipbuilding facilities in the world, Newport News Shipbuilding and Dry Dock Company has built Polaris submarines, the aircraft carriers *Enterprise* and *John F. Kennedy,* and the once-proud trans-Atlantic liners *United States* and *America.* You can see the retired *United States* at her berth from vantage points in the city or from the harbor tours that originate in the four cities.

Fort Monroe, at Old Point Comfort, was built in 1819 and is the largest stone fort in North America. It has been continuously occupied since 1823. Covering 63 acres and surrounded by a moat, the hexagonal-shaped fort was "home" to several distinguished prisoners during its lifetime, including Indian Chief Black Hawk and Confederate President Jefferson Davis.

Norfolk

If you've spent any time at all in the U.S. Navy, you've heard of Norfolk. It's one of the largest naval installations in the world—home port for 130 ships of the Atlantic and Mediterranean fleets and 45 aircraft squadrons—and NATO's Atlantic headquarters. March through November, air-conditioned buses leave the main gate for 55-minute guided tours, and on Saturdays and Sundays visitors are permitted to tour an "open house" ship. In the winter, a sailor-guide will ride in your car, for free, by advance request.

One of the newest attractions in Norfolk is Waterside, an exciting festival marketplace that is home to over 100 shops, galleries, bazaars, and boutiques. There are several major restaurants, many specializing in seafood, as well as smaller cafés with romantic harbor views. Patterned after Baltimore's Harborplace and New York's South Street Seaport, Waterside is the focal point for a variety of city celebrations.

The Douglas MacArthur Memorial, in downtown Norfolk, celebrates the general's illustrious career. On display is the collection of awards, gifts, papers, and mementoes from his life of service to his country. In the rotunda, his final resting place, the General lies surrounded by the words and banners of his glory.

The Adam Thoroughgood House is the oldest brick home in America. Constructed on the banks of the Lynnhaven River, it contains authentic 17th-century furnishings. Visitors marvel at the excellence of construction of this colonial home. Another old home, Moses Myers House, was built in 1792 by one of the first millionaires in America. It remains one of the most elegant townhouses in the country. Visitors stroll the halls once trod by President James Monroe, Daniel Webster, and the Marquis de Lafayette.

St. Paul's Church, built in 1739, is the lone survivor of the British bombardment and fiery destruction of the city by Lord Dunmore in 1776. A British cannonball fired during the attack is still embedded in the southeastern wall of the church. The interior displays several Tiffany stained-glass windows.

The Chrysler Museum was founded in 1933 as the Norfolk Museum of Arts and Sciences. In 1971, the magnificent art collection of Walter P. Chrysler, Jr., was donated and the museum renamed in his honor. In addition to the permanent collection, new and exciting loan exhibitions are placed on view throughout the year. The permanent collection represents the entire gamut of cultures and civilizations from ancient Greece and Rome to contemporary paintings and sculpture.

Virginia Beach

Just south of Norfolk, Virginia Beach is the prime seashore resort for the state as well as the largest city in both population and area. It's a total resort with 175 hotels providing over 10,000 rooms, half of them on the oceanfront, souvenir shops, and 28 blocks of boardwalk.

The Virginia Marine Science Museum is the most popular museum in the state and one of the newest. It contains 100,000 gallons of fresh and salt water and more than 200 exhibits about meteorology, submarine travel, and aquatic life. The adjacent salt marsh is a refuge for countless bird species.

Virginia Beach developed around a U.S. Lifesaving Coast Guard Station that is now the local Maritime Historical Museum. Built in 1903, the station houses photos, nautical artifacts, scrimshaws, ship models, and other maritime memorabilia from all over the world.

North of town is the Old Cape Henry Lighthouse authorized by America's first Congress. Built in 1791 to warn mariners of Virginia's treacherous capes, it is now open to visitors. Nearby, too, is the First Landing Cross where the Jamestown settlers first made landfall in the New World. They touched shore here on April 26, 1607, and then proceeded up the James River and their date with destiny. Both the lighthouse and the cross are located on the grounds of Fort Story military reservation.

Little Creek Amphibious Base is the largest of its kind in the world. It's open on Saturdays and Sundays, and you can visit one of the ships that calls this base home. There's also an amphibious museum to see. Oceana Naval Air Station has two observation areas—one on Oceana Boulevard, the other on London Bridge Road—from which you can watch takeoffs and landings of the latest U.S. Navy aircraft. The base, however, is closed to the public.

Eastern Shore

Virginia's Eastern Shore is at the very bottom of the Delmarva Peninsula and consists of two counties, Accomack and Northampton, which are isolated from the rest of the state. The landscape is flat and the country agrarian. Agriculture is the biggest business with nearly 120,000 acres under cultivation. The area leads the state in growing vegetables with the Irish potato the most important crop.

The main road, running north–south, is U.S. 13, which enters the Eastern Shore from Virginia Beach over the one-of-a-kind 17½-mile Chesapeake Bay Bridge-Tunnel, an engineering marvel that leaps across the bay entrance on a series of causeways and trestles. The road dives beneath the water at two points from man-made islands. Driving over the bridge-tunnel is akin to taking an ocean cruise in your automobile.

At the northern end of Virginia's Eastern Shore is Chincoteague Island. World famous for its oyster beds and clam shoals, the island is the gateway to a national seashore and wildlife refuge. The serene fishing village, seven miles long and 1½ miles wide, abounds with history and natural charm.

Protecting Chincoteague Island from the Atlantic is the barrier island of Assateague, which boasts more than 37 miles of isolated beaches. The rare beauty is protected by the Assateague Island National Seashore and Chincoteague National Wildlife Refuge. The two make up a birdwatcher's Eden. Over 260 species of birds can be found here, and as days get colder the arrival of Canada and snow geese herald the onset of winter.

The most popular inhabitants of the refuge, however, are the Chincoteague wild ponies that were made famous in the book *Misty of Chincoteague.* Legend has it that these ponies are descendants of horses that swam ashore from a wrecked Spanish galleon centuries ago. The famous Wild Pony Round-up and swim to Chincoteague Island for auction is held annually in late July.

A rocket launch site was established on Wallops Island, near Chincoteague, in 1945 by the Langley Research Center, then a field station for NASA. Today it is used primarily to obtain scientific data about the atmosphere and space. NASA operates a Visitor Center on VA 175, the road that leads from U.S. 13 to Chincoteague Island.

Tangier Island

In 1608, Captain John Smith sailed up Chesapeake Bay and landed on a small island which he named Tangier after the seaport in Morocco. For many years this was the hunting and fishing grounds for the Pocomoke Indians, but the rich oyster beds and crab grounds surrounding the island quickly attracted settlers to the remote spot.

Today, although modernization has come to the island, it has not lost its quaint charm. The people of Tangier, who speak with a lingering trace of Elizabethan accent, are warm, friendly, and proud of their island. A visit here is a truly unique experience.

Cruises to Tangier Island are available from Onancock, VA, on the Eastern Shore (804–787–8220) and from Reedville, on the Northern Neck (804–333–4656).

While in Onancock drop in at the Hopkins & Bro. Store, which dates back to 1842. One of the oldest general stores on the east coast, it is a Virginia and U.S. Historic Landmark. The store sells a variety of "general merchandise," groceries plain and fancy, dry goods, and quaint arts and crafts. It also sells tickets for the Tangier Island cruise.

PRACTICAL INFORMATION FOR VIRGINIA

Note: See also "The Southern Appalachian Mountains" chapter.

WHEN TO GO. Virginia has a mild climate making it a year-round tourist destination. Spring and autumn are particularly delightful while summer tends to be very hot. Winters are mild although an occasional snow or ice storm will whiten the landscape. Because of the proximity of Washington, D.C., probably the number one tourist destination in the country, summer finds crowds of families flocking to the nearby Virginia attractions. Spring and autumn, when the schools are in session, and the weather is pleasant, are ideal times to visit the Old Dominion.

HOW TO GET THERE. By plane. Washington, Richmond, Newport News (serving Williamsburg), Norfolk, Roanoke, and Charlottesville have major airports. There is also regular scheduled air service to other cities in the state. In the recent spate of airline buyouts, *USAir* (800–368–5425 or 800–428–4322) has taken over the old regional carriers and now serves more destinations than any other carrier in the state.

By car. I-95, which stretches from Maine to Florida, parallels old U.S.1 and runs north–south through Washington, Richmond, Fredericksburg, and Petersburg. In the western part of the state, I-81 runs southwest from Pennsylvania to Tennessee. I-66 and I-64 run east–west from the mountains to Norfolk-Newport News and Washington areas. U.S. 13 connects the Norfolk area with the Eastern Shore over and through the spectacular 17½-mile Chesapeake Bay Bridge-Tunnel. Major car rental companies with outlets around the state include *Thrifty* (800–367–2277), *Hertz* (800–654–3131), and *Avis* (800–331–3131).

By train. *Amtrak* serves 16 cities in Virginia (including Alexandria, Richmond, Williamsburg, Fredericksburg, and Charlottesville). There are direct trains from Florida, New York, Chicago, New Orleans, Boston, and Philadelphia. Connections from other cities can be made at Washington. *Auto-Train,* which carries personal cars along with passengers, operates between Lorton, VA, and Sanford, FL. For train information, call 800–USA–RAIL.

By bus. *Greyhound/Trailways* operates throughout the state. A wide variety of motor coach tours to and through Virginia are also available from many major cities in the East. Consult your travel agent.

TOURIST INFORMATION. *Virginia Division of Tourism,* 1021 E. Cary St., 14th Floor, Richmond, VA 23219 (804–786–4484 or, for a booklet, 800–847–4882). Travel information is also available at 10 highway stations operated by the state along the Interstates, generally at entry points into Virginia.

The following are good sources of information on the area you plan to visit.

Arlington County: *Arlington Visitors Center,* 735 18th St. South, Arlington, VA 22202 (703–358–5720).

Fredericksburg: *Visitor Center,* 706 Caroline St., Fredericksburg, VA 22401 (703–373–1776).

Richmond: *Richmond Visitors Center,* 1710 Robin Hood Rd., Richmond, VA 23220 (804–358–5511).

Charlottesville: *Thomas Jefferson Visitors Bureau,* Box 161, Charlottesville, VA 22902 (804–293–6789).

Petersburg: *Petersburg Information Center,* 425 Cockade Alley, Petersburg, VA 23803 (804–733–2400).

Appomattox: *Chamber of Commerce,* Box 704, Appomattox, VA 24522 (804–352–2621).

Williamsburg: *Colonial Williamsburg,* Box C, Williamsburg, VA 23187 (Toll-free, 1–800–HIS–TORY, for reservations and information). *Williamsburg Area Tourism and Conference Bureau,* Drawer GB, Williamsburg, VA 23187 (804–253–0192).

Jamestown and Yorktown: *Jamestown Festival Park,* Drawer JF, Williamsburg, VA 23187 (804–229–1607); *Yorktown Victory Center,* Box 1976, Yorktown, VA 23690 (804–887–1776); or *Colonial National Historic Park,* Box 210, Yorktown, VA 23690 (804–898–3400).

Hampton Roads: *Virginia Peninsula Tourism & Conference Bureau,* 8 San Jose Dr., Suite 3B, Newport News, VA 23606 (804–873–0092 or 800–333–RSVP).

Norfolk: *Norfolk Convention & Visitors Bureau,* Information Center, Ocean View, End of 4th View St., Norfolk, VA 23503 (804–588–0404).

Virginia Beach: *Virginia Beach Visitors Information Center,* 19th St. and Pacific Ave., Virginia Beach, VA 23456 (800–446–8038, toll-free).

Eastern Shore: *Eastern Shore Tourism Commission,* Box 147, Accomac, VA. 23301, 804–787–2460.

TELEPHONES. The state is covered by two telephone area code numbers. 703 serves northern Virginia and the mountain areas of the western part of the state; 804 is used in the southeastern portion of the state.

HINTS TO DISABLED TRAVELERS. The Virginia Division of Tourism has a 96-page book, *Virginia Travel Guide for the Disabled,* which lists special rates, accessible accommodations, accessible attractions, and support groups that can provide assistance in emergencies.

STATE PARKS. The Commonwealth of Virginia maintains 23 recreational and six historical state parks and six natural areas. Two state parks are under development. Portions of the Appalachian Trail, encompassing 795 acres, are also within the state park system.

Virginia's state parks are open year-round, although they are generally geared to seasonal operation. Visitors are welcome to enjoy many outdoor recreational activities during the off-season including boating, fishing, hiking, bicycling, nature observation, picnicking, and sightseeing. Seasonal facilities, open from Memorial Day weekend to Labor Day weekend, include swimming beaches, bathhouses, boat and horse rentals, restaurants, refreshment stands, and stores. Parking and admission fees are in effect during the regular operating season.

Campsites open for occupancy in late Mar. and close in late Dec. Exact opening dates vary slightly each year. For summer camping, it is recommended that reservations be made as early as possible. These can be made up to 90 days in advance, beginning in late Mar. Any campsites not reserved are available on a first-come, first-served basis.

Vacation cabins are located in eight of the state parks. Cabins are of concrete, frame, or log construction and may be reserved up to a year in advance. Cabins may be rented for a minimum of one week and, when space is available, for a maximum of two consecutive weeks at one park.

Reservations can be made in person at any state park with cabins and/or campsites and at the *Division of Parks & Recreation* Central Office in Richmond; or contact Ticketron Reservation Center, Box 62221, Virginia Beach, VA 23462 (804–490–3939).

More information on the state parks, as well a copy of the descriptive booklet, "Virginia State Parks," is available from the *Division of Parks & Recreation,* 203 Governor St., Capitol Sq., Richmond, VA 23219 (804–786–2134).

CAMPING. Besides the campsites in state parks, there are many private campgrounds located throughout the state. For information on these, write for "Virginia Campgrounds," from the *Virginia Travel Council,* 7415 Brook Rd., Richmond, VA 23227 (804–266–0444), and for "Virginia Campgrounds Directory," from the *Virginia Campground Assn.,* 300 W. Franklin St., Richmond, VA 23220 (804–648–4895).

FISHING AND HUNTING. Virginia is blessed with four great tidal rivers and the inland sea called Chesapeake Bay. Its agrarian Eastern Shore peninsula is flanked by a chain of marshy uninhabited barrier islands with their inlets and sounds and the proximity of the southbound Labrador Current and the northbound Gulf Stream out in the Atlantic. What this all adds up to is excellent saltwater fishing for channel bass, tarpon, spot, tautog, bluefish, marlin, yellowfin tuna, wahoo, amberjack, and swordfish. Fishing can be done from a private boat, from the beach or fishing pier, or from charter and head boats.

No license is required for saltwater fishing in the ocean, bay, or in rivers up to the freshwater line. Licenses are needed for freshwater fishing in rivers, lakes, and impoundments. Licenses cost $12 for residents, $30 for non-residents, and they are valid for the calendar year. An additional fee is charged for fishing in stocked trout waters.

Hunting licenses, which are good from July 1 to June 30, cost residents $12 and non-residents $60. The fees are doubled if you hunt for "big game," which includes bear, deer, and turkey.

More information on hunting and freshwater fishing from the *Virginia Commission of Game and Inland Fisheries,* 4010 W. Broad St., Richmond, VA 23230 (804–367–1000; ask for an Information Officer). More information on saltwater fishing from the Virginia Division of Tourism.

ACCOMMODATIONS. Hotels and motels in Virginia span a wide range. Generally, they are less expensive west of the Blue Ridge than those in the Piedmont and Tidewater areas. Prices in the suburbs surrounding Washington, D.C., are also more expensive. A competitive thrust, now extending along the East Coast to Texas, originated in Virginia with the Econo Lodge motels. There are now more than 70 units of that economical chain in Virginia.

Price categories in this section will average as follows: *Super Deluxe,* over $155; *Deluxe,* $100–$155; *Expensive,* $75–$100; *Moderate,* $60–$75; *Inexpensive,* under $60. Rates are based on peak season, double occupancy in mid-week. Many of the establishments offer reduced rates on weekends and in off-peak travel seasons.

Alexandria

Super Deluxe

Morrison House. 116 S. Alfred St. (703–838–8000). An intimate hotel of just 47 rooms built in Federal style. Excellent restaurant and grill. In Old Town.

Deluxe

Best Western Old Colony Inn. First and North Washington Sts. (703–548–6300 or 800–528–1234). Color TV. Pool. Restaurant. Shuttle to and from airport and Metro subway.

Guest Quarters Suite Hotel-Alexandria. 100 S. Reynolds St. (703–370–9600). One- and two-bedroom suites with kitchens. Hotel service.

Holiday Inn of Old Town. 480 King St. (703–549–6080 or 800–HOLIDAY). Colonial-style luxury in the heart of Old Town. Indoor pool.

Holiday Inn-Eisenhower Metro. 2460 Eisenhower Dr. (703–960–3400 or 800–HOLIDAY). Color TV. Pool. Pets. Several other Holiday Inns in the area.

Appomattox

Inexpensive

Traveler's Inn. U.S. 460 near VA 24 (804–352–7451). Attractive, clean rooms are offered at this place near the historic site.

Arlington

Super Deluxe

Hyatt Arlington at Key Bridge. 1325 Wilson Blvd. in Rosslyn. (703–525–1234 or 800–228–9000). Indoor parking. 303 rooms. Good dining facilities.

Sheraton National Hotel. Near Pentagon at Columbia Pike and Washington Blvd. (703–521–1900 or 800–325–3535). 431 rooms. Indoor pool. Indoor parking. Rooftop dining.

Stouffer's Concourse Hotel. Near National Airport on U.S. 1 at 2399 Jefferson Davis Hwy. (703–418–6800 or 800–468–3571). A full-facility hotel with 386 rooms; special weekend rates.

Expensive

Best Western Rosslyn Westpark Hotel. Junction U.S. 29 and George Washington Pkwy. (703–527–4814 or 800–528–1234). 308 rooms. One block to Metro subway. Rooftop restaurant. Heated indoor pool.

Quality Inn Iwo Jima. 1501 Arlington Blvd., on U.S. 50 (703–524–5000 or 800–228–5151). 142 rooms. Swimming pool. Restaurant.

Charlottesville

Expensive

Best Western Cavalier Inn. 105 Emmet St. (804–296–8111 or 800–528–1234). Near the University of Virginia. 118 rooms. Pool. Restaurant.

Boar's Head Inn. U.S. 250, west of Bypass U.S. 29–250 (804–296–2181). 175 rooms in 40-acre resort. Comfort and historic elegance. Health, tennis and squash courts, and fishing.

English Inn. Jct. Bus. 29 and Bypass U.S. 29–250 (804–971–9900). 88 units. King suites available with wet bars. Exercise room. Sauna. Airport limo. Indoor swimming pool. Breakfast included in room price.

Inexpensive

Best Western Mount Vernon. Jct. Bus. 29 and Bypass U.S. 29–250 (804–296–5501 or 800–528–1234). 110 rooms. Quiet and high above the road overlooking the mountains to the west. Fine restaurant.

Chincoteague

Expensive

Refuge Motor Inn. Maddox Blvd. (804–336–5511). 68 rooms. Overlooks the wildlife refuge. Pool and sauna. Open Apr.–Thanksgiving.

Moderate

Birchwood Motel. 573 S. Main St. (804–336–6133). 40 rooms in attractive, family-oriented property. Swimming pool. Convenient location. Open Apr.–Thanksgiving.

Fredericksburg

Expensive

Sheraton Fredericksburg Resort & Conference Center. VA 3 at I-95 (703–786–8321 or 800–325–3535). 195 attractive rooms with balconies or patios. Pool. Wading pool. Tennis. Golf.

Moderate

Howard Johnson's Motor Lodge. U.S. 1 at Massaponax exit from I-95 (703–898–1800 or 800–654–2000). 134 rooms. Restaurant nearby. Swimming pool.

Ramada Inn-Spotsylvania Mall. VA 3 and I-95 (703–786–8361 or 800–228–2828). 130 rooms. Near Civil War battlefields.

Inexpensive

TraveLodge. Exit 46 off I-95 at 605 Warrenton Rd. (703–371–6300 or 800–255–3050). Offered at this chain are 40 standard rooms.

Hampton

Deluxe

Radisson Hotel Hampton. 700 Settlers Landing Rd. (804–727–9700 or 800–333–3333). 174 oversized rooms. Swimming pool, exercise room, and an excellent restaurant.

Moderate

Holiday Inn. 1815 West Mercury Blvd. (804–838–0200 or 800–HOLIDAY). 325 rooms. Indoor and outdoor pools, fitness course, exercise room, Jacuzzi, game room. Restaurant and bar.

Inexpensive

Econo Lodge. Two locations at 1781 N. King St. (804–723–0741 or 800–446–6900), and at 2708 W. Mercury Blvd. (804–826–8970 or 800–446–6900).

Newport News

Expensive

Governor's Inn. 741 Thimble Shoals Blvd. (804–873–1701). A new hotel of 50 spacious units. Restaurant, steamroom, airport transportation.

Old London Inn (formerly Newport Inn). 950 Clyde Morris Blvd. (804–599–6193). Available here are restaurants, lounge, tennis court, and an indoor pool.

Moderate

Holiday Inn. 6128 Jefferson Ave. (804–826–4500 or 800–HOLIDAY). 162 rooms. Swimming pool. Restaurant. Airport transportation.

Inexpensive

Econo Lodge–Oyster Point. 11845 Jefferson Ave. (804–599–3237 or 800–446–6900). 110 rooms. Fifteen minutes from Colonial Williamsburg. One other Lodge in town.

Thr-rift Inn. U.S. 17 at 6129 Jefferson Ave. (804–838–6852). Complimentary coffee.

Norfolk

Deluxe

Omni International Hotel. 777 Waterside Dr. (804–622–6664 or 800–228–2121). 442 units, including some suites. Adjoins Waterside Festival Marketplace. Cocktail lounge. Award winning restaurant. Swimming pool. Entertainment.

Expensive

Holiday Inn–Waterside Area. 700 Monticello Ave. (804–627–5555 or 800–HOLIDAY). Adjacent to Scope Chrysler Hall. 317 rooms, some suites. Pool. Airport bus. Meeting rooms. Dining rooms and coffee shop.

Moderate

Econo Lodge Airport. 3343 N. Military Hwy. (804–855–3116 or 800–446–6900). 48 rooms. Convenient to bases, convention center. Seven others in city.

Petersburg

Moderate

Best Western of Petersburg. 405 E. Washington St. (804–733–1776 or 800–528–1234). 124 rooms. Comfortable and colorful. Traditional decor. Aunt Sarah's Pancake House, Hunan Restaurant, cocktail lounge.

Inexpensive

Econo Lodge South. 16905 Parkdale Rd. (804–862–2717 or 800–446–6900). 10 miles south of the city. 96 rooms. Laundromat, restaurant, game room. Pool; another in the area.

Portsmouth

Inexpensive

Imperial 400 Motor Inn. 333 Effingham (804–397–5806). Swimming pool. 24 rooms. Few efficiencies available. Coin laundry, pool.

Richmond

Deluxe

Hyatt Richmond. West Broad St. at I-64 (804–285–1234 or 800–233–1234). 372 large rooms, some suites. Heated indoor and outdoor pool. Three restaurants, cocktail lounge. Lighted tennis courts, playground, jogging track.

Moderate

Best Western Airport Inn. Opposite airport south of I-64 (804–222–2780 or 800–528–1234). 123 rooms. Restaurant, cocktail lounge. Shopping center and golf five minutes away. Senior citizen discount of 10 percent all year.

Best Western Governor's Inn. 9848 Midlothian Tpk. (804–323–0007 or 800–528–1234). This spiffy 86-room suburban motor hotel has a restaurant, lounge, and banquet, as well as facilities, and a pool.

Holiday Inn-Downtown. 301 W. Franklin St. (804–644–9871, 800–HOLIDAY). 220 rooms. Restaurant. Solarium, lounge, pool. Pet kennel.

Inexpensive

King's Quarter. I-95 and VA 30, Doswell (804–876–3321 or 800–528–1234). 248 rooms. Offered here are a restaurant and lounge, pool, game room, tennis, shuffleboard, and laundry. Senior-citizen discount.

Tysons Corner (Northern Virginia)

Deluxe

Embassy Suites. Exit 10B on VA 7, W from I-495 (703–883–0707 or 800–362–2779). All-suite hotel with 232 rooms facing a central atrium. Indoor pool. Super bargain rates, for up to four, on weekends, include breakfast.

Tysons Corner Marriott. Exit 10B on VA 7 at Jct. with 495 (703–734–3200 or 800–228–9290). 392 units, concierge level. Heated pool, sauna, two dining rooms, cocktail lounge. Convenient to one of the area's biggest shopping complexes.

Expensive

Ramada Hotel-Tysons. 7801 Leesburg Pike (800–272–6232 or 703–893–1340). 404 rooms, including some suites. Heated indoor pool; laundromat, restaurant.

Virginia Beach

Deluxe

Cavalier Resort Hotel & Tower. 42nd and Oceanfront (804–425–8555). Two buildings with 403 rooms make up the largest hotel in town. Tower dates back to 1927 but is completely modernized. Tennis, putting green, jogging track. This is the "Grand Dame" of the beach.

Holiday Inn on the Ocean. 39th St. and Oceanfront (804–428–1711 or 800–HOLIDAY). All 267 rooms here overlook the ocean. Pool, coffee shop, 39th Street Seafood Grille, lounge, coin laundry.

Radisson Hotel Virginia Beach (formerly Pavilion Tower Hotel). 1900 Pavilion Dr. (804–422–8900 or 800–333–3333). 282 rooms, some suites; adjacent to Virginia Beach Conference Center. Excellent meeting facilities, heated indoor/outdoor pool, sauna, tennis, health club, jogging track. Concierge floor. Airport transportation.

Expensive

Belvedere Motel. Ocean at 36th St. (804–425–0612). 50 rooms, some with rental refrigerators. Heated pool. Closed Dec.–Mar. Coffee shop open off-season. Three-day minimum.

Flagship. 512 Atlantic Ave. (804–425–6422). 55 rooms, all with refrigerators. Heated pool. Roof-top sun deck. Golf. Fishing. Efficiencies available. Open weekends only Dec.–Mar.

Inexpensive

Econo Lodge Expressway. 3635 Bonney Rd. (804–486–5711 or 800–446–6900). 53 rooms. Restaurant next door. Weekly rates, seniors discount. Two others of this chain in area.

Red Roof Inn. East of Jct. I-64 and VA 44 at 196 Ballard Ct. (804–490–0225 or 800–843–7663). 109 rooms. Restaurant next door. Pets accepted.

Williamsburg

Super Deluxe

Williamsburg Inn. Francis St. in historic area (800–447–8956 or 804–229–1000). 102 rooms in main building and beautifully restored 18th-century Colonial houses. Swimming pool. Two golf courses. Tennis. Lawn bowling. Operated by Colonial Williamsburg.

Deluxe

Williamsburg Lodge. South England St. near historic area (800–447–8956; 804–229–1000). Many of its 311 rooms have private terraces or balconies. Indoor pool and health club. Exercise room. Operated by Colonial Williamsburg. Reservations.

Expensive

Holiday Inn-1776. U.S. 60 Bypass Rd. (804–220–1776 or 800–HOLIDAY). 202 rooms. Spacious grounds. Tennis. Par 54 golf. Similar accommodations at Holiday Inn-Patriot, 3032 Richmond Rd. (804–565–2600 or 800–HOL–IDAY).

Motor House. Located at Visitor Center (804–229–1000 or 800–447–8956). Casual atmosphere and informal lodgings in 219 rooms. Pools for wading, swimming, and diving. Operated by Colonial Williamsburg.

Moderate

Williamsburg Westpark. 1600 Richmond Rd. (804–229-9631 or 800–446–1062/3). A mile from Colonial Williamsburg, this place has a restaurant, lounge, indoor pool, and game room.

Inexpensive

King William Inn. 824 Capitol Landing Rd. (804–229–4933). 183 family-sized rooms; new outdoor pool. Modern, quiet, and located centrally to major attractions. Restaurant adjacent.

Yorktown

Moderate

Duke of York Motor Hotel. 508 Water St. (804–898–3232). Overlooks scenic York river and is within walking distance of historic sites. 42 rooms. Pool, playground, restaurant nearby.

RESTAURANTS. Dining out in Virginia can be as varied as the state's topography. U.S. 460, from Petersburg to Suffolk, runs through peanut and ham country in southside Virginia. It's as if the traveler is passing a smorgasbord all the way. On the coast, around Norfolk, Newport News, the Northern Neck, and the Eastern Shore, fresh seafood—much of it from Chesapeake Bay—abounds. On the Peninsula, Colonial Williamsburg's seven dining facilities set a top-notch standard. The urban areas of Richmond and northern Virginia also stimulate fine cuisine.

Restaurant price categories are as follows: *Deluxe,* $30–$40; *Expensive,* $20–$30; *Moderate,* $10–$20; *Inexpensive,* $10 and under. The price categories reflect the cost for one person of a middle-of-the-menu meal consisting of an appetizer, entree, and dessert. Cocktails or wine are not included.

Alexandria

Deluxe

Two-Nineteen Restaurant. 219 King St. (703–549–1141). Elegant Creole cuisine. Specialty weekend brunch. Live jazz nightly in upstairs bar. Two blocks from the waterfront. AE, MC, V.

Expensive

Bilbo Baggins. 208 Queen St. (703–683–0300). Continental seafood and poultry are served in this cozy stone town house. A free loaf of homemade bread is available to take with you. L, Mon.–Fri., 11:30 A.M.–2:30 P.M., Sat., 11:30 A.M.–3 P.M.; D, Mon.–Sat., 5:30–10:30 P.M., Sun., 4:30–9:30 P.M.; Sun. brunch, 11:30 A.M.–2:30 P.M. AE, DC, MC, V.

Taverna Cretekou. 818 King St. (703–548–8688). An authentic Greek restaurant, outstanding quality. Dine in the garden, weather permitting. Tues.–Fri., 11:30 A.M.–2:30 P.M., 5–10:30 P.M.; Sat., noon–11 P.M.; Sun., 11 A.M.–3 P.M., 5–9:30 P.M. AE, DC, MC, V.

Moderate

Old Gadsby's Tavern. 138 N. Royal St. (703–548–1288). Historic tavern restored to the colonial period. Waiters and waitresses in 18th-century costumes. Colonial entertainment nightly. Open daily L, Mon.–Sat., 11 A.M.–3 P.M.; D, 5:30–10:30 P.M.; Sun. brunch, 11 A.M.–3 P.M.; D, 5:30–10 P.M. AE, MC, V.

Inexpensive

Hard Times Cafe. 1404 King St. (703–683–5340). Excellent Texas, Cincinnati, and vegetarian chili in a quaint café well away from Old Town. Open daily. L, D, Mon.–Thurs., 11 A.M.–10 P.M.; Fri. and Sat., 11 A.M.–11 P.M.; Sun., 4–10 P.M. MC, V.

Charlottesville

Deluxe

Boar's Head Inn. Two and one half miles west of city on U.S. 250 (804–296–2181). Old Mill Dining Room is the Inn's formal dining room with jackets required. Served is traditional American fare that includes prime rib, a catch of the day, and surf 'n turf. B, 7–10:30 A.M.; L, 11:30 A.M.–3 P.M.; D, 6–9:30 P.M. Also, **The Tavern** (*Expensive*), a more casual dining facility with music and dancing. Hours generally parallel those of the Old Mill Dining Room. AE, DC, MC, V.

Moderate

Ivy Inn. 2244 Old Ivy Rd., Ivy exit off U.S. 29 & 250 Bypass (804–977–1222). Most popular specialty here is a steaming "seafood kettle," in reality a heaping platter of clams, lobster, shrimp, and crab claws. L, Tues.–Sat., 11:30 A.M.–2 P.M.; D, Mon.–Sat., 5–10:30 P.M.; brunch Sun., 11 A.M.–3 P.M. AE, MC, V.

Inexpensive

Michie Tavern-The Ordinary. On VA 53, ½ mi. below Jefferson's Monticello (804–977–1234). One basic and tasty menu: Southern fried chicken, black-eyed peas, stewed tomatoes, cornbread, and biscuits. Choice of four salads. Open daily. 11:30 A.M.–3 P.M. MC, V.

Chincoteague

Expensive

Channel Bass Inn. 100 Church St. (804–336–6148). Seafood served with a European touch. Crab soufflé for two is the specialty of the house. Ten elegant rooms available at $100–$200 per night. D, Tues.–Sat., 6–9 P.M. AE, DC, MC, V.

Great Falls

Expensive

Falls Landing. 774 Walker Rd. (804–759–4650). Imaginative gourmet seafood (particularly the chowders) is served in a quiet setting here, a short drive from Washington. L, Mon.–Fri., 11:30 A.M.–2:30 P.M.; D, Mon.–Fri., 5:30–10 P.M., Sat., 5:30–10:30 P.M., Sun., 4–9 P.M. AE, DC, MC, V.

Hampton

Expensive

Mountain Jack's. 1123 W. Mercury Blvd. (804–827–1012). The Peninsula's beef and prime rib specialists. Also fresh seafood from the waters of the Chesapeake Bay. Open daily. L, D, Mon.–Fri., 11 A.M.–10 P.M.; Sat., D, 5–11 P.M.; Sun., L, D, noon–9 P.M. AE, DC, MC, V.

Norfolk

Expensive

Riverwalk Cafe. In the Omni International Hotel at 777 Waterside Dr. (804–622–6664). A romantic setting and excellent steaks and local seafood make this casual restaurant a favorite. Dinner only, Tues.–Sat., 6–11 P.M. AE, DC, MC, V.

Ships Cabin. 4110 E. Ocean View Ave., overlooking Chesapeake Bay (804–480–2526). Serves an array of sautéed, baked, and broiled seafood plates plus New York strip steaks and filet mignon. Specialty is fresh seasonal fish grilled over mesquite. Dinner only, Sun.–Thurs., 5:30–10 P.M., Fri.–Sat., 5:30–10:30 P.M. AE, DC, MC, V.

Moderate

Phillips Waterside. In the Waterside Festival Marketplace (804–627–6600). One link in the chain of fine Phillips restaurants that originated in Ocean City, Maryland. Cocktails, entertainment and excellent seafood. Open daily. L, D, Sun.–Thurs., 11:30 A.M.–9 P.M., Fri.–Sat., 11:30 A.M.–10 P.M.; restaurant closed weekdays 2–5 P.M. (lounge open). AE, DC, MC, V.

Richmond

Moderate

Tobacco Company. 1201 E. Cary St. (804–782–9555). Good food served in Victorian decor in a restored ex-tobacco warehouse. Open daily. L, Mon.–Sat., 11:30 A.M.–2:30 P.M.; Sun., brunch, 10:30 A.M.–2 P.M. D, Mon.–Fri., 5:30–10:30 P.M.; Sat., 5:30 P.M.–midnight; Sun., 5:30–10 P.M. AE, MC, V.

Inexpensive

Bill's Barbecue. Eight locations in town (804–272–9876). Established in 1930. Tasty minced pork and beef sandwiches. Varied menu with a full line of sandwiches. Open daily, hours depending on location. No credit cards.

Morrison's Cafeteria. 8220 Midlothian Tpk. (804–272–9314). A popular chain with good variety of food at economical prices. Open daily. L, D., Sun.–Thurs., 11 A.M.–8:30 P.M.; Fri.–Sat., 11 A.M.–9 P.M. V, MC.

New York Delicatessen. 2920 W. Cary St. (804–355–6056). A Richmond tradition for 30 years serving sandwiches, salads, and omelets. Open daily. 7:30 A.M.–8:30 P.M. MC, V.

Sally Bell's Kitchen. 708 W. Grace St. (804–644–2838). A lively, always busy Richmond institution serving box lunches, homemade bread, salads by the pound, sandwiches, cakes. Take outs only. No credit cards.

Tysons Corner

Expensive

Clyde's. 8332 Leesburg Pike (703–734–1901). A worthy counterpart to its namesake in Georgetown. Fine dining: a short and sophisticated menu and a long wine list. The decor's risqué murals suggest Las Vegas. L, D, Mon.–Sat., 11 A.M.–2 A.M., Sun., 10 A.M.–2 A.M. AE, DC, MC, V.

Smithfield

Expensive

Smithfield Inn and Tavern. 112 Main St. (804–357–0244). Southern cooking featuring, of course, Smithfield ham and fried chicken. Homemade pies and cobblers. L, daily, noon–2 P.M.; D, Fri.–Sat., 6–9 P.M., Sun., noon–7 P.M. MC, V.

Virginia Beach

Expensive

The Lighthouse. 1st St. and Atlantic Ave. (804–428–7974). Seaside location. Featuring fresh seafood specialties. Dinner only. Mon.–Fri., 5–10 P.M.; L, D, Sat.–Sun., 10 A.M.–10 P.M. AE, DC, MC, V.

Moderate

Three Ships Inn. 3800 Shore Dr., between Chesapeake Bay Bridge-Tunnel and Lynnhaven Bridge (804–460–0055). Good selection of steaks and seafood. Specialties include crab imperial, flounder à la Royster, duckling in a black cherry sauce, and steak à la Stephen. Open daily. D, 6–11 P.M. AE, MC, V.

Williamsburg

Deluxe

Williamsburg Inn. Francis St. (800–229–1000). The Regency Dining Room provides elegant dining and continental cuisine based on local products like crab, sausages, and Smithfield ham. The chef serves an excellent seafood ragout, a mixture of lobster, shrimp, scallops, and crab cooked in a tasty white sauce. Operated by Colonial Williamsburg. Reservations recommended. AE, MC, V.

Expensive

The Trellis. On Duke of Gloucester St. in Merchant's Sq. (804–229–8610). Regional American cuisine prepared from all fresh ingredients served in a contemporary setting. Open daily. Sun., brunch, 11:30 A.M.–2:30 P.M.; D, 5:30–9 P.M.; Mon.–Sat., L, 11:30 A.M.–2:30 P.M.; D, 5:30–9:30 P.M. AE, MC, V.

Moderate

Christiana Campbell's Tavern. Waller St. (804–229–1000). This was George Washington's favorite dining place in Williamsburg. It specializes in seafood such as Hampton crab imperial and a chilled shrimp salad. The Southern spoon bread is delicious. Operated by Colonial Williamsburg. Reservations recommended. AE, MC, V.

Josiah Chowning's Tavern. Duke of Gloucester St. (804–229–1000). Specialties include Brunswick stew and Welsh rarebit along with spareribs, prime ribs, and Chesapeake Bay crabmeat. Cocktails. Children's menu. Operated by Colonial Williamsburg. Reservations recommended.

King's Arms Tavern. Also on Duke of Gloucester St. (804–229–1000). Gracious dining with waiters in period costumes. Specialties are Virginia ham, fried chicken, English lamb chops, and roast beef. Try the peanut soup. Cocktails and children's menu. Operated by Colonial Williamsburg. Reservations recommended. AE, MC, V.

Yorktown

Expensive

Nick's Seafood Pavilion. Water St. at the York River (804–887–5269). Specialties are Greek seafood, lobster dien bien, seafood shish kabob, and crab meat salads. Also steaks and chops cooked to order. Open daily. L, D, 11 A.M.–10 P.M. AE, DC, MC, V.

LIQUOR LAWS. Hard liquor is sold only through Alcoholic Beverage Control (ABC) package stores except where prohibited by local option. Beer and wine are generally available in grocery and drug stores. Mixed drinks at licensed restaurants and hotels. Drinking age is 21 for all drinks.

THE SOUTHERN APPALACHIAN MOUNTAINS

by
EDGAR and PATRICIA CHEATHAM

Award-winning travel writers Edgar and Patricia Cheatham are based in Charlotte, North Carolina. They are members of the Society of American Travel Writers, American Society of Journalists and Authors, and the Authors Guild/Authors League of America.

The southern Appalachians, from the Virginias through eastern Kentucky, North Carolina, and fringes of Tennessee, are among the nation's treasure troves. The Shenandoah National Park with its Skyline Drive, the Blue Ridge Parkway from the Old Dominion to the Old North State, thence the Newfound Gap Road through the Great Smoky Mountains National Park to the Volunteer State, encompass vacation ventures second to none in the USA.

There are high places in these storied mountains where it seems as though surging seas, stretching endlessly toward hazy horizons, were eternally stopped in time. These southern Appalachians are intriguing domains, ever welcoming visitors who would savor their singular offerings. At the same time, fun-loving families with young children come and enjoy. Cool and comfortable during summer, vibrant in spring and autumn, these mountains have their own way of luring vacationers who come once, then return again and again.

In recent years, an exciting new dimension has been added, thanks to development of snow-making equipment. Lavish ski resorts flourish mid-

December through mid-March at high elevations in Virginia, West Virginia, North Carolina, and Tennessee. Many southerners, once rather languid about cold-weather vacations, now flock to favorite Appalachian slopes and join the ranks of confirmed snow bunnies.

In many mountain ranges around the world, jagged sawtooth peaks rise in solitary splendor against backdrops of cloudless skies, blue and lucid, to reveal in an instant their immense majesty. The southern Appalachians, though, are different. Here is a dominion of morning mists hovering in coves and hollows, clouds and haze enshrouding ridges and crests. A moist climate has produced verdant forests with stands of hardwood trees, hemlocks, pines, and spruce. There are more species of wildflowers in these highlands than the entire continent of Europe can boast. Brilliant colors of flame azalea, mountain laurel, rhododendron, and dazzling autumn foliage provide a captivating aura. The southern Appalachians only gradually, sometimes almost too begrudgingly, reveal their singular endowments, often moody and mysterious, to discerning visitors. This may well be the reason why they are so enchanting.

Cherokee Indians, the first human inhabitants, dominated considerable portions of the southern Appalachians. Their cultural institutions have generally been regarded as the finest among aboriginal tribes in the United States. When pioneer settlers came in, the Cherokee readily adapted to the new way of life by building cabins and living on farms and in small towns. Within a few months the Cherokee Nation became literate when Sequoyah devised his famed syllabary alphabet, which preserved the tribal language in writing. They were the only tribe in the United States with laws and a constitution written in their own language. The Cherokee Nation reached the nadir of its history with its removal to Indian territory along the tragic Trail of Tears during the severe winter of 1838. A few intrepid Indians refused to be driven from their ancestral homeland and sought refuge in remote mountain hideaways. Their descendants live today on North Carolina's Qualla Boundary Reservation in the shadow of the Great Smokies. They constitute the eastern band of the Cherokee Nation. The larger western band is based in Talequah, Oklahoma.

To westward-trekking pioneers seeking fertile lands and new opportunities in present-day central Tennessee and Kentucky's bluegrass country, the Appalachians became a barrier. One of the few viable overland corridors was low-lying Cumberland Gap, where the borders of Kentucky, Virginia, and Tennessee come together. In 1775, Daniel Boone led an expedition of 30 axmen who cut trees and blazed a trail, the storied Wilderness Road, which droves of settlers traversed and subsequently established the state of Kentucky.

Later, additional routes were opened to the Old West, a few by land, others along interconnecting rivers. Yet the Appalachian highlands, beautiful as they may be for present-day visitors, were scarcely appealing to early-era, upwardly mobile pioneers heading westward. Perhaps a broken wagon wheel, an unforeseen injury, or impending birth of a child rendered impossible a family's ability to continue with the pioneering expedition. So they were reluctantly left behind. These southern Appalachian folk struggled to survive and in so doing richly rewarded American life.

Fertile valleys lie here and there in the midst of the mountain masses. In the western portion of Virginia, between the Blue Ridge on the east and the Alleghenies to the west, is the extensive Shenandoah, reaching from north of Roanoke to Harpers Ferry in West Virginia. In contrast to the poverty found in some other areas of the southern Appalachians, the Shenandoah is a land of spacious farms, orchards, pastures, and forests. In prosperous, appealing towns such as Winchester, Staunton, Lexington, and Harpers Ferry, the present co-exists harmoniously with historic remembrances of great people and dramatic events in American history.

SOUTHERN APPALACHIAN MOUNTAINS
PENN.
WEST VIRGINIA
OHIO
75
KENTUCKY
CHARLESTON
Snowshoe
White Sulphur Springs
West Virginia Turnpike
LEXINGTON
Bert T. Combs Mountain Parkway
Beckley
Lewisburg
Hinton
Prestonburg
Berea
75
Daniel Boone Parkway
Hazard
Appalachian Trail
81
London
Corbin
Abingdon
Pineville
Big Stone Gap
Middlesboro
Cumberland National Historic Park
Cumberland Gap
Blue Ridge Parkway
TENNESSEE
81
Banner Elk
Boone
Blowing Rock
KNOXVILLE
40
Burnsville
Little Switzerland
40
85
Pigeon Forge
Gatlinburg
Asheville
Cherokee
Foothills Parkway
Waynesville
Hendersonville
Fontana Dam
Great Smoky Mountains National Park
Brevard
CHARLOTTE
SOUTH CAROLINA
GEORGIA

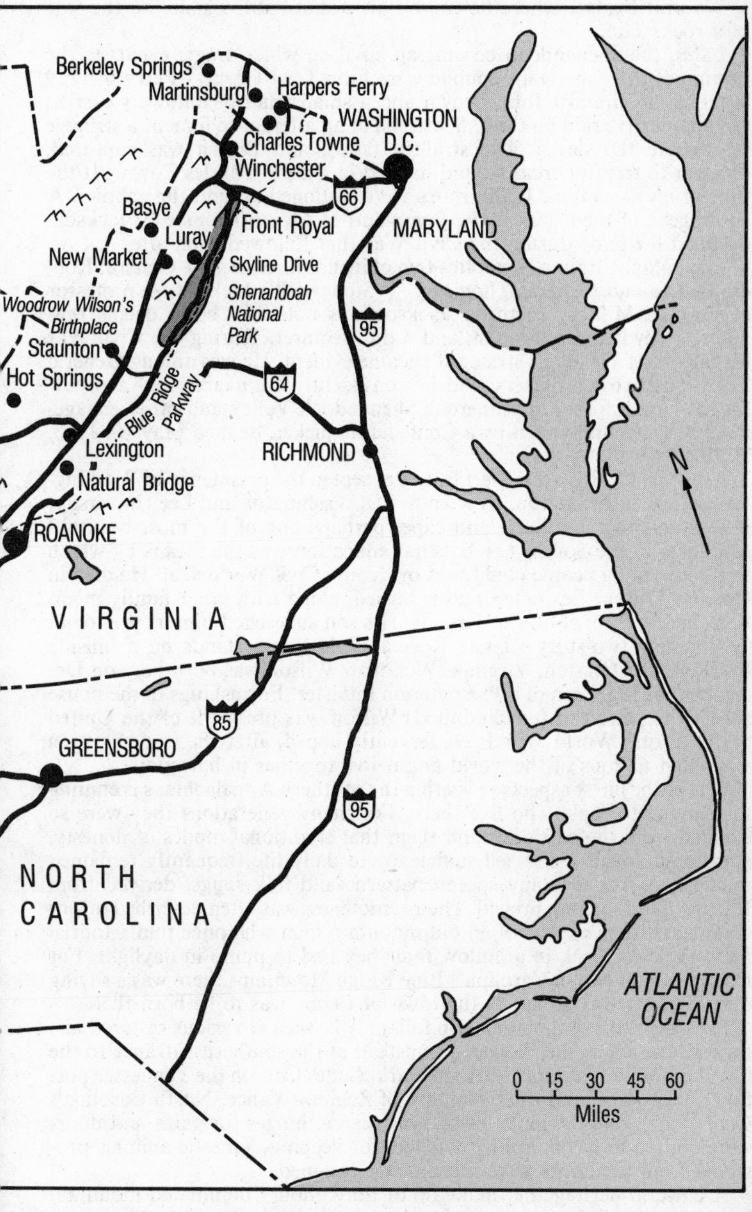
Berkeley Springs
Martinsburg
Harpers Ferry
WASHINGTON D.C.
Charles Towne
Winchester
66
Basye
Front Royal
MARYLAND
Luray
New Market
Skyline Drive
Shenandoah National Park
Woodrow Wilson's Birthplace
95
Staunton
Hot Springs
Blue Ridge Parkway
64
Lexington
RICHMOND
Natural Bridge
N
ROANOKE
VIRGINIA
85
GREENSBORO
95
NORTH CAROLINA
ATLANTIC OCEAN
0 15 30 45 60
Miles

As a young man, George Washington came to the Shenandoah Valley on surveying and military expeditions. His presence is esteemed at Winchester, where his rather primitive headquarters have been preserved, and at Natural Bridge, where he carved his initials, still visible, on the side of a rocky cliff.

Later, the Shenandoah became an anvil on which tragic events in the destiny of the American republic were forged. At Harpers Ferry in 1859 fanatical abolitionist John Brown and a small band of followers carried out an abortive raid on the U.S. arsenal in an attempt to foment a struggle to liberate the slaves. The strategy failed, and Brown was captured, brought to trial for treason, and hanged in nearby Charles Town. At the time of his execution, 1,500 troops were stationed around the gallows. A contingent of them was under command of Major Thomas F. Jackson, destined for fame during the Civil War that followed soon after.

Lexington, Virginia, venerates two of its finest residents—General Robert E. Lee and General Thomas F. ("Stonewall") Jackson. A professor at Virginia Military Institute, Jackson was noted for being deeply religious, a devoted family man, and a dull lecturer. During the Civil War his talents as a brilliant strategist became evident. He was among General Lee's most trusted officers, and he consistently outmaneuvered and outfought Union forces in numerous Shenandoah Valley and other engagements. Accidentally shot by a Confederate picket, he died May 10, 1863, at 39.

After the Civil War, Robert E. Lee accepted the presidency of Washington College in Lexington. Now known as Washington and Lee University, it is situated in a rolling landscape, perhaps one of the most beautiful campuses in the South. Lee felt that education was the means by which southern young people could best overcome Civil War defeat. He died in October 1870 at Lexington and is buried, along with other family members, in Lee Chapel on the campus. His son succeeded him as president.

A stately two-story Classic Revival–style house stands on a hillside overlooking Staunton, Virginia. Woodrow Wilson was born here on December 28, 1856, son of a Presbyterian minister. Furnishings in the house reflect the period of his childhood. Wilson was president of the United States during World War I. He fervently hoped, after the war had been won, that nations of the world might live together in harmony.

One of the finest aspects in visiting the southern Appalachians is coming to know the people who live there. For many generations they were so isolated from the world around them that traditional modes of honesty, sturdiness, loyalty, and self-sufficiency in daily life frequently remained unchanged. Today many speech patterns and folk songs, derived from Elizabethan England, prevail. Their remoteness was often described in wry comments, such as that of an old mountain man who once told a tourist he lived so far back in a hollow that they had to pump in daylight. For many years in North Carolina's Blue Ridge Mountains there was a saying that the only way to get to the town of Boone was to be born there.

Creative skills of the mountain folk may be seen at various restored historic sites such as the Pioneer Farmstead at the southern entrance to the Great Smoky Mountains National Park, Cades Cove in the Tennessee portion of the Park, and the birthplace of Zebulon Vance, North Carolina's Civil War governor. Since metal was scarce, hinges for gates and doors were crafted in wood. Split-rail fences for keeping domestic animals protected from predators were ingeniously designed.

A cultural heritage of "make do or do without" dominated mountain life. Virtually all the necessities for everyday living had to be hand crafted. Wooden tables, chairs, cabinets, bedsteads, and large dough bowls, still being made today by skilled artisans using traditional techniques, are much admired for their sturdy designs and clean-lined simplicity. Carding combs, spinning wheels, and hand looms became the tools for creating fabrics colored in warm earth tones with dyes extracted from a variety of plants. The antique methods are still being used in making bed coverlets, wall hangings, and clothing. To "pleasure the young 'uns" hand-dyed corn husks were fashioned into attractive dolls, and leftover bits of wood became gee-haw whimmydiddles, little toys with a small propeller attached to a handle and put in motion by quickly rubbing a stick over notches.

Beautifully crafted musical instruments, such as fiddles and banjos, provided lively entertainment to accompany dancing and singing. A favorite, though, has long been the oblong mountain dulcimer, its strings plucked with a goose quill or by hand to produce a gentle, plaintive tone. It's one of only two musical instruments native to New World pioneers. The banjo is the other.

Throughout the southern Appalachians today visitors quickly discover the richness of mountain craftsmanship. Earlier in the 20th century, as itinerant merchants began to bring in machine-made wares, many traditional crafts and folkways were threatened with extinction. But under the aegis of such organizations as the Southern Highland Handicraft Guild and programs at Berea College in Kentucky and elsewhere, revival came about. Mountain craftspeople, instilled with new pride and self-esteem, have come to realize that their one-of-a-kind creations are now valued for inherent beauty by many Americans and will become tomorrow's cherished heirlooms.

PRACTICAL INFORMATION FOR THE SOUTHERN APPALACHIAN MOUNTAINS

WHEN TO GO. The southern Appalachians contain some of eastern America's highest mountains. Here the seasons are different than in neighboring regions in lower latitudes. Winters tend to be severe, with average highs in the upper 40s, average lows in the upper 20s. In higher elevations, especially, snowfalls are frequently heavy, much to the delight of skiers, who flock to the slopes at popular resorts in the Virginias, North Carolina, and eastern Tennessee. The lowest rates of the year in many motels, hotels, and resort inns are very cost effective for visitors who don't mind wintry doldrums.

As an old mountain woman once proclaimed, "Spring comes in a glory!" In May, violets, dogwoods, trailing arbutus, crab apple, wisteria, and white and pale rose hues of rhododendron appear. June and July bring displays of mountain laurel, flame azalea, purple rhododendron, and magnolias. During summer, the primrose, sweet shrub, Indian paintbrush, Queen Anne's lace, Turk's cap lilies, and minuscule bluets last into Sept. These are among the most popular visitor seasons. Toward late Sept. along the higher slopes, the sumac turns deep scarlet, heralding the approach of autumn. Foliage generally peaks about mid-Oct. in higher altitudes, lasting into early Nov. along intermediate and lower slopes. Numerous varieties of hardwood trees produce brilliant colors—gold, red, russet, deep scarlet, dazzling yellow. Visitors come from near and far to enjoy the spectacle. Advance reservations are desirable in popular resort areas.

HOW TO GET THERE. The southern Appalachian mountains are a region essentially of villages, small towns, and a few intermediate-size cities. Highway construction, especially since the end of World War II, has helped bring once-remote communities closer to the mainstream of American life. But even now a few places are still relatively isolated and hard to reach. Roanoke, Virginia, and Asheville, North Carolina, are the leading urban centers in the most frequently visited vacation areas.

By plane. Roanoke Regional Airport is served by *USAir* and its *USAir Express* subsidiary from outside and within the state. Delta's *ComAir* affiliate connects Roanoke and Cincinnati. Delta's *Atlantic Southeast Airlines* connects Roanoke with Atlanta. American Airlines affiliate *American Eagle* offers scheduled direct service to Baltimore, Newark, Orlando, Philadelphia, and Washington's Dulles and National airports, as well as points inside Virginia.

The Asheville Airport is served by *USAir* and its *USAir Express* affiliate with scheduled flights within the state and nationwide. Delta Air Lines commuter affiliate *Atlantic Southeast Airlines* offers scheduled flights between Asheville and Atlanta. Via its affiliate, *American Eagle,* American Airlines has nonstop service from Asheville to Nashville, TN, and Raleigh/Durham, NC, for nationwide connections.

By bus. Roanoke is served by interstate *Greyhound.* Asheville is served by *Greyhound.*

By car. Roanoke is readily reached by I-81, running northeast to southwest from Maryland and West Virginia through the Shenandoah Valley, then into eastern Tennessee. The I-581 connector leads into Roanoke. Asheville's major east-west highway link is I-40, beginning in Raleigh and continuing over the Great Smoky Mountains into Tennessee and westward, terminating in Barstow, CA. I-26 begins in Charleston, SC, and terminates at Mars Hill, about 16 mi. north of Asheville.

TOURIST INFORMATION. West Virginia: *Travel West Virginia,* State Capitol Complex, 2101 Washington St., E. Charleston, WV 25305, provides general information for vacationers. Phone toll-free 800–CALL–WVA for a trip planning package. Also specify if you would like material about state parks and recreational opportunities. For data about hunting and fishing sites, regulations, and license requirements and costs, contact *Department of Natural Resources,* Wildlife Resources Division, State Capitol, Charleston, WV 25305 (304–348–2771).

Motorists entering the northeastern portion of the state should stop at the West Virginia Information Center in Harpers Ferry (304–274–2281) for folders, brochures, maps, and reservation assistance; open 8:30 A.M. to 5 P.M.; closed Jan. 1, Thanksgiving Day, Dec. 25.

For information about historic communities of Charles Town and Shepherdstown, contact *Jefferson County Convention and Visitors Bureau,* Box A, Harpers Ferry, WV 25425 (304–535–2627). *Chamber of Commerce,* 110 W. Burke St., Martinsburg, WV 25401 (304–267–4841); and *Southern West Virginia Convention and Visitors Bureau,* Box 1799, Beckley, WV 25802 (304–252–2244).

Kentucky: *Kentucky Department of Travel Development,* Capital Plaza Tower, Frankfort, KY 40601 (502–564–4930 or 800–225–8747), provides vacation information, for literature about the state and a listing of events. For recreational areas and parks contact *Department of Parks,* Capital Plaza Tower, Frankfort, KY 40601, 800–255–PARK. For data about hunting and fishing sites, regulations, and license requirements and costs, contact *Department of Fish and Wildlife Resources,* 1 Game Farm Rd., Frankfort, KY 40601 (502–564–4336).

Eastern Kentucky is served by tourist information centers at Florence, I-75 southbound and northbound and Williamsburg, I-75 northbound. Open daily, 8 A.M. to 8 P.M.

Local and regional information is available from *Berea Recreation, Tourism & Convention Comm.,* 105 Boone St., Berea, KY 40403 (606–986–2540); *Hazard-Perry County Chamber of Commerce and Tourism Commission,* 221 Memorial Dr., Hazard, KY 41701 (606–439–2659); and *Chamber of Commerce,* 102 E. Court St., Prestonsburg, KY 41653 (606–886–2185).

Virginia: *Virginia Division of Tourism,* 1021 E. Cary St., Richmond, VA 23219 (804–786–4484); *Virginia Division of Tourism,* 11 Rockefeller Plaza, New York, NY 10020 (212–245–3080); *Virginia Travel Council,* 7619 Brook Rd., Richmond, VA 23227 (804–266–0444); and the *Travel Development Department* of the Virginia State Chamber of Commerce, 611 E. Franklin St., Richmond, VA 23219 (804–644–1607) provide useful brochures, recreational data, maps, and events listings for vacationers. For hunting and fishing sites, regulations, and license requirements and costs contact *Commission of Game and Inland Fisheries,* Box 11104, Richmond, VA 23230 (804–257–1000).

Virginia Welcome Centers are situated on I-81 southbound, just south of the Virginia–West Virginia border near Clear Brook, and on I-81 northbound, just north of the Virginia–Tennessee border near Bristol. Open daily, 8:15 A.M. to 5 P.M. except Jan. 1, Thanksgiving Day, Dec. 25.

For regional information, contact *Shenandoah Valley Travel Association,* Box 1040, New Market, VA 22844 (703–740–3132), which has an information center on VA 211 just west of I-81, exit 67, near the entrance to New Market Battlefield Park. Regional information about Southwest Virginia is also available from *LENOWISCO (Lee-Norton-Wise-Scott) Planning District Commission,* Box 366, Duffield, VA 24244 (703–431–2206). For local information, contact *Washington County Chamber of Commerce,* 304 Depot, Abingdon, VA 24210 (703–628–8141); *Chamber of Commerce of Front Royal–Warren County,* 501 S. Royal Ave., Box 568, Front Royal, VA 22630 (703–635–3185); *Lexington Visitors Bureau,* 102 E. Washington St., Lexington, VA 24450 (703–463–3777); *Roanoke Valley Convention and Visitors Bureau,* Box 1710, 14 W. Kirk Ave., Roanoke, VA 24008 (703–342–6025); *Chamber of Commerce,* 30 N. New St., Box 389, Staunton, VA 24401 (Travel Information Service 703–885–8504); *Winchester–Frederick County Chamber of Commerce and Visitors Center,* 13605 Pleasant Valley Rd., Winchester, VA 22601 (703–662–4118).

North Carolina: *North Carolina Travel and Tourism Division,* 430 N. Salisbury St., Raleigh, NC 27611 (919–733–4171; in United States and Toronto, 800–VISIT–NC), provides attractive vacation materials. For data about state parks and recreational areas, contact *Division of Parks and Recreation,* Department of Natural Resources and Community Development, Box 27287, Raleigh, NC 27611 (919–733–4181). For hunting and fishing sites, regulations, license requirements, and costs, contact *NC Wildlife Resources Commission,* 512 N. Salisbury St., Archdale Bldg., Raleigh, NC 27611 (919–733–7291 out-of-state; 800–662–7350 in-state).

State welcome centers are at I-26 south near Tryon just north of the North-South Carolina border (704–894–2120) and I-40 west near Waynesville (704–627–6206), open daily, 8 A.M. to 5 P.M. Regional information is available from North Carolina High Country Host, 701 Blowing Rock Rd., Boone, NC 28607 (704–264–1299; in NC, 800–222–7515; in eastern U.S., 800–438–7500).

For information about local areas, contact *Asheville Convention and Visitors Bureau,* Box 1011, Asheville, NC 28802 (704–258–3916; in NC, 800–548–1300; in eastern U.S., 800–257–1300); *North Carolina High Country Host,* 701 Blowing Rock Rd., Boone, NC 28607 (704–264–1299 or 800–222–7515 in state; 800–438–7500 eastern U.S.); *Brevard Chamber of Commerce,* Box 589, Brevard, NC 28712 (704–883–3700); *Yancey County Chamber of Commerce,* 2 Town Sq., Room 3, Burnsville, NC 28714 (704–682–7413); *Cherokee Tribal Travel and Promotion,* Box 465, Cherokee, NC 28719 (704–497–9195; out of state, Apr.–Oct., 800–438–1601); *Franklin Chamber of Commerce,* 180 Porter St., Franklin, NC 28734 (704–524–3161); *Highlands Chamber of Commerce,* Box 404, Highlands, NC 28741 (704–526–2112). *Hendersonville Chamber of Commerce,* 330 N. King St., Hendersonville, NC 28739–0489 (704–692–1413); *Jackson County Travel & Tourism Authority,* 18 Central St., Sylva, NC 28779 (704–586–4887; 800–962–1911 nationwide). *Maggie Valley Chamber of Commerce,* Box 87, Maggie Valley, NC 28751 (704–926–1686; 800–334–9036 out of state); and *Greater Haywood County Chamber of Commerce,* Box 125, Waynesville, NC 28786 (704–456–3021).

Tennessee: *Tennessee Department of Tourist Development,* Box 23170, Nashville, TN 37202–3170 (615–741–7994), provides vacationers with brochures, state highway map, events listings, information about historic sites. For data about state parks and recreation opportunities, contact *Tennessee State Conservation Office,* 701 Broadway, Nashville, TN 37203 (615–742–6666 or 800–421–6683). For hunting and fishing sites, regulations, and license requirements and costs, contact *Tennessee Wildlife Resources Agency,* Box 40747, Ellington Agricultural Center, Nashville, TN 37220 (615–741–1512).

The state welcome center most convenient to the Great Smokies area is at I-81 just south of the Tennessee–Virginia border near Bristol, open daily 24 hours in summer, 8 A.M. to 6 P.M. rest of year. (615–764–5821).

Local and regional materials are available from *Gatlinburg Chamber of Commerce,* Box 527, 520 Parkway, Gatlinburg, TN 37738 (615–436–2392; 800–822–1998 nationwide). *Pigeon Forge Department of Tourism,* Box 1390, Pigeon Forge, TN 37868 (615–453–8574; outside TN, 800–251–9100); *Chamber of Commerce,* Box 66, Townsend, TN 37882 (615–448–6651).

TIME ZONES. The eastern areas of West Virginia, Kentucky, and Tennessee and the entire states of Virginia and North Carolina are in the eastern time zone and observe seasonal daylight-saving time.

TELEPHONES. Roanoke and western parts of Virginia are in area code 703. Asheville and western North Carolina are in area code 704. In both cities local pay-telephone calls are 25 cents with no time limit; dial 411 for local directory assistance; from outside the respective area codes, dial 1–area code–555–1212. To place station-to-station calls within the area code, dial 1 and the appropriate number; to place station-to-station long-distance calls outside the area code, dial 1–area code–number. To place long-distance operator-assisted calls, dial 0–area code–number, then give specifics when operator comes on the line.

The entire state of West Virginia is area code 304; eastern Kentucky is area code 606; eastern Tennessee is area code 615.

EMERGENCY TELEPHONE NUMBERS. In **Roanoke,** use the following emergency numbers: *Fire,* 344–5133; *Police,* 344–5133; *Ambulance,* 344–5111; *American Red Cross Disaster Services,* 982–2491; *Emergency Outreach Services,* 981–9351; *Roanoke Memorial Hospital,* 981–7000; *Community Hospital,* 985–8000; *24-hour pharmacy at Prescription Shoppes,* 2900 Peters Creek Rd., between Cove Rd and I-581, 366–3786. Roanoke has the 911 standard emergency number.

In **Asheville,** emergency numbers are: *Fire,* 255–5321; *Police,* 255–5211; *Ambulance EMS,* 255–5631; *Rescue Squad,* 253–1208; *Poison Control Center,* 255–4490; *Rape Crisis Center,* 255–7576; *State Patrol,* 298–4252; *St. Joseph's Hospital Emergency Room,* 255–4032; *TDD emergency for deaf,* police, 255–5231. Asheville does not yet have the 911 standard emergency number.

HOW TO GET AROUND. From the airport. Roanoke Regional Airport is 5½ mi. from downtown. *Airport Limousine* (345–7710), conveniently near the baggage-claim area, charges per person rates between airport and downtown. Inquire locally about base fare. **Asheville Airport** is about 20 mi. from downtown.

By bus. Roanoke's city bus service is operated by *Valley Metro* (982–2222), which has a route and schedule information center at 17–19 Campbell Ave. **Asheville**'s city bus service is operated by *Asheville Transit* (253–5691 for route and schedule information).

By taxi. In **Roanoke,** one-way taxi fare between airport and downtown is approximately $10–$11. Leading companies include *Yellow Cab* (345–7711) and *Willard's Taxi* in neighboring Salem (389–8131). Inquire about base and mileage rates. In **Asheville,** basic taxi rate is $1.05 plus $1 per mile. Operators include *Blue Bird Taxi* (253–1611), *Jolly Taxi Company* (253–1411), *Millers Cab Service* (252–6314), and *Yellow Cab Company* (253–3311).

By rental car. In **Roanoke,** auto-rental companies with airport locations include *Avis* (366–2436), *Budget* (362–1654), *Hertz* (366–3421), and *National* (345–7719). Advance reservations are desirable during late spring, summer, and the Oct. foliage season. Rental firms at convenient locations in the **Asheville Airport** terminal include *Avis* (684–7144) and *Hertz* (684–3131). *National* has an airport terminal counter (684–8572) and an in-town facility (254–7283). Firms with locations in vicinity of Asheville Airport include *Budget* (684–2272), *Dollar* (687–0222), and *Sears* (684–2891). *Deal* (253–5317) and *U-Save* (255–0133) advertise cost-effective rates. Comparison shopping, of course, is essential before signing any auto-rental contract. Advance reservations are desirable during the late spring, summer, and the Oct. foliage seasons.

HINTS TO MOTORISTS. The interstate highways and major routes in the southern Appalachians are well maintained. Pleasant roadways for scenic driving include the West Virginia Tpk., a toll road from Charleston southward to Princeton near the Virginia state line; two beautiful toll routes in upland Kentucky, the Bert T. Combs Mountain Pkwy. westward from Winchester and the Daniel Boone Pkwy. west from London; and Tennessee's Foothills Pkwy. in vicinity of Gatlinburg. Please see the Skyline Dr., Blue Ridge Pkwy., and Great Smoky Mountains section for motoring information about these well-known routes.

In varied parts of the southern Appalachians, two-lane highways with numerous twists and turns are still encountered in rugged terrain and higher elevations. These roads must be driven slowly and cautiously, especially around blind curves, where it's a good idea to sound your horn to alert oncoming traffic.

Maximum speed limit is 65 mph on certain stretches of interstate highways throughout the mountain region; be alert for lower limits posted on many highways, as well as in cities and towns. Efforts have been made in recent years to improve access to major vacation areas. Please inquire about road conditions at state visitor-information and welcome centers.

The AAA supernumber (800–336–HELP) is for emergency information about road services, available 24 hours a day for members traveling outside their local club area.

Roanoke (population 100,700) and neighboring Salem (population 24,000) lie at the southern end of the Shenandoah Valley. The urban area is easy to negotiate by automobile and presents no rush-hour problems. The in-town speed limit is 25 mph unless higher limits are posted. Downtown on-street parking spaces are generally metered; off-street parking lots and garages are plentiful, conveniently situated. Right turns on red are legal after stop unless posted otherwise.

Asheville, with a city population of about 58,600, ranks among the best-known resort communities in the southern Appalachians. Connecting thoroughfares from the Blue Ridge Pkwy. and I-40 lead into the city. A considerable number of major attractions lie outside the central business district. Although downtown and residential streets follow no set pattern, the city is not difficult to negotiate by auto. There are few rush-hour problems except when a main thoroughfare may be under repair. Speed limit is 35 mph, except where noted. Right turn on red is legal after stop unless otherwise posted. Most downtown on-street parking spaces are metered; garages and lots are conveniently situated, reasonably priced.

Motorists in North Carolina must observe the state law requiring front-seat passengers to wear seat belts. Also by law children under 3 must be secured in child safety seats, those 3 to 6 in safety seats or with seat belts. The state's drunk-driving laws are rigidly enforced, and violators can expect severe penalties.

HINTS TO DISABLED TRAVELERS. An increasing number of parks, historic sites, outdoor areas, attractions, and accommodation facilities in the southern Appalachians are providing for handicapped travelers. The *Virginia Tour Planners' Guide* lists over 160 attractions and more than 315 overnight accommodations statewide equipped for handicapped visitors. Please inquire at the state welcome centers. A free copy of "Tips for Physically Disabled Travelers" may be obtained from the Virginia Division of Tourism, 202 N. 9th St., Suite 500, Richmond, VA 23219 (804–786–4484). In Roanoke, parking spaces reserved for the handicapped are marked with the blue-and-white wheelchair symbol. In portions of the central business district and in major shopping centers, curbs have been ramped.

Tape recorders with Braille instructions and cassettes describing scenery and other highlights are available for sight-impaired visitors to the Blue Ridge Pkwy. in Virginia and North Carolina. Parking, restrooms, campgrounds, restaurants, and exhibit and sightseeing areas along the parkway are all wheelchair accessible.

Throughout North Carolina, parking spaces reserved for handicapped are noted by the wheelchair symbol. Public buildings and various private businesses such as stores and restaurants are required to provide access and specially equipped restrooms. Asheville has ramped curbs in the business district and major shopping centers. Please inquire at state welcome centers about provisions for handicapped in parks, attractions, and overnight accommodations. For users of telecommunications devices for the deaf the emergency number for Asheville police is 255–5231 (TDD only). For a free copy of *Access North Carolina,* phone toll free 800–847–4862, 8 A.M. to 5 P.M. weekdays.

The *Tennessee Group Travel Directory* lists parks, attractions, accommodations, and restaurants that provide for the handicapped. The listings include parking, ramps or curb cuts, special guest and meeting rooms, provisions for guide dogs, public restrooms, telephones, and facilities for hearing and visually impaired. Please inquire at state welcome centers. For further information about tour and travel opportunities for the handicapped, along with a guide for disabled travelers, contact Tennessee Department of Tourist Development, Box 23170, Nashville, TN 37202-3170 (615–741–7994).

SEASONAL EVENTS. West Virginia. January 2–December 20. *Charles Town Turf Club Thoroughbred Racing,* post times Fri.–Mon., 1:30 P.M., 7:15 P.M. (call to verify). Skyline Terrace, dining room at trackside, clubhouse, cafeteria, heated–air-conditioned grandstand, refreshment areas, pubs. Rates on request; write or phone Charles Town Turf Club, Box 551, Charles Town, WV 25414 (304–725–7001).

April. *House and Garden Tours* in Charles Town, Harpers Ferry, Martinsburg, and Shepherdstown, 2 days late month, 10 A.M. to 6 P.M. Rates on request; write or phone TOUR, Box 40, Shepherdstown, WV 25443 (304–876–2242).

June and September. *Mountain Heritage Arts and Crafts Festivals,* held near Harpers Ferry, celebrate Southern Appalachian culture with more than 160 talented craftspeople, lively mountain music, savory foods, second weekend in June, fourth weekend in Sept. For both events write or phone Jefferson County Chamber of Commerce, Box 426, Charles Town, WV 25414 (800–624–0577 or 304–725–2055).

October. *Mountain State Apple Harvest Festival* highlights the season with parades, demonstrations, sales of arts and crafts, and music and dancing, Civil War reenactments, 3 days mid-month. Write or phone Box 1362, Martinsburg, WV 25401 (304–263–2500 or 263–6414).

December. *Old Tyme Christmas* features caroling, decorative craft shops, Yule log, living nativity scene, special events for children, first and second weekends in month. Write or phone Harpers Ferry Merchants Association, Box 262, Harpers Ferry, WV 25425 (304–535–2372).

Kentucky

June. *Poke Sallet Festival,* gala events including sidewalk art shows, antique sales, home and garden tours, mountain food, sing-alongs, country music, pet show, last week in June. Write or phone Harlan Chamber of Commerce, Box 268, Harlan, KY 40831 (606–573–4717).

July. *Berea Craft Festival,* top quality craftspeople demonstrate and sell their products; regional foods, live entertainment, 3 days mid-July. Adults, $2.50; children (6–12), $1; under 6, free. For further information phone (606–986–3426).

October. *Daniel Boone Festival* features horse show, old-time fiddling, antiques, square dances, men with beards wearing coonskin hats, Cherokee Indians participating in festivities, first week in Oct. Write or phone Knox County Chamber of Commerce, 205 City Municipal Bldg., Daniel Boone Dr., Box 1000, Barbourville, KY 40906 (606–546–4300).

Virginia

March. *Highland County Maple Festival* shows how syrup is produced and features great country cookery, mountain music, dances, arts, crafts, 2 weekends mid- and late month, write or phone Highland County Chamber of Commerce, Box 223, Monterey, VA 24465 (703–468–2550).

April. *Historic Garden Week in Virginia,* a splendid statewide series of tours, now over 50 years old, involving more than 30 areas of the Old Dominion's treasured sites, including many in the Shenandoah Valley and Blue Ridge regions. For complete information write or phone Garden Club of Virginia, 12 E. Franklin St., Richmond, VA 23219 (804–644–7776).

May. *The Shenandoah Apple Blossom Festival* recognizes Winchester's apple industry amid such festivities as band concerts, crowning of a queen, world's largest fireman's parade, dances, music, concerts, grand feature parades that have included well-known figures such as Bob Hope, Billy Graham, President Gerald Ford, and Howard Cosell, has been nationally televised, lasts four days in early May. Write or phone Box 3000, Winchester, VA 22601 (703–662–3863). *Lonesome Pine Fine Arts and Crafts Show* presents some of most talented craftspeople in the southern Appalachian region, at Big Stone Gap, 2 days mid-month. Write or phone Box 285, Big Stone Gap, VA 24210 (703–523–0846). *Annual Reenactment of the Battle of New Market* authentically traces events in the 1864 engagement that brought fame to 264 Virginia Military Institute cadets, always on Sun. prior to May 15th. Write or phone New Market Battlefield Park, Box 1864, New Market, VA 22844 (703–740–3101).

June. *Roanoke Valley Horse Show,* one of the largest such events in the nation, shows a large variety of breeds, 6 days mid- to late month. Write or phone Box 886, Salem, VA 24153 (703–375–3004).

July. *Hungry Mother Arts and Crafts Festival,* quality handcrafted items on show and for sale, 3 days late month. Write or phone Box 924, Marion, VA 24354 (703–783–3505).

August. *Virginia Highlands Festival,* a celebration of Appalachian arts, crafts, music, with antique cars featured, 16 days early to mid-month. Write or phone Washington County Chamber of Commerce, Abingdon, VA 24210 (703–628–8141). *Annual Old Fiddlers' Convention* has been happening for over 50 years, the nation's largest such event featuring string music, folk songs, and dancing, admission fee, 4 days early month. Write or phone 328–A Kenbrook Dr., Galax, VA 24333 (703–236–6355). *Annual Jousting Tournament,* held at the Chimneys scenic rock formation, riders in medieval costumes and armed with steel-tipped lances compete with each other, event has been going on for over 165 years, one day mid-month. Write or phone Rte. 1, Mt. Solon, VA 22843 (703–350–2510).

September. *Annual Fincastle Festival,* exhibitions and sale of arts, crafts, quilts, photography, beer, and German foods, 2 days early month. Write or phone Historic Fincastle, Inc., Box 19, Fincastle, VA 24090 (703–473–2851). *Edinburg Ole Time Festival* features apple-butter making, quilting, broom tying, crafts, entertainment, pork-skin frying, 3 days mid- to late month. Write or phone Box 85, Edinburg, VA 22824 (703–984–8521).

October. *Festival of Leaves* showcases regional history, traditional arts, crafts, music, 2 days early month. Write or phone Warren Heritage Society, 101 Chester St., Front Royal, VA 22630 (703–639–1446). *Page County Heritage Festival,* held in Luray, features chili cook-off, music, dancing, "Oh Shenandoah" pageant, 2 days early month. Write or phone 45 Cave St., Luray, VA 22835 (703–743–6290).

December. *Annual Christmas Festival & Flower Show* highlights a community Christmas chorus, garden-club shows, refreshments, 3 days early month. Write or phone Box 326, Big Stone Gap, VA 24219 (703–523–2060). *Holiday in Lexington* celebrations feature a gala parade, tree-lighting ceremony, special Christmas events, 2 days early month. Write or phone 102 E. Washington St., Lexington, VA 24450 (703–463–3777).

North Carolina

March. *Cataloochee's Annual Spring Frolic* features music, food, costume contest, zany activities, classic series finals ski race, 2 days early month. Write or phone Cataloochee Ski Area, Rte. 1, Box 500, Maggie Valley, NC 28751 (704–926–0285).

April. *Festival of Flowers,* held at Biltmore House, celebrates spring with thematic floral displays in each room, gardens on grounds are at peak bloom, 19 days mid- to late month. Write or phone Marketing Dept., Biltmore Estate, 1 N Pack Sq., Asheville, NC 28801 (704–255–1700).

May. *Annual Ramp Convention,* over 50 years old, celebrates tradition of eating ramps, festivities also feature mountain music, fellowship, good times, 1 day early month. Write or phone Haywood Post 47, American Legion, Box 911, Waynesville, NC 28786 (704–456–8691). *Annual World Gee-Haw Whimmy Diddle Competition,* at Folk Art Center, features gee-haw whimmydiddle competitions, craft demonstrations, musical entertainment, storytelling, 2 days early month. Write or phone Southern Highland Handicraft Guild, Box 9545, Asheville, NC 28815 (704–298–7928).

June. *Annual Dillsboro Heritage Festival,* a celebration of mountain life with singing, dancing, spinning, weaving, and arts and crafts, 1 day mid-month. Write or phone Dillsboro Merchants Ass'n, Box 634, Dillsboro, NC 28725 (704–586–5244). *North Carolina Rhododendron Festival* showcases square dancing in the street, arts and crafts, a 10-km run, a golf tournament, beauty pageants, 4 days mid to late month. Write or phone NC Rhododendron Festival, Box 407, Bakersville, NC 28705 (704–688–3113).

July. *Frontier Days–Wagon Train,* a series of festive bluegrass music, food, and arts and crafts, climaxed by a gala parade featuring arrival of an authentic Daniel Boone wagon train, which begins in North Wilkesboro and ends in Boone, 2 days early month. Write or phone Wagon Train, Box 362, DTS, Boone, NC 28607 (704–

264–9357). *Annual Grandfather Mountain Highland Games and Gathering of Scottish Clans* attracts over 100 clans and societies for traditional athletic contests, Highland dancing and piping, ceremonial events, pageantry, 2 days mid-month. Write or phone Grandfather Mountain, Box 995, Linville, NC 28646 (704–733–2013). *Annual Guild Fair,* sponsored by Southern Highland Handicraft Guild, features top flight craftspeople demonstrating, exhibiting, and selling their wares, also folk and contemporary entertainment, 4 days mid- to late month. Write or phone Southern Highland Handicraft Guild, Box 9545, Asheville, NC 28815 (704–298–7928).

August. *Mount Mitchell Crafts Fair,* held in town square at Burnsville, is a festive gala of music, food, entertainment, games, and arts and crafts, 2 days early month. Write or phone Yancey County Chamber of Commerce, 2 Town Sq., Room 3, Burnsville, NC 28714 (704–682–7413). *Annual Asheville Mountain Dance and Folk Festival,* held in the civic center, features traditional clogging, figure and buck dancing, oldtime string bands, mountain-dulcimer playing, ballad singing, yarn spinning, band and dance competitions, 3 days early month. Write or phone Festival Manager, Asheville Chamber of Commerce, Box 1011, Asheville, NC 28802 (in East, 800–257–1300; in NC, 800–548–1300; elsewhere, 704–258–3916). *North Carolina Apple Festival* showcases apple cider, orchard tours, golf tournament, parade, arts and crafts, and pageants to select Apple Queen, Junior Princess and Petite Princess, 10 days late month into early Sept. Write or phone Apple Festival General Manager, 330 N. King St., Hendersonville, NC 28739 (704–693–6336).

October. *Cherokee Fall Festival,* held on Ceremonial Grounds, celebrates traditional Indian culture with athletic events, dancing, crafts, foods, 5 days early month. Write or phone Fall Festival, Box 104, Cherokee, NC 28719 (704–497–3157). *Annual Guild Fair,* held at Asheville Civic Center; leading artisans from southern Appalachians exhibit and sell their crafts, also folk and contemporary musical entertainment, 3 days mid-month. Write or phone Market Coordinator, Southern Highland Handicraft Guild, Box 9545, Asheville, NC 28815 (704–298–7928). *Woolly Worm Festival* offers worm races, forecast of winter weather by observing stripes on the famous worms, music, food, crafts, one day mid-month, write or phone Banner Elk Chamber of Commerce, Box 335, Banner Elk, NC 28604 (704–898–5605).

November–December. *Christmas at Biltmore,* held in Biltmore House, recalls Victorian Yuletide celebrations with over two dozen decorated live trees, candlelight evenings, holiday music commemorating Christmas Eve, 1895, when George W. Vanderbilt formally opened his mansion; festivities last from late November through all of December. Write or phone Marketing Director, Biltmore Estate, 1 N. Pack Sq., Asheville, NC 28801 (704–255–1700).

Tennessee

April. *Annual Spring Wildflower Pilgrimage* offers programs of nature walks, motorcades, photographic expeditions to wildflower areas in the Great Smoky Mountains National Park, 3 days late month. Write or phone Gatlinburg Chamber of Commerce, 520 Pkwy., Gatlinburg, TN 37738 (out of state, 800–251–9868; in TN, 800–824–4766; locally, 615–436–4178).

June. *Rhododendron Festival,* Roan Mountain State Resort Park, arts, crafts, gospel singing held in the beautiful 600-acre natural rhododendron gardens atop towering Roan Mountain during peak bloom, 2 days late weekend in month. Write or phone Roan Mountain State Resort Park, Hwy. 143, Rte. 1, Box 50, Roan Mountain, TN 37687 (615–772–3303). *Dollywood National Music Festival,* presented in the mountain village setting of Dolly Parton's popular theme park, showcases country and Bluegrass musicians, 16 days late June. Write or phone Dollywood, Dollywood Ln., Pigeon Forge, TN 37863 (615–428–9400).

July. *Gatlinburg's Summer Craftsman's Fair,* a mountain gala that attracts over 100 artisans from several states to exhibit and market their products; Cherokee Indian displays depict traditional life styles, 10 days late July–early Aug. Write or phone Gatlinburg Chamber of Commerce, Box 527, 520 Pkwy., Gatlinburg, TN 37738 (615–436–2392; 800–822–1998 nationwide).

November–December. *Great Smoky Arts and Crafts Community Christmas Show,* a 3-day event featuring handmade Yule season arts, crafts, gifts displayed and sold in a village market atmosphere, late Nov.; *Smoky Mountain Christmas* celebrates the festive season with such happenings as Yule log burnings, a living Christmas tree, madrigal feasts, seasonal crafts fair and Festival of Christmas Past, held during the four weekends prior to Christmas day. For information about both events, write or phone Gatlinburg Chamber of Commerce, Box 527, 520 Pkwy., Gatlinburg, TN 37738 (615–436–2392; 800–822–1998 nationwide).

NATIONAL PARKS AND SCENIC DRIVES. Shenandoah National Park and Skyline Drive (Virginia). Extending 80 mi. from north to south and 2 to 13 mi. east to west, the Shenandoah National Park encompasses extensive wildernesses, vast hardwood and conifer forests, cascading streams, and rugged cliffs. Abundant animal life includes bear, deer, fox, bobcats, groundhogs, chipmunks, and more than 200 species of birds. The variety of flowers is so plentiful that many have yet to be properly classified and listed.

From the northern end of the park at Front Royal, the 105-mi. Skyline Dr. passes along Blue Ridge Mountain crests southward to Waynesboro. It's a leisurely route with numerous overlooks for stunning panoramic views of the rolling Piedmont foothills to the east, the Shenandoah Valley and misty Alleghenies on the west. Footpaths and hiking trails lead from some of the overlooks and other sites into fascinating natural enclaves. A 94-mi. segment of the 1,028-mi. Maine to Georgia Appalachian Trail goes through the national park and criss-crosses the Skyline Dr. at several places. Speed limit along the winding roadway is 35 mph. Distances along the drive are measured by Mileposts numbered from north to south. Locations on park-service maps and guide materials are generally indicated by Milepost number. The Skyline Dr. remains open except when severe winter weather conditions require certain sections to be closed.

Detailed information about the Shenandoah National Park and Skyline Dr. is available from the *Harry F. Byrd Visitor Center* at Big Meadows, Milepost 51, where a film and museum displays describe the park; open daily, 9 A.M. to 5 P.M., except part-time in Jan. and Feb. The *Dickey Ridge Visitor Center* at Milepost 4.6 provides information and a film; open Apr.–Oct., daily 9 A.M. to 5 P.M. The Skyline Drive may be entered from U.S. 340 near Front Royal, from U.S. 211 at Thornton Gap, near Luray, from U.S. 33 at Swift Run Gap, near Elkton, and from U.S. 250 at Rockfish Gap, near Waynesboro. Admission to the park is $5 for each private non-commercial vehicle; $2 per person by other means of transportation.

Seasonal overnight accommodations are available on the Skyline Drive at Big Meadows Lodge near Luray (see Accommodations). Tent and trailer camping sites, without hookups, are at *Big Meadows Campground,* Milepost 51.3, open Mar.–Dec., 227 sites; *Lewis Mountain Campground,* Milepost 57.5, open late May–early Nov., 31 sites; *Loft Mountain Campground,* Milepost 79.5, open late May–Nov. 1, 221 sites; and *Matthews Arm Campground,* Milepost 22.2, open late May–Nov. 1, 186 sites. Daily rates per site, $7, $9 at *Big Meadows* 14-day stay limit; for further information call 703–999–2229.

Special naturalist-guided walks and campfire programs are presented regularly from mid-June to Labor Day and on limited schedules at other times. Check park headquarters, visitor centers, and concessions for events. For more information about the many offerings in the park, contact Superintendent, Shenandoah National Park, Rte. 4, Box 348, Luray, VA 22835 (703–999–2229).

The Blue Ridge Parkway (Virginia and North Carolina). Beginning at Rockfish Gap, where the Skyline Dr. ends, the Blue Ridge Pkwy. reaches toward the southwest, winding amid towering crests and along mountain ridges in Virginia and North Carolina. A magnificent roadway, 469 mi. in length, it terminates outside Cherokee, NC, near the southern entrance to the Great Smoky Mountains National Park. The north-to-south milepost system, patterned after the one on the Skyline Dr., provides a convenient means of designating locations. The well-engineered two-lane parkway has numerous overlooks for scenic viewing and in many areas has been beautifully landscaped. Trails lead to places of natural interest as well as historic relics of human habitation such as log cabins and old mills. Towns have been bypassed but are often in easy driving distance for overnight stays, automobile servicing, dining, and shopping. Designed for slow, leisurely driving, the parkway has a 45 mph speed limit. Motorists should always keep their gasoline tanks at least half full. Portions of the parkway are closed during severe winter weather.

Detailed information about the Blue Ridge Pkwy. is available from visitor and information centers. Those in Virginia are at *Humpback Rocks,* Milepost 5.8; *James*

River Wayside, Milepost 63.6; *Peaks of Otter,* Milepost 86; *Rocky Knob,* Milepost 169; and in North Carolina at *Cumberland Knob,* Milepost 217.5; *Moses H. Cone Memorial Park,* Milepost 294.1; *Museum of North Carolina Minerals,* Milepost 331; *Craggy Gardens,* Milepost 364.6. Gasoline stations, seasonal park-ranger programs, restaurants, and overnight lodging are available at Peaks of Otter, Milepost 86, and Rocky Knob (housekeeping cabins only, no restaurant), Milepost 169 in Virginia and at Doughton Park, Milepost 241.1, and Mount Pisgah, Milepost 408.6, in North Carolina. Peaks of Otter remains open year-round; the other areas May–Oct.

The nine campgrounds along the parkway are fully open May–Oct., have very limited facilities during winter. Tent and trailer sites are available, but there are no hookups. Drinking water, comfort stations, and in some instances sanitary disposal stations have been provided; there are no shower or laundry installations. Limited supplies may be purchased at gasoline stations and camp stores. Some of the campgrounds are near lodges or restaurants; others are in more remote locations. Sites are on a first-come, first-served basis, 14-day stay limit, daily fee, $6–$7. Virginia campgrounds are at *Otter Creek* (804–299–5941), 67 sites at Milepost 60.9; *Peaks of Otter* (703–586–4357), 148 sites at Milepost 86; *Roanoke Mountain* (703–982–6490), 105 sites at Milepost 120.4; and *Rocky Knob* (703–745–3451), 109 sites at Milepost 167.1. North Carolina campgrounds are found at *Doughton Park* (704–259–0701), 136 sites at Milepost 241.1; *Julian Price Memorial Park* (704–259–0701), 197 sites at Milepost 297.1; *Linville Falls* (704–259–0701), 75 sites at Milepost 316.3; *Crabtree Meadows* (704–259–0701), 93 sites at Milepost 339.5; and *Mount Pisgah* (704–259–0701), 140 sites at Milepost 408.6.

Highlights in the Virginia segment of the parkway include: *Otter Creek,* Mileposts 58 to 63.6, with a restaurant, a gasoline station, campground, lake fishing, an exhibit shelter depicting the James River and Kanawha Canal, a footbridge across the river to a restored canal lock, and a hiking trail along the River bluffs. *Onion Mountain,* Milepost 79.7, has a short loop trail through clusters of rhododendron and mountain laurel, which bloom in early June. *Peaks of Otter,* Mileposts 84 to 87, a complete destination with lodge, restaurant, campground, visitor center with exhibits, gasoline station, picnic area, hiking trails and a shuttle bus to scenic Sharptop. *Rocky Knob,* Mileposts 167 to 174, where rock formations resemble the crest of a wave, offers visitors a picnic area, housekeeping cabins, a campground, scenic hiking trails. *Mabry Mill,* Milepost 176.1, dating from 1910 and still operative, is in a lovely setting where visitors may also enjoy a sawmill, blacksmith shop, restaurant, and seasonal craft demonstrations.

The extensive North Carolina portion of the Blue Ridge Parkway showcases many highlights: *Cumberland Knob,* Milepost 217.5, delightful for walking in open meadows and forests, also has a picnic area, an information station, trails. *Doughton Park,* Mileposts 238.5 to 244.7, where visitors find a lodge, a restaurant, a gasoline station, a trail to scenic Wildcat Rocks, and demonstrating artisans and a craft shop at Brinegar Cabin. *Moses H. Cone Memorial Park,* Milepost 292.7 to 295, at the former estate of the late textile executive, now serves as the parkway craft center, where fine handmade items may be purchased; hiking trails, lakes, and carriage roads are also here. *Linville Falls,* Milepost 316.3, plunge into a rugged gorge in a vast wilderness area where hiking trails, a campground, and picnic tables are also found. *Crabtree Meadows,* Milepost 339, has a restaurant, a gasoline station, a campground, a picnic area, and a scenic trail to Crabtree Falls. *Craggy Gardens,* Mileposts 363.4 to 369.6, are scene of a visitor center, a picnic area, and trails among spectacular masses of purple Catawba rhododendron, which peak bloom in mid-June. *Mt. Pisgah,* Milepost 408.6, a popular stopover point, has an inn, a restaurant, a gasoline station, a spacious campground, and hiking trails into Pisgah National Forest and to the summit of the mountain. *Richland Balsam,* Milepost 431, with trails leading through a spruce-fir forest, is, at 6,053 ft., the highest point on the parkway. *Waterrock Knob,* Milepost 451.2, offers panoramic views of the Great Smoky Mountains and provides a comfort station, exhibits, and trails.

The Blue Ridge Parkway is administered by the National Park Service. For additional information, maps, and brochures, write or phone Superintendent, 200 BB&T Bldg., 1 Pack S., Asheville, NC 28801 (704–259–0701 or 259–0702). Free admission.

Great Smoky Mountains National Park (North Carolina and Tennessee). The southern Appalachians reach their ultimate grandeur in the Great Smokies, where

16 peaks soar more than 6,000 ft. in the national park, roughly about 60 mi. long and 20 mi. wide, straddling the border between North Carolina and Tennessee. The mountains received their name from the Cherokee Indians, who observed the smoke-like clouds often hovering about the peaks. The major highway through the Smokies is U.S. 441, traversing about 35 winding mi. between Cherokee, NC, and Gatlinburg, TN. Within the national park it is known as Newfound Gap Rd. These mountains, mysterious and haunting, are teeming with abundant wildlife, innumerable varieties of flora, and forests of spruce and hemlock characteristic of Canada. It is scarcely surprising that the Great Smoky Mountains National Park is the most-visited in the nation.

Maps, folders, literature, and detailed information about the park may be obtained at three visitor centers. The southern entrance is served by Oconaluftee, 4 mi. north of Cherokee, NC, on Newfound Gap Road (U.S. 441). Open daily year-round except Dec. 25; May–Oct., 8 A.M. to 6 P.M.; remainder of the year, until 4:30 P.M. Sugarlands, 2 mi. southwest of Gatlinburg, TN, on Newfound Gap Rd., is also the park headquarters. Open daily year-round except Dec. 25; May–Oct., 8 A.M. to 7:30 P.M.; remainder of year, to 4:30 P.M. Cades Cove center, 13 mi. southwest of Townsend, TN, off U.S. 321, is open mid-Apr.–Oct., 10 A.M. to 6 P.M.; closed remainder of the year.

The three largest and most popular developed campgrounds in the national park are open year-round; they provide basic amenities, other than showers, and naturalist programs and recreation. Fees are $7–$9 per site per day; 7-day stay limits during peak season. From May through Oct. reservations must be made through any of 600 nationwide Ticketron outlets at least one day in advance, or approximately six weeks in advance by mail from Ticketron Reservation System, Box 62429, Virginia Beach, VA 23462 or phone 900–370–5566. The all-year campgrounds are: *Smokemont,* 6 mi. north of Cherokee, NC, via Newfound Gap Rd., with 152 sites; *Elkmont,* 8 mi. west of Gatlinburg, TN, via Newfound Gap Rd. and Little River and Elkmont Rds., with 220 sites; and *Cades Cove,* 10 mi. southwest of Townsend, TN, via TN 73 and Laurel Creek Rd., with 160 sites. Fees and stay limits noted above apply to other campgrounds open only from May through Oct., but sites are on a first-come, first-served basis. These campgrounds are *Balsam Mountain,* 45 sites, and *Deep Creek,* 119 sites, in the North Carolina section of the park. Campgrounds open May through mid-Oct. are *Cosby,* 175 sites and *Look Rock,* 92 sites, in the Tennessee section of the park.

Nature's beauty and the impact of human habitation are dramatically revealed as one explores the Great Smoky Mountains National Park. At the southern entrance to the Park the *Oconaluftee Pioneer Farmstead* near the visitor center is a collection of vintage structures—main house, barn, storage bins, smokehouse—depicting the sturdy, self-sufficient lifestyle of mountain people during the late 19th century. Half a mile northward off Newfound Gap Rd., cornmeal produced the old-fashioned way by water-powered wheels may be purchased at Mingus Mill. North Carolina and Tennessee come together at Newfound Gap, situated on the crest of the Great Smokies in the midst of a spruce-and-hemlock forest reminiscent of Canada. The views from overlooks at the parking area are extraordinary. The Appalachian Trail crosses the highway here, and visitors often enjoy short hikes along nearby portions. A 7-mi. spur road from Newfound Gap leads to Clingmans Dome, soaring 6,643 ft., where an observation tower affords panoramas in all directions of spectacular mountain scenery unsurpassed anywhere.

In the Tennessee section of the park, Newfound Gap Rd. wends through rugged wilderness areas that reach a maximum of color when rhododendron and other flowering plants bloom in early summer. The visitor center at Sugarlands is situated in a woodland where bears would come to devour honey deposited in hollow logs—thus the name. At Cades Cove in a western enclave of the park, a loop road leads through a mountain farm community that has remained virtually intact. Small wooden churches, hewn-log farmhouses, massive barns, split-rail fences, beehives, cattle grazing in open meadows, and a still-operating old grist mill stand as remnants in a place once so remote that many of the people who lived there never left the quiet and peaceful valley.

Motorists must observe speed limits in the Great Smoky Mountains National Park and should *never* approach, annoy, or feed the bears that frequently congregate at overlooks and along the roadside. Violators are subject to severe penalties.

An informative Auto Tape Tour of the park provides a one-hour commentary about the scenery, fauna, flora, legends, lore, and history of the Cherokee Indians and pioneer settlers in the Great Smokies. Cassettes and a detailed map are available on a rental basis, $11.95, at the Log Cabin Trading Post and Qualla Gift Shop in Cherokee, NC, and at Christus Gardens in Gatlinburg, TN. Advance copies of the tape may be purchased for $11.95 each, plus $1 postage and handling, from Auto Tape Tours, Box 385, Scarsdale, NY 10583 (914–472–5133).

For additional information, maps, and brochures, write or phone Superintendent, Great Smoky Mountains National Park, Gatlinburg, TN 37738 (615–436–1200). Free admission to park.

PARTICIPANT SPORTS. Still relatively unspoiled in many areas, the southern Appalachians have great appeal to those who enjoy open spaces, wild and natural flowing rivers, hiking trails, wilderness domains—and even downhill and cross-country skiing.

Rafting and Canoeing

Trips range from rugged whitewater expeditions to journeys along more placid streams. Raft trips are generally guided, canoes often available on individual rental basis. Rates vary widely according to location, season, length of trips. Please inquire.

West Virginia. *Blue Ridge Outfitters* offers whitewater raft trips on Shenandoah and Tygart rivers, 4 to 5½ hours in length, also canoe rentals; outfitting-supply store open Apr.–Oct.; Box 750, Harpers Ferry, WV 25425 (304–725–3444). *Wildwater Expeditions Unlimited,* 15 mi. NE of Beckley, provides 1- and 2-day whitewater raft trips, expeditions to historic ghost towns, canoe trips of 1 to 4 days, all on the New and Gauley rivers; equipment and meals can be furnished, Dept. C.P.O., Box 55, Thurmond, WV 25936 (304–469–2551). *Whitewater Information, Ltd.,* offers whitewater rafting on New and Gauley rivers, also dory trips, fishing expeditions, 1 to 3 days, Apr.–Nov.; base camp 8 mi. north of Beckley, Drawer 243, Glen Jean, WV 25846 (304–465–0855; 800–782–7238 out of state).

Kentucky. *Renegade Rick's Rockcastle River Runners* offers three 42-mi. canoe, raft, and "funyak" trips Mar.–Nov.; 117 Hawkins St., Somerset, KY 42501 (606–597–5026; 800–782–7238 out of state). *Rockcastle Adventures* books canoe trips from 4 hours to 5 days on the Rockcastle and Cumberland rivers, and Rock and Wood creeks; canoe rentals also available; write or phone company at Box 662, London, KY 40741 (606–864–9407).

Virginia. *James River Basin Canoe Livery, Ltd.,* offers fishing, rafting on the rapids, picnicking.; Rte. 4, Box 125, Lexington, VA 24450 (703–261–7334). *River Wind Outfitters* provide canoe and kayak trips on the New River; inquire about rates and seasonal schedules; Rte. 5, Galax, VA 24333 (703–236–7580).

North Carolina. Among the swift-flowing mountain streams popular for canoeing and whitewater rafting are the French Broad, Little Tennessee, Nantahala, and Oconaluftee rivers and the south fork of the New River. Outfitters noted provide raft and canoe rentals, clinics, and guided trips. Since mountain rivers are very rugged, inexperienced canoers are advised to take caution. Please inquire about seasons, times, itineraries, and rates from the companies. *Carolina Wilderness Adventures, Inc.,* Box 488, Hot Springs, NC 28743 (704–622–3535). *Edge of the World Outfitters,* Rte. 3, Box 510–A, Banner Elk, NC 28604 (704–898–9550). *Nantahala Outdoor Center,* U.S. 19W, Box 41, Bryson City, NC 28713 (704–488–2175). *Nantahala Rafts,* Box 21, U.S. 19W, Bryson City, NC 28713 (704–488–2325). *Rolling Thunder River Co.,* Box 88, Almond, NC 28702 (704–488–2030).

Tennessee. *Big South Fork National River and Recreation Area* provides information about 80 mi. of streams, many in remote locations, suitable for beginning to skilled canoeists; send 35 cents for descriptive folder; Superintendent, Drawer 630, Oneida, TN 37841 (615–569–6963). *Ocoee Rafting, Inc.,* guided white-water trips on the Ocoee River, Apr.–Oct.; inquire about schedules and rates, Box 461, Ducktown, TN 37326 (615–496–3388 or 800–251–4800). *Pigeon River Outdoors,* guided raft trips on Big Pigeon River, numerous rapids, suitable for advanced paddlers, Apr.–Oct.; inquire about days of operation, rates, Box 592, Gatlinburg, TN 37738 (615–436–5008).

Skiing

Downhill and cross-country skiing have become immensely popular in the southern Appalachians during the past two decades. Snowmaking machines supplement what nature provides during the season, which generally lasts from about mid-Dec. to mid-Mar. Rates vary widely among the different ski areas, so please inquire. Virtually all the resorts offer rental equipment, instructional staff, dining, après-ski activities, and favorable package plans (see Accommodations section about facilities at or near some of the resorts).

West Virginia. *Canaan Valley State Park,* chairlifts, 6 slopes, 15 trails, overnight lodging, dining, Rte. 1, Box 330, Davis, WV 26260 (304–866–4121). *Snowshoe,* the South's largest ski area, chairlifts, 33 slopes and trails, 1,500-ft. vertical drop, restaurants, overnight lodging, Box 10, Snowshoe, WV 26209 (304–572–1000 or 304–572–5252).

Virginia. *Bryce Resort,* chairlifts, rope tow, four slopes, overnight lodgings, dining, Bryce Resort, Box 3, Basye, VA 22810 (703–856–2121). *Cascade Mountain,* chairlift, four slopes including one for novices, dining and overnight at inn, on VA 608 near Fancy Gap, VA off Blue Ridge Parkway (703–728–2300 for Cascade Inn reservations). *Homestead Ski Area,* chairlift, T-bar, rope tows, 700-ft. vertical drop on main slope, cross-country skiing, dining, overnight at the Homestead resort hotel, Homestead Ski Area, Hot Springs, VA 24445 (703–839–5079). *Massanutten Village Ski Resort,* chairlifts, J-bar, longest run 5,600 ft., dining, overnight at resort hotel, Massanutten Village, Box 1227, Harrisonburg, VA 22801 (703–289–9441 or 800–334–6086). *Wintergreen,* chairlifts, 12 slopes, longest vertical drop 1,003 ft., luxury spa, choice of dining, overnight at resort inn, chalets, Wintergreen, Wintergreen, VA 22958 (804–325–2200 or 800–325–2200 in eastern USA).

North Carolina. *Appalachian Ski Mountain,* chair- and surface lifts, 8 slopes, French-Swiss Ski College (South's largest ski school), new teaching hill for youngsters, dining, lodging, Appalachian Ski Mountain, Box 106, Blowing Rock, NC 28605 (704–295–7828). *Cataloochee Ski Area,* chair- and surface lifts, 8 slopes, NASTAR races three times weekly, nursery, dining, lodging, Rte. 1, Box 500, Maggie Valley, NC 28751 (704–926–0285). *Fairfield Sapphire Valley,* chair- and surface lifts, 4 slopes, downhill and cross-country, new health club, nursery, dining, lodging, Rte. 70, Box 80, Sapphire, NC 28774 (704–743–3441 or 800–222–1057 in NC; 800–438–3421 out-of-state). *Hound Ears,* 1,200-foot slope, chairlift, rope tow, dining, lodging, Hound Ears Lodge and Club, Box 188, Blowing Rock, NC 28605 (704–963–4321). *Ski Beech,* surface and chairlifts—including South's first detachable quad chair, 16 slopes—among them a meandering run into majestic "western bowl," nursery, shopping village, Bavarian atmosphere, varied choices for dining, overnight accommodations, Beech Mountain Resort, Box 1118, Banner Elk, NC 28604 (704–387–2011 or 800–222–2293 NC, 800–438–2093 out-of-state for snow reports). *Ski Hawksnest,* chair- and surface lifts, 6 slopes—including one new intermediate, noted for advanced terrain, limitation on ticket sales avoids overcrowding, dining, lodge, Hawksnest Ski Area, Rte. 1, Box 256, Banner Elk, NC 28604 (704–963–6561). *Ski Scaly,* chair- and surface lifts, 5 slopes—including new one for beginners. South's southernmost ski area is ideal for beginning and intermediate skiers, dining, lodging, Ski Scaly, Box 339, Scaly Mountain, NC 28775 (704–526–3737). *Sugar Mountain Resort,* chair- and surface lifts, 16 slopes, some especially designed for experts; 1,200-ft. vertical drop, one of longest in eastern U.S., provides for skiers of all ability levels, popular Switchback run recently expanded, new Eastman Kodak SNOMAX has increased snowmaking 20–50%, resulting in drier snow at higher temperatures; nursery, fine dining, overnight accommodations, Sugar Mountain Resort, Box 369, Banner Elk, NC 28604 (704–898–4521). *Wolf Laurel Ski Resort,* chair- and surface lifts, 9 slopes, special expert slopes, site of NASTAR races, nursery, dining, recently renovated lodge. Wolf Laurel Ski Resort, Rte. 3, Mars Hill, NC 28754 (704–689–4111).

Tennessee. *Ober Gatlinburg,* reached from downtown via aerial tramway or automobile; quad and double chairlifts lead to mountaintop, 10 slopes and trails ranging from novice to expert, shops, dining at resort, lodgings in town, Ober Gatlinburg, 1001 Parkway, Gatlinburg, TN 37738 (615–436–5423; out-of-state, 800–251–9202; in TN, 800–843–6237).

Hiking

The Appalachian Trail, stretching from Maine to Georgia, traverses wilderness areas of vast beauty along crests and ridges of high mountains. Veteran hikers often do the entire journey; others cover only segments. One of the most popular portions of the trail passes through the Great Smoky Mountains National Park. For detailed guidebooks, maps, other information about hiking conditions, shelters, highlights, availability of food and supplies, contact Appalachian Trail Conference Headquarters, Box 236, Harpers Ferry, WV 25425 (304–535–6331).

FAMILY ATTRACTIONS. Throughout the southern Appalachian region, a wide variety of lively attractions provides entertainment, outdoor activities, and good times for grown-ups and children alike. Here are some of them, listed according to state.

West Virginia

Cass Scenic Railroad State Park. Box 107, Cass, WV 24927 (304–456–4300). From Cass, once a bustling logging town, steam-powered Shay locomotives pull passengers over an old logging trail in Monongahela National Forest up steep slopes to the top of Bald Knob, second highest point in West Virginia. 4½-hour trip goes to top of Cheat Mountain; 2 hours to Whittaker Station. A restaurant, a large gift shop, 11 vacation cottages, and a museum are part of an 855-acre state-park complex at the departure point. Memorial Day–Labor Day, Tues.–Sun.; Labor Day–Oct., Sat.–Sun. Long trip leaves at noon; fare, adults, $11; children 5–11, $5; short trip at 11 A.M., 1 P.M., 3 P.M., fare, adults, $8; children 5–11, $4.

Virginia

Luray Caverns and Car & Carriage Caravan. U.S. 211 Bypass, Box 743, Luray, VA 22835 (703–743–6551). One of the southern Appalachians' most popular caves, highlighted by majestic spotlighted formations in rooms with 140-ft.-high ceilings. Great stalacpipe organ in Cathedral Room provides concert-quality music by musician striking stalactites with rubber-tipped plungers by remote control from special organ console. At the Luray Singing Tower, entrance to the caverns, a carillon of 47 bells is also played each Tues., Thurs., Sat., and Sun., early spring through late fall. Car & Carriage Caravan on premises showcases vintage automobiles, including Rudolph Valentino's 1925 Rolls-Royce. Caverns open daily year-round. Adults, $9; senior citizens, $8; children 7–13, $4.50 (includes both attractions). Singing Tower: free.

Mill Mountain Zoological Park. Atop Mill Mountain in city limits, Box 13484, Roanoke, VA 24034 (703–343–3241). Pleasant small zoo is open daily mid-Apr.–Oct. 10 A.M.–6 P.M. Mountain offers beautiful views of city, countryside; its 100-ft.-high electric star is illuminated at night. Inquire locally about nominal admission costs.

Natural Bridge of Virginia and the Caverns of Natural Bridge. U.S. 11, at junction VA 130, Box 57, Natural Bridge, VA 24578 (703–291–2121; 800–533–1410 in VA; 800–336–5727 out-of-state). Astounding 215-ft.-high limestone arch spans Cedar Creek and supports U.S. 11, which runs above it. Thomas Jefferson once owned the bridge, and George Washington as a young surveyor climbed the southwest wall to chisel his initials, still visible today. Impressive sound-and-light production, *The Drama of Creation,* is conducted beneath the bridge, 9 P.M., summer; 8 P.M., spring and fall; 7 P.M., winter. Adjacent Caverns of Natural Bridge, 34 stories underground, is highlighted by the Colossal Dome, Canyon Room, unusual formations. Natural Bridge open daily, 7 A.M.–dusk. Adults, $5, day or night visit; seniors, $4, children 6–15, $2.50; combination day and night visit, adults, $6; seniors, $5; children 6–15, $3. Caverns open daily Mar.–Nov. 30. 10 A.M. to 5:30 P.M., fall and spring; 10 A.M. to 8 P.M., summer. 1-hour guided tours. Adults, $4.50; children 6–15, $2; under 6, free; not recommended for seniors.

Shenandoah Caverns. I-81, Exit 68, 4 mi. north of New Market, Box 1, Caverns Rd., Shenandoah Caverns, VA 22847 (703–477–3115). Colorful caverns are highlighted by Rainbow Lake, Diamond Cascade, and eerily natural "bacon" formations. Convenient elevators—no hiking up and down steps. Coffee shop, picnic areas, gift and antique shops on premises. Open daily, 9 A.M.–6:30 P.M., mid-June–Sept. 1; to 5:30 P.M. mid-Apr.–mid-June, Sept. 2–mid-Oct.; to 4:30 P.M. rest of year. Adults, $7; seniors, $6; children 8–14, $3.50; under 8, free with parent.

Virginia Museum of Transportation, Inc. 303 Norfolk Ave. SW, Roanoke, VA 24011 (703–342–5670). Unique museum displays largest collection of railroad artifacts in the southeastern United States. Exhibits include railroad artifacts, steam locomotives; southwest Virginia railroading is depicted in model train layout. Youngsters enjoy miniature passenger train rides. Open Mon.–Sat. 10 A.M.–5 P.M., Sun., noon to 5 P.M. Adults, $3; over 60, $2.50; 13–18, $2; 3–12, $1.75; under 3, free.

Big Walker Lookout. Atop U.S. 21–52 N, 9 mi. south of Bland, 12 mi. north of Wytheville; Star Tour, Wytheville, VA 24382 (703–228–4401). Sky Lift leads to 3,405-ft. mountaintop picnic area surrounded by rhododendron, wildflowers in season. Lift reached via suspension bridge leading to 100-ft. lookout tower. Shops offer souvenirs, crafts, country foods, herb teas, spices. Skyride: open daily 9 A.M.–6 P.M., Memorial Day–Labor Day; 9 A.M.–5 P.M., Mar. 1–Memorial Day and Labor Day–Nov. 1. Adults, $3.50, 3–11, $2.25. Lookout open daily Memorial Day–Labor Day, 8 A.M. to 8 P.M., Mar. 1 to late May, after Labor Day–Oct. 31, 9 A.M. to 5 P.M.

North Carolina

The Blowing Rock. 2 mi. south on U.S. 321, Blowing Rock, NC 28605 (704–295–7111). Immense cliff 4,090 ft. above sea level offers majestic views of Johns River Gorge 3,000 ft. below. Rocky wall of gorge forms a flume through which the wind sweeps with such force that it returns light objects tossed from the crest. Beautifully tended garden grounds, with pools, waterfalls; snack bar, observation tower, gift shop. Open mid-May–Oct. 31, daily, 8 A.M. to 8 P.M.; mid-Apr.–mid-May and Nov. (weather permitting), 9 A.M. to 6 P.M. Adults, $3.50; children 6–11, $1; under 6, free.

Tweetsie Railroad. 4¼ mi. north on U.S. 321, Box 388, Blowing Rock, NC 28604 (704–264–9061). Theme park is highlighted by 3-mi. narrow-gauge railroad ride in antique coaches pulled by Tweetsie, historic steam-powered locomotive; passengers witness a train hold-up and an Indian raid. Chair lift to Mouse Mountain, with Mouse Mine Ride, gold panning, petting farm, Tweetsie Mining Co. 1900s Country Fair includes rides, arcades, shooting gallery. Tweetsie Junction, Tweetsie Square offer general store, ice-cream parlor, other shops, blacksmith, firehouse, Crafts Junction. Live entertainment at the Tweetsie Palace. Full operation: second Mon. in June to mid-Aug., daily, 9 A.M.–6 P.M. Partial operation (train rides, petting farm, shops only) Mon.–Fri. Memorial Day to second Mon. in June and mid-Aug. to Oct. 31, 9 A.M. to 5:30 P.M.; weekends, full operation. Adults, $10.95; seniors and children 4–12, $8.95; partial operation periods, $5.

Chimney Rock Park. U.S. 64 and 74, Chimney Rock, NC 28720 (704–625–9611). The Chimney, an astounding granite monolith, towers 315 ft. An elevator whisks visitors to trails that lead to the pinnacle. Observation lounge offers dramatic views of the Blue Ridge and Lake Lure. Miles of other beautiful trails include one to Hickory Nut Falls with a sheer drop twice that of Niagara. Picnic tables, grills, playground, gift shop, snack bar. Ticket office open mid-Mar.–mid-Nov. (weather permitting), daily, 8:30 A.M. to 5:30 P.M., June–Aug.; to 4:30 P.M., other times. Park remains open 1½ hours after ticket office closes. Adults, $7.50; children 6–15, $4; season pass, $12.

Cherokee's Magic Waters Park. U.S. 19, Box 337, Cherokee, NC 28719 (704–926–1922). Popular water park offers giant waterslides, tube slides, Blackbeard's Lagoon pool, splash pool for toddlers, Li'l Pirates Playground, adult and kiddie rides, shops, food stands. Ventriloquist-marionette entertainment, championship divers, musical variety shows, many special weekend events. Open daily, Memorial Day weekend to Sept. 2; inquire locally for hours, admission costs.

Oconaluftee Indian Village. Just off U.S. 441 near Mountainside Theater, Box 398, Cherokee, NC 28719 (704–497–2315). In living restoration of Cherokee community of 200 years ago, skilled craftsfolk demonstrate indigenous arts and crafts: beadwork, basketry, finger weaving, and canoe, pottery, and arrowhead making. Cherokee guides describe tribal lore, rituals, history and explain significance of seven-sided council house. Trails lead through Indian herb gardens, natural areas. Open mid-May–late Oct., daily, 9 A.M. to 5:30 P.M. Adults, $7; children 6–13, $3.

Santa's Land Park and Zoo. U.S. 19, 3 mi. east of town, Cherokee, NC 28719 (704–497–9191). Christmas Village includes 25 houses, amusement rides such as merry-go-round, race cars, miniature train, helicopter, moon walk. Petting zoo, gift-and-craft shops, picnic tables are also in the park. Open early May–late Oct., daily, 9 A.M. to 5 P.M., later, July–Aug. Adults, $8.95; children 2–12, $7.95; under 2, free.

Grandfather Mountain. 1 mi. south of junction U.S. 221 and Blue Ridge Pkwy., Linville, NC 28646 (800–438–7500 eastern U.S.; 800–222–7515, NC; 704–733–4337, elsewhere). Highest peak in Blue Ridge. North Carolina landmark resembling profile of a slumbering old man offers dramatic scenic vistas. Mile-high swinging bridge spans a deep gorge. Huge magnificent natural habitat is home to Mildred, a large friendly black bear, and various cubs and relatives. Another habitat houses herds of American white-tail deer. Visitor center features wildlife, wildflower, and mineral exhibits; restaurant, snack shop, crafts, souvenir shops. Site of world-renowned Sept. Masters of Hang Gliding Championship, other special events. Open Apr.–mid-Nov., daily, 9 A.M. to dusk; good weather weekends other times, 9 A.M. to 5 P.M. Adults, $7.50; children 4–12, $4.

Ghost Town in the Sky. U.S. 19, Maggie Valley, NC 28751 (704–926–1140). Rides, entertainment, and music highlight this mountaintop entertainment center, a Wild West village transplanted to the Great Smokies. Scenic chair lift and incline railway take visitors 3,364 ft. to the summit. Craft village, gift shops, restaurants, weekend country-music concerts by big-name entertainers—two shows daily. Open early May–late Oct., daily, 9 A.M. to 6 P.M. Admission, $12.95; children 3–9, $10.95; children under 3, free. $1 extra, dates of special concerts.

Tennessee

Gatlinburg Sky Lift. Pkwy. at Maples La., Gatlinburg, TN 37738 (615–436–4307). Chairlift leads up 2,300-ft. Crockett Mountain for splendid vistas of the Great Smoky Mountains. Apr.–Oct., daily 9 A.M. to 9 P.M., except June–Aug., 8:30 A.M. to 11 P.M. Adults, $5; children 3–11, $2.50.

Mysterious Mansion. River Rd. (behind McDonald's), Gatlinburg, TN 37738 (615–436–7007). A scary and fun-filled maze of adventure and excitement sure to thrill the entire family. Open daily 10 A.M. to 11 P.M., May through Oct. Call for winter hours. Adults, $3.50; children 7–12, $2.50; children 6 and under, free with adult.

Dollywood. 700 Dollywood Ln., Pigeon Forge, TN 37863 (615–428–9400; 800–433–6558 in TN; 800–433–6559 out of state). This theme park developed by Dolly Parton, native of nearby Sevierville, encompasses former Silver Dollar City park and is 50% larger. Highlights include the popular recreated 1880s mountain community with demonstrating craftspeople, theme rides, old-time shows, bluegrass, gospel, and country music, the new Apple Jack Mill, Dolly Parton Museum, River Raft thrill ride, Parton Family Back Porch Theatre with seating capacity of 1,000 for live shows, new Daydream Ridge addition, and Aunt Granny's Dixie Fixin's Restaurant; rip-roaring New Thunder roller coaster zips through dense backwoods setting. Open early May–late Oct. Schedule very complex; phone the park office before visit. One-day admissions, adults, $18.65; children 4–11, $13.15; under 4, free; tickets purchased after 3 P.M. are valid the next day as well.

Ogle's Water Park. 115 N. Pkwy., Pigeon Forge, TN 37863 (615–453–8741). 8-acre playground of exciting water activities including surfing, water slides, wave pool, as well as miniature golf, playgrounds, restaurants. Open June and July, daily, 10 A.M. to 8 P.M.; Aug., daily, 11 A.M. to 6 P.M.; May and Sept. 1–mid-Sept., Sat.–Sun., 11 A.M. to 6 P.M. Adults, $13.12; senior citizens, $11.15; children 4–11, $12.02.

Magic World. U.S. 441, Pigeon Forge, TN 37863 (615–453–7941). Guests take train through theme park's Dinosaur Valley and Haunted Castle, tour the Smokies with Martians on a flying saucer. Open early June–late Aug., daily, 10 A.M. to 10:30 P.M.; late Aug.–early Sept., daily, 10 A.M. to 7 P.M.; Sept.–Oct. Sat.–Sun. 10 A.M. to 5 P.M. Admission, $8.95; children 2 and under, free.

Tuckaleechee Caverns. 3 mi. south off U.S. 321, Townsend, TN 37882 (615–448–2274). Cave includes impressive formations of flowstone falls and one of the largest cavern rooms in the eastern U.S. One-hour guided tours every 15–20 minutes. Illuminated walkway leads over subterranean streams, past waterfalls. Open Apr.–Oct., daily, 9 A.M. to 6 P.M. Adults, $6; children 6–12, $3.

HISTORIC SITES AND MUSEUMS. The Southern Appalachians abound with national and regional treasures, inevitably intriguing to visitors from the U.S. and abroad. Some of the U.S.'s most valuable national parks, combined with regional and local historic points of interest, are included in the following listings. Museums are listed after the historic sites.

West Virginia

Harpers Ferry National Historical Park. On U.S. 340, in the scenic town of Harpers Ferry at confluence of the Potomac and Shenandoah Rivers, Box 65, Harpers Ferry, WV 25425 (304–535–6371). Historic old town in the eastern panhandle is site where abolitionist John Brown seized the U.S. Arsenal in 1859 in an attempt to free the slaves. Park is under continuing restoration; many historic buildings have been furnished in 19th-century period. Structures include blacksmith shop, provost office, dry-goods store, master armorer's house, tavern, post office, confectionery, pharmacy, Civil War museum, 1775–82 Harper House—oldest surviving structure in the park—and Stagecoach Inn, the park visitor center. The John Brown Museum houses a theater and exhibits about the raid. John Brown's Fort, a fire engine house used by Brown as a refuge, stands next to Arsenal Sq., with foundations of the Arsenal buildings that burned when Union troops evacuated the town at the beginning of the Civil War in 1861. During summer, conducted walks, demonstrations, and short talks by historians help visitors understand the complex. Park open daily except Jan. 1, Dec. 25. Admission, $2 individuals; $5 per car; group rates available.

Kentucky

Cumberland Gap National Historical Park. ½ mi. south of Middlesboro on U.S. 25 E, Box 1848, Middlesboro, KY 40965 (606–248–2817). Shared by Kentucky, Tennessee, and Virginia, 20,222-acre site is nation's largest historical park. A natural break in the Cumberland Mountain barrier, the gap, discovered by Dr. Thomas Walker in 1750, lies 800 ft. below surrounding peaks. Daniel Boone and a party of pioneers followed Walker's route in 1769 and spent two years exploring the wilderness, returning to mark the famed Wilderness Road through the gap. At Pinnacle Overlook, with awesome views of the Cumberland Valley and Mountains; the borders of the three states converge at Tri-State Peak. Visitor center–museum open daily, 8 A.M. to 6 P.M., mid-June–Labor Day; to 5 P.M., rest of year. Closed Dec. 25. Orientation programs in summer. Hiking trails, camping by permit only. Free. Campgrounds, $7 per night.

Virginia

Abram's Delight. 1340 S. Pleasant Valley Rd. Mailing address: Winchester-Frederick County Historical Society, Box 97, Winchester, VA 22601 (703–662–6519; 703–662–6550, historical society office). The oldest house in Winchester, 1754 limestone structure with 2½-ft.-thick walls was restored and furnished in period by the Winchester–Frederick County Historical Society, which administers it. It is a registered Virginia historic landmark. House was built by Isaac Hollingsworth; in 1800 a wing was added, and in 1830 the house was "modernized" in Federal style. A restored log cabin is on the grounds. Guided tours daily, Apr.–Oct., 9 A.M. to 5 P.M. Adults, $3.50; children 6–12, $1.75; combination, with Stonewall Jackson's Headquarters, George Washington's Office Museum, adults, $7.50; children 6–12, $4.

Belle Grove Plantation. 1 mi. south of Middletown on U.S. 11. Mailing address: Box 137, Middletown, VA 22645 (703–869–2028). Late 18th-century classical limestone mansion was built in 1794, during George Washington's presidency. Design reflects the influence of Thomas Jefferson. Surrounding farmland was site of the Battle of Cedar Creek, claiming the lives of over 6,000 American soldiers. Today, Belle Grove, a working farm in the heart of the Shenandoah Valley, is owned by the National Trust for Historic Preservation. Craftsfolk demonstrate during Farm

Craft Days, highlight of the summer season. A wheat harvest festival, traditional weaving and open-hearth cooking workshops, rail-splitting contest and old-fashioned Christmas celebration are also annual events. Open mid-Mar.–mid-Nov. Mon.–Sat., 10 A.M. to 4 P.M.; Sun., 1–5 P.M. Adults, $3; over 65, $2.50; 6–16, $2.

Booker T. Washington National Monument. Rte. 1, Box 195, Hardy, VA 24101 (703–721–2094). Site is birthplace and early home of famous black leader and educator Booker T. Washington. After stopping at visitor center, guests follow trail through a small 19th-century tobacco farm, the Burroughs Plantation. The 207-acre site is being restored as a working farm, with buildings, tools, crops, animals, and at times, people in dress of the period. Visitor center open and staffed 8:30 A.M. to 5 P.M., daily year-round, except Thanksgiving, Dec. 25, Jan. 1. Picnic facilities, nature trails. Adults $1; over 62 and under 17, free; families, $3.

John Fox, Jr., House. 117 Shawnee Ave., Box 1976, Big Stone Gap, VA 24219 (703–523–2747 or 703–523–2987). The brown-shingled two-story home of the author of the bestselling novels *Trail of the Lonesome Pine* and *Little Shepherd of Kingdom Come* is furnished as when the family lived here in the late 19th century. Open June through Labor Day (rest of year by appointment), Sun.–Sat., 2–5 P.M. Closed Mon. Adults, $1.50; students, 75 cents; under 5, free.

June Tolliver House (1890). Jerome and Clinton Sts., Big Stone Gap, VA 24219 (703–523–1235). Former residence of heroine of *The Trail of the Lonesome Pine* is furnished in period; regional handicrafts may be purchased. Restored 1890 one-room school and log cabin are on grounds. Guided tours July 1–Aug. 31, Tues.–Fri., 9:30 A.M. to 5 P.M.; Sat., 10 A.M. to 6 P.M.; Sun., 2–5 P.M.; Sept. 1–Dec. 19 and mid-May–June 30, Tues.–Sat., 10 A.M. to 5 P.M.; Sun., 2–6 P.M. Free.

New Market Battlefield Park. I-81, Exit 67, Box 1864, New Market, VA 22844 (703–740–3102). One of the Civil War's most remarkable battles took place here May 15, 1864. Some 247 young Virginia Military Institute cadets marched four days from their Lexington campus to join Confederate General Breckinridge's forces to help vanquish 6,000 troops of Union General Sigel. At the Hall of Valor Visitor Center, guests can view two award-winning films, extensive exhibits of Civil War relics, and living-history displays. On the grounds, the historic Bushong Farm, center of the battle's action, has been restored. Two rooms of the farmhouse are furnished in period, and various outbuildings recreate the original setting. Craftsfolk demonstrate during the July 4th Crafts Festival. Farm is starting point for a walking tour of the park.

Visitor center gift shop has excellent assortment of Civil War memorabilia. Park and Hall of Valor open daily, 9 A.M. to 5 P.M., except Dec. 25 and second Sun. after Labor Day, when reserved for VMI cadets. Park admission free. Hall of Valor: Adults, $4; senior citizens, $3.50; children 10–15, $1.50. Bushong House open June 15–Labor Day, 10 A.M. to 4:30 P.M. Free.

Stonewall Jackson's Headquarters. 415 N. Braddock St., Winchester, VA 22601 (703–667–3242; 703–662–6550, historical society office). The 1854 Hudson River Gothic Revival–style house, Nov. 1861–Mar. 1862 headquarters of General Thomas Jonathan "Stonewall" Jackson, is administered by the Winchester–Frederick County Historical Society. A registered Virginia and national historic landmark, it contains many of Jackson's possessions, original furniture, prints, Civil War items. Open Apr.–Oct., daily, 9 A.M. to 5 P.M. Adults, $3.50; children 6–12, $1.75; combination with George Washington's Office Museum, Abram's Delight, adults, $7.50; children 6–12, $4; children under 6 free.

Stonewall Jackson House. 8 E. Washington St., Lexington, VA 24450 (703–463–2552). Restored house is the only home the famed Confederate general ever owned. Here he lived a decade before the Civil War and taught at the Virginia Military Institute. Rooms include much of the Jacksons' own furniture as well as appropriate period pieces. Interpretive tours, slide-tape show, restored 19th-century garden. Gift shop has excellent assortment of small period items such as reproduction candlesticks, sconces. Open year-round, Mon.–Sat., 9 A.M. to 5 P.M.; Sun., 1–5 P.M.; inquire about extended summer hours. Closed Sun., Jan.–Feb., major holidays. Adults, $3.50; children 6–11, $2.

Woodrow Wilson Birthplace. 24 North Coalter St., Box 24, Staunton VA 24401 (703–885–0897). Wilson, 28th president of the United States, was born in this magnificent Greek Revival town house Dec. 28, 1856. The handsome house, built by the Presbyterians as a manse for their ministers, is restored to its appearance at the time the Rev. Joseph Ruggles Wilson and his family lived there. Trained guides escort visitors through 12 rooms containing many items that belonged to the Wilsons. Grounds include a Victorian town garden, reception center with exhibits, and documentary film about the Wilson era. Gift shop adjoins the garden. Open daily, 9 A.M.–6 P.M., Memorial Day weekend–Labor Day weekend; Mon.–Sat., 9 A.M.–5 P.M., Sun., 1–5 P.M., Memorial Day–Labor Day weekend. Closed major holidays. Adults, $3.50; over 62, $3; 6–12, $1; under 6 free.

North Carolina

Biltmore Estate House, Gardens, Winery. U.S. 25, 3 blocks north of I-40 exit 50 or 50 B, enter from Biltmore Village. For information: Marketing Dept., Biltmore Estate, 1 N Pack Sq., Asheville, NC 28801 (704–274–1776). 255-room French Renaissance mansion of the late George Washington Vanderbilt, patterned after great châteaux of the Loire Valley, is set on beautifully landscaped, wooded 12,000-acre tract. Rooms open to visitors display Old World treasures, antiques, tapestries, paintings. Included on self-guided tours are downstairs kitchens, servants' quarters, recreation rooms. Four-acre walled English garden has been called finest in America. Adjoining 20-acre Azalea Glen has many magnificent rare varieties, with peak bloom usually early May. Rose gardens bloom summer through fall. Visitors also welcome to adjacent Biltmore Estate Winery, in renovated dairy buildings. Tour includes audiovisual program, wine tastings. Champagnes and red, white, and rosé wines are produced, sold on premises. House and grounds open daily 9 A.M.–8 P.M., Memorial Day–Labor Day; daily 9 A.M.–5 P.M. rest of year. Closed Jan. 1, Thanksgiving, Dec. 25. Allow four hours to tour entire complex. Adults, $18.95; children 12–17, $14; under 12, free with adult.

Carl Sandburg Home National Historic Site. Little River Rd. west of U.S. 25, Flat Rock, NC 28731 (follow signs) (704–693–4178). Connemara Farm is restored home of the late poet-historian, who lived there the last 22 years of his life until his death in 1967. It is a wonderfully simple old house, where the visitor can sense the family's presence and lifestyle in every room. Sandburg's guitar is propped on a chair; upstairs in the study, his typewriter sits on an orange crate. Visitors may tour the grounds, where Mrs. Sandburg, sister of famed photographer Edward Steichen, was the farm manager. The heart of Connemara's operation was her registered, prize-winning Chikaming goat herd. Open daily, 9 A.M. to 5 P.M., except Jan. 1, Thanksgiving, Dec. 25. Admission, $1.

Cradle of Forestry in America National Historic Site. 14 mi. northwest of Brevard and 4 mi. southeast of Blue Ridge Pkwy., Milepost 412, in Pisgah National Forest. Information: CFA Interpretive Assoc., Box 8, Pisgah Forest, NC 28768 (704–877–3265). Unique complex is site where scientific forestry was first practiced and taught in America. In 1879 George Washington Vanderbilt purchased 100,000 acres of forested land around Mount Pisgah, adjoining his lavish Biltmore estate. To manage the property, he hired Gifford Pinchot, father of American forestry, who was succeeded by a German forester, Dr. Carl Schenck. In 1898 he launched the Biltmore Forest School, first in the nation. Re-created structures in midst of magnificent wilderness preserve include restored school, commissary, blacksmith shop, ranger's dwelling, student quarters, Schenck's office; portable sawmill, logging locomotive, other early equipment are displayed. Visitor center exhibits offer a walk-through history of the evolution of forestry; 18-min. film traces pioneering efforts of Pinchot and Schenck. Open May–Oct., daily, 10 A.M. to 6 P.M. Adults, $1; senior citizens and children 6–17, 50 cents; under 6 free.

Thomas Wolfe Memorial State Historic Site. 48 Spruce St., Box 7143, Asheville, NC 28807 (704–253–8304). As a youth, Thomas Wolfe, one of the eloquent voices of early-20th-century literature, lived in this rambling 29-room boardinghouse operated by his mother. It became Dixieland in his classic novel *Look Homeward, Angel.* House is preserved as a memorial to Wolfe's literary genius and is furnished with family possessions, portraits. Room of Wolfe's father, the book's stonecutter, remains much as he left it, with tools and examples of his trade. Open Apr.–Oct., Mon.–Sat., 9 A.M. to 5 P.M., Sun., 1–5 P.M.; Nov.–Mar., Tues.–Sat., 10 A.M. to 4 P.M., Sun., 1–4 P.M.; closed Thanksgiving, Dec. 24–25. Adults, $1; children through high school, 50 cents.

Zebulon B. Vance Birthplace State Historic Site. Rte. 1, Box 465, Weaverville, NC 28787 (704–645–6706). Reconstructed 1795 Appalachian Mountain birthplace of famed Civil War governor includes large post–Revolutionary War log house, various farm buildings. House in its sylvan setting includes pioneer furnishings, tools, utensils; it was a showplace of its day. Many historians consider Vance the most capable of all Confederate state governors; after bitter years of Reconstruction, he again served as governor, then as U.S. senator until his death. Visitor center; guided tours available. Open year-round, Mon.–Sat., 9 A.M. to 5 P.M.; Sun., 1–5 P.M. Apr.–Oct; Tues.–Sat., 10 A.M.–4 P.M., Sun., 1–4 P.M., rest of year. Closed Thanksgiving, Dec. 24–25. Free.

Tennessee

The Old Mill. Just east of U.S. 441, center of town, Pigeon Forge, TN 37863 (615–453–4628). One of Tennessee's finest landmarks, the Old Mill dates from 1830 and is still used to grind corn, wheat, rye, and buckwheat into flour. The mill also produces that southern staple, grits. Guided tours Mar.–Oct., Nov. if weather permits, daily except Sun., 8:30 A.M. to 6 P.M. Adults, $2; children 8–12, $1; under 8, free with adult. All its products are sold at the mill.

MUSEUMS

West Virginia

John Brown Wax Museum. High St., Harpers Ferry, WV 25425 (304–535–6342). Life-size animated wax figures in realistic settings trace the career of controversial abolitionist John Brown. Open Apr.–Dec., daily, 9 A.M. to 5 P.M.; Feb.–Mar., Sat.–Sun., 10 A.M. to 5 P.M. Closed Dec.–Jan., Thanksgiving. Adults, $2; 12–18, $1.50; 6–11, 75 cents.

North House Museum. 100 Church St., Lewisburg, WV 24901 (304–645–3398). Restored 19th-century house features historic objects from Greenbrier County, along with a collection of dolls. Open May–Oct., Tues.–Sat., 10 A.M.–4 P.M. Adults, $2; 6–12; $1.

Kentucky

Berea College Appalachian Museum, Box 2298, Jackson St., Berea, KY 40403 (606–986–9341, ext. 6078). Classic mountain craft exhibitions of works by finest artisans, demonstrations, visual programs, on-ground authentic buildings on campus of esteemed college devoted to education of young people from southern Appalachian region. Open Mon.–Sat., 9 A.M. to 6 P.M.; Sun., 1–6 P.M. Closed Easter, Thanksgiving, Dec. 25. Adults, $1.50; senior citizens, $1; children 6–12, 50 cents.

Virginia

George C. Marshall Museum and Library. West end of Parade Ground at Virginia Military Institute, Lexington, VA 24450 (703–463–7103). Exhibits include personal papers, possessions, General Marshall's 1953 Nobel Peace Prize, and electronic map and narration tracing events during World War II. Open Mar. 1–Oct. 31, Mon.–Sat., 9 A.M. to 5 P.M.; Sun., 2–5 P.M.; until 4 P.M. rest of year. Closed Jan. 1, Thanksgiving, Dec. 25. Free.

Lee Chapel. Campus of Washington and Lee University, Lexington, VA 24450 (703–463–8768). Chapel sanctuary on upper level contains dramatic Civil War painting and Edward Valentine's famed recumbent statue above General Lee's burial site. Lower-level museum displays Lee's office just as he left it on Sept. 30, 1870, and valuable collections of Lee, Custis, and Washington family objects. Open mid-Apr.–mid-Oct., Mon.–Sat., 9 A.M. to 5 P.M.; Sun., 2–5 P.M.; until 4 P.M. rest of year. Closed Jan. 1, Thanksgiving and day following, Dec. 24–26, Dec. 31. Free.

Natural Bridge Wax Museum. Natural Bridge, VA 24578 (703–291–2426). Historic regional characters and Indian and pioneer folklore displayed in lifelike scenes enhanced by special electronic, lighting, and sound techniques; also a vivid portrayal of the Last Supper, based on Da Vinci's famous painting. Open daily, May–Aug.,

9 A.M. to 9 P.M.; Mar.–Apr., Sept.–Nov., 10 A.M. to 6 P.M. Closed remainder of year. Adults, $5; senior citizens, $4.50; 6–15, $2.50; under 6, free with adult.

Roanoke Valley Museum of Fine Arts. Center in the Square, One Market Square, Roanoke, VA 24011 (703–342–5760). Exhibits include ancient Egyptian, Greek, Roman objects, 19th-century Japanese displays, historic glassware, vintage American paintings, works by contemporary regional artists, also traveling exhibits. Open year-round, Tues.–Sat., 10 A.M. to 5 P.M.; Fri., 10 A.M. to 8 P.M.; Sun., 1–5 P.M. Closed Mon., major holidays. Free.

Science Museum of Western Virginia and William B. Hopkins Planetarium. Center in the Square, One Market Sq., Roanoke, VA 24011 (703–343–7876). Designed for the entire family, the museum showcases hands-on experiences, computers, a walk-through coal mine, exhibits of fish, various reptiles; also laser shows, movies, explorations of the universe in the planetarium. Museum open Tues.–Sat., 10 A.M. to 5 P.M.; Fri., 10 A.M. to 8 P.M.; Sun., 1–5 P.M. Closed Mon., major holidays. Museum only, adults, $2; 6–12 and over 65, $1. Planetarium shows Tues.–Fri., 4 P.M., Sat.–Sun., 2 P.M. and 4 P.M., also special 7:30 P.M. show Thurs.–Sat. Combination museum and planetarium, adults, $3.50; 6–12 and over 60, $2.50.

Southwest Virginia Museum Historical State Park. W. First St. and Wood Ave., Big Stone Gap, VA 24219 (703–523–1322). Life among mountain people displayed in dioramas, miniature log houses, historical furnishings, folk arts and crafts. Open daily, Memorial Day–Labor Day, 9 A.M. to 5 P.M., after Labor Day–Dec. and Mar.–Memorial Day, Tues.–Sun., 9 A.M. to 5 P.M. Closed Jan.–Feb., Thanksgiving, Dec. 25, Mon. Labor Day–Dec. and Mar.–Memorial Day. Admission Memorial Day Weekend–Labor Day, adults $1.25; children 6–12, $1.

North Carolina

Asheville Art Museum. Asheville Civic Center, Haywood St., Asheville, NC 28801 (704–253–3227). Permanent exhibition showcases 20th-century American art; changing exhibits feature painting, sculpture, crafts, prints. Open Tues.–Fri., 10 A.M. to 5 P.M.; Sat.–Sun., 1–6 P.M. Closed Mon., major holidays. Free.

Colburn Mineral Museum. Asheville Civic Center, Haywood St., Asheville, NC 28801 (704–254–7162). Colorful displays of numerous minerals, gem stones found in the southern Appalachians. Open Tues.–Fri., 10 A.M. to 5 P.M., Sat.–Sun., 1–6 P.M. Closed Mon., major holidays. Free.

Folk Art Center. On Blue Ridge Pkwy., Milepost 382, about ½ mi. north of U.S. 70, just east of Asheville. Mailing address: Box 9545, Asheville, NC 28815 (704–298–7928). A major project of the prestigious Southern Highland Handicraft Guild, the center preserves and displays the finest native arts and crafts in the southern Appalachians; demonstrating craftspeople, films, music, dance, folklore; top-quality, handmade, one-of-a-kind items available at the craft shop. Open daily, 9 A.M. to 5 P.M. Closed Jan. 1, Thanksgiving, Dec. 25. Donations.

Museum of the Cherokee Indian. On U.S. 441 at Drama Rd., Cherokee. Mailing address: Box 770-A, Cherokee, NC 28719 (704–497–3481). Well-mounted exhibits trace 10,000 years of Cherokee history and culture, with emphasis on eastern band of the Cherokee Nation in North Carolina's mountains; audiovisual presentations, arts, crafts, special hands-on exhibits for children; beautiful stained-acrylic windows honor outstanding Cherokee men and women. Open mid-June–Aug., Mon.–Sat., 9 A.M. to 8 P.M.; Sun., 9 A.M. to 5:30 P.M.; Sept.–mid-June, daily, 9 A.M. to 4:30 P.M. Adults, $3.50; children 6–12, $1.75.

Tennessee

American Historical Wax Museum. 542 Pkwy., Gatlinburg, TN 37738 (615–436–4462). Over 100 life-size wax figures in authentic costumes and settings depict famous Americans. Open daily, Jun.–Aug., 8 A.M. to 11 P.M.; Apr.–May and Sept.–Oct., 9 A.M. to 10 P.M.; rest of year, 9 A.M. to 5 P.M. Closed Dec. 25. Adults, $4; children 6–12, $2.

Christus Gardens. 801 River Rd., Box 587, Gatlinburg, TN 37738–0587 (615–436–5155). A series of authentic biblical-era dioramas, lifelike wax figures, enhanced by special lighting, narration, music trace the ministry of Jesus; also fine collection of sculpture, early Christian-era coins. Open daily, Apr.–Oct., 8 A.M. to 9 P.M.; rest of year, 9 A.M. to 5 P.M. Adults, $5; children 7–11, $2.50.

Carbo's Police Museum. Pkwy. (U.S. 441), Pigeon Forge, TN 37863 (615–453–1358). Badges, uniforms, confiscated weapons and drugs, plus featured displays about *Walking Tall* Sheriff Buford Pusser, including 1974 Corvette in which he was killed. Open daily, May–Oct., 10 A.M. to 5 P.M., Fri., Sat., and Sun. only, Apr. Closed remainder of year. Adults, $4.50, children 4–10, $2.50; under 4 free.

MUSIC. Virginia. *Garth Newel Summer Music Festival,* early July–early Sept.; features chamber-music concerts by outstanding resident musicians and guest artists. Admission cost by request; write or phone Summer Music Festival, Box 427, Hot Springs, VA 24445 (703–839–5018). *Shenandoah Valley Music Festival,* 3 weekends late July, early Aug., early Sept., concerts of symphonic, choral, chamber, and big-band music. Admission costs by request; write or phone Music Festival, Box 12, Woodstock, VA 22664 (703–459–3396).

North Carolina. *Brevard Music Center,* late June through early Aug., offers a series of over 50 musical events including symphonic, chamber, and choral concerts, recitals, grand opera, musical comedies, appearances by nationally and internationally recognized guest artists. Performances Mon.–Sat., 8:15 P.M.; Sun., 3 P.M. Request full program, reservations information; write or phone Brevard Music Center, Box 592, Brevard, NC 28712 (704–884–2019).

STAGE. West Virginia. *Hatfields & McCoys and Honey in the Rock,* outdoor dramas presented mid-June–late Aug. at Cliffside Amphitheatre in Grandview State Park approximately 15 mi. east of Beckley; *Hatfields* depicts family feuding, *Honey in the Rock* traces founding of West Virginia; each summer, a third show, usually a popular contemporary musical, also plays in repertoire. Show time, 8:30 P.M.; picnic dinner served 7 to 7:45 P.M. Admission: adults, $10; senior citizens and 13–21, $8; 2–12, $5; dinner, $8. For schedule, reservations, write or phone Theatre West Virginia, Box 1205, Beckley, WV 25801 (304–253–8313 or June through Aug., 800–642–2766 in WV).

Kentucky

Jenny Wiley Theatre. Broadway musicals staged at amphitheater in Jenny Wiley State Resort Park near Prestonsburg, mid-June–late Aug. Inquire about evening show times and admissions. Write or phone Wiley Theatre, Box 22, Prestonsburg, KY 41653 (606–886–9274).

Virginia

Barter Theatre presents Broadway-caliber comedy and drama Apr. 1–mid-Oct., Tues.–Thurs. at 8 P.M.; Fri.–Sat. at 8:30 P.M.; Sun. at 7 P.M., matinees Wed.–Thurs. and Sat.–Sun. Playbills and admission costs upon request; write or phone Box 867, Abingdon, VA 24210 (703–628–2281; 800–572–2081 in-state; 800–368–3240 in neighboring states).

Trail of the Lonesome Pine, outdoor musical drama about forces of change in mountain life, presented July–late Aug. at **June Tolliver Playhouse,** Thurs.–Sat. at 8:30 P.M.; adults, $6; children, $4. Write or phone Tolliver Playhouse, Box 1976, Big Stone Gap, VA 24219 (703–523–1235).

Festival Theater at Rock Kiln Ruin, near Lexington, offers outdoor dramas, storytelling, performances of classic and folk music in unique setting of an old lime kiln, experimental theatrical presentations May–Sept. Inquire about various performances, time schedules and admissions. Write or phone Festival Theater at Rock Kiln Ruin, 27 W. Washington St., Box 663, Lexington, VA 24450 (703–463–7088). Picnickers welcome.

Henry Street Playhouse, summer theater with playbills of comedies, musicals, turn-of-the-century melodramas, mid-June–mid-Aug., inquire about programs, admissions, and curtain times. Write or phone the Henry Street Playhouse, Box 1087, Lexington, VA 24450 (703–463–8637).

Mill Mountain Theatre at Roanoke's Center-in-the-Square stages professional comedies, dramas, musicals, children's plays during regular season, Dec.–Aug., nightly except Mon.; matinees Sat.–Sun.; special programs, Sept.–Nov. Inquire about performances, times, and admissions. For playbills write or phone the Theatre at Center-in-the-Square, One Market Square, Roanoke, VA 24001 (703–342–5740).

The Long Way Home, outdoor historic drama based on true adventures of Mary Draper Ingles, who survived a 1755 massacre and walked 850 mi. to warn pioneers of Indian attacks, mid-June–late Aug. Thurs.–Sun., 8:30 P.M.; inquire about admission costs. Write or phone The Long Way Home, Box 711, Radford, VA 24141 (703–639–0679).

North Carolina

Flat Rock Playhouse, North Carolina's official state theater and home of the Vagabond Players, stages about nine Broadway- and London-caliber productions, late June through Aug., Tues.–Sat., 8:30 P.M.; Wed. and Sat., 2:30 P.M.; Inquire about playbills and ticket costs. Write or phone the Playhouse, Box 248, Flat Rock, NC 28731 (704–693–0731).

Horn in the West, outdoor drama about Daniel Boone, pioneers, Indians during Revolutionary War, presented late June–mid-Aug., nightly at 8:30 P.M. except Mon.; adults, $9; senior citizens, $7; children under 14, $4.50. Write or phone Box 295, Boone, NC 28607 (704–264–2120). *Unto These Hills,* vividly staged outdoor drama, traces history of the Cherokee Nation from arrival of De Soto to departure along the Trail of Tears, mid-June through late Aug., nightly except Sun., June–July, 8:30 P.M., Aug., 8:45 P.M.; tickets, $7.50–$9.50. Write or phone Director of Public Relations, Box 398, Cherokee, NC 28719 (704–497–2111).

Parkway Playhouse in Burnsville offers musical and dramatic productions by University of North Carolina Greensboro summer repertory theater company. Season is generally Wed.–Sat. evenings, July to late or mid-Aug., though it may vary. For latest playbills, schedules, admissions, please write or phone Director, Theatre Division, Communications and Theatre Department, University of North Carolina-Greensboro, Greensboro, NC 27412 (919–379–5562; or try Burnsville phone number 704–682–6151).

Tennessee

Archie's Playhouse features comedy and music by *Hee Haw* star Archie Campbell and his friends. For show times, admission costs write or phone Archie's Playhouse, Pkwy., Pigeon Forge, TN 37863 (615–428–3218).

The Smoky Mountain Passion Play, tracing the life of Jesus, is performed Mon., Wed., Fri., and Sat. evenings; *Damascus Road,* the story of Apostle Paul, is staged Tues., and Thurs. evenings, both at 8:30; early June–late Aug. in outdoor amphitheater at Townsend; adults, $10, reserved seats; senior citizens and 12–17, $7; under 12, $4. General admission $8, $5, and $3, respectively; write or phone Smoky Mountain Passion Play, Townsend, TN 37882 (615–448–2244, box office; 615–984–4111, year-round phone).

Sweet Fanny Adams Theatre offers original musical comedies, Gay 90s revue, old-fashioned sing-alongs, foot-stomping hilarity, mid-May–Oct., showtime 8 P.M. nightly except Sun. Inquire about admission costs. Write or phone the Sweet Fanny Adams Theatre, 461 Pkwy., Gatlinburg, TN 37738 (615–436–4038).

ACCOMMODATIONS—WEST VIRGINIA. In West Virginia, choices range from small, family owned establishments to chains and systems and elegant resorts, including one of the most renowned in the U.S. Price categories are based on double occupancy and except where noted do not include meals. In and near ski resorts, higher rates are effective during the season. These are average rates: *Deluxe,* $85–$190; *Expensive,* $50–$75; *Moderate,* $40–$50; *Inexpensive,* under $40.

Beckley. Glade Springs Resort. *Deluxe.* 5 mi. southeast of Beckley on WV 3, Box 185–D, Daniels, WV 25832 (304–763–2000). 4,200-acre resort-residential community has 2- and 3-bedroom rental villas. 18-hole championship golf course, clubhouse, tennis, swimming, horseback riding, health spa. Restaurant, coffee shop, lounge.

Holiday Inn. *Moderate–Expensive.* 1924 Harper Rd., Beckley, WV 25801 (304–255–1511, 800–465–4329). 105 rooms. Garden of Eden restaurant, Eden Lounge, heated pool, cable TV, in-room movies. Teens free.

Best Western Motor Lodge. *Inexpensive–Moderate.* 1939 Harper Rd., Beckley, WV 25801 (304–252–0671, 800–528–1234). 80 units. Cable TV, under 12 free. Near ski slopes, whitewater rafting. Western Steer Restaurant next door.

Comfort Inn. *Inexpensive–Moderate.* 1909 Harper Rd., Beckley, WV 25801 (304–255–2161, 800–228–5150). 130 units, some kitchenettes. waterbeds, nonsmoking rooms available. Game room, laundry, free HBO, free morning coffee and doughnuts. Restaurant near. Family, senior-citizen, government-military plans.

Berkeley Springs. Coolfont Resort, Conference Center, Health Spa. *Deluxe.* Cold Run Valley Rd., Berkeley Springs, WV 25411 (304–258–4500). 23 units in lodge, also cabins, chalets, camping. 1,200-acre wooded mountain, lake setting. Swimming, boating, fishing, full spa facilities, tennis, nature trails, riding stables. Cultural, educational events sponsored by Coolfont Foundation; classical, bluegrass concerts; dinner theater, dance workshops, art films, square dances. Restaurant, lounge with entertainment.

Cacapon Lodge. *Moderate.* Cacapon State Park, off U.S. 522, Berkeley Springs, WV 25411 (304–258–1022). 50 rooms in lodge, 30 cabins. Swimming, boating, fishing, championship golf course, tennis, lawn games, nature trails, horseback riding, picnicking. Restaurant, gift shop. Open May 1–Nov. 1.

Charles Town. Towne House Motor Lodge. *Inexpensive.* E. Washington St., 1 mi. east on U.S. 340, Charles Town, WV 25414 (304–725–8441). 107 rooms. Cable TV, pool; restaurant near. Close to famed Thoroughbred horse-racing track.

Harpers Ferry. Cliffside Inn and Conference Center. *Moderate–Expensive.* 1 mi. west on U.S. 340, Box 786, Harpers Ferry, WV 25425 (304–535–6302). 102 comfortable, spacious rooms with views of Shenandoah Valley or Blue Ridge Mountains. 12 conference rooms, complete audiovisual equipment—no charge. Special package plans. Outdoor pool, large enclosed indoor pool, tennis, excellent gift shop. Cable TV. Coffee shop, dining room (see Restaurants).

Hinton. Pipestem Resort State Park. *Moderate–Expensive.* 17 mi. southwest, then northwest, via WV 20, Pipestem, WV 25979 (304–466–1800). The 4,023-acre park has 113 lodge rooms, 25 deluxe kitchen cottages, tent-trailer sites. 18-hole championship golf course, tennis, indoor and outdoor pools, hiking, horseback riding, cross-country skiing, game courts and rooms, playgrounds. Social director, dancing. Fishing, boating, waterskiing at nearby Bluestone Public Fishing Area. Restaurant, snack bar.

Lewisburg. Budget Host Fort Savannah Inn. *Moderate.* 204 N. Jefferson St., Lewisburg, WV 24901 (304–645–3055, 800–835–7427, ext. 111). 67 rooms in two-story motor inn. Cable TV, pool, golf privileges. Senior-citizen plans, under 18 free in room with parents. Dining room adjoins (see Restaurants). Facilities for handicapped.

Martinsburg. The Woods Resort. *Expensive–Deluxe.* Mt. Lake Rd. off WV 9 E, Box 5, Hedgesville, WV 25427 (304–754–7977). 48 rooms, 24 have fireplace and whirlpool. TV in rooms only. Heated pool, indoor-outdoor lighted tennis, golf privileges, lawn games, nature trails, cross-country skiing, sports director; home of Eastern Fitness Institute. Grocery, package stores. Restaurant, lounge with entertainment. Modified American plan and European plan available.

Best Western Leisure Inn and Resort. *Inexpensive–Moderate.* Junction I-81, Exit 16 E and WV 9, Martinsburg, WV 25401 (304–263–8811, 800–528–1234).121 units. Cable TV, leisure atrium with dome-enclosed pool, wading pool, putting green, exercise room, shuffleboard, whirlpool, jogging track. Dining room, lounge, entertainment. Under 12 free, senior-citizen program. Facilities for handicapped.

Shepherdstown. Bavarian Inn and Lodge. *Expensive–Deluxe.* Rte. 1, Box 30, Shepherdstown, WV 25443 (304–876–2551). Four exquisite Bavarian Alpine chalets in scenic setting above Potomac River. 42 elegantly furnished rooms, all with balconies overlooking river; 18 have fireplaces, canopied beds; six suites have sunken whirlpool bathtubs. Swimming, sundeck, jogging; near golfing, tennis, horseback riding, white-water rafting. Owner-operated by Bavarian-born Erwin Asam and his British wife, Carol. Adjoins award-winning dining room (see Restaurants).

Snowshoe. Snowshoe Mountain Resort. *Inexpensive.* Snowshoe Mountain, Box 10, Snowshoe, WV 26209 (304–572–5252). On U.S. 219. 100 rooms in attractive mountain lodge. Dining room, lounge with entertainment. Skiing, tennis, horseback riding, fishing. Television. Limousine service.

White Sulphur Springs. The Greenbrier. *Super Deluxe.* Just off I-64, on U.S. 60, White Sulphur Springs, WV 24986 (800–624–6070; 304–536–1110, in WV). Renowned stately Georgian-style award-winning resort on 6,500 acres has 700 rooms, suites. Outdoor, indoor pools; 20 tennis courts; 3 golf courses; bowling, riding, skeet and trap shooting, carriage rides, platform tennis, mineral baths, par exercise courses, social director; theater, shops. Six-course gourmet dining in formal elegance of main dining room (see Restaurants); four other restaurants. Modified American plan. One of nation's grandest old resorts.

Best Western Old White Motel. *Inexpensive–Moderate.* 1 mi. east of downtown, on U.S. 60 at 865 E. Main St., Box 58, White Sulphur Springs, WV 24986 (304–536–2441, 800–528–1234). All 26 rooms at ground level with at-door parking. Pool, cable TV. Restaurant and lounge adjacent. Rates go up in summer.

Superior Colonial Court. *Inexpensive.* Box 188, 830 E. Main St., White Sulphur Springs, WV 24986 (304–536–2121). 18 units, all have TV. Pool, restaurant adjacent.

ACCOMMODATIONS—KENTUCKY. Lodging in Kentucky's southern Appalachians is most affordable. The state's resort-park lodges are notable for attractiveness and comfort. Accommodations are listed according to price category, based on double occupancy: *Moderate,* $40–$50; *Inexpensive,* under $40.

Berea. Boone Tavern Hotel. *Moderate.* Campus of Berea College, U.S. 25 and KY 21, 1½ mi. northeast of Junction I-75, Box 2345, Berea, KY 40404 (606–986–9358). Operated by Berea College, gracious Southern-style inn is staffed mainly by students. Most furniture in the 59 spacious, comfortable guest rooms and lobby was handmade by students, faculty, in college's woodworking program. Tavern gift shop off the lobby and nearby log-cabin salesroom offer fine student- and faculty-made ceramics, basketry, fabrics, woodcarvings, custom furniture, other distinctive handcrafts. Color TV, phones, combination or shower baths. Drugstore, barber and beauty shops. No-tipping policy. Dining room (see Restaurants).

Econo-Lodge. *Inexpensive.* I-75 and KY 21, Box 183, Berea, KY 40403-0183 (606–986–9323 or 800–446–6900). 48 units. No-smoking rooms, water beds available. Small pets allowed. Color TV, playground, restaurants near. Close to Berea College.

Corbin. Holiday Inn. *Moderate–Expensive.* Junction I-75 and U.S. 25 W, Corbin, KY 40701 (606–528–6301 or 800–465–4329). 156 rooms. Beautiful mountaintop setting. Color cable TV, showtime movies, tennis, indoor pool, playground. Handicapped facilities. Weekend package plans, teens free. Ivys Restaurant, gift shop.

DuPont Lodge. *Moderate.* In Cumberland Falls State Resort Park, 19 mi. southwest via U.S. 25 W, KY 90, Corbin, KY 40701 (606–528–4121 or 800–325–0063, reservations only). 52 rooms, suites in three-story lodge; also cottages with kitchens, refrigerators, fireplaces. Cable TV, movies, some radios. Pool, wading pool, tennis, social and recreational programs, playground, horseback riding, lawn games, hiking. Dining room (see Restaurants).

Days Inn. *Inexpensive.* Junction 25 W at I-75 S, Corbin Exit, Rte. 6, Box 10, Corbin, KY 40701 (606–528–8150 or 800–325–2525). 120 units. Gasoline service. Days Inn Travel Club discounts for senior citizens; under 12 eat free accompanied by adult guest. Free cribs; cable TV, pool, sundries shop.

Quality Inn. *Inexpensive.* Junction I-75 and U.S. 25 E, Corbin, KY 40701 (606–528–4802 or 800–228–5151). 119 rooms, some nonsmoking, king-size beds, some refrigerators available. Free HBO, acres of spacious grounds with 2 outdoor basketball courts, horseshoes, picnic tables. Dining room. Family, senior citizens, corporate, government-military rates; handicapped facilities.

Hazard. Buckhorn Lodge. *Moderate.* Buckhorn Lake State Resort Park, 25 mi. west on KY 28, Buckhorn, KY 41721 (606–398–7510 or 800–325–0058, reservations only). 36 handsomely furnished rooms in lodge overlooking lake. Cable TV, pool, wading pool, tennis, miniature golf, lawn games, recreation and games rooms, picnicking, beach. Restaurant. Closed mid–Dec. to Mar. 1.

La Citadelle Motor Inn. *Moderate.* 651 Skyline Dr., 2 mi. northeast off KY 15, Box 240, Hazard, KY 41701 (606–436–2126). 72 rooms, some suites, kitchen units; balconies offer fine views from mountaintop setting. Some oversize beds, cable TV, heated pool. Lounge, with entertainment, dancing Mon.–Sat. Weekend packages, under 18 free.

London. Best Western Harvest Inn. *Moderate.* I-75 Exit 41 at Daniel Boone Pkwy., Box 207, London, KY 40741 (606–864–2222 or 800–528–1234). 100 units. King-, queen-size beds. Cable TV, in-room movies, enclosed pools, therapy pools, Dining room. Senior-citizen program, under 12 free with parents.

Westgate Inn. *Inexpensive.* I-75 Exit 41, 254 West Daniel Boone Pkwy., London, KY 40741 (606–878–7330). At this family style motel, there are 44 well-maintained rooms, a heated pool, and a children's playground. A restaurant is nearby.

Middlesboro. Best Western Inn. *Inexpensive.* 1623 Cumberland Ave., Middlesboro, KY 40965 (606–248–5630 or 800–528–1234). Near Cumberland Gap National Historical Park. 100 units. Pool, cable TV; cafeteria open 6 A.M.–9 P.M. Senior-citizen program, under 12 free. Fishing, riding near.

Pineville. Evans Lodge. *Moderate–Expensive.* In Pine Mountain State Resort Park, 1 mi. south on U.S. 25 E, 6 mi. SW on KY 190, Box 610, Pineville, KY 40977 (606–337–3066 or 800–325–1712, reservations only). 50 units in lodge, housekeeping cabins with kitchens. Color cable TV, pool, wading pool; social, recreational, nature programs; playground; 9-hole and miniature golf; fishing, riding, waterskiing. Dining room. Rates drop Nov.–Apr.

Prestonsburg. May Lodge. *Moderate–Expensive.* In Jenny Wiley State Resort Park, 3 mi. south on U.S. 23-460, 4¼ mi. east on KY 3, Prestonsburg, KY 41653 (606–886–2711 or 800–325–0142, reservations only). 66 units in native-stone-and-timber lodge, family efficiencies. Restaurant. Pools (seasonal), rental boats, dock and ramp; fishing, waterskiing, playground, golf, miniature golf, horseback riding. Summer Broadway musicals in amphitheater.

Carriage House Motor Hotel. *Moderate.* 105 2nd St., off U.S. 23, at Paintsville, KY 41240 (606–789–4242). 150 rooms, suites, some with balconies. Cable TV, indoor-outdoor pools, whirlpool, sauna, valet service, coin laundry. Free airport transportation. Shops, putting green, miniature golf, games room, tennis and golf privileges. Rooms for handicapped.

ACCOMMODATIONS—VIRGINIA. Virginia's southern Appalachians offer lodgings for every budget. There are family-owned motor inns, city hotels, a good variety of chains and systems, and elegant mountain resorts, including one of the nation's most luxurious. Inquire about package plans and off-season rates, which may bring costs down considerably at even the famous resorts.

Accommodations are listed according to price category, based on double occupancy, and, except where noted, do not include meals: *Super Deluxe,* over $190; *Deluxe,* $85–$190; *Expensive,* $70–$85; *Moderate,* $45–$70; *Inexpensive,* $45 and under.

Abingdon. The Martha Washington Inn. *Expensive.* Box 1037, 150 W. Main St., Abingdon, VA 24210 (703–628–3161; toll free 800–533–1014 in VA). Classic inn, elegant accommodations in 150-year-old antiques-furnished Federalist mansion. 61 rooms, including five suites, and public areas impeccably renovated. No pets. Dining room. Golf, tennis packages.

Basye. Bryce Resort. *Deluxe.* 11 mi. west of I-81 Exit 69, on U.S. 263, Box 3, Basye, VA 22810 (703–856–2121). Year-round resort with snow and grass skiing, riding, golf, tennis, swimming, boating, picnic tables, grills. Ski lodge, boutique. Accommodations in fully equipped condominiums, town houses. Cable TV in condominiums. Fireplaces, private patios, balconies. Entertainment, dancing weekends. Modified American Plan.

Big Stone Gap. Trail Motel. *Inexpensive.* 509 Gilley Ave. E., Big Stone Gap, VA 24219 (703–523–1171). 40 rooms, some with balconies. Cable TV, senior-citizen program. Restaurant near.

Front Royal. Quality Inn Skyline Dr. *Moderate.* U.S. 522 Bypass, at northern end of Skyline Dr., Front Royal, VA 22630 (703–635–3161 or 800–228–5151). 107 rooms. Pool, family plan, golf and hiking nearby. Restaurant, lounge with live entertainment.

Cool Harbor Motel (formerly Cool Harbor Budget Host Inn). *Inexpensive–Moderate.* 1½ mi. north on U.S. 340, 15th and Shenandoah Ave., Front Royal, VA 22630 (703–635–2191). 41 units. Cable TV, pool, golf privileges. Senior-citizen program; handicapped facilities. Restaurant adjacent.

Hot Springs. The Homestead. *Super Deluxe.* Hot Springs, VA 24445 (703–839–5500 or 800–533–1747 in VA; 800–468–7747 out-of-state). 600 impeccably furnished rooms and suites in one of nation's premier luxury resorts nestled on 15,000 wooded acres of the Allegheny Mountains. Championship golf on three courses, tennis, outdoor swimming pools, fishing in mountain streams, horseback riding, skeet and trap shooting, nature trails. Complete health spa with health director, bowling lanes, indoor pools, movies, game room, social and children's programs. Winter skiing, ice skating. Quality shops, boutiques in main building, also Cottage Row. Modified American plan. Gourmet dining on Continental-American cuisine in the Grille or main dining room. Sumptuous buffet luncheon in the adjacent Casino. Dancing to Meyer Davis and Lester Lanin orchestras. Afternoon tea in the Great Hall, accompanied by string ensemble. Dress code. Special package, family plans.

Lexington. Best Western Keydet General. *Moderate.* U.S. 60 W, Exit 51W, I-81; Exit 12, I-64; Rte. 1, Box 10, Lexington, VA 24450 (703–463–2143 or 800–528–1234). 53 units in quiet hilltop setting with panoramic views of Shenandoah Valley. Satellite TV, king-size beds. Refrigerators, wet bars available. Handicapped facilities, senior-citizen discount. Dining room, lounge. Some units in *Inexpensive* category.

Holiday Inn Lexington. *Moderate.* U.S. 11 and I-64, Lexington, VA 24450 (703–463–7351 or 800–465–4329). 72 rooms, suites. Cable TV, movies, pool, golf privileges. Restaurant, lounge. Senior-citizen discount.

Econo-Lodge. *Inexpensive.* I-64 and U.S. 11, Box 1088, Lexington, VA 24450 (703–463–7371 or 800–446–6900). 48 units. Free color cable TV. Senior-citizen, family, frequent-traveler discounts. Restaurants near.

Luray. Luray Inn & Conference Center. *Moderate.* U.S. 211 Bypass, junction of U.S. 340 and U.S. 211 Bypass E., Box 389, Luray, VA 22835 (703–743–4521). Scenic views of the Blue Ridge Mountains are available from all 101 rooms of this inn, which also offers excellent meeting facilities as well as the Shenandoah Dining Room and Lounge and a pool. Pets are accepted at an extra charge. Restaurant near. Senior-citizen discount, handicapped facilities.

Big Meadows Lodge. *Inexpensive.* On the Skyline Dr., Milepost 51, 19 mi. south of U.S. 211, 15 mi. north of U.S. 33, Box 727, Luray, VA 22835 (703–999–2211 mid-May–Oct., 703–743–5108, 8 A.M.–5 P.M., Mon.–Fri., Nov.–mid-May). 93 units in attractive lodge, motel, cabins, with panoramic views of Shenandoah Valley at 3,640-ft. elevation. Also tent, trailer sites. Private patios, balconies, picnic tables, grills, playgrounds, horsedrawn-wagon rides. Dining room, box lunches; lounge, entertainment. Mountain-craft shop, newsstand, summer naturalist activities, playground, religious services. Closed Jan.–Feb. Some rooms in *Moderate* category.

Natural Bridge. Natural Bridge Hotel/Motor Inn/Motor Lodge. *Inexpensive.* Junction U.S. 11, VA 130, Exit 49, 50, Natural Bridge, VA 24578 (703–291–2121; 800–336–5727; 800–533–1410 in VA). At entrance to Natural Bridge. 144-room complex offers facilities to suit all budgets. All rooms have color cable TV, private bath; suites available. Pool, tennis, playground, game room; gift, candy shops. Jogging, hiking trails. Coin laundry, service station, post office on premises. Fully equipped convention center. Snack bar, cafeteria; Virginia specialties in elegant Colonial Dining Room; lounge. Package plans. Some rooms in *Moderate* category.

New Market. Quality Inn Shenandoah Valley. *Moderate.* I-81 Exit 67, Box 100, New Market, VA 22844 (703–740–3141, 800–228–5151). 100 rooms. Cable TV, free in-room movies, pool, sauna, playground, miniature golf, tennis, golf privileges at PGA course. Gift shop, dining room, lounge, coin laundry, handicapped facilities. Applecore Village Gift Shop.

Roanoke. Marriott Roanoke Airport. *Deluxe.* U.S. I-581, exit 3W, 2801 Hershberger Rd. NW, Roanoke, VA 24017 (703–563–9300 or 800–228–9290). Situated on beautifully landscaped grounds, this 320-room chain hotel has two pools, sauna, whirlpool, exercise room, and tennis courts. There is an elegant, intimate Remington's Restaurant as well as coffee shop. Transportation to the nearby airport is provided. Some rooms are in *Expensive* category.

Sheraton Airport Inn. *Expensive.* 2727 Ferndale Dr., I-581 Exit Hershberger Rd., Roanoke, VA 24017 (703–362–4500 or 800–325–3235). 148 rooms, extensive meeting facilities. Cable TV, indoor-outdoor pool, whirlpool, tennis, golf privileges. Airport limousine service, pets allowed. Dining room, 2 lounges; entertainment, dancing Mon.–Sat. nights. Some *Deluxe* rooms.

Holiday Inn Civic Center. *Moderate.* Williamson Rd. at Orange Ave., Jct. U.S. 460, 220 and I-581, Roanoke, VA 24012 (703–342–8961 or 800–465–4329). 153 units. HBO, golf privileges, indoor tennis, pool, wading pool. Oversize beds, senior-citizen rates, under 18 free. Ziggie's Restaurant and Lounge. Near Lancelot Sports Complex. Some rooms in *Expensive* category.

Peaks of Otter Lodge. *Moderate.* On the Blue Ridge Pkwy., milepost 86, 29 mi. northeast of Roanoke, via I-81 to VA 43 east to Parkway, then about 5 miles north. Box 489, Bedford, VA 24523 (703–586–1081 or 800–542–5927, VA). 62 rooms in elegantly furnished contemporary lakeside lodge nestled beneath mountain peaks. Spacious rooms have two double beds, fireplace, private balcony or terrace. Lobby TV, gift shop. Excellent dining room has varied menu: seafood, Virginia ham, other specialties. Friday seafood buffet. Nature trails, fishing.

Best Western Coachman Inn. *Inexpensive–Moderate.* Exit 44, I-81, at U.S. 220 N., Box 7329, Roanoke, VA 24019 (703–992–1234 or 800–528–1234). 98 units in quiet hilltop setting with fine views. Cable TV, movies, pool, wading pool. Dining room, 24-hour airport courtesy car. Fly-drive, senior-citizen programs, under 12 free.

Econo-Travel Civic Center. *Inexpensive.* 308 Orange Ave. N.W., Roanoke, VA 24016 (703–343–2413 or 800–446–6900). 48 units. Color cable TV, senior-citizen discounts, under 12 free. Picnic tables; restaurants near. Free morning coffee and sweet rolls.

Staunton. Holiday Inn. *Moderate.* Exit I-81 and Woodrow Wilson Pkwy., Exit 58, Box 2526, Staunton, VA 24401 (703–248–5111 or 800–465–4329). 100 units. Cable TV, Showtime movies. Pool, whirlpool, wading pool; racquetball, golf, tennis privileges at nearby health club. Coin laundry. Senior-citizen discount, teens free. Handicapped facilities. Lilly's Restaurant; Adjacent Lilly's is the Lounge which has live entertainment.

Ingleside Red Carpet Inn. *Inexpensive.* Rte. 11, 2½ mi. north on U.S. 11, ¾ mi. west of I-81, Exit 57, Box 1018, Staunton, VA 24401 (703–248–1201). 200 rooms in four-story resort motel on 200 landscaped acres. Elevators, large meeting capacity. Pools, wading pool, playground, gift shop. Lighted tennis, 18-hole golf course. Private patios, balconies overlook course. Valet service, coffee shop, dining room, lounge with nightly entertainment. Senior-citizen rates, under 12 free.

Winchester. Holiday Inn Winchester-East. *Moderate.* I-81 and U.S. 50 E.; north, Exit 80 on I-81; south, Exit 80E on I-81, 1050 Millwood Pike, Winchester,

VA 22601 (703–667–3300 or 800–465–4329). 175 rooms, some with refrigerators, oversize beds. Cable TV, pool, valet service, free airport-bus transportation. Tennis, golf privileges. Senior-citizen rates, under 18 free. Jimmy's Restaurant, Sir George's Lounge with live entertainment.

Quality Inn Boxwood South. *Moderate.* Exit 79 off I-81, 2649 Valley Ave., Winchester, VA 22601 (703–662–2521 or 800–228–5151). 73 rooms, some with refrigerators. Free HBO, in-room coffee. Pool, sauna; handicapped facilities. Senior, family, corporate, and government-military plans. Duff's Restaurant, Gaslight Lounge adjoin.

Best Western Lee–Jackson Motor Inn. *Inexpensive.* U.S. 50, 522, and 17 at I-81 Exit 80, 711 Millwood Ave., Winchester, VA 22601 (703–662–4154 or 800–528–1234). 138 rooms. Cable TV, pool, valet service, free airport-bus transportation. Picnic tables, tennis, golf privileges. Senior-citizen program, under 12 free; pets allowed. Adjacent to 80-store shopping mall. Dining room, lounge, entertainment. Some rooms in *Moderate* category.

Wintergreen. Wintergreen Resort. *Deluxe–Super Deluxe.* VA 664, 4½ mi. west of junction VA 151, Wintergreen, VA 22958 (800–325–2200; 804–325–2200, VA). 350 units in fully equipped efficiencies, apartments, houses, most with fireplaces. 10,600-acre wooded mountain resort–residential community has $3.5-million conference center. 18-hole championship golf course, 18 tennis courts, 3 pools, 10 ski slopes, 16-acre lake, equestrian center, outdoor center, playgrounds, hiking trails. 10-acre Shamakin Springs Nature Preserve is treasure trove of botanical rarities in natural setting. Luxurious Wintergarden Spa has indoor pool, whirlpool, hot tubs, saunas, exercise room. Modified American plan. Dining in Rodes Farm Inn (family-style meals), the Garden Terrace, the Copper Mine (see Restaurants). Three lounges, entertainment; many package plans.

ACCOMMODATIONS—NORTH CAROLINA. North Carolina's mountains offer landmark hotels, luxurious resorts, family motels, and a good choice of chain and system motor inns. Peak seasons vary widely, depending on location. In ski areas, costs decline after the season. In popular summer vacation areas, rates may go down after the peak of fall foliage until the beginning of the spring blooming season. Some facilities close in winter.

Accommodations are listed according to price category, based on double occupancy, and, except where noted, do not include meals: *Deluxe,* $105–$160; *Expensive,* $76–$96; *Moderate,* $50–$75; *Inexpensive,* under $50.

Asheville. The Grove Park Inn and Country Club. *Deluxe.* 290 Macon Ave., Asheville, NC 28804 (704–252–2711; 800–438–5800; 800–222–9793, NC). 342 rooms, including 22 parlors, in famed, beautifully restored 1913 stone resort lodge and adjoining new contemporary wing. 18-hole championship golf course, 8 indoor-outdoor tennis courts, indoor-outdoor pools, children's activity program, carriage and pony rides. 6 restaurants, 4 lounges, newsstand, gift shops, dry cleaning, laundry. One of the South's grandest resorts.

Comfort Inn. *Expensive.* 800 Fairview Rd., Asheville, NC 28803 (704–298–9141 or 800–228–5150). 176 units, including 12 kitchen suites with whirlpools. Color cable TV, movies, radio. Pool, sauna, lighted tennis courts. Cafeteria next door. Handicapped facilities. Family, senior-citizen, government-military plans.

Ramada Inn West. *Expensive.* Exit 44 of I-40, 435 Smokey Park Hwy., Box 6164, Asheville, NC 28816 (704–665–2161 or 800–272–6232). This contemporary inn has a welcoming atrium lobby that adjoins a pool. There are 156 rooms, some suites, a dining room, and a coffee shop. Fitness facilities include a sauna, whirlpool, and jogging track. Some rooms are in *Moderate* category.

Great Smokies Hilton Resort and Conference Center. *Moderate–Expensive.* One Hilton Dr., Asheville, NC 28806 (704–254–3211 or 800–445–8667). 280 units, including some suites, in spacious landscaped setting. Color cable TV, pools, wading pool, tennis, golf, airport transportation. Package plans. Coffee shop, dining room, lounge, entertainment.

Forest Manor Motor Lodge. *Moderate.* U.S. 25, 1 mi. south of junction of I-40, at exit 50, 865 Hendersonville Rd., Asheville, NC 28803 (704–274–3531). Nestled amid attractively landscaped grounds, this small motor lodge has 21 rooms, three with kitchens. Some rooms available for nonsmokers. Heated pool and complimentary morning coffee. Restaurants are nearby.

Sheraton Inn. *Moderate.* 22 Woodfin St., Box 7286, Asheville, NC 28801 (704–253–1851 or 800–325–3535). 150 units, some with refrigerators. Color cable TV, movies, heated pool. Dining room, lounge.

Ramada Inn Central. *Inexpensive–Moderate.* 180 Tunnel Rd. at I-240, Asheville, NC 28805 (704–254–7451 or 800–272–6232). 120 rooms, some suites. Pool, cable TV, free in-room movies. Senior-citizen discount. Golf, tennis packages, airport transportation. Dining room, lounge.

Best Western of Asheville. *Inexpensive.* Exit 53-B off I-40 to 240 W to Exit 7, U.S. 70 E ¼ mi., 501 Tunnel Rd., Asheville, NC 28805 (704–298–5562 or 800–528–1234). 90 units. Cable TV, pool, restaurant near.

Banner Elk. Holiday Inn Banner Elk–Beech Mountain. *Moderate–Expensive.* NC 184, Rte. 1, Box 1478, Banner Elk, NC 28604 (704–898–4571 or 800–465–4329). Near Beech Mountain, Sugar Mountain Ski Resorts. 102 rooms. Color cable TV, in-room movies, pool, wading pool, coin laundry. Dining room. Rates drop after winter ski season.

Blowing Rock. The Green Park Inn. *Deluxe.* 2 mi. southeast on U.S. 321, Box 7, Blowing Rock, NC 28605 (704–295–3141). 89 rooms, suites, many with poster beds, private balconies, in lavishly refurbished stately white-columned 1882 luxury hotel. Lawn games, tennis, golf privileges at adjacent Blowing Rock Country Club. Gourmet dining in elegant multilevel Allen's. Also 19-piece Big Band Orchestra, intimate Green Park Dinner Theatre with entertainment by resident repertory company. Open all year; modified American and bed-and-breakfast plans.

Hound Ears Lodge and Club. *Deluxe.* 7 mi. west, ½ mi. off NC 105, Box 188, Blowing Rock, NC 28605 (704–963–4321). 27 rooms in luxurious contemporary lodge in mountainside residential-resort community; also clubhouse suites, all with private balconies, panoramic views. All-weather tennis, heated pool, golf. Strict evening dining room dress code, 15% service charge. Modified American plan. "Dry" county—no alcohol service; guests may bring beverages for table service, locker storage, at no charge.

Cliff Dwellers Inn. *Moderate.* 1 mi. north junction U.S. 321 Bypass, U.S. 221, Box 366, Blowing Rock, NC 28605 (704–295–3121). 18 units, all with balconies, in scenic mountaintop setting with panoramic views. Color cable TV, radios, some refrigerators. Open Apr. 15–Oct. 31.

Azalea Garden Inn. *Inexpensive.* 3 blocks north on U.S. 221, 321 Bus., N. Main St., Box 165, Blowing Rock, NC 28605 (704–295–3272). 17 units on beautifully landscaped setting, 1 log cabin with fireplace, kitchen. Color cable TV, near restaurants.

Blowing Rock Inn. *Inexpensive.* 2 blocks north on U.S. 221, 321 Bus., N. Main St., Box 265, Blowing Rock, NC 28605 (704–295–7921). 24 units, including 4 efficiencies. Color cable TV, radios, heated pool, morning coffee. Restaurants near.

Boone. Holiday Inn. *Moderate.* U.S. 321 S, 710 Blowing Rock Rd., Boone, NC 28607 (704–264–2451 or 800–465–4329). 138 rooms. Color cable TV, movies, coin laundry, pool, restaurant. Near golf course, ski areas, trout fishing. Nonsmoking rooms available.

High Country Inn. *Inexpensive–Moderate.* NC 105 S, Box 1339, Boone, NC 28607 (704–264–1000; 800–334–5605; 800–438–0407, NC). 120 tastefully furnished rooms, suites, with fireplaces, efficiency apartments, in handsome stone-and-timbered contemporary lodge. Color TV, free movie channel. Sauna, hot tub, indoor-outdoor heated pool, weight-exercise room. Under 16 free. American-Continental cuisine.

Cardinal Motel. *Inexpensive.* 816 S. U.S. 321 (Blowing Rock Rd.), 2 mi. south on U.S. 221-321 Boone, NC 28607 (704–264–3630). 43 rooms in well-maintained facility convenient to *Horn in the West* outdoor drama. Cable TV, heated pool. Restaurant. Rates drop after summer, ski seasons.

Brevard. Imperial Motor Lodge. *Inexpensive–Moderate.* ¾ mi. north on U.S. 64-276, at 750 N. Caldwell St., Box 586, Brevard, NC 28712 (704–884–2887). 94

units, some refrigerators. Cable TV, free morning coffee, pool, lawn games, picnic tables; under 15 free. Restaurant near.

Cherokee. Best Western Great Smokies Inn. *Moderate.* 2½ mi. north, 1 block off U.S. 441 N, Box 1309, Cherokee, NC 28719 (704–497–2020 or 800–528–1234). 112 units in lodge-style inn with native landscaping. Color cable TV, movies, heated pool, playground. Handicapped facilities. Senior-citizen discount, under 12 free. Dining room, lounge with entertainment. Rates drop Nov., Apr. 1–May 31; closed Dec.–Mar.

Comfort Inn. *Inexpensive–Moderate.* 1 mi. west on U.S. 19 S, Box 132, Cherokee, NC 28719 (704–497–2411 or 800–228–5150). 54 rooms. Cable TV, in-room movies, pool, playground. Restaurant near. Handicapped facilities. Open mid–Apr.–Oct. 31. Family, senior-citizen, government-military plans.

Holiday Inn. *Inexpensive–Moderate.* U.S. 19, Box 648, Cherokee, NC 28719 (704–497–9181 or 800–465–4329). 154 units. Color cable TV, movies, coin laundry. Indoor, outdoor pools, whirlpool, sauna, playground, game room. Indian craft shop, trout fishing, tennis. Senior-citizen discount. Dining room.

Fontana Village. Fontana Village Resort. *Moderate–Expensive.* Fontana Village, NC 28733 (800–438–8080; 704–498–2211, NC). Varied accommodations adjoining Fontana Dam: 225 basic family cottages; 33-room rustic lodge; luxurious 94-room inn with pool, saunas, restaurant, lounge, gift shop, meeting facilities. Also 400-seat cafeteria in Village Center. Swimming, fishing, horseback riding, square dancing, boating, waterskiing, par-3 miniature golf, playground, archery, basketball, lawn games, renowned square-dance center. Crafts workshops, movies, coin laundry, post office, grocery store. Limited access for handicapped. Service stations, shops, game room, campground. Dry county; will serve guests from their own supply in the Inn. Rate structure based on Inn occupancy. Cottages closed Dec.–Mar.

Hendersonville. Holiday Inn. *Moderate.* U.S. 64 and I-26, Exit 18–A, at 201 Sugarloaf Rd., Hendersonville, NC 28739 (704–692–7231 or 800–465–4329). 150 rooms, some with refrigerators, oversize beds. Cable TV, HBO. Holidome with heated pool, sauna, whirlpool, hot tub; table tennis, playground. Dining room, lounge.

Ramada Inn. *Moderate.* I-26 and U.S. 64 E, Box 669, Hendersonville, NC 28973 (704–692–0521 or 800–272–6232). 99 rooms. Cable TV, free movies, in-room coffee. Gift shop, game room, restaurant, lounge with live entertainment. Free airport transportation.

Little Switzerland. The Chalet Lodge. *Moderate.* Milepost 334 on Blue Ridge Pkwy., Box 399, Little Switzerland, NC 28749 (704–926–0201). 63 rooms, suites in Alpine-style lodge nestled on scenic mountain ridge. Lobby TV, heated pool, putting green, tennis. Weekly, monthly rates also. Under 12 free. Dining room, coffee shop. Open May 1–Oct. 31.

Waynesville. Holiday Inn of Maggie Valley-Waynesville. *Moderate.* 6 mi. northwest, via U.S. 1, 19, and 276, Rte. 2, Waynesville, NC 28786 (704–926–0201 or 800–465–4329). 102 rooms, suites. Cable TV, free HBO. Heated pool, playground, game room, golf, ski packages; teens free. Nonsmoking rooms, free breakfast. Steakhouse Restaurant.

ACCOMMODATIONS—TENNESSEE. Tennessee's mountain-resort towns of Gatlinburg and Pigeon Forge are among the South's most popular family vacation spots. Rate structure is based on peak season; costs often drop sharply outside the popular summer and fall-foliage seasons. Many lodgings listed here would be rated in a lower category then. Some properties close off season.

Accommodations are listed according to price category, based on double occupancy: *Expensive,* $55–$80; *Moderate,* $45–$55; *Inexpensive,* $45 and under.

Cumberland Gap. Holiday Inn. *Moderate.* 1 mi. south on U.S. 25 E, ½ mi. south of junction U.S. 558, Box 37, Cumberland Gap, TN 37724 (615–869–3631 or 800–465–4329). 152 rooms, suites. Cable TV, coin laundry, heated pool. Dining room, lounge. Near Cumberland Gap National Historical Park. Airport transportation.

Gatlinburg. Best Western Zoder's Inn. *Expensive.* On U.S. 441, 402 Pkwy., Box 708, Gatlinburg, TN 37738-0708 (615–436–5681 or 800–528–1234). 87 rooms, suites, in idyllic 5-acre setting over stream. Many have fireplaces, refrigerators. Color cable TV, movies, coin laundry, heated pool, fishing.

Park Vista Hotel (formerly Sheraton Gatlinburg). *Expensive.* ¾ mi. east off U.S. 441 via Airport Rd., Box 30, Gatlinburg, TN 37738 (615–436–9211; 800–421–7275; 800–526–1235, TN). Lavish 315-unit circular tower hotel offers mountain views from private balconies. Color cable TV, heated indoor pool, wading pool, whirlpools. Dining room, lounge, nightclub, entertainment.

Best Western Fabulous Chalet Inn. *Moderate–Expensive.* Sunset Dr., Box 11, Gatlinburg, TN 37738-0427 (615–436–5151 or 800–528–1234). Scenic mountainside setting overlooking city. 38 rooms in lodge, town houses; all have refrigerators, in-room coffee, color cable TV, in-room movies, electronic security system; suites have whirlpool, fireplace. Complimentary Continental breakfast in season.

Best Western Twin Islands Motel. *Moderate–Expensive.* U.S. 441 downtown, Box 648, Gatlinburg, TN 37738 (615–436–5121 or 800–528–1234). 107 units include some suites, kitchens, fireplaces, hydro spas, waterbeds, balconies over stream. Heated pool, playground.

Comfort Inn. *Moderate–Expensive* (formerly Olde English Inn). 309 Oakley Dr., off Ski Mountain Rd., Box 138, Gatlinburg, TN 37738 (615–436–7813 or 800–228–5150). 54 rooms, suites with kitchenettes, fireplaces. Color cable TV, heated pool. Near restaurants, ski slopes. Senior-citizen, family, corporate, government-military plans.

Cox's Gateway Motel. *Moderate–Expensive.* U.S. 441, 1100 Parkway, Gatlinburg, TN 37738 (615–436–5656). 48 rooms, cottages, some fireplaces, refrigerators, kitchens. Color cable TV, heated pool, wading pool; caters to families.

Holiday Inn Gatlinburg Resort Complex. *Moderate–Expensive.* 333 Airport Rd., Gatlinburg, TN 37738 (615–436–9201 or 800–465–4329). 402 rooms, suites. Color cable TV, in-room movies. Holidome, indoor pool, exercise rooms, sauna, whirlpool, putting green, games room. Airport transportation. Louie's Restaurant, Sade & Dora's Lounge; Downunder Club has entertainment in season.

Ramada Resort Four Seasons and Conference Center. *Moderate–Expensive.* 756 Pkwy., Gatlinburg, TN 37738 (615–436–7881 or 800–272–6232). 148 rooms, suites. 2 to 5 stories, elevators. Color cable TV, oversize beds, balconies, some fireplaces, refrigerators, waterbeds. Indoor, outdoor pools, aquatic center, sauna, playground, whirlpools. Handicapped facilities. Pets accepted. Four Seasons Restaurant and Lounge, name entertainment June–Oct.

Brookside Resort. *Moderate.* U.S. 321 N, Rte. 4, Box 47, Gatlinburg, TN 37738 (615–436–5611; 800–251–9597; 800–362–9605, TN). 243 guest rooms, cottages, apartments, some with kitchens, fireplaces, steam baths, whirlpools, balconies; all have refrigerators. Color cable TV, movies, coin laundry, 2 heated pools, wading pools, playground, fishing. Quiet location 4 blocks from town center. Some rooms in *Expensive* category.

Rivermont Motor Inn. *Moderate.* U.S. 441, 293 Pkwy., Gatlinburg, TN 37738 (615–436–5047; 800–624–2929; 800–634–2929, TN). 69 rooms, suites, overlooking stream; private balconies. Color cable TV, in-room movies, free coffee bar, heated pool. Closed Dec.–Mar. Some rooms in *Expensive* category.

Creekstone Motel. *Inexpensive.* On U.S. 321, 1 mi. east of Jct. U.S. 441, Rte. 4, Box 14, Gatlinburg, TN 37738 (615–436–4628). 25 units in quiet wooded setting on mountain stream. Family owned. Color cable TV, heated pool, wading pool. Pets accepted.

Ogle's Vacation Motel. *Inexpensive.* 2 blocks east on U.S. 321 N, Pkwy. E. Rd., Rte. 2, Box 38, Gatlinburg, TN 37738 (615–436–5856). 47 large, comfortable rooms. Cable TV, in-room movies, pool. Popular with families. Some rooms in *Moderate* category.

Pigeon Forge. Best Western Plaza Inn. *Moderate–Expensive.* U.S. 441, Box 926, Pigeon Forge, TN 37863 (615–453–5538 or 800–528–1234). 140 rooms and town houses; some fireplaces, whirlpools, refrigerators, water beds. Cable TV, sauna, game room.

Colonial House Motel. *Moderate–Expensive.* 224 S. Pkwy., Pigeon Forge, TN 37863 (615–453–0717). 63 rooms with whirlpools, fireplaces, private balconies overlooking river, some kitchenettes. Cable TV, movies. Handicapped facilities. Heated pool, fishing. Restaurant on grounds.

Grand Hotel & Convention Center. *Moderate–Expensive.* U.S. 441, 500 N. Pkwy., Pigeon Forge, TN 37863 (615–453–1000). 425 designer-decorated rooms, efficiencies, suites, some with whirlpools, saunas, fireplaces, waterbeds. Satellite TV, movies; handicapped facilities. Heated pool, fishing; airport transportation. Senior-citizen and AAA-member discounts. Restaurant.

Holiday Inn. *Moderate–Expensive.* 413 N. Pkwy., Box 1383, Pigeon Forge, TN 37863 (615–428–2700 or 800–465–4329). 208 rooms, suites. Cable TV, movies. Holidome with indoor pool, whirlpool, sauna, exercise rooms. Game room, shops. Louie's Restaurant.

Rodeway Inn. *Moderate–Expensive.* U.S. 441, Box 1230, Pigeon Forge, TN 37863 (615–453–4707). 76 rooms, suites; some oversize, water beds. Cable TV, movies; handicapped equipped. Senior-citizen discounts.

Tennessee Mountain Lodge. *Moderate–Expensive.* Box 105, 228 S. Pkwy., Pigeon Forge, TN 37863 (615–453–4784, TN). 50 rooms, suites, all with oversize beds, refrigerators; some water beds. Color cable TV, heated pool, wading pool, fishing, elevator.

Bilmar Motor Inn. *Moderate.* 411 S. Pkwy., Box 118, Pigeon Forge, TN 37863 (615–453–5593). 52 rooms; king, queen, and water beds. Cable TV, heated pool, wading pool, playground, picnic tables, grills. Closed Nov.–mid Mar.

Family Inns of America West. *Moderate.* U.S. 441 at Pine Mountain Rd., Box 10, Pigeon Forge, TN 37863 (615–453–4905; 800–251–9752; 800–332–9909, TN). 95 rooms, suites; few kitchenettes, some waterbeds. Color cable TV, heated pool. Closed Dec.–Apr.

McAfee Motor Inn. *Moderate.* 407 S. Pkwy., Box 119, Pigeon Forge, TN 37863 (615–453–3490 or 800–548–4133). 103 units, some kitchenettes. In-town location. Cable TV, in-room movies, pool, playground, picnic area. Closed Jan.–Feb.

Mountain Breeze Motel. *Inexpensive.* ½ mi. north on U.S. 441, Pigeon Forge, TN 37863 (615–453–2659). 46 units, some kitchenettes. In-room coffee; color cable TV; pool, playground, lawn games.

RESTAURANTS—WEST VIRGINIA. Dining out in West Virginia offers an opportunity to sample country ham, grits, and other southern delicacies, as well as steaks and seafood. In the elegant dining rooms of luxurious resorts, continental and American cuisines are showcased. Casual good taste is usually the dress code, except in top resorts, where a strict dress code is observed. Some resort dining rooms are open to nonguests, space permitting, and reservations are mandatory.

Restaurants are listed according to price of a complete dinner; drinks, tax, and tip are not included. Desserts may also be extra. *Expensive,* $18–$30; *Moderate,* $7–$17.95. In order to serve liquor, dining rooms in West Virginia must have a club license.

Beckley. Glade Springs Golf Clubhouse Inn. *Moderate.* Glade Springs Resort, 5 mi. southeast on WV 3 (304–763–2000). Specialties are seafood, veal marsala. Reservations preferred for dinner. Attractive contemporary decor. Private club lounge. Open 7 A.M.–3 P.M., 6–10 P.M., daily. AE, DC, MC, V.

Berkeley Springs. Country Inn. *Moderate.* 207 S. Washington St. (304–258–2210). Two dining rooms, West Virginia Room and the Country Garden, are separated by glass wall. Latter, open seasonally, has translucent ceiling, outdoor garden setting. Music, dancing on weekends. Specialties include country ham, smothered chicken, seafoods. Wayfarer's Lounge adjoins. Open 7–11 A.M.; 11:45 A.M.–2 P.M.; 5–9 P.M.; to 10 P.M., Fri.–Sat. AE, DC, MC, V.

Treetop House. *Moderate.* In Coolfont's Woodland House Lodge. (304–258–4500). Lavish salad bar, sumptuous buffets, in idyllic setting high amidst the trees. Emphasis on low-calorie health-conscious menus. Squirrel's Nest Lounge adjoins. Open 8–10:30 A.M., 11:30 A.M.–2 P.M., 5:30–9 P.M., Mon.–Sat.; 8 A.M., –8 P.M. Sun. AE, MC, V.

Elkins. 1863 Tavern. *Expensive.* In Elkins Motor Lodge, Harrison Ave. (304–636–1400). Seafood, veal, steak specialties in colonial atmosphere, paintings of historic persons. Children's menu. Open 7 A.M.–10:30 A.M., 5:30 P.M.–10 P.M., Sun. 7–11 A.M., 4 P.M.–8 P.M. Closed Dec. 25. Some entrées in *Moderate* category. AE, CB, DC, MC, V.

Harpers Ferry. Cliffside Inn and Conference Center, main dining room. *Moderate.* 1 mi. west on U.S. 340 (304–535–6302). Attractive, locally popular dining room specializes in steaks, seafood, some Continental dishes. Weekend buffets. Cocktails. Live late-evening entertainment. Open 7 A.M.–9:30 P.M. AE, DC, MC, V. Reservations recommended when conventions are in session.

Hinton. Riverside Inn. *Expensive.* 14 mi. east via WV 3, at Pence Springs, WV (304–445–7469). Restored 1900s log structure has old-English country-tavern atmosphere. Specializes in colonial meat pie, fruit-stuffed duckling, roast goose with glazed grapes. Children's plates. Open 5–10 P.M., Tues.–Sat., Apr.–Oct.; Sat.–Sun., Mar., Nov.–Dec. Closed Jan.–Feb. CB, DC, MC, V. Some entrées in *Moderate* category.

Lewisburg. General Lewis Dining Room. *Moderate.* General Lewis Inn, 301 E. Washington St. (304–645–2600). Specialties include country ham, grilled pork chops, fried chicken, steaks. Open year-round, daily, 7:30–9:30 A.M.; noon–2 P.M.; 5–9 P.M. AE, MC, V.

The Woods. *Moderate.* Fort Savannah Inn, 204 N. Jefferson St. (304–645–3055). In the Old Stone House, restored 1700s structure now part of the inn. Colonial décor. Veal Oscar, quail baked in wine, steaks are specialties. Children's plates, senior-citizen discounts. Sun. buffet; lounge. Antiques, stone fireplace add to colonial aura. Evening piano entertainment. Open 6 A.M.–10 P.M. AE, DC, MC, V.

Shepherdstown. Bavarian Inn. *Moderate.* Adjoins Bavarian Inn and Lodge, Rte. 1 (304–876–2551). Fine German-American cuisine in elegantly decorated graystone mansion. Specialties include smoked loin of pork, roll roast of beef, veal cutlet with mushrooms and sour cream, tournedos Rossini, rack of lamb, Black Forest cake, apple strudel. Children's menu. Reservations requested on weekends. Open year-round 7:30–11 A.M.; 11:30 A.M.–2:30 P.M.; 5–10 P.M., Mon.–Sat.; 7:30–11 A.M., noon to 9 P.M., Sun. AE, DC, MC, V. Some entrées in *Expensive* category.

White Sulphur Springs. The Greenbrier Main Dining Room. *Expensive.* The Greenbrier Resort (304–536–1110). Open to nonguests, space permitting, by reservation only. Magnificent formal setting filled with antiques, original art, floral arrangements. Evening chamber music, strict dress code, formal service. Continental-American specialties include chicken Dijon, baked lobster with shrimp stuffing. *Prix fixe* menus, 15% service charge added. Open 7:30–9:45 A.M.; 7–9 P.M. AE, MC, V.

RESTAURANTS—KENTUCKY. Kentucky's regional specialties include such luscious delicacies as country ham, corn dodgers, Sally Lunn bread, and chess pie. In the mountains, costs remain surprisingly moderate. Restaurants are listed according to price of a complete dinner; drinks, tax, and tip are not included. Desserts are usually extra. *Moderate,* $10–$17; *Inexpensive,* $3.95–$9.95.

Berea. Boone Tavern Dining Room. *Moderate.* In Boone Tavern Hotel, Berea College campus (606–986–9358). Noted for its regional cuisine, featuring such specialties as spoon bread, plantation ham, blackberry dumplings, Jefferson Davis pie. Friendly service by Berea College students. No tipping. Dress code Sun., all evenings. Children's menu. Reservations preferred. Open 7–9 A.M., 11:30 A.M.–2 P.M. daily. Dinner seatings at 6, 6:45, 7:30 P.M., Sun.–Thurs.; 5:30–8 P.M. Fri.–Sat., with seatings every half hour. AE, DC, MC, V.

Corbin. DuPont Lodge Dining Room. *Inexpensive.* In Cumberland Falls State Resort Park, 19 mi. southwest of Corbin via U.S. 25, KY 90 (606–528–4121). Regional specialties, dinner buffets in peak season. Attractively decorated, overlooks river. Children's menu. Entertainment. Open 7–10:30 A.M., 11:30 A.M.–2:30 P.M., 5:30–9 P.M. AE, DC, MC, V.

Hazard. Skyline Dining Room. *Moderate.* La Citadelle Motor Inn, 651 Skyline Dr. (606–436–2126). Regional specialties include country ham, fresh-cut steaks, prime rib. Background music, outdoor dining in season. Entertainment, dancing, Tues.–Sat. Open 6:30 A.M.–1:30 P.M., 6:30–10:15 P.M.; winter, 6–9:30 P.M. Sun. brunch 11:30 A.M.–1:30 P.M. Closed Dec. 25. DC, MC, V. Some entrées in *Inexpensive* category.

Woodland Dining Room. *Moderate.* In Woodland Motel, 524 E. Main St. (606–439–4531). Chicken specialties, home-baked bread. Open 6 A.M.–midnight; Sun. 6 A.M.–4 P.M. Closed Dec. 25. MC, V. Some entrées in *Inexpensive* category.

Prestonsburg. Carriage House Restaurant. *Moderate.* In Carriage House Inn, 105 2nd St., Paintsville, KY (606–789–4242). Regional specialties, also seafood, steaks. Salad bar, own baking, children's plates. Open 6 A.M.–10 P.M.; Sun., 8 A.M.–8 P.M. Locally popular. AE, DC, MC, V. Some entrées in *Inexpensive* category.

May Lodge Dining Room. *Inexpensive.* In Jenny Wiley State Resort Park, 3 mi. south on U.S. 23,460, 4¼ mi. east on KY 3 (606–886–2711). Fine Kentucky specialties in attractive setting. Children's menu; luncheon buffet Mon.–Fri. Open 7 A.M.–9 P.M.; to 8 P.M., winter, Sun. Closed Dec. 23–29. AE, DC, MC, V.

RESTAURANTS—VIRGINIA. Dining out in Virginia can be as varied as the state's geography. In the mountains, southern-style cookery is showcased by such specialties as luscious Virginia cured ham, spoon bread, and peanut soup. Elegant resorts offer both Continental and American cuisines. Some resort dining rooms are open to nonguests, space permitting, and here reservations are a must. A strict dress code is observed in top resort and hotel dining rooms.

Restaurants are listed according to price of a complete dinner; drinks, tax, and tip are not included. Desserts may also be extra. *Expensive,* $10–$23; *Moderate,* $4.95–$10.

Abingdon. First Lady's Table. *Moderate.* Martha Washington Inn, 150 W. Main St. (703–628–3161). Attractive colonial setting. Specialties include crab and shrimp Norfolk, steak Diane. Cocktails, background music. Open 7–10 A.M., 11:30 A.M.–2 P.M., 5–10 P.M.; Sun., 5–9 P.M. AE, CB, DC, MC, V. Some entrées in *Expensive* category.

Hardware Company Restaurant. *Moderate.* 260 W. Main St. (703–628–1111). There is a turn-of-the-century ambience in this converted 1895 hardware store, which offers beef and seafood dishes as well as nightly specials. A children's menu is available. Open 11 A.M.–10 P.M. Mon.–Thurs., to 10:30 Fri. and Sat.; closed Sun. and major holidays. Cocktail lounge. AE, MC, V.

Front Royal. Constant Spring Dining Room. *Moderate.* Constant Spring Inn, intersection of U.S. 55 and 340, 413 S. Royal Ave. (703–635–7010). Hearty family-style dining; specialties include Virginia baked ham, baked chicken, fresh vegetables, home-baked desserts. Children's plates. Open 7:30–11 A.M., 5–8:30 P.M.; Sat., 11:30 A.M.–2:30 P.M.; Sun., 8–11 A.M., 12:30–3:30 P.M., brunch to 11 A.M. Closed Wed., holidays, 2 weeks in Jan. No credit cards.

My Father's Moustache. *Moderate.* 108 S. Royal Ave. (703–635–3496). In the Victorian Manor House, decorated with 1920s memorabilia. Fresh Maine lobsters, prime beef, deli sandwiches. Cocktails, beer, wine. Open 11:30 A.M.–3 P.M., 5:30–9 P.M.; Sun., noon–8 P.M. Closed Mon., Tues., and holidays and, from Dec. to Feb., Sun. AE, MC, V. Some entrées in *Expensive* category.

Lexington. Southern Inn. *Moderate.* 37 S. Main St. (703–463–3612). Lexington's family restaurant for more than half a century. Specializes in traditional southern-style cuisine, sandwiches, Greek and Italian dishes. Beer and wine. Open 7 A.M.–9:30 P.M., Tues.–Sun. Closed Mon. AE, MC, V.

Virginia House. *Moderate.* 722 S. Main St. (703–463–3643). Southern-style cooking—Virginia ham, steaks, seafood, excellent choice of vegetables, homemade desserts. Beer, wine. Open 9 A.M.–2 P.M., 5–8:30 P.M., daily. No credit cards.

Middletown. Wilkinson Tavern (formerly Wayside Inn Restaurant). *Expensive.* In 1797 Wayside Inn, crossroads of U.S. 11 and I-81, Exit 77, 7783 Main St. (703–

869–1797). Friendly service by colonial-costumed staff in 7 uniquely decorated period rooms. Specialties include Virginia pan-fried chicken, ham, spoon bread, peanut soup, carrot cake. Children's menu. Coachyard Lounge reminiscent of an English pub. Reservations suggested, locally popular. Open 7 A.M.–3 P.M., 5:30–9 P.M.; Sat., to 9:30 P.M.; Sun., 7–11 A.M., noon–8:30 P.M. AE, MC, V.

New Market. Johnny Appleseed Restaurant and Lounge. *Moderate.* Quality Inn, I-81 Exit 67 (703–740–3141). Economical family dining featuring full menu, salad bar, homemade breads, desserts such as apple fritters. Open daily, 7 A.M.–10 P.M. Closes at 9 P.M. in winter. AE, DC, MC, V.

Roanoke. Fesquet's Restaurant. *Expensive.* Main entrance to Crossroads Mall NW, ½ mi. east off U.S. I-581, Hershberger Rd., E exit (703–362–8803). Despite the name, both French and American cuisines are presented at this place, which has an elegant and intimate basement setting. Children's menu is available. Open 6–10 P.M. Mon.–Sat., closed Sun. and major holidays. Reservations suggested. AE, DC, MC, V.

The 4 Parrots. *Expensive.* Patrick Henry Hotel, 617 S. Jefferson St. (703–345–8811). Sun. brunch, daily breakfast and luncheon buffets; all you can eat prime-rib dinner, Mon.–Sat. Reservations required Fri.–Sat. P.M. Piano entertainment, Fri.–Sat. Open 7 A.M.–2 P.M., 5–9 P.M., Mon.–Fri.; 8 A.M.–10 P.M., Sat.; 8 A.M.–2 P.M., Sun. brunch. AE, DC, MC, V. Some entrées in *Moderate* category.

La Maison du Gourmet. *Expensive.* 5732 Airport Rd. (703–366–2444). Continental, American cuisine in beautifully restored historic mansion. Dress code; reservations suggested. Sat.-night piano entertainment, lounge, valet parking. Open 11 A.M.–11 P.M.; Sat., 5 P.M.–midnight. Closed Sun., major holidays. AE, DC, MC, V. Some entrées in *Moderate* category.

Ye Olde English Inn. *Expensive.* 6 mi. south on U.S. 221, 6063 Bent. Mt. Rd. (703–774–2670). Attractive Tudor atmosphere. Prime rib, steaks are specialties. Background music. Reservations necessary Fri.–Sat. nights. Open 11 A.M.–2 P.M., 5–9 P.M., Mon.–Thurs.; 6–10 P.M., Fri.–Sun. Closed holidays. Strict dress code, supper club atmosphere, adults only. MC, V. Some entrées in *Moderate* category.

Staunton. Lilly's. *Expensive.* Holiday Inn, I-81 at Exit 58 (703–248–5111). Dinner specialties include Polynesian dishes, steaks, seafood. Lounge adjacent. Open 7 A.M.–10 P.M. AE, D, DC, MC, V. Some entrées in *Moderate* category.

White Star Mills Restaurant. *Expensive.* 1 Mill St. (703–885–3409). This restored old flour mill in the center of the Historic District offers gracious dining on Continental cuisine and Cajun specialties. There is a raw bar. Dress is casual, but reservations are suggested. D only, 5–10 P.M. Closed Sun., major holidays. AE, DC, MC, V.

Edelweiss Restaurant. *Moderate.* Greenville Exit 55 S (340 N. and U.S. 11), next to Hessian House Motel (703–337–1203). Attractive log-cabin setting. Home cooked German foods include rindsrouladen, sauerbraten. Children's plates. Open 5–9 P.M., Tues.–Sat., 11:30 A.M.–3 P.M. Sun. Closed Mon., major holidays. Reservations requested. Chef-owned. MC, V.

Winchester. Duff's Restaurant. *Moderate.* 2655 Valley Ave., adjoining Quality Inn Boxwood South (703–667–8311). Full menu, Kentucky fried chicken a specialty. Entertainment in Gaslight Lounge. Open 7 A.M.–10 P.M. week nights, to 11 P.M. weekends. AC, CB, DC, MC, V. Some entrées in *Expensive* category.

The Elms. *Moderate.* 2011 Valley Ave., in the Elms Motel (703–662–2567). Family-style dining, daily L, D specials; extensive salad bar; homemade pies, rolls. Pennsylvania Dutch décor, menu. Open 7 A.M.–9 P.M., Tues.–Fri.; from 8 A.M. Sat.; 8 A.M.–3 P.M., Sun. Closed Mon., holidays. MC, V. Some entrées in *Expensive* category.

Wintergreen. The Copper Mine. *Expensive.* Wintergreen Resort, VA 664, 4½ mi. west of junction VA 151 (804–325–2200). Fine Continental, American specialties in a warm, relaxing atmosphere. Live entertainment in adjoining lounge. Open daily 7:30–10 A.M., noon to 2:30 P.M., 6–10 P.M. Lavish Sun. brunch. Dress code. Reservations requested; essential for nonguests, space-available basis. AE, MC, V.

Wytheville. The Manor House. *Moderate–Expensive.* 410 W. Main St. (703–228–6419). Ceiling fans whir in this cozy, colonial-style dining room specializing in Continental cuisine with American touches. Desserts and rolls are homemade. There's a children's menu along with early bird dinner specials. Open 11:30 A.M.–2 P.M. Mon.–Fri. and 5–9 P.M. Mon.–Sat. Closed Sun. MC, V.

RESTAURANTS—NORTH CAROLINA. Country ham appears on many North Carolina mountain menus. Each state of the southern Appalachians seems to have its own version, equally delicious. Trout, fresh from mountain streams, is another delicacy, as is barbecue; the state takes fierce pride in its expertise in this delicacy. Casual good taste is the usual dress code; in the top resorts and hotels, men should expect to wear coat and tie for dinner. Some of North Carolina's country inns are notable for not-to-be-believed tables groaning under a load of meats and fresh vegetables, served family style.

Restaurants are listed according to price of a complete dinner; drinks, tax, and tip are not included. Desserts are usually extra. *Moderate,* $10–$20; *Inexpensive,* under $10.

Asheville. Dynasty Restaurant. *Moderate.* Grove Park Inn and Country Club, 290 Macon Ave. (704–252–2711). Elegant dining room specializing in Oriental cuisine. Splendid view of city and mountains. Open 6:30 P.M.–10:30 P.M. Closed Mon. Reservations advised. AE, DC, MC, V.

Magnolia's Raw Bar & Grille. *Moderate.* 26 Walnut St. (704–251–5211). Seafood with Southern and Cajun-Creole accents as well as International specialties are offered at this place, where you dine either on a New Orleans style patio or in the elegant Magnolia Room. There's also a raw bar. Live entertainment is provided Mar.–Sept. Open 11 A.M.–midnight, to 1 A.M. Fri.; 3 P.M.–1 A.M. Sat. Reservations suggested. AE, DC, MC, V.

Bill Stanley's Barbecue and Bluegrass. *Inexpensive.* 20 S. Spruce St. (704–253–4871). Outstanding hickory-cooked barbecue, mountain smoked chicken, ribs, plus a great evening of bluegrass music Tues.–Sat. evenings. Area cloggers often entertain. Fun for entire family. Open 11 A.M.–1 A.M., Tues.–Thurs.; to 2 A.M. Fri.; 6 P.M.–2 A.M., Sat. Closed Sun.–Mon. Winter hours vary. AE, MC, V.

Banner Elk. Heidi's Swiss House. *Moderate.* 1½ mi. southeast on NC 184, Banner Elk. (704–898–5020). Superb specialties include Swiss fondue, sauerbraten. Swiss chalet decor, artifacts. Swiss owners-chefs. Open 6 P.M.–10 P.M. Sun.–Sat. Inquire locally about off-season hours. Reservations requested.

Blowing Rock. The Farmhouse. *Moderate.* S. Main St., overlooking Johns River Gorge, 1 mi. south on U.S. 321 Bus. (704–295–7361). A North Carolina institution. Popular Victorian-style restaurant features singing waiters, waitresses, musicians. Steak, seafood, prime rib; children's plates. Home baking. Al fresco dining at lunch. Open 11:30 A.M.–3 P.M., 5–11 P.M.; Sun., noon–11 P.M. Closed Labor Day–May. Some entrées in *Inexpensive* category.

Blowing Rock Café. *Inexpensive.* 1 block west of U.S. 321, Sunset Dr. (704–295–9474). Cozy, locally popular restaurant features mountain trout, homemade soups, desserts. Open 7–11 A.M., 11:30 A.M.–2 P.M., 5–8 P.M.; June 1–Nov. 15, 7 A.M.–9 P.M., 7–11 A.M. Sun. Closed holidays. AE, MC, V.

Boone. Dan'l Boone Inn. *Inexpensive.* 105 Hardin St., Jct. U.S. 221, 321, 421 (704–264–8657). Down-home atmosphere, family-style dining on country ham, fried chicken, and all the fixin's; children's plates. Open 11 A.M.–9 P.M.; from 4 P.M. Nov.–May; Sat.–Sun., from 7 A.M. Closed Christmas holidays. Regionally popular—lines form early.

Burnsville. Nu-Wray Inn Dining Room. *Inexpensive.* The Nu-Wray Inn, U.S. 19 E on town square (704–682–2329). Lavish family-style meals—turkey, country ham, fried chicken, fresh vegetables, hot breads, homemade desserts. Treasure trove of Americana, antiques, family owned since 1870. Sittings: 8:30 A.M., 6 P.M., 8:30 P.M.; Sun., 1 P.M., 2 P.M. Closed Jan.–Apr. Reservations essential for nonguests. No credit cards; personal checks, traveler's checks accepted.

Hendersonville. Woodfield Inn Dining Room. *Moderate.* The Woodfield Inn, 3 mi. south on U.S. 25, Flat Rock, NC (704–693–6016). Luscious regional specialties, home-grown fresh vegetables, own baking in exquisite ambience of antique-filled historic inn. Open 11:30 A.M.–2 P.M., 6–9:30 P.M.; 11:30 A.M.–2 P.M., Sun. brunch; children half price. Reservations essential for nonguests AE, MC, V. Some entrées in *Inexpensive* category.

Waynesville. Heath Lodge Restaurant. *Inexpensive.* Heath Lodge Motel, 900 Dolan Rd. (704–456–3333). Lazy-Susan tables laden with luscious southern food. Family-style dining in log-beamed room as fireplace flickers. Children half price. Buffet breakfast. Open 8–9 A.M.; dinner sittings 6 P.M., 7:30 P.M.; Sun., 12:30 P.M., 1:45 P.M. Closed Nov.–May. Dinner reservations for nonguests, 6 P.M. only.

RESTAURANTS—TENNESSEE. Freshly caught mountain trout and country ham with red-eye gravy showcase many Tennessee mountain menus. Home-baked biscuits, blueberry pie, and fruit cobbler are often luscious specialties. Even in the popular resorts, prices remain surprisingly modest. Restaurants are listed according to their price category. Not included are drinks, tax, and tip or, usually, desserts. *Moderate,* $10–$20; *Inexpensive,* under $10.

Gatlinburg. The Burning Bush. *Moderate.* On the parkway, entrance to Great Smoky Mountains National Park (615–436–4669). Evenings, dine by candlelight and soft music; specialties include filet of beef Rossini, brace of quail, mountain trout. Also bountiful breakfasts, hearty lunches. Children's plates. Open 7 A.M.–2 P.M., 5–10 P.M.; Jan.–Mar., 8 A.M.–2 P.M., 5–9 P.M. Reservations in season. AE, DC, MC, V.

The Open Hearth. *Moderate.* 1138 Pkwy. (615–436–5648). Candlelight dining in delightful atmosphere. Aged charcoal-broiled beef, rainbow trout, complete dinner menu, children's plates. Open 5–9:30 P.M., Mon.–Thurs.; to 11 P.M., Fri.–Sat.; noon–8 P.M., Sun. Closed Dec. 25. AE, DC, MC, V.

Pioneer Inn Restaurant. *Moderate.* 373 Pkwy., in town (615–436–7592). Charming atmosphere in restored rustic log cabin beside the river. Game pie, country pork chops, fried chicken, homemade soups with golden corn sticks. Open 7 A.M.–2 P.M., 5–10 P.M.; from 8 A.M. off season. Closed Dec., Wed.–Thurs. Nov. 1–Apr. 1. AE, DC, MC, V. Some entrées in *Inexpensive* category.

Ogle's Restaurant. *Inexpensive.* On the Pkwy. downtown, next to Best Western Twin Islands and Crossroads motor inns (615–436–4157). Lavish choice of meats, vegetables, 75 salad varieties. Children's plates to age 9. Dining patio over stream. Open 7 A.M.–9:30 P.M., Mon.–Fri.; 11:30 A.M.–9:30 P.M., Sat.; 11:30 A.M.–4P.M., Sun. Major credit cards.

Smoky Mountain Trout House Restaurant. *Inexpensive.* 410 Pkwy., in Best Western Zoder's Inn (615–436–5416). Fresh mountain trout prepared eight ways; also prime rib, country ham, luscious desserts. Children's plates. Open 5–10 P.M., Apr. 1–Nov. 30. AE, DC, MC, V. Some entrées in *Moderate* category.

The Teague Mill and Creekside Restaurant. *Inexpensive.* 13 mi. east on U.S. 321N. (615–436–8869). Located beside a stream where guests catch their own trout. Children's menu. Open May 15–Dec 1, 7 A.M.–8:30 P.M., to 11 P.M., Fri.–Sun. MC, V.

Pigeon Forge. Green Valley Restaurant. *Moderate.* In Green Valley Motel, 804 S. Pkwy. (615–453–9091). Country ham, fresh eggs, sausage, homemade biscuits for breakfast; family-style lunches. Dinner specialties include rainbow trout, seafood, lobster tails, homemade cobblers, pies. Open 7 A.M.–10 P.M.; closed Dec. 24–25. Senior-citizen discount. AE, MC, V.

Apple Tree Inn Restaurant. *Inexpensive.* Pkwy. and Frances Rd. (615–453–4961). B, L, D, in cozy, informal dining room with apple tree growing through ceiling. Soup, salad, breakfast and fruit bars; luscious spoon bread; complete menus. Open 6:30 A.M.–10 P.M. Closed Jan–mid-Feb. AE, MC, V.

Trotters. *Inexpensive.* 405 S. Pkwy. (615–453–3347). Family style dining, special menu for children; luscious down-home specialties include hot biscuits, ham 'n' gravy, homemade breads, desserts. Open 7 A.M.–9:30 P.M., Apr. 1–Oct. 31. AE, MC, V.

LIQUOR LAWS. West Virginia. Liquor is sold by the bottle in state stores. Some grocery stores sell beer and wine. The state has a uniform law allowing clubs, night spots, and restaurants to purchase liquor licenses entitling guests to consume alcoholic beverages. Check locally for availability and closing times. Legal age: 21.

Kentucky. Liquor by the bottle is sold in retail and drugstores, as well as by the drink on a local-option basis, with wide variations among different localities. Check locally for closing times. Legal age: 21.

Virginia. Liquor and wine by the bottle are sold in state liquor stores. Mixed drinks are served in licensed establishments on a local-option basis. Cocktails available in most larger cities and popular vacation areas. Closing times vary; check locally. Legal age: 21 for spirits, wine.

North Carolina. Where authorized by local option, liquor by the bottle is sold in state ABC (Alcohol Board of Control) stores. Wine and beer may be purchased in grocery stores. Mixed drinks in licensed establishments are generally available in larger cities and some resort communities such as Asheville. Certain restaurants in dry areas may sell set-ups to patrons who wish to bring their own bottles. Bars and lounges are usually open until 1 A.M. Legal age: 21.

THE SOUTHEAST COAST

by
EDGAR and PATRICIA CHEATHAM

The Southeast Coast spans North Carolina, South Carolina, and Georgia. It's quite distinct from the rest of the Atlantic seaboard. Here visitors discover historic communities seemingly lost in time, lively contemporary resorts, glowing gardens, wildlife refuges, and hideaway islands. Even the larger cities are only medium-sized by national standards. Along with many smaller communities they evoke a serene atmosphere, slow-paced and comfortable.

North Carolina

About four centuries ago the foundations of British America were established, albeit tenuously, when Sir Walter Raleigh, in 1587, sent a small contingent of men, women, and children to Roanoke Island in hopes of founding a permanent settlement. But faced with the threat of a massive invasion by Spain, the Mother Country could not spare even a single ship to supply the colony. Following England's defeat of the Spanish Armada, a ship was finally dispatched to Roanoke Island in 1590, only to discover that the colonists had vanished. Today the fate of "The Lost Colony" still remains mysteriously shrouded in history's shadows.

A short distance east of Roanoke Island, the Dare Coast resort towns of Kitty Hawk, Kill Devil Hills, and Nags Head border a wide, sandy beach. Southward the famed Outer Banks, narrow sandy barrier islands, extend toward the ocean, separating the Atlantic from Currituck, Albemarle, and Pamlico Sounds.

Cape Hatteras National Seashore occupies vast portions of Bodie, Hatteras, and Ocracoke Islands. Small fishing and vacation villages, mainly along the protected "sound side" of the islands, are surrounded by, but are not included in, the National Seashore. Prior to construction of bridges and causeways, these communities were long isolated from the mainland. Their inhabitants, who call themselves "Bankers," still retain distinctive folkways and speech patterns—"toime and toide wait for no one."

Some of the villages have distinct characteristics. Avon on Hatteras Island is an old-time fishing community where frame houses overlook a small harbor, delightful for late afternoon visits when trawlers return with their catches. Buxton lies near towering Cape Hatteras Lighthouse and the Buxton Woods, where nature trails wend through clusters of yaupon (a variety of holly) and shore and swamp vegetation. The village of Ocracoke is situated on the southern tip of the island by the same name. It is a quiet, isolated place (reachable only by auto ferries, private boats, or air) where weathered wooden houses line sandy streets, an 1823 lighthouse stands in a photogenic grove of cedars, and a Coast Guard Station–Visitor Center faces lovely Silver Lake harbor, a protected enclave for mariners.

Across Ocracoke Inlet, Cape Lookout National Seashore encompasses the southward-lying uninhabited Outer Banks, now being preserved as wilderness refuges. Portsmouth, at the northern tip of the National Seashore, once flourished as a shipping community, but today is a ghost town with an abandoned Coast Guard Station, church, burial ground, post office and a few houses. The towering Cape Lookout Lighthouse, with distinctive black and white diamond markings, stands watch at the southern edge of the Seashore.

Some of North Carolina's loveliest historic towns are located along the broad sounds and river estuaries that indent the coastland. The little village of Bath, earliest incorporated settlement in the state, and a favorite haunt of Blackbeard the Pirate, has been carefully preserved and restored. Edenton, among the oldest communities in North Carolina, is a living memorial to the past, considered by many travelers to be one of the South's most beautiful antebellum towns. Founded by a group of Swiss and German colonists in 1710, New Bern is an elegant showcase of Georgian and Federal period architecture. Its finest building is Tryon Palace completed in 1770 by Royal Governor William Tryon as a combined gubernatorial residence and colonial capitol. Prior to that time, North Carolina had no permanent seat of government—the colony was simply administered from wherever the governor chose to live. Sometimes called "the most beautiful building in colonial America," the Palace has been faithfully restored and reconstructed and is furnished in period. Beaufort (pronounced BOH fort), third oldest town in the state, was founded by British and French Huguenot merchants and mariners who built sturdy homes from timbers of sailing ships. Many of the preserved houses, dating from the late 18th and 19th centuries, are still occupied by family descendants.

From Morehead City to the Wilmington–Cape Fear area, the islands hover closer to the shoreline, their beaches often easy to reach by causeways. Wilmington, North Carolina's largest coastal city, serves as a major seaport and marketing center. In addition to a number of colonial and antebellum houses, it's also home of the heroic World War II battleship USS *North Carolina,* permanently moored beside the Cape Fear River. An antique wharf and historic Cotton Exchange along the riverfront have been converted to attractive market places with shops, boutiques, a nautical museum, and restaurants. The Cape Fear country, with its moss-laden live oaks, springtime gardens glowing with dazzling blooms, classic-columned homes, and former riverside rice plantations evokes a casual deep-South aura.

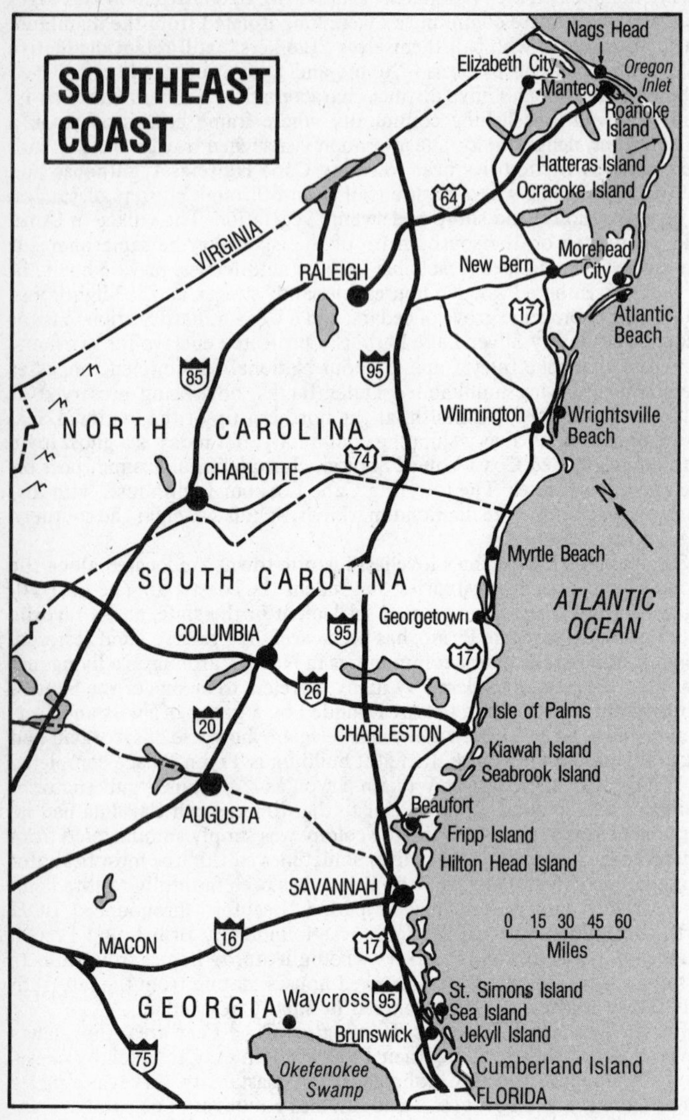
SOUTHEAST
COAST
Nags Head
Elizabeth City
Oregon
Inlet
Manteo
Roanoke
Island
Hatteras Island
Ocracoke Island
64
VIRGINIA
RALEIGH
New Bern
Morehead
City
17
Atlantic
Beach
85
95
Wilmington
Wrightsville
Beach
NORTH CAROLINA
74
CHARLOTTE
N
Myrtle Beach
SOUTH CAROLINA
Georgetown
ATLANTIC
OCEAN
COLUMBIA
95
17
26
Isle of Palms
20
CHARLESTON
Kiawah Island
Seabrook Island
AUGUSTA
Beaufort
Fripp Island
Hilton Head Island
SAVANNAH
0 15 30 45 60
Miles
MACON
16
17
St. Simons Island
GEORGIA
Waycross
95
Sea Island
Brunswick
Jekyll Island
75
Cumberland Island
Okefenokee
Swamp
FLORIDA

South Carolina

Smallest among the southern states in land area, South Carolina is also one of the most diverse, especially along the coast where a seemingly "foreign" atmosphere prevails in many places. Here life moves at a leisurely pace, the distinctive deep-South mode of living rooted in family traditions, large plantations, and small communities with Charleston as the focal point of social, cultural, economic, and political attitudes. Often as not, homes, churches, and public buildings are of mellowed brick or weathered wood, reminding the traveler that here past and present live in closer harmony than in many other places.

Visitors arriving in the state from the north will first encounter up-to-the-minute resort amenities at Myrtle Beach and nearby seaside communities along the 55-mile Grand Strand, one of the most extensive swatches of sand beach on the Atlantic coast. Immensely popular with summer vacationers, Myrtle Beach also appeals to winter-weary Canadians in early spring and savvy shoulder-season visitors during autumn. Abundant accommodations, restaurants, shops, carnival type amusements, fine golfing, tennis, and water sports keep peak-season family vacationers happily occupied.

From Myrtle Beach to Charleston, U.S. 17 wends southward through a coastland rich in natural endowments, history, lore, and legends. Its singular enchantments are revealed at such places as Brookgreen Gardens adorned with American statuary amid live oaks, floral displays and reflecting pools. Just across the highway, Atalaya, the winter home and studio of its founders, wealthy magnate Archer M. Huntington and his famed sculptress wife, Anna Hyatt Huntington, has been preserved. Historic nuances spring to life at Georgetown, a cultural and marketing center for colonial- and Federal-era rice and indigo planters whose opulent lifestyle may be savored at nearby Hopsewee Plantation home.

South of Georgetown, the Francis Marion National Forest extends inland from the coast. It was named in memory of the famed "Swamp Fox" of the Revolutionary War who elusively fought engagements here against the British. Many scenic roadways lead into the forest, once an important center of the "naval stores" industry, providing wood and tar for building and caulking sailing ships.

Farther south along U.S. 17, local inhabitants hand weave unusually beautiful baskets of palmetto fronds and marsh grasses. It's an age-old craft with roots in western Africa. The baskets are sold at stands along the roadside and appreciate in value since fewer and fewer young people are learning the craft.

Charleston has often been called "The Mother City of the South" because of its traditional influence on the manners, mores, and gentility of cultivated Southerners,wherever they may live. Historic portions of the city occupy a narrow peninsula overlooking the large natural harbor created by the confluence of the Cooper and Ashley Rivers—although some Charlestonians, keeping a perfectly straight face, have been known to tell visitors the two streams actually come together to form the Atlantic Ocean. Originally established in 1670 at Charles Towne Landing on the Ashley River, it was moved to its present location a decade later in accord with a master plan. Many of the earliest colonists came from the overcrowded Caribbean island of Barbados, bringing with them architectural styles still evident in the city.

In order to conserve space and take advantage of welcome sea breezes, Charlestonians often built two-storied open galleried homes at right angles to the sidewalks. Many of the houses face charming courtyard gardens. Singular delights of the historic city are best seen by strolling or riding in a horse-drawn carriage along such streets as Broad, Meeting, Tradd,

East Bay, Queen, and Legare (pronounced Le GREE), down narrow Prices Alley and on cobblestoned Chalmers. Today Charleston is a vibrant commercial, industrial, cultural, and educational center that has kept faith with its heritage. It was the nation's first city to establish, in 1931, a program of community-wide historic preservation. Unlike most American communities of comparable size (about 70,000 in the city, over 376,000 in the metropolitan area), the skyline is still dominated by church steeples, much as in colonial and antebellum times.

South from Charleston, the coastland has a distinct character with seaside islands separated from the mainland by extensive salt marshes. In earlier eras some of these islands were sites of prosperous long-staple cotton plantations which have since disappeared. But many of the Afro-American inhabitants still speak a difficult-to-understand Gullah dialect unique to the South Carolina coast. Several islands such as Kiawah, Seabrook, Fripp, and Hilton Head are now luxurious residential and resort communities complete with championship golf, tennis, inns, restaurants, club houses, and shopping centers. Others still exist in time-warps, but are gradually changing. Edisto Island was once famed for long-fiber cotton. Today, though, visitors see remnants of old plantation houses, lovely antebellum churches, a small fishing village, abundant wildlife and a shell-laden beach—along with a resort-land development project.

In 1956, once-remote Hilton Head Island was connected to the mainland by a causeway. Largest of the sea islands on the Southeast coast—containing more territory than Manhattan—it has a 12-mile expanse of pristine sand beach, a delightful semi-tropical climate, and one of the few unpolluted marine estuaries on the Atlantic seaboard. Happily, extensive resort, residential and commercial developments have been attentive to the inherent beauty of the island, with large segments of the natural environment carefully preserved. In many of the luxurious club colonies, architectural styles of private homes and condominiums blend harmoniously with their settings. Here visitors discover quiet and elegant accoutrements of the good life remote from outside interference. Hilton Head Island boasts some of the nation's finest golf, tennis, and water sports facilities along with a pleasing array of splendid hotels, rental villas, restaurants, shops, and quiet night clubbing.

About 43 miles north of Hilton Head Island, Beaufort (pronounced BEW fort) nestles in the midst of sea islands and coastal marshes. It is South Carolina's second oldest and one of its loveliest towns. Antique Colonial era and antebellum homes face shady streets; churches from Revolutionary and pre–Civil War days are still in use. It's a pleasant historic contrast to Hilton Head's spiffy contemporary resorts, most enjoyable for leisurely strolling, browsing, shopping for arts and crafts, and dining in restaurants featuring delectable coastal seafoods and other specialties.

Georgia

Britain's Thirteenth Colony in North America began on February 12, 1733 when General James Edward Oglethorpe and a group of settlers climbed to the top of the 43-foot Yamacraw Bluff on the south bank of the Savannah River and began construction of their colonial community. Some of the colonists were former imprisoned debtors looking toward a new start in life, others were Protestant separatists seeking religious liberty. Oglethorpe and his idealistic supporters in England envisioned the Georgia colony as a bold experiment based upon personal rehabilitation and economic growth in a society structured in accord with high moral principles. As a militarist, Oglethorpe also intended the colony to serve as a buffer zone to prevent the Spanish in Florida from attacking the British colonies.

Savannah became the second planned city in the Thirteen Colonies, the first being Philadelphia. Wary of possible Indian aggression, Savannah's master plan (based in part on an ancient map of Peking, China) provided for a series of stockade squares with walls, wells, and buildings where the inhabitants could quickly find refuge. As it happened, though, the Indians under their imposing, seven-foot-tall chief, Tomochichi, turned out to be friendly. So the squares were converted to parks and connected by wide, tree-lined boulevards.

Oglethorpe's social aspirations involved small farms, where slavery and consumption of rum were prohibited, and agrarian experiments in growing grapes for wine production and the cultivation of silk worms. None of these restrictions worked and were gradually lifted when many colonists fled across the river to South Carolina. The General's military plans, on the other hand, fared extremely well. He built massive Fort Frederica on St. Simons Island to the south, garrisoned it with Scottish Highlanders and lived at the adjoining post town. In 1742 his troops defeated a numerically superior force of Spanish invaders at the epic Battle of Bloody Marsh and foiled further aggressive attempts.

During the late colonial period Georgia began to prosper as rice plantations developed along the waterways and Savannah became an important commercial and shipping center. By the time of the Revolutionary War, a considerable number of Georgians, happy with the *status quo,* remained steadfast in their loyalty to the Crown.

Eli Whitney's invention of the cotton gin revolutionized agriculture in the South. Vast plantations flourished along the coast and rivers, and Savannah became a major port for marketing and shipping the "white gold." Cotton merchants, known as factors, established elaborate offices and warehouses beside the Savannah River bluff and built splendid mansions in the gardenlike city. But the Civil War brought this lifestyle to an end. General William T. Sherman's destructive "March to the Sea" ended at Savannah in December, 1864. The city had been evacuated to prevent bombardment. Sherman presented it, intact and untouched, to President Lincoln as a "Christmas present."

When the famed City Market was torn down in the mid-1950s and replaced with a hideous parking deck, there was an outcry of resentment. By 1955, when the splendid Federal style Davenport House became threatened with destruction, also to make way for a parking facility, a group of concerned—and outraged—citizens formed the Historic Savannah Foundation. The Davenport House was saved and restored, followed by the preservation of many other treasured structures. Today, the two-and-one-half-square-mile National Historic Landmark District is the nation's largest, with over 1,100 architecturally and historically significant buildings. Savannah residents proudly describe their cherished city as "The Past Preserved With Love."

Long before arrival of Europeans, Georgia's coastal Indians so revered the Golden Isles that they would go there only in peace, never allowing them to become battlegrounds in fierce tribal wars. Now connected by causeways in the vicinity of Brunswick, the gemlike islands still retain immense appeal. They're separated from the mainland by the glorious Marshes of Glynn, vividly depicted by Sidney Lanier in a long and spiritually haunting narrative poem of that name. Each of the major islands has distinctive appeal. Sea Island is famed for The Cloister resort hotel and beautiful private homes. St. Simons boasts General Oglethorpe's Fort Frederica, a charming church founded by John and Charles Wesley, an appealing village with some delightful shops, and a nearby lighthouse inhabited by a gentle ghost. During the late 1880's, Jekyll Island became an exclusive hideaway for a colony of millionaires who built lavish "cottages" now open to the general public. Jekyll has also become a favorite beach resort with modern hotels, restaurants, golf courses, water sports, and a convention center.

Cumberland Island National Seashore at the extreme southern end of Georgia's coastline is a blending of historic buildings, wildlife, sand dunes, and remote beaches. A few miles westward, the incomparable Great Okefenokee Swamp was once part of the Atlantic Ocean, but now rises about a hundred feet above sea level. Most of it has been preserved as the Okefenokee National Wildlife Refuge inhabited by alligators, bears, white-tailed deer, raccoons, numerous varieties of birds, and insects. Early Indians in the Swamp, fascinated by the many floating islands, provided its name, meaning "Land of Trembling Earth."

PRACTICAL INFORMATION FOR THE SOUTHEAST COAST

WHEN TO GO. Four distinct seasons prevail along the Southeast Coast. While winters are usually mild, occasional short cold snaps may produce freezing temperatures and dustings of snow, especially in the Carolinas, rarely in Georgia. Many hotels in the Myrtle Beach and Outer Banks resort areas close in winter. Those which remain open offer lowest seasonal rates. Spring arrives in full force during Mar. and Apr., luring vacationers to enjoy spectacular floral displays in Brunswick, Savannah, Charleston, Wilmington, and elsewhere. This is often the busiest visitor season in the historic cities along the Southeast Coast.

Family vacation times traditionally last from Memorial Day through Labor Day weekend in such popular resorts as the Outer Banks, Grand Strand, and Golden Isles. Midsummer days tend to be hot and humid, often hovering in the 90s, with evening lows in the 70s. From time to time brief, heavy thunderstorms bring some relief. Autumn asserts itself with balmier days and cooler evenings during Oct. into Nov., and even early Dec. in areas farther south. It's a quiet and lovely time to visit. Accommodation rates are lower and crowds have diminished.

HOW TO GET THERE. The larger cities and major vacation areas along the Southeast Coast are generally accessible by automobile and various modes of public transportation. Since numerous barrier and sea islands lie some distance from the mainland, transportation by auto ferries and passenger boats is used more frequently than in many parts of the country. Visitors who would venture to isolated and virtually uninhabited island retreats must often utilize private launches.

By plane. The closest commercial air service to the Dare Coast resorts is at Norfolk, 79 mi. northwest, which is served by *American, Continental, Delta, Pan Am, TWA, United,* and *USAir.* Wilmington, largest city on the North Carolina coast, is served by *American* and its *American Eagle* affiliate, and *USAir,* with service to and from Atlanta. South Carolina's popular Grand Strand–Myrtle Beach resort region is served by American's *American Eagle* affiliate, *Delta* and its *Atlantic Southeast Airlines* affiliate, and *USAir,* offering scheduled flights outside and inside the state. Charleston's contemporary new *International Airport Terminal* has service by *American, Continental, Delta, USAir,* and *United.* Hilton Head Island Airport is served by *USAir Express,* regional airlines under contract to the carrier. Most travelers, though, use the *Savannah International Airport,* about an hour's drive from Hilton Head via transfer bus or limousine services. *American, Continental, Delta, USAir,* and *United* serve Savannah. Brunswick, gateway city to Georgia's Golden Isles, has commercial air service to and from Atlanta provided by *Atlantic Southeast Airlines* (800–282–3424).

By bus. Wilmington, Charleston, Savannah, Brunswick, and various other communities on the Southeast Coast are served by *Greyhound.*

By train. *Amtrak*'s north–south passenger trains between New York–Miami and New York–Tampa have scheduled stops at Charleston and Savannah. The closest Amtrak station to Myrtle Beach is in Florence, SC, 70 mi. west, with convenient connecting bus services. Brunswick's nearest Amtrak station is at Jessup, GA, 40 mi. northwest.

By car. U.S. Hwy. 17 is the major north–south coastal route through the Carolinas and Georgia, in easy reach of virtually all the most popular visitor areas and attractions. Important east–west routes include U.S. 64 to the Dare Coast and Outer Banks, U.S. 74 to Wilmington, I-26 to Charleston, and I-16 to Savannah. From north to south, I-95 is the closest superhighway to the Carolina coastlands, though often 50 to 100 or more mi. removed from noteworthy seaside destinations. In Georgia it clings closer to river estuaries and coastal marshes between Savannah and Brunswick before turning inland to the Florida state line. The U.S. and state highways are generally well maintained, often bypass cities and towns, and range from two to four lanes depending upon traffic density.

By boat. Automobile ferry services connect North Carolina's widely scattered barrier islands with each other and the mainland. They're operated by the North Carolina Department of Transportation year round. Some are free, others charge tolls. In the extreme northeastern corner of the state, the *Currituck Sound Free Ferry* runs between Knotts Island and the mainland. On the Outer Banks, *Hatteras Inlet Free Ferry* links Hatteras Island and Ocracoke Island. Frequent summer schedules are arranged to handle peak crowds for the 40-minute crossing; even then there may be delays because of long lines.

The *Cedar Island-Ocracoke Toll Ferry* connects Ocracoke village with Cedar Island to the south. The *Ocracoke-Swan Quarter Toll Ferry* crosses Pamlico Sound, linking Ocracoke village with the westward-lying mainland town of Swan Quarter. Crossings take 2½ hours. One-way fare for both ferries is $10 for single vehicle or combination 20 ft. or less in length, $20 for vehicles or combinations 20 to 40 ft. in length. Reservations, especially during summer, are recommended for these services and may be made up to 30 days in advance of departure date. Reservations must be claimed at least 30 minutes prior to departure time; driver's name and vehicle license number are required when making reservations. For reservations on the Cedar Island-Ocracoke Ferry, phone 919–225–3551 for departures from Cedar Island, 919–928–3841 for departures from Ocracoke. For the Ocracoke-Swan Quarter Ferry, phone 919–928–3841 for departures from Ocracoke, 919–926–1111 for departures from Swan Quarter. Calls should be made between 6 A.M. and 6 P.M. Reservations may also be made in person at departure terminals during these same hours.

The *Southport-Fort Fisher Toll Ferry* crosses the estuary of the Cape Fear River, an hour-long journey. One-way fares are $3 for single vehicle or combination 20 ft. or less in length, $6 for single vehicle or combination from 20 ft. up to and including a maximum length of 35 ft.

For additional information about ferry schedules and rates, contact Director, Ferry Division, Room 116, Maritime Bldg., 113 Arendell St., Morehead City, NC 28557; phone (919–726–6446) or (919–726–6413). Rates and schedule information also appear on the 1986–87 North Carolina Transportation Map, available at visitor information centers throughout the state.

TOURIST INFORMATION. North Carolina: For folders, guide brochures, booklets, official map and special information about the Tar Heel State, contact *North Carolina Travel and Tourism Division,* 430 N. Salisbury St., Raleigh, NC 27611 (toll-free in U.S. and Toronto, Canada, 800–VISIT–NC; in Raleigh, 919–733–4171). Fishing and hunting regulations are available from *NC Wildlife Resources Commission,* Archdale Bldg., 512 N. Salisbury St., Raleigh, NC 27611 (919–733–3391). A useful brochure of state parks, recreation opportunities may be obtained from the *North Carolina Division of Parks and Recreation,* Department of Natural Resources and Community Development, 512 N. Salisbury St., Raleigh, NC 27611 (919–733–4181).

Eight North Carolina Welcome Centers at major interstate entrances into the state provide detailed information daily between 8 A.M. and 5 P.M. Those closest to the Southeast Coast are at I-95 North near Roanoke Rapids (919–573–9836) and I-95 South near Rowland (919–422–8314).

Additional information about the North Carolina coast may be requested from *Dare County Tourist Bureau,* Box 399, Manteo, NC 27954 (919–473–2138); the *Outer Banks Chamber of Commerce,* Box 90, Kitty Hawk, NC 27949 (919–261–3801); *Historic Edenton,* Box 474, Edenton, NC 27932 (919–482–3663); the *New*

Bern Chamber of Commerce, 211 Broad St., Drawer C, New Bern, NC 28560 (919–637–3111) which can provide information about audiotaped walking tours of the historic district and other aspects of the city; *Carteret County Chamber of Commerce,* Box 1198, Morehead City, NC 28557 (919–726–6831 or toll free in state, 800–682–3934) for information about Morehead City, historic Beaufort, Cape Lookout National Seashore, Harker's Island, Fort Macon, Atlantic Beach, and other "Crystal Coast" offerings; and the *New Hanover Convention and Visitors Bureau,* Box 266, Wilmington, NC 28401 (919–341–4030; 800–922–7117 in state; 800–222–4757 eastern U.S.).

South Carolina: For folders, guide brochures, booklets, state map, and any special information requests about the Palmetto State, contact *South Carolina Department of Parks, Recreation and Tourism,* 1205 Pendleton St., Columbia, SC 29201 (803–734–0122). Hunting and fishing regulations are available from the *S.C. Department of Wildlife and Marine Resources,* Box 167, Columbia, SC 29202 (803–734–3888). Helpful brochures about state parks and recreational opportunities can be provided by the *S.C. Division of State Parks,* PRT, Suite 110, Edgar A. Brown Bldg., 1205 Pendleton St., Columbia, SC 29201 (803–734–0159).

South Carolina maintains ten Welcome Centers on major highways. Those in proximity of the Southeast Coast are on U.S. 17 SC–NC Border near Little River (803–249–1111), and on I-95 SC–GA Border near Hardeeville (803–784–3275). Centers open daily, except Dec. 25, 8:30 A.M.–6 P.M. in summer, to 5:30 P.M. in winter.

Additional information about the South Carolina coast is available from the *Myrtle Beach Area Convention Bureau,* 710 21st. Ave. N, Suite J, Myrtle Beach, SC 29577 (803–448–1629 or 800–356–3016); *Georgetown County Chamber of Commerce,* 600 Front St., Box 1776, Georgetown, SC 29442 (803–546–8436); *Beaufort County Chamber of Commerce,* Box 910, Beaufort, SC 29901–0910 (803–524–3163); and the *Hilton Head Island Visitor & Convention Bureau,* Box 5647, Hilton Head Island, SC 29938 (803–785–3673).

Visitors to Charleston should stop first at the *Charleston Visitor Information Center,* 85 Calhoun St. (803–722–8338) for specific information about lodging, dining, and sightseeing. A 38-minute, multi-image, quadraphonic presentation, *Charleston Adventure,* is shown in a theater adjacent to the Center. For further information, contact *Charleston Trident Convention and Visitors Bureau,* 81 Mary St., Box 975, Charleston, SC 29402 (803–577–2510). Charleston information is also available at the *Preservation Society Visitor Center,* 147 King St., Box 521, Charleston, SC 29402 (803–723–4381) where an award-winning 42-minute film, *Dear Charleston,* is shown on a regular schedule. It is also screened at the Dear Charleston Visitor Center, 52 N. Market St., and the Old Exchange & Provost Dungeon, 122 E. Bay St.

Georgia: For folders, guide brochures, booklets, state map, and any special information requests about the Peach State, contact *Georgia Tourist Division,* Box 1776, Atlanta, GA 30301 (404–656–3545). For fishing and hunting regulations and recreational opportunities in state parks, address inquiries to the *Georgia Department of Natural Resources,* 205 Butler St., SE, Suite 1258, Atlanta, GA 30334 (404–656–3530; 800–342–7275 in-state; 800–542–7275 nationwide).

Ten Visitor Centers are located in various cities and towns throughout the state. Hours are 8:30 A.M.–7:30 P.M. during summer, until 5:30 P.M. remainder of the year. The coast is served by the *Georgia Visitor Center* (912–964–5094) on I-95 just south of the South Carolina-Georgia state line.

For a free visitor information packet, write or call the *Savannah Area Convention and Visitors Bureau,* 222 W. Oglethorpe Ave., Savannah, GA 31499 (912–944–0456, toll-free 800–444–2427 outside GA). The Savannah Visitors Center, at 301 W. Broad St., is open Mon.–Fri., 8:30 A.M.–5 P.M.; Sat., Sun., and major holidays, 9 A.M.–5 P.M. The Center is an ideal first stop for visitors. Trained hostesses provide information and literature and a complimentary 15-minute audiovisual presentation is shown on the hour and half-hour. There's ample free parking and the Center is accessible for the handicapped.

For information about other places along the Georgia coast, contact the *Brunswick–Golden Isles Tourist and Convention Bureau,* Box 250, 4 Glynn Ave., Brunswick, GA 31520 (912–265–0620); *Jekyll Island Convention and Visitors Bureau,* 1 Beachview Dr., Jekyll Island, GA 31520 (912–635–3400; 800–841–6586, nationwide; 800–342–1042, in state); and *St. Simons Island Chamber of Commerce,* Neptune Park, St. Simons Island, GA 31522 (912–638–9014 or –2172).

TIME ZONES. The entire Southeast Coast is in the Eastern Standard–Eastern Daylight time zone.

TELEPHONES. Southeast Coast area codes are 919 for coastal North Carolina, 803 for all of South Carolina, and 912 for coastal Georgia. In Wilmington, NC; Charleston, SC; and Savannah, GA, the cost of local pay-phone calls is 25 cents. For operator assistance with long distance, credit card, and person-to-person calls dial 0 before area code; for long-distance, station-to-station calls, dial 1 before area code; for toll-free calls, dial 1–800, then the number; for local directory assistance dial 411; for directory assistance from outside local areas dial 1, then the area code, followed by 555–1212.

EMERGENCY TELEPHONE NUMBERS. Wilmington, NC; Charleston, SC; and Savannah, GA, all utilize the universal 911 emergency number for police, ambulance, fire department, and paramedics. In **Wilmington,** other emergency numbers are *State Highway Patrol Division Headquarters* (791–5311), *Rape Task Force* (763–3695), *New Hanover Memorial Hospital* (343–7000), *Poison Control Center* (343–7046). In **Charleston,** other emergency numbers are *State Highway Patrol* (747–5705), *People Against Rape* 24-Hour Crisis Line (722–7273), *Charleston Memorial Hospital* (577–0600), *Poison Information Center* (800–922–1117, toll free). In **Savannah,** other emergency numbers are *State Highway Patrol* (232–6414), *Poison Control Regional Center* (355–5228), *Rape Crisis Center* (233–7273), *City Police* (233–4141). *Fire Department* (232–5121), *Ambulance* (352–8122), *Memorial Medical Center Hospital* (356–8000).

HOW TO GET AROUND. From the airport. Wilmington's *New Hanover County Airport* (919–763–1671) is approximately 2½ mi. from downtown. Limousine and taxi services are available at the terminal. Dedicated in Mar., 1985. *Charleston's International Airport* (803–767–1100) boasts a convenient new contemporary terminal 10 mi. from downtown. Transfer services are available by taxi and limousine. *Savannah International Airport* is approximately 11 mi. from downtown. Transfer services are available by *Coastal Express* limousines (912–964–0332), approximately $8–$15 round-trip, and approximately $8 one-way to downtown Historic District; taxi cabs charge about $15 per person, one way, $3 for each additional person.

By bus. Citywide bus service in Wilmington is operated by the *Wilmington Transit Authority.* Schedules and route information are available from the company at 1110 Castle St. (919–343–0106). Local fare is 50 cents. *Charleston's Downtown Area Shuttle (DASH),* utilizing new air-conditioned trolley-style vehicles, provides fast, convenient service weekdays only between major hotels, restaurants, Historic District, downtown, and nearby areas. Fare is 25 cents, exact change; 10 cents from 9:30 A.M.–3:30 P.M. for senior and handicapped citizens. Free transfers are available from drivers for other city buses operated by *South Carolina Electric and Gas Company.* For schedules, route information contact DASH (803–724–7368) and SCE&G (803–722–2226). Savannah's citywide bus service is operated by the *Chatham Area Transit* (CAT). Schedules and route information are available from the company at 900 E. Gwinett St. (912–233–5767). Fare is 75 cents, exact change required; transfers are 5 cents.

By taxi. In Wilmington, basic taxi rates are $1, plus $1.20 a mi.; there is a 50 cent surcharge for each trip in city from 6:30 P.M.–6:30 A.M. Companies include *Port City Taxi* (919–762–1165) and *Yellow Cab* (919–762–3322 or 919–762–4464). In Charleston, taxi fare between airport and city is approximately $13; fares within the city average $2–$3. Companies include *Everready Cab Co.* (803–722–8383), *North Area Taxi* (803–554–7575), *Yellow Cab* (803–577–6565), *Safety Cab* (803–722–4066), and *Limo-Taxi* (803–767–7111). In Savannah, taxi fare between airport and downtown is approximately $13–$14 for one person, $4 for each additional person. Companies include *Adam Cab Inc.* (912–927–7466), *Milton's Cab Co.* (912–236–2424), and *Taxi Service of Savannah* (912–352–9169, 912–944–9668 or 912–944–9669). *Coastal Express* (912–964–0332), with a counter at the airport, provides cost-effective transfer service.

By rental car. Driving is the most pleasant and comprehensive way to enjoy the Southeast Coast even if it means renting an automobile. Car-rental companies conveniently located near the baggage claim area in the terminal at **Wilmington's** New

Hanover County Airport include *Hertz* (912–762–1010), *Avis* (919–763–3346), *Budget* (919–762–8910), and *National* (919–762–8000). Locations near baggage claim in **Charleston's** International Airport include *Dollar* (803–774–3364), *Avis* (803–767–7030), *Budget* (803–763–3300), *Hertz* (803–554–6311), and *National* (803–723–8266). *American and International* (803–747–3606), located at 1818 Remount Rd. near the Airport Terminal, provides complimentary shuttle service. At the Sheraton Charleston Hotel, 170 Lockwood Drive, *Avis* has a reservations counter (803–722–2977), and *National* maintains an in-town rental facility at 252 Meeting St. (803–723–5729). Companies at the terminal baggage claim area in **Savannah** International Airport include *Hertz* (912–964–1220), *Avis* (912–964–1781), *Budget* (912–964–7111), and *National* (912–234–8913). *Alamo* maintains a rental facility near the terminal (912–946–1781) and provides convenient shuttle service. *Avis* has an in-town location at 210 Bernard St. (912–236–3096) across from the Ramada Inn.

HINTS TO MOTORISTS. In sandy beach areas, motorists must take care to stay on the pavement to avoid getting stuck in the sand. This is especially true on NC Hwy. 12 in the Cape Hatteras National Seashore along the Outer Banks. Certain other roads in particularly scenic areas, such as SC 61 from Charleston to the historic gardens and roadways in Georgia's Golden Isles, require more leisurely driving for maximum enjoyment and safety. The legal speed limit is 55 mph in the three states, unless lower limits are posted. Speed limits vary in different communities, so check signs carefully. The AAA supernumber (800–336–HELP) is for emergency information about road services available 24 hours a day for club members traveling outside their local club areas.

North Carolina strictly enforces a mandatory law requiring front seat passengers to wear seat belts; and a mandatory child restraint law requiring children three years old and under to be secured in a child safety seat, those three to six in a safety seat or seat belt. The state's drunk-driving laws are rigidly enforced; violaters receive severe penalties.

A *Guide Map* folder of Wilmington is available at State Welcome Centers and the Wilmington Chamber of Commerce. It includes an access map of the city environs, a detailed walking–driving tour map of the downtown Historic District, and useful descriptive information about sites and attractions. Laid out in an orderly grid pattern, the Historic District is easy to navigate. Most downtown on-street parking is metered; off-street lots and enclosed parking facilities are also available. Major hotels and motels provide on-premises parking. Right turns are permitted on red after a full stop unless noted otherwise. Local emergency road service is provided for members through the AAA Carolina Motor Club in Wilmington (919–763–8446).

South Carolina has a well-engineered highway system. The Ocean Hwy.—U.S. 17—is delightful for leisurely exploring of modern resorts, historic towns, antique homes, and wildlife habitats. Charleston, situated on a narrow peninsula, has historically conserved space for homes, parks, public buildings, and thoroughfares. It is connected on the north by two bridges across the Cooper River. The newer one for northbound traffic has wide lanes; the older bridge for southbound motorists, though, is a narrow lane and should be driven cautiously.

An 88-page booklet, *Charleston Area South Carolina Visitor's Guide,* with a map and information about the Historic District, may be obtained from state Welcome Centers, or the Charleston Visitor Information Center at 85 Calhoun St. Some of the major streets are sufficiently wide to handle automobile traffic comfortably enough; others are quite narrow, often one-way, and must be navigated with considerable care. During the popular spring season, the city becomes especially busy as visitors explore its manifold charms by tour buses, horse-drawn carriages, self-guided walking, and auto tours. So please be considerate. On-street metered parking is quite limited. Off-street lots and parking garages are available. Right turn on red after a full stop is legal unless otherwise noted. Major in-town hotels and motels provide on-premises parking. Local emergency road service is available for club members through the AAA Carolina Motor Club in Charleston (803–766–2394).

Georgia's federal, state, and county roads are of good quality. Interstate-95 parallels much of U.S. 17 and provides for time-saving driving as well as convenient access to major points of visitor interest.

Vacationers in Savannah can secure driving and walking tour maps, along with a copy of *The Savannah Guidebook,* at the Visitor Center, 301 W. Broad St. (912–944–0456). The city's Historic District consists of numerous park-like squares connected by thoroughfares. It's a beautiful instance of urban planning, but must be carefully navigated by motorists unfamiliar with the unique configuration. Here are some driving tips: when entering the squares, always yield to the LEFT; one-way streets follow no set pattern, so watch for and obey all traffic signs; if you want to pause for a closer look at an intriguing park or house, pull out of the traffic flow rather than slowing down or delaying other drivers; and be especially alert for tour buses, horse-drawn carriages, bicycle riders, and pedestrians. Rush hours are no problem in Savannah's Historic District. Most downtown streets have parking meters with maximum times of two hours and must be paid from 8 A.M.–6 P.M., except Sun. and holidays. Off-street parking is available in lots and enclosed garages; virtually all downtown hotels and motels provide parking facilities. Right turns on red, after stopping, are permitted throughout Georgia except where noted otherwise. Emergency road service in Savannah is available to AAA members through the Georgia Motor Club (912–352–8222).

HINTS TO DISABLED TRAVELERS. In many national and state parks on the Southeast Coast, as well as a variety of private attractions, efforts have been made to accommodate handicapped visitors. In some historic restorations, however, wheelchair and limited mobility access is often restricted or impossible because of flights of steps, interior designs with narrow doors, hallways, and crowded rooms.

North Carolina law requires reserved handicapped parking spaces, marked with white and blue wheelchair signs. Public buildings and certain private enterprises such as stores and restaurants must provide adequate access and specially equipped restrooms. Please inquire at state Welcome Centers and local tourist information offices about access to particular attractions. For a free copy of *Access North Carolina,* phone toll-free 800–VISIT NC, 8 A.M. to 5 P.M. weekdays.

Provisions for handicapped accessibility to a number of attractions in **South Carolina** are noted in the state's *Meeting and Tour Planning Guide,* a reference source that state Welcome Center consultants should have on hand. At Myrtle Beach, access to beach locations by ramps are located at 81st Ave., North; 75th Ave., North; 74th Ave., North; 73rd Ave., North; 71st Ave., North; 69th Ave., North; 67th Ave., North; 43rd Ave., North; 31st Ave., North; 23rd Ave., North; 19th Ave., South; and 11th Ave., South. Parking spaces for the handicapped are found in most areas of the Grand Strand. Look for signs with the wheelchair symbol. Such prime attractions as Brookgreen Gardens near Murrells Inlet and Fort Sumter National Monument in Charleston harbor provide facilities which enhance enjoyment by handicapped visitors.

A valuable booklet, *Access Charleston, a Guide for Persons with Mobility Difficulties* details places that offer assistance for those confined to wheelchairs, admission of seeing eye dogs, verbal presentations, special exhibits for touching, and, in some instances, provision for handicapped groups. For a copy, contact Charleston Trident Convention and Visitors Bureau, Box 975, Charleston, SC 29402 (803–577–2510). Reserved parking spaces in the city are noted by the blue and white symbol.

For information about provisions for the handicapped along the **Georgia** Coast, inquire at the state Visitor Center (912–964–5094) on I-95 just south of the GA–SC state line. In Savannah, information can be obtained from the Savannah Visitors Center, 301 Broad St. (912–944–0456). Throughout the city, parking spaces marked with the wheelchair symbol have been reserved for handicapped. Broughton St., the main downtown shopping thoroughfare, has ramped curbs. The Brunswick–Golden Isles Tourist and Convention Bureau, 4 Glynn Ave., Brunswick, GA 31520 (912–265–0620) can furnish information about attractions and lodgings with facilities for the handicapped.

SEASONAL EVENTS. North Carolina. APRIL. *NC Azalea Festival,* parade, concerts, pageant, nationally known entertainers; 4 days mid-month; write or phone Secretary, Box 51, Wilmington, NC 28402 (919–763–0905). JUNE. *Big Rock Blue Marlin Tournament,* boat parade, fish fry, beauty pageant, preteen fishing tournament, fashion show, pig pickin'; 7 days mid-month; contact Tournament Office, Box 1673, Morehead City, NC 28557 (919–247–3575). *Sound & Light Spectacular*

"The Immortal Showboat," outdoor presentation of World War II history of USS *North Carolina* at the Battleship Memorial, nightly 9 P.M.; early June–Labor Day, adults, $4, children 6–11, $2; write or phone Immortal Showboat, Box 417, Wilmington, NC 28402 (919–762–1829). *Outdoor Symphonic Drama "The Lost Colony,"* about Sir Walter Raleigh's ill-fated attempt to establish an English colony on Roanoke Island, nightly 8:30 P.M., Mon.–Sat.; mid-June–late Aug., adults, $10; senior citizens, handicapped, military, $9; under 12, $4; free on Mon.; write or phone Lost Colony, Box 40, Manteo, NC 27954 (919–473–2127). SEPTEMBER. *Annual Albemarle Craftsman's Fair,* a gala regional event for over 25 years, held in Elizabeth City's Knobb Creek Recreation Center; 4 days late month; contact Elizabeth City Area Chamber of Commerce, Box 426, Elizabeth City, NC 27909 (919–335–4365). OCTOBER. *Annual New Bern Chrysanthemum Festival,* featuring flowers, antiques, crafts at Tryon Palace Gardens; 2 days mid-month; contact Tryon Palace Restoration & Gardens Complex, Box 1007, New Bern, NC 28560 (919–638–1560). DECEMBER. *First Flight Commemoration,* held at Wright Brothers National Memorial, is a splendid gathering of vintage aircraft, period vehicles and upbeat people who venerate the beginnings of the Air Age; always held Dec. 17; contact First Flight Society, Box 1903, Kitty Hawk, NC 27949 (919–441–3761).

South Carolina. JANUARY. *Oyster Festival,* a Charleston extravaganza for the entire family, music, exhibits, contests, oysters galore; mid-month; contact Charleston Trident Convention and Visitors Bureau, Box 975, Charleston, SC 29402 (803–577–2510). MARCH. *Springfest,* Hilton Head Island's celebration of the season with seafood, films, sports events, entertainment; entire month; contact Springfest, Box 5278, Hilton Head Island, SC 29938 (803–842–3378). APRIL. *Flowertown Festival,* a family celebration in Summerville with parade, pageant, floral, and art displays, home tours; 3 days early month; contact Summerville Family YMCA, 900 Crosscreek Rd., Summerville, SC 29483 (803–871–9622). *MCI Heritage Classic:* more than 100 top professional golfers play Harbour Town Links in prestigious, nationally televised PGA tour event; 1 week, mid-month; contact 11 Lighthouse Lane, Hilton Head Island, SC 29928 (803–671–2448). MAY. *Lowcountry Shrimp Festival* in McClellanville with entertainment, foods, crafts, Blessing of the Fleet, 1 day early month; contact Lowcountry Shrimp Festival, Box 520, McClellanville, SC 29458 (803–887–3323). *Spoleto Festival U.S.A.,* among the world's greatest celebrations of the arts, was founded by famed composer–maestro Gian-Carlo Menotti in 1977 as a New-World counterpart to his esteemed festival in Spoleto, Italy. He personally chose Charleston as the location to showcase opera, dance, symphonic, and chamber music performances, drama, jazz, and the visual arts with festivities in concert halls, theaters, parks, churches, streets, and gardens throughout the city and environs; 17 days late May to early June; many events are free, tickets for others, in varying price ranges, are best ordered in advance; for schedules of events, admissions, contact Spoleto Festival U.S.A., Box 704, Charleston, SC 29402 (803–722–2764). JUNE. *Sun Fun Festival,* Myrtle Beach's annual gala with parades, concerts, beach games, beauty pageant, sports, 7 days early June; contact Myrtle Beach Area Convention Bureau, 710 21st. Ave. N., Suite J, Myrtle Beach, SC 29577 (803–448–1629). JULY. *Annual Beaufort County Water Festival,* features boat races, musical events, crafts, antique show; mid-month; contact Greater Beaufort Chamber of Commerce, Box 910, Beaufort, SC 29901 (803–524–3163) *July Fourth Celebration,* field day games, pony rides, sky divers, music, fireworks, in picturesque Low Country town of Summerville; contact Chamber of Commerce, Box 670, Summerville, SC 29484 (803–873–2931). *Art in the Park,* a juried art show, exhibitions and entertainment at Chapin Park in Myrtle Beach, 2 days in mid-month; contact Art Plus, 803 65th Ave., Myrtle Beach, SC 29577 (803–651–4771). DECEMBER. *Christmas at Middleton Place,* plantation dinners, candlelight tours of historic home, wreathmaking, bird walks, special events; entire month; contact Middleton Place, Rte. 4, Charleston, SC 29407 (803–556–6020). *Christmas in Charleston,* the antique city offers parades, caroling, concerts, tree lighting, and house tours; entire month; contact Charleston Trident Convention and Visitors Bureau, Box 975, Charleston, SC 29402 (803–577–2510).

Georgia. JANUARY. *Annual Blue Grass Festival,* Jekyll Island's celebration of sand, surf, family fun, lively music, and dancing; 3 days early month; contact Jekyll Island Convention & Visitors Bureau, 1 Beachview Dr., Jekyll Island, GA 31520 (912–635–3400). FEBRUARY. *Georgia Week,* Savannah's salute to the significance of historic preservation, highlighted by special tea and luncheon, arts and crafts exhibit, school children in costumes; 7 days early to mid-month; contact Historic Savannah Foundation, 41 W. Broad St., Box 1733, Savannah, GA 31402 (912–233–7787). MARCH. *Confederate Weekend at Fort Pulaski.* Continuous activities depict garrison life from Jan. 1861 to Apr. 1862. Musket, artillery drills; soldier-life demonstrations; guided tours 10 A.M. to 4 P.M. Candle Lantern Tour Sat. evening, reservation only. Mid-month weekend. Contact: Fort Pulaski National Monument, Box 98, Tybee Island, GA 31328 (912–786–5787). APRIL. *Night in Old Savannah,* a celebration of the many ethnic and nationality heritages that have enriched this gracious city; foods, entertainment, childrens' activities, delightful happenings for everyone; 3 days late month; write or phone Alee Shrine Temple, Box 14147, Savannah, GA 31416 (912–355–2422). MAY. *Savannah Scottish Games and Clan Gathering,* features athletic contests, Highland dancing, pipe bands, foods, clan societies, genealogy sources, Scottish heritage memorabilia on sale; one day early month; contact Savannah Scottish Games, 106 Halifax Rd., Savannah, GA 31410 (912–897–2327 or 598–0484). *Brunswick-Golden Isles Spring Fiesta* is a delightful celebration offering good fun for the family, culminating in a "Blessing of the Shrimp Fleet" at Brunswick; mid-month during Mother's Day weekend; contact Brunswick City Hall, 601 Gloucester St., Brunswick, GA 31520 (912–265–8210). JUNE. *Jekyll Island Musical Comedy Festival,* lively performances by the University of Georgia Festival Theater Company at Jekyll Island Musical Amphitheatre, 181 Stable Rd.; nightly late June–mid-Aug., except Sun., 8 P.M.; adults, $5; children 10–15, $4; under 10, free, rates subject to change without notice; contact Box 3144, Jekyll Island, GA 31520 (912–635–2504). AUGUST. *Georgia Sea Island Festival,* features traditional crafts and music on Casino Grounds, St. Simons Island, third weekend of month; contact Glynn County Department of Leisure Services, 30 Nimitz Dr., Brunswick, GA 31520 (912–264–1041). DECEMBER. *Christmas in Savannah,* a delightful array of seasonal happenings from tree-lighting and boat parade, decoration seminars, and special carriage tours to symphony concerts, jazz brunch, and holiday oyster roast; entire month; to request brochure listing all events and costs, contact Savannah Area Convention and Visitors Bureau, 222 W. Oglethorpe Ave., Savannah, GA 31499 (912–944–0456, toll free 800–444–2427 outside GA).

TOURS AND SPECIAL-INTEREST SIGHTSEEING. North Carolina. *Historic Bath Tour,* Box 124, Bath, NC 27808 (919–923–3971). An introductory film at the Visitor Center precedes the historic district tour Mon.–Sat., 9 A.M.–5 P.M.; Sun., 1 P.M.–5 P.M., Apr.–Oct.; Tues.–Sat., 10 A.M.–4 P.M., Sun.; 1–4 P.M., rest of year. Closed Thanksgiving, Dec. 24–25. Adults, $1 per building; children under 12, 50 cents per building.

Old Beaufort By The Sea Restoration Area Tour. Beaufort Historical Association, Box 1709, Beaufort, NC 28516 (919–728–5225). Self-guided tours begin at Josiah Bell House, 138 Turner St., include visits to Pigott House, Joseph Bell House (1767), historic courthouse, jail, Apothecary Shop, and Old Burying Grounds; English double-decker bus available. Mon.–Sat., 9:30 A.M. to 4:30 P.M.; Sun., 2 P.M.–4 P.M. Adults, $5; children 8–12, $1.50.

Historic Edenton Tour. Site Manager, Historic Edenton, Box 474, Edenton, NC 27932 (919–482–3663). Guided tours of the buildings noted begin at the 1782 Barker House Visitor Center on S. Broad St.; an audiovisual program introduces the area. Mon.–Sat., 10 A.M. to 4:30 P.M.; Sun., 2 P.M.–5 P.M. Closed Thanksgiving, Easter, Dec. 24–26, and New Years Day. Adults, $5; 6–18, $2.50, complete tour; adults, $3, 6–18, $1.50, to individual buildings.

Inside Old Wilmington Tour. Convention and Visitors Bureau, Box 266, Wilmington, NC 28402 (919–341–4030, 800–922–7117 in-state, 800–222–4757 Eastern U.S.). Guide service is provided in each building visited on the Historic District tour. Visitors begin at Thalian Hall, 305 Princess St., a magnificently restored mid-19th-century opera house, then continue to Burgwin-Wright House (see Historic Sites and Houses), and the Zebulon Latimer House, an ornate 1852 Italianate mansion. Tours scheduled Tues.–Sat., 10 A.M. to 4 P.M., or by appointment, except July 4, Thanksgiving, Dec. 24–Jan. 31. Tickets available at Convention and Visitors Bureau and each building. Single admission to each building: adults, $3; youths, $2; combination for all three: adults, $6; students, $2; under 6, free.

Captain J.N. Maffitt River Cruises. 2 Ann St., at Chandler's Wharf, Wilmington (919–343–1776). Narrated cruises of the Cape Fear River harbor include views of the historic Cotton Exchange, a Coast Guard icebreaker, and USS *North Carolina* Battleship Memorial. Operates May–Sept., daily departures 11 A.M. and 3 P.M. Closed remainder of year. Adults, $3; children 1–12, $1.50.

South Carolina. *Historic Tour Train.* Georgetown County Chamber of Commerce, Box 1776, Georgetown, SC 29442 (803–546–8436). The Tour Train departs from the Chamber of Commerce building at 600 Front St., wending its way along the tree-lined streets for views of historic homes, Prince George Winyah Church, and the Rice Museum. Also available are horse and carriage tours, Winyah Bay water tours. Operates Mar.–Oct., Mon.–Fri., hourly departures 10 A.M., 11 A.M., 1 P.M., 2 P.M., and 3 P.M., weather permitting. Closed remainder of year. Adults, $4–$8; students 6–12, $2–$5; children under 11 ride free.

Charleston Carriage Co. 96 N. Market St., Charleston (803–577–0042). Horse-drawn, narrated carriage tours of Historic District, 45–50 minutes. Daily 9 A.M.–dusk. Adults, $12; ages 3–12, $5; ages 2 and under ride free. Company also offers bicycle rentals, $2 per hour, $10 all day, deposit of $5; Historic District cassette tours, $7 per cassette; licensed guides for individual tours in visitors' automobiles, $35 per hour; and guided Historic District walking tours for groups up to 15 persons, adults, $10; children under 12 free.

Festival of Houses. Historic Charleston Foundation, 51 Meeting St., Charleston, SC 29401 (803–723–1623). Tour programs, late Mar. through mid-Apr., include afternoon and evening walking tours for visits to private homes open for the occasion; candlelight galas with wine, *hors d'oeuvres* and chamber music in the Foundation's two magnificent houses; sunset harbor cruise, Fort Sumter visit, wine and appetizers on return journey; and plantation oyster roasts on the grounds of Drayton Hall. Rates, $25 per person per event. AE, MC, V accepted. Write for detailed schedule of events; tickets may be ordered in advance. Direct inquiries to Festival of Houses at address above.

Starlight Dinner Cruise. Fort Sumter Tours, Inc., 205 Kings St., Suite 204, Charleston, SC 29401 (803–722–2628). The harbor cruise aboard the 110-passenger *Spirit of Charleston* includes dining, dancing, live entertainment, cocktail lounge aboard; yacht is heated, air conditioned. Nightly, 7 P.M., Apr.–Labor Day, sails from Municipal Marina at 17 Lockwood Blvd. Weekdays, $29.95; weekends, $32.50. Reservations required.

Kiawah Island Tours. Box 31485, Charleston, SC 29417 (803–768–1111). A 2-hour Jeep Safari Tour includes unspoiled portions of the island, wildlife refuge areas, forests, marshlands, isolated beaches, remnants of historic Vanderhorst Mansion; year-round, 12 daily departures. Visitors over age 12, $14.50; children 4–11, $7.25; senior citizens, $12.50. Marsh Creek canoeing, tour, 2 hours, departs 4 times daily, May–Sept.; each tour, adults, $13.50; children, $6.75; senior citizens, $1 discount.

Georgia. *Historic Savannah Foundation Tours.* William Scarbrough House, 41 W. Broad St., Box 1733, Savannah, GA 31402 (912–233–7703, for information; 912–233–3597, for reservations). Tours of Savannah historic district, Victorian district, gardens, or coastal Georgia's unique charms. Rates: $8–$11; children, $4.

Gray Line Savannah Landmark Tours, Inc. 215 W. Boundary, Savannah, GA 31401 (912–236–9604). City and low-country tours. $4.25–$14.50

Savannah Tours on Tape. 17 Price St., Savannah, GA 31401 (912–234–9992). Includes taped tours for drive in downtown Historic District and in countryside; walking tours on waterfront, around squares, in historic areas; tapes available from Visitors Center, DeSoto Hilton Hotel, Hyatt-Regency Savannah Hotel, Pirate's House Restaurant. Tape, cassette player, map, $6 plus deposit; 2 tapes, $10; 3 tapes, $12; tapes also available in some foreign languages.

Carriage Tours of Savannah. 522 Indian St., Savannah, GA 31401 (912–236–6756). Daytime and evening tours by horse-drawn carriages last about one hour, cover major Historic District sights. Tours operate daily except Mon. For all tours, adults, $9.50; children 12 and under, $4.50. Reservations desirable, but please check with drivers about space availability on short notice.

Old Town Brunswick Driving Tour. Old Town Brunswick Preservation Association, Old City Hall, Brunswick, GA 31520 (912–264–0442). Founded in 1771 and named for King George III's House of Brunswick, the city retains street names reminiscent of its British heritage. Many of the houses seen on the driving tour are in Victorian style architecture popular in the late 19th century. The Old City Hall, built in 1888, is a good example of Romanesque Revival design. A driving tour map with photographs and information about the buildings is available for $2.

Jekyll Island Club Historic District Tour. Macy Cottage, 375 Riverview Dr., Jekyll Island, GA 31520 (912–635–2762, 800–342–1042 GA, 800–841–6586 out of state). Between 1886 and 1942, isolated Jekyll Island was a winter vacation retreat for the very wealthy. They built a lavish clubhouse and a number of them constructed "cottages," often with 20 or more rooms. Such names as Rockefeller, Morgan, Goodyear, McCormick, Gould, and Pulitzer prevailed in the so-called "Millionaires' Village." Guided tours by motorized tram begin at the orientation center in old club stables on Stable Rd., where an orientation slide program is presented. Six of the cottages are open to the public, along with Faith Chapel noted for a fine Tiffany stained-glass window personally installed by the artist. From Memorial Day to Labor Day, tours depart Macy Cottage at 10 A.M., noon, 1, and 2 P.M.; remainder of the year at 10 A.M. and 1 P.M. Adults, $7; students 6–18, $5; children 5 and under, free. Cottage tours, adults, $5; students 6–18, $3.

PARKS AND GARDENS. North Carolina. *Orton Plantation Gardens.* Just off NC 133, 18 mi. south of Wilmington (919–371–6851). Overlooking the Cape Fear River, the gardens are site of a former 12,500-acre rice plantation. Age-old oaks draped with moss, gracious magnolias, many ornamental plantings, and flowering trees offer dazzling color. Visitors also see the eloquent antebellum classic revival style Orton House in the gardens, a private residence closed for public visits. Favorite times are Mar. through Apr. for flowering fruit trees, dogwoods, azaleas, camellias and roses; May through June for day lilies, rhododendron, oleander, gardenias, iris, and magnolias; and July through Sept. for crape myrtle, summer annuals. Open daily 8 A.M.–6 P.M., Mar.–Aug.; 8 A.M.–5 P.M., Sept.–Nov.; closed Dec.–Feb. Adults, $5; children 6–12, $2.50; under 6, free.

South Carolina. *Brookgreen Gardens.* Off U.S. 17, 4 mi. south of Murrells Inlet (803–237–4218). Situated on the grounds of a former rice and indigo plantation, the spacious gardens were established by late millionaire Archer M. Huntington and his wife, famed sculptor Anna Hyatt Huntington. Over 400 pieces of classic American statuary are exhibited among colorful floral displays, shrubs, flowering trees, moss-draped oaks, lakes, and reflecting pools. The Gardens are especially lovely during spring blooming season in Apr. The stunning art works range in size from intricate miniatures and life-size statuary to heroic equestrian sculptures. A wildlife park, an aviary, cypress swamp, nature trail, and picnic tables are also available. Ramps and specially equipped restrooms provided for handicapped. Open daily 9:30 A.M.–4:45 P.M. except Dec. 25. Adults, $5; children 6–12, $2; under 6, free; tape tours, $1.

Cypress Gardens. Just off U.S. 52, about 24 mi. north of Charleston. Mailing address: Cypress Gardens, Rte. 2, Box 588-A, Moncks Corner, SC 29461 (803–553–0515). The 160-acre gardens span an ancient water forest harboring vast cypress trees festooned with moss, blooming plants, abundant animal and bird life. The gardens may be toured by motorized sightseeing boats for stunning panoramas of floral color reflected in the dark waters. Visitors can then see the flowers at close range along winding pathways. The most dramatic season is spring, from late Mar. into Apr., when azaleas, camellias, daffodils, wisteria, and dogwood reach the peak of their splendor. There is a picnic area in the gardens; parking is free. Open daily 9 A.M.–5 P.M., Feb. 15–Apr. 30; 8 A.M.–4 P.M. remainder of year. Adults, $6 in spring, $5 rest of year; senior citizens, $5 in spring, $4 rest of year; children 6–16, $2; under 6, free. Boat ride with guide, $1 per person.

Magnolia Plantation and Gardens. Ten mi. northwest of Charleston via SC 61 (803–571–1266). These internationally famed informal gardens date from 1676 when the lands were acquired by the Drayton family, whose tenth-generation descendants still live there. Plantings include 950 species of camellias, about 250 varieties of azaleas, and hundreds of other plantings that provide year-round blooms. Mar.–Apr. spring season is most colorful, though other times offer singular beauty. Other highlights include tours of a historic plantation home with an art gallery, a waterfowl refuge, herb and Biblical gardens, boardwalk for exploring Audubon Swamp Garden, a mini-horse ranch, petting zoo, canoe and bicycle rentals, nature trails, and picnic areas. Also on the grounds are a snack bar, gift shop, Plantation Kitchen (open Mar. through May) and a 50-ft. observation tower for panoramic views of marshlands, a lake, and the Ashley River. The grounds are open Sun.–Wed. 8 A.M.–6:30 P.M., Thurs.–Sat. 8 A.M.–8 P.M. Gardens lighted several nights weekly for moonlight strolls. Admission to the grounds is adults, $7; over 65, $6.50; youths 13–19, $5; children 4–12, $3; 3 and under, free. Visits to the House and Gallery are $4 additional for each person.

Middleton Place Gardens, House and Plantation Stableyards. Just off SC 61, 14 mi. northwest of Charleston (803–556–6020). Dating from 1741, the formal gardens on the banks of the Ashley River took 10 years to complete, the handiwork of Henry Middleton, who later became President of the First Continental Congress. The beautifully designed gardens feature floral alleés; terraced lawns; and ornamental lakes to showcase magnificent plantings of camellias, magnolias, azaleas, roses, crape myrtles, and all-year seasonal flowers enhanced by ancient live oaks festooned with Spanish moss. Mar. and Apr. are the most dazzling months. Swans, peacocks, and other exotic fowls wander about the grounds. Middleton Place House, built in 1755, was largely destroyed during the Civil War; only one wing remains. Here visitors may tour various period rooms with family furniture, paintings, silver and historic documents. The Plantation Stableyards re-create 18th-and 19th-century Low Country rural life through exhibitions of tools, artifacts, and crafts people demonstrating spinning, pottery making, weaving, corn grinding, candle dipping, and other skills. Typical farm animals inhabit the Stableyards and visitors can ride in a vintage horse-drawn wagon. A restaurant serves distinctive regional specialties; gift shop features arts, crafts. Gardens and the Plantation Stableyards are open daily 9 A.M.–5 P.M. The House is open for tours Tues.–Sun., 10 A.M.–4:30 P.M., Mon., 1:30–4:30 P.M. and is closed during mid-Jan. Admission to gardens and stableyards, Mar. 1–mid-June is adults, $8; children 6–12, $4; house tours, $5 additional per person. Mid June–Feb., adults, $7; children 6–12, $3.50, Gardens and Plantation Stableyards tours.

Georgia. *Okefenokee Swamp Park.* Southeast of Waycross, 8 mi. on U.S. 1-23, then 4¾ mi. on GA 177 (912–283–0583). This northern gateway to the Great Okefenokee Swamp is in an 1,800-acre wildlife sanctuary developed to introduce visitors to the fascinating "land of trembling earth." An Interpretive Center features animated exhibitions, aquariums, dioramas tracing evolution of the Swamp, plus an Ecological Center devoted to fauna, flora, and insect life. Native animals, birds, and reptiles are exhibited in an outdoor museum where wildlife shows are presented on a daily schedule. Elevated boardwalks and a 90-ft. tower offer panoramic views of the Swamp. Guided boat tours, included in admission cost, provide close-up views of plant and animal life. Longer boat excursions are also available for $5 per person. Open daily 9 A.M.–6:30 P.M. during Daylight Savings period; 9 A.M.–5:30 P.M. rest of the year. Adults, $7; children 5–11, $5; over 61, $6.

NATIONAL AND STATE PARKS. North Carolina. *Cape Hatteras National Seashore.* Contact Superintendent, Rte. 1, Box 675, Manteo, NC 27954 (919–473–2111). Beginning just south of Nags Head, the National Seashore, served by NC 12, extends approximately 70 mi. and spans three narrow barrier islands. Northernmost is Bodie (pronounced "body"), connected by the Bonner Bridge to Hatteras, largest island in the Seashore. Free auto ferries link Hatteras with Ocracoke Island (see How to Get There). The Whalebone Junction Information Center at the northern entrance to the Seashore provides schedules of activities and brochures. Open daily Memorial Day–Labor Day, 9 A.M.–9 P.M.; inquire at Seashore Headquarters during remainder of the year. Visitor Centers, generally open daylight hours in summer, variable times remainder of the year, are located at the Bodie Island Lighthouse, Cape Hatteras Lighthouse near Buxton, and in Ocracoke village.

National Park Service campgrounds in the Seashore are located at Oregon Inlet, Cape Point, and Ocracoke Island (open mid–Apr. to Nov. 1) and at Frisco (in operation late May to Labor Day); reservations required mid-May through Labor Day by mail (Rte. 1, Box 675, Manteo, NC 27954) or in person (but not by telephone) at reservations offices in Whalebone Junction, Buxton, and at Ocracoke, only through Ticketron Reservation Office, Dept. R, 401 Hackensack Ave., Hackensack, NJ 07601. The campgrounds are in open, sandy areas without shade; supplies are available from stores in nearby villages. Fees are $8 per night for each site up to 6 persons. Time limit is 14 days, May–Aug.

Cape Lookout National Seashore. Contact Superintendent, Box 690, Beaufort, NC 28516 (919–728–2121). This National Seashore begins where Cape Hatteras

National Seashore leaves off. It's a veritable wilderness, extending about 55 mi. southward from Ocracoke Inlet to Beaufort Inlet, encompassing Portsmouth Island, Core Banks, and Shackleford Banks. Only access from the mainland is by boat and there are no roadways in the National Seashore. It's a fragile, splendid environment for day-long exploring, shelling, and observing nature. Campers must be prepared to carry their own tents, food, water, clothing and equipment—there are no campgrounds or concessions in the Seashore. All trash must be carried out—not buried—when campers leave. Passenger and four-wheel drive vehicle ferries serve the Seashore from Harkers Island and the towns of Atlantic and Davis during summer—but generally not in winter.

South Carolina. *Hunting Island State Park.* Sixteen miles east of Beaufort via U.S. 21 (803–838–2011). Situated on a semi-tropical barrier island once used by deer hunters, the park has a wide oceanfront beach, marshlands, and forests. Swimming, boating, pier fishing, hiking trails, carpet golf, picnic shelters, nature programs, playground, and concessions are among the recreational amenities. Visitors may also climb the 181 steps to the top of Hunting Island Lighthouse for stunning views of the island and ocean. Rental cabins and a campground with 200 sites are located in the park. Admission, $2 per car in summer; free remainder of year.

Huntington Beach State Park. Three miles south of Murrell's Inlet on U.S. 17, near Brookgreen Gardens (803–237–4440). Centerpiece in the park is Atalaya, the lavish winter home and studio of Archer M. Huntington and his wife, sculptress Anna Hyatt Huntington. Also in the park are an oceanfront beach, hiking, and nature trails, interpretive center, boardwalk into marshes, picnic shelters, playground, concessions, and a campground with 127 sites. Summer season admission to Atalaya: adults, 25 cents; children, 15 cents. Nominal parking fee during peak months.

Georgia. *Cumberland Island National Seashore.* Contact Superintendent, Box 806, St. Marys, GA 31558 (912–882–4335). Tours begin at the Cumberland Island Visitor's Center in St. Mary's with an orientation talk. A park ranger then accompanies visitors aboard the ferry for the 45-minute ride to the National Seashore. Highlights include the late 18th-century remains of Dungeness plantation house, which was built by the widow of Revolutionary War hero General Nathanael Greene, and remnants of Thomas Carnegie's late 19th-century mansion, which burned in the 1950's. Isolated dunes and white-sand beaches line the eastern side of the island. Just behind the dunes is a maritime forest of palmetto, pine, magnolia, and live oak trees. Only 300 persons are allowed to visit the island each day. Restricted camping is permitted. Visitors and campers must make reservations in advance in person or by telephone; requests by mail are not accepted. The ferry costs about $8 for adults.

Stephen C. Foster State Park. Eighteen mi. northeast of Fargo via GA 177; contact Stephen C. Foster State Park, Fargo, GA 31631 (912–637–5274). Located on Jones Island, the Park is in an especially beautiful area of the Okefenokee Swamp, where moss-strewn strands of cypress trees reflect in the black-mirror waters and flowers display seasonal colors. Rental boats, canoes, and guided tours are available for exploring the Swamp and for fishing expeditions. Open Mar. 1–mid-Sept., 6:30 A.M.–8:30 P.M.; mid-Sept.–Feb., 7 A.M.–7 P.M. Please inquire about camping, cottage fees, and reservations.

Suwannee Canal Recreation Area, Okefenokee National Wildlife Refuge. Eleven mi. southwest of Folkston off GA 23–121; contact about guided tours, boat or canoe rentals, and fishing: Concessionaire, Suwanee Canal Recreation Area, Folkston, GA 31537 (912–496–7836). Also known as Camp Cornelia, the Recreation Area provides access to fascinating Chesser, Grand, and Mizell prairies by following the Suwannee Canal for 11 mi. into the Okefenokee. These are among the most extensive open areas in the Swamp, where small lakes and 'gator holes provide excellent fresh water fishing. The prairies are also interesting to bird watchers, especially as they are home of the rare Florida sandhill crane. Other facilities in the Recreation Area are a 4.5-mi. Swamp Island Drive where visitors can see a reconstructed Chesser Island Homestead and follow a boardwalk to an observation tower. There are also picnic tables, a wildlife interpretive center, and a concessionaire for booking guided boat tours into the Swamp. Open daily Mar. 1–mid-Sept., 7 A.M.–7:30 P.M.; 8 A.M.–6 P.M. the remainder of year; closed Dec. 25. Free admission to Recreation Area, though some activities may involve fees.

HISTORIC SITES AND HOUSES—NORTH CAROLINA. Elizabeth II State Historic Site. Across from the waterfront, Manteo (919–473–1144). The *Elizabeth II* is a composite replica of the 16th-century sailing ships that were used in various expeditions sponsored by Sir Walter Raleigh to Roanoke Island. The Lost Colonists sailed aboard a ship similar to this one. Interpreters in Elizabethan costumes conduct tours and, in summer, present living history programs. Visitor Center provides historic exhibits, a 20-minute multimedia program, and a gift shop. Open daily 10 A.M.–6 P.M., Apr.–Oct. Tues.–Sun., 10 A.M.-4 P.M., Nov.–Mar. Closed Thanksgiving, Dec. 24–25. Adults, $3; over 65, $2.50; children 6–12, $1.50. Ramps and rest rooms for handicapped.

Fort Raleigh National Historic Site. On Roanoke Island, three mi. north of Manteo on U.S. 64–264 (919–473–2111); Lindsay Warren Visitor Center (919–473–5772). In 1685, Sir Walter Raleigh sent an expedition of 500 men in seven ships to Roanoke Island with the purpose of building a fort and establishing a colony. Slightly over a hundred men stayed at the settlement until the following year when they returned to England. The Lost Colonists occupied the Fort briefly in 1687 while building their town. The old Fort, surrounded by an earth embankment, has been excavated and restored. An orientation film and excellent exhibits in the Lindsay Warren Visitor Center include artifacts, historic maps, documents, and vivid paintings of the Indians by John White, who was appointed governor of the Lost Colony by Sir Walter. Governor White was the grandfather of Virginia Dare, first child of English parentage born in the New World. The Lindsay Warren Visitor Center is open daily except Dec. 25, 9 A.M.–6 P.M., mid-June–Labor Day; 9 A.M.–5 P.M., rest of year. Free.

Tryon Palace Restoration and Garden Complex. 610 Pollock St., at south end of George St., New Bern (919–638–1560). Completed in 1770 as the combined residence and colonial capitol building during the administration of Royal Governor William Tryon, the Palace was considered among the finest government structures in the Thirteen Colonies. Elaborate furnishings and accessories in the Palace are splendid American and British antiques based on an inventory of the Governor's possessions, which were lost in a warehouse fire after he returned to England. Accuracy of appointments extends even to titles of books on the shelves. Costumed hostesses guide visitors through the Palace, its two wings and beautifully planted grounds. Special historical drama tours during summer supplement the regular interpretation. Crafts demonstrations are presented daily. An 18-minute film at the visitor center provides interesting background. Also included in the Palace Complex are the restored Georgian-style John Wright Stanley House, built during the 1780's, and the Stevenson House, dating from about 1805. Both houses are furnished in period and open for tours. The Palace Complex is open daily except major holidays Mon.–Sat., 9:30 A.M.–4 P.M.; Sun., 1:30–4 P.M. with last tours departing at 4 P.M. Admission to Palace and Gardens; adults, $8; students through high school, $4. Gardens only for self-guided tour: adults, $4; students through high school, $3. Combination tickets for Palace, Gardens, Stanley House, and Stevenson House: adults, $12; students through high school, $6. Stanley and Stevenson Houses: adults, $8; students through high school, $4, for each house.

U.S.S. North Carolina Battleship Memorial. On west bank of Cape Fear River on U.S. 17–74–76–421 over the Cape Fear Memorial Bridge, Wilmington (919–762–1829). Commemorating all the men and women who served their country in U.S. military forces during World War II. Commissioned in 1941, this was the first modern American battleship, dubbed "The Showboat" by Navy personnel. A heroic participant in Pacific engagements from Guadalcanal to Tokyo Bay, the ship earned 15 battle stars. Visitor tours include the galley, engine room, wheelhouse, hospital, crew's quarters, mess hall, and gun turrets. An on-board museum has exhibits of wartime engagements. Also at the Memorial is a rare restored Vought Kingfisher World War II float plane, used in Pacific air-sea rescue missions. Open daily 8 A.M.–sunset. Adults, $5; children 6–11, $2.50.

Wright Brothers National Memorial. On U.S. 158 Bypass at Milepost 8, Kill Devil Hills (919–441–7430). An imposing memorial shaft atop a tall sand dune commemorates the point from which Orville and Wilbur Wright in Dec. 1903 successfully accomplished the first sustained flight in a craft heavier than air. Though others may have earlier accomplished similar feats, it was the Wright brothers of Akron, Ohio who pioneered the "air age." Visitor Center displays graphically describe their accomplishments and a replica of their first-flight aircraft, *The Flyer,* is also there—the original is in Washington, D.C.'s Smithsonian Institution. Also on the grounds are reconstructions of the Wright brothers' living quarters, complete with furnishings and canned foods. Open daily 9 A.M.–7 P.M., mid-June–Labor Day; 9 A.M.–5 P.M., rest of year; closed Dec. 25. Admission, $1; over age 62 and 1–16, free.

HISTORIC SITES AND HOUSES—SOUTH CAROLINA. Charles Towne Landing. 1500 Old Towne Rd. on SC 171, west bank of the Ashley River just outside Charleston (803–556–4450). Established in 1670, this was the original site of the Charleston settlement, earliest in South Carolina. It was occupied for 10 years until the city was permanently established in its present location. Highlights include replica fortifications, a reconstructed village, gardens, an animal park where species native to the region three centuries ago roam freely, nature and bicycle paths, a reconstruction of a 17th-century trading vessel, and a pavilion where museum exhibits and an orientation film introduce visitors to the coastal region. Also on the grounds are a snack bar, gift shop, picnic tables, and provisions for handicapped vacationers. Open daily, except Dec. 24–25, 9 A.M.–6 P.M., June 1–Labor Day; 9 A.M.–5 P.M., rest of year. Rental bicycles, $1 an hour; kayaks, $1 half an hour; cassette tours, $1; tram tours, $1 per seat. Adults, $5; senior citizens, $2.50; children 6–14, $2.50; handicapped visitors, free.

Drayton Hall. On SC 61, nine mi. north of Charleston (803–766–0188). Built in 1738 beside the Ashley River, Drayton Hall is considered the nation's finest example of unspoiled Georgian Palladian architecture. The house was never altered by plumbing, electricity, running water, or central heating. Now a property of the National Trust for Historical Preservation, the house is unfurnished so visitors can see original plaster moldings, woodwork, and paint. Guided tours conducted hourly. Open daily 10 A.M.–5 P.M., Mar. 1–Oct. 31; 10 A.M.–3 P.M., remainder of the year; closed major holidays. Adults, $6; children 6–18, $3.

Edmondston–Alston House. 21 East Battery, Charleston (803–722–7171 or 556–6020). Dating from about 1826, the eloquent two-story house, at a right angle with the street, overlooks the harbor. Furnishings in the Greek Revival mansion include lovely displays of china, silver, family portraits, antiques. Open daily, except Dec. 25., Mon.–Sat., 10 A.M.–5 P.M.; Sun. 1:30 P.M.–5 P.M. Admission, $4 or combination ticket including Nathaniel Russell House, $6; under 6 free.

Fort Sumter National Monument. In Charleston harbor, reachable only by Fort Sumter Tours excursion boats from Charleston City Marina, 17 Lockwood Blvd., Charleston, SC 29401 (803–722–1691). National Monument telephone (803–883–3123). Built on an artificial island between 1829–1860, Fort Sumter was garrisoned by a Union force in the spring of 1861. They refused a Confederate demand to evacuate. On Apr. 12th, the Confederates fired the first shots of the Civil War from the shore in a bombardment lasting two days before the Union troops surrendered. National Park Service guides conduct tours of the Fort, which also contains museum displays and a gift shop. Fort Sumter Tours offers excursions year round except Dec. 25 on varying seasonal schedules; please write or phone in advance. The Fort Sumter boat tours last 2¼ hours, with one hour at the Fort, remainder of time for a harbor excursion. Facilities for handicapped. Adults, $8; 6–11, $4; under 6, free. Fort admission, free.

Heyward-Washington House. 87 Church St., Charleston (803–722–2996). Completed in 1772, the fine town house was residence of Thomas Heyward, one of the signers of the Declaration of Independence. During his visit in May, 1791, President George Washington stayed in the home. Notable 18th-century furnishings include pieces by Thomas Elfe and other Charleston craftsmen. Tours also include kitchen and garden behind the house. Open Mon.–Sat., 10 A.M.–5 P.M., except holidays; Sun., 1–5 P.M. last tour at 4:30 P.M. Adults, $4; seniors, $3.60; children 3–12, $2. Combination tickets, including Charleston Museum and Joseph Manigault House, $10.

Hopsewee Plantation. On U.S. 17, 12 mi. south of Georgetown (803–546–7891). Dating from 1740, the two-story black cypress house overlooking the North Santee River is typical of South Carolina coastal and Low Country Colonial-era architecture. The Georgian staircase and period furnishings are especially beautiful. The house is surrounded by moss-draped live oaks, magnolias, and tree-sized camellias. Open Tues.–Fri., 10 A.M.–5 P.M., Mar.–Oct.; by appointment other times; closed

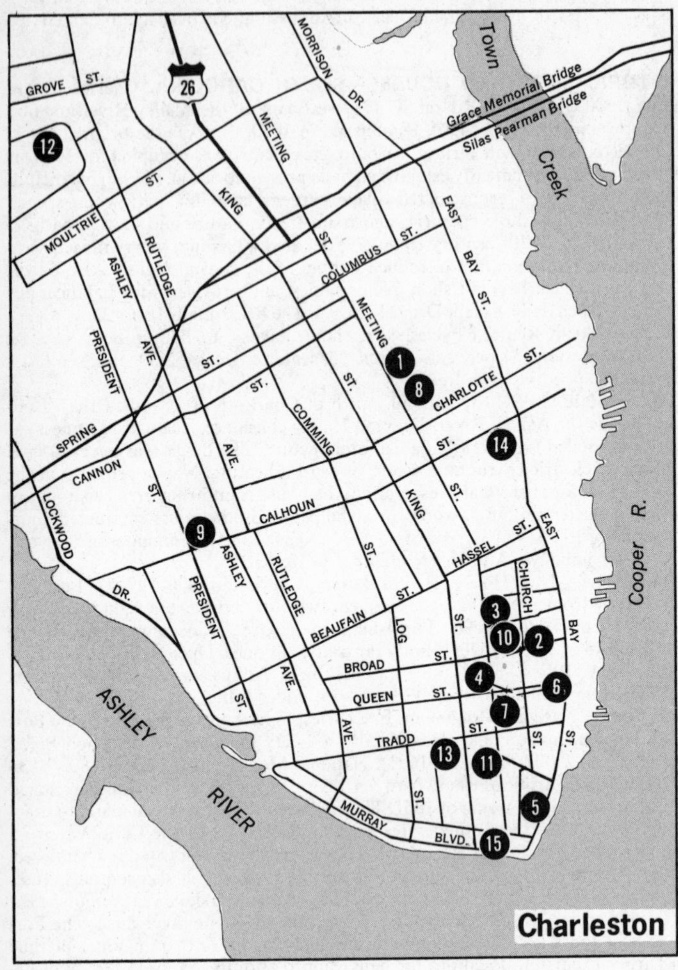

Points of Interest

1) Charleston Museum
2) City Hall
3) Confederate Museum
4) Dock Street Theater
5) Edmondston-Alston House
6) French Huguenot Church
7) Heyward-Washington House
8) Manigault House
9) Medical University of South Carolina
10) Old Powder Magazine
11) Russell House
12) Sunken Gardens
13) Sword Gates
14) Visitor Information Center
15) White Point Gardens

major holidays. Adults, $5; ages 6–18, $1; grounds only, including nature trail, $1 per car.

Huguenot Church. Church St., at Queen St., Charleston (803–722–4385). The present Gothic-style French Protestant Church dates from 1845, the fourth structure on the site. As early as 1687, many French Huguenots came to South Carolina to escape religious persecution. Quite a few of them settled on Cooper River plantations and came to Charleston by boat to attend services. An annual French Liturgy service is held each spring. Open Mon.–Sat., 10 A.M.–12:30 P.M. and 2–4 P.M., closed major holidays, Jan. 1–31. Donations.

John Mark Verdier House. 801 Bay St. in downtown Beaufort (803–524–6334). Dating from about 1790, the splendid Federal-style house was built by a wealthy merchant-planter. It is headquarters of the Historic Beaufort Foundation, which has furnished the mansion with pieces from the 1790s to 1825, when the Marquis de Lafayette was entertained there. Open Tues.–Sat., 11 A.M.–4 P.M., Feb. 1–mid-Dec.; closed Thanksgiving, mid-Dec.–Jan. Adults, $3; children under 15, $2.

Joseph Manigault House. 350 Meeting St., Charleston (803–722–2996). Completed in 1803, this was Charleston's first Adam-style house. It was designed by Charleston architect Gabriel Manigault for his brother Joseph. The imposing main house is in the shape of a parallelogram with half-moon bows at either end. It has an elaborate staircase and decorative Louis XVI motifs symbolic of the owner's French Huguenot heritage. Furnishings are fine examples of British, French, and Charleston antiques. Open Mon.–Sat., 10 A.M.–5 P.M.; Sun. 1–5 P.M. Closed major holidays; last guided tour at 4:30 P.M. Adults, $4; seniors, $3.60; children 3–12, $2. Combination ticket, including Aiken-Rhett House, Charleston Museum, and Heyward-Washington House, $10.

Nathaniel Russell House. 51 Meeting St., Charleston (803–723–3646 or 722–3405). Among Charleston's finest examples of the Adam style, this house was completed in 1808 as the home of a wealthy merchant. Its most notable features are a "free flying" circular staircase which spirals three stories with no apparent means of support, innovative elliptical designs in some of the rooms, splendid examples of period furniture, and accessories. The house is headquarters of The Historic Charleston Foundation. Open Mon.–Sat., 10 A.M.–5 P.M.; Sun. 2–5 P.M.; closed Dec. 25. Guided tours, $4; combination ticket with Edmonston-Alston House, $6. Children under 6 free.

St. Michael's Episcopal Church. Meeting at Broad Sts., Charleston (803–723–0603). Completed by 1761, the Church has a Palladian Doric portico and 186-ft. steeple. It's one of the few city churches in the nation to retain its original design. The ornate interior includes the original pulpit and box pews. Except for interruptions during the Revolutionary and Civil Wars, the bells in the steeple have been part of Charleston's life for over two centuries. George Washington worshipped here during his 1791 visit and climbed the steeple for a panoramic view of the city. Open Mon.–Fri., 9 A.M.–4:30 P.M., closes early on Wed. Sat. 9 A.M.–noon; closed some holidays. Free.

Thomas Elfe Workshop. 54 Queen St., Charleston (803–722–2130). The modest residence and workplace of one of Charleston's most talented furniture makers, this is a welcome change from elaborate mansions of the very wealthy. It's a charming two-story, four-room miniature of a Charleston "single house," adorned with beautiful cypress panels and collections of original and replica Elfe furniture. A small courtyard garden behind the house is especially delightful. A gift shop next door features hard-to-find Charleston-style household accessories and gift items. Open for conducted half-hour tours Mon.–Fri., 10 A.M.–5 P.M.; Sat., 10 A.M.–1 P.M.; closed Sun. and major holidays. Admission, $3.

HISTORIC SITES AND HOUSES—GEORGIA. **Davenport House.** 324 East State St. on Columbia Sq., Savannah (912–236–8097). Among Savannah's finest examples of Federal architecture, the house was completed in 1821 as the home of Isaiah Davenport, a prosperous master builder originally from New England. He designed the house himself and its richness of detail reflects his impeccable taste. Period furnishings include antiques from England and the United States, rich carpets and draperies, delicate wrought iron, and ornate plaster work. Open 10 A.M.–4 P.M., Mon.–Sat.; 1:30–4 P.M. Sun.; closed major holidays. Adults, $3; children 6–18, $2.

Fort Frederica National Monument. Twelve mi. northeast of Brunswick via Torras Causeway, on St. Simons Island (912–638–3639). Some standing remnants of the fortification established in 1736 by General James Oglethorpe and foundations of the garrison town are seen at the National Monument. The site borders the Frederica River. Visitor Center features displays, a diorama, excavated objects from the site, and an orientation film. Scene of the Battle of Bloody Marsh where Oglethorpe's forces ambushed and defeated Spanish invaders on July 7, 1842, is six miles south of the Fort. Visitor Center open daily, except Dec. 25, 9 A.M.–5 P.M.; to 6 P.M., Memorial Day–Labor Day. Admission, $1; maximum charge, $3 per vehicle; over 62 and under 16 free.

Fort Pulaski National Monument. Off U.S. 80, 15 mi. east of Savannah (912–786–5787). Named in honor of the famed Revolutionary War Polish hero who lost his life in the defense of Savannah against the British, this monumental fortress was built between 1829 and 1847 on Cockspur Island in the delta of the Savannah River. Brick and masonry work is distinctive, especially in archways. During the Civil War, Confederate forces held the fort until 1862 when they surrendered after a 30-hour Union bombardment. Faithfully restored, Fort Pulaski includes officers' rooms and mess, chapel, enlisted men's quarters, and medical dispensary. Various artillery pieces are on display. Visitor Center has historic exhibits and a book store. Guided tours and demonstrations are offered daily during summer, weekends rest of the year. All facilities available to handicapped. Open daily 8:30 A.M.–6:45 P.M. Memorial Day-Labor Day, 8:30 A.M.–5:15 P.M. rest of year; closed Jan. 1, Dec. 25. Admission, $1 per car Apr.–Oct.; rest of year, free.

Hofwyl-Broadfield Plantation State Historic Site. On U.S. 17, 10 mi. north of Brunswick (912–264–9263). A working rice plantation was established at Broadfield on the Altamaha River in 1806 by William Brailsford, whose family built Hofwyl house there during the 1850s. When the rice industry had collapsed by the early 1900s, the plantation was converted to a dairy farm, remaining in the family until 1973. Much of the land today is a wildlife preserve. Museum exhibits and slide show trace evolution of rice culture. Hofwyl House, a typical coastal-Low Country plantation residence, is furnished with many original family pieces. Open 9 A.M.–5 P.M., Tues.–Sat.; 2–5:30 P.M. Sun; closed Thanksgiving, Dec. 25, Adults, $1.50; children 6–12, 75 cents; under 6, free.

Juliette Gordon Low Birthplace. 142 Bull St. at Oglethorpe Ave., Savannah (912–233–4501). The splendid Regency mansion was designed by young English architect William Jay and completed by 1821. Here Juliette Gordon was born in 1860. After the death of her husband, William M. Low, she founded the first troop of Girl Guides in 1912. The organization became the nucleus of the Girl Scouts of America. The home is maintained by the Girl Scouts as a national program center and memorial to their magnificently restored mid-19th century opera house, then continue and furnished with many family originals. Open 10 A.M.–4 P.M., Mon.–Tues. and Thurs.–Sat.; 12:30 P.M.–4:30 P.M., Sun Feb.–Nov.; 10 A.M.–4 P.M. Mon.–Tues., Thurs.–Sat., rest of year. closed Wed., Jan. 1, Thanksgiving, Dec.–Jan. Adults, $3; students 6–18, $2.25; under 6, free.

Owens-Thomas House. 124 Abercorn St. on Oglethorpe Sq., Savannah (912–233–9743). This is considered by many architectural historians to be the finest English Regency house in the United States. It was designed by John Jay and completed in 1819. Distinctive highlights include the exterior color similar to Georgia's red clay soil, a side balcony from which Marquis de Lafayette delivered an address, interior columned foyers, a double stairwell spanned by a small second story bridge, and fascinating *trompe l'oeil* images in the salon. Miss Margaret Thomas, a granddaughter of the Owens family, faithfully preserved the house and gardens as a national treasure. Original family furnishings, including pieces by Duncan Phyfe and rare European and Chinese porcelains may be seen on guided tours. Open 10 A.M.–5 P.M., Tues.–Sat.; 2–5 P.M., Sun.–Mon.; closed major holidays, entire month of Sept. Adults, $4; senior citizens, children 12–18, $2; 6–11, $1; under 6 free with adult.

MUSEUMS. Charleston Museum. 360 Meeting St., Charleston (803–722–2996). Oldest museum organization in nation, dating from 1773, features archaeology, natural history, the arts, and historical exhibits of South Carolina, including replica of Confederate submarine *Hunley.* Open Mon.–Sat., 9 A.M.–5 P.M.; Sun. 1–5 P.M. Closed major holidays. Adults, $4; senior citizens, $3.60; children 3–12, $2; combination ticket, including Heyward-Washington House and Joseph Manigault House, $10.

Gibbes Museum of Art. 135 Meeting St., Charleston (803–722–2706). Excellent collections of South Carolina art, Southern historical portraits, sculpture, Japanese prints, miniatures. Concerts and lectures periodically. Open Tues.–Sat., 10 A.M.–5 P.M.; Sun.–Mon., 1–5 P.M.; closed major holidays. Adults, $2; students with ID and over 65, $1; under 18, 50 cents; under 12, free.

Savannah History Museum. 303 W. Broad St., adjoining Visitor Center, Savannah (912–238–1779). Housed in a massive former 19th-century railroad terminal, the museum offers a historical presentation using three-dimensional moving figures, a special effects program depicting the 1779 Siege of Savannah, and abundant museum displays, including Indian artifacts, model of Whitney's cotton gin, a vintage locomotive and autos, weapons, and illustrations. Gift shop and café also on premises. Open daily 8:30 A.M.–5 P.M. Closed Jan 1, Dec. 25. Adults, $3.75; over 55, $3.25; children 4–11, $2.50.

Museum of Coastal History. 610 Beachview Dr., St. Simons Island (912–638–4666). Displays, illustrations, furnishings, accessories in 1872 lightkeeper's house depict area's history. Visitors may climb to top of adjoining lighthouse for glorious views. Open Tues.–Sat., Memorial Day–Labor Day, 10 A.M.–5 P.M.; Sun. 1:30–5 P.M., remainder of year. Tues.-Sat., 1–4 P.M., Sun., 1:30–4 P.M. Closed Mon. and major holidays. Adults, $1.50; children, 6–12, $1.

Patriots Point Naval and Maritime Museum. Two mi. east of Charleston on U.S. 17 at north end of Cooper River Bridge (803–884–2727). Centerpiece is the World War II, Korean, and Vietnam era aircraft carrier USS *Yorktown;* also on exhibit are the nuclear merchant ship *Savannah,* a vintage World War II submarine, a destroyer, a former Coast Guard Cutter, missiles, airplanes, and weapons. Tours include working areas of all the ships. A film, *The Fighting Lady,* is shown regularly aboard the *Yorktown.* Open daily Apr.–Oct., 9 A.M.–6 P.M.; remainder of year 9 A.M.–5 P.M. Adults, $8; senior citizens 62 and over and military personnel in uniform, $7; children 6–11, $4.

Ships of the Sea Maritime Museum. 503 E. River St., Savannah (912–232–1511). Splendid collection housed on four floors of historic Factors Walk warehouse. Highlights feature ship models, scrimshaw, colorful figureheads from clipper ships, weapons, fine furniture, and accessories of early 19th-century seafarers brought to Savannah from journeys abroad. Internationally esteemed collection of ships in bottles includes models of General Oglethorpe's *Ann,* Columbus's *Santa Maria,* and a sinking *Titanic.* Open daily, 10 A.M.–5 P.M. Closed major holidays. Adults, $2; military personnel, senior citizens over 65, $1; children 7–12, 75 cents.

Telfair Mansion and Art Museum. 121 Barnard St., on Telfair Sq., Savannah (912–232–1177). Museum is housed in an 1818 Regency mansion used as governors' residence. It was designed by young English architect William Jay. The restored Octagon Room is considered by many to be one of the nation's finest period rooms. Collections include American and English antique furniture and accessories, American Impressionist paintings, sculpture, and Kahlil Gibran drawings and paintings. Guided tours are available. Open Tues.–Sat., 10 A.M.–5 P.M.; Sun., 2–5 P.M. Closed Mon. and major holidays. Adults, $2.50; over 65 and students $1; children 6–12, 50 cents.

ACCOMMODATIONS—NORTH CAROLINA. The North Carolina coast is especially popular with family vacationers, and offers a good choice of motels and motor lodges in every price category. State law prohibits admittance of dogs in lodging facilities unless accompanying a sight- or hearing-impaired individual. Rates are based on high season, which usually applies Memorial Day–Labor Day. During this time, reservations should be made well in advance. In the beach resorts, rates may drop considerably off season. Some establishments close at this time. Toll-free numbers are those of individual facilities. Call 800–555–1212 for toll-free numbers of national systems. Accommodations are listed according to category, in a geographical progression from north to south.

These are average rates, based on double occupancy: *Deluxe,* $90–$145; *Expensive,* $60–$90; *Moderate,* $50–$60; *Inexpensive,* under $50. Tax ranges from 4–6.5%.

Beaches North of Oregon Inlet

Deluxe

Best Western Armada Resort Hotel. Beach Rd., Milepost 17, Oceanfront, Box 307, Nags Head, NC 27959 (919–441–6315 or 800–528–1234, nationwide). 105 rooms, 3 efficiencies. Restaurant, lounge with ocean view, pool, golf privileges, tennis courts, playground. Cable TV. Handicapped facilities.

Holiday Inn. U.S. 158 Bus., Milepost 9½, Oceanfront, Box 308, Kill Devil Hills, NC 27948 (919–441–6333 or 800–465–4329). 105 rooms, restaurants, live entertainment in Madeline's Lounge. Handicapped facilities, pool, cable TV-HBO, golf privileges. Special golf, fishing, "getting away" value packages.

Expensive

Beacon Motor Lodge. 2617 S. Va. Dare Tr., Milepost 11, Oceanfront, Box 729, Nags Head, NC 27959 (919–441–5501) 48 units include 15 efficiencies, 5 apartments, 2 cottages. Also weekly rates. Pool, cable TV, golf privileges, recreational facilities, laundry. Daily maid service. Open late Mar.–late Oct.

Blue Heron Motel. Milepost 15–16, Oceanfront, Rte. 1, Box 741, Nags Head, NC 27959 (919–441–7447). 14 rooms, 10 efficiencies, heated indoor pool/spa, cable TV. Oceanfront balconies.

Cabana East Motel. U.S. 158 Bus., Milepost 11, Oceanfront, Box 395, Nags Head, NC 27959 (919–441–7106). Pool, cable TV/HBO, golf privileges, recreational facilities. 16 rooms, 22 efficiencies, 1 cottage.

Carolinian Hotel. Milepost 10½, Oceanfront, Box 370, Nags Head, NC 27959 (919–441–7171). Landmark hotel offers touches of Southern charm, showcases gourmet specialties in dining room. Ten percent off dinner entrées, free breakfast coffee for hotel guests. Comedy Club Mon.–Thurs., hotel guests half price. Packages, discounts for longer stays. Cable TV, golf privileges. Open mid-Mar.–Nov.

Days Inn. U.S. 158 Bypass, Milepost 4½, Box 1096, Kitty Hawk, NC 27949 (919–261–4888 or 800–325–2525). 98 units. Pool, cable TV, HBO. Free continental breakfast. Reservation deposit required. Nonsmoking rooms available. Some rooms in *Deluxe* category.

Ocean Veranda Motel. 2603 S. Va. Dare Tr., Milepost 11, Box 651, Nags Head, NC 27959 (919–441–5858). 31 units include some efficiencies. Cable TV, poolside gazebo, golf privileges, recreational facilities, family picnic area, free morning coffee. Some rooms in *Moderate* category.

Quality Inn John Yancey. U.S. 158 Bus., Milepost 10, Box 422, Kill Devil Hills, NC 27948 (919–441–7141 or 441–7727; 800–228–5151). 63 rooms, 45 efficiencies, pool, cable TV, rocking chair sundeck, refrigerators in all rooms, children under 12 free. Golf privileges, recreational facilities. Handicapped units. Restaurant open during season. Some rooms in *Deluxe* category.

Sea Foam Motel. U.S. 158 Bus., Milepost 16 ½, Oceanfront, RFD 1, Box 730, Nags Head, NC 27959 (919–441–7320). 30 rooms, 2 cottages, 18 efficiencies (some oceanfront). Pool, cable TV, daily maid service, golf privileges, shuffleboard.

Tanya's Ocean House. U.S. 158 Bus., Milepost 10, Oceanfront, Kill Devil Hills, Box 747, Kill Devil Hills, NC 27948 (919–441–2900). 42 rooms, all lavishly decorated in unique "themes." Refrigerators in all rooms, Cable TV–HBO, golf privileges. Open Apr. 1–Nov. 1.

Moderate

Tar Heel Motel. 7010 Va. Dare Tr., Milepost 16, Box 242, Nags Head, NC 27949 (919–441–6150). 33 rooms, 4 efficiencies. Cable TV. Open Apr.–Oct.

Inexpensive

Owens' Motel. U.S. 158 Bus, Milepost 16½, Rte. 1, Box 729, Nags Head, NC 27959 (919–441–6361). 26 rooms, 8 efficiencies. Pool, cable TV, oceanfront deck with rocking chairs, fishing pier, shops. Some rooms in *Moderate* category. Open Apr.–Nov. Next door restaurant features coastal cuisine in setting of artifacts and relics from sailing days. Station Keepers' Lounge has nightly entertainment.

Manteo, Roanoke Island

Moderate

Duke of Dare Motor Lodge. U.S. 64–264, Box 746, Manteo, NC 27954 (919–473–2175). 57 units, pool, cable TV.

Elizabethan Inn. U.S. 64–264, Box 549, Manteo, NC 27954 (919–473–2101). 65 rooms in 3 structures, to suit various tastes, budgets. Some rooms have refrigerators. Queen-size beds. Handicapped facilities. Pool, cable TV, picnic area. Some rooms in *Expensive* category. Restaurant features home-style cooking.

Hatteras Island

Moderate

General Mitchell Motel. NC 12, Oceanfront, Box 37, Hatteras, NC 27943 (919–986–2444). 49 rooms, 15 efficiencies. Pool, cable TV, boat ramp. Some rooms in *Expensive* category.

Hatteras Island Resort. NC 12, Oceanfront, Box 8, Rodanthe, NC 27968 (919–987–2345). 32 rooms, 35 cottages. Restaurant, pool, handicapped facilities, fishing, recreational facilities. Open all year.

Sea Gull Motel. NC 12, Box 280, Hatteras, NC 27943 (919–986–2550). 45-unit oceanfront facility on Hatteras Island has some apartments and efficiencies with kitchens. Pool, TV; some rooms equipped for handicapped. Open Mar.–Dec. 1. Restaurant nearby. Some rooms in *Expensive* category.

Ocracoke Island

Expensive

Anchorage Inn & Marina. On the harbor, Box 130, Ocracoke, NC 27960 (919–928–1101). 36 rooms. Pool, handicapped facilities, cable TV, boat ramp and docks, fuel.

Moderate

Harborside Motel. NC 12, Box 116, Ocracoke, NC 27960 (919–928–3111 or 919–928–4141). 18 rooms, 4 efficiencies, TV, recreational facilities, boat ramp. Open Mar. 15 through Nov. Some rooms in *Expensive* category.

Island Inn. NC 12, Box 9, Ocracoke, NC 27960 (919–928–4351). 37 rooms, 2 cottages. Heated pool, cable TV, island seafood in one of Ocracoke's most popular dining rooms. Front porch rocking; friendly, personalized service. Open Mar.–early Nov.

Pony Island Motel. NC 12, Box 309, Ocracoke, NC 27960 (919–928–4411). 31 rooms, 9 efficiencies, 2 cottages, Restaurant, cable TV, bike rentals. Open Mar.–Nov.

Elizabeth City

Expensive

Holiday Inn. 522 S. Hughes Blvd., Elizabeth City, NC 27909 (919–338–3951 or 800–465–4329). 158 rooms. Madeline's Steak and Seafood Restaurant, lounge. Playground, Showtime movies, cable TV, coin laundry. Teens free; weekly, monthly rates.

New Bern

Deluxe

Fairfield Harbour Resort. 750 Broad Creek Rd., New Bern, NC 28560 (919–638–8011 or 800–334–5739; 800–682–8140 in NC). 176 units, 36 condominiums,

74 efficiencies. Lounge, restaurant, cable TV. Laundry, pool, stables, mini golf, health club. Jacuzzi, sauna. Golf, tennis privileges. Some facilities for handicapped. Open all year. Some rooms in *Expensive* category.

Expensive

Ramada Inn. Jct. U.S. 70 Business & U.S. 70 Bypass, 101 Howell Rd., New Bern, NC 28562 (919–636–3637 or 800–272–6232). Offered here are 196 units, some suites. There are a restaurant, lounge with entertainment, pool, and airport transportation.

Morehead City and Its Beaches

Deluxe

Holiday Inn. Salterpath Rd., Box 280, Atlantic Beach, NC 28512 (919–726–2544 or 800–465–4329). 115 units, some with refrigerators. Restaurant, free movies, golf, tennis, pool. Oceanfront, with private beach. Near children's amusement park. Teens free. Some rooms in *Expensive* category.

Expensive

Best Western Buccaneer Motor Lodge. 2806 Arendell St., Morehead City, NC 28557 (919–726–3115 or 800–528–1234). 92 units. Cable TV, movies, restaurant. Pool, golf privileges. Some rooms in *Moderate* category.

Ramada Inn. Salterpath Rd., Box 846, Atlantic Beach, NC 28512 (919–247–4155 or 800–272–6232). 100 rooms. Restaurant, lounge, entertainment, dancing. Pool, handicapped facilities. Beach-front location. Some rooms in *Moderate* and *Deluxe* categories.

Wilmington and Its Beaches

Deluxe

Blockade Runner Resort Hotel & Conference Center. One-quarter mi. south on U.S. 76, Box 555, 275 Waynick Blvd., Wrightsville Beach, NC 28480 (919–256–2251; 800–722–5809 in NC), 150 units. Cable TV, pool, lifeguard, playground, sailboats, health club. Golf, tennis privileges. Private balconies, patios. Landmark property has been recently remodeled. Dining room, classical piano entertainment in lounge. Senior citizen rates, under 12 free. Some rooms in *Deluxe* category.

Expensive

Hilton Wilmington. 301 N. Water St., Wilmington, NC 28401 (919–763–5900 or 800–445–8667). 178 rooms, some 2-bedroom units, suites. Pool, wading pool, cable TV. Restaurant, lounge, entertainment. Golf privileges. Fee for movies, docking. Airport transportation.

Holiday Inn Wrightsville Beach (formerly Sheraton Wrightsville Beach). 1706 N. Lumina Ave., Wrightsville Beach, NC 28480 (919–256–2231 or 800–465–4329). 147 rooms; suites, studios available. Cable TV, pool, wading pool, golf privileges, game room. Restaurant, lounge, entertainment. Private balconies, beach. Senior rates, under 12 free. Some rooms in *Deluxe* category.

Moderate

Best Western Carolinian. 2916 Market St., Wilmington, NC 28403 (919–763–4653 or 800–528–1234). 61 units. Two restaurants adjacent. Cable TV, pool; nearby golf, fishing, beaches, tennis, horseback riding. Fly-drive program. Senior discount. Some rooms in *Expensive* category.

Comfort Inn Executive Center. 151 S. College Rd., Wilmington, NC 28403 (919–791–4841 or 800–228–5150). 149 units, suites, lounge, dining room, pool. Some rooms in *Expensive* category.

Holiday Inn. 4903 Market St., Wilmington, NC 28405 (919–799–1440 or 800–465–4329). 234 rooms. Adam's Restaurant and Lounge. Cable TV; golf, fishing nearby. Teens free. Some rooms in *Expensive* category.

Ramada Inn Conference Center. 5001 Market St., Wilmington, NC 28405 (919–799–1730 or 800–272–6232). 100 rooms; kings, suites available. Dining room, lounge, dancing. Handicapped facilities, playground. Seasonal golf packages; airport transportation. Corporate, government, and senior rates available.

Inexpensive

Comfort Inn. 2929 Market St., Wilmington, NC 28403 (919–763–3318 or 800–228–5150). 48 rooms. Restaurant within walking distance. Pool, handicapped facilities. Seniors, government and military plans available; fly-drive voucher. Some rooms in *Moderate* category.

Days Inn. 5040 Market St., Wilmington, NC 28405 (919–799–6300 or 800–325–2525). 122 rooms. Pool, cable TV. Restaurant. Handicapped, nonsmoking facilities available. Some rooms in *Moderate* category.

ACCOMMODATIONS—SOUTH CAROLINA. This hospitable state's coastland offers an amazing variety of lodging choices. Myrtle Beach, one of the Eastern Seaboard's most popular family vacation meccas, has everything from comfortable accommodations for the budget-minded to super-luxurious resort hotels. Serene old Charleston, a national treasure, provides an excellent choice of motels, motor lodges, and hotels; many are within, or near, the restored Historic District. Beautiful historic Beaufort has witnessed a motel "boom" in recent years. And several of the idyllic semi-tropical sea islands dotting the South Carolina coast are home to some of the nation's finest and most luxurious resort developments. A wide array of package plans makes them more affordable than you might imagine.

Accommodations are listed according to category, in a geographical progression from north to south. Rates are peak season which, strangely, varies greatly from one facility to another even in the same area. Generally, it spans the spring and summer vacation period; it's best to request current rates from the individual establishment. Even in the most luxurious resorts, rates can drop considerably during off season.

These are average rates, based on double occupancy: *Super Deluxe,* over $130; *Deluxe,* $80–$130; *Expensive,* $65–$80; *Moderate,* $45–$65; *Inexpensive,* under $45. Most facilities add 7% tax; a few charge 6%.

Myrtle Beach

Super Deluxe

Radisson Resort Hotel. At Kingston Plantation, 9800 Lake Dr., Myrtle Beach SC 29577 (803–449–0006 or 800–228–9822 except NE). 513 one-bedroom balconied suites with kitchen bar, refrigerator, in new luxury property set amidst 145 acres of beautiful oceanside woodlands. Casual dining in Azaleas, poolside Reflections, gourmet specialties at Carolinas. Live entertainment, dancing at Nightwatch; two additional lounges. Guests have privileges at sports/fitness complex offering racquetball, tennis, squash, aerobics, exercise equipment, sauna, whirlpool. Golf packages.

Deluxe

The Breakers Golf & Beach Lodge. 2006 N. Ocean Blvd., Box 485, Myrtle Beach, SC 29578–0485 (803–626–5000 or 800–845–0688). 391 spacious rooms and suites; new housekeeping units in Breakers North Tower. Oceanfront. Safari Restaurant and Lounge, coin laundry, children's programs. Golf, tennis privileges at the Dunes Club, 43 other courses. Some units in *Super Deluxe* category.

Captain's Quarters Motor Inn. 901 S. Ocean Blvd., Drawer 2486, Myrtle Beach, SC 29578–2486 (803–448–1404). Ocean front. Rooftop restaurant, indoor pools, whirlpool, free tennis, golf privileges, shuffleboard. All 210 units have color TV, refrigerator, microwave oven. Married couples and families only.

Days Inn Myrtle Beach Central (formerly Ocean Reef Motor Inn). 601 S. Ocean Blvd., Drawer 2485, Myrtle Beach, SC 29577 (803–448–1491 or 800–325–2525). 156 rooms, apartments, and efficiencies, all with refrigerators; 100 units are oceanfront. Pools, whirlpool, playground, free tennis, golf privileges, maid service. Restaurant adjacent. Near amusement park, shopping center. Married couples and families only. Ocean view rooms in *Expensive* category.

Holiday Inn Oceanfront (formerly Holiday Inn Downtown). 6th Ave. and Ocean Blvd., Box 1856, Myrtle Beach, SC 29577 (803–448–4481 or 800–845–0313). 310 spacious rooms. Convenient in-town oceanfront location. Holidome, tennis, golf privileges, pool, sauna, whirlpool, exercise rooms. Restaurant, lounges, live entertainment.

Landmark Best Western Resort Hotel. 1501 S. Ocean Blvd., Myrtle Beach, SC 29577 (803–448–9441 or 800–528–1234). 326 tastefully decorated oceanfront rooms, some with balconies. Pool, children's activity program, under 18 free. Dining rooms, lounges, nightclub, live nightly entertainment.

Myrtle Beach Hilton. In Arcadian Shores, Myrtle Beach, SC 29577 (803–449–5000 or 800–445–8667). Luxurious 392-unit oceanfront resort hotel has 14-story atrium lobby. Continental dining in elegant Alfredo's; lounges, entertainment. Shops, social program, tennis, golfing on championship course. Some rooms in *Super Deluxe* category.

Ocean Dunes Resort & Villas. 202 74th Ave., N., Box 2035, Myrtle Beach, SC 29578 (803–449–7441, collect in state or 800–845–0635, extension 9). 430 units oceanfront. Dining room, lounge, reciprocal dining at 15 area restaurants. Tennis courts, health center, indoor pool, game room, children's program. Golf privileges on more than 45 area courses. Airport transportation.

Sheraton Myrtle Beach Resort (formerly Sheraton Atlantic Shores Resort). 2701 S. Ocean Blvd., Myrtle Beach, SC 29577 (803–448–2518 or 800–325–2525). All 219 rooms and suites here have been renovated. Fully equipped health club, arcade, gift shop. Kokomo's Restaurant, serving B, L, D daily, is one of three new food and beverage areas. Oceanfront lounge, highlighted by tropical colors and rattan furnishings, is lively evening gathering spot. Seaside deck offers casual outdoor dining and drinks.

Expensive

Caravelle Resort Hotel & Villas. 6900 N. Ocean Blvd., Box 2065, Myrtle Beach, SC 29577 (803–449–3331; 800–845–0893, nationwide; 800–752–1444 in state). 428 rooms, suites and efficiencies, oceanfront villas. Quiet north beach location, fine dining in Santa Maria restaurant. Golf privileges, free tennis, 7 pools, Jacuzzis, saunas, children's program. Some rooms in *Deluxe* category.

The Driftwood on the Oceanfront. 1600 N. Ocean Blvd., Box 275, Myrtle Beach, SC 29578–0275 (803–448–7158 or 800–942–3456). All 90 units have refrigerators. Two pools, coin laundry, golf, tennis privileges. Packages, winter guest and discount plans. Popular with families. Some rooms in *Deluxe* category.

Jamaican Motor Inn. 3006 N. Ocean Blvd., Box 1267–A, Myrtle Beach, SC 29578–1267 (803–448–4321 or 800–732–6478; 800–258–1164 outside SC). 45-unit family motel on uncrowded beach has rooms, apartments, some connecting, all with refrigerators. Heated pools, golf, tennis privileges, laundry facilities. Restaurants near.

Sea Mist Resort. 1200 S. Ocean Blvd., Box 2548, Myrtle Beach, SC 29578–2548 (803–448–1551). 661 units. Family owned, caters to families. Seven adult, four kiddie pools; Jacuzzis; game room; children's program; tennis. Laundromat, ice cream parlor, doughnut shop. Minigolf, tennis, golf privileges. Most rooms have refrigerators.

Moderate

The Cherry Tree Inn. 5400 N. Ocean Blvd., Myrtle Beach, SC 29577 (803–449–6425 or 800–845–2036). 34 spacious rooms, efficiencies, bridal suite. Oceanfront, quiet residential section. Refrigerators; some efficiencies with total electric kitchen. Glass enclosed heated pool, laundromat. Discount after 7-day stay.

Swamp Fox Ocean Resort. 2311 S. Ocean Blvd., Box 1307, Myrtle Beach, SC 29577–1307 (803–448–8373 or 800–222–9894 outside SC). 380 rooms and efficiencies, all with balconies. Oceanfront. 4 pools, Jacuzzi, exercise room, coin laundry, golf privileges. Restaurant locally popular. Some rooms in *Expensive* and *Deluxe* categories. Senior citizens' discount.

Teakwood Motel. 7201 N. Ocean Blvd., Myrtle Beach, SC 29572 (803–449–5653 or 800–868–0046). This family-oriented place has 25 rooms, efficiency apartments, in Polynesian decor. All have refrigerators and balconies or patios. Heated pool, tennis, coin laundry, cookout areas, playground. Social lobby with free coffee.

Georgetown

Expensive

Carolinian Inn (formerly Best Western Carolinian). 706 Church St., Georgetown, SC 29440 (803–546–5191). 90 rooms. Cable TV, movies, pool, fishing, restaurant nearby. Seniors program, under 12 free. Golf privileges. Some rooms in *Moderate* category.

Moderate

Days Inn (formerly Holiday Inn of Georgetown). U.S. 17 N, Box 671, Georgetown, SC 29442 (803–546–8441 or 800–325–2525). 119 units. Pool, restaurant, lounge. Cable TV, Showtime movies. Dining room, lounge, entertainment, dancing. Coin laundry. Airport and bus depot transportation. Some rooms in *Inexpensive* category.

Isle of Palms

Deluxe

Wild Dunes. 12 mi. NE of Charleston via U.S. 17, SC 703, Box 338, Isle of Palms, SC 29451 (803–886–6000 or 800–845–8880). 1,500-acre resort has luxurious villa accommodations in 360 units. Championship golf course, Racquet Club, yacht harbor on IntraCoastal Waterway, bicycling, nature trails, surfcasting, water sports, children's programs. Beef specialties at The Club House; fresh seafoods at The Island House, where all dishes are created by one of 15 practicing French master chefs in the country. Family cookouts, lounge, entertainment. Some rooms in *Super Deluxe* category.

Charleston

Super Deluxe

Best Western King Charles Inn. 237 Meeting St., Charleston, SC 29401 (803–723–7451 or 800–528–1234). 91 rooms include some for handicapped. Dining room, cocktail lounge, entertainment, pool. Cable TV/in-room movies. In center of historic and business districts. Some rooms in *Expensive* category.

Omni Hotel at Charleston Place. 130 Market St., Charleston, SC 29401–3133 (803–722–4900 or 800–843–6664). This elegant new luxury hotel and conference center near the fine Old City Market is flanked by a four-story complex of 40 restaurants and specialty shops. Architecture reflects 18th- and 19th-century ambience. 443 rooms, including 46 suites, are decorated with handsome period reproduction furnishings. Formal dining room; casual meals in Charleston Place Cafe. Lounge, live late night entertainment. Health club.

Deluxe

Mills House Hotel. 115 Meeting St., Charleston, SC 29401 (803–577–2400 or 800–465–4329). 215 units include some suites. Antique furnishings, glowing chandeliers give unusual charm and ambience to historic hostelry, reconstructed with all 20th-century amenities. Beautifully furnished lobby, guest rooms. Dining room. Lounge, live entertainment, pool. Part of Holiday Inn system. *Super Deluxe* mid-Mar–early June, mid-Sept.–early Nov.

Sheraton-Charleston Hotel. 170 Lockwood Dr., Charleston, SC 29403 (803–723–3000 or 800–325–3535). 337 units, including suites. Luxury hotel is elegantly furnished, has concierge service. Heated outdoor pool, jogging track, lighted tennis courts, golf privileges. Dining rooms, entertainment in lounge.

Expensive

Heart of Charleston-Quality Inn (formerly Quality Inn Historic District). 125 Calhoun St., Charleston, SC 29403 (803–722–3391 or 800–228–5151). Available here are 126 rooms and suites, some with balcony, all decorated in Charleston tradition. Magnolia Restaurant and Lounge. Coin laundry, pool.

Moderate

Comfort Inn Riverview (formerly Days Hotel Riverfront Medical Center). 144 Bee St., Charleston, SC 29401 (803–577–2224 or 800–221–2222). Some of the 127 rooms and suites here have views of the Ashley River. Pool, exercise room, coin laundry.

Days Inn Historic District. 155 Meeting St. Charleston, SC 29401 (803–722–8411 or 800–325–2525). 124 units in well-maintained motor inn. Dining room, pool, golf privileges. Senior citizens' discount.

Inexpensive

Econo-Lodge. U.S. 17 N Bypass at E. Mathis Ferry Rd., Mt. Pleasant, SC 29464 (803–884–1411 or 800–533–2666). 124 rooms. Cable TV/movies, coin laundry, pool. Restaurant nearby. Facilities for handicapped. Senior citizens' program; government/military discounts.

Kiawah Island

Super Deluxe

Kiawah Island Resort. SC 20, 21 mi. from Charleston via SC 17 to SC 700, Box 12910, Charleston, SC 29412 (803–768–2121 or 800–654–2924 nationwide; 800–845–2471 in-state). Luxurious resort island offers 150 inn rooms; 48 suites; 500 1–4 bedroom, completely equipped villas. 2 complete resort villages on 10,000 wooded acres; magnificent broad beaches. 3 championship golf courses, 2 racquet clubs, jeep safaris, water safaris, land sailing, canoeing, off-beach sailing, surfcasting, fishing, extensive children's programs, many packages. General store, distinctive boutiques. Casual dining in the Sand Wedge, Sundancers, Jonah's; Low Country specialties in the Jasmine Porch and Veranda; Continental cuisine in The Charleston Gallery. Low Country cuisine at Indigo House; lagoonside dining at The Park Cafe.

Seabrook Island

Super Deluxe

Seabrook Island Resort. On Seabrook Island, 23 mi. from Charleston via U.S. 17 S, SC 171, to SC 700, Box 32099, Charleston, SC 29417 (803–768–1000 or 800–845–5531). 360 units, including 1–3 bedroom, fully equipped villas, cottages, or beachhouses. Beach Club and Island Club are center for dining, leisure activities. Championship golf, tennis center, water sports, pools, equestrian center, bicycling. Children's programs in season; many package plans. Lounges, entertainment. Some rooms in *Deluxe* category.

Fripp Island

Deluxe

Fripp Island Resort. 19 mi. S. of Beaufort, via U.S. 21, One Tarpon Blvd., Fripp Island, SC 29920 (803–838–3535 or 800–845–4100, outside SC, east of Mississippi River). 150 2- and 3-bedroom rental villas. Three restaurants, tennis courts, bicycle and jogging trails, pools, championship golf course, tennis, full service marina with rental boats. General store, design and gift shops. Coin laundry, children's program, nature trails. Some rooms in *Super Deluxe* category.

Beaufort

Moderate

Best Western Sea Island Motel. 1015 Bay St., Box 532, Beaufort, SC 29901 (803–524–4121 or 800–528–1234). 43 rooms. Cable TV, pool, restaurant, lounge. Senior citizens discount, under 12 free.

Comfort Inn. 2625 U.S. 21, I-95 exit 42, Beaufort, SC 29902 (803–525–9366 or 800–228–5150). 79 rooms; some with refrigerators, some equipped for the disabled. Cocktail lounge, pool, playground, in-room movies, free Continental breakfast. Family plan; AAA discount.

Holiday Inn of Beaufort. U.S. 21 & Lovejoy St., Beaufort, SC 29902 (803–524–2144 or 800–465–4329). 152 rooms in colonial atmosphere. Cable TV/movies, heated pool, tennis. Live Oaks Restaurant features Fri. night prime-rib special, Sun. buffet. Lounge, live entertainment.

Inexpensive

Days Inn. 1809 S. Ribaut Rd., Port Royal, SC 29935 (803–524–1551 or 800–325–2525). 150 units. Historic tours available. Near Parris Island Marine Corps Recruit Depot, Marine Corps Air Station, U.S. Naval Hospital. Restaurant. Facilities for handicapped; nonsmoking rooms available.

Lord Carteret Motel. 301 Carteret St., Beaufort, SC 29902 (803–524–3303). 25 rooms, including some kitchenette units with refrigerators. Restaurants near.

Hilton Head Island

Super Deluxe

Hyatt Regency Hilton Head at Palmetto Dunes. Box 6167, Hilton Head Island, SC 29938 (803–785–1234 or 800–233–1234). 505-unit oceanfront hotel recently completed $35-million renovation. Spacious rooms have private balconies, cable TV, in-room movies. Oceanfront. Indoor-outdoor pools, sailboats, bicycles, health club. Dining rooms, lounges, entertainment, dancing at Club Indigo. Guests enjoy 3 golf courses, Rod Laver Tennis Center at Palmetto Dunes Resort.

The Westin Resort, Hilton Head (formerly Hotel Inter-Continental Hilton Head). At Port Royal Resort, 135 S. Port Royal Dr., Hilton Head Island, SC 29928 (803–681–4000 or 800–228–3000). Island's newest luxury property, the 416-room, horseshoe-shape hotel offers pool and ocean swimming, water sports, health club. Golf, tennis, sports privileges of Port Royal Resort. Informal fare in the Brasserie, international specialties in the country French atmosphere of the Barony. Elegant lobby lounge with piano entertainment.

Deluxe

Holiday Inn. South Forest Beach Dr., Box 5728, Hilton Head Island, SC 29928 (803–785–5126 or 800–465–4329). Large motor hotel directly on the beach has 200 spacious rooms, gift shop, beauty salon, poolside bar, dining room, lounge. Boat, bicycle rentals, children's programs. Golf, tennis, marina privileges. Many packages. Some rooms in *Super Deluxe* category.

Mariners' Inn-A Clarion Hotel. 23 Ocean Lane, Box 6165, Hilton Head Island, SC 29938 (803–842–8000 or 800–845–8000). 324 oceanview accommodations, health club, pool, sauna, Jacuzzi, volleyball, canoeing, fishing, biking, sailing. Full resort privileges at Palmetto Dunes Resort. Some rooms in *Super Deluxe* category.

Marriott's Hilton Head Resort. 130 Shipyard Dr., Shipyard Plantation, Hilton Head Island, SC 29928 (803–842–2400 or 800–228–9290; 800–642–8008 in NE). 338 units. Spectacular 5-story atrium lobby, dining in The Veranda, Club de Mer; dancing, live entertainment in The Mockingbird Lounge. Pool, exercise rooms, sauna. Golf privileges at Shipyard & Port Royal Golf Clubs, tennis at Shipyard Racquet Club. Some rooms in *Super Deluxe* category.

Moderate

Red Roof Inn. U.S. 278, Long Cove, 5 Regency Pkwy., Hilton Head Island, SC 29928 (803–686–6808 or 800–843–7663). 108 rooms, 4 suites in comfortable motor inn popular with families. Color TV, movies. Shoney's Restaurant nearby.

ACCOMMODATIONS—GEORGIA. Lodgings along Georgia's blithe and spirited coastland range from family style motels to the elegant hotels and lodges of Savannah and the Golden Isles, and include one of the nation's most luxurious and renowned island hideaways, where rates include all meals. Otherwise, accommodations are based on double occupancy, peak season (early spring through summer), without meals. In Savannah, rates may also increase for St. Patrick's Day. Again, lodgings are listed in a north to south progression.

These are average rates, based on double occupancy: *Super Deluxe,* over $135; *Deluxe,* $90–$135; *Expensive,* $60–$90; *Moderate,* $37–$60; *Inexpensive,* under $37. Tax is 7 percent.

Savannah

Deluxe

DeSoto Hilton Hotel & Towers. Bull & Liberty Sts., Box 8207, Savannah, GA 31412 (912–232–9000 or 800–445–8667). 250 rooms, some suites. Elegant, refined atmosphere. Near historic district. Coffee shop, excellent Pavilion dining room, entertainment in The Lion's Den. Heated pool, cable TV. Parking garage. Weekend packages. Some rooms in *Expensive* category.

Hyatt Regency Savannah. 2 West Bay St., Savannah, GA 31401 (912–238–1234 or 800–233–1234). 346 rooms, suites. Choice location in historic district overlooking riverfront. Heated indoor pool, rental bikes. Dining in Patrick's Porch off the atrium lobby or in elegant ambience of The Windows. Live music, dancing in MD's Lounge. Parking garage (fee).

The Mulberry. 601 East Bay St., Savannah, GA 31401 (912–238–1200 or 800–554–5544 nationwide; 800–282–9198 in state). In this elegant small hostelry in the Historic District are 119 exquisitely furnished Georgian style rooms and some suites. Christopher's Restaurant and Mulberry Bar. Pool, rooftop whirlpool; pay garage.

Sheraton Savannah Resort and Country Club. 612 Wilmington Island Rd., Savannah, GA 31410 (912–897–1612 or 800–325–3535). On Wilmington Island, 11 mi. southeast of Savannah via U.S. 80, GA 367. 202 rooms, 29 suites. Landmark resort has Olympic pool, beach, tennis, 18-hole golf course, sailing, deep sea fishing, saunas, 2 dining rooms, lounge, entertainment. Limousine service.

Expensive

Days Inn Lodge of America. 201 W. Bay St., Savannah, GA 31401 (912–236–4440 or 800–325–2525). 196 units with 57 lodge suites. In historic district; offers modern conveniences in 19th-century reproduction structure. Free parking, 24-hour Daybreak Restaurant. Handicapped facilities. Airport transportation. Some rooms in *Moderate* category.

Quality Inn Heart of Savannah. 300 W. Bay St., Savannah, GA 31401 (912–236–6321 or 800–228–5151). 53 handsomely renovated rooms with individual HVAC units. Complimentary Continental breakfast. Family, senior-citizen, fly-drive plans.

Moderate

Best Western Savannah Riverfront Inn. 412 W. Bay St., Savannah, GA 31401 (912–233–1011 or 800–528–1234). In historic district, with 142 attractively renovated rooms. Dining room, pub lounge, pool, Cable TV. Senior citizen discount; 24-hour airport transportation.

Holiday Inn Downtown. 121 W. Boundary St., Box 1781, Savannah, GA 31401 (912–236–1355 or 800–465–4329). 205 rooms. Satellite dish, two outdoor pools. Bridges Restaurant and Lounge, dancing. Senior-citizen rates, under 18 free. Coin laundry.

Brunswick

Moderate

Comfort Inn (formerly Quality Inn). I-95, Exit 7B, 490 New Jesup Hwy., Brunswick, GA 31520 (912–264–6540 or 800–228–5150). 119 rooms. Dining room, lounge with entertainment, pool. Handicapped facilities. Family, senior-citizen, government, and military plans.

Days Inn Brunswick. I-95 & U.S. 341. Exit 7A, 409 New Jesup Hwy., Brunswick, GA 31520 (912–264–4330 or 800–325–2525). 158 units. Cable TV-HBO. Pool, restaurant. Pets allowed.

Holiday Inn. 3302 Glynn Ave., Brunswick, GA 31520 (912–264–9111 or 800–465–4329). 124 rooms. Cable TV-HBO. Lili's Restaurant (fresh local seafood) and Lounge. Teens free.

Ramada Inn Downtown. 3241 Glynn Ave. (U.S. 17), Brunswick, GA 31523 (912–264–8611 or 800–272–6232). 100 units. Pool, playground, tennis, seafood restaurant, lounge, live entertainment. Pets allowed. Laundry facilities. Cable TV. Senior's, weekend discounts.

Inexpensive

Best Western Brunswick Inn. Jct. 2 blocks W of I-95 on U.S. 341, Exit 7B, Brunswick, GA 31520 (912–264–0144 or 800–325–2525). 143 units. Restaurant, pool, pets allowed. Senior-citizen discount, under 12 free.

Knights Inn. I-95, Exit 7A, (U.S. 341), Brunswick, GA 31520 (912–267–6500). 110 rooms, some efficiencies. Cable TV, pool. Restaurant near. Senior-citizen discount.

Sea Island

Super Deluxe

The Cloister. Sea Island, GA 31561 (912–638–3611 or 800–732–4752). One of the nation's premier luxury resorts offers 264 units in main building, beach and guest houses. Magnificent garden grounds ring private beach. Racquet Club, putting green, croquet. Championship golf at Retreat Plantation. Children's program, horseback riding, social, recreational programs. Superb dining in formal setting, nightly dancing. Shops, auto rentals, laundry-cleaners, service station, photographer on premises. Many package plans. American Plan; children charged only for meals. No credit cards.

St. Simons Island

Deluxe

Sea Palms Golf & Tennis Resort. 5445 Frederica Rd., St. Simons Island, GA 31522 (912–638–3351 or 800–841–6268, nationwide; 800–282–1226, in-state). 800-acre compound has 300 deluxe hotel rooms, villas, and suites overlooking Marshes of Glynn. Golf course, Health & Racquet Club, three pools, beach playground, jogging, tennis. Continental-American cuisine, seafood in Oglethorpe's dining room, cocktail lounge, live entertainment.

Expensive

King & Prince Beach Hotel & Villas. 201 Arnold Rd., Box 798, St. Simons Island, GA 31522 (912–638–3631). 128 rooms, 35 villas. Pools, beach, tennis, rental bicycles. Dining room is one of island's most popular; lounge, entertainment. Some rooms in *Deluxe* category, some villas, *Super Deluxe.*

Moderate

Queen's Court. 437 Kings Way, St. Simons Island, GA 31522 (912–638–8459). In-town motel has 23 units, some efficiencies. Cable TV, pool. Restaurant near.

Sea Gate Inn. 1014 Ocean Blvd., St. Simons Island, GA 31522 (912–638–8661). 48 units in two segments, on oceanfront. Pool, cable TV, coin laundry. Some rooms in *Expensive* category, some apartments, *Deluxe.*

Jekyll Island

Deluxe

Holiday Inn Beach Resort. 200 S. Beachview Dr., Jekyll Island, GA 31520 (912–635–3311 or 800–465–4329). 205 units, some kitchenettes. Golf, indoor tennis, pool, ocean beach, deep-sea fishing, playground, gift shop. Teens free. Greenery Restaurant, Balloons Lounge, entertainment. Coin laundry. Pets allowed.

The Jekyll Island Club—A Radisson Resort. 371 Riverview Dr., Jekyll Island, GA 31520 (912–635–2600 or 800–822–1886 out of state; 800–843–5355 in GA). Renowned "millionaires' club" has been beautifully restored and transformed into a 136-room luxury hotel with Victorian ambience. Facilities for handicapped. Restaurant, pool, surfside beach cabana, putting green, croquet, bocci, shuffleboard. Golf, tennis packages. Some units in *Super Deluxe* category.

Expensive

Comfort Inn Island Suites. 711 N. Beachview Dr., Jekyll Island, GA 31520 (912–635–2211 or 800–228–5150). 180 ocean, lanai suites with whirlpool sauna. On beach, pools, playground. Restaurant, lounge, entertainment. Some rooms in *Deluxe* category.

The Jekyll Inn. 975 N. Beachview Dr. Jekyll Island, GA 31520 (912–635–2531). 188 rooms, 61 one- and two-bedroom villas. Cable TV, movies, pools, beach, playground, rental bicycles, mopeds. Pets allowed. Dining room, lounge, entertainment in season. Villas in *Deluxe* category.

Clarion Resort Buccaneer (formerly Quality Inn Buccaneer). 85 S. Beachview Dr., Jekyll Island, GA 31520 (912–635–2261). 209 rooms; many are efficiencies with refrigerator. On beach. Pools, playground, rental bicycles, mopeds, sailboats. Handicapped facilities. Restaurant, lounge, entertainment. Some rooms in *Deluxe* category.

Moderate

Seafarer Motel. 700 N. Beachview Dr., Jekyll Island, GA 31520 (912–635–2202). 71 units, including one- and two-bedroom apartments. Pools, playground, coin laundry. Restaurant near. Some rooms in *Expensive* category.

BED AND BREAKFASTS. These accommodations are relative newcomers to coastal North Carolina. Now there's a growing assortment in the Low Country and along the coast. For application and reservation forms or further information about lodging in the Outer Banks and Albemarle Sound communities, contact *Bed & Breakfast in the Albemarle,* Box 248, Everette, NC 27825 (919–792–4584). Some accommodations are in picturesque, sometimes historic structures.

The unique charm of historic **Charleston,** South Carolina, can be enhanced by a stay in one of its many inns, a number housed in fine restored structures. Some are full-scale hostelries, reminiscent of elegant vintage European establishments. For further information, reservation forms about rooms, cottages, and carriage houses in the Charleston area, contact *Charleston East Bed and Breakfast League,* Reservations Coordinator, 1031 Tall Pine Rd., Mount Pleasant, SC 29464 (803–884–8208); *Charleston Society Bed & Breakfast,* 84 Murray Blvd., Charleston, SC 29401 (803–723–4948); *Historic Charleston Bed and Breakfast,* 43 Legare St., Charleston, SC 29402 (803–722–6606).

Gracious old **Savannah,** Georgia, offers some of the Southeast's finest guest houses and inns. Most are in restored historic houses or new establishments designed to reflect the Colonial period.

For information about 12 choice Savannah Inns, contact *Savannah's Historic Inns and Guest Houses,* 147 Bull St., Savannah, GA 31401 (800–262–4667 nationwide, 912–233–7667 in town); phone between 8:30 A.M.–5 P.M., or leave message any time on answering machine.

RESTAURANTS—NORTH CAROLINA. Fresh local seafood highlights coastal North Carolina's menus. Don't miss the "lace cornbread" that's unique to the Outer Banks; it's crispy, thin, cooked quickly on a griddle, and absolutely delicious. East coast Tarheels take fierce pride in their barbecue. You can sample it throughout the area. Casual good taste is the dress code; men should expect to wear jackets for dinner in the more elegant hotels. Inquire locally about reservations.

Restaurants are listed according to the price of a complete dinner; drinks, tax, and tip are not included. *Expensive,* over $20; *Moderate,* $10–$20; *Inexpensive,* under $10.

Beaches North of Oregon Inlet

Moderate

J.K.'s Restaurant. Milepost 8.5 on U.S. 158 Bypass, 600 S. Croatan Highway, Kill Devil Hills (919–441–3021). Offered here are American specialties—prime rib, steaks, seafoods, lamb, barbecued ribs—broiled over mesquite coals. There is a comfortable, laid-back ambience, with a patio bar in season. Extensive wine list, children's menu. Open 5–10 P.M., to 9 P.M. off-season. AE, MC, V.

Owens Restaurant. Milepost 16.5, U.S. 158 Business, Nags Head (919–441–7309). This family-owned restaurant has been a regional favorite since 1946 for fresh seafood, roast beef, and mesquite-grilled specialties. Children's menu. D daily; closed major holidays. Some entrees in *Expensive* category. Cocktails, lounge. AE, DC, MC, V.

Port-O-Call Restaurant. Milepost 8.8, Kill Devil Hills (919–441–7484). Steaks, duck, seafood, and Continental specialties are offered at this place, with background music and Sat. night entertainment. AE, MC, V.

Queen Anne's Revenge. In village of Wanchese, 3 mi. west on U.S. 64 and 3 mi. south on NC 345 from Nags Head (919–473–5466). In a quiet wooded area, this popular hideaway restaurant serves fresh seafood and prime steaks. D, 5–9:30 P.M.; closed off-season. Beer, wine, no cocktails. MC, V.

Inexpensive

The Dunes. Milepost 16–5, U.S. 158 Bypass, Nags Head (919–441–1600). B, 5:30 A.M.–noon; D, 5–9 P.M. All you can eat specials. Open Mar.–Nov.

Roanoke Island

Inexpensive

Elizabethan Inn. U.S. 64–264, Elizabethan Inn Motor Lodge, Manteo (919–473–2101). Local seafood, home-style cooking. Open 6 A.M.–9:30 P.M. Closed Dec. 24–26. AE, C, DC, MC, V.

Hatteras Island

Inexpensive

Bubba's Bar-B-Q. 6 mi. S from Cape Hatteras Lighthouse, Frisco Village (919–995–5421). Spareribs, chicken, beef, and pork are cooked before your eyes at this place on open pit with hickory wood. Open year-round.

Channel Bass Restaurant. N on NC 12, Hatteras Village (919–986–2250). Fresh local seafood, hushpuppies, home-baked pies. Nautical atmosphere, long-time favorite. Open 5–9 P.M. Closed Dec.–Mar. AE, MC, V.

Ocracoke Island

Moderate

The Back Porch. ½ mi. N of ferry terminal, W on NC 1324 (919–928–6401). Fresh seafood and vegetables are served here on screened-in porch. Open 5:30–10 P.M., May through Oct. MC, V.

Inexpensive

The Island Inn Dining Room. NC 12, Island Inn Motel (919–928–4351). Fresh Island seafood and she-crab soup are the specialties here, in one of Outer Banks' most popular dining rooms. Open year round, 7 A.M.–9 P.M.; Fri., 7 A.M.–2 P.M., 5–9 P.M. MC, V.

Pony Island Restaurant. NC 12, Pony Island Inn (919–928–5701). Fresh seafood dinners, children's plates in this casual, family style restaurant. Open 6:30–11 A.M., 5–9 P.M., late Mar.–early Nov. MC, V.

Elizabeth City

Inexpensive

The Marina. Camden Causeway, U.S. 158 (919–335–7307). Seafood, steaks, home baking in picturesque setting overlooking Pasquotank River. Open 11 A.M.–9 P.M.; Sat., from 5 P.M. Closed Mon. and major holidays. No credit cards.

New Bern

Moderate

Henderson House. 216 Pollock St. (919–637–4784). Seafood, peanut soup, home baking in restored 1779 house in historic district. Child's portions. Open 11 A.M.–2 P.M.; also 6–9 P.M., Thurs.–Sat. Closed Sun.–Mon. and holidays. MC,V.

Morehead City

Inexpensive

Sanitary Fish Market & Restaurant. 501 Evans St. (919–247–3111). Don't be turned off by the name! This casual, 56-year-old, family-owned restaurant is one of the state's most popular. Serves lavish portions of fresh seafood straight from catches by own fishing fleet. Child's portions. Open 11:30 A.M.–9 P.M., May through Oct.; to 8:30 P.M., Feb.–Apr. and Nov. Closed Dec. and Jan. Nonsmoking area. Some dinners may edge into the *Moderate* category. MC, V.

Wilmington and Its Beaches

Moderate

The Bridge Tender. Airlie Rd., 1 block S of U.S. 76 and IntraCoastal Waterway drawbridge, Wrightsville Beach (919–256–4519). Casual dining on excellent seafood, steaks. Sun. buffet 11:30 A.M.–2 P.M. Open 11:30 A.M.–2 P.M., 5:30–10 P.M.; to 11 P.M., Fri.; Sat. 5:30–11 P.M.; Sun. 5:30 P.M.–10 P.M. Closed major holidays. AE, MC, V.

The Pilot House. 2 Ann St. (919–343–0200). This Chandler's Wharf establishment overlooking the Cape Fear River specializes in fresh seafood dishes, including Cape Fear crab and smoked peppered mackerel. Casual "back porch" atmosphere. Open 11 A.M.–3 P.M., 5–10 P.M. Mon.–Sat.; closed New Year's Day, Thanksgiving, Christmas. AE, MC, V.

Inexpensive

Skinner & Daniels. 5214 Market St., Wilmington (919–799–1790). Featured here are barbecue pork, beef, chicken, and Brunswick stew; take out orders. Open 10 A.M.–9 P.M., Mon.–Sat. No credit cards.

RESTAURANTS—SOUTH CAROLINA. Fine fresh seafood is abundant throughout coastal South Carolina. There's Continental and American cuisine to please the most discriminating palate in sophisticated city and resort dining rooms. She-crab soup originated in Charleston and the Low Country, and it's not to be missed. Neither are benne (sesame) seed wafers. Attractively boxed, they're good take-home gifts.

During peak vacation season especially, reservations should be made in Charleston and resort dining rooms. In most, men should expect to wear jackets at night.

Restaurants are listed according to price of a complete dinner; drinks, tax, and tip are not included. *Expensive,* over $20; *Moderate,* $10–$20; *Inexpensive,* under $10.

Myrtle Beach

Moderate

J. Edward's Great Ribs & More. Two locations: 29 Ave. N., U.S. 17 N., 2901 Kings Hwy., Myrtle Beach (803–448–4001) and 23 Ave. and U.S. 17, 2300 S. Kings Hwy., Myrtle Beach (803–626–9986). Barbecue ribs, steaks, prime rib, and seafoods are choices at these popular family-style restaurants with casual, laid-back atmosphere. Early-bird specials, children's menus. Open 4:30–10:30 P.M. daily. Cocktail lounge. AE, MC, V. Reservations preferred spring and fall.

The Library. 1212 N. U.S. 17 Bus., Myrtle Beach (803–448–4527 or 448–9242). Dover sole, rack of lamb, and other Continental specialties are on the menu at this place with a library decor and book collections in dining room. Open 6–10:30 P.M. Closed Sun. Some entrées in *Expensive* category. Reservations essential. AE, DC, MC, V.

Planter's Back Porch. U.S. 17 & Wachesaw Rd., Murrells Inlet (803–651–5263 or 803–651–5544). Sip cool libations in the Spring House, dine on fresh seafood specialties in garden setting reminiscent of a Southern plantation. Open 5–10 P.M.. Closed Thanksgiving, Dec.–mid-Feb. AE, MC, V.

Rice Planter's Restaurant. 6707 N. Kings Hwy., Myrtle Beach (803–449–3456 or 803–449–3457). Dine on fresh seafood, stuffed flounder, quail, and steak in charming setting enhanced by period antiques, candlelight. Open 5–10 P.M. Closed Thanksgiving, Dec. 25–26. AE, MC, V.

Sea Captain's House. 3002 N. Ocean Blvd., Myrtle Beach (803–448–8082). Seafood, crab casserole, steaks, own baking. Charming cottage-style restaurant with nautical decor; pleasant, relaxing, waterside setting. Informal. Open 11:30 A.M.–2:30 P.M., 5–10 P.M. Closed Dec.–Jan. AE, MC, V. Some entrées in *Expensive* category.

Slug's Rib. 9713 U.S. 17 N., Myrtle Beach (803–449–6419). Features only aged prime rib. Welcoming contemporary setting with outdoor lounge overlooking Intracoastal Waterway. Children's menu. Open 5:30–10 P.M.; 4:30–10 P.M. mid-May–mid-Sept. Closed Dec. 19–26. AE, DC, MC, V.

Inexpensive

The Beverage Station Cafe. U.S. 17 & Atlantic Ave., Garden City (803–651–3113). Lunch and dinner are served here in a relaxing, casual atmosphere with lots of brass, plants, antiques. Specialties include fresh grouper, French onion soup in bread bowl, fresh homemade desserts. Open 11 A.M.–11 P.M., Mon.–Sat.; to 11:30 P.M., Fri., Sat. Closed Dec. 25. Major credit cards.

Georgetown

Moderate

The Rice Paddy. 408 Duke St., Georgetown (803–546–2021). Homemade soups, salads and sandwiches are served at this place at lunch; dinner specialties are fresh seafoods, veal, steak. Open 11:30 A.M.–2:30 P.M., 6–10 P.M.

Charleston

Expensive

Restaurant Million. 2 Unity Alley, between 149 and 151 E. Bay St. (803–577–7472). This widely acclaimed French restaurant specializes in nouvelle cuisine. Prix fixe 7-, 8-, and 10-course dinners, also à la carte. Open 6:30–10:30 P.M. Mon.–Sat., closed Jan. and holidays. Reservations, dress code. AE, MC, V.

Moderate

Barbadoes Room. Mills House Hotel, Queen and Meeting Sts. (803–577–2400). Gourmet Continental–American cuisine is featured here in elegant surroundings. Lobster Calhoun and Mills House mud pie are specialties. Reservations, jacket and tie recommended for dinner. Open 7 A.M.–3 P.M., 5:30–10:30 P.M. AE, DC, MC, V. Some entrées in *Expensive* category.

The Colony House. 35 Prioleau St. (803–723–3424). Low Country specialties at this place include baked pompano, she-crab soup; also steaks, veal. Friendly, personalized service in handsomely restored 1830 warehouse. Open 11:30 A.M.–3 P.M., 5:30–10:30 P.M.; Sun., 5:30–9:30 P.M. Closed Dec. 25. Child's plates. AE, MC, V.

East Bay Trading Company. 161 E. Bay St. (803–722–0722). Fresh seafood, lamb, Carolina quail, international cuisine are the specialties in this former warehouse, which comprises three dramatic levels wrapped around skylight-topped atrium. Antiques, artifacts, lavish greenery lend warm, serene ambience. Open 11:30 A.M.–10:30 P.M. Mon.–Fri., 5:30–11 P.M. Sat., 1–9 P.M. Sun. Lounge has live entertainment. AE, MC, V.

82 Queen. 82 Queen St. (803–723–7591). Seafood, Low Country specialties in distinctive ambience of 19th-century town house. Indoor and outdoor dining. Open 11:30 A.M.–2:30 P.M., 6–10:30 P.M. Closed major holidays. Reservations required for dinner. AE, MC, V.

Trawler/Captain's Table. U.S. 17 N, Mt. Pleasant (803–884–2560). Family dining in nautical atmosphere; specialties include fish stew, shrimp à la Newburg. Open 5–10:30 P.M.; Sun., noon–9 P.M. AE, DC, MC, V.

Beaufort

Moderate

The Anchorage House. 1103 Bay St. (803–524–9392). International cuisine is featured in this 1765 structure with a pre-Revolutionary ambience. Open 11:30 A.M.–2 P.M., 6–9:30 P.M., Mon.–Sat. Closed Sun. and holidays. Cocktail lounge. AE, DC, MC, V.

Hilton Head Island

Moderate

Ed Murray's. The Gallery of Shops, 14 Greenwood Dr. (803–785–8502). Fresh broiled seafood, beef, veal, lamb, poultry in elegant setting. Free private limousine to and from area resorts. Jackets optional, reservations recommended. Open 6–10 P.M. AE, DC, MC, V.

Fulvio's. 33 New Orleans Rd., Shipyard Business Center (803–681–6001). Continental dining with emphasis on Italian specialties is featured at this place, which is one of the island's most popular and elegant dining rooms. Open 6–10 P.M.; Sat. to 11 P.M. Closed Sun., major holidays, and Jan. 1–15. AE, DC, MC, V. Some entrees in *Expensive* category.

Hemingway's. In Hyatt Regency Hilton Head Palmetto Dunes (803–785–1234). This new oceanfront restaurant serves fresh grilled seafood, steaks, in a relaxed Key West atmosphere. Adjoining Hemingway's Lounge offers live entertainment in a casually elegant setting. Open 6–11 P.M.; lounge 4 P.M.–midnight. AE, DC, MC, V.

Hudson's Seafood House on the Docks. 1 Hudson Rd. (803–681–2773). Lavish selection of fresh seafood caught daily from own boats. Oyster bar open 10 A.M.–10 P.M.; L, 11 A.M.–5 P.M.; D, 6–10 P.M. No reservations. AE, DC, MC, V. Adjacent, under same management, is companion family-style restaurant, Hudson's Landing (803–681–3363). Same hours. Both have popular area following.

Old Fort Pub. In Hilton Head Plantation overlooking Skull Creek (803–681–2386). Low Country dishes include oyster pie, grilled shrimp and oysters wrapped in Smithfield Ham, Savannah chicken fried steak with onion gravy and hoppin' john. L, Mon.–Sat.; D, daily. AE, DC, MC, V.

RESTAURANTS—GEORGIA. Again, fresh local seafood highlights coastal Georgia menus. Savannah's diverse ethnic heritage is reflected in its distinctive and varied cuisine. It's said if you dine here on red beans and rice on New Year's Day, you'll have good luck all year. Gourmet Continental and American cuisine is featured in many city and resort dining rooms. In many of these, jacket and tie are requested at night, and reservations should be made.

Restaurants are listed according to price of a complete dinner; drinks, tax, and tip are not included. *Expensive,* over $20; *Moderate,* $10–$20; *Inexpensive,* under $10.

Savannah

Moderate

The Boar's Head. 1 N. Lincoln St. at River St. (912–232–3196). French and local cuisines are offered here in candlelit atmosphere overlooking Savannah River. Open 11:30 A.M.–4 P.M., 6–10 P.M., daily in season. French, German, Dutch, Spanish also spoken. AE, DC, MC, V.

Elizabeth on 37th. 105 E. 37th St. (912–236–5547). This is a nationally heralded restaurant in old Savannah mansion. Freshly prepared seasonal foods; "Southern American" cuisine with Continental influences. Owner-chef acclaimed one of nation's best chefs. Open 11:30 A.M.–2:30 P.M., 6–10:30 P.M., Tues.–Sat. Reservations suggested. AE, DC, MC, V. Some entrees in *Expensive* category.

Johnny Harris Restaurant. 1651 E. Victory Dr. (912–354–7810). Great local favorite since 1924 for true Savannah cookery: ribs, steaks, seafood, out-of-this-world barbecue. Luscious onion, crab soups, home baked desserts. Children's menu. Open 11:30 A.M.–11 P.M.; to 12:30 A.M., Fri. and Sat. Closed Sun. and holidays. Jackets required in main dining room Fri., Sat. P.M. AE, DC, MC, V.

The Olde Pink House Restaurant & Tavern. 23 Abercorn St. (912–232–4286 or 912–232–4262). Fresh seafoods, Continental cuisine in lovely Colonial rooms of 1771 Georgian mansion, a National Historic Landmark. Jacket and tie requested for dinner. Open 11:30 A.M.–3 P.M., 5–11 P.M., Mon.–Sat. Sun. 5:30–9 P.M. Antique shop 11:30 A.M.–3 P.M. or by appointment. AE, MC, V.

The Pirates' House. 20 E. Broad at Bay St. (912–233–5757). One of the South's most famous restaurants, this large place features regional and Southern specialties in 23 colorful rooms. Spectacular Rain Forest Bar, sumptuous Sun. jazz brunch, 36 luscious "calorie-free" desserts. House in historic Trustees' Garden was supposedly setting for portions of R. L. Stevenson's *Treasure Island.* Open 11:30 A.M.–3 P.M., Mon.–Sat.; 5:30–10 P.M., Mon.–Fri.; to 11 P.M., Sat.; 11:30 A.M.–3 P.M. for Sunday Musical Brunch. AE, DC, MC, V.

River House Seafood. 125 River St. (912–234–1900). "Low Country cookin' " is offered in this 1810 cotton warehouse. Seafood handpicked daily at the docks. Home made desserts. Cheerful, informal atmosphere. Open 11 A.M.–10 P.M., Mon.–Thurs.; to 11 P.M., Fri.–Sat. Also open Sun. 12 noon–10 P.M., Mar. through Oct. AE, MC, V.

Inexpensive

Crystal Beer Parlor. 301 W. Jones St. at Jefferson (912–232–1153). Famous shrimp salad, "crystal burger," Southern fried chicken, gumbo, crab stew, homemade cornbread are the mainstays in this comfortable old tavern. Takeouts. Open 11 A.M.–9 P.M., Mon.–Sat. Closed Sun.

Mrs. Wilkes Boarding House. 107 W. Jones St. (912–232–5997). A famed Savannah institution. Homestyle cooking—all fresh vegetables, meats, served family style. No signs—just follow your nose—and the crowd. Open 8–9 A.M., 11:30 A.M.–3 P.M., Mon.–Fri. No reservations; lines form early!

Brunswick

Inexpensive

Captain Joe's Seafood Restaurant. New Jessup Hwy. (912–264–8771). Generous portions of fresh local seafood. Locally popular. Open 11 A.M.–10 P.M. Closed Dec. 25. MC, V.

Pier 17. Ramada Inn East, 3241 Glynn Ave. (912–264–8611). Seafood, salad bar, homemade soups. Entertainment, dancing, Mon.–Sat. Open 6 A.M.–10 P.M.; Sun. to 2 P.M. Sun. brunch from 11 A.M. AE, DC, MC, V.

St. Simons Island

Moderate

Blanche's Courtyard. 440 Kings Way, center of village. (912–638–3030). "Bayou Victorian" atmosphere prevails here, where fresh crabs, fish, shrimp, and oysters are cooked to order. Weekend entertainment by Good Ole Boys Ragtime Band. Open 5:30 P.M.–10:30 P.M. Mon.–Sat.; Closed Sun. and holidays. AE, DC, MC, V.

The Emmeline and Hessie. Overlooking IntraCoastal Waterway at Golden Isles Marina on causeway to Brunswick (912–638–9084). Seafood, steaks, unique casseroles, and lobster are featured at this place, which also offers pre-dinner entertainment in The Raw Bar and Lounge. Open 7 A.M.–10 P.M., Mon.–Sat.; Sun. from 5:30 P.M. Closed major holidays. AE, DC, MC, V. Some evening entrees in *Expensive* category.

Jekyll Island

Moderate

Saint Andrews Landing. Jekyll Inn, 975 N. Beachview Dr. (912–635–2531). Tempting fresh coastal seafood and beef are served in this attractive oceanfront inn. Entertainment in season. Open 7 A.M.–3 P.M., 5–10 P.M., Mon.–Sat.; 11:30 A.M.–3 P.M., Sun. brunch. AE, DC, MC, V.

LIQUOR LAWS. North Carolina's liquor laws are on a local-option basis for municipalities and counties with regard to package sales of distilled spirits, beer, wine, and mixed beverage service in licensed restaurants. Approximately half the coastal counties allow package purchases in state-operated ABC stores, generally open daily 9 A.M.–9 P.M., except Sun., major holidays, and election days. Wine and beer are sold in grocery stores and wine shops. Several major urban and resort areas permit cocktail, wine, and beer service in restaurants and dining rooms; a few establishments where only beer and wine are sold may allow the sale of setups for those who want to bring their own bottles. Some communities also permit Sun. sales of mixed beverages. Bars and lounges usually remain open until 1 A.M., but this might vary in different municipalities. Legal age in North Carolina is 21.

In **South Carolina,** bottled liquor is sold in state-licensed package stores open daily 9 A.M.–7 P.M., except Sun., major holidays, and election days. Beer and wine are available from some groceries and drugstores. Licensed restaurants and dining rooms serve mixed beverages, beer, and wine, Mon.–Fri., 10 A.M.–2 A.M., Sat. until midnight. Sun. service is only on a private, non-cash basis or in private clubs. Legal age in South Carolina is 21.

In **Georgia,** liquor is sold by the package in retail stores, generally open 8 A.M.–11:30 P.M. except major holidays, election days, and Sun. in most places. Liquor sales in lounges, restaurants, and dining rooms are on a local option basis. Coastal Georgia's main vacation areas, such as Savannah and the Brunswick–Golden Isles orbit, provide mixed beverages in restaurants and dining rooms during the week, and permit cocktail service only with meals on Sun. Bars and lounges must close at 2 A.M. Legal age in Georgia is 21.

FLORIDA

by
JOICE VESELKA and MOIRA BAILEY

Ms. Veselka is regional travel editor of Chevrolet Friends Magazine, *and for many years was travel editor and publicity director of the Florida Division of Tourism. Ms. Bailey is a reporter with the* Orlando Sentinel.

Florida, home and workplace for some 12.5 million people, is also a seasonal playground for four times that many visitors. They are all seekers of something: wildlife, high life, low life, the quiet or noisy, lively or sedate, simple or luxurious, or any combination—in sum, the good life.

Whatever their specific quests, nearly all visitors are drawn by the basic magnets of sun and surf. The climate, Florida's greatest single asset and sweetheart of its chambers of commerce, is a powerful lure to northerners who'd rather sit in the sun than shovel snow. The beaches' appeal, which transcends the seasons, is a temptress winter, summer, spring, and fall to the work-weary, the school-bored, the wanderlust-inclined.

Trying to describe the mystique and demeanor of all Florida's cities would take volumes. But each of the four cities we focus on here is a microcosm of the state, its individual highlights and idiosyncrasies part of the appeal called Florida.

Miami

To get to Miami, just go south. You can't miss it—and you shouldn't. There are Miami Beach and Coral Gables, Hialeah and Miami Springs, the core of Miami proper, and Key Biscayne, West Miami, North Miami,

Points of Interest

1) Aventura Mall
2) Bass Museum of Art
3) Bayfront Park; Bayside Marketplace and the *HMS Bounty* Exhibit; Torch of Friendship
4) Bayside Marketplace
5) Biscayne Kennel Club
6) Calder Race Track
7) City Convention Complex
8) Coconut Grove Exposition Hall
9) Fairchild Tropical Garden
10) Flagler Dog Track
11) Hialeah Park Race Course
12) Hotel Fontainebleau Hilton
13) Jai-Alai Fronton
14) Japanese Gardens
15) Joe Robbie Stadium
16) Lincoln Road Mall
17) Lowe Gallery
18) Marine Stadium
19) Little Havana
20) Metrozoo
21) Mayfair House/Shops
22) Miami Arena
23) Museum of Science and Natural History, Planetarium
24) North Shore Open Space Park
25) Omni International Hotel
26) Orange Bowl
27) Parrot Jungle
28) Planet Ocean
29) Seaquarium
30) South Florida History Museum, Arts Center
31) Theater of the Performing Arts
32) University of Miami
33) Vizcaya Art Museum

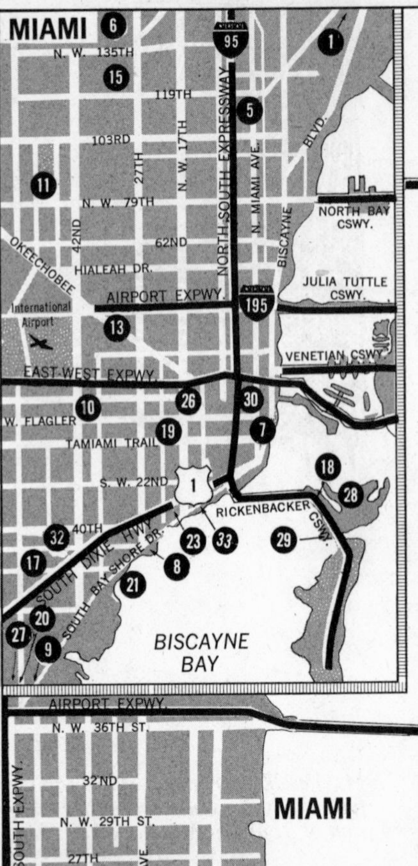

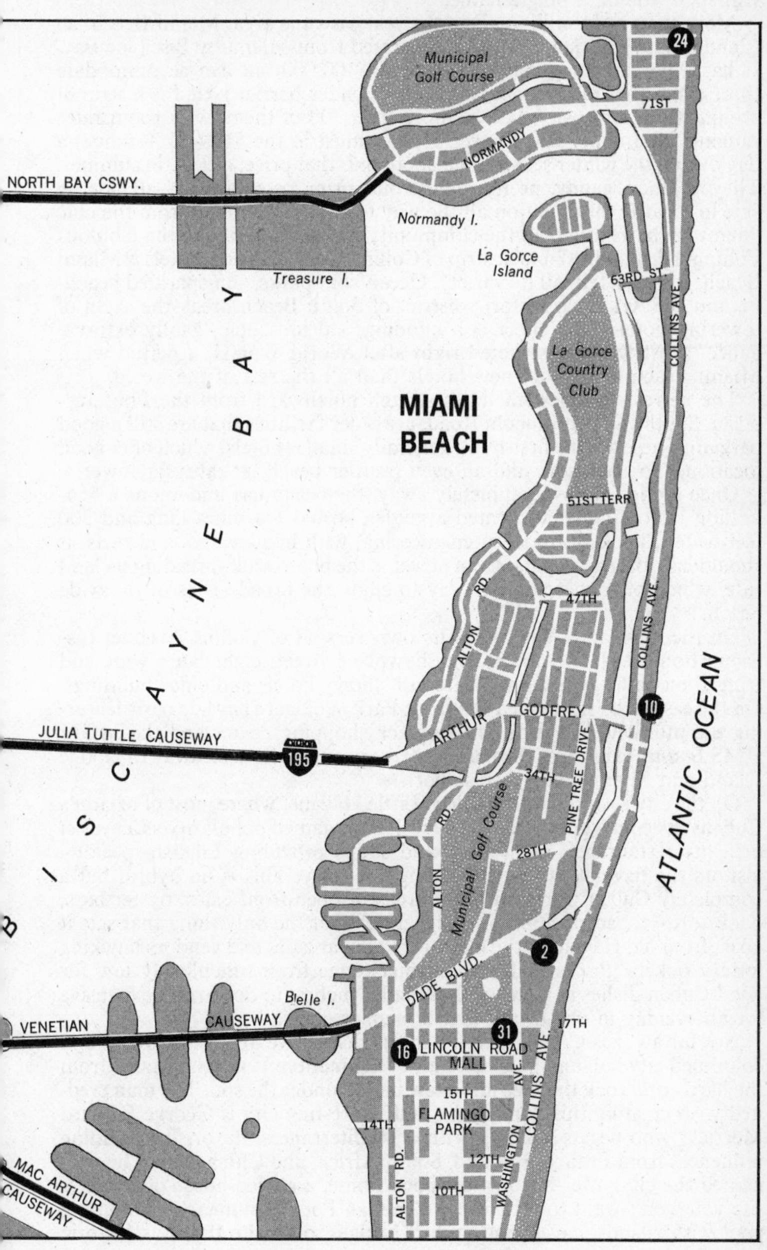
Municipal Golf Course
71ST
NORMANDY
NORTH BAY CSWY.
Normandy I.
La Gorce Island
Treasure I.
63RD ST.
COLLINS AVE.
La Gorce Country Club
MIAMI BEACH
BISCAYNE BAY
51ST TERR
ALTON RD.
47TH
COLLINS AVE.
ATLANTIC OCEAN
GODFREY
ARTHUR
JULIA TUTTLE CAUSEWAY
195
34TH
PINE TREE DRIVE
Municipal Golf Course
28TH
ALTON RD.
DADE BLVD.
Belle I.
VENETIAN
CAUSEWAY
17TH
LINCOLN ROAD MALL
15TH
FLAMINGO PARK
14TH
COLLINS AVE.
WASHINGTON AVE.
12TH
10TH
ALTON RD.
MAC ARTHUR CAUSEWAY
24
10
2
31
16

South Miami, Miami Shores, and others. Put them all together and they still spell Miami, a magic name.

More than eight million visitors a year visit the area. Miami Beach, an island of just 7.5 square miles, is separated from Miami by Biscayne Bay. It has a permanent population of about 100,000 but can accommodate three times that many visitors. On this slender barrier island is a strip of architectural virtuosity: hotels, more than 300 of them, with room rates ranging from under $50 to over $1,000 (most in the $100–$150 range) a day during the winter season, and about half that price, or less, in summer. They're fancy, gaudy, pretty, monstrous, prim, ostentatious—all side by side in a battle for attention all the way to the county line. From the chic Sheraton Bal Harbour in the community of Bal Harbour, to the fabulous Fontainebleau, the 87-block strip of Collins Avenue luxury hotels *is* Miami Beach, the resort, in all its variety. Oceanfront parks, sun-sparkled beaches, and the Art Deco historic district of South Beach break the skein of towering hotels. The effect is a blinding, kaleidoscopic, gaudy extravagance. Most were constructed right after World War II, a period when Miami Beach built more new hotels than all the rest of the world.

The newest, plushest facilities stretch northward from the Fontainebleau. Southward, to Lincoln Road, are older facilities that are still a good bargain. These are the first-built, generally smaller hotels, which offer good location, the same sun, and an even prettier beach, at rates far lower.

Once eroded almost completely away, the beach has undergone a $64-million restoration that created a golden strand ten miles long and 300 feet wide. Thanks to modern engineering, with breakwaters and reefs, it should last for many years. Even newer is the boardwalk threading its land side, which offers yet another way to enjoy the broad vistas of the wide beach.

On the mainland, Miami has its own version of Collins Avenue: Biscayne Boulevard, the downtown showplace street, eight lanes wide and fringed by palms. On the west are tall, showy hotels and office buildings. On the east is the revitalized Bayfront Park, a 62-acre bayside oasis featuring the multilevel Bayside Marketplace shopping center and the MGM HMS *Bounty* exhibit; at the park's northern end is the accessway to Dodge Island and Miami's busy cruise port.

On the city's southwestern side is Little Havana, where most of Miami's Cubans live and work. Since the 1960s, it has gained popularity as a tourist area, its restaurants, nightclubs, and shops providing English-speaking visitors the flavor and feel of a foreign country. This is no hybrid but a completely Cuban world with hundreds of open-front cafés, oyster bars, bookstores, tobacco shops, and grocers. About the only thing that sets it apart from old Havana is the lack of covered arcades and vendors hawking lottery tickets. Prices in Little Havana range from ridiculously low for good Cuban dishes in some of the smaller niches, to downright expensive for an evening in one of the fancier supper clubs.

Not far away is Coral Gables, with its distinctive Spanish-towered and columned city hall and an overall air of distinction. It takes its name from the hard coral rock that lies just a few inches under the soil. The man credited with creating this flamboyant and interesting city is George Edward Merrick, who began building with a Mediterranean flavor, later adding influences from France, Holland, South Africa, and China. It was he who named the city, after his own boyhood home, a gabled house of coral. A site you won't want to miss is the Venetian Pool, a municipal swimming pool with islands, caves, and arched bridges, on a site that's as historic as the city.

Key Biscayne, linked to Miami by a causeway, is a very reasonable facsimile of a South Sea island. It was a coconut plantation long before the postwar causeway was built and is a favorite of moviemakers because of its tropical lushness. When Richard Nixon was president, the winter

White House was here. County-owned Crandon Park, site of many special events, sprawls over much of the island's northern segment. At its southern end is another popular recreation site, a state park encompassing Cape Florida Lighthouse. And sandwiched in between is a residential area, with some houses boasting grounds that could double as a garden attraction.

Coconut Grove is Miami's Bohemian section but also the home of some of the area's oldest families, the original settlers and local aristocracy who came down before the boom eras. It is a village within the city—private, discreetly cosmopolitan, and charming, with elegant shopping, dining, and hotel facilities. It's part Greenwich, Connecticut, and part Sausalito, California, with overtones of Tahiti.

Orlando

Another Florida, distinctly different from the beach-keys-ocean experience, comes into view in the rolling hills and sparkling lakes of central Florida. You'll discover worlds of magic, entertainment, and family fun, spiced with adventure and variety. Several of Florida's early attractions opened prior to World War II. But the announcement by Walt Disney in the mid-1960s that this would be the site of his most ambitious project sparked the development of the tourist facilities that have catapulted this area into the world's premier vacation site.

There is actually too much to see and do here in a single trip. It could take weeks just to visit the major attractions. Walt Disney World officials advise that it takes four or five days to see what they term "a major share" of their four parks (each with separate admission): Magic Kingdom, Epcot Center, Typhoon Lagoon Water Park, and Disney–MGM Studio Theme Park. Adding to Orlando's emergence as a movie town is Universal Studios Florida, which, like the Disney–MGM Studio, combines production and entertainment facilities. Every year brings an array of new shows, new rides, new experiences as the area's many entertainment complexes continue to grow. Sea World, noted for its killer whales and shows in an innovative stadium, was the first to have a killer whale born in captivity (the first in 1985, another in 1988, and a third in 1989). It also features a Penguin Encounter with more than 200 penguins and other Arctic seabirds in their own, chilly environment.

This is an area where finding something to do is not the problem—the problem is finding enough time to do the things that hold the most appeal for you. Theme parks and entertainment complexes are literally everywhere, but if exploring on your own is more to your liking, there's a similar wide array of choices.

Orlando itself encompasses 81 city parks and recreation areas and has more than 50 lakes within its city limits. Winter Park, with an Old World charm left over from its New England settlers, has 84 city parks of its own. There are gardens that rival commercial attractions, and interesting museums of every sort. Winter Park has its own scenic boat tours of the area. An apprentice under Louis Comfort Tiffany now holds, and offers for the public's viewing, the world's largest collection of Tiffany art nouveau items. A shell museum contains an example of almost every known species of seashell.

Wekiwa Springs, a 6,400-acre state park east of Orlando, encompasses one of the numerous natural springs that exist throughout the central heartland. Lake Apopka, southwest of town, is the second largest in the state. Two major canoe trails, one on the Wekiwa River and the other on the Econlockhatchee River, offer a serene look at the wildlife and terrain. Other boating opportunities include leisurely cruises on the area's lakes and waterways.

This is also cattle country, supporting a major beef and dairy cattle industry. And where there are cows, there are cowboys. Kissimmee (pro-

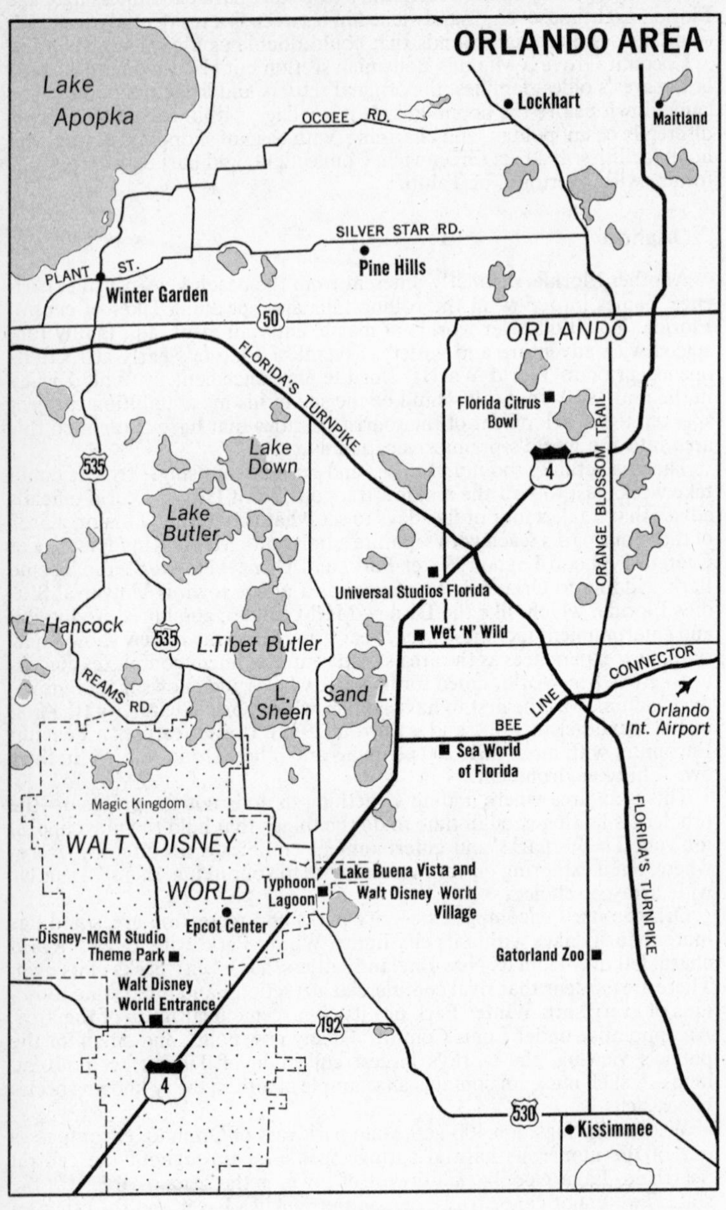
ORLANDO AREA
Lake Apopka
OCOEE RD.
Lockhart
Maitland
SILVER STAR RD.
Pine Hills
PLANT ST.
Winter Garden
50
ORLANDO
FLORIDA'S TURNPIKE
Florida Citrus Bowl
535
Lake Down
4
ORANGE BLOSSOM TRAIL
Lake Butler
Universal Studios Florida
L. Hancock
535
L.Tibet Butler
Wet 'N' Wild
CONNECTOR
REAMS RD.
L. Sheen
Sand L.
BEE LINE
Orlando Int. Airport
Sea World of Florida
Magic Kingdom
WALT DISNEY WORLD
FLORIDA'S TURNPIKE
Typhoon Lagoon
Lake Buena Vista and Walt Disney World Village
Epcot Center
Disney-MGM Studio Theme Park
Gatorland Zoo
Walt Disney World Entrance
192
4
530
Kissimmee

nounce it with the accent on the second syllable) continues to conduct business as usual at its weekly cattle auction but welcomes visitors who'd like to watch. The relaxed, friendly city is also site of the Silver Spurs Rodeo, the state's largest, in February and July.

For those who prefer to participate rather than watch, golf and tennis are a way of life in the area. Many top resorts are built around their sports programs and offer a number of attractive package plans for the active visitor. More than 3,000 eating establishments cater to varied tastes and offer some out-of-the-ordinary dining experiences: medieval banquets amid jousting tournaments, Polynesian luaus, bierhaus fare, hot-air balloon rides with champagne, and fine dining around the World (Disney's of course) within sight of each country's famous landmarks.

Tampa

The Tampa area is a region of contrasts. It's a major metropolitan center—largest on the state's west coast—but here, humans still reside in close proximity to the beauty and wonder of nature. Tampa's shining new structures herald the city's tomorrow, while stately historic structures whisper of its yesterdays.

When Henry Plant brought his railroad and steamship lines to Tampa in the 1880s, the city was little more than a minor port of call for schooners operating from Key West to Cedar Key. But his railroad and the magnificent Tampa Bay Hotel he constructed quickly transformed it into a fashionable resort. It's a legacy apparent to everyone, in the landmark onion domes and minarets that have long been a distinctive element of the city's skyline. The structure is now part of the University of Tampa campus, but tours are offered in the one wing housing the Henry Plant Museum.

The city's skyline is changing, reflecting the tremendous growth completed, in progress, and slated to continue throughout the 1990s. Among the completed developments, affording visitors some exciting new options are the billion-dollar Harbour Island complex, reached by monorail running from the downtown area on Franklin Street and the $57-million Tampa Bay Performing Arts Center, heart of the downtown arts district. The new $137-million Tampa Convention Center, which was completed in late 1990, is among the nation's largest. Ultimately, new docks and facilities for cruise ships will be located in the downtown area.

Additions to Harbour Island will continue through 1999, as the striking red-brick-and-bronze-glass complex reaches full development as a marketplace combining European charm and the festivity of an Old World street market.

But there's more to the city than its downtown developments. Its Latin Quarter, Ybor City, remains a major point of interest, and expanded facilities exist there as well. A major cigar-production center at the turn of the century, it is now a national historic site encompassing Ybor City State Museum; Ybor Square, a restored cigar factory now housing shops and restaurants; Ybor Preservation Park, restored houses; and Ybor Park and Farmers Market, a Cuban open-air market for ethnic food and imported produce. You can see cigars rolled by hand and watch Cuban bread-baking processes—but don't be surprised if the aromas tempt you into purchases.

Busch Gardens, second only to Walt Disney World in the number of guests it attracts, offers instant transport to the Dark Continent, where its 300 acres of African-theme sections teem with belly dancers, snake charmers, and enough other entertainment options to fill a full day. The attraction's Serengeti Plain, incidentally, is home to more than 3,000 animals—making it one of the five largest zoos in the world.

The city's fairgrounds are aswarm with people in February, both when the fair is in progress and earlier, when it ties in with the city's festive Gasparilla Pirate Invasion and Festival. The celebration, a week of rollicking

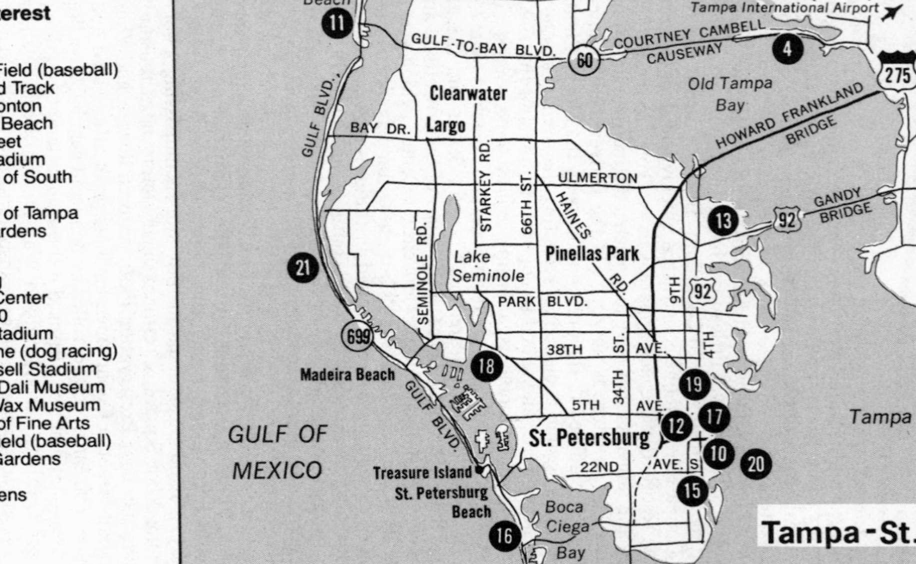

Points of Interest

Tampa
1) Al Lopez Field (baseball)
2) Greyhound Track
3) Jai Alai Fronton
4) Municipal Beach
5) Shrimp Fleet
6) Tampa Stadium
7) University of South Florida
8) University of Tampa
9) Busch Gardens

St. Petersburg
10) Bayfront Center
11) Big Pier 60
12) Al Lang Stadium
13) Derby Lane (dog racing)
14) Jack Russell Stadium
15) Salvador Dali Museum
16) London Wax Museum
17) Museum of Fine Arts
18) Payson Field (baseball)
19) Sunken Gardens
20) The Pier
21) Tiki Gardens

piratical fun, pays dubious homage to Tampa's raffish patron saint, José Gaspar, a cut-throat pirate about whom colorful tales are told. No one knows whether he really existed, but the lore provides reason enough for the people to get together and celebrate.

Jacksonville

Jacksonville, surrounded by historical and recreational highlights, keeps its biggest attraction close to its heart. This is a river's city—born of the river's strength, sustained by its commerce, and forever wed to its romantic aura. The mighty St. Johns River, one of the few rivers in the United States that flows south to north, winds through the downtown district, muscling its way past the city's landmark Friendship Fountain. Millions of dollars have gone into the river-development area in the city's midst, creating its appealing Riverwalk. Accessible through the park where the fountain is—St. Johns Riverpark—the Riverwalk is dotted with sidewalk cafés and kiosks with boardwalks along both banks and water taxis zipping back and forth. On the grassy commons of Metropolitan Park, another river facility, music enthusiasts gather for the annual Jacksonville and All That Jazz festival; at other times it is used for festivals and special activities.

The Jacksonville Zoo, beyond the river's north bank, is home to more than 700 animals, including a herd of rare white rhinos. Here, they offer what is known as the world's slowest thrill ride: rides on a lumbering elephant.

Historic sites abound, for this northeastern area is the historic cornerstone of the state. Fort Caroline National Memorial is a replica of the 1564 French Huguenot fort overlooking the river. Kingsley Plantation, a state historic site, preserves the state's oldest existing plantation site, dating back to 1792, when it was the center of a slave-trading empire. Neighboring Mayport, reputed to be the oldest fishing village in the nation, some 300 years old, is also site of Mayport Naval Station, with one of the U.S. east coast's largest aircraft-carrier basins. Free weekend tours are offered on a ship in port.

Jacksonville Beach and its neighboring communities of Atlantic Beach and Neptune Beach create an island of beaches whose hometown hospitality keeps visitors returning. Its popular fishing pier, just short of a thousand feet long, is the most popular gathering site, for watchers as well as doers.

Nearby are Fernandina Beach, a salty little seaport with a captivating Victorian historic district and pre–Civil War fort; Amelia Island Plantation, a plush resort on the southern tip of Amelia Island, where top women tennis stars gather each April to vie for one of pro tennis's largest purses, the WTA Championships; Ponte Vedra, site of two of the biggest draws for golfing visitors—Sawgrass resort, with its scenic, challenging courses, and the high-stakes Tournament Players Championship, held there annually the last week in March; and St. Augustine, the nation's oldest city, which has historic sites from the 1500s, 1600s, and 1700s.

PRACTICAL INFORMATION FOR FLORIDA

WHEN TO GO. Winter is peak season in Florida's southern reaches, when dropouts from icy winter climes congregate at the continent's balmiest sites. January temperatures hover in the 70-degree range. In summer, the 80- to 83-degree temperatures and undeniably high humidity are tempered by almost constant breezes and the pesky brief showers that come almost daily. This is when the northern sections

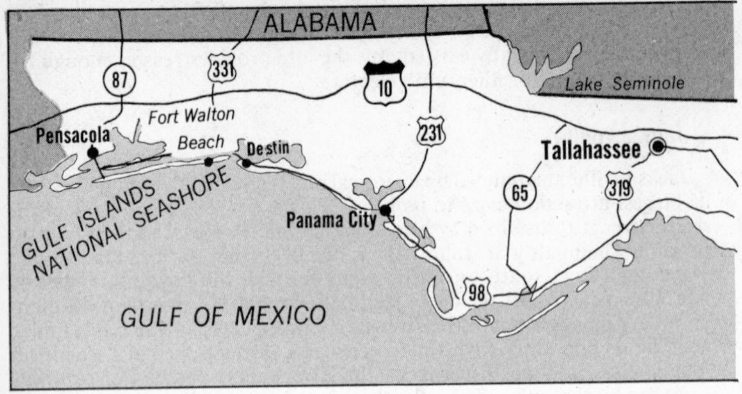

come into their peak season, as the school's-out family trade gravitates toward lively resorts along both coastlines and quieter inland areas rich in natural highlights and historic sites. Central Florida, the fun-tier attraction kingdom, has no clearly defined peak season, though its steady stream of visitors reaches the greatest proportions in summer and at major holiday periods throughout the year. In between are shoulder seasons—those inviting nontraditional travel periods when rates are lower, facilities less crowded, and weather just as pleasant. They've begun attracting their own growing number of seasonal visitors; perhaps one day there'll be a "peak off-season." Until then, best bets are late Apr. through May, when many of the subtropical flowers are at their showiest, and Oct. through Nov., when summer lags well behind summer visitors.

HOW TO GET THERE. Florida's popularity as a leisure and business destination translates into an abundance of transportation service, as well as frequent discounts on packages and promotional fares. Rates and routes change frequently, so consult several lines or a travel agent and shop around for the best deal.

By Plane

Miami. You can reach busy Miami International Airport on direct flights from all major American cities via *American, Continental, Delta, Midway, Northwest, Pan Am, USAir, TWA,* or *United.* Service is also offered by a number of regional carriers and intrastate airlines. Miami is an important international gateway, serving 31 certified foreign airlines and providing international service by U.S. carriers. It offers more than 400 flights weekly to the Bahamas and the Caribbean, 385 to Latin America, and 140 to European cities, including Concorde service by British Airways (to London, via Washington, three times weekly).

Orlando. Orlando International Airport, whose $1-billion expansion will add improvements through 1998, has 800 flights per day, with direct service from some 100 U.S. cities via *American, British Airways, Continental, Delta, Iceland Air, Midway, Northwest, Pan Am, TWA, United,* and *USAir.* Almost two dozen carriers offer international charter service.

Tampa. Tampa International Airport, consistently voted a favorite of the Airline Passengers Association, offers service by some two dozen national and international carriers, including *Air Canada, Air Jamaica, American, Bahamasair, British Airways, Condor, Continental, Delta, Midway, Northwest, Pan Am, TWA, United, USAir,* and *Ward Air.* International flights are offered to Europe, Canada, Mexico, and the Caribbean.

Jacksonville. Jacksonville International Airport serves as the transportation hub of Florida's northeast, with service by *American, Continental, Continental Express, Delta, TWA, United,* and *USAir.*

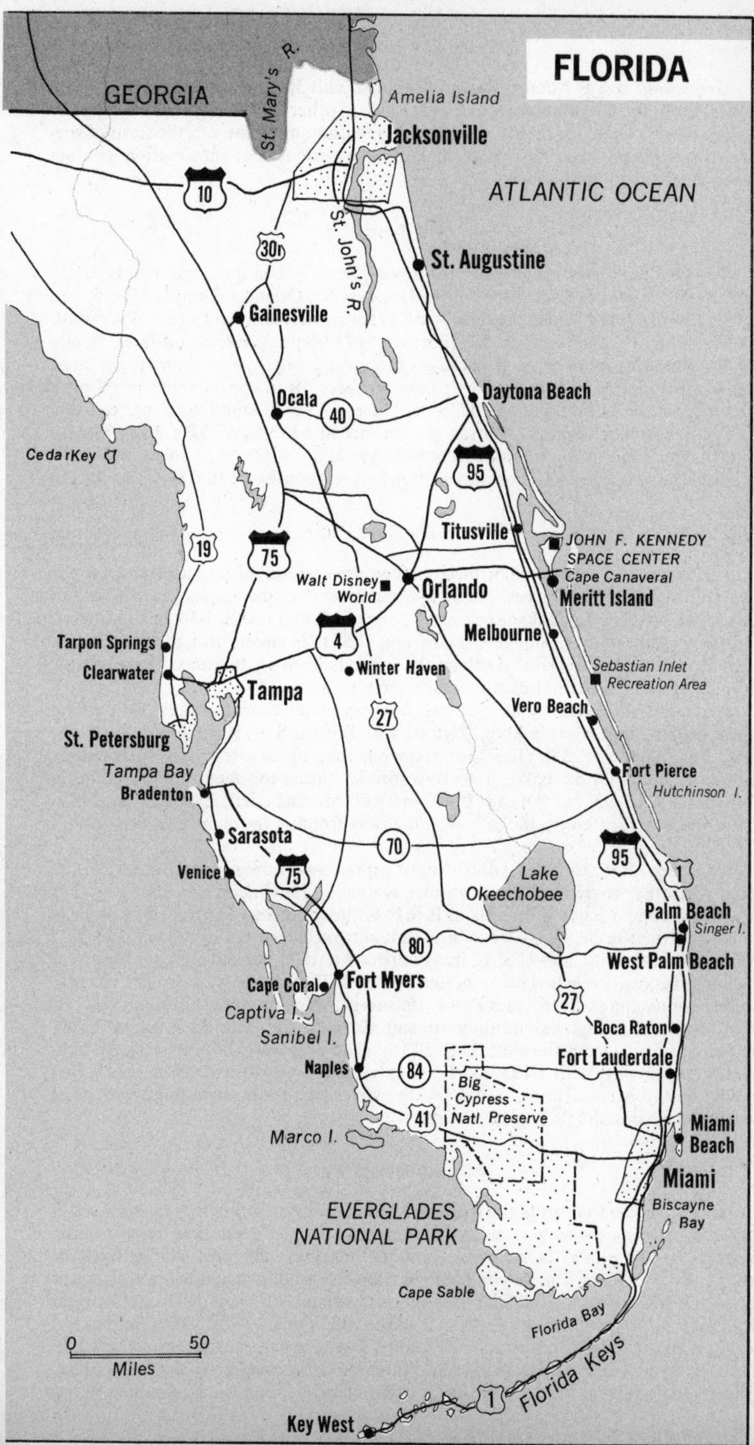
FLORIDA
GEORGIA
St. Mary's R.
Amelia Island
Jacksonville
ATLANTIC OCEAN
10
30
St. John's R.
St. Augustine
Gainesville
Ocala
40
Daytona Beach
Cedar Key
95
Titusville
JOHN F. KENNEDY SPACE CENTER
Cape Canaveral
19
75
Walt Disney World
Orlando
Meritt Island
Melbourne
4
Tarpon Springs
Clearwater
Winter Haven
Tampa
Sebastian Inlet Recreation Area
27
Vero Beach
St. Petersburg
Tampa Bay
Bradenton
Fort Pierce
Hutchinson I.
Sarasota
70
95
Venice
75
Lake Okeechobee
1
Palm Beach
Singer I.
80
West Palm Beach
Cape Coral
Fort Myers
Captiva I.
27
Sanibel I.
Boca Raton
Naples
84
Fort Lauderdale
Big Cypress Natl. Preserve
41
Marco I.
Miami Beach
Miami
Biscayne Bay
EVERGLADES NATIONAL PARK
Cape Sable
Florida Bay
0 50
Miles
Florida Keys
1
Key West

By Bus

Greyhound serves Miami, Orlando, Tampa, and Jacksonville, as well as those cities' suburban communities and a wide range of other Florida cities. The company offers express buses to specific destinations and discounted rates in the form of special travel passes covering regions and/or time periods. For information, contact your local Greyhound office.

By Train

Amtrak offers passenger service from New York–Washington and points south, via the *Silver Meteor* and *Silver Star* to Jacksonville, Orlando, Tampa, Miami, and other Florida cities. It also operates Auto Train service between Lorton, VA (south of Washington), and Sanford, FL (northeast of Orlando). Excursion fares, family plans, discounts for seniors, or packages can mean a big savings. Auto Train fares, regularly about $200 per car plus passenger fares, drop considerably in off-peak seasons, as low as $150 per car, $119 per passenger southbound; $114 per car, $69 per passenger northbound. Amtrak **stations** are at 8303 N.W. 37th Ave., Miami; 1400 Sligh Boulevard, Orlando; Nebraska Ave and Twiggs St., Tampa; and 3570 Clifford Ln., Jacksonville. For information and reservations, call 800–USA–RAIL.

By Car

All four cities, each a major metropolitan area, are laced by interstates for the traveler in a hurry and accessible by alternate scenic routes for those with time to savor the settings. In **Jacksonville,** I-95 runs north and south, I-10 east and west. I-295 loops the western side of the city, and U.S. 1/23 slices through to the southeast from the northwest. A1A, along the coast, is historic Buccaneer Trail, a slow but scintillating trek that can include a ferry crossing.

Orlando is threaded by at least half a dozen major thoroughfares: I-4 curving northeast to southwest, linking Daytona and Tampa; S.R. 50 running east to the Titusville area; S.R. 528 (Bee Line Expwy.), running east from I-4 to Kennedy Space Center; Florida Tpke., a northwest-to-southeast toll facility terminating in Miami; U.S. 17–92–441 (Orange Blossom Trail) running north and south; and U.S. 192 (Space Coast Pkwy.), the east–west highway fronting the main entrance to Walt Disney World.

In **Tampa,** I-75, the major north-south expressway, now runs to the east of the city; its former route through downtown is now I-175, which connects with I-275 spanning Tampa Bay via Frankland Bridge to the southwest and Sunshine Skyway Bridge to the southeast. I-4 leads into Tampa from the east, U.S. 41 parallels I-75 southeast of the city, and U.S. 19 leads north on a route just inland from the coast.

Miami is easily reached by numerous routes: I-75 from the west, via the recently added connector of Everglades Pkwy. (formerly Alligator Alley toll road); U.S. 1, the north-south highway leading to and through the Florida Keys; U.S. 41 (Tamiami Trail) from the west; U.S. 27 from the northeast; I-95, its major north-south expressway, with I-195 and I-395 extensions on eastward spans across Biscayne Bay to Miami Beach; and A1A, the water-rich route threading the edge of the Atlantic coastline's barrier islands.

By Boat

You can come to Florida the truly buoyant way: afloat, either in your own vessel or as a one-way passenger on commercial craft during a seasonal repositioning voyage. In Miami and Jacksonville, abundant marinas offer slips and facilities for waterway transients. Unless you come in from the islands, you'll utilize the Intracoastal Waterway, whose official terminus is in Miami—1,391 miles from its origin in Trenton, NJ, and 349 miles from Jacksonville. On the Gulf side, Tampa, not really a coastal city, revels in its own Tampa Bay, a broad expanse into which half a dozen rivers empty. Even land-locked Orlando is accessible, via the Okeechobee Waterway (which can be reached from either coastline) and the Kissimmee River.

For information on Florida's Intracoastal Waterway, write: U.S. Army Engineer District, Box 4970, Jacksonville, FL 32201, or Florida Inland Navigation District, 2725 Ave. E, Riviera Beach, FL 33404. *U.S. Coast Guard* numbers to keep handy: Jacksonville (Mayport Office)—904–247–7312; Miami—305–536–5641; Tampa (St. Petersburg office)—813–896–6187.

TOURIST INFORMATION. To get the most out of your visit, take advantage of the wide variety of material you can obtain in advance. For a free, 120-page guide to the whole state, which includes lists of information sources by geographic regions and gives addresses and phone numbers, contact *Florida Div. of Tourism,* Direct Mail, 126 Van Buren St., Tallahassee, FL 32301 (904–487–1462). (Tell them your destination, and they'll include brochures and other literature on that specific site as well.)

Miami. Miami area visitors may contact the Greater Miami Convention & Visitors Bureau. It offers maps, brochures, and literature in several languages, which you can obtain in advance or pick up after arrival at 701 Brickell Ave., Suite 2700, Miami, FL 33131 (800–641–1111 or 305–539–3000). For greater in-depth information, you may also want to write or visit offices in individual communities (Greater Miami encompasses 27 municipalities, and most have their own tourist information sources). Among them: *Coconut Grove Chamber of Commerce,* 2820 McFarlane Rd., Coconut Grove, FL 33133 (305–444–7270); *Coral Gables Chamber of Commerce,* 50 Aragon Ave., Coral Gables, FL 33134 (305–446–1657); *Hialeah–Miami Springs Area Chamber of Commerce,* 59 W. 5th St., Hialeah, FL 33010 (305–887–1515); *Key Biscayne Chamber of Commerce,* 95 W. McIntyre St., Key Biscayne, FL 33149, (305–361–5207).

Orlando. Orlando area visitors can utilize one or more of the following: *Orlando/Orange County Convention and Visitors Bureau,* 7208 Sand Lake Rd., Suite 300, Orlando, FL 32819 (407–363–5800 or 800–828–7776). *Kissimmee–St. Cloud Convention & Visitors Bureau,* Box 422007, Kissimmee, FL 32743 (800–327–9159 U.S.; 800–432–9199 in Florida); *Walt Disney World,* Guest Letters, Box 40, Lake Buena Vista, FL 32830 (407–824–4321). *The Kissimmee–Osceola County C&VB* maintains tourist information centers in several locations: Fort Liberty, 5260 W. Irlo Bronson Memorial Hwy., Kissimmee; in Lake City, at Rte. 13, Box 184-A, Lake City, FL 32055; and one in a central location at the main office in Kissimmee (1925 E. Irlo Bronson Memorial Hwy., 407–847–5000). All are open 8 A.M. to 6 P.M., seven days a week. *Orlando Tourist Center* (407–351–0412), 8445 International Dr. at Mercado, is open seven days a week, 8 A.M. to 8 P.M. *Orlando Area Chamber of Commerce* also operates a tourist center, near I-4 (75 E. Ivanhoe Blvd., 425–1234), open weekdays 8 A.M. to 5:30 P.M.

Tampa. Tampa visitors can obtain advance information from *Tampa/Hillsborough Convention and Visitors Association,* 11 Madison St., Suite 1010, Tampa, FL 33602 (800–826–8358 or 813–223–1111), or pick it up at *Tampa Chamber of Commerce,* (813–228–7777), 801 E. Kennedy Blvd. (open 9 A.M. to 5 P.M., Mon.–Fri.). The city's popular Latin Quarter, Ybor City, has its own chamber of commerce, which provides information and literature: *Ybor City Chamber of Commerce,* 1800 E. 9th Ave., Ybor City, Tampa, FL 33605 (813–248–3712). A literature section for visitors is in the front of the office, open 9 A.M. to 4 P.M., Mon.–Fri.

Jacksonville. For information on the Jacksonville–Jacksonville Beaches area, write or visit *Jacksonville Convention & Visitors Bureau,* 6 E. Bay St., Suite 200, Jacksonville, FL 32202 (800–733–2668 or 904–353–9736) (open 8:30 A.M. to 5 P.M., Mon.–Fri.). The bureau also has listings of events in the Jacksonville area. If you're primarily interested in the coastal section, contact or visit *The Beaches of Jacksonville Chamber of Commerce,* Box 50427, Jacksonville Beach, FL 32240 (904–249–3868) (at 413 Pablo Ave., open 8:30 A.M. to 5 P.M., weekdays). Auto travelers coming into the state via I-95 or U.S. 1–301 may want to stop at the state-operated *Florida Welcome Stations* at Yulee or Hilliard. They offer free grapefruit juice, maps and literature, and assistance by travel counselors.

TIME ZONES. Eastern Time is the correct setting for timepieces in Miami, Orlando, Tampa, and Jacksonville. Most of the state lies within this time zone. The only exception is the northwest panhandle area, from just east of Panama City westward to the Alabama border, which lies within the Central Time zone.

TELEPHONES. Miami. The area code for Miami and the southeastern quadrant of the state is 305. A pay-phone call is 25 cents, and there is no time limit. The local calling area covers most of the county, although calls between exchanges at the edges of the county may be long distance—a call to North Miami is local from the downtown area but long distance from the southern suburb of Perrine. Dial 411 for local directory assistance, which also can advise you whether the number you wish to call will be local or long distance.

Orlando. Orlando's area code was changed to 407 in spring 1988. This code is used in parts of Orange County, where Orlando is located, as well as in the adjacent Seminole and Volusia counties and in other communities southeast of Orlando. The area south of the Broward County/Palm Beach line uses area code 305. The charge for a pay phone call is 25 cents; no time limits are placed on pay-phone calls. The local calling area encompasses most of the metropolitan area including Kissimmee, Lake Buena Vista–Walt Disney World, Winter Park, and other communities. For local directory assistance, call 411.

Tampa. Tampa is within the 813 area code, covering Florida's southwestern quadrant. Pay-phone calls are 25 cents, with no time limit, and long distance calls to other 813 numbers may be dialed without the area code. The local calling area encompasses most of Tampa's metropolitan area but does not extend across Tampa Bay to the nearby coastal resort areas. Reach local directory assistance by dialing 411.

Jacksonville. Jacksonville is within the 904 area code, which includes the entire northern half of the state. Jacksonville and Jacksonville Beach, separate municipalities, both have 25-cent charges for pay phones (no time limit) and 411 as the number for local directory assistance. Jacksonville's local calling area takes in Jacksonville Beach, Ponte Vedra, Fort George, Orange Park, and other communities. From Jacksonville Beach, calls to communities other than Jacksonville Beach, Jacksonville, or Ponte Vedra are long distance.

EMERGENCY TELEPHONE NUMBERS. The standard emergency number for police, fire department, ambulance, and paramedic assistance in all four cities is 911, as it is in most communities throughout the U.S. Other important numbers are:

Miami. *Police,* 595–6263 (Miami Beach Police, 673–7900). *Fire Dept.,* 579–6300 (Miami Beach Fire Dept., 673–7111). *Ambulance,* 579–6111. *Florida Highway Patrol,* 470–2510. *Poison Control Center,* 325–7711. *U.S. Coast Guard,* 535–4314. *Miami Beach Lifeguard Service,* 673–7711.

Tampa. *Police,* 223–1112. *Fire Dept.,* 681–9927. *Ambulance,* 681–4422. *Florida Highway Patrol,* 272–2211. *Poison Control Center,* 253–4444 or 800–282–3171. *U.S. Coast Guard* (St. Petersburg office, long distance), 1–896–6187.

Orlando. *Police,* 849–2414. *Fire Dept.,* 849–2390. *Ambulance,* 298–6700. *Florida Highway Patrol,* 423–6400. *Poison Control Center,* 841–5222.

Jacksonville. *Police,* 633–4202 (Jacksonville Beach Police, 249–2531). *Fire Dept.,* 633–5457 (Jacksonville Beach Fire Dept., 249–2334). *Ambulance,* 633–2211 (Jacksonville Beach Ambulance, 733–6600). *Florida Highway Patrol,* 355–9981. *Poison Control Center,* 387–7500 (Jacksonville Beach Poison Control Center, 387–2422). *U.S. Coast Guard,* 247–7311.

HOW TO GET AROUND. As popular destinations for leisure and entertainment, Miami, Orlando, Tampa, and Jacksonville are well equipped to provide visitors with full access, both to and from the airports and around the towns.

Miami

From the airport. Miami International Airport is 7 mi. from downtown and about 15 from the beach's major hotels. *SuperShuttle Miami* serves Dade, Broward, and Palm Beach counties, with airport transfer service door to door 24 hours a day every day, at about $8 to downtown, $10 to the beach. Pickup at Van/Limo booth on airport's lower level; call 800–633–1915 or 305–871–2000. Many hotels provide free guest transportation; check hotel telephone boards to see whether your lodging site has this service or to call for pickup. Taxis, which are plentiful, charge about $15 to downtown, $20–30 to the beach; a $1 airport surcharge is added to the fare.

Metrobus (638–6700) offers two downtown routes and one to Coral Gables and Miami Beach, with frequent departures from clearly marked boarding sites; fares are $1, plus 25 cents for transfers. All major car-rental companies have airport facilities as well.

By bus. Miami's county-operated *Metrobus* runs local and express routes throughout the metropolitan area; you'll need exact change for the fares ($1, plus 25 cents for a transfer). For route information, contact Maps by Mail, (638–7460).

By Metrorail. The Metrorail, Miami's sleek elevated rapid-transit system, whisks passengers from downtown Miami west to Hialeah and south to Kendall. Stops, about 1 mi. apart, include some popular points of interest such as the Hialeah Race Track and Vizcaya. Operating hours are 6 A.M. to midnight daily. Fares are $1 (exact change only), with an additional 25 cents to transfer to Metrobus or mover. For information, call 638–6700.

By trolley. *Old Town Trolley* (374–8687) offers historical tours with on/off and start/stop privileges at any of its stops. It runs from Bayside Marketplace to Miami Seaquarium, Vizcaya, Mayfair Shops in Coconut Grove, and along Miracle Mile in Coral Gables. Adults, $12, children 3–12, $4.

By Tri-rail. This commuter rail service, begun in January 1989, links points in Palm Beach, Broward, and Dade counties (800–TRI–RAIL). It operates weekdays 5–9:30 A.M., noon–2 P.M., and 3:30–9 P.M.; newly added Saturday service operates between 6 A.M. and midnight, with different times for each city. Fare is $2 one-way.

By taxi. Miami's basic taxi rates, which have changed again, are $1.10 to set the meter, plus $1.40 per mile; airport surcharge has been dropped, but passengers pay for waiting time. Among major companies are *Metro Taxi* (888–8888), *Yellow Cab* (444–4444), and *Super Yellow Cab* (885–5555).

By rental car. More than a hundred rental-car companies serve the Miami area. Rates vary widely—with a complicated schedule of high and low and in-between seasons—but include some of the best bargains anywhere: Compacts rent for as little as $65 per week with unlimited mileage.

Orlando

From the airport. Orlando International Airport lies roughly 15 mi. from downtown, the same from Winter Park, Kissimmee, or the International Drive area, and about 20 from Walt Disney World. Transportation is readily available, ranging from taxis, shuttles, and buses to rental cars and chauffeured limousines. Taxi fare will run you approximately $30 to downtown, $25 to International Drive, or around $40 to Disney World. *Airport Limousine Service* (422–5466), which ferries to Disney World, offers a shuttle at $12 one-way, $21 round-trip (departing from second level outside baggage claim area), as well as town car service at $55 and limousine service at $90. Other chauffeured limousines, with prices varying according to amenities, include *American Limo Inc.* (629–5060) and *Florida Tour Lines* (841–6400). *Kissimmee-Orlando Airport Limousine* (933–5010) has shuttle rates of $9–$15 for parties of one to three, or $35 total for four, until 9 P.M.; from 9 to 11 P.M., rates are $35 per person, regardless of party size. Advance reservations required. City buses run at regular intervals from early morning to early evening; fare is 75 cents. Nearly all major rental-car companies have airport locations, and others are in sites along nearby access roads.

By bus. *Tri-County Transit* has routes throughout the metropolitan Orlando area, including Winter Park, Sanford, and the International Drive area. The downtown terminal is at 438 Woods Ave.; call 841–8240 for route and schedule information. *American Sightseeing Tours* (859–2250) and *Gray Line of Orlando* (422–0744) offer transport to major area attractions; rates vary by location of hotel and attraction.

By taxi. Basic taxi rates, set by the city, are $2.40 to set the meter plus $1.30 per additional mile. Among major operations are *AA Taxi & Tours* (851–3300), *Ace Taxi* (855–1111), *City Cab* (422–5151), and *Yellow Cab* (699–9999).

By rental car. It takes a lot of rental cars to meet the needs of this area's visitors, and Orlando's more than four dozen rental-car agencies are eager to provide them. Rates are seasonal and vary widely, with weekly rental for a compact ranging from $85 to $150. Most major companies, including *Avis, Budget, Dollar, Hertz, National,* and *Thrifty,* have locations within the terminal; others, including *Alamo* (800–327–

9633), *General* (800–327–7607), *American International* (800–527–0202), and *Payless* (800–641–2990), have locations nearby.

Tampa

From the airport. Tampa International Airport is roughly 5 mi. from downtown, reached by taxi, limo, hotel shuttle, or rental car. Taxi fare to the downtown area is about $12, limo service about $11 for either one or two passengers; to Pinellas County, the coastal resort area across Tampa Bay, the taxi fare jumps to the $30–$35 range. *Central Florida Limousine* (813–276–3730) provides service to points within the county in which Tampa lies, and *The Limo* (822–3333) serves the coastal area; both have booths outside the baggage-claim area of the airport. (Be advised that for transport back to the airport, you must make an advance reservation, preferably 24 hours in advance.) Also at the airport are numerous rental-car agencies.

By bus. Tampa has *Hillsborough Area Regional Transit Authority (HART)* buses covering routes within the city and county. For information and schedules, call 254–4278, 7 A.M. to 7 P.M., Mon.–Fri., 8 A.M. to 12 P.M., Sat.

By taxi. Tampa's basic taxi rates are 95 cents to set the meter and between $1.50 and $1.60 per additional mile. Among major companies are *Tampa Bay Cab* (251–5555), *United Cab* (253–2424), and *Yellow Cab* (253–0121).

By rental car. Tampa is served by some 100 rental-car companies, with rates below those in many parts of the nation; weekly rates on a compact start around $75 with unlimited mileage. Tampa rates are seasonal, with best bargains usually available in summer. *Hertz, Avis,* and *Dollar* have operations inside the airport terminal; among the many in peripheral locations (many with free transportation from airport to office) are *Budget, General* (800–327–7607), *National* (800–227–7368), and *Thrifty* (800–367–2277).

Jacksonville

From the airport. Jacksonville International Airport is about 15 mi. from the city's riverfront downtown area, about 25 minutes' driving time, and approximately $18–$22 by either taxi or limousine. Minibus service is offered by *Airport Limo Express* (739–3236) at $20 for one or two passengers. Limousine or van service to resorts in the Jacksonville Beaches area or Amelia Island are in the $35 range. Rental cars are a definite necessity here; several have airport locations.

By bus. Jacksonville's municipal bus service includes regular routes (60 cents), express routes (75 cents–$1.25), and a special express bus to the beaches ($1.10); all require correct change. Call Jacksonville Transportation Authority, 630–3100, for information or pick up a schedule at the downtown location, at Forsythe and Hogan.

By taxi. Jacksonville taxis charge $1.25 for the first one-eighth mi. and $1.25 for each additional mi. *American Cab* (764–1111) has an airport location; other companies include *Checker Cab* (764–2472) and *Yellow Cab* (354–5511).

By rental car. *Avis, Budget, Hertz,* and *Snappy* (800–321–7159) offer airport locations. Other companies with Jacksonville service include *Alamo, Budget, Dollar, General, Payless, National,* and *Value* (800–327–2501).

HINTS TO MOTORISTS. Miami. Getting around by auto in Miami, as in any large city, requires a good city map. Miami has a numbered road system, with streets, lanes, and terraces running east and west and avenues, courts, and places running north and south. Dividers are Flagler St. and Miami Ave. There are exceptions: roads and drives can go any direction, and both Coral Gables and Coconut Grove have their own systems.

Orlando. Orlando, dotted with 54 lakes and numerous separate municipalities, has no simple grid system that motorists may follow to get around easily. Generally, within Orlando proper, major avenues run north and south, major streets east and west, and circles encircle lakes. Courts, places, lanes, and roads go in any direction. Numbered streets are largely in the southwestern area (but do not continue into the southeastern part). Best bet is to pick up an area map at any of the tourist-information offices; major points of interest are clearly marked, and most are easily accessible via main thoroughfares. Rush hours—7:30 to 9 A.M. and 4:30 to 6 P.M.—bring heavy congestion to these thoroughfares.

Tampa. The Tampa Bay area sprawls over most of two counties: Hillsborough, in which Tampa is situated, and Pinellas, across the bay, site of the coastal resort communities. Two bridges and a causeway link the two areas. All three arteries bear heavy traffic at almost every hour, day and night, and it moves at a brisk pace—so save your leisurely looking for less-crowded roads. Tampa's downtown area is undergoing massive changes, so expect some driving inconvenience because of construction. Some of the major new developments are already completed—like the first phases of the $1-billion Harbor Island, the $48.5-million performing-arts center, and the $100-million Barnett Plaza (now the city's tallest structure)—but others will be in progress throughout the decade. The city's $120-million-dollar convention center was completed in late 1990 and an eagerly anticipated attraction on the downtown waterfront, the $84-million *Florida Aquarium,* will open in late 1994. Expansions to Harbor Island will continue through 1999.

Jacksonville. Jacksonville, on both banks of the northward-flowing St. Johns River, defies efforts to categorize it neatly into distinctive geographic segments. The river twists and turns all through the city, and there's no apparent pattern to the street system. Basically, the downtown area is on the northeastern side of the river (actually the south bank of the river's northern section); this is the site of the landmark Friendship Fountain and the city's Riverwalk. Downtown is practically all one-way streets, which at least will keep you from getting lost! Best bet is to stop by the convention and visitors bureau (see Tourist Information) to pick up a city map and study it, or simply stop and ask directions. You can even hail a city police car or a taxi—both keep maps and guides in their vehicles to give out to visitors (part of the southern hospitality for which the area is noted).

HINTS TO DISABLED TRAVELERS. Florida, as a destination state, takes special interest in meeting the needs of handicapped visitors. Although there is no statewide directory of accessible sites and facilities—it would be too voluminous, since all public facilities built after 1974 fall into that category—nearly all visitor-oriented sites, particularly attractions and hotels, have designed their facilities with these special guests' needs in mind. Major attractions either produce their own guides for the handicapped or include the information in their general visitor literature. You can contact each of the individual attractions you plan to visit, or request the same from local or area information sources, such as: City of Miami Dept. of Leisure Services, Program for the Handicapped, 2600 S. Bayshore Dr., Miami, FL 33133 (305–579–3431), and Orlando Visitor Information Center, Mercado Shopping Village, 8445 International Dr., Orlando, FL 32819 (407–363–5871).

The state also has seven *Centers for Independent Living* (CIL), which provide helpful information. The four major CILs are Dade County CIL, 1310 N.W. 16th St., Room 101, Miami, FL 33125 (305–547–5444); CIL of Central Florida, 720 N. Denning Dr., Winter Park, FL 32789 (407–623–1070); Self Reliance CIL, 12310 N. Nebraska Ave., Suite F, Tampa, FL 33612 (813–977–6368); Space Coast Assn. of the Physically Handicapped, 1127 S. Patrick Dr., Satellite Beach, FL 32937 (305–777–2964). Others are in Pensacola, Tallahassee, and Gainesville.

SEASONAL EVENTS—MIAMI. January: *Orange Bowl football game,* Miami, New Year's Night; *Art Deco Weekend,* Miami Beach, mid-Jan., '30s celebration with tours, art, and music (672–2014); *International Wine & Food Festival,* Miami (305–531–4851); *Taste of the Grove,* Coconut Grove, food fest benefit with 30 restaurants serving bite-size portions of noted specialties (624–2714). **February:** *South Florida Shakespeare Festival,* Miami, Feb.–Apr., classic theater in gardens of Vizcaya (446–1116); *Coconut Grove Arts Festival,* Coconut Grove, 3rd weekend, noted festival with outstanding works and outdoor entertainment (447–0401); *Doral-Ryder Open Golf Tournament,* Miami; *International Boat Show,* Miami Beach, last weekend, nation's largest public boat show (531–8410); **March:** *Carnaval Miami,* Miami, 1st and 2nd weekends, traditional Latin celebration in Little Havana district (324–7349). **April:** *Grand Prix Miami,* premiere car race in Camel GT Series, on Biscayne Blvd. (665–RACE); *River Cities Festival,* Hialeah–Miami Springs, entertainment and contests focusing on Miami River (887–1515); *Miracle Mile Festival,* Coral Gables, music, arts and crafts, entertainment (446–1657). **May:** *Coconut*

Grove Bed Race, Coconut Grove, zany benefit in Peacock Park (624–3714). **June:** *Miami-Bahamas Goombay Festival,* Miami, traditional islands celebration with guest Bahamian entertainers, in Coconut Grove (445–8292); *Dinner Key Summer Boat Show,* Miami, with entertainment and open boarding of all boats (764–7642). **July:** *Miccosukee International Crafts & Music Festival,* Miccosukee Indian Village, celebration with Indian foods, music, entertainment (223–8380). **August:** *International Festival,* Surfside, salute to international foods, music, and city's foreign visitors (864–0722). **October:** *Banyan Festival,* Coconut Grove, 2-day street food-and-art carnival (444–7270); *Baynanza,* Miami, outdoor celebration focusing on Biscayne Bay (662–4124). **November:** *Junior Orange Bowl Festival,* Coral Gables, Nov.–Dec., sports and cultural events for youngsters (662–1210). **December:** *Orange Bowl Festival,* Miami, one of nation's most celebrated festivals and sporting events, with televised King Orange Jamboree Parade on New Year's Eve (642–1515).

SEASONAL EVENTS—ORLANDO. January: *Florida Citrus Bowl,* Orlando, college bowl game (423–2476); *Scottish Highlands Games,* Orlando, including field events, dancing and piping competition, sheepdog demonstrations (644–0516). **February:** *WDW Village Wine Festival,* Lake Buena Vista, tastings by leading California wineries (828–3425); *Silver Spurs Rodeo,* Kissimmee, 3rd weekend, (363–5800). **March:** *Bach Festival,* Winter Park, 3-day musical event with 140-voice choir performing great choral compositions of Bach and other composers (646–2182); *Nestle Invitational,* Orlando, PGA Tour event at Arnold Palmer's course (876–2888); *Bluegrass Festival,* 3-day bluegrass and gospel-music event (847–5000); *Sidewalk Arts Festival,* Winter Park, 3rd weekend, national and international artists plus concerts, folk singing, and strolling musicians (644–8281). **May:** *Orlando Jazz Festival,* at Lake Eola Park (246–2555); *Airport Art Show* (825–2055). **September:** *Osceola Art Festival,* Kissimmee, last weekend, 2-day event at Lake Tohopekaliga (847–5000). **October:** *Pioneer Days Folk Festival,* Orlando, 3rd weekend, old-fashioned event with sugarcane grinding, bluegrass music, chair caning (855–7461). **November:** *Florida State Air Fair,* Kissimmee, 2-day show with top aerobatic pilots (847–5000); *Light Up Orlando,* Orlando, downtown street party extravaganza (849–2221); *Festival of the Masters,* Lake Buena Vista, art festival on Lake Buena Vista Lagoon (828–3425). **December:** *St. Cloud Country Art Festival,* 1st weekend, folksy show of crafts and arts, entertainment (847–5000); *WDW Christmas Celebration,* Lake Buena Vista, last 2 weeks and New Year's Day, special Christmas pageantry (824–2222).

SEASONAL EVENTS—TAMPA. February: *Florida State Fair,* Tampa, 12-day fair with free top-name entertainment plus grandstand shows, fair midway (621–7821); *Gasparilla Pirate Invasion and Festival,* Tampa, gala invasion, parade of pirates and fun and festivity throughout city (223–1111); *Fiesta Day,* Ybor City, gala fiesta in Tampa's Latin Quarter plus nighttime parade (248–3712). **March:** *Florida Strawberry Festival,* Plant City, early Mar., fair and festival at Winter Strawberry Capital (752–9194); *Gasparilla Sidewalk Art Festival,* Tampa, sidewalk show of local and regional artists (221–5333); *Winter Equestrian Festival,* Florida State Fairgrounds (623–5801). **April:** *Ybor City Folk Festival* (248–3712). **June:** *Charge of the Yellow Rice Brigade,* Ybor City, Teddy Roosevelt look-alike contest and other events salute the days when Rough Riders trained here (247–1434).

SEASONAL EVENTS—JACKSONVILLE. March: *Delius Festival,* Jacksonville, 1st full week, musical event honoring English composer (744–3950). **April:** *Riverfest,* Jacksonville, free two-day celebration on river, with entertainment, contests, special events (630–0837); *Beach Festival,* Jacksonville Beach, weekend of special events including parade, sandcastle contest, carnival, and art show (249–3868); *Country Music Fest,* Jacksonville (630–0837). **May:** *Riverwalk Arts & Crafts Festival* Jacksonville, visual and performing arts in Riverside Park (396–4900); *Annual Homes Tour,* Jacksonville, tours of restored riverside mansions (389–2449); *Isle of 8 Flags Shrimp Festival,* Fernandina Beach (261–7130); *Mug Race,* Palatka to Jacksonville, nation's largest inland sailboat race (264–4904). **September:** *Sandy Crafters Arts & Crafts Show,* Jacksonville Beach (249–2381). **October:** *Jacksonville Jazz Festival,* free jazz festival with top-name performers, arts-and-crafts and food booths (353–7770); *Seafest,* on Jacksonville's Riverwalk (396–4900). **December:** *Gator Bowl and Gator Bowl Hoedown,* Jacksonville, college football bowl game (396–1800) preceded by festive gathering with country-western and high school band entertainment, laser show, fireworks, and barbecue (633–2009).

TOURS AND SPECIAL-INTEREST SIGHTSEEING. Miami. *Amor Tours International* (146 Biscayne Blvd., Miami, FL 33132, 305–374–7512). Daily offerings of city sightseeing, attractions, and shopping tours ($23–$38), plus Everglades outing ($40).

Buffalo Tiger Airboats, Tamiami Trail (U.S. 41) about 25 mi. west of Miami (223–8380). Miccosukee Tribe-operated airboat rides, one of many ride operations along U.S. 41. Half-hour rides across Everglades terrain aboard flat-bottom boats powered by aircraft engines, $7.

Gold Coast Helicopters, 151st St. & Biscayne Blvd. (940–1009). Helicopter flights along areas of your choice; about $30 per person, for 8 mi. along beach. Operates daily 9:30 A.M. to 5 P.M. *Dade Helicopter Service,* at Watson Island on MacArthur Cswy. (374–3737). Operates daily, 8 A.M.–5 P.M.; about $60 per person.

Miami Design Preservation League (661 Washington Ave., Miami Beach, FL 33139, 305–672–2014). 1½-hour guided walking tours of Miami Beach's colorful Art Deco district, a national historic site. Conducted Sat. only, 10:30 A.M., departing from Welcome Center, $5.

Nikko Gold Coast Cruises, Haulover Park Marina, 10800 Collins Ave., Miami Beach (945–5461). Variety of daily cruises on Biscayne Bay or to Vizcaya or Miami Seaquarium; $7.95–$25.39. Day-long sailing to Fort Lauderdale and the Everglades offered Wed., Fri., and Sun. One-day advance reservations recommended. *Island Queen* (379–5119), sailing both from Bayside Marketplace and Hyatt Regency three times daily, offers 1¾-hour cruises to Millionaires' Row. $10 adults, $5 children.

Celebration Excursions (445–8456) also sails from Bayside Marketplace, with sightseeing and dinner/dance cruises ($10 and $29.95) aboard a 100-foot yacht.

SeaEscape (800–432–0900) offers evening cruises to nowhere aboard a full-size liner (Wed. 8 P.M.–12:30 A.M., Fri. till 1 A.M.), at $49 per person plus port charges.

Orlando. *Church Street Station* (129 W. Church St., Orlando, FL 32801, 407–841–8787). 1-hour hot-air balloon trips around the city, followed by champagne breakfast at Lily Marlene's within the Church Street Station complex; $150 per person, departs 6 A.M. from in front of Rosie O'Grady's. At least five other Orlando firms offer similar sunrise outings. *Balloons by Terry* (422–3529), $125 for one, less for multiple passengers (discount for cash); *Orange Blossom Balloons* (239–7677), $140 for one, $180 for two (includes breakfast at Fort Liberty); *Rise & Float Balloon Tours* (352–8191), $150 for one, $280 for two (discount for cash). Also within area are *Fab-Co Balloon Flights,* Longwood (407–862–7737); *Fantasy Ballooning,* DeLeon Springs (904–736–1010 or 800–255–1827 in FL); and *Wind Drifters Hot-Air Balloon Co.,* Ocoee (407–295–3689).

Gray Line of Orlando (4950 L.B. McLeod Rd., Orlando, FL 32811, 407–422–0744). Local and area excursions to Kennedy Space Center, Sea World, Cypress Gardens, Busch Gardens, Circus World, and Wet 'n Wild. Also offers frequent shuttle service daily to Walt Disney World, both Magic Kingdom and Epcot Center. Pickups at major area hotels for all outings. *Rabbit Bus Lines* (291–2424) offers similar service, for slightly less money.

Orlando Area Chamber of Commerce, 75 E. Ivanhoe Blvd. (425–1234), and Winter Park Chamber of Commerce, 150 N. New York Ave. (644–8281). Scenic drives through the individual cities. Routes, each of which begins at the respective chamber of commerce, are marked by signs on the street and lead past prominent points of interest within each community.

Scenic Boat Tours, from dock at end of E. Morse Blvd., Winter Park (644–4056). Narrated 1-hour small-boat tour of three lakes with connecting canals, going past Isle of Scily, Azalea Gardens, and Rollins College. Operates 10 A.M. to 4 P.M., daily; adults, $5; children, $2.50.

Tampa. *Tampa Tours* (621–6667). City tours two times daily except Sun. Price is $12 per person; advance reservations recommended. *Swiss Chalet Tours* (985–3601). Two-hour city tours by van twice daily, at $12 per person; or private tours of Tampa, St. Petersburg, and Clearwater by auto with lunch stop, at $40 per person.

McDill Air Force Base (830–2215). Guided tours of military base, Tues. and Fri. by advance reservation. Tours last approximately 1½ hours. Free. Early reservations a must; tours often filled 4–5 months in advance.

University of Tampa, 401 W. Kennedy Blvd. (253–3333, ext. 400). Guided tours of main building, the former Tampa Bay Hotel, an elaborate 1891 structure considered finest example of Moorish architecture in western hemisphere; recently completed $1.5 million refurbishing. Tours, which last 1–1½ hours, offered Tues. and Thurs. at 1:30 P.M.; donation requested. Evening candlelight tours during Christmas season, at small charge.

SeaEscape, 250 8th Ave., S.E., St. Petersburg (800–327–7400 U.S.; 800–432–0900 FL). 1-day Cruise to Nowhere with 3 meals and entertainment; 9 A.M. to 5:30 P.M. daily, at $39 plus $12 port charge. Evening cruises, 7 P.M. to 2 A.M., are offered during holidays, at $49 plus $12 port charge.

Seminole Indian Village, 5221 N. Orient Rd. (620–3077). Seminole Indian village with sewing, beadwork, and snake-handling demonstrations, museum, movie, and native animals. Admission $3.50 per person. Open 9 A.M.–5 P.M. Mon.–Sat., noon–5 P.M. Sun.

Villazon & Co., 3104 N. Armenia Ave., Ybor City (879–2291). Free ½-hour guided tours of cigar factory, where hand-rolling techniques are still in use. Conducted at 9:30 A.M. Mon.–Fri. *La Segunda Bakery,* 15th St. and 15th Ave., Ybor City (248–1531), offers tours where you can see how Cuban bread and other delicacies are made. Tours are short—about 15 minutes—and early in the morning, when the day's goods are being prepared; any time before 8:30 A.M. is recommended. Offered daily except Sun. (shop is open that day, but owner warns, "Everything is usually gone before 7:30 A.M.").

Ybor City Chamber of Commerce and Visitor Information Center, 1800 E. 9th Ave., Ybor City, FL 33605, (813–248–3712). Self-guided walking tours of the historic Latin Quarter, Ybor City. Based on free tour map distributed by chamber of commerce, which may be picked up in that office, open 9 A.M. to 4 P.M., Mon.–Fri; 10 A.M. to 3 P.M., Sat.

Jacksonville. *Annabelle Lee,* Civic Auditorium Dock downtown (396–2333). Dinner/dance cruises, 7–10 P.M. or 8–11 P.M., at $31.95 per person; or luncheon cruises, usually Wed. and Fri. 11:30 A.M.–2 P.M., at $15 per person. *First Lady* and *Viking Sun* (398–0797) each departs from both Riverwalk and The Landing, offering 2-hour luncheon cruises at $15 per person and 2½-hour dinner cruises at $26 per person. You can also zip around the river via *The Gondola* (642–6357), or the fleets of three water taxi companies: *Bass Marina* (730–8685), *PJ's Water Taxi* (771–6440), and *St. Johns River Taxi* (783–0875).

Mayport Naval Station, at end of Mayport Rd., Mayport (246–5440). Free weekend tour of one of the frigates, destroyers, cruisers, or aircraft carriers in port, in what is one of the nation's largest U.S. carrier basins. Offered 10 A.M. to 4:30 P.M., Sat., 1 to 4:30 P.M., Sun.; sailor at gate will direct you to the day's visit ship, where a crew member aboard will conduct tour.

Fernandina Beach (on Amelia Island). *Old Town Carriage Co.,* (635–3466). Offers 30-minute horse-drawn carriage tours of Centre St. historic district, giving history of town and island, at $5 per person. Day and evening tours, daily spring–summer, Wed.–Sun. during off season. *Hay Soose* (261–5897), at Fort Clinch State Park, offers 1-hour carriage tours through the park; $5 adults, $3 children. *Emerald Princess,* 11 S. 2nd St. (800–842–0115). Dinner cruises into the Gulf: 7 P.M.–1 A.M. Wed., Thurs., Fri.; 6 P.M.–midnight Sat.; and 1–6 P.M. Sun. Prices are $29.50 Wed. and Thurs., $45.39 Fri. and Sun., and $56 Sat.

PARKS AND GARDENS—MIAMI. Bayfront Park. Along Biscayne Blvd. from N.E. 5th St. to S.E. 2nd St., Miami (579–6939). This recently revitalized 62-acre park is a downtown oasis, fringed with royal and coconut palms and 21,000 tropical and subtropical plants. It offers a boardwalk along the bay, an amphitheater, areas for special events, and an elevated pedestrian walkway to the PeopleMover station across the street. Adjacent to the Bayside Marketplace shops. No set hours. Free.

A.D. Barnes Park. 3401 S.W. 72nd Ave., Miami (665–1626). A newcomer to Miami's parks, this one features special facilities for the handicapped: a solar-heated pool with hydraulic lift and nature trails with handrails for the blind. The 65-acre park is open for day use, dawn to dusk. Free park admission; pool $1.50 adult; $1 students (13–17), seniors, and handicapped; 75 cents children (3–12).

Fairchild Tropical Garden. 10901 Old Cutler Rd., Coral Gables (667–1651). More than 400 species of palms and thousands of species of tropical plants from around the world highlight this 83-acre pure botanical garden. Narrated tram tours are offered. Open daily (except Dec. 25) 9:30 A.M. to 4:30 P.M.; admission, $5 adult, children (to 13) free; tram tours $1 adult, 50 cents children.

Greynolds Park. 17530 W. Dixie Hwy., North Miami Beach (945–3425). Visitors to this heavily wooded 184-acre park can rent paddle boats to ride on the lagoon (Sat. and Sun. only, $3.50 per half hour), relax on its wading beach, fish, or play a round of golf on its 9-hole course. It also has picnic areas with shelters and an abundant bird population. Open 6 A.M. to sunset. Free admission; $1.50 parking fee.

Hialeah Park. 4 E. 21st St. and 4th Ave., Hialeah (887–4347). This is a Thoroughbred-race-track facility so beautifully landscaped and interesting that it attracts visitors even in nonracing periods. The 220-acre site, a national historic landmark, features pretty park areas, rare birds, a resident colony of flamingos, and an aquarium. Open daily, 9:30 A.M. to 5 P.M. during nonracing season. Free.

Miami Beach Garden Center Conservatory. Convention Center Dr. between 19th and 20th Sts., Miami Beach (673–7256). Horticultural complex with green and flowering plants, including an orchid collection, draws green-thumb fans to its recently remodeled, domed conservatory and outdoor Japanese garden with winding walkways, ponds, and statuary. Open 10 A.M. to 3:30 P.M., Mon.–Fri. Free.

Tropical Park. 7900 S.W. Bird Rd., Miami (226–8315). Horse-racing fans may remember this site from its earlier life as a major track, but today it's one of the most popular recreational sites within the county. There's a lake for swimming (May–Sept., $1), another for fishing and boating (including rental paddle boats in summer), picnic areas with grills, volleyball equipment loaned for a driver's license deposit, tot lots and playgrounds, a vita course, and concession stands. It has an equestrian center (where meets are often held), six baseball diamonds, a boxing center (where Louis Aguayo trained), a football stadium, basketball courts, and a community center. Its grounds are often the site of festivals. General park hours are 9 A.M. to 10 P.M., Mon.–Fri.; 9 A.M. to 8 P.M., weekends, although they vary for individual facilities within the complex and when special events are in progress.

PARKS AND GARDENS—ORLANDO. Though frequently overshadowed by attractions, scenic parks abound. Orlando, dotted with 54 lakes, has 81 city parks, and Winter Park—which uses an innovative concept that puts everyone within easy reach of a green oasis—offers 84 city parks, some no larger than your own yard. For information on sites with no telephone listing, contact the city park offices: Orlando, 849–2285; Winter Park, 623–3292.

Big Tree Park. General Hutchinson Pkwy. off U.S. 17–92, Longwood. This 12-acre county park showcases The Senator, one of the oldest (3,500 years old) and largest bald cypress trees in the nation. Includes picnic areas. Open 7 A.M. to sunset weekdays, 9 A.M. to sunset Sat.–Sun. Free.

Central Park. Park Ave., mid-city, Winter Park. This is a great people-watching site, nestled in the heart of the city's European-looking downtown area. It's 6 acres of tree-shaded walkways, a rose garden, and benches where you can relax, feed the birds, or join the many who lunch or snack al fresco. Because of its open access and busy location, it doesn't adhere to the city parks' usual sunset closing and may have people in it as late as 1 A.M.

Cypress Gardens. Off U.S. 27 near Winter Haven, in town of Cypress Gardens (800–282–2123). Exotic flowers and plants from around the world and spectacular seasonal displays are the traditional magnet for this Central Florida landmark attraction. Its list of highlights are an ice-skating show, a synchronized swimming-and-diving revue, an expanded animal collection, and a completely revamped water-ski show. Open 9 A.M. to 7 P.M. daily. Adults, $18.95; children (3–9), $12.95; half-hour cruise on Lake Eloise is $2.50 adults, $2 children.

Eola Park. At end of Central Blvd. on Eola, Robinson, and Rosalind Sts., Orlando. Most popular of all the city park facilities, this 11.2-acre park encircles Lake Eola, with 1 full mi. of walkways, nature trails, picnic areas, and lots of benches for watching the landmark fountain in the lake. The park was renovated in 1988 and features playground areas and paddle-boats in season. A new amphitheater was added in 1989. Open sunrise to 11 P.M. Free.

Fleet Peoples Park (formerly Lake Baldwin Park). S. Lakemont Ave., Winter Park. This 23-acre lakeside park ranks as the area's premier windsurfing site. Other recreational facilities include swimming and boating areas, picnic tables and pavilions, and a baseball field. Open 8 A.M. to sunset. Free.

Kraft Azalea Gardens. Alabama Dr. on Lake Maitland, Winter Park. City-owned 11-acre park whose focal point is its walk-through gardens, a colorful mass of azaleas and tropical plants. There are numerous benches, scenic lakefront areas, and a fishing dock. Open 8 A.M. to 8 P.M. in summer, 8 A.M. to 6 P.M. the rest of the year. Free.

Lake Fairview. U.S. 441 & Lee Rd., Orlando. One of the city's major recreational facilities, with 23 acres fronting the large lake. It offers a swimming beach, a boat ramp, a softball field, a playground, and picnic areas with tables, grills, and shelters. Open dawn to dusk daily. Free.

Leu Gardens. 1730 N. Forest Ave., Orlando (246–2620). City-owned 56-acre showplace of live oak and subtropical trees, azaleas, camellias, exotic plants, formal gardens, scenic walkways, and a garden shop, all on the shores of Lake Rowena. It also includes a restored Victorian manor (open 10 A.M. to 3:30 P.M., Tues.–Sat., 1 P.M. to 3:30 P.M., Sun. and Mon., with free guided tours). Gardens open 9 A.M. to 5 P.M., daily. General admission is $3 adults, $1 ages 6–16.

Loch Haven Park. Princeton Blvd. & Mills Ave., Orlando. City-owned 40-acre complex with picnicking areas and fishing facilities. Within the park are Orlando Science Center (896–7151), with science and natural-history displays and a planetarium with shows at 2:30 P.M. daily and 8 P.M. Fri.; and Orlando Museum of Art (896–4231), with permanent and changing exhibits. The science center is open 9 A.M. to 5 P.M., Mon.–Thurs.; 9 A.M. to 9 P.M., Fri.; noon-9 P.M., Sat.; and noon–5 P.M., Sun.; admission: adults, $4; children and senior citizens, $3; $1.50 for planetarium show. The museum is open 9 A.M. to 5 P.M., Tues.–Fri.; 10 A.M.–5 P.M., Sat.; and noon–5 P.M. Sun.; admission to the center is $3 adults, $2 senior citizens and students.

Mead Botanical Gardens. S. Denning Dr., Winter Park. Largest and prettiest of the Winter Park facilities, it covers 55 acres, with boardwalks over one of the last marshes within the city, plus a self-guided nature trail. There also is a picnicking area with grills. Open 8 A.M. to sunset. Free.

Turkey Lake Park. 3401 S. Hiawassee Rd., Orlando (299–5594). Major 300-acre recreational facility on Turkey Lake. It offers picnic areas, beaches, concessions, boating facilities, bike and roller-skating trails, a farm with a petting zoo, and special exhibits. Open 9:30 A.M. to 5 P.M., daily, with extended summer hours. $2 adult, $1 children (12 and under).

PARKS AND GARDENS—TAMPA. Busch Gardens. 3000 E. Busch Blvd. (971–8282). From its 1959 opening as a modest 15-acre free garden—a public-relations effort for a new brewery—this facility has grown into a 300-acre compound teeming with activities. The original gardens are still there, in today's Bird Gardens section, complete with colorful blossoms and foliage, lagoons, exotic birds, an aviary, the brewery tour, and the popular Hospitality House, where free Anheuser-Busch products are served. It's accessible only as part of the overall attraction, for an admission price of $24.95 (children 2 and under free) plus $3 parking fee. Open 9:30 A.M. to 6 P.M. daily, with extended hours in summer and certain holiday periods.

Eureka Botanical Gardens. Eureka Springs Rd. north of I-4 (626–7994). Within the 31 acres of this county botanical gardens are trellised walks, nature trails, boardwalks, a greenhouse, and picnic areas. Open daily, sunrise to sunset. Free.

Lettuce Lake Park. Fletcher Ave. at Hillsborough River (985–7845). Covering 240 acres, this county park offers wooded picnic areas, two boardwalks, an observation tower, bike and jogging trails, a fitness course, an interpretive center with exhibits, an open-space activities area, and a playground. Open daily, sunrise to sunset. Free.

Lithia Springs Park. Off U.S. 301 in Lithia (8 mi. from Brandon) (689–2139). A natural spring bubbles in the midst of this 160-acre county park, serving as its free swimming area. Other facilities include picnic grounds with grills and electricity, a playground, nature trails, and a 38-site campground ($12 nightly including hookups). Open 8 A.M.–6 P.M. Sat.–Thurs., 8 A.M.–7 P.M. Fri. (camping registration by 5 P.M.). Admission $1 per person.

Lowry Park. North Blvd. and Sligh Ave. (935–8552). This 20-acre city facility is on the Hillsborough River. It has a zoo, adult and children's rides ($1 and under), a miniature-train ride, and a novel storybook minipark known as Fairyland, with colorful life-size figures of Snow White, Little Red Riding Hood, and other fairy-tale characters. A new zoo opened in 1988 (now open 9:30 A.M.–5 P.M. daily; $4 adults, $2 children, $3 senior citizens). Park also includes picnic areas and concession stand. Open 10 A.M. to dark. Free.

Riverfront Park. 1111 North Blvd. (251–3742). This small city recreation area is more riverwalk than park. It covers 5 acres on the Hillsborough River, with landscaped walkways, a theater in the round, and facilities for tennis, racquetball, handball, and shuffleboard. Open daily, 6 A.M. to 10 P.M. Free.

Upper Tampa Bay Park. Double Branch Rd. (855–1765). Largest of the county's facilities, this park sprawls over 595 acres, most in its natural state. There are freshwater ponds, pine flatwoods, salt marshes, oyster bars, salt barrens, oak hammocks, and mangrove forests. For visitor enjoyment, it offers nature trails, picnic areas, a playground, primitive camping areas, and a study center. Open daily, sunrise to sunset. Free.

PARKS AND GARDENS—JACKSONVILLE. For more information on sites that do not have telephones, contact the Recreation and Parks Dept., 249–2381.

Kathryn Abbey Hannah Park. Off FL A1A north of Atlantic Beach (249–4700). This is the area's major municipal recreational facility, covering 450 acres of scenic beachfront. It offers 1½ mi. of beaches, lakes, miles of nature trails, picnicking areas, and a 300-site campground ($13.26 with hookups). Open 8 A.M. to sunset daily. Admission 50 cents per person.

Metropolitan Park. 1410 E. Adams St., behind Gator Bowl (630–0837). Newest of the city facilities, this 23-acre riverside park has landscaped grounds, a boardwalk along the St. Johns River, a dock, picnic areas, and a concert pavilion that is the site of the city's annual jazz festival. Open 9:30 A.M. to 10 P.M., daily. Admission to park is free, although many of the special events held there charge admission.

St. Johns River Park. Gulf Life Dr., near Main St. Bridge in downtown Southbank. This 10-acre park is site of the city's landmark Friendship Fountain, which gushes 17,000 gallons of computer-controlled dancing water per minute, in sprays as high as a 10-story building. The park recently underwent a face-lift; it is now main access point to the city's Riverwalk, an inviting area of landscaped walkways along the river's edge, dotted with sidewalk cafes and gazebos. Open 24 hours. Free.

Treaty Oak Park. Prudential Dr. in downtown Southbank. This tiny 1.85-acre park was created to preserve Treaty Oak, a magnificent oak tree estimated to be between 200 and 500 years old; according to local lore, Indians and early settlers met beneath its spreading branches to discuss treaties. The tree is 66 ft. tall, with a limb span of 180 ft. Park open 24 hours. Free.

CHILDREN'S ACTIVITIES, THEME PARKS, ZOOS. Florida is the family vacation destination par excellence. There are plenty of attractions to catch children's attention and start them clamoring for a visit. Luckily, many parents will find these places entertaining as well, or at least relatively painless.

Miami

Coral Castle, U.S. 1 at S.W. 286th St., Homestead (248–6344), is an open-air castle, a monument to unrequited love. It was hand carved by a 97-pound Latvian who hoisted into place coral blocks weighing up to 30 tons. Open 9 A.M. to 9 P.M., daily, closed Dec. 25; adults, $7.25; children (6–12), $4.50.

Malibu Castle Park, 7775 N.W. 8th St., Miami (266–2100), with its distinctive turreted-castle façade, houses an amusement center that draws kids of all ages. It features video-game arcades, miniature golf, bumper boats, go-carts, and other rides and activities. All are individually priced, with games operated on 25-cent tokens and others averaging $2–$3. No admission charge to center. Open Mon.–Thurs., 11 A.M.–11 P.M.; Fri.–Sat.; 11 A.M.–2 A.M.; Sun., 11 A.M.–midnight.

Metrozoo, 12400 S.W. 152nd, Miami (251–0400), boasts an impressive collection of animals in zoogeographical settings—individual cageless islands with topographical highlights resembling countries of origin. It covers 290 acres with 60 major exhibits, and a monorail (included in admission price) glides through the park offering unlimited on-off privileges. Open daily, 9:30 A.M. to 5:30 P.M. (box office closes 4 P.M.); adults, $8.25; children (3–12), $4.25.

Miami Seaquarium, on Virginia Key off Rickenbacker Cswy. (361–5703), is the most famous of Miami's entertainment sites. Among its offerings are a shark channel and shows featuring the antics of porpoises, killer whales, sea lions, and seals. Open daily, 9:30 A.M. to 6 P.M.; adults, $14.95; children (12 and under), $10.95; prices include monorail.

Miccosukee Indian Village, U.S. 41, 25 mi. west of Miami (223–8388), offers demonstrations and exhibits of woodcarving, patchwork, beadwork, and other traditional crafts, plus alligator-wrestling shows. There are an Indian museum with films and artifacts of various tribes, a crafts shop, and airboat rides. Open daily, 9 A.M. to 5 P.M.; adults, $5; children (3–12), $3.

Monkey Jungle. 3 mi. west of U.S. 1 in Goulds (235–1611). Visitors watch from enclosed walkways as monkeys roam free. Continuous shows include chimps performing in Monkey Theater. Open daily, 9:30 A.M. to 6 P.M. (gates close at 5); adults, $8.75; children (4–12), $4.75.

Parrot Jungle. 11000 S.W. 57th Ave. (666–7834). Let perky parrots pose on your arm and ponder the fact that most of the colorful birds could fly away but don't. Macaws and cockatoos star in shows, riding bikes and roller skating. Open daily, 9:30 A.M. to 6 P.M., later in holiday periods; adults, $10.50; children (3–12), $6.

Police Hall of Fame & Museum. 3801 Biscayne Blvd. (573–0700). More than 10,000 items of law enforcement equipment, from full-size squad car embedded on building's front to firearms, equipment, uniforms, photos, memorabilia. Open 10 A.M.–5:30 P.M. daily; $3 adults, $1.50 children (3–12) and senior citizens.

Venetian Pool, 2701 DeSoto Blvd., Coral Gables (442–6483), ranks as both one of Coral Gables' historic landmarks—where lots for the city were hawked by William Jennings Bryan in the 1920s—and the ultimate in swimming pools, a Venetian lagoon carved out of coral, with caves, stone bridges, and sandy beach areas. Open 11 A.M. to 4:30 P.M.; Tues.–Fri.; 10 A.M. to 4:30 P.M. weekends. Adults, $4; teens, $3.50; children (12 and under), $1.50.

Orlando

Central Florida Zoological Park, at I-4 & U.S. 17-92, Sanford (323–4450), covers 110 acres, with some 200 animals, including reptiles and birds, plus a petting zoo. Open 9 A.M. to 5 P.M., daily; closed Dec. 25. Adults, $5; children (3–12), $2; adults 60 and over, $3; ages 2 and under, free.

Cypress Gardens, off U.S. 27 near Winter Haven (800–282–2123), long noted for its gardens and ski shows and in recent years blossoming into a theme park with rides, animals, and other features, has now undergone further revision via a multimillion-dollar expansion. Among highlights: an ice-skating show and a high-diving and synchronized-swimming revue (each with three shows daily), a completely revamped ski show and stadium area, and special seasonal garden displays called Floral Magic. Open daily, 9 A.M. to 7 P.M. Adults, $18.95; children (3–9), $12.95; children 2 and under, free.

Elvis Presley Museum, 6544 Carrier Dr. (345–9427), displays the late singer's first jumpsuit, last Cadillac, private airplane, grand piano from Graceland, and other items. Open daily, 9 A.M. to 10 P.M. Adults, $4; ages 7–12, $3; age 6 and under, free.

Fun 'n Wheels, 6739 Sand Lake Rd.—International Dr. area—(351–5651) and at 3711 W. Vine St., Kissimmee (870–2222) are amusement centers with rides, video arcade, miniature golf, and go-cart tracks. All individually priced (most averaging $1–$3); no admission fee to centers. Open daily, 10 A.M. to midnight.

Gatorland Zoo, 14501 S. Orange Blossom Tr., Kissimmee (855–5496), showcases alligators and crocodiles, as well as pythons, giant tortoises, zebras, and other creatures, and offers a narrated minitrain tour of it all. Open 8 A.M. to 7 P.M., summer and holiday periods; 8 A.M. to 6 P.M., rest of year. Adults, $7.95; children (3–11), $4.95. **Gator Jungle Alligator Farm,** on FL 50 E in Christmas (568–2885), offers alligators, crocodiles, and other reptiles in their native habitat. Open daily, 9 A.M. to 6 P.M. Adults, $6; children (3–11), $3.

Medieval Times, U.S. 192, Kissimmee (239–0214), and **King Henry's Feast,** International Drive (351–5151), both offer multicourse banquets right in the midst of jousting matches and medieval tournaments. Prices average $26, adults; $18, children, including dinner and show. The former also offers **Medieval Life Village,** an 11th-century village from Spain where artisans and craftsmen demonstrate ancient skills. Admission $7 adults, $5 children, or combo ticket with dinner. **Arabian Nights,** U.S. 192, Kissimmee (351–5822) and **Fort Liberty,** U.S. 192, Kissimmee (351–5151), offer dinner shows with exotic horses and Wild West pageants, respectively.

Mystery Fun House. 5767 Major Blvd., in Orlando's Florida Center (351–3355). 15 chambers of fun, from laughing doors and magic floors to a mirror maze and games galore. Open daily, 10 A.M. to 11 P.M. (box office closes 9 P.M.). Admission $7.95 all ages.

Reptile World Serpentarium, on U.S. 192–441 3 mi. east of St. Cloud (892–6905), has educational exhibits of the reptile world and venom production for scientific research. Programs at 11 A.M., 2 P.M., 5 P.M. Open 9 A.M. to 5:30 P.M., daily. Adults, $3.75; students (6–17), $2.75; children, $1.75.

Sea World, 7007 Sea World Dr. (351–3600), is a sprawling marine park starring Shamu the killer whale—plus the three offspring that made big splashes. Shamu performs in the innovative Shamu Stadium with slide-out aisle that brings the creature right into the audience. The park also features seal, dolphin, and walrus shows, feeding and petting pools, ski show, and a Penguin Encounter. Operating hours cover 10 time periods in the year; generally, park opens at 8:30 or 9 A.M.; closing hours vary from 7 to 9 P.M. (most of year) to 10:30 P.M. (summer and select holidays). Adults, $25.50; children, $21.70; children under 3, free.

Tupperware World Headquarters, U.S. 441 south of Orlando, near Kissimmee (847–3111, ext. 2694, or 800–858–7221). Tours of exhibits (food containers, model kitchens). Mon.–Fri. from 9 A.M. to 4 P.M. Landscaped gardens and lakes. Free.

Universal Studios Florida. 1000 Universal Studios Plaza (800–BE A STAR). 444-acre complex with rides and entertainment focusing on *E.T., King Kong, Jaws,* and other movie favorites, plus tours to see filming in progress. Backlot stages, themed restaurants. Open 9 A.M.–7 P.M. weekdays, extended hours weekends and holidays. Admission $29 adults, $23 children.

Walt Disney World. Lake Buena Vista (824–4321). This superstar of attractions has a world of activities and entertainment within its Magic Kingdom (100 acres with 45 major shows and adventures); Epcot Center (260 acres with 9 theme pavilions in Future World and 11 minilands in World Showcase; Disney–MGM Studio Theme Park (52 acres of movie backstage magic); and Typhoon Lagoon (a 50-acre water park). All are separately gated. Open 9 A.M. daily with closing times varying and later closing hours in summer and peak attendance periods. One-day/one-park tickets $31 adults, $25 children (3–9); 4-day multiple-park tickets $107 adults, $83 children; 5-day plus Super Pass (good for 7 days) $135 adults, $108 children.

Wet 'n Wild. 6200 International Dr. (351–3200). A seasonal water park offering slipping and sliding good times with every conceivable kind of slide, ride, and tide activities. Open 10 A.M. to 5 P.M. Hours are seasonal. Adults, $17.95; children, $15.95; under 2, free; half-price specials during certain off-season periods.

Tampa

Busch Gardens/Dark Continent, 3000 Busch Blvd. (971–8282), teems with activity. Some 3,000 animals, including lions, zebras, rhinos, giraffes, and elephants, roam Serengeti Plain, traversed by monorail or skyride. In Moroccan Village, snake charmers, magicians, and belly dancers are just part of the entertainment. Dare to ride the Python or Monstrous Mamba thrill ride or opt for the White Water Rafting ride or Log Flume. Adults can tour the brewery and sample some free "suds" while the children enjoy, enjoy. Adjacent is Adventure Island (971–7978), the attraction's water park, with white sand beaches and pools topped by surf, with waterfalls. Park open daily, 9:30 A.M. to 6 P.M., with extended hours during summer and some holidays; $24.95 per person; 2 and under, free. Water park open 10 A.M. to 5 P.M., daily, Mar.–Oct.; $15.95 per person; 2 and under, free.

Lowry Park Zoo, North Blvd. and Sligh Ave. (932–0245), offers monkeys, lions, tigers, an elephant, and other animals within the 15-acre zoo area of this child-pleasing park. It also offers a train ride, amusements, and a fairyland section with statues of storybook characters. Open 9:30 A.M.–5 P.M. daily; $4 adults, $2 children.

Museum of Science and Industry. 4801 E. Fowler Ave. (985–5531). A child-oriented, nonstuffy museum with lots of hands-on exhibits. Kids can experience a hurricane, explore Dr. Thunder's Boom Room, and match wits against computers. Science demonstrations also are offered. Open 10 A.M. to 4:30 P.M., daily. Adults, $4; children (5–15), $2.

NATIONAL AND STATE PARKS. Biscayne National Park. On S.W. 328th St. near Homestead (park headquarters, 247–2044; boat tours, 247–2400). This mammoth 175,000-acre park—8,750 of which are land, the rest water—encompasses a chain of 45 keys between Key Biscayne and Key Largo and the tip of the coral reef that lies offshore from Key Largo. On Elliott Key offshore are a visitor center, boat docks, nature trails, and other facilities. Glass-bottom-boat tours run 10 A.M.–1 P.M. Mon.–Sat. and 1:30–4:30 P.M. daily, at $14.50 adults, $8 children; snorkeling trips 1:30–5:30 P.M. daily, at $21.50; and scuba trips 1:30–5:30 P.M. daily, at $30. Advance reservations. For details, write Biscayne Aqua-Center, Biscayne National Park, Box 1369, Homestead, FL 33039.

Cape Florida State Recreation Area. 1200 S. Crandon Blvd., Key Biscayne (361–5811). Covering 406 acres of Key Biscayne's southern end, this popular park offers Atlantic beaches fringed with lush foliage, a woodsy interior, a boardwalk, biking and nature trails, picnic areas, and concession stands. Historical focal point is the lighthouse and restored lighthouse keeper's house. Tours are offered at 10:30 A.M., 1 P.M., 2:30 P.M., and 3:30 P.M. Closed Tues. Park open 8 A.M. to sunset, daily; lighthouse open only during tour periods. Park admission, $1 driver plus 50 cents per passenger; historic site admission, $1 per person.

Everglades National Park. Main entrance southeast of Florida City, about 50 mi. from Miami (247–6211). Largest subtropical wilderness in the coterminous U.S., this 1.4-million-acre preserve covers most of the lower part of the state. It has been declared a world heritage site. Nine boardwalks offer great views of the abundant wildlife and birdlife, and a busy schedule of ranger-led outings includes canoe trips, hikes and bike hikes, bird walks, sunrise watches, night prowls, and even a 4-hour car caravan. Also within the park are restaurant, inn, lounge, camping facilities, canoe and bike rentals, marina, and boat and tram tours. The visitor center at the main entrance offers a short film, lots of literature, and schedules of activities. Recent modifications to facilities, programs, and services have made the park much accessible to handicapped guests. Free accessibility guides may be picked up at either of the park's two visitors centers or by writing Box 279, Homestead, FL 33090. Park open 24 hours daily, including holidays; visitor centers open 8 A.M. to 5 P.M. Entrance fee $5 per vehicle, or free if someone in your party is a U.S. citizen 62 or over. *Note:* Highway numbers have changed on route to main park entrance: SR 27 on your map from Florida City to the park is now Rte. 9336.

FISHING. Florida's waters, both fresh and salt, have long been touted as an angler's dream. Some 600 species of saltwater fish roam the coastal waters, and almost every kind of freshwater fish can be found in the state's 8,000 lakes, rivers, and streams. The question isn't where—because it's everywhere—but how. You can charter a boat to go out in search for trophy game fish, hire a knowledgeable guide to find just the right place, or go the boatless route and fish some of the many piers, beaches, bridges, canals, lakes, and impoundments. Another option is group fishing aboard party or head boats, a popular Florida method. Though individual prices vary, approximate averages are $30 for day trips aboard party boats and $500 for offshore charter trips (for up to six people). Licenses are now required for both saltwater and freshwater fishing. Residents pay $12 for 10-day or $14 for annual saltwater license, and $13.50 for annual freshwater license. Nonresidents pay $17 for 7-day or $32 for annual saltwater license, $16.50 for 7-day or $31.50 for annual freshwater license. For additional information on saltwater licenses, contact 904–487–3122; on freshwater licenses, contact 904–488–4676.

BOATING. There are 2,200 mi. of tidal shoreline and thousands of navigable lakes and rivers. Under the out-of-state reciprocity system, Florida grants full recognition to valid registration certificates and numbers from other states, for up to 90 days. Miami has berthing for over 4,000 boats and accommodates sizes up to 180 ft. Miamarina is a modern downtown facility with 178 slips for pleasure craft.

Central Florida, with its wealth of lakes—Orlando alone has 54 and the two-county area more than twice that many—is an inland boater's mecca. Although you can rent almost any type of craft, the most popular are canoes. Among operations are *Hidden River Park Canoe Livery,* 15295 E. Colonial Dr. (568–5346), which charges $5 for first hour and $2.50 for each additional hour and offers day trips up the Econlockhatchee River with prices varying by number of people per canoe and number of canoes but averaging $15–$18 for two people.

In the Tampa Bay–Gulf Coast area, canoe outfitters gain the bulk of the inland boaters, while sailing operations draw the largest numbers of the coastal visitors. *Nobleton Canoe Outpost,* a franchise operation of the pioneer canoe outfitter in the state, Box 188, Nobleton, FL 33554 (904–796–4343), operates on the Withlacoochee River and offers 5-, 10-, and 16-mile trips for $8.50, $10, $11.50 per person. St. Pete, "Sailing Capital of the South," maintains its title with a wealth of sailboat-rental operations and several sailing schools. You can rent a Sunfish for about $15 per hour or a 14-ft. Hobie for around $20; Anapolis Sailing School (867–8102) offers 2-day weekend courses for $185 beginners, $240 intermediate, and $300 advanced.

In the Jacksonville and northeast Florida area, major resorts often have their own rental concessions. Sawgrass, at Ponte Verdra Beach, offers catamarans for $28, or $40 with a skipper.

GOLF. Golfing in Florida is pursued with a passion. The more than 750 courses across the state attest to its popularity. Among the top courses are: Orlando's Grand Cypress Resort (800–835–7377); Miami's Doral Country Club (305–592–2000), with its five courses and the Doral-Ryder Open; the northeast's Sawgrass in Ponte Vedra Beach (904–285–7777), with 99 championship holes and the annual Tournament Players Assn. Championships; the Tampa area's Innisbrook Golf and Country Club in Tarpon Springs (813–937–3124), with its 63 great holes; central's WDW Golf Resort (305–824–2270), Lake Buena Vista, with two championship courses and the WDW Classic; and Arnold Palmer's Bay Hill course (407–876–2429), site of the Nestlé Invitational. PGA headquarters is in the Palm Beaches area (407–624–0071), in a sprawling complex with four courses and the PGA Sheraton Resort (407–627–2000). Six major LPGA tournaments are also held in Florida.

TENNIS. Florida tennis courts are busy and have been for some time, molding the likes of women's star Chris Evert-Lloyd. Primary focus is in the Jacksonville area, with Amelia Island Plantation's 21 courts and stadium the site of the annual WTA Championships (904–261–6161) and Sawgrass's 13-court Racquet Club, ranked as one of the top in the nation (904–285–2261). The Tampa Bay area boasts 123 public courts and is site of four major tournaments, including an international cup event and a celebrity open. Miami's Turnberry Isle Yacht and Country Club (305–932–6200) is site of a major invitational tour, and the tennis championships that are part of the Junior Orange Bowl Festival in Coral Gables (305–662–1210) offer a look at some of tomorrow's stars.

SPECTATOR SPORTS. Baseball. March visitors can see some early baseball at the training camp cities, as 18 major league teams warm up. Teams and cities are: *Atlanta Braves* and *Montreal Expos* in West Palm Beach (for ticket info, call 305–683–6100 and 305–684–6801, respectively), *Boston Red Sox* in Winter Haven (813–293–3900), *Chicago White Sox* in Sarasota (813–957–3190), *Cincinnati Reds* in Plant City (813–752–7337), *Detroit Tigers* in Lakeland (813–682–1401), *Houston Astros* in Kissimmee (407–933–5500), *Kansas City Royals* in Kissimmee (407–424–7211), *Los Angeles Dodgers* in Vero Beach (407–569–4900), *Minnesota Twins* in Orlando (407–849–6346), *New York Mets* in Port St. Lucie (407–879–7378), *New York Yankees* in Fort Lauderdale (305–776–1921), *Philadelphia Phillies* in Clearwater (813–442–8496), *Pittsburgh Pirates* in Bradenton (813–748–4610), *St. Louis Cardinals* in St. Petersburg (813–896–4641), *Texas Rangers* in Port Charlotte Beach (813–625–9500), and *Toronto Blue Jays* in Dunedin (813–733–0429).

Basketball. The *Orlando Magic,* an NBA franchise, competes in the new, 15,500-seat Orlando Arena. The arena opened in Jan. 1989. The *Miami Heat,* another NBA franchise, competes in the 16,000-seat Miami Arena which opened in July 1988.

Football, Soccer. In Miami, performing dolphins are not confined to marine attractions. Don Shula's *Miami Dolphins,* one of the National Football League's powers, continually pack their own show arena, the Joe Robbie Stadium (305–620–2578). The Orange Bowl (305–643–4700) is home to the University of Miami *Hurricanes* (305–284–2655), a top-ranked college team; each New Year's Day, the Orange Bowl is sold out for one of the nation's top bowl games.

The Tampa Bay *Buccaneers* (813–870–2700) perform before cheering crowds at Tampa Stadium during the NFL season. The Tampa Bay *Rowdies* (813–877–7800), one of the top NASL teams, play outdoor games in Tampa Stadium and indoor games across the bay in St. Petersburg. Jacksonville's Gator Bowl (904–630–3900) keeps football fever high in the northeast, with the highly heated Georgia-Florida matchup during college football season, and the Gator Bowl classic capping college play.

Racing. Southeast Florida has year-round racing with the combined seasons of its tracks. *Calder Race Course* (305–625–1311) operates two separate seasons (one Calder schedule, one Tropical Park schedule), May to early Jan., then again mid-Jan. to May; *Gulfstream Park,* Hallandale (305–454–7000), Jan.–May; and *Hialeah Park* in Hialeah (305–885–8000), Nov.–May. *Pompano Park,* in Pomano Beach (305–972–2000), presents harness racing Oct.–Apr. *Tampa Bay Downs* (813–855–4401), the state's only other track with a racing season, offers racing Dec.–May (Orlando has Ben White Raceway, where harness racing training is done, but it has no racing season.)

Seems as if everyone in Florida is going to the dogs—or to their tracks, to be more precise. Greyhound racing is offered in the southeast at Miami's *Biscayne Kennel Club* (305–754–3484), Nov.–Dec., and *Flagler Kennel Club* (305–649–3000), July–Sept., as well as at two neighboring tracks, *Hollywood Greyhound Track* (305–454–9400), Dec.–Apr., and *Palm Beach Kennel Club* (305–683–2222), Sept. to July. Tampa and the west coast region place wagers at *Tampa Greyhound Track* (813–932–4313), Sept.–Jan., *Derby Lane* in St. Petersburg (813–576–1361), Jan.–May, and *Sarasota Kennel Club* (813–355–7744), May–Sept. Central Florida racing is at the *Sanford-Orlando Kennel Club* in Longwood (407–831–1600), late Dec.–May, and at *Seminole Park* in Casselberry (407–699–4510), May–Sept. In the Jacksonville area racing is at *Jacksonville Kennel Club* (May–Sept.), *St. Johns Greyhound Park* (Mar.–May, Sept.–Oct.), and *Orange Park Kennel Club* (Dec.–Mar., Oct–Dec.). Call 904–646–0001 for information and hours at Jacksonville area tracks. Other tracks in Florida include three in panhandle locations, one in Fort Myers, and one in Key West.

Jai Alai. This dangerous Basque sport, a combination of handball, tennis, and lacrosse, requires great nerve, endurance, and savvy and draws crowds to 10 Florida frontons to bet on the fast-moving game. *Miami Fronton* (305–633–6400) features a Nov.–Apr. season. In West Palm Beach, *The Fronton* (407–844–2444) has a Sept.–July season. In the Orlando area, fans go to the *Jai Alai of Orlando-Seminole* (407–339–6221), which operates Sept.–Jan., and in Tampa, to the *Tampa Jai Alai Fronton* (813–831–1411), Nov.–Sept.

BEACHES. Beaches are what Florida and Florida vacations are all about. In heavily developed areas, don't be dismayed by a solid wall of beachfront hotels that cut off your access to their backdoor beaches. Beaches are public domain—in legal jargon it reads "all areas seaward of the mean high tide are sovereign lands"—and if you can find an access point between the structures, you gain entry to the whole sandy stretch, at least the part closest to the water. Since more than a thousand miles of Florida's coastline is inviting beach area, your choices are as wide as your travel plans. But in all coastal communities are some special beach sites.

Miami

Cape Florida State Recreation Area. 1200 S. Crandon Blvd., Key Biscayne (361–5811). This is a postcard park—the scenic palm-fringed and tropical foliage-backed beach usually on the other side of the message you send a friend. It has roughly 2 mi. of beach (see National and State Parks).

Crandon Park. Crandon Blvd., Key Biscayne (361–5421). Like its state park neighbor, this 898-acre park showcases the south Florida ambience, with coconut palms and dense thickets of sea grape and other tropical foliage. It has 3 mi. of well-kept beaches, bathhouse, cabana rentals, lifeguards, boardwalk (handicapped accessible), concession stands, amusement facilities, a golf course, and a marina.

Haulover Beach Park. A1A north of Bal Harbor (947–3525). Taking its name from people's hauling their boats across the beach to reach the waterway, this 177-acre park includes a marina that berths sightseeing and fishing boats, a golf course and tennis courts, a fishing pier, a picnicking area with grills, and other conveniences. Its oceanfront beaches stretch for almost 2 mi., and there are a bathhouse and a paved walkway.

North Shore Open Space Park. 79th St. to 87th St., Miami Beach. A multimillion-dollar program created this 32-acre oceanfront park with winding boardwalks, bike paths, and inviting picnic areas. Public access. Free.

Tampa

Ben T. Davis Municipal Beach. Courtney Campbell Cswy. Tampa brought the coast a little closer by establishing its own sandy beach alongside the causeway leading to St. Petersburg. Here you can swim, sun, fish, water ski, windsurf, or go boating. Picnic areas contain shelters and grills. Public access. Free.

Jacksonville

Kathryn Abbey Hannah Park. Off A1A north of Atlantic Beach (249–4700). This 450-acre oceanfront city park is the area's major recreational facility.

Parks and Gardens

Fort Clinch State Park. 2601 Atlantic Ave., Fernandina Beach (261–4212). More than 1,000 acres of beach, campgrounds, nature trails, and campsites make up Fernandina Beach's municipal swimming area, situated inside the state park property and covering the northeastern tip of Amelia Island. The swimming beach fronts the Atlantic and is so broad that parking facilities are right on the beach. Also within the park is Fernandina Beach's municipal fishing pier, extending alongside the jetties into the Atlantic, plus the park's focal point fort. State park entrance fee $1 for Florida drivers and 50 cents for passengers; $2 for out-of-state drivers, $1 for passengers; fort $1 per person Memorial Day to Labor Day (free rest of year).

Little Talbot Island State Park. On A1A about 3 mi. north of Mayport Ferry (251–3231). Beaches, picnic areas, and nature trails offer many ways to enjoy this popular island recreational facility. (See National and State Parks.)

HISTORIC SITES AND HOUSES. Miami. *Art Deco Historic District.* Miami Design Preservation League, 661 Washington Ave., Miami Beach, FL 33139 (305–672–2014). This 80-block, 800-structure district preserves the colorful art deco-style of South Miami Beach in the 1930s and '40s. To date, only a portion of the full district has been restored. Guided tours offered weekly (see Tours and Special-Interest Sightseeing).

The Barnacle State Historic Site. 3845 Main Hwy., Coconut Grove (448–9445). The restored 1891 bayfront home of early homesteader Commodore Ralph Munroe provides a glimpse of pre-Miami Coconut Grove. Tours are given at 10:30 A.M., 1 P.M., and 2:30 P.M., Thurs.–Mon. Open 9 A.M.–4 P.M. daily. Admission, $1 per person.

Cloisters of the Monastery of St. Bernard de Clairvaux. 16711 W. Dixie Hwy., North Miami Beach (945–1461). This ancient structure dates back to 1411 and its heritage to its original site in Segovia, Spain. The story of its relocation, from the time William Randolph Hearst purchased it in Spain to its reassembly at its present site, is amazing. Open 10 A.M.–5 P.M., Mon.–Sat.; noon–5 P.M., Sun. Admission: adults, $4; children (7–12) $1.

Vizcaya Museum and Gardens. 3251 S. Miami Ave. (579–2813). International Harvester magnate John Deering built this magnificent Renaissance-style palace in 1916 for his priceless European and oriental art treasures. Natural Florida jungle and 10 acres of formal gardens surround the structure, which overlooks Biscayne Bay. Guided tours are offered, and the Cafe Vizcaya serves some tempting, dainty delights. From mid-Feb. through mid-Apr., the museum hosts the annual South Florida Shakespeare Festival, and on Thurs. evenings during the festival, a spectacular sound-and-light show is presented. Open 9:30 A.M.–4:30 P.M. daily except Dec. 25. Adults, $8; children (6–18).

Orlando. *Church Street Station.* 129 W. Church St. (422–2434). Situated in Orlando's historic district, this nostalgic entertainment complex encompasses some historic restored structures, including the 1889 railroad depot and the railroad car formerly owned by the president of Southern Railway. No charge to enter complex before 4:30 P.M.; after that hour, cover charge of $14.95; $9.95 (ages 4–12); 3 and under free with parent.

Leu House. 1730 N. Forest Ave. (246–2620). Situated on the grounds of Leu Gardens (see Parks and Gardens), this recreated turn-of-the-century manor houses a museum depicting the lifestyle of successful farmers of 1910–1930. Free guided tours 10 A.M. to 3:30 P.M., Tues.–Sat.; 1–3:30 P.M., Sun.–Mon. House admission included in general admission to Leu Gardens: $3, adults, $1; children (6–16); ages 5 and under free.

Orange County Historical Museum. 812 E. Rollins St. (896–4231). Situated in Loch Haven Park (see Parks and Gardens), this museum traces the area's history through a variety of displays including a pioneer kitchen, an 1880 parlor, and other memorabilia. An 1863 slave cabin and a 50-year-old fire station are being restored on the grounds. Open 9 A.M. to 5 P.M., Tues.–Fri.; 10 A.M.–5 P.M. Sat., and noon to 5 P.M. Sun. Admission $3 adults, $2 for 18 and under.

Tampa. *Fort Foster State Historic Site.* Hillsborough River State Park, U.S. 301 N., Zephyrhills (986–1020). An 1837 fort and the bridge it protected during the Seminole wars has been reconstructed on its original site. Historical interpretations, presented on weekends and holidays (weather permitting), put you in the middle of garrison life in 1837. Free transportation to fort provided from main state park visitors' area 9 A.M. to 4 P.M. (excluding noon hour) on program days. is $1 for driver plus 50 cents per passenger for Florida residents, $2 driver and $1 per passenger for nonresidents; fort admission: adults, $1.50; children (12 and under), 75 cents.

University of Tampa. 401 W. Kennedy Blvd. (253–3333, ext. 400). The distinctive structure today housing the university's offices and the Henry Plant Museum is the former grand Tampa Bay Hotel built by Plant (see Tours and Special-Interest Sightseeing). The structure's unique onion domes and minarets have recently undergone a 16-month, $1.5-million restoration.

Ybor City. Bounded by I-4, 22nd St., 6th Ave., and Nebraska Ave. (248–3712). Tampa's historic Latin Quarter, established in 1885 by Vincente Ybor, grew into a major cigar-production center that, by the turn of the century, made 90 million cigars per year. Now a national historic site, the area encompasses Ybor City State Museum (see Museums), with historical exhibits; Ybor Square, a renovated complex within a restored cigar factory; Ybor Preservation Park, a permanent display of 6 restored, furnished turn-of-the century cigar workers' houses; and Ybor Park and Farmers Market, a park and open-air pavilion that sells locally grown produce and ethnic foods. The historic Cuban Club and Italian Club now serve as headquarters for performing-arts groups. Public access area. Free.

Jacksonville area. *Castillo de San Marcos National Monument.* 1 Castillo Dr., St. Augustine (829–6506). Landmark 1600s fortress that required a quarter century to construct. Admission $1, senior citizens and 16 and under free.

Fort Caroline National Memorial. 12713 Fort Caroline Rd. (641–7155). Replica of 1564 French Huguenot fort. Free.

Fort Clinch State Park. 2601 Atlantic Ave. (261–4212). Well-preserved 1864 fort on northern tip of Amelia Island. Park admission $2 driver, $1 per passenger for out-of-state residents, $1 driver, 50 cents per passenger for Florida residents; during peak months (Memorial Day–Labor Day), an additional charge of $1 per person is charged to enter fort.

Fort Matanzas National Memorial. A1A south of St. Augustine (471–0116). A 1740s fort erected to protect the flank of Castillo de San Marcos. Free.

MUSEUMS. Miami. *Bass Museum of Art.* 2121 Park Ave., Miami Beach (673–7530). Paintings, sculpture, vestments, and textiles from 14th through 20th centuries comprise this permanent collection, which includes outstanding oriental bronzes. Open 10 A.M. to 5 P.M., Tues.–Sat.; 1 to 5 P.M., Sun. Adults, $2; students, $1; under 16 free.

Center for the Fine Arts. In Dade Cultural Center, 101 W. Flagler St. (375–1700). Rotating exhibits are featured in this fine county facility, open only a couple of years. Open 10 A.M.–9 P.M., Tues.–Sat.; noon–5 P.M., Sun. Adults $5, children (6–12) $2.

Historical Museum of Southern Florida. 101 W. Flagler St. (375–1492). Exhibits in this Dade Cultural Center facility trace the history of south Florida over a period of 10,000 years. The museum also sponsors a regular schedule of imaginative outings to sites throughout South Florida, which are open to visitors. Open: 10 A.M.–5 P.M., Mon.–Sat., except Thurs., 10 A.M.–9 P.M., Sun., noon to 5 P.M. Adults $4, children (6–12) $2.

Lowe Art Museum. 1301 Stanford Dr., University of Miami campus, Coral Gables (284–3536). The Kress collection of old masters distinguishes this facility's holdings, which also include rotating exhibits. Open 10 A.M.–5 P.M., Tues.–Sat., Sun.; noon–5 P.M., Adults $4, senior citizens $3, children $2.

Orlando. *Beal-Maltbie Shell Museum.* Holt Ave., Rollins College campus, Winter Park (646–2364). Examples of all but 5 of the 100,000 known species of shells are represented in this collection. Some oddities, including the shell from a giant clam, are included. Open 10 A.M. to 5 P.M. (excluding noon hour), Mon.–Fri. Admission adults, $1; students and children, 50 cents.

Orlando Museum of Art. Princeton Blvd. and Mills Ave. (896–4231). In Loch Haven Park (see Parks and Gardens), the center houses a permanent collection of pre-Colombian, African, and 20th-century American art, plus changing exhibits. Open 9 A.M. to 5 P.M. Tues.–Fri.; 10 A.M.–5 P.M. Sat.; noon–5 P.M. Sun. Adults $3, 18 and under, $2.

Morse Gallery of Art. 133 E. Welbourne Ave., Winter Park (644–3686). This private collection is owned by a man who apprenticed under Louis Comfort Tiffany. It features 4,000 pieces of Tiffany art objects, making it the world's largest collection, and even includes some windows from Tiffany's summer home. Open 9:30 A.M. to 4 P.M., Tues.–Sat.; 1–4 P.M., Sun. Adults, $2.50; students, $1.

Tampa. *Henry B. Plant Museum.* 401 W. Kennedy Blvd., University of Tampa campus (253–3333, ext. 400). Named for the railroad tycoon who constructed the lavish 1891 Tampa Bay Hotel, the museum is housed in one wing of that historic structure (now the main administration building for the university). It includes complete room settings, personal items of the Plants, and other memorabilia. Guided tours Tues. and Thurs. 1:30 P.M., while school is in session. Open 10 A.M. to 4 P.M., Tues.–Sat. No entrance fee but $2 donation requested.

Tampa Museum. 601 Doyle Carlton Dr. (223–8130). This museum features rotating humanities and art shows. Its permanent collection includes more than 7,000 works of art, including Greek and Roman antiquities in the Joseph Veach Noble Collection. Open Tues. and Thurs.–Sat. 10 A.M.–5 P.M., Wed. 10 A.M.–9 P.M., Sun., 1 P.M.–5 P.M. No entrance fee, but $2 donation is requested.

Jacksonville. *Cummer Gallery of Art.* 829 Riverside Ave. (356–6857). Situated in the formal gardens of the former Cummer mansion, the museum offers 10 galleries of paintings and sculptures. The permanent collection, an outstanding assemblage of old masters and Meissen porcelain, is supplemented by rotating exhibits. Open 10 A.M. to 4 P.M., Tues.–Fri.; noon–5 P.M., Sat.; 2–5 P.M., Sun. Free.

Jacksonville Art Museum. 4160 Boulevard Center Dr. (398–8336). The permanent Koger Collection of oriental porcelain highlights the offerings of this facility. Open 10 A.M. to 4 P.M., Tues., Wed., and Fri.; 10 A.M. to 10 P.M., Thurs.; 1–5 P.M., Sat. and Sun.; closed Mon. Donation requested.

Jacksonville Museum of Science and History. 1025 Gulf Life Dr. (396–7062). This well-known facility offers permanent exhibits on Florida history and wildlife, Indians, and ancient Egypt, with a varied schedule of rotating exhibits, It also includes a science theater and the Alexander Brest Planetarium, both with shows that are included in admission price. Open 9 A.M.–5 P.M. Mon.–Fri., 10 A.M.5 P.M. Sat., 1–5 P.M. Sun. Admission: adults, $3; senior citizens, $2.50; children, $2.

New in Fernandina Beach on Amelia Island are *Amelia Island Museum of History* (261–7378), tracing the island's 8 flag periods; and *Faith Wick's World of Little People* (261–3127), an enchanting doll museum with backgrounds by Disney set designers. Open 10 A.M.–5:30 P.M. Mon.–Sat., 1–5:30 P.M. Sun. (hours extended to 9 P.M. during certain seasons). Admission $2 adults, $1 children.

ACCOMMODATIONS. In Florida more than any other state, your schedule of activities will probably revolve around where you stay. If you want active sports, you'll look for one kind of facility; for lazing on the beach, you'll want another.

Seasonal rates are used in most areas of the state, though Central Florida and inland areas in general are less affected than coastal resort areas. The exact months and days vary widely from city to city, and even from hotel to hotel within the same city, but the broad overview is that south Florida is busiest from Thanksgiving through Easter and north Florida from Easter through Labor Day. The peak seasons lie somewhere within those parameters and the off seasons outside them.

Room taxes also vary, primarily by county. Since resort areas often spread over more than one county, inquire when checking on room rates.

We have listed hotels and motels alphabetically, grouped according to the areas we've covered in this chapter—Jacksonville, Miami, Orlando, Tampa—in categories determined from double, peak-season rates: *Super Deluxe,* $100 and up; *Deluxe,* $80–$100; *Expensive,* $60–$80; *Moderate,* $40–$60; *Inexpensive,* $40 and under.

JACKSONVILLE AREA

Amelia Island

Super Deluxe

Amelia Island Plantation. Amelia Island, FL 32034 (904–261–6161; 800–358–3652, U.S.; 800–874–6878, FL). This luxurious resort has 625 units in the main hotel and villas; 16 pools; 5 restaurants and lounges, beach club, tennis center, marina, and stadium (WTA Championship site), championship golf course.

Amelia Surf & Racquet Club. 800 Amelia Pkwy. S., Amelia Island, FL 32034 (904–261–0511). Condo towers beachside. 67 units. Pool, tennis.

Expensive–Deluxe

Bailey House. 28 7th St., Fernandina Beach, FL 32034 (904–261–5390). This is a charming bed-and-breakfast inn converted from a restored, ornate Victorian manor that is a national register site, in the heart of the town's historic district.

1735 House. 584 S. Fletcher Ave., Fernandina Beach, FL 32034 (904–261–5878). This seaside bed-and-breakfast inn has one- and two-bedroom units and a separate lighthouse unit sleeping four persons.

Moderate–Expensive

Shoney's Inn. 2707 Sadler Rd., Fernandina Beach, FL 32034 (904–277–2300). Comfortable chain facility with 135 units including king, kitchenette, and handicapped units, plus restaurant.

Jacksonville

Super Deluxe

Omni Hotel. 245 Water St., Jacksonville, FL 32202 (904–355–6664 or 800–THE–OMNI). This luxury hotel near Riverwalk complex downtown has 354 units, concierge floor, heated pool, valet parking.

Expensive–Super Deluxe

Jacksonville Marriott. 4670 Salisbury Rd., Jacksonville, FL 32216 (904–739–5800 or 800–228–9290). Offered here are 256 units, indoor pool, sauna, whirlpool, and health club.

Marina Hotel. 1515 Prudential Dr., Jacksonville, FL 32207 (904–396–5100). 350-room hotel overlooking river. Two restaurants, lounges, entertainment, pool, tennis courts.

Expensive

The Inn at Baymeadows. 8050 Baymeadows Circle W., Jacksonville, FL 32216 (904–739–0739). This all suite facility at private golf club features a pool, Jacuzzis, jogging trails, tennis courts, and complimentary country club membership.

Moderate

Hampton Inn-Orange Park. 6135 Youngerman Circle, Jacksonville, Fl 32244 (904–777–5313). 122-unit property with suites, pool.

Hospitality Inn. 901 N. Main St., Jacksonvile, FL 32202 (904–355–3744). In heart of downtown, this remodeled inn has a restaurant, room service, pool.

Inexpensive

Economy Inn. 4300 Salisbury Rd., Jacksonville, FL 32216 (904–281–0198). 124 units. Heated pool, suites, movies.

Jacksonville Beach

Deluxe–Super Deluxe

Holiday Inn Oceanfront. 1617 N. 1st St., Jacksonville Beach, FL 32250 (904–249–9071 or 800–465–4329). Beachside property with 150 rooms. Pool, tennis, sailboats, restaurant, lounge, entertainment.

Expensive–Deluxe

Sea Turtle Inn. 1 Ocean Blvd., Atlantic Beach, FL 32233 (904–249–7402). This is a beachfront lodging site with 202 rooms, suites, pool, and one of the area's most noted restaurants. Health club privileges.

Expensive

Comfort Inn Oceanfront. 1515 N. 1st St., Jacksonville, FL 32250 (904–241–2311). This former Howard Johnson's, with beachfront setting, has 187 rooms, bar, boating, restaurant.

Ramada Resort. 1201 N. 1st St., Jacksonville Beach, FL 32250 (904–241–5333 or 800–2–RAMADA). This chain offers 142 rooms. Restaurant, lounge, entertainment. Sailboats, pool.

Moderate–Expensive

Days Inn Beachfront. 1031 1st St., S., Jacksonville Beach, FL 32250 (904–249–7231 or 800–633–1414). This beachfront place, formerly the Sheraton, has 156 rooms. Pool, volleyball, croquet. Live entertainment. Golf and tennis nearby.

Ponte Vedra Beach

Super Deluxe

Marriott at Sawgrass. 1000 TPC Blvd., Ponte Vedra Beach, FL 32082 (904–285–7777 or 800–228–9290). Luxurious 4,800-acre oceanfront golf and tennis resort. Permanent site of Tournament Players Championship and one of nation's top tennis resorts. Villas with 1 to 3 bedrooms. 99 holes of championship golf, 10 tennis courts. 7 restaurants and lounges, 5 pools, shops, grocery store, sailing, riding stable, bike rentals, fishing facilities.

MIAMI AREA

Coconut Grove

Super Deluxe

Grand Bay. 2669 S. Bayshore Dr., Coconut Grove, FL 33133 (305–858–9600). Shaped like a pyramid. Superb amenities; jet-setter Regine's nightclub on premises.

Coral Gables

Super Deluxe

The Colonade Hotel. 180 Aragon Ave., Coral Gables, FL 33134 (305–441–2600 or 800–533–1337). Part of a historic complex in the heart of the city, this Luxury facility has 157 units, restaurants, heated pool, Jacuzzi, fitness center.

Key Biscayne

Super Deluxe

Sonesta Beach Hotel and Tennis Club. 350 Ocean Dr., Key Biscayne, FL 33149 (305–361–2021 or 800–343–7171). This beautiful resort is situated on a private beach. Supervised children's programs, four dining rooms, golf nearby, 25 villas with indoor swimming pools. Sailboats, windsurfing.

Miami

Super Deluxe

Doral Country Club. 4400 N.W. 87th Ave., Miami, FL 33178 (305–592–2000). Elegant resort hotel that's almost a city in itself. Pools, tennis, golf, water sports, boating.

Hotel Intercontinental-Miami. 100 Chopin Plaza, Miami, FL 33131, at foot of Biscayne Blvd., part of Miami Center (305–577–1000). Grand hotel. 646 rooms.

Omni International Hotel. 1601 Biscayne Blvd., Miami, FL 33132 (305–374–0000 or 800–THE–OMNI). A 20-story megastructure on 10.5 acres. Self-contained restaurants, theaters, shops, tennis courts, pool, health club, and more. 535 rooms.

Sheraton River House. 3900 N.W. 21st St., Miami, FL 33126 (305–871–3800 or 800–325–3535). 408 rooms. Charming decor. Tennis courts, health club, pool, restaurant, lounge.

Deluxe–Super Deluxe

Hotel Riverparc. 100 S.E. 4th, Miami, FL 33131 (305–374–5100). Luxurious. All suites.

Hyatt Regency. 400 S.E. 2nd Ave., Miami, FL 33131 (305–358–1234 or 800–233–1234). Outstanding 615-room facility. Ultramodern. 2 restaurants, 2 lounges, huge ballrooms, shops and boutiques.

Miami Airport Hilton and Marina. 5101 Blue Lagoon Dr., Miami, FL 33126 (305–262–1000 or 800–HILTONS). This is a contemporary chain hotel with full facilities. 500 rooms.

Sheraton Brickell Point. 495 Brickell Ave., Miami, FL 33131 (305–373–6000 or 800–325–3535). 598 rooms. Beautiful facility on Biscayne Bay. Full service with all amenities.

Expensive–Deluxe

Best Western Marina Park. 340 Biscayne Blvd., Miami, FL 33132 (305–371–4400). 200-unit facility facing Bayside Marketplace and port. Suites, restaurant, limited parking.

Miami Beach

Super Deluxe

The Alexander Hotel. 5225 Collins Ave. Miami Beach, FL 33140 (305–865–6500). Oceanfront. Suites. Two heated pools. Restaurant.

Doral on the Ocean. 4833 Collins Ave., Miami Beach, FL 33140 (305–532–3600). Stunning highrise, decorated like a Fellini set. Rooftop supper club. Golf at Doral Country Club.

Eden Roc Hotel and Americana Resort. 4525 Collins Ave., Miami Beach, FL 33140 (305–531–0000). 351 rooms, all large and attractively furnished. Penthouse suites. EP available.

Fontainebleau Hilton Resort and Spa. 4441 Collins Ave., Miami Beach, FL 33140 (305–538–2000 or 800–HILTONS). 1,207 rooms. Refurbished at $25 million. Outstanding restaurants and bars. Total resort with constant action and a half-acre, free-form pool complete with waterfalls. Recently added spa complex.

Sheraton Bal Harbour. 9701 Collins Ave., Bal Harbour, FL 33154 (305–865–7511 or 800–325–3535). 675 rooms. One of the leading resort hotels. Nightclub with lavish shows. Conveniently close to chic Bal Harbour shops.

Expensive–Super Deluxe

Clarion Castle Hotel & Resort. 5445 Collins Ave., Miami Beach, FL 33140 (305–865–1500). 500 rooms/suites. Private beach, gourmet dining, nightclubs, 2 pools.

Holiday Inn Newport Pier Resort. 16701 Collins Ave. Sunny Isles, FL 33160 (305–949–1300). 350 rooms. Pool, fishing, tennis courts, jogging track. Oceanfront.

Expensive–Deluxe

The Palms Resort on the Ocean. 9449 Collins Ave., Miami Beach, FL 33140 (305–865–3551. This recently renovated place is near shopping area. Good facilities.

Moderate

Thunderbird Resort Hotel. 18401 Collins Ave. Miami Beach, FL 33160 (305–931–7700). Pool, tennis, social programs.

Miami Lakes

Super Deluxe

Miami Lakes Inn and Country Club. Main St., Miami Lakes, FL 33014 (305–821–1150). This elegant inn offers 305 country club–style rooms. Pool, restaurants, bar, golf, tennis, athletic club.

ORLANDO AREA

Cypress Gardens

Moderate

Quality Inn Town House. 975 Cypress Gardens Blvd., Winter Haven, FL 33880 (813–294–4104 or 800–228–5151). Located across from entrance to gardens. Cable TV. Coin laundry. Heated pool.

Kissimmee

Deluxe

Radisson Inn Main Gate. 7501 W. U.S. 192, Kissimmee, FL 32741 (407–396–1400 or 800–333–3333). Offered here are a whirlpool, two tennis courts, restaurant.

Ramada Resort Main Gate. 2950 Reedy Creek Blvd., Kissimmee, FL 32741 (407–396–4466 or 800–2–RAMADA). 384 rooms, This chain hotel has a restaurant, two heated pools, tennis courts, playground.

Expensive–Deluxe

Hilton Inn Gateway. 7470 W. U.S. 192, Kissimmee, FL 32741 (407–396–4400 or 800–HILTONS). 353 rooms. Restaurant, lounge, two pools, outdoor fitness center, playground, game room.

Moderate–Expensive

EconoLodge Main Gate East. 6051 W. U.S. 192, Kissimmee, FL 32741 (407–396–1748 or 800–533–2666). Featured here are 358 units, including some efficiencies, tickets, baby-sitting services, rooms for the handicapped, game room, playground, shuttle to Disney World.

Howard Johnson Main Gate. 7600 W. U.S. 192, Kissimmee, FL 32741 (407–396–2500 or 800–654–2000). Pool, putting green, playground, restaurant.

TraveLodge Main Gate West. 7785 W. U.S. 192, Kissimmee, FL 32741 (407–396–1828 or 800–255–3050). With 446 rooms, this eight-story facility is the largest in the TraveLodge chain. Free transportation to Disney World.

Moderate

Rodeway Inn East Gate. 5245 W. U.S. 192, Kissimmee, FL 32742 (407–396–7700 or 800–228–2000). 200 rooms. Games room, lounge, playground, heated pool. Pets allowed.

Lake Buena Vista

Super Deluxe

Hilton at Walt Disney World Village. 1751 Hotel Plaza Blvd., Lake Buena Vista, FL 32830 (407–827–4000 or 800–HILTONS). One of almost a dozen Disney-affiliate hotels within the village, this huge place has 814 rooms, many oversized for families, many equipped for handicapped guests. Youth Hotel for children 3–12 when parents are away from hotel. Three restaurants, self-service laundry, shops, tennis center, two pools, health club, whirlpool, steam room, sauna.

Marriott's Orlando World Center. 8701 World Center Dr., Lake Buena Vista, FL 32830 (407–239–4200 or 800–228–9290). This is a self-contained resort at entrance to Epcot Center. Ultramodern 27-story tower with 1,500 rooms, 10 restaurants, multiple pools, shops, free parking, outside dining area with barbecue pit. Outdoor activities terrace with three heated pools, Jacuzzis, waterfalls, and lagoon. Health club with pool and saunas. Tennis courts, golf course, putting green, driving range, club rentals. Tickets and transportation to area attractions.

WDW's Grand Floridian. This stately 900-room Victorian beauty is in the waterfront location and on the park's monorail route.

WDW's Yacht Club and **Beach Club.** The resort's two newest on-site lodgings are both nostalgic waterside complexes connected to Epcot by water taxi. For information, reservations at any Disney property, contact Central Reservations, Box 10100, Lake Buena Vista, FL 32830 (407–934–7639).

Expensive–Deluxe

WDW's Caribbean Beach Resort. This is Disney's first medium-priced on-site resort, a family-oriented complex of island-themed villages around a lake. 2,112 units. Pools, lagoon, recreational activities, food court.

Orlando

Super Deluxe

Embassy Suites. 8250 Jamaican Ct., Orlando, FL 32819 (407–345–8250 or 800–EMBASSY). 246 units, all suites. Complimentary full breakfast (cooked to order) and afternoon cocktail party. Indoor-outdoor pool, whirlpool, sauna, steam bath, exercise room, game room.

Hyatt Regency Grand Cypress Resort. 1 Grand Cypress Blvd., Orlando, FL 32819 (407–239–1234 or 800–233–1234. 750-room hotel and 24 two- and four-bedroom villas. 18-floor hotel has five restaurants, pitch 'n putt, tennis courts, bikes, jogging trail, golf, half-acre swimming pool with Jacuzzis, slides, and swing bridge. Also features a marina, health club, game room, and racquetball courts.

Omni International Hotel. 400 W. Livingston St., Orlando, FL 32801 (407–843–6664 or 800–THE–OMNI). 290 rooms. Located within walking distance of downtown, and across from Orlando's new arena, this place is also next door to Expo Center and serves as a convention facility.

Stouffer Orlando Resort. 6677 Sea Harbor Dr., Orlando, FL 32821 (407–351–5555 or 800–HOTELS–1). This 778-room hotel is next to Sea World. Atrium lobby with gardens, lounges, walkways, birds in free-flight aviary. Four restaurants, tennis courts, free-form pool, men's and women's health clubs.

Deluxe–Super Deluxe

Hilton Inn Florida Center. 7400 International Dr., Orlando, FL 32819 (407–351–4600 or 800–HOLIDAYS). 400-rooms. Offered at this inn are a playground, game room, laundry facilities, and sightseeing tours; rental cars available. Baby-sitting service, two pools, games room.

Park Suite Hotel. 8978 International Dr., Orlando, FL 32819 (407–352–1400). Here, there are 245 units, all suites with microwaves and refrigerators. Complimentary breakfast. Indoor pool, exercise room, sauna, steam room, Jacuzzi.

Deluxe

Holiday Inn International Drive. 6515 International Dr., Orlando, FL 32819 (407–351–3500). Across from Wet 'n Wild water park, this place has 657 rooms, restaurant, poolside snack bar, video lounge, games room, and a playground.

Expensive–Deluxe

The Floridian. 7299 Republic Dr., Orlando, FL 32819 (407–351–5009). One block off International Drive, this 300-room hotel has a warm atmosphere. Complimentary newspaper, coffee, and doughnuts daily; complimentary welcome cocktail.

Moderate–Expensive

Howard Johnson Florida Center. 5905 Kirkman Rd., Orlando, FL 32819 (407–351–3333 or 800–654–2000). Available at this recently renovated hotel are 260 rooms, restaurant and 24-hour coffee shop, adult and children's swimming pools.

Ramada Orlando Central. 3200 W. Colonial Dr., Orlando, FL 32808 (407–295–5270 or 800–2–RAMADA). At this chain are 319 rooms, two pools, sauna, playground, games room. Free cribs and cots.

Tampa Area

Plant City

Expensive–Deluxe

Holiday Inn Plant City. Rte 39, Plant City, FL 34289 (813–752–3141 or 800–465–4329). Near I-4. Award-winning restaurant, lounge with entertainment, pool, laundry facilities, gift shop. 281 units.

Tampa

Super Deluxe

Guest Quarters Hotel. 555 N. Westshore Blvd., Tampa, FL 33609 (813–875–1555 or 800–424–2900). 225 units. All suites, complete with living and dining rooms and fully equipped kitchens. Restaurant and lounge, 24-hour room service, valet parking, swimming pool, sauna, Jacuzzi.

Hyatt Regency Tampa. 2 Tampa City Centre, Tampa, FL 33602 (813–225–1234 or 800–233–1234). 540 rooms. Health club, Jacuzzi, sauna, pool, 2 restaurants, 2 lounges, ice-cream factory, shopping center at base of hotel. Adjoining Franklin St. Mall.

Wyndham Harbour Island Hotel. 725 S. Harbour Island Blvd., Tampa, FL 33602 (813–229–5000). In heart of city's glitzy waterfront section, this place is connected to the shops of Harbour Island. 300 rooms. Outdoor heated pool, marina, sail charters, athletic club privileges.

Deluxe–Super Deluxe

Bay Harbor Inn. 7700 Courtney Campbell Cswy., Tampa, FL 33607 (813–281–8900). Private beach with cabana, sailing, and free sailing instruction. Pool, lighted tennis courts, waterfront restaurant, lounge with entertainment. Rooms for handicapped. Complimentary airport transportation.

Deluxe

Riverside Hotel Tampa. 200 Ashley Dr., Tampa, FL 33602 (813–223–2222). Resort atmosphere in heart of downtown. Formerly a Hilton, this place has balconies overlooking river, plus variety of amenities.

Sailport Resort. 2506 Rocky Point Dr., Tampa, FL 33607 (813–281–9599). 237 units. Available here are one- and two-bedroom waterfront condos. Twenty-four-hour desk, grocery store, pool, lighted tennis courts, beach, fishing pier, grills.

Expensive–Deluxe

Holiday Inn Ashley Plaza. 111 W. Fortune St., Tampa, FL 33602 (813–223–1351 or 800–465–4329). This 322-unit riverside facility downtown is adjacent to Performing Arts Center. Gourmet restaurant, heated pool, whirlpool, exercise room.

Expensive

Ramada Hotel North. 820 E. Busch Blvd., Tampa, FL 33612 (813–933–4011 or 800–2–RAMADA). 260 rooms. Two heated pools, tennis, restaurant, coffee shop, lounge, whirlpools, sauna, exercise room.

Moderate–Expensive

Days Inn at Rocky Point Island. 7627 Courtney Campbell Cswy., Tampa, FL 33607 (813–281–0000 or 800–633–1414). 152 rooms. Solar-heated pool with poolside bar and entertainment. Lighted tennis courts, sauna, private beach, gourmet restaurant. Free airport transportation.

Moderate

Rodeway Safari Court. 4139 E. Busch Blvd., Tampa, FL 33617 (813–988–9191 or 800–228–2000). 100-room property opposite Busch Gardens. Heated pool, whirlpool, saunas, restaurant.

Inexpensive–Moderate

John Henry's Inn. 1701 E. Busch Blvd., Tampa, FL 33612 (813–933–7681). Rail cars used for dining rooms and public lounge. Coin laundry, heated pool. Some rooms with steambath or whirlpool.

Red Roof Inn-Fairground. 5001 U.S. 301, Tampa, FL 33610 (813–623–5245). Near fairground. 109 rooms. Extra-long beds, free morning coffee and daily newspaper. Children 18 and under free in parents' room; cribs and rollaways available.

RESTAURANTS. Eating your way across Florida may not be good for your waistline—or your budget. Every city has at least one outstanding dining spot. Restaurant categories in the listing below reflect the cost of a medium-priced dinner for one person, for food alone. Tax—which in Florida is 6%—and tip are not included. Price ranges are: *Deluxe,* $25 and up; *Expensive,* $15–$25; *Moderate,* $10–$15; *Inexpensive,* under $10.

JACKSONVILLE AREA

Fernandina Beach

Moderate–Expensive

Brett's Waterway Cafe. At Front and Centre Sts. (261–2660). Popular eatery in a waterfront setting in the new marina complex downtown. Fine fare of seafood, chicken, beef, and outstanding desserts. Open for L and D Mon.–Sat., closed Sun. AE, DC, MC, V.

1878 Steak House. N. 2nd St. (261–4049). Good steaks and seafood in a converted 18th-century warehouse. D, 5–10 P.M., Mon.–Sat.; L in summer and fall. AE, MC, V.

Sliders Seaside Inn. 1009 S. Fletcher Ave. (261–0954). American favorites, with emphasis on seafoods. D only. AE, MC, V.

Snug Harbor. 201 Alachua St. (261–8031). Here you can get crabs boiled, oysters roasted, and shrimp broiled. D only, daily. AE, DC, MC, V.

Inexpensive

Palace Oyster Bar. 117 Centre St. (261–9068). This is a new expansion to Florida's oldest saloon, offering oysters, shrimp, sandwiches, and daily luncheon specials. Food served 11 A.M.–11 P.M. daily; bar open 9 A.M.–2 A.M. MC, V.

Jacksonville

Expensive–Deluxe

Chart House. 601 Hendricks Ave., next to Sheraton St. Johns Pl. (398–3353). Unique design. Excellent seafood, steaks. D only, 5:30–10 P.M. weekdays; 5:30–11 P.M., weekends. All major credit cards.

Moderate–Expensive

The Water Garden. 1515 Prudential Dr., at Marina Hotel (396–5100). Gourmet dining is enjoyed here, in posh setting in heart of Riverwalk area. Exemplary service. Reservations. D only, 5–10 P.M. All major credit cards.

Inexpensive–Moderate

The Homestead. 1712 Beach Blvd. (249–5240). Great fried chicken and steak dinners. Rustic setting. Mon.–Sat., 5–11 P.M.; Sun., noon–10 P.M. Major credit cards.

Jacksonville Beach

Moderate–Expensive

Crustaceans. 2321 Beach Blvd. (241–8238). This bustling 2-story eatery on Intracoastal Waterway specializes in local seafoods. D, Mon.–Fri., 5–10 P.M.; Sat.–Sun., 1–10 P.M. AE, DC, MC, V.

MIAMI AREA

Key Biscayne

Moderate–Expensive

Ventana's. 6700 Crandon Blvd. (361–0496). Perched in the middle of Key Biscayne Golf Course, this place has a unique bay view. Pasta, veal, seafood, chicken; outdoor dining for lunch. Early-bird specials. L and D daily. Reservations. AE, MC, V.

Miami

Expensive

Cye's Rivergate. 444 Brickell Ave. (358–9100). Fine foods from steak to stone crab, plus special chicken dishes. L and D, 11:30 A.M.–midnight weekdays, D only on Sat., 5 P.M.–1 A.M. Reservations. AE, DC, MC, V.

Moderate–Expensive

Chez Vendome. 700 Biltmore Way, in David William Hotel, Coral Gables (443–4646). Great care in food preparation, including a terrific sole veronique. Intimate dining room. L and D. Major credit cards.

La Tasca. 2741 W. Flagler St. (642–3762). Long-time favorite. Paella valenciana and red snapper cataloman rate raves. Serving hours 11:30 A.M.–11 P.M., daily. Major credit cards.

Miami Beach

Deluxe

Cafe Chauveron. 9561 E. Bay Harbor Dr., Bay Harbor Islands (866–8779). Fine French cuisine is served here in a lush setting. Rack of lamb, veal Chasseur, and decadently rich chocolate mousse. L, 11:30 A.M.–2 P.M. weekdays, D, 6–11 P.M. daily; closed Aug.–Sept. Reservations and jackets required. All major credit cards.

Dominique's. 5225 Collins Ave., in Alexander Hotel (861–5252). Exotic foods prepared in an exquisite manner, under the eye of Washington, DC's famous Dominique D'ermo. D, 6–10 P.M., daily. Reservations necessary. All major credit cards.

Fontainebleau Dining Galleries. 4441 Collins Ave., at Fontainebleau Hilton (538–2000). Bountiful buffets with elegant ice and butter sculptures and grand à la carte dining with impeccable service. D, 6–11 P.M. nightly; Sun. brunch, 10 A.M.–3 P.M. Reservations a must. All major credit cards.

ORLANDO AREA

Lake Buena Vista

Moderate–Expensive

Walt Disney World Restaurants. (824–4321) for info on all WDW restaurants. Restaurants getting rave reviews at Disney-MGM studios are Brown Derby, a re-creation of Hollywood's famed '30s eatery; and Soundstage, filled with sets and props from actual movies. Among the stars at Pleasure Island, a glittery nighttime entertainment complex with more than 2 dozen restaurants and clubs, are Fireworks Factory, a lively place for barbecue; Portobello Yacht Club, for Italian specialties; Videopolis East, a teen's nonalcoholic nightclub; and Zephyr's a club with a skating rink. **Epcot Center restaurants** at WDW have outstanding food in all 10 World Showcase restaurants, plus 2 Future World restaurants (including Coral Seas Restaurant in Living Seas pavilion). Serving hours vary, but are around 11 A.M.–3 P.M. for lunch, 5–8 P.M. for dinner (extended hours during summer, generally until park closing time). Reservations essential. Major credit cards accepted.

Orlando

Deluxe

Medieval Times. U.S. Hwy. 192, Kissimmee (396–1518). Four-course meals in a castle, served during a jousting tournament and other activities. 8 P.M., weekdays; 6 and 8:30 P.M. Fri. and Sat. Reservations. Major credit cards.

Sea World Luau. 7007 Sea World Dr., at attraction (351–3600). Polynesian-style luau in lakefront area where ski show held. Includes Polynesian dancing show. Reservations. All major credit cards accepted.

Expensive–Deluxe

Maison & Jardin. 430 S. Wymore Rd., Altamonte Springs (862–4410). Garden-surrounded villa. Prize-winning dishes. Romantic. D only. Reservations recommended. Major credit cards.

Moderate–Deluxe

Bubble Room. 1351 S. Orlando Ave.; Maitland (628–3331). American cuisine served in rooms decorated in a unique, nostalgic style. Hearty servings. L and D. Major credit cards accepted.

Moderate–Expensive

Le Coq Au Vin. 4800 S. Orange Ave. (851–6980). Lunch served 11:30 A.M.–2 P.M., Tues.–Fri. Dinner is served Tues.–Sat., 5:30–10 P.M.; Sun. 5–9 P.M. Major credit cards.

Inexpensive–Moderate

Purple Porpoise. 220 N. Orlando Ave. (644–1861). Seafood, steaks, and prime rib are the specialties here. D only, daily. AE, DC, MC, V.

TAMPA

Moderate–Deluxe

Bern's Steak House. 1208 S. Howard Ave. (251–2421). Specialties include aged prime beef and selections from the largest wine list in the world—more than 6,000 selections. Even the vegetables are special—grown in Bern's own organic farm. The finest chateaubriand steak this side of Paris. D, daily. All cards.

CK's. Atop the Tampa International Airport's Marriott Hotel (879–5151). Features the best nonwater view in the Tampa Bay area from its revolving restaurant. Entrées vary from stir-fried shrimp to red snapper. If you're lucky enough to see one of the sun coast's famous afternoon thunderstorms roll in while visiting this high view, it's a sight you won't soon forget. L, D, daily. All cards.

Columbia. 2117 E. 7th Ave., Ybor City (248–4961). A landmark and a Spanish cuisine trademark in Tampa for decades. Chicken and rice are a specialty, and try the Columbia's 1905: the salad of ham, olive, and cheese named for the year this restaurant was founded. The building is charming, and singers and dancers entertain with gusto. L, D, daily. Reservations recommended. All cards.

Harbour View Room. In Wyndham Harbour Island Hotel (229–5000). Fine specialties here range from chicken breast cooked in coconut to grilled swordfish, lamb chops, prime rib, and veal. L (featuring a pasta bar) and D. Reservations advised. All major credit cards.

Inexpensive–Moderate

Colonnade. 3401 South Bayshore, at Julia Ave.; (839–7558). One of the most popular restaurants in town since 1935, it has an unparalleled and yet serene view of Tampa Bay, while serving good seafood in a pleasant atmosphere. Broiled steak and fried chicken as well. L, D. All cards. No reservations.

Selena's. 1623 Snow Ave. (251–2116). In historic Hyde Park Village, this place features seafood, beef, veal, and family specials—dinners of either Italian sausage (homemade) or stuffed eggplant. Valet parking. L and D, from 11 A.M. All major credit cards.

Valencia Garden. 811 W. Kennedy Blvd. (253–3773). Renovated in the past few years, the menu hasn't changed in decades: the Spanish bean soup is tops. This is one of downtown Tampa's oldest and most popular Spanish restaurants. D, daily. All cards.

LIQUOR LAWS. The drinking age is 21 in Florida. Local authorities establish their own closing times; some cities are "open" until 5 A.M.

THE GULF COAST

Coastal Hospitality, Southern Style

by
JOICE VESELKA and CAROL BARRINGTON

The Gulf of Mexico, fifth-largest sea in the world, laps at the shoreline of five states that rim it like jewels: Florida, Alabama, Mississippi, Louisiana, and Texas. Each glows with a special luster and boasts multifaceted highlights of history, topography, and visitor-interest sites. There is also an underlying characteristic common to the coastal regions of all five states. Call it spirit, flavor, ambience, whatever—it's a disarming blend of self-reliant independence and unpretentious southern hospitality.

Wherever you travel in this region, you'll find a wealth of things to do, places to see, and people to enjoy.

Florida's coastal region stretches along 673 miles of sandy beachfront (almost 100 miles more than on its Atlantic side). It harbors resorts of all kinds—some large, some small, some slick and sophisticated, some relaxed and casual, but all showcasing the state's most famous asset, its beaches. Lee Islands Coast, in the southwest, encompasses Fort Myers, which has shed its image as a retirement area and is now a major leisure destination, with emphasis on its Caribbean-like setting and natural highlights. St. Petersburg Beach, about midpoint in the state, has an easy familiarity that extends to its name, shortened to St. Pete Beach by those who frequent the area. A busy, cosmopolitan region, it and neighboring communities are the coastal-resort arm of the metropolitan Tampa Bay area. Pensacola, on Florida's western edge and anchor to its panhandle beaches, is a quiet, relaxed resort that takes equal pride in its national seashore, historic districts, and military heritage.

Alabama's broad girth narrows in its southern reaches, extending a small slip to the Gulf. Its short coastline radiates out from Mobile, with thirty miles or less of actual gulf beachfront and slightly more than that bordering Mobile Bay. Little of the coastal-resort atmosphere permeates Mobile itself; most beach activity focuses on Gulf Shores to the east and Dauphin Island to the west. Mississippi, on the other hand, revels in its narrow slip of gulf-coast, which measures approximately 65 miles. Laced by a major U.S. highway, it's an almost continuous string of resort communities, with the Biloxi–Gulfport area ranking as its major resort section. Relaxation and enjoyment are the key words here.

Louisiana's coastline border is about 400 miles, though its meandering shoreline measures more than 7,000 miles. Its coastal zone, constructed by thousands of years of delta growth of the Mississippi River and accounting for some 40 percent of all the coastal wetlands in the nation, lies below I-10 and I-12. New Orleans, Lafayette, and Baton Rouge are major access points for exploration along the fingerlike highways probing the coastal marshland.

From the Louisiana state line to the Mexican border, the Sabine River to the Rio Grande, the Texas gulf coast offers variety for 624 miles. No single road runs the full distance, and only a handful of communities mark the permanent presence of humans. For the most part, this quiet meeting of sand and water remains in its natural, rather wild state.

For considerable miles there actually are two coasts. A beautiful estuary called the Laguna Madre separates the mainland from a string of barrier islands and peninsulas thrown up by centuries of storms. A mix of lush wetlands and marsh with quiet bays, the Laguna Madre attracts one of the nation's largest collections of birds, many of them commuters on the central and Mississippi flyways. The Laguna Madre also acts as a breeding ground for fish and crustaceans, making both bay and gulf fishing popular and rewarding.

Playing in all its outdoor forms—from beachcombing to surfing—is available at various places on the coast, and crabbing is a popular lazy pastime. Numerous wildlife refuges conserve much of the coast's wilderness, and historical sites abound. Most of the fun is concentrated, however, in three areas: Galveston; Corpus Christi and neighboring Mustang and North Padre islands; and South Padre Island.

PRACTICAL INFORMATION FOR THE GULF COAST

WHEN TO GO. Gulf-coast regions offer a variety of experiences, with peak seasons at different times of the year in different areas. Southwest Florida, in the state's tropic zone, is a winter resort where Dec.–Jan. temperatures are 63 to 65 degrees Fahrenheit. Its peak season is Nov.–Apr. The St. Pete area is a spring break site, drawing its greatest number of visitors per single month in Apr. but also showing great popularity in June and July. Pensacola and the panhandle beaches are a summer resort area, busy from Easter through Labor Day but peaking in the summer months.

Mobile's major draws are Mardi Gras, in Feb., and the azalea-blooming season, generally Mar.–Apr., when large numbers of visitors come to view the city's noted Azalea Trail. Mississippi attracts its largest number of visitors during beach season, May–Sept. Louisiana's peak Mardi Gras period in Feb. is famed far and wide, but perhaps its busiest periods are summer and fall, when fairs and festivals are always in progress somewhere within the state.

Traveling the Texas coast is rewarding any time of year. Winter usually brings mild weather with temperatures in the 40- to 60-degree range, although some subfreezing days can be expected from late Dec. through Jan. on the upper coast. If you are looking for semireliable winter sunshine, the area from Rockport south is your best bet. This is "snowbird" country, and numerous low-cost, long-term lodgings are available to out-of-staters seeking winter warmth. Fishing is strong during the winter—the flounder runs off Port Aransas in Nov. and Dec. always draw crowds—and both beachcombing and birdwatching are outstanding.

Spring arrives in late Feb. on the south coast and mid-Mar. near Galveston, when the first wildflowers begin to color the sand dunes. The state highway department calculates that spring moves north from the Mexican border at the rate of 15 mi. per day, but by May the summer heat and humidity are firmly in charge. Temperature and humidity readings hover in the 80s and 90s, but there's often a cooling coastal breeze to keep beaching bearable. Be aware that hurricanes and tropical storms often bedevil the June–Aug. tourist season; Sept. usually has storms but no crowds. Oct. and Nov. are often the nicest months of the year.

HOW TO GET THERE. Gulf-coast regions are accessible by air via major airports in Tampa, New Orleans, Houston, and Corpus Christi and smaller regional airports, with scheduled service to smaller cities. But the practical way to explore is by auto—your own or rented—which will enable you to get into coastal areas not spanned by interstates or major highways.

In Florida, U.S. 41 traverses the southwestern coast, U.S. 19-98 the coast along the upper part of the peninsula, and U.S. 98—which would have to be underwater to be any closer to the gulf—the panhandle region. In Alabama, U.S. 98 skirts the eastern edge of Mobile Bay, feeding into U.S. 90, which runs through the city and slices back down to the coastline on the Mississippi side of the border. U.S. 90 provides oceanfront views and convenient beachside parking all the way through Mississippi and into Louisiana, then leads into New Orleans via the water-rich back door of the interstate route. From New Orleans, it threads through the coastal marshlands on the south before turning northwest to reach its east-west route, 40 mi. inland from the coast.

In Texas, the interstate highways all run a considerable distance inland. You will want to select a specific area to visit and then route your trip accordingly. Do not expect to jaunt from one part of the coast to another with speed and ease. Although the roads are good, most of them wander inland and don't connect communities along the coast.

Good maps are essential and available from state tourism offices.

TOURIST INFORMATION. Each of the states offers a variety of literature and information through their main offices in the state capitals or in the coastal regions through conveniently situated welcome or tourist-information centers.

Florida: Contact *Florida Div. of Tourism,* Direct Mail, 126 W. Van Buren St., Tallahassee, FL 32301 (904–487–1462), or drop in at its welcome center on I-10 in Pensacola, open 8 A.M.–5 P.M. daily.

Alabama: Contact *Alabama Bureau of Tourism & Travel,* 532 S. Perry St., Montgomery, AL 36104 (205–242–4169; 800–ALABAMA, U.S.; 800–392–8096, AL), or visit its eastern welcome center on I-10 in Baldwin County near the FL-AL border or its western welcome center on I-10 at Grand Bay near the AL-MS border, both open 8 A.M.–5 P.M. daily.

Mississippi: Contact *Mississippi Div. of Tourism,* Visitor Inquiry, Box 22825, Jackson, MS 39205 (601–359–3414; 800–647–2290, U.S.; 800–962–2346, MS), or visit its welcome centers on I-10 in both Pascagoula and Bay St. Louis, or its Pearl River center on I-59 in Nicholson near the MS-LA border; all are open 8 A.M.–5 P.M., Mon.–Sat.; 1–5 P.M., Sun.

Louisiana: Contact *Louisiana Office of Tourism,* Box 94291, (900 Riverside Dr.) Baton Rouge, LA 70804 (504–342–8119 or 800–33GUMBO, US), or visit its state tourist centers on I-10 in Vinton near the LA-TX border, on I-10 in Slidell near the LA-MS border, or on I-59 in Pearl River, all open 8:30 A.M.–5 P.M., daily.

Texas: Contact *Texas Div. of Tourism,* Box 12008, Capitol Station, Austin, TX 78711 (512–462–9199). The Texas highway department operates 10 tourist bureaus across the state on major highways; several are near the state lines. All are open daily, 8 A.M.–5 P.M., and offer free maps, brochures, and advice. You can receive help also from the *State Dept. of Highways and Public Transportation,* Travel and Information Division, Box 5064, Austin, TX 78763 (512–463–8585).

HINTS TO MOTORISTS. Expect heavy traffic congestion on coastal highways leading through major resort areas, during peak seasons for those resorts. Allow extra driving time on Florida's U.S. 19 along the St. Pete–Clearwater–Tarpon Springs area and on U.S. 98 through Panama City and Destin–Fort Walton Beach, as well as U.S. 90 in Mississippi's Gulfport–Biloxi area. Coastal fog is also a seasonal problem, most often appearing in late fall and winter. Fogs are usually confined to night and early-morning hours, however, and generally dissipate soon after sunrise. When fog is encountered, extreme caution should be exercised and highway speed kept to a safe minimum.

Officially, Texas observes the 55 mph speed limit. (Some rural sections of interstate highways observe a 65 mph speed limit.) In practice, however, Texans tend to drive as fast as traffic will allow. You can expect to be ticketed if you do the same or if you exceed the posted speed limits in residential areas, school zones, and business districts. Drivers must stop for school buses flashing red lights or when children are boarding or alighting. Seat belts and insurance are mandatory. If you drink, don't drive; 0.10% or higher level of alcohol in your blood is considered legally intoxicated, and even the first offender risks a stiff fine and/or jail sentence.

THE FLORIDA COAST

Lee Islands Coast

White sands and tropical breezes are probably the greatest magnets of the Lee County area of southwest Florida, now promoted as Lee Islands Coast. Primary focal points of the countywide resort area are Fort Myers, its major city and transportation hub; Fort Myers Beach, its coastal section on Estero Island; and Sanibel and Captiva Islands, the best known of its offshore islands.

The islands give you the best look at the natural Florida. Sanibel and Captiva, ranked by conchologists as among the best shelling sites in the western hemisphere, receive daily shell-rich tides. Shelling is such a popular pastime here that it has given rise to a malady called "Sanibel stoop." The islands also harbor an amazing variety of native plants and wildlife, much of it preserved within a 5,000-acre national wildlife refuge.

Fort Myers Beach enjoys a reputation as the nation's safest beach, with no undertow or steep drop and numerous schools of sociable porpoises who gather along the esplanade or at beachside attractions. One of the most popular recreational sites is a county park, where visitors are transported via tram over mangrove islands and clear tidal flats to one of the most secluded public beaches anywhere. Fort Myers, on the mainland, is site of the fascinating Thomas Edison Winter Home and Laboratory, where many of the inventor's original light bulbs still burn. The city is also noted for its lush foliage. The palms along one of its major boulevards were planted by Edison.

St. Petersburg Beach

St. Petersburg Beach, one of eight coastal communities comprising the resort area known as Pinellas Suncoast, bustles with the kind of resort activity for which many of the state's top beach destinations are noted: sailing, parasailing, sailboarding, jet skiing, and others. Its landmark structure, looking like an ornate pink wedding cake rising from the sand, is the grand old Don CeSar Hotel, a lavish 1928 structure that has hosted such illustrious guests as F. Scott Fitzgerald. Still an operating hotel, it is a national historic site, is listed by the National Archives as a historical monument, and is one of three building landmarks used by the National Maritime Association on its maps and navigational aids for sailors.

Pensacola and Pensacola Beach

Pensacola, Florida's gateway city from the west, flies its five flags proudly over the waters of Escambia Bay. (The area was ruled by the Spanish, British, French, Confederates, and United States since the first settlers landed in 1559. In its 300 years of settlement, it has seen 17 changes of government.) Across two bridges spanning Pensacola Bay is Pensacola Beach on Santa Rosa Island, whose soft, white gulf beaches vie with the mainland city's historic sites for visitor attention. They are part of Gulf Islands National Seashore, which stretches from the western edge of Santa Rosa Island, in the Fort Walton Beach–Destin area, all the way into the Gulfport–Biloxi area of Mississippi, taking in barrier islands in both states (the park passes, but does not include, Alabama coastal islands). Encompassed within Pensacola Beach's segment of the park is historic Fort Pickens, where Native American chief Geronimo was once held captive.

PRACTICAL INFORMATION FOR THE FLORIDA COAST

HOW TO GET THERE. Fort Myers. *By plane.* Southwest Florida Regional Airport, 10 mi. southeast, is served by *American, American Trans Air, Delta, Midway, Northwest, TWA, United,* and *USAir. Sun Lines Limousine Service* (768–0800) provides transportation to all Lee County areas. Major rental-car companies serve the area, and *Avis, Budget, Dollar, Greyhound, Hertz, National,* and *Sears* have airport locations.

By car. I-75 and U.S. 41 offer parallel north-south routes, and FL 80 is the major highway to the east. To reach Fort Myers Beach, on Estero Island offshore, take County 867 to San Carlos Blvd., which crosses Matanzas Pass and becomes the major beach thoroughfare. To reach Sanibel and Captiva islands, take County 867, which leads directly to the island, crossing San Carlos Bay.

St. Petersburg Beach. *By plane.* Major air service is through Tampa International Airport, about 30 mi. from St. Petersburg Beach and offering service by all major domestic carriers and numerous international lines. Airport limousine service to the coastal resort area is provided by The Limo (822–3333), which has a booth inside the terminal. All major rental-car companies have facilities in or around the airport.

By car. Access from the northern side is by U.S. 19 or Alt. U.S. 19, from the southern side by U.S. 19 feeding into I-275 to cross Tampa Bay via Sunshine Skyway Bridge. St. Petersburg Beach, on a barrier island, is connected to mainland St. Petersburg by Pinellas Bayway, running west off U.S. 19, or, within St. Petersburg, by 66th St., which branches off U.S. 19. The major thoroughfare through St. Petersburg Beach is Gulf Blvd., which connects the whole chain of barrier islands.

Pensacola. *By plane.* Pensacola Regional Airport, about 5 mi. from the city, is served by *Continental* and *Delta.* Numerous taxi companies meet incoming flights, and at least five rental-car companies, including *Avis, Budget,* and *Hertz,* offer airport locations.

By car. U.S. 98, the scenic coastal highway that hugs the shoreline leading to Pensacola from the east, parallels Santa Rosa Island and offers access to Pensacola Beach on the island or mainland Pensacola to the north. Western access is via U.S. 90 into Pensacola and U.S. 98 across Pensacola Bay to Pensacola Beach. I-10 travelers, or southbound motorists on U.S. 29, can connect with I-110 leading through the city and to U.S. 98 to Pensacola Beach.

TOURIST INFORMATION. Fort Myers area. *Lee County Visitor and Convention Bureau,* Box 2445, Fort Myers, FL 33902-2445 (813–335–2631; 800–237–6444,

U.S.; 800–237–6444, FL), offers some excellent guides and literature on the countywide resort area. The office, 2180 W. 1st St., Suite 100, is open 8:30 A.M.–5 P.M., Mon.–Fri. Individual local information sources include the *Chamber of Southwest Florida,* 1365 Hendry St., Fort Myers, FL 33902 (334–1133), open 9:30 A.M.–5 P.M., Mon.–Fri.; 10 A.M.–3 P.M., Sat.; *Fort Myers Beach Chamber of Commerce,* 1661 Estero Blvd., Fort Myers Beach, FL 33931 (463–6451), open 9 A.M.–5 P.M.,Mon.–Fri.; and *Sanibel-Captiva Islands Chamber of Commerce,* Causeway Rd., Sanibel Island, FL 33957 (472–3232), open 10 A.M.–9 P.M., Mon.–Sat.; 10 A.M.–5 P.M., Sun.

St. Petersburg Beach area. For a complete guide to the 8-community resort area, contact *Pinellas Suncoast Tourist Development Council,* 4625 E. Bay Dr., Suite 109, St. Petersburg, FL 34624 (530–6452). Local information sources include *St. Petersburg Beach Chamber of Commerce,* 6990 Gulf Blvd., St. Petersburg Beach, FL 33706 (360–6957), open 9 A.M.–5 P.M., Mon.–Fri.; 10 A.M.–5 P.M., Sat.; and *St. Petersburg Area Chamber of Commerce,* 100 2nd Ave. S, St. Petersburg, FL 33701 (821–4069), open 9 A.M.–5 P.M., Mon.–Fri.

Pensacola area. The *Pensacola Convention and Visitors Bureau* operates an efficient and helpful visitor information center at 1401 E. Gregory St., Pensacola, FL 32501 (904–434–1234; 800–874–1234, U.S.; 800–343–4321, FL), open 8:30 A.M.–5 P.M., daily, including weekends.

TELEPHONES. The area code for Florida's west coast, including both the Fort Myers area and the St. Petersburg Beach area, is 813. The local directory-information number for both cities is 1–411, and the number for emergencies is 911. Pensacola's area code is 904, covering the state's entire panhandle region. Dial 411 for local directory assistance and 911 for emergencies. For all long-distance calls, dial 1 before the area code and number.

HOW TO GET AROUND. Fort Myers area. Fort Myers, bounded on the west by the Caloosahatchee River, has four major thoroughfares that give easy access to most points of interest and facilities. McGregor Blvd. (County 867) is the scenic riverside drive, which continues past the Intracoastal Waterway and connects with County 869 leading to Sanibel and Captiva Islands. (At a fork in County 869, farther east, San Carlos Blvd. leads to Fort Myers Beach.) Colonial Dr. is a major east-west street connecting I-75 and McGregor Blvd., and Cleveland Ave. is U.S. 41 (also called the Tamiami Trail), the major north-south thoroughfare.

St. Petersburg Beach area. In St. Petersburg, streets and ways run north and south, beginning with First at the bay and increasing numerically outward toward the gulf. Avenues, places, and terraces run east and west, designated N. and S. from the dividing point of Central Ave. Central Ave. is the thoroughfare leading to the bayside waterfront area. St. Petersburg Beach—reached via Corey Cswy. (County 693), which intersects with Central, or via Pinellas Bayway (County 682) to the south—is across Boca Ciega Bay from the mainland. The major road through the slender barrier island is Gulf Blvd. (County 699).

Pensacola area. Major historic and entertainment sites in Pensacola are easily accessible from I-110, which roughly parallels a major city thoroughfare, Palafox St. Both the residential historic district, North Hill Preservation District, and the Seville Square historic district are just a few blocks from that interstate spur, and the city's quayside waterfront area is just beyond its terminus. On the city's western side, Warrington Rd. (Navy Blvd.) leads to the naval air station and popular Naval Aviation Museum. U.S. 98 spans Pensacola Bay and leads to Pensacola Beach, where Via de Luna (County 399) is the only major road.

TOURS AND SPECIAL-INTEREST SIGHTSEEING. Fort Myers area. Eight different cruises are offered by *Everglades Jungle Cruises* (334–7474), operating from Fort Myers Yacht Basin. Choices include jungle cruises on the Okeechobee or Orange rivers, Gulf of Mexico cruises, tropical-island buffet cruises, and dinner cruises 3 nights a week; prices range from $10 to $30. The chamber of commerce (334–1133) distributes a free walking-tour guide of historic Fort Myers.

On Sanibel Island, take island tours aboard the bright red open-sided *Sanibel Trolley,* departing from the chamber of commerce (for schedules on its 10-month operating period, contact the chamber, 472–3232). A circular route through Sanibel, running 9 A.M.–6 P.M., is free; a route through both Sanibel and Captiva, from 10 A.M. to 3 P.M., is $3 (with on-off privileges).

Sanibel–Captiva Conservation Foundation (472–2329) offers insight into the islands' delicate ecology, on 1-hour tours through portions of its 207-acre wetlands tract; offered 3 times daily, Mon.–Sat., $1; under 18, 50 cents.

Cruises from the Gulf (472–7549) offers breakfast, lunch, and dinner cruises, including some to offshore Useppa Island and Cabbage Key, site of a cozy inn built by playwright-novelist Mary Roberts Rinehart. Trips run $15–$30.

Capt. Mike Fuery's Shelling Charters (472–3459) has shelling tours to offshore barrier islands. Reservations required.

Fort Myers Beach is site of one of the nation's few true flotilla operations, offering week-long sailing excursions from Matanzas Inn Marina on Estero Bay (463–6171); also available for rent are blue-water cruising houseboats, by day, by week, or longer.

St. Petersburg area. *Gulf Coast Gray Line Sightseeing Tours* (822–3577) offers bus tours of city, with stops at Sunken Gardens, the waterfront, and area beaches.

Among vessels offering dinner-dance excursions are *Capt. Anderson* (367–7804), sailing from St. Petersburg Beach, and *Belle of St. Petersburg* (823–1665), sailing from Vinoy Basin, with rates of approximately $7.50 to $20; both operate seasonally.

Pensacola area. *Right This Way Pensacola* (434–0493) offers a 1-hour riding tour of Pensacola's three historic districts plus major museums and houses; and 2- and 3-hour tours to select sites within those areas, visiting major points of interest. Prices of these and other tours vary; winter rates are lower than summer rates.

Pensacola Naval Air Station offers self-guided tours of the facility, the nation's largest; it includes Sherman Field, home of the famed Blue Angels, a sea and land survival section, the Naval Aviation Museum, Naval Rework Facility, and historic Fort Barrancas; information on tours is available at main gate.

Walking and driving tours of the city's historic areas are outlined in a free brochure available from the visitor-information center, 1401 E. Gregory St. (434–1234).

BEACHES. Fort Myers area. For just relaxing, enjoy the beaches at *Fort Myers Beach,* called the safest because it has no undertow or steep drops. There's a well-maintained county beach with bathhouse on the main strip, and at the island's southern end is the unusual *Carl Johnson County Park,* a county park on its own little island, with a tram to transport guests across mangrove islands and tidal flats to reach one of the most secluded public beaches anywhere. The park also has nature trails, canoe rentals, snack bar, and restrooms. For shelling, try the bountiful shell-strewn shores of Sanibel and Captiva islands. A favorite site is *Blind Pass,* between the islands, where shells pile up in layers; best shelling time is at low tide (check with marinas for times). For soft, powdery beaches where you can shed your shoes, choose *Bowman's Beach* or the picturesque beach at *Sanibel Lighthouse,* on the island's southern tip.

St. Petersburg Beach. The island has 7½ mi. of white, sandy beaches. Public beaches at Upham Park and Pass-a-Grille offer complete facilities including snack bars and restrooms, and many of the oceanside resorts offer beach bars, a favorite with beach strollers looking for cooling refreshment.

Pensacola Beach. Santa Rosa Island and Perdido Key offer mile upon mile of the soft, dazzling white sand that prompted the area's nickname of Miracle Strip. Much of it lies within the boundaries of Gulf Islands National Seashore, including the major Pensacola Beach facilities and Johnson Beach at Perdido Key, all with parking, changing, and restroom facilities, plus seasonal lifeguard service.

NATIONAL PARK. Gulf Islands National Seashore, Box 100, Gulf Breeze, FL 32561–0100 (904–932–5302), extends from Santa Rosa Island in Florida to West Ship Island in Mississippi. Within its Pensacola-area bounds are peninsular beaches east of Gulf Breeze; gulf beaches, nature trails, a museum, a campground and historic Fort Pickens on the western end of Santa Rosa Island; beaches and jetties on Perdido Key; and the Naval Aviation Museum, Fort Barrancas, and Advanced Redoubt within Pensacola Naval Air Station on the western peninsula. Seasonal lifeguard service is offered at Johnson Beach on Perdido Key, at the Santa Rosa area, and at the Fort Pickens area; Santa Rosa has a bathhouse; Fort Pickens and Perdido Key have outdoor showers.

PARTICIPANT SPORTS. Fort Myers area. *Waterskiing* and *parasailing* instruction and equipment rental, as well as speedboat rides, are offered by Catherwood Waterski & Parasailing at three Fort Myers Beach locations: Royal Beach Club (463–9494), Breakers Econo Lux Motel (463–9759), and Holiday Inn (463–5711). *Golf courses* include Bay Beach Golf Club, Fort Myers Beach (463–2064); and Eastwood Golf Course (275–4848), Fort Myers Country Club (936–2457), Hideaway Country Club (275–4653), and San Carlos Golf Inc. (481–5121), all in Fort Myers. In addition, Sanibel Island offers two golf courses and Captiva Island one.

St. Petersburg area. *Sailing, sailboarding,* and *jet ski* rentals are offered by numerous resort facilities and private firms throughout the area. Among them, in St. Petersburg Beach, are the Don CeSar Beach Resort (360–1881) and Suncoast Boat Rentals (360–1822). *Golf courses* abound, with the Pinellas Suncoast region alone offering more than three dozen. Popular courses include Belleview Biltmore Country Club, Belleair (442–6171); Clearwater Golf Park, Clearwater (447–5272); Isla-del-Sol, St. Petersburg (864–2417); and Paradise Island Golf & Tennis Club, Treasure Island (360–6062).

Pensacola area. Rental and instruction facilities for *sailing, sailboarding, jet skiing,* and other water activities are concentrated near the causeway entrance to Pensacola Beach. One of them is Surf & Sail Boardsailing (932–7873). *Golf courses* include Carriage Hill Golf & Country Club (944–5497), Santa Rosa Golf Club (267–2229), and Tigerpoint Golf & Country Club (932–1333).

SPECTATOR SPORTS. March visitors to the St. Petersburg-Clearwater-Sarasota area can get a head start on baseball season, with exhibition games by major-league teams in Florida training sites: *St. Louis Cardinals* in St. Petersburg (896–4641); *Philadelphia Phillies* in Clearwater (442–8496); *Toronto Blue Jays* in Dunedin (733–0429); *Chicago White Sox* in Sarasota (957–3190); and *Pittsburgh Pirates* in Bradenton (748–4610).

SEASONAL EVENTS. Fort Myers area. Fort Myers, winter home of Thomas Edison, salutes its most famous resident with the *Edison Pageant of Light* each **Feb.,** a gala that's the area's largest event. Fort Myers Beach hosts the week-long *Island Shrimp Festival* in **Feb.** or **Mar.,** with fleet blessing, shell show, and other activities. The *Sanibel Shell Fair* in **Mar.** is the island's oldest and best-known event, but also slated is the now-traditional **July 4th** *Riverfest.* In **Oct.** is the month-long *Festival of the Islands.*

St. Petersburg area. St. Petersburg salutes its mixed heritage with the *International Folk Fair* in **Feb.** and holds nationwide high school band competition in the competitive, by-invitation-only *Festival of States* in **Mar.** It also hosts a special fishing tourney, this one for anglers 12 and under, at the *Fishathon* in **Aug.**—the same time the countywide *Tarpon Roundup* is drawing adult sportsfishers. Clearwater hosts the lively *Fun 'n Sun Festival* in **Mar.**

Pensacola. Florida's City of Five Flags revels in its own *Mardi Gras* celebration in **Feb.** and provides equal fun and festivities at its *Freedom Festival in Old Seville Square* celebration on **July 4th,** an old-fashioned picnic in the Seville Square historic area, featuring bands and turn-of-the-century costumes. On the last two weekends in **Sept.,** *Seafood Festival* brings a bounty of seafood, first to Pensacola Beach's Quietwater Boardwalk, then to Pensacola's Seville Sq.

CHILDREN'S ACTIVITIES. St. Petersburg area. Just across Tampa Bay is one of the state's premier attractions, Tampa's famous *Busch Gardens* (971–8282), with 300 acres of pure entertainment, open 9:30 A.M.–6 P.M. daily. Within the coastal area itself, however, are other child-pleasing sites. At the recently renovated *Pier,* the inverted pyramid-shaped structure on St. Petersburg's waterfront, watch sailboats in the bay and airplane traffic at the adjacent small-craft airport, buy a packet of fish to feed the ever-present comical pelicans, and browse in international shops with goods from around the world. At *Sunken Gardens,* 1825 4th St. N. (896–3186), children probably will be less interested in the exotic plants and flowers that are its hallmark than in its African pygmy goats, talking macaws, monkeys, and other furry and feathery creatures. The gardens are open 9 A.M.–5:30 P.M., daily.

Pensacola area. Children love the open, accessible displays at the interesting, free *Naval Aviation Museum* (453–NAVY) on Navy Blvd. (Warrington Rd.); 40

full-size aircraft dot the exterior and interior of the spacious structure, and kids can even try their hands at the control of a jet trainer. A recent million-dollar expansion created a new atrium section, with jets suspended as mobiles. On U.S. 98 in Gulf Breeze is *The Zoo and Botanical Gardens* (932–2229), with the largest gorilla in captivity.

MUSEUMS. Fort Myers. The museum and laboratory of *Edison Winter Home,* 2350 McGregor Blvd. (334–3614), showcases hundreds of the well-known and little-known discoveries by this famous inventor. Open 9 A.M.–4 P.M. Mon.–Sat. and 12:30–4 P.M. Sun. Connected by "Friendship Gate" is the newly added *Henry Ford Home,* restored to the period in which Edison and Ford wintered as neighbors. *Fort Myers Historical Museum,* 2300 Peck St. (332–5955), in an old railroad depot, has displays on Caloosas, cowmen, and Koreshans—all of whom played key roles in the area—plus other memorabilia; open 9 A.M.–4:30 P.M., Tues.–Fri.; 1–5 P.M., weekends.

St. Petersburg area. More than a dozen museums are situated within the coastal resort area. Among them are St. Petersburg's *Salvador Dali Museum,* 1000 3rd St. S. (823–3767), with the world's largest collection of the artist's distinctive, melting-watch-style works (open varied hours); *Museum of Fine Arts,* 225 Beach Dr. N. (896–2667), with period rooms and some fine permanent collections (open 10 A.M.–5 P.M., Tues.–Sat.; 1–5 P.M., Sun.); *Haas Museum,* 3511 2nd Ave. S. (327–1437), with restored structures in a nostalgic setting (open 1–5 P.M., Tues.–Sun.); and *St. Petersburg Historical Museum,* 335 2nd Ave. N.E. (894–1052), with collections from the past (open 10 A.M.–5 P.M., Tues.–Sat.; 1–5 P.M., Sun.). In Clearwater, *Yesterday's Air Force Museum,* on Fairchild Dr. near the St. Petersburg-Clearwater airport, features restored aircraft and aviation artifacts. Open weekends only.

HISTORIC SITES. The entire city of **Pensacola** ranks as one big historic site, its colorful history dating back to 1559, when the Spanish established their first New World colony here. By all rights, it is the nation's oldest city, but because the original settlement was destroyed by storm and later reestablished on another site, St. Augustine now lays claim to the title, since its sites have been continuously occupied since 1565. Whispers of the past still echo throughout Pensacola, from the site of *Fort George* in town to *Forts Barrancas, San Carlos,* and *Redoubt,* to *Fort Pickens,* now within the national seashore. Its Spanish street names, hundreds of historical landmarks, early-19th-century homes, a turn-of-the-century preservation area, and a historical district reflect the patina of well-preserved, well-used sites. Most of the historic sites, as well as 7 historical museums, are free. *Old Christ Church,* 405 S. Adams (433–1559), an 1830s national-register site, houses *Pensacola Historical Museum,* open 9 A.M.–4:30 P.M., Mon.–Sat. The *Lavalle House,* 203 E. Church St., is an early-1800s structure with apron roof and Bahamas railing. *Quina House,* 204 S. Alcaniz St., is an example of Creole architecture, one of the city's oldest houses on its original site.

ACCOMMODATIONS. Like nearly all sections of Florida, these three areas of the state offer lodging in a wide range of prices, from posh luxury resorts to budget mom-and-pop-operated facilities. Seasonal rates apply in all three areas, making off-season visits a time to find bargain rates. Although room taxes vary from county to county in Florida, each of these areas charges 7%. Price categories are based on peak-season, double-occupancy rates: *Super Deluxe,* $100 and up; *Deluxe,* $80–$100; *Expensive,* $60–$80; *Moderate,* $40–$60; *Inexpensive,* under $40.

Fort Myers Area

Super Deluxe

Casa Ybel Resort. 2255 W. Gulf Dr., Sanibel Island, FL 33957 (813–472–3145 or 800–282–8906, U.S.; 800–282–8906 FL). Luxurious oceanfront complex of 114 1- and 2-bedroom condos. Outstanding restaurant, lounge with entertainment, pool, tennis courts, playground, baby-sitting services.

Ramada Inn. 1231 Middle Gulf Dr., Sanibel Island, FL 33957 (813–472–4123 or 800–2–RAMADA). This is a waterfront motel with 98 rooms and efficiencies. Restaurant, lounge, pool, tennis courts, playground.

South Seas Plantation. Box 194, Captiva Island, FL 33924 (813–472–5111 or 800–282–3402). Major oceanside resort with 600 units, including rooms, efficiencies, and condo units. Restaurant, lounge, pool, marina, golf course, tennis courts, game room, beauty shop.

Deluxe–Super Deluxe

Holiday Inn. 6890 Estero Blvd., Fort Myers Beach, FL 33931 (813–463–5711). Beachfront resort with 103 rooms; efficiencies available. Restaurant, lounge, pool, tennis, playground, game room, baby-sitting service. Pets allowed.

Expensive–Deluxe

Eventide Resort Hotel 1160 Estero Blvd., Fort Myers Beach, FL 33931 (813–463–6158). On the gulf. 36 efficiencies. Small heated pool, beach.

Outrigger Beach Resort. 6200 Estero Blvd., Fort Myers Beach, FL 33931 (813–463–3131). 138 units. This Gulf-front facility has a heated pool, sun deck, coffee shop, lounge.

Moderate–Expensive

Rodeway Inn. 4760 Cleveland Ave., Fort Myers, FL 33907 (813–275–1111 or 800–228–2000). Available here are 140 rooms on 3 floors; door parking. Lounge, pool, whirlpool.

St. Petersburg Area

Super Deluxe

Don CeSar Registry Resort. 3400 Gulf Blvd., St. Petersburg Beach, FL 33706 (813–360–1881 or 800–237–8987). Posh 272-room grande dame hotel that is a national historic site. Stunning public rooms, gourmet dining in noted restaurant, lounge with entertainment. Pool complex with beach bar and sailboat and water-sport rentals. Shops, other services and amenities.

Holiday Inn. 5300 Gulf Blvd., St. Petersburg Beach, FL 33706 (813–360–6911). Gulf resort with 120 rooms; kitchenettes available. Rooftop dining in one of 3 restaurants; lounge with entertainment, sailboat and water-bike rentals, beach bar, heated pool, game room. Some rooms only *Deluxe.*

TradeWinds Beach Resort. 5500 Gulf Blvd., St. Petersburg Beach, FL 33702 (813–367–6461). 381 rooms, 114 suites. All rooms have refrigerator, wet bar, coffee-maker, toaster, remote-control TV; suites are 1, 2, or 3 bedroom, each with full kitchen. Concierge floors, 2 restaurants, 2 lounges, beach bar, 1 indoor and 3 outdoor pools, tennis and racquetball courts, exercise room, 2 saunas, 2 whirlpools, watersports facilities, playground, baby-sitting service.

Expensive

Trail's End. 11500 Gulf Blvd., Treasure Island, FL 33706 (813–360–5541). Gulf-front motel with 54 rooms including kitchen suites and efficiency apartments. Beach, pool, restaurant, lounge, facilities for handicapped. No pets allowed. No discounts or family plan.

Moderate

Days Inn. 1690 U.S. 19 N., Clearwater, FL 34625 (813–799–2678 or 800–325–2525). Amenities here include a pool and movies. Pets allowed at minimal extra charge.

Quality Inn. 2260 54th Ave. N., St. Petersburg, FL 33714 (813–521–3511 or 800–228–5151). 119 rooms. Complete health spa and exercise room, free in-room movies, restaurant, lounge, pool. Family plan; discounts for AAA members, seniors, and military.

Pensacola Area

Deluxe

Holiday Inn Pensacola Beach. 165 Fort Pickens Rd., Pensacola Beach, FL 32561 (904–932–5361). Gulf-front resort with 150 rooms. Rooftop lounge with entertainment, oceanfront restaurant. Pool, tennis courts, other guest amenities.

Expensive–Deluxe

Barbary Coast Motel. 24 Via de Luna, Pensacola Beach, FL 32561 (904–932–2233). This newly remodeled Gulf-front property has 24 large rooms, some 1- and 2-bedroom suites. Pool.

Howard Johnson's Gulfside. 14 Via de Luna, Pensacola Beach, FL 32561 (904–932–5331 or 800–654–2000). This is a Gulf-front resort facility with 100 rooms; suites available. Charter boats and rentals for sailboats, sailboards, jet skis, and bikes. Restaurant, coffee shop, lounge, game room, pool, tennis courts, guest laundry facilities.

Pensacola Hilton. 200 E. Gregory St., Pensacola, FL 32590-2148 (904–433–3336 or 800–HILTONS). A historic railroad depot was transformed into the striking one-story lobby for this modern high-rise hotel with 212 rooms. Two restaurants, two lounges, shops, room service, pool. Conveniently close to historic district and waterfront area.

Expensive

Holiday Inn Bay Beach. 51 Gulf Breeze Pkwy., Gulf Breeze, FL 32561 (904–932–2214). 168-room bayside resort. Boat dock, fishing pier, charter-boat and sailboat-rental facilities. Private beach, pool, other amenities.

Inexpensive

Comfort Inn. 6919 Pensacola Blvd., Pensacola, FL 32505 (904–478–4499 or 800–228–5150). 120 rooms. Pool, cable TV, family plan, senior and military discounts, facilities for the handicapped.

RESTAURANTS. Florida restaurants have lots of flavor—not only in their foods but also in their settings. Restaurant categories in the following listing reflect the cost of dinner for one person, for food alone. Tax (which in Florida is 5%) and tip are not included. Price categories are: *Deluxe,* $20 and up; *Expensive,* $15–$20; *Moderate,* $7–$14; *Inexpensive,* under $7.

Fort Myers Area

Expensive–Deluxe

Bubble Room. North end of Captiva Island (472–5558). Seafood, prime rib, chicken, and other entrées are featured, along with 5 or 6 fresh vegetables and homemade bread. Dress is casual, reservations a must (and waits not unusual, though a lounge and piano bar make the wait not-unpleasant). Open daily. L, 11:30 A.M.–2 P.M.; D, 5:30–10 P.M. All major credit cards.

Chadwick's. South Seas Plantation, Captiva Island (472–5111). Specialty buffets are the hallmark of this picturesque resort restaurant named for the pioneer islanders whose homestead is now the resort. L buffets, 11:30 A.M.–2:30 P.M., Mon.–Sat., Sun. buffet, 9 A.M.–2 P.M.; D, nightly, 5:30–9 P.M., with Polynesian buffet on Tues., seafood buffet on Fri. Reservations recommended. All major credit cards.

Nutmeg House. 2761 W. Gulf Dr., Sanibel Island (472–1141). A popular island standby for seafood and veal, its specialties, as well as for beef, duck, and other entrées. D, 5:30–9:30 P.M. daily L Sun. only, noon–2 P.M. Reservations recommended. AE, DC, MC, V.

Moderate–Expensive

Smitty's Beef Room. 2240 W. 1st St., Fort Myers (334–4415). Prime rib and steak are the stars here, although the seafood holds equal appeal for diners. L, 11

A.M.–2:30 P.M., Mon.–Sat.; D, 4–10 P.M., Mon.–Sat., 4–9 P.M., Sun. All major credit cards.

Thistle Lodge. Casa Ybel Resort, Sanibel Island (472–3145). This resort restaurant, in a historic reconstruction of an old island resort, specializes in New Orleans–style foods including crawfish, shrimp, oysters, and its noted specialty, blackened grouper. Also offers prime rib and a great beef Wellington. L, 11 A.M.–2 P.M., Mon.–Sat., 10 A.M.–2 P.M., Sun.; D 6–10 P.M., daily. AE, DC, MC, V.

St. Petersburg Area

Deluxe

King Charles Room. Don CeSar Registry Resort, 3400 Gulf Blvd., St. Petersburg Beach (360–1881). Fine dining amid an elegant and historic setting, in the beach's landmark structure. Continental cuisine of the highest caliber, including rack of lamb. D, 6–10 P.M., Mon.–Sat.; Sun. brunch, 10:30 A.M.–2:30 P.M. Reservations recommended. All major credit cards.

Wine Cellar. 17307 Gulf Blvd., North Redington Beach (393–3491). Noted as one of the top dining sites in the Tampa Bay area. Offers fresh and imported seafoods, plus beef, veal, chicken. D only, 4:30–10 P.M., Tues.–Thurs.; 4:30–11 P.M., Fri.–Sat.; 4–10 P.M., Sun. Major credit cards.

Moderate–Expensive

Siple's Garden Seat. 1234 Druid Rd., Clearwater (442–9681). A waterfront mansion setting with great Continental and American fare; seafoods are the specialty. Consistent winner of Golden Spoon awards. L, 11:30 A.M.–3 P.M., Mon.–Sat.; D, 6–9:30 P.M., Mon.–Fri., 5:30–10 P.M., Sat.; continuous serving Sun., 11:30 A.M.–8:30 P.M. All major credit cards.

Inexpensive–Expensive

Crab Trap. U.S. 19, Terra Ceia (722–6255). Unpretentious and delightful fish shack, widely famed for its seafood (even catfish trucked in from Lake Okeechobee) and wild pig, shark, and alligator tail. Open 11:30 A.M.–9:30 P.M., weekdays and Sun.; 11:30 A.M.–10 P.M. Fri.–Sat. MC, V.

Pensacola Area

Moderate–Expensive

Boy on a Dolphin. 400 Pensacola Beach Blvd., Pensacola Beach (932–7954). Seafood specialties. 11 A.M.–11 P.M. daily. Major credit cards

Jubilee. At Quietwater Beach Boardwalk (934–3108). Fresh local seafoods are offered here—fried, sautéed, mesquite-grilled, or blackened. L and D daily. Most major credit cards.

Liollio's. 1602 W. Garden St. (432–1113). A noted Pensacola dining landmark, with special Greek seafood and traditional steaks. L, D, Mon.–Sat. Major credit cards.

THE ALABAMA COAST

Mobile retains a Deep South antebellum air, with gracious old manors, wrought-iron-frilled balconies, and colorful gardens. The city boasts four historic districts, with some 250 architectural gems dating to the early nineteenth century. Oakleigh, a splendid 1830s mansion housing a museum, is a picturebook structure in the Victorian neighborhood district. Bellingrath Gardens, in neighboring Theodore, is a 65-acre postcard setting of showy flowering plants, including a quarter million azaleas. The city's official welcome center is Fort Conde in the heart of downtown, a reconstruction of the 1720s fort that was site of Alabama's first settlement, on its actual site (remains of the original fort were unearthed during construction of I-10).

Beach areas are on both sides of Mobile Bay, at Gulf Shores to the east and Dauphin Island to the west. Ferry service connects the two areas, with trips leaving every 40 minutes that provide excellent views of historic forts Gaines (on eastern end of Dauphin Island) and Morgan (on western end of the Gulf Shores peninsula). Gulf State Park, in the Gulf Shores area, also offers recreational facilities. Bayou la Batre, on the mainland across from Dauphin Island, is a picturesque fishing village where even the city hall is a shrimp boat.

PRACTICAL INFORMATION FOR THE ALABAMA COAST

HOW TO GET THERE. By plane. *Air New Orleans, American, Delta,* and *Northwest* serve Mobile. *Budget, Hertz, National,* and *Thrifty* are among the many rental-car companies that have local facilities.

By car. Major east-west access is by I-10 and U.S. 90, both of which feed into the two tunnels on Mobile's eastern side. U.S. 98 is the northwestern highway, connecting Hattiesburg and Mobile. U.S. 45 and U.S. 43 are major routes from the north; I-65 from the northeast crosses U.S. 43 before curving southward into Mobile.

TOURIST INFORMATION. For advance information, contact *Mobile Convention & Visitors Corp.,* One St. Louis Centre, Suite 2002, Mobile, AL 36602 (205–433–5100; 800–666–6282). Upon arrival, visit *Fort Conde,* the city's official welcome center in a reconstructed 1700s fort, 150 S. Royal St., across from City Hall (434–7304), open 8 A.M.–5 P.M., daily. (It is adjacent to the Conde-Charlotte House, built in 1824 as the city's first official jail. Now a restored house museum, the two-story structure is open Tues.–Sat., 10 A.M.–4 P.M.)

TELEPHONES. The area code for all of Alabama is 205. Dial 1 for all long-distance calls, but you needn't dial the area code if calling within the 205 area. The number for local directory assistance is 1411, and 911 is the emergency number for fire, police, or ambulance. Calls from pay phones, which have no time limits, are 25 cents.

HOW TO GET AROUND. As might be expected of a city whose downtown streets were laid out in 1711, Mobile has narrow streets. Congestion is alleviated, however, by numerous one-way streets, which alternate in direction. In the old part of town, all thoroughfares, regardless of direction, are called streets, so your best bet is to pick up a guide to the city, which contains an easy-to-use sightseeing map, from the welcome center or chamber of commerce. Should you encounter difficulty, just look for the city police—some are especially trained to provide visitor information and their patrol cars are so marked.

SEASONAL EVENTS. From the nationally televised *Senior Bowl* college football classic in **Jan.** to the *Holiday Flower Show* at Bellingrath Gardens in **Dec.,** Mobile offers a full year of festive events. **Feb.** is *Mardi Gras* time, a traditional celebration that predates even New Orleans's event. **Mar.** is especially busy, with the *Historic Homes Tour* of antebellum country mansions and townhomes, the *Azalea Trail Festival* with its 35-mi. floral route, and the *Sea Oats Jamboree* in Gulf Shores. *America's Junior Miss Pageant* is in **June,** and the *Blessing of the Shrimp Fleet* in Bayou la Batre in **July. Dec.** brings the *Candlelight Christmas* at Oakleigh, a delicate and historic finale.

TOURS AND SPECIAL-INTEREST SIGHTSEEING. *Gray Line of Mobile* (432–2229) offers four Mobile-area tours: Bellingrath Gardens and its historic home, homes and churches of Old Mobile (2 tours), and tours of the U.S.S. *Alabama* battleship and U.S.S. *Drum* submarine. Tours, which range from $7 to $20, include admissions and pickups at most area hotels. Special outings are offered in March, for the Historic Homes Tours and Azalea Trail.

ACCOMMODATIONS. The following list of accommodations is by no means complete. Full lists may be obtained from local visitor centers or chambers (see Tourist Information). Taxes in Mobile are 6% (5% in Point Clear). Seasonal rates apply to some facilities. Categories reflect double-occupancy, peak-season rates in the following price ranges: *Super Deluxe,* $100 and up; *Deluxe,* $80–$100; *Expensive,* $60–$80; *Moderate,* $40–$60; *Inexpensive,* under $40.

Super Deluxe

Marriott's Grand Hotel. Point Clear, AL 36564 (205–928–9201; 800–228–9290, U.S.; 800–826–7689 in-state). 308-room luxury grande dame resort on the bay. Beach, restaurant, lounge with entertainment, pool, golf, tennis, horseback riding, bicycling, skeet and trap shooting, sailing, deep-sea fishing, waterskiing. European plan and Modified American plan.

Deluxe–Super Deluxe

Stouffer's Riverview Plaza. 64 Water St., Mobile, AL 36602 (205–438–4000 or 800–468–3571). Bayside garden-style resort with 376 rooms, including suites and concierge floors. Restaurant, lounge, pool, complimentary coffee and newspaper with wake-up call. Free shuttle service to downtown district.

Moderate–Expensive

Bradbury Inn Best Western. 180 S. Beltline Hwy., Mobile, AL 36608 (205–343–9345 or 800–528–1234). 86-unit inn with 15 specialty rooms with unique decor (no children in this facility because of its special furnishings). Complex also includes pool, recliners and refrigerators in some rooms, free breakfast, free movies.

Days Inn. Box 2600, Gulf Shores, AL 36542 (205–981–9888 or 800–325–2525). This beachfront facility has 94 rooms, some efficiencies. Indoor pool, tennis courts, exercise equipment.

Holiday Inn I-10. 3527 Hwy. 90 W., Mobile, AL 36619 (205–666–5600 or 800–465–4329). New motel with 160 rooms near exit for Bellingrath Gardens. Restaurant, lounge, pool.

Radisson Admiral Semmes. 251 Government St., Mobile, AL 36602 (205–432–8000; 800–228–9822, U.S.). Landmark downtown luxury hotel; 170 rooms and suites, furnished in Chippendale and Queen Anne styles and with standard guest amenities of robe, umbrella, hair dryer, remote-control TV, and twice-daily maid service. Gourmet dining in Oliver's restaurant; lounge that resembles an admiral's library, plus a lobby bar. Heated pool, gazebo, Jacuzzi.

Moderate

Malaga Inn. 359 Church St., Mobile, AL 36602 (205–438–4701). Restored historic structure in heart of downtown historic district. 40 distinctively decorated rooms. Restaurant and lounge, walled-in pool, central garden and patio area.

RESTAURANTS. Seafood is good and fresh here. In the following list, price categories reflect the cost of dinner for one person, for food alone. The tax in Alabama is 7%. Price categories are: *Deluxe,* $20 and up; *Expensive,* $15–$20; *Moderate,* $7–$14; *Inexpensive,* under $7.

Deluxe

The Pillars. 1757 Government St. (478–6341). Fine Continental dining in a restored Southern mansion. Gulf Coast seafood specialties and Italian veal dishes. D only, 5–10:30 P.M., Mon.–Sat. Major credit cards.

Moderate–Expensive

Roussos. 166 S. Royal St. (433–3322). Greek salads, fried crab claws, and a wide range of steaks, chicken, and other entrées are on the menu, but the restaurant's speciality is seafood, with some 3 dozen choices. Open 11 A.M.–10 P.M., Mon.–Sat.; 11:30 A.M.–9:30 P.M., Sun. Major credit cards.

Weichman's All Seasons. 168 S. Beltline Hwy. (344–3961). This restaurant combines Old Mobile elegance with gulf-coast culinary art. Seafood, prime beef, and veal are specialties of this restaurant—one of 39 in nation singled out for designation in *A Taste of America.* Some *Deluxe* meals. Continuous serving, 11:30 A.M.–10:30 P.M., weekdays, 11:30 A.M.–11 P.M. weekends. All major credit cards.

Moderate

Korbet's. 2029 Airport Blvd. (473–3578). Quiet, comfortable atmosphere in 3-generation local restaurant. Varied menu with large selection of seafoods and beef, with fresh vegetables and homemade deserts. Open 7 A.M.–11 P.M., Mon.–Wed.; 7 A.M.–midnight, Thurs.–Sat. Major credit cards.

THE MISSISSIPPI COAST

The Biloxi–Gulfport area has long been star of Mississippi's sandy fun-in-the-sun strip, drawing plantation owners as early as the mid-19th century for a little seaside recreation. Today, U.S. 90 fronts the white sand beach all along the resort area. The beach is human-made, perhaps the nation's longest, created during the Truman administration with sand pumped in from the Gulf.

The western terminus of Gulf Islands National Seashore is here; the land-based park headquarters is at Ocean Springs, just east of Biloxi, and visitor facilities are on two of its four offshore islands, which are all accessible only by boat. Excursion boats offer seasonal service to the main island, West Ship Island. The historic Fort Massachusetts (1859–66) built on the orders of Jefferson Davis is on the island.

Ocean Springs, an integral part of the resort area and a favorite site for artists and craftspeople, was the site of the original Biloxi settlement in 1699 by French Canadian explorer Sieur d'Iberville. A festive celebration each April commemorates its historic beginning. Biloxi's points of historic interest include Beauvoir, home of Jefferson Davis, a striking architectural gem fronting the main highway; and the Biloxi Lighthouse, which was painted black upon the death of Abraham Lincoln (but later repainted its original white).

Gulfport is a port community, combining its resort facilities with some outstanding deep-sea sportfishing facilities. Its summer Mississippi Deep Sea Fishing Rodeo lays claim to the title of world's largest event of its type. Long Beach and Pass Christian—the latter a favorite hideaway site for late Presidents Grant, Jackson, Theodore Roosevelt, Taylor, Truman, and Wilson—offer additional resort facilities. The entire area's French and Spanish Creole heritage is reflected in the cuisine, annual fleet-blessing ceremonies, and Mardi Gras festivities that are offered by nearly all the communities. Historic homes are spotlighted in March, when the Mississippi Gulf Coast Council of Garden Clubs sponsors its annual Gulf Coast Pilgrimages, with each community spotlighted on different days.

PRACTICAL INFORMATION FOR THE MISSISSIPPI COAST

HOW TO GET THERE. By plane. You can reach the coastal resort area by *Northwest,* the only line serving the regional airport, or from the New Orleans airport via limo service offered by *Mississippi Coastliner* (601–432–2649; 800–647–3957, outside MS), which charges $33 per person or $56 per couple. Limo service from the Biloxi–Gulfport airport is offered by *C&E Limo* (601–432–8000) and by *Dial-a-Ride* (868–7433), which offers 24-hour service; fare is about $10. Most major rental-car companies serve the area; those with airport locations include *Budget, Hertz, National,* and *Thrifty.*

By car. I-10 is the fastest east-west route, U.S. 90 the most scenic. U.S. 49 is the only major highway from the north, dead-ending in Gulfport. I-110 leads from I-10 to Biloxi.

TOURIST INFORMATION. *Gulf Coast Convention & Visitors Bureau,* Box 6128, Gulfport, MS 39506 (601–896–6699; 800–237–9493, outside MS) provides a variety of helpful information. Other information sources include: *Biloxi Chamber of Commerce,* Drawer 1928, Biloxi, MS 39533 (601–374–2717), situated at 1036 Fred Haise Blvd., across from the Biloxi Lighthouse, and open 8:30 A.M.–5 P.M., Mon.–Sat.; and *Gulfport Chamber of Commerce,* Drawer FF, Gulfport, MS 39502 (601–863–2933), on 20th Ave., open 8:30 A.M.–5 P.M., Mon.–Fri.; 9 A.M.–1 P.M., Sat. There are also state welcome centers in Waveland (on U.S. 90; 467–4367) and Pearlington (on Hwy. 607; 533–5554).

TELEPHONES. All of Mississippi is within the 601 area code. Dial 1 before the area code and number for long-distance calls. The 911 emergency number reaches ambulance, highway patrol, fire, and Coast Guard assistance. The poison-control center, at Gulf Coast Community Hospital, is 388–1919. Pay-phone calls are 25 cents, and the local calling area covers not only Biloxi and Gulfport but also Bay St. Louis, Waveland, Ocean Springs, Pass Christian, and other area communities.

SEASONAL EVENTS. Feb. This coastal area also goes all out for *Mardi Gras,* with festive individual celebrations in Biloxi, Gulfport, Long Beach, and Pass Christian, all held two weeks prior to New Orleans's celebration. **Mar.** events include the tasty *Oyster Festival* in Biloxi and the elaborate *Spring Pilgrimage of Homes,* with historic homes in 11 separate communities spotlighted on different days. Ocean Springs reenacts the *D'Iberville Landing* in **Apr.** Bounties of the sea are the focus of spring–summer–fall festivities: Biloxi's *Crawfish Festival* in **May,** separate Blessing of the Fleet *Shrimp Festivals* in both Pass Christian and Biloxi in **June,** Gulfport's noted *Gulf Coast Deep Sea Fishing Rodeo* in **July,** and the expansive *Seafood Festival* in **Sept.,** headquartered in Biloxi but including participation by all area communities plus Mobile and New Orleans.

TOURS. Sightseeing excursions to area points of interest are offered by *Biloxi Shrimping Trip* (374–5718), at the city dock, and by *Mississippi Coastliner* (432–2649; 800–647–3957, outside MS), both in Biloxi; *Luxury Limousine Service* in Ocean Springs (875–1984); and *Coast Area Transit* (896–8080) and *Coasting, Inc.* (896–3044), both in Gulfport.

NATIONAL PARK. Gulf Islands National Seashore, 3500 Park Rd., Ocean Springs, MS 39564 (601–875–9057), encompasses a mainland park site bordering Davis Bayou, including park headquarters, a visitor center, a fishing pier, a picnic area, and nature trails; and four offshore islands including West Ship Island, its major visitor-use site, with swimming and picnic areas and historic Fort Massachusetts. Boat trips are offered from both Biloxi and Gulfport, Mar.–Oct., on varying schedules. Guided tours of the fort are offered in summer.

ACCOMMODATIONS. Because of the area's popularity as a resort destination, numerous facilities, in all price ranges, stand shoulder to shoulder. The ones listed, which are representative, are by no means the only facilities; complete lists may be obtained from local visitor centers or chambers of commerce (see Tourist Information). Room tax is 9%. Categories reflect double-occupancy, peak-season rates in the following price ranges: *Super Deluxe,* $100 and up; *Deluxe,* $80–$100; *Expensive,* $60–$80; *Moderate,* $40–60; *Inexpensive,* under $40.

Expensive–Super Deluxe

Broadwater Beach Resort. 3600 Beach Blvd., Biloxi, MS 39533 (601–388–2211 or 800–647–3964). Long one of the area's most popular and extensive resorts. Sprawling complex includes 360 rooms in 5 buildings, plus additional cottages. Full resort facilities and amenities, plus a marina with fishing and charterboat facilities.

Expensive–Deluxe

Biloxi Hilton. 1950 Beach Blvd., Biloxi, MS 39531 (601–388–7000 or 800–445–8667). This newly remodeled beachside resort facility has 530 rooms and suites. Two pools, golf, tennis, restaurant, lounge, other facilities.

Royal d'Iberville. 1980 Beach Blvd., Biloxi, MS 39531 (601–388–6610 or 800–647–3955). Newly remodeled, handsome resort facility with 263 rooms. Pool, tennis, whirlpool, many other guest amenities.

Moderate–Expensive

Biloxi Beach Resort Motor Inn. 2736 Beach Blvd., Biloxi, MS 39531 (601–388–3310; 800–345–1570, outside MS). Beach-side complex with 184 units; offers pool, restaurant, lounge, and meeting facilities.

Moderate

Beachwater Inn. 1678 Beach Blvd., Biloxi, MS 39531 (601–432–1984). 2-story facility with 31 balconied rooms nestled amid live oaks. Many rooms have cooking niches. Pool. Special packages available in off season.

RESTAURANTS. There's no mistaking that you're on the gulf coast: The seafood is so fresh that it slept in the gulf the night before. Price categories reflect the cost of dinner for one person, for food alone (tax is 6%). Price categories are: *Deluxe,* over $20; *Expensive,* $10–$20; *Moderate,* $7–$10; and *Inexpensive,* under $7.

Deluxe

White Pillars. 100 Rodenberg, Biloxi (432–8741). Gourmet seafood, prime rib, steak, duck, and veal are offered in this elegant restored southern mansion. Especially tasty is its eggplant Josephine, available either as an appetizer or as a main course. D, 5–9 P.M., Tues.–Thurs.; 5–midnight, Fri.–Sat.; Brunch, 11:30 A.M.–3:30 P.M., Sun. All major credit cards.

Expensive–Deluxe

Trilby's. 1203 U.S. 90, Ocean Springs (875–4426). Look for the old gray house with the awning if you're looking for great seafood. From shrimp and crab (hard- and soft-shell), to red snapper and flounder, they've got it all, served up fried, broiled, boiled, or in casseroles. L, 11:30 A.M.–2 P.M., Tues.–Sun.; D 6–10 P.M., Tues.–Sat. Restaurant seats less than 100, so reservations are recommended, especially for D. AE, DC, MC, V.

Inexpensive–Moderate

Broadwater Beach Marina Restaurant. 3600 Beach Blvd., Biloxi (388–2211). Daily specials are offered at this waterfront restaurant set within the marina of the Broadwater Beach Resort. Seafoods star, of course, and the stuffed flounder is a tasty favorite. Open 6 A.M.–10 P.M., daily. DC, MC, V.

The Landing. U.S. 90 and Hwy. 49, Gulfport (863–8312). Seafood and steaks reign supreme in this popular downtown-Gulfport facility. Chowders and gumbo are great appetizers before seafood platters, steak, or the popular surf-turf combo. Also offered are 5 vegetables, potato boats, and crepes. Open 11 A.M.–10 P.M., daily. AE, MC, V.

THE LOUISIANA COAST

Louisiana's bayou-laced, swamp-speckled coastal region reflects the state's most colorful and best-known heritage. It was settled in the mid-18th century by French Acadians fleeing persecution from Canada's eastern coast. This is Cajun country, where swamp boats traverse the back country, historic sites preserve Acadiene heritage, and festive annual celebrations offer a relaxed look at cultures and lifestyles. Here they say, "*Laissez les bon temps rouler!*"—Let the good times roll! It's also an area of gracious plantation homes, many on the mighty Mississippi River, which was the major highway to the great port cities.

Although almost every highway and road leads to interesting, hospitable communities, two major routes offer good representative samplings:

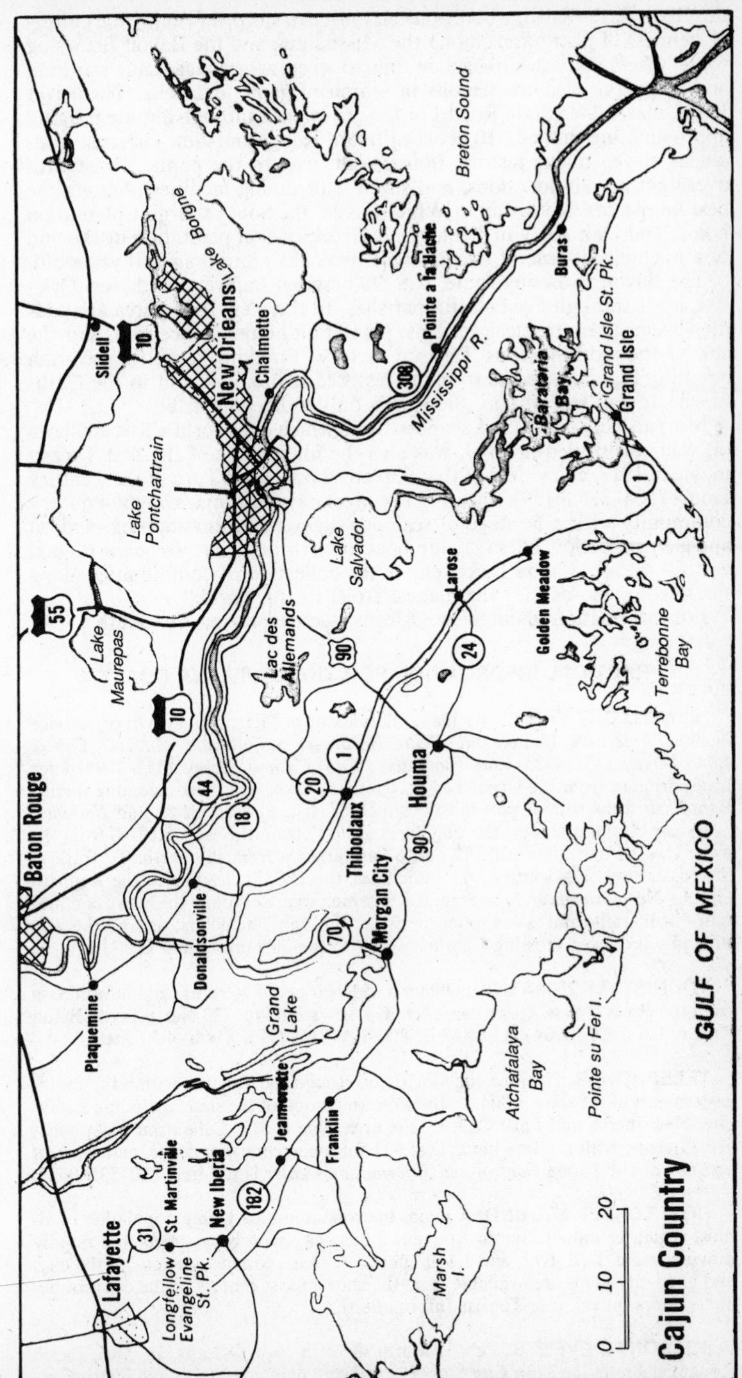
Cajun Country
0 10 20
GULF OF MEXICO
Baton Rouge
Lafayette
New Orleans
Slidell
Chalmette
Lake Pontchartrain
Lake Maurepas
Lake Borgne
Breton Sound
Pointe a la Hache
Mississippi R.
Buras
Grand Isle St. Pk.
Grand Isle
Barataria Bay
Lake Salvador
Lac des Allemands
Larose
Golden Meadow
Terrebonne Bay
Houma
Thibodaux
Morgan City
Donaldsonville
Plaquemine
Grand Lake
Jeanerette
Franklin
New Iberia
St. Martinville
Longfellow Evangeline St. Pk.
Marsh I.
Atchafalaya Bay
Pointe su Fer I.
10
55
10
44
18
20
1
90
24
308
1
90
70
182
31

the Great River Road, where you can tour, eat, sleep, and enjoy the cultural richness of plantations along the Mississippi; and the Bayou Browsing route, where you can slip back in time to an era when sugar cane was king and trappers poled the bayous in search of game and pelts. The River Road, reached via State Road 1 or U.S. 61, wends through a route roughly approximating that of I-10 between Baton Rouge and New Orleans. It includes eleven major historic homes—all open to the public, three with overnight accommodations, and seven with dining facilities. Among the best known are Nottoway in White Castle, the South's largest plantation home; and Oak Alley in Vacherie, a Greek-revival plantation at the end of a magnificent lane of twenty-eight live oaks more than 250 years old.

The Bayou Browsing route, U.S. 90 between Lafayette and New Orleans, leads through five colorful parishes. In the New Iberia area are paddlewheelers, semitropical gardens, plantation homes, a rice mill, and the site of the world-famous Tabasco factory. Franklin, a restful tree-rich community, offers access to many restored plantations and to the Chitimacha Indian reservation, the state's only indigenous tribe.

Morgan City, an island seaport from which the world's first offshore oil well was drilled in 1947, was also the filming site of the first Tarzan movie in 1917, and videos of that film are shown in its Turn of the Century House (504–385–6159), open 1–5 P.M., weekdays. Houma, a bayou-country community with a heritage of seafood, sugar cane, fur-trapping, and oil and gas production, offers swamp-boat tours through its *terrebonne* ("good earth") setting. Bayou Lafourche is the collection of communities along the bayou, who call it "the longest street in the world."

For information about New Orleans, see chapter on the South.

PRACTICAL INFORMATION FOR THE LOUISIANA COAST

HOW TO GET THERE. By plane. Baton Rouge Metropolitan Airport service includes *American, Continental, Delta, Northwest,* and *Royale. Mackie's Cab & Limo Service* (357–4833) and *Thompson's Cab & Limo Service* (357–7094) offer transportation from the airport, as do the many taxis that meet incoming flights. Rental-car firms with airport locations include *Avis, Budget, Hertz,* and *National.*

By car. Major east-west thoroughfares are I-12 from the east and I-10 from the west. U.S. 61 and State Rds. 19 and 67 are arteries from the north. To traverse the coastal wetlands south of the interstates, use U.S. 61, leading to the Kenner–Gretna–New Orleans area, or State Rd. 1, which wends through the many communities in Iberville and Assumption parishes, through Thibodaux, and all the way to land's end, even crossing Caminada Bay to the offshore Grand Isle.

TOURIST INFORMATION. Obtain a wide variety of literature and information from the *Baton Rouge Area Convention & Visitors Bureau,* 730 North Blvd., Baton Rouge, LA 70802 (504–383–1825 or 800–LA ROUGE), 8 A.M.–4:30 P.M.,

TELEPHONES. The area code for Baton Rouge and all cities within the southeastern part of the state is 504. In the western section of the state, including Lafayette, New Iberia, and Lake Charles, the area code is 318. Calls from pay phones are 25 cents, with no time limit. Dial 911 for *emergency fire, police,* and *medical assistance.* The *Poison Control and Information Center* is toll-free: 800–535–0525.

HOW TO GET AROUND. A major metropolitan area with a population of almost a quarter million, Baton Rouge is a busy city with busy streets and rapidly moving traffic. I-10, I-12, and I-110 offer easy access to most sections of the city, and good city maps are available from the state tourist centers or the convention-and-visitors bureau (see Tourist Information).

SEASONAL EVENTS. Feb. is Mardi Gras in New Orleans. In **Apr.,** Baton Rouge celebrates the *River City Blues Festival* with plantation tours and pilgrimages throughout the area, while Abbeville salutes its heritage with *French Acadian Music*

Festival. A sweet treat in **May** is the *Louisiana Praline Festival* in Houma. Kenner has the *Okra Festival* and Gonzales the *Jambalaya Festival.* In **June** are *South Lafourche Cajun Festival* in Galliano and *Bayou Lacombe Crab Festival* in Lacombe. You can pig out at Des Allemands' *Louisian Catfish Festival* or Galliano's *Louisiana Oyster Festival* in **July** or at *shrimp festivals* in Delcambre and Morgan City in **Aug.** Grande Isle, the sportfishing resort offshore, hosts the *International Tarpon Rodeo* in **July,** and Galliano its festive *Cajun Hunters Festival* in **Aug.** Lafayette salutes its heritage at the *Festivals Acadiens* in **Sept.,** while New Iberia's *Louisiana Sugarcane Festival,* staged by 16 sugar-producing parishes, showcases sugar production and includes a sugar-cookery contest. In **Oct.,** Franklin hosts the *International Alligator Festival* and Larose the *French Food Festival,* where you can eat your fill of shrimp creole, crawfish étouffée, seafood gumbo, and alligator sauce piquante. One of the most festive events of the year is *Bonfires on the Levee,* at **Christmas** time, when communities all along the banks of the Mississippi build and light huge bonfires, many in elaborate or whimsical shapes, accompanied by good food and good times. The greatest concentration is in the Lutcher-Gramercy area southwest of Baton Rouge.

TOURS. *Louisiana Lagniappe Tours*—pronounced lan-yap and operated by the *Foundation for Historical Louisiana*—offers 2-hour morning tours of Baton Rouge highlights and 4-hour afternoon tours of its river-country plantations, for about $20–$30. Advance reservations required. 900 North Blvd., Baton Rouge, LA 70802 (504–387–2464).

Norfolk Tours, 2354 S. Acadian Throughway, E–1, Baton Rouge, LA 70808 (504–383–2215; 800–626–6957, outside LA), offers standard half-day outings to area points of interest for $25 per person, or for the same price will provide a van and guide to take you to sites of your choice (full day's run $60 per person). They also offer a special *Louisiana Cajun Country Tour,* a 5-day trip to Houma, Franklin, New Iberia, Avery Island, St. Martinville, Lafayette, and St. Francisville, with tour time in Baton Rouge as well; shorter tours also are offered.

Unique swamp-boat tours are an interesting way to see the bayou backcountry. Tours vary greatly in both length and content, so be advised that you should inquire fully; among them: *Atchafalaya Basin Backwater Adventure,* Gibson (504–575–2371), *Basin Boat Tours,* near Henderson (318–228–8567), *Cypress Bayou Swamp Tours,* Houma (504–851–3569), *Lake des Allemands Swamp Tours,* Vacherie (504–265–3160).

Paddle-wheel riverboat cruises offer "big fun on the bayou": the *Vermilion Queen* in Lafayette (318–235–1776), and the *Samuel Clemens* in Baton Rouge (504–381–9606).

Allons à Lafayette (318–269–9607), which translates to "Let's go to Lafayette," conducts narrated tours of Lafayette and Acadian Cajun country.

Avery Island Jungle Garden (318–369–6243), southwest of New Iberia on LA 329, is filled with beautiful gardens and nearby is the McIlhenny Tabasco Sauce factory, which you can tour.

STATE PARKS. Coastal state park recreation areas include *Cypremort Point State Park* in Franklin and *Grand Isle State Park* on Grand Isle. Commemorative state park sites in the immediate coastal area include *Longfellow-Evangeline* in St. Martinville, *Edward Douglas White* in Thibodaux, and both the *Old Arsenal* and *Old State Capitol* in Baton Rouge.

ACCOMMODATIONS. This is only a sample of available accommodations. A complete list may be obtained from the local visitor center (see Tourist Information). We have included three historic plantations that offer guest accommodations. There is a 9% tax on rooms. Seasonal rates apply to some facilities, but differences are generally not as drastic as in Florida and Texas resort areas. Categories reflect double-occupancy, peak-season rates in the following price ranges: *Deluxe,* $75–$100; *Expensive,* $60–$75; *Moderate,* $40–$60.

Deluxe

Embassy Suites. 4914 Constitution Ave., Baton Rouge, LA 70808 (504–924–6566 or 800–EMBASSY). This 8-story all-suite hotel is near I-10, 2 mi. from downtown. 224 suites. Complimentary cooked-to-order breakfast, complimentary cocktail party daily. Wheelchair units, concierge, valet, laundry service.

Expensive–Deluxe

Lafayette Hilton Towers. 1521 Pinhook Rd., Lafayette, LA 70505 (318–235–6111 or 800–33CAJUN). This 15-story high rise has 328 rooms, 2 restaurants, pool, lounge.

Sheraton Baton Rouge. 4728 Constitution Ave., Baton Rouge, LA 70808 (504–925–2244). 300-room hotel near I-10. Restaurant, lounge, nightly Las Vegas–style entertainment, jazz brunch on Sun., daily international lunch buffet.

Moderate–Expensive

Baton Rouge Hilton. 5500 Hilton Ave., Baton Rouge, LA 70808 (504–924–5000 or 800–HILTONS). 300 rooms. Restaurant, lounge with entertainment, pool, 24-hour room service.

Moderate

Holiday Inn Holidome. 210 S. Hollywood Rd., Houma, LA 70360 (504–868–5851). 200 rooms including bilevel suites. Health and fitness facilities, putting green, pool, game room.

Historic Plantation Houses

Nottoway Plantation. *Super Deluxe.* Box 160, White Castle, LA 70788 (504–545–2730). South's largest plantation house, with 53,000 square feet in a magnificently restored 1859 riverfront mansion. 8 guest rooms in main house, 4 rooms in cottage; restaurant 11–3 daily. Priced at $115–$200; includes tour of house, bottle of sherry, and full breakfast.

Oak Alley. *Expensive.* Rte. 2, Box 10, Vacherie, LA 70090 (504–265–2151). Fine example of Greek-revival architecture, approached by canopied lane of live oaks. Guest facilities in 4 cabins (2- and 3-bedroom) on grounds. Breakfast in the historic site's restaurant is included.

Tezcuco. *Moderate–Expensive.* 3138 Hwy. 44, Darrow, LA 70725 (504–562–3929). 1855 raised cottage in Greek-revival style, with wrought-iron-trimmed galleries, ornate friezes and medallions. Restaurant. 13 cottages, all in restored slave quarters. Breakfast served if requested, at $5 per person.

RESTAURANTS. There's no mistaking where you are when you enter restaurants in the coastal Louisiana region. The food has Cajun and Creole flavors and utilizes *fresh* seafood. Price categories reflect the average cost of the least expensive dinners for one person, for food alone; all the restaurants serve more costly items. Tax is 7%, although it may vary outside the metropolitan Baton Rouge area. Price categories are: *Deluxe,* $20 and up; *Expensive,* $15–$20; *Moderate,* $7–$15; *Inexpensive,* under $7.

Expensive

Nottoway Plantation. River Rd., White Castle (504–545–2730). This national historic site includes a restaurant offering fine dining amid gracious surroundings. À la carte menu. Open daily, L, 11 A.M.–3 P.M.; D, 6–9 P.M. Reservations required. AE, MC, V.

Moderate

The Cabin Restaurant. Junction of Hwys. 22 & 44, Burnside (504–473–3007). Collection of restored 100-year-old slave cabins. Seafood dinners, chicken and andouille gumbo, and generous po-boys. Open 8 A.M.–3 P.M., Mon.–Wed.; 8 A.M.–9 P.M., Thurs.; 8 A.M.–10 P.M., Fri.–Sat.; 8 A.M.–6 P.M., Sun. AE, MC, V.

Cafe Vermilionville. 1304 W. Pinhook Rd., Lafayette (318–237–0100). Casually elegant restaurant in 1800s former Acadian inn of cypress and handmade bricks. Garconniere is now a bar, and glassed dining room overlooks courtyard. Menu of award-winning dishes of Cajun and Creole cuisine. Open daily, L, 11 A.M.–2 P.M.; D, 6–10 P.M.; Sun. jazz brunch, 10:30 A.M.–2 P.M.

Mulate's Restaurant. 325 Mills Ave., Breaux Bridge (318–332–4648). Authentic Cajun restaurant with casual dining in family atmosphere. Specialties include stuffed crab, stuffed mushrooms, fried catfish. Live Cajun music daily, 8–11 P.M. Continuous serving, 7 A.M.–10:30 P.M., Mon.–Sat., 11 A.M.–10:30 P.M., Sun. AE, MC, V.

Patout's. 1846 Center St., New Iberia (318–365–5206). Combining 3 generations of expertise in Creole cookery with local seafood, the restaurant is unmatched in fine Creole culinary arts. Restored 1920s structure with ceiling fans, stained-glass windows, and authentic New Orleans bar. L, 11 A.M.–2 P.M., Mon.–Fri.; D, 5–10 P.M., Mon.–Sat. All major credit cards.

Ralph and Kacoo's Seafood Restaurant. 7110 Airline Hwy., Baton Rouge (504–356–2361). Lousiana seafood restaurant seating more than 500, and serving a wide variety of Gulf specialties. Open Mon.–Thurs., 11:30 A.M.–2 P.M. and 5–10 P.M.; Fri., 11 A.M.–2 P.M. and 5–10:30 P.M., Sat., 5–10 P.M.; and Sun., 11:30 A.M.–9 P.M. AE, MC, V.

THE TEXAS COAST

Port Arthur to Galveston

Exploring the Texas coast from northeast to southwest, the first major stop is Galveston. Consider, however, beginning where Texas begins, at Lake Sabine. One of the best sailing lakes in Texas, it's also renowned for freshwater fishing at its northern end and saltwater fishing near its outpour into the gulf. Port Arthur provides access via a bridge to 3,500-acre Pleasure Island. You'll find four fishing piers, picnic and camping areas, playgrounds, and marinas here, plus an outdoor amphitheater with a full summer schedule of productions and the Pleasure Island Hotel. For information, contact the Port Arthur Convention and Visitors Bureau, 3401 Cultural Center Dr., Port Arthur, TX 77642 (409–985–7822).

Swinging on to the coast via TX 87, don't miss Sartin's Restaurant in Sabine Pass. This Texas institution is known for its barbecued crab and its fresh-fish dinners and is open daily from 11 A.M. to 9 P.M. (409–971–2158).

Next stop is the 15,000-acre Sea Rim State Park, the third-largest in the state and the only one with both a beach unit and a pristine marsh unit. If you don't want to canoe into the wetlands, a 3,640-foot boardwalk covers a smaller marsh area behind the dunes, and there are campsites, restrooms, and an outstanding interpretive center. Egrets, herons, alligators, wild geese, and ducks are here in abundance. For information, contact Sea Rim State Park, Box 1066, Sabine Pass, TX 77655 (409–971–2559 or 971–2781).

Unless wiped out by recent storms, TX 87 flirts with the edge of the gulf as it continues southwest from Sea Rim to Bolivar, where you can catch a free ferry to Galveston. This is one of the best drives in the state, and picnics on the open beach are memorable. If you prefer a seafood feast, try the Stingaree Restaurant, 12 miles east of the Bolivar Ferry in Crystal Beach (409–684–2731).

Beyond Gilchrist, TX 87 threads the length of the Bolivar Peninsula, and the beaches are open and unspoiled, much like those of the Padres farther south on the coast. Cars are permitted to drive on the sand—convenient for some but dangerous to small children and sunbathers. Another warning: Riding the free ferry to Galveston is scenic and fun—bring some bread to feed the gulls—but on weekends the lines of waiting cars often stretch for miles.

Galveston

Discovered by the Spanish in 1528, this sliver of sand some 60 miles south of Houston has had a colorful past. Pirate Jean Lafitte used it as home base, and many still search for his treasure, reputed to be buried and lost in the island's sand. Soon after the Republic of Texas was established in 1836, Galveston applied for a city charter, and it quickly became the prime point of entry for colonists. By the 1880s its streets were lined with magnificent homes and its docks heavy with cotton bales, grain, and supplies for and from the ever-expanding economy of Texas. Its main business district centered on the Strand, one block from the bay, which soon became known as the Wall Street of the Southwest.

In 1900 a killer hurricane wiped away the city and more than 6,000 of its citizens, leaving the 32-mile-long sandbar in shambles. Realizing that Galveston was in the gulf's hurricane alley, the islanders began construction of a massive seawall as a bulwark against the relentless and unpredictable storms. The land behind the seawall then was raised with sand dredged from nearby channels and bayous, 17 feet on the south side of the city and 6 feet near the bay. The first seawall was less than 4 miles long; today it extends more than 10 miles and provides the longest continuous sidewalk in the world.

Today, Galveston is again in renaissance. Massive restorations have revitalized the Strand neighborhood, and new hotels and condominium projects line Seawall Boulevard. There are beaches galore, historic sites and homes to visit, outstanding and unusual museums, plenty of fishing, and a variety of lodgings and restaurants. Plan at least two days here, more if possible. There is plenty for "swinging singles" to enjoy, but the entire island is geared for family entertainment.

PRACTICAL INFORMATION FOR GALVESTON

HOW TO GET THERE. By plane. The *Galveston Limousine Service* (765–5288 or 713–223–2256, from Houston) runs shuttle vans between Galveston and Hobby Airport and Houston Intercontinental Airport approximately every 1½ hours. Time between destinations ranges from 1½ to 3 hours because of intermediate stops. A personal car is recommended, and all national rental-car agencies are represented at both airports; most have agencies in Galveston.

By car. Officially, Galveston is 51 mi. south of Houston via I-45. A double causeway connects the mainland with the island. On the eastern end, Galveston is accessed by TX 87 and the Bolivar ferry, on the western end by a toll bridge that spans San Luis Pass. Approximate driving times: from Corpus Christi, 4 hours; Houston, 1 hour; Dallas, 6 hours; San Antonio, 5 hours.

By bus. Call *Texas Bus Lines,* 765–7731.

TOURIST INFORMATION. The *Galveston Convention and Visitors Bureau* is located at 2106 Seawall Blvd., Galveston, TX 77550 (763–4311; 800–351–4236, in TX; 800–351–4237, outside TX). It is open daily. The *Strand Visitors Center,* operated by the Galveston Historical Foundation, is open daily, 2016 Strand, Galveston, TX 77550 (765–7834 or 713–488–5942). Make this your first stop when touring the city. They offer numerous free brochures and suggestions on historical sightseeing, portable cassette recorders for audio-walking tours (fee), and an activity-guide book for children (fee). The *Galveston Chamber of Commerce,* 621 Moody, Suite 300, Galveston, TX 77550 (763–5326), is another source for advance information.

TELEPHONES. Galveston's area code is 409. You need not dial the area code if it is the same as the one from which you are calling. Dial 1 first if you are calling outside the city to other 409 areas. For information, dial 1411. In case of emergency, dial 911.

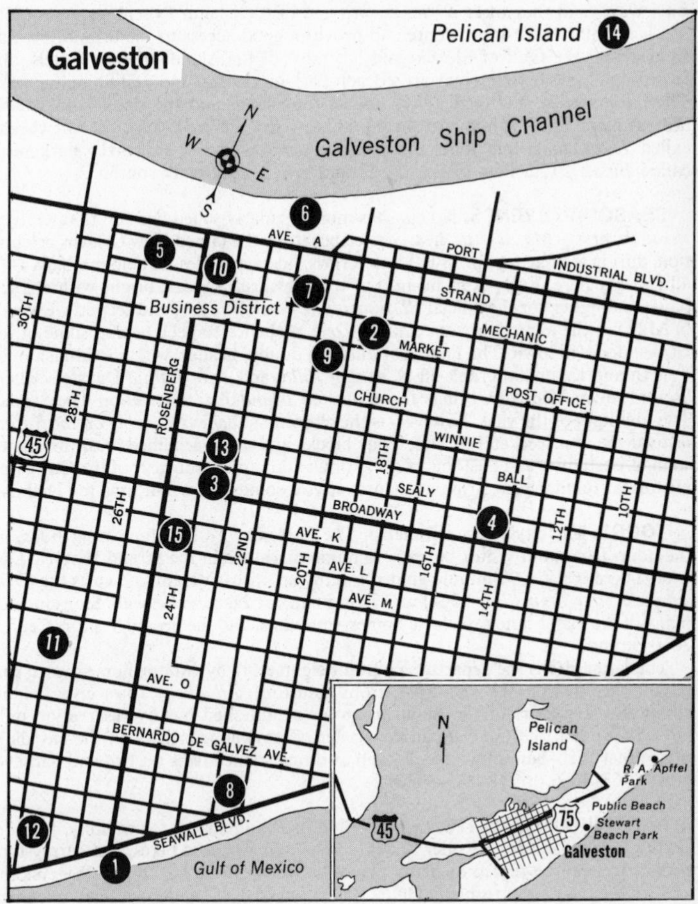

Points of Interest

American National Insurance Co. Tower, 2
Ashton Villa, 3
Bishop's Palace, 4
Center for Transportation and Commerce, 5
The Elissa and The Colonel, 6
Fishing Jetty, 1
Galveston Arts Center. 7
Galveston Convention and Visitors Bureau, 8
Grand Opera House, 9
Kempner Park, 11
Menard Park, 12
Rosenberg Library, 13
Seawolf Park, 14
Strand Historic District, 10
Sweeney-Royston House, 15

HOW TO GET AROUND. The city is easy to navigate. Most streets running east and west are labeled alphabetically (Avenues A, B, & O½, for example), and those going north and south are numbered. Seawall and Broadway are the primary length-of-the-island arterials—I–45 swings onto Broadway at the island end of the causeway—and they meet at the eastern end of the island. Rosenberg Ave. (25th St.) is a major north-south route and provides good access to the Strand. Seawall Blvd. fronts the Gulf of Mexico and has most of the island's hotels, motels, and recreational toys between Stewart's Beach Park on the east and 81st St. on the west. The harbor is on the north (bay) side of the island, and the smaller boat basin around piers 19–22 is home to shrimp boats, party fishing boats, a paddlewheeler called *The Colonel* that tours the bay, and a restored and seaworthy barkentine called *Elissa.* From Pier 19–22, the Strand is a 2-block walk south.

SEASONAL EVENTS. No city has more regularly scheduled fun than Galveston. **Feb.** brings *Mardi Gras,* nearly as elaborate as the famed New Orleans celebration, during the ten days prior to Lent. Krews, floats, parades, doubloons, balls—it's all lavishly here. **Early Apr.** brings out the isle shrimp boats, bright with colored paper and lights, for the official *Blessing of the Fleet.* The first and second weekends in **May** are the annual *Historic Homes Tour,* a chance to peek behind some of the ritziest doors in town. The **Fourth of July** is a double-header, with an old-fashioned Fourth and ice cream crank-off at *Ashton Villa,* and *Jean Lafitte* Days elsewhere around town. **Mid-Nov.** brings the *Galveston Island Jazz Festival* on The Strand. The highlight of the year, however, is the charming *Dickens Evening on the Strand* festival the first weekend in **Dec.** Four blocks and more are filled with the sights, sounds, costumes, and customs of a Victorian Christmas, courtesy of the Galveston Historical Foundation. Bring a costume if you come to town in time for Dickens.

TOURS. The city's new rail metro, *The Galveston Trolley,* runs every hour, on the hour, from both visitor bureaus to numerous stops in the Strand Historic District. There is also a 90-minute guided tour by an open-air tram known as the *Treasure Isle Tour Train* (765–9564) which originates at 21st and Seawall. Stops include many of the major hotels, historic homes, museums, and the Strand Visitors Center, 2010 Strand.

The latter also is the departure point for sightseeing by antique horse-drawn carriage (765–7834 or 713–488–5942, from Houston). *All About Town* gives 2-hour comprehensive tours of the island in an air-conditioned bus by reservation only (765–7834), and the *Colonel* paddlewheeler offers 2-hour cruises on the bay daily in summer, Fri.–Sun. in winter, as well as dinner-dance trips on Fri. and Sat. evenings (763–4666 or 713–280–3980).

PARTICIPANT SPORTS. Seawall Blvd. is headquarters for walking, jogging, skating, and bike riding. Roller skates, single- and 10-speed bikes, and surrey-type pedal carts can be rented at many places between 6th and 20th Sts. Waterskiing and windsurfing are possible in Offats Bayou, off 61st St., and horses can be rented for west beach rides at Sandy Hoof Stables, FM 3005 between 7 and 8 Mile Rds. You'll find free tennis courts at Menard Park, Seawall Blvd. between 27th and 28th Sts.; fee tennis at the private Galveston Racquet Club, 83rd and Airport (765/744–3651). There are two golf courses. Pirates Golf Course, 1700 Snydor Lane, west of Stewart Rd. (765/744–2366), is 18 holes and public; The Galveston Country Club, 9 mi. west of Stewart Rd. (765/737–2040), is private.

BEACHES. Galveston has more than 32 mi. of beaches, so you can choose between concessions-crowds and extreme solitude. Best bet if you have small children is either *Stewart's Beach Park,* at the end of Broadway on the east end of the island, or one of the three *beach pocket parks* run by Galveston County off FM 3005 (extension of Seawall Blvd.) on the western end of the island. All have changing rooms, showers, concessions, picnic areas, parking (fee), and lifeguards. Stewart's is far more crowded and commercial; the pocket parks more natural, with boardwalks through the dunes and an unspoiled landscape.

There also are numerous tidal beaches tucked between the jetties along Seawall Blvd. Most are more convenient than pleasant. A far better choice is the newly refurbished *R. A. Apffel Park,* at the end of East Beach. Another possibility is *Galves-*

ton Island State Park, west of downtown at the intersection of FM 3005 and 13 Mile Rd. In addition to picnicking, beaching, and camping here, there's also a series of nature trails and observation platforms for birding on the north side of the park facing Galveston Bay.

Vehicular traffic is restricted on the beaches year-round. Parking lots are provided, some free, some fee.

HISTORIC SITES AND MUSEUMS. The many historic homes as well as the Strand district are living museums. There are more than 500 structures of historical significance and three historic districts on the island. Brochures detailing walking and biking tours are available at the Strand Visitors Center. For a short stroll or windshield tour, try Sealy, Ball, and Winnie streets between 12th and 19th Sts.

The Strand is downtown on the bay side of the island between 20th and 25th Sts. The center of Galveston's commerce during the golden years of the late 19th century, it's now a national historic landmark and has one of the finest concentrations of iron-front commercial buildings in the country. Most have been restored and now house eateries, galleries, businesses, shops, etc.

Three blocks north, at 2020 Postoffice (Ave. F), is the **1894 Grand Opera House,** now back in gleaming condition and host to a constant stream of dramatic and musical events. Self-guided tours are available; performance tickets can be reserved at box office (765–1894 or 713–480–1894).

Also well worth seeing is **St. Joseph's Church,** 2206 Ave. K, built by German immigrants in 1859 and noted for its rich Victorian Gothic interior. Tours are available through the Galveston Historical Foundation.

Ashton Villa, 2328 Broadway (762–3933), is a red-brick Italianate beauty built before the Civil War. Tours begin in the restored carriage house with a multimedia presentation on the 1900 storm. Children with adults are welcome; the Victorian dollhouse in one of the bedrooms fascinates them. The **Antique Auto Museum,** 1309 Tremont (765–5801) shows vintage Mercedes to Model Ts in a 20,000 sq. ft. showroom, more than 90 rare and beautiful exhibits.

The **Bishop's Palace,** 1402 Broadway (762–2475), was designed by noted architect Nicholas Clayton, opened in 1893, and now is considered among the top 100 homes in America for architectural significance. Design aside, it's a lavish mansion that gives a penetrating glimpse of what upper-class life was like in Galveston's heyday; an outstanding tour.

The 1839 **Samuel May Williams Home,** 3601 Bernardo de Galvez (Ave. P) (765–1839), is one of the two oldest structures surviving in the city. Built in 1839 from prefab parts shipped from Maine, its rooms have been furnished to the 1854 period and tell the story of the Williams family, complete with audio dramas.

Completed at a cost of $5.5 million in 1982, the inventive **Center for Transportation and Commerce** traces the island's growth and heritage from the mid-1600s to the present with a series of light and sound shows unequaled in America. It's housed in what was the old train depot, and the waiting room has been recreated with life-size sculptures of travelers frozen in a moment of 1932. Visitors can listen to their conversations before moving outside to tour an assortment of steam locomotives, railroad cars, etc. Open daily, except Thanksgiving and Dec. 25, at Shearn Moody Plaza, 25th and Strand (765–5700).

The *Elissa* is a towering survivor of the Age of Sail, the only tall ship in Texas. It is the oldest ship in Lloyd's Register. A film, public tours, and exhibits tell the story, and a shoreside playground delights small children. Built in 1877 and restored by the Galveston Historical Foundation between 1975 and 1981, *Elissa* sails daily on guided tours (765–7834).

ACCOMMODATIONS. Lodgings come in many guises in this beach city. From bed-and-breakfast to condominiums, swanky hotels to vacation houses on the sand, there's something for everyone. Conventions are becoming big business here year-round, so don't just drop in expecting to find a room at your hotel of choice. Festival weekends often are sell-outs also. Be aware that there is a 13% combination room and sales tax and that reservations are strongly suggested. Rates often dip in winter and on weekdays; those quoted are for the peak summer season, double occupancy, European plan (no meals): *Deluxe,* $120–$160; *Expensive,* $90–$120; *Moderate,* $60–$90; *Inexpensive,* under $60.

For information on condominiums, bed-and-breakfast lodgings (many in Victorian-style homes), and beach or bay rental homes, contact the Galveston Convention and Visitors Bureau (see Tourist Information).

Deluxe

The San Luis on Galveston Isle. 5222 Seawall Blvd. (at 53rd St.), Galveston, TX 77550 (744–1500; 800–392–5937, TX; 800–445–0090, outside TX). This $20-million hotel has 244 well-appointed rooms with balconies overlooking the gulf and the outdoor courtyard with its swaying palms and serpentine swimming pool. They've even hauled in sand to create a beach beyond the seawall across the street. One of the newest luxury hotels in town, it's popular with the CEO-conference trade and is headquarters for the annual Mardi Gras celebration. Condos are also available.

The Tremont House. 2300 Ship's Mechanic Row, Galveston, TX 77550 (763–0300; 713–480–8201, from Houston; 800–874–2300). One of the most elegant hotels in Texas, this historical restoration has 108 rooms, complete with specially designed furniture from Baker, butler at the door, and antique ambience. The Strand is one street away, the staff parks your car at no extra charge, and the lobby with its evening pianist and the adjacent restaurant are two of the city's best. Tremont shares the chef of the popular Wentletrap Restaurant, across the back alley and directly accessible from the hotel.

Expensive

Flagship Hotel. 2501 Seawall Blvd., Galveston, TX 77550 (762–9000; 800–392–6542, in TX; 800–231–7128, outside TX). Although the 220 rooms and suites of this hotel may not be the quietest in town, they certainly have the best view (most have balconies), and the sound of the waves will help lull you to sleep. The hotel sits on its own pier extending into the gulf from the heart of the seawall's action district. Although the hotel overlooks beaches, the swimming is best in the hotel pool.

Hotel Galvez. 2024 Seawall Blvd., Galveston, TX 77550 (765–7721; 713–480–2640, from Houston). Although many of the rooms tend to be small, they are well appointed, and the vintage atmosphere of this superbly restored island queen sets it apart. The dining room and lounge usually have crowds, and the indoor and outdoor pools provide year-round swimming.

Key Largo Resort Hotel. 5400 Seawall Blvd., Galveston, TX 77550 (744–5000; 713–480–2801, from Houston; 800–833–0120, in TX). Well priced and appointed, this 150-room resort hotel overlooks the gulf, and its show lounge, Hemingway's, is one of Galveston's hottest night spots. Expect a 3000-sq.-ft. swimming pool, plus hot tub, exercise room, sauna, lighted tennis court and putting green. Junior suites with small parlors are available at increased price.

Moderate

Seawall Blvd. is lined with motels, most of them charging between $60 and $80 double per night. Ask about amenities, complimentary services, swimming pools, and multinight or family packages, and weekly rates when reserving. Among the best are:

The Commodore. 37th and Seawall Blvd., Drawer N, Galveston, TX 77552 (763–2375; 800–231–9921, outside TX).

Gaido's Motor Inn. 3800 Seawall Blvd., Galveston, TX 77550 (762–9625; 713–488–7005, from Houston).

La Quinta Motor Inn. 1402 Seawall Blvd., Galveston, TX 77550 (763–1224 or 800–531–5900).

Ramada Inn. 59th & Seawall Blvd., Galveston, TX 77552 (740–1261 or 800–2–RAMADA).

TraveLodge. 23rd and Seawall Blvd., Galveston, TX 77550 (765–9535; 800–255–3050, nationally; 800–268–3330, Canada).

RESTAURANTS. From fish and chips on the seawall to French cuisine amid damask and crystal, Galveston's restaurants tend to feature fresh seafood prepared a variety of ways. Shrimp and oyster lovers will be in heaven, but most of the following offer a varied menu as well. Price classifications are based on the cost of an average three-course dinner for one; beverages, taxes, and tips would be extra. *Expensive,* $20 and up; *Moderate,* $10–$20; *Inexpensive,* less than $10. The following are among the best in town in their price categories.

On the Strand

Competition keeps the prices low and quality high in this historic district.

The Wentletrap. *Expensive.* 2301 Strand (765–5545). Memorable Continental dining in an elegant and historic setting; one of the best restaurants in Texas. Sunday brunch is exceptional. Jacket for men required at dinner. Mon.–Sat., 11:30 A.M.–2:30 P.M., 6–10 P.M.; Sun., 11:30 A.M.–2:30 P.M. Reservations strongly advised. AE, DC, MC, V.

Lone Star Steak House. *Moderate.* 2122 Strand (762–2200). Texas-style steaks with more trimmings than most tummies can take. Mon.–Fri., 11 A.M.–10 P.M.; Sat.–Sun., noon–10 P.M. AE, DC, MC, V.

Fullen's Waterwall. *Inexpensive–Moderate.* 2110 Strand (765–6787). Tasty steaks, homemade soups, salad, hamburgers, etc., in a deli atmosphere, plus an outside courtyard with waterfall wall for summer dining al fresco. Open daily 11 A.M.–5 P.M. AE, MC, V.

Nash D'Amico's Pasta and Clam Bar. *Inexpensive–Moderate.* 2328 Strand (763–6500). If you love seafood, pasta, and desserts, you are in triple trouble here; all are outstanding. Mon.–Thurs. 11 A.M.–10 P.M.; Fri.–Sat.; 11 A.M.–11 P.M.; Sun., noon–10 P.M. AE, MC.

Scattered around Town

Maximilian's. *Expensive.* 5222 Seawall, in the San Luis Hotel (744–1500, ext. 7326). Formal—men will need jackets—and known for its outstanding and inventive Continental offerings, this is the only serious competition for the Wentletrap. Mon.–Sat., 6:30–11 P.M. AE, DC, MC, V.

Dinner on the Diner. *Moderate–Expensive.* In the Center for Transportation and Commerce, 25th and Strand (763–4759). Tasty lunches and dinners are served railroad-style in a restored Silver Hours Club Car, circa 1940. Reservations necessary. Mon.–Sat., 11 A.M.–2 P.M., dinner from 5 P.M.; Sun. brunch during special events and summer. AE, CB, DC, MC, V.

Gaido's Seafood Restaurant. *Moderate–Expensive.* 39th and Seawall (762–9625). Outstanding pisces here; check to see what's fresh off the boat. If it's oyster season, these usually are the tastiest in town. Mon.–Thurs., 11:30 A.M.–9 P.M.; Fri., noon–10 P.M.; Sun., Noon–9 P.M. AE, MC, V.

Benno's. *Inexpensive–Moderate.* 1200 Seawall (762–4621). For fresh crab, crawfish, shrimp, etc., when you don't want to dress up or even change out of your bathing suit, this is a good bet. Open Sun.–Thurs., 11 A.M.–9 P.M.; Fri. and Sat., to 10 P.M. MC, V.

Hill's Pier 19. *Inexpensive.* 20th and Wharf Sts. (763–7087). Near the *Elissa,* this cafeteria-style café serves fresh fish, salads, gumbo, and some of the best poorboys in Texas. The roof dining deck overlooks the small boat harbor. Open daily. Winter: 10:30 A.M.–8 P.M. Summer: 10:30 A.M.–9 P.M., until 10 P.M. weekends. AE, CB, DC, MC, V.

Shrimp & Stuff, #1. *Inexpensive.* 3901 Avenue O (763–2805). When you are beach-weary and hungry for a good shrimp poorboy or platter, come here. Mon.–Wed., 10:30 A.M.–7:30 P.M.; Thurs.–Fri., 10:30 A.M.–8:30 P.M.; Sat., 11 A.M.–8:30 P.M.; Sun., 11 A.M.–7 P.M. AE, DC, MC, V.

Rockport

Tucked within 20,000 acres of landlocked bays and graced with windswept oak trees and a curving beach along Aransas Bay, this small town of approximately 6,000 is a fishing and birding paradise 35 miles northeast of Corpus Christi via TX 35. Also a growing artists' colony, Rockport sports a number of galleries and boutiques, and a small but active art museum that catches a number of major traveling exhibits.

Following Fulton Beach Road brings you to the newly restored Fulton Mansion, a historic home operated by the Texas Parks and Wildlife Department. Built in the mid-1870s in French Second Empire styling, it is furnished to the period; guided tours are given Wednesday through Sunday.

A drive north of town on TX 35 brings you first to 8,700-foot Copano Bay State Fishing Pier and Goose Island State Recreation Area. The pier is lighted for night fishing, and the park has camping, picnicking, fishing, children's play area, and the "Big Tree," officially the largest live oak in the state. Some 38 miles north of town is Aransas National Wildlife Refuge, a naturalist's paradise. Birding is outstanding here; the endangered whooping cranes arrive in November and leave in March, and some 350 other species of songbirds and waterfowl winter here. An interpretive center is open daily, and 16 miles of road roam through 54,829 acres of blackjack oaks, grasslands, and tidal marsh. For boat tours to see the whooping cranes, inquire at the Chamber of Commerce (see below). Two of the tour companies offering such trips are *Bay Princess* (512–729–4975) and *Captain Ted's* (512–729–9589).

Dotted with mom-and-pop lodgings, neat motels, and luxury homes and condominiums, Rockport is a good destination, particularly for winter Texans. For information, contact the Chamber of Commerce, Box 1055, Rockport, TX 78382 (512–729–6445; 800–242–0071, in TX; 800–826–6441 outside TX). Special annual events include the Fulton Oysterfest the first weekend in March; the Rockport Art Festival on the July 4 weekend; and Seafair on the weekend before Columbus Day in October.

Corpus Christi

The pivot of the "Texas Riviera," this clean and inviting city of 276,000 looks as if it belongs in California. Palm trees, slowly recovering from the 1984 Christmas freeze, line Shoreline Drive, and downtown literally begins at the edge of sparkling and vast Corpus Christi Bay. A two-mile promenade stretches from the convention center and museums of Bayfront Plaza at the north end of Shoreline Drive to beyond Magee Beach on the south, ideal for pedaling a surrey, roller skating, or just strolling. Everything from sailboats to water trikes can be rented at the water-recreation basin next to the Peoples Street T-head marina.

Corpus Christi is the kind of place that turns out for band concerts in the park on Sundays and to watch the yacht-club sailboat races late on Wednesday afternoons. Casual outdoor living is a way of life here.

Corpus Christi Bay was named by the Spanish in 1519, and the town acquired the name when a trading post was established about mid-bay in 1839. Today, Corpus Christi's port is the ninth largest in the nation, a major outlet for the state's huge cotton, oil, grain, and chemical industries. Yet it is consistently rated one of the least polluted cities in the nation. Pollution controls are stringent, but they get a little help from Mother Nature. A steady offshore breeze keeps the air clear, and because no rivers empty silt into the bay, the waters are the cleanest along the coast.

Blessed with an average temperature of 71 degrees, 255 days of sunshine, and less than 28 inches of rainfall annually, Corpus Christi has a tropical flavor. Overall, it's a low-key, friendly place with a rapidly climbing recreation and entertainment level. Two new major hotels have brought some needed glitz to the bayfront, and new restaurants seem to open monthly.

Exploring the coastal bend territory around the city takes you to the artist-and-fishing colony of Rockport, a ramshackle fishing community called Port Aransas on the northern tip of Mustang Island, and the wild scenery of North Padre Island National Seashore. You also can jaunt in less than an hour to the famous King Ranch, southwest of town.

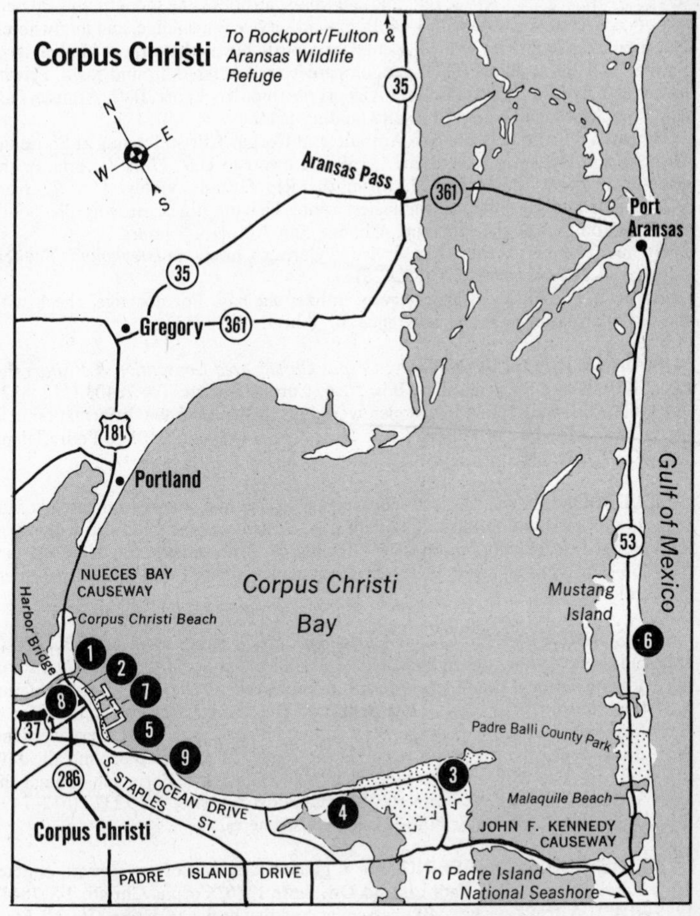

Points of Interest:

1) Bayfront Arts and Sciences Park, including the Corpus Christi Museum, Art Museum of South Texas, and Harbor Playhouse
2) Bayfront Plaza Auditorium and Convention Center
3) Corpus Christi Naval Air Station
4) Corpus Christi State University
5) Memorial Coliseum
6) Mustang Island State Park
7) T-heads and L-head Marina (off Shoreline Blvd.)
8) Heritage Park
9) Cole Park

PRACTICAL INFORMATION FOR CORPUS CHRISTI

HOW TO GET THERE. By plane. Corpus Christi International Airport is served by *American, Continental,* and *Southwest* airlines. The modern and efficient airport is west of downtown on I-44. Limo-van service is available, and many hotels and motels have pickup service. Rental cars available at the airport include *Avis, Budget,* and *Hertz.* Local rental-car companies are scattered around town. Private planes also fly into Aransas County Airport north of Rockport. Both Aransas Pass and Port Aransas have paved public landing fields.

By car. I-37 runs between San Antonio and Corpus Christi, ending at Shoreline Drive. From Houston, use either U.S. 59 southwest to U.S. 77 in Victoria, or the close-to-the-coast route, TX 35. From the Rio Grande Valley, U.S. 77 from Brownsville and Harlingen is the fastest route. Driving times: Brownsville–South Padre Island, 3.5 hours; Houston, 4 hours; San Antonio, 3 hours.

By bus. There is excellent bus service to Corpus Christi via *Greyhound.* The terminal is at 702 N. Chaparral (882–2516).

By boat. The intracoastal waterway utilizes the bay. For dockage, check with the city marina office at the Lawrence St. T-head (882–7333).

TOURIST INFORMATION. The *Corpus Christi Area Convention & Visitors Bureau,* 1201 North Shoreline Dr., Box 2664, Corpus Christi, TX 78403 (512–882–5603; 800–221–SURF in TX), is open weekdays, 8:30 A.M.–5 P.M. Information centers at 6667 Hwy. 77 in Nueces River Park (241–1464) and 9401 S. Padre Island Dr. (937–6711) and open daily, 8:30 A.M.–6 P.M.

TELEPHONES. The area code for Corpus Christi and surrounding area is 512. You do not need to dial the area code if it is the same as the one from which you are calling. For information, dial 1411 locally or, from outside the 512 area, dial 512–555–1212. For all emergencies (fire, ambulance, police), dial the general emergency number 911.

SEASONAL EVENTS. Corpus Christi becomes a pirate town with *Buccaneer Days* at the end of **Apr.**—even the mayor walks the plank—and the *Texas Jazz Festival* featuring national headliners is on a mid-**July** weekend. *Bayfest,* an annual family festival, keeps things busy in late **Sept.** and **Dec.** brings *Harbor Lights.* Nearby Port Aransas on Mustang Island hosts a fishing tournament almost every weekend from **June–Sept.,** the biggest of which is the *Deep Sea Roundup* around the July 4th weekend. The latter attracts more than 600 contestants. For a list, contact the Port Aransas Chamber of Commerce, Box 356, Port Aransas, TX 78373 (512–749–5919; 800–242–3084 in TX; 800–221–9198 elsewhere).

TOURS AND SIGHTSEEING. For a guided look at Corpus Christi, contact *Gray Line Tours,* 5488 S. Padre Island Dr., Suite 1386, Corpus Christi, TX 78411 (993–7042). A triple-decked, 400-passenger paddlewheeler, *Captain Clark's Flagship,* 202 Shore Dr., Portland, TX 78374 (643–7128) has harbor and bay cruises, plus day and moonlight trips with live bands; it anchors at the People's Street T-head on the bayfront.

If it is winter, catch the *Lucky Day* at Rockport's harbor to see the rare whooping cranes at the Aransas Wildlife Refuge (729–6351; 800–852–FISH). Half-day shrimping trips usually are available from either the Rockport or Fulton Beach marinas. Check with the Rockport Chamber of Commerce (512–729–6445; 800–242–0071 in TX; 800–826–6441 elsewhere).

It's fun to explore **Port Aransas,** particularly if you catch the free (and very short) ferry ride from the mainland via TX 361. This quiet fishing village has hit the touristic big time lately, attracting condos, resorts, and crowds. Drop in at the Tarpon Inn for a look at the autographed fish scales that line its lobby walls—the restaurants and lounge out back are recommended—and wander around the docks. Shrimp boats unload their catches here, providing an interesting look at a coastal industry. You'll find good fishing yourself either on a party-boat cruise or from the new 1,240-ft. fishing pier that juts out into the gulf.

The 826,000-acre **King Ranch** is 40 mi. southwest of Corpus Christi via U.S. 77. Stop first at the Kingsville Visitor Center, 101 N. 3rd St., Box 1562, Kingsville, TX 78363 (592–8516) for a brochure and directions on how to reach the 12-mi. loop that shows off the ranch. Cassettes (fee) are available. If time permits, stop at the John E. Conner Museum at Texas A&I University in Kingsville.

A fun and nostalgic train excursion, the **Tex-Mex Express,** runs between Corpus Christi and Laredo on the Mexican border. Inaugurated in early 1986, it's the first passenger service between those two cities since 1947. At press time service had been suspended, but operators hope to reinstate it in the near future. For details call: 289–1818 in Corpus Christi; 722–6411 in Laredo; 800–221–3182 in TX.

NATIONAL AND STATE PARKS. Padre Island National Seashore covers 80.5 mi. of a slim barrier island that stretches 113 mi. from Corpus Christi almost to the Mexican border. The human-made Mansfield Cut divides the island into North and South Padre. Considered by environmentalists to be the most outstanding stretch of natural seashore left in America, the national seashore has a large day-use area and pavilion at Malaquite Beach, a ¾-mi. nature trail through grasslands, camping and picnic areas, and miles of undeveloped beach. Conventional cars can be driven on the beach for about 12 mi. beyond the end of the road; four-wheel drive is a necessity to go the length of North Padre Island. The shelling and solitude are outstanding on the most southern beaches. From Corpus Christi, take South Padre Island Dr. over the J. F. Kennedy Causeway and swing south on Park Rd. 22. Contact Superintendent, 9405 S. Padre Island Dr., Corpus Christi, TX 78418 (937–2621); ranger station, 949–8173; surf and driving conditions, 949–8175).

Mustang Island State Park. Mustang Island seems to be the northern extension of North Padre, so closely linked are these strands. Now bustling with condo development, Mustang's beauty can best be enjoyed at this 3,704-acre state park that fronts directly on the gulf. Swimming, picnicking, showers, rest rooms, etc., are here, and Port Aransas is 14 mi. north on the island's only road. Box 326, Port Aransas, TX 78373 (749–5246).

FISHING. Game fish, often of record size, thrive in the gulf waters offshore from both Mustang and North Padre islands. The red snapper banks lie 40 mi. out, but there's plenty of good fishing closer in. Party-boat trips for sailfish, blue and white marlin, tuna, jewfish, jack, dorado, gafftop, sheepshead, black drum, and pompano are easily arranged on the docks at Port Aransas.

The bays offer year-round fishing for redfish, speckled trout, sand trout, and flounder. Bay fishing trips run from marinas along Corpus Christi's bayfront and from the boat basin in Rockport, or you can drop a line at any number of places in town. Best bets: the barge dock next to the art museum, at the Channel View parks at each end of the Harbor Bridge, at the lighted breakwater at Magee Beach, and at the lighted pier off Cole Park. Gulf surf fishing is also popular from any island beach. Licenses are usually necessary and can be bought at most bait–tackle–sporting goods stores and at convenience stores.

BEACHES. Gulf beaches in Texas are public, and many allow automobile traffic. If you don't want to risk tire marks on your anatomy, head for *Mustang Island State Park* or the *Padre Island National Seashore;* both restrict cars to parking lots. Mustang Island also has *Nueces County Park,* with special swimming and surfing areas, fishing jetties, rest rooms, showers, ranger and first aid and *J. P. Luby Youth Park,* with a pavilion and specially-designed surfer's pier. The latter is on Access Road 3A-1 from Park Rd. 53.

In Corpus Christi, families usually head for *Magee Beach,* downtown on Shoreline Drive; it's shallow and fun for children. Sailors and surfers head for *Corpus Christi Beach* (also called North Beach), a 300-ft.-wide stretch of sand that goes for 1.5 mi. No driving is allowed on the beach. Concessionaires rent everything from umbrellas to catamarans (lessons available), and there are new rest rooms and picnic areas. Numerous motels line the back of the beach.

ACCOMMODATIONS. The convention and visitors bureau has an extensive list of accommodations in Corpus Christi, Rockport, North Padre, and Port Aransas. *Sand Dollar Hospitality,* 3605 Mendenhall, Corpus Christi, TX 76415 (853–1222), arranges bed-and-breakfast accommodations. *Padre Isles Rentals* (Box 8809, Corpus Christi, TX 78412 (949–7036; 800–234–0117 in TX; 800–531–1030 U.S.) is a clearing house for condo rentals. The following listings will give some idea of what is available. All are air-conditioned and have free parking. Price categories, based on double-occupancy rates, peak season, European plan (no meals), are *Expensive,* $85–$110; *Moderate,* $65–$85. Ask about special packages. Be aware there is a 13% room/sales tax.

Corpus Christi Bayfront

The Marriott. *Expensive.* 707 N. Shoreline, Corpus Christi, TX 78401 (882–1700 or 800–228–9290). New and beautifully decorated, this 346-room hotel is across from the water recreation area at People's T-head marina. Its high-energy nightclub swings until 2 A.M.

The Wyndham. *Expensive.* 900 N. Shoreline, Corpus Christi, TX 78401 (887–1600 or 800–533–3131). The city's newest luxury hotel has 474 guest rooms with view balconies, pool with lounge, sundeck, health club, and the best Sun. brunch in town in its rooftop restaurant. Good nightclub also.

Holiday Inn-Emerald Beach. *Moderate–Expensive.* 1102 S. Shoreline, Corpus Christi, TX 78401 (883–5731 or 800–465–4329). Extremely popular with families, this 368-room hotel is adjacent to McGee Beach and has a heated pool, fun center, and two restaurants.

Royal Nueces Day's Hotel. *Moderate.* 601 N. Water, one block from Shoreline Dr., Corpus Christi, TX 78401 (888–4461 or 800–325–2525). Some of the 200 rooms are for nonsmokers, and there's a rooftop swimming pool plus dining, dancing, and entertainment nightly.

Sheraton Marina Inn. *Moderate.* 300 N. Shoreline, Box 2687, Corpus Christi, TX 78403 (883–5111 or 800–325–3535). Refurbished in 1984, this 175-room hotel has pool, valet service, and on the top floor, one of the city's most popular nightclubs.

Corpus Christi Beach

Villa del Sol Hotel Condominium. *Moderate–Expensive.* 3938 Surfside, Corpus Christi, TX 78402 (883–9748 or 800–242–3291). These 1-bedroom, 1-bath units on the beach have kitchens, and there are a pool, a laundry, and 3 spas.

Best Western-Sandy Shores Resort. *Moderate.* 3200 Surfside, Box 839, Corpus Christi, TX 78403 (883–7456 or 800–528–1234). One of the largest and nicest fronting on the sand, this 250-unit resort has two swimming pools, a guest-activities desk, saunas, restaurants, and a nightclub.

RESTAURANTS. Corpus Christi is not New Orleans or San Francisco, but its dining star is on the rise. An increasing number of young immigrants are bringing talent and taste to the city's restaurant scene, giving flair to the local seafood and more than a Texas twist to Mexican fare in particular. Those listed below are among the best in town and are listed according to the price of a complete dinner for one (drinks, tax, and tip not included). *Expensive,* $18 and up; *Moderate,* $10–$18; *Inexpensive,* under $10.

Expensive

Reflections. In the Wyndham Hotel, 900 N. Shoreline (887–1600). Seafood specialties are featured in this chic rooftop eatery with a panoramic view of bay water and city lights. D, Mon.–Sat. AE, DC, MC, V.

Uncle Chester's Old Crab House. 6810 Saratoga Blvd. (991–8730). Nothing on the menu except fresh seafood and fine steaks. Eat one or the other, or try one of the combination plates with steak, shrimp, lobster, or king crab. Nautical decor throughout. D, daily; Sun. brunch. AE, DC, MC, V.

Moderate

Baja Coast. 5253 S. Staples (992–3474). Fresh seafood grilled over a mesquite fire, plus an oyster bar and house specialties from the Baja region of Mexico. Fresh fish-market atmosphere with a piano accompaniment, and you can watch the chefs at work. D, daily. AE, DC, MC, V.

Lighthouse Bar & Grill. Lawrence St. T-head marina (883–3982). The view is swell—boats go swooping by almost within touching distance—and the inventive menu features fresh gulf seafood. Oyster bar too, in a Sausalito-café atmosphere. Open daily, 11–2 A.M. daily. AE, DC, MC, V.

Water Street Oyster Bar. 309 N. Water St. (881–9448). This high-tech but low-key eatery serves outstanding fresh seafood fixed the Cajun way. Fresh oysters a good bet here. Families as well as dating couples enjoy the lively atmosphere. Open daily, 11 A.M.–11 P.M. AE, MC, V.

Inexpensive

Five cafeterias offer excellent selection and low prices, nice when you have children in tow. One of the best is *Luby's,* which has two locations: 3217 S. Alameda (854–4373) and 5411 S. Padre Island Dr. (991–5761). Both are open from 10:45 A.M.–8 P.M., daily, have nonsmoking sections, and do not accept credit cards. Other good bets:

Casa de Roy. 5838 S. Staples (993–1911). Fajitas and homemade tortillas are house specialties, along with caldo, a hearty beef-and-vegetable soup. B, L, daily; D, Mon.–Sat. AE, MC, V.

Howard's Bar-B-Que. 200 N. Staples (882–0312). Locals consider this one of the best barbecue places in town. Open Mon.–Fri., 11 A.M.–5:30 P.M. No credit cards.

Rusty's Burgerfactory, Bakery & Bar. 1645 Airline (993–5000). Steaks and hamburgers from their own butcher shop (buns from their bakery too) are cooked to your order; then you add what you want from the condiments bar. Live entertainment on Fri. and Sat. evenings. Open daily, 11 A.M.–11 P.M. AE, MC, V.

South Padre Island

Discovered by a Spanish explorer in 1519 and named in honor of an early missionary, South Padre Island has been a retreat for beach-loving Texans for generations. The opening of the causeway from the mainland replaced a ferry service and brought the world here in 1954, and now the island enjoys an international reputation for its vast sandy beaches, good and well-priced accommodations, and great fishing. The beach is manicured daily, the shelling is excellent, and Mexico is just a splash away.

Separated from North Padre by the human-made Mansfield Cut, South Padre refers to both the small town and its long, narrow island. The Laguna Madre, the slender bay between the island and the mainland, cools off summer days and provides warming breezes during the winter, moderating the average annual temperature to a pleasant 74 degrees. Because the humidity usually is lower here than in the rest of the coast and southwest Texas, summer is high season. You'll find good weather and lower prices in spring and fall. Also be aware that Easter week and/or spring break is no time for the average traveler to come to the island. Thousands of college students from throughout the Midwest congregate here like lemmings for the rites of spring.

Connected to the mainland by the two-mile Queen Isabella Causeway, the developed area is less than a half mile wide and just under five miles long, a somewhat unsightly mix of highrise condos and hotels with strip business centers and small beach shacks. Beyond the northern limits of the town of South Padre Island lie some 30 miles of undeveloped beach, an isolated and commercially untouched stretch of sand. A land of crashing waves and 25-foot-high dunes, it is accessible by dune buggy and four-wheel drive; rentals and guided day trips can be arranged. Although conventional cars are permitted to drive on the gulfside beach, beware of being forced into the soft sand by high tide. Many rental-car companies will assess penalties for driving their cars on the beach.

Enroute to South Padre, stop in Port Isabel to see the historic lighthouse. Situated in the middle of the main street and noted as the state's

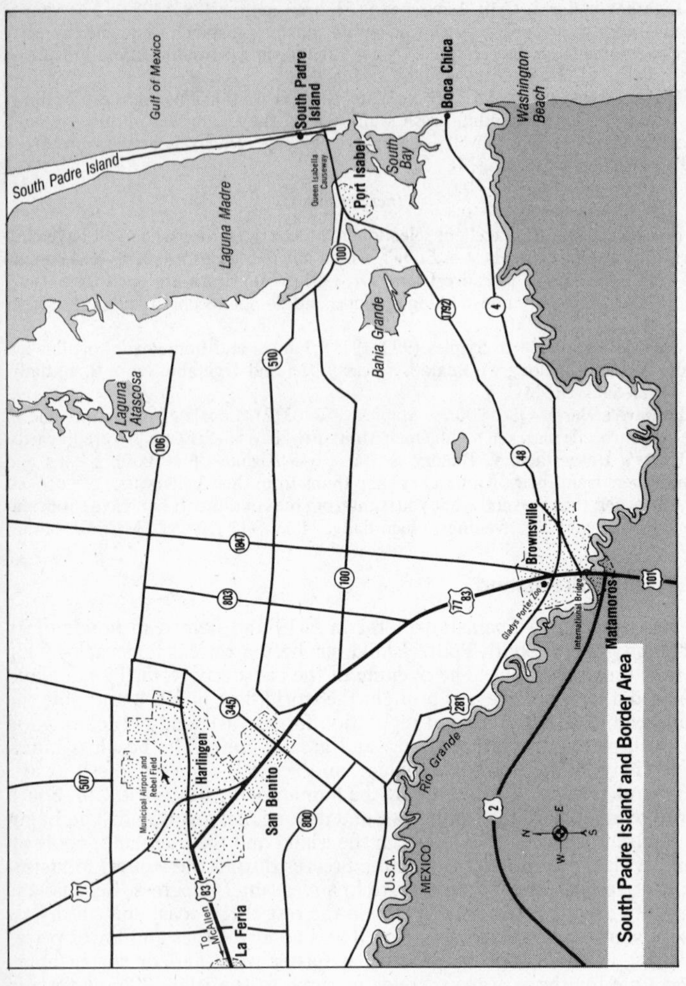

smallest historic site, the 60-feet-high lighthouse gives a grand view, not only of the Laguna Madre and South Padre but of the local (and mammoth) shrimp fleet. Dinner at the Yacht Club Hotel and Restaurant in Port Isabel, 700 Yturria St. (943–1301), is another custom.

The overriding reason to come to South Padre Island is to enjoy the endless beach. The area north of "hotel row" often is thick with sand dollars and other exotic shells, and the multiline breakers make for good body surfing. Two suggestions: there is natural oil seepage offshore, so wear an old bathing suit and bring liquid shampoo to clean the tar off your feet. Also bring some meat tenderizer, good for treating stings from the Portuguese man-of-wars that often float just offshore in the early fall.

PRACTICAL INFORMATION FOR SOUTH PADRE ISLAND

HOW TO GET THERE. By plane. Three international airports (Brownsville–South Padre Island, McAllen, and Harlingen) provide daily air service to the Rio Grande Valley. There is no commercial air service to the island proper. Rental cars are available at all three airports, as is bus service.

By car. Three major highways, U.S. 77, 83, and 281, lead to the Rio Grande Valley, which is the gateway to South Padre Island. From U.S. 77–83, take TX 100 to Port Isabel and then cross the causeway to the island.

TOURIST INFORMATION. The *South Padre Visitor and Convention Bureau* provides information on hotels, sightseeing, activities, fishing, etc. If you are already in town, stop at their building at 600 Padre Blvd. (761–6433). For advance information contact them at Box 3500, South Padre Island, TX 78597 (800–343–2368). Many South Padre Island events are planned by the South Padre Island Chamber of Commerce, Box 2098, South Padre Island, TX 78597 (943–2262).

TELEPHONES. The area code for South Padre Island and the Rio Grande Valley is 512. For information, dial 1411. For *police, fire department,* or *ambulance,* dial 761–2236 or 761–5454; for the *coast guard,* dial 761–2668; for poison control, dial 1–423–1224. The 911 emergency number is in effect; give it a try first.

HOW TO GET AROUND. Padre Boulevard, also known as Park Road 100, will take you right through the center of town. Parallel to it, and next to the shore is Gulf Blvd., running from Harbor St. to just south of the Bahia Mar Resort. Street maps are in the front of the local telephone book.

SEASONAL ACTIVITIES. *Give Your Sweetheart the Island* celebration kicks off the year's fun on the weekend closest to Valentine's Day in **Feb.** Early **May** brings the surfers to town for the annual *Boardsailing Blow-Out,* a series of contests and hijinks that test the best. Late **June** features annual windjammer and Hobie-Cat races among other special events, followed by a major fireworks display over the water on the **Fourth of July. August** is the *Texas International Fishing Tournament,* and **Oct.** brings the 3-day **Tarpon Fishing Classic,** followed by *Queen Isabella Days,* a community-wide festival. *Christmas by the Sea,* a 3-day festival in **Dec.,** includes a lighted boat parade and sandman building contest.

TOURS. The 250-ft. *Le Mistral* operates gambling cruises Wed.–Sun. with full casino, buffet, and live entertainment (761–7992). *Gray Line* has guided tours of the island and Port Isabel and two trips to Mexico. The first is a day-long sightseeing-shopping-fiesta trip over the border to Matamoros; the second is a multi-day excursion to Tampico and Veracruz on the Mexican gulf coast (761–2124; 761–2111; 800–321–8720).

PARKS. Both ends of town are anchored by parks. *Isla Blanca County Park* at the southern tip of the island offers good surfing near the jetties; excellent shelling, particularly in winter and after a storm; bathrooms and showers; concessionaires; and 4 mi. of manicured beach for swimming and sunning. This is a good spot to watch the boat traffic in the channel of Santiago Pass; it's also a favorite hangout for the young and lithe. *Andy Bowie Park* is on the north end of town and is far more natural and undeveloped. Snorkeling is good here on calm days, and the beach is closed to vehicular traffic. Construction on South Padre's new convention center was due to begin on the bayside of this park in 1991.

FISHING. The lighted fishing pier south of the causeway accesses the Laguna Madre and is one of the world's longest lighted piers. Contented anglers may be seen here at all hours of the day and night, fishing for redfish, trout, croaker, flounder, etc. This bay has the heaviest fish population of any bay along the gulf or Atlantic coasts; the ocean floor is unusually steep offshore, so good catches of marlin, swordfish, bonito, sailfish and tuna are common close-in. South Padre currently holds the state record for blue marlin, bluefin tuna, mako shark, and tarpon. If you've never cleaned a fish before, you'll find instructions on how to fillet one in the front of the local telephone book. Most of the major hotel restaurants will cook your catch on request.

A list of charter fishing boats is available through the tourist bureau.

ACCOMMODATIONS. There are a number of rental agencies specializing in condo and beach-house rentals; many have toll-free telephone numbers. A list is available from the tourist bureau (see Tourist Information). Be aware that winter is low season, summer is high season, and spring break (one week in Mar.–Apr.) is very very high season—prices often triple. Winter rates are usually very reasonable. Note, too, that many of the hotels also rent condominium units, that swimming pools and air conditioning are generally givens, and that many lodgings have a restaurant either on the premises or nearby. Double-occupancy rates are classified (high season) as: *Deluxe,* $150–$175; *Expensive,* $90–$150; *Moderate,* $70–$90; *Inexpensive,* $50–$70. A 13% room/sales tax is added.

Deluxe

Bridgepoint. 333 Padre Blvd., Box 3590, South Padre Island, TX 78597 (761–7969; 800–221–1402, nationwide). This 29-story luxury condominium has a limited number of rental units. A full-service resort, on the beach, with tennis, Jacuzzi, exercise area, and pool.

Expensive

Holiday Inn Beach Resort. 100 Padre Blvd., Box 2125, South Padre Island, TX 78597 (761–5401; 800–292–7506, in TX; 800–531–7405, elsewhere). Some 228 units ranging from doubles to family suites here, about one third overlooking the gulf. Planned children's activities in summer.

Sheraton South Padre Island. 310 South Padre Blvd., Box 3380, South Padre Island, TX 78597. (761–6551; 800–672–4747 in TX; 800–222–4010 elsewhere). This new high rise brings luxury and "concierge" travel to the isle.

South Padre Radisson Resort. 500 Padre Blvd., Box 2081, South Padre Island, TX 78597 (761–6511; 800–292–7704, nationwide). This 310-room resort has pools, tennis courts, restaurants, nightclub lounge, whirlpools, plus accommodations in either highrise units or around the garden pools.

Sunchase IV Condominiums. 1000 Padre Blvd., Box 2820 South Padre Island, TX 78597 (761–5521; 800–292–7520 in TX; 800–531–4540 elsewhere). Anchored by the Sunchase Mall (some of the best shopping on the island), this 120-unit condominium has tennis and racquetball courts, exercise center, etc., on the beach.

Moderate

Bahia Mar Resort Village. 6300 Padre Blvd., P.O. Box 2280, South Padre Island, TX 78597 (761–1343; 800–292–7502, in TX; 800–531–7404, elsewhere). Some 347 units, either high-rise or scattered around grassy grounds. Swimming pool. On the beach.

Fiesta Isles–Best Western. 5701 Padre Blvd., Box 3079, South Padre Island, TX 78597 (761–4913 or 800–528–1234). On the bay side of the island, this 58-room motel also has condo units and a swimming pool.

Holiday Inn. 100 Padre Island Blvd., Box 2125, South Padre Island, TX 78597 (761–5401). This beach resort features 227 units, pools, tennis, and a restaurant.

Inexpensive

Days Inn. 3913 Padre Blvd., Box 2400, South Padre Island, TX 78597 (761–7831). This 59-unit motel has kitchenettes, swimming pool, and Jacuzzi.

RESTAURANTS. You'll find good dining in many of the hotel restaurants, from Continental cuisine to fresh local seafood. The following are among the best bets elsewhere on the island. Ratings are for the price of a complete dinner for one (drink, tax, and tip not included). *Expensive,* $18–$30; *Moderate,* $10–$18; *Inexpensive,* under $10; Listings are alphabetical.

Louie's Backyard. *Expensive.* 2305 Laguna Blvd. at Ling (761–6406). What was a small, laid-back café is now a large, laid-back restaurant, noted for its dinner buffet and six bars. Catching the sunset from Louie's is an island tradition. Open Tues.–Sun., 4:30 P.M.–2 A.M. AE, MC, V.

Blackbeard's Restaurant. *Inexpensive–Moderate.* 103 E. Saturn, across from City Hall (761–2962). Very casual and popular with families, this place serves sandwiches, salads, seafood, hamburgers, and steaks. Open daily, 11 A.M.–11 P.M. AE, DC, MC, V.

Rossi's Ristorante. *Inexpensive–Moderate.* 2412 Padre Blvd. (761–9361). This is a new island favorite for pizza and seafood with Italian touch. AE, DC, MC, V.

Jettie's Restaurant. *Inexpensive.* In Isla Blanca Park at the southern tip of the island (761–6461). An island standby, this informal place is known for its seafood. The raw-oyster cocktails are memorable. Open daily, noon–9 P.M. AE, MC, V.

Naturally's Casa de Nutricion & Oasis Cafe. *Inexpensive.* 2600 Padre Blvd. (761–5332). Light breakfasts and nutritious lunches are the game here. There's always a hot soup, along with a salad bar, hearty sandwiches, fresh fruit smoothies, etc. The café is open daily from 8 A.M.–4:30 P.M., the adjoining store until 6 P.M. MC, V.

The Pantry and Grill Room. 708 Padre Blvd. (761–9331). There's casual dining during the day in The Pantry, and more formal settings at night in the upstairs Grill Room. Steak and seafood dishes are best bets. The Pantry is open for lunch daily, except Mon. The Grill Room is open for dinner Wed.–Sun. AE, CB, DC, MC, V.

Ro-Van's Restaurant and Bakery. *Inexpensive.* 5304 Padre Blvd. (761–6972). All pastries here are made from scratch, including 16 kinds of cookies, apple fritters, and real old-fashioned waffles for breakfast. No fancy food nonsense; expect plate lunches, chili, hamburgers, steaks, etc., just right for filling up for a day at the beach. Open Wed.–Mon., 6 A.M.–6 P.M. V.

THE SOUTH

by
KAREN LINGO and WILLIAM SCHEMMEL

Ms. Lingo, who lives in Birmingham, Alabama, is the Southeast travel editor at Southern Living *magazine and a member of Society of American Travel Writers.*

GEORGIA

If the South begins anywhere, it begins in Atlanta, transportation hub of the region. The standing joke among southerners is that if you want to get anywhere in the world, you first have to go through Atlanta's Hartsfield International Airport. And if you're driving eastward, most of the interstate highways feed into . . . Atlanta.

Atlanta—The South's Premier City

It began as a railroad terminus in 1837, and in almost a century and a half since, Atlanta has grown to a metropolitan area of nearly two million people. More than 450 of the Fortune 500 companies have offices here, including Coca-Cola, Delta Airlines, and Georgia-Pacific. And millions of visitors each year come to enjoy the sophisticated shopping found at such places as Lenox Square, which has a branch of Neiman Marcus; Phipps Plaza, which includes branch stores of Lord & Taylor, Saks Fifth

Avenue, and Tiffany's; and the more recently opened Galleria, connected to the Waverly Hotel.

Cultural opportunities await at the Atlanta Memorial Arts Center, a modern $13 million complex that houses the Atlanta Symphony, High Museum of Art, Alliance Theatre, Children's Theatre, and the Atlanta College of Art. There's also a theater district on Peachtree Street, anchored by the wonderful old Fox Theatre, built in 1929 in the Moorish style and designated a national landmark.

If visitors come for the sophistication of Atlanta, they also come for, or discover while they're in town, the southern charm that still exists in places like the Tullie Smith House, an 1840s Georgia farmhouse that is part of the Atlanta Historical Society complex. Also in the complex are McElreath Hall, which houses an extensive collection of area historical items, and the Swan House, a 1928 Palladian-style mansion. Another noteworthy house is the Tudor-style mansion that houses Callanwolde Arts Center. And of course, no trip is complete without at least a glimpse of the Georgia State Capitol, whose dome is sheeted in gold; and the governor's mansion, a Greek-revival-style mansion furnished with a fine collection of Federal period antiques.

For a taste of Civil War history, there's the famous three-dimensional panoramic painting of the Battle of Atlanta, at the Cyclorama in Grant Park. A more romantic, fictional view of the war rests in the Gone with the Wind Museum, which includes 53 first editions of the book, as well as letters, original book reviews, and posters and programs from the various world premieres of the movie. Reality, though, lies 19 miles northwest of the city, at the Kennesaw Mountain National Battlefield. This is the site of one of the most crucial skirmishes in the Civil War Battle of Atlanta. It includes a museum with slide presentation and exhibits and 18 miles of hiking trails.

Opened in 1986, the Carter Presidential Center, near downtown, welcomes visitors to its Jimmy Carter Library and Museum. The Center's four contemporary circular buildings are set among 30 acres of trees, gardens, lakes and waterfalls. Inside are thousands of documents, photos, gifts and memorabilia from Jimmy Carter's White House years. The Center is also a tribute to all who have served in our nation's highest office.

One of the city's newest major attractions, the $140 million restored Underground Atlanta, a Rouse Company project, opened in 1989 on the historic downtown site of the original Underground Atlanta. It's a lively "town center" of upscale shops, specialty stores, pushcart vendors, restaurants, and nightclubs, geared to lure locals and visitors back to the heart of the city. Unlike its predecessor, the sprightly, cheery indoor-outdoor complex is not actually underground.

Adjacent to Underground's Kenny's Alley entrance is The World of Coca-Cola pavilion, which was opened in 1990 as Atlanta's newest major visitor attraction. The three-story structure pays homage to Coca-Cola products and events that shaped the last century. It includes innovative displays and multimedia exhibits, along with 1,200 artifacts from 1886 to the present. Visitors can walk into giant "Coke" cans, press soda "bubbles" to see videos, and listen to radio jingles at a vintage soda fountain as they enjoy free samples of the world-renowned soft drink.

Beyond Atlanta

A more entertaining bit of Civil War memory is carved into the side of Stone Mountain, 825-feet high and the world's largest mass of exposed granite. About 20 miles east of Atlanta, the monolith bears the likenesses of Confederate Generals Robert E. Lee and "Stonewall" Jackson and Confederate President Jefferson Davis. Lee's likeness alone is 138 feet from the top of his head to his horse's hoof. His nose measures five feet long, and the stars on his collar are bigger than dishpans. Surrounding the mountain is a 3,200-acre family amusement park that includes steamboat and locomotive rides, a skylift to the top of the mountain, a game ranch, a complex of antebellum buildings moved in from other areas of the state, an antique automobile museum, a carillon with daily concerts, a museum, golf, and a lake for fishing, swimming, and boating.

For pure amusement, though, there's Six Flags over Georgia, about 10 miles west of Atlanta. It covers 331 acres and includes more than 100 rides, shows, and attractions, all for one admission price. There's something for every member of the family, from kiddie rides for the very young to stomach-churning rides for the older visitor. Among the latter are the all-time favorite Great American Scream Machine roller coaster and the hair-raising Mind Bender, a triple-loop roller coaster. In 1982, the park introduced Thunder River, a raft trip down a whitewater river. The next year, a freefall ride was added. And the next, the Looping Star Ship, with heart-stopping loops that turn riders upside-down. One of the most successful additions, though, has been the Looney Tune Shows, with costumed characters Bugs Bunny and friends, who delight young and old alike.

Other Georgia Cities

Southeast of Atlanta, via I-85 and I-185, lies Columbus. Situated on the banks of the Chattahoochee River, it is a city with a past. But it uses that past in very modern ways. The convention and trade center, for instance, was once an old ironworks, and exposed beams, old brick walls, and many artifacts are used in the décor. The Chattahoochee Promenade, along the banks of the river, is an outdoor historical museum developed as the city's permanent observance of the national bicentennial. It ties together such points of interest as the convention center and the Confederate Naval Museum, the only one of its kind in the world. The museum houses the hull of the iron-clad Civil War gunboat *Muscogee,* which was raised from the bottom of the Chattahoochee River.

In the historic district, one of the attractions is the Pemberton House, once occupied by Dr. John Styth Pemberton, who originated the Coca-Cola formula. Downtown, the Springer Opera House is a restored Victorian theater where many famous people appeared, including Edwin Booth and Franklin D. Roosevelt.

North of Columbus lies Pine Mountain, home of Callaway Gardens, a beautiful resort with gardens that bloom with azaleas in spring and seasonal flowers the rest of the year. The 2,500-acre resort offers miles of garden drives, walking trails, display greenhouses, the spectacular new Day Butterfly Center, 63 holes of golf, a 175-acre fishing lake, tennis, horseback riding, a beach, and quail hunting in season.

Nearby, Warm Springs holds the memories of Franklin D. Roosevelt. After he contracted poliomyelitis, F.D.R. came to bathe in the mineral springs here. The cottage he built became known as the Little White House. It remains just the same as on the day President Roosevelt died here in 1945, and an adjacent museum includes a 12-minute movie of his life.

Macon lies very near to the geographic center of the state. In spring, cherry blossoms seem to float like pink clouds along the streets, thanks to an extensive planting program financed by a local citizen. Later in the season, the entire central area of the state is covered with peach blossoms. For preservation buffs, Macon has 46 individual structures listed in the National Register of Historic Places such as the Hay House and The Grand Open House.

Savannah, founded in 1733, was laid out on a grid of garden-like public squares, adorned with fountians, flowers and stately mansions. Since the

1950s, a zealous campaign has restored more than 1,200 historic structures in the downtown National Historic District. With its hundreds of romantic old buildings, the city is an excellent place for walking and horsedrawn carriage rides. Most visitors wind up at the seafood restaurants and pubs in the old cotton warehouses along the Savannah River. Youngsters especially enjoy the miniature ships in glass bottles, ornate figureheads, and other sailing artifacts in the Ships of the Sea Museum.

At one time, Augusta was the largest inland cotton market in the world. Today, it's best known as the home of the world-famous Master's Golf Tournament, played each April at the Augusta National Golf Club. The setting for the tournament seems perfect, for the area is characterized by a lush green landscape dotted with foothills that descend toward the coast, some 125 miles away. Aside from golf, Augusta has homes that date from the 18th and 19th centuries, the remains of a Confederate powder works, and monuments both to Georgia's signers of the Declaration of Independence and to its heroes of the Civil War.

Athens, the site of the nation's first state-chartered university and America's first women's garden club, is aptly named. Its Greek Revival homes, built in the 1800s, are a delight to see on a self-guided driving tour. One, the Taylor-Grady House, is an outstanding example and is open to the public. If your interest lies in horticulture, the state headquarters of the Garden Club of Georgia is housed in an 1857 brick home filled with 18th- and 19th-century antiques. Around it are a series of gardens, including a formal boxwood garden. Also, the University of Georgia Botanical Gardens offer nature trails and outstanding examples of native plants of the Georgia piedmont.

The Crowning Jewels of Georgia

North of Atlanta, stretching like a rainbow across the upper reaches of the state, are those delightful out-of-the-way places that embody the character of Georgia. The eastern anchor of the rainbow is Gainesville, with its Green Street Historical District, featuring Victorian and Neoclassical revival houses as well as Green Street Station, which displays historical and arts and crafts exhibits of the area. The western anchor is Rome, home of Berry College, with its Martha Berry Home and Museum. In between lie places like Chatsworth, with the Vann House, once the showplace of the Cherokee Nation. Dahlonega, rich with its history of a gold rush in the 1800s, has a gold museum and commercial mine open to the public. Helen, a bit of Bavaria tucked into the Appalachians, is a shopper's delight. Nearby are the Old Sautee Store, a 110-year-old country store and museum, and Mark of the Potter, a restored gristmill that serves as a crafts center. In this area lie the beginning of the Appalachian Trail and Brasstown Bald, Georgia's highest peak, with a view of four states. And, spreading like a many-fingered oasis, is Lake Sidney Lanier. Created by the U.S. Army Corps of Engineers, it is home of Lake Lanier Islands, a 1,200-acre state-operated resort with hotel, golf, tennis, horseback riding, boating, swimming, and some of the best fishing in the state.

PRACTICAL INFORMATION FOR GEORGIA

WHEN TO GO. Any time is a good time to visit Georgia. Winter weather can be pleasant or cold, but the average daytime temperature is around 47° F. Spring is the best time to visit many areas, particularly in Mar. and Apr., when the dogwoods and azaleas are blooming in Atlanta and at Callaway Gardens. Summer months can be hot, but temperatures usually average around 80° F. during the day.

HOW TO GET THERE. The transportation hub of the state, indeed of the region, is Atlanta. By air or automobile, even on *Amtrak* trains, you'll usually find yourself routed through Atlanta on your way to or from most cities in the South.

THE SOUTH
KANSAS
MISSOURI
ILLINOIS
ARKANSAS
OKLAHOMA
MISSISSIPPI
LOUISIANA
TEXAS
GULF
Eureka Springs
Fayetteville
Mountain View
Jackson
Fort Smith
Memphis
LITTLE ROCK
Russellville
Hot Springs
Pine Bluff
Greenwood
Columbus
Greenville
Texarkana
El Dorado
Yazoo City
Shreveport
Monroe
Vicksburg
JACKSON
Meridian
Laurel
Natchez
Hattiesburg
Alexandria
BATON ROUGE
Bogulusa
Opelousas
Biloxi
Pascagoula
Lake Charles
Lafayette
NEW ORLEANS
Galveston
Mississippi River
Yazoo River
Red River
Sabine River
Tombigbee River
Scale of Miles
0
100
200

KENTUCKY
TENNESSEE
NORTH CAROLINA
SOUTH CAROLINA
GEORGIA
ALABAMA
FLORIDA
ATLANTIC OCEAN
OF MEXICO
CUMBERLAND GAP
Great Smoky Mtns. Nat. Park
NASHVILLE
Albany
Knoxville
Columbia
Florence
Huntsville
Decatur
Cullman
Chattanooga
Dahlonega
Greenville
Athens
Rome
ATLANTA
Decatur
Gadsden
Anniston
BIRMINGHAM
Tuscaloosa
Alexander City
La Grange
Columbus
Montgomery
Macon
Augusta
COLUMBIA
Savannah
Savannah River
Chattachoochee River
Alabama River
Apalachicola River
Albany
Waycross
Brunswick
Dothan
Okefenoke Swamp
JACKSONVILLE
Mobile
Pensacola
TALLAHASSEE
Gainsville
Tampa
75
41
65
40
24
64
72
72A
27
59
85
26
77
74
20
95
19
80
16
82
301
55
43
84
10
98

By plane. Most major airlines fly into Atlanta's Hartsfield International Airport, including *American, Bahamasair, British Caledonian, Continental, Delta, Japan Airlines, Lufthansa, KLM, Northwest, Pan Am, Sabena, Swissair, TWA, United,* and *USAir.*

By bus. *American Coach, Greyhound, Gray Line,* and *Southeastern Stages,* serve Atlanta and the state.

By car. Interstates 20, 75, and 85 criss-cross the state, giving access from every bordering state.

TOURIST INFORMATION. *Tourist-Communications Division,* Georgia Department of Industry & Trade, 230 Peachtree St., N.W., Box 1776, Atlanta, GA 30301 (404–656–3590); *Athens Convention & Visitors Bureau,* 300 N. Thomas St., Box 948, Athens, GA 30601 (404–549–6800); *Atlanta Convention & Visitors Bureau,* 233 Peachtree St., N.E., Suite 2000, Peachtree Harris Tower, Atlanta, GA 30303 (404–521–6600); *Augusta Convention & Visitors Bureau,* Box 657, Augusta, GA 30913 (404–722–0421); *Columbus Convention & Visitors Bureau,* Box 2768, Columbus, GA 31902 (404–322–1613); *Dahlonega-Lumpkin County Local Welcome Center,* Public Square, Dahlonega, GA 30533 (404–864–3711); *Gainesville-Hall County Tourism & Convention Bureau,* Box 2553, Gainesville, GA 30503 (404–536–5209); *Greater Helen Local Welcome Center,* Main St., Helen, GA 30545 (404–878–2521); *Macon-Bibb County Convention & Visitors Bureau,* 200 Coliseum Dr., Macon, GA 31210 (912–743–3401); *Greater Rome Convention & Visitors Bureau,* Box 5823, Rome, GA 30161 (404–295–5576). *Savannah Convention & Visitors Bureau,* 222 W. Oglethorpe Ave., Savannah, GA 31499 (912–944–0456 in GA; toll free, 800–444–CHARM outside GA).

In addition, visitor-information centers, operated by the Tourist Division of the Georgia Dept. of Industry and Trade, are open daily at the following locations: Lavonia, I-85, ½ mi. south of South Carolina line; Columbus, intersection of U.S. 280 and U.S. 27; Ringgold, I-75, 2 mi. south of Tennessee line; Sylvania, U.S. 301, ¼ mi. southwest of South Carolina line; Valdosta, I-75, 2 mi. north of Florida line; Augusta, I-20, ½ mi. west of South Carolina line; I-95 at Kingsland; I-85 at West Point; I-20 near Tallapoosa, east of Alabama line; Hartsfield International Airport, Atlanta; U.S. 80, Plains; and I-95, Savannah.

Additional information is available from the *Game & Fish Div., Dept. of Natural Resources,* 205 Butler St., SE., Suite 1258, Atlanta, GA 30334; *Georgia Chamber of Commerce,* Commerce Building, Atlanta, GA 30334; *U.S. Forest Service,* 1720 Peachtree Rd., N.W., Room 816, Atlanta, GA 30367.

TELEPHONES. The area code for Atlanta and northern Georgia is 404. For south Georgia, the area code is 912. The cost of local telephone calls is 25 cents, and there is no time limit. Dial 411 for information. In Atlanta and most larger cities, you can direct-dial credit, collect, or person-to-person calls by dialing 0 before the area code. In some smaller towns, you dial the number and wait for your party to answer before depositing the coin, so be sure to read directions on public telephones before making a call. In an *emergency,* dial 911.

HOW TO GET AROUND. By plane. Automobile is the best way to get around in many areas of the state, but commercial flights are available from Atlanta to some of the larger cities. *Atlantic Southeast, Delta,* and *USAir* airlines serve the various cities.

By bus. *American Coach Lines,* Norcross (404–449–1806); *North Georgia Bus Lines,* Atlanta (404–753–2160); *Greyhound* (404–522–6300).

By subway. In Atlanta, the *Metropolitan Atlanta Rapid Transit Authority (MARTA)* is a combined rail and bus system. It serves the airport, as well as many areas of the city. Fare is $1; transfers are free. For information and schedules, call 404–848–4711, Mon.–Fri., 6 A.M.–10 P.M.; Sat. and Sun., 8 A.M.–4 P.M.

By taxi. In Atlanta, *Checker* (351–1111) and *Yellow* (525–0200) are the largest companies. In Macon, *Yellow Cab* (742–6964).

By rental car. In Atlanta: *Avis* (530–2720); *Budget* (252–4234); *Hertz* (659–3000); *National* (530–2800); *Alamo* (768–1892); *General* (763–2035); *Payless* (763–2038); and *Airport Rent-a-Car* (768–5000). Most have offices at Hartsfield International Airport. In other cities, Avis and Hertz are major companies serving the airports. Reservations aren't always necessary in Atlanta but are a good idea in other cities.

HINTS TO MOTORISTS. Interstates make travel among all areas of the state convenient. In the northern reaches of the state, many of the smaller highways are winding, twisting trails that require a driver's strict attention.

Strict attention is an asset in driving in Atlanta. Every street seems to be named Peachtree, and finding the one you need can be a confusing task. The ramps onto the interstate system running through the city give no room for error, often merging directly into traffic.

For road conditions in the state, contact the *Georgia Dept. of Transportation-Road Conditions,* 2 Capitol Sq. S.W., Atlanta, GA 30334 (404–656–5267). For weather conditions that may affect driving, phone 404–294–6027; toll-free, 800–722–6617.

ACCOMMODATIONS. We have listed Georgia accommodations alphabetically by city, and under the city according to price categories, based on the cost of a double room. The categories are: *Deluxe,* $145–$250; *Expensive,* $100–$145; *Moderate,* $50–$100; *Inexpensive,* $50 and under.

Athens

Moderate

Holiday Inn. Broad at Hull St., 30603 (404–549–4433 or 800–465–4329). Has 237 rooms, restaurant, pool, jogging paths. Some rooms in *Expensive* category.

Quality Inn History Village. 295 E. Dougherty St., 30601 (404–546–0410 or 800–228–5151). Has 115 rooms, restaurant, pool, lounge with entertainment.

Ramada Inn. 513 W. Broad St., 30601 (404–546–8122 or 800–2–RAMADA). Has 160 rooms, restaurant, pool, lounge with entertainment.

Inexpensive

Days Inn. 2741 Atlanta Hwy., 30606 (404–546–9750 or 800–325–2525). Has 60 rooms, pool, restaurant.

Atlanta

Deluxe

Atlanta Hilton & Towers. 255 Courtland and Harris Sts., N.W., 30043 (404–659–2000 or 800–445–8667). Has 1,250 rooms, including 60 suites. Tennis courts, a health club, a variety of restaurants and lounges, including the popular Nikolai's Roof, a sumptuous, glass-enclosed restaurant on the top floor.

Atlanta Marriott Marquis. 265 Peachtree Center Ave., N.W., 30303 (404–521–0000 or 800–228–9290). Has 1,674 rooms (one of the largest hotels in the southeast), 5 restaurants, shops, pool, health facilities, lounges with entertainment.

Atlanta Perimeter Center Marriott. 246 Perimeter Center Pkwy, N.E., 30346 (404–394–6500 or 800–228–9290). Has 402 rooms, restaurants, lounges with entertainment, pool, tennis, health facilities.

Colony Square Hotel. Peachtree & 14th Sts., N.E., 30361 (404–892–6000; 800–422–2527 in GA; 800–422–7895 out of state). Has 466 rooms in a contemporary office-residential-shopping complex, restaurants, lounges with entertainment, health facilities.

Hyatt Regency Atlanta. 265 Peachtree St., N.E., 30303 (404–577–1234 or 800–233–1234). Has 1,279 newly renovated rooms, pool, spectacular lobby atrium, variety of restaurants and lounges, including the Polaris dining room, which revolves as you dine.

Omni Hotel at CNN Center. 100 CNN Center, Atlanta, GA 30335 (404–659–0000 or 800–843–6664). 470 rooms, some for mobility impaired. Two restaurants, three lounges, live entertainment. Pool, racquetball, health club; baby-sitting, valet services.

The Ritz Carlton Atlanta. 181 Peachtree St., N.E., 30303 (404–659–0400 or 800–241–3333). Has 454 elegantly appointed rooms, restaurants, shopping, lounges with entertainment.

The Ritz-Carlton Buckhead. 3434 Peachtree Rd., N.E., 30326 (404–237–2700 or 800–241–3333). Has 553 attractive guest rooms with bay windows, restaurants, lounges with entertainment, shopping, pool, health facilities.

Stouffer Waverly Hotel. 2450 Galleria Pkwy., I-75 & U.S. 41 N.W. (404–953–4500 or 800–468–3571). Luxurious hotel with 521 rooms, restaurants, health club, lounges with entertainment.

Westin Peachtree Plaza. Peachtree at International Blvd., 30303 (404–659–1400 or 800–228–3000). A towering 73-story hotel with 1,074 rooms, 7-story atrium lobby with half-acre lake, restaurants, lounges with entertainment, health facilities.

Expensive

Atlanta Airport Marriott. 4711 Best Rd., College Park 30337 (404–766–7900 or 800–228–9290). Has 640 rooms, restaurants, entertainment, lounges, meeting rooms, pool, tennis.

Sheraton Parkway 75 Hotel. I-74 and S 120 Loop, Marietta, GA 30067 (404–428–4400 or 800–325–3535). 221 rooms, some handicapped accessible. Nonsmoking rooms available. Heated outdoor pool; pets accepted. Julia's Restaurant; Randolph's Lounge, entertainment. Full American breakfast buffet included with room. Call toll-free number for information on three other area Sheraton facilities.

Terrace Garden Inn Buckhead. 3405 Lenox Rd., N.E. Across from Lenox Square Shopping Center, 30326 (404–261–9250 or 800–241–8260). 360 rooms, restaurant, lounge with entertainment, health facilities.

Moderate

Courtyard By Marriott. Several locations, including 5601 Peachtree-Dunwoody Rd., 30342 (404–843–2300); 2045 S. Park Pl., 30339 (404–955–3838; 3000 Cumberland Circle 30339 (404–952–2555); 1236 Executive Park Dr., 30329 (404–728–0708); and eight others. A new concept in lodging, in residential area. Restaurant, pool. Call toll-free 800–321–2211 for complete roster of these Atlanta area properties.

Days Inn Downtown. 300 Spring at Baker Sts., 30308 (404–523–1144 or 800–325–2525). Has 262 rooms, restaurant, pool.

Holiday Inn Atlanta Airport North. 1380 Virginia Ave. (404–762–8411 or 800–465–4329). 500 rooms, including some suites. Dining room; lobby bar, live entertainment. Teens and under stay free in parents' room. Free 24-hour airport transportation. Sauna, golf, tennis, exercise room, pool, whirlpool, coin laundry. Pay movies, ESPN, FAX service. Weekend packages. Call toll-free for information about 15 other area Holiday Inns.

Howard Johnson's Motor Lodge. Three locations in city: 1377 Virginia Ave., at I-85 S. (404–762–5111); 1569 Phoenix Blvd., College Park, GA 30349 (404–996–4321); and 2700 Curtis Dr., Smyrna, GA 30080 (404–435–4990). Toll-free, all locations, 800–654–2000.

Quality Inn Habersham-Downtown. 330 Peachtree St., N.E., Atlanta, GA 30308 (404–577–1980 or 800–228–5151). This recently renovated European-style hotel has 91 king and double bed executive rooms, kitchenettes (unfurnished), in-room coffee makers; HBO, free parking, complimentary daily newspapers, and health spa privileges. Dining room and lounge.

Radisson Inn Dunwoody. I-285 N. at Chamblee-Dunwoody Rd., 30338 (404–394–5000 or 800–288–9822). Has 391 rooms, restaurants, lounges with entertainment, pool, tennis. Some rooms in *Moderate* category.

Sheraton Inn Southwest-Atlanta Airport (formerly Harley Hotel). 3601 N. Desert Dr., East Point, GA 30344 (404–762–5141; 800–325–3535 or 800–325–3535). Has 184 rooms, restaurant, lounge with entertainment, pool, health facilities.

Inexpensive

Knights Inn-Atlanta East. 2942 Lawrenceville Hwy., Tucker, GA 30084 (404–934–5060 or 800–722–7220). This member of the fast-growing new economy system has 95 rooms; 14 are efficiencies. Pool, restaurant nearby. Member of fast-growing new economy system has 106 comfortable rooms, all ground level; 22 have refrigerators, 11 are efficiencies. Color cable TV, movies, pool; pets accepted; restaurant adjacent. Other locations at 5230 S. Cobb Dr., Smyrna, GA 30080 (404–794–3000); 2608 Bouldercrest Rd. (404–243–3515); and 3860 Flat Shoals Rd., College Park, GA (404–969–0110).

Bed & Breakfast

Bed and Breakfast Atlanta. 1801 Piedmont Ave., N.E., Atlanta, GA 30324 (404–875–0525). This professional reservations service will arrange lodging in carefully selected private homes, inns, guest cottages, or condominiums. Transportation, language needs, preferences, considered in placement. Continental breakfast included; long-term rates available. For information, reservations, call or write, enclosing stamped self-addressed envelope.

Columbus

Moderate

Columbus Hilton. 800 Front Ave., edge of historic district, across from convention center, 31901 (404–324–1800 or 800–445–8667). Has 178 rooms, restaurant, lounge with entertainment, pool.

Courtyard By Marriott. 3501 Courtyard Way, 31909 (404–323–2323 or 800–321–2211). Has 138 rooms, restaurant, pool. Some rooms in *Inexpensive* category.

Holiday Inn South (Fort Benning area). 3170 Victory Dr., Columbus, GA 31902 (404–689–6181 or 800–465–4329). 176 rooms. Playground, pool. Teens and under stay free in parents' room. Government discounts. Pipers Restaurant, Connexions Lounge. Some rooms in *Inexpensive* category. Also 2800 Manchester Expwy. 31904 (404–324–0231).

Inexpensive

Days Inn. 3452 Macon Rd., 31907 (404–561–4400 or 800–325–2525). Has 125 rooms. Pool, restaurant next door. Free cable TV, HBO, local calls.

La Quinta Inn. (Fort Benning area). 3201 Macon Rd. and I-185, 31906 (404–568–1740 or 800–531–5900). Has 122 rooms, pool. 24-hour Denny's Restaurant, Bombay Bicycle Club, Morrison's Cafeteria nearby.

Helen

Moderate

Comfort Inn. Rte. 75, New River Rd. 30345 (404–878–8000 or 800–221–2222). Recently opened, this well-maintained property has 60 rooms; two have whirlpools. Some have microwaves and refrigerators (extra charge). Pool.

Helendorf Inn. Box 305, 30545 (404–878–2271). Has 82 rooms, 40 are efficiencies; coin laundry, pool; restaurant next door.

Inexpensive

Unicoi State Park Lodge—Conference Center. Box 849, Hwy. 356, 30545 (404–878–2824). This lodge has 100 rooms in rustic lodge in the mountains. Restaurant, lake, swimming, boating, tennis. Summer social, recreational programs.

Macon

Moderate

1842 Inn. 353 College St., 31201 (912–741–1842). This place in downtown historic district has 22 rooms furnished in 19th-century style. Four have whirlpools.

Inexpensive

Best Western Riverside. 2400 Riverside Dr., 31204 (912–743–6311 or 800–528–1234). Has 124 rooms, restaurant, pool, coin laundry. Summit Restaurant specializes in down-home Southern cooking.

Holiday Inn. I-475 & U.S. 80, 4775 Chambers Rd., Macon, GA 31206 (912–788–0120 or 800–465–4329). Has 182 rooms, Cedar Dining Room, Chesterfield's Lounge, pool. Some rooms in *Moderate* category.

Pine Mountain

Expensive

Callaway Gardens Inn and Cottages. U.S. Hwy. 27 S., 31822 (404–663–2281 or 800–282–8181). Has 793 units, three restaurants, coffee shop, two lounges, pool, golf, tennis, horseback riding, bicycling, fishing. One of the South's finest family resorts.

Rome

Moderate

Holiday Inn Skytop Center. Exit U.S. 411 E. at Chateau Rd., Rome, GA 30161 (404–295–1100 or 800–465–4329). 197 units in hilltop setting overlooking valley. Coin laundry. Indoor/outdoor pool, sauna, whirlpool. Senior discounts. Hackett's Restaurant, Topper's Lounge, live entertainment.

Savannah

Deluxe

Gastonian Inn. 220 E. Gaston St., Savannah, GA 31401. (912–232–2869). 13 guest rooms in a pair of 19th-century town houses, graced with antiques and modern luxuries. Some rooms in *Expensive* category.

Moderate

Days Inn. 201 W. Bay St., downtown, Savannah, GA 31401 (912–236–4440 or 800–325–2525). 253 attractive rooms in heart of historic Savannah, adjacent to Riverfront Plaza; 24-hour restaurant, pool in the historic district.

Unique Lodging in North Georgia

Big Canoe. Big Canoe, GA 30143 (404–268–3333; 800–652–6091 outside state). A resort and second-home community with par-72 golf course, fishing, boating, swimming in three lakes.

Clermont Hotel. 107 Dean St., Clermont, GA 30527 (404–983–3516). Renovated 1912 hotel with 6 rooms furnished in antiques that are for sale.

Cohutta Lodge. 5000 Cochise Trail, GA 52, Chatsworth, GA 30705 (404–695–9601). Three-story lodge with 60 rooms (42 with refrigerators), restaurant with magnificent view of mountains, near Fort Mountain State Park. Heated indoor pool, tennis courts, nature trail. No elevators.

The Smith House. 202 S. Chestatee, Dahlonega, GA 30533 (404–864–3566). Has 19 rooms but is best known for the food and family-style dining in its restaurant.

The Stovall House. Rte. 1, Box 103-A, Sautee, GA 30571 (404–878–3355). 5 mi. east of Helen, this 1837 house has 5 rooms and an excellent restaurant.

RESTAURANTS. Cuisine in Georgia ranges from the Continental fare you'll find in most large cities to the southern-style foods that seem most at home in informal settings. Atlanta has a number of cosmopolitan restaurants, but it also has some that feature down-home cooking in comfortable surroundings. Our price categories for a complete dinner (drinks, tax, and tip not included) are: *Super Deluxe,* $30 and up; *Deluxe,* $25–$30; *Expensive,* $20–$25; *Moderate,* $12.50–$20; *Inexpensive,* under $12.50.

Athens

Moderate

Ginkgo Tree Restaurant. Holiday Inn, Broad and Hull Sts. (549–4433). Steaks, chops, and seafoods are served in a cheery setting at this lively, locally popular place; lounge adjoins. AE, DC, MC, V.

The Lighthouse. 1653 S. Lumpkin St. (613–6061). Excellent steaks, seafoods, in comfortably casual atmosphere. Lounge, nightly entertainment. Major credit cards.

Inexpensive

Morrison's Cafeteria. 3700 Atlanta Hwy. (353–0030). Specialty is roast beef, fried chicken, own baking. L, 11 A.M.–2:30 P.M.; D, 4:30–8:30 P.M.; to 8 Sun. MC, V.

Atlanta

Super Deluxe

Nikolai's Roof. Atop Atlanta Hilton Hotel (659–2000). Floor-to-ceiling wine vault and outstanding French-Czarist menu. Beautiful rooftop setting overlooking city. Reservations, jacket, and tie required. 5-course dinner served at 6:30 and 9:30 P.M. AE, DC, MC, V.

Deluxe

The Abbey. 163 Ponce de Leon Ave., N.E., at Piedmont Rd. & North Ave. (876–8831). French-Continental cuisine is served in this converted church. D, 6–10 P.M. Closed major holidays. AE, DC, MC, V.

Bugatti. In Omni International Hotel (659–0000). Northern-Italian menu, own baking. L, 11:30 A.M.–2 P.M. D, 6–10:30 P.M.; Sat.–Sun., from 6 P.M. Reservations recommended. AE, DC, MC, V.

Coach and Six. 1776 Peachtree Rd., NW. (872–6666). Specialties, prime beef, lobster, lamb chops, own baking. L, 11:30 A.M.–2:30 P.M.; D, 6–11 P.M.; Sat., 6 P.M.–midnight; Sun, from 6 P.M. Closed major holidays. AE, DC, MC, V.

The Dining Room. Ritz-Carlton Buckhead Hotel, 3434 Peachtree Rd. (237–2700). *Nouvelle cuisine* prepared by a European master chef, in a darkly romantic dining room, enriched by English hunting portraits and Waterford chandeliers. D, 6–11 P.M. Mon.–Sat., closed Sun. AE, D, MC, V.

Hedgerose Heights Inn. 490 E. Paces Ferry Rd., N.E. (233–7673). Outstanding European dishes, elegant setting in restored 1915 home. Reservations and jacket required. D, 6:30–10 P.M.; Fri., Sat. to 11 P.M. Closed Sun., Mon., and major holidays. AE, DC, MC, V.

103 West. 103 W. Paces Ferry Rd. (233–5993). Lavish American and Continental cuisines, wines, in an extravagant Victorian decor. D, 6–11 P.M., Mon.–Sat. AE, DC, MC, V.

The Restaurant. Ritz-Carlton Atlanta Hotel, 181 Peachtree St., N.E. (659–0400). Nouvelle cuisine with fresh market ingredients highlights this elegant Edwardian dining room. Formal service, dress code. Reservations requested. L, 11:30 A.M.–2:30 P.M. Mon.–Fri.; 10:30 A.M.–2 P.M. Sun.; D, 6:30–11 P.M. Mon.–Sun. Cocktail lounge. AE, DC, MC, V.

Expensive

Bone's Steaks & Seafood. 3130 Piedmont Rd. N.E., (237–2663). This clubby, popular New York-style steak-and-seafood house specializes in aged prime beef, own baking. L, 11:30 A.M.–2:30 P.M.; D, 6–11 P.M.; Fri., Sat., to midnight Sun., from 6 P.M. Closed major holidays. Reservations, jacket, and tie recommended. AE, DC, MC, V.

Pano's and Paul's. 1232 W. Paces Ferry Rd. (261–3662). Continental cuisine. Specialties include medallions of veal, own baking. D, 6–10:30 P.M.; Sat., 5:30–11 P.M. Closed Sun., major holidays. AE, DC, MC, V.

Savannah Fish Company. In Westin Peachtree Plaza Hotel (589–7456). Fresh seafood in a sophisticated setting. Menu changes daily, own baking. L, 11:30 A.M.–2:30 P.M.; D, 5:30–11 P.M. AE, DC, MC, V.

Trotters. 3215 Peachtree Rd., N.E. (237–5988). A nostalgic 1920s country-club setting for northern-Italian style pastas, veal, own baking. L, 11:30 A.M.–2:30 P.M.; D, 6–11 P.M.; Fri., to midnight; Sat., 6 P.M.–midnight. Closed major holidays. AE, DC, MC, V.

Moderate

Dante's Down the Hatch. 3380 Peachtree Rd., N.E. (266–1600). Across the street from Lenox Sq., in a building used as a hospital during the Civil War. Specialties include cheese trays, fondue dinners, homemade stew, own baking. D, 4 P.M.–midnight; Fri., Sat., to 1:30 A.M.; Sun., from 5:30 P.M. Closed major holidays. AE, DC, MC, V.

Gene and Gabe's. 1578 Piedmont Ave., N.E., at Monroe St. (874–6145). Veal is the prime attraction, and the fresh seafood is well prepared. D, 6 P.M.–midnight. Closed major holidays. AE, DC, MC, V.

McKinnon's Louisiane Restaurant. 3209 Maple Dr. (237–1313). Fresh Cajun, Creole seafoods. An Atlanta favorite with nationwide reputation. New grille room now open. Piano bar. D, 6–10 P.M. Mon.–Sat.; to 10:30 Fri.–Sat.; closed Sun. AE, DC, MC, V.

Pittypat's Porch. 25 International Blvd., N.W. (525–8228). The Old South is proudly reproduced in food, service and decor. Seven-course meal includes renowned "endless appetizer" salad buffet. D, daily from 4:30 P.M. Reservations, validated parking after 6 P.M. AE, DC, MC, V.

Inexpensive

The Colonnade. 1879 Cheshire Bridge Rd. (874–5642). An Atlanta favorite for 30 years, serving American and Southern dishes to full houses, daily. B, 7–10 A.M.; L, 11 A.M.–2:30 P.M.; D, 5–9 P.M. No credit cards.

Touch of India. 970 Peachtree St. (876–7777). Curries, tandooris, and other spicy Indian favorites. L, 11:30 A.M.–2:30 P.M., Mon.–Fri.; D, daily 5–11 P.M. AE, MC, V.

The Varsity. 16 North Ave., N.W. (881–1706). Large fast-food drive-in next to Georgia Tech. Chili dog, frosted orange, onion rings. Open 7 A.M.–12:30 A.M., Sun.–Thurs.; to 2 A.M. Fri., Sat. No credit cards.

Augusta

Moderate

Town Tavern. 17 7th St. (724–2461). Specialties are steaks, seafood, own baking, in renovated old warehouse. L, 11:30 A.M.–2:30 P.M.; D, 5–10 P.M.,; Mon.–Sat.; closed Sun., major holidays. AE, DC, MC, V.

Columbus

Moderate

Bludau's at the 1839 Goetchius House. 405 Broadway (324–4863). In old home in historic district. Continental cuisine, with veal specialties, own breads. D, 5–10 P.M., Mon.–Thurs.; to 11 Fri.–Sat.; closed Sun., major Holidays. AE, MC, V.

Dahlonega

Inexpensive

Smith House. 202 S. Chestatee (864–3566). Old-fashioned mountain boarding house serves all you can eat, family style. No credit cards.

La Grange

Moderate–Expensive

In Clover. 205 Broad St. (882–0883). Continental cuisine specializing in beef Wellington, veal, own baking. In a beautifully restored Victorian mansion. L, 11:30 A.M.–2 P.M.; D, 6–10 P.M. Closed Sun., major holidays. AE, DC, MC, V.

Macon

Moderate

Beall's 1860. 315 College St. (745–3663). In restored home. Specialties are prime rib, seafood, own baking. Jacket and tie recommended at dinner. L, D, 11 A.M.–10 P.M. Closed Sun., major holidays. AE, DC, MC, V.

Savannah

Moderate

The Chart House. 202 W. Bay St. (233–6686). Cozy seafood house overlooking the Savannah River, features local oysters and shrimp. D, 5:30–10 P.M. Mon.–Thurs.; 5–11 P.M., Fri.–Sat. AE, DC, MC, V.

Inexpensive

Crystal Beer Parlor. 301 W. Jones St. (232–1153). Friendly old tavern is famous for huge hamburgers, chowder and fried oyster sandwiches. L, D, 11:30 A.M.–10 P.M., Mon.–Sat. MC, V.

LIQUOR LAWS. In Georgia, a person must be 21 years of age or older to buy or drink alcoholic beverages. Alcohol may be purchased by the bottle at retail package stores 8 A.M.–11:45 P.M. except Sun. and during voting hours on Election Day. Bars are closed on Sun. and during voting hours on Election Day, except in Atlanta, and various other areas by local option.

WHAT TO SEE AND DO IN ATLANTA

TOURS. Guided tours of Atlanta and the surrounding areas are offered by *Northside Charter Tours & Sightseeing* (768–7676), *Gray Lines of Atlanta* (767–0594), and *Presenting Atlanta* (231–0200). *Pegasus* has city tours by horse-drawn carriage; call 373–9726. *TourGals* (262–7660), offers specially tailored tours with multilingual guides. Guided and self-guided tours of the city's historic areas are offered through the *Atlanta Preservation Center* (522–4345). For guided tours of the *Martin Luther King Jr. National Historic Site,* call 331–3919; donations accepted. Biking tours are available through the *Southern Bicycle League* (594–8350).

PARKS AND GARDENS. Chattahoochee River National Recreation Area. U.S. 41 and I–75, about 12 mi. north of downtown (394–8324, 394–7912). A popular area for rafting and inner-tubing over mild rapids, picnics and hiking. Open daily.

Fernbank Science Center. 156 Heaton Park Dr. N.E., near Decatur (378–4311). A must-see for families. The large complex includes a planetarium with seasonal shows, natural history museum, greenhouses, botanical gardens, and nature trails. Admission fee only for planetarium shows ($2 adults, $1 students). Open Mon., 8:30 A.M.–5 P.M.; Tues.–Fri., 8:30 A.M.–10 P.M.; Sat., 10 A.M.–5 P.M.; Sun., 1–5 P.M.

Grant Park. 800 Cherokee Ave. (624–1071). The highlight of the park, about 3 miles from downtown, is the Cyclorama, a dramatic circular painting, 50 ft. high

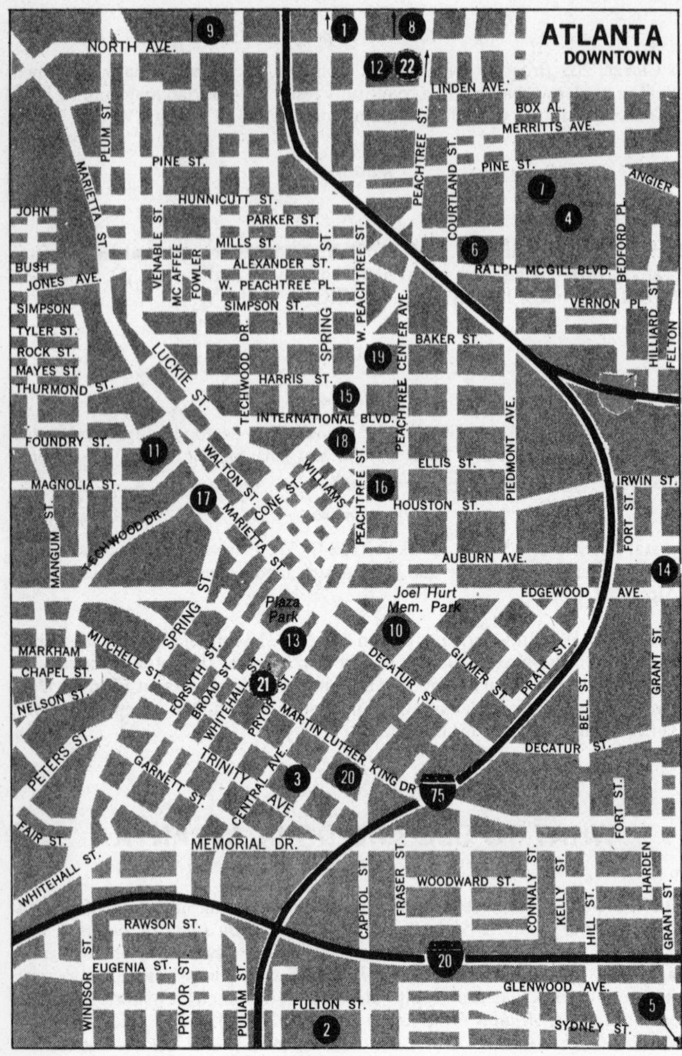

Points of Interest

1) Atlanta Historical Society
2) Atlanta Stadium
3) City Hall
4) Civic Center
5) Cyclorama
6) Emory University School of Dentistry
7) Exhibition Hall
8) Fox Theater
9) Georgia Institute of Technology
10) Georgia State University
11) Georgia World Congress Center
12) High Museum of Art
13) Five Points Rapid Rail Station
14) Martin Luther King grave
15) Merchandise Mart
16) Georgia-Pacific Center
17) Omni Hotel and Megastructure
18) Peachtree Plaza Hotel
19) Hyatt Regency Atlanta Hotel
20) State Capitol
21) Underground Atlanta
22) Woodruff Arts Center

by 400 ft. in circumference, depicting the most crucial hour in the 1864 Battle of Atlanta. Adults $3.50, senior citizens $3, ages 6–12 $2, under age 6, free. Open daily, 9:30 A.M.–5:30 P.M. There is a museum, housing the locomotive "Texas," which took part in the Civil War's "Great Locomotive Chase," as well as photographs, uniforms, and other memorabilia. After a rash of bad publicity, the Atlanta Zoo in the same park has made some noticeable improvements.

Piedmont Park. Off Piedmont Ave., between 10th and 14th Sts. Has softball fields, tennis courts, a swimming pool, picnic pavilions, jogging trails, and botanical gardens and greenhouses. Open daily, 6 A.M.–1 A.M. Small fee for some facilities.

Six Flags Over Georgia. Off I-20, 12 mi. west of downtown (739–3400). An immaculately maintained theme park with something for every taste, from roller coasters to tame rides and live shows. All-inclusive admission is $17.50; small children and 55 and over $10.95; under 2 free. All-inclusive 1-day admission $20. Parking $3.

Stone Mountain Park. Off U.S. 78, 16 mi. east of downtown (498–5600). Centerpiece is the granite monolith, 825 ft. high and 5 mi. around, carved with images of three Confederate heroes. Other amusements include a Swiss skylift to the mountaintop, a steam locomotive ride, an antebellum plantation, an 18-hole golf course, swimming, fishing, camping, boating, and even ice skating. The park is 16 mi. east of the city and served by MARTA buses from downtown. Admission $5 per car, with additional charges for rides and attractions. Open daily, 6 A.M.–midnight. Attractions open June–Aug. 10 A.M.–8:30 P.M.; Sept.–May to 5:30 P.M.

HISTORIC SITES AND HOUSES. Atlanta's rich and varied array of attractions includes Civil War battlefields, historic homes, and magnificent residential neighborhoods.

Atlanta Historical Society, Swan House, and Tullie Smith Plantation. 3101 Andrews Dr. (261–1837). Even jaded jet-setters gasp in astonishment as they drive past French chateaus, Spanish and Italian villas, Tudor manors, and white-columned Greek Revival mansions in the Buckhead section of northwest Atlanta, along West Paces Ferry, Habersham, Blackland, Andrews, and other tree-lined thoroughfares. For an inside peek at privilege, visit the Swan House, an Italianate villa filled with European and Oriental furnishings and antiques. By contrast, the Tullie Smith House on the same grounds is furnished with simple handicrafted furnishings from the 1830s. Both are maintained by the Atlanta Historical Society. All-inclusive ticket, $6 adults; $4 over 60 and students with ID; $3, 6–17; under 6 free; family rate, $10. Mon.–Sat. 9 A.M.–5:30 P.M.; Sun., noon–5:30 P.M.

Fox Theatre. Peachtree St. at Ponce de Leon Ave. (881–1977). One of the last of the 1920s picture palaces, a fantasy of Moorish arches, minarets, and Egyptian hieroglyphics that now hosts Broadway shows, concerts, and special films.

The Georgia Governors Mansion. 391 W. Paces Ferry Rd. (261–1776). Near the Historical Society, this is a modern-day Greek Revival building with Federal period furnishings and antiques; it is open free of charge Tues.–Thurs., 10–11:30 A.M.

Georgia State Capitol. Downtown on Capitol Hill (656–2844). Gleams with a dome of north Georgia gold. Inside are state offices, Confederate Battle flags, and museums. There's an inexpensive underground restaurant across the street in Georgia Plaza Park. Mon.–Fri., 9 A.M.–4:30 P.M. Sat., 10 A.M.–2 P.M.; Sun., 1–3 P.M. Free.

Kennesaw Mountain National Battlefield Park. Off I–75 near Marietta (427–4686). This area saw some of the fiercest fighting of the 1864 Battle of Atlanta campaign. Stop at the National Park Service Visitors Center and then hike or take a shuttle bus to the crest, view the earthworks, and have a picnic lunch. Free. **The Big Shanty Museum** (427–2117) in the nearby town of Kennesaw houses the locomotive "General," subject of a Civil War spy chase re-created in Disney's *The Great Locomotive Chase.* Adults, $2.50; over 65, $2; children 7 to 15, $1. Family rate $10. Mon.–Sat., 9:30 A.M.–5:30 P.M., daily, noon–5:30 P.M., Mar.–Nov. 30; daily, noon–5:30 P.M., rest of year.

The Martin Luther King Jr. Memorial Historic District, near downtown, includes the civil rights leader's birthplace home, the Ebenezer Baptist Church where he preached, his tomb, museums, and memorials. There is no charge to see the tomb or to take a walking tour with National Park Service rangers. Phone 524–1956 for the center; phone the National Historic Site at 331–3919. Daily, 10 A.M.–5 P.M. Free.

The Wren's Nest. 1050 Gordon St. S.W., (753–8535). The former home of author Joel Chandler Harris, filled with memorabilia of Br'er Fox, Br'er Rabbit, and others made famous in the Uncle Remus tales. Tues.–Sat., 10 A.M.–5 P.M.; Sun., 1–5 P.M. Adults, $3; teenagers and senior citizens, $2; ages 4–12, $1.

MUSEUMS AND GALLERIES. Atlanta's importance as the visual arts center of the Southeast is reflected by the opening in 1983 of its spectacular new High Museum of Art and by the number and variety of galleries. The "Weekend" tabloid section of Sat.'s Atlanta *Journal-Constitution* carries news about exhibitions and galleries.

Atlanta Museum. 537 Peachtree St. (872–8233), is for admirers of the offbeat. The eight-room Queen Anne-style brick mansion is filled with antiques and curiosities from around the world, including Hitler's hat and coat, Civil War artifacts, and Indian relics. Antiques are for sale in a separate area of the house. Adults, $2; children, $1. Mon.–Sat., 9 A.M.–5 P.M.

The Catherine Waddell Gallery. Trevor Arnett Library, Atlanta University (681–0251). Has one of the nation's largest collections of Afro-American paintings, sculpture, and graphics. Daily, 9 A.M.–5 P.M.

The High Museum of Art. 1280 Peachtree St. N.E. (892–3600). Moved into its new home in 1983; along with permanent collections of European, American, and African paintings, sculpture, and decorative arts, it hosts a continuous schedule of important traveling exhibitions. Designed by world-famed architect Richard Meier, the museum is a dazzling high-tech masterpiece with a light-flooded central atrium. Admission is adults, $4; seniors, college students with ID, $2; 6–17, $1; free Thurs., 1–5 P.M. Tues., Thurs.–Sat., holidays, 10 A.M.–5 P.M.; Wed., 10 A.M.–9 P.M. Closed major holidays.

Jimmy Carter Library and Museum. North Highland and Cleburne Aves. (331–3942). Photos, memorabilia from Jimmy Carter's presidency. Adults, $2.50; seniors, $1.50; under 16, no charge. Mon.–Sat., 9 A.M.–4:45 P.M. Sun., noon–4:45 P.M.

The Margaret Mitchell Collections at the Atlanta Public Library, downtown at Peachtree and Forsyth Sts., will appeal to *Gone with the Wind* buffs who want to see displays of memorabilia of the movie and editions of the book in many languages. Mitchell is buried in Oakland Cemetery, a landmark in its own right, on Memorial Dr., near the state capitol. Loew's Grand Theatre, where the movie had its stupendous 1939 premiere, was on the site of the Georgia-Pacific Tower, downtown. Mon.–Sat., 9 A.M.–6 P.M.; Sun., 2–6 P.M.

Nexus Gallery. Forsyth St. (688–1970). Photography and local, regional and national experimental art are displayed by a consortium of independent artists with studios in a former school building.

MUSIC. The **Atlanta Symphony Orchestra** is the keystone of the city's cultural life. Regarded as one of the nation's leading symphonies, ASO performs its regular season at Woodruff Arts Center, 1280 Peachtree St. (892–2414), with outstanding artists as guest performers. In the summer the orchestra puts on a series of free concerts Sunday nights in Piedmont Park as well as pops concerts at Chastain Park. Other highlights of the ASO year include the Christmas concerts, winter pops series, and children's concerts.

Other organizations performing regularly include the **Atlanta Boy Choir** (378–0064), **Choral Guild of Atlanta** (435–6563), **Atlanta Chamber Players** (892–8681), **Atlanta Opera,** (872–1706), and **Atlanta Virtuosi** (938–8611).

DANCE. Atlanta's dance scene is headed by the highly acclaimed **Atlanta Ballet** (873–5811). The 65-year-old company is nationally known for its presentations of classical works as well as highly innovative new programs. Most programs are at the Atlanta Civic Center. Other excellent companies include **Celeste Miller and Company** (524–3399), **Atlanta Dance Theatre** (872–2887), the **Carl Ratcliff Dance Theatre** (266–0010), and the **Ruth Mitchell Dance Company** (237–8829), a 20-year-old group that performs originally choreographed ballet and jazz dancing. Ticket prices vary with the event, but rarely exceed $12 to $15.

STAGE. Regional theater is thriving in Atlanta, with nearly a score of professional companies presenting traditional, modern, and experimental plays. Several of the largest companies are on Peachtree St. between 10th and 15th Sts., convenient to downtown hotels and public transportation. Most theaters offer discounts to senior citizens, students, and groups. For current offerings, check the "Weekend" tabloid section of Sat.'s Atlanta *Journal-Constitution.*

Alliance Theater. Arts Alliance Bldg., Peachtree and 15th Sts. (892–2414). Presents a balanced repertory of new and standard plays to one of the nation's largest season-ticket audiences. Also in the Woodruff Center, the **Studio Theater** presents new and experimental works, while the **Atlanta Children's Theatre** presents classic and contemporary plays for the younger set.

The Center for Puppetry Arts. 1404 Spring St. (873–3391). Offers regularly scheduled plays with an all-puppet cast as well as a puppet museum and a school for puppetry.

Theatre of the Stars, in the Atlanta Civic Center (252–8960), presents touring musicals with big-name stars during the summer and, in winter, straight drama and comedy, often fresh from Broadway.

ALABAMA

Alabama offers a surprising variety of terrain and attractions. The foothills of the Appalachians dominate the northern portion of the state and fade into the rich black loam of the blackbelt just below Montgomery, the state capital. The heritage of cotton is strong, but a new history of industry and medicine is taking over, especially in Birmingham, the state's largest city.

Birmingham—From Iron Age to Modern Age

Birmingham, Alabama's largest city, has become one of the region's most progressive metropolitan areas. The changes began more than a decade ago, starting with Birmingham Green, a landscaping project along the main business street that won an All America City Award in 1971. Then, rapidly, Birmingham added a new civic center with exhibition hall, concert hall, coliseum, and theater; new hotels and office buildings in the downtown area; expanded facilities at the University of Alabama in Birmingham; a new wing to the museum of art; and a new museum devoted to the unique geology of the area.

More recently, the pace picked up with the renovation of the old Sloss Furnaces into a museum of iron-and steelmaking history; renovation and reopening of the old Redmont Hotel downtown; construction of a horse-racing track; and the opening of a 164-acre complex south of town that includes the posh Wynfrey Hotel, a 17-story office building, and a galleria with more than 130 stores, including a branch of Macy's.

Among all the new, though, Birmingham still holds onto its old. One familiar landmark is Vulcan, a 55-foot cast-iron statue of the god of the forge that sits on a 124-foot pedestal atop Red Mountain, overlooking the city. For a bit of antebellum tradition, there's Arlington Antebellum Home and Gardens, an 1822 house turned into a museum. The Birmingham Museum of Art has a Kress collection, as well as one of the world's finest displays of Wedgwood pottery and a fine collection of Remington bronzes.

Geology buffs head for the Red Mountain Museum. Next door sits Discovery Place, a hands-on museum for children. Those interested in iron-and steelmaking visit Sloss Furnaces. Sports fans enjoy the memorabilia housed in the Alabama Sports Hall of Fame Museum at the civic center. And anyone who has ever gazed in awe at the sight of a plane overhead can find more than a few interesting displays at the Southern Museum of Flight, near the Birmingham airport.

Birmingham's botanical gardens are 67 acres of horticultural heaven and include a formal Japanese garden. The nearby Birmingham Zoo, the largest in seven southeastern states, houses some of the world's most unusual animals. Many live in the zoo's new, modern predator house.

Beyond Birmingham

Close enough to the city to make a delightful day or half-day trip are Oak Mountain State Park and Tannehill Historical State Park. Oak Mountain, 15 miles south of town via U.S. 31 or I-65, is the largest in the state-park system. Within its 9,940 acres are mountains, lakes, beaches, tennis courts, hiking trails, a demonstration farm, picnic areas, cabins, and campgrounds. Tannehill, 30 miles southwest of Birmingham via U.S. 78 or I-20, is built around the site of a pre–Civil War iron furnace. It includes hiking trails, an iron- and steelmaking museum, a country store, a gristmill, a picnic area, a train ride, and campgrounds.

Other Alabama Cities

Montgomery, state capital of Alabama, wears the face of a sleepy southern town. But don't let the image fool you. Not only does the city have much of historical value, but it's made great strides in the cultural field as well. Recently, it became the home of the Alabama Shakespeare Festival Theatre. Opened in late 1985, the new octagon-shaped theater is the home for year-round productions of plays performed by a resident repertory company. The theater traces its roots to the annual Shakespeare festival, which originated in the smaller city of Anniston.

For a taste of the past, there's the state capitol, with Alabama's history depicted in paintings around the inside of the dome. At the top of the west portico steps, a brass star marks the spot where Jefferson Davis took the oath of office as president of the Confederate States of America. Nearby is the first White House of the Confederacy, an 1835 Italianate-style house that served as the home of President and Mrs. Jefferson Davis while the capital of the Confederacy was in Montgomery.

Founded in 1711 by French explorer Jean Baptiste LeMoyne, Mobile is Alabama's oldest city, its major seaport, and a treasury of Old South heritage and architecture. Shaded by moss-veiled live oaks and banks of azaleas, Mobile's lovely old residential districts are resplendent with white columns and wrought iron. The city of 200,000 is especially lively in March and April, when America's oldest Mardi Gras winds through the streets, and mansions and gardens are open for the month-long Azalea Trail Festival. The city's many attractions include 800-acre Bellingrath Gardens, the Battleship USS *Alabama* Memorial Park, and Fort Conde, a re-creation of an 18th-century French fortress. Gulf Shores, south of the city on the Gulf of Mexico, has beautiful sand beaches and vacation accommodations.

Selma, 50 miles west of Montgomery, serves as a good example of the many small Alabama towns with antebellum history and heritage. It sits high on a bluff above the Alabama River and still has many antebellum homes of architectural interest.

In addition to being the home of the University of Alabama, Tuscaloosa has several historic houses. One, the Gorgas House, was built in 1829 and houses memorabilia of William Crawford Gorgas, an Army doctor credited with conquering yellow fever. Another, the Battle-Friedman House, was built in 1835 and is now the city cultural center and museum.

The undisputed giant of north Alabama, Huntsville is the home of the Alabama Space and Rocket Center, billed as the largest space museum in the world. Here, you can become an astronaut for the day. Activities include the simulated firing of a rocket engine, guiding spacecraft by computer, and experiencing the sensation of weightlessness on a zero-G machine. One of the latest additions to the center, a spectacular 67-foot movie screen, surrounds and covers the audience in a tilted 280-seat theater. Space-flight films are shown throughout the day. Also available are escorted bus tours of the NASA-Marshall Space Flight Center.

As important as the space center is to Huntsville, it isn't the only show in town. There's the Twickenham Historic District, a living museum of antebellum architecture and the state's largest district of antebellum homes. There's also Constitution Hall Park, commemorating the site of the meeting place of Alabama's first constitutional convention. Here are an early 19th-century cabinetmaker's shop, print shop, theater, library, and post office. From April through October, period folklife demonstrations are given. Area museums include the Huntsville Museum of Art and the Burritt Museum, built in the shape of a Maltese cross and displaying exhibits of archaeology, antiques, and minerals.

Nearby, Decatur is the home of the Wheeler Wildlife Refuge, the state's oldest and largest refuge. An interpretive center contains displays of native animals, and an observation platform allows you to see the waterfowl that migrate through the area from September through May. The greatest number can be seen from November to January.

The home of "Fighting" Joe Wheeler of Civil War fame, for whom the refuge is named, is 17 miles west of Decatur on State Highway 20. It is open during summer months and contains period antiques and rare china that was buried for protection during the Civil War.

More wildlife can be seen at Cook's Natural Science Museum. A privately owned museum, it features an extensive collection of insects, beetles, birds, and mounted animals.

For sheer entertainment, Decatur has Point Mallard Park. The main draw here is an aquatic center with a wave pool and an Olympic diving pool. There are also a campground, a golf course, nature trails, and in winter an ice-skating rink.

Tucked into the far northwestern corner of Alabama, Florence and Tuscumbia pay tribute to two notable figures in American history. In Florence, the W. C. Handy Home and Museum is dedicated to the man known as the Father of the Blues. It contains Handy's trumpet, the piano he used in composing the "St. Louis Blues," and other memorabilia. In Tuscumbia, Ivy Green is the birthplace of Helen Keller. Left both deaf and blind at an early age, Keller overcame her handicaps and devoted her life to the service of humankind. You can see the pump where young Helen learned her first word, "water," from teacher Anne Sullivan. And during the summer, an outdoor drama on the grounds tells the story of Helen Keller's life.

Florence also has Pope's Tavern Museum, which has served as stagecoach stop, Confederate hospital, and private residence since it was built in 1811. The largest Indian mound on the Tennessee River rises at the end of South Court Street.

In Anniston, the museum of natural history presents more than 100 mounted African animals in authentic settings. Nearby, Cheaha State Park sits atop Cheaha Mountain, the highest point in Alabama. And in Talladega, the Alabama International Motor Speedway roars with the excitement of auto races in spring. The International Motorsports Hall of Fame there gives a glimpse into the history of the sport.

For a pleasant day trip into North Alabama, Cullman has much to offer. The trip can begin at Ave Maria Grotto, which has more than 125 miniature churches, shrines, and famous buildings constructed of materials donated from throughout the world. Clarkson Covered Bridge, one of the longest two-span covered bridges standing in the Deep South, is the focal point of a rustic park with a shady picnic area. And Hurricane Creek Park, about 7 miles north of Cullman, is the perfect place to end the day, with a walk across a swinging bridge or a hike over the 4 miles of nature trails.

PRACTICAL INFORMATION FOR ALABAMA

WHEN TO GO. Any time is a good time to visit Alabama, for the weather is seldom extreme. Spring is a particularly good time, for the state seems to burst with azaleas and dogwoods in Mar. and early Apr. Fall is an excellent time to head for the northern stretches of the state, where the Appalachian foothills put on a colorful show.

HOW TO GET THERE. Birmingham is the largest city and has the largest airport. Centrally located, it is an excellent starting point for a visit to any part of the state.

By plane. Birmingham may be reached on *American, Continental, USAir, Delta,* and *United;* Huntsville-Decatur on *American, Delta, Continental,* and *United;* Montgomery on *American, Continental,* and *Delta;* Dothan on *Delta;* Anniston and Tuscaloosa on *Delta;* Mobile by *American, Delta,* and *TWA.*

By bus. *Greyhound.*

By train. *Amtrak* trains go into Birmingham, Anniston, and Tuscaloosa. The new *Gulf Breeze* recently began service between Birmingham and Mobile, with stops at Montgomery, Greenville, Evergreen, and Atmore. It joins in Birmingham with the daily northbound *Crescent* to Atlanta, Washington, New York, and intermediate points.

By car. I-59 runs from Chattanooga, TN, to Birmingham and Tuscaloosa; I-20 from Atlanta, GA to Anniston and Birmingham; I-65 from Tennessee passes through Decatur, Cullman, Birmingham, and Montgomery; I-85 comes from Atlanta, via LaGrange, GA, to Auburn and Montgomery.

By boat. The Tennessee-Tombigbee Waterway has recently been opened to boat traffic, allowing craft to travel from the southern reaches of the state up to the Tennessee River.

TOURIST INFORMATION. *Alabama Bureau of Tourism and Travel,* 532 S. Perry St., State Highway Bldg., Montgomery, AL 36130; *Alabama Division of Parks,* 64 N. Union St., Montgomery, AL 36104; *Alabama Travel Council,* 427 Interstate Park Dr., Montgomery, AL 36109; *Forest Supervisor,* U.S. Forest Service, Box 40, Montgomery, AL 36130, for detailed information on recreational facilities in national forests. *Alabama Department of Conservation and Natural Resources,* Information and Education Section, 64 N. Union St., Montgomery, AL 36130, for fishing, hunting, and camping.

Alabama Mountain Lakes Association, Box 1075, Decatur, AL 35602; *DeKalb County Tourist Association,* Box 125, Fort Payne, AL 35967; *Greater Birmingham Convention & Visitors Bureau,* 2027 1st Ave. N., Birmingham, AL 35203; *Tallacoosa Highland Lakes Association,* Box 97, Westover, AL 35186; *Historic Chattahoochee Commission,* Box 33, Eufaula, AL 36027.

For toll-free information from out-of-state (except Alaska and Hawaii), call 800–252–2262. In Alabama, call 800–392–8096.

In Birmingham, *Travelers' Aid* is at 624 19th St. N. (251–6400).

TELEPHONES. The area code for Alabama is 205. The cost of local calls is 25 cents, with no time limit. In most areas, you can direct dial credit, collect, or person-to-person calls by dialing 0 before the area code. For *emergency* assistance, dial 911.

HOW TO GET AROUND. The interstate system in Alabama, which was only recently completed around Birmingham, gives excellent access to all areas of the state.

Rental cars: *Hertz, National, Budget, Dollar, Thrifty, Sears,* and *American International* have offices in Birmingham. Most major companies serve other cities as well.

By plane. Local flights are provided by *American, Continental,* and *Delta.*

By bus. *Greyhound* (800–241–0396); *American Charters & Tours, Inc.,* Mobile (433–2684); *Ingram Buslines,* Tallassee (283–2750); *Joiner Transit Company,* Florence (764–8627); *Basden Transportation,* Tuscumbia (383–6220); *Alabama Stage Coach Lines,* Inc., Ozark (774–3471); *Johnson Bus Service,* Huntsville (539–0448).

By taxi. In Birmingham, *Yellow Cab* (252–1131) and *Veteran Cab* (328–1301). Limousine service available from *Royal Limousine* (979–7900).

HINTS TO MOTORISTS. Speed limits in the state, particularly in small municipalities, are strictly enforced. A right turn on red is permitted, except where posted. In Birmingham, rush hour can be frustrating, so if possible, plan your driving time to avoid the 7:30–8:30 A.M. and 4–6 P.M. rush.

ACCOMMODATIONS. Alabama accommodations, which range from the luxurious to the simple, are listed in categories based on the price of a double room: *Deluxe,* $95–$150; *Expensive,* $65–$95; *Moderate,* $40–$65; and *Inexpensive,* under $40.

Alexander City

Moderate

Horseshoe Bend. AL 22 and U.S. Hwy. 280 (205–234–6311). Has 50 rooms, restaurant, pool, lighted tennis, boating, and fishing facilities.

Anniston

Moderate

Hampton Inn. 1600 Hwy. 21 S., Oxford, AL 36203 (205–835–1492 or 800–426–7866). 130 rooms, some handicapped accessible, nonsmoking. Pool. Free Continental breakfast, local phone calls, in-room movies. 18 and under stay free in parents' room. Pets accepted.

Holiday Inn Anniston-Oxford. Jct. U.S. 78, 431, AL 21 and I-20, Box 3308, Anniston, AL 36203 (205–831–3410 or 800–465–4329). 237 rooms, some nonsmoking. London House Rest Restaurant, Cambridge Pub Lounge. Spa, outdoor whirlpool, game room, playground, picnic area, coin laundry. Teens and under stay free in parents' room. Free airport transportation. Some rooms in *Expensive* category.

Inexpensive

Carriage House Inn. 300 Quintard Ave. 36201 (205–237–0301). Has 98 guest rooms, pool, restaurant, lounge with entertainment.

Knights Inn-Anniston South. North of junction of I-10 and AL 21, exit 185, 25 Elm St., Oxford, AL 36203 (205–831–9480 or 800–722–7220). Offered here are 114 rooms, 12 of which are efficiencies. Pool, cable TV.

Birmingham

Deluxe

Embassy Suites Hotel. 2300 Woodcrest Pl. 35209 (205–879–7400 or 800–362–2779). There are 243 units, including 14 2-bedroom suites, in this property with expansive public areas in gardenlike atrium. Complimentary evening cocktails, breakfast, airport transportation. Coin laundry, indoor pool, sauna, whirlpool, health-club privileges. Restaurant, cocktail lounge.

Wynfrey Hotel. 2084 Valleydale Rd., at the Riverchase Galleria (205–987–1600 or 800–476–7006). Has 329 rooms, restaurant, lounge with entertainment, health facilities, shopping in adjacent mall. Weekend packages available.

Expensive

Courtyard By Marriott. 500 Shades Creek Pkwy. Homewood, AL 35209 (205–879–0400 or 800–321–2211). 142 guest rooms, restaurant, lounge, meeting facilities.

Holiday Inn Airport. 5000 10th Ave. N., Birmingham, AL 35212 (206–591–6900 or 800–465–4329). I-59 & I-20, Airport exit. 224 rooms, some nonsmoking. Color cable TV, pool, exercise room. Free in-room coffee. Jackson Square Restaurant,

Hooters Lounge, live entertainment. Teens and under stay free in parents' room. Complimentary airport transportation. Three other area Holiday Inns are at 7941 Crestwood Blvd. (205–956–8211); 1548 Montgomery Hwy. (205–822–4350); Medical Center Downtown, and 260 Oxmoor Rd. (205–942–2041).

Mountain Brook Inn. 2800 U.S. Hwy. 280 S. (205–870–3100). Has 162 rooms, restaurant, pool, lounge with entertainment. Complimentary airport transportation.

Radisson Birmingham (formerly Birmingham Hilton). 808 S. 20th St. (205–933–9000 or 800–282–5806). Has 298 rooms, restaurant, lounge with entertainment, pool, health facilities. Some rooms in *Deluxe* category.

Sheraton Perimeter Park South. 8 Perimeter Park Dr. (205–967–2700 or 800–325–3535). Has 209 rooms, restaurant, pool, health facilities. Some units equipped for mobility-impaired. Some rooms in *Deluxe* category.

Moderate

Days Inn-Civic Center. 2230 10th Ave. N., Birmingham, AL 35203 (205–328–6320 or 800–325–2525). This 200-room property adjoins the downtown Civic Center. Restaurant, cocktail lounge, color cable TV, pool.

Hampton Inn South. 1466 Montgomery Hwy., Birmingham, AL 35216 (205–822–2224 or 800–426–7866). 123 rooms, some nonsmoking, handicapped accessible. Pool; free Continental breakfast, local phone calls, in-room movies. 18 and under stay free in parents' room. Pets accepted.

La Quinta Inn. 905 11th Court, West, Birmingham, AL 35204–1806 (205–324–4510 or 800–531–5900). 106 rooms, some nonsmoking. Free copy of *Newsweek,* color cable TV, local calls, morning coffee. Pool. Government, military discounts. 24-hour Kettle Restaurant adjacent.

Motel Birmingham. 7905 Crestwood Blvd. (205–956–4440 or 800–338–9275). Restaurant, pool, play area, new garden rooms recently added, facing spacious courtyard. Free Continental breakfast, airport shuttle.

Inexpensive

Econo Lodge. Two locations: 103 Greensprings Hwy., at Valley Ave. (205–942–1263); 1813 Crestwood Blvd. (205–956–3650).

Red Roof Inn. 151 Vulcan Rd. Birmingham, AL 35209 (205–942–9414 or 800–843–7663). Member of fast-growing economy chain, this place has 97 well-maintained units. Color cable TV; restaurant next door.

Cullman

Moderate

Holiday Inn. 4½ mi. south on AL 69 (205–734–8484 or 800–465–4329). Has 126 rooms, Apples Restaurant, indoor pool with Hydro-Spa.

Decatur

Moderate

Days Inn Conference Center (formerly Decatur Inn-Master Hosts). 810 N. 6th Ave., Hwy. 31 N at Church St. near I-65 (205–355–3520 or 800–325–2525). 121 units, some king/leisure. Restaurant, Olympic pool, wading pool.

Holiday Inn. 1101 6th Ave., N.E. (205–355–3150 or 800–465–4329). Has 225 rooms, some studio rooms, Louie's Restaurant, Sade & Dora's Lounge, indoor/outdoor pools, whirlpool, electronic games. Some rooms in *Expensive* category. Lovely location on shores of Tennessee River and Lake Wheeler.

Quality Inn (formerly Ramada Inn). 3439 U.S. 31 S. (205–355–0190 or 800–228–5151). Has 92 rooms, two swimming pools. Restaurant and cocktail lounge; playground. Pets accepted.

Inexpensive

Econo Lodge. 1317 Hwy. 67, Box 5007, Decatur, AL 35602 (205–353–0333 or 800–446–6900). 84 units. Pool; free cribs, ice, local phone calls, color TV/movie channel. Restaurants near.

Dothan

Moderate

Comfort Inn Carousel. 3591 Ross Clark Circle (205–793–9090 or 800–228–5151). Has 90 rooms, restaurant, pool, playground, lounge.

Holiday Inn. 3053 Ross Clark Circle (205–794–6601 or 800–465–4329). Has 157 rooms, Veranda Restaurant, Duke's Lounge, pool, wading pool. Teens and under stay free in parents' room.

Olympia Motel & Conference Center. Hwy 231 S. (205–677–3321). Has 96 rooms, restaurant, pool, indoor hot mineral pool, lighted tennis, golf, health facilities.

Ramada Inn. 3001 Ross Clark Circle W. (205–792–0031 or 800–272–6232). Has 159 rooms, restaurant, lounge with entertainment, pool, wading pool. Some rooms in *Expensive* category.

Sheraton Motor Inn. 2195 Ross Clark Circle, S.E. (205–794–8711 or 800–325–3535). Has 151 rooms, restaurant, lounge with entertainment, pool.

Inexpensive

Days Inn. 2841 Ross Clark Circle, S.W. (205–793–2550 or 800–325–2525). Has 120 rooms (some handicapped-accessible); restaurant next door.

Florence

Moderate

Best Western Executive Inn. 504 S. Court St. (205–766–2331 or 800–528–1234). Has 120 rooms, restaurant, lounge with entertainment, pool, whirlpool.

Joe Wheeler State Resort Lodge. 20 mi. east on U.S. 72, then 4 mi. south at Rogersville (205–247–5461). Has 75 units, restaurant, pool, playground, lighted tennis, golf, state-park facilities.

Fort Payne

Moderate

Best Western Fort Payne. 1828 N. Gault Ave. (205–845–0481 or 800–528–1234). Has 66 rooms (some handicapped-accessible), restaurant, pool. Idyllic setting with panoramic views. Some rooms in *Inexpensive* category.

Gadsden

Moderate

Days Inn. I-759 and U.S. 411, Rainbow City exit, 1600 Rainbow Dr. (205–543–1105 or 800–325–2525). 103 units in attractive new lakeside inn. Outdoor pool, free cable TV, HBO. Many restaurants nearby.

Holiday Inn. 801 Cleveland, S.E. Attalla 35954 (205–538–7861 or 800–465–4329). Has 143 rooms, The Cafe Restaurant, Duke's Lounge with dancing, entertainment, pool, wading pool. Teens and under stay free in parents' room.

Huntsville

Expensive

Huntsville Hilton & Towers. 401 Williams Ave. (205–533–1400 or 800–445–8667). Has 284 rooms, restaurant, lounge with entertainment, pool, jogging track. Some rooms in *Deluxe* category.

Sheraton Inn Huntsville. 4404 University Dr., N.W. (205–837–3250 or 800–325–3535). Has 203 rooms, restaurant, lounge with entertainment, outdoor Olympic pool. Some rooms in *Deluxe* category.

Skycenter Airport Hotel & Conference Center. 10001 Hwy. 20 W. (205–772–9661 or 800–241–7873). Has 151 rooms, restaurant, lounge with entertainment, pool, health facilities, golf, tennis. In the airport terminal.

Moderate

Hampton Inn. 4815 University Dr., Huntsville, AL 35816 (205–830–9400 or 800–426–7866). 128 rooms. Heated pool, whirlpool, exercise room. Color cable TV. 1 mi. to Alabama Space and Rocket Center. Restaurant near. Airport transportation.

Holiday Inn Space Center. 3810 University Dr. (205–837–7171 or 800–465–4329). Has 180 rooms, The Garden Room Restaurant, Galaxy Lounge, racquetball, sauna, pool, jogging track, health facilities. Complimentary *USA Today;* king, female executive traveler rooms available.

Ramada Inn. 3502 Memorial Pkwy. S.W. (205–881–6120 or 800–272–6232). Has 141 rooms (some handicapped accessible), restaurant, pool, wading pool. Pets accepted.

Mobile

Deluxe

Stouffer's Riverview Plaza. 64 Water St. 36652 (205–438–4000 or 800–468–3571). 375 first-class rooms and suites, dining, entertainment, meeting and recreation facilities. In downtown historic district.

Moderate

Malaga Inn. 359 Church St. 36602 (205–438–4701). 40 elegantly furnished rooms in restored antebellum mansion with antiques, private balconies, gardens. Dining room is locally popular.

Montgomery

Expensive

Governor's House Hotel & Conference Center. 2705 E. South Blvd. (205–288–2800). Has 201 rooms, restaurant, pool, lounge, executive amenities.

The Madison Hotel. 120 Madison Ave. (205–264–2231; 800–356–1744, in AL). This 190-room hotel in heart of downtown historic district is centered by six-story atrium with exotic plants and tropical birds. Two restaurants, cocktail lounge with live entertainment. Pool, garage, parking lot, and airport transportation.

Moderate

Holiday Inn. Three locations: 9 mi. west on I-65 at Millbrook-Prattville exit (205–285–3420); 1100 W. South Blvd., at airport (205–281–1660); 1185 Eastern Bypass (205–272–0370). (Toll-free number for all three Holiday Inns: 800–465–4329.) Some rooms in *Expensive* category.

Riverfront Inn. 200 Coosa St., downtown (205–834–4300 or 800–325–3535). Has 130 rooms in a renovated railroad freight depot, restaurant, lounge with entertainment, pool.

Inexpensive

Best Western Montgomery Lodge. 977 W. South Blvd. (205–288–5740 or 800–528–1234). Has 100 rooms, restaurant, lounge, pool.

Days Inn. 1150 W. South Blvd. (205–281–8000 or 800–325–2525). Has 176 rooms, restaurant, pool. Also at 7725 Mobile Hwy., Hope Hull, AL 36043 (205–281–7151). 125 rooms, restaurant, pool.

Peddler's Motor Inn Best Western. 4231 Mobile Hwy. (205–288–0610 or 800–528–1234). Has 253 rooms, restaurant, lounge, pool.

Tuscaloosa

Moderate

Best Western University Inn. 1780 McFarland Blvd. N. (205–759–2511 or 800–528–1234). Has 106 rooms, restaurant, lounge, pool.

Shoney's Inn. 3501 McFarland Blvd. E. (205–556–7950 or 800–222–2222). Has 113 rooms, restaurant next door, pool.

Inexpensive

Days Inn. 3600 McFarland Blvd. (205–556–2010 or 800–325–2525). 152 rooms, restaurant next door, pool.

RESTAURANTS. In Alabama, you'll find barbecue, catfish, and Southern-fried chicken the backbone of many menus. Our price categories for a complete dinner (drinks, tax, and tip not included) are: *Expensive,* $20–$25; *Moderate,* $12.50–$20; and *Inexpensive,* under $12.50.

Anniston

Inexpensive

The Anniston. 1709 Noble (236–5156). Specialties are steaks, seafood. D, 4–10 P.M.; closed Sun., major holidays. AE, DC, MC, V.

Morrison's Cafeteria. 700 S. Quintard Ave., Oxford (831–7470). Good chain cafeteria with its own baking. L, D, 11 A.M.–8:30 P.M. MC, V.

Birmingham

Expensive

Dexter's. 354 Hollywood Blvd., Homewood (870–5297). French cuisine with a hint of Creole influence. Gumbo and mesquite-grilled entrées are popular. L, D. Open 11 A.M.–10 P.M.; to 11, Fri.–Sat.; 10:30 A.M.–10 P.M., Sun.; closed major holidays. Reservations recommended for dinner. AE, DC, MC, V.

Highlands, a Bar & Grill. 2011 11th Ave. S., in recently renovated Five Points South area (939–1400). L, D. Cuisine has a French influence and includes lamb, veal, fish, and steak. Reservations recommended. AE, MC, V.

Meadowlark Restaurant. 534 Industrial Rd., Alabaster (663–3141). Lovely country inn with charming setting featuring European cuisine. D, Mon.–Sat. AE, MC, V.

Michael's Sirloin Room. 431 S. 20th St. (322–0419). Superb steaks, with seafood and lamb as other specialties. L, D, 11 A.M.–11 P.M.; closed Sun., major holidays. AE, DC, MC, V.

Winston's. Wynfrey Hotel, 2084 Valleydale Rd., at the Riverchase Galleria (205–987–1600). Distinctive American, Continental cuisines in elegant formal setting. Jackets and ties, reservations, required. Cocktail lounge has entertainment. Open Mon.–Sat., 5:30–11 P.M.; closed Sun., major holidays. AE, DC, MC, V.

Inexpensive

Golden Rule Barbecue. 2520 Crestwood Blvd., U.S. 78 E., in Irondale (205–956–2678). A beloved Birmingham institution, the restaurant has been serving its renowned "loin" pork ribs and Brunswick stew since 1891. Inquire locally for hours.

Lloyd's. 5301 Hwy. 280 S. (991–5530). Specialty is barbecue in a casual atmosphere. Limited other dishes available, including chicken, shrimp. All fried. L, D. No credit cards.

Cullman

Inexpensive

All Steak. 414 2nd Ave., S.W. (734–4322). B, L, D. Open 6 A.M.–9 P.M., Mon.–Thurs.; to 10, Fri.–Sat.; 6:30 A.M.–4 P.M., Sun.; closed major holidays. Specializes in steak, seafood, own baking, Sun. buffet. No credit cards.

Decatur

Inexpensive.

Lyons Dining Room. In Decatur Inn Motel, 810 6th Ave., N.E. (355–3520). Specializes in steak, seafood, own baking. B, L, D. AE, DC, MC, V.

Morrison's Cafeteria. Beltline Mall (350–0190). L, D. One of good-quality chain cafeterias specializing in roast beef, seafood. L, D. MC, V.

Dothan

Inexpensive

Garland House. 200 N. Bell St. (793–2043). L, D. Specializes in crepes, own baking. In turn-of-the-century home. MC, V.

Spinnaker's. U.S. 231 N., in Wiregrass Commons Mall (205–794–8629). Seafoods, steaks, sandwiches, good selection of Mexican specialties are served here in a cozy, publike setting. L, D; open daily. AE, MC, V.

Florence

Inexpensive

Dale's. 1001 Mitchell Blvd. (766–4961). D, 5–10 P.M., closed Sun., major holidays. Specialties are steak and seafood. AE, DC, MC, V.

Morrison's Cafeteria. Regency Square Mall (766–2227). L, D. Open 11 A.M.–8:30 P.M.; Sun., to 7. One of chain, with own baking. MC, V.

Huntsville

Expensive

Skycenter Rib Cellar. In Skycenter Airport Hotel & Conference Center, 1001 Hwy. 20 W. (205–772–9661). D; closed Sun., major holidays. Well-prepared beef and lobster specialties. Jacket, tie, and reservations recommended. AE, DC, MC, V.

Inexpensive

Michael's. 3502 Memorial Pkwy. (881–6120). B, L, D; closed major holidays. Specializes in steak, with own baking. AE, DC, MC, V.

Morrison's Cafeteria. 5901 University Dr., in Madison Square Mall (830–2198). L, D. Varied selection of entrées, salads, vegetables; own baking. MC, V.

Mobile

Expensive

The Pillars. 1757 Government St. (478–6341). Stylish restaurant features Gulf seafood, Continental dishes, wines. D, 5–10 P.M. Mon.–Sat. AE, DC, MC, V.

Montgomery

Moderate

Bacchus Ristorante. The Madison Hotel, 120 Madison Ave. (264–2231). This stylish, locally popular dining room features northern Italian and regional American specialties in a sophisticated setting. Dress code. D, 6–10 P.M., Mon.–Fri.; to 11 Sat.; closed Sun., major holidays. Reservations requested. AC, DC, MC, V.

Mr. G's Gourmet. 3080 McGehee Rd. (281–1161). L, 11 A.M.–2 P.M., D, 5–10 P.M.; Fri., to 10:30; Sat., 5–10 P.M. closed Sun., major holidays. Prime rib, seafood, baking on premises. AE, DC, MC, V.

Sahara Restaurant. 511 E. Edgemont (262–1215). L, D. Open 11 A.M.–10 P.M.; closed Sun., major holidays. Music accompanies special fares of beef and seafood. AE, DC, MC, V.

Inexpensive

Morrison's Cafeteria. Eastdale Mall (227–8640). L, D. Open 10:45 A.M.–8:30 P.M.; Sun., to 7:30. One of chain, with own baking. MC, V.

Tuscaloosa

Inexpensive

The Landing. 2100 McFarland Blvd. E. (205–349–1803). Locally popular for superb prime rib, steaks, fresh seafoods. Children's menu. Open Mon.–Sat., 11 A.M.–2:30 P.M., 5–9:30 P.M.; Fri.–Sat., to 10; Sun., to 2:30 P.M. Closed major holidays. Lounge. AE, DC, MC, V.

Morrison's Cafeteria. University Mall (205–556–4960).One of chain, with good food. L, D. MC, V.

LIQUOR LAWS. In Alabama, a person must be 21 or older to buy or drink alcoholic beverages. Alcohol is sold by the bottle at state stores and in bars with licenses, daily until 2 A.M. There are no Sun. sales except in private clubs, and in Madison County (Huntsville).

MISSISSIPPI

If you've ever dreamed of the sweet scent of magnolias, of a riverboat paddling gently down the river, or of a dusky Delta morning with only the sounds of the birds coming out of the mist, you've dreamed of Mississippi.

Jackson—Journey to Mississippi's Heartland

A crossroads for the interstates that slice through Mississippi, Jackson has been the State Capital for as long as there has been a state. Typical of most southern capitals, it has a small-town feeling, with more than a touch of sophistication lying beneath the surface.

The State Capitol is patterned after the nation's capitol in Washington, D.C., and is well worth a tour. So, too, is the governor's mansion. Built in 1842, the exterior resembles the White House, and it is furnished with antiques and period pieces.

An older State Capitol, an impressive Greek-revival building used for legislative purposes from 1839 to 1903, now houses the state historical museum. Here are dioramas and exhibits tracing state history, as well as a collection of Jefferson Davis memorabilia. Other museums downtown include the Mississippi Museum of Art, with 19th- and 20th-century works by local as well as national artists. The Mississippi Museum of Natural Science features WPA dioramas, as well as aquariums that tell the ecological story of the state. One of the most popular places in town is the Russell C. Davis Planetarium, with everything from astronomy shows to starlight concerts.

For sports fans, the Dizzy Dean Museum displays memorabilia of the famous baseball player. And the Mississippi Agriculture and Forestry Museum includes a 1920s living history farm and town, along with an exhibit center and a forest trail.

Beyond Jackson

Just a short 4 miles west of Jackson, Mynelle Gardens provides an escape to nature, with 6 acres of botanical plantings, including flowers and blooming shrubs, water plantings, and Japanese and tropical areas. About 10 miles northeast of town, off I-55, Ross E. Barnett Reservoir offers outdoor recreation in the form of fishing, boating, swimming, and camping. And little more than 20 miles to the northwest, near Flora, the Mississippi Petrified Forest represents a geologic oddity. Giant petrified trees, dating back 36,000,000 years, were deposited here by a prehistoric river. The site includes a nature trail, a geographical museum, and a lapidary shop.

Branching off I-20 to the west, and again off I-55 to the north, just at the Jackson city limits on both interstates, is the Natchez Trace Parkway. One of the country's earliest major highways, the trace once stretched from Natchez to Nashville, Tennessee. It was heavily traveled in the early 1800s by boatmen who floated their goods down the Mississippi River, sold them and the boats, and returned home overland. The parkway you travel today crosses and recrosses the old trace and is operated by the National Park Service.

Other Mississippi Cities

Jackson may lie in the state's heartland, but the heart of Mississippi lies in its antebellum towns. One of the loveliest is Vicksburg. Perched like a crown atop a bluff above the Mississippi River, Vicksburg is a city of brick streets, lovingly tended gardens, antebellum homes, and gaslights. An important fact to remember is that when Mississippi took a vote on secession at the beginning of the Civil War, Vicksburg voted against it. But the citizens were caught up in the war anyway. Memories of the siege on the town are found at the Vicksburg National Military Park. It has been estimated that if you were to read every word on every marker and monument there, it would take about three weeks of eight-hour days.

After, or even before, visiting the National Military Park, you should stop at the Old Courthouse Museum in Vicksburg. Here, memorabilia of the siege and the town's beginnings are displayed. Another place to visit is the Biedenharn Candy Company. The museum here reveals that it was Joseph Biedenharn who had the innovative idea of bottling Coca-Cola so it could be transported to workers in the Mississippi cotton fields. For a nostalgic trip on the Mississippi River, hop aboard the *Spirit of Vicksburg,* an authentic paddlewheel boat that leaves the downtown dock daily. Or you can see a scale model of the Mississippi at the Waterways Experiment Station, where the Army Corps of Engineers studies navigation and flood control.

Among the antebellum homes open for tours are Anchuca, Balfour House, Cedar Grove, and McRaven. Some also offer bed-and-breakfast accommodations.

Another delightful antebellum town is Natchez, with nearly 600 historic structures. The names roll off the tongue like drops of honey—Longwood,

Dunleith, Arlington, Melrose, Rosalie, and Auburn. Most date from the early to mid-1800s. Connelly's Tavern was built around 1798 and is owned and operated by the Natchez Garden Club. Stanton Hall, perhaps the most famous landmark, was completed in 1857 and is owned and operated by the Pilgrimage Garden Club. Many of the homes are open during the annual pilgrimages, in March and October.

A part of Natchez that has developed over the past decade is Natchez-under-the-Hill. This historic district, below the high bluff on which the town sits, was once a thriving entertainment center for 19th-century boatmen. The remaining buildings now house a variety of shops and restaurants.

All in Natchez isn't from the 19th century, though. The Grand Village of the Natchez Indians features archaeological artifacts from the years 1682 to 1729. And nearby on the Natchez Trace Parkway, Mount Locust was built around 1789 and served as an inn for travelers.

Columbus claims more than 100 antebellum homes, many of which are open for tours. Among them are Amzi Love, Barry House, Rosedale, Shadowlawn, and Temple Heights. Another, Waverly Plantation, is about 10 miles northwest of town. Built in 1852, Waverly has beautiful twin circular self-supporting stairways leading to a 65-foot-high octagonal observation cupola.

Another delightful but smaller town of architectural importance is Holly Springs, in the north-central part of the state. Founded by William Randolph, a descendant of Virginia's John Randolph, Holly Springs never went through the frontier era of log cabins. Instead, its first structures were Georgian-colonial and Greek-revival mansions. One is Melrose, a Greek-revival brick home built in 1858.

A half hour's drive south of Holly Springs lies Oxford, home of the University of Mississippi. Here are the Center for the Study of Southern Culture, a research center for southern music, folklife, and literature; and the Department of Archives and Special Collections, with a permanent exhibit on author William Faulkner. Of special interest is Rowan Oak, the home where Faulkner lived from 1930 to 1962. It remains much as it was during Faulkner's lifetime.

Although it is more industrial than historic, Meridian does have its famous house. Merrehope is a stately 26-room mansion begun in the mid-1800s and enlarged and remodeled in 1904. It is furnished with Empire-style antiques. Also in Meridian is the Jimmie Rogers Museum, which honors the Father of Country Music and displays Rogers's personal effects and memorabilia.

The Smaller Jewels of Mississippi

Some of the best things in the South aren't in the larger metropolitan areas. They're often tucked away in small towns or along the back roads and off major highways. So it is with the Cottonlandia Museum in Greenwood. This regional historical museum depicts the history of the Delta over the past 10,000 years. Also in Greenwood is Florewood River Plantation State Park, with museum displays and living-history presentations of lifestyle typical of an antebellum cotton plantation. Find tiny Philadelphia on the map, northwest of Meridian via State Highway 19, and you'll find the Choctaw Museum of the Southern Indian, with exhibits and archives detailing the culture of Indians in the region. Stop in Laurel, halfway between Meridian and Hattiesburg, and you'll find the Lauren Rogers Library and Museum of Art, with one of the best collections of international baskets you'll find anywhere.

Travel to tiny Lorman, northwest of Natchez on U.S. 61, and the Old Country Store will delight with merchandise dating back a century or more. And just a few miles up the road, Port Gibson is the home of the

Grand Gulf Military Park Museum, a 400-acre park with Civil War artifacts. Here, also, are the ruins of Windsor, the remains of a Greek-revival mansion built in 1861 and destroyed by fire in 1890. Several homes in Port Gibson may be toured, and some offer overnight accommodations.

For railroad buffs, there's Vaughn, about an hour's drive north of Jackson via I-55. Here, the Casey Jones Museum State Park commemorates the legendary railroad engineer killed in a train wreck in 1900.

PRACTICAL INFORMATION FOR MISSISSIPPI

WHEN TO GO. Any time. Mississippi has a moderate climate year-round, which accounts for its lush landscape. Although the state is known for a mild climate, it is not exempt from winter storms that occasionally dip into the South, and into northern areas of the state.

HOW TO GET THERE AND AROUND. Jackson is the gateway to the state and has good air service from other parts of the region. It is also a crossroads for the interstates coming into the state.

By plane. *American, United,* and *Delta* into Jackson. *Royale* (601–354–2813 in Jackson) connects New Orleans, Jackson, and Natchez.

By bus. *Greyhound* offers statewide service. *Gulf Transport* (601–234–4313) operates from Mobile through eastern Mississippi to Memphis.

By train. *Amtrak* from Chicago to New Orleans runs over Illinois Central Gulf rails from north to south. Amtrak's *Crescent* runs from New Orleans through Picayune, Harrisburg, Meridian and Laurel on the way to Atlanta.

By car. I-55, U.S. 45, and U.S. 61 run from north to south; U.S. 82, I-20, U.S. 84, I-10, and U.S. 90 run from east to west.

TOURIST INFORMATION. *Mississippi Department of Economic Development–Tourism Division,* Box 849, Jackson, MS 39205 (601–359–3414; 800–647–2290, out-of-state). For **hunting and fishing information:** *Department of Wildlife Conservation,* Box 451, Jackson, MS 39205 (601–961–5300). For **state park information:** *Department of Natural Resources,* Bureau of Recreation & Parks, Box 20305, Jackson, MS 39209 (601–961–5099. For **national-forest** information: *National Forests in Mississippi,* 100 W. Capitol St., Suite 1141, Jackson, MS 39269 (601–960–4391). For information about **bicycle tours:** *Governor's Council on Physical Fitness & Sports,* 723 N. President St., Suite 450, Jackson, MS 39201 (601–354–6344). For the **Natchez Trace Parkway:** *Tupelo Visitor Center,* Natchez Trace Pkwy., RR #1, NT-143, Tupelo, MS 38801 (601–842–1572).

Individual city chambers of commerce: *Greenville,* Drawer 933, Greenville, MS 38701 (601–378–3141); *Holly Springs,* Box 12, Holly Springs, MS 38635 (601–252–2943); **Visitor Bureaus:** *Columbus–Lowndes Convention & Visitor Bureau,* Box 789, Columbus, MS 39701 (601–392–1191; 800–327–2686 outside MS); *Jackson Convention & Visitors Bureau,* Box 1450, Jackson, MS 39205–1450 (601–960–1891; 800–354–7695 outside MS); *Meridian/Lauderdale County Tourism Commission,* Box 5866, Meridian, MS 39302 (601–483–0083); *Natchez Convention and Visitor Commission,* Box 794, Natchez, MS 39120–0794 (601–446–6345; 800–647–6724 outside MS); *Vicksburg–Warren County Tourism Commission,* Box 110, Vicksburg, MS 39180 (601–636–9421; 800–221–3536 outside MS).

TELEPHONES. The area code for Mississippi is 601. The cost of local pay-telephone calls is 25 cents, and there is no time limit. You can direct-dial credit, collect, or person-to-person calls in many areas of the state by dialing 0 before the area code. In some less-populated areas, you must dial the operator and give your number and billing information.

EMERGENCY TELEPHONE NUMBERS. In case of an emergency, dial 911. To call the *Mississippi Highway Patrol,* call: Batesville, 563–4651; New Albany, 534–4755; Greenwood, 453–4515; Starkville, 323–5314; Meridian, 693–1026; Jackson, 982–1212; Brookhaven, 833–7811; Hattiesburg, 264–3529; Gulfport, 864–1314.

WATER TRAVEL. The luxury **riverboats** *Delta Queen* and *Mississippi Queen* dock in Natchez and Vicksburg. For cruise information, call the Delta Queen Steamboat Company (800–543–1949).

Pleasure boats. The 234-mi.-long Tenn-Tom Waterway, opened in early 1985, flows through northeast Mississippi. One section begins its Mississippi sojourn just south of Columbus and goes to Amory. A 46-mi.-long canal section extends from Amory north to Bay Springs Lock and Dam; and a 39-mi.-long divide section goes from Bay Springs Lock and Dam to the Tennessee River. The waterway is in operation 24 hours a day, 7 days a week. Pleasure craft can lock through quickly and safely. Clearance for masthead is a minimum of 52 ft. above normal flood elevation, or 40 ft. above high water.

HINTS TO MOTORISTS. The interstate system in Mississippi is well developed, with good east-west and north-south connections. In winter, Jackson and points north are occasionally subject to freezing rains, sleet, or snow. When that happens, the interstates close, and traffic comes to a virtual standstill. Traffic laws and speed limits are enforced, especially in smaller municipalities.

ACCOMMODATIONS. Mississippi accommodations are listed by city and price categories. Rates are for double occupancy, and categories are *Expensive,* $55–$80; *Moderate,* $35–$55; and *Inexpensive,* $20–$35.

Biloxi

Expensive

Royal D'Iberville. 3420 W. Beach Blvd. 39531 (601–388–6610). This is a lavish beachfront resort, with 264 rooms, dining, entertainment, recreation. Some rooms in *Moderate* category.

Moderate

Howard Johnson's. 3920 W. Beach Blvd. 39531 (601–385–5555 or 800–323–9164). At this 225-room beachfront hotel you'll find a pool, dining room, entertainment. Some rooms in *Expensive* category.

Columbus

Moderate

Columbus Ramada Inn (formerly Hilton Inn.) 1200 Hwy. 45 N. (601–327–7077 or 800–272–6232). Has 121 rooms, restaurant, lounge with entertainment, pool. Some rooms in *Expensive* category.

Holiday Inn. 5th St. at 5th Ave. N. & Hwy 45 N. (601–328–5202 or 800–465–4329). Has 155 rooms, pool, Annabelle's Restaurant, Good Times Bar & Grille. Teens and under stay free in parents' room.

Inexpensive

Passport Inn (formerly Columbus Motel). 2400 Hwy. 82 E. at 24th St. (601–328–2551). Has 55 rooms, lounge, pool.

Greenville

Moderate

Hampton Inn. 2701 U.S. 82 E. (601–334–1818 or 800–426–7861). 120 rooms, some handicapped-accessible, nonsmoking. Pool, whirlpool, sports court, exercise room. Free Continental breakfast, local phone calls, in-room movies. 18 and under stay free in parents' room. Restaurant near.

Ramada Inn. 2700 U.S. 82 E. (601–332–4411 or 800–272–6232). Has 121 rooms, restaurant, lounge, pool. Buffet breakfast, free airport transportation.

Greenwood

Moderate

Ramada Inn. 900 W. Park Ave. (601–455–2321 or 800–272–6232). Has 149 rooms, restaurant, lounge, pool, whirlpool, video game room.

Gulfport

Moderate

Holiday Inn Beachfront. U.S. 90 39501 (601–864–4310 or 800–465–4329). 229 rooms, across from beach, with pool, restaurant, entertainment. Some rooms in *Expensive* category.

Inexpensive

Best Western Seaway Inn. I-10 at U.S. 49 39503 (601–864–0050 or 800–528–1234). 170 rooms, pool, restaurant, lounge.

Hattiesburg

Expensive

Holiday Inn. Hwy. 49 N. 39401 (601–268–2850 or 800–465–4329). Has 125 rooms, pool, wading pool. Louie's Restaurant and Lounge with live entertainment.

Moderate

Hampton Inn. 4301 Hardy St., I-59 and U.S. 98 (601–264–8080 or 800–426–7861). 116 rooms, some handicapped accessible, nonsmoking. Pool, free Continental breakfast, local phone calls, in-room movies. 18 and under stay free in parents' room. Restaurant nearby.

Inexpensive

Peddler's Motor Inn (formerly Best Western Peddler's Motor Inn). 900 Broadway Dr. 39401 (601–582–7101). Has 112 rooms, all ground floor, restaurant, lounge with live entertainment, dancing, pool.

Days Inn. I-59 and U.S. 49, Exit 67-A, 3320 Hwy. 49 N., 39401. (601–268–2251 or 800–325–2525). 181 rooms (some handicapped-accessible), nonsmoking. Restaurant, free movies (news/sports channels), gift and craft shop, pool.

Jackson

Deluxe

Ramada Renaissance Hotel. 1001 County Line Rd. (601–957–2800 or 800–272–6232). Has 300 rooms, restaurants, lounge with live entertainment, pool, executive suites.

Expensive

Holiday Inn. Four locations: 200 E. Amite St. (601–969–5100); 2375 N. State St., at Medical Center (601–948–8650); U.S. 55 N. Frontage Rd. (601–366–9411); 2649 U.S. 80 W. (601–355–3472). Toll-free reservations number is 800–465–4329. Some rooms in *Moderate* category.

Moderate

Best Western Metro Inn. 1520 Ellis Ave. (601–355–7483 or 800–528–1234). Has 160 rooms, restaurant, pool, hot tub, exercise room.

La Quinta Motor Inn. 150 Angle St., I-20 at Terry Rd. (601–373–6110 or 800–531–5900). Has 101 rooms, restaurant, pool. Airport transportation may be arranged.

Passport Inn. 5035 I-55 North 39206 (601–982–1011). Has 145 guest rooms, pool, restaurant, exercise room, coin laundry. Some rooms in *Inexpensive* category.

Inexpensive.

Days Inn. Three locations: I-20 at Hwy. 80 E. (601–939–8200 or 800–325–2525); I-55 N. & Briarwood (601–957–1741 or 800–325–2525); I-20, U.S. 80 and Ellis Ave., Exit 42B (601–948–0680 or 800–325–2525). Some rooms in *Moderate* category.

Laurel

Moderate

Sawmill Ramada Inn & Convention Center. Hwy. 1105 Sawmill Rd. (601–649–9100 or 800–272–6232). Has 206 rooms, restaurant, lounge with entertainment, pool.

Inexpensive

Days Inn (formerly Quality Inn). I-59 and U.S. 11 N (601–428–8421 or 800–325–2525). Has 140 rooms—some nonsmoking—restaurant, lounge with live entertainment, pool.

Town House Motel. 340 Beacon St. (601–428–1527). Has 87 rooms, pool, Continental breakfast in sitting room. Seniors' discount.

Meridian

Moderate

Days Inn. 1521 Tom Bailey Dr., at I-59 (601–483–3812 or 800–325–2525). Has 122 rooms, restaurant, pool.

Holiday Inn. Two locations: Jct. I-59, I-20, U.S. 11 and Hwy. 19 (601–485–5101); Hwy. 45 S. at I-20 and I-59 (601–693–4521). Toll-free reservations number is 800–465–4329. Restaurants, lounges, pools. Teens and under stay free in parents' room.

Inexpensive

Best Western Meridian. I-20 and 59 S. Frontage Rd., at airport (601–693–3210 or 800–528–1234). Has 120 rooms, restaurant, lounge with entertainment, pool.

Natchez

Expensive

The Natchez Eola Hotel. 110 N. Pearl St., downtown (601–445–6000). Has 126 rooms in restored hotel, restaurant, lounge with entertainment.

Ramada Hilltop. 130 John R. Junkin Dr. (601–446–6311 or 800–272–6232). Has 163 rooms, restaurant, pool, coin laundry. Some rooms in *Moderate* category.

Riverpark Hotel (formerly Sheraton Natchez). 645 S. Canal St. (601–446–6688). This place has 148 rooms, restaurant, lounge with entertainment, pool.

Moderate

Best Western Prentiss. Hwy. 61 S. (601–442–1691 or 800–528–1234). Has 128 rooms, restaurant, pool, golf, tennis, jogging track.

Days Inn. Hwy. 61 S. (601–445–8291 or 800–325–2525). Has 120 rooms, restaurant, tennis court, pool.

Bed & Breakfast

The Briars. 31 Irving La. (601–446–9654; 800–634–1818 out of state). Overlooking Mississippi River, this magnificent antebellum home was the setting for the 1845 wedding of Jefferson Davis to Varina Howell. 13 rooms; pool, whirlpool. Complimentary evening beverages; sumptuous plantation breakfast served in dining pavilion overlooking the river.

Burn. 712 N. Union St. 39120 (601–442–1344 or 800–654–8859). This Greek-revival plantation home was built in 1822. Six antique-rich guest rooms, pool and gardens.

Dunleith. 84 Homochitto St. (601–446–8500). Greek-revival home built in 1856. Lodging is in slave quarters, where rooms have fireplaces.

Linden. 1 Linden Pl., one block off John A. Quitman Pkwy. (601–445–5472). Seven antiques-furnished rooms in gracious 1800 antebellum home owned by Connor family since 1849. Each has private bathroom; central air-conditioning and heat. Hearty Southern breakfast. No pets or children under 10. No credit cards.

Monmouth. John A. Quitman Pkwy. (601–442–5852 or 800–828–4531). This is one of Natchez's grandest mansions, built in 1818. Some rooms in main house, others in slave quarters.

Oxford

Moderate

Best Western Oxford Inn. 1101 Frontage Rd. (601–234–9500 or 800–528–1234). Has 100 rooms, restaurant, lounge with entertainment, pool.

Holiday Inn. 400 N. Lamar (601–234–3031 or 800–465–4329). Has 101 rooms, Victoria's Restaurant and Lounge with entertainment, pool, racquetball, golf, tennis. Free HBO, airport transportation. Teens and under stay free in parents' room.

Vicksburg

Moderate

Best Western Magnolia Motor Inn. 4155 Washington St. (601–636–5145 or 800–528–1234). Has 118 rooms, restaurant, pool.

Days Inn. 8260 Pemberton Blvd. (601–634–1622 or 800–325–2525). Has 65 rooms, all poolside, some nonsmoking, handicapped-accessible. Recreation room, sauna, Jacuzzi, 24-hour day care. Restaurant nearby.

Holiday Inn. U.S. 80 & I-20 (601–636–4551 or 800–465–4329). Has 325 rooms, restaurant. Holidome recreation area with atrium, poolside lounge, indoor-outdoor pools, lighted tennis courts, jogging trail, game room, exercise room, whirlpool, golf privileges, coin laundry.

Quality Inn (formerly Comfort Inn). I-20 Frontage Rd. (601–634–8607 or 800–228–5151). Has 70 rooms, pool, health facilities. Restaurant nearby.

Bed & Breakfast

Anchuca. 1010 First East St. (601–636–4931 or 800–262–4822, out of state). Nine rooms available. Swimming pool, whirlpool; Southern breakfast.

Cedar Grove. 2200 Oak St. (601–636–1605 or 800–862–1300, out of state). Has 18 rooms, including a carriage house. Decorated with period antiques, some original furnishings.

The Duff Mansion. 1114 1st St. E., in Historic District (601–636–6968). Eight rooms, elegantly furnished with antiques and period furniture. This 1856 mansion is listed in National Registry of Historic Places. Pool; pets accepted.

RESTAURANTS. Good regional cuisine is the keynote to most Mississippi restaurants. Our price categories for a complete dinner (drinks, tax, and tip not included) are: *Expensive,* $20–$25; *Moderate,* $12.50–$20; and *Inexpensive,* under $12.50.

Biloxi

Expensive

Mary Mahoney's Old French House. 138 Rue Magnolia (374–0163). This lovely restored home, circa 1737, is renowned for Gulf seafoods with a distinctive Creole touch. D, Mon.–Sat. AE, DC, MC, V.

Moderate

Fisherman's Wharf. 1020 E. Beach Blvd. (436–4513). Casual beachside seafood house is a landmark for red snapper, oysters, flounder, and shrimp. L, D, daily. AE, DC, MC, V.

Inexpensive

McElroy's Harbor House. 695 Beach Blvd., Biloxi Small Craft Harbor (601–435–5001). This casual, family-style seafood restaurant specializes in broiled stuffed flounder, shrimp, oysters, catfish; chicken, steaks, and children's plates are also available. B, L, D; closed major holidays. AE, DC, MC, V.

Columbus

Moderate

The Depot. 1302 Main St. (329–6612). L, D; closed Sun., major holidays. In old railroad depot; specialties are prime rib, seafood, own baking. AE, MC, V.

Hattiesburg

Inexpensive

Morrison's Cafeteria. 999 Broadway Dr., in Cloverdale Mall (545–3241). L, D. One of regional chain, with own baking. MC, V.

Wagon Wheel Restaurant. 3 mi. south on U.S. 49 (545–2323). L, D; closed Mon., major holidays. Specialties are barbecue, homemade bread, desserts. AE, MC, V.

Jackson

Moderate

The Cafe. Radisson Walthall Hotel. 225 E. Capitol St. (601–948–6161). Specializes in American Regional/Southern cookery. B, L, D daily; also luncheon buffet. Lavish Sun. brunch highlighted by classical chamber music. Lounge, entertainment. AE, DC, MC, V.

Silver Platter. 219 N. President (969–3413). L, D; closed Sun., Mon., major holidays. Reservations recommended. Specialties are lamb, shrimp, own baking. MC, V.

Inexpensive

Cerami's. Rice Rd., I-55 at Natchez Trace Exit (856–8469). D; closed Mon., major holidays. Specialties are homemade pasta, other Italian dishes. AE, DC, MC, V.

Cock of the Walk. 1 Dyke Rd., Madison (856–5500). D; closed major holidays. Specializes in catfish, chicken dinners, skillet bread. AE, MC, V.

1001 Restaurant. 1001 County Line Rd. (601–956–1001). Mesquite-grilled specialties are featured here in a charming, airy, and garden-like atmosphere. Open 6–10:30 P.M. Mon.–Sat.; closed Sun. and major holidays. Cocktail lounge; reservations suggested Fri. and Sat. AE, DC, MC, V.

Meridian

Inexpensive

Weidman's. 208 22nd Ave. (693–1751). L, D. Special lobster and steam items, plus black-bottom pie. AE, DC, MC, V.

Natchez

Inexpensive

Carriage House. 401 High St., on grounds of Stanton Hall. (445–5151). L, D; closed major holidays. Specialties are southern-fried chicken, ham, own baking. AE, MC.

Cock of the Walk. 15 Silver St. (446–8920). D; closed Sun, major holidays. Specialties are catfish, hush puppies, fried dill pickles. Overlooking Mississippi River. AE, MC, V.

Vicksburg

Inexpensive

Garnett's. I-20 and Hwy. 80 E., in Holiday Inn of Vicksburg. (636–4551). B, L, D. Three buffets offered daily, with special emphasis on dinner buffet of seafood or prime rib. AE, MC, V.

Maxwell's. 4207 Clay St. (636–1344). L, D. Creole cooking, seafood, steaks, prime rib. AE, DC, MC, V.

Walnut Hills Roundtables & Tearoom. 1214 Adams St. (638–4910). L, D; closed Sat., major holidays. Specialties are rib-eye steak, home-style vegetables served family style. AE, MC, V.

LIQUOR LAWS. In Mississippi, a person must be 21 or older to buy or drink alcoholic beverages. Almost half of the state's counties are dry. Alcohol may be purchased by the bottle, daily except on Sun. (when there may be sales by local option in some resort areas). on Christmas, and on Election Day while voting stations are open.

LOUISIANA

There's more to Louisiana than just New Orleans, but no one can deny that the Crescent City is the number one destination for visitors to the state.

New Orleans—an Old Charmer

Even a world's fair in 1984 couldn't change the basic character of New Orleans. The fair came and went, leaving behind some good times and more than a few memories, as well as a number of new hotels and restaurants. But the spirit of the city remains the same. She's a lady with a past, and proud of it.

The most famous area of New Orleans is the French Quarter, a 100-square-block district of shops, nightclubs, hotels, restaurants, and history. The best place to begin a tour is at 525 St. Ann Street, Visitor Information Center, the Greater New Orleans Tourist and Convention Commission. Then, armed with information on places to see, including a brochure that outlines a walking tour of the quarter, you can explore to your heart's content. One logical place to start is at Jackson Square, which in pleasant weather is filled with artists, mimes, musicians, and sightseers. St. Louis Cathedral dominates one side of the square. It's a beautiful structure, built in 1794. To either side of the cathedral, the Pontalba Apartments face each other across the square. They were built in 1849 and are now owned by the city and the Louisiana State Museum. Across Decatur Street from the square, the French Market begins. Here, the Café du Monde is as much a tradition as the farmers' market that has been on the site for more than two centuries. No visit to New Orleans is complete without a cup of café au lait (half chickory coffee and half hot milk) and a square type of doughnut called a beignet. Between the Café du Monde and the farmers' market, a number of shops have moved into the old buildings, including one that makes and sells the delicious praline candy that is indigenous to the city.

If you're in the mood for a bit of river watching, the Moon Walk is also just across the street from Jackson Square. It's a block-long promenade right down to the river's edge, with benches to encourage sitting and watching the traffic of tankers, towboats, and barges. Another place from which to see the river is the Jax Brewery, renovated from an old brewhouse into a festival marketplace. It's at the corner of Decatur and Toulouse streets and has benches and tables spread out along six levels of outdoor terraces that face the river. Yet another place to see the river is from the 31st-floor observation deck of the World Trade Center at the end of Canal Street.

To actually capture the spirit of the Mississippi River, though, you have to get out on it. A free ferry leaves from the wharf at the end of Canal Street every 15 minutes between 5:45 A.M. and 9:30 P.M. Or you can choose from six riverboats that offer sightseeing cruises.

Back in the French Quarter, there's still plenty to see. The Presbytere, next to the cathedral, is a part of the Louisiana State Museum complex and contains maps, Audubon's *Birds of America,* and numerous artifacts of Louisiana history. Yet another part of the museum is Madame John's Legacy, at 632 Dumaine Street. This is one of the oldest buildings in the Mississippi Valley, built in 1727 and rebuilt in 1788. Many other buildings worth a visit include the Hermann-Grima House, with furnishings typical of the period from 1830 to 1860; the Old Absinthe House, a tavern where Andrew Jackson and Jean Lafitte supposedly met to plan the defense of New Orleans in 1815; and the Gallier House, the 1860–68 residence of architect James Gallier, Jr.

Not to be forgotten are the shopping opportunities in the French Quarter. There are a number of boutiques and gift shops, but the antique shops along Royal and Magazine streets are excellent. Also a must is a visit to Preservation Hall, where traditional New Orleans jazz is played nightly. It's often crowded, but admission is a small donation, and the music is perhaps the most authentic in the city.

Stepping out of the French Quarter is like stepping into another era. The St. Charles Streetcar offers a nostalgic ride to the Garden District, the city's most elegant section. Here, lovely Greek-revival homes are surrounded by magnolia trees, palms, and live oaks. Farther out of downtown is Audubon Park and Zoological Gardens, a 400-acre park with a recently renovated zoo that features natural habitats for the animals. One of the more modern aspects of New Orleans, though, is the Superdome, the world's largest enclosed stadium-arena. The Sugar Bowl is played here, as are home games of the Saints and the Tulane University football team.

Beyond New Orleans

Just 6 miles south of the city, the Chalmette National Historical Park commemorates the 1815 Battle of New Orleans. There's a national cemetery here, along with a museum and visitor center with audiovisual presentation. In Slidell, across the mouth of Lake Pontchartrain via I-10, lies Fort Pike Commemorative Area. It was built not long after the War of 1812 to protect the navigational channels into New Orleans.

Travel the Great River Road west of New Orleans, and you find a number of beautiful old plantation homes. Only 8 miles from New Orleans's Moisant International Airport, on State Highway 48, is Destrehan Plantation. Built in 1787, it is an interesting blend of West Indies and Greek-revival architecture. Farther west, 2½ miles beyond Reserve on state highway 44, San Francisco Plantation was recently completely restored. It features five painted ceilings, ornate grillwork, gingerbread trim, and authentic furnishings. Crossing the river to Vacherie, you find Oak Alley Plantation. A fine example of Greek Revival architecture, it is famous for its alley of 28 live oaks. Crossing back over the river, there are three homes near Convenant. One, Judge Poche Plantation, is a Victorian-Renaissance-revival house built in 1870. Another, Tezcuco Plantation, is an 1855 raised cottage of Greek-revival style with ornate friezes and galleries trimmed with wrought iron. West from here, Houmas House Plantation is a magnificent Greek-revival mansion built in 1840 and furnished with period antiques. And Nottoway Plantation, across the river in White Castle, is believed to be the largest plantation home in the South, with 64 major rooms.

Other Louisiana Cities

Less than 20 miles north of Nottoway Plantation lies Baton Rouge, State Capitol of Louisiana. It is a mixture of history, industry, and plantation heritage. The State Capitol is an imposing 34-story building with an observation tower that affords a great view of the city and surrounding area. Nearby, the Old Arsenal Museum houses historical exhibits of Louisiana under the rule of ten flags. The old State Capitol is one of the most interesting-looking structures in town, resembling a Gothic-revival castle. It has a beautiful stained-glass dome and a spiral staircase. Across River Road from the old capitol is the Louisiana Arts and Science Center, once a railroad station and now a museum of art, history, and hands-on experiences for children. On the grounds of the Louisiana State University in Baton Rouge is the Rural Life Museum, a complex of plantation buildings and museum displays (see also The Gulf Coast chapter).

North of Baton Rouge via U.S. 61 is tiny St. Francisville. The annual pilgrimage here each March is one of the highlights of the region, but many of the plantation homes can be toured at any time of year. Among the more popular are Oakley, where John James Audubon once lived; Rosedown, with 17th-century-style French gardens; the Myrtles; Catalpa; the Cottage, which was begun during the Spanish occupation of the area; Rosemont Plantation, the restored boyhood home of Jefferson Davis; and Afton Villa Gardens, all that remains of a beautiful antebellum plantation house that burned more than a decade ago.

Lafayette sits in the middle of Cajun country, and the attractions here reflect its heritage. One of the most popular is the Acadian Village, five miles south via U.S. 167. It looks like a small Acadian bayou town. The only thing that gives it away as a museum complex is that no one lives here. Back in town, the Lafayette Natural History Museum, Planetarium, and Nature Station gives a more educational look at the geology of the area and the wildlife unique to it. At the Lafayette Museum, you'll find a display of carnival costumes, for New Orleans isn't the only city to celebrate Mardi Gras.

Lake Charles also reflects the Acadian culture. Items of local history are housed in the Imperial Calcasieu Museum. And about 15 miles southwest of town, the Creole Nature Trail offers views of several bayous, as well as migrating waterfowl and one of the largest alligator populations in the country.

Alexandria marks the geographic center of the state, and one of the best reasons for stopping here is the Kent House, a restored French-colonial plantation home. Completed in 1800, it contains period furnishings and has many interesting outbuildings to explore. Other attractions in the area include the Marksville prehistoric Indian Park and Hot Wells Health Resort, which features mineral baths and recreation facilities.

In Monroe, the Bible Research Center and Elsong Gardens features rare Bibles, including an original Danish 1550 Martin Luther Bible and a 1617 King James Bible. Louisiana Purchase Gardens and Zoo are a popular place for children, with 70 acres filled with formal gardens and zoo animals. A worthwhile side trip takes you 35 miles east of the city to Poverty Point State Commemorative Area, in Eppes. Here, displays document the earliest aboriginal culture group yet found in the lower Mississippi Valley, dating from 700 to 1700 B.C.

The largest city in north Louisiana is Shreveport, home of the American Rose Center. Here, also, is the R. W. Norton Art Gallery, with American and European paintings, including a large collection of western art by Frederick Remington and Charles Russell. The Louisiana State Exhibit Museum contains dioramas, historical murals, and archaeological displays. The R. S. Barnwell Memorial Garden and Art Center is a combination art and horticultural facility. For entertainment, Shreve Square has a variety of restaurants, nightclubs, and shops. Next door to Shreveport, Bossier City offers Thoroughbred racing from late spring into fall, and the live radio show "Louisiana Hayride" on weekends all year.

The Smaller Jewels of Louisiana

Places not to be overlooked on a visit to Louisiana include the smaller towns of Natchitoches, Many, and St. Martinsville. Natchitoches, the oldest permanent settlement in the Louisiana Purchase territory, has several fine historic structures, as well as the Bayou Folk Museum. Situated 20 miles south of town on State Highway 1, this museum is housed in the restored home of short-story writer Kate Chopin and includes exhibits dealing with the history of the area. Many, southwest of Natchitoches via State Highway 6, offers the beautiful Hodges Gardens, one of the largest privately operated gardens and wildlife refuges in the country. A 10-mile driving trail loops through the gardens and around a 225-acre lake, offering ample opportunities to stop along the way and get a closer look at the plantings. The best time of year to visit is spring, when hundreds of azaleas bloom along hillsides and around garden borders. Farther south, St. Martinville is on the banks of peaceful Bayou Teche. It is the home of the Evangeline Oak, believed to be the meeting place of the real Evangeline and Gabriel, made famous in Longfellow's poem. The Longfellow-Evangeline Commemorative Area, with Acadian House Museum, is north of town.

PRACTICAL INFORMATION FOR LOUISIANA

WHEN TO GO. Any time is a good time to visit Louisiana, with one exception. In July and Aug., the heat in New Orleans can be almost unbearable, except in the hotels, all of which are air-conditioned. If you enjoy crowds and merrymaking, Feb. is the time to visit, when Mardi Gras is in full swing. Accommodations can be difficult to find at this time and around Jan. 1, when the Sugar Bowl college-football classic is played at the Superdome.

Spring is probably the best time to visit, when the entire state blooms with flowering trees and bulbs. The plantations are especially pretty then.

The northern area of Louisiana, especially around Shreveport, is subject to the same weather as Dallas, TX, which lies to the west, and Jackson, MS, to the east. Usually mild winters can turn unexpectedly harsh when winter storms sweep across this area, but they seldom last more than a few days or a week at the most.

HOW TO GET THERE. By plane. New Orleans is the transportation gateway to southern Louisiana, and Shreveport and Monroe are the gateways to northern Louisiana. New Orleans International Airport, about 17 mi. west of the French Quarter, is the main airport for New Orleans and surrounding area. Shreveport Regional Airport is 5 mi. from Shreveport–Bossier City. Monroe Regional Airport, near downtown, serves Monroe. Serving New Orleans are *American, Delta, Continental, United, TWA, Southwest,* and *USAir.* Regional airlines include *Royale.* Serving Shreveport are *American, Delta,* and the commuter airline *Royale.* Serving Monroe are *Delta,* and *Royale.* Alexandria is served by *Delta* and *Royale;* and Lake Charles has flights on *Royale.*

By bus. *Greyhound.*

By train. *Amtrak* has three major lines that connect New Orleans with the west and east coasts and the north-central states.

By car. From Picayune, MS, you can reach New Orleans via I-59. I-55 takes you from McComb, MS, south to Kentwood and Hammond. I-20 comes in from Vicksburg, MS, and cuts through the state west to the Texas state line. I-10 enters the state at Vidor, TX, and leads across to Slidell. In the north, I-20 comes into Shreveport from Texas and continues east. U.S. 71 comes in from Texarkana, AR, and goes south to Shreveport and then southeast to Alexandria and New Orleans. U.S. 61 enters the state at Woodville, MS, and goes south to Baton Rouge and then east to New Orleans. Note: Highway 1 is the best way to go from Shreveport to Alexandria.

By river boat. See above, under "Mississippi."

TOURIST INFORMATION. *Louisiana* **Office of Tourism,** Box 94291, Baton Rouge, LA 70804–9291 (504–925–3858). For **hunting and fishing** information: *Louisiana Dept. of Wildlife and Fisheries,* Box 15570, Baton Rouge, LA 70895 (504–925–3617). For **national forest** information, *Forest Service,* Southern Region, 50 7th St., N.E., Atlanta, GA 30323.

For information on individual cities, contact the following. *Greater New Orleans Tourist & Convention Commission,* 1520 Sugar Bowl Dr., New Orleans, LA 70112 (504–566–5011). *Shreveport-Bossier Convention & Visitors Bureau,* Box 1761, Shreveport, LA 71166 (318–222–9391; 800–551–8682); *Baton Rouge Convention & Visitors Bureau,* Drawer 4149, Baton Rouge, LA 70821 (504–383–1825); *Lafayette Convention & Visitors Commission,* Box 52066, Lafayette, LA 70505 (318–232–3737); *Monroe–West Monroe Convention & Visitor Bureau,* 1333 State Farm Dr., Monroe, LA 71202 (318–387–5691); *Rapides Parish Convention & Visitors Bureau,* Box 8110, Alexandria, LA 71306 (318–443–7049). *Southwest Louisiana Convention & Visitors Bureau,* Box 1912, Lake Charles, LA 70601 (318–436–9588).

TELEPHONES. The area code for New Orleans and the "toe" of Louisiana is 504. The area code for the entire western portion of the state is 318. You can direct dial credit, collect, or person-to-person calls by dialing 0 before the area code from most areas of the state. The cost of a local pay-phone call is 25 cents, and there is no time limit. For *emergency* assistance, dial 911.

HOW TO GET AROUND. The interstate system in Louisiana serves east-west traffic well in both the northern and southern parts of the state, but it does not connect the northern to the southern area. So unless you're making a special trip to New Orleans or are driving across the Deep South anyway, New Orleans is out of the way. Three interstates do converge in New Orleans: I-59 from Birmingham, AL; I-55 from Chicago and St. Louis; and I-10 from Jacksonville, FL.

By plane. *Delta* and *Royale* airlines service cities within the state.

By bus. *Greyhound,* as well as *Arrow Coach, Central Texas Bus Lines, Inc., Great Southern Coaches, Inc., Orange Belt States,* and *Salter Bus Lines* serve some cities within the state. In New Orleans, the Union Passenger Terminal, 1001 Loyola Ave., about a 10-minute walk from Canal St., handles *Greyhound* (504–525–4201). *Amtrak* departs from here also (504–528–1610; 800–872–7245).

By taxi. Taxi fares are $1.10 initially, and 20 cents each ⅕ mi. From New Orleans International Airport, *Airport Rhodes Limousine Service* (464–0611, 24-hour reservation service) offers transportation between the airport and hotels, ranging generally $7–$8 per person.

By ferry. The Mississippi River may be crossed by ferry at New Orleans, Plaquemine, White Castle, Reserve, Luling, Belle Chase, St. Francisville, or Lutcher.

HINTS TO MOTORISTS. Driving in the French Quarter of New Orleans is somewhat like trying to thread a needle with a piece of almost-too-big string. The streets are narrow and crowded, and at some hours some streets are blocked to all but pedestrian traffic. Walking is easy here and taxis plentiful, so once you arrive, it's best to park your car and leave it until you're ready to depart the French Quarter.

Leaving the interstate in southern Louisiana, you'll find yourself at times on narrow roads, often bordered by bayous and with little or no shoulder to the road, so there's no margin for driving errors. This is especially true in the extreme southern areas.

Driving between southern and northern areas of Louisiana is time consuming because of the lack of interstate connections. But such a trip can be rewarding if you look for out-of-the-way attractions and enjoy seeing the countryside.

ACCOMMODATIONS. Hotels, motels, and inns are listed alphabetically, by city and by price category, based on double occupancy. Categories are: *Super Deluxe,* \$125 and up; *Deluxe,* \$95–\$125; *Expensive,* \$65–\$95; *Moderate,* \$50–\$65; and *Inexpensive,* \$50 and under.

Alexandria

Expensive

Alexandria Hilton & Convention Center. 4th & Jackson Sts. (318–442–9000 or 800–445–8667). Has 174 rooms, restaurant, lounge with entertainment,

Moderate

Best Western of Alexandria. 2720 W. MacArthur Dr. (318–445–5530 or 800–528–1234). Has 154 rooms, restaurant, lounge with entertainment, pool.

Holiday Inn (formerly Sheraton Inn). 2716 W. MacArthur Dr. (318–487–4261 or 800–465–4329). Has 127 rooms, restaurant, lounge with entertainment, pool.

Inexpensive

Days Inn. 2300 N. MacArthur Dr. (318–443–7331 or 800–325–2525). 150 rooms, some nonsmoking, handicapped accessible. Restaurant, Back Door Lounge.

Motel 6. 546 MacArthur Dr. (318–445–2336). 113 rooms. Free TV, local calls. Pool. Restaurants near.

Rodeway Inn. 742 MacArthur Dr. (318–448–1611; 800–228–2000). Has 121 rooms, pool, coin laundry. Restaurant nearby.

Baton Rouge

Deluxe

Embassy Suites Hotel. 4914 Constitution Ave. (504–924–6566 or 800–362–2779). Has 224 rooms, restaurant, lounge with entertainment, pool, health facilities.

Expensive

Baton Rouge Hilton. 5500 Hilton Ave., at Corporate Sq. (504–924–5000 or 800–445–8667). Has 298 rooms, restaurant, lounge with entertainment, pool, tennis, jogging path, health facilities.

Bellemont Hotel. 7370 Airline Hwy. (504–357–8612 or 800–535–8486). Has 300 rooms, restaurant, lounge with entertainment, pool, jogging path. Some rooms in *Moderate* category.

Sheraton Baton Rouge Hotel. 4728 Constitution Ave. (504–925–2244 or 800–325–3535). Has 290 rooms, restaurant, lounge with entertainment, pool.

Moderate

Best Western Monarch Inn. 10920 Mead Rd. (504–293–9370 or 800–528–1234). 150 rooms, some are king suites. Restaurant; lounge, entertainment. Free HBO, morning coffee. Pool.

Holiday Inn. Three locations: Siegen Lane and I-10 E (504–293–6880); 9940 Airline Hwy. (504–924–7021), and Exit 151, Port Allen, LA 70767 (504–343–4821).

Toll-free reservations number is 800–465–4329. Pools, restaurants, lounges. Some rooms in *Expensive* category.

Lafayette

Expensive

Lafayette Hilton & Towers. 1521 Pinhook Rd. (318–235–6111 or 800–445–8667). Has 328 rooms, restaurant, lounge with entertainment, pool, jogging path.

Moderate

Best Western Evangeline. 108 Frontage Rd. Hwy. 167 N. (318–236–3584 or 800–528–1234). Has 194 rooms, restaurant, pool. Golf, tennis nearby. Some rooms in *Inexpensive* category.

Days Inn. 1620 N. University (318–237–8880 or 800–325–2525). 120 rooms, some handicapped accessible, nonsmoking. Restaurant, pool, coin laundry. Government, military, senior discount plans.

Holiday Inn Central. 2032 N.E. Evangeline Thruway (318–233–6815 or 800–465–4329). Has 244 rooms, restaurant, lounge with entertainment, Holidome recreation area with indoor pool, tennis, jogging path, health facilities, sauna, game room. Some rooms in *Expensive* category.

Holiday Inn North. 2716 N.E. Evangeline Thruway (318–233–0003 or 800–465–4329). This chain has 184 rooms, with a coin laundry, pool, and wading pool. Bonaparte's Dining Room, Sassy's Lounge. Teens and under stay free in parents' room. Some rooms in *Expensive* category.

La Quinta Motor Inn. 1810 Hwy. 167 N. at I-10 (318–233–5610 or 800–531–5900). Has 139 rooms, restaurant, pool.

Lake Charles

Expensive

Lake Charles Hilton. 505 N. Lakeshore Dr. (318–433–7121 or 800–445–8667). Has 267 rooms, restaurant, lounge with entertainment, pool. On Lake Charles.

Moderate

Howard Johnson's Motor Lodge. I-10 and Hwy. 171 (318–433–5213 or 800–654–2000). Has 140 rooms, restaurant, lounge with live entertainment, pool, jogging path. Free in-room movies, guest laundry, playground.

Inexpensive

Best Western Belmont. 2700 Broad St. (318–433–8291 or 800–528–1234). 85 rooms; in-town location. Restaurant, lounge, pool, satellite TV, exercise facilities. Children under 12 stay free in parents' room. Small pets only.

Econo Lodge. 1101 W. Prien Lake Rd. (318–474–5151 or 800–446–6900). 104 rooms. Free HBO; restaurant and boat slip on premises. On shores of scenic Contraband Bayou.

Monroe

Expensive

Holiday Inn Civic Center Holidome. I-20 at 1051 U.S. Hwy. 165 Bypass (318–387–5100 or 800–465–4329). 259 rooms. Concierge floor facing atrium. Fun center, sauna, whirlpool, indoor pool. Bobbisox and French Market cafés; lounge. Airport, mall transportation. Teens and under stay free in parents' room.

Moderate

Best Western Monroe Motor Lodge. 610 Civic Center Expwy. (318–323–4451 or 800–528–1234). Has 92 rooms, restaurant, pool. Newly remodeled. Some rooms in *Inexpensive* category.

La Quinta Airport Inn. 1035 U.S. 165 Bypass S. (318–322–3900 or 800–531–5900). 130 rooms, some nonsmoking. Pool. 24-hour Kettle Restaurant adjacent. Government, military discounts. Free local phone calls, morning coffee, color cable TV, free *Newsweek* magazine.

New Orleans

Super Deluxe

Bourbon Orleans. 717 Orleans St. (504–523–2222 or 800–521–5338). With a lobby like a French drawing room, this historic hotel has 164 rooms and 47 suites with Queen Anne furnishings; most king-size beds have canopies. Restaurant, 1815 ballroom, lounge with entertainment, pool, parking, valet service.

Fairmont Hotel. University Pl. (504–529–7111 or 800–446–6900). Has 730 rooms, restaurant, lounge with entertainment, pool, tennis.

Hotel Meridien New Orleans. 614 Canal St. (504–525–6500 or 800–223–9918). Has 497 rooms, restaurant, lounge with entertainment, pool, health facilities.

Hyatt Regency New Orleans at Louisiana Superdome. 500 Poydras Plaza & Loyola Ave. (504–561–1234 or 800–228–9000). Has 1,193 rooms, restaurant, lounge with entertainment, pool.

Inter-Continental New Orleans Hotel. 444 St. Charles Ave. (504–525–5566 or 800–327–0200). Has 497 rooms, restaurant, lounge with entertainment, pool, health facilities.

Marriott Hotel. Canal and Chartres Sts. (504–581–1000 or 800–228–9290). Has 1,290 rooms, restaurant, lounge with entertainment, pool, jogging path.

Monteleone Hotel. 214 Royal St. (504–523–3341 or 800–535–9595). Has 600 rooms, restaurant, lounge with entertainment, pool.

New Orleans Hilton Riverside & Towers. Poydras St. at the Mississippi (504–561–0500 or 800–445–8667). Has 1602 rooms, restaurant, lounge with entertainment, pool, tennis, jogging path, health facilities.

Pontchartrain Hotel. 2031 St. Charles Ave. (504–524–0581 or 800–952–8092). Has 100 rooms, restaurant.

Royal Orleans—An Omni Classic Hotel. 621 St. Louis St. (504–529–5333 or 800–843–6664). Has 351 rooms, restaurant, lounge with entertainment, pool.

Royal Sonesta Hotel. 300 Bourbon St. (504–586–0300 or 800–343–7170). Has 500 rooms, restaurant, lounge with entertainment, pool.

Sheraton New Orleans Hotel & Towers. 500 Canal St. (504–525–2500 or 800–325–3535). Has 1,200 rooms, restaurant, lounge with entertainment, pool.

Westin Canal Place. 100 Rue Iberville (504–566–7006 or 800–228–3000). Has 438 rooms, restaurant, pool.

Windsor Court. 300 Gravier St. (504–523–6000 or 800–266–2662). Has 310 rooms, restaurant, lounge with entertainment, pool, health facilities.

Deluxe

Dauphine Orleans Hotel-Master Host. 415 Dauphine St. (504–586–1800 or 800–521–7111). Has 109 rooms, pool.

Holiday Inn Crowne Plaza. 333 Poydras (504–535–9444 or 800–465–4329). Has 441 rooms, restaurant, lounge with entertainment, pool. Some rooms in *Super Deluxe* category.

Maison Dupuy. 1001 Toulouse St. (504–586–8000). 194 rooms in beautifully restored French Quarter hotel. Dining room, lounge. Heated pool, exercise room, valet garage (fee). Airport transportation.

Expensive

Holiday Inn—French Quarter. 124 Royal St. (504–529–7211 or 800–465–4329). Has 252 rooms, restaurant, indoor pool, indoor parking. Some rooms in *Deluxe* category.

Lamothe House. 621 Esplanade Ave., in the French Quarter (504–947–1161). An inn with 20 rooms. Some rooms in *Deluxe* category.

Le Pavillon Hotel. Baronne at 833 Poydras St. (504–581–3111 or 800–535–9095). Has 220 rooms, restaurant, lounge with entertainment, pool.

Prytania Park Hotel. 1525 Prytania St. (504–524–0427 or 800–862–1984). 62 rooms, 13 in restored Victorian town house. Charming hotel in Garden District.

Refrigerators, color cable TV. Free parking, breakfast. Some rooms in *Deluxe* category.

Moderate

Days Inn Read Blvd. 5801 Read Blvd. (504–241–2500 or 800–325–2525). Here, there are 143 rooms, some nonsmoking, with balcony or patio. Across street from Lake Forest Plaza, two minutes from Lake Pontchartrain. Color TV with HBO and ESPN; pool, playground. Full service restaurant.

La Quinta Airport Inn. 5900 Veterans Memorial Blvd., Metairie (504–456–0003 or 800–531–5900). 153 rooms, some nonsmoking. Government, military discounts. 24-hour Denny's Restaurant adjacent. Free local phone calls, morning coffee, color cable TV, free *Newsweek* magazine.

The Warwick Hotel. 1315 Gravier St. (504–586–0100 or 800–535–9141). Has 175 rooms, restaurant, lounge with entertainment.

Shreveport

Expensive

Regency Hotel of Shreveport. 102 Lake St., I-20 at Spring St. (318–222–7717). Has 190 rooms, restaurant, lounge with entertainment, pool, jogging path. Some rooms in *Deluxe* category.

The Residence Inn by Marriott. 1001 Gould Dr., Bossier City, LA 71111 (318–747–6220 or 800–331–31310). Available in this two-story inn are 72 one- and two-bedroom housekeeping suites with living room; many have fireplaces. Coin laundry, pool, whirlpool, sports court.

Sheraton Bossier Inn. 2015 Old Minden Rd., Bossier City (318–742–9700 or 800–325–3535). Has 212 rooms, restaurant, pool, health facilities. Some rooms in *Moderate* category.

Sheraton Pierremont Hotel & Towers. 1419 E. 70th St. (318–797–9900 or 800–325–3535). Has 280 rooms, restaurant, lounge with entertainment, pool. Some rooms in *Deluxe* category.

Moderate

Bossier City Luxury Inn (formerly Hilton Inn Bossier). 3033 Hilton Dr., Bossier City (318–747–2400). Has 246 rooms, restaurant, lounge with entertainment, pool. Some rooms in *Expensive* category.

Days Inn. I-20 Exit 13, 4935 W. Monkhouse Rd. (318–636–0080 or 800–325–2525). 148 rooms, some nonsmoking, handicapped-accessible. Restaurant, pool, picnic ground, and tables. Government, military, senior discount plans.

Holiday Inn Financial Plaza. 5555 Financial Plaza (318–688–3000 or 800–465–4329). Has 207 rooms, restaurant, lounge with entertainment, Holidome recreation area with indoor/outdoor pools, whirlpool, sauna, exercise room; jogging path. Teens and under stay free in parents' room.

Ramada Inn. 5116 Monkhouse Dr. (318–635–7531 or 800–272–6232). 258 rooms, some nonsmoking. Atrium dining room, 24-hour coffee shop; lounge, dancing, live entertainment. Fitness center; transportation to Louisiana Downs racetrack.

RESTAURANTS. Louisiana cuisine has a Cajun flair that's irresistible. New Orleans offers some of the finest dining you'll find anywhere, but some of the smaller towns hold dining surprises as well. Our price categories for a complete dinner (drinks, tax, and tip not included) are: *Super Deluxe,* $30 and up; *Deluxe,* $25–$30; *Expensive,* $20–$25; *Moderate,* $12.50–$20; and *Inexpensive,* under $12.50.

Baton Rouge

Moderate

Chalet Brandt. 7655 Old Hammond Hwy. (927–6040). L, D; closed Sun., Mon., major holidays, also last week in July, first two weeks in Aug. French cuisine, with Medallions de veau a local favorite. AE, MC, V.

Lafitte's Landing. "In the shadow of the Sunshine Bridge," Donaldsonville. (504–473–1232). Internationally renowned Chef John Folse works his singular magic, blending "*haute* Creole" and Cajun cuisines. Historic structure reputedly was haunt of pirate Jean Lafitte. Reservations required. D, daily. AE, DC, MC, V. Chef Folse also manages the Pilot House Restaurant on grounds of Tezcuco Plantation.

Ralph & Kacoo's. 7110 Airline Hwy. (356–2361). L, D; closed major holidays, Mardi Gras. Specialties are seafood, crawfish dishes in season, steak. AE, MC, V.

The Village. 8464 Airline Hwy. (925–2551). L, D; closed Mon., major holidays. Italian and American menu, with homemade pasta dishes. AE, DC, MC, V.

Inexpensive

Piccadilly Cafeteria. 7169 Florida Blvd. (924–6535). L, D. Regional chain, own baking. Three other locations in the area. No credit cards.

Lafayette

Moderate

Café Vermilionville. 1304 Pinhook Rd. (237–0100). L, D; closed major holidays. Reservations recommended. Specialties include red fish, own baking. AE, MC, V.

Chez Pastor. 1211 Pinhook Rd. (234–5189). L, D; closed Sun., major holidays. Creole, Acadian menu. AE, DC, MC, V.

La Fonda. 3809 Johnston St. (984–5630). L, D; closed Sun., Mon., July 3–11, major holidays. Mexican food. AE, MC, V.

Prejean's. Hwy. 167 North (896–3247). A Lafayette landmark for crayfish, oysters, shrimp, gumbo, and live Cajun music. L, Mon.–Fri; D, daily. AE, DC, MC, V.

Lake Charles

Moderate

Chez Oca. 815 Bayou Pine Dr. (439–8364). L, D; closed Sun, major holidays. Reservations recommended. Owned by a former New Orleans chef. Continental cuisine with specialties such as Louisiana turtle soup, fresh fish amandine. Jacket and tie required for dinner. AE, MC, V.

New Orleans

Super Deluxe

Antoine's. 713 St. Louis St. (581–4422). L, D; closed Sun., Mardi Gras, major holidays. French, Creole cuisine. Specialties include oysters Rockefeller, pompano en papillote, and tournedos. AE, DC, MC, V.

Broussard's. 819 Conti (581–3866). D; closed major holidays. Reservations recommended; jacket required. Specialties are duck Nouvelle Orleans, chicken ratatouille, oysters Gresham, trout Conti. AE, DC, MC, V.

Caribbean Room. In the Pontchartrain Hotel. (524–0581). L, D. Reservations recommended; jacket required. Menu is eclectic, and specialties include shrimp saki, trout Veronique, steak Diane, and mile-high ice-cream pie. AE, DC, MC, V.

Commander's Palace. 1403 Washington Ave., in Garden District (899–8221). L, D; closed Mardi Gras, major holidays. Reservations required. French, Creole menu, excellent Sun. jazz brunch. Outdoor dining. AE, DC, MC, V.

Galatoire's. 209 Bourbon St. (525–2021). L, D; closed Mon., Mardi Gras, major holidays. French, Creole menu. Excellent seafood includes trout Marguery, trout meuniere amandine, and broiled pompano. Jacket and tie at dinner.

Le Ruth's. 636 Franklin St., Gretna. (362–4914). D; closed Sun., Mon., major holidays. Reservations recommended; jackets required. The limited French menu perfectly complements the intimate environment. AE, MC, V.

Expensive

Arnaud's Restaurant. 813 Bienville St., at Bourbon St. (523–5433). L, D; closed major holidays. Reservations, jacket required. Wide selection of delectable dishes, including oysters Bienville, shrimp Arnaud, and filet mignon Clemenceau. AE, DC, MC, V.

Bon Ton. 401 Magazine St. (524–3386). L, D; closed Sat., Sun., major holidays. Reservations required for dinner. Creole cuisine, with excellent turtle soup, redfish Bon Ton. AE, MC, V.

Brennan's. 417 Royal St. (525–9711). B, L, D; closed Christmas. Creole menu, with seafood specialties, but best known for its breakfasts. AE, DC, MC, V.

Court of Two Sisters. 613 Royal St. (522–7261). B, L, D; closed Christmas. Reservations recommended. French, Creole menu in a beautiful garden setting. AE, DC, MC, V.

Kolb's. 125 St. Charles (522–8278). L, D. Authentic Bavarian décor. Schnitzel à la Kolb, imported draft beer. AE, MC, V.

K-Paul's Louisiana Kitchen. 416 Chartres St. (524–7394). The fiery Cajun blackened seafood cooking craze began in Paul Prudhomme's French Quarter kitchen. No reservations, and lines are usually lengthy. D, Mon.–Fri. AE, MC, V.

Mosca's. On Hwy. 90 in Waggaman (436–9942). D; closed Sun., Mon., month of Aug. Reservations required, except none taken for Sat., Thanksgiving, Christmas. Italian cuisine with emphasis on seafood.

Tujagues. 823 Decatur St. (525–8676). L, D. French, Creole menu. AE, MC, V. The quintessential neighborhood restaurant, its low-key, laid-back ambience makes it a favorite with locals and celebrities alike.

Moderate

Dooky Chase. 2301 Orleans (822–9506). L, D. Excellent Creole restaurant but in high-crime area, so it's best to take a cab to and from front door. AE, MC, V.

Felix's. 739 Iberville St., between Bourbon and Royal (522–4440). L, D; closed Sun. Nationally famous for oysters on half shell. AE, MC, V.

Inexpensive

Acme Oyster House. 724 Iberville (522–5973). L, D; Closed Sun., Mardi Gras, major holidays. The granddaddy of local oyster bars; good po-boy sandwiches also. No credit cards.

Camellia Grill. 626 S. Carrollton (866–9573). B, L, D; closed major holidays. Specializes in gourmet sandwiches, own baking. No credit cards.

The Jackson Brewery. Decatur St. facing Jackson Sq. (529–1211). In renovated turn-of-the-century brewhouse. New Orleans and Louisiana cuisine, from gumbo to meat pies. B, L, D. No credit cards.

NOTE: This is only a sample of the dining experiences New Orleans has to offer. For a dining guide to the city, contact the *Greater New Orleans Tourist & Convention Commission,* 1520 Sugar Bowl Dr., New Orleans, LA 70112 (504–566–5011).

Shreveport

Moderate

Brocato's Restaurant. 189 E. Kings Hwy. (865–2352). Family-owned since 1924, this locally popular establishment specializes in Italian dishes and also offers American-style steaks and seafoods. Children's menu available. D, Tues.–Sun., closed Mon., major holidays. AE, DC, MC, V.

Don's Seafood and Steak House. 3100 Highland Ave. (865–4291). L, D; closed major holidays. Specializes in steak, seafood, Cajun dishes. AE, D, DC, MC, V.

Sansone's. 701 E. Kings Hwy. (865–5146). L, D; closed major holidays. Steak, seafood, and Italian dishes highlight the American and Continental menu here. AE, DC, MC, V.

Smith's Crosslake Inn. 5301 Lakeshore Dr. (631–0919). D; closed Sun., major holidays. Seafood, steak, and Crosslake catfish attract locals as well as visitors. AE, MC, V.

LIQUOR LAWS. In Louisiana, a person must be 18 or older to buy or drink alcoholic beverages; some establishments may set 21 as age for admission. Some parishes in north Louisiana are dry. Alcohol is sold by the drink or bottle in many establishments. Days and times of sales vary with locality. New Orleans has the most liberal ordinances.

WHAT TO SEE AND DO IN NEW ORLEANS

TOURS. Tourism is one of New Orleans's major industries, and practically every type of touring service has popped up. There are bus tours, walking tours, and steamboat tours. There are tours of restaurants and bars, plantations, the French Quarter, the Mississippi River, museums, houses, and graveyards.

River and Bayou Cruises. For one-day or half-day excursions on the Mississippi River and connecting waterways, the New Orleans Steamboat Company has the *Steamboat Natchez* (about as authentic a steamboat as one can get), the *Bayou Jean Lafitte* (travels the Mississippi to Bayou Barataria, once the stronghold of the infamous pirate, Jean Lafitte), and the sternwheeler *Cotton Blossom.* The *Natchez* has two trips daily at 11:30 A.M., and 2:30 P.M. Adults, $11.75; children 6 to 12, $5.50; children under 6 free. Evening-dinner jazz cruises depart daily at 6:30 P.M.; cruise, $13.75; cruise with dinner, $29.75. The *Bayou Jean Lafitte* makes one trip each day, 11 A.M. to 4 P.M.; the charge is $13.75 for adults, half price for children. The *Natchez* and *Bayou Jean Lafitte* are moored on the river at the foot of the Toulouse Street Wharf at Jackson Sq. The *Cotton Blossom* also offers a "Zoo Cruise" round-trip from the Toulouse Street Wharf upriver to the Audubon Park Zoo. Sailing time each way is about an hour. Departures daily at 9:30 A.M., 12:30, and 3:30 P.M.; departs from zoo at 11 A.M., 1:45, and 4:30 P.M. The round-trip cruise only is $8.50 for adults, $4.25 for children 2 to 12. One-way cruise only is $5.50 for adults, $3.25 for children 2 to 12. Children under 2 and younger may travel free on all cruises. For further information, call 586–8777.

The **Canal Street ferry** crosses the river from the foot of Canal St. to Algiers Point. It's a great ride (about 40 min. round-trip) and it's free.

City and Plantation Tours. Several of the larger sightseeing companies offer a variety of bus tours in New Orleans and to the plantation houses up and down the Mississippi River. *Gray Line Tours of New Orleans,* for example, offers three daytime tours of the city, including a riverboat ride, the French Quarter, Garden District, cemeteries, lakefront, and St. Charles Ave. It also offers a tour of plantation houses along the old River Rd. and five after-dark tours of the city's nightlife. The daytime tours begin between 9 A.M. and 11 A.M. and last from 3 hours on. The tours depart from several of the leading hotels; prices range from $16–$32 (add another $20 if you take the dinner tour). For reservations, check with the hotel desk or call 587–0861 or 800–535–7786. Several other large sightseeing companies offer similar tours. Sometimes the choice comes down to convenience and price. Others include *American Sightseeing International* (246–1991), and *New Orleans Tours* (482–1991). *Gay 90s Carriage Tours* (482–7013) offers a horse-drawn carriage tour of the French Quarter. Tours are available throughout the day at Jackson Sq. and other French Quarter locations.

Friends of the Cabildo, a nonprofit volunteer affiliate of the Louisiana State Museum system in the French Quarter, offers a walking tour of the Quarter at 9:30 A.M. and 1:30 P.M. Tues.–Sat.; 1:30 P.M. Sun.; closed Mon., major holidays, Mardi Gras. The $5 charge is tax-deductible. Children under 12, free; senior citizens, $2.50. For further details, call 523–3939.

National Park Service guides give free walking tours of the French Quarter in the morning and afternoon (times may vary), except New Year's Day, Mardi Gras, and Christmas. They also give tours of St. Louis Cemetery No. 1 at 1 P.M. (reservations required) and of the Garden District at 3 P.M. All tours begin at the Jean Lafitte National Historical Park Visitor and Folklife Center, 916 N. Peters St. (589–2636).

The Preservation Resource Center, 604 Julia St. (581–7032), is dedicated to the preservation of old New Orleans. Throughout the year the PRC offers walking tours

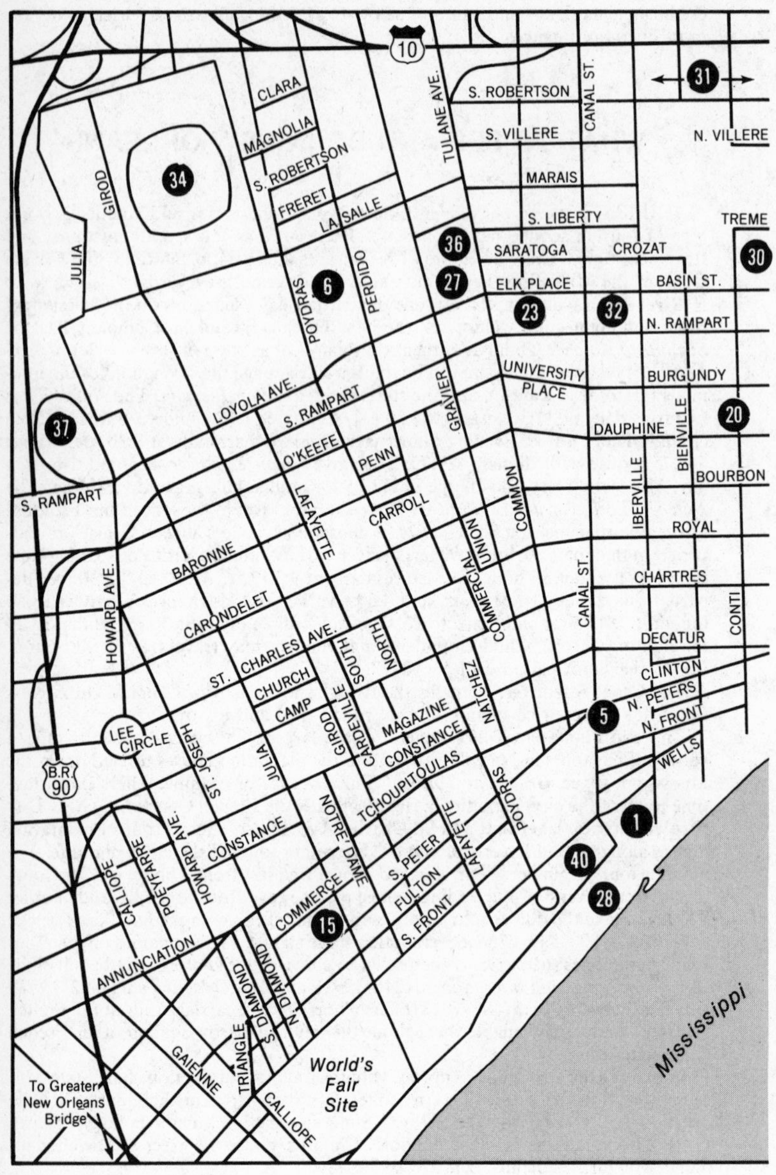
10
31
S. ROBERTSON
CANAL ST.
S. VILLERE
N. VILLERE
CLARA
MAGNOLIA
S. ROBERTSON
TULANE AVE.
34
MARAIS
FRERET
LA SALLE
S. LIBERTY
TREME
GIROD
36
SARATOGA
CROZAT
30
JULIA
6
PERDIDO
27
ELK PLACE
BASIN ST.
POYDRAS
23
32
N. RAMPART
UNIVERSITY PLACE
BURGUNDY
GRAVIER
LOYOLA AVE.
S. RAMPART
20
37
DAUPHINE
BIENVILLE
O'KEEFE
PENN
IBERVILLE
BOURBON
S. RAMPART
COMMON
CARROLL
LAFAYETTE
UNION
ROYAL
BARONNE
COMMERCIAL
CHARTRES
CANAL ST.
HOWARD AVE.
CARONDELET
CONTI
DECATUR
NORTH
ST. CHARLES AVE.
SOUTH
CLINTON
CHURCH
NATCHEZ
N. PETERS
5
CAMP
GIROD
MAGAZINE
N. FRONT
LEE CIRCLE
ST. JOSEPH
JULIA
CARDEVILLE
CONSTANCE
WELLS
TCHOUPITOULAS
B.R. 90
NOTRE DAME
POYDRAS
LAFAYETTE
1
POEYFARRE
CONSTANCE
HOWARD AVE.
S. PETER
40
CALLIOPE
COMMERCE
FULTON
28
S. FRONT
15
ANNUNCIATION
S. DIAMOND
N. DIAMOND
DIAMOND
TRIANGLE
GAIENNE
Mississippi
World's Fair Site
To Greater New Orleans Bridge
CALLIOPE

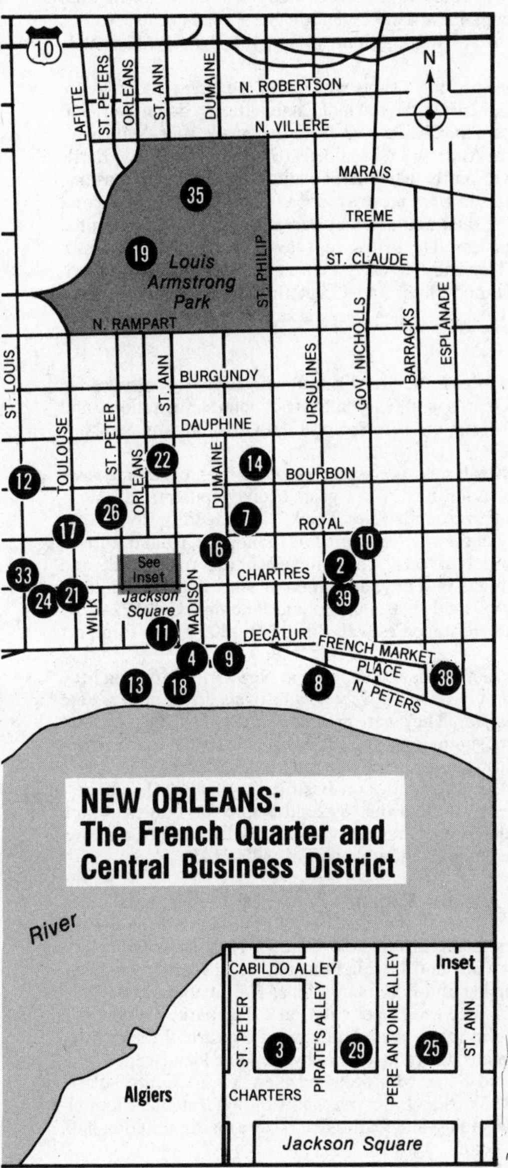

Points of Interest

1) Aquarium of the Americas
2) Beauregard House
3) Cabildo
4) Café du Monde
5) Canal Place
6) City Hall
7) Cornstalk-Iron Fence
8) Farmer's Market
9) French Market
10) Gallier House
11) Greater New Orleans Convention and Visitors Bureau
12) Hermann-Grima House
13) Jackson Brewery
14) Lafitte's Blacksmith Shop
15) Louisiana Children's Museum
16) Madame John's Legacy
17) Merieult House
18) Moon Walk
19) Municipal Auditorium
20) Musée Conti Wax Museum
21) Napoleon House
22) New Orleans Spring Fiesta Mid-19th Century Town House
23) Orpheum Theater
24) Pharmacy Museum
25) Presbytere
26) Preservation Hall
27) Public Library
28) Riverwalk
29) St. Louis Cathedral
30) St. Louis Cemetery 1
31) St. Louis Cemetery 2
32) Saenger Performing Arts Center
33) State Wildlife and Fisheries Building
34) Superdome
35) Theatre for the Performing Arts
36) Trailways Station
37) Union Station (Amtrak and Greyhound)
38) U.S. Mint
39) Ursuline Convent
40) World Trade Center

of New Orleans neighborhoods. The tours are given irregularly during the year, so check with the center for prices (which are quite reasonable) and schedules.

Louisiana Superdome. Guided tours of the world's largest building of its kind are given 10 A.M., noon, and 2 and 4 P.M. daily except during special events. Adults, $5; senior citizens, $4; children 5 to 12, $3; infants 4 and younger free. Call 587–3808.

For those who do not mind venturing a short way out of the city, the **Chalmette Battlefield** will prove interesting. It is in the town of Chalmette just downriver, and you can get there by driving down St. Claude Ave. from Esplanade Ave.—you can't miss it. It was here that General Andrew Jackson defeated the British in the Battle of New Orleans in January 1815 on the Chalmette plantation. The battle was one of the last dramatic performances in what most American historians call the second war of independence. When the dust and smoke cleared, the Americans counted 13 dead, 39 wounded, and 19 missing. The British reported 858 killed, 2,468 wounded, and many others missing. Ironically, in early February the British and Americans received word that the United States and Great Britain had signed a peace treaty at Ghent, Belgium, on Dec. 24, 1814—two weeks before the Battle of New Orleans had taken place.

FESTIVALS. Spring Fiesta begins the first Fri. after Easter and continues for 19 days, with tours of French Quarter and Garden District homes, plantations, and patios by candlelight. Call 581–1367 or write Spring Fiesta, 526 St. Ann St., New Orleans, LA 70116.

The Jazz and Heritage Festival, held the last week of Apr. and the first week of May, has become world famous for music (jazz, gospel, folk, popular) and Louisiana food. It takes place at the Fairgrounds Race Track, 1751 Gentilly Blvd. Anything you have heard in the way of New Orleans music is found here, from traditional New Orleans jazz and gospel to early rhythm and blues, rock'n'roll, and bluegrass. There are dozens of acts in a day, at numerous stages outdoors and in tents, and an immense variety of food that is cheap and fabulous. Call 522–4786 or write: New Orleans Jazz and Heritage Festival, Box 2530, 1205 North Rampart St., New Orleans, LA 70116.

After the jazz festival closes, not much else happens in New Orleans during May and June. But in late June and July two relatively new festivals crank up: **La Fête** and the **New Orleans Food Festival.** They were created in the late 1970s to attract visitors to the city during the hot summer months. The city bills La Fête as an annual family summer festival, featuring special events in the French Market, a fireworks display on the River on July 4, and festivities on Bastille Day (July 14). The best part of La Fête is the Food Festival, held the weekend before the Fourth, where for the price of a reasonable admission charge one gets to sample the best Louisiana food prepared by the best Creole and Cajun chefs. Call 525–4143.

PARKS AND GARDENS. Audubon Park and Zoological Garden, 6800 block of St. Charles Ave. (861–2537), is one of the most beautiful urban parks in the nation. It encompasses 400 acres in the fashionable Uptown New Orleans area on St. Charles Ave. across from Tulane and Loyola universities. The land making up the park originally was the Foucher and Bore plantations. The city bought the land from speculators in 1871 and created the Upper City Park. The park was renamed Audubon Park for naturalist John James Audubon around the turn of the century and redesigned partially from plans drawn up earlier by the famed landscape architect Frederick Law Olmsted and Sons, who designed New York's Central Park. It was the site of the 1884–1885 World's Industrial and Cotton Centennial Exhibition—New Orleans's first world's fair—and featured a 31-acre main exhibition hall. All traces of the fair are now gone.

Aside from the 18-hole golf course, Audubon Park offers a public swimming pool, tennis courts, picnicking throughout the park, and jogging paths. There is also a 1¾-mile jogging path with exercise stations along the way. The park is closed to automobile traffic on weekends. There is plenty of parking throughout the park. Mon.–Fri., 9:30 A.M.–5 P.M.; Sat.–Sun., till 6 P.M. The magnificent Audubon Zoo also is located here (see Zoos).

City Park, located in the Midcity area at Esplanade and City Park Aves., about 3 mi. from the French Quarter, was once the sugar plantation of Louis Allard.

Today the 1500-acre park is the fifth largest urban park in the nation. The park is closed from 10 P.M. until sunrise. The grounds, with their magnificent live oaks and network of man-made lagoons, are well worth seeing. Located in City Park is the New Orleans Museum of Art. On the south side of the museum are the majestic 19th-century dueling oaks where many scores were settled and honor upheld. Much of the park was built or improved under the aegis of the Works Progress Administration during the Depression of the 1930s. Evident everywhere are signs left by the WPA, including the Beaux Arts-style pavilion that stands near the Casino (1914). The Casino has an information office, concessions, and bicycle and boat rentals. The bronze statue of New Orleans-born Confederate General P. G. T. Beauregard stands at the main entrance to the park at Esplanade Ave. (Beauregard's forces fired the first shot opening the Civil War at Fort Sumter, South Carolina.)

City Park also features three 18-hole golf courses, tennis courts, canoes and paddle boats, picnic grounds, horseback riding, fishing, an amusement park, a beautiful carousel (built in 1904), a petting zoo and storyland for children, and a miniature train.

Longue Vue House and Gardens, 7 Bamboo Rd, off Metaire Rd. (488–5488), once was the 8-acre private estate of Edith and Edgar B. Stern. It is now open to the public. The 45-room house and five surrounding English and Spanish gardens are exquisite. The formal English gardens complement the great country house, and the Spanish "water" gardens with their 25 fountains provide a soothing treat for eye and ear. The house was built in the late 1930s in the Classical style. Admission to house and garden: adults, $5; seniors, $5; children over 2 and students, $3. Gardens only, $2 and $1. Tues.–Sat., 10 A.M.–4:30 P.M. Sun., 1–5 P.M. Closed Mon. and holidays.

Louisiana Nature and Science Center, located in eastern New Orleans, 11000 Lake Forest Blvd. (246–5672), is an 86-acre wilderness park in the middle of suburban New Orleans. The center is a nonprofit private institution dedicated to preserving what little is left of the natural environs that once surrounded the city. Contains exhibitions on south Louisiana flora and wildlife, media center, lecture hall, and gift shop. The center also offers woodland trails and bird-watching classes, nighttime canoe trips through swamplands, craft workshops, and field trips. Adults, $3; senior citizens, $2.50; children 3 to 14, $1; family rate, $6; children under 3 free. Open Tues.–Fri., 9 A.M.–5 P.M.; Sat. and Sun., noon to 5 P.M. Closed Mon.

ZOOS. The 58-acre **Audubon Zoo,** 6500 Magazine St., is in a state of ongoing expansion, and in recent years it has become one of the finest zoos in the nation. The main entrance is off Magazine St. behind Audubon Park near the river. Visitors can stroll through the picturesque setting and see over a thousand animals kept in natural settings or take the Mombasea Railway ($1) for a guided tour. You catch the train inside the zoo. The zoo is divided into various sections—Asian Domain, World of Primates, African Savannah, North American Grasslands, South American Pampas, Louisiana Swamps, and Australian exhibits—that feature animals native to those parts of the world. Also has a sea lion pool, reptile aquarium, elephant rides, and children's petting zoo.

The zoo is open Mon.–Fri., 9:30 A.M.–4:30 P.M., Sat. and Sun. to 5:30 P.M.; closes one hour earlier during Daylight Saving Time. Adults, $6.50; children 2–12, and seniors, $3; children under 2 free. Tram and elephant rides, $1 each. Call 861–2537. You can get there by Magazine bus, St. Charles streetcar (ask driver for transfer at Broadway), by car up St. Charles Ave., or *Steamboat Cotton Blossom* (see Tours).

HISTORIC SITES AND HOUSES. The Gallier House, 1118–1132 Royal St., in the French Quarter (523–6722), is one of the finest historic houses in the city. It was built around 1858 by James Gallier, Jr., and has been lovingly restored to its state at the time when the notable architect lived there. This house shows how the wealthy lived in mid-19th-century New Orleans. Adults, $4; over 65, $3; 13–18, $3; 6–12, $2.25; family rate, $9. Docent tours. Open 10 A.M.–4:30 P.M. Mon.–Sat.

Historic Hermann-Grima House and Courtyard. 820 St. Louis St., in the French Quarter (525–5661). The local headquarters of the Christian Women's Exchange. It was built in 1831 for a wealthy New Orleans merchant. The historic house contains a gift shop, Creole kitchen, and courtyard *par-terre.* The courtyard, one of the largest in the French Quarter, has been replanted in the early 19th-century style. Adults, $3; 8–18 and over 62, $2. Open weekdays and Sat. 10 A.M.–3:30 P.M.

Le Carpentier or Beauregard-Keyes House. 1113 Chartres St., in the French Quarter (523–7257). Built in 1827. During the winter of 1866–67 Civil War General P. G. T. Beauregard rented a room here and then lived here after the war. The house later became the residence of the novelist Frances Parkinson Keyes, who wrote many novels about the region. The historic house boasts lovely French Quarter gardens. Adults, $4; over 62 and 13–17, $2; children 2–12, $1. Open 10 A.M.–3 P.M. Mon.–Sat.

New Orleans Spring Fiesta Mid-19th-Century Town House. 826 St. Ann St., in the French Quarter (581–1367). Furnished with early 19th-century and Victorian pieces and *objets d'art.* Admission $3. Group tours arranged. Docent guides. Open 11 A.M.–4 P.M., Mon.–Fri.

St. Louis Cathedral, on Jackson Sq., (861–9521), is the oldest active Roman Catholic cathedral in the United States (1793). The present cathedral (built in the 1790s and remodeled in the 1850s) is the third church to occupy this site since New Orleans was founded in 1718. The cathedral was named for Louis IX of France. Free guided tours daily Mon.–Sat., 9 A.M.–5 P.M.; Sun., 1 P.M.–5 P.M.

Jackson Square, in the heart of the French Quarter, was first established in 1721 as a drill field for soldiers. Known first as the Place D'Armes under the French and then the Plaza de Armas under the Spanish, the square was renamed in honor of General Andrew Jackson in 1851. The focal point of the square is the large bronze equestrian statue of Jackson by Clark Mills. During the summer free concerts are held on Sat. afternoon. The park is open to the public from sunup to sundown.

St. Louis Cemeteries No. 1 and 2. St. Louis No. 1 is located on Basin and St. Louis Sts., and No. 2 can be found between St. Louis and Iberville Sts. along North Claiborne Ave. Both are located behind the French Quarter in Faubourg Tremé. Established in 1796, St. Louis No. 1 is the oldest extant graveyard in the city. These cemeteries, like others in the city, are famous for their ornate aboveground tombs. They have been called cities of the dead. Local legend has it that New Orleans cemeteries are built aboveground because some parts of the city are just at or below sea level, and to dig into the ground would mean coming up with water. It's a nice story, but the city's Mediterranean and southern European heritage probably had more to do with the custom of aboveground tombs. St. Louis No. 2 dates from the 1820s and was laid out in the same general style as its predecessor. New Orleanians from all walks of life were buried here during the 19th century; white, black, slave, and free, from the city's most prominent citizens to its lowliest. Some of those buried in these two cemeteries include Voodoo Queen Marie Laveau (notice *gris gris* X's marked on her tomb) and Paul Morphy (renowned 19th-century world chess champion from New Orleans). A word of caution: The best and safest way to visit these cemeteries is by guided tour and in large numbers.

MUSEUMS. Because of the city's preoccupation with its past, most New Orleans museums are historical in nature. The two largest, the Louisiana State Museum and the New Orleans Museum of Art, both of which have recently staged major exhibits, have gained impressive national reputations. With the New Orleans Symphony and Mardi Gras, they form the nucleus of the city's cultural life.

Louisiana State Museum. Jackson Sq. in the French Quarter (568–6968). Has eight historical buildings. One of the buildings, the historic Cabildo Museum, was recently heavily damaged by fire. Along with the Arsenal and Jackson House, it was closed at press time for renovation. The others are open, with varying hours and rates. Call 568–6968 for information.

New Orleans Museum of Art. City Park (488–2631). The permanent collection ranges from pre-Columbian and Far Eastern to European and African art. Since the 1960s, the museum has been building a special collection devoted to the Arts of the Americas: North, Central, and South. Tues.–Sun., 10 A.M.–5 P.M., closed Mon., holidays. Adults, $4; senior citizens and ages 3–17, $2; under 3, free.

Historic New Orleans Collection. 533 Royal St. in the French Quarter (523–4662). Ten galleries featuring the history of New Orleans in maps, charts, paintings, and historical documents. Tues.–Sat., 10 A.M.–3:15 P.M. Docent tour, $2.

Confederate Memorial Museum. 929 Camp St. near Lee Circle (523–4522). Adults, $2; students and senior citizens, $1; children under 12, 50 cents. Mon.–Sat., 10 A.M.–4 P.M.

Pharmacy Museum, 514 Chartres St. in the French Quarter (524–9077). "La Pharmacie Française" resembles a 19th-century New Orleans apothecary. Tues.–Sun., 10 A.M.–5 P.M. Admission, $1.

Middle American Research Institute. Fourth floor, Dinwidde Hall, Tulane University, facing St. Charles Ave. (865–5110). Pre-Columbian Mayan artifacts. Mon.–Fri., 8 A.M.–4 P.M. Admission free.

Musée Conti Historical Wax Museum. 917 Conti St. in the French Quarter (525–2605). New Orleans historical exhibits and people. Adults, $5; senior citizens, $4.50; children 4 to 17, $3; family rate, $16. Open daily 10 A.M.–5:30 P.M. Closed Mardi Gras Day, Dec. 25.

Aquarium of the Americas and Woldenburg Riverfront Park. Mississippi Riverfront at Canal St. (861–2537). Opened in 1990, the park and aquarium are designed to revitalize the riverfront at the area of new Orleans' "crescent." The 12-acre park includes over 600 different trees and 1,400 shrubs. The aquarium, operated by the Audubon Institute, highlights aquatic life indigenous to the Western Hemisphere. Displays include 132,000-gallon Caribbean Reef exhibit, mist-filled Amazon River Basin display, re-creation of Mississippi River Delta wetlands, and 500,000-gallon Gulf of Mexico tank. Adults, $7.50; seniors, $6; children 2–12, $4. Open Sun.–Thurs. 9:30 A.M. –5 P.M., Thurs. till 8, Fri. and Sat. till 6; closed Mardi Gras, Dec. 25.

ARKANSAS

Arkansas is one of the richest states in the South, if you count such things as beautiful mountain scenery, music, crafts, history, and of course the region's only diamond mine.

Little Rock—A Capital Place to Begin

From the state capital, right in the middle of all Arkansas has to offer, it's only a matter of deciding which way to go. But first, Little Rock and its twin sister, North Little Rock, bear some close investigation. The most obvious place to start is with a tour of the State Capitol, a scaled-down replica of the nation's capitol in Washington, D.C. But the heart of the city lies in the Quapaw Quarter Historic Neighborhoods. This area covers the original town of Little Rock and includes three historic districts. It has a handsome collection of Greek-revival and Victorian structures, and one of the restored buildings is the old State House. This Greek-revival building served as the state capitol from 1836 to 1911. Its legislative chambers have been restored, and museum exhibits detail Arkansas history. Also in the Quapaw Quarter is the Arkansas Territorial Restoration, a fine complex of homes and outbuildings depicting pre–Civil War history here. Here, you can visit the home and print shop of the founder of the *Arkansas Gazette,* the oldest newspaper west of the Mississippi River.

Two places of note are in MacArthur Park. The former Little Rock Arsenal, birthplace of General Douglas MacArthur, now houses the Arkansas Museum of Science and History. Next door, the Arkansas Arts Center offers a variety of cultural programs, including performances by the Arkansas Opera Theater, Community Theater, and Children's Theater.

Beyond Little Rock

For a taste of Indian history, you can travel 10 miles south of Little Rock via U.S. 165 to the Toltec Mounds State Park. The guided archaeological tour takes about an hour, after which you can see the archaeological lab and audiovisual programs. This is one of the largest prehistoric religious ceremonial sites in the United States.

Pinnacle Mountain State Park lies less than 10 miles west of town, via State Highways 10 and 300. This is a place to get away to nature, to hike the trails, do a little fishing, and camp. And if you're really in the mood for getting away for the day or weekend, there's Petit Jean State Park, about an hour's drive northwest via I-40. This 3,471-acre park is named for a French young woman who, legend says, disguised herself as a boy in order to accompany her sailor boyfriend to America. There are cabins, a lodge, campgrounds, picnic areas, hiking trails, and canoe rentals. Adjacent to the park is the Museum of Automobiles, with some antique vehicles from the collection of former Arkansas governor Winthrop Rockefeller.

Other Arkansas Cities

The second city of Arkansas is Hot Springs, much of it encompassed in Hot Springs National Park. Hernando de Soto is credited with discovering the area in 1541 and staying awhile to bathe in some of the valley's 47 thermal springs. Approximately a million gallons of water flow from these springs each day, with an average temperature of 143 degrees Fahrenheit. Today, visitors come not only to "take the waters," but to watch Thoroughbred-horse racing from February to mid-April at Oaklawn Race Track, to browse through the auction houses downtown, and to explore the principles of life and energy at the hands-on Mid-America Museum. For pure entertainment, there's Magic Springs Family Fun Park, a theme park with rides, music, and crafts. For the rockhound, there's Coleman's Crystal Mine, 15 miles north on State Highway 7, where you can dig for quartz crystals.

Take a side trip south via U.S. 70 and State Highway 27 to Murfreesboro, and you can dig for diamonds at the Crater of Diamonds State Park. The largest diamond ever found by a tourist at the park is the 16.37-carat Amarillo Starlight, which was unearthed in 1975. The largest ever found, when this was a commercial mine, weighed 40.42 carats.

Up on the Arkansas and Oklahoma border, Fort Smith was once a frontier outpost that served as a supply center and starting point for prospectors headed for the gold fields of California. It also became a center of activity for bandits and gamblers. Judge Isaac C. Parker, known as the hanging judge, was sent to clean up the place, and today you can see the courtroom where he sentenced so many men to the gallows. It is part of the Fort Smith National Historic Site. Nearby is the Old Fort Museum, filled with pioneer exhibits from the region's past.

The undisputed Queen of the Ozarks is Eureka Springs. A resort since 1879, this Victorian village twists and winds up and down the mountain slopes, making you think there isn't a level spot in town. The last home of Carrie Nation is here, with her personal memorabilia on display. Rosalie House, built in 1880, housed the first telephone company in town, and an old telephone switchboard is still inside. The Hammond Museum of Bells traces the history and geography of bells from 800 B.C. And the Miles Musical Museum, just west of town, has one of the better collections of nickelodeons, music boxes, and hand organs you'll find anywhere.

Blue Spring, about 5 miles west of town, claims one of the largest natural springs in the Ozarks. Nearby, too, is the amphitheater where the Great Passion Play is performed from April to late October. Traveling westward, you find numerous other small towns with *springs* attached to their names.

The largest city in this part of the state, though, is Fayetteville, home of the University of Arkansas. On campus are Hotz Hall, a museum with science and natural-history exhibits; and the Fine Arts Center, with a theater, a concert hall, and an exhibition gallery. Ten miles west of town via U.S. 62, Prairie Grove Battlefield commemorates a battle of the Civil War.

Mountain View, in north central Arkansas, is the cradle of Ozark music and crafts. The Ozark Folk Center is a state-park-operated facility, a kind of showcase for the arts as well as for the lore and architecture of the area. In period buildings, with tools and materials of the 19th and early 20th centuries, craftspeople demonstrate such skills as basketmaking, quilting, woodcarving, and musical-instrument making. Music is an integral part of this region, and musicians from the area come to perform regularly in the conference center.

PRACTICAL INFORMATION FOR ARKANSAS

WHEN TO GO. Spring is the most popular time of year to visit Arkansas, with summer coming in a close second. Fishing and boating, two popular activities, are at their best in these two seasons. Fall is the time to visit the Ozark region, though, when the mountains are flooded with the colors of changing leaves. Winter can see snow on the ground around Jan. and Feb.

HOW TO GET THERE. By plane. The transportation center of the state is Little Rock, but airports are also in Fayetteville, Fort Smith, Harrison, Hot Springs, Camden, El Dorado, Jonesboro, and Texarkana. *American, Delta, TWA, United, Northwest, Southwest,* and *Air Midwest* airlines fly into Little Rock.

By bus. Major bus line serving the state is *Greyhound.*

By train. *Amtrak* serves Little Rock (372–6841) and a number of smaller towns within the state.

By car. I-40 enters the state from Memphis on the east and Fort Smith on the west. I-30 comes into the state at Texarkana.

TOURIST INFORMATION. *Arkansas Department of Parks and Tourism,* 1 Capitol Mall, Little Rock, AR 72201 (501–371–7777 or 800–643–8383). *Eureka Springs Chamber of Commerce,* Auditorium Bldg., Box 551, Eureka Springs, AR 72632 (253–8737; 800–643–3546). *Fayetteville Chamber of Commerce,* Box 4216, Fayetteville, AR 72702 (521–1710). *Fort Smith Chamber of Commerce,* 613 Garrison Ave., Fort Smith, AR 72901 (783–6118). *Hot Springs Chamber of Commerce,* Box 1500, Hot Springs, AR 71902 (321–1700; 800–643–1570, outside AR; 800–272–2081 in AR). *Little Rock Bureau for Conventions and Visitors,* Box 3232, Statehouse Plaza, Little Rock, AR 72203 (376–4781). *Mountain View Chamber of Commerce,* Box 133, Mountain View, AR 72560 (269–8068).

An information center at the Little Rock Municipal Airport, open 24 hours a day, provides free tourist information. In addition, there are state tourist-information centers in Bentonville, Hwy. 71 S.; Blytheville, I-55 S.; Corning, Hwy. 67 S.; Van Buren, I-40 E.; El Dorado, Hwy. 167 N.; Helena, Hwy. 49 W.; Lake Village, Hwy. 65 N.; Texarkana, 2222 I-30 E.; and West Memphis, I-40 W.

TELEPHONES. The area code for Arkansas is 501. The cost of a local telephone call is 25 cents, with no time limit. In many places, you can direct dial credit, collect, or person-to-person calls by dialing 0 before the area code. In smaller towns, and in rural areas, the phone system may not be so advanced. In an *emergency,* dial 0 for an operator, who will assist.

HOW TO GET AROUND. By plane. It is easier to fly between some cities in Arkansas than to drive. *Air Midwest* flies into Little Rock (372–3920), Fayetteville (442–7484), Fort Smith (646–4581), Harrison (741–6500), Hot Springs (623–8233), El Dorado (862–0189), and Jonesboro (932–4403). *Camden Flying Service* serves Camden (574–0598), and Texarkana is reached via *Rio* (800–233–5746) and *American Eagle* (800–433–7300).

By bus. Companies operating within the state are: *Arkansas Bus Tours* (Little Rock, 376–2535), *Arrow Coach Line* (Little Rock, 663–6002), *Diamond Bus Lines* (Little Rock, 821–4141), *Greyhound Bus Lines* (Little Rock, 372–2226), *Gray Line of Eureka Springs* (253–9540), *Great Southern Coaches* (Jonesboro, 935–5569), *Jef-*

ferson Tours (Fort Smith, 783–8991), and *National Park Tours* (Hot Springs, 623–2527, 623–1111).

By rental car. Many of the major rental-car companies, including *Avis, Budget, Hertz,* and *National,* are at the Little Rock Municipal Airport. Rental-car facilities are more limited in other cities in the state.

In Little Rock, public transportation is provided by *Central Arkansas Transit* (375–1163). For a taxi, call *Black and White Cab* (374–0333). If you're driving, Markham St. and Broadway are the two main arteries.

HINTS TO MOTORISTS. The interstates within Arkansas are complete and convenient. Speed limits are enforced, so it's wise to obey them. When traveling off the interstate, particularly in the northern portion of the state, travel time between destinations can be misjudged. It takes longer to travel over the winding roads in the northern part of the state than over the straighter ones in the Delta region.

ACCOMMODATIONS. Most accommodations in the state are chain operations, moderately priced. The selection here is listed alphabetically by city. Price categories are: *Deluxe,* $90–$160; *Expensive,* $50–$90; *Moderate,* $35–$50; and *Inexpensive,* $35 and under.

El Dorado

Kings Inn Best Western. *Moderate.* 1920 Junction City Rd., 71730 (501–862–5191 or 800–528–1234). 8 mi. from the El Dorado Airport. Has 132 rooms, restaurant, indoor and outdoor pools, racquetball courts, tennis, sauna, gift shop. Some rooms in *Expensive* category.

Comfort Inn. *Inexpensive.* 2302 Junction City Rd., 71730 (501–863–6677 or 800–228–5150). 70 rooms, some handicapped accessible. Pool, Jacuzzi, cable TV. Restaurant; free Continental breakfast. Seniors, family plan, government/military discounts. Some rooms in *Moderate* category.

Eureka Springs

Palace Hotel & Bath House. *Deluxe.* 135 Spring St. 72632 (501–253–7474). Beautifully restored Victorian inn. Eight guest rooms furnished with antiques.

Best Western Inn of the Ozarks. *Expensive.* Box 431, 72632 (501–253–9768 or 800–528–1234). 1 mi. west on U.S. 62. 122 rooms. Heated pool, lighted tennis courts, café, senior citizen rates.

1876 Inn. *Expensive.* Rte. 1, Box 247, 1 Van Buren St. 72632 (501–253–7183). ½ mi. east, on U.S. 62 and AR 23 S. Has 72 rooms, restaurant, computerized wake-up calls, package tours, heated swimming pool, and Jacuzzi.

Eureka Inn. *Expensive.* Hwy. 62 & 23 N., 72632 (501–253–9551). 1 mi. southeast. Has 85 rooms, restaurant, lounge, large outdoor pool, racquetball court, exercise room.

Swiss Village Motel. *Expensive.* Rte. 1, Box 5, U.S. 62 E., 72632 (501–253–9541). This place has 54 rooms, six with private whirlpool. Heated pool; complimentary Continental breakfast. Restaurants nearby. Closed mid-Nov.–mid-Mar.

Alpen-Dorf Motel. *Inexpensive.* Rte. 4, Box 580, 72632 (501–253–9475). 3½ mi. east on U.S. 62 E. Small motel, with 29 rooms. Pool, playground; pets allowed.

Colonial Inn. *Inexpensive.* Box 527, 72632 (501–253–7300). On State Hwy. 23 S. 27 rooms. Closed Nov. through Mar. Pool; café nearby.

Fayetteville

Fayetteville Hilton. *Expensive.* 70 N. East St., 72701 (501–442–5555 or 800–445–8667). 234 rooms. Café, indoor-outdoor pool, gift shop, entertainment in lounge.

Best Western Inn. *Moderate.* 1000 U.S. 71 Bypass, 4 mi. SW at U.S. 71 and 62 (501–442–3041 or 800–528–1234). 105 rooms. 1 mi. from University of Arkansas. Heated pool, complimentary Continental breakfast, exercise room; restaurant adjacent.

Mountain Inn. *Moderate.* 21 S. College, 72701 (501–521–1000). 60 rooms. Café, lounge with entertainment, health club, pool; pets allowed.

Park Inn. *Moderate.* 1255 S. Shiloh Dr., 72701 (501–521–1166). 197 units, 10 with refrigerators, in attractive new inn nestled on landscaped grounds. Heated indoor pool, sauna, whirlpool, exercise room, recreation area. Dining room, lounge. Airport transportation.

Fort Smith

Fifth Season Inn. *Expensive.* 2219 S. Waldron Rd., 72903 (501–452–4880). Has 139 rooms, restaurant, indoor atrium pool, whirlpool, sauna.

Holiday Inn Downtown Civic Center. *Expensive.* 700 Rogers Ave., 72901 (501–783–1000 or 800–465–4329). 255 rooms, some nonsmoking. Nine-story open atrium centered around five-story waterfall. Two restaurants, 2 nightclubs. Indoor pool, whirlpool, sauna, cable TV. Teens and under stay free in parents' room.

Sheraton Inn. *Expensive.* 5711 Rogers Ave., 72901 (501–452–4110 or 800–325–3535). Has 244 rooms, restaurant, pool, lounge with entertainment.

Best Western Kings Row Inn. *Inexpensive.* 5801 Rogers Ave., 72903 (501–452–4200 or 800–528–1234). Available here are 110 rooms with small refrigerators. Free coffee in lobby; coin laundry, pool. Restaurants, cocktail lounge near.

Regency Red Carpet Inn (formerly Best Western Regency). *Inexpensive.* 2301 Towson, 72901 (501–785–1401). Has 91 rooms, café, pool, barber and beauty shops, 2 private clubs with entertainment.

Hot Springs

Lake Hamilton Resort and Conference Center (formerly Sheraton Hot Springs Lakeshore Resort). *Deluxe.* 3501 Albert Pike, Box 2647, 71914 (501–767–5511). Has 105 rooms, restaurant, nature walk, sauna, 3 restaurants, lounge, indoor-outdoor pool, tennis courts, private beach on Lake Hamilton, boat dock, and launching ramp.

Arlington Resort Hotel & Spa. *Expensive.* Central at Fountain Sts., 71901 (501–623–7771 or 800–643–1502). Has 488 rooms, 3 restaurants, 2 lounges, thermal waters piped into some rooms, privileges at Hot Springs Country Club, 2 heated pools, arcade shopping. Some rooms in *Deluxe* category.

Avanelle Motor Lodge. *Expensive.* Grand and Central Aves., Box 1088, 71902 (501–321–1332). This place, in hub of city, has 88 rooms, including 16 efficiencies. Heated pool, cable TV, and HBO. Popular Sirloin Room noted for charcoal-broiled steaks and chops.

Buena Vista Resort. *Expensive.* 71901 (501–525–1321). Cottage colony with tennis, waterskiing, fishing, boating on Lake Hamilton.

Downtowner Motor Inn & Baths. *Expensive.* 135 Central Ave., 71901 (501–624–5521 or 800–238–6161). Has 150 rooms, restaurant, thermal-bath house, whirlpool; within walking distance of national-park visitor center. Some rooms in *Moderate* category.

Holiday Inn—Lake Hamilton. *Expensive.* Box 906, 71902 (501–525–1391 or 800–465–4329). Located on Hwy. 7 S. Has 151 rooms, restaurant, boat-launching facility, docks, fishing, tennis courts.

Majestic Resort-Spa. *Expensive.* Park & Central Aves., 71901 (501–623–5511 or 800–643–1504). Has 270 rooms, restaurant, thermal-bath house, largest year-round heated pool in the area; golf and tennis at Hot Springs Country Club. Some rooms in *Moderate* category.

Ramada Inn Towers. *Moderate.* 218 Park Ave., 71901 (501–623–3311 or 800–272–6232). Has 191 rooms, restaurant, health club, pool; within walking distance of downtown shopping. Some rooms in *Expensive* category.

Little Rock

The Capital Hotel. *Deluxe.* 111 W. Markham St., 72201 (501–374–7474 or 800–643–6456). Has 123 rooms in a century-old restored hotel, restaurant, lounge with entertainment.

Camelot Hotel. *Expensive.* Broadway & Markham Sts., 72201 (501–372–4371 or 800–331–4428). Has 303 rooms, restaurant, pool, lounge with entertainment; connected to Robinson Center.

Holiday Inn Little Rock City Center. *Expensive.* 617 S. Broadway, 72201 (501–376–2071 or 800–465–4329). Has 280 rooms, restaurant, lounge with entertainment, pool; free health club adjacent to hotel with indoor pool and jogging track.

Holiday Inn-West. *Expensive.* I-430 and I-630, 201 S. Shackelford, 72211 (501–223–3000 or 800–465–4329). Has 205 spacious rooms. Sauna, hot tub, exercise room, Holidome, indoor/outdoor pool, coin laundry. Restaurant, Reunion Night Club. In-room movies. Free airport transportation.

Little Rock Excelsior. *Expensive.* 3 Statehouse Plaza, 72201 (501–375–5000). Has 420 rooms, on the banks of the Arkansas River, 3 restaurants, 3 lounges, shopping arcade, 18-story glass atrium, luxury-level rooms. Some rooms in *Deluxe* category.

Little Rock Hilton Inn. *Expensive.* 925 S. University Ave., 72204 (501–664–5020 or 800–445–8667). Has 270 rooms, across street from zoo and 2 shopping centers, restaurant, lounge, pool.

Radisson Legacy Hotel & Motor Inn. *Expensive.* Capitol Ave. at Gaines St., 72201 (501–374–0100). Has 114 rooms, 2 restaurants, pool, lounge with entertainment. Some rooms in *Deluxe* category.

Best Western Cottontree. *Moderate.* I-40 Protho Jct., Exit 157, One Gray Rd., North Little Rock, 72117 (501–945–0141 or 800–528–1234). 90 rooms. Dining room, lounge, pool. Free local phone calls.

La Quinta Motor Inn West. *Inexpensive.* 200 Shackleford Rd., 72211 (501–224–0900 or 800–531–5900). 106 rooms, some nonsmoking. Free local phone calls, morning coffee, *Newsweek* magazine. Seniors, family, government/military plans. Julie's Place Restaurant and Lounge adjacent.

Mountain View

Ozark Folk Center Lodge. *Moderate.* 1 mi. north of AR 14, ¼ mi. west of AR 382 (501–269–3871). Has 60 rooms, pool, café, game room.

Inn at Mountain View. *Inexpensive.* (501–269–4200). Historic inn, built in 1885, furnished with Ozark Mountain antiques, handicrafts.

RESTAURANTS. Arkansas fare ranges from fresh mountain trout to barbecue, with restaurants in larger cities offering the regular selections of steaks and seafood. Many bake their own desserts, so watch for fresh blueberry and apple pies in season. Price categories for complete dinner (drinks, tip, and tax not included): *Expensive,* $20–25; *Moderate,* $12–$20; *Inexpensive,* under $12.

Eureka Springs

Crest Restaurant. *Inexpensive.* Hwy. 62 W. and Hwy. 187 (253–9113). Salad bar, fresh seafoods, charbroiled steaks, "all you can eat" catfish filets. D, 5–9 P.M.; closed Sun. except holiday weekends. MC, V.

David's Place. *Inexpensive.* In the 1876 Inn, ½ mi. east at U.S. 62 and AR 23 South (253–7033). Specialties are regional dishes and own baking. B, 6:30–11 A.M.; D, 5–9 P.M.; closed Dec., Jan., Feb. AE, MC, V.

Plaza Restaurant. *Inexpensive.* 55 S. Main (253–8866). Specialties are steak and lobster, own baking. L, 11:30 A.M.–2:30 P.M.; D, 5:30–10:30 P.M.; closed Mon.–Fri. in Jan., Feb. No credit cards.

Fayetteville

The Old Post Office. *Moderate.* 1 Center Sq. (443–5588). Specialties are seafood, own baking, in former post office decorated with brass and oak. L, 11 A.M.–2 P.M.; D, 5–10 P.M.; to 11 P.M., Fri., Sat.; to 2 P.M., Sun.; closed major holidays. Reservations recommended. AE, DC, MC, V.

Fort Smith

Furr's Cafeteria. *Inexpensive.* 4 mi. south on U.S. 71, in Phoenix Village Mall (646–4374). Specialties are steak, seafood, own baking. L, 11 A.M.–2 P.M.; D, 4:30–8 P.M.; to 7 P.M., Mon.–Fri.; 11 A.M.–8 P.M., Sat.–Sun. No credit cards.

Lewis Cafeteria. *Inexpensive.* 3400 Rogers Ave., in Park Plaza Shopping Center (783–4569). Good fried chicken, roast beef; own baking. L, 11 A.M.–2 P.M.; D, 4:30–8 P.M.; to 7:30 P.M. Sun. No credit cards.

Taliano's. *Inexpensive.* 201 N. 14th St. (785–2292). Specialties are veal scaloppini, pasta, own baking. In an old Victorian mansion. D, 5:30–9:45 P.M.; closed Sun., major holidays. AE, MC, V.

Hot Springs

Hamilton House. *Moderate–Expensive.* 130 Van Lyell Dr. (525–2727). Specialties include leg of lamb, seafood, steak, own baking. In 1929 mansion on Lake Hamilton. D, 5:30–9:30 P.M., Mon.–Fri.; to 10 Sat.; closed Sun., Thanksgiving, Christmas, first two weeks in Jan. Reservations recommended. AE, D, MC, V.

Coy's Steak House. *Moderate.* Cypress & Reserve Sts. (321–1414). Specialties are steak, seafood, oyster bar. A comfortable, Old English decor. D, 5–10 P.M.; to 11 Fri.–Sat.; closed Thanksgiving, Christmas Eve, Christmas, New Years. AE, DC, MC, V.

Mrs. Miller's Chicken & Steak House. *Inexpensive–Moderate.* 5 mi. south on AR 7 (525–8861). Specialties are fried chicken, catfish, own baking. D, 5–10 P.M. Closed Dec., first two weeks in Jan. MC, V.

Little Rock

Ashley's. *Expensive.* 111 W. Markham St., in Capital Hotel (374–7474). Continental specialties in elegant atmosphere; small, intimate dining room. Lounge. Reservations requested. B daily, 6:30–10:30 A.M.; L, 11:30 A.M.–2:30 P.M.; D, 6–11 P.M. AE, DC, MC, V.

Anderson's Cajun Wharf. *Moderate.* 2400 Cantrell Rd. (375–5351). Cajun specialties, including crawfish étouffée, snapper du lac. Own baking. In old warehouse overlooking Arkansas River. D, 5–10:30 P.M.; to 11 P.M., Fri., Sat.; closed Sun., major holidays. AE, DC, MC, V.

Chili's Restaurant. *Moderate.* 10700 Rodney Parham Rd. (224–0455). Mexican cuisine. Open 11 A.M.–11 P.M., Mon.–Thurs.; 11 A.M.–midnight Fri.–Sat.; 11:30 A.M.–10:30 P.M., Sun. Major credit cards.

Coy's Steak House. *Inexpensive–Moderate.* 11400 Rodney Parham Rd. (224–2000). Specialties are steak, prime rib, seafood, own baking. D, 5–10 P.M.; to 11 P.M., Sat.; 9 P.M., Sun.; closed major holidays. AE, DC, MC, V.

Franke's Cafeteria. *Inexpensive.* 300 S. University, in University Mall (666–1941). Delicious vegetables, desserts. Family-owned. L, 11:15 A.M.–2:30 P.M.; D, 4–7:45 P.M.; Sat. & Sun., 11:15 A.M.–7:45 P.M.; closed major holidays. No credit cards.

LIQUOR LAWS. In Arkansas, persons must be 21 or older to buy or drink alcoholic beverages. Liquor is sold in package stores and by the drink in licensed hotels, motels, and restaurants. Beer and wine may be purchased in grocery stores, except on Sun., during polling hours on Election Day, and other days at local option.

NASHVILLE AND MEMPHIS

by
WILLIAM SCHEMMEL

William Schemmel is a freelance travel writer and photographer and a regular contributor to Fodor's guides.

NASHVILLE

"Athens of the South" . . . "Insurance and Investment Banking Capital of the Southeast" . . . "America's Printing Center" . . . "Buckle of the Bible Belt" . . . and, to be sure, "Music City USA." All these sobriquets lend their influences to make up today's Nashville. With a metropolitan population sprinting toward one million, Nashville is Tennessee's state capital, the cultural, commercial, communications, and transportation hub of much of the booming mid-South, and a refreshing marriage of Old South traditions and All-American hustle-bustle.

For millions of music-lovers the world over, Nashville means only Music City, and its holy of holies, the fabled Grand Ole Opry. By the hundreds of thousands every year, they pilgrimage here from small towns in Oregon and Alabama, and from as far away as Japan and Australia, Canada, and Western Europe, to bask in the aura of their idols performing on the Opry House boards.

Like Nashville itself, the Opry changes with the times. In 1974, the then 50-year-old show bid a tearful farewell to creaking old Ryman Auditorium in downtown Nashville and moved to the suburbs as centerpiece of a bright new complex called Opryland U.S.A. Its companions there are a 120-acre theme park, a hotel bigger than some Tennessee towns, and a TV network where guests are invited to sit in on variety and game shows hosted by country music personalities.

Something new and dazzling seems to join the Opry family every year. In 1985, Opryland took a cue from Mark Twain and put its paddlewheel showboat, *General Jackson,* in the Cumberland River. A sparkling new musical extravaganza called "Music! Music! Music!" has taken over the park's Roy Acuff Theater.

In the age of mass communications, the Grand Ole Opry may not be the dominant force in country music it was of yore. Many of today's headliners reach the pinnacle without the blessing of the Opry House gods. But its traditions run strong and deep, all the way back to 1925, when it debuted as WSM's Radio Barn Dance, and no serious student of our folk culture should miss the chance to join the fun.

Before leaving town, Opry fans usually make a point of visiting the Country Music Hall of Fame and Museum, taking a nostalgic trip down the aisles of Ryman Auditorium, and bus tours past the homes of the stars, and visiting assorted wax museums, and shops specializing in records, souvenirs, and western wear. They'll wait patiently outside the Music Row recording studios for a glimpse, and maybe an autograph, from a Dolly Parton, Ricky Skaggs, Randy Travis, or Barbara Mandrell.

Many people have a wonderful time here without ever touching on country music at all. Fishing, swimming, water skiing, and boating lure leisure-lovers to the shores of nearby Percy Priest and Old Hickory Lakes. You may browse battlefields where some of the Civil War's fiercest fighting took place, and walk through the peaceful rooms of The Hermitage, the Doric-columned mansion Andrew Jackson built in 1819 for his beloved Rachel. The neighboring little town of Franklin is crammed with antiques and historical landmarks. A little farther on, in the lush Tennessee Walking Horse Country, the Brigadoonish village of Lynchburg welcomes you to the parklike grounds of the Jack Daniels Distillery.

Nashville's antebellum heritage shines at Belle Meade. "The Queen of Tennessee Plantations," Belle Meade once presided over one of America's most famous thoroughbred farms. Contemporary visitors come to admire the pastoral landscape, and a horde of art and antiques in the elegant main house. The Cheekwood Fine Arts Center and Tennessee Botanical Gardens include another dreamlike mansion with 60 rooms of paintings, sculpture, and decorative arts in the center of 55 acres of gardens and trees.

Movie fans will recall the last tragic scene of "Nashville," played on the steps of the Parthenon. Located in Centennial Park, the world's only full-scale replica of the famed Athenian temple was originally built for the Tennessee Centennial of 1897, and later permanently reconstructed in sandstone. Along with Vanderbilt University and other area colleges and universities, the Parthenon symbolizes Nashville's standing as, "Athens of the South." The monumental temple houses an art gallery and is the focus of several yearly outdoor festivals. No matter where you look, you'll find no more dramatic backdrop for a picnic or for kite-flying.

For entertainment somewhat afield from the Grand Ole Opry, Nashvillians come downtown to the strikingly contemporary Tennessee Performing Arts Center, home of the Nashville Symphony Orchestra, dance and theater groups, and touring shows of all sorts. The Arts Center is one of the anchors of an ongoing downtown renaissance that has swept away hundreds of acres of worn out buildings and replaced them with parks, office buildings, deluxe hotels, restaurants, and entertainment areas.

Crowned by its distinctive 80-foot round tower, the Grecian-style Tennessee State Capitol has been set off by plazas with plenty of trees, fountains, and benches. Also downtown, a string of Victorian brick warehouses

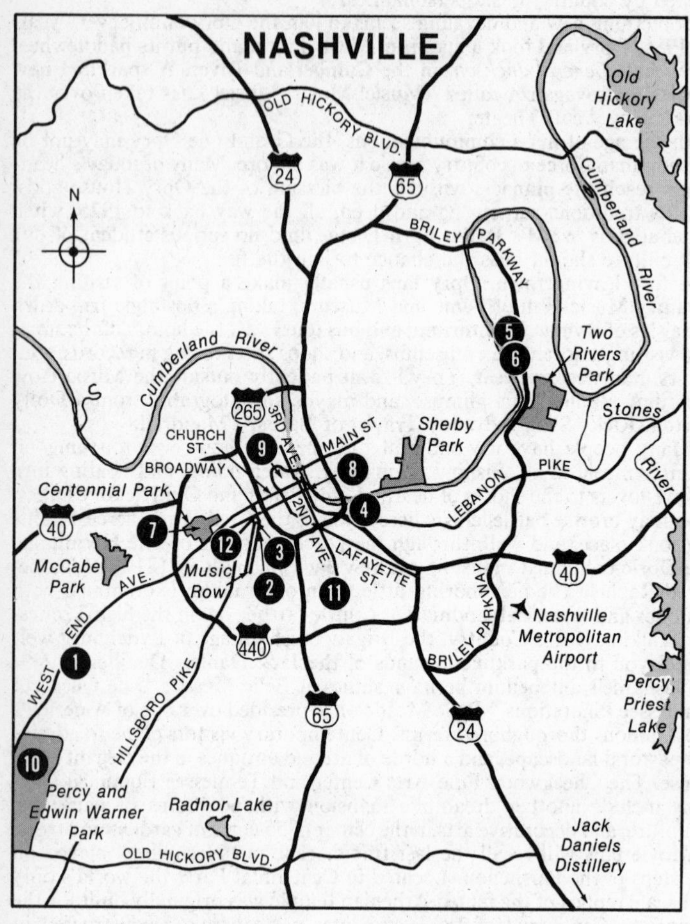

Points of Interest

1) Belle Meade Mansion
2) Country Music Hall of Fame Museum
3) Elvis Presley Memorial
4) Fort Nashboro
5) Grand Ole Opry
6) Opryland U.S.A.
7) Parthenon
8) Riverfront Park
9) State Capitol
10) Tennessee Botanical Gardens
11) State Fairgrounds
12) Vanderbilt University

on Second Avenue near the Cumberland River has come back to life as restaurants, shops, and offices. Riverfront Park, an open-air musical theater, is another big draw, as is the string of brightly neon-lit nightclubs and restaurants on Printers Alley. In days of yore, this area was home of Nashville's printing industry. Moved to more modern facilities elsewhere around the city, the industry produces millions of Bibles, religious and secular books, and has a larger payroll than country music.

Nashville's urban glitter and gleam would assuredly flabbergast Colonel James Robertson, whose expedition of North Carolina frontiersmen crossed the Cumberland River and established Fort Nashboro on Christmas Day, 1779, as protection against contentious Indians. The city's evolution is illustrated by a replica of the fort near the original site. Nashboro became Nashville in 1784, and was chosen as Tennessee's permanent capital in 1843.

PRACTICAL INFORMATION FOR NASHVILLE

WHEN TO GO. Nashville has a temperate climate year-round. Spring and Fall are the most pleasant times of year. The summer months, especially July and Aug., can be very hot and humid. Winters usually are not severe, but Jan. and early Feb. can produce bone-rattling cold and enough snow to shut down the city. The primary tourist season runs Apr. 1–Oct. 30, but Nashville's second season offers many of the same attractions without the multitudes.

HOW TO GET THERE. By plane. Airline deregulation and the tremendous growth in the convention and tourist business have opened up a major network of U.S. routes with connections to Nashville. Most major U.S. carriers service the city. Nashville has achieved the status of a gateway city, meaning that it is eligible for the heavily discounted fares that are accorded to cities with high-volume traffic. The Nashville International airport is conveniently located off Briley Parkway near I-40, about eight mi. southeast of the downtown area. The airport is served currently by *American Airlines,* which has a major hub in Nashville, as well as *Delta, Pan American, Northwest,* and *USAir,* and several regional commuter lines.

By bus. *Greyhound* (256–6141 or 800–528–0447) travels to Nashville from nearly all states in the continental U.S. Also, a number of regional bus lines specialize in tours, which may include sightseeing, nightlife, entertainment packages, fly and drive packages, ground transportation, and other custom features. Check with your travel agent for current specialty tours and prices.

By car. A network of three interstate systems converges on Nashville, linking cities north and south on the I-65 route and east and west on I-24 and I-40. Tennessee highways are in very good condition and well maintained unless you are unlucky enough to arrive during one of the two or three snowstorms that hit most winters.

TOURIST INFORMATION. *Nashville Area Chamber of Commerce,* 161 Fourth Avenue, N., Nashville, TN 37219 (615–259–3900). Newcomers to Nashville should stop first at the *Tourist Information Center* (242–5606), also operated by the Chamber of Commerce. The center downtown is located at I-65 and James Robertson Parkway, Exit 85. Look for the big green sign with the white question mark. The center is open seven days a week, year-round, during daylight hours. It is staffed by courteous and knowledgeable chamber employees. Free maps and brochures are available. Tennessee's welcome centers provide helpful maps and tourist and sightseeing brochures to motorists entering the state at 10 Interstate locations. Centers are operated and staffed by the State Department of Tourist Development seven days a week year-round.

TELEPHONES. The area code for Metro Nashville is 615. Local directory assistance is 411; for long distance within the area code, call 555–1212. An operator will assist on person-to-person, credit-card, and collect calls if you dial 0 before the number. Local pay telephone calls are 25 cents, no time limit. The front of the telephone book provides information on prefixes that fall within the toll-free local area.

EMERGENCY TELEPHONE NUMBERS. In any emergency, the number for police, fire, and ambulance is 911. For other police assistance, call 385–8600. The Poison Control Center is at 322–6435. Crisis Call Center, for personal and domestic crises, is at 244–7444.

HOW TO GET AROUND. From the airport. A taxi from Metro Nashville Airport to downtown costs $12–$14. Cabs run 24 hours a day and are always available at the airport. *Gray Line* runs a limousine service from the airport to the downtown area and most hotels for $8 and up, per person, depending on the destination (downtown is $8). Call 367–2305 for reservations and information. Most major hotels offer regular courtesy van service from the airport to the hotel, some free of charge. An automated dialing system in the baggage claim section connects you with the hotel for ride schedule information. Reservations for return trips should be made at one of the participating hotels. Opryland Hotel operates its own courtesy van dispatched from a separate airport counter. Limos and vans depart from a designated passenger pickup area.

By bus. Metropolitan Transit Authority buses cover the entire Davidson County area daily. Most routes begin between 4 A.M. and 5 A.M. and run until 11:15 P.M. The fare is 75 cents within the central downtown zone and 5 cents for each additional zone traveled up to $1.05. Correct change is required. For schedule information, call 242–4433.

By taxi. Cabs run 24 hours a day. Regulated fares have ceilings of $1.50 for entry and 10 cents each additional ¼ mi. Taxi companies include *Yellow* (256–0101), *Checker* (254–5031), *Nashville* (242–7070), and *Rivergate* (865–4100). Hailing a cab from downtown is not impossible, but there are so few unoccupied taxis roaming around that it's best to phone for cab service.

By rental car. Major car rental firms (Hertz, Avis, Budget, Dollar, and National) have leasing desks both at the airport and downtown. It's best to make reservations to avoid the shortages that can occur on busy tourist weekends. Avis and Hertz have discounts for AAA members, and all offer discount weekend rates. The numbers, local and toll-free, for these agencies are as follows: *Hertz,* 361–3131, 800–654–3131; *Avis,* 361–1212, 800–331–1212; *Budget,* 366–0800, 800–527–0700; *Dollar,* 366–0449, 800–421–6868; and *National,* 361–3131, 800–328–4567.

HINTS TO THE MOTORIST. Nashville's streets and highways are easy to get around except at peak morning (7:30–8:30 A.M.) and evening (4:30–5:30 P.M.). The Interstate system (I-40, I-65, I-24, I-440) crisscrosses and encircles the metropolitan area, delivering motorists within a few mi. of any destination. Nashville's primary streets are laid out in a spoke pattern leading out from the downtown area. Other major roads, such as Old Hickory Blvd. and Briley Pkwy., cover vast arcs around the city. The names of Nashville streets, in tribute, apparently, to its many prominent citizens, can change within short distances. The direction can, too. A good road map and careful instructions can be invaluable.

Traffic laws contain no unusual prohibitions. Right turns on red are permitted after stopping except where marked. Coins are required for parking meters, Mon.–Fri., 8 A.M.–6 P.M. and Sat. until noon. Holidays and Sun. are exempt. The overtime parking law prohibits meter feeding, or parking for periods of time that exceed the meter's limit. Speed limits in the city are clearly posted.

The AAA office is within one mile of downtown at 1121 Church St. (244–8889).

A word of caution to motorists who drink and drive: Tennessee has a tough drunken driving law, with mandatory jail and fine penalties on conviction. For first offenders, the jail time and fine is a minimum two days and $250. Metro police occasionally set up roadblocks to screen drivers for intoxication. If they suspect you've been drinking, you'll be asked to pull off the road and take a breath test. You have the right to refuse, but that gives the police probable cause to believe that you are intoxicated. They can and will charge you with DWI.

HINTS TO DISABLED TRAVELERS. Much work has been accomplished to accommodate handicapped people. Residents are issued special license plates allowing parking privileges in designated spaces nearest the entrances to virtually all public facilities. Park here without special tags and you will be subject to the city's tow-in ordinance. Additionally, curbs downtown and in many suburban areas have ramps to facilitate street crossings near public buildings, and most public rest rooms also accommodate wheelchairs. For the blind, many elevators are equipped with Braille floor indicators.

The Metro Office for Handicapped Persons publishes "Accessibility Guidebook," detailing accommodations for the handicapped at restaurants, hotels, churches, and other facilities. For a free copy, write the *Office for Handicapped Persons,* 214 Stahlman Building, Nashville, TN 37201 (615–259–6676).

TOURS AND SPECIAL-INTEREST SIGHTSEEING. Nashville has a wealth of bus tours offered by several large sightseeing companies. They cover virtually everything you could want to see in Nashville, from the stars' homes, the Grand Ole Opry, and Music Row to President Andrew Jackson's Hermitage. Most tours last 3–4 hours and cost $11 to $17 for adults and half price for children. Most run daily; a few are closed Sun. and Mon. Call for times and reservations.

The major tour companies are: *Captain Ann & Music City Queen Riverboat Cruises,* Broadway near Fort Nashboro Nashville, TN (244–3430; 800–342–2355); *Custom Tours,* 1108 Gallatin Rd., Nashville, TN 37206 (256–1200); *Grand Ole Opry Tours,* 2810 Opryland Dr., Nashville, TN 37214 (889–9490); *Gray Line Tours,* 314 Hermitage Ave., Nashville, TN 37210 (244–7330 or 800–251–1864); *Johnny Walker Tours,* 97 Wallace Rd., Nashville, TN 37211 (834–8585); *Nashville Tours,* 2626 Music Valley Dr., Nashville, TN 37214 (889–4646); and *Stardust Tours,* Box 120396, Nashville, TN 37212 (244–2335).

Downtown walking tours are outlined in a free brochure prepared by the Historical Commissions of Metropolitan Nashville and Davidson County, in the Customs House, 701 Broadway, Nashville, TN 37203 (259–5027).

Historic home tours. Features elegantly refurbished late 19th-century and early 20th-century homes in renovation districts near downtown. Scheduled on occasional weekends throughout the summer and fall. Admission $2 to $5. For dates, call the Metro Historical Commission at 259–5027.

Self-guided driving tours also are outlined in a free brochure entitled *The Civil War Battle of Nashville.* This covers the major points of battle between Union and Confederate troops. Brochures are available at the Nashville Area Chamber of Commerce, 161 Fourth Ave., N., Nashville, TN 37219 (259–3900).

Jack Daniels Distillery is 65 mi. southeast of Nashville but is easily accessible by I-24, East. A free 1-hour tour of the facility is offered 7 days a week year-round, except major holidays. See the making of the world-famous brand of Tennessee sour mash whiskey. Write Jack Daniels Distillery, Lynchburg, TN 37352. For lunch, Miss Mary Bobo's Boarding House in Lynchburg serves home-cooked fried chicken and vegetables, family style, Mon.–Sat. at 1 P.M. Reservations required. Adults, $8.75; children under 12, $4; no tipping. Call 759–7394.

PARKS AND GARDENS. Metro Nashville has 70 public parks, in keeping with the tradition of spending time outdoors from early spring until late fall. The parks department maintains an active schedule of sports and entertainment events as well as gyms, game rooms, art classes, summer concerts, and outdoor art shows. For information regarding all parks activities, call 259–6399.

Centennial Park, near downtown, on West End Ave. (259–6399), is home for the Parthenon replica (see Historic Sites). Lush acreage, shady, grassy, and beautifully landscaped with elaborate floral designs and ponds. Summer bandshell events and festivals. A great place to take the children for scheduled activities ranging from kite flying to outdoor theater.

Percy Warner and **Edwin Warner parks,** 7311 Hwy. 100 (259–5218), are Nashville's largest. Rolling hills, woods, and picnic areas are ideal for nature lovers. The adjacent Warner parks have a nature center, gardens, and nature trails with self-guided tours (booklets available at the nature center) or guided tours by reservation; call 352–6299. They also include picnic shelters, soccer fields, and playground equipment. Everything is free with the exception of the two golf courses. The parks are open year-round from daybreak until 11 P.M. Call for picnic shelter reservations and fees.

Riverfront Park, downtown, where Broadway meets the Cumberland River, is the concrete crown jewel of the park system. It offers a quiet waterfront setting for downtown brown bag lunchers who want to watch the barges move along the

Cumberland River. During summer months, there's a steady schedule of free concerts and dances.

The **Tennessee Botanical Gardens and Fine Arts Center** at Cheekwood, Forest Park Dr., is the former home of the Cheek family of Maxwell House Coffee fame. The grounds consist of nearly 30 acres of artfully manicured and landscaped gardens. Botanic Hall features botanical art exhibits adjacent to four public greenhouses of wild flowers, herbs, and Japanese gardens. (Fine Arts Center, see Museums and Galleries.) Open Tues.–Sat., 9 A.M.–5P.M.; Sun., 1–5 P.M.; closed major holidays. Adults, $4; college students and senior citizens, $3; 7–18, $1; children under 7 free. Group rates available. Call 356–8000.

Other parks and wildlife preserves that offer excellent scenic and sporting opportunities (see Participant Sports) include **Old Hickory Lake,** at the Old Hickory Dam on the Cumberland River (822–4846); **Center Hill Lake,** at the Center Hill Dam on the Caney Fork River (1–858–3125); **Percy Priest Lake** (several federal parks), picnics and sailboat races on Sun. (259–6735); and **Radnor Lake,** a state natural area with "Turtle's Eye View" guided nature trips by canoe, Sat.–Sun. in the fall and spring. Also free weekend guided walking tours during fall and spring. For reservations, call 377–1281.

PARTICIPANT SPORTS. Nashville is made to order for the outdoor enthusiast, with long, mild spring and autumn seasons, hilly and scenic terrain, plenty of lakes, and public tennis courts and golf courses.

Jogging maintains its hold as one of the more popular outdoor pastimes, and Nashvillians have discovered a number of beautiful jogging sites, including Centennial Park, Vanderbilt University running track, Percy and Edwin Warner parks, and Radnor Lake. *The Nashville Striders Club,* affiliated with the downtown YMCA, can recommend choice spots and provide information on the many races that take place during the summer, such as their own fun runs twice a week in Centennial Park; call 254–0631.

Many of the places that provide joggers with running room also give **bicyclers** plenty of space for serious workouts or leisurely pedaling amid scenic backdrops. Most notable perhaps are the Percy Warner and Edwin Warner parks, easily accessible from Highway 100 and Belle Meade Blvd. Miles of paved roads wind around beautiful hills, past remote picnic settings, and through dense woods.

Nashville has seven public **golf courses,** six of which are open year-round. Fees are $7.50 for 18 holes, $3.75 for 9 holes at the following courses: *Harpeth Hills,* an 18-hole, par-72 layout, 2424 Old Hickory Blvd. (373–8202); *McCabe,* 27 holes, pars 35, 35, and 36, 46th Ave. N, and Murphy Rd. (297–9138); *Percy Warner,* 9 holes, par 34, Forrest Park Dr., (352–9958); *Rhodes,* 9 holes, par 36, 2400 Metrocenter Blvd. (242–2336); *Shelby,* 18-hole hangout for big money players, par 72, South 20th and Fatherland Sts. (227–9973); and *Two Rivers,* the newest 18-hole, par 72 course, McGavock Pike and Briley Pkwy., (889–9748). Tee times may be required on weekends. Starters will help the lone golfer hook up with other players. *Nashboro Village,* 2250 Murfreesboro Rd. (361–3242), has a challenging 18-hole, par-72 golf course (367–2311). Fee for 18 holes is $12.

Many of Nashville's public parks have outdoor **tennis** courts, some of which are lighted. All are free to the public with the exception of the *Centennial Park Tennis Center,* which charges a nominal fee. For locations, check the blue pages of the telephone book under Metro Parks and Recreation or call 259–6399.

Several indoor **roller skating** rinks located in suburban areas include the *Rivergate Skate Center* (868–3692) and *Brentwood Skate Center* (373–1827). Call for times and charges (generally $1.75 to $3.75). Skate rentals are available. Other rinks are listed in the Yellow Pages under "Skating Rinks."

For **ice skating,** *Ice Centennial* 333 23rd. Ave., N., off Elliston Place, operates Sept. through Apr. except Christmas Day. Adults, $3; children, $2.25; skate rental, $1. Call 320–1369 for information.

Fishing and boating. A wide variety of outdoor water activities is available at the many lakes in and around Nashville and Middle Tennessee. At *Old Hickory Lake,* Old Hickory Dam on the Cumberland River (822–4846), there's a boat ramp for sailboats and motor-powered craft. No rentals. At *Center Hill Lake,* between Nashville and Cookeville (858–3125), launching ramps are provided, and houseboats, small fishing boats, and pontoon boats can be rented from *Cove Hollow Boat*

Dock (548–4315). These and other lakes also host summertime weekend sailboat races. Old Hickory, Percy Priest, and Center Hill lakes are operated by the U.S. Army Corps of Engineers. For maps and information on these and other waterways ($1.50 to $8 fees), write Natural Resources Management Branch, U.S. Army Corps of Engineers, Box 1070, Nashville, TN 37202.

HISTORIC SITES AND HOUSES. Belle Meade Mansion, 110 Leake Ave., Nashville, TN 37205 (356–0501). A taste of the grand old South is evident in this early 19th-century "Queen of the Tennessee Plantations" mansion built by General William G. Harding on what was then a 5,300-acre farm and famous thoroughbred nursery. Open with guided tours Mon.–Sat., 9 A.M.–5 P.M.; Sun., 1–5 P.M. Closed major holidays. Adults, $4; 13–18, senior citizens, $3.50; 7–12, $2; under 7, free.

Fort Nashborough. Adjacent to Riverfront Park, 170 First Ave., N. (255–8192). Five reconstructed log cabins, with costumed staff depicting late 18th-century frontier life. Colonel James Robertson and a band of settlers built the original Fort Nashboro in 1789, just a few hundred yards north of the current site, on the limestone bluff overlooking the river. Tues.–Sun., 9 A.M.–4 P.M., Apr.–Nov. Closed Sun., Mon., and all legal holidays. Adults, $2; 4–17, and over 62, $1.

The Hermitage, 4580 Rachel's La., Hermitage, TN 37076, 12 mi. east of Nashville (889–2941). Well-informed tour guides take visitors through the estate of President Andrew Jackson. Features include original slave cabins, furnishings, and gardens. Gift shop on the premises. Open daily 9 A.M.–5 P.M. Closed Thanksgiving, Dec. 25, and third week in Jan. Adults, $7; over 65, $6.50; 6–18, $3.50; under 6 and servicemen on active duty free.

The Parthenon, Centennial Park, West End Ave., Nashville, TN 37203 (259–6358). The world's only exact-size replica of the Greek Parthenon. It was constructed in the 1930s to replace a temporary structure built for the Tennessee Centennial Exposition in 1897. Casts of original Greek sculpture fragments line the interior. Art shows in four galleries change monthly. Open Tues.–Wed., Fri.–Sat., 9 A.M.–4:30 P.M.; Thurs., 9 A.M.–8 P.M. Adults, $2.50; over 62 and 6–17, $1.25.

James K. Polk residence, 301 W. Seventh St., Columbia, TN 38401, about 40 mi. south of Nashville (388–2354). Ancestral home of the 11th president of the United States. Original furnishings, clothing, china, and crystal used in the White House. Open Mon.–Sat., 9 A.M.–5 P.M., Apr.–Oct.; Mon.–Sat., 9 A.M.–4 P.M., Sun., 1–5 P.M., rest of year. Closed major holidays. Adults, $2.50; over 60, $2; 6–18, $1; under 6, free.

Ryman Auditorium. 116 Opry Pl. (Fifth Ave. N), Nashville, TN 37219 (254–1445). Built by riverboat captain Tom Ryman as a tabernacle, the auditorium was home for the WSM Grand Ole Opry from 1943 to 1974. The building is the sacred fount of Nashville's country music industry. Open daily, 8:30 A.M.–4:30 P.M., except major holidays. Adults, $2; 6–12, $1; under 6 free.

Tennessee State Capitol. Downtown on Charlotte between Fifth and Seventh Aves. (741–2692). Designed by Philadelphia architect William Strickland. Free guided tours conducted 7 days a week, except major holidays, every hour, 9 A.M.–4 P.M.

MUSEUMS. Carl Van Vechten Gallery at Fisk University (329–8543). Restored gallery is the permanent home for the Alfred Stieglitz collection donated to the historic black university by Stieglitz's widow, Georgia O'Keeffe. The collection features 101 pieces of 19th- and 20th-century European and American art, including paintings, watercolors, drawings, lithographs, photographs, bronze sculpture, and African sculpture. A second gallery features changing exhibits. Also on campus is the Rinold Reiss permanent collection in the Fisk Library. The school administration building houses the Cyrus Leroy Baldridge permanent collection. Murals painted by Aaron Douglas dot the campus. Gallery hours are Tues.–Fri., 10 A.M.–5 P.M., Sat.–Sun., 1–5 P.M. from Sept. through June. Closed Mons. Adults, $2.50; children, 6 to 18, $1; children under 6 free. Administration building and Jubilee Hall hours 8 A.M.–5 P.M. daily, year-round. Library hours vary. Free.

The Country Music Hall of Fame and Museum, 4 Music Sq. E. (255–5333), offers the old and new in country music, instruments, costumes, and photos. Memorable special exhibits. Two theaters show movie clips. Gift shop. Daily, 9 A.M.–5 P.M.; June–Aug., 8 A.M.–8 P.M. Closed on major holidays. Adults, $6.50; children 6 to 11, $1.75; under 6 free. Call 256–1639.

The Fine Arts Center at Cheekwood (Tennessee Botanical Gardens) hosts permanent collections of 19th- and 20th-century American art, particularly the work of leading southern artists, Worcester porcelain, and Old Sheffield silver plate, shown in the exquisitely restored Cheek mansion. Admission to Gardens and art center: adults, $4; seniors and college students, $3; 7–18, $1; children under 7 free. Open Tues.–Sat., 9 A.M.–5 P.M.; Sun., 1–5 P.M. Closed Mon. and major holidays. Call 356–8000.

Nashville Artist Guild. 100 Second Ave., N., at Broadway in the Silver Dollar Saloon (242–5002). Exhibits by artist guild members plus special exhibits of guest artists. Tues.–Sat. noon–4 P.M.; Sun. 1–4 P.M.

Tennessee State Museum. 505 Deaderick St. (741–2692). Exhibits depicting life in Tennessee, art gallery, visiting exhibits. Mon.–Sat., 10 A.M.–5 P.M.; Sun., 1–5 P.M. Across the street in the 1925 War Memorial Building, the museum's military branch illustrates Tennessee's role in wars; Mon.–Sat., 10 A.M.–4 P.M., Sun. 1–4 P.M. Both museums free.

OPRYLAND U.S.A. Opryland is a musical show park for families that is in a class by itself. The theme park features 21 rides, 12 stage shows ranging from musical reviews to fully staged musical productions, strolling musicians and singers, mimes, and clowns. One-day ticket, $21.50; two-day ticket, $26.88; children under 4 free. Opryland U.S.A. Passport, $51.50, includes 3-day Opryland ticket, Grand Ole Opry matinee, day cruise aboard the *General Jackson* riverboat, and sightseeing tours, and discount coupons for Opryland and Opryland Hotel. Open 7 days and evenings a week from Memorial Day through Labor Day weekends. Open weekends Apr. and May, Sept., and Oct. Call 889–6700.

Grand Ole Opry. Legendary showcase of country music greats and new rising stars now performed in new theater at Opryland U.S.A. Fri. and Sat. nights year-round. Special Tues., Thurs., Sat., and Sun. matinees in summer months. Prices, $9.70–$14 plus tax; no discounts. For weekly roster, consult Fri. and Sat. morning "Arts and Leisure" section of the *Tennessean.* Reservations recommended; call 889–3060.

General Jackson riverboat. A new 272-foot paddle wheel showboat with four decks, three lounges, snack bar, and Victorian dinner theater cruises the Cumberland River from Opryland to Nashville's Riverfront Park. Morning and afternoon cruises. Adults, $13.95; children under 4 free. Optional meal service available. Dinner dance and theater cruises, $32.95 adults; $25.95 ages 4–11. Call 889–6611.

ACCOMMODATIONS. Catering to hundreds of thousands of budget-conscious tourists every year, as well as an increasingly sophisticated corporate and convention clientele, Nashville now offers a very impressive selection of hotel, motel, bed-and-breakfast, and all-suite accommodations in all prices categories and levels of luxury. Although some establishments increase rates slightly during the peak summer travel season, most maintain the same rates year-round. Some downtown luxury hotels offer special weekend rates to attract guests to otherwise vacant rooms. Your hotel bill will include a 4% state hotel/motel tax, as well as a 7.75% state sales tax. The following categories are based on double occupancy: *Deluxe,* $90–$170; *Expensive,* $65–$90; *Moderate,* $50–$65; *Inexpensive,* under $50.

Deluxe

Doubletree Hotel at Commerce Pl. 2 Commerce Pl., Fourth Ave., N., and Union St., Nashville, TN 37219 (800–528–0444 or 615–244–8200). In a glass-sheathed, high rise in the center of the downtown commercial and governmental area, the Doubletree has 337 guest rooms, and 26 suites on its luxury Plaza Club level. The Hunt Room specializes in classical French and Continental cuisine.

The Hermitage. 231 Sixth Ave., N., downtown, Nashville, TN 37219 (800–251–1908 or 615–244–3121). Ensconced in any of the 112 suites of this restored 1910 Beaux Arts-style hotel, guests might well imagine themselves in a time warp. Suites have living rooms, dressing areas, and wet bars. Amenities include concierge service, restaurants, and lounges. Near the State Capitol and Tennessee Performing Arts Center.

Hyatt Regency Nashville. 623 Union St., Nashville, TN 37219 (800–233–1234 or 615–259–1234). Located near the State Capitol and downtown shopping, the

478-room, 31-suite Hyatt has glassed-in elevators, a huge skylighted lobby, and a big choice of dining and entertainment.

Marriott Nashville Hotel. Briley Pky. at I-40, 8 mi. east of downtown, Nashville, TN 37210 (800–228–9290 or 615–889–9300). The 18-floor, 399-room Marriott is 5 minutes from Metro Airport, and about 10 minutes from downtown and Opryland. Facilities include several restaurants and lounges, large meeting and exhibition space, indoor-outdoor pool, lighted tennis, free airport transportation.

The Maxwell House Clarion. 2025 MetroCenter Blvd., 1 mi. east of downtown, Nashville, TN 37228 (615–259–4343). With 289 deluxe rooms and suites, the Maxwell House is the essence of good living, Nashville-style. The Crown Court is one of Tennessee's most outstanding restaurants; Pralines is also excellent for breakfast, lunch, and dinner. Other facilities include lighted tennis, health club, meeting rooms, live entertainment, and airport transportation.

Opryland Hotel. 2800 Opryland Dr., Nashville, TN 37214 (615–883–2211). Adjacent to the Grand Ole Opry House, the Opryland theme park and *General Jackson* paddle-wheel showboat, the 1891-room Opryland Hotel is a bonafide attraction in its own right. The glass-roofed Conservatory Wing has 2 acres of gardens, gazebos, walkways, waterfalls, and fountains. The Old Hickory Dining Room is one of Nashville's best restaurants. Live entertainment is featured in several lounges. There's also lighted tennis, heated pools, enormous meeting space. "Christmas at Opryland" package includes accommodations, live holiday shows, tickets to Grand Ole Opry, sightseeing. Hotel has more meeting, exhibit, and banquet space than any in the country.

Park Suite Hotel. 10 Century Blvd., Nashville, TN 37214 (615–871–0033 or 800–432–7272). 296 multiroom suites with wet bar include 15 handicapped-accessible units. Indoor pool, sauna, whirlpool, health club. Fine dining in The Plaza on the Green; live entertainment in Aviators. Free buffet breakfast. 25% discount to AAA members.

Stouffer Nashville Hotel. 611 Commerce St. (615–255–8400 or 800–468–3571). 673 units. Luxurious facility has heated indoor pool, sauna, whirlpool, sundeck, health club. Parking garage, airport transportation. Dining room, lounge.

Union Station Hotel. 1001 Broadway, Nashville, TN 37203 (615–726–1001). "New" 127-room luxury hotel, painstakingly restored, was once Music City's opulent railroad depot. Dining in elegant Arthur's and another restaurant; entertainment in lively piano lounge. 24-hour room service, valet parking, complimentary airport shuttle. Health club (fee).

Expensive

Ramada Inn Across From Opryland. 2401 Music Valley Dr., Nashville, TN 37214 (615–889–0800 or 800–272–6732). 307 rooms, 4 for handicapped. Briley's Restaurant; Pennington's cocktail lounge, live entertainment. Heated indoor pool, whirlpool, sauna; shuttle service to airport, Opryland. Call toll-free number for information about five other area Ramada Inns.

Shoney's Inn of Music Valley. 2420 Music Valley Dr., Nashville, TN 37214 (615–885–4030 or 800–222–2222). This 185-room inn offers heated indoor pool, whirlpool, parking garage. Restaurant next door.

Moderate

Best Western at Opryland. 2600 Music Valley Dr., Nashville, TN 37214 (615–889–8235 or 800–528–1234). 212 rooms include 2 handicapped-accessible units. Restaurant, coffee shop; cocktail lounge, live entertainment, band, dancing nightly in season. Call toll-free number for information about seven other area Best Western Inns. Some rooms in *Inexpensive* category.

Days Inn Downtown Convention Center. 711 Union St., Nashville, TN 37219 (615–242–4311 or 800–325–2525). This place has 100 rooms, with a deli and convenience market on premises and a coffee shop adjacent. Free parking. Walking distance to State Capitol, auditorium, convention center.

Holiday Inn. I-24 E. Airport Area. 350 Harding Pl., Nashville, TN 37211 (615–834–0620 or 800–465–4329). 217 rooms, 2 are handicapped accessible. Adjacent American Fitness Club free to guests over 18. Restaurant; cocktail lounge has live entertainment Tues.–Sat. Airport courtesy van. Call toll-free number for information about five other area Holiday Inns.

Howard Johnson's Motor Lodge-North. I-65 and I-24 (800–654–2000 or 615–226–4600). **Howard Johnson's Motor Lodge-West,** I-40 West at Charlotte Pike (800–654–2000 or 615–352–7080). Modern lodges with restaurants, lounges. North locations has fitness center with saunas, whirlpool. Some rooms in *Expensive* category.

Quality Inn-Hall of Fame. 1407 Division St., on Music Row, Nashville, TN 37203 (615–242–1631 or 800–228–5151). 103 rooms. Restaurant, cocktail lounge; entertainment nightly, live music, dance floor. Call toll-free number for information about five other area Quality, Comfort, Clarion Inns.

Shoney's Inn. 1521 Demonbreun St., Nashville, TN 37203 (800–222–2222 or 615–255–9977). 147 rooms, restaurant, pool. In heart of Music Row, near downtown, walking distance of many popular attractions.

Inexpensive

Fiddlers Inn-North. 2410 Music Valley Dr., Nashville, TN 37214 (615–885–1440). **Fiddlers Inn-South,** I-40 and Briley Pkwy., Nashville, TN 37217 (367–9202). Both inns have pools, restaurants. North Inn is near Opryland, and has live entertainment.

Knights Inn-North. I-65 and Long Hollow Pike, Goodlettsville, TN 37072 (615–859–4988). **Knights Inn-South,** I-24 at Harding Pl., Nashville, TN 37211 (615–834–0570). Comfortable rooms, some with kitchenettes. Restaurants or coffee shops nearby.

La Quinta MetroCenter Motor Inn. 2001 MetroCenter Blvd. Nashville, TN 37228 (800–531–5900 or 615–259–2130). **La Quinta South Motor Inn.** 4311 Sidco Dr., Nashville, TN 37204 (800–531–5900 or 615–834–6900). Restaurant nearby.

Motel 6. 323 Cartwright St., Goodlettsville, TN 37072 (615–859–9674). 94 units; pool, free local calls, TV, in-room movies. 18 and under stay free in parents' room. Also at 311 W. Trinity Ln., Nashville, TN 37207 (615–227–9696); 95 Wallace Rd., Nashville, TN 37211 (615–333–9933).

Red Roof Inn. 110 Northgate Dr., Goodlettsville, TN 37072 (615–859–2537 or 800–848–7878); I-65, Exit 78A Harding Pl., 4271 Sidco Dr., Nashville, TN 37204 (615–832–0093 or 800–848–7878). Senior discounts, restaurants near both properties.

BED AND BREAKFASTS. Nashville has a growing network of private homes that are open to visitors. In the best tradition of Southern hospitality, all homes are carefully screened for comfort and cleanliness. They are available in the city and out in the country. A Continental breakfast is included in double occupancy rates, ranging from $25–$80. Kitchen facilities available at some locations. For information and reservations write to: Bed and Breakfast Host Homes of Tennessee, Box 110227, Nashville, TN 37222 (615–331–5244); Bed and Breakfast of Middle Tennessee, Box 40804, Nashville, TN 37204 (615–297–0883).

RESTAURANTS. Almost overnight, Nashville has turned into a diner's adventure. The city is still full of small, unpretentious hideaway cafés where fried chicken, catfish and hushpuppies, salty country ham, and barbecue and buttermilk biscuits reign supreme. But as it swiftly spreads its wings from a mid-sized regional hub into a national metropolis, Music City is becoming equally well-versed in suave gourmet dining, as well as Oriental, Middle Eastern, Asian, and other exotic cuisines. Restaurant categories, based on the cost of an average three-course dinner for one, not including cocktails or wine, taxes, or tips, are as follows: *Expensive,* $20 and up; *Moderate,* $10–$20; *Inexpensive,* under $10.

Expensive

Arthur's of Nashville. Union Station Hotel, 1001 Broadway (255–1494). Sophisticated dining room features a prix fixe seven-course dinner that changes daily; impressive wine list, plush decor, and professional service add up to one of Nashville's leading establishments. L, Mon.–Fri.; D, daily; Sun. brunch 11:45 A.M.–3 P.M.

Crown Court. Maxwell House Hotel, 2025 MetroCenter Blvd. (259–4343). Steak Diane, chateaubriand, fresh seafoods, an excellent wine list, and panoramic views of downtown Nashville. L, D, daily.

Hermitage Dining Room. Hermitage Hotel, 231 Sixth Ave., N., downtown (244–3121). Classical gourmet cuisine, fine wines, a soft piano, in a gorgeous Beaux-Arts Dining room. B, L, D, daily.

Julian's Restaurant Français. 2412 West End Ave. (327–2412). Intimate French restaurant, long a favorite of sophisticated Nashvillians. Specialties include veal aux champignons, pheasant, rack of lamb, and dessert soufflés. D, only, Mon.–Sat.

Mario's. 1915 West End Ave. (327–3232). Superb Northern Italian veal, pasta, and seafood dishes, served by a very polished staff, make this a very "in" place for local and visiting celebrities. D, only, Mon.–Sat.

Mère Bulles, The Wine Bar and Restaurant. 152 2nd Ave., N. (615–256–1946). Aura of casual elegance prevails in this chic, popular establishment where three intimate dining areas in artfully restored warehouse offer river views. Live entertainment nightly, usually jazz or folk music. Specialties include veal saltimbocca, which is stuffed with honey-cured ham and Swiss cheese and topped with Chef Chris's special sauces. Excellent wine selection, by glass or bottle. L, D daily. Reservations suggested. AE, CB, DC, MC, V.

Old Hickory Restaurant. Opryland Hotel, 2800 Opryland Dr. (889–1000). One of Nashville's finest dining experiences. Excellently prepared French, Continental, and American dishes in a lovely atmosphere of flickering candles, antiques, and piano music. Specialties include rack of lamb, chateaubriand, fresh seafoods, veal scaloppini forestiere, and Viennese and French pastries. D, only.

The Stock Yard. 901 Second Ave., N., downtown (255–6464). Succulent aged western beef and fresh seafoods are the specialties of this handsomely restored 1920s stockyards building. Live entertainment comes with nightly dinner.

Moderate

Faison's. 2000 Belcourt Ave. (298–2112). Veal, chicken, seafood, pasta, and beef attract local Yuppies to this attractively renovated bungalow for lunch and dinner.

Hachland Hill Country Inn. 1601 Madison St., Clarksville, TN 37043 (615–647–4084). Located 35 mi. northwest of downtown Nashville, attractive inn has been one of state's most popular for over 30 years. Luscious Southern-style "down-home" cookery. Handicapped accessible; dance floor. Reservations required. B, L, D.

Kobe Steaks. 210 25th Ave., N. (327–9081). Hibachi-grilled steaks, seafoods, chicken in a lovely Japanese atmosphere. D, only.

Maude's Courtyard. 1911 Broadway (320–0543). Seafoods, steaks, chicken, veal, lamb in a beautifully restored house, with an enclosed courtyard. Sun. Bourbon Street Brunch features a Dixieland band. L, D., Sun. brunch

Old Spaghetti Factory. 160 Second Ave., N. (254–9010). Spaghetti with a big choice of sauces in a restored riverfront warehouse crammed with antiques and oddities. D, only. No credit cards.

106 Club. 106 Harding Pl. at Belle Meade, five mi. west of downtown Nashville (356–1300). Creative Continental cuisine is served in an elegant Art Deco setting here, with intimate small dining rooms. Piano nightly. Reservations advised. D only; open 5 P.M.–1 A.M. AE, DC, MC, V.

Peking Garden. 1923 Division St. (327–2020). Many regional styles of Chinese cooking, and a bargain-priced Sun. brunch buffet.

West End Cooker Restaurant & Bar. 2609 West End Ave. (327–2925). Casual place near Vanderbilt University; specializes in American and regional cooking. L, D.

Inexpensive

Amanda Sue. 2201 Bandywood Dr. (297–1993). Bright little café specializes in gourmet deli items, salads, sandwiches, soups, and carry-outs. L only.

The Bluebird Cafe. 4104 Hillsboro Rd. (383–1461). Casual European-style coffee house and bistro serves imaginative sandwiches, salads, meats, vegetarian dishes, and rich house-baked desserts. L, D.

Le Bon Vivant. 231 Franklin Rd. (377–1058). French bakery and cafe offering salads, quiches, sandwiches, fresh breads, and pastries. L, only. No credit cards.

Cawthons's Famous Bar-B-Que. 4121 Hillsboro Rd., at Armory Dr. (256–8045). Spicy barbecued pork, with all the hearty trimmings. L, D. No credit cards.

El Chico. 21 Rivergate Mall, Goodlettsville (859–3913); 1132 Murfreesboro Rd. (366–6002). This is a popular destination for Tex-Mex cooking.

Ciraco's. 212 21st Ave., S. (329–0036). Casual trattoria serving generous portions of pasta, pizza, veal. L, D.

Duncan's Diner. On Blythe St., Gallatin TN, 25 mi. northeast of downtown Nashville (452–5618). The essential homecooking hideaway, well worth the trip. B, L, D. No credit cards.

Elliston Place Soda Shop. 2111 Elliston Pl. (327–1090). A landmark for generations of Vanderbilt students, features hamburgers, sandwiches, sodas, plate lunches, and breakfasts in booths and at an old-fashioned soda fountain. B, L, D. No credit cards.

Loveless Motel & Cafe. Rte. 5, Hwy. 100, 20 mi. southwest of downtown (646–9700). An institution as renowned as the Opry and the Parthenon, the Loveless attracts hordes of city folks for fried chicken, country ham, vegetables, and buttermilk biscuits. B, L, D.

Miss Daisy's. 126 Church Street Mall (242–8585). Served here are Southern dishes, imaginative casseroles in Colonial Williamsburg motif. L, D.

The Pineapple Room at Cheekwood. Forrest Park Dr. (352–4859). Salads, sandwiches, luncheon plates in a glass-enclosed dining room overlooking the Tennessee Botanical Gardens and Cheek mansion. L, only. Closed Mon. CB, DC, MC, V.

Satsuma Tea Room. 417 Union St., (256–0760). Simply wonderful little downtown retreat, a bit like eating at grandma's house. Fresh vegetables, soups, meats, breads, and desserts all have a just-made taste. L, only. No credit cards.

LIQUOR LAWS. The drinking age in Tennessee is 21. Clubs that serve liquor by drink are required to serve food. Beer-only taverns are not subject to this law. Drinks cannot be served past 2 A.M., and glasses must be off the tables by 3 A.M.

NIGHTLIFE AND BARS. With a few exceptions, Nashville nightlife bargains exist outside the central business district, either near downtown or in suburban locations. With a rekindled interest in nighttime activities downtown comes the promise of a new variety of eating and drinking establishments. Lounges in established hotels offer entertainment possibilities, but Printer's Alley between Third and Fourth Aves., North, and Church and Union Sts. remains the undisputed center of downtown nightclub activity. It is expensive and mostly overrun with tourists. The Alley offers floor shows, house bands, and exotic strippers. Established recording giants and songwriters have been known to show up in the Alley and even give impromptu performances. Dozens of established night spots exist outside downtown in no particular district. Many out-of-the-way places have worthwhile live entertainment, and those cherished by the locals feature some of Music City's best songwriters, musicians, and singers.

Nashville's talented musicians, singers, and songwriters seek exposure as well as income. An abundant talent pool lends itself nicely to bars and lounges in need of live entertainment. Several establishments showcase a variety of musical styles. The best overview of the music and entertainment scene from week to week is the "Showcase" section of the Sun. *Tennessean* newspaper. Cover charges at the untouristy places generally are nominal ($2 to $5) but are considerably higher if a big name is booked for performances. Dress is casual, but patrons are comfortable in anything from jeans to jackets and ties. Some clubs do not allow jeans, so ask before arriving.

The Bluebird Cafe. 4104 Hillsboro Rd. (383–1461). A variety of music styles, occasionally by name talent, offered 7 nights a week in a cozy café atmosphere. Sunday night is songwriter's night for established and amateur writers. Sun.–Mon., no cover; Tues.–Sat., $3 to $5.

Boots Randolph's. 209 Printers Alley, between Third and Fourth Aves. (615–256–5500). A sophisticated supper club, this is one of city's landmark night spots. It features Boots ("Mr. Yakkety Sax") at 9:30 and sometimes at 11:30 P.M., Mon.–Sat., 9–11 P.M. or later.

Bullpen Lounge. Second Ave., N., and Stockyard Blvd. (255–6464). A big basement lounge beneath the popular Stockyard Restaurant seats 500 for country music entertainment. Special name acts are featured occasionally, and country music stars have been known to show up and sit in with the house band. A convivial setting in the renovated cattle stockyard building. Mon.–Sat. Cover, $4 to $7 for special acts.

Ernest Tubb Record Shop Midnight Jamboree. 2208 Elliston Rd. (615–889–2474). A live radio show that's much like the Opry, with performances by Opry stars and new talent. Each Sat. at midnight (arrive by 11:30 P.M.). No cover charge.

Nashville Palace. 2400 Music Valley Dr. (885–1540). Nightclub-style showcase for country entertainment. Located very near the Opryland Hotel and Park.

Printer's Alley. Between Third and Fourth Aves., N., and Church and Union Sts. A descendant of Nashville's 19th-century saloon district. The cobbled alley is lined with restaurants and clubs that feature country and pop entertainment: Captain's Table, Boots Randolph's, Western Room, Embers Showcase, and others. Ideal location for club hopping. Dinner reservations may be required at some establishments. Dinners are expensive, although entertainment covers are moderate (about $5). Clubs are closed Sun.

The Station Inn. 402 12th Ave., S. (255–3307). A lively no-frills hideaway where some of Nashville's best down-home bluegrass is played and sung. Bluegrass jam sessions on Sun. bring together some of the genre's best talents. Opens at 7 P.M. Tues.–Sat. Music begins at 9 P.M. Cover, $4 to $6.

The World's End. 1713 Church St. (329–3480). A contemporary bistro featuring Sun. night jazz ($5 minimum) and weekend dinner theater ($16 includes dinner and show). For Sun. brunch, it's live classical music (very economical).

Zanie's. 2025 Eighth Ave., S. (269–0221). Stand-up comedy is the attraction at this stop on the national circuit. A popular local feature is amateur night on Tues. Professional talent performs Wed.–Sun. nights, at 8:30 P.M. Late shows begin at 10:45 P.M. Fri. and Sat. Menu includes hamburgers, sandwiches, and munchies. Admission varies.

MEMPHIS

Memphis conjures up languid pictures of paddlewheelers churning on the muddy Mississippi, of blues wailing out of Beale Street honky-tonks, of cotton, and Elvis Presley, pampered ducks strutting through the lobby of the Peabody Hotel, and a tempo of life still rooted in the Old South.

Tennessee's largest city—16th largest in America—Memphis is a gracious, easy-going metropolis, that belies its population of nearly one million in a metropolitan area that includes parts of Mississippi and Arkansas. Perched on bluffs above the river, laced by tree-shaded boulevards and a wealth of parks and open spaces, it bears a closer kinship to the cottonlands of the Mississippi Delta than it does to Nashville, or to faraway Knoxville and the Smoky Mountains.

This grande dame of the river bluffs has had many important men in her life. Spanish explorer Hernando DeSoto first crossed the Mississippi here in 1541, during a search for gold in the wilds of the Southeast. In 1819, Andrew Jackson, inspired by the rich, black soil of the Mississippi bottomlands, named the new city for Memphis, the ancient Pharaoh's capital of Egypt. The name means, "Place of Good Abode."

Along with reigning as the world's largest spot cotton market, modern Memphis is a hardwood and soybean capital, and a major river port. Its Medical Center is one of the nation's largest. Don't litter or make undue noise while you're here. The city is proud of its annual awards for cleanliness, safety, and serenity.

The distinctive Memphis tempo can be largely attributed to a pair of colossal musicians, who first made an impact here and then on the nation and the world, a half-century apart. William Christopher Handy, a black man born in a northern Alabama log cabin, was the first. Elvis Aron Presley, a young white man from nearby Tupelo, Mississippi, followed in Handy's giant steps.

After Handy published his "Memphis Blues" in 1912, followed by the "St. Louis Blues," "Beale Street Blues" and many others, Beale Street, on the edge of downtown Memphis, almost overnight became one of the most famous streets in America.

Prosperity lasted until the late 1920s. The Great Depression virtually closed down the flourishing musical life, turning rowdy-raucous Beale into another grimy gray byway of pawn shops, used clothing stores, and cheap saloons. But W. C. Handy's music lived on, and influenced a gifted truck driver named Presley, who blended some of the deep, rich flavors of the old black musicians into his own hip-grinding revolutionary style.

Every year, thousands of pilgrims travel to Memphis from around the world to hear blues and rockabilly at their fountainhead. The largest numbers stream up the driveway of Graceland, to pay homage to "King" Elvis, who died in the mansion on Aug. 16, 1977.

While they're reveling in music and memories, these out-of-towners find that Memphis has much more to offer. After a long, quiet period when her Southern sisters raised taller skyscrapers, wider freeways, and more deluxe hotels and restaurants, Memphis has come back to life. Nowhere is its surging revitalization more evident than a once-moribund downtown. Beale Street is in the forefront of this new energy. Three blocks of the legendary thoroughfare once again bristle with offices, restaurants, nightclubs, and small shops and museums. Many of the old cotton warehouses along the Mississippi bluffs have been turned into luxury condos and wining and dining establishments.

Also downtown, a five-mile Mississippi mudflat called Mud Island has been transformed into a $60-million complex of museums and displays honoring the river's legends, history, and heritage.

Memphis cherishes its traditions, and one of the most beloved has been miraculously restored. The ducks are once again splashing in the tiered Italian marble fountain of The Peabody, part of a top-to-bottom resurrection that has returned this grand old hotel to the glory days of the '20s, '30s, and '40s.

Almost anytime is a good time to visit Memphis. But May is the best time of all. Throughout the month, the annual "Memphis In May" celebration puts on free outdoor concerts, an international barbecue cooking contest, and scores of special events and festivities. While "Memphis In May" is in full swing, the city's traditional Cotton Carnival also packs the month, into early June, with Mardi Gras-like parades and pageantry, concerts, and sporting events.

Whatever the duration of your stay, let the blues and the river get into your bloodstream. It's what this laid back old city is all about.

PRACTICAL INFORMATION FOR MEMPHIS

WHEN TO GO. Spring and fall are the ideal times for Memphis. With its two major festivals, May is especially delightful. The city's river location tends to make summers hot and humid. Winters are generally mild, although winds off the river can be painfully reminiscent of Chicago.

HOW TO GET THERE. In far western Tennessee, Memphis is about 200 mi. from Nashville, 300 from St. Louis, and 400 from New Orleans. The city is served by several airlines, and by bus and train, and is a port for steamboat tours on the Mississippi.

By plane. *Memphis International Airport* is 9½ mi. south of downtown. Domestic carriers include *Air Midwest, Delta, American, Northwest, TWA, United, USAir,* and *Air Atlanta.*

By bus. *Greyhound* (800–528–0447) has frequent service into Memphis terminals.

By train. Amtrak's *City of New Orleans* offers service between Memphis and New Orleans and Chicago.

By steamboat. The paddle-wheel steamboats *Delta Queen* and *Mississippi Queen* stop at Memphis on excursions between New Orleans, St. Louis, Cincinnati, and St. Paul. Phone 800–543–1949 for schedules.

By car. Memphis is served by three Interstate highways: I-55 north to St. Louis and south to Jackson, MS; I-40 east to Nashville and Knoxville; I-240, an intracity freeway loop. The city is also served by U.S. Hwys. 51, 61, 64, 72, and 78.

TELEPHONES. Memphis's area code is 901. Local calls are 25 cents, with no time limit. In an *emergency* contact police, fire, and ambulance by dialing 911. Otherwise, phone *police* at 528–2222; *fire department* at 458–8281; *ambulance* at 458–3311.

TOURIST INFORMATION. Visitors should stop first at the *Memphis Convention & Visitors Bureau,* Morgan Keegan Tower, 50 N. Front St., Suite 450, Memphis, TN 38103 (901–576–8181). Maps, brochures, information, and tours are available Mon.–Sat. 9 A.M.–5 P.M.

TOURS. You can tour Memphis in an air-conditioned bus, van, private car, or limo; in a horse-drawn carriage; or on a Mississippi River paddlewheeler. Contact *Carriage Tours of Memphis,* 422 S. Main St., Memphis, TN 38103 (527–7542); *Cottonland Tours,* 255 N. Main Memphis, Suite 101, TN 38103 (774–5248); *Gray Line of Memphis,* 2050 Elvis Presley Blvd., Memphis, TN 38106 (942–4662); *Memphis Queen Cruise Line,* Box 3188, Memphis, TN 38173–0188 (527–5694); *Rivertown Tours,* 2035 Madison Memphis, TN 38104 (683–1518).

PARKS AND GARDENS. Dixon Gallery and Gardens. 4339 Park Ave. (761–2409). Lovely house museum set among 17 acres of woodlands and formal gardens has collections of French and American Impressionists; 18th- and 19th-century British antiques and paintings. Open Tues.–Sat., 10 A.M.–5 P.M.; Sun. 1–5 P.M. Adults, $2.50; students, senior citizens, $1; free to all on Tues.

Libertyland. 940 Early Maxwell Blvd. (274–1776). Small theme park at Mid-South Fairgrounds with rides, live shows, petting zoo. mid-Apr.–mid-June, weekends only; mid-June–Aug., daily. Gate fee $6; 4 and under, free; over 55, $2. General admission $3 after 4 P.M. Rides extra.

Meeman-Shelby Forest State Park. U.S. 51, Millington, TN, 16 mi. north of Memphis (876–5201). On the Mississippi, 12,500-acre park has two lakes, swimming pool, fishing, boating, biking and horseback trails, and camping areas. Open year-round. Fees for some facilities.

Memphis Botanic Garden. 750 Cherry Rd. (685–1566). Several areas include dogwood and azalea trails, Japanese gardens, and Arboretum with many varieties of flowers and trees. Open daily 8 A.M.–dusk. Goldsmith Civic Garden Center and adjacent conservatory open Tues.–Sat., 9 A.M.–dusk; Sun. from 11 A.M. Adults, $2; senior citizens, $1.50; 6–17, $1.

Memphis Zoo & Aquarium. Overton Park (726–4775). Large well-maintained zoo has hundreds of animals, birds, and reptiles from every continent, and an aquarium with fishy creatures great and small. Open daily 9 A.M.–5 P.M.; closed Thanksgiving, Dec. 24–25. Adults, $3.50; 2–11 with adult, $2; free to all 3:30–5 P.M. Mon. Aquarium: adults, 25 cents; children, 10 cents.

Overton Park. Off Poplar Ave. and N. Parkway, about 10 minutes from downtown. A 350-acre retreat with a zoo, major art museum, golf course, picnic grounds, lake, and wooded walking trails. Open daily.

SPECTATOR SPORTS. *Southland Greyhound Park.* Box 2088, 1550 Ingram Blvd., West Memphis, AK 72301. (501–735–3670). The nation's foremost greyhound racing track, with parimutuel betting, restaurants. The season is Apr.–Nov.

HISTORIC SITES AND HOUSES. Chucalissa Indian Museum. 1987 Indian Village Dr., off U.S. 61, 6 mi. south of downtown (785–3160). Re-created 1,000-year-old Choctaw village, with craft demonstrations and a museum of unearthed artifacts. Open Tues.–Sat., 9 A.M.–5 P.M.; Sun., 1–5 P.M. Adults, $3; 4–11, over 60, $1.50. T.O. Fuller State Park, adjoining the village (785–3950) is believed the site where Hernando DeSoto crossed the Mississippi. Facilities include swimming pool, fishing, picknicking, and 18-hole golf course. Open year-round. Fees for some facilities.

Graceland. 3717 Elvis Presley Blvd. (332–3322; 800–238–2000, outside TN). For legions of Elvis fans, this tree-shaded Southern mansion is the holy of holies, the realization of an impossible dream of wealth and fame. They walk through the musical gate notes by the hundreds every day, through the garishly furnished rooms of the mansion, and place flowers at his grave. A museum has his gold and platinum records, photos, show costumes. Home tour admission, adults, $7.95; ages 4–11, $4.75; 3 and under, free. Combination tour, including mansion, airplanes, museum, tour bus: adults, $15.95; 4–12, $10.95. Parking $2. Open daily 9 A.M.–5 P.M. Reservations a must.

Lorraine Motel/Martin Luther King Jr. Memorial. 406 Mulberry St. (525–6834). Dr. King's room and the balcony where he was assassinated in 1968 have been preserved as a memorial to the civil rights champion. Open daily 8 A.M.–7 P.M. Donations accepted.

Mud Island. On the Mississippi, downtown (576–7241). This fascinating 50-acre park, museum, and entertainment complex salutes Ole Man River and Memphis's colorful musical heritage. Music rooms feature Dixieland, jazz, blues, gospel, and Elvis; "Mark Twain" speaks from a replica of a riverboat. Outside, a 5-block River Walk traces the Mississippi from Cairo, IL, to New Orleans. Top names perform in a 4,000-seat amphitheater. You'll also find playgrounds, picnic areas, restaurants, gift shops, and summertime outdoor performers. Open daily, May–Oct. All-inclusive admission, adults $6; seniors, ages 4–12, disabled, $4; under 4, free. Groups of 25 and more, $3.50 adults, $2.25 ages 4–12. Grounds admission only, adults $3; ages 4–12 and over 60, $2.

A. Schwab's Department Store. 163 Beale St. An old-fashioned emporium crammed with voodoo love potions, 99-cent neckties, 1940s and 1950s suits and dresses, and other marvels. Worth a nostalgic browse through.

Victorian Village. 100 to 700 block of Adams Ave., near downtown. Nearly two dozen restored Victorian, French, Italianate, Neoclassical, Gothic, and other style homes. Open daily are: French-Victorian Fontaine House (526–1469), $4 adults; $3, over 60 and military; $2 students and 6–18; Italianate Mallory-Neely House (523–1484); $4 adults $3, over 62 and under 17; and clapboard cottage Magevney House (526–4464), no admission charge.

MUSEUMS. Memphis Brooks Museum of Art. In Overton Park (722–3500). Permanent collection includes works by Renoir, Corot, Sir Joshua Reynolds, Gainsborough, Andrew Wyeth, Jackson Pollock, and Georgia O'Keefe; also Kress Collection of Italian art; decorative arts; Chinese and Japanese porcelains. Open Tues.–Sat., 10 A.M.–5 P.M.; Sun. 1–5. Donation.

Memphis Pink Palace Museum and Planetarium. 3050 Central Ave. (320–6320). Eclectic pink Georgia marble museum houses scores of exhibits on mid-South geology, frontier life, birds and animals, commerce, and Civil War history. Planetarium offers seasonal looks at the heavens. Open Tues.–Sat., 9:30 A.M.–4 P.M.; Sun. 1–5 P.M. Adults, $3; senior citizens and ages 4–18, $2.

ACCOMMODATIONS. Memphis hotels are especially busy during the entire month of May, for the Memphis In May Festival and Cotton Carnival; and in mid-Aug. when pilgrims observe Elvis Presley's death. Tennessee's 4% hotel/motel tax, and a 7.75% state sales tax will be added to your bill. The following categories are based on double occupancy: *Deluxe,* $95–$135; *Expensive,* $60–$95; *Moderate,* $40–$60; *Inexpensive,* $40 and under.

Deluxe

Holiday Inn Crowne Plaza. 250 N. Main St., Memphis, TN 38103 (901–527–7300 or 800–465–4329). Flagship hotel has 406 rooms on 18 floors. Two full-service restaurants; lounge, live music, dancing. Indoor pool, health club, whirlpool, in-room movies. Airport courtesy car. Some rooms in *Expensive* category.

Omni-Memphis (formerly Hyatt Regency Memphis). 939 Ridge Lake Blvd., Memphis, TN 38119 (901–684–6664 or 800–843–6664). In the flourishing eastern suburbs, this circular 27-story glass tower has 380 guest rooms, health club, swimming pools, restaurants, entertainment.

The Peabody. 149 Union Ave., downtown, Memphis, TN 38103 (901–529–4000 or 800–732–2639). One of the South's grand, legendary hotels—originally opened in 1925—this standby has been given a $20-million rejuvenation and once more reigns as a *grande dame* supreme. The Renaissance-style lobby, the ornate ceilings and woodwork are a joy to the eye; the famous ducks frolicking in the lobby's travertine marble fountain, a pure delight. Each morning they come down from their penthouse "apartment" and parade across a red carpet to Sousa marches. Classical cuisine is served in Chez Philippe; light fare (not including duck) at Dux. There's music and dancing at the rooftop Skyway. The 454 guest rooms and suites are handsomely furnished.

Expensive

Brownestone Hotel (formerly Sheraton Memphis). 300 N. Second St., downtown, Memphis, TN 38105 (901–525–2511 or 800–325–3535). 250 guest rooms, 25 on Executive Level with special amenities and service.

Holiday Inn Overton Square. 1837 Union Ave. at McLean Ave., Memphis, TN 38104 (901–278–4100 or 800–465–4329). There are 174 rooms in this recently renovated inn with convenient mid-city location. Coin laundry, pool, garage. Bluff City Bar and Diner. Hometown of Holiday Inns, Memphis has other representatives of the chain at Poplar Ave. and I-240; Airport I-55 (Graceland area); 5795 Poplar Ave.; 6101 Shelby Oaks Dr.; I-55 and Ingram Blvd., West Memphis.

Marriott Residence Inn. 6141 Poplar Pike, Memphis, TN 38119 (901–685–9595 or 800–331–3131). 105 1- and 2-bedroom suites, with kitchen and wood-burning fireplace. Some units in *Deluxe* category.

Memphis Airport Hilton Inn. 2240 Democrat Rd., Memphis, TN 38132 (901–332–1130 or 800–445–8667). Adjacent to the international airport, with 380 rooms, restaurants, lounges, health clubs, meeting facilities.

Radisson Memphis Hotel, 185 Union Ave., downtown, Memphis, TN 38103 (901–528–1800 or 800–228–9822, except NE). Spectacular new luxury hotel, with 283 guest rooms, gourmet dining, and live entertainment.

Ramada Inn Convention Center. 160 Union Ave., downtown, Memphis, TN 38103 (901–525–5491 or 800–272–6232). 186 guest rooms, including 18 deluxe rooms and suites in the Executive Level. Restaurants, lounges.

Moderate

Best Western Riverbluff. 340 W. Illinois Ave., Memphis, TN 38106 (901–948–9005 or 800–528–1234). 99 rooms, restaurant, entertainment.

Days Inn Downtown. 164 Union Ave., Memphis, TN 38103 (901–527–4100 or 800–325–2525). 106 guest rooms, suites, studios. Restaurant, lounge service. Handicapped facilities. Cable TV. Phone toll-free reservations number for information about other area Days Inns.

Ramada Inn-Southwest Airport. 1471 E. Brooks Rd., Memphis, TN 38116 (901–332–3500 or 800–272–6232). Offered here are 250 guest rooms. Restaurant, cocktail lounge with live entertainment. Coin laundry, pool, complimentary airport transportation.

Inexpensive

Lakeland Inn-Best Western. 9822 Huffnpuff Rd., Arlington, TN 38002, 16 mi. east of downtown (901–388–7120 or 800–528–1234). 91 rooms, café on a resort lake.

Red Roof Inn. 3875 American Way, Memphis, TN 38118 (901–363–2335). 110 guest rooms on three floors. Pets accepted. Restaurant nearby.

RESTAURANTS. Memphis proclaims herself the pork barbecue capital of the universe, and invites you to taste-test its claim at more than 100 homey emporiums. Upriver from New Orleans, the city also serves Cajun and Creole specialties, as well as French, Italian, Greek, Mexican, and Oriental dishes. Restaurant categories, based on an average three-course dinner for one, not including cocktails, wines, tips, or taxes, are: *Expensive,* $20 and up; *Moderate,* $10–$20; *Inexpensive,* $10 and under.

Expensive

Chez Philippe. The Peabody Hotel, 149 Union Ave. (529–4188). Elegant French cuisine, fine wines, European service. D, only. Closed Sun.

Folk's Folly. 551 Mendenhall Rd. (762–8200). Huge steaks, Cajun-style vegetables, music in unique and friendly surroundings. D, only.

Grisanti's. 1489 Airways Blvd. (458–2648). Owner John Grisanti is a Memphis legend, and so is his Northern Italian cooking, lengthy wine list, and hospitality. Moderately priced lunch; dinner expensive.

Justine's. 919 Coward Pl. (527–3815). Another revered Memphis tradition. Superb French cuisine in an historic antebellum mansion. D, only.

Moderate

Captain Bilbo's River Restaurant. 263 Wagner Pl., downtown (526–1966). Enormous converted warehouse overlooking the Mississippi serves oysters, shrimp, steaks, drinks, and music from several dining rooms and bars. D, only.

Chervil's. In Holiday Inn–Crowne Plaza, next to Memphis Convention Center, 250 N. Main St. (527–7333). *Nouvelle American* cuisine. Coat and tie suggested; reservations advised. B, L, D, Mon.–Sat., closed Sun.

Jim's Place East. 5560 Shelby Oaks Dr., off I-40 at Sycamore View (388–7200). Steaks, seafood, and Greek specialties in congenial, down-home atmosphere. Fervent local following. L–D, Mon.–Fri.; D, Sat.; closed Sun.

Paulette's. 2110 Madison Ave., Overton Square. (726–5128). Lovely small restaurant with French, Continental dishes, wines. L, D.

Ruby Tuesday. 3092 Poplar Ave., in Chickasaw Oaks Village Mall (327–9355). This branch of a popular nationwide chain offers predictably eclectic, lively atmosphere. Fare ranges from soups, burgers, and quiche to hearty, well-prepared seafood, chicken, and steaks. Children's plates, L, D, daily. Also cocktail lounge. AE, MC, V.

Inexpensive

Anderton's East and Oyster Bar. 1901 Madison Ave. (726–4010). Superbly prepared fresh Gulf Coast seafood, steaks, veal, chicken. Friendly, informal atmosphere, great local favorite. L, D., Mon.–Fri.; D, Sat.; closed Sun.

Charlie Vergos Rendezvous. Across from The Peabody, in Gen. Washburn Alley (523–2746). In a back alley basement, this wonderful place is crammed with antiques and what many experts swear are the choicest barbecued ribs in creation. L, D.

Coletta's. 1063 S. Parkway. (948–7652). Only in barbecue-crazy Memphis would you expect to find an Italian restaurant specializing in barbecued pizza. L, D.

Dixie Cafe. 1733 Sycamore View (377–2211); 3500 Park Ave. (324–3644). Down-home, Southern-style cookery is offered here in casual, rustic settings. Children's menu. L, D daily; closed major holidays. AE, MC, V.

Leonard's. 1140 Bellevue Blvd. S., (948–1581). Specializing in barbecue pork, shoulders and ribs since 1922. Ask for "outside brown," (crusty, chopped pork) to be transported to barbecue heaven. A cherished Southern institution. Call for daily hours.

The Little Tea Shop. 69 Monroe Ave., downtown (525–6000). First-rate Southern home cooking. Mon.–Fri. L, only. No credit cards.

Piccadilly Cafeteria. Two locations: 2055 Exeter Rd., in Exeter Village (755–5603); 3968 Elvis Presley Blvd., in Whitehaven Plaza (398–5186). These locally popular cafeterias feature good choices of entrees, vegetables, salads, homemade desserts. L, D. No credit cards.

Rum Boogie Cafe. 182 Beale St. (528–0150). Memphis music and barbecue.

Shelby Place Restaurant. 107 S. Germantown Rd., Cordova, TN, at Shelby Farm Show Place Arena (756–8207). The only thing "country" about this popular new dining room is the drive out. Excellent pasta, fresh seafood, steaks, chicken, in attractive casual setting. L, D, daily.

NIGHTLIFE. The largest concentrations of dining and nightlife are downtown in the Beale St. area, and at Overton Sq., at Madison and Cooper, a short drive from downtown. Blues and Dixieland are the city's musical hallmarks, but you'll also find jazz, rock, country, and other musical expressions in clubs and lounges all over town. See prior listings for Folk's Folly, Captain Bilbo's, and Rum Boogie Cafe.

THE MIDWEST

by
CAROLYN R. LANGDON

Ms. Langdon, a freelance writer, lived on both coasts before settling in Kansas City, where she has worked on the Kansas City Star.

The Midwest is the country's middle of the road, a mixture of great expanses of farms and concentrations of heavy industry, of huge skyscrapers representing urban commerce and isolated, pristine forests unchanged for 200 years. It was a muddy wilderness with Indian and French names when Boston was founded. Its values are "Midwestern." Its history is of two great struggles, the westward migrations and the Civil War. Its fortunes rise and fall a few years after the rest of the country; recessions start sooner and end later. But it has the ability to change quite rapidly. The nation's rust belt in the 1970s became America's revitalized manufacturing and service sector in the 1980s.

As seen by Easterners, the area is the middle ground between the East Coast and the Great Plains States to the west. The Midwest then is the bulwark between the Great Northern states of Wisconsin and Michigan and the Mid-South and Appalachian Mountains.

Seen from the East, the Midwest begins in Ohio, and "Buckeyes" consider themselves closer in sentiment to the East as they're on Eastern time, an hour ahead of the rest of the Midwest. Ohio ranges from the shores of Lake Erie to the Ohio River, from the Pennsylvania steel towns and West Virginia mill towns to the Indiana line.

Indiana bridges the northern gap between Lakes Erie and Michigan—where steel, refining, and industrial wealth reside—to the rich woodland beauty of the Cumberland Mountains winding along the Ohio River to the south. Resembling the design of the state's central and capital city, Indianapolis, roads in the Hoosier State spread out to all corners like wagon wheel spokes.

If there were a hub to the Midwest, indeed to the nation, it would be that city of "big shoulders" resting on a small niche of Lake Michigan's southern shore: Chicago. Dominating Illinois and the Midwest in population, Chicago is the center of the area's commerce, art, transportation, and international trade. Chicago's daily influx of two million commuters comes from as far away as Illinois's northern lakeside border with Wisconsin. An hour south or west of Chicago is where Illinois begins, and it extends southwest past Abraham Lincoln's home in Springfield to the river delta lands, aptly named Cairo, abutting Missouri.

Missouri, home of Harry Truman and Mark Twain, is the thriving countryside between urbane St. Louis and Kansas City, the East and West gateways. Along the area's southern borders, the Ozark mountains and lakes are a key tourist attraction and a major industry, in contrast to the farm lands that spread northward into Iowa.

If one Midwestern state epitomizes agriculture, it is Iowa. Iowa could be described as unbroken expanses of corn surrounding a few large cities. Agriculture covers the state northward, and the mighty Mississippi and Missouri rivers border on the east and west. Each fall, great rivers of Iowa corn and grain flow southward to world markets. Iowa industries such as implement production, insurance, and kitchen appliances carry on regardless of the ebb and flow of the state's agricultural economy.

OHIO

Ohio offers a surprising diversity of geography, culture, and lifestyle: historical villages and aerospace museums, bustling metropolises and quiet farming villages, heavily industrialized areas and verdant countryside with 40,000 miles of streams and rivers, galleries of classical art and amusement theme parks.

The eastern portion of the state, anchored by Akron and Youngstown, tends to be industrialized; Dayton in the west with Wright Patterson Air Force Base is an aviation center (the Wright brothers' first experiments with flying were in Dayton); and there are the three Cs: Columbus, Cincinnati, and Cleveland.

Columbus has experienced rapid growth of late. Civil War vintage buildings have been torn down to make room for new structures. The limestone state capitol, however, remains a monument to the past, considered the purest example of Greek-revival architecture in the U.S.

Cincinnati came to life in the early 19th century as steamboats began to ply the waters of the Ohio River. Today Cincinnati is conservative politically and cosmopolitan socially; the early German influence is still strong in the Ohio Valley. The city has fine restaurants and museums.

The Civil War launched Cleveland as a great city. When iron ore in the upper Great Lakes and coal in nearby fields were in great demand the industrialists of Cleveland answered the call. Today the nation's 11th largest metropolitan area sprawls 45 miles on either side of the Cuyahoga River.

Long before the white man came to Ohio, Indian tribes such as the Iroquois were there. The Iroquois War Trail east of what is now Cleveland along the shores of Lake Erie on U.S. 20 or I-90 was used by the tribes of the Iroquois Confederacy of upper New York. Later these foot paths

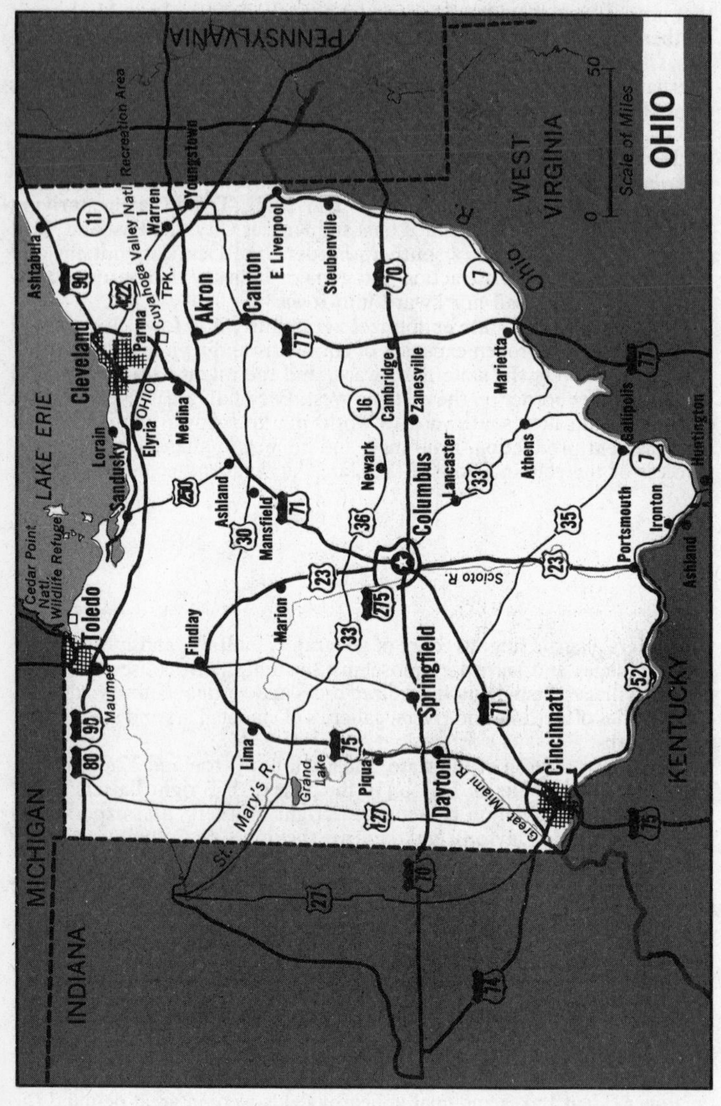

OHIO
Scale of Miles
0
50
LAKE ERIE
MICHIGAN
INDIANA
PENNSYLVANIA
WEST VIRGINIA
KENTUCKY
Cedar Point Natl. Wildlife Refuge
Toledo
Maumee
Sandusky
Lorain
Elyria
Cleveland
Parma
Ashtabula
Cuyahoga Valley Natl Recreation Area
Warren
Youngstown
TPK.
OHIO
Medina
Akron
Canton
E. Liverpool
Steubenville
Cambridge
Zanesville
Marietta
Gallipolis
Huntington
Athens
Lancaster
Newark
Columbus
Ashland
Mansfield
Findlay
Marion
Lima
Grand Lake
St. Mary's R.
Piqua
Springfield
Dayton
Great Miami R.
Cincinnati
Scioto R.
Portsmouth
Ironton
Ashland
Ohio R.
90
80
11
422
77
70
7
16
250
30
71
36
33
35
23
275
75
127
52
27
74

were used for travel and to settle northern Ohio. As villages grew up quickly, immigrants, many from New England, incorporated some of the characteristics of the villages they left behind. City squares and the general layout of towns such as Hudson, Burton, and Painesville remain today as reminders of New England.

PRACTICAL INFORMATION FOR OHIO

HOW TO GET THERE. By plane. Major carriers serve Toledo, Akron, Columbus, Dayton, Cleveland, and Cincinnati. *Greater Cincinnati International Airport* is about 12 mi. from downtown, across the Ohio River and the Kentucky border. A taxi downtown costs about $14. The *Cleveland Hopkins International Airport* is about a 20-minute and $15 cab ride from downtown.

By bus. *Greyhound-Trailways* serves cities in Ohio.

By train. *Amtrak* trains stop at Cleveland and Cincinnati as well as other Ohio towns.

By car. The major east-west highways into Ohio are I-90, I-80, and I-70. On the north-south axis, the routes are I-77, I-71, and I-75.

TOURIST INFORMATION. *Ohio Office of Travel and Tourism,* Box 1001, Columbus, OH 43216 (800–BUCKEYE, nationwide; 614–466–8844, in state). Listings and calendars of events also are maintained by the following: *Ohio Arts Council,* 727 E. Main St., Columbus, OH 43205 (614–466–2613); *Ohio Festivals and Events Association,* Box 303 Utica, OH 43080 (614–892–3728); *Ohio Historical Society,* 1985 Velma Ave., Columbus, OH 42311 (614–297–2300); and *Ohio Travel Association,* Box 2675, Columbus, OH 43216–1200 (614–469–1200).

Information about events in and around Ohio's 3 largest cities is available from the *Greater Cincinnati Convention Bureau,* 300 W. Sixth St., Cincinnati, OH 45601 (513–621–2142); *The Convention and Visitors Bureau of Greater Cleveland,* 50 Public Sq., Cleveland, OH 44113 (216–621–4110); and the *Greater Columbus Convention and Visitors Bureau,* 10 W. Broad St., Columbus, OH 43215 (614–221–6623).

TELEPHONES. The area code for Cleveland and the surrounding area is 216. For local directory assistance dial 411. The area code for Cincinnati and the surrounding area is 513. Dial 1–555–1212 for directory assistance within the 513 area code. The cost of a local call is 25 cents, and there is no time limit.

EMERGENCY TELEPHONE NUMBERS. Cincinnati. Most of greater Cincinnati is served by 911. The universal *police* emergency number is 765–1212. To report a *fire,* call 241–2525. Some other numbers: fire department *life saving squad,* 241–2525; *Ohio State Highway Patrol* (Hamilton County), 863–4606; *Drug and Poison Information Center,* 558–5111; *Suicide Prevention,* 281–2273.

Cleveland. The *police* emergency number is 911. To report a *fire,* call 911. Some other numbers: *Poison Control,* 231–4455; *Suicide Prevention,* 229–2211; *emergency ambulance* (Cleveland and Cuyahoga County), 911.

HOW TO GET AROUND. Cincinnati. The *Queen City Metro* (621–4455) provides regularly scheduled bus service with almost 400 buses throughout most of the metropolitan area. Taxi companies include: *Center Cab Co.* (761–5007), *Radio and Diamond Cab Co.* (681–5100 or 681–2500).

Cleveland. Most of the metropolitan area is covered by buses and rapid transit lines run by the *Regional Transit Authority* (621–9500), located across from Terminal Tower. The Rapid costs $1, with free transfers to users; buses cost 85 cents. Taxi companies: *Yellow-Zone Cab* (623–1500), *Americab* (881–1111), *Lakewood Cab* (331–5000), and *Southwest Cab* (237–3100).

HINTS TO DISABLED TRAVELERS. Specially marked parking spaces for the handicapped can be recognized by blue and white signs. Transit districts in Cleveland and Cincinnati offer special pickup and delivery bus services for the handicapped. For information or to summon a bus, call the *Regional Transit Authority in Cleveland* (216–621–9500) and the *Queen City Metro Access Program in Cincinnati* (513–621–9450).

SPECIAL-INTEREST SIGHTSEEING. Ohio has the world's largest Amish population, situated mainly in several counties in the northeast area of the state.

Among these Amish communities are: **Berlin,** Holmes County, offering tours of a working farm, restaurants, furniture makers, quilt and fabric shops, and Ohio's only working woolen mill; **Middlefield,** Geauga County, offering cheese house, largest producer of Swiss cheese in Eastern U.S. and area history museum; **New Philadelphia,** Tuscarawas County, offering Amish-style restaurant and shops; and **Sugarcreek,** Tuscarawas County, offering cheese factory, quilt and craft shops, and historical museum.

PARKS AND GARDENS. Northeast: *Fellows Riverside Gardens.* Mill Creek Metropolitan Park, Youngstown, OH 44502 (216–743–7275). Ten-acre formal garden open year-round. Rose Garden design in English style and collection of rhododendrons, dwarf evergreens, and 20,000 tulips.

Garden Center of Greater Cleveland. 11030 E. Blvd., Cleveland, OH 44106 (216–721–1600). Open year-round, closed Sat. Variety of outdoor gardens and indoor displays and horticultural library and classes.

Kingwood Center & Gardens. 900 Park Ave. W., Mansfield, OH 44906 (419–522–0211). Open Tues.–Sat. year-round. Display gardens, greenhouse, nature trails, and bird sanctuary; 27-room French Provincial mansion home of the late Charles Kelley King.

Rockfeller Park City Greenhouse. 850 E. 88 St., Cleveland, OH 44108 (216–664–3103). Open year-round daily. Tropical, fern, cacti, and orchard areas and landscaped grounds.

Stan Hywet Hall & Gardens. 714 N. Portage Path, Akron, OH 44303 (216–836–5533). Open year-round; closed Mon. and major holidays. Garden architect Warren Manning designed this 70-acre natural garden environment around a Tudor-revival mansion.

Central: *Battelle Riverfront Park.* 25 Marconi Blvd., Columbus, OH 43215 (614–645–7410). Open year-round daily. Five-acre park along the Scioto River features walkways and ramps leading to Riverfront Amphitheater, fishing pier, and pontoon and pedal boats.

Southwest: *Cincinnati Nature Center.* 4949 Tealtown Rd., Milford, OH 45150 (513–831–1711). 12 mi. of wooded trails, lakes, and ponds.

ZOOS. Cleveland Metroparks Zoo. 3900 Brookside Park Dr., Cleveland, OH 44109 (216–661–6500). Open daily year-round. 125-acre zoo with about 1,300 animals including 2 walk-through aviaries and 6-acre African exhibit.

Cincinnati Zoo. 3400 Vine, Cincinnati, OH 45220 (513–281–4700). Open daily year-round. Includes famous collection of white tigers, reptiles, and children's zoo.

Columbus Zoo. 9990 Riverside Dr., Powell, OH 43065 (614–645–3550). 100-acre zoo with 40 buildings. New North American exhibit and 4 generations of gorillas.

STATE PARKS. Ohio has a network of state parks with amenities such as lodges and rental cabins. For a complete list write *Ohio State Parks,* Division of Parks and Recreation, Fountain Square Building C, Columbus, OH 43224 (614–265–7000).

SPECTATOR SPORTS. Sports enthusiasts have a choice of several professional teams in Ohio, including football, baseball and basketball: *Cleveland Browns,* Cleveland Stadium (216–696–3800), National **Football** League. *Cleveland Cavaliers,* Box 355, Richfield (216–659–9100), Oct.–May season, National **Basketball** Association. *Cleveland Indians,* Cleveland Stadium (216–861–1200), American League **Baseball,** Apr.–Oct. season. *Cincinnati Bengals,* 200 Riverfront Stadium (513–621–3550), National **Football** League. *Cincinnati Reds,* 100 Riverfront Stadium (513–421–4510), National League **Baseball.**

HISTORIC SITES AND HOUSES. Grant Birthplace. Point Pleasant, OH 45103 (513–553–4911). Open Wed. through Sun. in summer; closed in winter. Restored 1817 cottage, the birthplace of Civil War General and 18th U.S. President.

Rutherford B. Hayes Presidential Center. Spiegel Grove, Fremont, OH 43420 (419–332–2081). Open daily year-round. 25-acre presidential estate, including family residence, museum, research library, and tomb.

Sherman House. 137 E. Main St., Lancaster, OH 43130 (614–687–5891). Open Mar.–Dec.; closed Mon. Restored home of Civil War General William T. Sherman and Senator John Sherman, built in 1871.

Stowe House State Memorial. 2950 Gilbert Ave., Cincinnati, OH 45214 (513–632–5120). Open Tues.–Thurs. 10 A.M.–4 P.M. year-round. Restored 1833 home of author Harriet Beecher Stowe; cultural and educational center promoting black history.

Thomas Edison Birthplace. 9 N. Edison Dr., Box 451, Milan, OH 44846 (419–499–2135). Open daily in summer; afternoons only in winter. Closed Dec. Edison's inventions and family furnishings are displayed in this 1841 furnished brick cottage.

Ohio also has a rich historical heritage preserved in several restored communities throughout the state.

Ohio Village. 1985 Velma Ave; I-71 at 17th Ave., Columbus, OH 43211 (614–297–2300). Closed Jan.; limited hours rest of winter. Reconstructed mid-19th-century village with working craftspeople; restored inn with restaurant.

Roscoe Village. 381 Hill St., Coshocton, OH 43812 (614–622–9310). Open year-round; limited days Jan.–Mar. Restored 1830s Ohio and Erie Canal town; encourages visitor participation.

Zoar Village. SR 212, Box 404, Zoar, OH 44697 (216–874–3011). Musuem open Apr.–Oct. and one weekend in Dec.; closed Mon. and Tues. 8 buildings built by Zoar separatists, a German religious communal group, from 1817–1898. Tours led by costumed guides.

MUSEUMS AND GALLERIES. Air Force Museum. Wright-Patterson Air Force Base, Dayton, OH 45433 (513–255–3284). Open daily year-round. Oldest and largest military aviation museum in the world. Artifacts, antique planes, photographs.

Cincinnati Art Museum. Eden Park, Cincinnati, OH 45202 (513–721–5204). Open year-round; closed Mon. General art museum with permanent and temporary exhibits.

Cleveland Museum of Art. 11150 E. Blvd., Cleveland, OH 44106 (216–421–7340). Open year-round; closed Mon. Collection includes more than 45,000 objects.

Cleveland Museum of Natural History. Wade Oval, University Circle, Cleveland, OH 44106 (216–231–4600). Open daily year-round. Mounted dinosaurana exhibits of prehistoric and North American Indian life are among this large collection.

Columbus Museum of Art. 480 E. Broad St., Columbus, OH 43215 (614–221–4848). Closed Mon. Large collection of fine art works from Old Masters to contemporary; new sculpture park and garden. Free Fri.

Pro Football Hall of Fame. 2121 Harrison Ave. N.W., Canton, OH 44708 (216–456–8207). Open daily year-round. 4-building complex of football history and displays.

Taft Museum. 316 Pike St., Cincinnati, OH 45215 (513–241–0343). Noted art collection housed in historic 1820s mansion. Open daily.

MUSIC. Cleveland Opera, 1438 Euclid Ave., Cleveland, OH 44115 (216–575–0903). The season is Oct.–May for these classical and light opera performances in the Hanna Theatre.

Cleveland Orchestra. Severance Hall, 11001 Euclid Ave., Cleveland, OH 44106 (216–231–7300). Symphony orchestra presents a variety of concerts year-round.

Ohio Light Opera. University and Beaver Sts., College of Wooster, Wooster, OH 44691 (216–263–2345). Performances June–Aug. except Mon. 68 light operas featuring Gilbert and Sullivan and others.

Columbus Symphony Orchestra. 55 E. State St., Columbus, OH 43215 (614–224–5281). Year-round. Full orchestra and chamber concerts and other events in the historic Ohio Theatre; outdoor concerts in summer.

Opera Columbus. 50 W. Broad St., Columbus, OH 43215 (614–461–0022). Year-round fully staged operas in the restored Ohio Theatre.

Cincinnati Opera. 1241 Elm St., Cincinnati, OH 45210 (513–621–1919). Year-round except June. America's second-oldest opera company performing Grand Opera, operettas, and musicals.

Cincinnati Symphony Orchestra. Music Hall, 1241 Elm St., Cincinnati, OH 45210 (513–621–1919). 48 concerts each season, often with internationally known guest conductors and artists.

DANCE. Ballet buffs will find lots of pleasure in Ohio.

Cleveland Ballet. 1 Playhouse Sq., Cleveland, OH 44115 (216–621–2260). Fri.–

Sun. year-round. Professional repertory ballet, featuring modern and classical works.

Ohio Ballet. 354 E. Market St., Akron, OH 44325 (216–972–7900). In residence at the University of Akron. Feb.–May, Sept.–Dec. Touring repertory ballet company.

Ballet Metropolitan. 78 Jefferson Ave., Columbus, OH 43215 (614–224–1672). Sept.–May season. Professional repertory ballet presenting a variety of original and premiere works.

Cincinnati Ballet Company. 1216 Central Pkwy., Cincinnati, OH 45210 (513–621–5219). Sept.–Apr. season with varying schedule. Repertory dance company performing contemporary and classical ballets.

Dayton Ballet. 125 E. First St., Dayton, OH 45402 (513–222–3661). Year-round performances of contemporary ballet with narratives.

STAGE. Great Lakes Theatre Festival. 1501 Euclid Ave., Cleveland, OH 44115 (216–241–5490). June–Oct. and Dec. Ohio's only professional, classical repertory company.

Cleveland Play House. 8500 Euclid Ave., Cleveland, OH 44106 (216–795–7000). Jan.–June and Oct.–Dec. season. 3 theaters make up this complex where live performances are presented.

Hanna Theatre. 2067 E. 14th St., Cleveland, OH 44115 (216–621–5000). Year-round. Daily performances of touring Broadway shows.

Ohio Theatre. 39 East State St., Columbus, OH 43215 (614–469–0939). Year-round. Ornate 1920s movie theater with a variety of events such as ballet, opera, popular and classical music, and summer movie series. Tours available.

ACCOMMODATIONS. Hotels and motels are listed alphabetically under the two major cities we have covered. The price categories (for double rooms) are: *Deluxe,* over $125; *Expensive,* $75–$125; *Moderate,* $50–$75; *Inexpensive,* under $50. Lower weekend rates available at some hotels.

Cincinnati. Hyatt Regency–Cincinnati. *Deluxe.* 151 W. 5th St. (513–579–1234). 484 guest rooms. Cable television, in-room movies. Indoor pool, cafe, shopping arcade, health club.

The Westin. *Deluxe.* Fountain Square, 5th and Vine Sts. (513–621–7700). Cable television. Indoor pool, whirlpool, sauna and sundeck, cafe, shopping gallery, health club.

The Harley. *Expensive.* 8020 Montgomery Rd. (513–793–5450 or 800–321–2323). 153 rooms. Cable television. Two swimming pools, whirlpool, playground. Putting green and rec/game room.

Holiday Inn-Downtown. *Expensive.* 800 W. 8th St. (513–241–8660 or 800–465–4329). 246 rooms. Cable television, in-room movies. Pool, cafe, barber.

Best Western Mariemont Inn. *Moderate.* 6880 Wooster Pike (513–271–2100 or 800–528–1234). 62 rooms. Cable television. Cafe and bar.

LaQuinta. *Inexpensive.* 11335 Chester Rd. in suburban Sharonville (513–772–3140). 144 rooms. Cable television. Heated swimming pool, health club privileges. Tennis and racquetball.

Red Roof Inn. *Inexpensive.* 11345 Chester Rd. in suburban Sharonville. (513–771–5141). Television, 24-hour cafe nearby.

Cleveland. Sheraton Cleveland City Center. *Deluxe.* 777 St. Clair Ave. (216–771–7600). Renovated in 1990.

Stouffer's Inn on the Square. *Deluxe.* 24 Public Sq. (216–696–5600 or 800–HOTELS–1). 511 rooms, 38 suites, 2 lounges. Free morning coffee and newspaper. Oversize beds, some refrigerators. Health club privileges.

Hilton-Cleveland South. *Expensive.* 6200 Quarry Lane, Independence 44131 (216–447–1300 or 800–HILTONS). 197 rooms and 3 suites. Restaurant and lounge. Cable television, in-room movies. Indoor and outdoor pools, whirlpool and sauna, game room.

Holiday Inn-Lakeside. *Expensive.* 1111 Lakeside Ave. (216–241–5100 or 800–465–4329). 382 rooms, 18 stories. In-room movies. Indoor pool, sauna, cafe, health club.

Harley Hotel-West. *Moderate.* Rte. 71 and Bagley Rd. in suburban Middlebury. (216–243–5200 or 800–321–2323). 245 rooms, 2 swimming pools. Playground, sundries, rec room, library. 5 minutes from Hopkins International Airport.

Quality Inn-East. *Moderate.* 28600 Ridgehills Dr., Wickliffe 44092. (216–585–0600 or 800–228–5151). 100 rooms. Cable television. Indoor pool, cafe, health club. Entertainment in the lounge.

Ramada Inn-Southeast. *Moderate.* 24801 Rockside Rd. (216–439–2500 or 800–2–RAMADA). Lounge, games room.

RESTAURANTS. Restaurants are listed alphabetically under the two major cities we are covering, Cincinnati and Cleveland. The price categories reflect the cost of a three-course meal for one (excluding beverage, tax, and tip): *Deluxe,* over $20; *Expensive,* $15–$20; *Moderate,* $8–$15; *Inexpensive,* under $8.

Cincinnati. Bacchus Restaurant. *Deluxe.* 1401 Elm St. (513–421–8314). This place has an "artsy" atmosphere with an upscale menu of nouvelle cuisine. Next to Music Hall. Lunch and dinner. Major credit cards

Del's Steaks and Chops. *Deluxe.* In the Westin Hotel, Fountain Sq., 5th and Vine Sts. (513–621–7700). Dinners here begin with a bucket of shrimp. Dinner daily 6:30–10 P.M.; lunch buffet daily 11:30A.M.–1:30 P.M. Major credit cards.

Maisonette. *Deluxe.* 114 E. 6th St. (513–721–2260). French cuisine, elegant dining, French decor. Jacket and tie required. Specialties include tournedos sautes aux lancs de poireaux and fresh baked pastries. Mon.–Fri., 11:30 A.M.–2:30 P.M. and 6–10:30 P.M.; Sat. 5:15–11 P.M. Closed Sun. AE, DC, MC, V.

The Golden Lamb. *Expensive.* 27 S. Broadway, Lebanon (513–621–8373). Ohio's oldest inn and restaurant. 10 U.S. presidents enjoyed the American fare here. Call for hours. AE, DC, MC, V.

Montgomery Inn. *Moderate.* 9449 Montgomery Rd. (513–791–3482). Specialized in barbecue ribs. Celebrity and sports theme. Call for hours. MC, V.

Camp Washington Chili. *Inexpensive.* Hopple and Colerain, off I-75 (513–541–0061). Known for its chili and nostalgia; jukebox selector at each booth. Mon.–Sat., 24 hours a day; closed Sun. No credit cards.

Schoolhouse Restaurant. *Inexpensive.* 8031 Glendale-Milford Rd., Rte. 126 (513–831–5753). A family-style restaurant that serves American fare. AE, DC, MC, V.

Skyline Chili. *Inexpensive.* 30 locations throughout the city. Everybody in Cincinnati knows where the closest Skyline is located; just ask. No credit cards.

Cleveland. The Parthenon. *Deluxe.* 1612 Euclid Ave. (216–241–7119). Truly authentic Greek cuisine. Open daily till midnight. AE, DC, MC, V.

Top of the Town. *Deluxe.* 100 Erieview Plaza (216–771–1600). Continental cuisine and casual elegance from atop 38 stories. AE, DC, MC, V.

Bali Hai. *Moderate.* 25649 Euclid Ave., Euclid 44132 (216–731–4800). Chinese cuisine and decor. Raw seafood bar. Mon.–Thurs., 11 A.M.–10:30 P.M.; Fri. till 12:30 A.M.; Sat., noon to 1:30 A.M.; Sun., noon to 9:30 P.M. AE, DC, MC, V.

James Tavern, *Moderate.* 28699 Chagrin Blvd., Woodmere Village (216–464–4660). Early-American menu. 11:30 A.M.–2:30P.M. 5:30–10 P.M. Fri, Sat. to 11 P.M. Special Sun. brunch and child's plates. Major credit cards.

Sweetwater's Cafe Sausalito. *Moderate.* E. 9th St. at St. Clair in the Galleria at Erieview. (216–696–2233). Featured here are seafood, pasta, and Continental dining. Try the famous Chocolate Death dessert. Lunch and dinner; late-night dining on weekends. Major credit cards.

Houlihan's Old Place. *Inexpensive.* Pavilion Mall on Chagrin Blvd. (216–464–7544) and Parmatown Shopping Center on Ridge and Ridgewood (216–842–8310). American cuisine. Specialties include steak, seafood, and quiche, with a moderate wine list. AE, DC, MC, V.

LIQUOR LAWS. In Ohio, a person must be 21 years of age or older to buy or drink alcoholic beverages, and 19 years to consume and purchase beer. The state operates and franchises to private operators liquor stores, hours of which vary depending on location. Liquor is available for on-premises use, by the drink, 5:30 P.M.–1 A.M. or 2:30 A.M., Mon.–Sat.; and 1 P.M.–midnight (1 A.M. or 2:30 A.M. for beer) on Sun. Open containers of alcoholic beverages are prohibited in all public places.

INDIANA

The Hoosier state has a rich historical heritage that is reflected in some familiar sayings. It was at Fort Ouiatenon, for instance, that the Indian warrior Pontiac ended his rebellion in 1766 by "burying the hatchet," thus originating the phrase.

Another phrase famous in Indiana is "Gentlemen, start your engines," uttered yearly by the clear-voiced announcer at the start of the Indianapolis 500 car race. The Indianapolis Motor Speedway Hall of Fame Museum (see "Special-Interest Sightseeing") attracts thousands of visitors for a bus ride around the world-famous 2½-mile track and for a display of classic and antique race cars.

There are several theories as to how the Hoosier nickname was acquired, but the most plausible concerns a contractor named Samuel Hoosier who was working on the Ohio Falls canal in 1826. It seems that he gave employment preference to men living on the Indiana side of the river. Soon the men in his work gang were called Hoosier's men, later shortened to Hoosiers.

Indiana is a diverse state historically and geographically. Between the white sand dune beaches on Lake Michigan in the north and the rolling hills in the south are charming river towns and bustling cities, and each area has contributed to the history and lifestyle of the state.

It's the state that was once the automotive capital of the world (and fascinating museums contain the "evidence"); the state that claims to have the Circus Capital of the World; the state that has turn-of-the-century wooden barns and a contemporary edifice with glass walls; the state that has the largest children's museum in the world; and the state that has the "greatest spectacle in racing."

Like her sister states in the Midwest, Indiana has a large Amish colony. Many of the well-kept farms in the lake country of the northeast belong to the Amish. Also in northeast Indiana are charming towns that give a glimpse of life a century ago. History buffs will want to wander through such towns as Anderson, with its historic West 8th Street district featuring Newport-style gas lights and restored 1890s homes, and Huntington, with its fine examples of Romanesque Revival architecture. In Wabash, see the Courthouse noted for its "Wabash Light" and one of the original electric Brush lamps which illuminated the dome. Wabash was the first town in the world to be wholly lighted by electric light.

History of a much earlier era is alive at Historic Fort Wayne (see Historic Sites and Houses) where visitors get a feel of what life was like at Indiana's military outpost. Fort personnel speak and dress in the style of 1816.

Throughout northwest Indiana are picturesque communities dominated by the town square. One of the most quaint examples is in Crown Point at the Old Lake County Courthouse. In 1896, William Jennings Bryan campaigned for the presidency on the steps of this building, and in 1909, an unknown car designer, Louis Chevrolet, accepted the winner's cup for the first major auto race, the forerunner of the Indy 500.

You will still find quaint round barns in northwest Indiana. Throughout Fulton County almost a dozen of these turn-of-the-century wooden structures dot the countryside surrounding Rochester. Farther south, in the hill country, Parke County claims to have more covered bridges than any other U.S. county. These bridges and backroads are fun to explore by car or bike.

Wandering through other towns in the southwest hills, you will turn up numerous architectural reminders of life in the last century. Especially

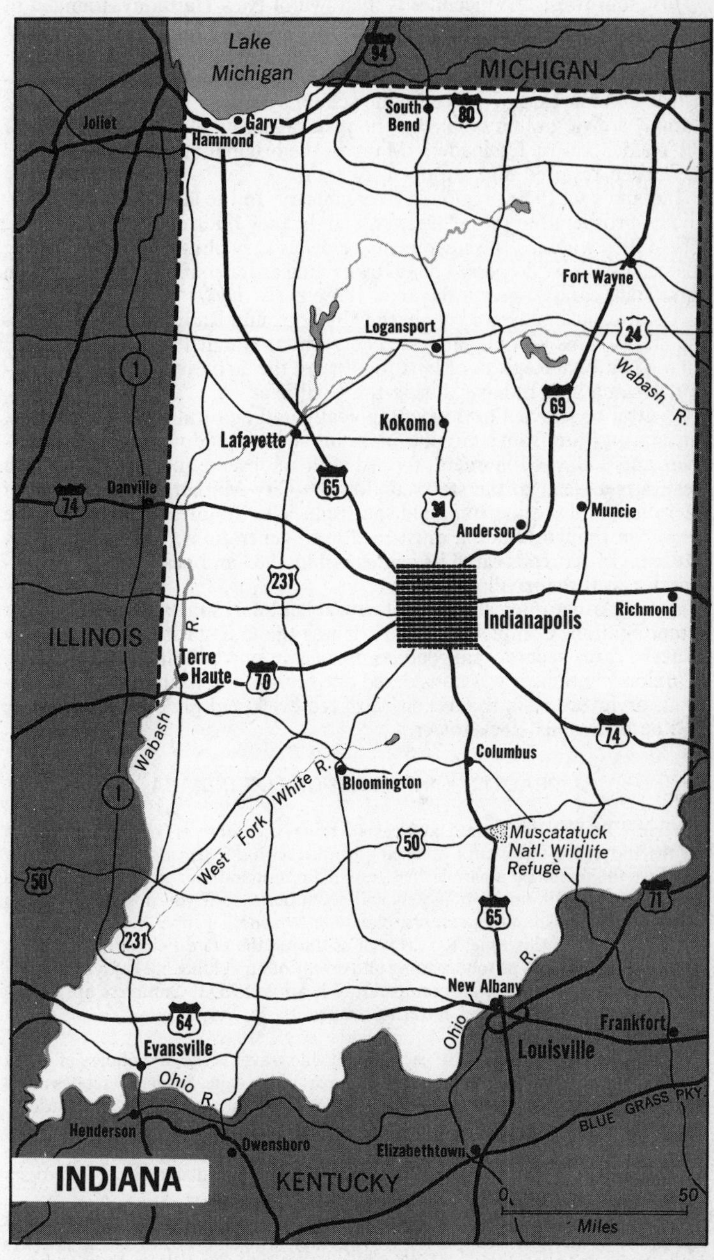
Lake Michigan
MICHIGAN
Joliet
Gary
Hammond
South Bend
Fort Wayne
Logansport
Wabash R.
Kokomo
Lafayette
Danville
Muncie
Anderson
Indianapolis
Richmond
ILLINOIS
R.
Terre Haute
Wabash
Columbus
Bloomington
White R.
West Fork
Muscatatuck Natl. Wildlife Refuge
New Albany
R.
Ohio
Frankfort
Louisville
Evansville
Ohio R.
Henderson
Owensboro
Elizabethtown
BLUE GRASS PKY.
INDIANA
KENTUCKY
0
50
Miles

picturesque is Evansville, with its Riverside Historic District and Old Vanderburgh County Courthouse.

Just southwest of Vincennes is the town of New Harmony, founded in 1814 by Father Rapp's New Harmony Society and hailed as that "wonder of the wilderness." To create "utopia," the founders brought in distinguished educators, scientists, artists, and social reformers. They established a kindergarten, a free public school system, a trade school, a free library, a civic drama club. But the plan failed, in part because many of the residents were freeloaders. Many of the original buildings and homes have been restored and are open for tours.

Indiana's southeast region is river country. In the last century, as merchants prospered in these "western" lands, they built mansions on bluffs. There they watched the steamboats below as they chugged along, helping to open up the wilderness. Today towns such as Jeffersonville and Corydon (first state capital) give a flavor of those early days.

The area also played a role in the Underground Railroad to help escaping slaves. This is commemorated at Vernon, founded in 1816 and listed on the National Register of Historic Places, the farthest north the Confederates came into Indiana during the Civil War.

Central to Indiana both geographically and culturally is Indianapolis. Jutting skyward from a circular plaza in the heart of downtown is the Soldiers and Sailors Monument, topped with an observation platform. From here, streets lead to the state capitol, the City Market, the mansions of Meridian, and the charming old southside. The Children's Museum is the largest in the world and a must-see for all generations. The Indianapolis Museum of Art celebrated its centennial in 1983 and has noteworthy collections in three pavilions.

Among other interesting architectural landmarks in Indianapolis is the Union Station. Completed in 1888, it was the first station in the country to serve three separate railroad companies in one building, thus forming a "union" station. It was considered one of the finest examples of Romanesque architecture in the nation, with red brick and pink granite exterior and an enormous clock tower.

PRACTICAL INFORMATION FOR INDIANA

WHEN TO GO. Memorial Day weekend brings thousands of fans to Indianapolis for the Indy 500. The month preceding is filled with a frenzy of events called the 500 Festival, including a parade, arts festival, mini-marathon, and parties. All this adds up to brisk business for hotels and restaurants, so if you don't like crowds or are not interested in these events, plan your trip another time. Motel rates often are higher during this time, too, as well as during the State Fair in mid Aug.

Winter sports such as tobogganing and cross-country skiing are enjoyed in Indiana, where the average winter temperature is around 25° F. Summers are on the mild side, with temperatures hovering around 75° F.

HOW TO GET THERE. By car. Automobile travel is the first-choice of many travelers in order to have access to remote areas of the state. Seven interstates crisscross Indiana, making the state motto appropriate: "The Crossroads of America." I-64 runs east–west in the southern tip of the state, with I-80 and I-90, called the Toll Rd., along the north. Also running east–west and crossing in Indianapolis are I-70 and I-74. I-65 and I-69 run north–south through Indianapolis. I-94 crosses extreme northern Indiana.

By plane. *Indianapolis International Airport* brings visitors to the state, and is served by the major carriers, as is Ft. Wayne. Smaller cities with regional airports have service by other lines.

By train. Several *Amtrak* trains pass through Indianapolis daily at the Amtrak Transportation Center, 350 S. Illinois St., behind the Union Station. In Ft. Wayne, the station is located at 231 West Baker St.

TOURIST INFORMATION. For brochures and a map write to *Tourism Development Division* of the Indiana Department of Commerce, One North Capitol, Suite 700, Indianapolis, IN 46204 (317–232–8860). For specifics on Indianapolis, contact the *Indianapolis Convention and Visitors Association,* One Hoosier Dome, Indianapolis, IN 46225 (317–237–5206 or 800–323–4639).

If you want to explore round barns, maps are available from the *Fulton County Round Barn Festival Committee,* Box 512, Rochester, IN 46975 (219–223–4436). For a map of covered bridges spanning Raccoon and Suger Creeks, contact the *Parke County Tourist Information Center* (E. Ohio St., Rockville, IN 47872 (317–569–5226) and then drive or bike through the backroads to find them.

HINTS TO MOTORISTS. Right-turn-on-red is permitted after a full stop, unless otherwise indicated. The national speed limit is enforced on interstate highways, where the minimum speed is 40 mph.

SEASONAL EVENTS. Indianapolis 500. Held Memorial Day, this car race draws nationwide attention to the 2½ mi. track situated 5 mi. west of the center city. For ticket information, contact the Indianapolis Motor Speedway, 4790 W. 16 St., Speedway, IN 46224 (317–241–2500).

Circus City Festival. Peru, IN. This mid-July celebration features 10 performances and a parade in the "Circus Capital of America." Contact Circus City Festival, Broadway at Seventh St., Peru, IN 46970 (317–472–3918).

Indiana State Fair. 1202 E. 38 St., Indianapolis, IN 46205 (317–923–3431). In mid to late Aug. the fairgrounds come alive with exhibits, contests, and more.

SPECIAL-INTEREST SIGHTSEEING. The Hoosier State once was hailed as the automotive capital of the U.S. Numerous automotive museums will interest car enthusiasts.

Elwood Haynes Museum. 1915 S. Webster, Kokomo, IN 46902 (317–452–3471). Home of the inventor of America's first successful commercial automobile. (Haynes also invented stainless steel and stellite.) Open 1–4 P.M., Tues.–Sat.; 1–5 P.M. Sun.

Studebaker Exhibit. 520 S. Lafayette, South Bend, IN 46601 (219–284–9108). Includes vintage cars, Studebaker archives, and the carriage Lincoln took to the Ford Theatre. Open Mon.–Sat., 10 A.M.–4 P.M.; Sun., noon–4 P.M.

Indianapolis Motor Speedway and Hall of Fame Museum. 4790 W. 16th St., Speedway, IN 46224 (317–241–2500). View 25 winning Indy 500 race cars and other classic and antique race cars, and ride a bus around the famous 2½ mi. track. Open 9 A.M.–5 P.M.

Indiana Transportation Museum. Forest Park, Noblesville, IN 46060 (317–773–0300). Take a trolley ride through Forest Park, and then view displays of buggies, wagons, automobiles, trucks, fire engines, and trains. Open weekends, noon–5 P.M. Apr.–Nov.

PARKS AND GARDENS. Eagle Creek Park. 7840 W. 56 St., Indianapolis IN 46254 (317–293–4827). Open dawn to dusk all year. Visit the Nature Center and the Indian Heritage Museum, or hike, swim, golf, or horseback ride. Boat and bicycle rental. Ice skating, sledding, and cross-country skiing in winter.

Mary Gray Bird Sanctuary. R. R. 6, Box 165, Connersville, IN 47331 (317–825–9788). Owned by the Indiana Audubon Society, this preserve contains over 6 mi. of trails.

Hayes Regional Arboretum. 801 Elks Rd., Richmond, IN 47374 (317–962–3745). This 355-acre nature preserve includes a forest, fern garden, children's garden, bird sanctuary, and hiking trails. The Nature Center, in a 130-year-old pioneer dairy barn, contains exhibits. Open seasonally; call for hours.

Hillsdale Rose Gardens. 7800 N. Shadeland, Indianapolis, IN 46250 (317–849–2810). The gardens are prettiest from Apr.–Oct., when over 200,000 rose blooms may be seen. Open 9 A.M.–4 P.M. daily.

ZOOS. Ft. Wayne Children's Zoological Gardens. 3411 Sherman Blvd., Ft. Wayne, IN 46808 (219–482–4610). Animals run free on the 22-acre African veldt. Open Apr.–Oct. daily. **Indianapolis Zoo.** 1200 W. Washington St., Indianapolis, IN 46218 (317–630–2030). 500 exotic and domestic animals, including a bald eagle.

Open weekdays, 10 A.M.–5 P.M.; weekends 10 A.M.–6 P.M. during the summer. Winter hours, 10 A.M.–4 P.M.

STATE PARKS. An array of facilities is offered at various parks, including bicycle rental, horseback riding, tobogganing, camping, cabins, inns. Sports include: swimming, boating, and fishing. Write for a copy of the "Recreation Guide" from the *Indiana Department of Natural Resources,* Division of State Parks, 616 State Office Building, Indianapolis, IN 46204. Among the state parks are:

Indiana Dunes State Park. 1600 N. 25 E., Chesterton, IN 46304 (219–926–4520). Swim, sun bathe, make sand castles, hike, or bicycle along the 9-mi. Calumet Trail. In winter cross-country ski. Open daily 7 A.M.–11 P.M.

Pokagon State Park. Rte. 2, Box 29C, Angola, IN 46703 (219–833–2012). In Steuben County in northeastern Indiana, this park features a toboggan run, snowmobiling, and cross-country skiing. Summer activities include swimming, boating, fishing on Lake James, and camping or staying at the Inn. Open year-round, 7 A.M.–11 P.M.

Tippecanoe River State Park. Rte. 4, Box 95A, Winamac, IN 46996 (219–946–3213). This park in Pulaski county was once the home of the Potawatomi Indians. The Tippecanoe River flows along the border of the park. Camping, swimming, hiking, boating, fishing for bluegill and bass, and horseback riding. Cross-country skiing in winter. Open year-round, 7 A.M.–11 P.M.

CAMPING. Indiana has an excellent network of campgrounds, some in state parks and some privately run. The Indiana Department of Commerce puts out a listing. Write: Tourism Development Division, One North Capitol, Suite 700, Indianapolis, IN 46204.

HUNTING AND FISHING. These sports are permitted on certain state facilities. Check with the *Division of Fish and Wildlife,* 607 State Office Building, Indianapolis, IN 46204 (317–232–4080). Resident license costs $8.75; a 5-day nonresident hunting license is $13.75. A nonresident fishing license is $15.75, a resident fishing license is $8.75.

HISTORIC SITES AND HOUSES. Amish Acres. 1600 W. Market, Nappanee, IN (219–773–4188). Visitors can wander through a restored Amish farmhouse and barns in this restored living-history farm.

Conner Prairie Pioneer Settlement. 13400 Allisonville Rd., Noblesville, IN 46060 (317–776–6000). Explore the 55 acres to see what life was like in 1836. Woodworkers, blacksmith, schoolmarm, doctor, and pioneer women who cook, spin, dye, and weave are among the people you will encounter. You may visit the 1823 Federal-style brick mansion built by Indian trader William Conner. Open daytime Apr.–Nov. (call for hours) and by appointment for candlelight tours in Dec.

Fort Ouiatenon. S. River Rd., West Lafayette, IN (317–742–8411). Today's visitors to the fort get a glimpse of what life was like in 1719 at the trading post built across the Wabash River from a Wea Indian Village. Open noon–5 P.M. daily in summer except Mon.; open weekends only in spring and fall.

Hillforest Mansion. 213 Fifth St., Aurora, IN 47001 (812–926–0087). This 1852 Italianate villa resembles a steamboat with its suspended staircase and gothic design. Overlooking Ohio River, it was built by Thomas Gaff, a prominent industrialist and shipping magnate. Open May–Dec., Tues.–Sun., 1–5 P.M.

Historic Ft. Wayne. 107 S. Clinton St. (Visitor Center 211 S. Barr St.), Ft. Wayne, IN 46802 (219–424–3476). Explore log barracks and Indian encampment and talk to French traders, British soldiers and settlers of the 1816 period. Open mid-Apr.–Oct., 7 days a week, 9 A.M.–5 P.M.

James Whitcomb Riley Home. 528 Lockerbie St., Indianapolis, IN (317–631–5885). The poet and humorist lived in this house, which is now one of the finest Victorian preservations in the U.S. Open Tues.–Sat., 10 A.M.–4 P.M.; Sun., noon–4 P.M.

Kemper House. 1028 N. Delaware, Indianapolis, IN 46202 (317–638–5264). Nicknamed "The Wedding Cake House," it is considered one of the finest examples of High Victorian architecture in the state. Built in 1873 by Charles Pierson as a gift for his bride. Open Mon.–Fri., 9 A.M.–5 P.M.

New Harmony. Town founded in 1814 by Father Rapp's Harmony Society. Historic New Harmony Tour includes 12 exhibition buildings. Also visit restored turn-of-the-century commercial district and visitor's center to see film. Open daily 9 A.M.–5 P.M. Visitor center phone, 812–682–4474.

Tippecanoe Battlefield and Museum. Prophet Rock Rd., just off I-65 in Tippecanoe County (317–567–2147). A dramatic battle was fought here between William Henry Harrison's troops and the Indian warriors led by Tecumseh's brother, the Prophet. The museum presents the historic battle from both points of view. Open daily, 10 A.M.–5 P.M.

Union Station. 39 Jackson Place, Indianapolis, IN 46204 (317–267–0700). Completed in 1888, this was the first station in the country to accommodate three railroad companies, thus forming a "union" station. Good example of Romanesque architecture, with red brick and pink granite exterior with clock tower. Interior features 7-ft.-high, barrel-vaulted ceiling with skylight and large rose windows.

Whitewater Canal Historic Site. Box 88, Metamora, IN 47030 (317–647–6512). Take a 30-minute cruise in a horse-drawn canal boat through the Whitewater Valley and across the only covered aqueduct in existence. Then wander through the 1838 canal town of Metamora, including the first mill and many pre–Civil War buildings. Canal ride summers only.

MUSEUMS. The Children's Museum. 30th and Meridian Sts., Indianapolis, IN 46208 (317–924–5431). The largest children's museum in the world gives visitor a hands-on experience by exploring a simulated cave, visiting a log cabin, looking inside a Sioux tepee or stepping into the tomb of an Egyptian mummy. Open Mon.–Sat., 10 A.M.–5 P.M.; Sun., noon–5 P.M. Closed, Mon., Sept.–May.

Fort Wayne Museum of Art. 1202 W. Wayne St., Ft. Wayne, IN 46804 (219–422–6467). An old Victorian mansion houses over 1,000 works of 19th- and 20th-century European and American art. Open Tues.–Fri., 10 A.M.–5 P.M.; Sat. till 8 P.M.; Sun., noon–5 P.M.; closed Mon.

Indianapolis Museum of Art. 311 E. Main St., Indianapolis, IN 46204 (317–923–1331). 3 pavilions of art in 140-acre park west of the city house dazzling collections of treasures. Open Tues.–Sat., 10 A.M.–5 P.M.; Thurs. til 8:30 P.M.; Sun., noon–5 P.M. Closed Mon.

Clark Historical Society/Howard Steamboat Museum. 1101 E. Market St., Jeffersonville, IN 47130 (812–283–3728). This Victorian mansion contains the original furnishings of the Howard family, who for 107 years built the finest steamboats of North and Central America. Furnishings from the 1890s plus navigational equipment, paddle wheels, and steamboat replicas are on display. Open Tues.–Sat., 10 A.M.–3 P.M.; Sun., 1–3 P.M.; closed Mon. and holidays.

Old Jail Museum. 225 N. Washington St., Crawfordsville, IN 47933 (317–362–5222). Listed on the National Register of Historic Places, this jail was built in 1882 with a circular set of cell blocks arranged so that, with the turn of a crank, they would rotate around the jailer. He could check prisoners without ever taking a step. Today the Old Jail is the only operating rotary cell block known. Open Apr.–Dec., Thurs.–Sun., 2–4:30 P.M.

ACCOMMODATIONS. It's best to make reservations as soon as you are sure of your travel plans. Reservations at least a year in advance are a must in Indianapolis during the "500." Price categories are based on least expensive double occupancy: *Deluxe,* over $75; *Expensive,* $50–$75; *Moderate,* $40–$50; *Inexpensive,* below $40.

French Lick. French Lick Springs. *Deluxe.* On IN 56, 2 mi. S. of U.S. 150, French Lick, IN 47469 (812–936–4255). Large resort and convention center nestled on 2,600 acres of rolling hills in southern Indiana. Country-estate setting has all amenities, including golf and tennis.

Ft. Wayne. Marriott. *Deluxe.* 305 E. Washington Center Rd., Ft. Wayne, IN 46825 (219–484–0411 or 800–228–9290). Large facility with indoor and outdoor pool, lighted tennis, playground, whirlpool.

Don Hall's Guesthouse. *Moderate.* 1313 W. Washington Center Rd., Ft. Wayne, IN 46825 (219–489–2524). 130 rooms. Close to Glenbrook Mall and Children's Zoo.

Signature Inn. *Moderate.* 1734 W. Washington Center Rd., Ft. Wayne, IN 46818 (219–489–5554). Free crib and Continental breakfast. Game room.

Indianapolis. Sheraton Inn Northeast. *Expensive.* 465 Pendleton Pike in northeast suburbs. (317–897–4000 or 800–325–3535). Usual amenities.

Howard Johnson's Speedway. *Moderate.* 2602 N. High School Rd., Indianapolis, IN 46224 (317–291–8800; 800–654–2000). Heated pool, playground. Free airport transportation.

Indianapolis Motor Speedway. *Moderate.* 4400 W. 16 St., Indianapolis, IN 46222 (317–241–2500). At gateway to 500 track and adjacent to Hall of Fame Museum. Cafe, room service. 27-hole golf course.

Motel 6–Speedway. *Moderate.* Rtes. I-465 and 74 W., Indianapolis, IN 46224 (317–293–3220). 164 rooms. Entertainment. Airport transportation available.

Lafayette. Prestige Inn. *Inexpensive.* 1217 Sagamore Pkwy. W., Lafayette, IN 47906 (317–463–1531). Smaller operation with pool, game room. Free cribs. Café adjacent.

RESTAURANTS. In Indiana, you have a choice of fare that includes everything from fried fish to Continental cuisine. Generally dress is informal, except in the larger cities, where a jacket may be required, depending on the establishment and time of day. Price categories are as follows: *Expensive,* $15–$20; *Moderate,* $10–$15; *Inexpensive,* $10 and below. These are based on the price of a single dinner excluding tax, tip, and beverage.

Bloomington. Tradewinds. *Expensive.* At Fourwinds Resort, on Lake Monroe. (812–824–9904) Antique country French decor with Continental menu. Outdoor dining overlooking lake. 7 A.M.–10 P.M. Sun. brunch 11:30 A.M.–2:30 P.M.

Ft. Wayne. Cafe Johnell. *Expensive* 2529 S. Calhoun. (219–456–1939). French specialities served in Victorian atmosphere. Jacket at dinner. Dinner only. Closed Sun and major holidays. Major credit cards.

Don Hall's–The Factory. *Inexpensive.* 5811 Coldwater Rd., Ft. Wayne, IN 46825 (219–484–8693). Steak, prime rib, Greek salad. 11 A.M.–11 P.M., Mon.–Thurs.; until midnight, Fri. and Sat.; to 8 on Sun. Closed holidays.

Indianapolis. Hollyhock Hill. *Moderate.* 8110 N. College Ave., Indianapolis, IN 46240 (317–251–2294). Fried chicken, seafood, and steak served in a tearoom atmosphere. Children's plates. Tues.–Sat., dinner only, 5–8 P.M.; Sun., noon–7 P.M. Closed Mon. AE, MC, V.

Iron Skillet. *Moderate.* 2489 W. 30 (317–923–6353). Family style dining in converted century-old homestead. Skillet fried chicken and pan fried walleye pike. D, only, Wed.–Sat., 5:30–8:30 P.M.; Sun., noon–7:30 P.M. Closed Mon. and Tues. Major cards. Reservations a must on weekends.

Jonathan's Restaurant and Pub. *Moderate.* 96th and Keystone Crossing (317–844–1155). English country atmosphere serving beef specialties. Open 11 A.M.–2:30 P.M., 4:30 P.M.–2 A.M., Mon.–Sat.; Sun., brunch 10:30 A.M.–2:30 P.M. Major credit cards.

The Teller's Cage. *Moderate.* 1 Indiana Sq., 35th floor of Indiana National Bank Tower (317–266–5211). American cuisine served in publike atmosphere. Free parking after 5 P.M. Mon.–Fri. 11 A.M.–8:30 P.M.

South Bend. Tippecanoe Place. *Expensive.* 620 W. Washington (219–234–9077). Many antiques grace this establishment in the former Studebaker mansion. Lamb and chateaubriand are specialties. 11:30 A.M.–2 P.M., 5–10 P.M., Mon.–Thurs.; Fri. to 11 P.M.; Sat. 4:30–11 P.M.; Sun., 10 A.M.–2 P.M., 4–9 P.M. AE, MC, V.

LIQUOR LAWS. Liquor by the drink or bottle may be purchased 7 A.M.–3 A.M. except on Dec. 25 and on election days during polling hours. Sunday sales by the drink only at certain hotels, restaurants, and clubs, noon–12:30 A.M. No children are allowed where liquor is served, except in establishments with a "family room." Minimum drinking age is 21.

ILLINOIS

Speeches, steel, and soybeans; manufacturing, Mormons, and earth movers; coal mining and commodity trading make up the Midwest's midpoint, Illinois. From the restored 19th-century homes of Galena in the extreme northwest corner to Cairo at the alluvial delta in the extreme south, Illinois encompasses a variety of lifestyles over its 56,400 level acres of land. The Prairie State's capital, Springfield, was home to President Abraham Lincoln, who practiced law there until his election to the presidency in 1860. Joining Lincoln among the state's great speakers were William Jennings Bryan, Adlai Stevenson, Everett Dirksen, and the writers Carl Sandburg and Ernest Hemingway.

Chicago

Chicago, once "Hog butcher to the world," is now hog trader to the world with its premier commodity trading markets. Illinois is first in the nation as a producer of soybeans and second in production of corn.

Chicago reigns as the nation's transportation hub for rail and truck shipments, the hub of Great Lakes shipping traffic, a gateway to the Mississippi River system, and home of the world's busiest airport, O'Hare International. Spreading out from Chicago are the nation's interstates: I-80 (east–west), I-90 and I-94 (north), I-55 and I-57 (south).

The city is home to more than three million people speaking as many as 54 languages and dialects. It is a most diverse and livable city, its front door the southern end of Lake Michigan with more than 26 miles of beachfront and parks. Downtown, what Chicagoans call The Loop, is the center of shopping, commerce, politics, hotels, museums, great architecture, and a world record.The world's tallest building, a tribute to Chicago's merchandising legend, the Sears Tower soars 110 stories to 1,454 feet—100 feet taller than the New York World Trade Center. Its observation deck is a must see on a clear day. (There are sometimes clouds and fog on the mammoth building's upper floors.) North of the Loop—across the Chicago River—are the Near North and Gold Coast areas, the swank places to live and shop.

The suburbs of Chicago teem with activity. Just north of Chicago is Evanston, home of Northwestern University and the development of nuclear fission as well as the home of the Women's Christian Temperance Union. Northwest of Chicago is the lovely village of Long Grove, dating back to the early 1800s. Cobblestone streets lead to some 80 shops (food, books, crafts, antiques, linens, pewter) that will keep even the kids happy watching apple cider being made or looking at the doll houses. Chocolate-covered strawberries are a local delicacy. (Take I-94 North to Lake Cook Road, west to Route 83 to Coffin Road, north and follow signs.)

Just 15 minutes west of Chicago is Oak Park, the suburban home of the architect Frank Lloyd Wright and authors Ernest Hemingway and Edgar Rice Burroughs. (East off I-290, the Eisenhower Expressway westbound from Chicago's Loop, exit at Harlem Avenue.) Wright developed his low, expansive prairie style of architecture in Oak Park, lovingly preserved by residents and the Frank Lloyd Wright Prairie School of Architecture National Historical District.

Points of Interest

1) Adler Planetarium
2) Art Institute and Goodman Theater
3) Auditorium Theater
4) Blackstone Theater
5) Buckingham Fountain
6) Chicago Civic Center (Richard J. Daley Center)
7) Chicago Theater
8) City Hall
9) Civic Opera House
10) Sears Tower
11) DePaul University (Downtown Campus)
12) Field Museum
13) Fort Dearborn original site
14) John Hancock Tower
15) Lakefront Tower
16) Water Tower Place
17) Chagall Mosaic (First National Plaza)
18) Tribune Tower
19) Orchestra Hall
20) Roosevelt University
21) Shedd Aquarium
22) Soldier Field
23) Navy Pier
24) University of Illinois

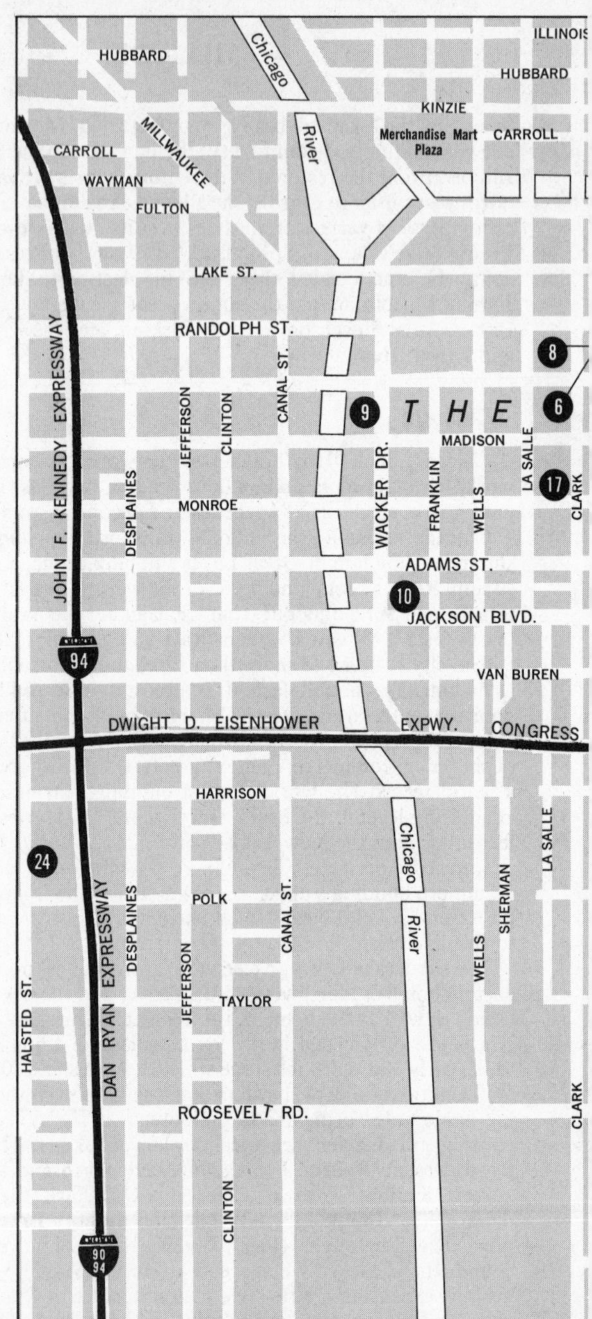

14
16
18
15
23
Ogden Slip
WATER
Chicago River
13
WACKER DR.
LAKE ST.
7
RANDOLPH DR.
WASHINGTON BLVD.
L O O P
DEARBORN
WABASH
MONROE DR.
2
STATE
19
DRIVE
JACKSON DR.
CHICAGO
HARBOR
11
SHORE
20
3
PARKWAY
CONGRESS
5
LAKE
PLAZA
Easterly Breakwater
MICHIGAN
DEARBORN
4
Grant
BALBO
BALBO DR.
Park
PLYMOUTH
FEDERAL
8TH
9TH
11TH
MICHIGAN AVE.
COLUMBUS DR.
41
Southerly Breakwater
LAKE
Illinois Central
Station
WEST
21
STATE
12
ACHSAH BOND DR.
1
LAKE SHORE DR.
WABASH
13TH
MC FETRIDGE DR.
Northerly Island
Park
14TH
22
CHICAGO
DOWNTOWN

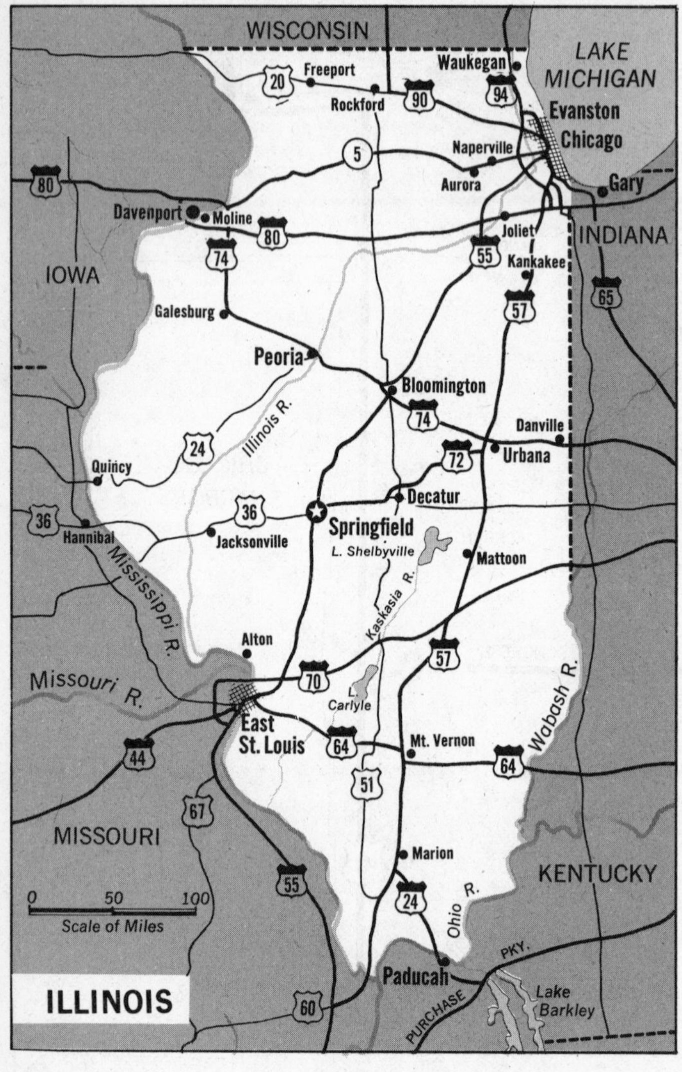
WISCONSIN
LAKE MICHIGAN
Freeport
Rockford
Waukegan
Evanston
Chicago
Naperville
Aurora
Gary
Davenport
Moline
Joliet
INDIANA
Kankakee
IOWA
Galesburg
Peoria
Bloomington
Illinois R.
Danville
Urbana
Quincy
Decatur
Springfield
L. Shelbyville
Hannibal
Jacksonville
Mattoon
Mississippi R.
Kaskasia R.
Alton
Wabash R.
Missouri R.
L. Carlyle
East St. Louis
Mt. Vernon
MISSOURI
Marion
KENTUCKY
Ohio R.
0 50 100
Scale of Miles
Paducah
PKY.
PURCHASE
Lake Barkley
ILLINOIS

Illinois Touring

West along I-90 is Rockford, Illinois's second city on the Rock River, with the Burpee Art Gallery, a Civil War–period preserved home. Northward is Galena, a Victorian city of delightful homes of the 1860s and 1890s. Rich with antique shopping and autumnal colors, the town perched on the hills is an excellent getaway, just two hours from Chicago's bustle. At the western edge of I-80 in Illinois, along the Mississippi, are the river towns of Moline and Rock Island.

To the east are Tampico and Dixon, the boyhood homes of President Ronald Reagan. Back to the Mississippi River, southward, is the Great River Road passing through Nauvoo, once the 1839 capital of the Church of Jesus Christ of Latter Day Saints (Mormons). Religious intolerance led the community and its leader, Brigham Young, to resettle in Salt Lake City, Utah.

From Alton to Chester is America's fertile plain winding down to Cairo where the wealth of river commerce flourished in the late 1800s. Magnolia Manor, a Victorian era showplace, sits atop the convergence of the Ohio and Illinois rivers.

Nowhere else in the state is American history so ingrained as in Springfield, the state capital and home of young attorney, congressman, and finally president, Abraham Lincoln. Even the state license plates proudly proclaim: Land of Lincoln.

The 16th president's story starts here near Decatur, now the Lincoln Homestead State Park. South in Charlestown is the Lincoln Log Cabin State Park, where a reproduction of the family's two-room cabin is maintained. The village of New Salem, now Lincoln's New Salem State Park, knew Lincoln as a young man who tended store in 1837, studied law and surveying, and went on to the legislature before practicing law, in Springfield.

His tomb in Springfield's Oak Ridge Cemetery is open to the public, for Lincoln does indeed "belong to the ages," as his Secretary of War, Edwin M. Stanton, said.

PRACTICAL INFORMATION FOR CHICAGO

HOW TO GET THERE. By plane. Chicago has three airports. *O'Hare International Airport,* on the city's far northwest side, is by far the busiest. O'Hare is served by 20 major domestic carriers (with *United Airlines* making this its home and hub) as well as many foreign lines. *Chicago Midway Airport,* 5700 S. Cicero, on the city's near southwest side, is Chicago's original airport, now offering fewer flights but is always less crowded and usually easier and cheaper to get to. The airport is served by *Northwest Orient, Midway Airlines* (flying to New York), *Midway Express* (to Florida), and two regional airlines, *Alliance* and *Air Midwest.* Right downtown on the lakeshore, next to the Shedd Auditorium, is *Meigs Field,* a general aviation field. *Britt* and *Missouri Valley* (MVA) airlines make scheduled flights from here to the state capital, Springfield.

By train. Chicago is the connecting point for most transcontinental *Amtrak* service. More than 50 trains come and go daily at Chicago's granite and marble Union Station (210 S. Canal St.) from the East, South, and West coasts (plus *The International* from Toronto). From the West, Chicago is a two-day trip; from the Southwest, South, and East, it's a one-day trip. Call 800–USA–RAIL for information.

By bus. Chicago is also a national hub for bus travel and less than two days by bus from anywhere in the U.S. The *Greyhound* depot is at 79 W. Randolph (781–2900).

By car. I-80, which bypasses Chicago 40 mi. to the south, is the most direct route from Iowa and other states to the west and Indiana and the eastern states. I-55 and I-57 connect I-80 with Chicago and bring traffic from the southern states. I-94 and I-90 approach Chicago from Wisconsin and states farther northwest.

WHEN TO GO. Chicago is a year-round city; the lakefront is the city's country club in the summer and the place for restful solitude or cross-country skiing in the winter. June and July, Sept. and Oct. are favorite months to visit Chicago. Chicago is hot towards the end of July and through mid Aug. and very, very cold in Jan. and Feb. "Injun Summer" brings mild weather and turning leaves in Oct. and by Dec. 25th, the snow and ice are frozen for the winter. By New Year's, the temperatures reach 22 degrees (F) and 50 degrees below (windchill factor). Mar. is still cold and windy but Apr. can signal an early summer. Spring is a fleeting season and May can be cool.

TOURIST INFORMATION. *Office of Tourism.* Department of Commerce and Community affairs, 222 S. College St., Springfield, IL 62706 (217–782–7500; from Illinois, 800–252–8987). The *Chicago Visitors Center,* Illinois Office of Tourism, 310 S. Michigan Ave., Suite 108, Chicago, IL 60604 (312–793–2094), will prepare a tour for the visitor. Housed in the historic Water Tower (the sandstone remains of the Great Chicago Fire of 1871) at 806 N. Michigan is the Chicago Visitor Information Center. Open 7 days a week; multilingual. Language problems can be overcome by the *International Visitors Center* at 520 N. Michigan, 645–1836. Travelers Aid has offices at 327 S. LaSalle (435–4500) and O'Hare International Airport (686–7562).

The best sources of information on what's going on in Chicago are newspapers and magazines: the Chicago *Sun Times* and *Tribune;* the free *Chicago Reader,* the best for arts and entertainment; and *Chicago* magazine.

TELEPHONES. The area code for downtown Chicago is 312; suburbs, 708. Calls made from pay telephone to telephones in the city cost 25 cents for unlimited time. The number for directory assistance is 411.

911 is the main *emergency* number in Chicago to reach the police, fire, ambulance, and paramedics. There are two 24-hour *poison control* numbers serving Chicago: 800–252–2022 and 942–5969.

HOW TO GET AROUND. From the airport. The subway now connects downtown and O'Hare International Airport with fast (35 minutes), cheap ($1.25), frequent (every 20 minutes), and convenient service. Pickup the subway at Terminal 4 on the lower level. From the city, catch the AIRPORT train at Dearborn Street Station.

From O'Hare to the Loop, the fastest way to make the 18-mi. trip is the Kennedy Expressway (I-90 to I-94). Public transportation leaves from the lower (baggage claim) level. Many hotels and motels have telephones for courtesy bus service. The Airport Express Continental bus to downtown and near north side hotels is $10.75 one way, $19 round-trip. Cabs cost about $25.

From Midway Airport to the Loop, turn north on Cicero Ave. to I-55 and then I-94 North for the 11-mi. trip. Bus service is available but slow. Taxis cost about $15 to downtown hotels. Limos are likewise $45.

By taxi. Taxis currently charge $1 as the base fare with 90 cents for each additional mile. Additional riders means an extra 50 cents added to the meter fare. Avoid the SHARED CAB in downtown areas, but it's not a bad idea from the airports. Maximum shared fare is $12. The major cab companies are *Yellow and Checker* (829–4222), *American United* (248–7600), and *Flash Cab* (561–1444).

By rental car. *Avis* (782–6825), *Dollar* (782–8736), *Budget* (800–527–0700), *Hertz* (372–7600), *National* (686–7722), and *Rent-A-Wreck* (585–7300) have counters at the airports and downtown. Rentals are as low as $17 a day with free miles.

HINTS TO MOTORISTS. Morning rush hour going downtown starts at 6:30 A.M. from the South Expswys. (Dan Ryan, Eisenhower, and Stephenson) and 7 A.M. from the North (Kennedy and Edens Expressways). Traffic clears up by 10:30 A.M. unless there's construction. The evening rush starts by 3:30 P.M. in both directions (earlier on Fri.).

Once in the city, the grid-system applies. It begins downtown at the intersection of State and Madison, which is zero-zero. From this center the numbers go up, roughly 100 numbers per block. If you're looking for 2800 N. Halsted, for example, that's roughly 28 blocks North of the Loop (Diversey Ave.) and 8 blocks west (Halsted). Eight city blocks usually equals a mile.

There's right turn on red in Chicago (unless posted), and U-turns are permitted in the middle of the block, not within 100 ft. of an intersection. The maximum speed limit on city roads is 30 mph and 45 mph on Lake Shore Dr. Expressways vary between 45 mph (Kennedy downtown) and 50 mph (Dan Ryan). Overnight parking is banned on some major streets, and a 2-in. snowfall on marked streets will eliminate more spaces.

HINTS TO DISABLED TRAVELERS. Chicago's various private and public agencies offer art, culture and a helping hand to the disabled visitor. *Silent Sounds,* 1528 W. Adams, Chicago, IL (829–7631), is a nonprofit arts agency bringing arts to all people through sign language. "Access Chicago," a disabled person's guide to the city highlighting parks, museums, shows, motels, and restaurants that are access oriented, is available for a small fee from the *Rehabilitation Institute of Chicago* (Division of Education and Training), 345 E. Superior St., Chicago, IL 60611 (908–6000). *Access Living,* a private agency, offers help at 226–5900. The City of Chicago sponsors a referral service through the *Schwab Rehabilitation Center* at 522–2010. It maintains a list of independent living centers and an access directory of Chicago. The City of Chicago maintains a 24-hour TTY (teletype) number 744–5699 to relay messages for travel arrangements, etc. The Chicago Hearing Society also maintains a TTY line at 427–2166.

Unfortunately, travel for the disabled in Chicago is expensive as there's currently no public transportation for visitors. Call *Cook DuPage Transportation Company* (521–1150) at least one day before arrival.

TOURS AND SPECIAL-INTEREST SIGHTSEEING. To get the big picture try the world's tallest building at the *Sears Sky Deck,* 233 S. Wacker Dr. (875–9696), 9 A.M.–midnight; adults, $3.75; children, $2.25; or the slightly shorter *John Hancock Center Observatory,* 875 N. Michigan (751–3681), adults, $3.65; children, $2.35.

To get a feel for the city, from the lakeside neighborhoods to out in Lake Michigan, try the organized bus and lake tours: *American Sightseeing Tours,* 520 S. Michigan Ave., Chicago, IL 60605 (427–3100); *Gray Line of Chicago,* 33 E. Monroe, Chicago, IL 60603 (346–9506).

You can see the city from the lake (summer only, weather permitting). Both *Wendella Streamliners,* Michigan Ave. at Wacker Dr., Chicago, IL 60601 (337–1446), and *Mercury Sightseeing Boats,* Michigan at Wacker Dr., Chicago, 60601 (332–1353), leave on 1-, 1½-, and 2-hour cruises from beneath the Michigan Avenue Bridge at the Chicago River. In addition to a short cruise up (west) the Chicago River, the ride takes the visitor through the locks at the river's mouth and out for a panoramic view. $6–$9; reduced prices for children.

Year-round, the *Chicago Architecture Foundation,* 1800 S. Prairie, Chicago, IL 60616 (326–1393), offers a one-hour walking tour showing off Chicago and Oak Park's wood and brick past, illuminating such names as Frank Lloyd Wright, Mies van der Rohe, and Louis Sullivan. $6 per person; tours leave every day at 1:30 P.M. from 330 S. Dearborn.

Railroad and sociology buffs can walk around America's first company town, *Pullman Community,* 614 E. 113th St., Chicago, IL 60628 (785–8181), on 90-minute guided tours, the first Sun. of the month, May–Oct. for $3.50; student and senior discount. Or call the *20th Century Railroad Club,* 509 W. Roosevelt Rd., Chicago, IL 60607 (829–4500) and arrange for a stop at their free library right in the Amtrak yards.

PARKS AND GARDENS. Chicago overflows with more than 600 parks including eight verdant lakeshore expanses serving as summer resorts and winter playgrounds. Park hours are from 6 A.M.–11 P.M., unless there is a special program. **Lincoln Park** (294–4750), the largest, extends from 5800 North to the Near North Side. In balmy months, joggers, bike riders, strollers, and picnickers populate the 20 mi. coursing through Lincoln Park. Within it are the *Lincoln Park Zoo,* a small farm, tennis courts, horseshoe pits, an archery and skeet range, an outdoor theater, baseball fields, golf courses, small boat harbors, and lazy lagoons.

Grant Park (294–2420), although missing a statue of General Ulysses S. Grant (it's in Lincoln Park), is a grand respite along the lake just east of the Loop between

Randolph St. and Roosevelt Rd. on the south. In addition to the city's largest public parking garage (underground), a yacht club, hidden tennis courts, and some fine gardens, Grant Park shelters some of the city's great showcases: the Buckingham Fountain, the Petrillo Music Shell at the South End, the Monroe Street Harbor along the lake, The Field Museum, Adler Planetarium, Shedd Aquarium, and The Art Institute of Chicago.

Slightly west of the Loop in the 4½-acre **Garfield Park Conservatory,** 300 N. Central Park Blvd. (533–1281), is the world's largest conservatory under one roof. In addition to a 175,000 sq. ft. formal garden, the conservatory features a special Garden for the Blind. The Conservatory is open daily from 9 A.M.–5 P.M. and always free.

Burnham Park (294–2200) bridges Grant and the south side's Jackson Park and the smaller Washington Park. Burnham was the site of the 1932–33 Century of Progress World's Fair, leaving behind Soldier Field, home of the Chicago Bears. Farther south, starting at 5600 South is **Jackson Park** (643–6363), site of the grand Columbian Exposition of 1893 and the current home of the Museum of Science and Industry. The **Midway Plaisance** (pleasure), a double boulevard, was the center midway of the exposition leading to **Washington Park** (684–6530). Farther south is **Rainbow Beach Park** (734–5976) from 7500 South and **Calumet Park** (721–3925) at 8900 South near the city's south boundary.

SPECTATOR SPORTS. The *Chicago Bears* **football** team plays at Soldier Field, Sept.–Dec. (663–5100). The **baseball** *Cubs* finally got permission in 1988 to install lights for night games at Wrigley Field, 1060 W. Addison at N. Clark St., Apr.–Oct. (404–2827). The *White Sox* play on the South Side of Comiskey Park, 35th and Shields, off the Dan Ryan Expressway (924–1000). The National **Basketball** Association pro team *Chicago Bulls* play Oct.–Apr. at the Chicago Stadium, 1800 W. Madison (943–5800). The Chicago *Blackhawks* play **hockey,** also at the Chicago Stadium (943–5800). There is **harness racing** at Maywood Park in the western suburb of Maywood (708–343–4800), 45 minutes from the Loop, and **thoroughbred** racing at Arlington Park Race Track (708–255–4300), one hour from the Loop, in the northwest suburb of Arlington Park.

BEACHES. Chicago is blessed with wide sand beaches and the fresh waters of Lake Michigan (60 to 70 degrees F at summer's peak). Hours are 9 A.M.–9:30 P.M. Lifeguards are on duty from Memorial Day–Labor Day. The most popular is the **Oak Street Beach** near the Gold Coast hotels and the **North Avenue beaches** (stretching to Fullerton Ave.). There are concession stands along the beachfront, picnic tables, grills at some beaches, and changing rooms at the North Avenue beach. The Chicago Park District's beach information number is 294–2333.

HISTORIC SITES AND HOUSES. Probably nowhere else is the feeling of Chicago's many generations of immigrants more keenly represented than at **Hull House,** a restoration of Jane Addams's social settlement house on the campus of the University of Illinois at Chicago, 800 S. Halsted St. (413–5353). Open 10 A.M.–4 P.M. and Sun. noons in summer.

The Great Chicago Fire of 1871 left just a few buildings. Mrs. O'Leary's cow started the blaze by kicking over a lantern, or so the fable goes, at the scene of today's **Chicago Fire Department Academy** at 558 W. DeKoven on the near South Side. You can start your look at Chicago sights at the **Water Tower** at Michigan and Chicago Aves., one of the few structures to survive the inferno. It's also the Chicago Visitor's Center. Across the street is the historic **pumping station** which today brings water into the city from Lake Michigan. Admission to the *Here's Chicago* show at the pumping station is $4.75 for adults, discount for seniors and kids. Open at 10 A.M.; closing varies by season.Multimedia shows and memorabilia.

Fort Dearborn, the original location of Chicago dating back to the 1700s, is depicted on bronze plaques on the bridge towers and sidewalks south of the Michigan Ave. bridge at the Chicago River. To get a fuller history, stop by the **Chicago Historical Society** on Mon. when admission is free, Clark St. and North Ave. (642–4600) 9:30 A.M.–4:30 P.M. Exhibits on Chicago pioneer life, the Great Fire, Indians of Chicago and Illinois, and Abraham Lincoln. The **Chicago Public Library,** 78 E. Washington Blvd., at Michigan Ave. (269–2900), has its impressive Tiffany glass domes, grand staircases, and 19th-century Italian Renaissance palazzo. Mon.–Thurs., 9 A.M.–7 P.M.; Fri. until 6, and Sat. until 5.

Guided tours are available by the *Chicago Architectural Foundation* through the 35-room Romanesque Glessner House and the Widow Clarke House, in the **Prairie Historic District** south of the Loop, 1800 S. Prairie, Chicago, IL 60616 (326–1393). These are the surviving homes of the great opulence Chicago enjoyed as a commercial center in the 1800s. Daily tours in winter and summer.

MUSEUMS. Adler Planetarium. 1300 S. Lake Shore Dr. (322–0304). Located on a spit of land called Northery Island Park on the lakefront. Antique astronomical items and space age hardware mingle in this museum and working observatory. Mon.–Thur., 9:30 A.M.–4:30 P.M.; Fri., 9:30 to 9; Sat., Sun., and holidays, 9:30 to 5. Sky show, a true percursor to Star Wars, is $3; $1.50 for children over 6 (under 6 not permitted in the sky show). Check schedule for regular show times, and Christmas and holiday shows.

Art Institute. In the Loop at Michigan at Adams (443–3600). Also home of Art Institute School. Always stunning and world-known Impressionist collection, Renaissance oils, Thorne miniature rooms, children's museum; garden restaurant and gift shops. Permanent collection of works by masters like Monet and Picasso, and "American Gothic" by Grant Wood. Oriental art, sculpture rooms, decorative arts, textiles, photography, primitives, Chinese pottery, windows by Marc Chagall, modern art and sculpture; special exhibits are not free. Donation: $6, adults; $3, seniors and kids. 10:30 A.M.–4:30 P.M., Tues. until 8; Sat., 10 to 5; Sun. and holidays, noon to 5. Parking is either public meter on the adjacent streets or in the underground city lot.

Chicago Academy of Sciences. 2001 N. Clark (549–0606). Oldest science museum in Midwest features the natural history of the Midwest and current plant and animal ecology. Winter lecture series on Tues. and field trips to nearby Indiana Dunes and state parks. Emphasis on children's exhibits. Normally $1, adults; 50 cents, kids and seniors. Free on Mon. Open daily 10 A.M.–5 P.M.

Field Museum of Natural History. In Grant Park at 12th St. 922–9410. Largest collection of natural history exhibits in the world housed at the 1893 Columbian Exposition site. From huge dinosaurs and the 550-lb. stuffed gorilla Bushman (long-time favorite in life at the Lincoln Park Zoo) to the smallest diamonds and precious stones makes this an awesome exhibit of the natural world around us. Excellent exhibits on American Indian, Chinese, and Tibetan cultures in lifelike exhibits. Restaurant and gift shop. Normally, $3 adults; $2 kids and seniors; and reduced family rate. Free admission on Thurs. Open daily, 9 A.M.–5 P.M. Much free and public metered parking.

John Shedd Aquarium, Lake Shore Dr. at 12th St., across from Field Museum of Natural History, (939–2438). Summer daily, 10 A.M. to 5 P.M. Other months vary. Special exhibits and regular population of 5,000 fish of more than 560 species. No goldfish bowl is the 90,000 gallon Coral Reef where divers feed the competitive (especially the tortoise) inhabitants daily at 11 and 2. Gift shop. Normally, $3, adults; $2, children and seniors. Free Thurs.

Museum of Contemporary Art. 237 E. Ontario (280–2660). Chicago artists' rooms and contemporary art exhibits from around the world; dance, theater, video library, music, German expressionism. Tues.–Sat., 10 A.M. to 5 P.M.; Sun., noon to 5. Gift shop. Suggested donation: $4 adults, $2 seniors and children. Tues. free.

Museum of Science and Industry. Jackson Park at 57th St. (684–1414). As the name implies, this is a push-button and high-tech museum with most exhibits sponsored by Chicago or area companies in what was the Palace of Fine Arts during the 1893 Columbian Exposition. Many hands-on features plus the always popular WWII German submarine, the U-505, and the coal mine, a simulated ride down into a mile-deep mine shaft. Special exhibits during the year; city favorite is Christmas Around The World with decorated trees, native dress, and traditions from around the world; antique and space-age cars; walk through a 19th-century street. Restaurant and gift shops. Free parking. Open daily 9:30 A.M.–5:30 P.M. in summer, and to 4 P.M. in winter.

Oriental Institute. University of Chicago, E. 58th St. and S. University Ave. (702–9521). Ancient history from 5000 B.C. lives again in free tours at 10, 11:30, 1, and 2:30; always free films on ancient civilizations. Pieces of the Dead Sea Scrolls and artifacts from archeological digs in Egypt, Persia, Syria, Mesopotamia, Memphis, Thebes, and elsewhere. The Near East focus features a reproduction of the 9,000 year old house of Jarmo in what is now Iraq. Tues.–Sat., 10 A.M.–4 P.M.; Sun., noon to 4 P.M.

ARTS AND ENTERTAINMENT. Music: Whether it's the mournful blues, folk, or lyric opera, it beats here. Starting with the grand: *Chicago Symphony Orchestra* under the leadership of Music Director Daniel Barenboim in the fall and winter at Orchestra Hall, 220 S. Michigan (435–8122). The symphony's string quartet breaks off for free concerts at the Public Library Cultural Center during the year (346–3278). The *Civic Orchestra* conducted by Margaret Hillis (chorus director of the Chicago Symphony) appears at Orchestra Hall (435–6666). The *Lyric Opera of Chicago,* 20 N. Wacker Dr. (332–2244), has a fall–New Year season of world famous performers. For a variety of concert tastes, check with the *Auditorium Theater,* 50 E. Congress (922–2110), a gilt and granite fortress with unmatched acoustics.

The sublime includes the *Old Town School of Folk Music* for the Sun. broadcast of the National Public Radio 'Folk Sampler' show, 909 W. Armitage (525–7793), $2, 5–7 P.M.

Dance: The Auditorium Theater, 50 E. Congress (922–2110), has its share of visiting dance companies (Twyla Tharp). The neighborhood's major attraction (with diversity and price) is the *Mo Ming Dance and Arts Center,* 1034 W. Barry (472–7662). Showcases Chicago artists and visiting ensembles. Resident companies, sans permanent homes, are the *Ballet Chicago* (993–7575), which performs in the spring at the Civic Opera, 20 N. Madison, and the ascending *Hubbard Street Dance Theater* 218 S. Wabash (663–1642).

Films: With first show daily and weekend discounts (often half-price), first-run films and even revivals are easily affordable. Neighborhood theaters are as low as $1.75 for first runs. November is the *Chicago International Film Festival* month. Foreign and art films are usually at the famous *Biograph Theaters* where John Dillinger met a fatal fusillade of gunfire, 2433 N. Lincoln (348–4123), with neighborhood and street parking; the *Fine Arts,* 418 S. Michigan (939–3700), with parking at Grant Park underground; and the *Music Box,* 3733 N. Southport (871–6604), with neighborhood and street parking. The strictly offbeat and arty foreign films come to *Facets Multimedia,* 1517 W. Fullerton (281–4114), with neighborhood and street parking. The neighborhood surrounding Facets is in transition so be careful.

Theater: You'll find the "names" and New York productions downtown at the remaining "Broadway" stage: *The Shubert,* 22 W. Monroe St. Chicago, IL 60603 (977–1710). Wed., Sat. and Sun. matinees. The captive Mayfair Theater, Blackstone Hotel, 636 S. Michigan (786–9120). Operating year-round is the *Goodman Theater,* at the Art Institute's east entrance, 200 S. Columbus Dr. (443–3800). Excellent children's and American debut theater offering a fine package dinner and show. The *Arie Crown Theater,* at McCormick Place, 23rd and the lake (791–6000), underground city parking, hosts a few Broadway shows during the year.

Don't miss the biting satire of Chicago's *Second City,* 1616 N. Wells (337–3992), lot parking, the original improv stage that brought out the late John Belushi, Mike Nichols, Elaine May, and Alan Arkin. If you're taking in Old Town and Wells Street on a weeknight, drop by at 11 P.M. for a free improv show after the main show. See a Second City touring company show for $9.50 ($10.50 Fri. and Sat.). No credit cards. Reservations are a good idea since most shows do sell out ahead of time.

The "off-Loop" stage outshines and outprices the Loop legit productions. Shakespeare is on some stage at all times and famous Chicago playwrights (e.g., Pulitzer Prize winner David Mamet) and also unknown authors and actors keep the seats full. Stages in the neighborhoods are: *Apollo Theater,* 2540 N. Lincoln (935–6100), neighborhood parking; *Steppenwolf,* 2851 N. Halsted (472–4141); *Wisdom Bridge,* 1559 W. Howard Street—Rogers Park (743–6000). *Huron,* 1608 N. Wells, *Kuumba,* 1900 W. Van Buren (243–2294); *Victory Gardens,* 2261 N. Lincoln Ave. (871–3000); *Immediate Theater Company,* Theater Building, 1225 W. Belmont (929–1031); *Court Theatre,* University of Chicago, 5535 S. Ellis (753–4472); the *Organic Theater Co.,* 3319 N. Clark (327–5588); and the *Chicago Theater Company,* Parkway Playhouse, 500 E. 67th St. (443–1130).

If the prospect of $20 tickets frightens and $10 is palatable for an evening or afternoon of theater or concert at more than 40 theaters, half-price tickets are available at 11 A.M. the morning of a production through **HOT TIX,** 24 S. State St.; Mon. noon to 6; Tues.–Fri. 10 to 6; Sat. 10 to 5. Locations in Oak Park and Evanston. HOT TIX also sells full-price advance seats. *Cash only.* Call 977–1755 for 24-hour theater information, availability, prices, and times. You can charge tickets on Visa, MasterCard, and American Express for a small fee through **Theater Tix,** 10 A.M. to 8 P.M. (902–1919).

ACCOMMODATIONS. Chicago is blessed with hotels ranging from glitz and gilt to plain and simple. Chicago nurtures every type and price hotel that either a traveler or conventioner could want; from aged beauties with great lobbies to small, European-type hotels serving just petit dejeuner off a small lobby to just run-of-the-mill motels. All have amenities like air conditioning and most have cable and movies. All hotels charge 10.1% room tax and 8% on food and beverage items. Because Chicago is a major business and convention town, Mar.–June and Aug.–Nov. are the traditionally busy seasons. Accommodations are listed under categories reflecting the cost of a double room: *Super Deluxe,* over $200; *Deluxe,* $125–$200; *Expensive,* $100–$125; *Moderate,* $65–$100; *Inexpensive,* under $65.

Super Deluxe

Ambassador West. 1300 N. State Pkwy., Chicago, IL 60610 (312–787–7900). Best neighborhood in the Gold Coast area; aristocratic clientele, excellent restaurants (Pump Room), valet parking.

The Drake. 140 E. Walton Place, Chicago, IL 60611 (312–787–2200). Grand hotel along the lake; no pets; several dining rooms, cocktails, and tea. The weekend special makes this most elegant Chicago landmark affordable. No free parking.

Hyatt Regency Chicago. 151 E. Wacker Dr., Chicago, IL 60601 (312–565–1234 or 800–233–1234). Glitzy lobby and cocktail area with entertainment, garage, shops. This huge convention center and multilevel hotel offers a reasonably priced weekend package with deluxe double occupancy and free parking. Lots of entertainment and weekend bustle. Children under 19 and cribs are free.

The Mayfair Regent. 181 E. Lake Shore Dr., Chicago, IL 60611 (312–787–8500). Lovely grand hotel. Rooftop dining, second dining room, afternoon tea, cocktails, lake view. 213 rooms.

The Ritz Carlton. 160 E. Pearson, Chicago, IL 60611 (312–266–1000). With its lobby nestled on the 12th floor of Water Tower Place, the Ritz Carlton is a cut above. Grand foyer, cocktails, entertainment, restaurants, 400 rooms, indoor pool, health club, recreational facilities.

The Westin. 909 N. Michigan Ave., Chicago, IL 60611 (312–943–7200). All the amenities, including health club. One block south of Water Tower Place.

Deluxe

Chicago Marriott. 540 N. Michigan Ave., Chicago, IL 60611 (312–836–0100 or 800–228–9290). Indoor pool, putting green, cable, tennis, health club, garage, 3 dining rooms.

Palmer House. 17 E. Monroe St., Chicago, IL 60690 (312–726–7500 or 800–HILTONS). Truly a grand old hotel, now a Hilton property. 1,800 units, small pool. 4 dining rooms and coffee shop; Trader Vic's restaurant in the hotel. Pets allowed. Free health club facilities.

The Raphael. 201 E. Delaware Place, Chicago, IL 60611 (312–943–5000). European atmosphere in this small hotel. 175 rooms, cocktail lounge.

Expensive

Allerton Hotel. 701 N. Michigan Ave., Chicago, IL 60611 (312–440–1500). An older, nicely renovated 450-room hotel well placed along the city's most expensive district. Excellent dining at L'Escargot (very expensive). Use of health club 3 blocks away. Weekend rate is deeply discounted.

Days Inn. 644 N. Lake Shore Dr. Chicago, IL 60611 (312–943–9200 or 800–633–1414). This chain outfit is right on the lake. Parking and cribs available.

Holiday Inn. Mart Plaza, 350 N. Orleans St., Chicago, IL 60654 (312–836–5000). Atop the Apparel Center at the Merchandise mart, 524 rooms. Indoor pool; dining room, and cafeteria; cocktails and entertainment.

Intercontinental Hotel. 525 N. Michigan Ave., Chicago, IL 60611 (312–944–4101). Excellent location for shopping and business. 875 units, indoor pool, sauna, dining rooms, and coffee shop.

The Midland. 172 W. Adams, Chicago, IL 60603 (312–332–1200). An established hotel in the heart of the city's financial district; dining room and coffee shop. Complimentary limo service to businesses and shopping in the Loop and N. Michigan Ave., even to jogging paths at 6:30 A.M. Weekend specials.

Moderate

Best Western River North Hotel. 125 W. Ohio St., Chicago, IL 60611 (312–467–0800 or 800–328–1234). Just 7 blocks from the Loop and 5 blocks from N. Michigan Ave. shopping. Rooftop swimming pool. Midweek specials based on availability make this place a bargain. Weekend rates are higher.

Blackstone Hotel. 636 S. Michigan Ave., Chicago, IL 60605 (312–427–4300 or 800–622–6330). This older hotel overlooks Lake Michigan and Grant Park. Prime location for visits to Art Institute and other museums. Home of jazz showcase.

Essex Inn. 800 S. Michigan Ave., Chicago, IL 60605 (312–939–2800 or 800–621–6909, nationwide). While slightly away from the downtown bustle, this inn is convenient to McCormick Place Convention Center. Cribs free. Pets allowed. Free parking. Delicatessen restaurant.

Inexpensive

Best Western Grant Park Hotel. 1100 S. Michigan Ave., Chicago, IL 60605 (312–922–2900 or 800–528–1234). Large motel 11 blocks south of the Loop and the best jumping-off point for visits to the Alder Planetarium, Field Museum, Shedd Aquarium, or McCormick Place Exposition Center. Outdoor heated pool.

Comfort Inn of Chicago. 601 W. Diversey, Chicago, IL 60614 (312–348–2810 or 800–228–5150). Although north of downtown this renovated, 100-room inn is a prime location in the Lincoln Park neighborhood. Excellent jumping off place for enjoying nearby neighborhoods. Free parking, complimentary Continental breakfast, children under 12 free.

Lakeside Motel. 5440 N. Sheridan Rd., Chicago, IL 60640 (312–275–2700). While well away from downtown, it's 2 blocks from the public Bryn Mawr beach and a good jumping-off point for exploring the Rogers Park neighborhood and nearby Evanston. Chinese restaurant; free parking.

LaSalle Motor Lodge. 720 N. LaSalle St., Chicago, IL 60610 (312–664–8100). North of the Loop but well situated just a few blocks away from N. Michigan Ave. shopping areas. Restaurant and free parking. Children under 16 free, cribs free; movie channel.

BED AND BREAKFASTS. *Bed & Breakfast, Inc.,* Box 14088, Chicago, IL 60614–0088 (312–951–0085), is the reservation service for lodging in 64 private homes from Victorian city homes to high-rise condos. Most recent prices were $25 for budget singles to $120, with most in the $45–$65 range. Rates vary by season.

RESTAURANTS. The Loop and North Michigan Ave.'s Gold Coast present some of Chicago's finest and best known restaurants—the Cape Cod Room, the Pump Room, The Chestnut Street Grill to name a few. As much as meat and potatoes, Chicago is a seafood town, enjoying the fresh water lake catches along with the salt water exotics flown in fresh daily. Variety is the spice of Chicago's ethnic restaurants, normally neighborhood establishments and away from downtown. Jackets in the better establishments downtown are expected; it is less formal out of the Loop. There are thousands of restaurants to choose from; the list here is a mere sample. Restaurants are listed according to categories based on the price of a three-course meal for one (excluding beverages, tax, and tip): *Deluxe,* more than $40; *Expensive,* $20–$40; *Moderate,* $12–$20; *Inexpensive,* $5–$12.

Deluxe

Le Français. 269 S. Milwaukee, Wheeling, IL (708–541–7470). Reservations months in advance suggested. The best kitchen in the Midwest for French cuisine. Exquisite pâtés, massive entrees, and unhurried atmosphere if you choose a second seating, after 9 P.M. Tues.–Sun., 5:30–9:30 P.M. AE, DC, MC, V.

Nick's Fishmarket Restaurant. 1 First National Plaza, Chicago (621–0200). Amid the sculptures and mosiacs of First National Plaza, Nick's offers 100 fish dishes on the menu with desserts and expansive ambience to match. Lunch 11:30 A.M.–3 P.M. Mon.–Fri.; dinner 5:30 P.M.–11 P.M. Mon.–Thurs., until 11:30 Fri. and Sat. Major credit cards.

Le Perroquet. 70 E. Walton (944–7990). Quiet and relaxed establishment in the Gold Coast area, this place features nouvelle cuisine presented in an elegant manner. Excellent seafood and grilled roasts with salads and cheese before desserts. Mon.–Fri., noon–3. D, Mon.–Sat., 6–10 P.M. AE, DC.

Expensive

Cape Cod Room. Drake Hotel, 140 E. Walton (787–2200). Reservations a must for this venerable seafood restaurant still serving the basic bests: fine service, a moderate costing wine list, dependable Bookbinder red snapper soup and inventive entrees. Mon.–Sun., noon–11 P.M. AE, DC, MC, V.

Chestnut Street Grill. Water Tower Place, Michigan and Chestnut sts., (280–2720). Although the menu features grilled meats, the Grill is known for its seafood—from trout to shark and excellent bowls of calamari. Soups and salads round out the grill. Mon.–Thurs., 11:30 A.M.–10:30 P.M.; Fri. and Sat. until 11:30 P.M.

Jackies. 2478 N. Lincoln, Chicago (880–0003). Small and intimate, this nouvelle-cuisine restaurant in the Lincoln Park neighborhood is a jewel of fine service and excellent food. A hot seafood salad is an excellent opener, with roasts, sauces, and vegetables to follow. Tues.–Sat., 11:30 A.M.–1:30 P.M.; Tues.–Thurs., 5:45–8:30 P.M.; Sat. and Sun. till 9:30 P.M.

Morton's. 1050 N. State St., Chicago (266–4820). Main courses of thick cuts of meat and baked or hash brown potatoes are first rate in Chicago, with lobsters there a close second. Mon.–Sat., 5:30–11 P.M. AE, DC, MC, V.

Moderate

The Courtyards of the Plaka. 340 S. Halsted, Chicago (263–0767). Greek specialties in Chicago's old Greek neighborhood off the Loop. Noted for its flaming saganaki and garlic-yogurt-cucumber tzatziki dip, along with Greek lamb and seafood dishes. Good selection of Greek wines. Sun.–Thurs., 11 A.M.–midnight; Fri. and Sat., to 1 A.M. AE, DC, MC, V.

On the Tao. 1218 Morse, Chicago (465–3257). Well north of downtown, this fine Chinese cuisine restaurant features the modern recipes with fresh seafood, poultry, and meats from crispy duck and hen to veal in ginger. Tues.–Sat. 5–11 P.M.; until 10 P.M. Sun. MC, V.

Inexpensive

Ed Debevic's. 640 N. Wells, Chicago (664–1707). Absolutely the best fun and food since 1950; 50's entrees like meat loaf or hamburgers, chili dogs with mashed potatoes, jello and chocolate pudding match period ambience and service. A smattering of 90s "healthy" foods is also offered. Mon.–Thurs., 11 A.M.–midnight; Fri., and Sat., to 1 A.M. Sun., 10 A.M.–11 P.M. No reservations, expect a short wait. No cards.

Pizzeria Due. 619 N. Wabash, Chicago (943–2400). Along with Pizzeria Uno, a block away at 29 E. Ohio (321–1000), the Chicago style, deep-dish pizza started here. A medium sausage pizza, with rich sauce, large pieces of fresh tomatoes, and what seems like layers of sausage and cheese, is enough for four. Uno's is more crowded than the newer Due's, but Uno's has better atmosphere. Good spots to catch a bite from lunchtime to late at night. Major credit cards.

LIQUOR LAWS. You must be 21 to drink in Illinois. Sold in liquor stores; available by the drink in most restaurants from 9 A.M. to 3 A.M., depending on the establishment's license.

MISSOURI

The "Show Me" state stretches across several hundred miles of middle America and offers attractions that are both cosmopolitan and wholly American. On its east and west boundaries, the state is anchored by two great cities: St. Louis, with its 630-foot-high Gateway Arch that symbolizes the gateway to the West, and Kansas City, with its miles of boulevards with parks and fountains. In between are villages, middle-sized cities, and miles of countryside to explore.

Interwoven in Missouri's history are the names of famous statesmen, politicians, authors, artists, and even a notorious outlaw or two. Tributes to Harry Truman, General John J. Pershing, Mark Twain, Eugene Field, and Jesse James attract visitors to various corners of the state. Festivals are another way Missouri celebrates its Old World past and American present.

To please country music fans, there are a multitude of toe-tappin' revues in the Ozark region. Nightly shows provide a blend of country, gospel, and other styles, plus a hint of hillbilly humor. The hottest areas for this type of entertainment are the Lake of the Ozarks area in south central Missouri, and Branson, in the southwestern Ozark Mountain Country. It is said there are more seats for country music fans (30,000) in Branson than in Nashville.

When Missouri tires of its Show Me nickname, it could adopt the legend Cave State, as it has more known caves than any other state. Some 45,000 caves have been recorded in Missouri, and others are discovered yearly. Visitors are advised to carry along sweaters or jackets because of the caves' constant low temperatures and damp, environment, which has preserved fossils and other artifacts. These crevices also provided shelter for the likes of Jesse James and the Dalton Gang. The writings of Mark Twain and Harold Bell Wright also bring the caves to life.

You may want to visit one of Missouri's 30 wineries in production. Before prohibition, Missouri was the second-largest wine producer in the U.S., and in those years Missouri's vines were so strong and disease-resistant that huge shipments were sent to France where they were grafted onto French vines to keep Europe's vineyards producing for years. But Missouri's wineries suffered a turn-of-the-century decline that, combined with prohibition, nearly meant the end of Missouri's wine industry until the 1960s. Today's wineries, scattered throughout the state, are backed by research at the University of Missouri-Columbia. Many of the wineries are family operated and owned, and they welcome visitors with tours and tasting. Two of the best known are in Hermann: the Stone Hill Winery and the Hermannhof Winery.

Fans of outdoor recreation will find a haven in the Lake of the Ozarks region that winds through south central Missouri. Only 15 people lived in the town of Old Bagnell in 1929 when the Union Electric Company decided to dam the Osage River for its hydroelectric power, thereby creating the lake. Since the completion in 1931 of the Bagnell Dam, the area has steadily grown and developed, and today more than three million tourists yearly visit the area to take advantage of the 1,300 miles of wooded shoreline. Countless coves offer opportunities for swimming, skiing, boating, and fishing.

In the Ozark Mountain Country of southwest Missouri, Table Rock Lake forms the center of a chain of lakes on the Missouri–Arkansas line. Bull Shoals, Norfolk, and Taneycomo are particularly popular with an-

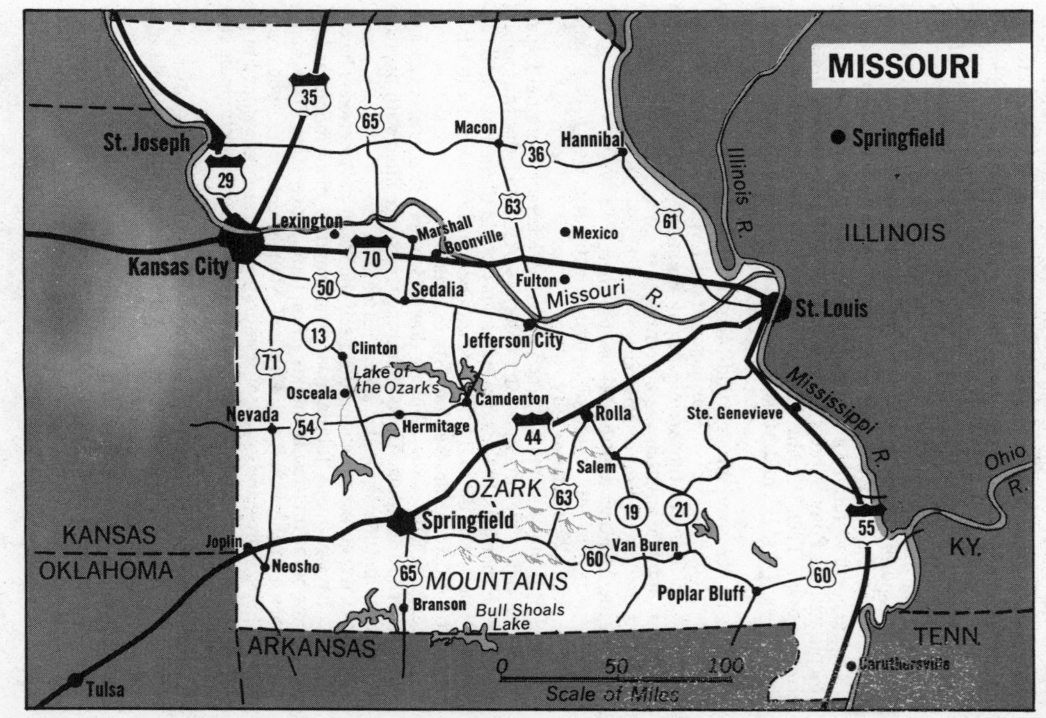
MISSOURI
Springfield
ILLINOIS
Illinois R.
St. Louis
Mississippi R.
Ohio R.
KY.
TENN.
Caruthersville
Ste. Genevieve
Poplar Bluff
Van Buren
Salem
Rolla
Hannibal
Mexico
Fulton
Missouri R.
Jefferson City
Camdenton
OZARK
MOUNTAINS
Springfield
Bull Shoals Lake
Branson
Hermitage
Lake of the Ozarks
Clinton
Sedalia
Boonville
Marshall
Macon
Lexington
Osceala
Nevada
Neosho
Joplin
Kansas City
St. Joseph
KANSAS
OKLAHOMA
ARKANSAS
Tulsa
61
36
63
65
35
29
70
50
13
54
71
44
19
21
60
55
0 50 100
Scale of Miles

glers, and each seems to be noteworthy for a different species: Table Rock, bass; Taneycomo, trout; Stockton, walleye; and Bull Shoals, white bass.

Missouri's geography is crisscrossed with a network of rivers, most notably the Mississippi and the Missouri. Indians, explorers, traders, and settlers used rivers as transportation, and the first settlements grew up along the rivers. The explorers Lewis and Clark and Marquette traveled the rivers, and today travelers can follow the water for modern excursions.

As the Mississippi flows south into Missouri, it takes you to Hannibal, the town immortalized by Mark Twain. Continuing south, the river flows into St. Louis, where the most historic part lies along the riverfront. Past St. Louis, the mighty river flows through Ste. Genevieve, Missouri's oldest town, to Cape Girardeau, founded in 1792. Next you'll be in the Old South region of Missouri in river towns such as New Madrid and Caruthersville.

On the northwestern edge of the state, the Missouri River runs past St. Joseph, with its Pony Express heritage, and Weston, the historic tobacco-growing town. Then the Missouri flows through Kansas City and meanders eastward through mid-Missouri on its way to join the Mississippi near St. Louis.

Following the river through mid-Missouri will take you on a journey to the past. You'll find Civil War memories in Lexington, frontier history in Arrow Rock, interesting architecture in Boonville, German heritage in Hermann and Washington, the current seat of government in Jefferson City, and the first capital of Missouri in St. Charles. Shortly beyond St. Charles, the Missouri and the Mississippi merge.

No visit to Missouri would be complete without a visit to her major cities, St. Louis and Kansas City.

One of St. Louis's primary attractions is the Jefferson National Expansion Memorial, which includes the Gateway Arch and the Museum of Westward Expansion. In the same vicinity is the Old Cathedral, the Basilica of St. Louis, and the Old Courthouse, where in 1847 Dred Scott's lawyers first pleaded for his freedom from slavery.

On the north side of the 12-block downtown area is a revitalized area called Laclede's Landing. The cobblestone streets are filled with bars and restaurants, and it's a popular spot with natives.

Kansas City, across the state, calls itself the Heart of America. The city claims to have as many fountains as Rome and as many boulevards as Paris. Some of the prettiest fountains are on the Country Club Plaza, south of downtown in the vicinity of 47th and Main streets. This spot boasts elegant shops, stores, and excellent restaurants. The area, developed in the 1920s using Spanish architecture, is hailed as America's first shopping center.

North of the Plaza on the way downtown is the multi-acre Crown Center complex developed by Hallmark; it contains a hotel, shops, restaurants, and apartments.

Downtown Kansas City is experiencing a building boom that promises to create ample office space and a revitalized downtown area.

PRACTICAL INFORMATION FOR MISSOURI

HOW TO GET THERE. By plane. Kansas City and St. Louis have international airports and are served by major carriers. Smaller airports served by regional airlines are in Columbia and Springfield.

By bus. In St. Louis *Greyhound-Trailways* has a terminal in downtown near the Arch, and Kansas City is served by the same line. Deregulation of airlines has cut into some bus service.

By train. Missouri is on the *Amtrak* line with stops at small cities and metropolises of St. Louis, where service is not always punctual, particularly in winter, and Kansas City.

By car. I-70 runs through Missouri from Kansas on the west and Illinois in the east (thus Kansas City and St. Louis are connected by I-70). I-35 runs north–south through western Missouri and Kansas City, and I-55 runs through St. Louis north–south.

WHEN TO GO. Missourians definitely get to experience all four seasons, but maybe not on schedule. It's not unusual for Mother Nature to tease by providing sunny, mild days in Feb. and blustery, snowy days in Mar. Or she may toy with the clock by granting balmy temperatures and blooming roses in Nov. But, by-and-large, you can count on temperatures in the 20s in winter, and in the upper 80s or 90s in summer, with a large dose of humidity. Spring and fall are the glorious seasons. Lots of travelers enjoy visiting the Ozarks during the fall for a kaleidoscope of foliage that is breathtaking.

TOURIST INFORMATION. Write to the *Missouri Division of Tourism,* Truman State Office Building, Box 1055, Jefferson City, MO 65102 for brochures and maps detailing the state's attractions (314–751–4133). For specifics on Kansas City, contact the *Convention and Visitors Bureau,* 1100 Main St., 64108 MO (816–221–5242). For tips on St. Louis, contact the *Convention and Visitor's Bureau,* 10 S. Broadway, Suite 300, 63102, MO (800–325–7962, nationwide; 421–1023, in the city).

TELEPHONES. Missouri has 3 area codes: 816, 417, and 314. You do not need to dial the area code if it is the same from which you are calling. To dial most out-of-state regions from Missouri, dial 1 plus the area code and number. Directory assistance can be reached at 411 from a pay phone, otherwise 1411. A phone call from a phone booth costs 25 cents.

EMERGENCY TELEPHONE NUMBERS. In St. Louis and Kansas City, *fire, police,* and *paramedics* can be reached by dialing 911.

HOW TO GET AROUND. From the airport. *St. Louis:* Taxis from the airport to downtown will run about $15; to midtown or Clayton, a little less. Driving time by expressway to downtown is about 20 minutes. *Kansas City:* Cab fare is about $20 for the 30-minute ride downtown from the airport.

By bus. Bus service in the major cities is not exceptionally good, and residents generally prefer to drive. *St. Louis:* Bi-State Transit (314–231–2345) charges about 85 cents within a region with additional 15 cents for transfers. *Kansas City:* Kansas City Area Transportation Authority (816–221–0660) operates buses, and their fares start at 75 cents.

By rental car. Major firms have outlets in Kansas City and St. Louis, where cars may be picked up at the airport, or other location. Options in St. Louis include *Dollar Rent-A-Car* (314–434–4004) and *Avis* (314–426–7766). Among agencies in Kansas City are *Hertz* (800–654–3131) and *National Car Rental* (800–227–7368).

HINTS TO MOTORISTS. Right turn-on-red is permitted unless otherwise posted. Missouri enforces the national highway speed limit; in most metropolitan areas the speed limit is 35 mph. A good street map is essential in St. Louis, as the streets radiate like spokes from downtown. Also, one-way streets downtown can be confusing. Kansas City is a bit easier to get around in, as most streets run north–south or east–west; generally, numbered streets run east–west, and named streets run north–south. Recent construction downtown has caused some traffic rerouting, so allow extra time. In both cities, snow tires or chains are necessary during heavy snows on streets designated "Snow Emergency Route."

HINTS TO DISABLED TRAVELERS. Parking spaces for handicapped should be marked with a blue and white sign or yellow paint on the road surface; you need to display an authorization sign in your vehicle. For information about access to buildings in Kansas City, contact the *Whole Person, Inc.,* 6301 Rockhill Rd., Suite 305 E, Kansas City, MO 64131 (816–361–0304). The St. Louis Convention and Visitor's Bureau (see Tourist Information) offers information on a particular attraction's accessibility.

SEASONAL EVENTS. German heritage is remembered in mid-**May** with the *Maifest* and Oct. weekends with Oktoberfest in the little Missouri River town of

Hermann. Contact Hermann Chamber of Commerce, 115 E. 3rd St., Hermann, MO 65041 (314–486–2313). There is dancing, German food and costumes.

Folks in southwest Missouri make the most of their hillbilly reputation with several celebrations, such as *Hillbilly Days* in Bennett Spring State Park, in **June** (800–334–6946) and the *Mountain Folks Music Festival* at Silver Dollar City in Branson (417–338–8210).

The antics of a mischievous little boy are re-created yearly in early **July** with the *National Tom Sawyer Days* in Hannibal. Contact Tourism Commission, Box 624, Hannibal, MO 63401 (314–221–1570). Raft racing, frog jumping, and a fence painting contest are part of the fun.

The quaint city of Ste. Genevieve, south of I-55 on U.S. 61, is Missouri's oldest city. Founded in the 1720s by the French, it yearly commemorates its past with the *Jour de Fete* in mid-**Aug.** Contact Ste. Genevieve Chamber of Commerce, Box 166, Ste. Genevieve, MO 63670 (314–883–5750).

Every **Nov.** Kansas City celebrates its agribusiness heritage with the *American Royal Livestock, Horseshow and Rodeo,* a 3-week spectacle that includes a parade through downtown. Stockmen "drive" their prize cattle, sheep, or hogs to Kansas City to compete for grand champion, and top horsemen from across the country are drawn to Kansas City to show their steeds at the American Royal—some events are even national championships. Another week is filled with the fun and thrills of a rodeo.

CAVES. Fantastic Caverns. Rte. 20, Box 1935, Springfield, MO 65803 (417–833–2010). Jeep-drawn trams take you on a 1 mi., 45-min. tour. $4–$8.50. **Mark Twain Cave.** Box 913, Hannibal, MO 63401 (314–221–1656). See where Tom Sawyer and Becky Thatcher got lost in this cave opened in 1886. $3–$6. **Meramec Caverns.** La Jolla Natural Park, Stanton, MO 63079 (314–468–3166). Open daily except Thanksgiving, Christmas, and Jan. and Feb. See Jesse James's Hideout or attend Easter Sunday nondenominational church service.

PARKS AND GARDENS. Faust Park. Olive Street Rd. at Arrowhead Estates, St. Louis, MO (314–532–7298). Restored home and granary of Missouri's second governor, Frederick Bates. Bright Dentzel carousel made in Philadelphia in the early 1920s features carved and painted wooden animals. Park is free, but there is a charge for carousel rides.

Forrest Park. St. Louis. Located on west side of the city, the 1,300 acres stretch from Kingshighway on the west to the city limits at Shinker Blvd. on the east, and from Lindell Blvd. on the north to Hwy. 40 on the south. Includes the *St. Louis Zoo* and the *Jewel Box Floral Conservatory* that has displays throughout the year; particularly pretty at Christmastime.

Loose Park. 51st St. and Wornall Rd., Kansas City, MO. A few blocks south of the Country Club Plaza, this park borders on some of the city's most exclusive residential neighborhoods. The park has open expanses of rolling terrain, a jogging path, duck pond, tennis courts, and a renowned rose garden. Closes 10 P.M.

Missouri Botanical Gardens. 4344 Shaw Blvd., St. Louis, MO (314–577–5143). Begun in 1859 by Henry Shaw, this 79-acre showplace houses the Climatron, a tropical greenhouse geodesic dome with sections for cacti and orchids. Also feature prize-winning rose gardens, splendid Japanese garden, and English woodlands. Open daily except Christmas until dusk. Admission is $2.

Swope Park. Meyer Blvd at Swope Pkwy, Kansas City, MO (816–444–3113). You could easily spend a day at this vast park, the nation's third largest municipal park, with 1,769 acres. Includes the *Kansas City Zoo,* two 18-hole golf courses, an outdoor theater, two fishing lakes, a nature center, 10 shelters and numerous athletic fields. Always open, but it's wise to avoid the area after dark unless you're attending a performance at Starlight Theatre.

STATE PARKS. Nature is preserved in 46 state parks operated by the Missouri Department of Natural Resources. Camping is allowed in most state parks, and some have backpacking trails, nature education centers, plus facilities for boating, fishing, and picnicking. Camping fees range from $5 per night for a basic campsite to $10 for a site with full hookups. Some parks have dining lodges, cabins, and even motels that are open from Apr. 15–Oct. 31. Lodging at trout fishing parks (Bennett

Spring, Montauk, and Roaring River) is open Mar. 1–Oct. 31. For information on specific parks, contact the *Missouri Department of Natural Resources,* Box 176, Dept. MT 85, Jefferson City, MO 65102 (314–751–3443 or 800–334–6946).

FISHING AND HUNTING. Nearly 200 species of fish swim the million acres of water in Missouri, including 50,000 mi. of rivers and streams. The popular Midwestern game fish such as bass, bluegill, crappie, and catfish lure anglers, as do northern pike, walleye, muskie, and striped bass. A fishing license for residents costs $6; non-resident licenses range from a 3-day permit for $5 to a year-long license for $15.

Deer, turkey, rabbit, squirrel, upland game birds, and migratory waterfowl hunting are permitted in some areas with proper license during certain seasons. Resident licenses for small game cost $8, and deer or turkey licenses cost $10. Nonresidents pay $50 for a small game license, $100 for deer, and $100 for turkey. For more information on fishing or hunting, write the *Missouri Department of Conservation,* Box 180, Dept. MT-85, Jefferson City, MO 65102 (314–751–4115).

PARTICIPANT SPORTS. In addition to the usual sports of **golfing, jogging,** and **tennis,** Missourians love to take **float trips** on the numerous scenic rivers. Some travel by canoe, and other adventurers like simply to relax in an innertube. If you don't have your own equipment, outfitters will provide nearly everything such as canoe or other boat, life jackets, and camping gear. Some outfitters even provide guides and can set up campsites. Favorite rivers for floating include the Current, Jacks Fork, Eleven Point, and Meramec. Summertime is the best time for a novice because the waters are placid, although there may be exposed sandbars or other obstructions. Rivers can be dangerous in the spring when they are full and rushing. For a list of outfitters and river information write Missouri Department of Conservation, Box 180, Jefferson City, MO 65102 (314–751–4115).

SPECTATOR SPORTS. With two major cities, Missouri has a lot to offer in professional sports, especially baseball. The 1985 World Series pitted the state's two teams, St. Louis Cardinals and Kansas City Royals (who won) in a classic dubbed the Show-Me Series.

Baseball: *Kansas City Royals* (816–921–8000) and *St. Louis Cardinals* (314–421–3060). **Football:** *Kansas City Chiefs* (816–924–9300). **Hockey:** *St. Louis Blues* (314–781–5300).

HISTORIC SITES AND HOUSES. Arrow Rock. 13 mi. north of I-70 on Missouri 41, 15 miles east of Marshall. The Santa Fe Trail crossed the Missouri River here, and the sites in this historic town remain much as they were in the pioneer days. Sites include the house of Missouri artist George Caleb Bingham; the Arrow Rock Tavern, built in 1834; the old courthouse; and Dr. Matthew Walton Hall House. Lots of antique shopping in vicinity.

Chatillon–DeMenil Mansion. 3552 DeMenil Pl., St. Louis, MO 63118 (314–771–5828). Farmhouse built in 1848 with addition in 1856. Guided tours Tues.–Sat., 10 A.M.–4 P.M. Closed Sun. and Jan. Adults, $2.50; children, 50 cents. The DeMenil Carriage House restaurant is open for lunch.

Felix Valle Home, At Merchant and Second Sts. in Ste. Genevieve, MO (314–883–7102). Built in the American Federal Style it served as headquarters and storage for a company that controlled Indian trade through Missouri and Arkansas. Also see Ste. Genevieve Museum (314–883–3461).

Mark Twain Birthplace. In Mark Twain State Park near Perry and Paris off Missouri 107 (314–565–3449). Boyhood home and museum in Hannibal (314–221–9010). The museum encloses the 2-room cabin in which Samuel Clemens was born in 1835. Many of his personal items and books are displayed, such as an early handwritten manuscript of "Tom Sawyer."

Watkins Woolen Mill. 6½ mi. north of Excelsior Springs on U.S. 69 (816–296–3357). Woolen mill built in 1869 still contains original machinery. Steam engine power plant, family home, smokehouse, and cemetery on the site.

MUSEUMS. Kansas City Museum. 3218 Gladstone Blvd. (816–483–8300). This museum originally was the 70-room ornate home of lumber magnate R. A. Long.

Among the exhibits of frontier life and early regional history are replicas of a trading post and store in Westport. Open 9:30 A.M.–4:30 P.M., Tues.–Sat.; noon–4:30 P.M., Sun. Suggested donation: $3 for adults.

Museum of Westward Expansion. Ground floor of the Gateway Arch, 702 N. First St., St. Louis. Overview of pioneer days. Rides up to the Arch's observation room. Daily, 9 A.M.–6 P.M., winter; 8 A.M.–10 P.M., summer.

Nelson–Atkins Museum of Art. 4525 Oak St., Kansas City, MO (913–561–4000). One of the nation's top galleries, it is internationally renowned for its Chinese collection, although it contains art from every period. Open 10 A.M.–5 P.M., Tues.–Sat.; 1–5 P.M., Sun. Adults, $4; under 19 and full-time college students, $1. Free on Sat. except for special exhibits on the first floor.

St. Louis Art Museum. In Forest Park (314–721–0072). Outstanding collection of pre-Columbian art and vast collection of German-born painter Max Beckmann's works. Also art of other periods from throughout the world. Closed Mon.; Open 10–A.M.–5 P.M. other days, except Tues., when hours are 1:30–8:30 P.M., and Fri., when hours are 10 A.M.–8:30 P.M. Free except for occasional special exhibits, when a donation is requested.

Harry S. Truman Library and Museum. Independence, MO (816–833–1400). Reproduction of Truman's White House office, United Nations Charter Table, and state gifts. Film programs. Open year-round. $2 adults, children free.

ARTS AND ENTERTAINMENT. Music: *Kansas City Symphony Orchestra.* At the Lyric Theatre, 1029 Central (816–471–4933). Since 1933, this orchestra has been playing, and is now conducted by William McGlaughlin. Concerts Fri. and Sat. nights, Nov.–Mar. $10–$22. *Conservatory of Music.* University of Missouri–Kansas City, 4949 Cherry (816–363–4300). Programs include concerts, recitals, and workshops. Student events generally are free, but there may be a fee for professional performances. *St. Louis Symphony Orchestra.* Powell Hall, 718 N. Grand (314–523–2500). Performances twice weekly Sept.–Apr. and summer pops concerts in Queeny Park.

Dance: *Kansas City Ballet.* Lyric Theatre, 1029 Central (816–931–2232). Now performs as the State Ballet of Missouri since the recent merger with Dance St. Louis. First-rate professional company started 25 years ago and well supported by dance patrons in the area. Season Oct.–May. Tickets $10–$30.

Dance St. Louis. 8338 Big Bend Blvd. (314–986–3770). Winter season with performances in differing locations. Both experimental and classical dance. Officially called the State Ballet of Missouri since its merger several years ago with the Kansas City Ballet.

Stage: *Lyric Opera.* 1029 Central, Kansas City (816–471–7344). Opera in English in Apr., Sept., and Oct. Prices range from $5–$32.

Missouri Repertory Theatre. 50th and Cherry Sts., on the University of Missouri–Kansas City campus (816–276–2727). First-rate productions are staged by this professional resident company. Season Jan.–Mar., July–Sept. $10–$19.

Repertory Theater of St. Louis. 130 Edgar Rd., Webster Groves, MO (314–968–4925). Eclectic offerings from Shakespeare to avant-garde plays. Early Sept.–mid-Apr. $7–$21.50.

ACCOMMODATIONS. If you're planning an excursion to coincide with one of Missouri's many festivals or a city's major event, you should book hotel accommodations as soon as your travel plans are firm; it is best to book a year in advance for events such as the Veiled Prophet Fair in St. Louis, the Plaza Lighting Ceremony or the American Royal in Kansas City, or a football weekend in Columbia. The entire summer (and often fall weekends) in the Ozarks region are busy, so again, advance planning will pay off.

Double-occupancy lodgings are categorized as follows: *Deluxe,* $75 and up; *Expensive,* $60–$75; *Moderate,* $40–$60. Tax is added to all bills, and in some places it will be nearly 10 percent. Categories are based on least expensive rooms.

Hannibal. Mark Twain Motor Inn. *Moderate.* 612 Mark Twain Ave., Hannibal, MO 63401 (314–221–1490). Heated outdoor pool. Walking distance to historic area.

Kansas City. Ritz Carlton. *Deluxe.* Wornall Rd. at Ward Pkwy., Kansas City, MO 64112 (816–756–1500). Total renovation was completed in 1990 of this hotel, which overlooks Country Club Plaza.

Raphael Hotel. *Deluxe.* 325 Ward Pkwy., Kansas City, MO 64112 (816–756–3800). 123 rooms. Charming European-style hotel overlooking Country Club Plaza. Free Continental breakfast served in room.

Westin Crown Center. *Deluxe.* One Pershing Rd., Kansas City, MO 64108 (816–474–4400). All the amenities of a large downtown hotel. 5-story terraced garden. Specialty shops.

Americana City Center Hotel. *Expensive.* 1301 Wyandotte, Kansas City, MO 64105 (816–221–8800). Downtown near Municipal Auditorium and Bartle Hall. 500 rooms. Restaurant and coffee shop.

Budget Luxury. *Moderate.* I-35 and North Antioch Rd., Kansas City North, MO 64117 (816–453–6550). Restaurant and lounge.

Drury Inn–KC Stadium. *Moderate.* 3830 Blue Ridge Cut-off, Kansas City, MO 64129 (816–923–3000). Close to sports complex. Under 18 free. Nonsmoker rooms available. Breakfast included.

Stadium Inn. *Moderate.* 7901 E. 40 Hwy., Kansas City, MO 64129 (816–921–9400). Jct. of I-70 and I-435, 1 mi. from sports complex or 10 min. from Worlds of Fun.

Ozarks Region. Lodge of the Four Seasons. *Deluxe.* Lake Road HH, Box 215, Lake Ozark, MO (800–392–3461). 320 rooms. All the amenities of a large resort including 27-hole Robert Trent Jones Golf course and trap shooting. Nightly entertainment.

Marriott's Tan-Tar-A Resort and Golf Club. *Deluxe.* State Hwy KK, Osage Beach, MO 65065 (314–348–3131 or 800–228–9290). 900 rooms. Lots of sports: tennis, golf, bowling, billiards, swimming, boating. 4 restaurants, 5 lounges.

Best Western Mountain Oak Lodge. *Moderate.* Hwy. 76W., Box 1106, Branson, MO 65616 (417–338–2141 or 800–528–1234). Restaurant, lounge, pool. Next door to Silver Dollar City. Closed Nov.–May.

Kimberling Arms Resort Best Western. *Moderate.* Hwy 13, Box 925 H, Kimberling City, MO 65868 (417–739–2461). 33 rooms. On Table Rock Lake. Restaurants nearby. Closed Nov.–March.

Kirkwood Inn at Kirkwood Center. *Moderate.* Hwy. 76 West. Box 1166, Branson, MO 65616 (417–334–4177). Indoor and outdoor pools, sauna, whirlpool. Live entertainment in Branson Opry House.

St. Louis. Chesire Inn and Lodge. *Deluxe.* 6300 Clayton Rd., Clayton, MO 63117 (800–325–RESV). 108 rooms. Near jogging trails and golf. Bus to summer Muny Opera. Two restaurants.

Marriott's Pavilion Hotel. *Deluxe.* One S. Broadway, St. Louis, MO 63102 (314–421–1776; 800–228–9290). Built at site of former Spanish Pavilion moved from the N.Y. World's Fair. Lounge, restaurants, health club.

Holiday Inn Southwest. *Expensive.* 10709 Hwy. 366, St. Louis, MO 63127 (314–821–6600 or 800–465–4329). Equidistant (17 mi.) from Six Flags and downtown, this place was renovated in 1989.

Country Hospitality Inn. *Moderate.* 2750 Plaza Way, St. Charles, MO 63303. (314–949–8700). Off I-70, 7 mi. from airport.

St. Louisian. *Moderate.* 1133 Washington Ave., St. Louis, MO (314–421–4727). Renovated in 1990. Downtown location near Arch, stadium, and Laclede's Landing.

Springfield. University Plaza Holiday Inn. *Expensive.* John Q. Hammons Pkwy., Springfield, MO 65806 (417–864–7333). 275 rooms, 41 are *deluxe* and poolside suites; 9-story atrium, 2 lounges and restaurants. Tennis, game room, Jacuzzi.

Drury Lodge of the Ozarks. *Moderate.* I-44 and Glenstone, Springfield, MO 65803 (417–866–3581). 135 rooms. Restaurant, lounge, outdoor pool, indoor recreation area. 30 mi. to Silver Dollar City; 2 mi. to Fantastic Caverns.

RESTAURANTS. Dining out in Missouri can mean anything from Continental cuisine to a juicy Kansas City Strip steak to a succulent barbecue or a crispy fried chicken. Jackets and ties are generally required at the deluxe establishments in cities, where reservations also are suggested. Tax is added to all meals, and the amount varies depending on locale. Expect 6–10 percent. Price categories are based on the average price for one dinner, excluding taxes, tip, and alcoholic beverage. *Super Deluxe,* over $30; *Deluxe,* $20–$30; *Expensive,* $15–$20; *Moderate,* $10–$15; *Inexpensive,* below $10.

Kansas City. American Restaurant. *Super Deluxe.* 25th and Grand Ave., top floor of Hall's Bldg., Kansas City, MO 64108 (816–471–8050). Bentwood oak and shaped network of glass create elegant, contemporary atmosphere. Salmon poached with vegetables, veal in cream sauce, Maple mousse, and other delicacies rotate on and off menu. Mon.–Thurs., 6–10 P.M.; Fri. and Sat., until 11 P.M. Closed Sun. Major credit cards.

Fedora Cafe. *Deluxe.* 210 W. 47 St., on Country Club Plaza, Kansas City, MO 64112 (816–561–6565). Trendy pasta and other Italian specialities. Also seafood, such as blackened redfish. Banquettes and white tile floor. L, 11:30 A.M.–3 P.M.; D, 5:30–11 P.M.; Mon.–Thurs.; until midnight, Fri. and Sat. Major credit cards.

La Méditerranée. *Deluxe.* 4742 Pennsylvania, on Country Club Plaza, Kansas City, MO 64112 (816–561–2916). Excellent choice of French cuisine in this small establishment. L, 11:30 A.M.–2 P.M.; D, 6–10 P.M. Closed Sun. Major credit cards.

Plaza III—The Steakhouse. *Deluxe.* 4749 Pennsylvania, on Country Club Plaza, Kansas City, MO 64112 (816–753–0000). This long-established eatery recently renovated its menu and interior to become a "classy" steak house. Famous steak soup still served. L, 11:30 A.M.–2:30 P.M.; D, 5:30–10 P.M., until 11 P.M. Fri. and Sat., Sun., 5–9 P.M.

Savoy Grill. *Deluxe.* 9th and Central, Kansas City, MO (816–842–3890). This historic landmark has been operating since 1903. White tile floor and crisp white linen. Lobster specialty, flown in daily. Open daily at 11 A.M., except open at 4 P.M. Sun. Major credit cards.

Starker's. *Expensive.* 200 Nichols Rd., on the Country Club Plaza, Kansas City, MO 64112 (816–753–3565). Eclectic menu including seafood and steaks. Recently redecorated. L, 11 A.M.–3 P.M.; D, 5–11 P.M., daily except major holidays. No lunch on Sun. Major credit cards.

Golden Ox. *Moderate.* 1600 Genessee St., Kansas City, MO 64102 (816–842–2866). In the stockyards district, **the** place to go for famous Kansas City beef. Packed during the American Royal and major events at the adjacent Kemper Arena. Open, Mon.–Sat., 11:20 A.M.–10 P.M.; Sun., 4–10 P.M.; Major credit cards.

Princess Garden. *Moderate.* 8906 Wornall Rd., Kansas City, MO (816–444–3709). Mandarin, Szechwan, and Hunan foods. Families and singles alike are comfortable here. Walnut chicken and steamed dumplings are superb. L, 11:30 A.M.–2 P.M.; D, 5–10 P.M., Tues.–Thurs.; till 11 P.M., Fri. and Sat., Sun., noon–10 P.M. Closed Mon.

Arthur Bryant's Barbecue. *Inexpensive.* 1727 Brooklyn (816–231–1123). Even presidents have eaten the fare from this establishment that Calvin Trillin raved about. Lunch is the best time to come. 10 A.M.–9:30 P.M. Mon–Thurs.; Fri and Sat. til 10 P.M.; Sun 11 A.M.–8 P.M.

St. Louis. Anthony's. *Super Deluxe.* 10 S. Broadway, in Equitable Bldg. St. Louis, MO 63102 (314–231–2434). Specializes in milk-fed veal, fresh seafood, and baby lamb. Free valet parking. Reservations required. D only, 5:30–10:30 P.M., Mon.–Sat. Closed Sun. and major holidays. All major credit cards.

Tony's. *Super Deluxe.* 826 N. Broadway, St. Louis, MO 63102 (314–231–7007). Prime veal and beef, homemade pasta. Elegant atmosphere. Semi-à la carte. D only. Closed Sun. and major holidays. All major credit cards.

Nantucket Cove. *Expensive.* 40 N. Kingshighway, St. Louis, MO 63108 (314–361–0625). In fashionable Central West End. New England seafaring atmosphere in which to dine on red snapper, lobster, and other seafood. D only, 5:30–10:30 Mon.–Fri., until 11:30 Sat. Closed Sun. Major credit cards.

Port St. Louis. *Expensive.* 15 North Central Ave., St. Louis, MO 63105 (314–727–1142). French and American dining in Victorian atmosphere. Major credit cards.

Miss Hulling's Cafeteria. *Inexpensive.* 1103 Locust St. St. Louis, MO 63101 (314–436–0840). Tempting desserts and home-style cooking. Daily specials. Open 6 A.M.–8:15 P.M., Mon.–Sat.

Old Spaghetti Factory. *Inexpensive.* 727 N. First St., St. Louis, MO 63101 (314–621–0276). In Laclede's Landing. Huge portions of pasta. Popular spot, long waits sometimes. Open, 5–10 P.M., Mon.–Thurs.; till 11:30 P.M., Fri; 4 P.M.–11:30 P.M., Sat; 3:30 P.M.–10 P.M., Sun. No credit cards.

LIQUOR LAWS. Liquor may be purchased by the package or by the drink, Mon.–Sat., 6 A.M.–11:30 A.M. Certain qualified establishments in convention trade areas may remain open and sell liquor by the drink until 3 A.M. except Sun. No sales on election days until one half hour after the polls close. Minimum age is 21.

IOWA

The "land between two rivers" holds delights and surprises for the tourist willing to taste them. Not the least of these is the lush, rolling countryside. (And you thought everything was flat between the Missouri River bluffs on the west and the Mississippi River's bluffs in northeast Iowa.)

The Hawkeye State—somehow, they say, the name seems to have evolved from James Fenimore Cooper's *The Last of the Mohicans*—can pleasantly take as much of your time as you'd like to spend exploring it. Count some of the ways, and what you might sample.

Travel I-80, east to west, from the Quad Cities to Council Bluffs, leaving the superhighway now and then for attractions within 30 miles or so—at West Branch, the Herbert Hoover National Historic Site, including the restored birthplace and home of the first President born west of the Mississippi, and the Hoover Presidential Library and Museum; at Iowa City, the University of Iowa and the Old Capitol, seat of Iowa government when the state was admitted to the Union in 1846; the museums, woolen mill, family restaurants, and furniture and other shops of the seven villages of the Amana Colonies, settled in the 1850s by Europeans seeking religious freedom and people today by their descendants; at Tama, the Mesquakie Indian Settlement (and its Pow Wow in August); at Indianola, the National Balloon Museum and summertime hot-air balloon competition; at Ames, Iowa State University; at Boone, the birthplace of first lady Mamie Doud Eisenhower and the Kate Shelley High Bridge, longest and highest double-track railroad bridge in the world; at Winterset, the birthplace of actor John Wayne (and the town is the gateway to six 100-year-old covered bridges nearby and host to the Covered Bridge Festival in October); at Elkhorn, an 1848 Danish windmill in one of the largest Danish settlements in the United States; at Council Bluffs, the home of Civil War General Grenville Dodge, chief construction engineer for the Union Pacific Railroad.

In the middle of the state, skirted by I-80 and I-35, is the State Capitol, Des Moines. This is where we focus our attention for practical information.

PRACTICAL INFORMATION FOR DES MOINES

HOW TO GET THERE. Once a jewel of a maze of railroads, Des Moines now finds its nearest passenger service reduced to an east–west Amtrak line at an impractical 40 mi. south—at Osceola, IA. The convenience of a choice of airlines, bus companies, and the Interstate highway system makes up for the loss of passenger trains.

By plane. Major domestic airlines operating through *Des Moines International Airport* are *American, United, Republic, TWA, Ozark, Frontier,* and *America West.* Smaller lines offer more limited service.

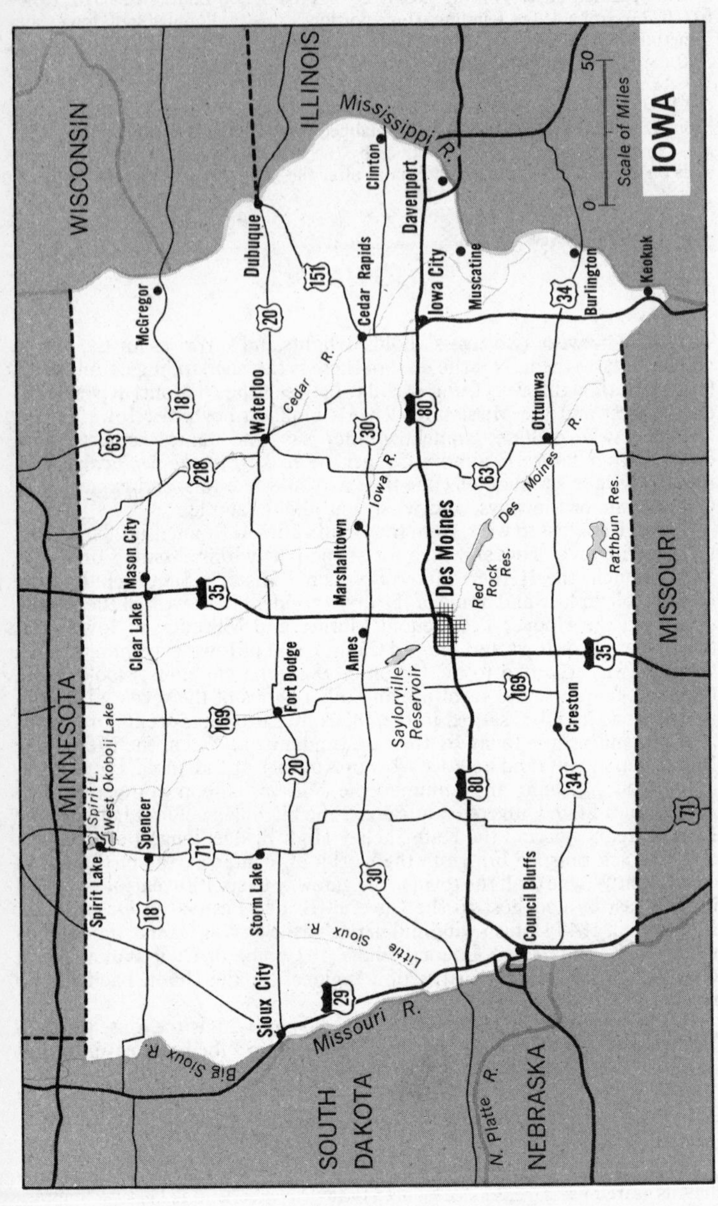
IOWA
Scale of Miles
0
50
WISCONSIN
ILLINOIS
MINNESOTA
SOUTH DAKOTA
NEBRASKA
MISSOURI
Mississippi R.
Missouri R.
Big Sioux R.
Little Sioux R.
N. Platte R.
Cedar R.
Iowa R.
Des Moines R.
Spirit L.
West Okoboji Lake
Saylorville Reservoir
Red Rock Res.
Rathbun Res.
Sioux City
Spirit Lake
Spencer
Storm Lake
Clear Lake
Mason City
Fort Dodge
Ames
Marshalltown
Des Moines
Council Bluffs
Creston
McGregor
Waterloo
Dubuque
Cedar Rapids
Iowa City
Clinton
Davenport
Muscatine
Ottumwa
Burlington
Keokuk
18
71
30
29
20
169
35
80
34
63
218
151

By bus. *Greyhound* and *Trailways* provide nationwide service through terminals in or near the downtown area.

By car. I-80 and I-35 skirt Des Moines to the north and west, with I-235 (MacVicar Frwy.) as the access from both; it runs from a mixmaster exchange north and east of the city, through the downtown area and on west to another exchange just west of suburban West Des Moines. For more leisurely approaches to the city, try U.S. Hwys. 65-69 or 6.

WHEN TO GO. Spring and fall offer the most pleasing temperatures. But the summer months bring special outdoor activities—especially the storied Iowa State Fair in mid-Aug. (it's a cosmopolitan extravaganza, far more than a mere reflection of a corn, hog, and soybean state). And don't overlook winter attractions in sports and the lively arts. The city's elaborate downtown skywalk system tames the sometimes subzero cold of Jan. and Feb. and the high 90s temperatures of July and Aug. The skywalks link virtually everything of importance in the hub of the city and provide immediate access to all manner of shops and other business outlets arrayed along the system.

TOURIST INFORMATION. *Visitors and Tourism section,* of the Iowa Development Commission, Suite A, 600 E. Court Ave., Des Moines, IA 50309 (515–281–3100). *Greater Des Moines Convention and Visitors Bureau,* 309 Court Ave., Des Moines IA 50309 (515–286–4960).

If you're arriving by plane, the airport's Iowa Realty Service Center and the Greater Des Moines Convention and Visitors Bureau booths can help you. Or, if you're driving on the Interstate system, look for a Welcome Center—8 are open at rest centers around the state, usually mid-May–mid-Sept.

Best bet for the week's events in Des Moines, plus tips on movies and where to eat and drink: Pick up "Datebook," published each Thurs. morning in The Des Moines *Register.* You can also try the T.I.P.S. number, (286–4991).

TELEPHONES. Des Moines' area code, 515, applies to the vertical middle third of Iowa (to the west, the code is 712; to the east, 319). A local call costs 25 cents from a pay telephone, with no time limit. The local calling area covers Des Moines and its suburbs, plus 23 other communities, including a number in 3 adjoining counties. In Des Moines, dial 1411 for directory assistance; from elsewhere, dial 515–555–1212.

EMERGENCY TELEPHONE NUMBERS. The main emergency number for *police, fire department, county sheriff,* and *ambulance* is 911. The *Iowa State Highway Patrol Helpline* is 800–362–2200. *Poison* information is available at 283–6254. Other numbers: *Crisis Line counseling* (244–1000); *Rape Crisis Center* (286–3838).

HOW TO GET AROUND. Driving yourself is preferable, although buses (information, 283–8100) serve much of the city (but not the airport) and taxicab service is available. A taxi ride to the downtown area from Des Moines International Airport is about 6 mi. and about $7. A *Twin Rivers Limousine* (288–1110) frequently is waiting at the airport, or one can be summoned by phone; the fare downtown is $4. *Carey Limousine* (244–0101) is by phone only.

HINTS TO MOTORISTS. Numbered streets in Des Moines run north and south. Westward from the Des Moines River downtown, the streets are 1st to 63rd; eastward from the river are E. 1st to E. 43rd. West of 9th St. in the downtown area, only two streets give access to the south side of the city: Fleur Dr. (at about 17th St.), which is the route to the airport, and 63rd St.

If cross traffic permits, turning right at a red light (after a full stop) is all right at an intersection unless a sign forbids it. Many major intersections include left-hand turn lanes, with green-arrow signals. Rush hours are 7–9 A.M. and 4–6 P.M. During those hours, parking is forbidden on one or both sides of major streets, including many parking meter areas downtown.

TOURS. Guided tours by vehicle, on foot, specialized sightseeing, or any kind of tour you wish, for a small group or large, can be tailored by *Des Moines Tours* *and Convention Services, Inc.,* 309 Court Ave., Suite 224, Des Moines, IA 50322 (515–246–5825); multilingual service is available. Another services is *Kaleidoscope World Ltd.,* 3908 Greenwood Drive, Des Moines, IA 50312 (515–279–1766).

PARKS AND GARDENS. A dozen large parks and more than a dozen smaller parks give the city of Des Moines major areas of green space, and parks in suburbs continue the trend. Hours for Des Moines's parks are generally 6 A.M.–10 or 11 P.M., and admission to the parks themselves is free. Where shelters are available, reservations can be made by calling 271–4719.

Greenwood Park (81 acres), 48th St. and Grand Ave. (271–4708), and adjoining **Ashworth Park** (66 acres) embrace the Des Moines Art Center, the Des Moines Center of Science and Industry, and the city's finest rose garden. Also included are a lagoon and excellent picnic facilities.

Water Works Park (1,500 acres), accessible from Fleur Dr. or Valley Dr. (283–8755), explodes into color when the flowering crab trees bloom in the spring. The Raccoon River provides fishing.

Waveland Park (193 acres) includes an observatory, tennis courts at 928 Polk Blvd. (277–9063), and one of the United States's highest-rated municipal golf courses at 4908 University Ave. (271–4705). **Birdland Park** (70 acres), E. 29th St. and Arthur Ave. (265–4464), includes golf (265–4136) and tennis, plus athletic fields. **Blank Park** (190 acres), 711 County Line Rd., gives golfers another test of skills (285–0864).

Ewing Park (357 acres), 5100 Indianola Ave. (285–4301), is a mecca for lilac lovers in the blooming season. **Grays Lake Park** (164 acres), 1631 Fleur Dr., is a center-of-the-city spot to boat, swim, hike, picnic, or just relax for a couple of hours.

Des Moines Botanical Center. 909 E. River Dr., Des Moines, IA 50316 (515–283–4148). The nearly 1,000 species and cultivars from all over the world live in a controlled atmosphere under a crystogon dome. In addition about 4,000 ornamental foliage or flowering plants make up each of six seasonal displays. Open daily 10 A.M.–5 P.M.

State Parks. These parks have a daily vehicle admission fee of $2, or a season fee of $5.50. *Walnut Woods State Park* (285–4502), on S.W. 52nd Ave.—an east–west road—southwest of Des Moines, is situated along the Raccoon River and offers camping (for an extra fee), hiking, fishing, and groves of the trees for which the park was named. *Big Creek State Park* (984–6473), on Iowa Hwy. 415 northwest of Polk City, which is north and west of Des Moines, does not permit camping, but you can picnic, hike, or go for the big attraction: big fish.

Saylorville Lake, a 5,400 acre, 16-mi.-long body, offers a sand beach with restrooms and a large parking lot at the Oak Grove Recreation Area on the east side of the lake. But the U.S. Army Corps of Engineers, which administers this Des Moines River flood-control reservoir, permits swimming everywhere in the lake except where specifically prohibited. There are also 4 *campgrounds* with 450 sites. For details on camping—and Saylorville's many other activities—contact Saylorville Lake, Rte. 3, Johnston, IA 50131 (515–276–4656).

HISTORIC SITES AND HOUSES. Hoyt Sherman Place. 1501 Woodland Ave. (243–0913). Home (built in 1877) of the city's foremost pioneer businessman, it is the focal point of the Sherman Hill area. Included are original furnishings in the dining room, an art museum, and an array of antiques, statuary, paintings, and cut glass. Call to arrange guided tours.

Iowa Capitol. This statehouse, bounded by E. 10th and 12th Sts. and by Grand Ave. and Walnut St., dominates other buildings in the 165-acre, state-office complex. The Capitol's gold-leafed dome commands the view east from Locust St. in downtown Des Moines. The building was begun in 1871 and completed in 1886. Twenty-nine varieties of marble and more than a dozen different woods went into the construction. Building hours are 8 A.M.–4:30 P.M., Mon.–Fri.; 8 A.M.–4 P.M., Sat., Sun., and holidays. Guided tours are available on weekdays—call 515–281–5591, or stop at the visitor information center in the rotunda on the first floor. Stroll the grounds to see the complex's memorials.

Salisbury House. 4025 Tonawanda Dr. (279–9711). A 42-room castle on 10 acres of woodland, this 1920s replica of King's House in Salisbury, England, is now the home of an art collection, library of rare books, and the Iowa State Education Association. Call about tours.

Terrace Hill. 2300 Grand Ave. (281–3604). This 20-room mansion built in 1869 and now the home of Iowa's governor, has been called "the finest example of Victorian architecture west of the Mississippi River." Tours, Mon.–Thurs., 10 A.M.–1:30 P.M.; Sun., 1–4:30 P.M. Closed holidays and Jan.–Feb.

Valley Junction. In the early 1900s, the Junction was a major railroad center. Today, the venerable buildings on and near lower 5th St. in West Des Moines (the modern name) house a noteworthy collection of two dozen antique shops, plus arts and crafts and other specialty shops.

MUSEUMS AND GALLERIES. Des Moines Art Center. 4700 Grand Ave., Des Moines, IA 50312 (515–277–4405). The center's exhibits include paintings, prints, and sculpture from its permanent collection as well as shows from elsewhere. Museum shop, restaurant. Tues., Wed., and Fri. 11 A.M.–5 P.M., Thurs. until 9 P.M., Fri. and Sat. 11 A.M.–5 P.M.; Sun. noon–5 P.M.

Iowa Historical Building. E. Sixth and Locust Ave., Des Moines, IA 50319 (515–281–5111). Some 1.3 million items of artifacts and documents in four floors of this stately old structure tell Iowa's history. (To house the growing collection, a new building near the Capitol opened in 1987.) Hours are 9 A.M.–4:30 P.M., Tues.–Sat.; noon–4:30 P.M., Sun. Admission free.

Living History Farms. Off I-35 and I-80 at Exit 125; the mailing address is 2600 N.W. 111th St., Urbandale, IA 50322 (515–278–5286). This 600-acre, open-air, agricultural museum tells the story of Midwest farming from the Ioway Indians to the solar farm home of today. Interpreters in historical clothing re-create the farming routine of bygone days. No two days are alike, and special events are frequent. Open May–Oct., 9 A.M.–5 P.M., Mon.–Sat.; 11 A.M.–6 P.M., Sun.—plus a week of Christmas activities in mid-Dec. $4–$6.

ARTS AND ENTERTAINMENT. Music. *Des Moines Symphony* concerts are at the Civic Center of Greater Des Moines, 221 Walnut St., Des Moines, IA 50309. Call 515–244–0222 for schedule and ticket information. The *Drake University Symphony* and other Drake musical organizations—concert band, jazz band, choir, chamber chorale—present concerts in the Hall of the Performing Arts in Harmon Fine Arts Center, 26th St. and Carpenter Ave., Des Moines, IA 50311 (515–271–3841).

Dance. The *Des Moines Ballet* performs at both the Civic Center (243–1120) and Harmon Fine Arts Center (271–3841); at Drake University; the ballet's office is at 4333 Park Ave., Des Moines, IA 50321 (515–282–3480). Occasional performances of *Dance Co'motion,* 129 E. 7th St., Ames, IA 50010, are in Des Moines.

Opera. The *Des Moines Metro Opera,* 106 W. Boston Ave., Indianola, IA 50125 (515–961–6221), performs in the Blank Performing Arts Center at Simpson College in Indianola, a few miles south of Des Moines. June–July.

Stage. The Civic Center of Greater Des Moines, 221 Walnut St., Des Moines, IA 50309 (515–243–1120) is the site for major road shows, as well as individual performers in comedy and music. The *Des Moines Community Playhouse,* 831 42nd St., Des Moines, IA 50312 (515–277–6261) stages musicals and more popular plays on its main stage, offbeat plays in its arena theater and children's shows on the main stage. The *Ingersoll Dinner Theater,* 3711 Ingersoll Ave., Des Moines, IA 50312 (515–274–4686), throughout the year stages locally produced popular shows, plus special performances by touring entertainers.

ACCOMMODATIONS. All hotel and motel room charges are subject to the state's 4 percent sales tax, plus a locally levied 7% hotel–motel tax. Double-occupancy lodgings are categorized this way: *Expensive,* $60 and higher; *Moderate,* $35–60; *Inexpensive,* under $35. These categories do not include the 11% tax. Bargain weekend rates are available at a very few motels, and a very few also offer lower Oct. 1–Apr. 30 rates. Many places offer senior discounts.

Expensive

Adventureland Inn. Box 3355, Des Moines, IA 50316 (515–265–7321). 130 units, at Adventureland Park (off I-80 at Exit 142 just northeast of Des Moines). Indoor courtyard, swimming pool, restaurants and lounge.

Des Moines Airport Hilton. 6111 Fleur Dr., Des Moines, IA 50321 (515–287–2400 or 800–HILTONS). 225 units, indoor pool, sauna, fitness center, restaurant, lounge, across from airport.

Des Moines Marriott Hotel. 700 Grand Ave., Des Moines, IA 50309 (515–245–5500 or 800–228–9290). 416 units, downtown, city's newest hotel, swimming pool, game room, 2 restaurants, 3 lounges.

Hotel Fort Des Moines. 10th and Walnut Sts., Des Moines, IA 50309 (515–243–1161). 240 units, downtown, free parking, restaurant, lounge, game room, movies.

Savery Hotel and Spa. 4th and Locust Sts., Des Moines, IA 50309 (515–244–2151). Connected to downtown skywalk system. Health spa, jogging track, restaurant, lounge.

Moderate

Best Western Des Moines International. 1810 Army Post Rd., Des Moines, IA 50321 (515–287–6464 or 800–528–1234). 150 units, restaurant and lounge, indoor pool, sauna, enclosed courtyard.

Super Eight Westmark. Ashworth Rd at I-80, West Des Moines, IA 50265 (515–223–6500). 165 units, restaurant, lounge, indoor pool, outdoor tennis.

Inexpensive

Blue Bird Motel. 6501 Hickman Rd., Des Moines, IA 50322 (515–276–6721). 18 units, kitchenettes.

Econo Lodge. 5626 Douglas Ave., Des Moines, IA 50310 (515–278–1601 or 800–533–2666). 50 units, HBO, restaurant, lounge, outdoor pool.

SPECIALTY LODGING. If the thought of Iowa conjures up images of tall corn and quaint farmhouses, you may opt for a sample of country living at one of the state's farm or ranch facilities. **Little House in the Woods** (319–783–7774), near Elkader, offers a stay in a Victorian house amid a 1,000-acre farm. Another option is lodging at one of Iowa's historic homes converted to a bed and breakfast. **The Redstone Inn,** 504 Bluff, Dubuque, IA 52001 (319–582–1894), features overnight accommodations and English afternoon tea in a mansion (1894) listed on the National Register of Historic Places.

RESTAURANTS. The restaurants of Des Moines offer menu variety that has been considerably amplified in recent years, particularly for oriental tastes. Generally, casual dress is acceptable. There's no general rule for reservations, so inquiring before you arrive at a particular place is advisable. Cocktail service is generally available except where noted.

Restaurants are listed according to the price of a three-course dinner (excluding the 4% sales tax, beverage, and tip): *Expensive,* $12 and higher; *Moderate,* $6–$12; *Inexpensive,* under $6.

Expensive

Crystal Tree. 6111 Fleur Dr., at Airport Hilton (287–2032). General menu, "Fabulous salad bar." B, L, Mon.–Fri. D, daily. Sun. brunch. AE, CB, DC, MC, V.

Mandarin. 3520 Beaver Ave. (277–6263). Mandarin and Szechwan cuisine. L, Mon.–Fri. and Sun. D, daily. AE, CB, DC, MC, V.

Shogun Steak House of Japan. 2900 University Ave., West Des Moines (225–3325). Steak, chicken, shrimp prepared at tableside. D, daily. AE, DC, MC, V.

Moderate

Colorado Feed and Grain Co. 1925 Ingersoll Ave. (244–4450). Saloon and vittles in an old-West setting. L, D, daily; Sun. brunch. AE, DC, MC, V.

Gino's. 2809 6th Ave. (282–4029). Genuine Italian specialties, steaks, seafood. D, Mon.–Sat. AE, DC, MC, V.

Waterfront Seafood. 2900 University Ave., West Des Moines (223–5106). Fresh seafood, oyster bar; wine and beer only. L, D, Mon.–Sat. MC, V.

Inexpensive

Boswell's Select Foods. 1409 Harding Rd. (243–9518). Hash brown potatoes a specialty. Beer only. B, L, daily. No credit cards.

Julio's. 308 Court Ave. (244–1710). Tex-Mex food, and gourmet burgers are served in this renovated turn-of-the-century storefront building. L, D. All major credit cards.

A Taste of Thailand. 215 E. Walnut St. (243–9521). Traditional Thai cooking. Beer and wine only. L, D, daily. AE, MC, V.

LIQUOR LAWS. The minimum age for drinking or buying alcoholic beverages is 21. Mon. through Sat., the sale of alcohol is permitted from 6 A.M. until 2 A.M., and bars and restaurants generally are open until that hour, though most do not serve food as late as that closing hour; on Sun., alcohol cannot be sold before 10 A.M. or after midnight. Package liquor is sold only in state-owned stores; seven such stores are in Des Moines, and three more in suburbs; the closing hours of the stores vary, but all are much earlier than the bar and restaurant liquor-sales deadline. Supermarkets and other grocery stores usually sell wine, although the selection is narrower than in the state liquor stores. Beer for consumption off the premises is for sale in supermarkets and other grocery stores, convenience stores, and some service stations.

THE UPPER GREAT LAKES

Michigan, Wisconsin, Minnesota

by
JERRY MINNICH and DON DAVENPORT

Mr. Minnich is a freelance writer in Madison, Wisconsin. He has published four books and has written for a number of magazines and newspapers on gardening, food, and travel. Mr. Davenport is a Madison-based freelance writer/photographer. He is the author of four books, including Fodor's Michigan, Wisconsin, Minnesota, *and writes for a number of magazines and newspapers on travel and Great Lakes subjects.*

The Upper Great Lakes region hugs the largest concentration of fresh water in the world. The total surface area of Lakes Superior, Huron, and Michigan is 77,000 square miles—an area almost as great as the land area of the entire state of Minnesota. In addition, Minnesota is proud to call itself "the land of 10,000 lakes," and the surface area of the Michigan and Wisconsin lakes together almost equals that of the Minnesota lakes. Moreover, the great Mississippi River cuts through Minnesota and runs alongside Wisconsin, connecting the region with the river ports of St. Louis, Memphis, and New Orleans.

The lakes dominate nearly every aspect of life in this area—its economic base, its industry and agriculture, its climate, and the very way of life of its people.

Long before the development of railroads and highways, the Great Lakes provided a transportation system between the populous east coast and the great plains and forests of the Midwest. First plied by fur traders, the region later yielded its enormous reserves of lumber and fish, then became host to major agricultural enterprises.

Today, with the completion of the Saint Lawrence Seaway, goods can be transported from Duluth 2,342 miles to the Atlantic, and from there to the rest of the world. The Illinois Waterway provides passage for small vessels from Lake Michigan to the Mississippi River, and then to New Orleans and the Gulf of Mexico. Ships carrying lumber, grain, and iron ore sail from Duluth to Sault Ste. Marie, through the Soo locks and into Lake Huron, around Detroit and on to the Atlantic. Ore ships move constantly across the water, carrying millions of tons of iron ore from the shores of Lake Huron, through the Straits of Mackinac and down Lake Michigan to the roaring steel mills of Gary, Indiana. Wheat grown in the western plains is milled into flour in Minneapolis, then shipped by ocean-going freighters through the St. Lawrence to the ports of Europe and Africa. Minneapolis alone has a grain storage capacity of 124 million bushels, largest in the U.S. Duluth can store another 76 million bushels. The numbers are staggering—but fully in keeping with the scale of the lakes themselves. Both the industrial and the agricultural vitality of the entire Midwest stem directly from its greatest resource, the gray-blue waters of the Great Lakes.

"Say yes to Michigan." "You're among friends" in Wisconsin. "Explore Minnesota." The tourism divisions of the three states urge vacationers to do these things, and vacationers seem to be responding in record numbers. The tourism industry is an important part of the region's economic base, accounting for $11 billion in annual spending by out-of-state visitors. Wisconsin accounts for more than half of this total and has succeeded with a minimum of promotion but with solid delivery of the things tourists value most: good, toll-free highways, an excellent state park system, and some of the lowest vacation costs of any region in the nation.

This is north woods country, the land of Hiawatha and Gitche Gumme, where pine forests encircle clean, sparkling lakes. It is a place to get away from the crowds, not to compete with them.

The fishing here is some of the best anywhere, offering every freshwater experience from big-water coho salmon fishing on a charter boat in Lake Michigan to lazily dipping a line from a pier in backwoods Minnesota. For biking, hiking, skiing, backpacking, and other low-key, nature-oriented pursuits, you can indeed say yes to Michigan, escape to Wisconsin, and explore Minnesota.

History

The real pioneers of the upper Great Lakes were not the French fur traders and missionaries who explored the region in the mid-17th century but the various Indian peoples who, archaeologists tell us, roamed the area as far back as 9500 B.C., thousands of years before the development of civilization in ancient Egypt. By A.D. 1668, when Father Jacques Marquette and his Jesuit band established the first white settlement where Sault Ste. Marie now stands, Indian peoples occupied all the territory around the lakes. The Chippewa held the entire northern region, including all of Lake Superior. Southern regions were occupied by the Miami, Fox, Sauk, Winnebago, Menominee, Huron, Ottawa, Potawatomi, and other peoples.

Unique to this area are the Effigy Mound builders, who were concentrated in what is now Wisconsin, from Green Bay south to Beloit. For burials they constructed low mounds in the shapes of buffalo, bears, lizards, and various birds. Most of these mounds, built before A.D. 1300, have now been destroyed, but hundreds have survived and are now protected. Visitors may see 31 examples of mounds at Lizard Mound State Park, near West Bend, Wisconsin, and another 18 at Indian Mound Park, near Sheyboygan, Wisconsin, at the intersection of County Highways KK and EE.

Voyageur
National Park
ONTARIO
Isle Royale National
Superior
National
Forest
Lake
Chippewa
National
Forest
Apostle Islands
National
Lakeshore
Duluth
MINNESOTA
Madeline Island
Mississippi River
35
WISCONSIN
Minneapolis
Stillwater
St. Paul
94
Eau Claire
Wabasha
Winona
Mankato
Rochester
La Crosse
90
Horicon
Wildlife
and
90
Austin
Madison
IOWA
N
0
100

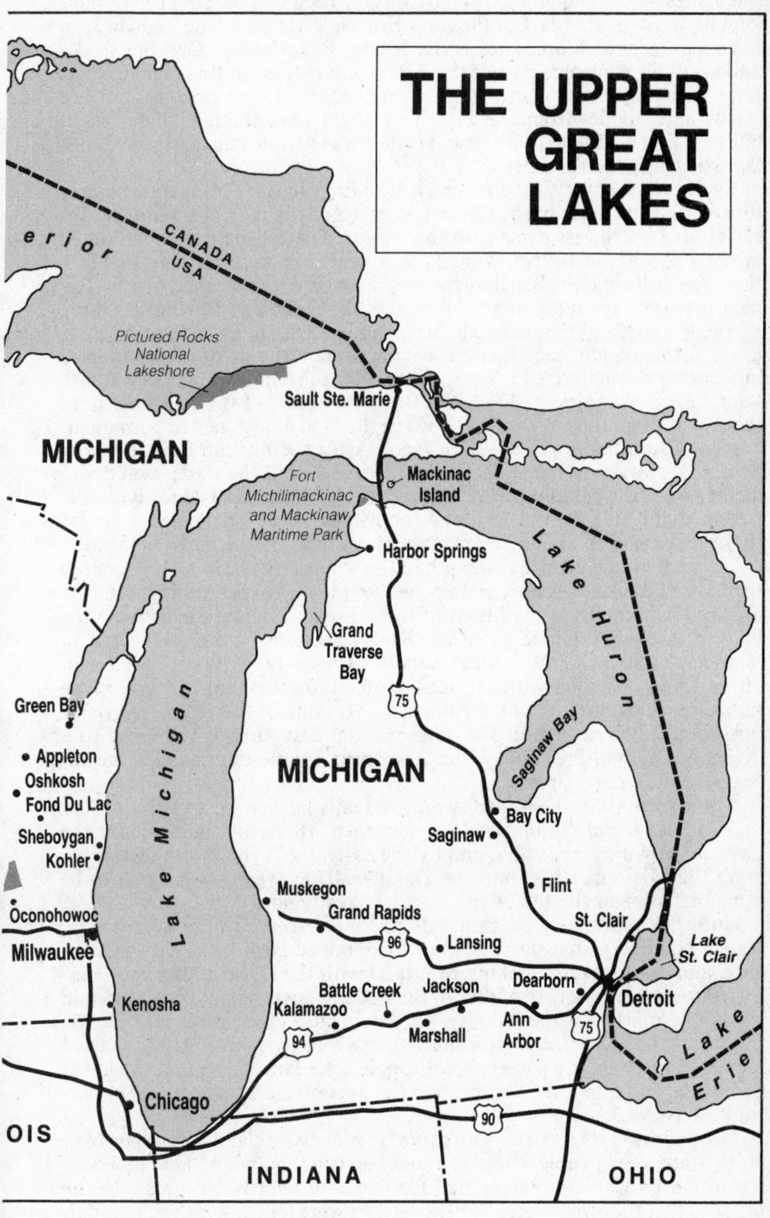
THE UPPER GREAT LAKES
erior
CANADA
USA
Pictured Rocks National Lakeshore
Sault Ste. Marie
MICHIGAN
Fort Michilimackinac and Mackinaw Maritime Park
Mackinac Island
Harbor Springs
Lake Huron
Grand Traverse Bay
75
Green Bay
Appleton
Oshkosh
Fond Du Lac
Sheboygan
Kohler
Lake Michigan
MICHIGAN
Saginaw Bay
Bay City
Saginaw
Flint
Muskegon
Grand Rapids
96
Lansing
St. Clair
Lake St. Clair
Oconohowoc
Milwaukee
Battle Creek
Jackson
Dearborn
Detroit
Kenosha
Kalamazoo
Marshall
Ann Arbor
94
75
Lake Erie
Chicago
90
OIS
INDIANA
OHIO

The coming of the French marked the beginning of the end of the Indian way of life as it had been practiced for thousands of years. In the histories, the names of key Indian figures have largely been lost because the Indians kept no written records. But the early French leaders are well known: Jean Nicollet, Jacques Marquette, Louis Jolliet, Rene-Robert Cavelier de La Salle—all have become part of the permanent culture of this region. Some have national forests named after them, others federal prisons, and not a few, automobiles from Detroit. (You might have thought that Detroit built the first Cadillac. In historical fact, it was Antoine de la Mothe Cadillac who built the first Detroit.)

By the 18th century, the French and the English were competing heavily for the rich fur trade in the Great Lakes region, as they also searched for the elusive northwest passage to the Orient. The competition culminated in the French and Indian War of 1754, which came to an end in 1763, the French losing all their North American territory to the British. The next twenty years, including the period of the American Revolution, were marked by further friction and fighting among British, French, and Americans in this region, each faction seeking to gain the favor of the Indians in securing the lucrative fur trade. Even after they finally made peace with their former colonies, in 1783, the British dominated the fur trade until the conclusion of the War of 1812, when the U.S. finally gained permanent control. From that point on, John Jacob Astor's American Fur Company held total sway over the Great Lakes fur trade, until the trade itself dwindled toward the middle of the 19th century. Mackinac Island, lying between Michigan's upper and lower peninsulas, is the best historic site for those interested in seeing remnants and artifacts of the early fur trade.

The victory and growing strength of the young American nation secured the entire Great Lakes area and opened up the region for mining, lumbering, and fishing. Then the thrust of the railroads opened the gates to the flood of westward-bound pioneers. Rich lead mines were discovered in Wisconsin and vast iron ore deposits in Minnesota. Millions of acres of virgin forest, coupled with the ideal water transportation system, made lumbering king throughout the northern sections of the region. Agriculture soon followed. Wheat was important at first, then it gave way to a diversified agriculture. Today, the Wisconsin–Minnesota region is the nation's leading dairy area.

At the same time, the Indians were gradually pushed westward. By 1855 the Chippewa had relinquished most of their Minnesota lands under the pressure of white expansion, and by the early 1860s they were driven beyond the Missouri River into the Dakotas. They were never again to be a major factor in the life of the Great Lakes region.

Until the building of the railroads, the major route to the west was by water. The Erie Canal, completed in 1825, linked New York City to Lake Erie, and another route linking Montreal with the Great Lakes was completed four years later. In addition, the Federal government began to build roads—primarily for the military—in Michigan's lower peninsula. By the middle of the 1830s the Detroit harbor was a lively place. Ships departed almost daily, carrying passengers through Lake Huron, around the lower peninsula, and into Lake Michigan to the western lands, where new opportunities awaited.

Most of the early settlers, who came from New England and upper New York State, were people whose fortunes had run thin, whose land had been worn out, or who simply yearned for new and uncrowded areas. In the decades that followed, these Yankee settlers were joined—rather, inundated—by wave after wave of European immigrants, most from central, northern, and western Europe. By 1890 the region was populated mostly by immigrants and the children of immigrants. One 19th-century diary reported the scene from the port of Milwaukee: "The torrent of emigration swells very strongly toward this place. During the fine weather, the poor refugees arrive daily in their national dresses all travel-soiled and worn . . . . Here, on the pier, I see disembarking the Germans, the Norwegians, the Swedes, the Swiss. . . . "

Today, the ethnic heritage of these European forebears permeates every aspect of life and culture in the region. Later immigrations of groups such as Poles, Italians, and Irish settled largely in the major urban centers. In the rural Great Lakes, however, it is the northern and western Europeans who dominate the culture today. The legend of Paul Bunyan still lives in Minnesota. Old World Wisconsin, near Eagle, celebrates 19th-century farm life on a Yankee, German, Norwegian, Danish, and Finnish farm. Norwegian Independence Day (*Syttende Mai*) is the biggest holiday of the year in Stoughton, Wisconsin. Even in the Italian-sounding town of Milan, Minnesota, the big community event of the holiday season is "Norwegian Christmas."

Cities

The Upper Great Lakes region is still largely rural. With a tristate population of about 18 million, there is only one city—Detroit—that has more than a million people. Milwaukee and the twin cities of Minneapolis and St. Paul still retain a small-town character despite their populations of more than a half-million each.

Detroit. Settled by the French in 1701 because of its strategic position in the Great Lakes chain, Detroit seemed destined to remain a small town whose main industry was carriage-making until a man named Henry Ford came to town with a new idea for manufacturing cars on an assembly line. As the automobile took America by storm, Detroit prospered as "the Motor City," one of America's industrial giants. Today the city, still preeminent in automobile manufacturing despite stiff foreign competition, is also a leading producer of office equipment, television components, pharmaceuticals, marine engines, meat products, and paints. It is one of the busiest ports in the nation, strategically located on the Canadian border between Lake Erie and Lake St. Clair.

In sharp contrast to the rest of the region, the pace of life in Detroit is definitely quick and businesslike. Like Chicago and New York, this is a working city with a certain hard edge. And like other great cities, Detroit offers a broad range of cultural opportunities. Its citizens are justly proud of the Detroit Civic Center, covering 75 acres along the downtown riverfront. The Center comprises Cobo Hall and Arena, the Joe Louis Sports Arena (home of the Detroit Red Wings hockey team), the historic Old Mariners' Church, and the impressive Renaissance Center, five glass towers that hold thousands of offices as well as restaurants, shops, theaters, and a major hotel.

Visitors seeking to soak up the region's history will definitely want to visit the Detroit Historical Museum, where exhibits trace the history of the city from earliest times. Other must-see features of Detroit include the Detroit Science Center (featuring a space theater) and the Henry Ford Museum and Greenfield Village in nearby Dearborn, two of the most popular tourist attractions in the entire region.

Milwaukee. Despite its population of more than 600,000, Milwaukee seems to be less a big city than a collection of small towns. Loyalties here are often to neighborhoods first, the city second. German neighborhoods, Black neighborhoods, Polish, Irish, Norwegian, Serbian—all have contributed to the ethnic diversity of this city, making it a very interesting place to live and work in or to visit.

Here, on the western shore of Lake Michigan only 93 miles north of Chicago, three rivers converge to flow into Lake Michigan. Again, the site of a major city was determined by its water location. In the 17th century

Milwaukee was a trading post, and before that it was an important gathering place for various Indian peoples.

In the 19th century Milwaukee grew at a very rapid pace, along with Chicago and other favored settlements of the region, as the European immigrants streamed westward. The key element in Milwaukee was the arrival, in 1848, of many German families who, having failed to dislodge monarchies at home, decided to flee to the New World. These were not, generally, your typical "poor and wretched." Many were highly educated families of substance, and they quickly became the dominant, if not the most numerous, ethnic group in the city. Where there are Germans, of course, there is beer (including beer gardens and breweries), polkas, dancing, and hearty food. There are still all these things in Milwaukee. Although the city's reputation as the beer capital of America has suffered in recent years, the German influence is still very strong. There are reminders of it everywhere, from the Pabst Theater to the Schlitz Audubon Center to the famous Mader's and Karl Ratzsch restaurants, even all the way out to Milwaukee County Stadium, home of the Milwaukee Brewers baseball team. This is still Beer Town, USA.

The visitor to Milwaukee generally feels instantly at ease because the city lacks the frenzied pace of some large cities and because the people are friendly and easygoing, especially in "the neighborhoods." When in Milwaukee, don't miss the Pabst Mansion, a 37-room Flemish Renaissance home built in 1893 for the beer baron. Other top attractions include the Schlitz Audubon Center, the Milwaukee County Zoo, and the Milwaukee Public Museum. Brewing giants like the Miller and Pabst breweries offer tours daily. Smaller breweries like Sprecher and the Water Street Brewery also welcome visitors.

Minneapolis and St. Paul. Many American cities began as military forts, which encouraged settlers to live in the nearby protected lands. So it was with St. Paul, which was born as Fort Snelling, at the fork of the Mississippi and Minnesota rivers. (Fort Snelling State Park marks the spot today.) As in other prime locations throughout the region, the big influx of European settlers arrived in the mid to late 19th century. The French Canadians were first on the scene, soon to be followed by large numbers of Swedes and Norwegians and, later, Germans, Czechs, Poles, and Finns. Minneapolis–St. Paul became a flour-milling center quite early in its history, and it remains one to the present day. Major plants of Pillsbury, General Mills, and Nabisco are still located here, alongside the high-tech plants of Honeywell and Control Data Corporation.

Running counter to the recent economic troubles of America's industrial belt, the twin cities of Minneapolis and St. Paul have prospered. Minneapolis is a major industrial city, enjoying the latest in high-tech research. The downtown area has been revitalized by the demolition of 17 blocks of old buildings, making room for new glass office towers and hotels, tree-lined plazas, fountains, miniparks, and—to make the snowy winters more navigable—enclosed pedestrian skywalks.

St. Paul, the State Capitol, is the beautiful and sedate twin, a city of hills, trees, and stately homes. The metropolitan area is full of parks, small lakes, and recreation areas. In the estimation of many, Minneapolis–St. Paul offers the perfect combination of big city culture and small town friendliness, cleanliness, and affordability.

Education and the arts are both very important here. The area is home to more than a dozen institutions of higher learning, anchored by the Minneapolis–St. Paul campus of the University of Minnesota and its more than 50,000 students. This is also the home of the internationally famous Tyrone Guthrie Theater, one of America's premier repertory companies.

When in the area, be sure to see the Minneapolis Society of Fine Arts Park, covering 17 acres; the Walker Art Center, which displays modern American and European art; and the Science Museum of Minnesota, which has outstanding space exhibits. The Minnesota Zoo houses more than 1,700 animals and 2,000 varieties of plants.

Fishing the Great Lakes

For the last 150 years, the history of fishing in the western Great Lakes has been one of legislative battles, court trials, and sharp accusations. Commercial fishermen maintain that government regulation deprives them of a livelihood. Sport anglers complain that the greed of the commercial fisheries is ruining fishing here forever. Both sometimes grumble that Indian treaty rights are unfair to the rest of the population. And the federal and state governments—not to mention the Canadian national and provincial governments—are caught somewhere in the middle. This controversy is not likely to be resolved in the near future.

The Indian peoples who lived on the shores of the lakes depended on fish as a major food source at all seasons of the year. Fishing with nets and spears, they easily harvested enough whitefish, sturgeon, and trout to supply their families. The early French fur traders and missionaries also depended heavily on fish from Huron, Michigan, and Superior.

The potential for trouble began around 1830, when some of the first permanent settlers tapped into the wealth to be derived from the lake fish when harvested and shipped to urban markets. The first commercial fishing operation was established on Lake Michigan, at Two Rivers. Three partners collected fish at a number of Lake Michigan stations, salted them, and delivered them to markets in Detroit. Soon they were packing 2,000 barrels of fish yearly. Later in the 1830s, as the immigration wave began, demand for the succulent whitefish grew along with it. More commercial fishermen joined the industry, selling to urban markets in Milwaukee and Chicago, where wholesalers redistributed the fish by rail to the entire Midwest. Pressure on the fish population increased.

By 1875, Chicago markets alone were handling 12 million pounds of fish a year, and still the demand outstripped the supply. The pressure increased. Three years later, more than 23 million pounds—mostly the favored whitefish—were removed from Lake Michigan alone. By this time the efficient gill net was in use and gill-net steamers were a frequent sight on the lakes. By 1885, more than 1,400 commercial fishing boats were working Lake Michigan and the market area had extended to the east coast and far into the west. Sturgeon—formerly considered a trash fish—were sought for their eggs, which when processed into caviar were in demand throughout the country and in Europe.

It was at about this time that the whitefish population began to decline. The commercial fisheries, however, merely filled the void by catching more trout and herring. The last great year of commercial fishing on Lake Michigan was 1908, when a record 47 million pounds was harvested. All fishing declined gradually after that, as governments argued for regulation, and the fisheries, fiercely resisting any form of regulation, complained that government failed in its restocking programs.

The problem, however, was not simply one of overfishing. Cities and towns along the shoreline used the lakes for drinking water and also as sewers. Industrial plants and lumbermills flushed all their wastes into streams feeding the lakes. Clear cutting of timber to increase farmland caused the erosion of millions of tons of soil into the lakes.

Then, in the 1930s, the dread sea lamprey made its way from the Atlantic into the Great Lakes. This eellike parasite attaches itself to a larger fish and sucks its host's blood until it dies. Then the lamprey moves on to find another host. By 1945, the lampreys had decimated the trout population in Lake Michigan and seriously reduced it in the other lakes. State, federal, and Canadian governments at last responded to the crisis and managed to control the lampreys with chemicals. By then, alewives—the favorite food of lake trout—had expanded wildly in Lake Michigan. To control the alewives, coho salmon were stocked in the mid-1960s.

Today there is a careful, government-controlled balance between commercial and recreational fishing on the Great Lakes. Commercial fishing, if not thriving, is at least surviving, on catches of yellow perch, whitefish, and chub. Salmon and lake trout are reserved for sport fishermen.

Sport fishing in the Great Lakes today is an angler's dream come true. Six species of trout and salmon are available in addition to yellow perch, walleye, and smallmouth bass. Catching a lake trout or salmon can be the thrill of a lifetime, for, if these fish have any one thing in common, it's size. Trophy fish are the star attraction, but they aren't the only thing drawing people to the Great Lakes. Trolling, surf casting, and stream, pier, and breakwater fishing are popular choices, each with its own appeal. Dipping for smelt is also popular in the spring.

The Call of the Wild

Most visitors come to the Upper Great Lakes not to experience urban life but to escape it. And here, particularly on the southern and western shores of Lake Superior, is perhaps the ultimate place to get far, far away. There are hundreds of thousands of acres that have not changed basically since the first Europeans set foot on our Atlantic shores. Here you can hear the call of the loon, experience the soft bed of a primeval forest, go fishing all day and see a moose but not another person, or go backpacking in the woods and find nothing but yourself.

Fortunately, too, both the federal and the state governments have preserved many of these acres and made them more accessible for those of us who enjoy at least a minimum degree of comfort and safety. There *are* bears here. There *are* wolves. When visiting these northern reaches, the first thing to remember is that you are invading nature's preserve. You are a visitor, and there are rules to be followed, for your own safety as well as for the preservation of the land.

Isle Royale National Park. To get to the park you leave your car and take a ferry to Isle Royale either from Duluth, Minnesota, or from Houghton or Copper Harbor, Michigan. Any of these ferries will deposit you at Rock Harbor Lodge, on the eastern tip of the island.

The lodge is the only one there, and the rates are not cheap, but from this outpost of civilization you can explore one of America's great natural preserves. Isle Royale is the largest island in Lake Superior, 45 miles long and 9 miles wide, with 99 percent of it wilderness. Here you will find acres of pine and hardwood forests, wildflowers, jagged bluffs along the shoreline, and all the rocks you will ever hope to see. You will be sharing all this grandeur with moose, beaver, red foxes, loons, and wolves. Once you hear, in the distance, the nighttime cry of the wolf, you will know you have experienced the North Woods.

There are 175 miles of hiking trails on the island, winding through some incredibly beautiful scenery. Do wear heavy hiking boots because the trails are rocky and often slippery. In most areas, camping is allowed but campfires are not. Get a camping permit from the ranger station and return it when you leave the park. This is a precaution because more than one camper has been lost in this vast wilderness.

A few more cautions: Swimming is not recommended because of Superior's cold water—and the possibility of encountering inland lake leeches. Boats smaller than 20 feet in length are not recommended for crossing Superior's unpredictable waters; however, small boats and canoes can be transported by the park service out of Houghton, Michigan. Pets are not allowed. There are no admission or camping fees.

Apostle Islands National Lakeshore. Just as beautiful as Isle Royale, and a little more tame, are the Apostle Islands, off the tip of Bayfield, Wisconsin. Indians had fished and hunted among these islands some 3,000 years before a group of 17th-century white missionaries, thinking there were 12 islands, named them after the apostles of Christ. In fact, there are 22 islands in the group, 21 of which are now protected as a national lakeshore. The islands suffered greatly at the hands of the early white settlers, who cut thousands of acres of big timber, did a big business in trapping animals for furs, and dug huge sandstone quarries. A few stands of virgin timber remain to remind us of how the islands looked in precolonial times, and the rest of the land is gradually being restored under protection of the federal government.

Indian legend says that the Apostle Islands were created when the "original man" threw clods of mud at a retreating deer. Geologists say that they were created when an enormous glacier scooped up part of the mainland and deposited it randomly into Lake Superior.

The Apostles offer plenty of opportunity for fishing, hiking, boating, and nature walks. Swimming is possible, but again the water is often too cold for any but members of the Polar Bear Club.

Visitors to the islands should begin in Bayfield. There, in the Old County Courthouse, is the headquarters of the National Park Service which oversees the Apostles. The park ranger and his staff will provide plenty of information about the islands, and the Service offers special evening campfire programs so that visitors can get the most out of their visit.

Madeline Island, the largest of the Apostles, is not part of the National Lakeshore. Here there is a well-maintained state park, Big Bay, that offers camping, hiking, picnicking, and swimming on 2,300 acres. Ferries leave for Madeline Island about every half hour during the peak summer season. The ferries operate from May through November, or whenever the lake freezes, running between Bayfield and La Pointe. (In winter the island's 165 permanent residents simply drive their cars over the ice to the mainland and back.)

Boundary Waters Canoe Area and Voyageurs National Park. Picture yourself gliding along a silent stream in your canoe, with only the sounds of your paddle and of the wilderness breaking the silence. This is prime canoe country, an enormous area covering hundreds of square miles east of International Falls between Minnesota and Ontario. Virtually all of it is pristine, a near paradise of lakes, rivers, and streams broken by rocky hills and bluffs; stands of pine, balsam, birch, and aspen; and an abundance of fish and wildlife. These are the routes traveled by the Indians for thousands of years and the very trails used by the French fur traders who paddled and portaged enormous loads from these waters to the rich markets of Montreal.

The Boundary Waters Canoe Area, known as the BWCA, is located in the Superior National Forest in northeast Minnesota on the Canadian border, adjoining Quetico Provincial Park. More than a million acres in size, the BWCA extends 150 miles, encompassing 1,200 miles of canoe trails. It is a protected wilderness area, and boat motors of any kind are prohibited. Camping is allowed only at the 2,000 designated camping sites, and no bottles or cans may be brought into the area. These restrictions are tough, but they protect the wilderness and offer a kind of primitive recreation not found in many places.

Voyageurs National Park is located on the Canadian border just east of International Falls. It is a waterbased park open to motorized boats as well as canoes. There are 30 lakes within its borders, separated by forested rocky knobs and ridges. Canoeists share the lakes with fishing boats, houseboats, runabouts, cabin cruisers, and sailboats. Kabetogama Peninsula, the center of the park, can be reached only by water or air, and both water routes involve short portages. There are about 100 designated campsites on islands and on lakeshores in the park. Access to the park is from

Island View, Kabetogama, Ash River, Kabetogama Narrows, and Crane Lake.

Because of the vast sizes of these wilderness areas, all but the most experienced of north woods canoeists are advised to join a trip organized by one of the local canoe outfitters.

Camping Rough or Easy

The beauty of vacationing in the Great Lakes area—aside from the welcome chance to reconnect with nature—lies in its remarkable affordability. The entire region is geared to recreation on a budget. Consider, for example, that Michigan, Wisconsin, and Minnesota together have more than 200 state parks that offer camping, boating, swimming, fishing, nature trails and educational programs, and—in winter—skiing, snowmobiling, and ice fishing. A reserved campsite costs only a few dollars a day, food costs are those of the grocery store, and nearly everything else is free. These are vacation opportunities available to everyone; traveling with a heavy purse is not necessary.

In summer, camping is clearly the focus of the family vacation. A typical pattern is to gather together the family camping and fishing gear, pile into the car, and head as far north as possible. After the tents are set up and the food is secured from bears and raccoons, the vacation begins. Whether for a weekend or a week, the campground serves as home base, leading to day trips to nearby attractions. There are no Walt Disney Worlds here, but there is plenty of nearby entertainment for every member of the family. Historical sites and local museums rarely charge more than minimal fees, and even the amusement centers in the region are budget-priced, compared to those in more populous areas.

The camping itself can be rough or easy. There are plenty of campgrounds accessible only by backpacking into the wilderness. Then there are those—including hundreds of private campgrounds—that offer every modern convenience: showers, restaurants, amusement centers, and cable TV for the family RV. In between, there are campgrounds for every possible taste, most of them offering lake or river recreation opportunities, all of them eminently affordable.

PRACTICAL INFORMATION FOR THE UPPER GREAT LAKES

WHEN TO GO. The Upper Great Lakes region has long been a favorite summer tourist spot, especially for residents of the lower (and hotter) Midwest. In recent years, however, Michigan, Wisconsin, and Minnesota all have made great strides in promoting themselves as winter havens as well. Summer temperatures are generally moderate (the average July spread ranges from about 83 to 60 degrees Fahrenheit in most of the region). In the northern reaches of all three states, however, night temperatures often plunge into the 40s. On the other hand, periods of hot and humid weather are not uncommon, even in the north. In summer, then, the wise traveler brings enough clothes to meet the unexpected.

The winter climate is similar to that of New England. Depending on the area and the particular day, Jan. temperatures may be anywhere from pleasantly brisk to downright dangerous. Once the snows come in Nov. and Dec., the ground is often covered until spring—much to the delight of ski enthusiasts.

HOW TO GET THERE. By plane. All major airlines serve Chicago's *O'Hare International Airport,* the nation's busiest. From there, you may make connections on a number of airlines to all parts of the Upper Great Lakes region. Other major air approaches are through the Minneapolis–St. Paul *International Airport* and the Detroit *Metropolitan Airport.* Government deregulation of the airlines has led to a proliferation of small commuter lines serving virtually any city of more than 25,000 in the region.

By bus. *Greyhound* is the major bus lines serving the region. In addition, there are smaller intrastate lines connecting many smaller cities and towns in all three states.

By train. *Amtrak* serves all three states. In Michigan the train stops at Detroit, Flint, East Lansing, Ann Arbor, Jackson, Battle Creek, Kalamazoo, Niles, St. Joseph and Lapeer. In Wisconsin the stops are at Sturtevant, Milwaukee, Columbus, Portage, Wisconsin Dells, Tomah, and La Crosse. In Minnesota, Amtrak serves Winona, Red Wing, St. Paul, St. Cloud, Staples, and Detroit Lakes before going on to North Dakota. For schedules, call Amtrak at 800–872–7245.

By car. Most traveling in this region is done by car. The Interstate System provides eight major highways through the area, and other roads and highways are well maintained in all three states. Auto ferries cross Lake Michigan in both summer and winter. The *Michigan–Wisconsin Ferry Service* runs between Ludington, MI, and Kewaunee, in northern Wisconsin. Service varies annually and seasonally. Schedules are dependent upon weather and will change without notice. Before driving any distance be sure to confirm the day's schedule. Michigan–Wisconsin Ferry Service, Box 279, Ludington, MI 49431 (616–843–2521). For information only, not reservations, call 800–253–0094.

TOURIST INFORMATION. All three states will be happy to send a complete vacation package to you, free of charge. They also will send a calendar of special events, for either the spring–summer or the fall–winter season. For the *Michigan* packet, contact Travel Bureau, Michigan Dept. of Commerce, Box 30226, Lansing, MI 48909 (800–543–2937). For *Wisconsin,* contact Division of Tourism, Box 7606, Madison, WI 53707 (800–432–8747). And for *Minnesota,* it's Minnesota Office of Tourism, 250 Skyway Level, 375 Jackson St., St. Paul, MN 55101 (800–657–3700).

TELEPHONES. The area code for eastern Michigan, including Detroit, is 313; for central Michigan, 517; and for western Michigan, 616. Area code for the Michigan upper peninsula is 906. The area code for eastern Wisconsin, including Milwaukee, is 414; for south-central and southwestern Wisconsin, including Madison, 608; and for northern Wisconsin, 715. Minnesota's area codes are 507 in the south, 612 in the center, including Minneapolis–St. Paul, and 218 in the north. The cost of a local call in most areas is 25 cents, with no time limit. Directory assistance procedures vary from town to town and are explained in local directories.

EMERGENCY TELEPHONE NUMBERS. In Detroit, Milwaukee, and Minneapolis–St. Paul, the emergency number is 911. The *Michigan State Police* number is 800–525–5555; the *Wisconsin State Patrol,* 608–246–3220; the *Minnesota State Highway Patrol,* 612–452–7473. Emergency numbers vary throughout the region. However, dialing "0" will bring an operator onto the line.

HOW TO GET AROUND. Except for the very few heavily urban areas, driving is the usual and recommended mode of transportation in the Upper Great Lakes region. The highway system is excellent in all three states, and even most remote roads are paved and well maintained, summer and winter.

By rental car. Visitors arriving through the major airports in Detroit, Chicago, Milwaukee, or Minneapolis–St. Paul may reserve a car through any of the major agencies, including *Avis* (800–331–1212), *Hertz* (800–654–3131), *National* (800–227–7368), *Budget* (800–527–0700), and *Thrifty* (800–367–2277). Growing in popularity also is *Rent-A-Wreck,* which offers older but safe cars at budget rates. (800–421–7253.) In most larger cities, also, visitors may rent cars at bargain rates from local car dealers. Check the telephone Yellow Pages for local information.

By bus. Public transportation between points within the region is often available but sometimes inconvenient. *Greyhound* provides bus service to the larger cities and towns, and several smaller bus lines operate within each of the states.

By train. *Amtrak* serves the more populated areas in the southern parts of the three states, and airlines of every size provide service to most areas. Still, for ease of getting from here to there, the automobile is still king in the Upper Great Lakes region.

HINTS TO MOTORISTS. This region, having virtually no true mountains, is easy on both cars and drivers. Winter driving, however, can be hazardous, especially for the driver not used to snowy highway conditions. The minimum driving age in all three states is 16.

Michigan, Wisconsin, and Minnesota all enforce the 55 mph speed limit quite rigorously. All three states have gotten tougher on drunk drivers, too, increasing law enforcement efforts and stiffening penalties. Do not speed. Do not drink and drive.

Vacationers who bring dogs more than six months old into Wisconsin must be prepared to show an interstate health certificate and proof of rabies vaccination. For more information, call the *Wisconsin Dept. of Agriculture,* Animal Health Div. (608–266–3481).

The AAA Emergency Road Service number is listed in local telephone directory white pages; if no number is listed, call 800–336–4357.

HINTS TO DISABLED TRAVELERS. All three states have, by passage of new laws, made public areas far more accessible to handicapped citizens. In addition, both Minnesota and Wisconsin's tourism divisions have published accessibility guides for handicapped travelers. Minnesota's guide (available free from the *Minnesota Office of Tourism,* 250 Skyway Level, 375 Jackson St., St. Paul, MN 55101) lists more than a hundred public attractions, museums, state parks, and other facilities and provides keys to ten different handicap-related features for each. In addition, the guide provides information on special transportation, programs, events, and facilities and lists of organizations and sources of further information.

A new brochure from Wisconsin rates several campsites in state parks and forests on accessibility. The author of the brochure—himself confined to a wheelchair—recommends nine sites as excellent for a first-time camping experience for wheelchair users and the mobility-impaired. Write to the *Wisconsin Dept. of Natural Resources,* Box 7921, Madison, WI 53707.

Individual and group tours for handicapped people may be arranged through *Flying Wheels Travel,* Box 382, Owatonna, MN 55060 (507–451–5005 or 800–535–6790).

Practical Information for Michigan

SEASONAL EVENTS. What follows is only a sampling of the hundreds of festivals and other special events held throughout the year in Michigan. For further information on any of them, write to *Travel Bureau, Michigan Dept. of Commerce,* Box 30226, Lansing, MI 48909.

January. *Michigan Tech Winter Carnival,* in Houghton, late month. *Plymouth Ice Sculpture Spectacular,* Plymouth, mid-month.

February. *Pine Mountain International Ski Jumping Tournament,* at Iron Mountain, mid-month. *Suicide Hill Ski Jumping Tournament,* in Ishpeming, mid-month. *Winter Carnival,* in Petoskey, mid-month. *Winter Sports Carnival,* in Grayling, mid-month.

April. *Maple Syrup Festival,* in Shepherd, late month. *Blossomtime Festival,* in Benton Harbor–St. Joseph, late month to early May.

May. *Mushroom festivals,* in Lewiston, Harrison, and Mesick, early to mid-month. *National Mushroom Hunting Championship,* in Boyne City, early to mid-month. *Fiddler's Jamboree,* in Port Huron, mid-month. *Holland Tulip Festival,* in Holland, mid-month. *Fort Michilimackinac Pageant,* in Mackinaw City, late month. *Highland Festival and Games,* in Alma, late month.

June. *World's Longest Breakfast Table,* in Battle Creek, mid-month. *Rose Festival,* in Jackson, early to mid-month. *Bavarian Festival,* in Frankenmuth, mid-month. *Asparagus Festival,* in Shelby & Hart, mid-month. *Thimbleberry Festival,* on the Keweenaw Peninsula, mid- to late month. *Seaway Festival,* in Muskegon, late month to early July.

July. *Stone Skipping Contest,* on Mackinac Island, early month. *National Cherry Festival,* in Traverse City, early month. *National Soaring & Hang Gliding Festival,* in Frankfort and Elberta, early month. *Hot Air Balloon Festival,* in Plymouth, mid-month. *National Blueberry Festival,* in South Haven, mid-month. *Port Huron–Mackinac Island Yacht Race,* in Port Huron, mid-month. *Old French Town Days,* in Monroe, late month. *Michigan Steam Engine & Threshers Reunion,* in Mason, late month to early Aug. *Ann Arbor Art Fairs,* late month.

August. *Coast Guard Festival,* in Grand Haven, early month. *Michigan Indian Art Festival,* Mt. Pleasant. *Danish Festival,* in Greenville, late month. *Melon Festival,* in Howell, late month. *Upper Peninsula State Fair,* in Escanaba, late month. *Yesteryear Heritage Festival,* Ypsilanti, late month. *State Fair,* in Detroit, late month through Labor Day.

September. *Carry Nation Festival,* in Holly, early month. *Mackinac Bridge Walk,* St. Ignace–Mackinaw City, early month. *Montreux Jazz Festival,* in Detroit, early month. *Peach Festival,* in Romeo, early month. *Riverfest,* in Lansing, early month. *Wine Festival,* in Paw Paw–Kalamazoo, early month. *Log-Jam-Boree,* in Ewen, late month.

October. *Viking Festival,* in Cadillac, early month. *Red Flannel Festival,* in Cedar Springs, early month.

December. *Mardi Gras Festival,* in Harrison, late month. *Snowmobile Safari,* in Curtis, late month.

TOURS AND SPECIAL-INTEREST SIGHTSEEING. Beaver Island. Round-trip boat excursions from Charlevoix to Beaver Island are offered daily, late June through Aug. During the spring and fall, one-way trips are offered, the boat returning the following day. Call 616–547–2311 for schedules and fares.

Detroit. Several bus tours of the Detroit metropolitan area, lasting from three to seven hours, are offered by *Gray Line.* Call 313–833–7692 for complete information.

Greenfield Village and the Henry Ford Museum. The two are adjacent to each other, in Dearborn, MI, only a 15-minute drive from Detroit Metro and International Airports, two mi. from the Detroit Amtrak station, near I-94 and I-75. Together, these two institutions form one of the greatest tourist attractions in the entire region. While the Henry Ford Museum displays artifacts and implements used in earlier times, Greenfield Village demonstrates how these items were used and how they affected lifestyles through the years. Scores of historic homes and other buildings on 240 acres hold fascination for everyone. Horse-drawn carriages and (in winter) sleighs are available. Call 313–271–1620 for fares and schedules.

Mackinac Island. Carriage tours of the island are offered throughout the day, mid-May to mid-Sept. The tours, lasting about 1½ hours, include stops at Fort Mackinac, Skull Cave, and the Beaumont Memorial. For schedules and fares, call 906–847–3573.

Pictured Rocks Cruises. At Munising, three-hour cruises are offered into Lake Superior and the spectacular rock formations in the area. Cruises leave five times daily in July and Aug., less often in spring and fall. Call 906–387–2379 for schedules and fares.

Soo Locks Boat Tour. If you've ever wanted to go through one of the giant locks, as the giant oceangoing ships do, here is your chance. Tour boats operate through the summer season, leaving from Sault Ste. Marie. The two-hour tour is narrated and includes good views of both the U.S. and Canadian waterfronts.

STATE AND NATIONAL PARKS. Many of Michigan's greatest natural attractions, such as the *Porcupine Mountains, Tahquamenon Falls, Hartwick Pines,* and the *Lake Michigan sand dunes* are in Michigan **state parks.** Seventy-one of the 94 state parks and recreational areas welcome camping and offer more than 14,000 campsites ranging from rustic to modern. Fees vary accordingly. Most campsites may be reserved in advance. Brochures and applications for reservations may be obtained by writing to the address in Tourist Information. The state park campsite reservation system has also been expanded to accept telephone reservations at most campgrounds. A state park motor vehicle permit is necessary to enter most state parks. Annual and daily permits are sold in the offices of state parks where they are required.

Within Michigan's six state forests are 155 campgrounds with more than 3,000 rustic campsites. These remote forest campgrounds are often the principal access to some of the best fishing waters in the state. All but two campgrounds have some campsites available on a first-come, first-served basis. There is a modest daily fee for all state campsites.

Within **Sleeping Bear Dunes National Lakeshore,** on the northwest coast of Michigan's lower peninsula, the National Park Service operates two campgrounds with 250 campsites. Spectacular views, marked trails along beaches and dunes, and a seven-mile scenic drive highlight this scenic wonder. For further information, contact Superintendent, Sleeping Bear Dunes National Lakeshore, Box 277, Empire, MI 49630 (616–326–5134).

Isle Royale National Park in northwestern Lake Superior contains one large island and more than 200 smaller islands and is accessible only by boat or float plane. A wilderness haven, the park contains 31 lakeside or trailside campgrounds, a lodge, housekeeping cottages, and extensive hiking trails. Further information is available from Superintendent, Isle Royale National Park, 87 N. Ripley St., Houghton, MI 49931 (906–482–0984).

Pictured Rocks National Lakeshore, just northeast of Munising, features magnificent sites and wind- and wave-carved sandstone cliffs lining the Lake Superior shore for 35 miles. The National Park Service is currently developing the area, so camping is limited to primitive campsites. For further information, contact Superintendent, Pictured Rocks National Lakeshore, Box 40, Munising, MI 49862 (906–387–2607).

The prime recreational season in Michigan's **national forests** is usually from Memorial Day to Labor Day. Camping is rustic and remote. Many campgrounds are situated on lakes or rivers and have fewer than 50 campsites. For further information, contact the forest supervisor of the appropriate forest: *Hiawatha National Forest,* 2727 N. Lincoln Rd., Escanaba, MI 49829 (906–786–4062); *Huron–Manistee National Forests,* 421 S. Mitchell St., Cadillac, MI 49601 (616–775–2421); *Ottawa National Forest,* 2100 E. Cloverland Dr., Ironwood, MI 49938 (906–932–1330).

In addition, Michigan has hundreds of private campgrounds with tens of thousands of campsites. These parks range from wilderness sites to plush modern campgrounds with all the amenities of a resort. For a directory of private campgrounds throughout the state, contact Michigan Association of Private Campground Operators, Box 68, Williamsburg, MI 49690.

FISHING AND HUNTING. The Great Lakes offer some of the greatest fishing opportunities in the world. Chinook and coho salmon are taken from Apr. through early autumn. The lakes also offer brown, rainbow, brook, and lake trout, walleye, perch, and smallmouth bass. Inland waters hold perch, pike, bluegill, walleye, trout, bass, and muskie. The annual spawning run of salmon in the fall is a spectacular sight. Many towns have built fish ladders in the waterways to help the salmon over the rough spots. Spring smelt dipping, sucker netting, and winter ice fishing are also popular. The National Trout Festival is held here, late each Apr., in Kalkaska. There are two bass tournaments in early June, one in Houghton Lake, the other in Manistee. There is also a mid-July bass festival held in Crystal Falls, and other fishing festivals and contests run from Apr. through Oct.

Whitetail deer, small game, partridge, pheasant, and waterfowl are abundant, especially in the rugged upper peninsula, where there are more than six million acres of open hunting ground, most of it owned by governments or by paper, timber, or mining companies. For information on fishing and hunting regulations, write the Dept. of Natural Resources, Information Services Center, Box 30028, Lansing, MI 48909.

PARTICIPANT SPORTS. With 3,000 mi. of shoreline, 11,000 inland lakes, and 36,000 mi. of rivers and streams, it's safe to say that many of Michigan's sporting and recreational opportunities are water-related. **Boating, sailing, swimming,** and **fishing** are integral parts of summer life in this state. Internationally renowned annual **yacht races** run from Chicago and Port Huron to Mackinac Island every summer. Charter boats go after salmon that may weigh 40 pounds or more. **Scuba** divers explore new worlds in Michigan's underwater parks, such as the one near Alpena which protects a shipwreck as an underwater museum. But most of the water fun is of a lower key, centered on dipping a line in a quiet lake and tuning out the rest of the world.

Hiking enthusiasts will have no trouble in finding terrain to their liking in Michigan. With 3.8 million acres, Michigan has the largest state forest system in the country. Four national forests cover an additional 2.7 million acres. In winter, the same landscape offers pleasures of a different kind. **Cross-country skiing, downhill skiing,** and **ice fishing** are all popular here.

Local governments own and operate most of Michigan's 65 public docks and harbors. More than half of all dock space is available on a first-come basis. Inland, and on the Great Lakes, about 1,000 launching sites are equipped for **boaters.** Although some charge a fee, most are free. The *Michigan Harbors Guide* and the *Michigan Boat Launching Directory* provide specific information and are available free from the Dept. of Natural Resources, Information Services Center, Box 30028, Lansing, MI 48909 (517–373–1220).

For a free list of **canoe** liveries, write to the Recreational Canoeing Association, Box 668, Indian River, MI 49749 (616–238–7868).

For information about which public areas permit **snowmobiling,** and for a book listing **alpine** and **cross-country** ski resorts, write the Travel Bureau, Michigan Dept. of Commerce, Box 30226, Lansing, MI 48909.

SPECTATOR SPORTS. Detroit is the major league city in Michigan, offering professional sports year-round. Fans can see the Tigers **baseball** team at historic Tiger Stadium (313–962–4000) from Apr. through Oct. The Lions **football** team (313–335–4131) plays indoors, in the Pontiac Silverdome. The Pistons **basketball** team plays in the Palace, Auburn Hills (313–337–0100). The Red Wings **hockey** team (313–567–6000) plays at the Joe Louis Sports Arena. Always call for information on ticket availability before planning to attend any specific event.

HISTORIC SITES AND HOUSES. Greenfield Village. Village Rd. and Oakwood Blvd. in Dearborn. One of the most popular tourist attractions in the state—located right next to the Henry Ford Museum—Greenfield Village covers 240 acres and houses scores of restored historic buildings. The village demonstrates how everyday life was lived in earlier times. Visitors see how, in an 18th-century home, life centered around the hearth, food was grown in the garden, and almost everything was made by hand. Next door, in a late 19th-century home, visitors can see the vast improvements effected by the Industrial Revolution. They enter into the homes of famous Americans, watch craftspeople blow glass, make pottery, and forge tools. In a single day, Greenfield Village lets the visitor travel back in time and return to the 20th century with a new understanding of the progress of a nation. Open daily 9 A.M.–5 P.M.; closed New Year's Day, Thanksgiving, and Christmas. Adults, $10.50; age 5–12, $5.25; senior citizen discount. Call 313–271–1620 for information (or 271–1976 for a 24-hour recorded message).

Fort Michilimackinac and Mackinaw Maritime Park. Mackinaw City (616–436–5563). This 1715 French fort has been reconstructed authentically. Included are various housing units, blockhouses, guardhouse, church, and blacksmith shop. Blacksmithing and cooking demonstrations are given daily. Uniformed soldiers, cannon firings, and colonial music demonstrations add to the fun at Fort Michilimackinac. Open daily 9 A.M.–7 P.M., June 15–Labor Day; 9 A.M.–5 P.M. May 15–June 14 and after Labor Day to mid-Oct. Adults, $5.50; ages 6–12, $2.75; family, $16.50. Fee includes admission to the reconstructed ship *Welcome,* when it is in port.

Historic White Pine Village, three mi. south of Ludington at 1687 Lakeshore Dr., includes 19 restored buildings that might have been found in a pioneer logging area. Included are a blacksmith shop, courthouse, school, and store. Craftsmen give demonstrations. Open Tues.–Sun. 10 A.M.–5 P.M. Memorial Day to Labor Day weekends. Adults, $3; over 65 and ages 8–17, $2. MC, V. Call 616–843–4808 for information.

Meadow Brook Hall, in Rochester, is a 100-room Tudor manor built by the widow of John Dodge of automobile fame. An unusual and most welcome feature of the Sun. tour is the opportunity to take tea and dine in the mansion. Guided tours Mon.–Sat. 10:15 A.M.–3:45 P.M., July–Aug.; self-guided tours Sun. 1–5 P.M. (last tour at 4 P.M.) the rest of the year. Open also the first week in Dec., when the manor is decorated for the Christmas season. Adults, $5; over 64, $4; ages 4–13, $3. Call 313–370–3140 for information.

MUSEUMS. Cranbrook, in Bloomfield Hills near Detroit (313–645–3149), is a complex built around the historic manor of George G. Booth, turn-of-the-century publisher of the *Detroit News.* Included are a 40-acre garden, three schools, and two museums. The Cranbrook Academy of Art Museum houses an impressive modern art collection. Open Tues.–Sun. 1–5 P.M.; closed on major holidays. Adults, $2.50; students and senior citizens, $1.50, under 7 free.

The *Cranbrook Institute of Science* includes an impressive mineral collection and a planetarium. Open Mon.–Thurs. 10 A.M.–5 P.M.; Fri.–Sat. 10 A.M.–10 P.M.; Sun. 1–5 P.M. Closed major holidays. Adults, $3; ages 3–17 and over 65, $2. Call for planetarium show schedule (313–645–3200).

Detroit Institute of Arts, at Kirby and Woodward Ave., in Detroit (313–833–7900), is an outstanding museum featuring a comprehensive collection of art from ancient times to the present. The famous William Hearst armor collection is on display here, as well as the G. Mennen Williams African art collection. Open Tues.–Sun. 9:30 A.M.–5:30 P.M.; closed major holidays. Contributions accepted.

Detroit Science Center, at John R. St. and Warren Ave., in Detroit (313–577–8400), features a space theater and dome and more than 50 scientific exhibits and demonstrations. Open Tues.–Fri. 9 A.M.–4 P.M.; Sat. 10 A.M.–6 P.M.; Sun. noon–6 P.M. Closed major holidays. Adults, $5; ages 6–12 and over 60, $4; ages 4–5, $2; family, $9. Parking, $1.25.

Henry Ford Museum. Located at Village Rd. and Oakwood Blvd., in Dearborn (313–271–1620 or 313–271–1976 for 24-hour recorded message). When he built this very American museum, Henry Ford wanted to create one that would contain artifacts not usually found in museums and use them to show how profoundly and rapidly life in America changed because of the technological innovations of a few people. The result is a lively and educational presentation of the American experience. Included are a duplicate of Philadelphia's Independence Hall and fully 12 acres of exhibits that help to trace the changes technology has wrought through the everyday tools and implements used by Americans for over 300 years. This is one of the finest museums in the country, always popular with visitors of all ages. Open daily 9 A.M.–5 P.M. Closed New Year's Day, Thanksgiving, and Christmas. Adults, $10.50; age 5–12, $5.25, senior citizen discount.

The **University of Michigan,** Ann Arbor, has several fine museums open to the public. The *Museum of Art,* in Alumni Memorial Hall at S. State St. and S. University Ave. (313–763–1231), has a fine collection of European art dating back to the 6th century, as well as collections from Asia and Africa. Open Tues.–Fri. 10 A.M.–4 P.M.; Sat.–Sun. 1–5 P.M. Free. The *Exhibit Museum,* located in the Museums Building at Geddes and N. University Ave. (313–764–0478), features archaeological exhibits, as well as those on astronomy, anthropology, and the natural sciences. Open Tues.–Sat., 9 A.M.–5 P.M.; Sun. 1–5 P.M. Donations. Planetarium, $2. The *Kelsey Museum of Archaeology,* in Newberry Hall, 434 State St., houses artifacts uncovered by the university's archaeological teams in various sites in the Mediterranean and Near East. Open Mon.–Fri. 9 A.M.–4 P.M.; Sat.–Sun. 1–4 during school year; Tues.–Fri. 11 A.M.–4 P.M., Sat.–Sun. 1–4 P.M. in summer. All university museums are closed when school is not in session.

ACCOMMODATIONS. Hotels and motels throughout the state offer clean and comfortable lodging at very reasonable rates. Although luxury accommodations are available in many areas, the going rate for a standard motel room is still under $40 in Michigan. A 180-page *Guide to Hotels and Motels* is available free from the Michigan Travel Bureau, Box 30226, Lansing, MI 48909 (800–543–2937).

More fun is to explore some of the hidden-away country inns that are now appearing throughout the state. Most of these are restored 19th-century manors, often with a great deal of interesting history behind them. In Dearborn, for instance, adjacent to Greenfield Village and the Henry Ford Museum, is the **Dearborn Inn,** a stately colonial re-creation with 207 rooms, 18th-century charm, and modern conveniences. Behind the inn are reproductions of five more historic homes, including Walt Whitman's birthplace, Edgar Allan Poe's cottage, and Patrick Henry's home. As it takes two full days to see everything in Greenfield Village and the Henry Ford Museum, a stay in one of these historic reproductions will greatly enhance the experience. Rooms at the Dearborn Inn, which recently became a Marriott Hotel, range from $120 to $190 per night. For reservations, write 20301 Oakwood Blvd., Dearborn, MI 48124, or call 313–271–2700 (800–228–9290 nationwide).

Another good alternative to standard motels is the **National House Inn,** in Marshall, between Battle Creek and Jackson. This inn, which traces its beginnings to 1830, has 15 rooms, each featuring antiques of the period, including a brass or fine wood bed. Continental breakfast is served every morning. Room rates are moderate. For a brochure and current rates, write National House Inn, 102 S. Parkview, Marshall, MI 49068 (616–781–7374).

Other noted country inns of Michigan include the **St. Clair Inn,** 500 N. Riverside Ave., St. Clair, MI 48079 (313–329–2222), a 90-room Tudor-style inn built in 1926; the **Island House,** Mackinac Island, MI 49757 (906–847–3347), a restored 1848 hotel; and the **Birchwood Inn,** Lake Shore Dr., Harbor Springs, MI 49740 (616–526–2151), a lovely, rambling motel built into the rolling hills near Traverse Bay. Perhaps the most famous hotel in all of Michigan—it's much too large to be called an inn, but it's just as charming—is the **Grand Hotel on Mackinac Island.** The hotel, with 311 rooms, is said to have the longest front porch in the world. It sits proudly on a hill overlooking the Straits of Mackinac. The hotel offers a swimming pool, tennis courts, sauna, whirlpool, nine-hole golf course, and other fine amenities. There is a strict dress code after 6 P.M., and rooms go for $200 to $400 a night. Everyone should stay at the Grand Hotel at least once in a lifetime. Call 906–847–3331 for reservations.

Families planning to vacation in one area for a week or more might consider renting a cabin or cottage. There are hundreds of them scattered throughout the more popular vacation areas, and most are listed in the state's *Guide to Cabins and Cottages,* a free 100-page book available from the Michigan Travel Bureau, Box 30226, Lansing, MI 48909.

RESTAURANTS. There are good restaurants throughout Michigan, ranging from the fashionable urban dining rooms of Detroit to the rustic country hotels of the upper peninsula. The following suggestions represent only a small sampling of the quality of cuisine—and the modest prices—to be found throughout the state. Restaurants are listed according to the price of a complete dinner (drinks, tax, and tip not included). *Expensive,* $20–$25; *Moderate,* $12–$20; *Inexpensive,* under $12.

Ann Arbor. Gandy Dancer. *Moderate.* 401 Depot St. (313–769–0592). Good standard fare served in a refurbished old train depot. Cocktail lounge. Open 11:30 A.M.–4 P.M. and 5–11 P.M., Fri. to midnight; Sat. 5 P.M.–midnight; Sun. 3–10 P.M. Closed New Year's Day, Thanksgiving, and Christmas. Reservations strongly advised. AE, DC, MC, V.

The Great Lakes Shipping Company. *Moderate.* 3965 S. State St. (313–994–3737). Noted for good steaks and seafood, served in a nautical decor. Cocktail lounge. Open 11 A.M.–2 P.M. and 5–10 P.M.; Fri. to 11 P.M.; Sat. 5–11 P.M.; Sun. 10:30 A.M.–2 P.M. and 3–10 P.M. AE, MC, V.

Battle Creek. Countryside Inn. *Inexpensive.* Michigan Ave. at I–94 (616–965–1247). Good family restaurant with an extensive menu. Children's menu. Cocktail lounge. Open 11 A.M.–9 P.M.; Fri. and Sat. to 11 P.M.; Sun. to 8 P.M. Closed Mon.; closed Christmas. AE, MC, V.

Benton Harbor. Bill Knapp's Restaurant. *Inexpensive.* 848 Ferguson Rd. (616–925–3212). Family dining featuring homemade specialities. Children's menu. Open 11 A.M.–10 P.M.; Fri. and Sat. to 11 P.M.; weekends to midnight from Memorial Day to Labor Day. Closed Thanksgiving and Christmas. MC, V.

Detroit. London Chop House. *Expensive.* 155 W. Congress (313–962–0277). Excellent Continental food, fine service. Dress code, cocktail lounge, entertainment. Open 11:30 A.M.–3 P.M. and 5–11 P.M. Mon.–Fri.; 5 P.M.–2 A.M. Sat.; closed Sun. and major holidays. Reservations advised. AE, DC, MC, V.

Carl's Chop House. *Moderate–Expensive.* 3020 Grand River Ave. (313–833–0700). A Detroit institution, featuring some of the best steaks in town. Valet parking. Cocktail lounge. Open 11:30–12:30 A.M.; Sun. 2–10 P.M. Closed Christmas. Reservations advised. AE, DC, MC, V.

Little Harry's. *Moderate–Expensive.* 2681 E. Jefferson Ave. (313–259–2636). Great food served in elegant surroundings. Dress code. Entertainment. Cocktail lounge. Valet parking. Children's menu. Open 11A.M.–midnight; Fri. to 2 A.M.; Sat. 5 P.M.–2 A.M. Closed Sun., Mon., and major holidays. AE, DC, MC, V.

Flint. Amigo's Mexican Restaurante. *Inexpensive.* 3539 S. Dort Hwy. (313–743–5840). True Mexican cuisine, as well as Tex-Mex chili. Cocktails. Open 11 A.M.–11 P.M.; Fri. and Sat. to 1 A.M.; Sun. noon–10 P.M. Closed Easter, Thanksgiving, Dec. 24–25. MC, V.

Grand Rapids. 1913 At the Plaza. *Expensive.* Pearl St. at Monroe St., in the Amway Grand Plaza Hotel (616–776–6426). Superb food served in a Victorian decor. Dress code. Cocktails. Valet parking. Reservations suggested. Open 11:30 A.M.–2 P.M.; and 5:30–11 P.M.; Sat. 5:30–11 P.M. Sun. 10 A.M.–3 P.M.; closed Sun. mid-May–mid-Sept. closed major holidays. AE, DC, MC, V.

Granny's Kitchen. *Inexpensive–Moderate.* 613 28th St., S.E. (616–241–5944). A no-nonsense family restaurant with good food and reasonable prices. Bring the kids. Cocktails served. Open 7 A.M.– 9:30 P.M.; Fri. and Sat. to 10:30 P.M.; Sun. 8 A.M.–9:30 P.M. AE, MC, V.

Jackson. Schuler's. *Moderate–Expensive.* 6020 Ann Arbor Rd. (517–764–1200). The decor is Old English and the food is well-prepared American. Cocktail lounge. Open 11 A.M.–10 P.M.; Fri. and Sat. to 11 P.M.; Sun. noon–9 P.M. Closed Christmas. AE, DC, MC, V.

Kalamazoo. Black Swan Inn. *Moderate.* 3501 Greenleaf Blvd. (616–375–2105). Excellent American and Continental cuisine served in a dining room overlooking a lake. Cocktails. Valet parking. Reservations advised. Open 11:30 A.M.–2:45 P.M. and 4–9 P.M.; Fri. till 10 P.M.; Sat. 5–10 P.M. Closed Sun.; closed major holidays. AE, DC, MC, V.

Lansing. The Pretzel Bell. *Inexpensive–Moderate.* 1020 Trowbridge Rd. (517–351–0300). Good food, pleasant modern dining room. Children's menu, cocktail lounge. Open Mon.–Fri. 11:30 A.M.–10 P.M.; Sat. 11:30 A.M.–2 and 5–11 P.M.; Sun. 10:30 A.M.–9 P.M. Reservations advised. AE, MC, V.

Marquette. Northwoods Supper Club. *Moderate–Expensive.* 3½ mi. west on U.S. 41 and SR 28 (906–228–4343). Smorgasbord Tues. night; Sun. brunch 10:30 A.M.–2 P.M., children's menu, cocktail lounge. Open 11:30 A.M.–11 P.M.; Fri. and Sat. to 1 A.M.; Sun. 10:30 A.M.–10 P.M., closed Dec. 24–26. AE, DC, MC, V.

Muskegon. Maxie's Restaurant & Night Spot *Inexpensive–Moderate.* 576 Seminole Rd. (616–733–3134). American and Mexican food; becomes a nightclub after 9:30 P.M. Children's menu, cocktails and lounge. Open 11:30 A.M.–10 P.M., Sun. 11 A.M.–3 P.M. Closed Christmas and New Year's Day. AE, MC, V.

Saginaw. Casa del Ray. *Inexpensive–Moderate.* 2945 Bay Rd. (517–792–8787). An extensive menu of Mexican foods, attractively prepared and served. Children's menu. Cocktail lounge. Entertainment. Open 11 A.M.–midnight, Tues.–Sat. to 2 A.M. Closed July 4, Thanksgiving, and Christmas. AE, MC, V.

LIQUOR LAWS. Liquor is sold by the package in state liquor stores and by licensed package dealers. It is available for purchase by the drink in licensed establishments only. Sunday sales by the drink are available from noon until 2 A.M. at local option. Legal drinking age is 21. Interstate import limit is one quart.

Practical Information for Wisconsin

SEASONAL EVENTS. The following is only a sampling of the many fairs, festivals, shows, and displays conducted annually in the state. For a calendar of events, write to the *Division of Tourism,* Box 7606, Madison, WI 53707 (800–432–8747). Be sure to confirm actual dates before traveling long distances for any specific event.

January. *Little Switzerland Winter Festival.* Parade, sleigh rides, arts and crafts. Contact Tourism, Box 713, New Glarus, WI 53574 (608–527–2095). *World Championship Snowmobile Derby,* third week. Contact *Municipal Information Bureau,* Eagle River, WI 54521 (715–479–8575).

February. *American Birkebeiner,* third week. The largest cross-country ski race in the U.S. draws 8,000 contestants annually. Contact Chamber of Commerce, Hayward, WI 54843 (800–472–3474 in state; 800–826–3474 nationwide).

April. The *Milwaukee Brewers* open their home baseball season at Milwaukee County Stadium. Call 414–933–9000 for information.

May. *Syttende Mai,* third week. This colorful event (pronounced Sitten-day-my) is Norwegian and means "the 17th of May," which is Norwegian independence day. Residents celebrate their ethnic heritage with parades, art and craft fairs, and ethnic foods. Contact the Stoughton Chamber of Commerce, 220 W. Main St., Stoughton, WI 53589 (608–873–7912).

Memorial Day Weekend. *Great Wisconsin Dells Balloon Rally.* This spectacular event, featuring more than 90 colorful hot-air balloons, celebrates the summer opening of this popular vacation area. Contact Wisconsin Dells Visitors Bureau, Box 390, Wisconsin Dells, WI 53965 (800–223–3557).

June. *Walleye Weekend Festival and National Walleye Tournament,* first or second weekend, on Lake Winnebago. Festivities include the self-proclaimed "world's largest fish fry" in Lakeside Park, Fond du Lac. Contact Convention & Visitor's Bureau, 207 N. Main St., Fond du Lac, WI 54935 (414–923–3010). *Lakefront Festival of Arts,* on the Lake Michigan shoreline in downtown Milwaukee. One of the largest outdoor art shows in the region. Write for dates—Milwaukee Art Museum, 750 N. Lincoln Memorial, Milwaukee, WI 53202 (414–271–9508). *Polish Fest,* Milwaukee (414–529–1140), mid-month, features music and dances, polka bands, contests, great food, and cultural demonstrations. *Summerfest,* last week and into July. Milwaukee's greatest summer celebration, featuring two weeks of jazz, country, ethnic, and rock music. Contact Summerfest, 200 N. Harbor Dr., Milwaukee, WI 53202 (414–273–3378).

July. *Song of Norway,* last three weekends. The famous light operetta, based on the life of Norwegian composer Edvard Grieg, is presented outdoors on the grounds of the Cave of the Mounds. Write Box 132, Mt. Horeb, WI 53572 (608–437–3038). *Festa Italiana,* third week. One of the nation's largest Italian festivals. Contact Italian Community Center, 2648 N. Hackett Ave., Milwaukee, WI 53211 (414–963–9613). *Lumberjack World Championships,* fourth week, in Hayward. Log-rolling, sawing, tree-chopping, tree-climbing contests, and more. Contact Hayward Chamber of Commerce, Hayward, WI 54843 (800–472–3474, in state; 800–826–3474, nationwide).

August. *EAA Fly-In,* first week, in Oshkosh. The Experimental Aircraft Assn. hosts the largest aviation event of its kind in the world. Contact EAA, Wittman Airfield, Oshkosh, WI 54903 (414–426–4800). *Sweet Corn Festival,* third week, in Sun Prairie, near Madison. Representative of many festivals celebrating the arrival of the sweet corn season. Tons of the succulent ears are consumed annually. Contact Sun Prairie Chamber of Commerce, 133 W. Main St., Sun Prairie, WI 53590 (608–837–4547). *Wisconsin State Fair,* West Allis (414–257–8800).

Labor Day Weekend. *State Cow Chip Throwing Contest* (608–643–4168), Sauk City and Prairie du Sac. *Wilhelm Tell Festival,* New Glarus (608–527–2095). Schiller's drama presented both in English and in German.

September. *Watermelon Seed-Spitting Championship,* second week, in Pardeeville (608–429–2442). "Pucker up and hope for a tail wind!" *Wine & Harvest Festival,* Cedarburg (414–377–9620).

October. *World Dairy Expo,* first week, Madison (608–251–3976). Large exposition featuring dairy animals and products. *Sister Bay Fall Festival,* second week, in Sister Bay (414–854–2812). *Apple Festival,* Bayfield (715–779–3335), autumn harvest celebration. *Fall Flower Show,* fourth week, in Milwaukee's Mitchell Park Horticultural Conservancy (414–649–9800).

November. *Spirit of Christmas Past,* Heritage Hill State Park, Green Bay (414–436–3010). *Holiday Folk Fair,* fourth week, in Milwaukee (414–933–0521). Cultural exhibits, ethnic foods, folk dances, Old World beer garden.

December. *Christmas Flower Show,* first week through New Year's Day, in Milwaukee's Mitchell Park Horticultural Conservatory (414–649–9800). *Annual Christmas Open House,* second week, in Oshkosh (414–235–4530). Historic displays from Christmases past. *Christmas Kohler,* mid-month–Jan. 1, traditional holiday celebration at famed American Club, Kohler (414–457–8005 or 800–344–2838).

TOURS AND SIGHTSEEING. Apostle Islands National Lakeshore. Sightseeing boat tours leave from the Bayfield city dock daily, mid-June to early Oct. Other cruises are available for Sand, Stockton, and Raspberry islands. Water taxis to other islands are offered to campers and hikers. Schedules and fees vary. Call 715–779–3925 for information and fares.

Madeline Island. A 90-minute bus tour of the island departs from the La Pointe pier four times daily, early June to early Oct. Call 715–747–2051 for information and fares.

Milwaukee. Sightseeing tours of Milwaukee's major attractions are offered during the summer by the *County Transit System.* Stops include the Mitchell Park Conservatory, the lakefront, and one of Milwaukee's famous breweries. Departures are from major hotels. Call 414–344–6711; for schedule. Architectural tours are offered by *ArchiTours* (414–277–7795). The *Miller Brewing Company* 4251 W. State St. (414–931–2337) offers free one-hour tours throughout the day, Mon.–Sat, 10 A.M.–3:30 P.M., mid-May–mid-Sept; Tues.–Sat. 11 A.M.–2 P.M. rest of the year. No reservations needed. Summer cruises of the Milwaukee Harbor are offered by the *Emerald Isle Boat Line* (414–786–6886) and *Iroquois Harbor Cruises* (414–332–4794). Reservations required.

PARKS AND GARDENS. Boerner Botanical Gardens. 5879 S. 92nd St., Hales Corners, WI 53130 (414–425–1130). Located in Whitnall Park, in suburban Milwaukee, the gardens feature spectacular floral displays during the entire summer and into early autumn. The entrance is on 92nd St., ½ mi. south of Grange Ave.

Horicon National Wildlife Refuge and Marsh. The marsh is located along Highway 33, between Horicon and Waupun (414–387–2658). Hundreds of thousands of migrating Canada geese stop here each Oct., drawing equal numbers of tourists carrying binoculars and cameras. Call for current information on geese concentrations.

Mitchell Park Horticultural Conservatory. 524 S. Layton Blvd., Milwaukee, WI 53215 (414–649–9800). It's hard to miss the three, seven-story geodesic domes along Layton Blvd. One simulates a tropical climate, another a desert climate, and the third provides a setting for changing floral displays, spectacular around the Christmas and Easter seasons. Open daily 9 A.M.–5 P.M. Adults, $2.50; ages 7–17, $1. Send a self-addressed and stamped envelope for a calendar of events.

Storybook Gardens. See Children's Activities.

University of Wisconsin Arboretum, 1207 Seminole Hwy., Madison, WI 53711 (608–263–7888). Eleven hundred acres of this impressive outdoor teaching laboratory are devoted to restorations of ecological communities native to Wisconsin. Included are two prairies, several pine forests, an oak forest dating back to presettlement times, and marsh areas along Lake Wingra. Another 140 acres feature landscaped areas and horticultural displays, including an impressive lilac collection. Ideal for biking, running, bird-watching, and cross-country skiing. No camping, no picnicking. The arboretum is open all year. No admission fee, free parking, free guided tours.

ZOOS. Milwaukee County Zoo. Intersection of I–94 and Hwy. 45 (414–771–3040). One of America's outstanding zoos displays animals in five continental groupings in simulated natural habitats. The use of moats allows an unobstructed view of the animals. Many special events are scheduled throughout the year. Both the rubber-tire Zoomobile and the Zoo Train provide frequent transportation from area to area. The Children's Zoo is one of the nation's best, allowing children to pet and feed a variety of baby animals. Open Memorial Day to Labor Day, 9 A.M.–5 P.M.; Sun. and holidays 9 A.M.–6 P.M. After Labor Day to Memorial Day, 9 A.M.–4:30 P.M. Admission fee.

Henry Vilas Park Zoo. On Drake St., at Lake Wingra, in Madison (608–266–4732). A modest-size zoo that the family can cover in a single afternoon. Picnic areas. Adjacent swimming beach. Open all year, 9:30 A.M.–4:45 P.M. The Shriners give free camel rides to children each Sun., in summer, 10:30 A.M.–noon. No admission fee.

PARKS AND CAMPING. The Wisconsin state park system is extensive, well developed, and well maintained, offering visitors a wide variety of recreational experiences in every region, throughout the year. In all, there are 71 state parks, recreational areas, and forests, providing camping, biking, hiking, swimming, canoeing, boating, water skiing, fishing, and—in winter—cross-country skiing, ice fishing, and snowmobiling. The camping experience can be easy (about 20 parks have showers and electrical hookups for RVs) to primitive: some areas accessible only by backpacking long distances.

Rock Island State Park (40 units), off the tip of the Door Peninsula in Lake Michigan, offers perfect solitude, while nearby *Peninsula State Park* (472 units) in Fish Creek, on the shore of Green Bay, is popular with teenagers and young adults. In between, there are parks for every taste, featuring waterfalls, big water areas, river gorges, virgin pine forests, spring-fed lakes, glacial formations, and clean sandy beaches.

In addition, there are 12 state trails, all built on old railroad grades, that are perfect for biking in the summer, snowmobiling in the winter. The longest—32 miles—is the Elroy-Sparta trail, which has 30 camping units. Daily camping rates are modest. Reservations are recommended, especially for the Memorial Day, Fourth of July, and Labor Day weekends. A daily or seasonal admission sticker is required for cars to enter the parks.

A chart listing all 71 areas, and giving separate features for each area, is included in the state's spring and summer tourism guide. Contact the *Wisconsin Division of Tourism,* Box 7606, Madison, WI 53707 (800–432–8747). You may also write for a free state park visitor guide and campsite reservation application: *Bureau of Parks & Recreation,* Box 7921, Madison, WI 53707 (608–266–2181). A 128-page parks guide in color is available for a moderate fee.

As an alternative to public parks and campgrounds, there are many private campgrounds, and these offer features not found in the public sites: restaurants, snack bars, swimming pools, laundry rooms, amusement centers, etc. For a booklet, send $2 to the *Wisconsin Assn. of Campground Owners,* Box 1770, Eau Claire, WI 54702 (715–839–9226).

National Forests and Recreation Areas. Most camping in national areas is on a first-come, first-served basis. There are three national areas in Wisconsin: *Apostle Islands National Lakeshore,* Rte. 1, Box 4, Old Courthouse Bldg., Bayfield, WI 54814 (715–779–3397); *Chequamegon National Forest,* 1170 S. 4th Ave., Park Falls, WI 54552 (715–762–2461); and *Nicolet National Forest,* 68 S. Stevens St., Federal Bldg., Rhinelander, WI 54501 (715–362–3415). Or write to U.S. Forest Service, Eastern Region, 310 W. Wisconsin Ave., Suite 500, Milwaukee, WI 53203 (414–297–3693).

FISHING. Bordered by the Mississippi River on the west, Lake Michigan on the east, Lake Superior to the north, and dotted with thousands of cold-water lakes and fast-running streams, Wisconsin properly qualifies as an angler's paradise. Three of the largest and most prized gamefish are the muskellunge, the northern pike, and the walleye pike, and all are abundant throughout the state. Plentiful also are yellow perch, smallmouth, largemouth, and white bass, sunfish, bluegills, black crappies, and brown, rainbow, and brook trout. The big waters of the Great Lakes hold giant lake trout, coho, and chinook salmon. Channel catfish inhabit most streams in the southern half of the state. Lake sturgeon is the oldest and longest-lived fish in Wisconsin's waters, but is not fished much these days. For current license fees, rules, and regulations, contact the *Dept. of Natural Resources,* Box 7921, Madison, WI 53707 (608–266–2105). Names of local guides are provided by local chambers of commerce. A list of the chambers is included in the state's spring-summer tourism guide. Write *Division of Tourism,* Box 7606, Madison, WI 53707 (800–432–8747).

HUNTING. Wisconsin's hunting highlights include deer, ruffed grouse, and waterfowl. Bow hunting for deer generally opens in late Sept., stops during the traditional Thanksgiving week nine-day gun season, and then continues to the end of Dec. Deer success is highest in the state's central counties. Ruffled grouse are common in the northern, central, and western parts of Wisconsin. Grouse seasons begin in mid-Sept. and continue to as long as the end of Jan. in southern regions. Goose hunting is excellent, but be sure to contact the Dept. of Natural Resources by July for instructions on how to apply for a permit to hunt the prime goose areas. The state's prime duck areas are the Mississippi River and the east-central counties. The best duck shooting takes place during the opening week in early Oct. and during the "northern flight" which traditionally takes place about Nov. 1st. There are approximately 300 public hunting grounds in Wisconsin, plus many national forests, state forests, and county forests open to gunning. For the latest information on hunting regulations and license fees, call the Department of Natural Resources at 608–266–2105, or write to the DNR at Box 7921, Madison, WI 53707.

SPECTATOR SPORTS. The Milwaukee Brewers **baseball** team occupies the scene from the late snows of Apr. until the first frosts of Oct., playing in Milwaukee County Stadium on the city's western edge, along I-94. For ticket information, call 414–933–9000. The Green Bay Packers **football** team also plays several exhibition and regular-season games at the stadium. Call 414–342–2717 for ticket information. (The stadium, incidentally, is very close to the Milwaukee County Zoo, opening up options for split family entertainment.) Packer tickets for games in Green Bay are virtually impossible to get. The Milwaukee Bucks of the National **Basketball** Assn. play at the Bradley Center, 4th and State Sts. (414–227–0500). Tickets are usually available. Tickets for all three teams may also be ordered through local Ticketron offices or through major Milwaukee hotels.

Big Ten college **football** may be seen five or six times during the autumn at Camp Randall Stadium in Madison, home of the University of Wisconsin Badgers. Fans often overflow the stadium's 77,000 seats, so it is best to write for a ticket application as early as May. UW Athletic Ticket Office, 1440 Monroe St., Madison, WI 53706 (608–262–1440). Include a self-addressed stamped envelope.

PARTICIPANT SPORTS. Bicycling. Wisconsin's gentle terrain and varied scenery offer the best bicycling opportunities. Eight state bike trails range in length from 13 to 32 mi. (See Parks and Camping.) A comprehensive touring guide, *Best Wisconsin Bike Trips,* ($9.95) is published by *Wisconsin Trails* magazine, Box 5650, Madison, WI 53705.

There are some 50 **downhill ski** areas in Wisconsin, and thousands of miles of **cross-country trails.** A good book on the Badger ski scene is *Skiing into Wisconsin,* ($10.95) published by Pearl-Win Publishing Co., Box 300, Hancock, WI 54943.

Golf and tennis are popular in Wisconsin. Most towns and cities of more than 10,000 have public facilities for both. The best area for private resorts offering these two sports is the Door Peninsula, a popular summer vacation spot.

The peninsula has public and private facilities for **horseback riding, bicycling,** and all **water activities.** Contact the *Door County Chamber of Commerce,* Box 346, Sta. A, Sturgeon Bay, WI 54325 (414–743–4456). The other major tourist area—this one more attuned to children and young adults—is Wisconsin Dells, in the south-central part of the state. Call the *Wisconsin Dells Regional Visitor & Convention Bureau* at 800–223–3557. For a list of golf courses, write the *Milwaukee Journal Travel Bureau,* Box 661, Milwaukee, WI 53201, and enclose a self-addressed and stamped business-size envelope.

CHILDREN'S ACTIVITIES. Wisconsin Dells. In summer, this town of 2,500 becomes a virtual children's paradise. Ride the duck boats, challenge the Tidal Wave Pool, go on one of dozens of waterslides. Try the bumper boats, take a real helicopter ride. Go to Robot World, take in the Standing Rock Indian Ceremonials, visit the Royal Wax Museum, or take a whitewater tube ride—you get the idea. One of the best attractions in "the Dells" is *Storybook Gardens,* a beautifully landscaped attraction with pools, waterfalls, children's book characters, baby animals to pet, boats, little trains and trams, a carrousel, a restaurant, and daily shows from 10 A.M. to 5 P.M. Admission fee. Call 608–253–2391 for daily schedule of events.

Cave tours are often popular with children—and, especially on hot days, with parents as well. A good one is the *Cave of the Mounds,* near Blue Mounds off U.S.-18/151 (and well marked by road signs), giving tours 9 A.M.–7 P.M. Memorial Day through Labor Day, varying hours the rest of the year. Another is *Crystal Cave,* near Spring Valley on Hwy. 29. Tours are given 9:30 A.M.–6 P.M. Memorial Day to Labor Day. Both caves charge admission.

HISTORIC SITES AND HOUSES. Old Wade House. Kettle Moraine Scenic Dr. at Hwy. 23 (414–526–3271). A mid-19th-century stagecoach inn, fully restored. Tours are conducted by costumed guides. Includes the Jung Carriage Museum, featuring more than 100 carriages, sleighs, and wagons. Open daily 9 A.M.–5 P.M. May–Oct. Adults, $4; over age 65, $3.20; ages 5–17, $1.50; family $10. Carriage rides: $1.

Old World Wisconsin. On Hwy. 67 near Eagle (414–594–2116). Nearly 50 restored and reconstructed buildings display the varied ethnic heritage of Wisconsin. Costumed guides explain the roles played by German, Norwegian, Danish, Finnish, and other immigrant groups. Considerable walking is required to cover the entire museum, but tram service is available for $1. Open daily 10 A.M.–5 P.M. May–Oct. Ticket sales stop one hour before closing. Adults, $6; over age 65, $4.80; ages 5–17, $2.50; family, $17. MC, V.

Stonefield Village and State Farm Museum. On County Rd. VV near Cassville, in Nelson Dewey Memorial State Park (608–725–5210). Reconstructed home of the state's first governor, a museum of mostly 19th-century farm implements, and a reconstructed village of the late 19th century, including a blacksmith shop, newspaper office, bank, and saloon. Open daily 9 A.M.–5 P.M., June 1 through Labor Day. Adults, $4; over age 65, $3.20; ages 5–17, $1.50; family, $10. Admission includes entrance to state park.

Villa Louis. 521 Villa Louis Rd., Prairie du Chien (608–326–2721). A mansion built in 1870 (on the site of an older family mansion) by the Dousman family, fur traders. The Victorian furniture, rugs, paintings, and rich decorations date from 1843 to 1913. Costumed guides explain the major features of each part of the house, and place the famous Dousman family into regional historical context. A great opportunity to see how the other half lived during frontier days. Open daily 9 A.M.–5 P.M. (the last tour begins at 3:45) May through Oct. Also open the first two weekends in Dec., when the house is decorated for Christmas. Adults, $4; over age 65, $3.20; ages 5–17, $1.50; family, $10.

MUSEUMS. The Circus World Museum. 426 Water St., Baraboo, WI 53913 (608–356–8341). The original winter quarters of Ringling Bros. Circus. Outstanding collection of circus wagons and memorabilia. Admission includes circus performance and parade. Open early May–mid-Sept., 9 A.M.–6 P.M. daily, to 9 P.M. mid-July–mid-Aug. Adults, $8.95; over age 65, $7.95; ages 3–12, $5.50; under age 3, free.

The Experimental Aircraft Association Air Museum. 3000 Poberezny Rd. (Jct. of U.S. 41 and SR 44), Oshkosh, WI 54901 (414–426–4800). 100 flyable aircraft including military, antique, and aerobatic planes. Exhibits include art gallery and two theaters. Open Mon.–Sat, 8:30 A.M.–5 P.M.; Sun. and holidays 11 A.M.–5 P.M. Closed major holidays. Adults, $5; ages 8–17 and 65 and over, $4; family, $15.

The Manitowoc Maritime Museum. 75 Maritime Dr., Manitowoc, WI 54220 (414–684–0218). Depicts the history of shipping on the Great Lakes with displays ranging from ship models to a replica of the Port of Old Manitowoc and the USS *Cobia,* a World War II submarine. Open 9 A.M.–5 P.M., daily. Admission, adults $5.50, children $3.25; family $14.50; includes submarine tour. Closed major holidays.

The Mid-Continent Railway Museum. North Freedom, WI 53951 (608–522–4261). Features a 9-mi. ride on a turn-of-the-century train pulled by steam locomotives, an 1894 depot and train yard, and railroad equipment displays. Open 10:30 A.M.–5:30 P.M., daily mid-May–Labor Day; weekends only early May, Sept.–mid-Oct. Train trips at 10:30 A.M., 12:30, 2, and 3:30 P.M. Adults, $6; over age 65, $5; ages 5–15, $3; family, $18. MC, V.

The Milwaukee Public Museum. 800 Wells St. in the Civic Center (414–278–2702). Exhibits include the streets of Old Milwaukee and a European village, as well as collections of fine arts and pre-Columbian artifacts. Open Mon. noon–8 P.M.; Tues.–Sun. 9 A.M.–5 P.M. Adults, $4; ages 4–17, $2; family, $10.

ACCOMMODATIONS. Wisconsin has its share of first-class hotels—from the elegant Pfister Hotel & Tower in Milwaukee to the unusual Mansion Hill Inn in Madison and the comfortable Clarion Hotel in Fond du Lac or the scenic Chequamegnon Hotel in Ashland—but for the most part, travel and life in the Badger State is informal and inexpensive. You can find comfortable lodgings in motels for under $40 in every area of the state.

More fun is to search out those hidden-away country inns, many of them now offering bed and breakfast at very reasonable rates. A sterling example is the *White Gull Inn,* in Fish Creek, Door County (414–868–3517). This white clapboard 1896 inn offers nine lodge rooms, some with private baths, some furnished with antiques. There are also housekeeping cottages for weekly rental. The ample dining room serves three meals a day, but the big attraction at the White Gull is the evening fish boil, long a Door County tradition. Behind the inn, the master boiler heats water in a giant cauldron, then cooks a basket of red potatoes. The basket is then filled with whitefish steaks (the whitefish caught that day) and is lowered again into the cauldron, where it stays for eight minutes. The master boiler then dumps a container of kerosene into the fire, causing flames to roar 12 ft. into the air. The resulting intense heat causes the cauldron to boil over, carrying away much of the fish fat. The succulent whitefish is then brought to the serving area (outdoors, weather permitting) and the inn guests line up for plates of fish with melted butter, potatoes, coleslaw, home baked goods, and Door County cherry pie. Is this more fun than eating in a typical hotel dining room? It certainly is—and it is fully typical of the Wisconsin approach to fun and relaxation.

There are several other good country inns in Door County, including the *Landmark Resort* in Egg Harbor (414–868–3205), and the *White Lace Inn* in Sturgeon Bay (414–743–1105). For a list of inns in this region, contact the *Door County Chamber of Commerce,* Box 346, Sta. A, Sturgeon Bay, WI 54235 (414–743–4456). *Bed and Breakfast Inns, Homes and Little Out of the Way Places* lists 145 such establishments. For a copy, send $8.95 to Bed & Breakfast Directory, 458 Glenway St., Madison, WI 53711.

For a complete guide to accommodations in Wisconsin, contact the *Wisconsin Innkeepers Assn.,* 509 W. Wisconsin Ave., Suite 622, Milwaukee, WI 53203 (414–271–2851). Enclose $2 for postage and handling. Students may receive information from *Wisconsin Youth Hostels,* 1417 Wauwatosa Ave., #102, Wauwatosa, WI 53213.

RESTAURANTS. It is not only possible to get a good, honest meal for under ten dollars, anywhere in Wisconsin, it is almost impossible *not* to get one. Coats and ties are seldom required, and in fact might set you apart from the crowd, especially in summer. On the other hand, there are exceptional dining experiences to be had, both in country inns and urban settings. The following suggestions, far from comprehensive, will give you some idea of the kind of food to be found in this state. Restaurants are listed according to the price of a complete dinner (drinks, tax, and tip not included). *Deluxe,* $25–$30; *Expensive,* $20–$25; *Moderate,* $12–$20; *Inexpensive,* under $12.

Appleton. The Captain's. *Moderate.* 3730 W. College, in Woodfield Suites hotel (414–734–9892). Good American fare served in nautical setting. Children's menu, cocktail lounge. Open 11 A.M.–11 P.M.; Fri.–Sat. to midnight. AE, MC, V.

Seigo's Japanese Steak House. *Moderate.* 1101 Westland Dr., west of U.S. 41 (414–739–6057). Both American and Japanese cuisines, the latter cooked at the table. Cocktail lounge. Open 5–10 P.M.; Sun. 4–10 P.M. Closed July 4th, Thanksgiving, and Dec. 24–25. AE, DC, MC, V.

Beloit. Butterfly Club. *Moderate.* On Hwy. 15, 1½ mi. east of I-90, Exit 185B (608–362–8577). Standard American fare in a rustic setting. Cocktail lounge. Entertainment. Open 5–10:30 P.M.; Sun. noon–8:30 P.M. Closed Mon.; closed New Year's Day and Dec. 24–25. Reservations required. AE, MC, V.

Eau Claire. Stafne's Sunset Inn. *Moderate.* An extensive variety of American fare served in a relaxing dining room. Children's menu. Cocktails. Open 11 A.M.–2 P.M. and 4–10:30 P.M.; Sat 4–11:15 P.M.; closed Sun. and major holidays. AE, DC, MC, V.

Fond Du Lac. Schreiner's Restaurant. *Inexpensive.* 168 N. Pioneer Rd. (414–922–0590). Family dining, good food and pie specialties, excellent pecan rolls. Cocktails. Open 6:30 A.M.–9 P.M.; Closed Thanksgiving and Christmas. AE, MC, V.

Green Bay. Rock Garden Supper Club. *Moderate.* 1951 Bond St. (414–497–4701). Extensive menu features steaks, seafood, much more. Cocktail lounge. Open 11 A.M.–2 P.M. and 5–10 P.M.; Fri. and Sat. 5–11 P.M.; Sun. 10 A.M.–2 P.M. and 4–9 P.M. Closed Mon. and major holidays. AE, MC, V.

Kenosha. Oage Thomesen's. *Moderate.* 2227 60th St. (414–657–9314). A Kenosha tradition since 1939. Varied menu. Children's menu. Cocktail lounge. Open 4–9 P.M.; Sat. 5 P.M.–11 P.M.; Sun. noon–9 P.M. Closed Mon.; closed Dec. 24–25. AE, DC, MC, V.

Kohler. American Club. *Expensive.* On Hwy. 23, ½ mi. west of I–43 (414–457–8000). Exceptional dining in sumptuous surroundings—part of the American Club Resort. Cocktail lounge. Open 5:30–11 P.M. AE, DC, MC, V.

La Crosse. Freight House Restaurant. *Moderate.* 107 Vine St. (608–784–6211). Varied American cuisine served in a renovated railroad building. Cocktail lounge. Entertainment. Open 5:30–10:30 P.M., Fri. and Sat. to 11 P.M.; Sun. 5–9:30 P.M. Closed Easter, Thanksgiving, Dec. 24–25. AE, DC, MC, V.

Madison. Fess Hotel Dining Room. *Moderate.* 123 E. Doty St. (608–256–0263). Elegant dining in a restored Victorian hotel. Garden dining in summer. Excellent Continental and American cuisine. Cocktail lounge. Open 11:30 A.M.–2:30 P.M. and 5–9:45 P.M.; Sat. and Sun. 10:30 A.M.–3 P.M. and 5–9:45 P.M. Closed Christmas Day. AE, MC, V.

Cafe Palms. *Inexpensive–Moderate.* 636 W. Washington Ave. (608–256–0166). American and European cuisine served in a refurbished historic hotel. Cocktails. Open 11 A.M.–2:30 P.M., and 5–9:30 P.M. Tues.–Fri.; dining until 2:30 A.M., Sat.; brunch 10:30 A.M.–2:30 P.M. Sat. and Sun. AE, MC, V.

Dotty Dumpling's Dowry. *Inexpensive.* 1441 Regent St. (608–255–3175). The ultimate in gourmet fast food—world-class hamburgers, championship chili, etc. German beers on tap. Open 11 A.M.–9 P.M.; Sun. noon–8:30 P.M.; Dec. 24, 11 A.M.–2 P.M. Closed New Year's Day, Easter, Thanksgiving, Christmas. No credit cards.

Manitowoc. The Breakwater. *Moderate–Expensive.* 101 Maritime Dr. in Inn on Maritime Bay. Good food, nautical atmosphere, dining room has marvelous view of harbor. Open 6:30 A.M.–10 P.M. Reservations suggested. AE, DC, MC, V.

Milwaukee. English Room. *Deluxe.* 424 E. Wisconsin Ave. (in the Pfister Hotel & Tower; 414–273–8222). Superb food served in a luxurious atmosphere. Cocktail lounge. Excellent wine list. Open 11:30 A.M.–2 P.M. and 6–11 P.M.; Fri. and Sat. to midnight, Sun. 5–11 P.M. Closed major holidays. AE, DC, MC, V.

Karl Ratzsch's Restaurant. *Moderate–Expensive.* 320 E. Mason St. (414–276–2720). A true Milwaukee landmark, in the Ratzsch family since 1904. Great German food in an Old World atmosphere. Cocktail lounge. Entertainment. Open 11:30 A.M.–10:30 P.M.; Fri., Sat. 11:30 A.M.–11:30 P.M.; Sun. 11 A.M.–10:30 P.M. Closed Dec. 24 and major holidays.

Mader's German Restaurant. *Moderate–Expensive.* 41 N. Third St. (414–271–3377). Milwaukee's other outstanding German restaurant, in the family since 1902. Outstanding menu, authentic Old World atmosphere. Cocktail lounge. Children's menu. Open 11:30 A.M.–11:30 P.M.; Mon. to 9 P.M.; Sun. 10:30 A.M.–9 P.M. Closed Dec. 24. AE, DC, MC, V.

Oconomowoc. Olympia Resort. *Expensive.* 1350 Royale Mile Rd. (414–567–0311). Superb American food served in this first-class resort. Cocktails. Entertainment. Open 6 A.M.–10 P.M.; Fri. and Sat. to 11 P.M. AE, DC, MC, V.

Oshkosh. Butch's Anchor Inn. *Inexpensive–Moderate.* 225 W. 20th St. (414–236–5360). Good standard fare served in a seafaring atmosphere. Cocktail lounge. Open 11 A.M.–11 P.M.; Sun. 10:30 A.M.–10 P.M. AE, DC, MC, V.

Sheboygan. City Streets. *Moderate.* 607 N. 8th St. (414–457–9050). Standard American menu. Good view of downtown Sheboygan and the Lake Michigan shoreline. Cocktail lounge. Open 11 A.M.–2 P.M. and 5–9 P.M.; Sat. 5–10 P.M. Closed Sun. MC, V.

LIQUOR LAWS. The legal drinking age in Wisconsin is 21. Both package goods and drinks are sold in private licensed establishments. Liquor is sold on Sun. Bar closing time is by local option, although most taverns close at 1 A.M.

Practical Information for Minnesota

SEASONAL EVENTS. Minnesota offers a wide variety of festivals, fairs, and other special events throughout the year. Theater, music, and dance thrive in the twin cities of Minneapolis–St. Paul. Following is just a sampling of the thousands of special events held throughout the year across the state.

January. *Winter Sports Festival* in Duluth, second week. Sled dog races, ski races, celebration of winter for people of all ages. Contact Duluth Convention & Visitors Bureau, 100 Lake Place Rd., Duluth, MN 55802 (218–722–4011). *St. Paul Winter Carnival.* Held annually for more than a century, the carnival is an event not to be missed. Features a giant ice palace, parades, pageantry, winter sports, events, and much more. Late month to early Feb. Contact Winter Carnival Assn., North Central Life Tower, 445 Minnesota, Ste. 600, St. Paul, MN 55101 (612–297–6053).

February. *Cabin Fever Days,* Cannon Falls, early month. Sled dog races, beauty pageant, arts and crafts fair. Contact Chamber of Commerce, Box 2, Cannon Falls, MN 55009 (507–263–2289). *Fasching,* in New Ulm. Traditional German winter celebration with costume ball, German food, refreshments, and entertainment. Contact Box 492, New Ulm, MN 56073 (507–354–4217). *Minnesota Sit 'n' Spit Annual Convention & Cherry Pit Spitting Contest.* Mid-month, in Mankato. The competition is open to the public, and "ya have to sit when ya spit." Contact Sit 'n Spit Club, 45 N. Hill, Mankato, MN 56001 (507–625–3347).

March. *Trout-O-Rama.* Early month, in Barnum. Annual fishing contest held on Bent Trout Lake. Prizes, no license required. Write Box 132, Barnum, MN 55707 (218–389–6941). *St. Patrick's Day Parade,* mid-month, in St. Paul. Nation's third largest St. Patrick's Day celebration draws more than 100,000 participants. Contact Northstar Adjustmen, 200 Degree of Honor Bldg., St. Paul, MN 55101 (612–224–5891).

April. *Festival of Nations,* late month, in St. Paul. *Swayed Pines Folk Fest,* Collegeville. Old time fiddle contest and craft fair. Call 612–363–2594/253–3620 for dates. *Minnesota Twins baseball* opens at the Hubert H. Humphrey Metrodome. Call 612–375–7444 for ticket information.

May. *Syttende Mai Fest,* mid-month, in Spring Grove and several other communities. Celebrate Norwegian independence day. *Smelt Fry,* Hanley Falls. Annual fire department fish fry, great eating (507–768–3510). *St. Paul Scottish Country Fair,* in St. Paul. Scotting costumes, dances, music, foods, and more. Call 612–696–6239 for dates.

June. *Turtle Fest,* Perham. Turtle races, art and craft show, parades. Third week. Contact Chamber of Commerce, Box 234, Perham, MN 56573 (218–346–6370). *Cottage Grove Strawberry Festival,* mid-month in Cottage Grove (612–459–8442). *Steamboat Days,* Winona. Late month into early July. One of the largest outdoor festivals in Minnesota. Contact Winona Area Jaycees, 507–454–3079.

July. *St. Paul North Star Morgan Horse Show.* Mid-month, at the State Fairgrounds in St. Paul (612–941–4625). *Hopkins Raspberry Festival,* mid-month, in Hopkins. Write Festival Director, Box 504, Hopkins, MN 55343. *Muskie Days,* 2nd Tues.–Wed., in Nevis. Fishing contest, parades, street dances. Write Box 268, Nevis, MN 56467.

August. *Fur Trade Rendezvous,* Grand Rapids (218–327–4482). *Minnesota State Fair,* late month to early Sept., at State Fairgrounds (612–642–2200). *Uptown Art Fair,* Minneapolis, early month, (612–827–8757).

September. *Jesse James Days,* Northfield. Enactment of James Gang bank robbery, parades, rodeo, tractor pulls. Write Box 198, Northfield, MN 55057 (507–645–5604).

October. *Riverton Fall Colors Festival,* Stillwater. Early month. Canoe races, apple ball, contact Chamber of Commerce, 423 Main St., Stillwater, MN 55082. *Oktoberfest,* New Ulm and other communities (800–657–3700).

November. *Deer season* opens, early month. *Norsefest,* in Madison. Your chance to experience Norway's favorite fish dish in the "Lutefish Capital of the USA" (612–598–7373, 3785).

December. *Folkways of Christmas,* Shakopee. All month Historic homes feature ethnic customs as practiced by Minnesota pioneers. Contact Mariann Reid, Murphy's Landing, 2187 Hwy. 101, Shakopee, MN 55379 (612–445–6900). *Victorian Christmas,* Winona, early month. Tours of historic homes, holiday festivities (507–452–2272). *Christmas in a 1900 Logging Camp.* Costumed interpreters and tour guides demonstrate cooking, baking, singing, story telling, as they were practiced in old logging camps. Free horse-drawn sleigh rides. Contact Forest History Center, 2609 Co. Rd. 76, Grand Rapids, MN 55744.

PARKS AND CAMPING. Budget-priced vacations are no problem in Minnesota, where the vast and well-maintained state park system makes the living easy—on the pocketbook. Whether your pleasure comes from exploring backcountry solitude on foot while pitching your tent with only the chatter of a red squirrel for company, or whether it comes from enjoying the comfort of a semi-modern campsite with a large groups of friends, the Minnesota parks have a place for you.

Campside reservations are accepted 15 days in advance and can be made by contacting the park between 8 A.M. and 4 P.M. Mon. through Fri. Weekend site reservations must include both Fri. and Sat. nights. For large gatherings, some of the parks offer large sites separated from the family camping areas. The group campsites are classified as modern (buildings provided for lodging, dining, and sanitation), semi-modern (buildings for dining and sanitation), or primitive (pit toilets). There are also horse sites, where trail riders may camp with their horses.

Vehicle permits which are required to enter any Minnesota state park may be purchased at the point of entry on a daily or annual basis. Fees are also charged for camping and for certain other services, such as boat, canoe, and ski rentals, depending on availability. For all the information you'll need about Minnesota's state parks, write to the *Dept. of Natural Resources Information Center,* Box 40, DNR Building, 500 Lafayette Rd., St. Paul, MN 55155 (612–296–4776, in the Twin Cities; 800–652–9747, in the rest of Minnesota. You may receive a state park guide, maps and individual guides to any of the 64 parks, information on group camping, and other valuable information. The state park guide lists all 64 parks and notes 28 special features for each of them.

Chippewa National Forest covers millions of acres of north central Minnesota. There are many trails in this forest, some with campsites for backpackers. Backpackers, however, may camp anywhere within the forest. Maps and other trail information are available from the Chippewa National Forest, Supervisor's Office, Cass Lake, MN 56633 (218–335–2226).

Superior National Forest covers an extensive area of northeast Minnesota and includes the popular Boundary Waters Canoe Area. Camping is permitted only at designated campsites on some trails; others allow camping anywhere more than 100 ft. from water. Trails within the Boundary Waters area require permits for both day and overnight use. For maps, permits, and other information, contact the U.S. Forest Service, Superior National Forest, Box 338, Duluth, MN 55801 (218–720–5324; ask for the Forest Service).

In addition to state and federal campgrounds, there are hundreds of private campgrounds throughout Minnesota, many featuring amenities and services not available at public grounds. For a list, write to the *Minnesota Assn. of Campground Owners,* 1000 E. 146th St., Suite 121G, Burnsville, MN 55337 (612–432–2228).

FISHING AND HUNTING. From its deep crystal lakes to its gentle streams, Minnesota offers more waters, and more kinds of fishing, than any other place in America. Lunker walleye, acrobatic bass, trophy pike, world-class muskies, magnificent trout—they're all here. Each year, more than a million anglers await the mid-May opening of walleye season. On Memorial Day weekend, bass anglers swing into action. And the arrival of muskie season in June brings forth thousands of dedicated trophy hunters.

Minnesota is definitely walleye country, where lunkers of ten pounds or more are not uncommon. The best-known walleye waters are lakes Millie Lacs, Leech, Winnibigoshish, Upper Red, and Lake of the Woods, and the Mississippi, and St. Louis rivers. The Minnesota Dept. of Natural Resources insures the walleye population by stocking more than a quarter-billion fingerlings and fry each year.

An index to more than 3,500 Minnesota lake maps is available from the Minnesota State Documents Center, 117 University Ave., St. Paul, MN 55135. Maps are $3 each, plus 6% sales tax and $1.50 postage and handling. Several free trout stream information guides are available on a county-by-county basis from the Minnesota Office of Tourism, 250 Skyway Level, 375 Jackson St., St. Paul, MN 55101.

Fishing licenses are sold by each County Auditor and his or her agents (resort operators, bait dealers, sporting goods stores, etc.) and a synopsis of fishing laws is delivered with each license.

Big game opportunities lie awaiting in the Minnesota wilderness, where deer, moose, bear, and elk may be taken in season. Small game birds include quail, grouse, pheasants, ducks, and geese. For further information on hunting rules, regulations, and license fees, write the *Minnesota Dept. of Natural Resources,* Information Center, 500 Lafayette Rd., Box 40, St. Paul, MN 55155.

PARTICIPANT SPORTS. With more than 12,000 lakes and streams, it's not surprising that Minnesota is a mecca for the serious canoeist and backpacker. But this is a prime region also for swimming, golf, and tennis in the summer—ice fishing, cross-country and alpine skiing, and snowmobiling in the winter.

Canoeing. Exploring the backwoods of Minnesota by canoe is a rare delight. The rivers and streams abound with walleye, northern pike, trout, bass, and other fish. Moose, deer, black bear, timber wolves, fox, coyote, raccoon, and beavers thrive in these habitats. Alert bird-watchers can spot bald eagles, hawks, loons, warblers, woodpeckers, owls, and a variety of ducks and other birds. The state has classified its rivers and streams according to the level of difficulty and danger for canoeists, ranging from Class I (easy, small waves, few obstructions) all the way to Class VI (great risk to life). Publications on canoeing, hiking and backpacking are available free from the Minnesota Office of Tourism, 250 Skyway Level, 375 Jackson St., St. Paul, MN 55101.

Day trips are ideal on the Cannon, Minnesota, North Fork Crow, Root, Zumbro, Rum, and Straight rivers. Extended wilderness trips may be taken on the Big Fork, St. Louis, Little Fork, Cloquet, and Vermillion rivers. But the favorite canoeing area, which draws aficionados from across North America, is the *Boundary Waters Canoe Area (BWCA),* located in the Superior National Forest in northeast Minnesota on the Canadian border. Over one million acres in size, the BWCA extends 150 miles, encompassing 1,200 mi. of canoe routes. For more information on the BWCA, write to the U.S. Forest Service, Box 338, Duluth, MN 55801, or call 218–720–5324.

Hiking & Backpacking. With 64 state parks, 55 state forests, state trails, hundreds of city and county parks, and vast Federal reserves, including the Superior National Forest and Voyageurs National Park, Minnesota is made for hiking and backpacking. There are more than 70 trails for backpackers, each trail with its own unique character and highlights.

Golf and tennis. Avid golfers will have little trouble finding a suitable (and uncrowded) course in Minnesota. There are more than 300 courses throughout the state, many of them attached to resorts, while others are municipal courses open to the public. For a booklet describing more than 500 Minnesota resorts, write the Minnesota Resort Assn., 871 Jefferson Ave., St. Paul, MN 55102.

Skiing. You may choose from 30 downhill areas, over 300 cross-country areas, and 2,500 mi. of cross-country ski trails. The ski season in Minnesota usually extends from Nov. through Mar. For a booklet listing and describing both downhill and cross-country ski areas, write to the Minnesota Travel Information Center, 250 Skyway Level, 375 Jackson St., St. Paul, MN 55101. Maps of ski trails and snowmobile trails in Minnesota state parks and state forests are available free by writing the Outdoor Recreation Information Center, Minnesota Dept. of Natural Resources, 500 W. Lafayette Rd., St. Paul, MN 55155. Statewide winter road conditions are available by calling the Minnesota Dept. of Transportation at 612–296–3076; 800–542–0220 elsewhere in Minnesota. For ski reports, call 612–296–5029, in the Twin Cities; 800–657–3700, nationwide.

SPECTATOR SPORTS. The Twin Cities are of major league calibre when it comes to football, baseball, basketball, and hockey. The Hubert H. Humphrey Metrodome, 900 S. 5th St., Minneapolis, MN (612–332–0386) is home to the Minnesota Twins **baseball** team (612–375–1366 for ticket information), the Minnesota Vikings **football** team (612–828–6500), and the University of Minnesota **football** team. The Minnesota North Stars professional **hockey** team plays at the Met Center, 7901 Cedar Ave., Bloomington, MN 55420 (612–853–9300).

HISTORIC SITES AND HOUSES. Minnesota is justifiably proud of its pioneer heritage, and has done much to preserve it. Following are a few of the many historic sites that have been restored or re-created to bestow a sense of living history for both residents and visitors.

Julien Cox Home. 500 N. Washington St., St. Peter, MN 56082 (507–931–2160). Built in 1871, the Cox home was once the center of a lively social life in the frontier town of St. Peter. Restored in 1971, the house has period furnishings, some of them original. The window glass, curved stairway, and woodwork are in their original state. Open June 1–Labor Day, Tues.–Fri. 1–4 P.M. and weekends through Sept. Decorated for the Christmas season and open first two weekends of Dec., 11 A.M.–4 P.M. Admission fee. Group tours by appointment.

Historic Fort Snelling. St. Paul, MN 55111 (612–726–1171). Historic fort built in the 1820s, now fully restored and staffed with costumed guides playing the roles of soldiers and civilians. Military drills and demonstrations, crafts, special events span the summer. Open daily 10 A.M.–5 P.M., May–Oct. History Center Nov.–Apr., Mon.–Fri. 9 A.M.–4:30 P.M. Admission fee.

Minnesota Pioneer Park. Hwy. 55, Annandale, MN 55302 (612–274–8489). Largest park of its kind in the entire region. Thirty structures house five different museums; pioneer village, 1886 church. 1850 and 1884 log houses, pioneer women exhibit, artifacts, nature trails, animals for children to pet. Open 10 A.M.–4:30 P.M.

Mon.–Fri., weekends and holidays 1–5 P.M. Memorial Day–Labor Day. Admission fee.

Village of the Smoky Hills. Box 282, Osage, MN 56570 (218–573–3000). A reconstructed old village featuring the human skills of yesteryear: pottery, woodworking, candledipping, quilting, stenciling, stained-glass making. Visitors can participate in some of these crafts. Open Memorial Day–Oct., daily 10 A.M.–5 P.M. Admission fee. Group tours.

MUSEUMS AND GALLERIES. There are hundreds of museums and art galleries throughout Minnesota, including many specialized ones in the Twin Cities. Following are some of the more notable of them. Publications on Minnesota arts and attractions are available from the Minnesota Office of Tourism, 250 Skyway Level, 375 Jackson St., St. Paul, MN 55101.

Canal Park Marine Museum. Duluth, MN 55802 (218–727–2497). Operated by the U.S. Army Corps of Engineers, the most visited museum on the Great Lakes; exhibits and programs on upper lakes commercial shipping, Duluth ship canal and aerial bridge. Open Memorial Day–Labor Day, 10 A.M.–9; P.M.; spring and fall, 10 A.M.–6 P.M.; Dec. 1–Apr. 30, Fri.–Sun. 10 A.M.–4:30 P.M. No admission fee. Call for group tours. Boatwatcher's Hotline (24–hr. tape), 218–722–6489.

Lake Superior Museum of Transportation. 506 W. Michigan St., Duluth, MN 55802 (218–727–8025). Railroad equipment and history occupy the spotlight here. The collection includes the first locomotive in Minnesota. Open May.–Oct. daily 10 A.M.–5 P.M.; Nov.–Apr. Mon.–Sat. 10 A.M.–5 P.M.; Sun. 1–5 P.M. Adults, $4; over 60, $3; ages 6–17, $2.

Minneapolis Institute of the Arts. 2400 Third Ave., S., Minneapolis, MN 55404 (612–870–3140). A showcase of world art with a vast collection of early and modern masterpieces and a lively schedule of exciting exhibitions. A spectacular building houses three floors of galleries, a museum shop, and a restaurant. Open Tues., Wed., Fri., and Sat. 10 A.M.–5P.M.; Thurs. 10 A.M.–9 P.M., Sun. noon–5 P.M. Free.

Minnesota Museum of Art, 205 Landmark Center, 5th & Market; and Jemne Bldg., St. Peter & Kellogg, St. Paul, MN 55102 (612–292–4355). Changing exhibitions of regional and national importance; emerging artist exhibition space; and art exhibitions for children. An extensive permanent collection of American and non-Western art is housed in the Hemne Bldg. Open Tues.–Fri. 10:30 A.M.–4 P.M.; Thurs. to 7:30 P.M. Sat.;–Sun. 1–4:30 P.M. Closed major holidays.

Science Museum of Minnesota. 30 E. 10th St., St. Paul, MN 55101 (612–221–9400). An exciting blend of two traditions in museums: a science/technology center and a natural history museum with a focus on participatory exhibits; the domed Omnitheater has the world's largest and most sophisticated film projection system. Museum exhibits and Omnitheater admission; adults, $5.50; under age 12 and over age 65, $4.50.

ARTS AND ENTERTAINMENT. Nearly 1,300 arts organizations thrive in Minnesota. The Minneapolis–St. Paul area is the center for upper midwest art groups. About 50 theaters, scores of galleries and museums, and more than 10 dance companies make their homes in the Twin Cities. Orchestra Hall in Minneapolis houses the *Minnesota Orchestra,* one of the nation's finest. St. Paul's Ordway Music Theatre is home to one of the top chamber orchestras in the country, and also the *Minnesota Opera.* The *Guthrie Theater* and the *Children's Theater* are nationally known.

Guides to Minnesota arts and attractions are available from the *Minnesota Office of Tourism,* 250 Skyway Level, 375 Jackson St., St. Paul MN 55101. Concerts, plays, and other cultural events in the Twin Cities are well covered by the daily *Minneapolis News-Tribune & Herald,* and by the *St. Paul Pioneer Press & Dispatch.*

ACCOMMODATIONS. Outside of the Twin Cities, there are no major urban areas in all of Minnesota—not one city, in fact, with a population as large as 100,000. The accommodations pattern, then, changes sharply once you leave the Twin Cities metro region. In Minneapolis–St. Paul, there is a wide choice of hotels and motels, ranging from budget chain motels to super-deluxe hotels such as the new Whitney and the Saint Paul hotels, where single rooms run more than $100 a night. Most motels are in the $40–$60 range. And new lodgings are continually being added in the bustling Twin Cities.

Outside of the Twin Cities, the only lodging choice is often the basic American roadside motel—clean and comfortable, but with no frills. Pleasant alternatives, however, are the bed-and-breakfast inns that are now growing in popularity throughout the region. Several suggestions include the **Lowell Inn,** in Stillwater (612–439–1100); **Archer House,** in Northfield (507–645–5661); the **St. James Hotel,** in Red Wing (612–388–2846); **The Hotel,** in Winona (507–452–5460); and the **Anderson House,** in Wabasha (612–565–4524). A call to any of these inns will bring a brochure with current rates.

Most tourists in Minnesota, in fact, do not stay in motels and hotels, but in cabins and tents in campgrounds or at resorts. There are hundreds of resorts throughout Minnesota, many of them specializing in one or more activities such as fishing, hunting, skiing, golf, and tennis.

For a free 100-page Minnesota resort guide, contact the *Minnesota Resort Assn.,* 871 Jefferson Ave., St. Paul, MN 55102 (612–222–7401). If camping is your preference, write for a free state park guide—*Minnesota's State Parks,* Box 40, DNR Bldg., 500 Lafayette Rd., St. Paul, MN 55155; or for a free 50-page private campground guide, contact the *Minnesota Assn. of Campground Operators,* 1000 E. 146th St., Suite 121G, Burnsville, MN 55337 (612–432–2228).

A free 38-page hotel guide is available from the *Minnesota Hotel & Motor Hotel Assn.,* 871 Jefferson Ave., St. Paul, MN 55102, and a free 58-page motel guide may be had by contacting the *Minnesota Motel Assn.,* 1000 E. 146th St., Burnsville, MN 55337 (612–432–2224).

RESTAURANTS. The Twin Cities have hundreds of good restaurants, offering standard American and Continental cuisine and ethnic foods from nearly every region in the world. In most of the rest of the state, restaurants are more apt to be more wholesome and economical than exotic and adventuresome. Here are some suggested restaurants in the larger cities and towns. They are listed according to the price of a complete dinner (drinks, tax, and tip not included). *Deluxe,* $25–$30; *Expensive,* $20–$25; *Moderate,* $12–$20; *Inexpensive,* under $12.

Austin. The Old Mill. *Inexpensive–Moderate.* Todd Park Rd., 2 mi. north of I–90 (507–437–2076). Good standard American fare served in an 1864 building that once was a flour mill. Cocktails. Open 11:30 A.M.–2 P.M. and 5:30–11 P.M.; Sat. 5:30–11 P.M. Closed Sun., major holidays. MC, V.

Duluth. Pickwick Restaurant. *Inexpensive–Moderate.* 508 E. Superior St. (218–727–8901). Excellent food served in historic building owned and operated by the same family since 1914. Children's menu, cocktail lounge. Open 11 A.M.–midnight; closed Sun. and major holidays. AE, MC, V.

Mankato. The San Paugh Dining Room. *Moderate.* 101 E. Main St. in the Holiday Inn-Downtown (507–345–1234). Varied menu here features steaks and seafood. Children's menu, cocktail lounge, entertainment. Open 6 A.M.–10 P.M.; Sun. 7 A.M.–9 P.M. AE, DC, MC, V.P.M.–10 P.M. MC, V.

Minneapolis. The Fifth Season. *Deluxe.* In the Marriott City Center Hotel, 30 S. 7th St. (612–349–4000). Fine dining in an elegant atmosphere. Dress code, valet parking, reservations required. Open 6–11 P.M.; closed Sun. and major holidays. AE, DC, MC, V.

The Whitney Grille. *Expensive.* 150 Portland Ave., in the Whitney Hotel (612–339–9300). Fine American and international cuisines are served in an elegant atmosphere overlooking the Mississippi River. Cocktail lounge, entertainment, valet parking. Open 6:30 A.M.–10:30 P.M.; Fri. and Sat to 11 P.M. AE, DC, MC, V.

Fox & Hounds. *Moderate.* Rte. 35E at Larpenteur Ave. (612–488–0565). Continental menu plus prime rib, seafood, and stir-fry dishes. Children's menu. Cocktail lounge. Entertainment. Open 11 A.M.–3 P.M. and 5–10 P.M. Closed Sun.; closed major holidays. AE, MC, V.

Reinhaus. *Inexpensive–Moderate.* 811 Hennepin Ave. (612–338–2812). Good German and American food, cocktail lounge. Open 11 A.M.–10 P.M.; Fri.–Sat. to 11 P.M.; closed Sun. and major holidays. AE, MC, V.

Rochester. Henry Wellingtons. *Inexpensive–Moderate.* 216 First Ave., S.W. (507–289–1949). Specializing in Wellingtons, beef and otherwise, but also offering a full standard menu. Beer and wine. Open 11 A.M.–midnight; Sun. to 11 P.M. Closed major holidays. MC, V.

Michael's Restaurant. *Inexpensive–Moderate.* 15 S. Broadway (507–288–2020). Well-prepared food in inviting atmosphere. Cocktail lounge, valet parking. Open 11 A.M.–11 P.M., closed Sun. and major holidays. AE, DC, MC, V.

St. Cloud. D.B. Searle's. *Inexpensive–Moderate.* 18 S. 5th Ave. (612–253–0655). Family dining in an old bank converted to a restaurant. Children's menu, lounge. Open 11 A.M.–10 P.M.; Fri. and Sat.–11 P.M.; Closed Christmas and New Year's Day. AE, DC, MC, V.

St. Paul. The Blue Horse. *Expensive–Deluxe.* 1355 University Ave. (612–645–8101). Continental cuisine. Specializing in fresh seafood, aged steaks, and veal entrees. Extensive wine list. Cocktails. Valet parking. Open 11 A.M.–11 P.M.; Fri. to 11:30 P.M.; Sat. 4–11:30 P.M. Closed Sun.; closed major holidays. AE, DC, MC, V.

Winona. Zack's on the Tracks. *Moderate.* 58 Center St. (507–454–6939). Children's menu, cocktail lounge. Open 11:30 A.M.–2:30 P.M. and 5–9:30 P.M.; Fri. and Sat.–10 P.M.; Sun. 10:30 A.M.–2 P.M. AE, MC, V.

LIQUOR LAWS. Liquor package goods are sold in municipal or private stores. Liquor by the drink is sold in licensed establishments. Sunday sales of liquor by the drink are allowed in hotels, restaurants, and clubs from 10 A.M. to midnight, local laws permitting. The legal drinking age is 21. No more than one quart of liquor may be brought in from out of state.

THE DAKOTAS

by
BOB KAROLEVITZ

Mr. Karolevitz is a professional writer with 28 books and more than 2,000 magazine and newspaper articles to his credit.

North and South Dakota entered the federal union as so-called "twin states" on the same day: November 2, 1889. By alphabetical order, North Dakota is generally recognized as the 39th state and South Dakota as the 40th, but no one knows for sure which of the two was first admitted. In signing the statehood proclamations, President Benjamin Harrison covered the texts of the documents with paper. He had them shuffled several times until he could not determine which was which. After he had affixed his signature to the bottom of the unidentifiable proclamations, they were shuffled again in order to hide for all time the progression of entry.

The two states may have been born on the same day, but they definitely are not identical twins. Geographically they are of the same general size and shape; their climates are not unalike (give or take a few degrees); their topography is similar; and they are each bisected and to a great extent influenced by the Missouri River. Both are partially in Central and Mountain time zones, creating some minor problems in east- and west-river communications. Beyond that, though, their citizens emphasize and occasionally boast of their individualism and "differentness."

The fact that the two states do not look to one another for major buying or selling markets is an important consideration. Since the earliest days of settlement (other than during a brief period of steamboat transportation on the Missouri a century or more ago), traffic patterns generally have run east and west. Consequently, interchange between the two states is surprisingly limited. Tourists and truckers travel across North Dakota from Minneapolis to Montana and the Pacific Northwest on Interstate 94. In South Dakota they go primarily from Iowa to the Black Hills and beyond via Interstate 90. North-south commercial and personal travel is largely confined to Interstate 29 along the eastern borders of the two states and to the two-lane U.S. Highway 281 some 90 miles west.

Airline, bus, and railroad routes are also part of the east-west pattern. Today South Dakota has no passenger train service whatsoever. The transcontinental Amtrak line runs through North Dakota, although relatively few stops are made. Flight connections to the two states are likewise limited, and visitors who want to travel by air are urged to check schedules and availabilities.

Despite curtailed public transportation, both Dakotas are much-favored vacation destinations, with guests coming principally by private auto, recreational vehicle, and tour bus. Travel accommodations are geared to those modes of transportation, and there is quite heavy tourist traffic from early May through September.

NORTH DAKOTA

North Dakota is a land of wide open spaces, offering visitors the opportunity to stretch out and breathe free. On its eastern border, the Red River of the North flows into Canada through an expansive, fertile flatland, source of mountains of potatoes and sugar beets. Farther to the west is the so-called Drift Prairie where mammoth tractors work some of the nation's largest wheat farms.

Next come the rolling bluffs of the Missouri River plateau, featuring the 11,300-foot long Garrison Dam, one of the world's largest rolled earth river barriers, which creates Lake Sakakawea. Honoring the famed Bird Woman of the Lewis and Clark Expedition (in other states the Shoshone Indian girl's name is spelled Sacajawea and Sacagawea), the 200-mile long impoundment is a major recreational attraction, teeming with fish and offering boating, water-skiing, and virtually endless camping opportunities.

In the southwestern corner of the state are the North Dakota Badlands created by the meandering Little Missouri River. This is the Roughrider Country where Teddy Roosevelt found his "perfect freedom" before he became the 26th president of the United States. The Theodore Roosevelt National Park—divided into two units—is a spectacular wilderness area, home of wild horses, bighorn sheep, bison, deer, and antelope. Park headquarters are at Medora, a unique rebuilt Old West cowtown. Here a restored chateau is evidence of the short-lived but pretentious cattle dynasty of the fabled Marquis de Mores.

Elsewhere in the state are other natural and man-made sites of interest. On the Canadian border, not far from the geographical center of North America near Rugby, is the beautiful and symbolic 2,000-acre International Peace Garden, which proudly emphasizes "the longest undefended international border in the world."

North of Jamestown, the Arrowwood National Wildlife Refuge is the nesting and feeding ground for millions of waterfowl and other species of birds and animals. Twice a year the skies over the region are almost blackened by huge flights of ducks and geese. To the southwest, Gackle is known as the Mallard Capital of the World.

In the northwestern part of the state, oil wells and extensive open-pit lignite coal mining operations are attractions of interest in an energy conscious era. There are five Indian reservations within the North Dakota borders: Fort Berthold, Fort Totten, Sisseton-Wahpeton, Standing Rock, and Turtle Mountain. Ironically, four miles south of Mandan is the reconstructed Fort Abraham Lincoln from which Lt. Col. George A. Custer

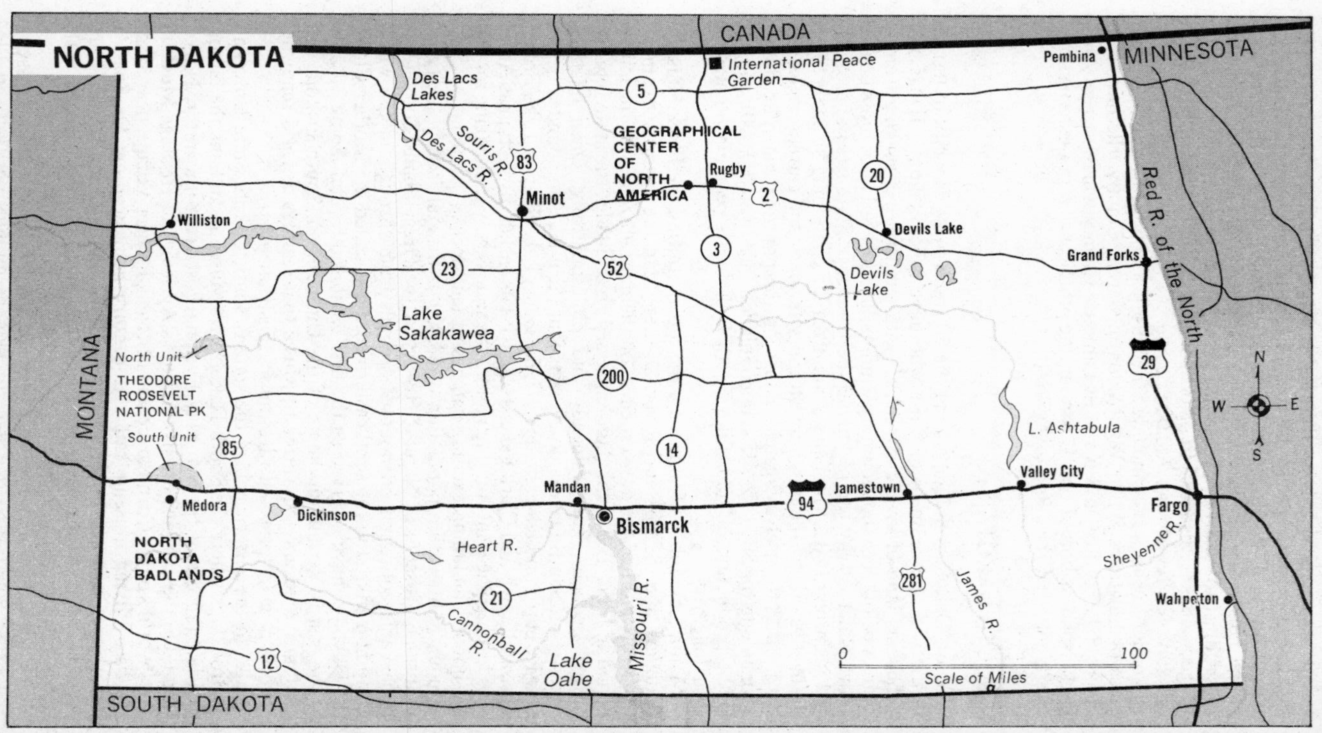
NORTH DAKOTA
CANADA
MINNESOTA
MONTANA
SOUTH DAKOTA
Pembina
International Peace Garden
Des Lacs Lakes
Souris R.
Des Lacs R.
GEOGRAPHICAL CENTER OF NORTH AMERICA
Rugby
Minot
Williston
Devils Lake
Devils Lake
Grand Forks
Red R. of the North
Lake Sakakawea
North Unit
THEODORE ROOSEVELT NATIONAL PK
South Unit
Medora
Dickinson
NORTH DAKOTA BADLANDS
Heart R.
Cannonball R.
Lake Oahe
Missouri R.
Mandan
Bismarck
Jamestown
Valley City
L. Ashtabula
James R.
Fargo
Sheyenne R.
Wahpeton
N
W
E
S
0
100
Scale of Miles
5
83
2
20
3
23
52
200
14
85
21
12
94
281
29

and the Seventh Cavalry began their ill-fated march to disaster at Little Big Horn in 1876. The fort is one of nine major state parks.

The state capital is located at Bismarck. The unique 18-story capitol building is a skyscraper by Dakota standards. Other principal cities are Fargo, home of North Dakota State University, and Grand Forks, site of the University of North Dakota. Travelers from metropolitan areas must adjust to relative population figures. "Big" in North Dakota means Fargo at 66,000, Bismarck at 48,000, and Grand Forks at 44,000. The entire state has fewer than 700,000 people.

Smaller towns of note include Strasburg in Emmons County, the birthplace of Lawrence Welk; Wimbledon in Barnes County, the hometown of singer Peggy Lee; and Kulm in Lamoure County where actress Angie Dickinson was born. Louis L'Amour, the prolific writer of western stories, was a native of the Jamestown area.

SOUTH DAKOTA

South Dakota is unique among the 50 states in its capacity to test the mettle and temperament of those who have called it home. It has been dubbed a "land of savage extremes," with temperatures ranging from 40 degrees below zero (not counting wind-chill factor) to 112 or more degrees above. That is why the nickname the Challenge State is so appropriate and inspiring: It describes and dramatizes the continuing struggle for an unshackled life by Indians, homesteaders, farmers, and entrepreneurs who have pitted themselves against nature on the prairie arena. The state is 16th among the 50 in size, 45th in population (just over 700,000), and first in the production of gold. Like North Dakota, its people are noted for their longevity.

Major geographical features are the broad prairies, the Black Hills, the Badlands, and the Missouri River. Of these four, the historic stream undoubtedly has had the greatest effect on the most citizens over the longest period of time. Today the dam-harnessed river divides the state into two distinct sections, geographically and philosophically. Once relatively water-poor, South Dakota now boasts four great lakes impounded behind massive earth-and-concrete dams: Lake Oahe, Lake Sharpe, Lake Francis Case and Lewis and Clark Lake. To go with its earlier distinction as America's leading pheasant-hunting region, the state is now challenging for fishing honors, including exciting catches of land-locked salmon.

Sioux Falls, with a population of 88,000, is the state's largest city. Its Delbridge Museum of Natural History at the Great Plains Zoo offers a remarkable collection of mounted animals from throughout the world. Historic Yankton in the southeastern corner is called the Mother City of the Dakotas, having served as the first territorial capital. Some 25 miles to the east is Vermillion, home of the University of South Dakota with its domed stadium and Shrine to Music that features a world-renowned collection of historic and rare musical instruments.

Also in the eastern half of the state is South Dakota State University at Brookings where the South Dakota Art Museum contains the famous prairie paintings of the Saturday Evening Post artist-illustrator, Harvey Dunn. On the campus, too, is the state's Agricultural Heritage Museum. The "world's only" Corn Palace is at Mitchell; Pioneer Village, near Madison, is a "living museum" of 19th-century homesteading; De Smet in Kingsbury County is the location of Laura Ingalls Wilder's "Little House on the Prairie" of children's book and television fame; and Huron is the site of the annual State Fair.

In the lake region in the northeastern corner of the state is Fort Sisseton State Park where the stone structures of the military post built in 1864 are reminders of past conflicts between natives and newcomers. There are

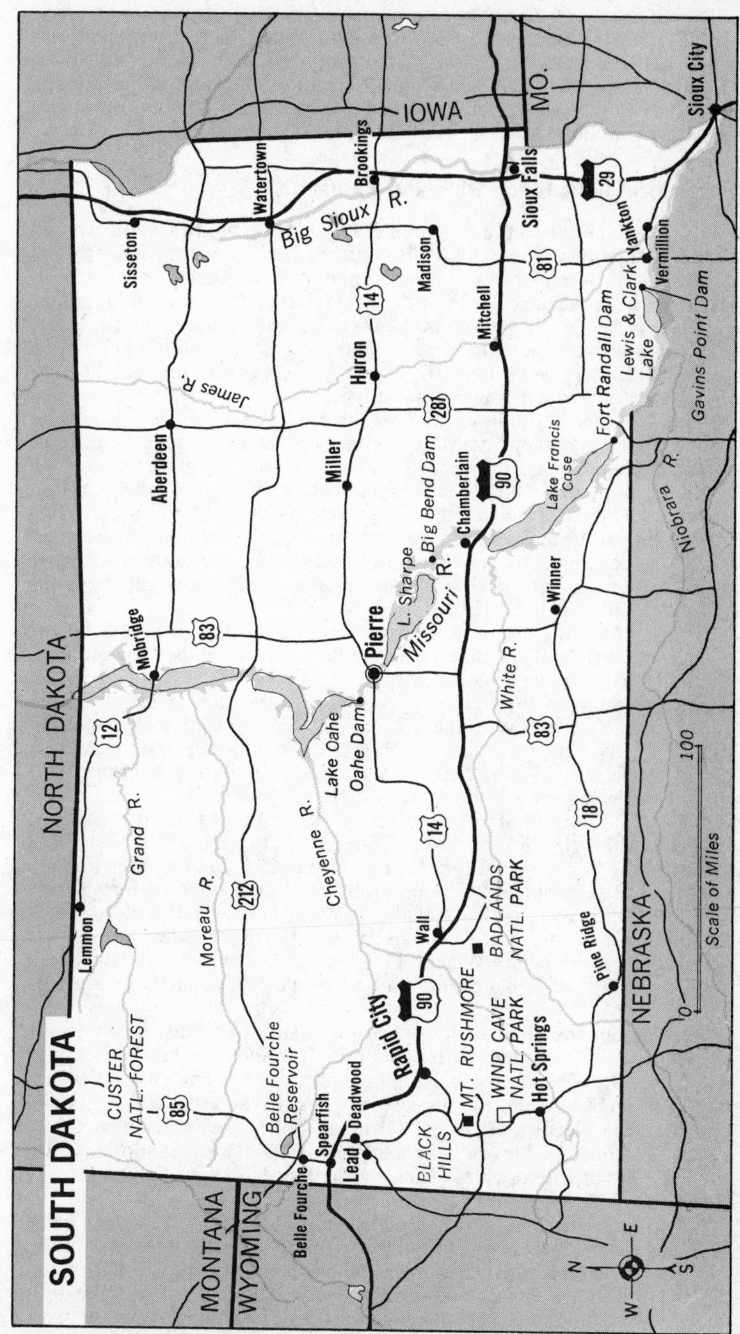
SOUTH DAKOTA
NORTH DAKOTA
MONTANA
WYOMING
NEBRASKA
IOWA
MO.
Lemmon
Mobridge
Aberdeen
Sisseton
Watertown
Brookings
Sioux Falls
Sioux City
Yankton
Vermillion
Madison
Mitchell
Huron
Miller
Pierre
Chamberlain
Winner
Wall
Rapid City
Pine Ridge
Hot Springs
Belle Fourche
Spearfish
Lead
Deadwood
CUSTER NATL. FOREST
Belle Fourche Reservoir
BLACK HILLS
MT. RUSHMORE
WIND CAVE NATL. PARK
BADLANDS NATL. PARK
Grand R.
Moreau R.
Cheyenne R.
Lake Oahe
Oahe Dam
L. Sharpe
Big Bend Dam
Missouri R.
White R.
Lake Francis Case
Fort Randall Dam
Lewis & Clark Lake
Gavins Point Dam
Niobrara R.
James R.
Big Sioux R.
12
83
212
85
90
14
18
281
81
29
Scale of Miles
0
100
N
E
S
W

six Indian reservations in South Dakota: Standing Rock, Cheyenne, Lower Brule, Crow Creek, Pine Ridge (site of Wounded Knee), and Rosebud.

North of Sioux Falls, near Garretson, is the Earth Resources Observation Systems headquarters (EROS), a data center for recording and disseminating information received from orbiting satellites. Located on the Missouri River near the geographical center of the state is Pierre (pronounced "Peer"), the state capital with typical seat-of-government attractions and the impressive Cultural Heritage Center.

Exploring the Black Hills and Badlands

The Black Hills and the Rushmore Memorial are South Dakota's major tourist attractions. The Black Hills National Forest consists of nearly 1¼ million acres, accented by towering granite spires and magnificent coniferous trees from whose dark hues the hills (or more correctly, mountains) get their name. Harney Peak, at 7,242 feet, is the highest summit. Rapid City, hub of the area, is the state's second largest city, with a population of 50,000. Ellsworth Air Force Base nearby offers guided tours of the Strategic Air Command's bomber and missile facility.

Visitors from throughout the world are drawn to the spectacular "Shrine of Democracy" at Mount Rushmore, some 25 miles southwest of Rapid City. The masterpiece of sculptor Gutzon Borglum features 60-foot high stone likenesses of U. S. Presidents Washington, Jefferson, Lincoln, and Theodore Roosevelt. A nighttime patriotic program preceding the lighting of the massive carving is a dramatic and emotional experience. Extensive parking is available at the site, as well as restaurant facilities, special viewing points, a museum, and a large souvenir and gift shop, one of the best in the Black Hills.

South of Mount Rushmore is Custer State Park where one of the largest bison (popularly called buffalo) herds in the country can be seen and photographed (though caution is advised). The Game Lodge, once President Coolidge's Summer White House, is located in the park. West of Custer, Jewel Cave National Monument is a 1,307-acre recreational area, highlighted by the subterranean chambers of the mammoth cave itself. It is one of numerous caves in the Hills available for exploring, a special treat for speleologists being Wind Cave near Hot Springs.

Another important stop is the Homestake Mine at Lead (pronounced "Leed"). Since the historic Gold Rush of '76, the Homestake has been a continuing bonanza, still producing more gold than any other mine in the Western Hemisphere. Ground level tours are conducted for visitors. Just four miles away is the "naughty" city of Deadwood, with legalized gambling, a main street still reminiscent of an earlier heyday, and Mount Moriah Cemetery where Wild Bill Hickok, Calamity Jane, Potato Creek Johnny Perrett, Preacher Smith, and other Old-West characters are buried.

Throughout the Hills a wide spectrum of sights and diversions awaits the visitor. They include the two-hour 1880 train ride from Hill City to Keystone, the Chapel in the Hills (a replica of Norway's 800-year-old, nail-less Stavkirke), and two especially scenic drives up Spearfish Canyon and over the Needles Highway. Of note, too, is the in-progress Crazy Horse Monument some six miles north of Custer. This gargantuan sculpture of a Sioux Indian chief begun by the late Korczak Ziolkowski will some day rival Rushmore.

A trip to the Badlands National Park east of the Black Hills can be as eerie and inspiring as a visit to the moon or a return to prehistoric times. This unique natural phenomenon can be reached from Wall (home of one of the world's most remarkable and popular drug stores) and via an eastern portal some 18 miles west of Kadoka on I-90. Headquarters for the park are at Cedar Pass, nine miles south of the interstate.

Millions of years ago this jagged and desolate area was a flat grassland, home to such prehistoric beasts as saber-toothed tigers and hairy mammoths. Then the earth's crust rose and volcanic ash drifted down. Rivers carved gorges, and the winds of thousands of centuries slowly wore away the softer rock and left sharp spires, rounded cones, and other baroque designs. The strange formations exhibit subtle colorations, especially striking in early morning and late afternoon, to intrigue and challenge amateur and professional photographers alike. The Badlands are a rich fossil bed, but it is illegal to remove specimens, many of which can be seen under plexiglas covers along walking trails. South Dakota is often referred to as the Land of Infinite Variety. The contrast between the Badlands and the state's other attractions emphasizes that nickname.

PRACTICAL INFORMATION FOR THE DAKOTAS

WHEN TO GO. The best time to visit the Dakotas is from mid-May to mid-Sept., with late spring and early autumn most ideal. It can get quite hot in July and Aug., with temperatures in the 90s and low 100s F. The Black Hills and the Missouri River lakes provide a respite from the heat of the open prairies, however.

Many tourist facilities shut down during the winter season or have curtailed activities so current schedules should be checked with the state tourism offices, chambers of commerce, or individual attractions. Both states offer winter sports accommodations for snowmobiling, slope and cross-country skiing, and ice-fishing. Hunting seasons are generally confined to the fall months before heavy snows set in. Winter travelers on the interstates and highways should be prepared for emergency conditions.

A pointed reality about travel in the two Dakotas is the great distance between attractions (the Black Hills being an exception). The states are basically rural in character with relatively small populations. This sparseness limits facilities and accommodations to some degree, but at the same time it offers uncluttered relaxation to go with a prevailing western hospitality.

HOW TO GET THERE. Private autos, recreational vehicles, and tour buses provide the principal means of access to the Dakotas. Accommodations are geared more to those transportation modes than to other kinds of public transportation.

By plane. *Northwest, Continental, TWA, United,* and *Delta* are the major airlines with connections into the Dakotas, but much of the service is confined primarily to Sioux Falls and Rapid City in South Dakota and to Fargo and Bismarck in North Dakota. Smaller commuter-type planes serve some of the larger towns. Airline ticket offices or travel agents should be consulted for current flight and route details. Many hunting and fishing parties fly into the two states by private plane, often using the dozens of secondary airports with turf runways or farm-and-ranch strips.

By bus. *Central Greyhound Lines* is the principal carrier in North Dakota, while *Jack Rabbit Lines* serves the key cities and towns of South Dakota. Travel off the interstates is limited, however, so prospective passengers should obtain up-to-date information before each trip.

By train. South Dakota has no rail passenger service. A transcontinental *Amtrak* line runs through North Dakota with stops at Fargo, Grand Forks, Devils Lake, Rugby, Minot, Stanley, and Williston.

By car. The Dakotas are served by three interstate highways: I-29 runs along the eastern border of both states and connects, via Canadian highway 75, to Winnipeg; I-94 crosses North Dakota from east to west, entering at Fargo and departing beyond Medora and the Badlands; I-90 similarly bisects South Dakota from Sioux Falls to Rapid City and the Black Hills. Two-lane U.S. 2 in North Dakota and 12, 14, 18, and 212 in South Dakota provide east-west connections, while U.S. 83, 85, and 281 are principal north-south roads crossing the two states.

HOW TO GET AROUND. With public conveyance considerably limited, rental cars are the best bet for Dakota visitors who don't arrive by private vehicle. *Hertz,*

Avis, Budget and *National* rental outlets are located in the larger cities, and local auto dealers offer rental services in some of the smaller communities. However, it is best to check with your nearest office of one of the national firms for specific information and/or advance reservations.

Only the larger cities offer regular taxi service.

HINTS TO MOTORISTS. The speed limit is 65 mph on interstate highways and 55 mph on all other routes unless otherwise posted. Sixteen is the minimum driving age in the two states, both of which also enforce strict drunken driving statutes. On cross-state travel, it is a good idea to keep gas tanks reasonably well filled as there are occasionally long stretches between facilities. Both states have good, hard-surfaced secondary roads, but sometimes the shoulders are inadequate.

In the Black Hills and North Dakota Badlands, special caution should be taken when driving. Drivers often stop suddenly (and unwisely) to watch or photograph bison, deer, antelope, bears, or other wild animals. Elsewhere deer-crossing signs should be strictly heeded because both states boast large deer populations from border to border. Also in the Black Hills, hairpin curves on the Needles Hwy. and other scenic roads demand alertness at the wheel.

The main office of the *North Dakota Automobile Club* is at the intersection of I-29 and I-94, Fargo, ND 58108 (701–282–6222). The *South Dakota Automobile Club* is headquartered at 1300 Industrial Ave., Sioux Falls, SD 57104 (605–336–3690).

HINTS TO DISABLED TRAVELERS. A continuing effort is being made to improve access for the disabled to both indoor and outdoor attractions. Specially marked parking places are common at city malls, most large hard-surfaced lots, and interstate rest stops. The latter also have accommodating restroom facilities. To plan a trip geared to the needs of handicapped individuals, contact the tourism offices in the two states (see addresses and phone numbers in the Tourist Information sections below).

LIQUOR LAWS. Liquor may be purchased in either North or South Dakota by the bottle in liquor stores or by the drink in licensed establishments. There are no sales on Sun. The minimum drinking age is 21.

Practical Information for North Dakota

TOURIST INFORMATION. Travel literature and maps are available from *North Dakota Tourism Promotion Division,* Liberty Memorial Building, Bismarck, ND 58505 (in-state toll free 1–800–472–2100, national toll free 1–800–437–2077). Hunting and fishing information is obtainable from *North Dakota Game and Fish Department,* 100 N. Bismarck Expwy., Bismarck, ND 58501 (701–221–6300). For other recreational information, contact *North Dakota Parks and Recreation,* 1424 W. Century Ave., Bismarck, ND 58502 (701–224–4887). Visitors to Canada may call the U. S. Customs District Office at Pembina, ND 58271 (701–825–6201), for up-to-date American customs information.

TELEPHONES. The area code for North Dakota is 701. Local calls cost 25 cents, and there's no time limit. For information within the 701 area, dial 1–555–1212. For long distance calls out of North Dakota, dial 1 before the area code. Dial 0 before the area code for operator assistance on credit card and long-distance calls.

EMERGENCY TELEPHONE NUMBERS. For fire, police, sheriff, ambulance, and highway patrol, dial 911 in major cities; otherwise you must consult the local directory. For emergency assistance and road conditions, call 1–800–472–2121. The *North Dakota Highway Department* is reached at 701–224–2500. The *North Dakota Poison Information Center* number is 1–800–732–2200.

SEASONAL EVENTS. Most events in North Dakota occur in the summer and fall, but there are year-round activities. Contact the *North Dakota Tourism Promotion Division* for specific dates and details (address and phone numbers in *Tourist Information* section above).

January. *Winterfest* at Minot, includes jazz festival and the *Regina (Canada)–Minot International 250 Snowmobile Cross Country Race.*

March. *North Dakota Winter Show,* Valley City, includes livestock, farm and home exhibits, plus indoor rodeo.

June. *Fort Seward Wagon Train,* Jamestown. Week-long authentic trail ride. *Old Time Fiddlers' Contest,* International Peace Garden.

June through Labor Day. *Medora Musical* in the Badlands; a nightly show in an outdoor theater, with western music and a patriotic salute.

July. *Governor's Cup Walleye Fishing Tournament,* Lake Sakakawea; two-day competition for approximately 200 two-person teams. *North Dakota Prison Rodeo,* State Penitentiary, Bismarck; a two-day cowboy competition within the walls. *North Dakota State Fair,* Minot; a nine-day exhibition with big-name concerts.

August. *Pioneer Days,* at Bonanzaville, USA, West Fargo; a weekend festival at a restored pioneer village, including parades and pioneer crafts demonstrations.

September. *United Tribes Powwow,* Bismarck; Native American singing and dancing competitions, Indian foods and costumes.

October. *Makoti Threshing Bee,* Makoti; exhibit and demonstrations of antique farm machinery, including a fiddlers' contest.

December. *"Little Christmas on the Prairie"* at Bonanzaville, USA, West Fargo; an old-fashioned Christmas celebration in a pioneer village setting.

NATIONAL AND STATE PARKS. North Dakota has one national park, nine major state parks, and numerous all-season recreation areas. Detailed information is available from *North Dakota Parks and Recreation,* 1424 W. Century Ave., Bismarck, ND 58502 (701–224–4887).

Theodore Roosevelt National Park, Box 7, Medora, ND 58645 (701–623–4466), offers sightseeing, hiking, camping, and picnicking in the rugged 70,436-acre wilderness areas. There is a 49-mi. circle drive through spectacular scenery in the South Unit. Admission $3 per vehicle (free in winter). Be sure to stop at the Visitor Center for the inexpensive guide to the auto tour.

FISHING AND HUNTING. Lakes Sakakawea and Oahe are the state's primary fishing attractions, with walleyes and northern pike being especially large and plentiful. North Dakota is on a major waterfowl flyway, so ducks and geese provide excellent hunting, as do pheasants and grouse. Deer and antelope challenge both gun and bow hunters. For current regulations, contact *North Dakota Game and Fish Dept.,* 100 N. Bismarck Expwy., Bismarck, ND 58501 (701–221–6300).

HISTORIC SITES. In North Dakota, many sites and remnants of forts remain from the Indian wars of the 19th century. Most are open to tourists from mid-May to mid-Sept. Three of the most notable are:

Fort Buford. A state historic site southwest of Williston near the Montana border. Built in 1866, it was the scene of Sitting Bull's surrender in 1881. Call 701–572–9034.

Fort Lincoln. Five mi. south of Mandan, now in a state park. Has interpretive center and reconstructed Mandan Indian earth lodges. Call 701–663–9571.

Fort Union Trading Post National Historic Site. Off State Road 1804, 17 mi. southwest of Williston near the Montana border. Founded in 1833, the fort was the largest fur trading post on the northern Missouri. Has visitors' center.

MUSEUMS. There are numerous county and local museums of varying quality in addition to larger ones at forts and other historic sites throughout the state. Watch for signs or inquire locally. Particularly noteworthy are:

Bonanzaville, USA. Six mi. west of West Fargo off I-94. This reconstructed pioneer village and farm includes the *Regional Museum of the Red River and Northern Plains.* Admission to museum and village: adults, $3.25; children 6–16, $1.25. Call 701–282–2822.

Museum of the Badlands. At Medora. Features fur-trade items and Indian artifacts. Adults, $2.50; children 6–16, $1.25. Call 701–623–4444.

North Dakota Heritage Center. On state capitol grounds in Bismarck. This museum offers the most thorough depiction of state history and development. Closed New Year's Day, Easter, Thanksgiving, and Christmas. Free. Call 701–224–2666.

ACCOMMODATIONS. North Dakota has good motel service along the interstates in addition to those listed below. In general, price categories for double occupancy average as follows: *Deluxe,* $60 and up; *Expensive,* $45–$60; *Moderate,* up to $45. Rates are year-around. Seniors should ask for discounts. Not listed are a number of economy motels of good quality such as *Super 8, Motel 6, Kelly Inn,* and *Days Inn* in or near the larger cities. Most facilities have winter plug-ins.

Bismarck. Radisson Inn Bismarck. *Deluxe.* 800 S. Third St., Bismarck, ND 58501 (701–258–7700 or 800–333–3333). More than 300 rooms with elegant Bavarian decor. Includes restaurant, lounge, indoor pool, other plus services.

Sheraton Bismarck Galleria. *Deluxe.* Sixth and Broadway, Box 2718, Bismarck, ND 58501 (701–255–6000 or 800–325–3535). Downtown facility with 223 rooms, convention center, and all accessory services; has retail shops, a rooftop park, and covered parking for 710 cars.

Best Western Doublewood Inn. *Expensive.* 1400 E. Interchange Ave., Bismarck, ND 58501 (701–258–7000 or 800–528–1234). 148 units not far from state capitol; has indoor pool, dining room with cocktails, playground.

Holiday Inn. *Expensive.* West on I–94, Box 1015, Bismarck, ND 58501 (701–223–9600 or 800–450–4329). Typical Holiday Inn accommodations with 259 rooms, lounge, restaurant, indoor pool.

Best Western Fleck House. *Moderate.* 122 E. Thayer Ave., Bismarck, ND 58501 (701–255–1450 or 800–528–1234). Smaller, comfortable facility with 58 units, 20 with kitchens; outdoor pool, restaurant, and lounge nearby; free coffee.

Bottineau. Norway House. *Moderate.* Hwy. 5, E., Bottineau, ND 58318 (701–228–3737). A 46-room motel with restaurant and lounge; one of few facilities within 30 miles of International Peace Garden.

Devils Lake. Trails West Motel. *Moderate.* Box 1113, Devils Lake, ND 58301 (701–662–5011). 74 comfortable units south on U.S. 2; restaurant adjacent.

Dickinson. New Oasis Motel. *Moderate.* 1000 W. Villard, Dickinson, ND 58601 (701–225–6703). 37 units on I-94 route to North Dakota Badlands; restaurant, outdoor pool.

Select Inn. *Moderate.* 642 12th St., W., Dickinson, ND 58601 (701–227–1891). Year-round facility with 59 units. Restaurant opposite.

Fargo. Radisson Hotel Fargo. *Deluxe.* 201 5th St., N., Fargo, ND 58102 (701–232–7363 or 800–333–3333). This is a highly rated city center hotel with 151 units. Has parking ramp, exercise room, outstanding Passages Cafe.

Best Western Doublewood Inn. *Expensive.* 3333 13th Ave., S., Fargo, ND 58103 (701–235–3333 or 800–528–1234). A highly rated motor inn with 170 rooms, restaurant, lounge, casino, and indoor pool.

Holiday Inn. *Expensive.* 3803 13th Ave., S., Fargo, ND 58103 (701–282–2143 or 800–465–4329). This is typically full-service facility of the chain, with 300 units; opposite city's largest indoor shopping mall.

Motel 75. *Moderate.* 3402 14th Ave., S., Fargo, ND 58103 (701–232–1321). Good family accommodations with 101 rooms, outdoor pool; free Continental breakfast and coffee; restaurant opposite.

Oak Manor Motel. *Moderate.* Junction I-94 and U.S. 81, Box 7328, Fargo, ND 58108 (701–235–3141). 116-room well-kept motel with lounge, restaurant, outdoor pool.

Garrison. Garrison Motel. *Moderate.* On SR 37, Garrison, ND 58540 (701–463–2858). 30 units; one of a limited number of facilities near Lake Sakakawea.

Grand Forks. Ramada Inn. *Expensive.* 1205 N. 43rd, Grand Forks, ND 58201 (701–775–3951 or 800–2–RAMADA). A top-rated Ramada with 99 units; restaurant and lounge with entertainment; indoor pool.

Ambassador Motel. *Moderate.* 2021 S. Washington, Grand Forks, ND 58201 (701–772–3463). Small economical 30-room facility with waterbeds and free coffee; restaurant nearby.

Roadking Inn. *Moderate.* 1015 N. 43rd St., Grand Forks, ND 58201 (701–775–0691). Good quality for the money; 100 rooms with sauna and exercise room; Continental breakfast; restaurant and lounge nearby.

Jamestown. Dakota Inn. *Moderate.* Hwy. 281, S. and I-94, Jamestown, ND 58401 (701–252–3611). 125 rooms; indoor pool; restaurant; entertainment; bowling alley connected by underground tunnel.

Gladstone Inn. *Moderate.* 111 Second St., N.E., Jamestown, ND 58401 (701–252–0700). 118 rooms downtown adjacent to Civic Center; indoor pool, restaurant, cocktails, entertainment.

Mandan. Best Western Seven Seas Motor Inn. *Expensive.* Exit 31 at I-94, Box 749, Mandan, ND 58554 (701–663–7401 or 800–528–1234). Excellent accommodations with award-winning dining room; 104 units, king- and queen-size beds, indoor pool, lounge, and entertainment.

Medora. Badlands Motel. *Moderate.* Box 198, Medora, ND 58645 (701–623–4422). Western style facility with 120 rooms in unique Badlands town; outdoor pool, miniature golf; restaurant and lounge nearby.

Minot. (Special note: Minot has two dozen motels but travelers are advised that during the State Fair in mid-July all accommodations are booked months in advance.)

Sheraton Riverside Inn. *Expensive.* 2200 Burdick Expressway E., Minot, ND 58701 (701–852–2504 or 800–325–3535). A multistoried, full-service facility with 176 units; indoor pool, game room, beauty and barber shops, restaurants, and casino bar; children under 18 free.

Thunderbird Motel. *Moderate.* 1900 4th Ave., S.E., Minot, ND 58701 (701–852–4488). Small but well-maintained 32-room facility near state fairgrounds.

Wahpeton. Travel Host Motel. *Moderate.* 995 21st Ave., N., Wahpeton, ND 58075 (701–642–8731). Offered here are 59 well-kept units with dining room and coffee shop. Available to State School of Science.

Williston. El Rancho Motor Hotel. *Moderate.* 1623 2nd Ave. W., Williston, ND 58801 (701–572–6321). This quality motor inn with 92 units is located near business loop and historic sites; it has cable TV, in-room movies, casual coffee shop, and cozy dining room.

RESTAURANTS. Dining in North Dakota ranges from highly sophisticated to simple ranch-country fare. Restaurant price categories are as follows: *Expensive,* $10 and up; *Moderate,* under $10. Not included are drinks, tax, and tip. Numerous fast-food chain facilities are available along interstates and in larger cities and towns. Holiday Inns, Ramada Inns, and similar quality establishments, whether listed or not, usually offer recommendable dining. Most have no-smoking sections.

Bismarck. Caspar's East 40. *Expensive.* 1401 E. Interchange Ave., Bismarck, ND 58501 (701–258–7222). Features prime rib in Early American decor. Cocktails. L, D, 11:30 A.M.–2 P.M., 5 P.M.–10:30 P.M. Closed Sun. AE, MC, V.

Der Mark. *Expensive.* 800 S. Third St., Bismarck, ND 58501 (701–258–7700). In Radisson Inn Bismarck. Seven days a week, B, L, D. Excellent food in a Bavarian setting. Cocktails. AE, DC, MC, V.

Dickinson. Good Earth Eating & Drinking Establishment. *Expensive.* I-94 and ND 22 junction, Dickinson, ND 58601 (701–227–1853). In Hospitality Inn. Varied fare with some moderate items on menu. B, L, D, seven days a week, 6 A.M.–10 P.M. Cocktails. AE, DC, MC, V.

Fargo. The Grainery. *Expensive.* West Acres Shopping Center, Fargo, ND 58102 (701–282–6262). Beef and chicken featured in yesteryear agricultural motif.

Children's menu. Cocktails. L, D, 11 A.M.–11 P.M. Closed Sun. and holidays. AE, DC, MC, V.

Paradiso. *Moderate.* 801 S. 38th St., Fargo, ND 58102 (701–282–5747). A touch of Mexico in northern climes. Children's menu, cocktails. Seven days a week. L, D, 11 A.M.–11 P.M.; additional hour Fri., Sat. Closed Thanksgiving and Christmas. AE, MC, V.

Grand Forks. The Peartree Restaurant. *Moderate–Expensive.* Junction I-29 and Hwy. 2, W., Jamestown, ND 58201 (701–772–7131). In Holiday Inn. Cocktails. Seven days a week, B, L, D, 6:30 A.M.–10 P.M. Sunday brunch 10 A.M.–2 P.M. AE, DC, MC, V.

Mandan. Captain's Table. *Expensive.* Exit 31, I–94, Mandan, ND 58554 (701–663–3773). In Best Western Seven Seas Motor Inn. Steaks and seafood in nautical decor. Cocktails. Some moderately priced items on menu. Seven days a week. B, L, D, 6:30 A.M.–11 P.M.; additional hour Fri., Sat.; 6:30 A.M.–9 P.M., Sun. AE, DC, MC, V.

Williston. Trapper's Kettle. *Moderate.* Junction of U.S. 2 and ND 85, Williston, ND 58801 (701–774–2831). Features home-style cooking amid artifacts of fur-trade era. Some menu items at higher price range. Open 24 hours, seven days a week. Closed Christmas Eve and Christmas. AE, DC, MC, V.

Practical Information for South Dakota

TOURIST INFORMATION. Travel literature and maps are available from *South Dakota Tourism,* Box 1000, Pierre, SD 57501 (in-state toll free 1–800–952–2217; national toll free 1–800–843–1930). Hunting and fishing information is obtainable from the *South Dakota Game, Fish and Parks Dept.,* 445 E. Capitol, Pierre, SD 57501 (605–773–3485). Other information sources are *Black Hills, Badlands and Lakes Association,* 900 Jackson Blvd., Rapid City, SD 57701 (605–341–1462); *Great Lakes of South Dakota Association,* Box 786, Pierre, SD 57501 (605–224–4617); and *Glacial Lakes Association of South Dakota,* Box 244, Watertown, SD 57201 (605–886–7305).

TELEPHONES. The area code for South Dakota is 605. Local calls cost 25 cents, and there's no time limit. For information within the 605 area, dial 1–555–1212. For long-distance calls out of South Dakota, dial 1 before the area code. Dial 0 before the area code for operator assistance on credit card and long-distance calls.

EMERGENCY TELEPHONE NUMBERS. For fire, police, sheriff, ambulance, and highway patrol, dial 911 in major cities; otherwise you must consult the local directory. Road conditions can be obtained by calling 605–773–3536. Other numbers are *South Dakota Department of Transportation* (605–773–5106); *Poison Control Center,* Sioux Falls (1–800–952–0123).

SEASONAL EVENTS. Contact the various South Dakota tourist information sources for specific dates and details. (Addresses and phone numbers are listed above in the *Tourist Information* section.)

January. *Snow Queen Festival* and *Winter Carnival* at Aberdeen, featuring snowmobile competitions and other sports events.

March. *Schmeckfest* at Freeman, a German food and heritage festival.

May. *Black Hills Hot Air Balloon Rally* at Fort Meade near Sturgis; a most colorful and exciting event.

June. *Czech Days* at Tabor in Yankton County, featuring ethnic food, dances, and Old Country charm.

Early June to late August. *Black Hills Passion Play* at Spearfish, a renowned theatrical production in a natural amphitheatre.

Late June to mid-July. *Laura Ingalls Wilder Pageant* at De Smet, recalling the author's "Little House on the Prairie" books.

July. *Black Hills Roundup* at Belle Fourche, a wild-and-woolly western celebration with parades and rodeo. *Brookings Summer Festival,* at Brookings, fun in the park with arts, crafts, and music.

August. *Black Hills Motorcycle Rally* at Sturgis attracts thousands of bikers for a week-long event. *Governor's Cup Walleye Tourney* at Pierre, a major fishing competition on Lake Oahe. *Yankton Riverboat Days,* with concerts and aquatic fun on the Missouri River at the Mother City of the Dakotas.

September. *South Dakota State Fair* at Huron, a typical state fair with all the trimmings. *Corn Palace Festival* at Mitchell, featuring name entertainers at the only arena of its kind.

October. *Hobo Day* at Brookings, South Dakota State University's homecoming, one of the nation's most unusual.

December. *State Capitol Christmas Exhibit* at Pierre, an unusual display of uniquely decorated trees.

TOURS AND SPECIAL-INTEREST SIGHTSEEING. *Gray Line* (605–342–4461), *Stagecoach West* (605–343–3113) and *Jack Rabbit Lines* (605–348–3330) offer tours of the Black Hills and Badlands, including the Passion Play. *Golden Circle Tours* (605–673–4349) visits points of interest in the southern Black Hills, including an evening schedule of the lighting program at Mount Rushmore.

Other points of interest are *Dinosaur Park* on Skyline Dr. in Rapid City, with seven life-size prehistoric reptiles; *Bear Butte,* near Sturgis, a huge volcanic bubble that rises abruptly 1,400 ft. above the plains; and the *Dells of the Sioux* near Dell Rapids in eastern South Dakota with picturesque craggy formations of red rock known locally as "Sioux Falls granite."

NATIONAL PARKS. **Badlands National Park,** Box 6, Interior, SD 57750 (605–433–5361). Open year-round. *Cedar Pass Lodge* open May 1–Oct. 15. More than 100 campsites, some primitive.

Wind Cave National Park, Hot Springs, SD 57747 (605–745–4600). Open year-round. Camping. Wind Cave is one of the largest caverns in the world. Above ground, the park is primarily prairie land, at the foot of the Black Hills.

For information about state parks, contact the Dept. of Game, Fish, and Parks, 445 E. Capitol, Pierre, SD 57501 (605–773–3485).

FISHING AND HUNTING. In addition to its long-time reputation as the Pheasant Capital of the World, South Dakota has added a claim to the walleye fishing honors on its four great lakes. Land-locked salmon, sauger, catfish, northern pike, and the prehistoric paddlefish (which must be snagged) are also taken in large numbers. The state also has excellent grouse, dove, turkey, and waterfowl shooting, along with deer, antelope, and elk hunting. For regulations and other information, again contact the Dept. of Game, Fish and Parks noted in the preceding section.

PARTICIPANT SPORTS. The four dam-created lakes on the Missouri River and numerous natural lakes in the northeast corner of the state offer a wide variety of **boating, swimming, water-skiing,** and other water-related activities. The state has numerous **golf courses,** although many are 9-hole, and some still have sand greens. **Gold-panning** and **rock-collecting** are interesting diversions in the Black Hills.

GAMBLING. The state constitution has been amended to allow gambling in the historic city of Deadwood only, although the state has lotteries. High-stake bingo is available on some Indian reservations (check locally).

HISTORIC SITES AND HOUSES. The **Cramer-Kenyon Heritage Home** at 509 Pine St., Yankton, is a three-story Queen Anne house (1886) containing original furnishings, fine woodwork, and unusual chandeliers.

Fort Sisseton, an 1864 military installation in the northeastern corner of the state, has a visitors' center and is the site of an annual festival in early June featuring cavalry, fiddling, and even tomahawk throwing.

The **Mammoth Site,** five mi. west of Hot Springs on U.S. 18, is a 10-acre graveyard of ancient elephants which is gradually being unearthed since its discovery in 1974.

The **Sitting Bull Monument,** on a hill near Mobridge overlooking the Missouri River, marks the controversial burial site of the famous Sioux leader.

MUSEUMS AND GALLERIES. The **Museum of Geology** in O'Harra Memorial Building on the campus of South Dakota School of Mines and Technology in Rapid City has excellent exhibits of rocks, minerals and fossils from the Black Hills and Badlands.

The **Cultural Heritage Center** in Pierre, built as a memorial to the state's centennial in 1989, has pioneer, Indian, and other historic exhibits and houses the *State Historic Resource Center,* a repository for genealogical study.

The **Shrine to Music,** Vermillion, contains the nationally renowned Arne B. Larson collection of antique and unusual musical instruments. The **South Dakota Art Museum** in Brookings features the prairie and World War I paintings of artist-illustrator Harvey Dunn. The major collection of works by the Sioux artist, Oscar Howe, is at the **W. H. Over Museum** in Vermillion.

Not to be overlooked are the **Blue Cloud Abbey Museum,** Marvin (in a Benedictine monastery); **Buechel Memorial Lakota Museum** at St. Francis (on the Rosebud Indian Reservation); the **Agricultural Heritage Museum,** Brookings; and the **Dahl Art Center,** Rapid City.

ACCOMMODATIONS. Hotels and motels in South Dakota, because they are generally smaller than those in the East or Far West, offer a homey, friendly atmosphere. A tip: when traveling in the sparsely populated interior or in the Black Hills during the peak tourist season (May–Sept.), make advance reservations. Off-season rates are usually available in the Black Hills.

Price categories listed in this section, for double occupancy, will average as follows: *Deluxe,* $60 and up; *Expensive,* $45–$60; *Moderate,* under $45. Not listed are a number of economy motels such as *Super 8, Kelly Inn, Motel 6,* and *Days Inn* which offer good inexpensive accommodations in or near the larger cities. Most facilities listed have winter plug-ins.

Aberdeen. Best Western Ramkota Inn. *Expensive.* 1400 8th Ave., N.W., Aberdeen, SD 57401 (605–229–4040 or 800–528–1234). A highly rated 154-unit facility with dining room, lounge, indoor pool, and exercise room.

Breeze-Inn Motel. *Moderate.* 1216 6th Ave., S.W., Aberdeen, SD 57401 (605–225–4222). 22 units, small but comfortable; restaurants nearby.

Brookings. Holiday Inn. *Expensive.* 2500 E. 6th St., Brookings, SD 57006. (605–692–9471 or 800–465–4329). Well-managed facility with 125 units; near campus and famed McCrory Gardens.

Staurolite Inn. *Expensive.* Junction U.S. 14 and I-29, Box 522, Brookings, SD 57006 (605–692–9421). A Best Western motel with 80 units, dining room and bar, indoor pool and sauna; near South Dakota State University.

Chamberlain. Best Western Lee's Motor Inn. *Moderate.* 220 W. King St, Chamberlain, SD 57325 (605–734–5575 or 800–528–1234). Pleasant mid-state stop, close to good fishing on Lake Sharpe of the Missouri; 60 units; restaurant and lounge.

Custer. State Game Lodge. *Expensive.* Mailing address: Custer, SD 57730 (605–255–4541). Enjoy the charm of the old lodge or the convenience of newer motel units in the heart of the 73,000-acre Custer State Park. Dining room features buffalo steaks. Reservations advised.

Bavarian Inn Motel. *Moderate.* One mi. north on U.S. 16–385, Box 152, Custer, SD 57730 (605–673–2802). Old World decor on heights above historic city; 52 units with pool, sauna, lighted tennis court; restaurant and lounge adjacent.

Dakota Cowboy Inn. *Moderate.* 208 Mt. Rushmore Rd., Custer, SD 57730 (605–673–4659). 33 units with restaurant, heated pool, playground; caters to families; has special 3-day rates.

Deadwood. Best Western Motor Inn. *Expensive.* 137 Charles St., Deadwood, SD 57732 (605–578–1611 or 800–528–1234). 41 units; best accommodations in historic mining town; restaurant.

Hot Springs. Best Western Hickock House. *Moderate.* 902 N. River St., Hot Springs, SD 57747 (605–745–3187 or 800–528–1234). Small historic hotel with 12 units; listed on *National Historic Register;* within walking distance of famed *Evans Plunge;* restaurant.

Huron. The Crossroads Hotel & Convention Center. *Expensive.* 100 4th St., S.W., Huron, SD 57350 (605–352–3204). This downtown facility has 100 units, dining room, and heated pool. These are the best accommodations in the State Fair city.

Kadoka. Cuckleburr Motel. *Moderate.* Exit 150, I-90, Box 575, Kadoka, SD 57543 (605–837–2151). A 34-unit facility near the entry to the Badlands; small heated pool, playground; restaurant nearby.

Keystone. Four Presidents Motel. *Expensive.* Box 690, Keystone, SD 57751 (605–666–4472). A Best Western facility downtown, with 30 units in the colorful tourist-oriented Black Hills town nearest to Mount Rushmore.

Madison. Lake Park Motel. *Moderate.* Box 47, Madison, SD 57042 (605–256–3524). Offered here are 41 units, with restaurant adjacent. Best facility available to Dakota State University.

Milbank. Manor Motel. *Moderate.* Box 26, Milbank, SD 57252 (605–432–4591). This small, well-operated, 30-unit facility has a restaurant adjacent. The motel is located in far northeastern city noted for its granite quarries.

Mitchell. Holiday Inn. *Expensive.* Box 458, Mitchell, SD 57301 (605–996–6501). 155 units near exit 330 of I-90; indoor pool, saunas, putting green; restaurant and lounge with entertainment.

Coachlight Motel. *Moderate.* 1000 W. Havens St., Mitchell, SD 57301 (605–996–5686). A small, well-rated 20-unit facility not far from the "world's only" Corn Palace.

Mobridge. Wrangler Motor Inn. *Moderate.* 820 W. Grand Crossing, Mobridge, SD 57601 (605–845–3641). This 58-unit motel overlooks Lake Oahe on the Missouri; has indoor pool, sauna, exercise room, and racquetball courts; restaurant adjacent.

Pierre. Best Western Kings Inn. *Moderate.* 220 S. Pierre St., Pierre, SD 57501 (605–224–5951 or 800–528–1234). A very popular 104-room facility, especially when the state legislature meets; has restaurant and busy cocktail lounge.

State Motel. *Moderate.* 640 N. Euclid Ave., Pierre, SD 57501 (605–224–5896). Comfortable but with no frills for an economical visit to the state capital.

Rapid City. Rapid City has dozens of motels with a wide range of quality to serve the heavy traffic to the Black Hills during the summer season. Reservations or early arrivals are advised.

Alex Johnson Hotel. *Expensive.* 523 6th St., Rapid City, SD 57701 (605–342–1210). Fine old downtown hotel restored with 121 rooms; valet parking; excellent restaurant.

Best Western Gill's Sun Inn. *Expensive.* 1901 W. Main St., Rapid City, SD 57709 (605–343–6040 or 800–528–1234). 84 attractive and varied units; heated pool; restaurant and lounge.

Big Sky Motel. *Moderate.* 4080 Tower Rd., Rapid City, SD 57701. 31 units on Skyline Drive with expansive view on main road to Mt. Rushmore.

Garden Cottages Motel. *Moderate.* 4030 Jackson Blvd., Rapid City, SD 57701 (605–342–6922). Only 13 units for those who want to depart from the conventional motel; four units with kitchens.

Lake Park Motel. *Moderate.* W. Hwy. 44, Rapid City, SD 57701 (605–343–0234). On the shores of Canyon Lake in a woodsy setting, this motel has 20 units.

Lamplighter Inn. *Moderate.* 27 St. Joseph St., Rapid City, SD 57701 (605–342–3385). A well-maintained 27-unit facility; heated pool; waterbeds available.

Town House Motel. *Moderate.* 210 St. Joseph St., Rapid City, SD 57701 (605–342–8143). 40 units with reputation for good housekeeping; small heated pool; restaurant opposite.

Sioux Falls. Best Western Ramkota Inn. *Expensive.* 2400 N. Louise Ave., Sioux Falls, SD 57101 (605–336–0650 or 800–528–1234). One of South Dakota's largest convention centers with 240 units; two heated pools, restaurant, lounge, miniature golf, and racquetball courts.

Holiday Inns. *Expensive.* City Centre: 100 W. 8th St., Sioux Falls, SD 57102 (605–339–2000), and Airport: 1301 W. Russell St., Sioux Falls, SD 57104 (605–336–1020 or 800–465–4329 for each). City Centre has 313 units and Airport 144; both have a full range of services, including indoor pools, restaurants, lounges, and entertainment.

Kelly Inn. *Moderate.* 3101 W. Russell St., Sioux Falls, SD 57104 (605–338–6242). A comfortable well-rated, 42-unit facility; has sauna and whirlpool; restaurant adjacent.

Pine Crest. *Moderate.* 4501 W. 12th St., Sioux Falls, SD 57106 (605–336–3530). Economical accommodations in a 34-unit motel with heated pool, playground, waterbeds, and free coffee.

Valley Inn. *Moderate.* 1000 S. Grange, Sioux Falls, SD 57105 (605–335–3040). A 30-unit motel in a quiet residential location; restaurant nearby.

Spearfish. Spearfish Holiday Inn. *Deluxe.* Exit 40, I-90 Box 399, Spearfish, SD 57783 (605–642–4683 or 800–465–4329). A highly rated luxury inn on the edge of the Black Hills; excellent accommodations, including indoor pool, restaurant, lounge, and entertainment.

Royal Rest Motel. *Moderate.* 444 Main St., Spearfish, SD 57783 (605–642–3842). Easily accessible 21-unit facility. Special note: Heavily booked during Passion Play season (early June to late Aug.).

Vermillion. Tomahawk Budget Motel. *Moderate.* SD 50W, Vermillion, SD 57069 (605–624–2601). An economical 20-unit motel near the campus of the University of South Dakota. Air conditioned, TV.

Wall. Sands Motel. *Moderate.* 804 Glenn St., Wall, SD 57790 (605–279–2121). A 49-unit motel, one of several of similar quality in a small town famous for the unique Wall Drug Store; also at the western portal to the Badlands. Air conditioned, TV.

Watertown. Best Western Ramkota Inn. *Expensive.* 2001 9th Ave., S.W., Watertown, SD 57201 (605–886–8011 or 800–528–1234). Attractive facility with 103 units; lounge, restaurant, indoor pool. In the heart of the state's northeast lake country.

Yankton. Yankton Inn. *Expensive.* 1607 E. Hwy. 50, Yankton, SD 57078 (605–665–2906). Fine accommodations with 125 units on the edge of the historic Mother City of the Dakotas; indoor pool, sauna, and exercise room; restaurant and lounge with entertainment. Air conditioned, TV.

RESTAURANTS. Heavy summer tourist traffic in South Dakota has been responsible for the development of a wide range of eating establishments, many in connection with motels. Numerous fast-food chain facilities are available in the larger cities and towns and along the interstates. Holiday Inns, and similar quality establishments, whether listed or not, usually have good dining accommodations. Restaurant price categories are as follows (although some menus span both levels): *Expensive,* $10 and up; *Moderate,* under $10. Not included are drinks, tax and tips. Most have no-smoking sections.

Aberdeen. The Lumber Company. *Expensive.* 815 6th Ave., S.E., Aberdeen, SD 57401 (605–226–2124). As the name implies, this is a converted lumberyard. Featured are three separate restaurants: the Lumberjack, the Aspen, and the Stake House. Menus range from inexpensive to expensive. Seven days a week, 24 hours a day in at least one facility. Two bars and an entertainment center are included. AE, MC, V.

Brookings. The Ram Pub. *Moderate.* 327 Main Ave., Brookings, SD 57006 (605–692–2485). A popular restaurant in a converted bank building. Cocktails. L, 11:30 A.M.–2 P.M.; D, 5–9:30 P.M.; additional hour, Fri., Sat. Closed Sun. and major holidays. MC, V.

Chamberlain. Al's Oasis. *Moderate.* 2½ mi. west on I–90, Box 128, Chamberlain, SD 57325 (605–734–6054). A much patronized mid-state stop, featuring five-cent coffee, homemade pie, and a menu ranging from inexpensive to expensive. B, L, D, 6 A.M.–10:30 P.M. seven days a week. MC, V.

Custer. Bavarian Inn Restaurant. *Moderate.* One mi. north on U.S. 16–385, Box 152, Custer, SD 57730 (605–673–4412). German specialties featured on general menu, with some items expensive. Cocktails. B, L, D, 7 A.M.–10 P.M. seven days a week. Reduced hours in off-season. MC, V.

Custer State Park. Pheasant Dining Room. *Moderate.* In State Game Lodge (605–255–4541). Old resort atmosphere; menu includes buffalo, pheasant, and native trout; some items expensive. Cocktails. B, L, D, 7 A.M.–8:30 P.M. in tourist season. Reduced hours in off-season. No credit cards.

Huron. Hangar Cafe. *Moderate.* Huron Regional Airport, Huron, SD 57350 (605–352–7576). Varied, interesting menu, from steaks to catfish; World War I aviation decor. Cocktails. B, L, D, 6 A.M.–11 P.M. daily. MC, V.

Keystone. Ruby House Restaurant. *Moderate.* Main St., Keystone, SD 57751. (605–666–4404). 1890 decor; in small resort town near Mount Rushmore. Open from mid-May to mid-Oct.; B, L, D, 7 A.M.–9:30 P.M. (one hour earlier and later from June 1 to Sept. 1). AE, DC, MC, V.

Mitchell. Chef Louie's. *Moderate.* 904 E. Havens St., Mitchell, SD 57301 (605–996–7565). Serving dinners only 4:30 P.M.–11 P.M. Closed Sun. Pheasant a specialty. Some items expensive. Cocktails. Reservations advised. AE, DC, MC, V.

Mobridge. The Wheel Family Restaurant. *Moderate.* 820 W. Grand Crossing (605–845–7474). B, L, D, 6 A.M.–10 P.M. Closed Christmas. AE, DC, MC, V.

Pierre. Kings Inn. *Moderate.* 220 S. Pierre St., Pierre, SD 57501 (605–224–5951). Features walleye, Alaskan King Crab, and South Dakota beef. B, L, D, 6:30 A.M.–midnight, Mon.–Sat.; 7 A.M.–9 P.M., Sun. AE, MC, V.

Rapid City. 1915 Firehouse Company. *Expensive.* 610 Main St., Rapid City, SD 57701 (605–348–1915). Dining treat in old remodeled fire station. Cocktails. Reservations advised. L, D, 11 A.M.–2 P.M., 5:30 P.M.–10 P.M. Closed Sun. AE, DC, MC, V.

Landmark Restaurant. *Moderate to Expensive.* In Alex Johnson Hotel. 523 6th St., Rapid City, SD 57701 (605–342–1210). Fine dining in relaxed classic hotel atmosphere. Cocktails, entertainment. B, L, D, 7 A.M.–10 P.M. Closed Christmas Eve and Christmas. AE, DC, MC, V.

Tally's. *Moderate.* 530 6th St., Rapid City, SD 57701 (605–342–7621). Family-style restaurant with children's menu. B, L, D, 7 A.M.–7:30 P.M. Closed Sun. No credit cards.

Sioux Falls. Lafayette. *Expensive.* 228 N. Phillips Ave., Sioux Falls, SD 57102 (605–332–2383). French cuisine in a Continental style. Cocktails. Reservations advised. L, D, 11 A.M.–2 P.M., 6–10 P.M. Closed Sun. and major holidays. AE, DC, MC, V.

The Northlander. *Expensive.* 4200 S. Minnesota Ave., Sioux Falls, SD 57105 (605–334–2727). Outstanding menu, including beef, seafood, and game fowl; the building itself is worth a visit. L, D, 11:30 A.M.–2 P.M., 5–10 P.M., Mon.–Fri.; 5–11 P.M., Sat.; 10 A.M.–2 P.M., 5–9 P.M., Sun. AE, DC, MC, V.

Minerva's Corner Creperie. *Moderate.* 3015 S. Phillips Ave., Sioux Falls, SD 57101 (605–334–0386). Specializes in Brittany crepes. Some items expensive. Cocktails. L, D, 11 A.M.–2:30 P.M., 5:30–10 P.M. Closed Sun. Reservations advised. AE, DC, MC, V.

Spearfish. The Sluice Restaurant *Expensive.* Heritage Dr., Spearfish, SD 57783 (605–642–5500). Highly recommended dining amid gold mining decor; extensive menu; cocktails. L, 11 A.M.–2:30 P.M.; D, 5–10 P.M.; Sun. brunch, 11 A.M.–3 P.M.; Sun. dinner buffet, 5–8 P.M.. Closed Mon., Christmas Eve, and Christmas. Reservations recommended. AE, DC, MC, V.

Wall. Elkton House Restaurant. *Moderate.* On South Blvd. off I-90 Exit 110, Wall, SD 57790 (605–279–2152). Home-style cooking in family atmosphere. B, L, D, 6 A.M.–10 P.M. Closed Thanksgiving, Christmas. AE, MC, V.

Yankton. The Black Steer. *Moderate.* 300 E. Third St., Yankton, SD 57078 (605–665–5771). Known for its hickory smoked ribs and open-pit charcoal-broiled steaks. Cocktails. L, D, 11 A.M.–2 P.M., 5–11 P.M.; till midnight Fri., Sat. MC, V.

Happy Jack's. *Moderate.* East Hwy. 50, Yankton, SD 57078 (605–665–7626). Where celebrities go for outstanding steaks. Cocktails. Some items expensive. D, 6–11 P.M., Wed.–Sun. Closed Mon., Tues. No credit cards.

THE CENTRAL PLAINS

by
JAKE THOMPSON

Mr. Thompson is a reporter for the Kansas City Star.

NEBRASKA

The heritage of the Wild West is commemorated time and again in Nebraska's museums, parks, historic sites, and official state functions. Here the prairie pioneer and cowboy struggled to survive as they traveled the Oregon Trail, the Mormon Trail, and the Lewis and Clark Trail. Those nomads often struck out for Chimney Rock or Scotts Bluff on the state's western edge, which also guided riders of the Pony Express.

William F. "Buffalo Bill" Cody held his Wild West show in North Platte, and Wild Bill Hickock, Chief Red Cloud, and Jesse James roamed through.

Nebraska became a state in 1867, and the frontier town of Lincoln, now a city of 180,000, was chosen as state capital. The Platte River, which is formed from the confluence of the North and South Platte rivers east of North Platte, is the state's largest river, eventually feeding into the Missouri. Near Grand Island in early spring one can see a spectacle of thousands of Sand Hill cranes soaring down to rest along the river and in the fields as they migrate south.

Another sort of migration, that of the railroad, connected Nebraska with America; in 1863 ground was broken for the transcontinental railroad. Today, the Union Pacific Railroad Co. is headquartered in Omaha and operates a museum explaining the railroad's vital importance to the state.

Omaha also houses the Joslyn Art Museum, an awesome structure containing the state's most diverse collection of art. Former President Gerald Ford's birthplace is in a downtown Omaha residential area. Whenever the weather is nice, Omahans gather at the Central Park Mall, with its concrete fountains, for lunch and then walk over to the Old Market area for shopping. The Old Market area is also the center of Omaha nightlife.

South in Bellevue is the Strategic Air Command Museum, presenting the history of the nation's military, which is located near the Strategic Air Command base, a top-secret installation. On Omaha's western outskirts, Boys Town, the famous City of Little Men, has been known to many since its story was told in a movie starring Spencer Tracy and Mickey Rooney. Opened in 1917 by Father Edward Flanagan, Boys Town today includes girls and provides hope for disadvantaged or neglected youths.

Traveling 50 miles southwest on Interstate 80, one will see the tall spire of the state capitol in Lincoln, long recognized as one of the most impressive state houses in the nation. It is more than 400 feet tall and is topped by a sculpture of a farmer sowing grain, a symbol of hope for the entire state. The University of Nebraska is here, as are the Cornhuskers, the football team that fills sports fans with pride. The Nebraska State Historical Society is near the campus and contains the state's largest collection of its history. Sheldon Art Gallery is known for modern art and has a movie theater that shows art films and foreign films. The famous orator William Jennings Bryan lived in Lincoln.

West of Lincoln in Minden is Pioneer Village, an extraordinary collection of original pioneer artifacts, antiques, and western lore kept in 24 buildings.

To the north of Lincoln in Grand Island is the Stuhr Museum of the Prairie Pioneer. This museum, surrounded by a moat and designed by the famous architect Edward Durell Stone, houses collections of pioneering and Americana. On the same grounds, a restored railroad town with original buildings moved to the site includes a post office, a general store, a church, homes, Henry Fonda's birthplace, and a depot which a steam train passes on a 1½-mile loop.

Military posts constitute an important part of Nebraska's attractions. Fort Kearney, near Kearney, west of Grand Island, is a reconstructed post where Indian-fearing wagon trains stopped. Fort McPherson, farther west near Maxwell, is a national cemetery, and in the northwest tip of the state Fort Robinson, where the famous Sioux chief Crazy Horse was killed, is now one of the state's top attractions. The fort offers overnight accommodations in restored original barracks, horseback riding, and singing around the campfire. Real buffalo stew is served.

Along the state's northern border near Valentine, Fort Niobrara is a national wildlife refuge that offers a rugged sage-and-cactus landscape spliced by the Niobrara River, a prime canoeing waterway.

Nebraskans are proud of an unusual Bicentennial project that placed a dozen abstract sculptures in a state-long sculpture garden along the 450 miles of Interstate 80.

An area often overlooked is perhaps the state's hidden jewel, the Sandhills. A vast, undulating, and nearly treeless terrain of sand, scrubby bushes, and blowing tumbleweeds, the Sandhills cover 20,000 square miles roughly from Loup City to the border, somewhat north of Interstate 80. This is solemn and serene cattle country; the soil is too sandy to support crops. In the heart of the Sandhills, in Hyannis, aging and weathered cowboys meet during the fall to test their roping, riding, and calf-tying skills one more time at the Oldtimers' Rodeo. In the Sandhills the mystique of the cowboy lives.

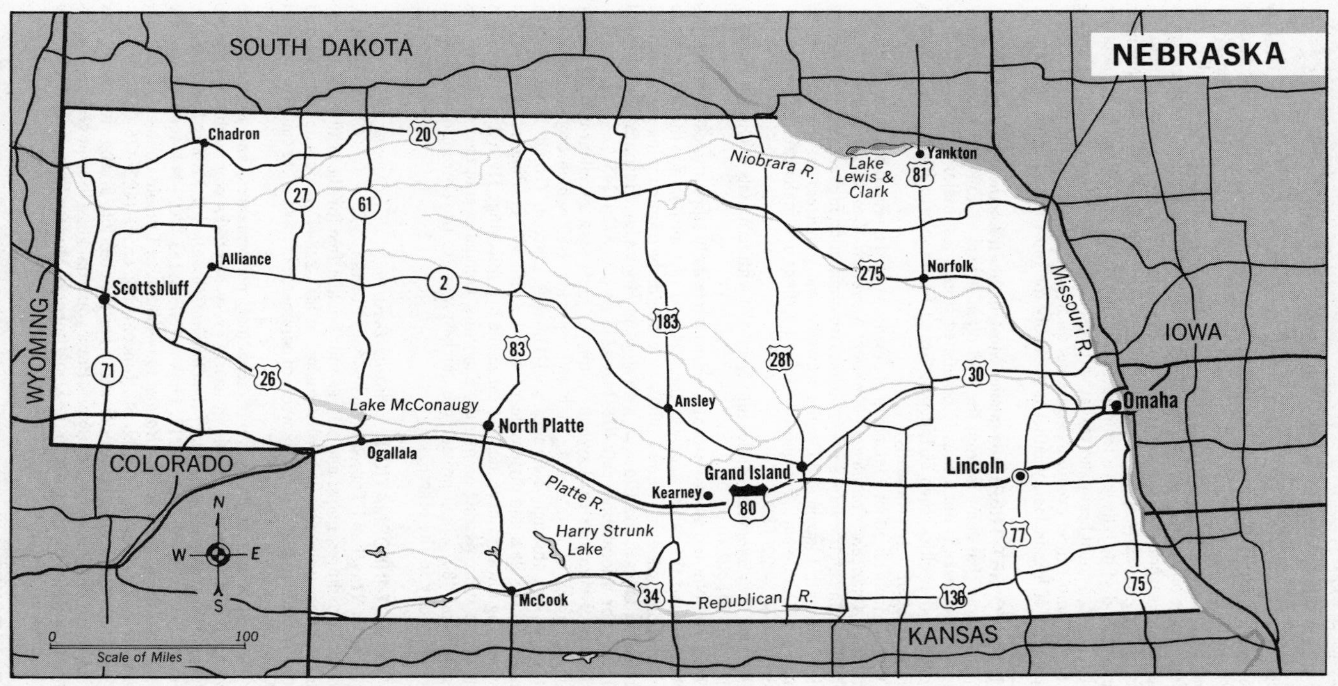
NEBRASKA
SOUTH DAKOTA
IOWA
WYOMING
COLORADO
KANSAS
Chadron
Alliance
Scottsbluff
Yankton
Norfolk
Omaha
Lincoln
Grand Island
Kearney
Ansley
North Platte
Ogallala
McCook
Niobrara R.
Missouri R.
Platte R.
Republican R.
Lake Lewis & Clark
Lake McConaugy
Harry Strunk Lake
20
27
61
2
71
26
83
183
281
275
81
30
80
77
75
136
34
N
E
S
W
0
100
Scale of Miles

PRACTICAL INFORMATION FOR NEBRASKA

WHEN TO GO. The nation's western midsection has a large variance in weather that keeps Nebraskans and their visitors amused and challenged, with summer days turning furnace-like as temperatures rise over 100° F. and cold winter days that push the temperatures well below zero. Be forewarned, summers are tolerable, and a few recent ones have been rainy and relatively cool, but winters are often arctic and require several layers of your warmest clothing. The state's rainy weather concentrates in the early spring, turning the land a lush green by June; its summers are usually dry; its falls have temperatures from the 30s to 60s; and its winters are noted for occasional heavy snows that will close highways and some schools, however briefly, and cancel events. Nebraskans do not let a little weather disrupt their enjoyment of life; in fact, weather is probably the most talked-about subject.

HOW TO GET THERE. By plane. Most flights from the east make stops in Omaha; those that come in from the west often stop at various other destinations. Because Nebraska is not a heavily populated state, most major airlines serve only Omaha—other cities, such as Lincoln, Grand Island, North Platte, and Ogallala, can be reached only erratically.

Epply Airport is about 3 mi. north of downtown and is served by about 15 airlines including *American, Continental, Frontier, Northwest, Ozark, TWA,* and *United.* Travelers can catch several smaller airlines for connecting flights to other Nebraska cities from both Lincoln and Omaha, as well as daily charters between those cities, which are 60 mi. apart. For questions about airlines in Omaha call the airport authority at 402–422–6800.

By bus. *Greyhound* has service into Nebraska with terminals in Omaha and Lincoln (402–341–1900).

By train. Not too many years ago, trains made daily stops at most communities statewide, and the rail system was the lifeblood of transport for the state's grain crops. Today, though, *Amtrak* offers only one daily train running east and west connecting Denver and Chicago, with stops in Holdredge, Hastings, Lincoln, and Omaha. For information, call 402–342–8333 or 800–872–7245.

By car. Nebraska's road system is, for the most part, excellent and the major mode of travel in a state more than 450 mi. wide. I-80, which crosses the entire nation, swings through Nebraska past Omaha, Lincoln, Grand Island, North Platte, and Ogallala and divides near Ogallala, with I-76 heading into Denver and I-80 leading toward Cheyenne. A great scenic trip rolls along Hwy. 2 in the western part of the state, passing among the Sandhills. Omaha is encircled by Interstates 80, 680, and 480, which provide the quickest ways to travel from one end of the sprawling city to the other.

TOURIST INFORMATION. *Nebraska Department of Economic Development,* Division of Travel and Tourism, Box 94666, Lincoln, NE 68509 (402–471–3111), provides brochures, maps, and a large tour booklet free for the asking. A toll-free tourist-information hotline can be reached at 800–228–4307 outside the state and 800–742–7595 in Nebraska. Chambers of commerce in most cities can provide local information for free.

The best source of daily events, schedules, performances, and theater is the *Omaha World-Herald,* available in nearly every Nebraska community. For more information about Omaha contact the *Omaha Convention & Visitors Bureau,* Civic Center, 1819 Farnam, Suite 1212, Omaha, NE 68183 (402–444–4665). For daily events dial the *Omaha Events Hotline* (444–6800). In Lincoln contact the *Lincoln Chamber of Commerce,* 1221 N. St., Lincoln, NE 68508 (402–476–7511).

The state travel-and-tourism office also has the ability to arrange for translators to help overcome language differences. But if you would like to arrange for a translator you may also call or write to the Department of Modern Languages, University of Nebraska-Lincoln, 1111 Oldfather Hall, Lincoln, NE 68588 (402–472–3745).

TIME ZONES. A change in time occurs along a jagged line that passes through the western part of the state, a few mi. west of Valentine, Thedford, North Platte, and McCook. The eastern side is on Central Time, an hour later than the western, which is on Mountain Time.

TELEPHONES. The area code for the eastern third of the state, including Lincoln, Omaha, Fremont, Norfolk, and Nebraska City, is 402. For the western two-thirds of the state, which covers Grand Island, Hastings, Kearney, North Platte, Ogallala, Scottsbluff, and Chadron, the area code is 308. Dial the pertinent area code and 555–1212 for directory assistance. There is no charge for directory assistance within the state. Dial zero before the area code for operator-assisted or credit-card and long-distance calls. Local calls in the state may be 20 or 25 cents.

EMERGENCY TELEPHONE NUMBERS. Nebraska widely uses the universal number 911 as its emergency telephone number, but you can also dial 0 and ask the operator to put you immediately in touch with the *fire department, police, ambulance dispatch,* or *paramedics.* In Omaha, the nonemergency police number is 593–2288. There are Nebraska *Highway Patrol* officers statewide, and their headquarters in Lincoln (471–4545) can provide emergency help. In Omaha, *Bergan Mercy Hospital* is 398–6060; *St. Joseph's Hospital,* 449–4000. *St. Elizabeth Community Health Center* in Lincoln is 489–7181. A statewide 24-hour *poison-control center* is at 800–642–9999.

HINTS TO MOTORISTS. Nearly every town is laid out in a square of streets, which makes getting lost in smaller communities difficult and finding your way in larger cities easy. In Omaha the main east and west streets are Douglas and Dodge, and the main north and south streets are 12th, 24th, and 72nd. I-80 and its counterparts 480 and 680 encircle the city and are a quick way to cross Omaha. In Lincoln, streets run north-south and east-west, and the main streets are 0 running east and west and 10th, 27th, 48th, and 84th running north and south. Rush-hour traffic is a problem on Omahas and Lincolns Sts. only beginning at 4:30 P.M. Traffic in Omaha during the early morning hours also slows with commuters, so leave early if you can. Right turn on red signals is permitted statewide unless otherwise posted. Nebraska, like most states, adheres to stiff policies against drunk driving and the federal speed limit on interstates and major highways.

The *Cornhusker Motor Club* in Omaha is Nebraska's member of the American Automobile Association and can help with travel plans, motel accommodations, airline flights, and maps for members. Call for information at 402–390–1000. Emergency road service is available for members by calling 800–390–1010.

HINTS TO DISABLED TRAVELERS. Nebraska's parks, restaurants, motels, and attractions are, for the most part, accessible to those who use wheelchairs. The *State Division on Travel and Tourism,* Box 94666, Lincoln, NE 68509 (402–471–3796) can help with tours and advice.

SPECIAL-INTEREST SIGHTSEEING. Omaha. *Boys Town,* 136th W. Dodge St., Omaha, NE 68010 (402–498–1111). This famous City of Little Men was founded in 1917 by the late Father Edward Flanagan for abandoned, neglected, or otherwise underprivileged boys. It was opened to girls in 1979. It provides an intensive living and teaching program renowned for helping youth.

DeSoto Bend National Wildlife Refuge–Steamboat Bertrand, Rte. 1, Box 114, Missouri Valley, IA 51555 (712–642–4121). Yes, the address is officially in Iowa, but this is a Nebraska refuge in which to watch migrations of thousands of snow geese, ducks, and other wildfowl. On the site of the large refuge also is a recently excavated and restored display of artifacts from the *Bertrand,* which sank into the muddy Missouri River in the 1860s. It features some of 2 million items recovered such as clothing, weapons, glassware, and gold coins.

Neligh. *Neligh Mills,* Box 271, Neligh, NE 68756 (402–887–4303). This is a working display of an 1870 flour mill listed on the National Register of Historic Places. Open daily, May–Nov.

Minden. *Harold Warp's Pioneer Village,* Box 68, Minden, NE 68959 (308–832–1181). Situated 12 mi. south of I-80 on Hwy. 10 in central Nebraska, this privately operated exhibit has an impressive collection of pioneer memorabilia and traces the nation's growth since 1830. Open daily 8 A.M. to sundown.

ZOOS. The *Henry Doorly Zoo,* Deer Park Blvd. and 10th St., Omaha, NE 68107 (402–733–8400). A high percentage of the zoo's inhabitants are in danger of becoming extinct. Most animals are in outdoor pens that resemble natural environments. The zoo features a Great Cat Complex housing lions, cheetahs, jaguars, leopards, tigers, and one of the few Indian white tigers in the nation. One can also enjoy a 2-mi. guided tour on a steam train. Open daily, 9:30 A.M.–4 P.M. in winter; till 5 in summer. Adults (12 and over), $5.25; children, $2.75.

CAMPING. There are roughly 60 state recreation areas and many other special-use areas. *Fort Robinson State Park,* Box 392, Crawford, NE 69339 (308–655–2660). Lodge, cabins, chuckwagon cookout, horseback rides, historical tours. Reserve early. *Indian Cave State Park,* Rte. 1, Shubert, NE 68437 (402–883–2575). Southeast corner of state, good cross-country skiing in winter, Adirondack shelters, backpacking on hiking trails. *Niobrara State Park,* Niobrara, NE 68760 (402–857–3373). Pool, camping, cabins.

LAKES. *Branched Oak Lake,* 17 mi. northwest of Lincoln; *Fremont Lakes,* 3 mi. west of Fremont; *Lake McConaughy State Recreational Area,* northwest of Ogallala; *Lewis & Clark,* 15 mi. north of Crofton.

FISHING AND HUNTING. Everyone 16 or older must have a fishing or hunting license to partake in those sports. Be forewarned that Nebraska has become aggressive concerning hunting and fishing out of season or in nondesignated areas through a statewide hotline, Operation Game Thief, 800–742–SNAP. Fishing is allowed year-round on Nebraska's many rivers, streams, and human-made lakes. The state is popular for deer, pheasant, antelope, and quail hunting. Fishers seek trout, large- and small-mouth bass, sunfish, catfish, and pike.

Hunting fee for residents is $8.50 annually plus a habitat stamp for $7.50; for nonresidents the fee is $40 to hunt small game. Deer permits for residents are $20 and for nonresidents, $100. Antelope permits for residents cost $20; $100 for nonresidents.

Fishing licenses for residents cost $11.50 annually; $25 for nonresidents. A 3-day license may be purchased for $7.50. To fish for trout you must pay an additional fee of $5.

For information on seasons and public and private hunting and fishing grounds contact the *Nebraska Game and Parks Commission,* Box 30370, Lincoln, NE 68503 (402–464–0641).

CANOEING. *Dismal River,* most ill-named pretty stream in the state. *Niobrara River,* northern clear river cutting through sandstone bluffs near Sandhills. Waterfalls, camping.

For both, contact *Wilson Outfitters,* 1329 Dawes Ave., Lincoln, NE 68521 (402–489–6241; 402–467–2300).

SPECTATOR SPORTS. *Rodeo,* across Nebraska all summer and fall, particularly the *Oldtimers Rodeo,* Hyannis, fall, and the *North Platte Buffalo Bill Rodeo* and *Nebraskaland Days.* These real Wild West rodeos are held in the third week of June and are among the state's biggest annual events.

Horse racing. Pari-mutuel thoroughbred racing begins in Grand Island in early Mar. and gallops east to AK-SAR-BEN, Omaha, in May–Aug.; ATOKAD in South Sioux City, May–July; Columbus, Aug.–Sept.; and Lincoln, Sept.–Nov.

HISTORIC SITES AND HOUSES. Agate Fossil Beds National Monument. Harrison, NE 69346 (308–668–2211). 34 mi. north of Mitchell on U.S. 29. Fossils dating back 20 million years.

Arbor Lodge State Historical Park and Museum. Rte. 2, Nebraska City, NE 68410 (402–873–3221). State's oldest park, named for founder of tree-planting Arbor Day, J. Sterling Morton. 52-room neocolonial mansion near hearty apple orchards.

Ash Hollow State Historical Park. Box A, Lewellen, NE 69147 (308–778–5651). Wagon ruts of Oregon Trail; visitor center in a cave. 28 mi. northwest of Ogallala.

Buffalo Bill Scouts Rest Ranch State Historical Park. R.R. 1, North Platte, NE 69101 (308–535–8035). See where Buffalo Bill lived, during the Wild West Rodeo Days held in North Platte.

Chadron Museum of the Fur Trade. Rte. 2, Box 18, Chadron, NE 69337 (308–432–3843). 3 mi. east of Chadron on U.S. 20. A beautiful drive. Traces fur trade through 1800s.

Fort Kearney State Historical Park. R.R. 4, Kearney, NE 68847 (308–234–9513). Important rebuilt stop along Oregon Trail.

Gerald Ford's Birthplace. 3202 Woolworth Ave., Omaha, NE. No phone.

Great Plains Black History Museum. 2213 Lake St., Omaha, NE 68110 (402–345–2212). Depictions of both pioneer and modern blacks, such as Omaha native Malcolm X.

Homestead National Monument. Rte. 3, Beatrice, NE 68310 (402–223–3514). 4 mi. west of Beatrice. Site of first homestead claim in U.S.

Scotts Bluff National Monument. Box 427, Gering, NE 69341 (308–436–4340). 3 mi. west of Gering in western edge of state. 800-ft. guidepost monolith used by settlers crossing the plains. Climbing, exploring. Road access to top.

Toadstool Park. spectacular rock formations in northwestern corner of state, similar to the Badlands.

Willa Cather Historical Center. c/o Nebraska State Historical Society, 338 N. Webster, Red Cloud, NE 68970 (402–746–3285). Home of Willa Cather society; museum.

William Jennings Bryan Home. 4900 Sumner, Lincoln, NE 68510. For information phone the Nebraska State Historical Society, 402–471–3270.

MUSEUMS AND GALLERIES. Hastings Museum. 1330 N. Burlington St., Hastings, NE 68901 (402–463–7126). Extensive pioneer and natural history displays and planetarium.

Joslyn Art Museum. 2200 Dodge St., Omaha, NE 68102 (402–342–3300). Impressive marble edifice with western art and classics, rotating exhibits, concert series.

Sheldon Memorial Art Gallery. 12th and R Sts., Lincoln, NE 68588 (402–472–2461). Excellent modern exhibits and fine-art film series. Sculpture garden.

State Historical Society Museum. 1500 R St., Lincoln, NE 68508 (402–471–3270).

Stuhr Museum of the Prairie Pioneer. 3133 W. Hwy. 34, Grand Island, NE 68801 (308–384–1380). Main building designed by Kennedy Center architect. Rebuilt house on grounds; restored pioneer railroad town with operating steam train and 60 original buildings.

ACCOMMODATIONS. We have listed Nebraska hotels and motels alphabetically by city and town. The price categories reflect the cost of a double room. They are: *Expensive,* \$45–\$80; *Moderate,* \$35–\$45; and *Inexpensive,* \$20–\$35. Although not always necessary, a reservation may be a good idea.

Alliance. West Way Motel. *Moderate.* 1207 W. 3rd, Box 765, Alliance, NE 69301 (308–762–4040 or 800–528–1234). 44 rooms.

Bellevue. White House Inn. *Moderate.* 305 N. Fort Crook Rd., Bellevue, NE 68005 (402–293–1600). 40 rooms, queen-size beds, water beds.

Chadron. West Hills Inn Best Western. *Moderate.* 1100 W. 10th, Chadron, NE 69337 (308–432–3305).

Grand Island. Holiday Inn. *Expensive.* I-80 and Hwy. 281, Box 1501, Grand Island, NE 68801 (308–384–7770 or 800–465–4329). 2 pools, sauna, whirlpool.

Riverside Inn. *Moderate.* Hwy. 34 and S. Locust, Grand Island, NE 68801 (308–384–5150). 182 rooms, indoor pool, games room, Jacuzzi, sauna.

Kearney. Holiday Inn. *Expensive.* I-80 Interchange, Kearney, NE 68847 (308–237–3141 or 800–465–4329). 210 rooms, indoor pool and recreation area, sauna, playground.

Fort Kearney Inn. *Moderate.* I-80 Interchange, Box 1688, Kearney, NE 68847 (308–234–2541). 107 rooms, outdoor pool.

TelStar Best Western Motor Inn. *Moderate.* 1010 3rd Ave., Kearney, NE 68847 (308–237–5185 or 800–528–1234). 63 rooms, outdoor pool, playground, queen-size beds.

Lincoln. Clayton House. *Expensive.* 10th and O St., Lincoln, NE 68508 (402–476–0333 or 800–233–7778). In heart of downtown.

The Cornhusker. *Expensive.* 333 South 13 St., on Cornhusker Sq., Lincoln, NE 68508 (402–474–7474).219 rooms, 2 restaurants, indoor pool, exercise rooms.

Lincoln Hilton, *Expensive.* 141 N. 9th St., Lincoln, NE 68508 (402–475–4011 or 800–HILTONS). 233 rooms, indoor pool.

Airport Best Western Inn. *Moderate.* I-80 Airport Exit, Lincoln, NE 68521 (402–475–9541 or 800–528–1234). 127 rooms, outdoor pool.

Best Western Villager Motor Inn. *Moderate.* 5200 O St., Lincoln, NE 68510 (402–464–9111 or 800–528–1234). 190 rooms, outdoor pool, putting green.

Days Inn Motel. *Moderate.* I-80 Airport Exit, Lincoln, NE 68521 (402–475–3616 or 800–633–1414). 142 rooms.

Ramada Inn. *Moderate.* 2301 N.W. 12th, Lincoln, NE 68501 (402–475–5911 or 800–2–RAMADA). 140 rooms, in-room movies.

Harvester Motel. *Inexpensive.* 1511 Center Park Rd., Lincoln, NE 68512 (402–423–3131). 81 rooms, restaurant.

Nebraska City. Stephenson Inn. *Inexpensive.* 502 S. 11th, Nebraska City, NE 68410 (402–873–5959).

North Platte. Best Western Circle C South. *Moderate.* 1211 S. Dewey, North Platte, NE 69101 (308–532–0130 or 800–528–1234). 77 rooms, heated indoor pool, queen-size beds.

Motel Nebraska. *Inexpensive.* I-80 and U.S. 83, North Platte, NE 69101 (308–534–3120). 80 rooms, pool.

Ogallala. Stagecoach Inn. *Moderate.* I-80 Interchange, Ogallala, NE 69153 (308–284–3656). 100 rooms, outdoor pool, playground.

Omaha. Marriott Hotel. *Expensive.* 10220 Regency Circle, Omaha, NE 68114 (402–399–9000 or 800–228–9290). Heated indoor-outdoor pool, saunas, restaurants.

Red Lion Inn. *Expensive.* 1616 Dodge, Omaha, NE 68102 (402–346–7600). Restaurants, saunas, indoor pool. Remodeled.

Best Western Immanuel Plaza. *Moderate.* 6901 N. 72nd, Omaha, NE 68124 (402–571–6161 or 800–528–1234). 47 rooms, indoor pool, sauna, whirlpool.

Days Inn. *Moderate.* 7101 Grover, Omaha, NE 68106 (402–391–5757 or 800–325–2325). I-80 at 72 St. Convenient to Ak-Sar-Ben and Old Market district.

La Quinta Motor Inn. *Moderate.* Maple and I-680, Omaha, NE 68124 (402–493–1900). 130 rooms, pool.

New Tower Best Western. *Moderate.* 7764 Dodge St., Omaha, NE 68114 (402–393–5500). 336 rooms, pool with solar heat dome, sauna, whirlpool, suites.

Oak Creek Inn. *Moderate.* 2808 S. 72nd, Omaha, NE 68124 (402–397–7137). 104 rooms, suites, indoor pool, sauna, whirlpool.

Scottsbluff. Candlelight Inn. *Moderate.* 1822 E. 20th Pl., Scottsbluff, NE 69361 (308–635–3751). 56 rooms, heated outdoor pool.

South Sioux City. Marina Inn. *Expensive.* 4th and B Sts., South Sioux City, NE 68776 (402–494–4000). Sauna, queen and king beds. Across the Missouri River from Iowa.

BED AND BREAKFASTS. North Platte, *Watson Manor Inn,* 410 S. Sycamore, North Platte, NE 69103 (308–532–3511). Old Nebraska home with comfortable features. Continental breakfast included.

Lincoln, *The Rogers House,* 2145 B St., Lincoln, NE 68502 (402–476–6961). Few blocks from state capitol. Hardwood floors, sunrooms, library. Locally historic 1914 home.

Omaha, *Bed and Breakfast at Offutt Mansion,* 140 N. 39th, Omaha, NE (402–553–0951).

RESTAURANTS. In Nebraska you are in the heart of cattle country, so if you like juicy steaks, ribs, or filets you will be pleased. Lincoln and Omaha also offer French cuisine and varieties of Old World food because many settlers in the region came from European countries and brought their rich heritage in food with them. Price categories are listed for a complete meal, not including drinks, tips, or tax: *Deluxe,* $25–$30; *Expensive,* $20–$25; *Moderate,* $12–$20; *Inexpensive,* under $12.

Grand Island. Atch's Restaurant. *Moderate.* 2610 S. Locust (308–384–1080). Hearty steaks.

Driesbach's. *Moderate.* 1137 S. Locust (308–381–7272). Steaks are supreme at this pleasant eatery.

Kearney. Cattleman's Mining Company. *Moderate.* 121 W. 46th St. (308–234–4215). Go for thick steaks and the best salad bar in miles.

Grandpa's Steak House. *Inexpensive.* Rte. 4 (308–237–2882). Steaks and seafood in family atmosphere.

Lincoln. Misty's. *Expensive.* 6235 Havelock (402–466–8424). Juicy and delicious steaks are the staple in a hushed decor.

The Rotisserie. *Expensive.* 11th and 0 Sts. (402–475–9475). Elegantly prepared Continental cuisine in high-tech decor.

K's Restaurant. *Moderate.* 1275 S. Cotner Blvd. (402–483–2858). Excellent breakfasts served all day; health foods and good sandwiches served where *Terms of Endearment* was filmed.

Lee's Restaurant. *Moderate.* 1940 Van Dorn (402–477–4339). Delicious chicken served in family atmosphere.

Spike & Olly's. *Moderate.* 5200 O St. (402–467–0560). A bistro atmosphere prevails at this place, which offers a Sun. brunch.

Sadies. *Inexpensive.* 5200 O St. (402–467–0565). Pan-fried chicken served family style. Dinner only.

Nebraska City. The Embers. *Moderate.* 1102 4th and Corso (402–873–6416). Steaks and seafoods.

Norfolk. The Brass Lantern, *Expensive.* 1018 S. 9th (402–371–2500). Elegant dining and American cuisine.

Omaha. Maxine's. *Deluxe.* Atop the Red Lion Inn, 1616 Dodge St. (402–346–7600). Excellent Continental cuisine. Reservations on weeknights.

The French Café. *Expensive.* 1017 Howard St. (402–341–3547). Elegantly prepared French cuisine in restored downtown market district with brick streets. Sun. brunch.

Mister C's. *Moderate.* 5319 N. 30th St. (402–451–1998). Italian and beef specialties in a year-round Christmas and Old World atmosphere complete with strolling strings players.

M's Pub. *Moderate.* 422 S. 11th St. (402–342–2550). Stylish decor in Old Market area featuring soups and sandwiches.

Neon Goose Café. *Moderate.* 1012 S. 10th St. (402–341–9980). Continental dining and especially fresh seafood are highlighted in eclectic setting here.

Old Vienna Café. *Moderate.* 4829 S. 24th St. (402–733–7491). Old World atmosphere; specializes in sauerkraut, dumplings, veal, sausages, and imported German beer.

Ross' Steak House. *Moderate.* 909 S. 72nd St. (402–393–2030). Long famed as having Omaha's finest steaks.

Yen Ching Chinese Restaurant. *Moderate.* 8809 W. Dodge (402–392–2550). A wide variety of Mandarin, Szechuan, and Hunan dishes along with homemade noodles served here.

Grandmother's Restaurant and Lounge. *Inexpensive.* 4712 S. 82nd St. (402–339–6633). As though it were your grandmother's cooking and her homemade breads.

Julio's. *Inexpensive.* 513 S. 13th St. (402–345–6921). Tasty Mexican food in cozy atmosphere. In the Old Market district.

LIQUOR LAWS. Liquor stores are privately owned and may open at the discretion of their owners but are required to close at 1 A.M. Beer can be purchased in many rural counties on Sun. but not inside Lincoln's city limits, where the liquor stores are closed and groceries are not allowed to sell it to you. One can purchase liquor by the drink in many Lincoln and Omaha restaurants on Sun., however. The minimum drinking age is 21.

KANSAS

The Wheat State lies in the heart of the nation, and in fact the exact geographic center of the coterminous forty-eight United States is two miles northwest of Lebanon in north-central Kansas, a few miles east of where the state song, "Home on the Range," was written.

Kansas has a colorful history dating to the 1500s. The Spanish conquistador Francisco Vásquez de Coronado marched north from Mexico in search of the seven golden cities of Cibola, and by 1541 he had reached the Dodge City area, whereupon he turned around because no gold had been discovered. In 1854 Kansas became a territory and was home to the Wichita, Osage, Kansa, and Pawnee Indians, who remained in the region when explorers and pioneers rolled west along the Oregon and Santa Fe trails.

Kansas became a state in 1861, just as the nation's unity was disintegrating; it entered the union a free state even though pro-slavery forces were strong. Kansas experienced only one large battle during the Civil War, the Battle of Mine Creek, on October 25, 1864, in Linn County. About 25,000 men fought, and the Confederate troops were defeated. This ended the threat of southern invasion.

Kansas gave women the right to vote in school elections in 1861, far ahead of most of the nation, and that right was extended to municipal elections in 1867. Susanna Madora Salter of Argonia was promptly elected the first woman mayor in the United States. Another woman who drew national attention to Kansas at the turn of the century was Carry Nation, whose fierce temperance sentiment was displayed vigorously as she traveled about smashing up illegal saloons with hatchets.

Today, the largest cities in the state are Kansas City, Kansas, just over the Missouri River from the Missouri city of the same name, with 177,000 residents, and Wichita, about 200 miles southwest, home to 270,000 residents. Near Kansas City, Leavenworth is the state's oldest city and site of the oldest army post west of the Mississippi. The post was established in 1827 to protect settlers and pioneers from Indians, and today one can visit the Post Museum, which houses pioneer artifacts and displays of the opening of the west. Leavenworth, the boyhood home of Buffalo Bill Cody also has a national cemetery and a federal prison.

Sixty miles west is Kansas's capital, Topeka, and the state's impressive capitol building. The capitol, an example of French renaissance architecture, was begun in 1866, and additions to it were gradually made until it took on its present appearance in 1903. The capitol has murals depicting the state's history by John Steuart Curry and ornate house and senate chambers.

Topeka, with a population of 120,000, has the state historical museum and the world-famous Menninger Clinic and Foundation, a research, teaching, and treatment center for mental illness.

West of Topeka is Manhattan, the state's first territorial capital, where Kansas State University has attained a national reputation for agricultural

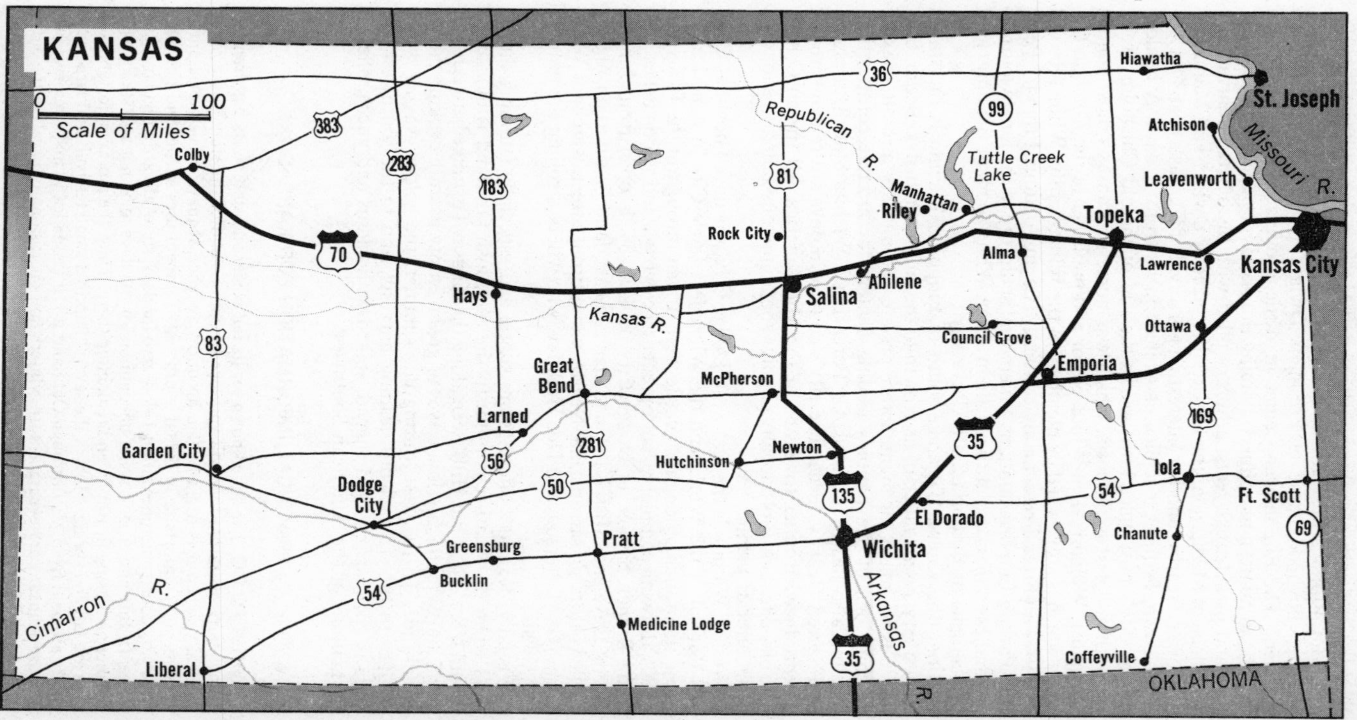
KANSAS
0
100
Scale of Miles
Colby
383
283
183
36
Hiawatha
St. Joseph
Atchison
Missouri R.
Leavenworth
Republican R.
99
Tuttle Creek Lake
81
Manhattan
Riley
Topeka
Kansas City
Rock City
70
Alma
Lawrence
Hays
Salina
Abilene
Kansas R.
83
Ottawa
Council Grove
Emporia
Great Bend
McPherson
Larned
169
35
Garden City
56
281
Hutchinson
Newton
Iola
50
54
Ft. Scott
Dodge City
135
El Dorado
69
Chanute
Pratt
Wichita
Greensburg
Bucklin
Arkansas R.
Cimarron R.
Medicine Lodge
Liberal
Coffeyville
OKLAHOMA

research. Between Manhattan and Junction City is Fort Riley, which houses a museum of military history and U.S. cavalry artifacts.

About 40 miles west of Manhattan along Interstate 70 is the town of Abilene, boyhood home of President Dwight D. Eisenhower and his brothers. The Eisenhower Center in Abilene offers the late president's childhood home, a museum containing thousands of papers from his military and presidential years, a library filled with his official archives, and the Place of Meditation, the final resting place of Dwight and Mamie Eisenhower. Nearby, another interesting portrayal of Kansas's past, Old Abilene Town, features a replica of Abilene in its frontier days. A boulder on the city's post office lawn marks the end of the old Chisholm Trail.

South and east is Emporia, which was home to Kansas's most famous journalist, William Allen White, editor and publisher of the *Emporia Gazette,* which is still owned by members of the White family. White received the 1923 Pulitzer Prize for his editorial "To an Anxious Friend." Peter Pan Park in Emporia contains a memorial sculpture to the famed journalist, and his papers are in the William Allen White room at the library on the campus of Emporia State University.

Along the Kansas Turnpike south of Emporia, Wichita is the state's largest city, owing much of its growth to the aircraft industry. Beech, Boeing, Cessna, and Lear manufacture private and military aircraft, making Wichita one of the nation's leading centers for aircraft construction. Wichita also has McConnell Air Force Base, Wichita State University, and Sacred Heart College. The city's cow-town days are remembered at a reproduced frontier town and at the Mid-America All Indian Center. The city offers visitors a locally popular zoo, numerous galleries, and tours of its aircraft plants.

West of Wichita is the real west. Dodge City was once known as Cowboy Capital of the World and the Wickedest Little City in America because thousands of longhorn cattle were driven through in the 1870s and 1880s, drawing commerce, entrepreneurs, cowboys, and saloon belles. The Long Branch Saloon, in Dodge City on U.S. 54, is open from June to Labor Day, and Miss Kitty and her can-can dancers entertain nightly while visitors sip sarsaparilla. Nearby along Front Street, watch for Wyatt Earp, Bat Masterson, and Doc Holliday, who will be strolling the restored boardwalk.

Visually, Kansas's offerings are subtle and especially stunning during days when the weather is mild. In the east, lush farmland is blocked in by tall trees. The Flint Hills, seen along the Kansas Turnpike between Emporia and Wichita, are low waves of green, empty pasture evoking moods of solitude. To the west, during late summer, the golden waving wheat testifies to the state's world-leading harvests, and to the southwest, the state is open, sparse, and rugged, spiked with cactus and yucca, offering intimations of the American Southwest.

PRACTICAL INFORMATION FOR KANSAS

WHEN TO GO. The state known for its tall wheat and sunflowers has dramatic swings in temperature that will vary even from one end of the state to the other. Typically, when it is frigid in Jan. around Lawrence, it may be fairly pleasant in Wichita and comfortable in the far southwest. Temperatures in Jan. and Feb. tend to be very cold, sometimes falling below zero for days; snowfalls are a regular occurrence. In July and Aug. it is not uncommon for the days to be hot and sticky, with the mercury rising to 100° F. and remaining there. Thus, the most comfortable seasons are fall and spring. Most of the several hundred small festivals and large-scale affairs are held from May through Oct., and it is a good idea to make reservations, because Kansans are eventgoers. In winter snows occasionally paralyze the entire state for a day or two, but road crews work all night to reopen major highways and interstates.

HOW TO GET THERE. By plane. Many major airlines serve Wichita's Mid-Continent Airport, which then serves as a jumping-off point to other Kansas cities and those in surrounding states. Because Wichita is in the center of a fairly well served region, fare wars can be found, though not as often as at other larger cities. The other Kansas cities are smaller still, though they are served by *Frontier, Ozark,* and private charter companies.

By bus. *Greyhound* does not travel to all the small communities in Kansas that they used to stop at before deregulation, but it does cover the entire state, and smaller companies have come in to pick up some of the slack.

By train. *Amtrak* makes a daily swing through Kansas, stopping in Garden City, Dodge City, Hutchinson, Newton, Emporia, and Kansas City, Mo. For information call 800–872–7245.

By car. Kansas has a road every square mile of land, though it is wise to stay on major highways to cover long distances. The major roadways: I-70, which goes east-west through the northern third of the state, passes Lawrence, Topeka, Salina, Hays, and Goodland; the Kansas Turnpike–I-35 goes from Kansas City to the southern border past Emporia and Wichita.

TOURIST INFORMATION. *Kansas Department of Economic Development,* Travel and Tourism Division, 400 S.W. 8th St. Topeka, KS 66603–3450 (913–296–2009; 800–742–7595). The best sources of information about daily events in Kansas can be found in the *Kansas City Star* or the *Wichita Eagle Beacon,* both of which list art, music, and entertainment events in Thurs. and Fri. editions.

For more local information: *Wichita Area Chamber of Commerce,* 111 W. Douglas, Suite 804, Wichita, KS 67202 (316–265–2800). *Lawrence Chamber of Commerce,* 823 Vermont, Lawrence, KS 66044 (913–843–4411). *Manhattan Chamber of Commerce,* Box 998, 505 Poyntz, Manhattan, KS 66502 (913–776–8829). For the far western area of the state contact the *Pioneer Country Travel Council,* Box 248, Hill City, KS 67642 (913–674–2151).

TIME ZONES. Out in Kansas wheat country, an invisible time line exists where you pass into the Mountain Time zone. The line runs through I-70 at Brewster, 20 mi. west of Colby, then goes south just east of Sharon Springs and Tribune. It then jumps east near Garden City, then west to the state border. To the west of the line, the time is one hour earlier than on the eastern side. If in doubt check a Kansas highway map and look for a small, jagged line of red Ts.

TELEPHONES. The area code for roughly the northern half of the state, including Lawrence, Kansas City, KS, Topeka, Salina, Hays, and Goodland, is 913. The area code for the southern half, including Wichita, Great Bend, Hutchinson, Garden City, and Dodge City, is 316. For directory assistance dial the area code and 555–1212 if you are in the other area code; otherwise just dial 555–1212. In very small communities, just dial 0 and the operator will provide directory assistance.

EMERGENCY TELEPHONES. The universal number 911 serves all major Kansas cities for *police, fire department, ambulance,* and *paramedics.* Some other numbers: *Stormont-Vail Regional Medical Center,* Topeka, 913–354–6000; *Wesley Medical Center,* Wichita, 316–688–2468; *Kansas Highway Patrol,* 913–296–3102; and *poison control,* 800–332–6633. For emergency services for the hearing-impaired, call 800–432–3959.

HINTS TO MOTORISTS. Almost every square mi. of Kansas has a road to get you from one place to another, and most towns are laid out in a grid system, at the center of which you will find a courthouse, a jail, and historical buildings. You may turn right on red in Kansas unless otherwise posted. Kansas's drunk-driving penalties have become tougher in recent years. Kansas follows the federal speed limit law on interstates and major highways.

Traffic in Lawrence runs smoothly all day; in Topeka rush hour begins about 4:30 P.M. and travel is slow while state employees make their way home; Wichita streets are often busy, and rush hour begins around 4 P.M. It will be slower during rush hour to go east or west across Wichita, but north and south highways and interstates allow freer flow of traffic.

The *AAA Automobile Club of Kansas* can help provide travel distance information and emergency road service at 913–272–6360. Their travel agency can help develop itineraries at 913–272–3600. Both are available to members of the American Automobile Association.

HINTS TO DISABLED TRAVELERS. Most rest areas, restaurants, hotels, museums, and attractions in Kansas are accessible, and some areas offer special services. For further information contact the *Kansas Department of Economic Development's* Travel and Tourism Division (see Tourist Information).

MUSEUMS AND SPECIAL-INTEREST SIGHTSEEING. Agricultural Center. 630 N. 126th, Bonner Springs, KS 66012 (913–721–1075). The hall honors the individuals and unheralded farmers who have made American agriculture such a powerful force in the world. Three buildings house exhibits on the evolution of farm life and tools. Hours: Apr.–Dec., daily 9 A.M.–5 P.M.; Sun., 1–5 P.M. Adults, $3; kids, $1.50.

Boot Hill Museum, 500 Wyatt Earp, Dodge City, KS 67801 (316–227–8188). Besides the museum, there is a reconstructed and authentic version of Front St. from Dodge City's days as the Wild West's most famous cowboy town. The Long Branch Variety Show is performed nightly, and gunfights are staged on the street during the summer. The Kansas Teachers Hall of Fame is housed in a one-room schoolhouse on the grounds. Summer hours and fees: 8 A.M.–8 P.M.; $4.50 adults and $4 children. Winter hours and fees: 9 A.M.–5 P.M.; $3.25 adults and $3 children. Guided tours every 90 minutes. Inquire about family rate.

Dalton Gang Hideout Tunnel & Museum. Box 332, Meade, KS 67864 (316–873–2731). The actual Dalton Gang hideout in southeast Kansas with underground tunnel connecting buildings. Hours: Sept.–May, Mon.–Sat., 9 A.M.–5 P.M.; June–Aug., 9 A.M.–6 P.M.; Sun 1–5 P.M.

Garden of Eden. 2nd and Kansas, Lucas, KS 67648 (913–525–6395). This one is worth the drive 15 mi. north of I-70, about 45 mi. west of Salina. It features a Garden of Eden created by hand by a "disabled" Civil War veteran. Summer, daily, 9 A.M.–6 P.M.; winter, daily, 10 A.M.–4 P.M.

Kansas Cosmosphere and Discovery Center. 1100 N. Plum, Hutchinson, KS 67501 (316–662–2305). The center houses an Omnimax movie projector, one of only 12 of the huge projectors in the United States. The center has an intriguing collection of space memorabilia, a reconstructed lunar lander, actual space uniforms, and displays tracing human voyages into space. Open daily except Sept.–May when it's closed Mon. Call for show times and reservations. Adults, $4.50; children and seniors, $3.25.

Lindsborg, Kansas. Called Little Sweden by many Kansans, Lindsborg is a quiet, picturesque town that showcases Swedish traditions and art. Visit the Birger Sandzen Memorial Gallery, 401 N. 1st, Lindsborg, KS 67456 (913–227–2220), which honors the internationally known Swedish-American painter. Wed.–Sun., 1–5 P.M. Adults, $1; children, 25 cents. Each year during Holy Week, Lindsborg presents its now world-famous Messiah Festival.

ZOOS. The **Topeka Zoo,** 635 Gage Blvd., Topeka, KS 66606 (913–272–5821), is Kansas's largest zoo, featuring a tropical rain forest with exotic birds in free flight and more than 400 species of animals, many in natural settings. The zoo adjoins the city's largest park, Gage Park, which has softball diamonds, a large public pool, playgrounds, and picnic tables. Zoo hours: daily, 9 A.M.–4:30 P.M.

HUNTING AND FISHING. Hunters flock to western Kansas during deer season. They also come for quail and pheasant, which fill the harvested wheat fields. The state has 300,000 acres of public land, much of it managed by the Kansas Fish and Game Commission for wildlife protection. Many hotels in smaller western communities offer discounts for hunters, who fill the rooms and cafés when their prey is in season. Nonresident hunting licenses are required for all who live outside of the state (except military personnel) and cost $50.50. Resident fees for those 16 to age 65 are $10.50. Kansas is abundant in deer, quail, wild turkey, and pheasant.

Some of the largest bass in the Midwest are pulled from Kansas's reservoirs and lakes. Fishers also come seeking crappie, walleye, smallmouth bass, and rainbow trout, found in 150 lakes and about 55,000 ponds. For more information about hunting season and fishing spots contact the *Kansas Fish and Game Commission,* Box 54A, Rte. 2, Pratt, KS 67124 (316–672–5911).

HISTORIC SITES AND HOUSES. Abilene. *Eisenhower Center,* S.E. 4th, Abilene, KS 67410 (913–263–4751). The center consists of Dwight D. Eisenhower's boyhood home, a museum featuring his military career and presidential years, a library, and the Place of Meditation, final resting place of Dwight and Mamie Eisenhower. Open year-round except holidays. Daily 9 A.M.–5 P.M. Adults, $1.50.

Council Grove. *Hays House,* 112 W. Main St., Council Grove, KS 66846 (316–767–5911). Used continuously as a restaurant since 1857; in its early days, the Hays House was also used for distribution of mail, U.S. Government court hearings, theater productions, church services, and newspaper printing. Open year-round except the first two weeks in Jan.

Larned. *Fort Larned National Historic Site,* Rte. 3, Larned, KS 67550 (316–285–6911). Fort Larned was a major post on the Santa Fe Trail and the Indian frontier from 1859–78. Four of the original nine military buildings are open and restored: barracks with museum, hospital, commissary, and officer's quarters. Films and historic programs. Open June–Aug. 8 A.M.–7 P.M.; Sept.–May 8 A.M.–5 P.M.

Oberlin. *Last Indian Raid Museum,* 258 S. Penn Ave., Oberlin, KS 67749 (913–475–2712). Museum is built on the site of the last Kansas Indian raid, the 1878 killing of 40 settlers by the North Cheyenne Indians. Museum houses Native American artifacts, country store, sod house, quilt collection, and period rooms. Pioneer Family Statue, a native-stone sculpture by Kansas sculptor Pete Felten, pays homage to the pioneer struggle to survive. Guided tours. Adults, $3; children, $1.50. Closed in winter.

ACCOMMODATIONS. We have listed Kansas hotels and motels alphabetically according to their city or town. The price categories reflect the cost of a double room: *Deluxe,* over $65; *Expensive,* $50–$65; *Moderate,* $30–$50; *Inexpensive,* under $30. Reservations, although not always necessary, are advisable.

Abilene. Best Western Inn. *Moderate.* 2210 N. Buckeye, Abilene, KS 67410 (913–263–2050 or 800–528–1234). 64 rooms.

Dodge City. Best Western Silver Spur Lodge. *Moderate.* 1510 W. Wyatt Earp, Dodge City, KS 67801 (316–227–2125 or 800–528–1234). 122 rooms. Accommodations for handicapped persons.

The Dodge House. *Moderate.* 2408 W. Wyatt Earp Blvd., Dodge City, KS 67801 (316–225–9900 or 800–553–9901). 170 rooms. Indoor pool and recreation area.

Emporia. Ramada Inn. *Moderate.* 1839 Merchant, Emporia, KS 66801 (316–342–8850 or 800–228–2828, out of state). 62 rooms.

Garden City. Wheatlands Best Western. *Moderate.* E. Fulton, Box 438, Garden City, KS 87846 (316–276–2387). 86 rooms.

Great Bend. Holiday Inn. *Moderate.* 3017 W. 10th, Great Bend, KS 67530 (316–792–2431 or 800–465–4329). 225 rooms.

Hays. Hampton Inn. *Moderate.* I-70 and U.S. 183 N., Hays, KS 67601 (913–625–8103). 118 rooms. Free Continental breakfast.

Hutchinson. Holiday Inn Holidome. *Expensive.* 1400 N. Lorraine, Hutchinson, KS 67501 (316–669–9311 or 800–465–4329). 220 rooms; facilities for handicapped.

Junction City. Days Inn. *Moderate.* 1024 S. Washington, Junction City, KS 66441, 1 block West of I-70 (913–762–2727 or 800–633–1414). 108 rooms. Continental breakfast.

Kansas City–Overland Park. Doubletree Hotel. *Deluxe.* 10100 College Blvd., Overland Park, KS 66210 (913–451–6100). 357 rooms. Indoor pool whirlpool, racketball courts, four restaurants, and lounge.

Lawrence. Holiday Inn Holidome. *Expensive.* 200 W. Turnpike Access Rd., Lawrence, KS 66044 (913–841–7077 or 800–465–4329). 192 rooms, restaurants, lounge, indoor pool, exercise room, putt-putt, sauna, whirlpool, convention center.

Days Inn. *Moderate.* 2309 Iowa St., Lawrence, KS 66044 (913–843–9100 or 800–325–2325). 113 rooms. Near the University of Kansas.

Manhattan. Days Inn. *Moderate.* 1501 Tuttle Creek Blvd., Manhattan, KS 66502 (913–539–5391 or 800–325–2325). 120 rooms, near Kansas State U.

Salina. Best Western Heart of America Inn. *Moderate.* 632 Westport Blvd., Salina, KS 67401 (913–827–9315 or 800–528–1234). 100 rooms with handicapped accessibility.

Topeka. Ramada Inn Downtown. *Expensive.* 420 E. 6th St., Topeka, KS 66601 (913–233–8981 or 800–2–RAMADA). 405 rooms. Restaurant, pool, private club.

Wichita. Ramada Hotel at Broadview Place. *Expensive.* 400 W. Douglas, Wichita, KS 67202 (316–262–5000). 275 rooms; restored hotel downtown.

Wichita Royale. *Deluxe.* 125 N. Market, Wichita, KS 67202 (316–263–2101). 134 rooms; superior accommodations.

RESTAURANTS. The following (a mere sampling) lists establishments alphabetically by city or town. The price categories reflect the cost of a 3-course dinner, without drinks, tax, or tips: *Expensive,* \$10–\$15; *Moderate,* \$5–\$10; *Inexpensive,* under \$5.

Council Grove. Hays House. *Moderate.* 112 W. Main (316–767–5911). Marvelous home-cooked meals, breakfasts, Sun. dinner. Try Beulah's ham. Worth a trip! Serving since 1857, Hays House claims to be the oldest restaurant west of the Mississippi.

Dodge City. Dodge House Restaurant. *Moderate.* 2408 W. Wyatt Earp (316–225–4188). Enjoy steaks and seafood here in a Wild West atmosphere.

Emporia. New China Restaurant. *Moderate.* 607 Merchant St. (316–342–1729). Chinese cooking.

Fairway (greater Kansas City). **Leona Yarbrough's.** *Moderate.* 2800 W. 53 St. (913–722–4800). Just across the state line from Missouri. Homecooked, family style meals: fried chicken, brisket, roast pork.

Great Bend. Black Angus Steak Ranch. *Moderate.* 2900 10th St. (316–792–4386). Famous for charcoal-broiled steaks.

Hays. Vernie's Hamburger House. *Inexpensive.* 527 E. 17th St. (913–628–1462). Best hamburgers around.

Hutchinson. Dutch Kitchen. *Inexpensive.* 6803 W. Hwy. 61 (316–662–2554). Amish home-style cooking.

Junction City. Cohen's Chicken and Steak House. *Moderate.* 104 Flint Hills Blvd. (913–238–6031). Travelers along I-70 make a special stop at Cohen's for great chicken dishes, barbecued ribs, desserts; quaint decor.

Lawrence. Nabil's Restaurant. *Expensive.* 925 Iowa (913–841–7226). Well-presented Continental cuisine, wine selection, piano music.

S.C. Pomeroy's. *Expensive.* 701 Massachusetts St., in the historic Eldridge House Hotel (913–841–8349). American regional specialties. Menu changes seasonally.

Cornucopia. *Moderate.* 1801 Massachusetts St. (913–842–9637). Natural foods, homemade breads, soups, desserts. Large, imaginative salad bar.

Paradise Café. *Moderate.* 728 Massachusetts St. (913–842–5199). "Good real food" is the motto here. Homemade pasta and seafood are served daily.

Manhattan. Continental Inn. *Expensive.* 100 Bluemont (913–776–4771). Steaks and seafood.

Osage House. *Moderate.* 2605 Stagg Hill Rd. (913–776–1234). Mainstays at this place are steaks, seafood, and chicken.

Overland Park (greater Kansas City). **Hayward's Barbecue.** *Moderate.* 11051 Antioch Rd., Overland Park (913–649–8005). Establishment famous for Kansas City barbecue.

KC Masterpiece Barbecue and Grill. *Moderate.* 10985 Metcalf (913–345–1199). Featured here is classic barbecue, from ribs to chicken, in good-size portions.

Salina. Brookville Hotel. *Moderate.* 15 mi. west on Hwy. 140 (913–225–6666). Country chicken dinners in restored hotel. A Kansas legend. Even the ice cream is homemade. Reservations suggested.

Red Coach Inn Restaurant. *Moderate.* 2110 Crawford Ave. (913–825–2166). Steaks, family dining.

Stanley (greater Kansas City). Joe's Barn. *Moderate.* 150th and Metcalf (913–681–2556). Family dining served buffet style. Chicken dishes, barbecue, country vegetables. Barn décor.

Topeka. McFarland's. *Moderate.* 4133 Gage Center Dr., in Gage Shopping Ctr. (913–272–6909). Prime rib, sauterbrauten. Third-generation family-owned.

Pore Richard's Cafe and Lounge. *Moderate.* 707 S. Kansas Ave. (913–271–6890). Steaks, chicken sandwiches, hamburgers. Booths with jukeboxes.

Wichita. Angelo's 1. *Moderate.* 3105 E. Harry (316–682–1473). Fine Italian dining.

Spears Restaurant. *Inexpensive.* 1930 S. Oliver (316–686–1211). Family dining, homemade pastries.

LIQUOR LAWS. There are about 1,000 privately owned liquor stores in Kansas, open from around 9 A.M.–11 P.M., Mon.–Sat. Liquor is sold by the drink or bottle in more than 1,200 private clubs. Tourists can obtain temporary memberships at clubs inside hotels and motels where they are staying and on the property owned or operated by a municipal airport authority. Liquor is not sold on Sun., except in some private clubs. The minimum drinking age is 21. A liquor-by-the-drink bill was recently passed by voters on a county option basis; soon the private club system will be phased out in those counties.

OKLAHOMA

Suddenly, in one day, Oklahoma and Oklahoma City sprang into being. On April 22, 1889, thousands of settlers flooded over the border to stake claims in a land run created when the U.S. government seized Indian land from the Five Civilized Tribes because they had supported the Confederacy. By nightfall, Oklahoma City surged from a small prairie town to a village of 10,000 residents. Oklahoma City thrived and today has a population of nearly one million. Oklahoma became our 46th state in 1907; Oklahoma City became the capital three years later. The name *Oklahoma* came from two Choctaw words meaning land of the red people, and today there are about 67 Native American tribes represented in Oklahoma City's population. Much of the state's present outlook evokes memories of its two most familiar elements, the Indians and the cowboys, from Pawnee Bill's Wild West Show in Pawnee to the annual Indian powwow south of Oklahoma City in Anadarko and Indian City, USA.

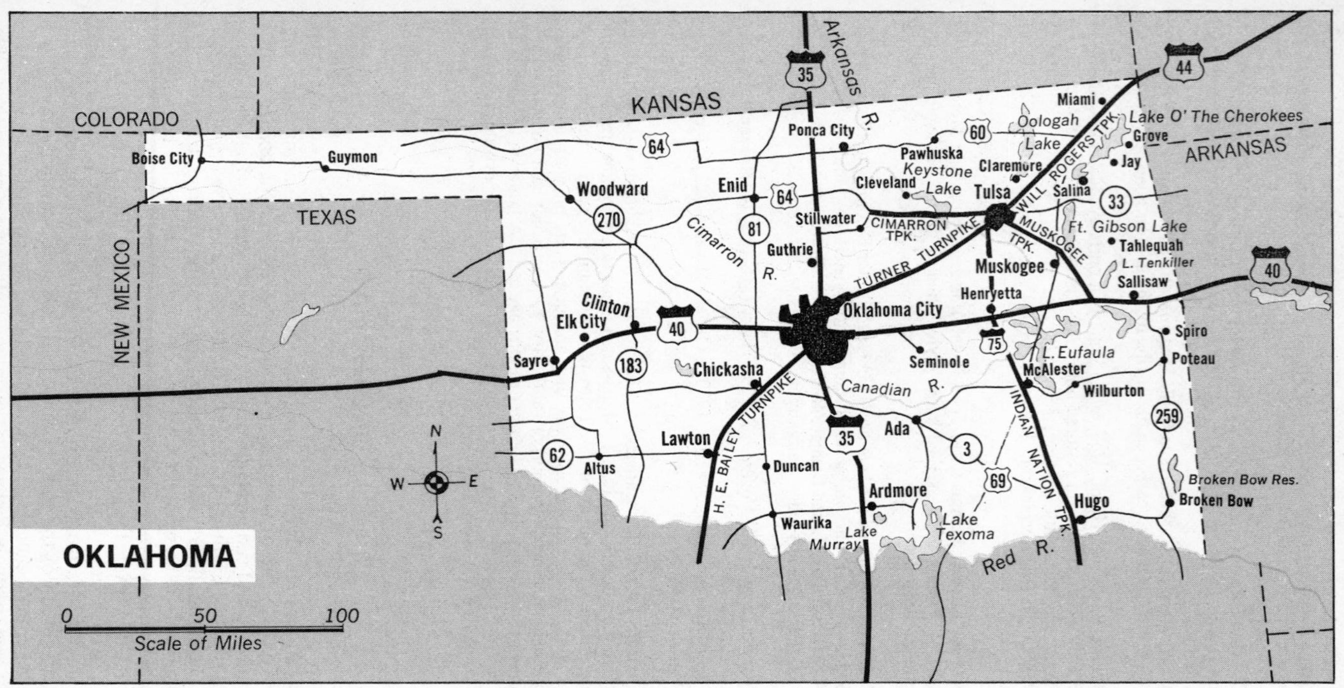
KANSAS
COLORADO
NEW MEXICO
TEXAS
ARKANSAS
Boise City
Guymon
Woodward
Enid
Ponca City
Pawhuska
Miami
Oologah Lake
Lake O' The Cherokees
Grove
Jay
Claremore
Keystone Lake
Cleveland
Tulsa
Salina
Stillwater
CIMARRON TPK.
WILL ROGERS TPK.
MUSKOGEE TPK.
Ft. Gibson Lake
Tahlequah
L. Tenkiller
Sallisaw
Guthrie
Cimarron R.
Arkansas R.
TURNER TURNPIKE
Muskogee
Henryetta
Oklahoma City
Clinton
Elk City
Sayre
Chickasha
Seminole
L. Eufaula
McAlester
Wilburton
Spiro
Poteau
Canadian R.
H. E. BAILEY TURNPIKE
INDIAN NATION TPK.
Ada
Lawton
Altus
Duncan
Ardmore
Waurika
Lake Murray
Lake Texoma
Hugo
Broken Bow Res.
Broken Bow
Red R.
N
W
E
S
OKLAHOMA
0
50
100
Scale of Miles
35
44
60
64
81
270
33
40
183
75
3
69
62
259

Oklahoma again underwent sudden change at the turn of the century, from its base of agriculture and livestock to a petroleum economy when oil was discovered across the state. Few sites were off-limits. Oil wells pump along today inside Oklahoma City's limits, and wells surround the state capitol at 23rd and Lincoln Boulevard. One well is drilled at an angle to remove oil from a pool directly under the substantial Corinthian-style state capitol building.

Indian artifacts and western memorabilia are found at the State Museum of Oklahoma, and the city offers an alluring variety of exhibits in its northeast quadrant. There you will find the Oklahoma City Zoo; the Kirkpatrick Center, which houses the International Photograph Hall of Fame; Omniplex, a hands-on science museum; the Kirkpatrick Planetarium and the Air Space Museum; and the African Gallery and galleries of Japanese art, U.S. Naval history, and artwork by Oklahomans. One should plan to visit the National Cowboy Hall of Fame and Western Heritage Center, where the world's most extensive collection of western art and history is gathered.

The city has other unusual museums, including the Firefighter's Museum, the National Softball Hall of Fame, the Oklahoma Museum of Art, and the Oklahoma Art Center.

In Tulsa, often in rivalry with Oklahoma City, there is a vibrant spirit of industry, artistic appreciation, and history. One of the city's eeriest sights is Oral Roberts University, a college named for the Christian evangelist, with its golden spires, and the adjoining City of Faith Medical Center. There, a metallic-looking 60-story clinic, 20-story research building, and 30-story hospital stand beside clasping hands that reach from the earth. The Philbrook Art Center and the Gilcrease Institute of American History and Art were both built with bequests from Tulsa oilmen and feature modern art and collections of artifacts tracing the development of the United States from prehistory to western times, in scenes captured by Frederick Remington. Tulsa has a nationally recognized ballet company, the Tulsa Ballet, the Tulsa Opera, and the Tulsa Philharmonic, all of which perform often in the theaters of the Tulsa Performing Arts Center.

Many associate Oklahoma with its most famous humorist, Will Rogers, whose rope tricks and plainspoken jabs at those in authority taught the nation to take itself less seriously. Asked once what inspired his humor, he said, "I don't make jokes—I just watch government and report the facts." His life and works are exhibited at the Will Rogers Memorial and at the Will Rogers Hotel, both in Claremore.

Oklahoma's largest lakes are tourist attractions, resorts, and havens for outdoor enthusiasts who like sunning, swimming, boating, camping, or fishing. The largest is Lake Eufaula in the eastern regions of the state, with 102,500 acres. On the southern border adjoining Texas are Lake Texoma and Lake Texoma State Park, a 93,000-acre lake and large park with a resort.

The Oklahoma panhandle has grown as a tourist lure in recent years for those who are attracted to the open expanses, low mesas, and amateur archaeological exploration. Oklahomans are proud of their western heritage, sprung from a culture steeped in Native American traditions.

PRACTICAL INFORMATION FOR OKLAHOMA

WHEN TO GO. The Sooner State, considered a part of the Southwest, has a sunny climate with hot summers, mild winters, and long, pleasant fall days. It is not unusual for July and Aug. daytime temperatures to soar over 105° F., but the air tends to feel drier than in upper-midwestern states. Tulsa and Oklahoma City are growing in their convention business and are quite busy during the spring, summer, and fall; they also have numerous small festivals and local events. Winter days are bitterly cold only infrequently. Flurries are punctual, and a few larger snowstorms surprise the state every few years.

HOW TO GET THERE. By plane. Tulsa and Oklahoma City are served by most major airlines, including *Frontier, Delta, Ozark, TWA, United,* and *Western.* Several smaller companies offer flights within Oklahoma also. Travelers should often be able to take advantage of fare wars because of the keen competition for air service.

By bus. *Greyhound* offers bus services to most cities and towns in Oklahoma, with connecting buses to other states.

By car. I-40 crosses the state's midsection east to west, meeting in Oklahoma City with north- and south-running I-35, which connects Wichita and Dallas. The Turner Tpk. connects Oklahoma City and Tulsa, and the Will Rogers Tpk. connects Tulsa with Joplin, Missouri. The H. E. Bailey Tpk. connects Oklahoma City and Lawton, and the Muskogee Tpk. links Tulsa and Muskogee.

TOURIST INFORMATION. *Oklahoma Division of Tourism,* 500 Will Rogers Bldg., Oklahoma City, OK 73105 (405–521–3553; 800–652–6552). *Oklahoma City Convention & Tourism Bureau,* One Santa Fe Plaza, Oklahoma City, OK 73102 (405–278–8912). *Tulsa Chamber of Commerce,* 616 S. Boston, Tulsa, OK 74119 (918–585–1201). For travel reservations in six foreign languages—French, German, Italian, Japanese, Portuguese, and Spanish—call 800–356–8392.

The best sources of daily information can be found in the *Daily Oklahoman,* published in Oklahoma City, and the Tulsa *World* and *Tribune.*

For information about Norman, home of the University of Oklahoma, contact their *Chamber of Commerce* (405–321–7260), and in Stillwater, where Oklahoma State University is found, contact their *Chamber of Commerce* (405–372–5573).

TELEPHONES. The area code for the northeastern sliver of the state, including Bartlesville, Tulsa, Miami, and Muskogee, is 918. For the rest of the state, including Oklahoma City, Stillwater, Norman, Guthrie, and Enid, the area code is 405. For directory assistance in most places dial 555–1212. If in Tulsa you want an Oklahoma City number, dial 405–555–1212. Dial 0 before the area code for operator assistance or credit-card long-distance calls. Local telephone calls are 25 cents statewide.

EMERGENCY TELEPHONES. The nearly universal emergency number, 911, is employed in most of Oklahoma's larger cities for emergency *fire, police, paramedic,* and *ambulance.* The regular police number in Oklahoma City is 405–232–5311; in Tulsa it is 918–588–9222. A 24-hour *poison-control office* is at 405–271–5454. *Baptist Medical Center* in Oklahoma City is 949–3011; Oklahoma Children's Memorial Hospital in Oklahoma City, 271–4371. If you are elsewhere and 911 does not work, dial 0 and ask the operator to put you in immediate contact with medical personnel or law-enforcement officers.

The state also has a statewide *poison-control number,* 800–522–4611.

HINTS TO MOTORISTS. Most of Oklahoma is laid out in north-south and east-west roads and highways. Oklahoma City basically follows the pattern with east-west thoroughfares marked by numbers and north-south thoroughfares by names. The state capitol is at the intersection of Lincoln Blvd. and 23rd St. In Tulsa, the main downtown streets are off-angle from a true compass scheme, though the core streets are First St. and Main St. Traffic can get congested during the day in Tulsa and Oklahoma City, especially during morning and evening rush hours, so it is wise to travel the breadth of the cities on major interstates that pass through and around each city.

Oklahoma aggressively enforces the federal speed limit on federal highways and interstates. Law-enforcement officials are tough on drunk drivers. For information about highway distances statewide, members of the American Automobile Association may call their headquarters in Oklahoma City, 405–943–9922. Emergency road help can be obtained for members at 405–943–9100.

HINTS TO DISABLED TRAVELERS. The state's museums, parks, restaurants, motels, and attractions are accessible for the most part. Persons who are disabled may qualify for reduced rates at certain attractions. For reservations or more information contact the *Oklahoma Tourism and Recreation Department* (405–521–2464).

ZOOS. The **Oklahoma City Zoo** is the oldest zoo in the Southwest and receives about 500,000 visitors a year, many of whom come to see the 500 species of mammals, birds, reptiles, and fish, often seen in re-created natural habitats. A quick way to see a lot of this sprawling zoo is on the Safari Tram or the zoo railroad. The zoo is renowned for its golden lion marmosets, its Indian rhinos, and an aquarium that opened in 1985. Open in the winter, 9 A.M.–5 P.M., daily; in the summer, 9 A.M.–6 P.M., daily. It is at 2101 N.E. 50th St., Oklahoma City, OK 73111 (405–424–3343).

Tulsa has the **Tulsa Zoological Park,** 5701 E. 36th St. N., Tulsa, OK 74115 (918–596–2400). The park has a large collection of exotic animals in natural settings, a life-size reproduction of a dinosaur, earth-science displays, a walk-through cave, a 10,000-gal. coral reef tank, and underwater viewing of ever-amusing polar bears. The park is open 10 A.M.–5 P.M. in spring and fall, and until 6 in summer. Closes at 4:30 in winter. Sea lions are fed daily at 2 P.M. The park also has a special children's area with a chimpanzee colony and a petting zoo.

STATE PARKS. Besides those listed below, Oklahoma has more than 100 smaller state and private resorts, campgrounds, and parks. For information and reservations for cabins and resorts, call 405–521–2464.

Beavers Bend State Park. 7 mi. north of Broken Bow (405–494–6538). Wilderness along Mountain Fork River. 3,500 acres; beach, canoeing, trout fishing.

Keystone State Park. 16 mi. west of Tulsa (918–865–4991). 715-acre park on southeast shore of Lake Keystone. Skiing, bass fishing, beaches. Discoveryland stages *Oklahoma!* in summer.

Lake Murray State Park and Resort. 2 mi. east of I-35 and 7 mi. north of Ardmore (405–223–6600). State's largest park; 12,496 acres around Lake Murray. Resort on eastern shore; scuba diving, sailboat, paddle boat, beaches. Park naturalist at Tower Nature Center.

Roman Nose State Park and Resort. West-central Oklahoma (405–623–7281). On 25-acre Lake Boecher, a retreat with lodge, golf, paddleboats, and unusual, natural-rock swimming pool.

Sequoyah State Park–Western Hills Guest Ranch. Northeast Oklahoma (918–772–2545). 2,800-acre park in Cookson Hills along East Gibson Lake. Stagecoach rides, cookouts, horseback rides, beach, marina, nature center.

Wister State Park. Southeastern Oklahoma (918–655–7212). 3,040-acre park near Quachita National Forest. Piney mountains, beach, marina on Lake Wister.

HUNTING AND FISHING. For hunters the state has 28 game birds including Rio Grande wild turkeys, pheasant, quail, dove, prairie chickens; and deer, pronghorn antelope, and elk are often found in its 40 wildlife-management areas or the national forest that offers a total of 850,000 acres of public hunting land.

Perhaps surprisingly, given Oklahoma's Dust Bowl legacy, there is a lot of fishable water in the state these days. With more than 600,000 acres of reservoirs, ponds, and lakes and 8,500 mi. of streams and rivers, the state ranks third in the amount of fishable fresh water. Striped bass, largemouth bass, walleye, catfish, and sunfish are popular.

Licenses are required. For more information about hunting season and fishing conditions contact the *Oklahoma Department of Wildlife Conservation,* 1801 N. Lincoln Blvd., Oklahoma City, OK 73105 (405–521–3851).

MUSEUMS AND SPECIAL-INTEREST SIGHTSEEING. Claremore. *Will Rogers Memorial,* Box 157, Claremore, OK 74018 (918–341–0719). Rogers memorabilia, saddle collections, photographs, manuscripts, clothing, family tree and more of the state's best-known citizen. There are also Rogers's tomb and a 178-seat theater with daily films illustrating Rogers's inimitable wisdom. Hours: Daily 8 A.M.–5 P.M.

Guthrie. *Oklahoma Territorial Museum,* 406 E. Oklahoma, Guthrie, OK 73044 (405–282–1889). The late Victorian-style museum attached to a Carnegie library, where the last territorial and first state governors were inaugurated, relates the state's territorial life from 1889–1907. It also has artwork by Frederick Olds. Hours: Tues.–Fri., 9 A.M.–5 P.M.; Sat., 10 A.M.–4 P.M.; Sun., 1–4 P.M.

Muskogee. *Five Civilized Tribes Museum,* Honor Heights Dr., Agency Hill, Muskogee, OK 74401 (918–683–1701). The original Union Indian Agency built in 1875 houses trading post, a gallery of original art, a library, a print room, and Native American artifacts. Hours: Mon.–Sat., 10 A.M.–5 P.M.; Sun. 1–5 P.M.

Oklahoma City. *National Cowboy Hall of Fame,* 1700 N.E. 63rd, Oklahoma City, OK 73111 (405–478–2250). Corrals the world's largest exhibition of western lore, art, and memorabilia. Includes paintings by Russell, Remington, Moran, and Fraiser, a collection of Native American art, and John Wayne's Kachina-doll collection. Open daily 9 A.M.–5 P.M. Adults $5; children, $2; senior citizens, $4.

National Softball Hall of Fame, 2801 N.E. 50th, Oklahoma City, OK 73111 (405–424–5266). Offers every imaginable aspect of softball in interesting displays. Hours: late Mar.–Oct., Mon.–Fri., 8:30 A.M.–5 P.M.; Sat., 10 A.M.–4 P.M.; Sun., 1–4 P.M.

Oklahoma Firefighters Museum, 2716 N.E. 50th, Oklahoma City, OK 73136 (405–424–3440). Houses an extensive collection of firefighting equipment through the years. Hours: Daily 10 A.M.–5 P.M.

Omniplex Science Museum, 2100 N.E. 52nd St., Oklahoma City, OK 73111 (405–424–5545). Has 200 hands-on exhibits of science, art, and history. Hours: Mon.–Fri., 9:30 A.M.–5 P.M.; Sat., 9 A.M.–6 P.M.; Sun., noon–6 P.M.

State Museum of the Oklahoma Historical Society, Historical Building, Oklahoma City, OK 73105 (405–521–2491). Depicts Oklahoma's diverse history from prehistoric Indian times to the present. Hours: Mon.–Sat., 8 A.M.–5 P.M.

Tahlequah. *Cherokee Heritage Center,* Box 515, Tahlequah, OK 74465 (918–456–6007). This unique center houses the Adams Corner Village, a reconstructed 1875 community; Cherokee Nation Museum, presenting the Cherokee story; "Trail of Tears" Outdoor Drama, a portrayal of Indian hardships, performed June–Aug.; and Tsa-La-Gi, a fascinating re-creation of 17th-century Cherokee villages, staffed by Cherokees in the dress of that time. Check each attraction for hours.

Tulsa. *Fenster Gallery of Jewish Art,* 1223 E. 17th Pl., Tulsa, OK 74120 (918–582–3732). The third-largest collection of Judaic materials in the United States. Includes objects of ritual and ceremony and aesthetic art of the Jewish faith dating from 5000 B.C. to present. Hours: Tue.–Fri., 10 A.M.–4 P.M.; Sun., 1–4 P.M.

Thomas Gilcrease Institute of American History and Art, 1400 Gilcrease Museum Rd., Tulsa, OK 74127 (918–582–3122). Art and artifacts documenting western Americana with works by such artists as Remington, Russell, Audubon, and Moran. Hours: Mon.–Sat. 9 A.M.–5 P.M.; Sun. 1–5 P.M.

Philbrook Museum of Art. 2727 S. Rockford, Tulsa, OK 74152 (918–749–7941). Art collection spans ancient Egypt, Italian Renaissance, contemporary American, Native American art. Hours: Tues.–Sat., 10 A.M.–5 P.M.; Thurs., 5–8 P.M.; Sun, 1–5 P.M. Adults, $3; senior citizens and students, $1.50; children, free.

ARTS AND ENTERTAINMENT. For information on what's happening in the arts statewide, call the *State Arts Council of Oklahoma* (405–521–2931). In Oklahoma City, for 24-hour information on arts events, dial 236–ARTS. The following is a sampling of some of the cultural events in the state:

Bartlesville. *Bartlesville Community Center.* 308 S.E. Adams Blvd., Bartlesville, OK 74003 (918–337–2787). Spectacular performing-arts facility showcasing both local and imported arts groups. Annual summer Mozart Festival.

Oklahoma City. *Black Liberated Arts Center.* 1901 N. Ellison, Oklahoma City, OK 73106 (405–528–4666). BLAC, Inc., was founded to showcase black culture, dance, music, theater.

Carpenter Square Theater. 840 Robert S. Kerr Ave., Oklahoma City, OK 73102 (405–232–6500). Theater in an old warehouse.

Lyric Theater. 2501 N. Blackwelder, Oklahoma City, OK 73106 (405–528–3636). At the Kirkpatrick Fine Arts Auditorium at the Oklahoma City U. campus.

Myriad Convention Center. 1 Myriad Gardens, Oklahoma City, OK 73102 (405–236–2333). Rock concerts, rodeo events.

Oklahoma City Philharmonic Orchestra. Civic Center Music Hall, 201 Channing Sq., Oklahoma City, OK 73102 (405–843–0900). Sept.–May season, classic and pops concerts with popular guest artists.

Tulsa: *Harwellden,* 2210 S. Main, Tulsa, OK 74114 (918–584–3333). Home of the Tulsa Arts and Humanities Council. Chamber music.

Tulsa Performing Arts Center. Williams Center, downtown Tulsa (918–596–7122). Multitheater facility stages fine-arts performances. Tulsa Philharmonic, Tulsa Ballet, Tulsa Opera all perform here.

ACCOMMODATIONS. We have listed hotels and motels in Oklahoma alphabetically, by town or city (with the most listings in Oklahoma City and Tulsa). The price categories reflect the cost of a double room: *Deluxe,* over $100; *Expensive,* $70–$100; *Moderate,* $50–$70; *Inexpensive,* under $50. Three chains well represented throughout the state are: **Holiday Inns** (800–HOLIDAY), **Ramada Inns** (800–2–RAMADA), and **Howard Johnson** (800–654–2000).

Bartlesville. Hotel Phillips. *Moderate.* 222 S.E. Washington, Bartlesville, OK 74005 (918–336–5600). 111 rooms; named after the city's largest employer, Phillips Petroleum Company.

Clinton. Granada Inn. *Inexpensive.* 1200 U.S. 66, Clinton, OK 73601 (405–323–5550; 800–654–4556, out of state). Club, pool, restaurant.

Enid. Midwestern Inn. *Inexpensive.* 200 N. Van Buren, Enid, OK 73702 (405–234–1200 or 800–541–1947). Meeting rooms, pool, sports court, whirlpool.

Guthrie. Territorial Inn. *Moderate.* 2323 Territorial Trail, Guthrie, OK 73044 (405–282–8831).

Lawton. Montego Bay Motor Hotel. *Inexpensive.* 1125 E. Gore, Lawton, OK 73502 (405–353–7177). 150 rooms; Captain's Cabin Café, suites, 3 pools, sauna.

Norman. Residence Inn by Marriott. *Expensive.* 2681 Jefferson, Norman, OK 73069 (405–366–0900; 800–228–9290). This place underwent complete renovation in 1988. All suites. Complimentary breakfast.

Oklahoma City. Waterford Hotel. *Deluxe.* 6300 Waterford Blvd., Oklahoma City, OK 73118 (405–848–4782). 197 rooms, dining room, pool, live entertainment.

Sheraton Century Center Hotel. *Expensive.* One N. Broadway (405–235–2780; 800–325–3535). This is a large inn with meeting rooms, entertainment, etc.

Skirvin Plaza Hotel. *Expensive.* One Park Ave., Oklahoma City, OK 73102 (405–232–4411). 209 rooms, pool, airport limo, spa.

Hilton Inn West. *Moderate.* 401 S. Meridian, Oklahoma City, OK 73108 (405–947–7681 or 800–HILTONS). Featured here are 509 rooms, tennis, movies, spa, airport limo, pool.

Lincoln Plaza Hotel and Conference Center. *Moderate.* 4445 N. Lincoln Blvd., Oklahoma City, OK 73106 (405–528–2741 or 800–654–8419, out of state). 330 rooms, convention center, live entertainment, suites, sauna.

Comfort Inn. *Inexpensive.* 2200 S. Meridian, Oklahoma City, OK 73139 (405–681–9000 or 800–228–5150). Free Continental breakfast is offered at this place.

Howard Johnson. *Inexpensive.* 400 S. Meridian (405–943–9841). This place, typical of the chain, offers transportation to the airport.

La Quinta Inn. *Inexpensive.* 8315 S. I-35, Oklahoma City, OK 73149 (800–531–5900 or 800–531–5900). Featured here are morning coffee and a pool.

Sands Motel. *Inexpensive.* I-40 at Rockwell Ave., Oklahoma City, OK 73128 (405–787–7353). Pool, playground, and laundry are featured here.

Shawnee. Cinderella Motor Hotel. *Moderate.* 623 Kickapoo Spur, Shawnee, OK 74801 (405–273–7010).

Tahlequah. Lodge of the Cherokees. *Inexpensive.* Box 948, Tahlequah, OK 74465 (918–456–0511). South of the city on Hwy. 62. Owned and operated by the Cherokee Nation of Oklahoma.

Tulsa. The Doubletree at City Center. *Deluxe.* 616 W. 7th, Tulsa, OK 74127 (800–223–5672). 418 rooms, near Assembly Center; spa, restaurant.

Westin Hotel Williams Center. *Deluxe.* 10 E. 2nd St., Tulsa, OK 74103 (918–582–9000). 450 rooms, dining rooms, lounge, tennis, indoor-outdoor pool. Walkway connects hotel to mall with restaurants, shops, ice skating.

Camelot Hotel. *Moderate.* 4956 S. Peoria, Tulsa, OK 74105 (800–331–4428). 300 rooms, suites.

The Lexington Hotel Suites. *Moderate.* 8525 E. 41st., Tulsa, OK (918–627–0030). 168 rooms. Free Continental breakfast.

Park Plaza. *Moderate.* 5000 E. Skelly, Tulsa, OK 74135 (918–622–7000). Available here are 400 rooms, lounge, 2 restaurants.

Ramada Inn. *Moderate.* 11521 E. Skelly, Tulsa, OK 74128 (918–438–7700). Available at this chain are 119 rooms.

Wagoner. Western Hills Guest Ranch, see State Parks.

Woodward. Best Western Wayfarer Inn. *Inexpensive.* U.S. 183 (405–256–5553; 800–528–1234). Featured here are a playground, café, and meeting rooms.

RESTAURANTS. As with accommodations, we have listed establishments alphabetically, by city or town. The price categories reflect the cost of a 3-course dinner for one, without beverage, tax, or tip. They are: *Deluxe,* over $20; *Expensive,* $15–$20; *Moderate,* $10–$15; *Inexpensive,* under $10.

Bartlesville. Marie's Steak House. *Expensive.* Adams and Silver Lake Rd. (918–333–8700). Chicken, seafood, steak dinners.

Guthrie. Sand Plum. *Moderate–Expensive.* 202 W. Harrison (405–282–7771). Continental fare in restored 19th-century building.

Lawton. Martin's. *Expensive.* 2107 Cache (405–353–5286). Seafood, ribs.

Norman. Legend's. *Moderate.* 1313 W. Lindsey (405–329–8888). Seafood, choice beef, pasta; pastries baked on premises.

Oklahoma City. Haunted House. *Expensive.* Must call for directions (405–478–1417). Steaks, seafood, fowl in out-of-the-way cozy country-inn atmosphere.

The Painted Desert. *Inexpensive.* 3700 N. Shartel (405–524–5925). Sandwiches, soups, salads for lunch; seafood, steaks, pasta for dinner. Colorful atmosphere.

Pryor. J. L.'s Barbecue. *Inexpensive.* 3 mi. south on Hwy. 69 (918–825–1829).

Tahlequah. Restaurant of the Cherokees. *Inexpensive.* Hwy. 28 S. of Tahlequah (918–456–0511). Owned and operated by the Cherokee Nation. Country fried steak and smoked chicken dinners.

Tulsa. Montagues. *Deluxe.* Williams Center, 2 W. 2nd (918–582–9000). Beef Wellington, Pheasant Vinter, stuffed lobster tail, and other fine cuisine.

15th Street Grill. *Expensive.* 1542 E. 15th St. (918–583–0571). Creative chef finds unusual touches for fish, lamb, veal. Menu changes seasonally.

The French Hen Restaurant. *Expensive.* 7143 S. Yale (918–492–2596). Game birds, pasta, seafood, and veal with French flair.

Chimi's. *Inexpensive.* 1413 E. 15th St. (918–587–4411) and 6709 E. 81st St. (918–495–1162). Mexican place that makes its own tortillas and tamales.

Ri-Le. *Inexpensive.* 71st St. and Lewis Ave. (2nd floor) (918–496–7638). Vietnamese specialties. Unusual fare in out-of-the-way spot.

Tules de Santa Fe, Restaurant y Cantina. *Inexpensive.* 424 S. Main (918–599–8080). Santa Fe-style Mexican food.

Woodward. Buffy's Buffet. *Moderate.* 2704 Williams (405–256–5873). Roasted chicken a specialty.

LIQUOR LAWS. The state has an unusual blend of laws within its boundaries. The minimum drinking age is 21. Liquor by the drink is sold in Oklahoma City, Tulsa, Norman, Bartlesville, and a number of other large cities, because of a special vote taken in 1985. Some areas of the state sell liquor by the drink in private clubs, of which you can become a temporary member if you are staying in a motel with a club. In some counties, you must bring your own bottle to a private club. The easiest way to find out the rules is to ask just about anyone; Oklahomans enjoy talking about their colorful battles over drinking.

TEXAS

by
CAROL BARRINGTON

Carol Barrington, an award-winning travel writer and photographer and the author of Day Trips from Houston, *lives in Houston and specializes in magazine and newspaper articles on Texas. This article is based partly on work by Omega Clay, Judy Williamson, Teresa Hurst, Nancy Haston Foster, and Ted J. Simon that originally appeared in* Fodor's Texas.

The Lone Star state is known for bigness, more than 2,675,300 acres, larger than the entire country of France. You will appreciate this vastness when you drive across the state. It is 821 miles from Texarkana in the northeast to El Paso in the west, and 872 miles from Dalhart in the far north of the Panhandle to Brownsville at the southernmost tip in the Rio Grande Valley. More than 70,000 miles of highway thread the state.

The state's population was officially counted at more than 14 million in the 1980 census, making it the third largest state in the nation. Fifteen Texas cities have more than 100,000 inhabitants, and Houston is the fourth largest city in the country. Four of its largest metro areas have detailed chapters in this section.

Do not succumb to the Hollywood-fostered stereotype of Texas being an arid wasteland populated primarily by cowboys and sagebrush. With more than 624 miles of coastline and 6,000 square miles of inland freshwater lakes and streams, water sports flourish through the summer and much of the moderate winter. Mountains more than 8,000 feet high dominate the skyline in West Texas, and in East Texas are some of the thickest, marshiest forests in America. In contrast, the flat brush country south of San

Antonio is almost devoid of high trees. Diversity is the keyword for the whole of the state.

Austin

Settled in 1839 on the banks of the Colorado River, Austin grew from the frontier villages of Waterloo and Montopolis. It was named for Stephen F. Austin, the entrepreneur who was responsible for bringing the first Anglo settlers to what is now Texas. The third Congress of the Republic of Texas made Austin state capital on the basis of its central location, mild climate, beautiful rolling terrain, and the availability of water, stone, and timber.

More than a hundred years later, in spite of a rapidly increasing population (485,000 in a recent census), Austin retains its mild climate, its clean water, and much of its beautiful land. The rolling Hill Country to the west of town remains largely undeveloped and is considered by Texans to be some of the most handsome land in the state. From the northwest, the Colorado River (*not* the same one that flows through the Grand Canyon) winds through the city, forming Lake Austin on the west and Town Lake in the south-central business district.

Austin's extensive park system contributes to the city's livability, forming greenbelts in every part of town. The capitol grounds themselves are favorites for strolls and picnics; Zilker Park, the city's largest and most used recreation area, is only five minutes from downtown. If the weather is warm, don't miss a swim-and-sun session here at Barton Springs Pool, fed by natural springs that originate in the surrounding Hill Country. The park also has a beautiful Japanese garden, azalea and rose gardens, special programs at the Austin Nature Center, and a miniature train for children. You also can rent canoes here to paddle on Town Lake.

The heart of the downtown business district is dominated by the state capitol building, on Congress Avenue between 11th and 14th streets. Built on what was thought to be the highest rise in town, it faces south to Town Lake. That corridor currently is a madhouse of construction, as new office buildings and hotels mix with more historic structures.

Another downtown area you won't want to miss is 6th Street, running west from I-35 to Congress Avenue. Fun for lunch and shopping during the day, it comes alive with people after dark, especially on weekends. Many of the city's most trendy cafes, restaurants, and bars are here; reservations are strongly suggested. The unrestrained nightlife on 6th Street has given it the nickname of "a little Bourbon Street"—when you are looking for action, start here.

Central Austin also includes the University of Texas campus, north of the capitol complex. Guadalupe Street, better known as "the Drag," runs on the western edge of campus north from Martin Luther King (called MLK locally) to 29th Street. Like most campus commercial districts, this area is full of small clothing shops, bookstores, eateries, and theaters, and on weekends the street vendors are out in force, selling everything from handcrafted jewelry to clothing and leather items.

Visitors are welcome on the handsome UT campus, but parking can be a problem. Try the new parking garage at 2500 San Jacinto (fee). The UT Visitor Center (471–1420) is open weekdays in the Little Campus area at the southwest corner of MLK and I-35. On the west side of campus, a good stopping place is the General Information and Referral Service on the ground floor of the Tower Building. A student-guided walking tour of campus leaves from here twice a day on weekdays, once on Saturdays (471–7601). Of special note are the Lyndon Baines Johnson Library and Museum, one of seven presidential libraries administered by the National Archives; the Harry Ransom Center, internationally recognized for its rare books and manuscripts, icon and photography collections; and one of the five extant editions of the Gutenberg Bible. Both libraries are also museums and open to the public.

Austin serves as a fertile ground for the arts. There may be more potters, painters, writers, sculptors, dancers, actors, singers, and musicians per square inch there than anywhere else in the state. And, whereas other Texas cities may raze old downtown structures to make room for reflecting-glass boxes, Austin's cityscape integrates the old with the new, making it a comfortable place to live and a unique place to visit in Texas.

Dallas

Within the state, Dallas is known for its diversified economic, civic, and cultural interests. It's young, vivacious, urbane—and fun. There are no natural resources to boast of—no mountains, lapping oceans, or mighty rivers. To use a whopping cliché, Dallas' greatest natural asset is its people: an alert, progressive, and friendly citizenry.

Most relics of Dallas' relatively short history are clustered in the west end of the thriving central business district. Here, perched on a concrete plaza, is the primitive log cabin that John Neely Bryan built in 1841, putting the city officially on early maps of Texas. Bryan allegedly chose this spot for its proximity to the Trinity River so that he could trade with Indians and the westbound wagon trains.

The name Dallas wasn't used until 1843, and the city's origin still is in doubt. Some say it was named for George Mifflin Dallas, vice-president of the United States. Others say it was named for a friend of Bryan's, one Joseph Dallas. The aggressive pioneer efforts that enabled the settlement to survive some difficult early days have since been duplicated time after time. Successive generations, equally spirited, have attained their respective goals: making the town the center of the state's emerging highway network; digging a new channel for the unruly Trinity River, thereby reclaiming 10,000 acres of land for the central business district; achieving a dominant position in the nation's airline transportation system (Dallas–Fort Worth Regional Airport is the nation's second largest and fourth busiest); and implementing a series of farsighted master plans for the practical and aesthetic development of the city.

Simply stated, Dallas works. In 1986 it was fifth-largest in terms of the number of million-dollar companies, according to Dun and Bradstreet's ratings. Of the famed Fortune 500 industrial firms, 309 have offices in Dallas and 13 others make it their headquarters. Although precise statistics are not available, Dallas is thought to be second only to Hartford (CT) in numbers of insurance companies who make it their home office.

Both downtown and North Dallas gleam with tall, glass-sheathed towers—you'll want to sample the upscale shopping of the new Dallas Galleria and view the area lights from the top of Hyatt Regency's Reunion Tower. But the city's character lies in its small-town neighborhoods. Mention Greenville Avenue to a Dallasite, and they'll tell you of a singles strip stretching north from University to Meadow Road. South from there, Lower Greenville, is a neighborhood in renaissance, the kind that features home delivery by groceries and shop owners who know their customers by name.

New restorations on Lower Greenville are similar to others on McKinney Avenue and in the West End Historic District downtown. Rickety old buildings are being reborn as chic restaurant–bars, and old storefronts are getting face-lifts and new identities.

Cross busy Central Expressway and you come to Highland Park, today one of the loveliest small towns in America. It's incorporated, but still is very much a neighborhood and still more a state of mind. Southern Methodist University is here, along with some of the state's most pricey real estate.

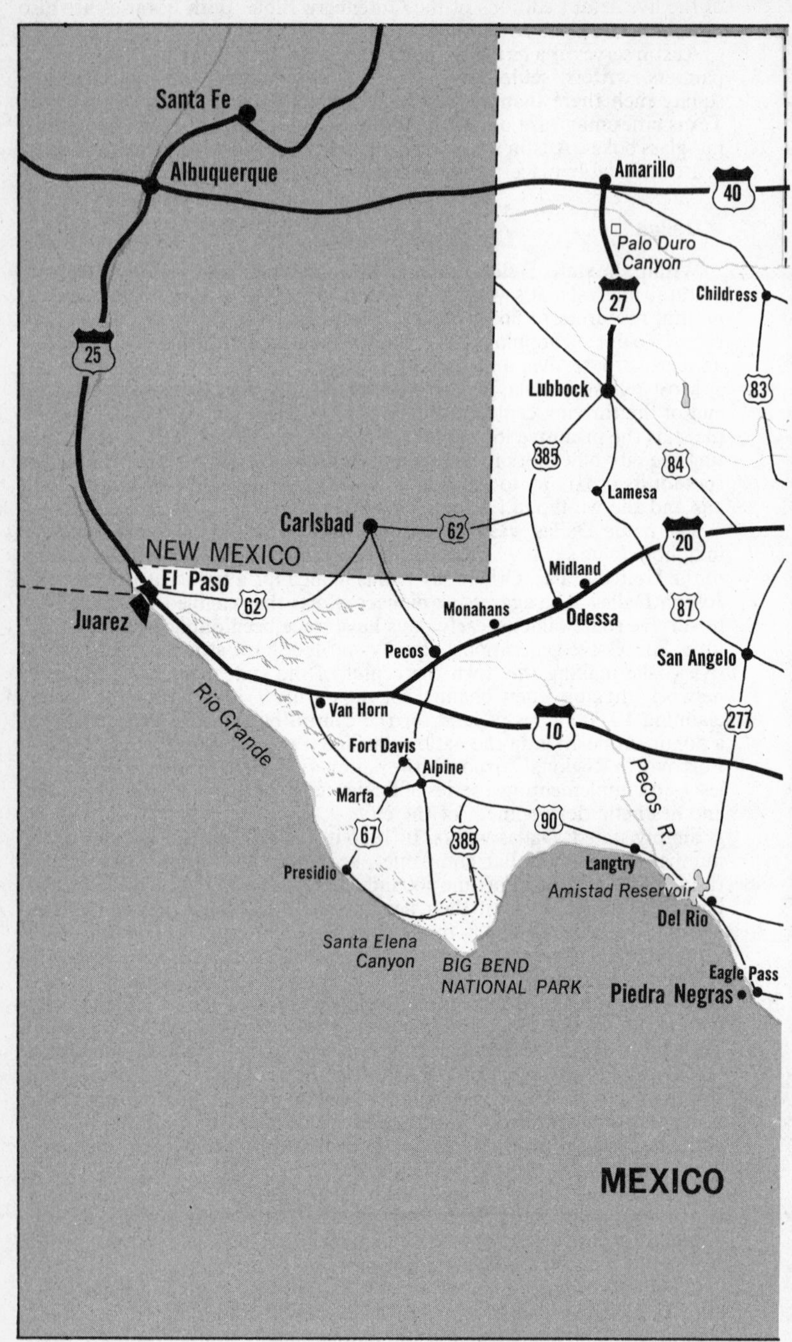
Santa Fe
Albuquerque
Amarillo
40
Palo Duro Canyon
27
Childress
25
Lubbock
83
385
84
Lamesa
Carlsbad
62
20
NEW MEXICO
Midland
El Paso
62
Juarez
Monahans
Odessa
87
Pecos
San Angelo
Van Horn
10
277
Rio Grande
Fort Davis
Alpine
Pecos R.
Marfa
90
67
385
Langtry
Presidio
Amistad Reservoir
Del Rio
Santa Elena Canyon
BIG BEND NATIONAL PARK
Eagle Pass
Piedra Negras
MEXICO

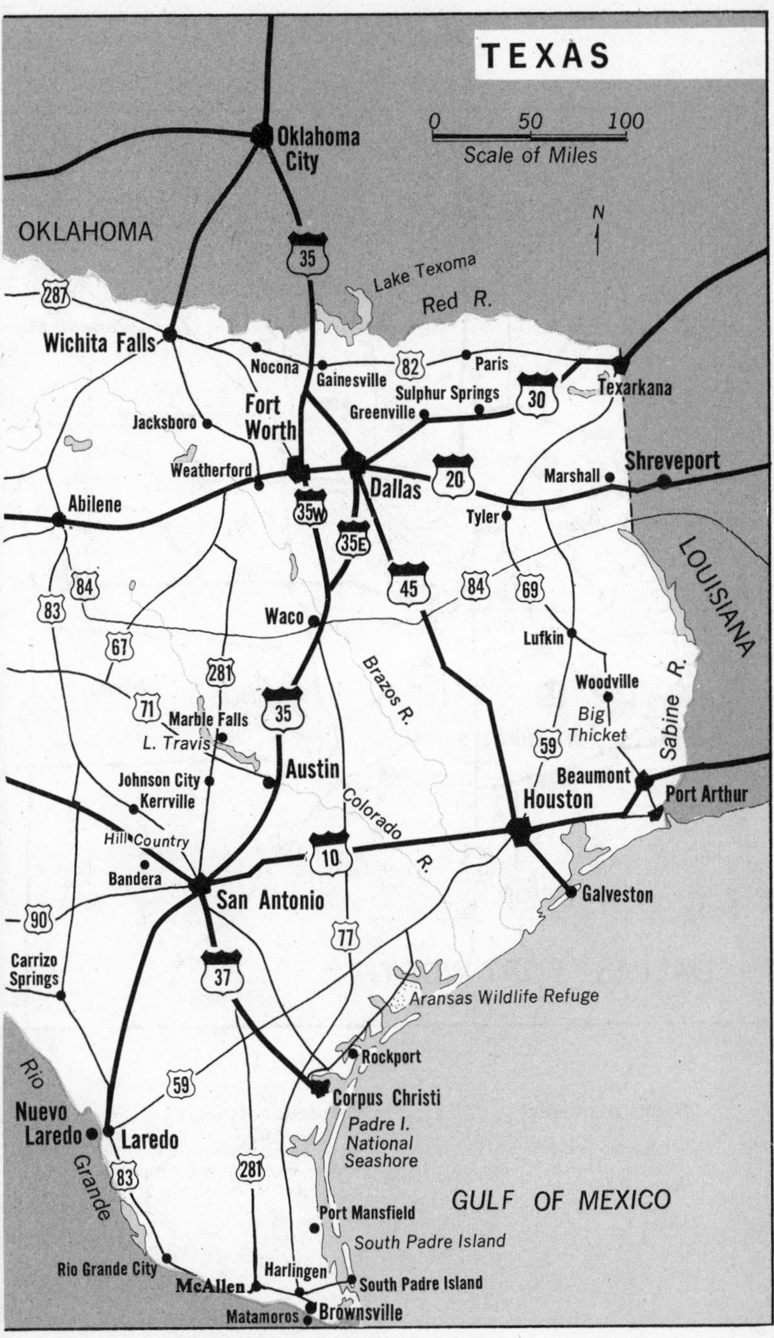
TEXAS
0 50 100
Scale of Miles
N
Oklahoma City
OKLAHOMA
35
Lake Texoma
Red R.
287
Wichita Falls
Nocona
Gainesville
82
Paris
30
Texarkana
Sulphur Springs
Greenville
Jacksboro
Fort Worth
Weatherford
Dallas
20
Shreveport
Marshall
Abilene
35W
35E
Tyler
LOUISIANA
84
83
45
84
69
Waco
Lufkin
67
Brazos R.
281
Woodville
71
Marble Falls
35
Sabine R.
Big Thicket
L. Travis
59
Austin
Beaumont
Johnson City
Kerrville
Colorado R.
Houston
Port Arthur
Hill Country
10
Bandera
San Antonio
Galveston
90
77
Carrizo Springs
37
Aransas Wildlife Refuge
Rio
Rockport
59
Corpus Christi
Nuevo Laredo
Laredo
Padre I. National Seashore
Grande
83
281
GULF OF MEXICO
Port Mansfield
South Padre Island
Rio Grande City
Harlingen
McAllen
South Padre Island
Brownsville
Matamoros

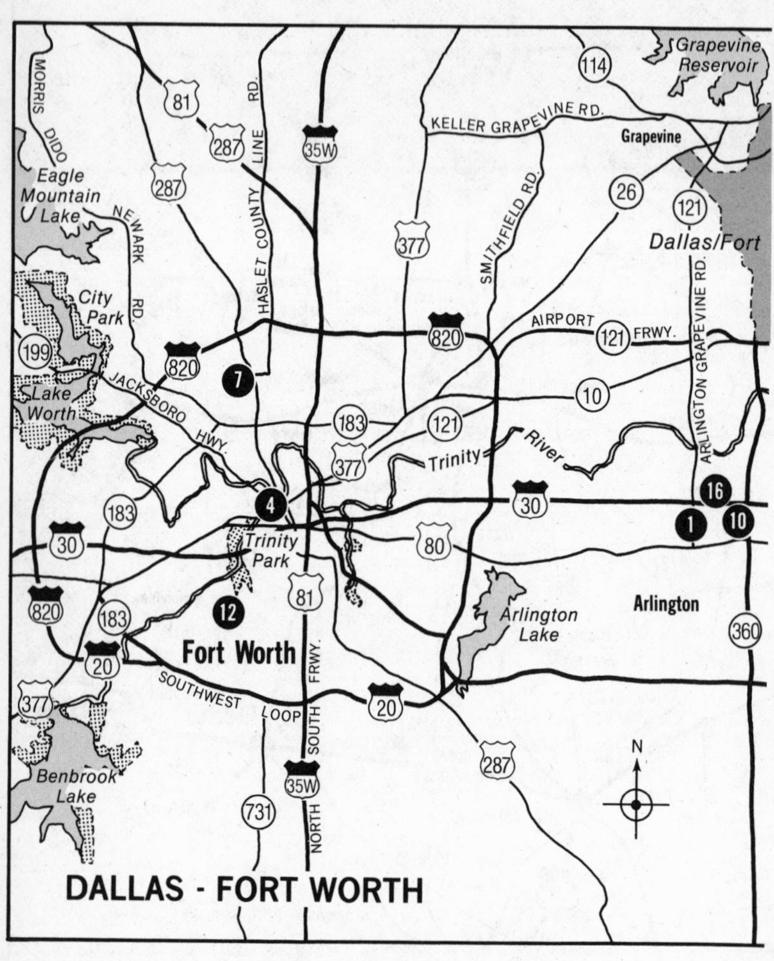

Points of Interest

Arlington Stadium, **1**
Dallas Love Field, **2**
Downtown Dallas, **3**
Downtown Fort Worth, **4**
The Galleria, **5**
International Wildlife Park, **6**
Meacham Field Municipal Airport, **7**
Prestonwood Town Center, **8**

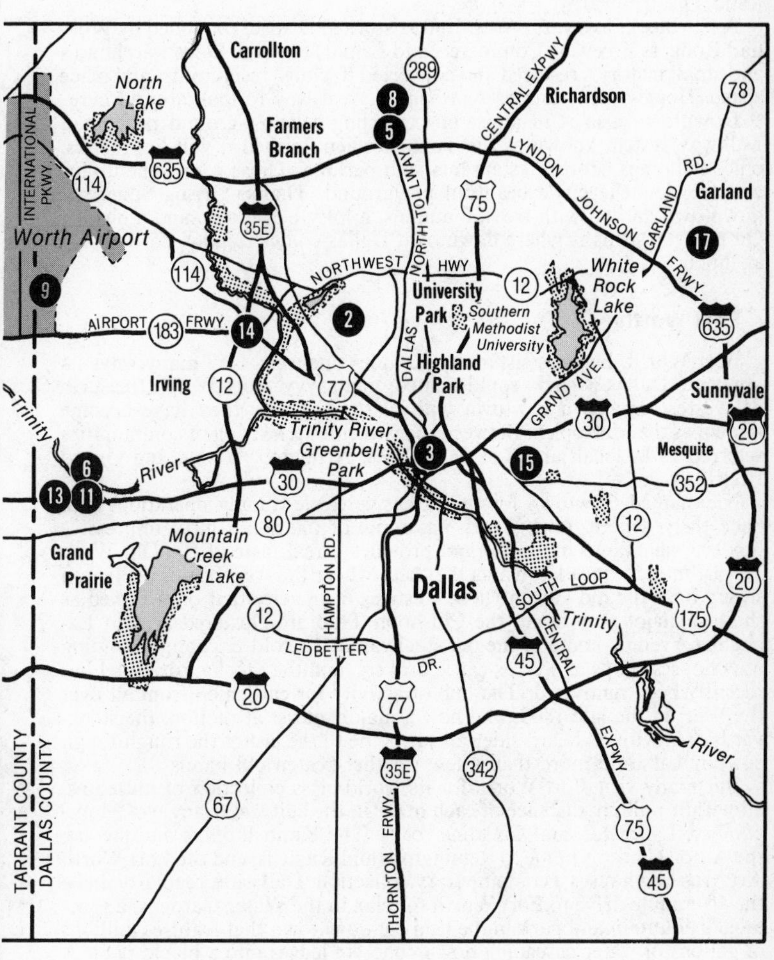

Six Flags Over Texas, **10**
Texas Christian University, **12**
Texas Sports Hall of Fame, **13**
Texas Stadium, **14**
Texas State Fair Grounds, **15**
Wax Museum of the Southwest, **11**
Wet 'n Wild, **16–17**
Dallas/Fort Worth Airport, **9**

The new centerpiece of the downtown business district is the Dallas Museum of Art next door to the Fairmont Hotel. Opened in November, 1984, it is the cornerstone of a 60-acre arts district which now also includes a new symphony hall. Don't miss catching a show at the newly restored Majestic Theatre nearby.

A few blocks away, the West End Historical District (bounded by Woodall Rodgers Freeway, Commerce, and Lamar) features 1920s warehouses and small factories restored and converted to clubs, restaurants, and office space. Horse-drawn carriages provide a great way to look around here.

Downtown also is in midst of expanding a below-ground pedestrian walkway system known as the Tunnel; when finished it will link banks, office buildings, stores, restaurants, and parking. Those who come up for air can view the city's beautiful playground, Thanks-Giving Square, a downtown garden with trees, fountains, a lofty bell tower, and a chapel. On nice days this is where downtown Dallas comes to play, particularly at lunch.

Fort Worth

Fort Worth, Dallas's sister city 30 miles due west, is in many ways its opposite. Dallas is slick, sophisticated, and savvy. Fort Worth treasures its western image, a cowtown with class. Together they have become known as the Metroplex. Between the two cities is a string of communities referred to in local jargon as Mid-Cities: Arlington, Irving, and Grand Prairie.

Nicknamed Cowtown for the extensive cattle-trading operations that once thrived here, Fort Worth has some of the area's most impressive modern sights and museums and provides a real taste of the Old West. It was, in fact, once known as the "city where the west begins." Plan on seeing both the old and the new. Vestiges of the city that once served as the last major stop along the Chisholm Trail are clustered around Exchange Avenue, home to the old stockyards. The old Exchange Building now houses shops as well as cattle brokers, and the Stockyards Hotel has recently been renovated. The hub of activity for cattlemen from all over the West in the late 1800s and now a major tourist attraction, the stockyards area with its board sidewalks is home to the last of the rough-tough cowboy bars and more than a few weather-beaten old hands.

But many visit Fort Worth for its world-class collection of museums, all within walking distance of each other in the cultural triangle of Montgomery, Lancaster, and Crestline roads. The Kimbell offers antique art; the Amon Carter is home to Remingtons and Russells; and the Fort Worth Art Museum houses a contemporary collection. Dallasites regularly make the 40-minute drive to Fort Worth to relax in the Water Gardens, a spectacular fountain and park in the heart of downtown that features millions of gallons of water cascading down concrete ledges into a placid pool. A series of steps takes visitors below street level to its very heart.

Houston

Houston began at Allen's Landing, where the Allen brothers stepped off a boat in 1836. Capitalizing on the then recent victory of Texas over Mexico at the battle of San Jacinto, they named their new town after the victorious General Sam Houston, the hero of Texas independence. They paid about $1.40 per acre for 6,642 acres of coastal prairie near the headwaters of Buffalo Bayou. The site was chosen because it was as close to Stephen F. Austin's central Texas colonies as shallow-draft boats could travel from the Gulf of Mexico.

The muddy, mosquito-infested settlement rapidly developed into a timber, cotton, and cattle-shipping town that served as the capital of the Texas

Republic from 1837 to 1840. In 1901, the Spindletop discovery in nearby Beaumont set off an oil boom that became the mainstay of Houston's economy for the 20th century. The 1914 opening of the manmade Houston Ship Channel was the realization of the Allen brother's dream of Houston as a major port. Today it is the nation's fourth largest, and visually it has fulfilled its early promotion as the "City of the Future."

Visitors marvel at how clean and modern the city is. That's because almost everything, including the downtown skyline, is less than 20 years old. Aggressively future-oriented, Houston has scant respect for tradition or the past. The tendency is to tear down and build anew, rather than to preserve and restore.

This is the most air-conditioned city in the world. Residents can get in their cars, drive to work or play, and then arrive home again without once stepping out into the heat and humidity. A vast underground tunnel system replete with restaurants connects most of the buildings downtown—you can take your own walking tour of underground Houston by using maps available at local banks and from the Houston Convention and Visitors Center.

Little remains of the city's past except in the downtown area of Old Market Square. Now bounded by Milam, Congress, Travis, and Preston streets, this once was the site of cattle drives, ox caravans bringing cotton to waiting barges, saloons, gambling houses, and an opera house. Today, the square is primarily a lunch restaurant district catering to downtown office workers. The city's oldest commercial structure still stands here. Now a bar called La Carafe, it was built in the 1860s and has served over the years as an Indian trading post, a stagecoach stop, and a brothel.

These remnants of the past are dwarfed by the gleaming glass and steel skyscrapers of the present. A good vantage point to see many of Houston's new buildings is Tranquillity Park (bounded by Smith, Walker, Bagby, and Rusk). This is the city's Bicentennial project which commemorates man's first landing on the moon. From there you can see the red granite Gothic spires of the Republic Bank Building; the white marble of One Shell Plaza, at one time the tallest reinforced concrete building west of the Mississippi; the curving glass facade of Allied Bank Plaza; the top of the Texas Commerce Tower, which at 75 stories is the world's tallest composite tube tower; and the distinctive black glass Pennzoil Towers, which are twin trapezoids.

The famed Texas Medical Center is directly south of downtown via Fannin or Main streets. The center consists of 37 colleges, schools, institutes, and hospitals, including the world famous M.D. Anderson Cancer Center.

The Astrodome, the world's first indoor, air-conditioned stadium, is south of the Medical Center and home to major league baseball and football teams. Adjacent are the Astrohall and the Astro Arena, which house the Houston Livestock Show and various conventions. Across the I-610 loop lies Astroworld amusement park and Waterworld, an aquatic playground.

West of downtown lies another world. Following Allen Parkway out of downtown brings you to River Oaks, bastion of the ultrarich and Houston's Beverly Hills. Generally, the area is bounded by I-10, Shepherd, San Felipe, and Memorial Park. Curving streets are lined with mansions owned by oil tycoons, politicians, celebrities, and even a few scions of continental and middle east nobility.

The Galleria, a lavish three-story mall with department stores, boutiques, restaurants, luxury hotels, and an ice-skating rink, gives its name to an area west of the I-610 West loop. The landmark for the area is the Transco Tower, a spectacular grey-black skyscraper with a rotating beacon on top. It's tall enough to be seen from almost every part of town. The Galleria offers the most expensive shopping in the city, plus world-

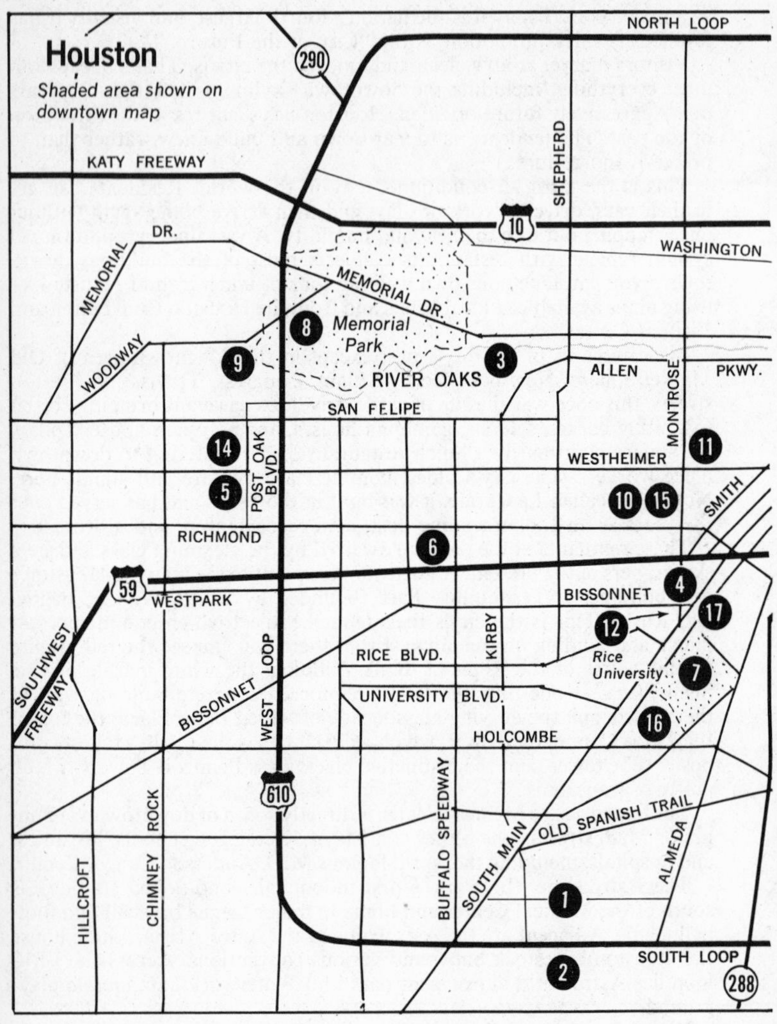

Points of Interest

1) Astrodome
2) Astroworld
3) Bayou Bend Branch, Museum of Fine Arts
4) Contemporary Arts Museum
5) Galleria
6) Greenway Plaza
7) Hermann Park, including the Museum of Medical Science, Museum of Natural Science, Hermann Park Zoo, and Hermann Park Garden Center

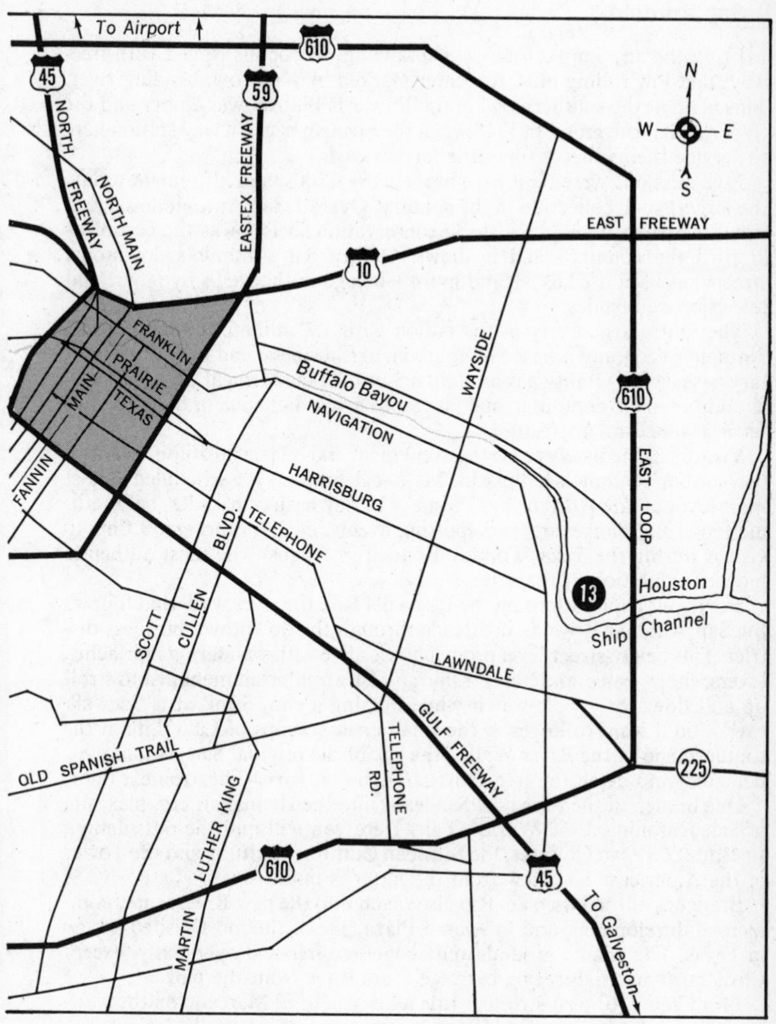

8) Houston Arboretum and Nature Center
9) Inn on the Park Hotel
10) Menil Collection
11) Montrose Neighborhood
12) Museum of Fine Arts
13) Port of Houston
14) Post Oak Shopping Sector
15) Rothko Chapel
16) Texas Medical Center
17) Warwick Hotel

class browsing because the mall is the gathering place for Houstonians as well as international travelers.

San Antonio

From the air, San Antonio is a sprawling metropolis ringed with freeways and low rolling hills, its center marked by a narrow, bending river. This plain at the southern end of the Edwards Plateau was empty and the river much more grand in 1718 when the Spanish began a way station here to service their other settlements farther east.

Five missions were built here in the early 1700s, and all remain today, the largest such collection in the country. Overall, San Antonio has a passion for preservation—its historic conservation society was the first of its kind in the country—and it shows. One of San Antonio's downtown streets has been used as a stand-in for Chicago in the 1930s by movie and television companies.

The ninth largest city in the nation with 1.2 million population, San Antonio's economy is based on tourism, agribusiness, and five active military bases. New vitality has brought a South Texas Medical Center as well as additional oil, computer, and insurance firms, and a major bio-tech center is planned for the future.

Visitors immediately sense the excitement and relaxed attitude that have become San Antonio's hallmarks. Major celebrations are scheduled almost monthly, but late April brings Fiesta, a 10-day bash of parades, balls, ethnic foods and dance, art, and sporting events, etc. Another good time to visit is during the Texas Folklife Festival in August, the most authentic pioneer exhibition in the state.

Start your explorations on the Paseo del Rio, the river walk that follows the San Antonio River as it threads through the downtown business district. This below-street-level promenade is alive with wandering mariachis, lovers, shops, cafes, and fun. It's fine and cheap entertainment just to stroll up and down or people-watch while nursing a cool drink at a sidewalk cafe. You'll want to linger in the small artisan shops of La Villita at the southern end of the River Walk—the site of the original San Antonio settlement—and catch the free shows at Arneson River Theatre next door.

One branch of the Paseo del Rio leads into the HemisFair complex, site of San Antonio's 1968 World's Fair. Here you will find the outstanding Institute of Texan Cultures, the Mexican Cultural Institute, and the Tower of the Americas. The view from the latter is impressive.

Branches of the Paseo del Rio also reach into the new Rivercenter commercial development and to Alamo Plaza, site of the most visited shrine in Texas. The Alamo grounds and chapel are free and open daily, except Christmas, and sightseeing carriage tours leave from the plaza.

From here a 10-cent streetcar ride takes you to El Mercado on the western side of downtown. En route, you can stop off at the San Fernando Cathedral, Southwest Craft Center, the Spanish Governor's Palace, and Navarro State Historic Site.

Although San Antonio has a strong Spanish flavor, many heritages have combined to build this interesting city. Walking tours will take you through the fine Victorian homes built by the city's German aristocracy in the King William District, and the Spanish missions are nearby. If you can visit only one besides the Alamo, make it Mission San Jose. The mariachi masses on Sunday at noon are open to all.

Whatever you see and do in San Antonio, you probably will end up agreeing with Texans: it's the most romantic, enjoyable, and affordable city in the Lone Star state.

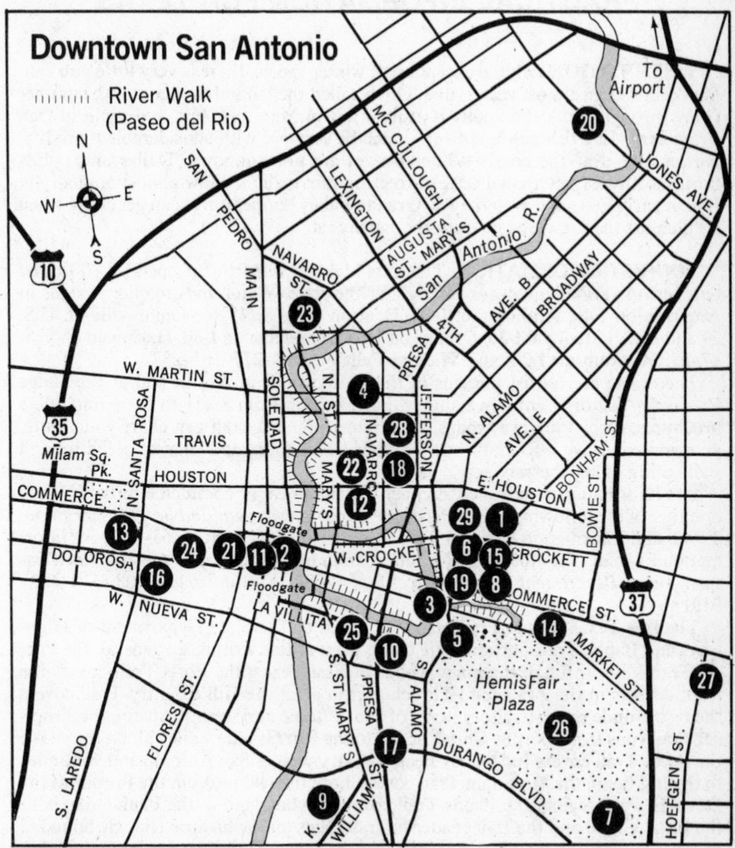

Points of Interest

1) Alamo
2) Alamo National Bank Building
3) Arneson River Theater
4) Bus Station
5) Hilton Palacio del Rio Hotel
6) Hyatt Regency Hotel
7) Institute of Texan Cultures
8) Joske's
9) King William Historic Area
10) La Villita
11) Main Plaza
12) La Mansion del Rio Hotel
13) Market Square
14) Marriott Hotel
15) Menger Hotel
16) Navarro State Historic Site
17) Plaza San Antonio
18) St. Anthony Inter-Continental Hotel
19) San Antonio Convention Center
20) San Antonio Museum of Art
21) San Fernando Cathedral
22) The Sheraton Gunter
23) Southwest Craft Center
24) Spanish Governor's Palace
25) Tower Life Building
26) Tower of the Americas
27) Train Station
28) Travis Park
29) Visitor Information Center

PRACTICAL INFORMATION FOR TEXAS

WHEN TO GO. With the exception of winter sports, there is very little you cannot do in Texas, almost year-round. Often called the land of the six-month summer (May through Oct.), it actually is at its prime in Mar. and Apr. and again in Oct. From early July through mid-Sept., it can be very *hot* with considerable humidity, particularly near the coast. Winter freezes are not unknown. Dallas and points north-northwest get a good dose of freezing rain or light snow almost annually in Jan. or early Feb., and even the Rio Grande Valley temperatures can get chilly when a "blue norther" sweeps in from the northwest.

TOURIST INFORMATION. The state highway department operates 10 tourist bureaus on various highways throughout the state. Watch for directional signs in Amarillo on I-40; Anthony on I-10; Denison on U.S. 75–69; Gainesville on U.S. 77 and I-35; Laredo on I-35; Orange on I-10; Texarkana on I-30; Harlingen on U.S. 77–83; Waskom on I-20; and Wichita Falls on U.S. 277–281–287.

There also are tourist bureaus in the state capitol in Austin and at the Judge Roy Bean Visitors Center in Langtry. Each is open from 8 A.M. to 5 P.M. and offers brochures, official highway maps, and counseling. The staff can chart your route, give you extensive information about your destination, and suggest activities and sightseeing along the way.

For information in advance, contact the chambers of commerce on your route or either of the following: *State Department of Highways and Public Transportation,* Travel and Information Division, Box 5064, Austin 78763 (512–465–7401 for information by mail; 512–463–8585 for information by telephone) or the *Tourism Division, Texas Department of Commerce,* Box 12008, Austin 78711–2008 (512–462–9191).

The free Texas Travel Trail maps published by the State Department of Highways and Public Transportation are out of print at this writing. In general, the Forest Trail loops through the piney woods of East Texas; the Forts Trail covers the frontier forts in the Abilene-to-Throckmorton area; the Hill Country Trail covers the resort-dude ranch territory north of San Antonio and west of Austin; the Tropical Trail runs from Corpus Christi south to the Rio Grande Valley along the coast; the Pecos Trail covers Judge Roy Bean Country west of San Antonio and continues to the Big Bend; the Mountain Trail covers more than 90 peaks in the Presidio-Fort Davis-El Paso region; the Plains Trail covers cowboy land in the Panhandle; both the Brazos Trail and the Independence Trail focus on the historic triangle bounded by Austin, Houston, and San Antonio; and the Lakes Trail features the many lakes around Dallas–Fort Worth.

For current information on what to see and do in the major cities, check the listing sections of *Texas Highways* and *Texas Monthly* magazines.

HINTS TO MOTORISTS. Because of the fine highways, a wide variety of landscape, and limited rail and bus routes, traveling by automobile is definitely the way to see Texas. You will find that your pleasure will increase if you drive some of the farm-to-market (F.M.) and ranch (R.M.) roads that crisscross major routes.

Although sometimes you may doubt it, Texas observes the national 55-mph speed limit unless other speeds are posted. You must slow down to the posted speed in school zones and stop when school buses are flashing lights or loading/unloading students.

Be alert to game and livestock on roads, particularly in rural areas and at night. Also be aware that both Central and West Texas are subject to flash floods. If water covers the road at any low crossing, do not attempt to reach the other side; water depth can be deceptive, and levels can rise swiftly.

Towed vehicles or trailers more than 55 ft. long or 8 ft. wide require special permits. Each permit is good for single trips not exceeding 10 days. They are available from the tourist bureaus and the State Department of Highways and Public Transportation district offices.

Texas has a mandatory seat belt law, so buckle up or face a stiff fine. Children under four also must be secured regardless of where they are in the car. New laws and heavy enforcement are aimed also at getting drunk drivers off the roads. If you drink, don't drive. A .10 percent or higher level of alcohol in your blood is considered legally intoxicated, and even the first time offender risks a stiff fine and/or jail sentence.

Unless otherwise posted, right turns on red are allowed statewide.

LIQUOR LAWS. The minimum age in Texas for consumption and possession of alcoholic beverages is 21. Other liquor laws vary from county to county. Out of 254 Texas counties, 62 are wholly dry—that is, no alcoholic beverages are sold. In 17 counties, only beer or beer and wine are marketed. In 175 counties, which include all the major cities, the status is wet, at least in part.

Bottled distilled liquor must be purchased in state-licensed package stores, which may be open from 10 A.M. to 9 P.M. except on Sun. and certain holidays. Beer and wine can be bought in liquor stores, supermarkets, and convenience stores between 7 A.M. and midnight, except on Sun., when beer and wine sales begin at noon.

Practical Information for Austin

HOW TO GET THERE. By plane. Austin's *Mueller Municipal Airport* recently completed an $8-million expansion and improvement program. The airport is framed by I-35 and U.S. 290 and surrounded by residential areas, which may make the descent into the airport a little hair-raising; on the plus side, it makes for a conveniently short ride between the airport and downtown.

Most out-of-state visitors will have to change planes in Dallas or Houston and then continue on to Austin. Currently, the city is served by *American, Continental, United, Pan Am, Southwest, Delta, America West, TWA, Northwest,* and *USAir.* Rental cars and recreational vehicles are widely available, with offices at the airport.

By bus. *Greyhound* connects Austin to most Texas cities and points beyond. Both lines use terminals at 916 Koening and 403 E. Ben White Blvd. Call 474–1200 for Capitol Metro bus advice from those points.

By train. The *Amtrak* passenger station is near downtown at 250 N. Lamar. Passenger service to and from Austin is limited to Amtrak's *Eagle Line,* which passes through daily enroute to Chicago and San Antonio; Mon., Wed. and Sat. enroute to Los Angeles. For schedules, fares, and information, call 476–5684 in Austin or 800–872–7245 elsewhere.

By car. I-35 cuts through Austin from the north (Dallas–Fort Worth and Waco). U.S. 290 runs east and west through the north part of town.

TOURIST INFORMATION. For brochures, maps, and friendly advice, contact the *Austin Convention and Visitors Bureau,* Box 2990, Austin, TX 78701. Request "A Driving Tour of Austin," which covers 30 historical, cultural, and recreational points of interest. *The Visitor Information Center* is located at 412 E. 6th St. (512–478–0098). *The Austin Chamber of Commerce,* 400-B S. First St. (at Palmer Auditorium), is another good source. For restaurants and current events, check the listings section of *Texas Monthly* magazine.

TELEPHONES. The area code for Austin, parts of central Texas, and all of south Texas is 512. You do not need to dial the area code if it is the same as the one from which you are calling. For directory assistance in Austin, dial 1411; for directory assistance within the 512 area code, dial 1–555–1212. For numbers outside the 512 area, dial 1–(area code)–555–1212. In case of emergency, dial 911.

HOW TO GET AROUND. From the airport. A taxi from the airport to downtown is about $8, plus tip. A free city bus leaves from downtown every 35–40 minutes on weekdays. There also are courtesy limousines to the major downtown hotels; inquire when you reserve.

By bus. The *Capitol Metro* bus system is comfortable and a good way to get around town. Some 48 routes serve almost all the city, and each has a printed schedule and map. For specific directions from where you are to where you want to go, call 474–1200. As of this writing, fares have been suspended, and everyone can ride the buses for free. The 'Dillo Express trolley-styled buses hit the downtown highlights from a free parking lot at City Coliseum, W. Riverside at Bouldin. 'Dillo stops also are well-marked at various intersections around town. Some 'Dillo routes operate Mon.–Thurs., others run on Fri. and Sat. There is no charge. For general bus information, write Box 1943, Austin TX 78767 (474–1200) or stop at the Capitol Metro Information Center, 504 Congress.

By taxi. Cabs can only be hailed at the airport. Otherwise, you must telephone one of several companies operating in town. Among them are *American Cab Co.,* 10315 McKalla Pl. (452–9999); *Harlem Cab Co.,* 2416 Webberville Rd. (474–2404); *Yellow Cab Co.,* 2943 E. 12th St. (472–1111); and *Yellow-Checker Cab Co.,* 1302 Glenview Cove (225–8040).

SPECIAL-INTEREST SIGHTSEEING. Texas State Capitol. Built in 1888 of native pink granite and sited on 25 wooded acres in the center of downtown, this handsome building's architectural style bears more than a passing resemblance to that of the nation's capitol. In true Texas fashion, however, the height of the dome is 309 ft., 8 in.—seven ft. higher than that of its prototype. The building is open from 6 A.M. to 11 P.M. daily, and tours are given every 15 minutes from 8:30 A.M. to 4:30 P.M., daily. A Capitol visitor booth and tourist information center is open daily in the south foyer from 8 A.M. to 5 P.M., a good place to get free information and maps and plan your Austin sightseeing (463–8586). When the legislature is in session, visitors may view the House and Senate proceedings from chamber balconies on the third floor. Free visitor parking is provided in designated lots on the southeast corner of 11th St. and Congress Ave., and in the mid-1500 block of Congress.

The Governor's Mansion. 11th and Colorado Sts. (463–5518). Built in 1855, this 20-room mansion is the oldest building in the capitol complex. Its Corinthian columns and wide verandas typify the antebellum style of the Texas Republic. The first floor has furnishings of Texas' past governors and an outstanding collection of antique furniture and art. Admission is free. Tours are conducted Mon. through Fri., every 20 minutes from 10 A.M. to noon.

The French Legation. 802 San Marcos St. (472–8180). Built in 1840 by Comte Alphonse Duboise de Saligny, French Ambassador to the Republic of Texas, the legation contains a beautiful collection of imported period French furniture. Outbuildings include an authentic French country kitchen. This is the only foreign legation ever built outside Washington, DC. Admission is $2 for adults, 50 cents for children. Open 1–5 P.M., Tues.–Sun.

The Bremond Block. Bounded by 7th, 8th, San Antonio, and Guadalupe Sts. These houses are representative of Austin's architecture from 1850 to the end of the century.

MUSEUMS. Elisabet Ney Museum. 44th St. and Ave. H (458–2255). Ney, a prominent German sculptor before coming to Texas, built this fortresslike studio-home in 1892 after receiving a commission for statues of Stephen F. Austin and Sam Houston. The museum houses many of her works in plaster, marble, and bronze, and some historic memorabilia. Admission free. Open Wed.–Sat., 10 A.M.–5 P.M.; Sun., 12–5 P.M.

Laguna Gloria Art Museum. 3809 W. 35th St. (458–8191). Housed in a 1916 Mediterranean-style villa on 29 acres fronting Lake Austin, this museum focuses on American art since 1900. Admission is $2 for adults (free, Thurs., 5–9 P.M.). Open Tues., Wed., Fri., Sat., 10 A.M.–5 P.M.; Thurs., 10 A.M.–9 P.M.; Sun., 1–5 P.M.

O. Henry Home and Museum. 409 E. 5th St. (472–1903). Short-story writer William Sydney Porter, known by his pen name O. Henry, lived in this small Victorian house in 1893 when it was on 4th St. It is furnished with period pieces, and O. Henry's personal effects are displayed. Rooms are not roped off, so visitors may walk freely through the house and browse. Admission free. Open Wed.–Sun., 12–5 P.M.

ACCOMMODATIONS. Austin lodgings range from functional motels along the major highways and interstates to handsome hotels downtown. Most of the latter are quite luxurious, and several have strong historic ties. The mid-price places are concentrated along I-35, many with free transportation to the nearby municipal airport. Most of the downtown hotels charge more for river or hill country views. You should inquire about special weekend, summer, and family packages that can lower your costs considerably. Also be aware that rooms can be hard to get in Austin on UT football weekends. The following price categories are based on double occupancy: *Expensive,* $100 and up; *Moderate,* $75–$100; and *Inexpensive,* under $75. The hotel tax currently is 13%.

Expensive

Driskill Hotel. 604 Brazos at 6th St., Austin, TX 78701 (512–474–5911 or 800–252–9367). This Austin institution is riding high after a quality restoration in 1986. Built by a cattle baron who made his fortune by selling beef to the Confederate Army during the Civil War, it has both traditional rooms (antiques, 19-ft. ceilings; recommended) or more standard rooms in a modern-style tower built in 1929. Historic tours can be arranged through the sales department, plus you can join the state's wheeler-dealers for either lunch in the dining room or some socializing at the swinging lobby bar.

Four Seasons Hotel. 98 San Jacinto Blvd., Austin, TX 78701–4039 (512–478–4500 or 800–332–3442). When you want luxury and service, this new 292-room hotel is a fine choice. Designed and furnished on a Southwestern theme, it is centrally located downtown near everything touristy, plus it has an in-house health club, outdoor heated swimming pool, 24-hour room and valet service, and such niceties as thick robes in the closet and hair dryers in the baths. Weekend packages can cut costs significantly.

Hyatt Regency. 208 Barton Springs Rd. (at S. Congress) Austin, TX 78704 (512–477–1234 or 800–228–9000). Situated on the south shore of Town Lake and convenient to downtown, this 448-room contemporary high-rise features a 17-story atrium lobby. Its lounge and restaurant are favorite Austin spots for watching night lights and the sunset. The VIP floor has concierge, complimentary wine and breakfast, and assorted other deluxe amenities. In addition to the heated pool and spa, the jogging and cycling trails of Town Lake are just outside the door.

Moderate

The Radisson Plaza Hotel at Austin Centre. 700 San Jacinto, Austin, TX 78701 (512–476–3700 or 800–228–9822). A new and glitzy addition to the downtown hotel scene, this 314-room glass box is in the heart of everything. Sixth St.'s pleasures are one block away, the state capitol is a four-block stroll. Rooms are cushy—go high for views. Aimed at the business traveler, this hotel may make the perfect weekend getaway. Ask about weekend packages.

The Residence Inn. 4020 I-35 S., Austin, TX 78704 (512–440–7722 or 800–331–3131). All 128 suites, from the studio size to the bilevel penthouse (great for families), have fully equipped kitchens, fireplaces, and oversized beds, plus there's a complimentary breakfast and happy hour. Add to that a pool, spa, sport court, and putting green as well as free transportation to the airport, and you have an outstanding place to stay.

Inexpensive

Hampton Inn North. 7619 I-35 N., Austin, TX 78752 (512–452–3300 or 800–HAMPTON). One of the best low-cost chains, this has nonsmoker rooms and free Continental breakfast, as well as free in-room movies, fitness room and local calls.

The Quarters Motor Inn. 9102 Burnet Rd. at Hwy. 183, Austin, TX 78758 (512–835–7070). This no-nonsense but comfortable place includes a free breakfast and newspaper each morning. There's also whirlpool baths, king-size beds, refrigerators, and free local calls.

Check also with the following chains: *Best Western Inns,* 800–528–1234; *Holiday Inns,* 800–HOLIDAY; *Howard Johnson,* 800–654–2000; *La Quinta,* 800–531–5900; *Marriott,* 800–228–9290; *Ramada,* 800–2–RAMADA; and *Rodeway Inn,* 800–228–2000.

RESTAURANTS. Austin has a number of exceptional eateries, often costing less than the going prices in other American cities of similar size. Whether it's the influence of the UT intellectual community or sheer luck, there's a lot of creativity in the assorted commercial kitchens. The following have stood the test of time and are recommended. However, check the current listings in *Texas Monthly* for what's new and offbeat. If all else fails, take a stroll on Sixth St. Price classifications are based on the cost of a typical meal for one person, exclusive of drinks, tax, or tip. *Expensive,* $18 and up; *Moderate,* $10–$18; *Inexpensive,* under $10.

Expensive

Courtyard Grill. 1205 N. Lamar (476–7095). This is a good place for an elegant, romantic dinner. Menu ranges from abalone and other seafoods through veal and such delights as filet mignon Montrachet. Reservations are essential; consider ordering one of the epicurean dinners at least 24 hours in advance. D, Mon.–Sat. AE, MC, V.

Green Pastures. 811 W. Live Oak (444–4747). Austin's grande dame restaurant, this place is housed in an old mansion on the south side of town. Outside you get peacocks and oaks; inside you get classic Continental choices. Coat and tie recommended. L, Mon.–Sat., D nightly, brunch, Sun. AE, MC, V.

Jeffrey's. 1204 W. Lynn (477–5584). When you want inventive American (translate Californian) and Continental food, come here, but early. Crowds have been known to hang around outside on the sidewalk, or at Jeffrey's Bar next door, just hoping to snag a table. No reservations taken. D, Mon.–Sat. DC, MC, V.

Moderate

Chez Nous. 510 Neches (473–2413). Around the corner from Sixth St., this tiny place features French country dishes, served with care. D, Mon.–Sat.

County Line. 6500 W. Bee Cave Rd. (327–1742). That Texas staple, barbecue, is served here with an inspiring view of the rolling hill country. The home-baked bread isn't bad either. D, daily. MC, V.

Hudson's On The Bend. 3509 Ranch Rd. (266–1369), 1.5 mi. southwest of Mansfield Dam. Game-lovers make the half-hour drive to feast here on wild boar, mallard, pheasant, rabbit, and venison dishes. D, Tues.–Sun. AE, DC, MC, V.

Inexpensive

El Azteca. 2600 E. 7th St. (477–4701). A little bit of everything Mexican is on the menu here, including 10 vegetable plates, chicken molé, beef ribs, and flautas. The Guerra family has operated this popular restaurant for more than 20 years. L, D, Mon.–Sat. AE, MC, V.

The Hofbrau. 613 W. 6th (472–0822). One of the old-timers, this is a reliable place for good steaks and home fries. L, D, Mon.–Fri. No credit cards.

Threadgills. 6416 N. Lamar (451–5440). A Texas classic, this honky-tonk café serves giant servings of typical Southern-style food. When you want fried catfish, black-eyed peas, or a slab of meat loaf, this is the place. B, L, D, daily. MC, V.

Practical Information for Dallas–Fort Worth

HOW TO GET THERE. By plane. Located 18 mi. west of Dallas and 15 mi. east of Fort Worth, the *Dallas–Fort Worth International Airport* serves both. More than 20 major carriers serve Dallas–Fort Worth from all parts of the country. A second airport, *Love Field* near downtown Dallas, is used primarily by regional airlines such as *Southwest.*

By bus. *Greyhound* provides regularly scheduled service to both cities.

By train. *Amtrak* serves both Dallas and Fort Worth. For information about schedules and programs call 800–USA–RAIL.

By car. Dallas sits like a hub on seven spokes of the interstate highway system. Fourteen additional major highways feed the city which also is circled by two giant highway loops. You have to be quick reading signs to be sure you are going where you desire.

Fort Worth is served east and west by Interstates 20 and 30, and from north to south by I-35W. Interstate 820 connects with I-20 to encircle the city.

TOURIST INFORMATION. Pretrip literature can be obtained from the *Dallas Convention and Visitors Bureau,* 1201 Elm St., Suite 2000, Dallas, TX 75270, 214–746–6702 and from the *Fort Worth Convention and Visitors Bureau,* 100 E. 15th St., Suite 400, Fort Worth, TX 76102, 817–336–8791 or 800–433–5747. Both are open weekdays, 8:30 A.M.–5 P.M. Another good source is the *Dallas/Fort Worth Area Tourism Council,* Box 836167, Richardson, TX 75083. You'll also find visitor information centers in the Love Field Terminal lobby and in the lobby of Union Station in downtown Dallas.

The *Dallas Committee for Foreign Visitors* provides help to non-English-speaking visitors by telephone: 214–744–3109.

TELEPHONES. The area code for Dallas is 214, for Fort Worth 817. In order to place a long-distance call to any number within area code 214, it is necessary to dial 1 (or 0) and 214 and then the 7-digit telephone number. A pay telephone call is 25 cents. Local directory assistance in either city is 1–411. From elsewhere, Dallas directory assistance is 214–555–1212; Fort Worth, 817–555–1212.

EMERGENCY TELEPHONE NUMBERS. The city of Dallas emergency number is 214–744–4444. In Fort Worth, dial 817 and then 332–2131 for *fires,* 335–4222 for *police assistance,* and 335–4357 for an *ambulance.* The 911 emergency number is in service in both cities.

HINTS TO MOTORISTS. Neither Dallas nor Fort Worth is laid out in a grid fashion. Many major roads follow early trails and cattle paths that radiate from the downtown areas. First-time visitors to Dallas may want to pick up a copy of a *Mapsco,* a heavily detailed road handbook available at bookstores. The freeway signs can be confusing, so chart your course in advance, and avoid the Central Expwy. at peak traffic times.

HOW TO GET AROUND. From the airport. *Super Shuttle* provides door-to-door service from both Dallas–Fort Worth Airport or Love Field 24 hours a day, seven days a week. Fares vary by zone; from Dallas–Fort Worth, it's $10 to downtown Dallas. From Dallas–Fort Worth, call 817–329–2020; from Love Field, call 817–329–2025; or use airport courtesy phones. Within that metro region, call 817–329–2000. Several other companies have regular service from Dallas–Fort Worth to Dallas hotels. One of the best is *TBS* (817–267–5150). Service is every 30 minutes and the fare is $9. Fort Worth is served by the "T" (817–870–6200); fare is $6. Both operate from approximately 6 A.M.–11 P.M.

By taxi. There are three taxi companies in Dallas: *State Cab Co.* (214–371–0777); *Terminal Cab Co.* (214–350–4445); and *Yellow Cab Co.* (214–426–6262). Within that city, the basic fare is $1.30–$2.10 for the first ⅒ mi., $1 for each additional mile. Average fares to downtown Dallas hotels are $10 from Love Field, $25 from Dallas–Fort Worth Airport.

Fort Worth is served by three cab companies: *Yellow Checker Cab* (817–534–5555); *American Cab Co.* (817–332–1919); and the *Greater Fort Worth Transportation Co.* (817–332–3137). Rates are $2.05 for the first mi., $1 for each additional mile.

By bus. In Dallas, *DART* buses cover most of the town. For routes and fare information, call 214–979–1111. *Hop-A-Buses,* recognizable by their display (#17, Hop-A-Bus), cover three downtown routes for a 35-cent fare. *Park & Hop* runs between Reunion Arena and downtown Dallas are $1.50 per round-trip.

A city-wide transportation system called the "T" covers Fort Worth, with free rides in the downtown zone. For information on routes and fares to other zones of the city, call 817–870–6200.

By train. *Amtrak* makes the Dallas-to-Fort Worth run every day. The fare currently is $6 one-way, $9 round-trip.

By rental car. All major car rental agencies are represented in the metroplex; most have offices at the airports.

On foot. A word to the wise about walking around downtown Dallas. Walking against the "Do Not Walk" flashing signs is considered jaywalking and draws a ticket.

HINTS TO DISABLED TRAVELERS. In Fort Worth, the *Mobility Impaired Service,* 2304 Pine St., outside the central business district (817–335–6487), provides a van service for handicapped and elderly people. In Dallas, a publication called *Access Dallas* lists city facilities and has maps denoting curb cuts. Request from the *Texas Easter Seal Society,* 3724 Executive Center Dr., Austin, TX 78731 (512–794–8890). For city transport information, call the *Dallas Transit System* (214–979–1111).

TOURS AND SPECIAL-INTEREST SIGHTSEEING. Walking tour brochures are available from the tourist information sources in both cities. *Gray Line* also covers the territory (214–824–2424 in Dallas. Among the Dallas sites you will want to see are **Southfork Ranch** (800–527–1624), the TV home of the Ewings; **Old City Park** (214–421–5141), a collection of restored buildings from the city's past; the **Swiss Avenue Historic District,** a collection of restored private homes in the city's best neighborhood of 1911-20; the **West End Historic District,** a revived warehouse region now lively with unique restaurants and shops (pushcart vendors and surrey rides also); the **Museum of Art** (214–922–1220); and the **Biblical Arts Center** (214–691–4661).

Sightseeing in Fort Worth includes the **Amon Carter Museum** (817–738–1933); the **Fort Worth Art Museum** (817–738–9215); and the **Kimbell Art Museum** (817–332–8451). The **Fort Worth Museum of Science and History** also is part of the complex (817–732–1631). Downtown fun includes carriage rides through quaint *Sundance Square* (you also can visit the horses and carriages at the stables; 817–870–1464), and nearby are *Log Cabin Village,* where costumed docents demonstrate old crafts against a backdrop of 1850s log cabins (817–926–5881); *Thistle Hill,* a restored mansion built by a cattle baron (817–336–1212); and the *Fort Worth Botanical Garden* with its lovely Japanese Garden section (817–870–7686).

CHILDREN'S ACTIVITIES. The Mid-Cities area between Dallas and Fort Worth is a kid's paradise. Here you will find the *International Wildlife Park,* an outstanding zoo you can drive through (214–263–2201); *Six Flags Over Texas,* a family amusement park with rides and entertainment (817–640–8900); *Wet 'n' Wild,* a giant water park across from Six Flags (214–840–0600); and the *Wax Museum of the Southwest* (214–263–2391). In Dallas, the Zoo is a great outing (214–946–5154), and in Fort Worth, try ice skating at Tandy Center Mall (817–878–4800). The *Mesquite Championship Rodeo* is family fun on Fri. and Sat. nights, Apr.–Sept., in Mesquite (214–285–8777).

ACCOMMODATIONS. Almost every budget and national chain is well represented in the Dallas and Fort Worth areas; call the toll-free reservation number of your favorite. A complete list of lodgings is available from the official information sources for both cities. Those listed below are pricey, but unique—places you will find nowhere else. Categories below are for two persons: *Super Deluxe,* $200 and up; *Deluxe,* $175–$200; *Expensive,* $140–$175; and *Moderate,* $100–$140. A 13% hotel tax is added in both Dallas and Fort Worth.

Super Deluxe

The Adolphus. 1321 Commerce St., Dallas, TX 75202 (214–742–8200; 800–441–0574 in state; 800–221–9083 nationwide). Built by brewer Adolphus Busch in 1912, this rococo beauty was restored to grandeur with $45 million and now is marketed as a "beautiful lady with a past." Downtown location is convenient also.

Hotel Crescent Court. 400 Crescent Court, Dallas, TX 75201 (214–871–3200 or 800–654–6541). This 218-room accommodation is Rosewood Hotel's latest entry in the Dallas luxury hotel competition. If you've always wanted to live the grand drawing-room-style life, this is the place. Outstanding service and comforts, plus pool, health club, and two restaurants worth a special trip.

The Mansion on Turtle Creek. 2821 Turtle Creek Blvd., Dallas, TX 75219 (214–559–2100; 800–442–3408 in state; 800–527–5432 nationwide). This 143-room hotel, also conceived and managed by the Rosewood Hotel Corp., is sited on a 4.5-acre tree-covered estate along Turtle Creek. Rooms featured in *Architectural Digest.* Restaurant is one of the city's best and most frequented.

Deluxe

Loew's Anatole-Dallas. 2201 Stemmons Frwy., Dallas, TX 75207 (214–748–1200 or 800–223–0888). A trio of glass pyramids covers two atria of trees and tapestries at this grand place of marble and space, accented with outstanding art. The health club is in separate quarters, plus there are nine restaurants tucked away here and there.

Expensive

Hyatt Regency DFW, In the center of the Dallas/Fort Worth airport. Box 619014, Dallas–Fort Worth Airport, TX 75261-9014 (214–453–8400 or 800–228–9000). Considered by many the world's finest airport hotel, it also is the world's largest, with 1,392 luxury and soundproof rooms in two towers. You can check your luggage through to your flight with the bellman and travel lightly on the way home. Four restaurants, three bars, and adjacent to the Bear Creek Golf and Racquet Center in case you feel like swinging something between flights.

The Worthington Hotel. 200 Main St., Fort Worth, TX 76102 (817–870–1000; 800–772–5977 in state; 800–433–5677 nationwide). Formerly the Americana Hotel-Tandy Center, this 509-room beauty sets the standard for luxury in downtown Fort Worth. It's connected to the good shopping of Tandy Center.

Moderate

The Stockyards Hotel. 109 E. Exchange Ave., Fort Worth TX 76106 (817–625–6427 or 800–423–8471). Built in 1907 and now restored into a very luxurious 52-room hotel with four types of sleeping rooms. Take your choice between Indian, Western, Mountain Man, or Victorian decors. Tucked into the historic stockyards area, it's within walking distance to Billy Bob's, the Exchange, and the Coliseum and on the trolley route to downtown.

RESTAURANTS—Dallas. Beware of glitz in this multirestaurant city. The quality of the food often doesn't equal the size of the check. Also be aware that some parts of Dallas are "dry"; you may have to join a "club" to buy a drink or bring your own in a brown bag and buy setups. The following generally can be depended upon to give good value for your money and good food as well. Price classifications are based on the cost of a typical meal for one person, exclusive of drinks, tax, and tip. *Inexpensive,* less than $10; *Moderate,* $10–$18; *Expensive,* $18 and up, sometimes way up.

Expensive

French Room at the Adolphus Hotel. 1321 Commerce (742–8200). This is the most luxurious restaurant in town: stunning baroque decor and fantastic nouvelle cuisine. Langoustine bisque as an appetizer and the feuilletee of seasonal fruit for dessert are musts. D, Mon.–Sat. Coat and tie required. AE, DC, MC, V.

Old Warsaw. 2610 Maple (528–0032). If you're ready for a big splurge, you couldn't have a nicer place. The service is outstanding, and the game dishes, in particular, follow suit. The sous chef is of genius quality. Dress code; reservations necessary. D nightly. AE, DC, MC, V.

Routh Street Cafe. 3005 Routh St., at Cedar Springs (871–7161). A creative, changing menu is offered here in one of the trendiest settings in town. The desserts are incredible, the entrees memorable. Don't bother to come if you haven't a reservation. Even though the sought-after prix fixe dinners are no longer available, the crowds never stop. D, Tues.–Sat. AE, DC, MC, V.

Moderate

Baby Routh. 2708 Routh (871–2345). Chic eats in high-tech setting, but don't let that fool you. The chef has a way with South/Southwestern foods with the accent on unusual combinations. L, Mon.–Fri.; D, daily; BR, Sat. and Sun. AE, DC, MC, V.

Campisi's Egyptian Restaurant. 5610 Mockingbird (827–0355). This is a Dallas favorite for Italian food and pizza. L, D, daily. No credit cards.

Chez Gerard. 4444 McKinney (522–6865). French bourgeois classics done with a contemporary hand are featured in this outstanding bistro. L, Mon–Fri; D, Mon–Sat. AE, MC, V.

Inexpensive

Chiquita. 4514 Travis (521–0721). Some of the best Mexican food in Dallas is served here. L, D., Mon.–Sat. AE, MC, V.

Highland Park Cafeteria. 4611 Cole (526–3801). Even Dallas' upper crust thinks this is the best cafeteria in the world. The fried chicken is a sure bet. L, D., Mon.–Sat. No credit cards.

Sonny Bryan's. 2202 Inwood Rd, west of Dallas North Tollway near Harry Hines Blvd. (357–7120). The sweet-and-sour barbecue sauce, which is legendary in Dallas, is the thing here. A cross-section of Dallasites always crowds the tiny, dingy interior where school desk tops serve as tables. Go early; the place closes when the meat is all gone. If you can't find the address, just follow the rich dusky smell of smoking meat. L, daily. No credit cards.

Fort Worth. You are about to enter hallowed country when it comes to Tex-Mex and CFS, which is Tex-talk for Chicken-Fried Steak. But, as cowtown has experienced gentrification, some extremely good French, Continental, and Italian restaurants have opened and been welcomed by local residents.

Expensive

Cattlemen's. 2458 N. Main (624–3945). Where else would you find the city's leading steak restaurant? Why, in the Stockyards area, of course. L, Mon.–Fri.; D, Mon–Sun. AE, DC, MC, V.

Crystal Cactus. Hyatt Regency Hotel, 815 Main (870–1234). American–International food is served with care and flair in this lovely restaurant, sort of the standard bearer for good food in the downtown area. L, Mon.–Fri.; D, Mon.–Sat. AE, DC, MC, V.

Reflections. 200 Main in the Worthington Hotel (870–1000). Grand food is served here in a dressy setting, so come slicked up and hungry. Reservations recommended. D, Mon–Sat. AE, DC, MC, V.

Moderate

Joe T. Garcia's. 2201 N. Commerce (626–4356). The city's most famous purveyor of Tex-Mex is an institution, not a mere restaurant. Joe. T.'s gives everyone "the dinner" which includes nachos, enchiladas, guacamole, rice, beans, and tortillas. You can wash it all down with pitchers of margaritas or a cold cerveza. This is Tex-Mex as it was meant to be served. L,D, daily; No credit cards.

On Broadway. 6306 Hulen Bend Blvd. (346–8841). This cozy Italian restaurant prepares an abundance of pizzas and pastas topped with fresh ingredients. L, Mon.–Fri.; D, daily. AE, DC, MC, V.

Inexpensive

Carshon's. 3133 Cleburne Rd. (923–1907). This outstanding deli features sandwiches, salads, and a vast array of domestic and imported beers and wines. L, Tues.–Sun. No credit cards.

Massey's. 1805 8th Ave. (924–8242). Chicken-fried steak here, plus seafood and Mex. Go with the CFS or go somewhere else. The cream gravy and biscuits are supreme of their kind. B, L, D, daily. AE, MC, V.

Paris Coffee Shop. 700 W. Magnolia (335–2041). For breakfast or lunch on the south side of town. Food like Mom would fix when she was having a great day. The chicken and dumplings will make you wonder what you ever saw in nouvelle cuisine. B, Mon.–Sat.; L, Mon.–Fri. No credit cards.

Practical Information for Houston

WHEN TO GO. Houston really has only two seasons, summer and winter. Blink and you may miss the few days in Apr. and Nov. that pass for spring and fall. Humidity often is high, thanks to the nearby Gulf of Mexico. Whichever season you come, be prepared for anything; Houston weather changes rapidly.

The long sauna of summer begins in earnest around the first of May and extends into Oct.; temperatures range from the mid-80s to the high 90s. During hurricane season—June through Aug.—heavy rains frequently inundate the city, flooding streets, and snarling traffic.

Winter comes about mid-Dec. and lasts through Mar., with moderate temperatures in the 40s and 50s. The thermometer can dip below freezing, however, when cold winds called blue northers whip through town. Snow is rare, and sunbathing on Christmas Day is not unheard of.

HOW TO GET THERE. By plane. Two airports serve the city, so confirm in advance which you will be using. Some airlines have flights into both.

W.P. Hobby Airport is 9 mi. southeast of downtown via I-45 and Broadway Blvd. There's ample parking; for long term, use the lots outside the airport proper. In addition to many national flights, Hobby is used by most of the commuter airlines serving Texas and surrounding states.

Houston Intercontinental Airport is 16 mi. north of downtown via I-45 or U.S. 59 and the North Belt. The least expensive long-term parking is at the City of Houston Satellite lot at the corner of Greens Rd. and Kennedy Blvd. Courtesy buses then take you and your luggage to the terminals.

In all, Houston is served by 22 domestic and international airlines. Check with your travel agent for the latest in discount or promotional fares.

By train. *Amtrak* passenger service connects Houston three times a week (Mon., Wed., and Sat.) with San Antonio, New Orleans, and Los Angeles. The station is downtown at 902 Washington (at Bagby) (800–872–7245).

By bus. Houston is served by *Greyhound Bus Lines,* 2121 Main (222–1161).

By car. Three major highways crisscross Houston. I-10 cuts through Texas from the Louisiana border on the east to the New Mexico border on the west. U.S. 59 runs northeast to southwest, and I-45 runs northwest to southeast.

TOURIST INFORMATION. The Greater Houston Convention and Visitors Council publishes free maps and an excellent series of multilingual brochures on local attractions, lodgings, downtown walking tours, shopping, restaurants, entertainment, and general public information. It also prepares a monthly "Day and Night" calendar with detailed schedules of sports, theater, and special events going on in the city and surrounding area.

Most of the brochures are available at the information booths in both airports; the "Day and Night" brochure is widely distributed by restaurants, hotels, and businesses throughout the city. All are available by advance mail from the *Greater Houston Convention and Visitors Council,* 3300 Main St., Houston, TX 77002 (523–5050; 800–392–7722 in state; 800–231–7799 nationwide). There also is a drive-in information booth with a multilingual staff at that location, open Mon.–Fri., 8:30 A.M.–5 P.M.; Sat., 9 A.M.–3 P.M.

Current events are covered in *Texas Monthly* magazine and both of Houston's daily papers.

TELEPHONES. The area code for the Houston metropolitan area is 713. You do not need to dial it within the area. Some 713 numbers in outlying areas, however, require that you dial 1 first, and then the seven digit calling number. Nearby cities are covered by the area code 409. Dial 409–555–1212 for information on those numbers and any toll-free metropolitan number available. Pay telephone calls are 25 cents.

EMERGENCY TELEPHONE NUMBERS. The universal emergency number, 911, is in effect in Houston. You also can dial 0 for operator and ask her to connect you to the appropriate agency. Or, you can dial the following numbers: *Houston Police* (222–3131); *Houston Fire Department* (227–2323); *Houston Ambulance* (221–6000); *Poison Control Center* (654–1701); and the *State Highway Patrol* (681–1761). Please note that several of those Houston numbers may not provide service to Harris County. Ask for a referral number if necessary.

HOW TO GET AROUND. Don't try to explore without a car. The Metro public transportation is improving, but it still is impractical for sightseers and those unfamiliar with the city.

From the airport. The *Airport Express* (523–8888) provides shuttle service between Houston Intercontinental Airport and downtown passenger terminals for $9.70 (adult), $4.35 (child). Departures are every 30–40 minutes, 6:15 A.M.–8:45 P.M. and intermittently thereafter. Departing passengers should allow one hour in-transit time. The *Hobby Airport Limousine* (644–8359) shuttles between downtown and Hobby Airport for a $6 fare. Downtown service begins at 5:30 A.M. and continues every 30–40 minutes until 11:30 P.M.

From Intercontinental, approximate taxi cab rates are: downtown, $26; Astrodome, $30; Galleria, $30; and Greenway Plaza, $28. There is an additional $1.20 per person charge from Intercontinental. From Hobby, approximate fares are: downtown, $13; Astrodome, $12; Galleria, $19; Greenway Plaza, $17. Look for "Ground Transportation" signs at both airports.

At both airports look for "Ground Transportation" signs both inside and outside the terminals.

By taxi. Several taxi companies operate in and around the city, among them: *Yellow Cab* (236–1111); *Liberty Cab* (695–6700); and *United Cab* (699–0000). Although they are permitted to cruise and can be hailed from the street, most line up outside major hotels and airports. Rates are $2.45 for the first mi., $1.20 for each additional mi., and up to four persons can ride for the price of one. Some credit cards are accepted by United Cab.

By rental car. Houston has scores of car-rental companies, both at the airports and scattered around the city. Check the yellow pages or call your favorite brand.

By bus. The *Metropolitan Transit Authority (Metro)* operates a city-wide bus system on a zone basis: 70 cents for local buses, $1 for express buses. Two shopper specials, marked with red and blue flags, circle the downtown area; fare is 35 cents. Exact change is required at all times. For routing and information, call 635–4000.

HINTS TO MOTORISTS. Texas has a mandatory seat-belt law, so buckle up—see Hints to Motorists at the beginning of the Practical Information for Texas section.

Native Houstonians attribute the erratic local driving habits to the influx of "foreigners." Actually, its basically a result of frustration; there are too many cars on too few roads. Ask a Houstonian for his definition of hell and he'll say any of the freeways at 5 P.M. If possible, avoid driving during the peak times of 3:30–6 P.M. and 7–9 A.M.

On-street parking is limited, particularly downtown, but there are many garages. Illegally parked cars get towed away and impounded until fines and storage charges (often very high) are paid. If in doubt, don't take a chance; head for a commercial garage. Also be careful of parking after hours on shopping center parking lots. A "tow away" sign may be tacked to an obscure post, which makes such areas happy hunting grounds for Houston's ever-eager towing firms.

When getting directions that involve using one of the freeways, confirm the freeway's name and number; locals sometimes call them by unusual names. Also check which off-ramp you are to use.

HINTS TO DISABLED TRAVELERS. You will find both marked parking spaces and specially equipped bathrooms city-wide. An accommodations pamphlet is available from the Visitors Council that indicates which hotels and motels have facilities for the handicapped.

TOURS AND SPECIAL-INTEREST SIGHTSEEING. One of the best ways to get your bearings and see most of the sights is to tour the city with *Gray Line Tours,*

602 Samson, Houston, TX 77003 (223–8800). Free pick-up at major hotels can be requested.

The following offer tours to the general public: **Astrodome** (799–9544), the first indoor sports stadium in America; **Walking Tours of Downtown** by the Greater Houston Preservation Alliance (861–6236 or 956–0480) on the third Wed. of every month; and the **Texas Medical Center** (790–1136).

The **Port of Houston,** Box 2562, Houston, TX 77252 (225–4044) offers free 90-minute tours aboard the *MV Sam Houston* at 10 A.M. and 2:30 P.M. Tues, Wed., Fri., and Sat; and at 2:30 P.M. on Thurs. and Sun. No trips in Sept. Reservations must be made far in advance.

The **Lyndon B. Johnson Space Center (NASA)** is at the top of every visitor's sightseeing list. About 25 mi. south of the city via I-45, it is the headquarters for the U.S. manned space-flight program. Free tours are self-guided, beginning at Rocket Park alongside the parking lot and continuing through museum buildings. Sign up at the Information Desk as soon as you arrive for the tours of the Mission Control Center (483–4321).

HISTORIC SITES AND HOUSES. **Sam Houston Park,** bounded by Bagby, McKinney, and Dallas streets in downtown, preserves a handful of the city's old homes and other historic structures in a small, rolling green. Entrance to the park is free, and tours can be arranged at the tour office (655–1912) in the Long Row, a small clapboard building on Bagby St. A museum of Texas history, housing three galleries, is also located on Bagby St., adjoining the Long Row. It is open daily and admission is free.

San Jacinto Battleground State Historic Park, 22 mi. southeast of downtown via TX 225 from I-45 south, marks the site where a ragged band of Texans led by Sam Houston defeated the mighty Mexican army led by General Santa Anna, thus winning independence for Texas in 1836 and establishing the Republic. The 570-foot high San Jacinto Monument has the story chiseled around its stone base, plus there's an excellent museum inside (479–2421). The USS *Texas* is permanently moored nearby and open for tours (479–2411).

MUSEUMS. As Houston's cultural consciousness has risen and expanded in the past decade, so have the quality and fortunes of its museums, concentrated primarily in the Hermann Park–Montrose–Rice University area south of downtown. A list of current exhibits is published in both newspapers. The following are among the city's best.

The Museum of Fine Arts. 1001 Bissonnet (639–7300). With more than 11,000 works in its collections, this rather eclectic house covers a vast range of art history, plus playing host to outstanding traveling shows. Primarily it is noted for its photography collection; the Straus Collection of Renaissance and 18th-century works; the Beck Collection of Impressionist and Post-Impressionist paintings; and the Kress collection of Italian and Spanish Renaissance works. There's a new sculpture garden across Bissonnet.

Across town in the River Oaks area is a branch of the MFA known as **Bayou Bend,** 1 Westcott St., off Memorial Dr. (529–8773). Formerly the home of Miss Ima Hogg, daughter of noted Texas Governor Jim Hogg, Bayou Bend now houses an outstanding collection of American antiques and art from 1650–1870. Surrounded by 14 acres of oaks and azaleas, it can be toured only by reservation except in Mar. and on the second Sun. of the month when the gardens and the main hall of the house are free and open to the public. Closed in Aug.

The Contemporary Arts Museum. 5216 Montrose. (526–3129). Across from the Museum of Fine Arts, this aluminum wedge of a building is home to the city's avant-garde art. The gift shop is outstanding.

The Houston Museum of Natural Science, Burke Baker Planetarium, and the Museum of Medical Science. Facing Hermann Park from the north, this trio can keep you and assorted children happy for hours with everything from dinosaur skeletons to talking exhibits that explain human anatomy and physiology. For information on the Planetarium, call 639–4630, for the Museum of Medical Science and the Museum of Natural Science, call 639–4600.

ARTS AND ENTERTAINMENT. Rich with outstanding symphony, ballet, and opera companies, Houston provides good theatre nearly year-round. Major fine arts choices include the *Houston Ballet* (523–6300); *Houston Symphony Orchestra* (227–ARTS); *Houston Grand Opera* (546–0200); and the *Nina Vance Alley Theater* (228–8421). Performances by *Theatre Under the Stars* and the *Society for the Performing Arts* add to the fun scene, as does the *Houston Pops Orchestra,* three professional sports teams, nightclubs, music group concerts, and numerous touring companies.

Unfortunately, no one ticket outlet handles all. *Houston Ticket Center* (227–ARTS) handles ballet, opera, symphony, and major fine arts events. *Ticketron* (526–1709) and *Allstar Tickets* (6632 Southwest Freeway, 222–7469) sell tickets to movies, sporting events, opera, ballet, symphony, concerts, roadshows, and Gray Line Tours. *Rainbow Ticketmaster* (977–3333) specializes in sporting events (Oilers, Rockets), concerts, and some plays. Most ticket agencies will take your booking over the phone with a major credit card such as Visa, MasterCard, and American Express, and your tickets will be waiting for you at the box office. Some businesses will arrange delivery to your hotel. Be sure to inquire about half-price specials for day-of-performance tickets.

ACCOMMODATIONS. Almost every budget and national lodging chain is represented in Houston; call the toll-free number of your favorite for specifics. A complete list of lodgings is available from the Convention and Visitors Bureau (see Tourist Information section). Those listed below are pricey but very special—places that may be the highlight of your trip to Houston. Price categories are for two persons: *Super Deluxe,* $150–$220; *Deluxe,* $100–$150; *Moderate,* $70–$100. Expect a 14% room tax on top of the room rate. If you will be here over a weekend, ask about lower weekend rates and special packages.

Super Deluxe

Four Seasons Hotel, Houston Center. 1300 Lamar, Houston, TX 77010 (650–1300 or 800–332–3442). Contemporary and outstanding, this high rise in downtown Houston is connected to the Houston Center shopping mall and athletic club. Each of 399 guest rooms has custom-made furniture, fresh flowers, and other luxury touches, and the lobby is rich with fine woods, marble, and art. Designed with the traveling executive in mind, yet strongly residential in feel; superb service.

The Lancaster. 701 Texas Ave. (downtown), Houston, TX 77002 (228–9500 or 800–231–0336). Directly across from both the Alley Theatre and Jones Hall, this elegant, European-style hotel is a favorite with visiting artists and celebrities. Only 94 guest rooms, each with fine furniture, marble baths, flowers, and original art—a one-of-a-kind place.

Ritz-Carlton Houston. 1919 Briar Oaks La. (inside the I-610 loop near the Galleria), Houston, TX 77027 (840–7600; 800–241–3333, nationwide). Designed for the upper limits of the carriage trade, this handsome residential-style hotel sits on a three-acre site facing Post Oak Park. Each of the 248 rooms was developed at a cost of $200,000, so expect a designer's best. Service may be the best in town.

Deluxe

The Houstonian Hotel and Conference Center. 111 N. Post Oak Lane (Galleria), Houston, TX 77024 (680–2626; 800–392–0784 in state; 800–231–2759 nationwide). Nestled in a 22-acre pocket of forest, this in-city resort also has a health-and-fitness facility that includes a preventive-medicine center. A women's health-and-beauty spa called the Phoenix is adjacent. The 247 rooms are quiet and well-appointed, and guests can use the indoor and outdoor running tracks, two swimming pools, and assorted sport courts.

Moderate

Hotel Luxeford. 1400 Old Spanish Trail (Medical Center), Houston, TX 55403 (796–1000 or 800–662–3232). The first of what may be the hottest hotel concept in the country, this contemporary place has 191 designer suites done in an Art Deco motif. Each has a kitchenette with microwave oven among the gadgets. Amenities also include complimentary Continental breakfast, overnight shoe shines, fitness center, and outdoor pool. Nice, whether you are staying one night or 10.

RESTAURANTS. Whatever you want, it's here, somewhere. Houston is incredibly spread out, so look for a good place near your lodgings unless you feel like a long drive. If none of those listed here excite you, check the most recent listings in either *Texas Monthly* magazine or the city papers; all keep their food critics on the move. The restaurant scene changes almost by the month, so don't rely on a previous trip's experience to lead you to a good place. The following currently are on top of the heap and can be relied on to give good value for the size of the check. Price classifications are based on the cost of dinner for one, without tax, drink, or tip: *Expensive,* $18 and up; *Moderate,* $10–$18; *Inexpensive,* under $10. Tips of 15–20% are expected nearly everywhere, unless the service has been deplorable. In that case, tell the management and do us all a favor.

Expensive

Cafe Annie. 1728 Post Oak Blvd. (840–1111). What a delightful surprise for adventurous palates! Chef-owner Robert Del Grande makes miracles on basically American cuisine, and you'll leave wondering how he ever thought of using sweet blueberry sauce on tender pheasant or pepper soup laced with cilantro cream. L, Tues.–Fri; D, Tues.–Sat. Reservations essential. AE, DC, MC, V.

La Colombe d'Or. 3410 Montrose (524–7999). Housed in the antiquely elegant Fondren mansion, this basically French restaurant cum small, très chic hotel traditionally has gifted chefs, grows its own herbs, smokes its own fish, and searches out the best suppliers in town for staples, which is why eating here is a memorable experience. L, Mon.–Fri.; D, Mon.–Sat. Jacket requested; dinner reservations strongly suggested. AE, DC, MC, V.

Tony's. 1801 Post Oak Blvd. (622–6778). Ask any of Houston's cognoscenti where the best food in town is, and Tony's is the unanimous vote. From the complimentary pâté to the chocolates at the end of the meal, the inventive Continental food is served with perfection. L, Mon.–Fri.; D, Mon.–Sat. Dress code; reservations required. AE, DC, MC, V.

Moderate

Damian's Cucina Italiana. 3011 Smith (522–0439). Outstanding Italian food unlike any you've ever had before is served here, from the fettuccine topped with crab and tomato and laced with cream sauce to the gnocchi verde or tagliarini. L, Mon.–Fri.; D, Mon.–Sat. AE, DC, MC, V.

Ninfa's. 2704 Navigation (228–1175). Tacos al carbon—charbroiled beef wrapped in a soft flour tortilla—made Ninfa's famous, but that's just the start of an extensive Mexican menu. Be sure to ask about off-the-menu specials, and avoid the Ninfarita's—they are potent. L, D, daily. Numerous locations around town. AE, DC, MC, V.

Inexpensive

Butera's. 4621 Montrose (523–0722), plus a second location at 2946 S. Shepherd (528–1500). Butera's on Montrose is smack in the middle of the Chelsea Market, the trendiest neighborhood in town. Both locations are great for sandwiches as you like them, and an incredible array of salads, imported beers and soft drinks tops off the menu. Both are good spots to assemble a picnic. L, D, daily. AE, DC, MC, V.

Captain Benny's Half Shell. 7409 Main (795–9051) and other locations around Houston. When you want fresh oysters or shrimp, this is the place to go. Price can escalate if you get carried away with the tasty goodies. Counter service. L, D, Mon.–Sat. No credit cards or checks.

Glatzmaier's Seafood Market. 809 Congress (223–3331). A downtown institution serving weekday lunch only on Old Market Sq., this place is known for well-filled fish plates and a relaxed atmosphere. L, Mon.–Fri.

Goode Company. 5109 Kirby (522–2530). About as country Texas as you can get, this place is known for its barbecued smoked chicken, beans, and pecan pie. Some locals modestly think the latter is the best in the world. L, D, daily. No credit cards.

Kim Son. 1801 St. Emanuel (222–2461). Chinese and Vietnamese menus are offered here, and there is a cheap Chinese lunch buffet. L, D, daily. AE, MC, V.

Souper Salad. 5469 Wesleyan (660–8950) and other locations. Your choice of what must be the longest salad bar in town, plus four soups. Polish off your meal with cornbread and gingerbread and still have money left in your jeans. L, D, Mon.–Sat. No credit cards.

Practical Information for San Antonio

HOW TO GET THERE. By plane. San Antonio's two terminals are served by *American, American Eagle, Continental, Mexicana, USAir, Pan American, TWA, Delta, Southwest,* and *United* airlines.

By car. Access from east or west is via I-10, and from north or south by Interstates 35 and 37. Interstate 410 circles the city. Driving times from other cities: Austin, 1.5 hours; Dallas–Fort Worth, 5 hours; El Paso, 12 hours; Laredo, 3 hours; Corpus Christi, 3 hours; Houston, 4 hours.

By bus. *Greyhound* has heavy service into San Antonio. The terminal is at 500 N. St. Mary's St. (270–5800). *Kerrville Bus Co.* has service to many of the smaller cities and towns within the state, such as Ft. Stockton, San Angelo, Big Spring, and Austin. That terminal is at 1430 E. Houston (226–7371).

By train. *Amtrak* connects the city with New Orleans, Los Angeles, and Chicago three times weekly. The train station is at 1174 E. Commerce. For toll-free information, call 800–872–7245.

TELEPHONES. The area code for San Antonio and Bexar (pronounced Bear) County is 512. If calling from outside San Antonio for directory assistance, dial 512–555–1212; if calling within San Antonio, dial 1411. For assistance in emergencies, dial 911.

TOURIST INFORMATION. For information in advance, contact the *San Antonio Convention & Visitors Bureau,* Box 2277, San Antonio, TX 78298 (270–8700; 800–447–3372, nationwide). Once in town, you can get brochures, maps, and information at the *Visitor Information Center* at 317 Alamo Plaza, across from the Alamo.

HOW TO GET AROUND. By trolley. Although a car will be needed to see some of the sights, you can park it once you are in downtown and either walk or ride the *VIA* motorized streetcars. A 10-cent fare will take you on either of the two loops that cover most of the major sights.

By car. To see the missions, however, you will need a car. Most national rental car companies are at the airport; check with your favorite for unlimited mileage rates.

By bus. The VIA public bus system also covers most areas of the city. Call 227–2020 for routing information.

By taxi. Taxi rates are $2.45 for the first mi., $1 for each additional mi. A taxicab from the airport to downtown hotels will cost about $11 plus tip for a 15-minute ride. Super Van Shuttle (344–7433) provides service between the airport and downtown hotels, 24 hours a day, for a $7 fare. The VIA public bus system, bus #12, operates Mon.–Fri. Fare is 75 cents. Many hotels, particularly those on the outer loops and suburban areas, run shuttles to the airport also.

HINTS TO MOTORISTS. Traffic is much lighter in San Antonio than in other cities. Downtown traffic lights are not well synchronized, so be patient. Free parking is widely available except downtown (prices range from $1.50–$4 per day). Good tip: park at El Mercado and use the VIA motorized streetcar to cover downtown. Use a street map at all times; San Antonio's streets not only change name on whim, they wander all over, the sign of a very old town.

HINTS TO DISABLED TRAVELERS. Write the *San Antonio Handicapped Access Office,* Box 9066, San Antonio, TX 78275, for a downtown ramp map and other information. Refer also to the access symbols in the Weekender supplement in the Fri. editions of the *San Antonio Express News.*

ACCOMMODATIONS. San Antonio is a popular destination, even for Texans, so you will find many hotels in the downtown tourist area. Weekend and special packages can knock as much as 50 percent off the room rates, so be sure to inquire; competition is keen. For less expensive lodgings, check out the numerous name brand chain hotels–motels that line the freeways, particularly the I-410 loop near the airport on the north side of town. From there, it is about a 15-minute drive into downtown. The following hotels carry the standard for the city and most are in the Paseo del Rio–Alamo area. All rates carry an additional 13% room tax. Price categories are based on a room for two persons: *Deluxe,* $125–$175; *Moderate,* $85–$125.

Deluxe

Hilton Palacio del Rio. 200 S. Alamo, San Antonio, TX 78205 (222–1400 or 800–445–8667). For a bird's-eye-view of River Walk action, request a balcony room overlooking the river. Popular as a convention hotel, this was the first on the River Walk and has held its style and action. Nice pool and roof garden.

Hyatt Regency. 123 Losoya, San Antonio, TX 78205 (222–1234 or 800–228–9000). The newest hotel on the River Walk modifies the atrium lobby with a small tributary of the river. Comfortable rooms and great location across from the Alamo.

La Mansion del Rio. 112 College, San Antonio, TX 78205 (225–2581 or 800–531–7208). Although there is another location north of town, this is the original: a classy reconstruction of an old school on the quiet portion of the River Walk. Mexican atmosphere, from the courtyard swimming pool to the balconies overlooking the river.

Plaza San Antonio. 555 S. Alamo, San Antonio, TX 78205 (229–1000 or 800–421–1172). Old-World, south-of-the-border charm plus individual attentiveness makes this one of the nicest hotels in town. Rooms are large, and the grounds include a beautifully landscaped pool, tennis courts, and several historic houses turned into bars and restaurants. The Anaqua Room restaurant has good food and ambience, and there's also a health club and sauna.

St. Anthony San Antonio. 300 E. Travis, San Antonio, TX 78205 (227–4392). This 1909 classic hotel has been restored to quiet elegance. Within walking distance of the Alamo and the River Walk, this hotel has a lovely lobby with antiques and hosts a pleasant happy hour.

Moderate

Crockett Hotel. 320 Bonham St., San Antonio, TX 78205 (225–6500; 800–292–1050 in state; 800–531–5537 nationwide). A $15 million restoration has created a stylish inn with atrium lobby, swimming pool, and roof deck. Almost in the backyard of the Alamo and an easy walk to the river and the convention center.

Emily Morgan Hotel. 705 E. Houston, San Antonio, TX 78205 (225–8486; 800–356–5683 in state; 800–824–6674 nationwide). Named for the Yellow Rose of Texas, this classy, romantic hotel has beautifully decorated rooms, two with private Jacuzzis. Across from the Alamo and within an easy walk of the river. Great honeymoon spot.

Sheraton Gunter. 205 E. Houston, San Antonio, TX 78205 (227–3241 or 800–325–3535). Both comfortable and historic, this freshly redone hotel is well-located and has a lovely glass enclosed lounge overlooking the street. The vintage decorations in the lobby are authentic and add an old San Antonio touch missing in some of the newer hostelries.

RESTAURANTS. You'll find food in San Antonio reasonably priced, and sometimes the best of it in the least likely no-frills places. That's part of the city's unpretentious charm. Price categories are for dinner for one person, not including drinks, tax, or tip. *Expensive,* $18 and up; *Moderate,* $10–$18; *Inexpensive,* less than $10.

Expensive

Anaqua Room. Plaza San Antonio Hotel. 555 S. Alamo downtown (229–1000). An elegant dining room currently serving outstanding American fare with flair. There's afternoon tea also, plus music in the adjacent bar in the later evening. Reservations recommended. B, L, D, daily; Sun. brunch. AE, DC, MC, V.

Chez Ardid. 1919 San Pedro at Woodlawn (732–3203). Out-of-towners who love good food find out when there's an open table here and then book their hotel rooms accordingly. This is outstanding French cuisine in a territory that calls it "quizeen." The reason? The owner-chef commands the kitchen, from the mussels in cream appetizer to the floating island dessert. Worth every sou of its very high cheque. Reservations essential. L, Mon.–Fri; D, Mon.–Sat. AE, MC, V.

La Louisiane. 2632 Broadway (225–7984). Coat and tie are required in this formal Louisiana-style French dining room. The dishes, from appetizers to the main course, are rich and extravagant. Reservations recommended. L, D, Tues.–Sat. AE, DC, MC, V.

Moderate

County Line. 606 W. Afton Oaks near FM 1604 and U.S. 281 (496–0011). This popular barbecue spot is a good place to tuck in some vittles enroute to or from LBJ-land and Fredericksburg in the Hill Country. On Thurs. quail is on the menu. D, nightly. AE, MC, V.

Hueys. 2734 N. St. Mary's at Russell (736–6666). Cajun cooking à la New Orleans is served in this 19th-century structure. L, Mon.–Sat.; D, daily. AE, DC, MC, V.

Liberty Bar. 328 E. Josephine (227–1187). While the ambience and service are far from supreme, the outstanding southern and regional dishes make up for any lack. Menu changes daily, depending on what is fresh and what the cook wants to fix. Bar serves Bass and Guinness on draft and a wide selection of choice wines by the glass. L, D, daily. AE, MC, V.

Little Rhein Steak House. 231 S. Alamo (225–2111). Tucked between La Villita and the Hilton, this is a long-time local favorite, known for its outstanding steaks and seafood. If you get carried away, the check may escalate into the expensive category. D, daily. Reservations suggested. AE, DC, MC, V.

Inexpensive

Copper Kitchen. 300 Augusta in the Southwest Craft Center (224–0123). Good soups and sandwiches are offered in this self-serve eatery, tucked away inside one of the best art experiences in town. L, Mon.–Fri. No credit cards.

La Fogata. 2427 Vance Jackson in northwest part of town (340–1337). To some aficionados, this small no-frills place has the most authentic Mexican food in town. Some outdoor seating, uneven service. B, L, D, Tues.–Sun. AE, DC, MC, V.

Mi Tierra. 218 Produce Row in El Mercado (Market Sq.) (225–1262). It's Christmas all year at this low-key place, known for its Mexican breakfasts, margaritas, and beers. Strolling mariachis add a nice touch, plus the all-night bakery fills the bill for late snacks. Open 24 hours a day, seven days a week. AE, MC, V.

Viet Nam. 3244 Broadway at Natalen (822–7461). A student crowd frequents this low-key restaurant known for Oriental tasties like spring rolls, glass noodles, and crab and chicken dishes. L, D, daily. AE, MC, V.

OTHER POINTS OF INTEREST IN TEXAS

Texas is such an enormous state with such a wealth of attractions to fascinate visitors that we cannot hope to cover thoroughly all that the state has to offer in this one chapter. The rest of this section therefore will cover some of Texas's most outstanding points, with the realistic aim of being suggestive rather than exhaustive.

Big Bend National Park

Far from major population areas, at the southwest point of Texas, is the state's last great wilderness area. Taking its name from the Rio Grande's bending from a southward course toward the north, the Big Bend area is a study in contrasts. There are peaks, deep canyons, vast desert areas, hidden waterfalls, and sun-drenched vistas. If time permits, don't miss exploring this rugged and almost spiritual place.

Abused before it came under the protection of the national park service, this 741,000-acre preserve is regaining its natural beauty. In the span of seasons, it is home to more than 67 species of mammals, 400 species of birds—including the majestic golden eagle—and 1,100 different kinds of plants.

Because elevations vary from 1,850–7,835 feet, camping can be enjoyed all year. The desert is popular in winter, and the high mountain basin offers an alpinelike retreat during the summer months. Orientation exhibits at Panther Junction, 29 miles south of the park's entrance on U.S. 385, introduce you to the park's treasures. You can headquarter at one of the following:

Chisos Basin has a small store, restaurant, a motel with a limited number of comfortable rooms (reserve well in advance), and campsites for tent and trailer. Trailers longer than 20 feet should not attempt the steep and twisting road into the basin.

Rio Grande Village and *Castolon,* both on the river and within the park, have visitor facilities. Rio Grande Village, 20 miles southeast of Panther Junction, has tent-and-trailer campground, store, showers, and laundromat. Castolon, 36 miles southwest of Panther Junction, has tent-and-trailer facilities, store, and a preserved army outpost used to thwart Pancho Villa in 1920.

The basin offers horseback riding and three outstanding hiking trails: Lost Mine, South Rim, and the Window. The latter gives panoramic views across West Texas and New Mexico; mornings are best.

You can hike to and through two of the park's scenic river canyons. *Santa Elena* is near Castolon, beautiful with 1,500-foot limestone walls and tiny rubber rafts bobbing in the slow current. *Boquillas* is near Rio Grande Village, and you can cross the river here, either by burro, when water is low, or by a small wooden skiff–ferry, hand-hauled by rope across the river when the water level is high.

Floating these Rio Grande canyons can be the highlight of a trip to the Big Bend. Park naturalists occasionally conduct flow trips, and there are commercial river-guide services at *Lajitas* and *Terlingua,* both outside the park boundaries. Lajitas is booming, with the Cavalry Post Motel, Badlands Hotel, restaurant, and condominium. The Lajitas Trading Post is the real McCoy, a ramshackle store and meeting spot that still serves its original purpose. Terlingua, in contrast, is a ghost town, a quicksilver settlement of the 1890s that now has less than two dozen residents. It has acquired world-wide fame, however, as the site of the World's Championship Chili Cook-Off annually on the first Saturday in Nov.

The Hill Country

When Texans play, they head for the Hill Country, an upthrust of the Balcones Fault that runs from the northern limits of San Antonio to the top of the chain of lakes on the Colorado River northwest of Austin. River floating is one of the big attractions—from inner tubes on the spring fed Comal River in *New Braunfels* and the San Marcos River in *San Marcos* to rubber rafts and canoes on the upper and lower Guadalupe River. The Frio River Canyon near Uvalde is another delight, best sampled at *Garner State Park.*

Blanco and *Wimberley* also are good bets. The former has a state park along the Blanco River and Wimberley has both the Blanco and Blue Hole on Cypress Creek, the classic American swimming hole.

This also is cave country; one of the most beautiful is *Natural Bridge Caverns,* southeast of New Braunfels on F.M. 3009.

With its panoramas of quiet hills, beautiful lazy valleys, bubbling streams, and variety of flora and fauna, the Hill Country is the perfect setting for dude ranches, and the small town of *Bandera* is the heart of the action. Located 50 miles northwest of San Antonio (about a 90-minute drive), Bandera is known as the Cowboy Capital of the World, and it actually is home to many working ranches and championship riders. It's basically a one-street Western-style town that really jumps from Easter through Thanksgiving, with rodeos twice a week in summer. Accommodations range from simple rooms at mom-and-pop motels to comfortable digs with meals at professional dude ranches. For information, contact the *Bandera Chamber of Commerce,* Box 171, Bandera, TX 78003 (512–796–4312). There also are dude ranches as well as water fun along the Guadalupe River at nearby *Kerrville* (Cur-vul in Texas talk). For information, contact the *Kerrville Convention and Visitors Bureau,* 1200 Sidney Baker Street (if you already are in town), Kerrville, TX 78028 (512–896–1155). Ask also about tours of the famous YO Ranch, a short drive northwest of Kerrville in Mountain Home.

Another major Hill Country destination is the *Lyndon B. Johnson State Park and National Historic Site,* 50 miles west of Austin in Johnson City (512–644–2252). This is a triple prize. Start at the Visitor's Center in Johnson City and then tour LBJ's boyhood home and the Johnson settlement, the original log-cabin home of the family when they came to Texas in the mid-1800s. The ranch unit is in two parts and is 14 miles west in Stonewall. Here you find the State Park, with its visitor center, swimming pool, tennis courts, and the turn-of-the-century Sauer-Beckman farm. The LBJ ranch is adjacent, and a tour bus covers his birthplace, the ranch in general, a one-room school, and LBJ's grave in the Johnson family cemetery. All of the park is open daily from 8 A.M. to 5 P.M.; tours are from 10 A.M. to 4 P.M. daily. For information, contact Box 238, Stonewall, TX 78671 (512–644–2252).

The *Highlands Lake* region of the Hill Country also is rewarding. Six beautiful lakes extend north from Austin along 80 miles of the Colorado River. Each is dotted with resorts and campgrounds, and the water sports are outstanding. For information, contact LCRA, Box 220, Austin, TX 78767 (512–473–3200); or the Highland Lakes Tourist Association, Box 1967, Austin, TX 78767 (512–793–6666).

If you are planning a spring trip to this region, be aware that the wildflowers are outstanding, particularly along U.S. 87–377 between Mason and Brady.

The Panhandle

The Northwest and Panhandle sections of Texas are rich with scenery associated with the Old West, as dramatized by movies and television. The *Panhandle* is known for its flat terrain, often called "the floor of the sky."

When the Spanish conquistadores explored this portion of the great plains of North America, they referred to it as the Llano Estacado—the staked plains. According to one legend, the term evolved when the explorers stuck bleached buffalo bones into the treeless prairie to serve as guide posts. No other natural landmarks were available.

Today, U.S. 87 and I-27 make an almost arrow-straight line down the length of the Panhandle to the South Plains region, the best route from Amarillo to Lubbock. Both were settled late in the history of the state. Amarillo was settled in 1887, Lubbock in 1891. Consequently both sites were laid out with parallel streets (most running north–south and east–west) and with uniform blocks. While unimaginative, it makes for easy exploring.

Amarillo

With a population of approximately 162,000, Amarillo is the commercial, cultural, and recreational center for the Panhandle, a region larger than Connecticut, Massachusetts, and Vermont combined. Originally a railroad town, Amarillo soon became the "world's greatest cattle shipping market," with as many as 50,000 head within sight of downtown.

The city's name, which is Spanish for "yellow," was taken from the color of a nearby creek bank. Today, local residents refer to their town as the "Yellow Rose of Texas."

There's a great deal to do here, from nightclubs and western dance hall entertainments to golf, fishing, etc. The *Amarillo Art Center* hosts fine arts, music, and drama year-round on the campus of Amarillo College in the heart of the city. Visitors also are welcome at the *Western Stockyards* at East Third and Stetson streets, one of the world's largest cattle auctions. Thousands of dollars and cattle change hands with a nod or a tip of a Stetson. The auctions are free and held on Tuesday, year-round, and either breakfast or lunch at the Stockyards Cafe is an absolute must. Locals claim the T-Bone is the best steak in Texas.

Also of interest is Discovery Center, near I-40 on the western edge of the city. Planetarium shows are held nightly in summer and on weekends year-round and the adjacent physical sciences museum is free and open daily.

For local color, don't miss *Stanley Marsh's Cadillac Ranch.* Featured photographically in numerous national publications since its "unveiling" more than a decade ago, this presents 10 vintage Cadillacs from the 1950s fin period nosed into a large grain field at a 40-degree angle. Marsh is one of Amarillo's home-grown characters; his latest patronage of "pop art" is "Floating Mesa," visible enroute to *Cal Farley's Boys Ranch and Old Tascosa,* another place to visit northwest of Amarillo.

Two special tours alone make the trip to Amarillo worthwhile. The first is "Cowboy Morning," a sunrise jaunt across a historic and a working ranch to breakfast at the rim of Palo Duro Canyon. The second is an excursion into the beautiful Palo Duro Canyon and its state park plus an evening at the production of "Texas," a musical drama about the settling of the area in the 1880s. Both can be combined with a trip to the stockyards and to the outstanding *Panhandle Plains Historical Museum* in Canyon, thanks to a special "Day or Two in the Old West" tour available from the *Amarillo Convention and Visitors Bureau,* 1000 Polk St., Amarillo, TX 79105 (806–374–1497; 800–692–1338 in TX; 800–654–1902 elsewhere).

Lubbock

During frontier times, this city's site was headquarters for buffalo hunters and trail drivers. According to local legend, the famed song, "Oh, Bury Me Not on the Lone Prairie," originated around a cowboy campfire on the plains near today's Lubbock.

For a look at the old times, don't miss the *Ranching Heritage Center* on the north side of the 1,800-acre campus of Texas Tech. Scattered around the outdoor setting are more than 30 authentic historic structures, ranging from a primitive dugout to an elegant home. They have been brought in from around the state, restored, and furnished. Open daily; call 806–742–2498 for information.

Adjacent to the 12-acre center is the *Museum of Texas Tech,* with exhibits covering arts, humanities, and the social and natural sciences. The museum's Moody Planetarium has programs throughout the year.

Everyone loves *Prairie Dog Town* in Mackenzie State Park, a large walled-in area that's home to one of the few remaining colonies in the country. They are showmen of the first quality, so bring some bread to tempt them out of their holes. The park also includes part of Yellow House Canyon that was the site of a fight between buffalo hunters and Indians in 1877. Today, the canyon has a string of four small lakes and man-made waterfalls, paths, and picnic facilities.

Downtown, near the Memorial Civic Center, is a statue of rock 'n' roll star Buddy Holly, one of Lubbock's most famous sons. You'll also find boating, fishing, waterskiing, and horseback riding at Buffalo Springs Lake, 5 miles southeast on F.M. 835. This 225-acre lake also has tent and trailer sites with full hookups and is open year-round.

For information on Lubbock and a list of lodgings and restaurants, contact the *Lubbock Visitors and Convention Bureau,* Box 561, Lubbock, TX 79408 (806–763–4666 or 800–692–4035 in TX). Also, you will want to stop at the Llano Estacado Winery, one of the leaders in the state's advancing viticulture industry. Opened in 1976, it grows the classic wine grape, vitus vinifera, and the tasting room allows viewing of the winery operations. Located 3.2 miles east of U.S. 87 on F.M. 1585, it is open daily.

Rio Grande Valley

This fertile river bottom land in the toe of Texas is the fruit and vegetable basket for much of America. Primarily agricultural, the valley has a strong Mexican flavor, ideal for a bi-nation experience. Three international airports, at *Brownsville, McAllen,* and *Harlingen,* have daily air service from many parts of the state, and rental cars can be reserved at all airports.

This also is prime territory for winter Texans, snowbirds fleeing the harsh winters north of the Mason-Dixon line. Their winter addresses can be found in any one of the numerous small towns that start at Brownsville and extend beyond Falcon (Fal-Cone) Lake at Rio Grande City. Laredo, 202 miles northwest of Brownsville and also a border town on the Rio Grande, gets its share of warmth-seekers.

Brownsville, Matamoros, and Harlingen

Right on the border between the United States and Mexico, **Brownsville** is a fun place to go for a taste of authentic Mexican charm and romance. Some 80 percent of the city's population have Hispanic surnames. The town's second claim to fame is the outstanding *Gladys Porter Zoo.* Even if you don't much care for zoos, don't miss it. This 31-acre botanical garden and zoological park specializes in endangered species and houses more than 1,800 mammals, birds, reptiles, amphibians, and invertebrates.

In Brownsville, TX 48 turns into International Boulevard which leads to the new International Bridge over the border into *Matamoros,* considered the cleanest and most enjoyable of the Mexican communities along the Rio Grande. No currency exchange is needed for shopping, nor is a passport required. But you must show proof of U.S. or Canadian citizenship at the border upon your return. Best bets in Matamoros for shopping are the Mercado (bargaining possible and expected) and better shops (set prices) such as Las Dos Republicas, Barbara's on Obregon Street, and the ProNaF building shops, also on Obregon. Liquor is relatively inexpensive over the border—Garcia's and Arti are good spots—and a favorite souvenir. In addition to U.S. Custom regulations on the importation of liquor, you will have to pay a small Texas tax on each bottle. For good food in Matamoros, try the *Drive-Inn* at 6th and Hidalgo (lunch and dinner daily), or *Garcia's* at Obregon and Margaritas. Both serve lunch and dinner daily and take credit cards. Border town water generally is safe to drink, but Tecate beer, served in the can with salt and a cut lemon, is the local drink of choice. Matamoros also has a swimming beach 20 miles east of town via Avenida Lauro Villar. The surf fishing is good, but the small seafood restaurants at the beach are not recommended.

One note of importance: Mexico does not observe Daylight Saving Time.

Getting to Matamoros is a breeze. If you don't want to fuss getting the essential Mexican automobile insurance, turn left just before crossing the bridge and park your car in the Civic Center parking lot, across from the Brownsville Chamber of Commerce, 1600 E. Elizabeth Street To walk across the bridge is 25 cents, and taxis and guides eagerly clamor for your business as soon as you step foot on the other side. Confirm rates before hiring either. There's also a Mexican tourism office, good for maps and advice.

Harlingen is of interest to tourists primarily because it is home to the Ghost Squadron of the Confederate Air Force (CAF). Even if you are not a World War II veteran or an aircraft buff, a visit to Rebel Field (adjacent to the Harlingen Airport) is a must. In addition to a museum concerning all branches of the service, there are three hangars of vintage aircraft. More than 70 are on display, representing a collection of the more prominent types of American combat planes of the World War II era. Volunteer Ghost Squadron members also have rounded up some of the British and German fighting aircraft, along with training planes and transports. All are in flying condition and show off at the annual airshow the second week in October. You are welcome to photograph the planes and talk with volunteers, many of whom will be working on the planes while you are there. The CAF is open daily. For information, contact Box CAF, Rebel Field, Harlingen, TX 78551 (512–425–1057).

Birdwatchers will be glad to learn that the Rio Grande Valley, especially around Brownsville and Harlingen, attracts a large variety of exotic bird species. The *Santa Ana National Wildlife Refuge* is the southernmost in the U.S. and has birds found in no other U.S. refuge. The *Laguna Atascosa Refuge* is home to coastal birds and mammals.

For further information on the valley, contact the *Brownsville Chamber of Commerce,* Box 752, Brownsville, TX 78522 (512–542–4341); the *Harlingen Chamber of Commerce,* Box 189, Harlingen, TX 78551 (512–423–5440); or *Adventures in Travel,* 1008 S. 77 Sunshine Strip, Harlingen, TX 78550 (512–428–0217).

Laredo

First-time visitors to Laredo may think they are in Mexico, so pervasive is the south-of-the-border influence. The music heard from the stores, the language spoken in the streets, even the aroma of food from the cafés—all are Mexican.

More than 90% of the population is of Mexican descent and the remaining citizens are for the most part bilingual. Laredo is a town where you get refried beans instead of hash browns with your breakfast.

Laredo was founded in 1775 as a Mexican frontier town on a site near the present-day San Augustine Plaza in downtown Laredo. After the Mexican War of 1846 firmly established the border at the Rio Grande, a group who preferred to remain Mexican citizens established Nuevo Laredo on the opposite bank of the river. Today, the two towns combine for an interesting travel experience.

The downtown area between Iturbide and Water streets is designated as the Villa de San Augustine Historical Zone, and walking tour maps are available from the *Chamber of Commerce,* 2310 San Bernardo. Don't miss either the *Museum of the Republic of the Rio Grande,* next to La Posada Hotel on Zaragoza Street, or *Saint Augustine Church,* facing the plaza on the east. The latter has fine stained-glass windows.

Laredo is a great shopping town—it is one of the busiest ports of entry in the U.S.—and many of the stores handle imported goods from around the world. Try the 1400 block of Zaragoza on the American side, and both Marti's and Deutsche's on Guerrero on the Mexican Side. If you don't want to drive, park at the Riverdrive Mall and walk across; there's a 20-cent toll. The Maclovio Herrera Market, a block of tiny stands and tourist goodies, is farther down on Guerrero.

When you are ready for a break, hunt up the *Cadillac Bar* at Belden and Ocampo, famous for its Ramos gin fizzes. The margaritas are also made by hand, not a blender, which is part of the bar's mystique. This classic watering hole has been copied in many other cities, but they never come close to the original.

This is Charro country, the Mexican equivalent of the American cowboy only more elegant, and good hunting territory as well. Webb County consistently produces some of the largest whitetail bucks in the state, and the whitewing dove season in early September brings hunters to the border in huge numbers.

Horse and greyhound racing are featured March to September at Nuevo Laredo Downs, opened in 1985 and a 15-minute drive south of the International Bridge. Wagering is allowed in either dollars or pesos and announcements are made in both English and Spanish. No limit bets are possible at off-track betting parlors in Nuevo Laredo, Reynosa, and Matamoros.

For further information, contact the *Laredo Chamber of Commerce,* Box 790, Laredo, TX 78042 (512–722–9895 or 800–292–2122).

THE SOUTHWEST

by
RUTH ARMSTRONG

Ms. Armstrong, now retired, has written about all of the West, specializing in New Mexico. In addition to travel articles for newspapers and magazines, she has written several books.

At the close of the War with Mexico, 1848, most of the Southwest was ceded to the U.S. It included what we know today as Arizona and New Mexico. A strip of land across the bottom of both states was bought by the U.S. in the Gadsden Purchase of 1853, which fixed the continental boundary of the U.S. Over the next 50 years many bills were introduced in Congress to admit both territories as states—one was proposed to admit them as one state. Finally New Mexico achieved statehood on January 6, 1912, the 47th state in the Union, and on February 14 Arizona was admitted, the last of the Lower 48.

New Mexico and Arizona are the real heart of the Southwest. Both have mild but invigorating climates, a lot of sunshine, great variety of terrain, and fascinating histories ranging from ancient Indian cultures through Spanish conquest to American exploration and settlement. Though Arizona and New Mexico are alike in many ways and are often treated together, they have many differences, both subtle and obvious.

Elevation in Arizona drops almost to sea level at Yuma and rises to Humphries Peak, 12,633 feet, north of Flagstaff. The lowest point in New Mexico is 2,817 feet near Carlsbad, and the highest point is Wheeler Peak near Taos, 13,161 feet With the somewhat lower elevations in Arizona, it has more true desert and warmer temperatures, which makes it possible for dude ranches and resorts in the southern part of the state to promote winter vacations in the sun. While both states have around 80 percent of all possible sunshine, because of higher elevation New Mexico is a little cooler. Humidity is fairly low in both states, but because of increased irrigation, lawns in rapidly growing Phoenix and Tucson, and the effects of the El Niño cycles, humidity and precipitation have increased in Arizona in recent years. Rainfall in both states occurs mostly during the summer thundershower season lasting from mid-July through September. Heaviest snowfall occurs in January and February, but ski seasons usually last from around Thanksgiving to Easter. Weather is not ordinarily a reason to postpone travel in the Southwest.

Prehistoric Indians made their way into the Southwest toward the end of the Ice Age, at least 15,000 years ago. They were hunters who followed bison and mammoths and gathered seeds to supplement their meat diet. Spear points and other artifacts dating to these prehistoric people have been found at Folsom, Clovis, the Sandia Mountains of New Mexico, and Ventana Cave near Tucson.

With the slow development of agriculture, life became more settled. The people left their caves and lived in small villages of pithouses and wood-and-mud surface dwellings. Communal life gave rise to crafts such as basketry and pottery-making.

The Basketmaker Period was followed by the Great Pueblo Periods, the zenith of prehistoric life. At Chaco Canyon in northwestern New Mexico, the Anasazis ("ancient ones," a name given them by the later Navajos) built huge dwellings of stone up to five stories high and containing hundreds of rooms. Pottery, baskets, road-building, crafts, governmental systems, and ceremonial rites all reached a high point at Chaco in the 11th and 12th centuries.

Toward the end of the 13th century, for reasons still unclear, the Anasazis began a dispersement to the middle and upper Rio Grande Valley. Others drifted south to found Zuni villages in western New Mexico, and west to establish the Hopi villages in Arizona.

The Hohokam culture (a Pima word meaning "those who have vanished") in Arizona, also descendants of Ice Age man, reached its peak earlier than the Anasazis, around A.D. 800. The Pima and Papago Indians of southern Arizona, believed to be descendants of the Hohokam Indians, live today on large reservations south of Tucson and Phoenix.

By the 16th century, when the Spaniards entered the Southwest, these ancient people were established in agricultural communities pretty much where they are now located. They were named Pueblo Indians by the Spaniards because they lived in villages, to distinguish them from the nomadic and warlike tribes of Athabascan Indians who had drifted down from Canada. These were the Apaches, who have large reservations in both states, and the Navajos, whose 16-million-acre reservation lies two-thirds in Arizona and one-third in New Mexico.

Nineteen Pueblos are in New Mexico, in the Rio Grande Valley and the western part of the state. Visiting their villages, learning about their arts and crafts, and observing their spectacular ceremonial dances are experiences you won't forget.

Spanish explorers entered the Southwest in 1540, but they did not colonize until 1598. Their first capital was at San Juan Indian Pueblo in New Mexico, which they moved to Santa Fe in 1610. Santa Fe was the seat of authority for the entire Spanish Southwest, a land so vast and unexplored that even the Spaniards did not know its boundaries. Spain ruled until 1822, when Mexico won its independence, and the Province of Nuevo Mejico became a Department of Mexico. After the U.S. won the Southwest in 1848, the history of New Mexico and Arizona became part of the history of the westward movement of the U.S. Ghost mining towns, ruins of forts, and tales of cattlemen and outlaws remind us of that period. Arizona made the transition to an American style of life a little more easily than New Mexico because there was not a deeply rooted Spanish civilization already there.

PRACTICAL INFORMATION FOR THE SOUTHWEST

WHEN TO GO. If you are interested in a specific sport, activity or special event, go when that's available, and don't worry about the weather. Both states have snow and ski seasons, both have outdoor recreation of almost every kind, both have desert flowers and cacti that bloom in the spring, and both have a wealth of scenic, historic, and geological attractions.

If you're a snowbird from the north seeking winter warmth, head for Arizona. New Mexico will be a lot warmer than Minnesota, but you won't be able to lie around a pool. In Phoenix, Tucson, and all of southern Arizona, the season is from Nov. through Mar. Guest ranches, resorts, trailer villages, and motels are busiest then, and rates are highest. Flagstaff in northern Arizona has a good ski season, and there's even skiing at Mt. Lemmon near Tucson. Most major events in Arizona are in the winter.

Most major events in New Mexico are geared toward summer and fall, though the season at the 12 developed ski areas usually lasts from Thanksgiving to Easter. Most Indian ceremonials are in the summer, not because it's the tourist season, but because they have to do with rain, crops, and a good harvest. Winter dances are animal dances, related to hunting.

Summer and fall in both states is the time for mountain hiking and camping, stream and lake fishing, boating and wind surfing on lakes, and most other outdoor activity. Fall days are glorious, golden and benign, with crisp, blanket-worthy nights. Mar. and Apr. are the best times to see cacti and wild flowers in bloom, especially in Arizona. Any time is a good time to go to the Southwest, whether you want sunshine or snow, desert heat or mountain-meadow coolness—it's there.

HOW TO GET THERE. By plane. Albuquerque, Phoenix, and Tucson are served by most major airlines and several regional lines. Southern New Mexico is best served by air service to El Paso, Texas.

By bus. *Greyhound* serves major towns in both states. Smaller feeder lines serve other towns in a network of routes from metropolitan centers. Local depots provide information, fares, and schedules.

By train. *Amtrak* goes through Albuquerque every afternoon, stopping at Gallup, Lamy (for Santa Fe), Las Vegas, and Raton, NM. Amtrak also serves Phoenix, Tucson, Flagstaff, and Kingman, AZ. Toll free number for Amtrak is 800–USA–RAIL.

By car. I-40 bisects both states, east–west. I-10 crosses half of southern New Mexico, and I-10 and I-8 cross southern Arizona. I-25 runs north–south down the middle of New Mexico, and I-17 runs down the middle of Arizona connecting with I-40 and I-10 and I-8. A good system of U.S. highways connect all major towns in both states, and state and county roads serve smaller towns. If you live anywhere in the general area, you will probably want to drive your own car, since these states are places that need to be explored at your own pace and whim. If you live too far away to consider driving, perhaps a fly-drive vacation would suit you. All major car rental companies have offices near all major airports, but if your visit is to be during a heavy tourist season, please make reservations in advance.

TOURIST INFORMATION. Stretch out the pleasure of your trip to the Southwest by ordering informational brochures and pretty picture books ahead of time. **In Arizona:** *Arizona Office of Tourism,* 110 W. Washington, Phoenix, AZ 85007 (602–542–0687). *Phoenix Convention and Visitors Bureau,* 505 N. Second St., Suite 300, Phoenix, AZ 85004 (602–254–6500). *Tucson Convention & Visitors Bureau,*

130 Scott Ave., Tucson, AZ 85701 (602–624–1889). *Grand Canyon National Park Lodges,* Box 699, Grand Canyon, AZ 86023 (602–638–2401). They can also provide information on river rafting trips, sightseeing tours, and mule back trips into the canyon. *Visitors Information Centers* are located in terminals 2 and 3 at Sky Harbor Airport in Phoenix, and downtown Phoenix at the corner of Adams and 2nd. **In New Mexico:** *N.M. Tourism & Travel Division,* Joseph M. Montoya Bldg., 1100 St. Francis Dr., Santa Fe, NM 87503 (800–545–2040). *Albuquerque Convention & Visitors Bureau,* Box 26866, Albuquerque, NM 87125 (505–243–3696). *Santa Fe Convention & Visitors Bureau,* Box 909, Santa Fe, NM 87504 (800–528–5369). *Taos Chamber of Commerce,* Drawer 1, Taos, NM 87571 (800–732–8267).

TELEPHONES. Area code for all of New Mexico is 505; for Arizona it is 602, necessary only when calling from out of state. For information (directory assistance) to find a number, call 1411 in either state. To call long distance dial 1 before the area code. Long distance is anything outside the city you are in. For operator assistance in making a credit card or collect call, dial 0 before the area code.

EMERGENCY TELEPHONE NUMBERS. The universal number for emergency police or ambulance service (not for ordinary information) is 911. **In Arizona:** *Poison Control* (800–326–0101). *Highway Patrol,* to report an accident (223–2000). *Weather and Road Conditions* (256–7706, Phoenix; 294–3113, Tucson). **In New Mexico:** *Poison Control* (843–2551). *State Police* in Albuquerque (841–8066), in Santa Fe (827–9300), in Taos (758–8878). *Weather and Road Conditions* (841–9256).

TIME ZONES AND BUSINESS HOURS. New Mexico is on Mountain Standard Time except from the first Sun. in Apr. to the last Sun. in Oct. when it is on Mountain Daylight Time, one hour earlier. Arizona stays on Mountain Standard Time all year, with the exception of the Navajo Reservation which goes to DT with the rest of the nation. New Mexico banking hours (for money exchange) are generally open weekdays from 9 A.M. to 3 P.M. Drive-up windows are open two or three hours later and sometimes on Sat. morning. Banking hours in Arizona are usually from 10 A.M. to 5 P.M., weekdays. Retail stores vary widely, but generally independent stores are open from 8:30 A.M. to 5:30–6 P.M. Large department stores in shopping centers stay open from 9 A.M. to 9 P.M., closing a little earlier on Sat. and Sun. Many large supermarkets (grocery stores) are open 24 hours a day, seven days a week. Most government offices are open from 8 A.M. to 5 P.M., week days. Any private business may elect to change its hours any time, so check locally.

LIQUOR LAWS. The legal age to drink or have alcohol in one's possession in both states is 21. Liquor is sold by package in liquor or grocery stores and by the drink in licensed establishments. Sunday sales are noon to 2 A.M. in New Mexico, noon to 1 A.M. in Arizona, but hours may vary by locality. Drunk driving in either state carries stiff penalties and a mandatory jail sentence.

HOW TO GET AROUND. By auto is the most satisfactory way to explore the Southwest; in some areas special tours and excursions are available by auto, limousine, plane, helicopter, and balloon. These options, plus various methods of in-city transportation, will be discussed in the section on each city or location.

HINTS TO MOTORISTS. If you have the notion that all of the Southwest is desert, and that all desert is flat, you're due for a surprise. Both Arizona and New Mexico have thousands of acres of mountains, mesas, canyons, and rough terrain. When driving in the mountains, stay on your side of the highway. Obey all posted speed limits, especially on curves. When coming down grade, shift to lower gears instead of riding the brake. A car going uphill has right-of-way. Don't tailgate the car in front. Avoid driving on unpaved roads when it is raining or threatening rain; caliche in the soil makes the dirt slick as butter when it's wet. Never drive or walk into an arroyo (natural gully) when the sky is dark upstream. It may be dry where you are, but a sudden thundershower 15 mi. away can send a flash flood crashing down the arroyo with killing speed. Away from towns and cities much of these two states is sparsely populated, so try to travel on the top half of your gas tank. If you plan to explore the deserts of southern Arizona, especially if you plan to walk much, take plenty of water, at least a gallon a day per person.

Both states observe the 55 mph speed limit and have been known to set radar or speed traps to catch unwary motorists. In inhabited areas, speed limits range from 25 to 45 mph, and down to 15 mph in school zones when children are present. More than 40 Indian reservations are in the two states, and each has its own law enforcement officers, and speed limits vary according to terrain and road condition. Just watch for signs.

Good highway maps may be obtained by writing the *Arizona Dept. of Transportation,* 2039 W. Lewis Ave., Phoenix, AZ 85009. Or *N.M. Tourism Division,* Joseph M. Montoya Bldg., 1100 St. Francis Dr., Santa Fe, NM 87503 (800–545–2040).

HINTS TO DISABLED TRAVELERS. Three helpful booklets published by the *Arizona Easter Seal Society* cover most of the state and are available by writing Arizona Easter Seal Society, 702 N. 1st St., Phoenix, AZ 85004. Tell them the area you plan to visit. For a listing of hotels and motels throughout the state that have facilities for the handicapped write the *Phoenix C&VB,* 505 No. 2nd St., Suite 300, Phoenix, AZ 85004 (602–254–6500). Similar books are not available in New Mexico, but state law requires that any new building include plans for access by the handicapped in its construction. Almost all newer hotels and motels have some rooms especially equipped for use by handicapped persons.

THE GRAND CANYON

Most people are rendered silent by the size and beauty of the earth formations banded in shades of purple, mauve, salmon, and gray that descend into the depths of the canyon. You can explore bits of it, learn about it, become familiar with parts of it, yet the Grand Canyon remains a magnificent, overpowering work of natural art that will always remain aloof, making man seem puny and fragile in comparison.

The Canyon was once under a vast sea, but as it was lifted to form the Kaibab Plateau, faults and cracks appeared, and down one of them a great river found its way. Over millions of years the river has ground its way through the canyon, revealing rock formations that reach back to the beginning of the earth, an open book of geological records.

The river is as abrasive as sandpaper, rubbing against the canyon walls. Until Glen Canyon Dam was built in 1963, it carried a half million tons of silt through the canyon every 24 hours! The figure is now 80,000 tons a day.

The canyon is 190 air miles long, 277 by river. It is 10 miles across, a 216-mile drive around the eastern end of the gorge, or a 21-mile hike for an experienced and fit hiker. The lowest part of the canyon is 2,400 feet above sea level, 4,500 feet below the south rim and 5,400 feet below the north rim, averaging about a mile in depth. Hiking from the south rim to the floor of the canyon, one passes through the same vegetation zones one would encounter going from Canada to Mexico.

Archaeologists have found evidence of human occupation of the canyon at least 4,000 years ago. The first non-Indians to see it was a detachment of conquistadores commanded by Garcia Lopez de Cárdenas, a lieutenant of the Coronado Expedition of 1540. They climbed down the canyon a little ways, realized it was deeper and the river bigger than they had thought, and realized they could not cross it. No other European saw it until 1776, when another Spanish explorer made his way up the canyon to the Havasupais, then climbed to the rim.

During the early 1800s a few American explorers found their way into the canyon, but the first real exploration of the Colorado River and the Grand Canyon was in 1869, led by Maj. John Wesley Powell, a one-armed

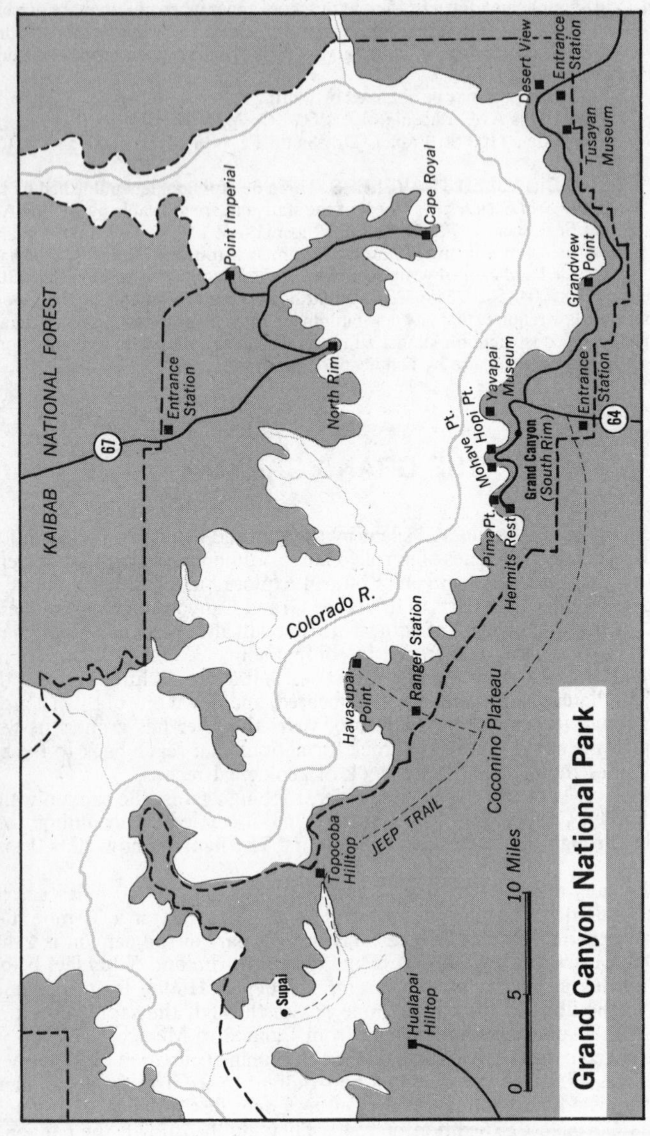

Grand Canyon National Park
KAIBAB NATIONAL FOREST
67
Entrance Station
Point Imperial
Cape Royal
North Rim
Colorado R.
Desert View
Entrance Station
Tusayan Museum
Grandview Point
Entrance Station
64
Yavapai Museum
Hopi Pt.
Mohave Pt.
Grand Canyon (South Rim)
Pima Pt.
Hermits Rest
Ranger Station
Havasupai Point
Coconino Plateau
JEEP TRAIL
Topocoba Hilltop
Supai
Hualapai Hilltop
0
5
10 Miles

Civil War veteran and professor of geology at Illinois Wesleyan University. Some of the men abandoned the expedition, climbed out of the canyon, and were killed by Indians, but six came through to where the Virgin River runs into the Colorado below the canyon. Powell led other expeditions down the Colorado and to the country to the north of the canyon. In one of these groups was the artist Thomas Moran, one of whose paintings of the Grand Canyon was bought by Congress for $10,000 to hang in the Capitol. This began the popularization of Grand Canyon. In 1919, under President Wilson, 1,211,104 acres were set aside as a National Park. It has now achieved World Heritage status. Each year the Park is visited by more than two million people, about a third of whom are from foreign countries.

Exploring the South Rim

The South Rim, the most accessible part of the canyon, is visited by far more people than any other part. Near the entrance to the Park are several motels and other businesses. A few miles beyond the entrance station is Grand Canyon Village where you will find park headquarters, a ranger station, visitor center, seven lodges, and hotels, a trailer village, campground, museums, restaurants, gift shops, stores, service station, pharmacy, clinic, ambulance, barber and beauty shop, post office, and even a bank. The first thing everyone does is get out of the car and go to the edge of the canyon as quickly as possible for that first thrilling look. A nature trail runs along this rim of the canyon for nine miles and is paved in the area of the Village.

West Rim Drive goes west of the Village 7.5 miles, past several scenic overlooks. To reduce traffic in summer, this is closed to private autos and access is by canyon shuttle. East Rim Drive goes east from the Village 25 miles past more overlooks, past the Tusayan Ruins and Museum, to Lipan Point, which some consider the finest view of the canyon.

On trips to the inner canyon—by foot, mule, or boat—you will get a more intimate view of the canyon's rich natural beauty and a truer appreciation of its size. Trails lead down to Plateau Point, to Phantom Ranch on the Colorado River, and to the Havasupai Indian Reservation; river rafting trips take you through the canyon. Helicopter and airplane rides may be available for a bird's eye view.

Exploring the North Rim

Getting to the North Rim is an adventure in itself. From the South Rim, drive 216 miles around the east end of the canyon on AZ 64, north on U.S. 89, west on U.S. 89A, and south on AZ 67. You cross the Colorado River at Marble Canyon, part of Glen Canyon Recreation Area, where the river slices through 800-foot cliffs of many colors. The route turns west at Marble Canyon and goes along the Vermillion Cliffs until it reaches the Kaibab Forest. This area, north of the Grand Canyon and west of the Colorado River to the boundary of Utah and Nevada, is known as the Arizona Strip. It is virtually unpopulated and inaccessible to the rest of Arizona except by the one route just described. Routes from Nevada and Utah converge at Jacob Lake and become AZ 67 for the last 45 miles to the visitor facilities at the North Rim. A thousand feet higher than the South Rim, all this country is deep within a magnificent forest of tall ponderosa pine and aspen trees with cool green lakes in flower-spangled meadows. It is quiet and inspiring, one of the most natural and remote recreation areas in the country. Deer, wild turkeys, squirrels, and other creatures are fairly common. Two nature trails and several scenic drives lead to vista points on the North Rim. The view is different here—the canyon seems wider because you are back farther from the edge, and you see more freestanding rock formations and promontories. Visitor facilities include a campground, cabins, and a big rustic lodge in the grand old style of lodges that were hallmarks of affluent vacation spots a couple of generations ago.

PRACTICAL INFORMATION FOR THE GRAND CANYON

WHEN TO GO. Summer is the height of the tourist season. There are lines for just about everything, and unless you have reservations, you probably will not be able to find a place to stay. During the winter, the Canyon puts on a fabulous show. Snow often lies deep and soft on the rim but disappears a mi. or two down the trails. Colors of the formations in the canyon are even more startling when wet or contrasted with snow. Few people are there in the winter, and you can enjoy the Canyon in virtual solitude and leisure. Rates at the lodges are lower during off-season, and there is no trouble getting a reservation. They open as many lodges as are needed, usually from among the four directly on the rim which have the best view. Fall is an excellent time to go, but storms can strike anytime from Sept. through the winter. The highways to the South Rim are kept open all year but are sometimes closed temporarily because of a storm. The highway from Jacob Lake to the North Rim is open only from late May through early Oct.

CLIMATE AND CLOTHING. Because of changes in elevation and effects of the canyon itself, weather conditions can vary dramatically. Summer temperatures can reach 100 degrees in the bottom of the canyon at Phantom Ranch, but on either rim they are more likely to be in the 70s or 80s. As in the rest of the Southwest, summer sun is direct and hot but the air is cool and dry. Nights are always comfortable.

Summer thunder and lightning storms are frequent in the Park. The canyon rim is a natural target for lightning bolts. If the hair on your head starts to stand on end and you detect a smell of ozone, an electrical charge is building up around you. Immediately move back from the rim and lie flat on the ground. Lightning strikes the tallest object, usually trees.

In winter, snow accumulates from four to ten ft. on the North Rim and temperatures drop below zero. On the South Rim, snow is seldom over two ft. deep. Clothing should be casual but sensible.

In the winter, dress as if you were going skiing. In the summer, wear cool cotton pants and shirts and comfortable walking shoes or boots if you plan to hike down the trails—but always have a jacket. A thunder shower can drop the temperature 20 or 30 degrees. Shorts are fine in the Village, but don't try to backpack or ride muleback in them. Some mule trip operators will refuse to take anyone dressed in shorts or open sandals. Jeans and long-sleeved cotton shirts are most practical.

HOW TO GET THERE. By plane. *Scenic Airlines* and *Air Nevada* operate from Las Vegas, Nevada, to Grand Canyon.

By car. The South Rim can be reached by turning north from I-40 at Flagstaff on U.S. 180 (81 mi.), or from Williams on AZ 64 (58 mi.). The North Rim is reached by leaving U.S. 89 at Kanab, UT, or Page, AZ and driving on U.S. 89A to Jacob Lake, then south on AZ 67.

By bus. *Greyhound* serves Flagstaff, and *Nava-Hopi Bus Line* goes to the Canyon. Call 774–5003 for information.

By train. *Amtrak* stops in Flagstaff, where connections can be made to the Canyon with the Nava-Hopi Bus Line. There is no bus or train service to the North Rim.

TOURIST INFORMATION. South Rim: *National Park Service Visitor Activities and Programs,* recorded message (638–9304). *Weather and Park information,* recorded message (638–2245). *Emergencies.* (doctor, ambulance, rangers) (dial 911, 9911 from hotel rooms). *Park Headquarters* (638–7888). *Central Reservations* (638–2401) for advance reservations. *Transportation information* at Bright Angel Lodge (638–2631). *Backcountry reservations,* information only (638–2474). **North Rim:** *Grand Canyon Lodge* (801–586–7686). *Grand Canyon Trail Rides* (638–2292).

HOW TO GET AROUND. By plane. Grand Canyon Airport, eight mi. south of the Park on AZ 64, is open year-round, providing scenic flights over the Canyon (see "Tours") and service to the North Rim if conditions permit. *Air Grand Canyon,* Box 3028, Grand Canyon, AZ 86023 (638–2686).

By car. You can drive your car on main access roads, but May through Oct. only the park shuttle is allowed on part of the West Rim Dr. You may drive anytime on the East Rim Dr.

By shuttle. A courtesy shuttle bus runs every 30 minutes from 9 A.M. to 8:30 P.M., stopping at all designated shuttle stops in the village. From 6 to 9 A.M. and 8:30 P.M. to midnight the shuttle will pick up passengers at any lodge. Call 638–2631.

TOURS. Helicopter tours. *Grand Canyon Helicopters,* Box 455, Grand Canyon, AZ 86023 (638–2419; 800–528–2418). **Airplane flights.** *Air Grand Canyon,* Box 3028, Grand Canyon, AZ 86023 (638–2686). *Scenic Airlines,* 241 E. Reno Av., Las Vegas, NV 98119 (702–739–1900), offers tours including hotel and airport transfers and a scenic flight through the canyon, with individual headsets with taped commentary. Cost ranges from $69 to $259. **Bus tours.** *Fred Harvey Transportation Co.* has tours going to all scenic points on the South Rim. *Indianlands Tours* goes to Monument Valley. For information on any tour, check at the *Transportation Desk* at Bright Angel Lodge or write or call *Grand Canyon National Park Lodges,* South Rim Reservations, Box 699, Grand Canyon, AZ 86023 (638–2401).

Rafting. Rafting through the Grand Canyon on the Colorado River has become extremely popular in recent years. More than 20 concessioners are licensed to operate river tours. Reservations should be made at least six months in advance. For information and a list of river operators, contact Grand Canyon National Park Lodges, Box 699, Grand Canyon, AZ 86023 (638–2401).

Horseback rides and wagon rides. Contact *Moqui Lodge,* Box 369, Grand Canyon, AZ 86023 (638–2424).

Canyon mule trips. On the South Rim a one-day trip goes to Plateau Point, which has a great view of the river, 1,400 feet below. A two-day trip goes down to the river, spending the night and having dinner and breakfast at Phantom Ranch. These are offered all year. Reservations, recommended at all times, are mandatory May–Oct. Contact Grand Canyon National Park Lodges, Box 699, Grand Canyon, AZ 86023. From the North Rim mule trips are offered by *Grand Canyon Trail Rides,* Kanab, UT 84741 (602–638–2292, summer). These trails are rougher than those on the South Rim and regulations are stiffer. Neither company will take anyone weighing more than 200 lbs, or shorter than 4 ft. 7 in.

CAMPING. Mather Campground at Grand Canyon Village and Desert View Campground, 25 mi. east of the Village are under jurisdiction of the National Park Service. At Mather reservations are strongly recommended from mid-May through Sept., and the rest of the year are first-come, first-served. Reservations can be made through any Ticketron outlet. For information contact *Mather Campground* (602–638–7851). A trailer village is located in the Village, operated by Grand Canyon National Park Lodges, Box 699, Grand Canyon, AZ 86023 (638–2401). All hookups are available. Commercial campgrounds are at the town of Tusayan, seven miles south of the Village, outside park boundaries. Camping at the North Rim is available at three campgrounds and one trailer campground, located between Jacob Lake and the rim. Write *North Rim,* Grand Canyon National Park, Box 129, Grand Canyon, AZ 86023.

HIKING. This is the second most important reason most people go to Grand Canyon (first is to look). Trails vary from easy, paved nature trails at the Village to rugged backcountry trails that require experience and stamina. These latter have fairly stringent regulations to protect the environment as well as the hiker. Contact Superintendent, Grand Canyon National Park, Box 129, Grand Canyon, AZ 86023 (638–2474). Trail maps are available at the visitor center.

MUSEUMS. Yavapai Museum, ½ mi. east of the visitor center, has exhibits, nature walks, and talks by rangers dealing with the geology of the canyon. **Tusayan Museum,** 21 mi. east of the visitor center on East Rim Drive, is located next to an Anasazi ruin occupied around A.D. 1185.

ACCOMMODATIONS. You can choose from a turn-of-the-century lodge, a cabin, campground, or a motel. Reservations for North Rim lodges may be made through TW Services, Inc., Box 400, Cedar City, UT 84720 (801–586–7686); for Grand Canyon National Park lodges on the South Rim contact Box 699, Grand Canyon, AZ 86023 (602–638–2401). Other motels and lodges are outside park boundaries. Facilities listed here are divided by price category: *Deluxe,* $90 and up; *Expensive,* $70–$90; *Moderate,* $50–$70. Prices are based on summer, or high season, rates, double occupancy.

South Rim

Deluxe

Kachina Lodge and **Thunderbird Lodge** are on the canyon rim and half of the rooms look over the canyon. Lodges are alike, contemporary style. Open year-round.

El Tovar Hotel. Built of native stone and logs, this grand old lodge has been refurbished and retains its air of gentility. Some rooms have canyon views. Open year-round. Continental dining room serves breakfast, lunch and dinner. Lounge and gift shop.

Expensive

Best Western Canyon Squire Lodge (638–2681 or 800–528–1234) is seven mi. from park entrance, free shuttle bus. Western decor, facilities for conventions and groups. Dining room, lounge, recreational facilities.

Red Feather Quality Inn. (638–2673 or 800–228–5151.) This inn is near the airport at the entrance to the park; restaurant, lounge.

Yavapai Lodges, is located in the woodlands between Yavapai Point and El Tovar. Rooms are spacious.

Moderate

Bright Angel Lodge, built of native stone. This and El Tovar were the original accommodations at the Canyon. Rooms are not large, but adequate. Some share bath. Has character. Good dining room.

Maswik Lodge is located a short distance from the rim. Rustic cabins with modern accommodations.

Moqui Lodge is just outside the park boundary. Dining room, lounge, tennis courts, horseback riding in season. Open Mar.–Dec.

North Rim

Expensive

Grand Canyon Lodge. Lodge is an elegant old log and stone building, beautiful views, Continental dining room. Separate cabins have somewhat lower rates.

Moderate

Jacob Lake Inn. 45 mi. from the North Rim features a restaurant, gas station, grocery store.

Kaibab Lodge. 18 mi. north of North Rim, closed in winter. Full-service restaurant.

RESTAURANTS. In addition to the following restaurants, there are cafeterias and small eateries where a quick meal may be found at an inexpensive price. The restaurants are listed by price of a meal for one: *Deluxe,* over $15; *Expensive,* $10–$15; *Moderate,* below $10.

Deluxe

El Tovar. On the South Rim. Excellent Continental-American menu, elegantly served.

Expensive

Bright Angel Lodge. Has a dining room and a cafeteria where prices are less. Good food.

Grand Canyon Lodge. North Rim. Excellent Continental-American food, well served. Lovely vistas.

Moqui Lodge. Located outside park boundary. Mexican and American food.

Moderate

Yavapai Lodge. In the Village, not on the rim. American menu.

PHOENIX

Almost a million people live in Phoenix, Arizona's capital and largest city. It is a center of business, government, and the tourist industry, especially for winter vacations in the sun. Remember the advertising campaign the state conducted a generation ago, "Bring your sinuses to Arizona"? People did just that and found it was a marvelous escape from the cold dampness of the Midwest and Great Lakes areas. Today Arizona is synonymous with winter warmth and sunshine.

Incorporated in 1881 as a farming community in the Salt River Valley, Phoenix is on the site of an ancient Hohokam Indian civilization which disappeared about the 15th century. They too were farmers, and they developed a sophisticated system of irrigation canals to water crops with diversions from the Salt River. Early settlers used the same canals dug by the Hohokams. Phoenix was named for the mythological bird that was destroyed by fire and rose again from its own ashes—a fitting name for a new city rising on the site of an ancient culture.

Elevation at Phoenix is 1,083 feet above sea level, a low desert land cut by a river. When Theodore Roosevelt Dam was built in the mountains 50 miles northeast of Phoenix early in the century, it became possible to store water and stabilize the year-round supply. Irrigation made the desert blossom into a rich Garden of Eden. With a year-round season, citrus fruits, cotton, and other warm climate crops produced abundantly. From farming community to trade center to health center for tuberculosis patients to tourism mecca, the growth of Phoenix has been remarkable, especially since World War II. Phoenix is national headquarters for many businesses, especially in the electronics and high-tech industries. It is a bright and airy city spread out over 351 square miles that seems to sit, smiling, in the sun.

Exploring Phoenix

Camelback Mountain is a virtual logo for the city; 1,800 feet high and visible from almost any part of the city, it really does look like a reclining camel. You can reach Camelback Road by going north from downtown on almost any main north–south street. A scenic drive, hiking trails, and picnic areas are on Camelback.

Phoenix is a city of verdant parks and golf courses, proof that all the desert needs to bloom is water. *Encanto Park,* near the intersection of Highways 89, 60, and 93 with Interstates 10 and 17, is a midtown oasis of palm-bordered lagoons, golf courses, tennis courts, flowers, and facilities for boating, picnicking, and shuffleboard.

On the east edge of town on Business Route I-10 is *Papago Park.* Hiking and riding trails wind through red sandstone formations and desert terrain. A public golf course, the city zoo and botanical garden are in the

PHOENIX

CAMELBACK RD.
INDIAN SCHOOL RD.
THOMAS RD.
McDOWELL RD.
VAN BUREN
WASHINGTON
BUCKEYE RD.
MARICOPA FREEWAY
UNIVERSITY DR.
BROADWAY ROAD
SOUTHERN AVE.
BASELINE RD.
GRAND AVE.
BLACK CANYON HWY.
35TH AVE.
27TH AVE.
19TH AVE.
7TH AVE.
CENTRAL AVE.
7TH ST.
16TH ST.
24TH ST.
24TH
32ND ST.
32ND
40TH ST.
48TH ST.
Papago Park
SCOTTSDALE ROAD
RURAL RD.
MILL AVE.
HAYDEN RD.
GRANITE REEF
PIMA FREEWAY
SALT R. BED
17
10

Points of Interest

1) Arizona Historical Society Museum
2) Arizona Museum
3) Arizona State University
4) Art Museum
5) Capitol Building
6) City-County Complex
7) Civic Plaza
8) Desert Botanical Garden
9) Grady Gammage Memorial Auditorium
10) Greyhound Park (Dog Racing)
11) Heard Museum
12) Mineral Museum
13) Municipal Stadium
14) Pueblo Grande
15) State Fairgrounds
16) Veteran's Memorial Coliseum
17) Phoenix Zoo

park which lies on the site of an ancient Hohokam village. Pottery shards can still sometimes be found (but not taken).

South Mountain Park, at the south end of Central Avenue, covers more than 17,000 acres of desert mountain terrain, the largest city park in the nation. Picnic sites along a scenic drive are available. A half dozen other parks in the metropolitan area all have public facilities for visitors and residents.

Civic Plaza, downtown on Van Buren and 7th, hosts dozens of events through the year: exhibits, demonstrations, fiestas. Nearby at Symphony Hall, the Phoenix Symphony performs. The Plaza is the focal point of a city that has kept its downtown area a vital part of city life. Municipal buildings, museums, hotels, and office buildings are in the area.

The State Capitol Complex, 17th and Washington, downtown, includes, in addition to many new buildings, the old capitol, finished in 1901 and built of native stone. The four-story rotunda and the rest of the building have been carefully restored, and tours Monday–Friday let visitors learn the history of Arizona.

As the nation's ninth largest city, Phoenix is a sophisticated metropolitan area, but underneath it is committed to the casual lifestyle of the Old West. With all its amenities, it is also the starting point for recreational adventures that are not far away in the mountains of Tonto National Forest. It is a city of wide, clean thoroughfares, verdant lawns and gardens, backyard pools, and beautiful homes. A good drive is north on Central Avenue to Lincoln Drive; east on Lincoln through the foothills of the Phoenix Mountains to Scottsdale Road. From there turn south to Camelback Road, then west to downtown Phoenix again.

PRACTICAL INFORMATION FOR PHOENIX

WHEN TO GO. From Oct. to May is "the season," but if you enjoy warm temperatures and activities, you will find the off-season rates and less crowded conditions appealing. Everything is air conditioned here, swimming pools are common, and summer is an informal season.

HOW TO GET THERE. By plane. *Phoenix Sky Harbor International Airport* is one of the busiest in the nation, and is served by most major airlines.

By train. *Amtrak* serves Phoenix (800–USA–RAIL).

By bus. *Greyhound* serves Phoenix on regular routes, and also have many tours to major attractions such as Grand Canyon and Lake Powell. Contact your travel agent.

TOURIST INFORMATION. *Phoenix and Valley of the Sun Convention and Visitors Bureau, (C&VB),* 505 N. 2nd St., Suite 300, Phoenix, AZ 85004, (602–254–6500). *Arizona Office of Tourism,* 110 W. Washington, Phoenix, AZ 85007 (602–542–8687). Visitor information booths are at terminals 2 and 3 at the airport, and downtown at 2nd and Adams.

HOW TO GET AROUND. By taxi. Taxis in Phoenix are not regulated and fees vary greatly. They do not cruise the streets but are usually near the airport and other pickup points.

By bus. City buses serve Phoenix and the suburbs. Adults, 85 cents; children and seniors, 40 cents; exact change is necessary. One-day passes available. No Sun. service. Phoenix Transit System (602–253–5000). At least 75 tour and charter bus companies have offices in Phoenix, serving both the city and state.

By car. Either your own or a rental car is the best way to get around a spread-out city like Phoenix. All major rental car companies have offices in Phoenix, most near the airport. Streets are laid out in a grid pattern, the center of which is Central and Washington. Expressways going through the city are I-10 and I-17, and U.S. 60–89 and AZ 93. Morning and afternoon rush hours are congested. Street parking downtown is often difficult. Some streets enforce restricted parking during business hours. City speed limit is 25 mph unless posted otherwise.

TOURS. *State Capitol Walking Tour* includes historic Old Capitol Bldg., Capitol Museum, 1700 W. Washington (542–4581). Two trolley companies provide casual pickup and drop-off in central Phoenix–Scottsdale–Mesa areas. About 75 tour and charter companies are in Phoenix. For a complete list write for Visitors Guide, Phoenix and Valley of the Sun C&VB, 505 N. 2nd St., Ste. 300, Phoenix, AZ 85004 (602–254–6500).

PARTICIPANT SPORTS. Golf. More than 80 golf courses are in Phoenix, ranging from little pitch-and-putts to challenging championship courses where some of our most famous tournaments are held every year. A few public courses are: *Ahwatukee Lakes Country Club,* 13431 S. 44th St. (275–8099). *Cave Creek Golf Course,* 15202 N. 19th Av. (866–8076). *Papago Golf Course,* Papago Park (495–0555). *Arizona Golf Resort,* 425 S. Power Rd., Mesa (832–3202). For a complete list, write the Phoenix and Valley of the Sun C&VB, 505 N. 2nd St., Ste. 300, Phoenix, AZ 85004. **Tennis.** Most city parks have public courts, many lighted for night use. Major hotels, motels, and all resorts also have courts; some, such as *John Gardiner's Tennis Ranch,* specialize in tennis packages with instruction by top pros. **Boating, waterskiing,** and **sailing** are available at six large lakes within a 60-mi. radius of the city.

SPECTATOR SPORTS. Phoenix is a sports town with its own professional **basketball, baseball,** and **football** teams, plus collegiate teams from ASU. The Chicago Cubs, Oakland Athletics, San Francisco Giants, Milwaukee Brewers, and Seattle Mariners have spring training here. Big time auto racing is at three tracks, and horseracing season is from Oct. through May.

HISTORIC SITES AND HOUSES. *Heritage Square,* 6th & Monroe, downtown (262–5071), a block of restored homes from late 1800s, on National Register. Only remaining homes from original townsite. *Taliesen West* (860–2700), winter home of late architect Frank Lloyd Wright.

MUSEUMS. *Arizona Museum,* 1002 W. Van Buren, historical exhibits from prehistoric to present. 11 A.M.–4 P.M. Wed.–Sun., closed holidays. Donation. *Heard Museum of Anthropology and Primitive Art,* 22 E. Monte Vista Rd., downtown. 10 A.M.–5 P.M. Mon.–Sat.; 1–5 P.M. Sun. Closed holidays. Admission. *Central Arizona Museum of History Museum on Wheels,* 1120 N. 3rd., 11 A.M.–3 P.M. Thurs.–Sat. *Phoenix Art Museum,* 1625 N. Central. 10 A.M.–5 P.M. Tues.–Sat.; 10 A.M.–9 P.M. Wed.; 1–5 P.M. Sun. Closed Mon. and holidays. Admission. *Pueblo Grande Museum,* 4619 E. Washington, preserves ruins of Hohokam culture, occupied from around 200 BC to AD 1400. 9 A.M.–4:45 P.M. Mon.–Sat.; 1–4:45 P.M. Sun. Admission. *State Capitol Museum,* 1700 W. Washington, original capitol. Weekdays 8 A.M.–5 P.M. Free. *Arizona Mineral Museum,* State Fairgrounds, 1826 W. McDowell. 8 A.M.–5 P.M. Mon.–Fri.; 1–5 Sat. Free. *Arizona Museum of Science and Technology,* 80 N. 2nd St. 9 A.M.–5 P.M. Mon.–Sat.; 1–5 P.M. Sun. and holidays. Admission. *Desert Botanical Garden,* 1201 N. Galvin Pkwy. in Papago Park. 9 A.M.–sunset, Sept.–June. 7 A.M.–sunset July, Aug. Admission.

Many smaller, specialized museums are in the Phoenix metropolitan area. For a list write Phoenix & Valley of the Sun C&VB, 505 N. 2nd St., Suite 300, Phoenix, AZ 85004.

ARTS AND ENTERTAINMENT. Music. The *Phoenix Symphony* season is from Oct. through mid-May in Symphony Hall, Civic Plaza. The *Arizona Opera* and the *Chamber Music Society* also perform at Civic Plaza, May through Oct. **Stage.** *Phoenix Little Theatre, Stagebrush Theatre, Arizona Theatre Co., Celebrity Theatre,* are live theater companies in the metropolitan area. Most have seasons Oct. through May. **Galleries.** Phoenix and its suburban neighbor, Scottsdale, have become leading art centers with many galleries representing distinguished artists of the world, and especially of the West. The fact that these are affluent winter resort cities make them a good market, and institutions such as the *Phoenix Art Museum* have fostered interest. The annual *Cowboy Artists of America* sale and exhibition in Oct. is one of the most prestigious shows in the country.

ACCOMMODATIONS. Almost all hotels and motels have pools, cabanas, and poolside service. Types of establishments here vary from mobile home parks and mom-and-pop motels to elegant resorts and guest (dude) ranches. Many chains have motels in Phoenix (e.g., Rodeway, Motel 6, Regal 8, Days Inn, Quality Inn, La Quinta). We list only a few options, in order of price category: *Super Deluxe,* over $200; *Deluxe,* $150–$200; *Expensive,* $100–$150; *Moderate,* $70–$100; *Inexpensive,* under $70. Price is based on double occupancy, highest season (winter), and does not include taxes.

Super Deluxe

Arizona Biltmore. 24th & Missouri, Phoenix, AZ 85016 (602–955–6600). Still the queen of resorts, this old standby features golf, pools, shops, tennis. American and European plans.

Ritz Carlton. 2401 E. Camelback Rd., Phoenix, AZ 85016 (602–468–0700). Luxury hotel with full fitness center, tennis, two restaurants, lounge.

The Wigwam. Litchfield Park, AZ 85340 (602–935–3811). Golf on three courses, tennis, pools, horseback riding, trap and skeet shooting, restaurants, secluded park-like setting.

Deluxe

Hotel Westcourt. 10220 N. Metro Pkwy. E (602–997–5900 or 800–858–1033). Lush courtyard; adjacent to shopping, restaurants, nightlife, new.

Hyatt Regency. 122 N. 2nd St., Phoenix, AZ 85004 (602–252–1234 or 800–233–1234). Mobil 4-Star, AAA Diamond A. Restaurant on roof. Also in Scottsdale.

InnSuites. 3101 N. 32nd St., Phoenix, AZ 85018 (602–956–4900). All suites, complimentary breakfast and cocktail hour each day.

Les Jardins. 3738 N. 4th Ave., Phoenix, AZ 85013 (602–234–2464). Garden hotel, exercise room, spa, kitchenettes.

Expensive

Best Western Phoenix InnSuites. 1615 E. Northern, Phoenix, AZ 85020 (602–997–6285 or 800–528–1234). Includes complimentary breakfast, cocktails.

La Mancha. 100 W. Clarendon, Phoenix, AZ 85013 (602–279–9811). Hotel and athletic club.

Sheraton Greenway. 2510 W. Greenway Rd., Phoenix, AZ 85023 (602–993–0800 or 800–325–3535). Tennis, Jacuzzi, saunas. Close to shopping.

Moderate

Courtyard by Marriott. 9631 N. Black Canyon Hwy., Phoenix, AZ 85201 (602–944–7373). A pool and restaurant are offered at this chain hotel.

Howard Johnson Plaza Hotel. 1500 N. 51st Ave., Phoenix, AZ 85043 (602–484–9009 or 800–654–2000). Indoor pool, sauna, restaurant.

Inexpensive

Comfort Inn. 1711 W. Bell Rd., Phoenix, AZ 85023 (602–866–2089 or 800–228–5150). Close to horse racing, shopping.

Econoline Convention Center. 401 N. 1st St., Phoenix, AZ 85004 (602–258–3411). Pool, courtesy van.

Kon Tiki. 2364 E. Van Buren, Phoenix, AZ 85006 (602–244–9361). A bit of Polynesia. Free Continental breakfast.

RESTAURANTS. Many restaurants specialize in western fare like barbecued ribs and steak and beans, but there are those which serve the most delicate gourmet food, nouvelle cuisine, and ethnic foods of many countries, especially Mexican. A few are listed here by price category: *Deluxe,* over $20; *Expensive,* $14–$20; *Moderate,* $10–$14; *Inexpensive,* below $10. This does not include alcoholic beverages, tax or tip. Almost all accept credit cards.

Deluxe

La Champagne, 7171 N. Scottsdale Rd., Scottsdale (991–3800). Elegant dining, creative Continental cuisine. Live harp music.

Orangerie. In Arizona Biltmore, 24th and Missouri (955–6600). International cuisine, formal service.

Expensive

Garcia's Las Villas. 4420 E. Camelback Rd. (952–8031). Mariachis, margaritas, and good Mexican food.

The Golden Eagle. 37th floor of Valley Center Bldg., Van Buren and Central (257–7700). Formal service and great city views are available at this dining room.

Timothy's. 6335 N. 16th St. (277–7634). A cottage-turned-restaurant; live jazz every night.

Moderate

Beside the Pointe. 7677 N. 16th St. (997–2626). Garden setting, backgammon lounge. Reservations suggested.

Hunan. 1575 E. Camelback Rd. (265–9484). Hot, spicy Chinese food.

Mother Tucker's Food Experience. 3113 E. Lincoln Ave. (957–8416). Nestled in foothills. Steaks, seafood, and city view. L, D, daily.

Inexpensive

The Eggery. 5109 N. 44th St. (840–5734). If your cholesterol is also on vacation, this is the place to come for egg specialties. B, L, daily.

Red Apple Restaurant. 10402 N. Black Canyon (997–6529). Casual, rustic; features daily all-you-can-eat specials. B,L,D.

TUCSON

Tucson is a lovely, lively city that, despite rapid growth, honors its roots. Its Indian, Spanish, Mexican, and pioneer American influences have endured. Indian arts and crafts, pioneer homes, and Mexican food and architecture are part of the ambience a visitor enjoys.

The first recorded visit by people of European descent was in 1687 by Father Kino, a Jesuit missionary who found two Indian tribes there. No permanent settlements were attempted until the next century when the Spaniards established a presidio, or walled garrison, to protect missionaries and settlers. In 1776 soldiers were assigned to the presidio, known as the Old Pueblo or Tucson, which sounded like what the Indians called it. The existence of the settlement was precarious because of raids by nomadic, warlike Apaches who roamed the mountains of eastern Arizona.

When the United States secured the Southwest in 1848, the land where the Old Pueblo lay became a territory of the U.S. From 1867 to 1877, Tucson was the Territorial Capital of Arizona. In 1891 the University of Arizona was built as an agricultural school, and Tucson began a slow and solid growth. The University excels now in medicine, where important research is done in the fields of cancer and heart surgery.

Tucson remained a health and university town until World War II when Davis-Monthan Air Force Base was located here. The Air Base and University are still major contributors to Tucson's economy, which is augmented by tourism, state and federal offices, and headquarters for several industries related to aviation. The elevation of Tucson is 2,410 feet, which gives it a pleasant climate. It can be hot in Tucson, but the air is dry and there are cooling high-desert breezes. Mountains on all sides offer unlimited outdoor recreation and have an important effect on the weather. Tucson is a wonderful winter vacation destination, especially for a western vacation at one of its many guest (dude) ranches.

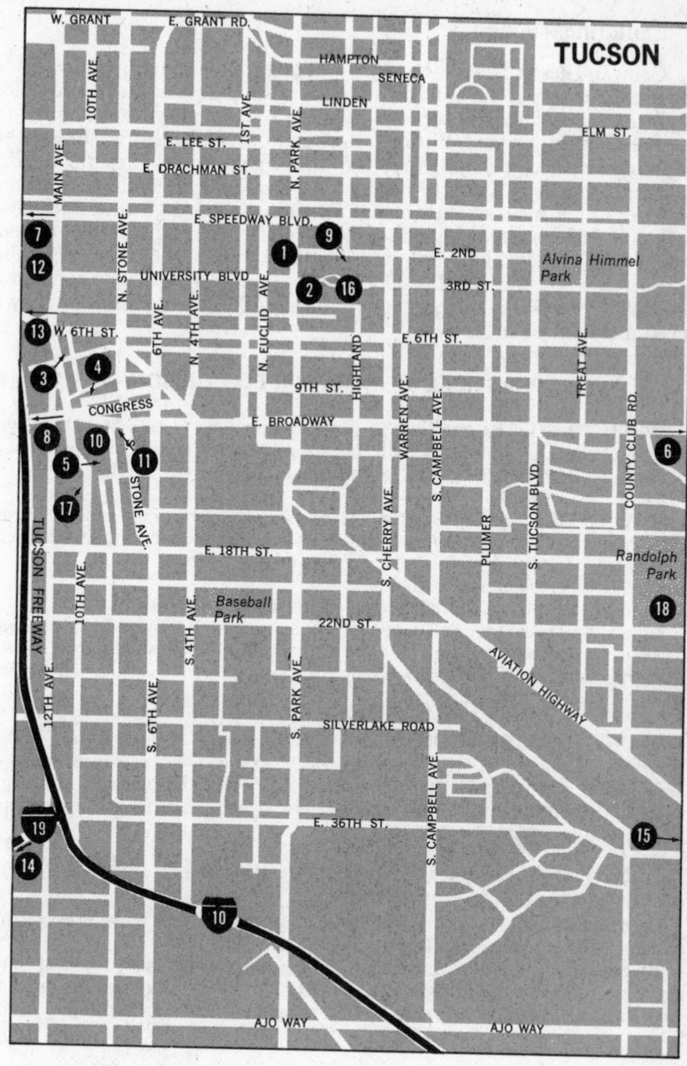

Points of Interest

1) Arizona Historical Society
2) Arizona State Museum
3) Art Center
4) City Hall
5) Community Center
6) Colossal Cave
7) Desert Museum
8) Garden of Gethsemane
9) Mineralogical Museum
10) Music Hall
11) Old Adobe
12) Old Tucson
13) Pima College
14) San Xavier Mission
15) Tucson Botanical Gardens
16) University of Arizona
17) Wishing Well
18) Zoo

Exploring Tucson

Central Tucson is best seen by a walking tour beginning on W. Paseo Redondo in La Placita Village, a cluster of shops, restaurants, and offices built in the Old Pueblo section. Maps and information can be obtained at the Convention and Visitor's Bureau to several historic sites within walking distance, including the site of the original walled presidio, historic homes of pioneers, the Art Museum, and the Mexican Heritage Museum. Two or three blocks south of the Presidio is St. Augustine Cathedral, begun in 1896, an adobe building modeled after the cathedral in Queretaro, Mexico. The walking tour ends at the Community Center, which has a sports arena, concert hall, and a convention center. Tucson's population of around 600,000 is spread out over nearly 500 square miles, so you will need a car to see most of it.

PRACTICAL INFORMATION FOR TUCSON

WHEN TO GO. The season in Tucson is winter, from Oct. to May, but if you don't mind heat, summer is all right too. At a 2,410-ft. elevation, with mountains nearby, and with little humidity, the heat is not oppressive.

HOW TO GET THERE. By plane. *Tucson International Airport* is six mi. south of downtown, and is served by most major airlines, and connects with several Mexican flights.

By bus. *Greyhound* serves Tucson.

By train. Served by *Amtrak* whose toll free number is 800–872–7245.

By car. I-10 goes through Tucson, turning northwest to Phoenix, 111 mi. away, where it connects with I-17 and other major highways. I-19 goes south from Tucson to the Mexican border at Nogales, 63 mi. Numerous car rental agencies have offices in Tucson, many at the airport.

TOURIST INFORMATION. *Tucson Convention and Visitors Bureau,* 130 S. Scott Ave., Tucson, AZ 85701 (602–624–1889). *Arizona Office of Tourism,* 110 W. Washington, Phoenix, AZ 85007 (602–542–0687). Watch for blue and white signs along I-10, indicating state information centers, a good source for information and brochures.

HOW TO GET AROUND. By taxi. *Allstate Cab Co.* (881–2227); *Yellow Cab* (624–6611); *Checker Cab* (623–1133).

By bus. City buses cover the metropolitan area. Fare is 60 cents; exact change required. Passes available to seniors and students. Call 792–9222.

By car. You will need a car to see the area. All major and many local car rental agencies are located here. Tucson is laid out in an easy grid system for the most part. Parking is not difficult except downtown and university areas during working hours.

PARKS AND RECREATION SITES. Santa Catalina Mountains in Coronado National Forest are a mountain playground in Tucson's back yard. Skiing on Mt. Lemmon, 9,157 ft. high, and other winter activities offer a recreational option not found at many southern desert cities. The rest of the year, hiking, picnicking, and nature study can be enjoyed. **Sabino Canyon,** also in the Santa Catalinas, but farther south and closer to town, is a year-round recreation area for picnicking, hiking, bird-watching, an aerial tram. Sabino Canyon Shuttle (749–2861) runs regular tours to the area.

Colossal Cave (791–7677), 20 mi. southeast in the Rincon Mountains, a large cave of limestone formations. Open Oct. through Mar., 9 A.M.–5 P.M., Sun. until 6 P.M. Apr. through Sept., 8 A.M.–6 P.M., Sun. until 7 P.M. Guided tours, admission. **Old Tucson** in Tucson Mtn. Park (883–0100), famous location for hundreds of western movies, 12 mi. west of town. Live gunfights, entertainment, tours, restaurants, shops; open 9 A.M.–5 P.M. daily.

Reid Park Zoo, Randolph Way and E. 22nd St. (791–3170), animals from around the world, exotic and familiar, well displayed in natural settings. Adults, $2; children, 50 cents. Winter hours, 9:30 A.M.–5 P.M. Summer hours, 8 A.M.–6 P.M. weekdays, till 6 P.M. Fri.–Sun.

Saguaro National Monument (296–8576), 17 mi. west of town, preserves outstanding examples of the stately saguaro cactus, the blossom of which is Arizona's state flower. Saguaro grows in only two states. Hiking trails and picnic tables. Free.

Tucson Botanical Gardens, 2150 N. Alvernon Way (326–9255), landscaped with desert plants and all familiar greenhouse plants, tropical gardens. Mon.–Fri., 9 A.M.–4 P.M. Sat., 10 A.M.–4 P.M. Sun., noon–4 P.M. Call for summer and holiday hours. Admission.

PARTICIPANT SPORTS. Golf. A popular winter activity, Tucson has four municipal courses. All have putting greens, driving ranges, electric and pull carts. For tee times and information, call 791–4336. *El Rio,* 1400 W. Speedway, was the original home of the Tucson Open. *Fred Enke,* 8500 E. Irvington Rd., a new and challenging course, large greens, semi-arid limited turf course. Grass on tees only. *Randolph North and Randolph South,* 702 S. Alvernon Way, includes two 18-hole courses. Longest in city, scenic, many trees, lush fairways. *Silverbell,* 3600 N. Silverbell Rd., near Santa Cruz River, has nine lakes, big, grassy fairways. For a complete list of golf courses, tennis courts and stables, write Tucson Convention and Visitors Bureau, 130 S. Scott Ave., Tucson, AZ 85701.

Skiing. *Mt. Lemmon Ski Valley,* 35 mi. north of downtown, is the southern-most ski area in North America. Season lasts from late Dec. through Mar.; facilities include ski school, rentals, tram, three lifts, restaurant, snack bar. Snow averages about 150 in. a year. Open in summer for chair lift, mountain hiking.

Tennis. *Randolph Tennis Center,* 100 S. Randolph Way, 24 courts, most lighted for night playing, municipally owned, small fee.

Horseback riding. *Pusch Ridge Stables,* 11220 N. Oracle, trail rides, hayrides, pack trips into Santa Catalinas. *Tucson Mountain Stables,* 6501 W. Ina Rd, guided rides in Tucson Mtns. and Saguaro National Monument.

HISTORIC SITES. Fort Lowell Park and Museum, Craycroft & Ft. Lowell Rds., preserves ruins of original cavalry post. **Fremont House,** 151 S. Granada Av., built in 1856 for John C. Fremont, famous military governor of Arizona. Open Wed.–Sat., part of Walking Tour of Tucson. Free. **Mission San Xavier del Bac,** (294–2624), 10 mi. south, a historic landmark. Mission established in 1691 by Fr. Kino, building completed a hundred years later, a combination of Moorish, Byzantine, Mexican, and Indian architecture. Active parish church of Papago Indians. **Tubac,** now a state park, site of oldest European settlement in Arizona. Established as Spanish presidio in 1752. Arts and crafts center, art colony. About 40 mi. south of town. Open daily except Christmas. Admission. **Tumacacori,** about 45 mi. south of town is another Spanish mission, founded in 1691 by Fr. Kino. Now a national monument, but much is gone. Open daily except Christmas. Admission $3 per car.

MUSEUMS. Tucson Museum, 949 E. 2nd St., has historical exhibits. **Arizona-Sonora Desert Museum,** 14 mi. west of town (883–1380), a living museum and zoo of native flora and fauna. Open winter, 8:30 A.M.–5 P.M.; summer 7:30 A.M.–6 P.M. Adults, $6; children, $1. **Arizona State Museum,** U of A campus. Prehistoric Indian culture, contemporary and changing exhibits. 9 A.M.–5 P.M., Mon.–Sat.; 2–5 P.M., Sun. Closed major holidays. Free. **De Grazia Gallery and Museum,** 6300 N. Swan Rd. (299–9191). Tucson's most famous artist has originals on exhibit depicting historic people and legends. Adobe construction studio. 10 A.M.–4 P.M., closed major holidays. Grounds and gallery tours. Free.

Flandrau Planetarium, U of A campus (621–4515). 16-in. telescope. Free admission to exhibit halls, fee for shows. Mon.–Fri., 10 A.M.–5 P.M.; Tues.–Sat., 7–9 P.M.; Sat. and Sun., 1–5 P.M. **Kitt Peak National Observatory,** 56 mi. southwest of town, part of the National Optical Astronomy Observatories. This is the world's largest astronomical facility. For tour information, call 620–5350. Visitor Center and three telescopes open to the public, 10 A.M.–4 P.M. daily except Dec. 24 and 25. Free.

Mexican Heritage Museum (La Casa Cordova), 173 N. Meyer Av., an old adobe home restored by Junior League, using traditional materials and styles. 10 A.M.–5 P.M., Tues.–Sat.; 1–5 P.M., Sun. Free.

Tucson Museum of Art, 140 N. Main Ave. (624–2333), contemporary and traditional art, sculpture garden. 10 A.M.–6 P.M., Tues.–Sat.; 1–5 P.M., Sun. Adults, $2; children, $1.

University Museum of Art, U of A campus (621–7567), art from middle ages through contemporary. Seasonal hours. Free.

ARTS AND ENTERTAINMENT. Music. *Arizona Opera Co.,* 3501 N. Mountain Ave. (293–4336). Arizona's only resident opera company. Oct.–Mar. Four performances. *Tucson Symphony Orchestra,* 443 S. Stone Av. (792–9155). Three series of concerts include classics, pops, and family entertainment, Oct.–May.

Stage. *Arizona Theatre Co.,* 56 W. Congress (622–2823). State's only professional resident company. Performances Tues.–Sun., Nov.–mid-May, at Leo Rich Theatre. Admission: $10.50–$19.50.

Simon Peter Easter Pageant of Tucson, Box 42103 (327–5560). Musical drama of life of Christ, Community Center Music Hall, free. Full orchestra.

ACCOMMODATIONS. Tucson is best known for its guest ranches, but there is a wide choice in motels, hotels, resort hotels with country club amenities, small lodges, and mobile home and trailer parks. The Tucson Visitors Guide, published by the C & VB, 130 S. Scott Ave., 85701, lists dozens. These listed here are by price category: *Super Deluxe,* $150 and up; *Deluxe,* $100–$150; *Expensive,* $80–$100; *Moderate,* $60–$80; *Inexpensive,* under $60.

Super Deluxe

Lazy K Bar Guest Ranch. 8401 N. Scenic Dr., Tucson, AZ 85743 (744–3050). Tennis, riding; situated at base of Tucson Mountains.

Loews Ventana Canyon Resort. 7000 N. Resort Dr., Tucson, AZ 85715 (299–2020). Golf, tennis, health club, lounge, dining room, and three restaurants.

Sheraton Tucson El Conquistador Golf & Tennis Resort. 10000 N. Oracle Rd., Tucson, AZ 85704 (742–7000). Golf, tennis, pools, riding, three restaurants, lounges, Sun. brunch.

Tanque Verde Guest Ranch. Rte. 8, Box 66, Tucson, AZ 85748 (296–6275). Gourmet dining, tennis, spa, open all year. American plan.

Westin La Paloma. 3800 E. Sunrise Dr., Tucson, AZ 85718 (742–6000). Tennis, golf course, restaurants, lounges, spa.

Deluxe

Arizona Inn. 2200 E. Elm St, Tucson, AZ 85719 (325–1541). Historic landmark, Spanish design and decor, relaxed ambiance, listed as one of the best hotels in world. Full dining room service, lounge, entertainment, Sun. brunch.

Doubletree Hotel. 445 S. Alvernon Way, Tucson, AZ 85711 (881–4200). Central location, next to golf and tennis. Two restaurants, bar.

Westward Look Resort. 245 E. Ina Rd. (297–1151). On 84 acres of high desert, in Catalina foothills. Great views, 4-star restaurant.

Expensive

Best Western Aztec Inn. 102 N. Alvernon Way, Tucson, AZ 85711 (795–0330). Midtown, large pool, dining room, lounge.

Days Inn Downtown. 88 E. Broadway, Tucson, AZ 85701 (622–4000). Historic downtown landmark, pool, golf, tennis, restaurant, lounge.

Embassy Suites. 5335 E. Broadway, Tucson, AZ 85711 (745–2700). All suites with kitchen. Rates include breakfast and cocktails.

Moderate

Best Western Tucson InnSuites. 6201 N. Oracle Rd., Tucson, AZ 85704 (297–8111). All suites, lighted tennis, coffee shop adjacent.

Tanque Verde Inn. 7007 E. Tanque Verde Rd., Tucson, AZ 85715 (298–2300). Heart of restaurant and entertainment area. Complimentary cocktails each evening. Movies in room.

Inexpensive

Desert Inn. 1 N. Freeway, Tucson, AZ 85745 (624–8151). Full service hotel, pool, 24-hour coffee shop, weekend entertainment.

Vista del Sol Motel & Trailer Park. 1458 W. Miracle Mile, Tucson, AZ 85705 (293–9270). Off I-10. Walking distance to bus, restaurants, shopping.

Wayward Winds Lodge. 707 W. Miracle Mile, Tucson, AZ 85705 (791–7526). Friendly, family atmosphere. Kitchens, garden setting.

RESTAURANTS. Though Tucson gets kudos for Mexican food, you can also find restaurants featuring almost all kinds of ethnic foods, American, Continental and gourmet cuisine. All listed here accept credit cards. All major hotels, resorts, and motels have restaurants on the premises, others are within easy walking distance. The following are listed by price category: *Deluxe,* $22 and up; *Expensive,* $16–$22; *Moderate,* $10–$16; *Inexpensive,* under $10. Price does not include tax, tip or alcohol.

Deluxe

Charles Restaurant. 6400 E. El Dorado Circle (296–7173). Distinctive gourmet food, is offered in this picturesque stone mansion. L, D, reservations required.

Janos Restaurant. 150 N. Main, 884–9426. In historic district, in landmark building. Nouvelle cuisine. L, D, reservations required.

Penelope's. 3619 E. Speedway (325–5080). Country French cuisine. Menu changes weekly. Closed Mon. L, D, reservations required.

The Tack Room. 2800 N. Sabino Canyon Rd. (722–2800). Tuxedoed waiters. Gourmet food. Prix fixe dinners. D, reservations required.

Expensive

Las Campanas de las Catalinas. 6440 N. Campbell Ave. (299–1771). Elegant setting with city view.

Jerome's. 6958 E. Tanque Verde Rd. (721–0311). Fresh fish and regional cuisine, featuring Creole and Cajun. L, D, Closed Mon.

Silver Saddle Steakhouse & Lounge. I-10 and 4th Ave. (622–6253). Mesquite-broiled steak, ribs, chicken, seafood. L, D.

Moderate

Cafe Magritte. 254 E. Congress St. (884–8004). This stylish, informal downtown cafe serves innovative dishes. L, D.

El Charro. 311 N. Court Ave. (622–5465). Tucson's oldest Mexican restaurant, in historic home, downtown. Patio dining. L, D.

Pinnacle Peak Steakhouse. 6541 E. Tanque Verde Rd. (296–0911). Mesquite-broiled cowboy steak. D only, daily; full bar.

Triple C Ranch. 8900 W. Bopp Rd. (883–2333). Authentic chuckwagon dinners are served here with western entertainment. D; closed Sun., Mon.

Inexpensive

El Adobe. 40 W. Broadway (791–7458). Authentic Mexican food served in garden patio or adobe dining rooms. In historic district. L, D;

Good Earth Restaurant & Bakery. 6366 E. Broadway (745–6600). Fresh fish, American menu. Fresh pastries. Beer and wine. B, L, D.

Millie's West Pancake Haus. 6530 E. Tanque Verde Rd. (298–4250). Pancakes, blintzes, Belgian waffles, omelets.

SANTA FE

The word "unique," diluted by overuse, really does apply to Santa Fe. There is no other city like it, not even in New Mexico. It appeals to all the senses: brilliant sunlight in high, cool mountain air; the smell of burn-

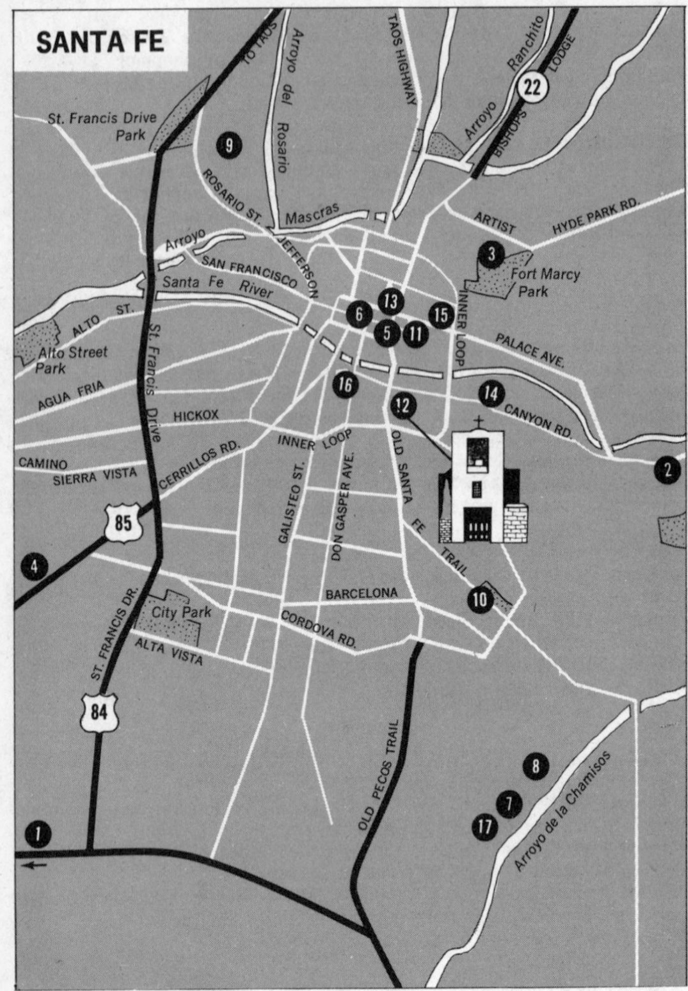

Points of Interest

1) College of Santa Fe
2) Cristo Rey Church
3) Fort Marcy Park
4) Institute of American Indian Arts
5) La Fonda Hotel
6) Museum of Fine Arts
7) Museum of International Folk Art
8) Museum of Indian Art and Culture
9) National Cemetery
10) Old Santa Fe Trail
11) St. Francis Cathedral
12) San Miguel Mission
13) Santa Fe Plaza
14) Santa Fe River State Park
15) Sena Plaza
16) State Capitol
17) Wheelwright Museum

ing piñon wafting over snowy streets; the taste of piquant food; flat-roofed architecture in golden earth tones on winding, secluded streets. The musical and artistic environment is as fine as can be found in the nation. Languages from all over the world are heard on the streets, blending with lilting Spanish and guttural, breathy Indian languages.

Steeped in history, Santa Fe rests like an aging queen, secure in her position, confident of her ability to charm. In 1610 Spanish officials moved the provincial capital to Santa Fe from San Juan Indian Pueblo, where it had been established in 1598, a decade earlier than the English settlement at Jamestown and 22 years before the Pilgrims landed at Plymouth Rock. They built a long adobe building on the north side of the plaza which served as the seat of government until 1913, when it became part of the state museum system. This old building has seen much history: the Pueblo Revolt in 1680 when every Spaniard was killed or driven out; the reconquest 12 years later by a Spanish nobleman; the government change from Spanish to Mexican in 1822 and then to American in 1846. It saw great caravans of covered wagons after crossing the Santa Fe Trail sweep into town and circle the plaza with a flourish. Santa Fe is a city of romance, mystery, and power.

Cheerful cynics, Santafeans have maintained both traditions and eccentricities in the face of economic, political, and social pressures to conform with the rest of the country. They grant visitors or residents the right to privacy and freedom.

The Historic Central Area

With a population of 52,000, Santa Fe is a fairly compact city. It is clustered around the old plaza portion of the city and along the old Santa Fe Trail, and it should be explored on foot.

On any sunny day in the plaza, you may see youngsters break dancing, oldsters feeding pigeons, artists sketching patrons, Indians selling jewelry, and people hurrying to work. Three sides of the plaza are lined with shops, galleries, stores, and restaurants, while on the north side is the Palace of Governors, oldest seat of government in the U.S. Along its covered portal, Pueblo Indians spread jewelry and crafts on colorful squares of cloth. Across from the southeast corner of the plaza is La Fonda, the last of several inns that have marked the end of the Santa Fe Trail since 1822. Across from the opposite corner is the Museum of Fine Arts, part of the state museum system. Built in 1919, extensively enlarged and remodeled in 1982, the building is a classic example of Pueblo architecture at its best, with massive adobe walls, viga ceilings, carved corbels, enclosed patios, flowing horizontal lines, and earth tones. It houses both permanent and changing exhibits of paintings by New Mexico's most respected and recognized artists, living and dead. St. Francis Auditorium in the west end of the building presents concerts throughout the year.

A block east of the Plaza on San Francisco Street is St. Francis Cathedral, begun in 1869 by Archbishop Jean Baptiste Lamy, made famous by Willa Cather's novel, *Death Comes for the Archbishop.* He built it in Romanesque style of native stone to remind him of churches in his native France. If it looks unfinished to you, it is. The two 160-foot stone steeples he planned were never added.

A block east of the plaza on Palace Avenue is Sena Plaza, built in 1831 as a private residence. It is a large adobe complex flush with the street, enclosing a private courtyard. Shops and restaurants of considerable interest are housed in the old adobe home.

Old Santa Fe Trail. The street follows almost exactly the old trail, which ended at La Fonda on the plaza. A block south of La Fonda is Loretto Chapel, built by the Sisters of Loretto in 1878 and based on Sainte-Chapelle in Paris. It was the first gothic structure west of the Mississippi.

A beautiful hand-carved stairway leading to the choir loft was believed by the sisters to be of miraculous origin, and the rose window on the west side is a jewel.

A little farther up Old Santa Fe Trail is San Miguel Mission, built in 1610, destroyed in 1680 in the Pueblo Revolt, and rebuilt in 1710. To the side of the church is The Oldest House in America, which it may or may not be. It was built in 1740 of materials and in the style of colonial New Mexico. These buildings are owned by the church and are open to the public. Old Santa Fe Trail continues another block to the State Capitol Complex. The Capitol itself is built in the shape of the Indian Zia (sun) symbol. The street continues out of town and around the southern spur of the Rocky Mountains.

East of the Capitol, off Paseo de Peralta, is *Canyon Road,* one of the most picturesque streets in the U.S. It follows an old Indian trail that came from the mountains along the banks of Santa Fe Creek. Since 1916, when Santa Fe became established as an art colony, this is where most of the artists lived. It is a street of galleries, studios, shops, and restaurants. At the east end of the street is El Cristo Rey Church, built in the 1940s, the largest adobe pueblo-style church in existence. Epicures should note that *Holiday* magazine considers The Compound at 653 Canyon Road one of the hundred most distinguished restaurants in the U.S.

PRACTICAL INFORMATION FOR SANTA FE

WHEN TO GO. All seasons are good in Santa Fe. At Santa Fe's 7,000-ft. elevation at the base of the Sangre de Cristo Mountains, summers are delightful. Skiing is excellent at several ski areas in the vicinity from Thanksgiving to Easter most years.

HOW TO GET THERE. Santa Fe is the only state capital in the country without jet or train service, and that's the way Santa Feans want to keep it. You can fly your own plane into Santa Fe or fly into Albuquerque on almost any major line.

By car. Santa Fe is on I-25 and U.S. 84–285. Rental cars available at Albuquerque Airport, 62 mi. south.

By bus. *Shuttlejack* runs regular service every two hours from Albuquerque Airport to Santa Fe and return, picking up passengers in Santa Fe at Hilton Inn or Inn at Loretto. Fare is $15 one way; call 243–3244 in Albuquerque, 982–4311 in Santa Fe. *Greyhound* provides service to Santa Fe. The terminal is at 858 St. Michael Dr., 2 mi. from downtown; call 471–0008.

By train. *Amtrak's* closest stop is Lamy, 14 mi. away. The Lamy Shuttle will transport passengers to most hotels and motels in Santa Fe. Fare is $9 one way, reservations required. Call 982–8829.

HOW TO GET AROUND. You'll need a car, as there is no public transportation. There are two cab companies: *Capital City Cab* (988–2090) and *Village Taxi* (982–9990). Rental car companies: *Avis* (982–4361), *Hertz* (982–1844), and *Budget* (984–8028). Street parking is difficult to find in downtown, so the best bet is one of 3 close-in municipal lots.

TOURIST INFORMATION. *Santa Fe Convention & Visitors Bureau,* Box 909, Santa Fe, NM 87504 (800–528–5369). *Santa Fe Chamber of Commerce,* 200 W. Marcy, Santa Fe, NM 87501 (983–7317). *N.M. Tourism Division,* Joseph M. Montoya Bldg., 1100 St. Francis Dr., Santa Fe, NM 87503. Every Fri. the local paper publishes a good list of the coming week's activities. Write: *The New Mexican,* 202 E. Marcy St., Santa Fe, NM 87501. The Newsstand at La Fonda Hotel is a good source of guides and books on the area.

TOURS. *Santa Fe Detours,* La Fonda Hotel, offers a short and a long walking tour around plaza and central area 983–6565. *Art Tours of Santa Fe,* 301-B E. Alameda, Santa Fe, NM 87501 (988–3527). *Discover Santa Fe,* Box 2847, Santa Fe,

NM 87504 (982–4979), and *Rocky Mountain Tours,* 102 W. San Francisco St., Santa Fe, NM 87501 (984–1684), offer a variety of group tours around the city.

NATIONAL AND STATE PARKS. *Santa Fe River State Park* follows 3 blocks of the stream as it runs through downtown. Picnic tables and benches. *Hyde Memorial State Park,* 350 acres in the mountains, surrounded by Santa Fe National Forest, is open all year for picnicking and camping with hookups. $5. Used as base camp for backpack trips. *Santa Fe National Forest* includes the Sangre de Cristo Mountains which come almost to the city limits. Hiking, backpacking, picnicking, fall-color watching, fishing, and skiing are all available in season.

SKIING. *Santa Fe Ski Area,* 1210 Luisa St., Suite 10, Santa Fe, NM 87501 (982–4429). For current ski conditions, call 983–9155. It lies 17 mi. from Santa Fe, in the Santa Fe National Forest. Shuttle buses run from several hotels to the ski area. Area has 36 runs, 40% advanced. Base elevation is 10,200 ft., rising to 12,000. Four chairlifts, 3 surface lifts, more than 100 instructors, rentals, children rates, restaurant, bar. *Sipapu Ski Area,* Rte. 29, Vadito, NM 87579 (587–2240), halfway to Taos. Mostly family area, cross-country, 50% intermediate, 1 triple chair, 2 Pomas, lodging, restaurant, lounge.

WATER SPORTS. Cochiti Lake, 25 mi. southwest, water skiing, wind surfing, fishing. White water rafting is great on the Rio Grande west of Santa Fe where it goes through deep volcanic gorges, May–July. *New Wave Rafting Co.,* Rte. 5, Box 302-A, Santa Fe, NM 87501 (984–1444 summer, 455–2633 offseason); *Rio Bravo River Tours,* 1412 Cerrillos Rd., Santa Fe, NM 87501 (988–1153 or 800–451–0708); *Santa Fe Detours,* La Fonda Hotel lobby, Santa Fe, NM 87501 (983–6565, 800–DETOURS).

MUSEUMS. The following four museums are part of the State Museum System. For information about any contact Museum of N.M., Box 2087, Santa Fe, NM 87504 (827–6460). **Museum of Fine Art,** Palace Ave. off northwest corner of Plaza. The building is a classic example of fine pueblo architecture. Permanent and changing exhibits of the best New Mexican artists, photographers. **Museum of International Folk Art,** on Camino Lejo, south part of town. Largest collection of folk art in the world, dolls, toys, costumes, jewelry, arts and crafts 1800 to present. **Palace of the Governors,** on the plaza. Oldest continuously used public building in U.S. Built 1610. Historic exhibits, prehistoric Indian through Territorial days. **Museum of Indian Art and Culture,** extensive exhibits on southwestern Indian culture, especially New Mexico. On Camino Lejo next to Folk Art Museum (827–8941). All museums are open 10 A.M.–5 P.M. daily, closed major holidays and Mon. during Jan. and Feb. Admission (each museum) adults, $3.50; under 16, free. A two-day pass is $6.

El Rancho de las Golondrinas, in village of Cienega, 7 mi. southwest, off I-25. 400-acre site with reconstructed Spanish colonial farm, hacienda, gristmill, morada. Costumed villagers at Spring and Fall Fiesta. Open May–Oct. Admission. Write Rte. 14, Box 214, Santa Fe, NM 87501, or call 471–2261.

Wheelwright Museum of the American Indian. 704 Camino Lejo, Santa Fe, NM 87505 (982–4636). Extensive exhibits of southwest Indian arts and crafts, traditional and contemporary. Old West Trading Post, good quality merchandise. Privately endowed, contributions. Open daily, closed Mon. except in summer.

GALLERIES. Los Cinco Pintores (five painters) established Santa Fe as an art colony in 1916, and it has achieved international status. The international avant-garde came a few years later, bringing such artists as Georgia O'Keeffe and Andrew Dasburg to Santa Fe and Taos. The number of resident artists has continued to grow steadily, and many of them live, work, and exhibit in Santa Fe. Well over a hundred galleries are in Santa Fe—on the plaza, on Canyon Rd., and on any street in town. Most feature Native American and Southwestern paintings, pottery, baskets, weavings, and other crafts.

ARTS AND ENTERTAINMENT. Music. *Santa Fe Opera,* Box 2408, Santa Fe, NM 87504 (982–3855). Season lasts July–Aug. Located 7 mi. north on U.S. 84–285 in a beautiful building partially open to the sky. It features old favorites with usually one premiere of an unknown opera each season. Performing more than 30 years, the opera has achieved international recognition. If coming to Santa Fe during opera season, make hotel reservations 6 months in advance. *Santa Fe Chamber Music Festival,* Box 853, Santa Fe, NM 87504. Six concerts in July, Aug. Mostly New York and European artists who spend the summer in Santa Fe. Concerts in St. Francis Aud., Museum of Fine Art. Daily rehearsals there are free to the public. *Orchestra of Santa Fe,* winter season, write Box 2091, Santa Fe, NM 87504 (988–4640). Festivals in Feb. are sponsored by Orchestra of Santa Fe with guest artist.

Stage. A variety of theater groups and dance companies schedule seasonal and year-round performances. For an up-to-date events calendar, contact *Santa Fe Convention and Visitors Bureau,* Box 909, Santa Fe, NM 87504 (800–528–5369).

ACCOMMODATIONS. Advance reservations should be made for summer vacations in Santa Fe. Weekends during the height of the ski season (Dec.–Mar.) may also be full. Occupancy varies greatly according to local activity, such as legislative sessions in Feb. and Mar., Indian Market in Aug., and the opera. Most larger hotels are in the downtown historic district, within 6 or 8 blocks of the Plaza, shops, restaurants, galleries and museums. More inexpensive motels are on Cerrillos Rd. (Hwy. 85) going south to Albuquerque. This partial list is arranged by price category: *Super Deluxe,* $150 and up; *Deluxe,* $100–$150; *Expensive,* $80–$100; *Moderate,* $60–$80.

Super Deluxe

Bishop's Lodge. Box 2367, Santa Fe, NM 87501 (505–983–6377). This is a gracious, well established resort 3 mi. north of town in wooded foothills. Families, repeat clientele. Dining room, outdoor activities. Quiet, genteel. Closed Nov. thru Mar.

El Dorado. 309 W. San Francisco St., Santa Fe, NM 87501 (505–988–4455). Santa Fe's newest and biggest, 5 stories, opened 1986. Eclectic Southwestern decor, original art, two dining rooms, one deli, small pool and hot tub on roof—spectacular views of city and mountains. Some suites with fireplaces.

Picacho Plaza Hotel. 750 N. St. Francis Dr., Santa Fe, NM 87501 (505–982–5591). Two mi. north of Plaza. Spacious grounds, Spanish architecture, dining rooms, views are all available here.

Rancho Encantado. Rte. 4, Box 57C, Santa Fe, NM 87501 (505–982–3537). Eight mi. north, in sunny piñon-juniper hills, spacious, pueblo-style cabanas and main lodge. Dining room, outdoor activities, privacy. Often the choice of celebrities.

Deluxe

Best Western Inn at Loretto. 211 Old Santa Fe Trail, Santa Fe, NM 87501 (505–988–5531 or 800–528–1234). This four-story building resembles a Taos Pueblo. Many artistic touches in decor. Named for and situated next to Loretto Chapel of the Miraculous Stairway. Dining room, coffee shop, galleries, shops.

Hilton Inn. 100 Sandoval St., Santa Fe, NM 87501 (505–988–2811 or 800–336–3676). Three-story building, wrought iron, beamed ceiling, tile add Southwestern flavor to this place. Dining room is in 200-year-old adobe house incorporated in building. Some rooms with mountain view.

Inn of the Governors. 234 Don Gaspar, Santa Fe, NM 87501 (505–982–4333). In the heart of town. Pool, fireplaces, restaurant, lounge.

Expensive

La Fonda. 100 E. San Francisco St., Santa Fe, NM 87501 (505–982–5511). Located in this historic heart of Santa Fe, and sooner or later everyone comes through the lobby of this colorful well-known place. Dining room, coffee shop, shops, galleries, popular lounge.

Moderate

Garrett's Desert Inn. 311 Old Santa Fe Trail, Santa Fe, NM 87501 (505–982–1851). Heated pool, restaurant adjacent

La Posada de Santa Fe. 330 E. Palace Ave., Santa Fe, NM 87501 (505–983–6351). Old estate and grounds adapted to lodge.

Quality Inn. 3011 Cerrillos Rd., Santa Fe, NM 87501 (505–471–1211). Four miles south of Plaza. Comfortable amenities are available at this chain adapted to the mission style.

BED AND BREAKFAST INNS. Several are in Santa Fe, homey and elegant. Contact Santa Fe Convention and Visitors Bureau, Box 909, Santa Fe, NM 87504 (800–528–5369).

RESTAURANTS. They run the gamut from nouvelle cuisine to native. Try some real New Mexican food—vastly different from "Mexican" and light-years away from "Tex-Mex." All listed here accept credit cards unless noted; liquor will be noted as FL (full license) or LL (beer and/or wine). Santa Fe is an eating-out place—part of the fun of discovering the city. Price ranges are: *Expensive,* over $18; *Moderate,* $10–$18; *Inexpensive,* under $10. Does not include tax, tip, or alcohol.

Expensive

The Compound. 653 Canyon Rd. (982–4353). Best known in Santa Fe, winner of awards. Continental menu. Daily specials, extensive wine list. Superbly designed old adobe bldg. L, D. FL. Closed Mon. Reservations.

Julian's. 221 Shelby (988–2355). Fresh ingredients are used to prepare Italian specialties here. Reservations strongly suggested on weekends. L, D, daily. FL.

The Palace. 142 W. Palace Ave. (982–9891). Continental cuisine. L, D, FL. Closed Sun.

Moderate

La Casa Sena. 123 E. Palace Ave. (988–9232). New Mexican and Continental cuisine. B, L, D, and serves snacks throughout the day. Singing staff entertain in the Cantina.

Legal Tender. In Lamy, near Amtrak depot (982–8425). Steaks and seafood are featured in this 1881 building. D. Closed Mon.

La Tertulia. 416 Agua Fria (988–2769). In restored convent, native New Mexican food. L, D. FL. Closed Mon.

Pink Adobe. 406 Old Santa Fe Trail (983–7712). Charming old favorite. Continental, seafood and Mexican entrées. L, D. FL.

Inexpensive

The Shed. 113½ Palace Ave. (982–9030). L only, no reservations. Always full. Superb New Mexican food, desserts. No credit cards.

Tecolote Cafe. 1203 Cerrillos Rd. (988–1362). Funky ambience, most popular with locals for breakfast. B, L. Closed Mon., Tues.

ALBUQUERQUE

Albuquerque is one of the oldest cities in the U.S., yet it exudes energy and youth. Around 400,000 people, a third of the state's population, live here. It is the transportation and business center of the state. Like most of the Southwest, Albuquerque has seen rapid growth since World War II. The climate is invigorating and pleasant, and so are its people. Official elevation at the airport is 5,312 feet, but it varies within the city from 4,800 to 6,500 feet.

Albuquerque was founded in 1706 as a farming community on the Rio Grande. A small adobe chapel was built on one side of a plaza surrounded by small adobe homes on the others. Old Town is still here, healthy and active, an island of the past surrounded by a sea of city that flowed around it years ago.

World War II brought military bases and related research and development industries, and the population exploded ten times over in 40 years,

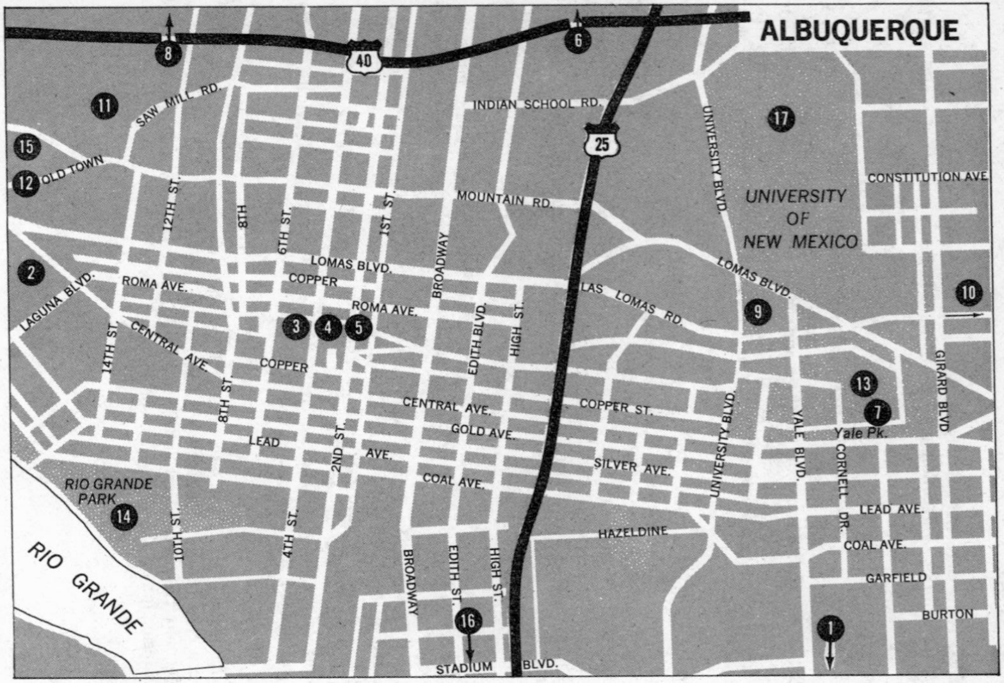

ALBUQUERQUE

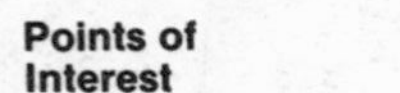

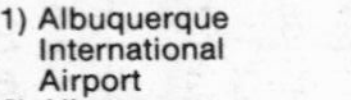

Points of Interest

1) Albuquerque International Airport
2) Albuquerque Little Theater
3) City Hall
4) Civic Plaza
5) Convention Center
6) Coronado State Park
7) Fine Arts Museum
8) Indian Pueblo Cultural Center
9) Maxwell Museum of Anthropology
10) New Mexico State Fairgrounds
11) Old Town
12) Plaza
13) Popejoy Hall
14) Rio Grande Zoo
15) San Felipe de Neri Church
16) University Arena
17) University of New Mexico

but its historic heritage is still very much part of the city's charm and appeal.

Exploring Albuquerque

Old Town Plaza and San Felipe Church are in the same place as in 1706. The Plaza is a grassy park with a bandstand in the middle where things have a way of happening. Wrought iron benches invite you to sit in the sun, whittle, visit, or people-watch. San Felipe Church is on the north side of the Plaza, and studios, galleries, specialty shops, and restaurants extend one or two blocks in each direction. The Albuquerque Museum is a block to the east, and across the street from it on Mountain Road is the New Mexico Museum of Natural History. Old Town is made for leisurely walking and browsing.

Civic Plaza is the heart of downtown, 20 blocks east of Old Town. It is often filled during the week with people from offices, eating lunch or listening to an impromptu concert. South from Civic Plaza one block on 4th Street is Crossroads Mall, an inviting area of trees, benches, and flowers. It extends to Central Avenue, old U.S. 66, the main street of America until it was superseded by I-40. The Convention Center is on one side of Civic Plaza, municipal buildings, shopping malls, hotels, and office buildings on the others.

Twenty blocks east of downtown is the University of New Mexico, the cultural heart of the city with concerts, plays, lectures, museums, and galleries, all open to the public. Architecturally, the UNM campus shows the evolution and adaptability of Pueblo architecture from the traditional features of buttressed corners, protruding vigas, portals, and flowing, horizontal lines to modern adaptations with angular lines and glass, but which still blend into the landscape of mesas and earth tones.

Continuing east, as the city has grown, about five miles to Louisiana Boulevard are Albuquerque's two largest shopping centers, Coronado and Winrock, just north of I-40. Most of the new high-rise office buildings, luxury hotels, restaurants, and night clubs are in this area.

Close against Albuquerque's eastern city limits are the Sandia Mountains and Cibola National Forest. The side of the mountains facing the city is steep and rugged, a wall of granite that changes character and color with every change of light. The name, which means "watermelon," was probably taken from the color they turn at sunset. The Sandias affect every aspect of life in Albuquerque. Aesthetically they are a constant source of inspiration and beauty. They are a moderating influence on the climate, blocking the storms that sweep down from Canada across the midwest. They provide miles of hiking trails, nature walks, rock climbing, skiing, snowshoeing, picnicking, and backpacking, within minutes from any part of town. Rising up the western face is Sandia Peak Tram, longest aerial tramway in North America.

PRACTICAL INFORMATION FOR ALBUQUERQUE

WHEN TO GO. Albuquerque is an all-season city, and hotel rates do not usually fluctuate. Winters are generally on the mild side, though storms do strike sometimes. Summers are fine. The sun is hot, but at an altitude of over 5,000 ft. the air is invigorating. Rainfall and humidity are low. Mid-July through Sept. is the rainy season, falling in brief thundershowers. Even on a hot day, nighttime temperatures drop at least 30 degrees Fahrenheit.

HOW TO GET THERE. By plane. Albuquerque is served by most major and several regional carriers. The airport is at the south end of Yale Blvd., 5 mi. from downtown, and about the same, but in the opposite direction, from the uptown district of new hotels, office buildings, shopping centers, restaurants, and night clubs.

By bus. *Greyhound* serves Albuquerque.

By train. The main line of *Amtrak* goes through Albuquerque. The depot is downtown on First St., five blocks from the Convention Center.

By car. I-40 (east–west) and I-25 (north–south) intersect in downtown Albuquerque.

TOURIST INFORMATION. *Albuquerque Convention and Visitors Bureau,* Box 26866, Albuquerque, NM 87125 (243–3696). Free maps to city, guides to attractions, accommodations, restaurants, events, cultural and other attractions. *Chamber of Commerce,* Convention Center, 402 2nd St. NW, Albuquerque, NM 87102 (842–0220), has brochures and information slanted toward moving and business inquiries. For maps and information about the state, contact *N.M. Tourism & Travel Division,* Joseph M. Montoya Bldg., 1100 St. Francis Dr., Santa Fe, NM 87503 (800–545–2040).

HOW TO GET AROUND. By car. I-40 runs east–west. I-25 runs north–south. Except for rush hours, the freeways are the fastest way to get from one part of town to another. Right turns are permitted on red after stopping. School zones are 15 mph when yellow lights are flashing. Residential areas vary from 25 to 35 mph. Many downtown streets are one-way.

Rental cars cost from $30 to $50 per day. All have offices at or near the airport, and most will deliver to hotels–motels. **Cabs** are usually standing at the airport and at major hotels. Fare is around $12 from airport to downtown or midtown hotels.

By bus. City buses serve the airport every 15 minutes, and all other parts of town on varying schedules. Schedule and routes available from drivers, or call *SunTran* at 843–9200.

Most major hotels and motels have **free van service** to and from the airport. **Albuquerque Trolley** operates small motorized trolleys in the midtown–downtown–Old Town area, stopping at major hotels, shopping centers, museums, zoo; call 242–1407 for information.

TOURS. *Walking tour of Old Town,* Wed.–Sun. led by docent from Albuquerque Museum, 2000 Mountain Rd. NW (243–7255). Fee includes museum admission. *Tours of Enchantment* (831–4285) will pick up at hotel for tours of city, state, Indian Pueblos, special balloon rides, tours lasting from half day to several days, beginning at $15. *Jack Allen Tours* (266–9688) and *Okupin Tours* (867–3817) offer personalized tours to major points of interest. Reservations. *Albuquerque Trolley* operates three little motorized trolleys between hotels and shopping centers in the mid-heights to downtown, Old Town, museums, and the zoo. Fare is $1. Ask your hotel or call 242–1407 for routes and stops.

PARKS. Coronado State Monument & Park, 15 mi. north of town on I-25, one mile west of Bernalillo on NM 44 (867–5351), preserves ruins of a large prehistoric Indian pueblo. 9 A.M.–5 P.M. daily, except holidays. Adults, $2; under 16, free. **Indian Petroglyph State Park** on the volcanic escarpment on the west side of town (west of Coors Rd., on Unser Blvd.). Trail up the escarpment leads to hundreds of Indian rock carvings. 8 A.M.–5 P.M. daily except holidays. $2 per car. **Rio Grande Nature Center** 2901 Candelaria Blvd. NW (344–7240). Trails and partially underground building offer close-up view of migratory waterfowl and other birds. 10 A.M.–5 P.M. daily except holidays. 25 cents per person. **Rio Grande Zoological Park,** 903 10th St. SW (843–7413). More than 1,200 animals are well displayed in large, natural settings. Children's petting zoo, picnic tables, snack bar. 9 A.M.–5 P.M. daily, adults, $4; children and seniors, $2.

PARTICIPANT SPORTS. Skiing. *Sandia Peak Ski Area* has 25 runs, 35 percent for beginners, 55 percent intermediate and 10 percent advanced. Season usually lasts from Dec. through Mar. Take Sandia Peak Tram up the west side (north on Tramway Blvd.) and be at the top of the mountains in 20 minutes; or drive around to the base of the runs (east on I-40, north on NM 14) in 45 minutes. Contact 10 Tramway Loop, Albuquerque, NM 87122 (296–9585).

Golf. It is sometimes possible to ski and golf on the same day. There are 11 courses in the city, but we list only the public courses: *Ladera,* 3401 Ladera Dr.

NW (836–4449) has 18 holes, 9-hole executive course, pro shop. *Arroyo del Oso,* 7001 Osuna NE (884–7505) has 18 holes, driving range, putting green, pro shop. *Los Altos,* 9717 Copper Ave. NE (298–1897) has 18 holes, 9 holes, driving range, putting green, pro shop, and restaurant. *Puerto del Sol,* 1600 Girard Blvd. SE (265–5636) has 9 holes, driving range, chipping greens. These are city-owned courses, and charge nonresidents varying greens fees of about $10 (18 holes) and $6 (9 holes). *University of New Mexico South Course,* I-25 to Rio Bravo, east to golf course (277–4546), has 18 holes, three regulation practice holes, putting greens, chipping area. Greens fee $16. Five private golf courses are in the city, most of which have reciprocal arrangements, or sell a guest privilege card.

Tennis. There are a total of 140 public tennis courts, and most are open to the public free of charge. *Albuquerque Tennis Complex* and *Sierra Vista* can be reserved in advance for a small fee (291–6281).

Horseback riding. *Los Amigos Roundup* on the Sandia Indian Reservation (898–8173) offers instruction and can arrange local guides for hayrides, trail rides, and pack trips to various destinations.

MUSEUMS. Albuquerque Museum. 2000 Mountain Rd. N.W., in Old Town (243–7255). Permanent history exhibit covering 400 years of New Mexico history; permanent art exhibits; changing exhibits of art, history, science. Open daily, 9 A.M.–5 P.M. Free admission.

Fine Arts Museum. UNM campus (277–4001). Changing art exhibits, mostly contemporary. Tues.–Fri., 9 A.M.–4 P.M.; Tues., 5–9 P.M.; Sun., 1–4 P.M. Summer hours. Free.

Indian Pueblo Cultural Center. 2501 12th St. N.W. (843–7270). Each of the NM pueblos has a separate exhibit area, with exhibits pertaining to their history, arts, and crafts. Museum contains combined exhibit of pueblo history, executed by the Indians themselves. Gift shop, restaurant. Weekends during the summer various tribes perform dances in the patio which may be photographed. This is a good place to become familiar with pueblo culture. Open Mon.–Sat., 9 A.M.–5:30 P.M. summer (restaurant opens at 7:30 A.M.). Closed Sun., Sept.–Apr. Adults, $2.50; senior citizens, $1.50; students, $1.

Maxwell Museum of Anthropology. UNM campus, Redondo Dr. at Ash St. N.E. (277–4404). Prehistoric and historic Indian culture exhibits, changing exhibits of contemporary anthropological interest. Gift shop. Mon.–Fri., 9 A.M.–4 P.M. Sat. 10 A.M.–4 P.M. Closed Sun. Free.

National Atomic Museum. Kirtland AFB, on Wyoming Blvd. (844–8443). Hardware from atomic weapons, energy, fuels. 9–5 daily; closed holidays. Free.

New Mexico Museum of Natural History. 1801 Mountain Rd. N.W. (841–8837). Opened in 1986, first major natural history museum built in this century anywhere in U.S. Exhibits cover geology, paleontology, flora, and fauna from pre-Cambrian to Pleistocene. 9 A.M.–5 P.M. daily, closed Christmas. $4, adults; $3, ages 12 to 16; $1, ages 3–11. A new feature is the in-house Dynamax movie theater, with changing programs. $7, adults; $3, under 16.

ARTS AND ENTERTAINMENT. Music. *The New Mexico Symphony Orchestra* is headquartered in Albuquerque. Concerts, often featuring world famous artists, are at Popejoy Hall, UNM campus, single tickets are sometimes available. Call 842–8565. *June Music Festival,* Woodward Hall, UNM campus (881–0844). Features the Guarneri String Quartet in eight concerts through the month. Single tickets sometimes available. *The Chamber Orchestra of Albuquerque,* Albuquerque Little Theater, 224 San Pasquale SW (242–4750). *Albuquerque Civic Chorus,* Kimo Theatre downtown (848–1370 or 848–1374). *Albuquerque Civic Light Opera,* 4201 Ellison NE (345–6577). One of the largest community theaters in the country; five major musicals each year.

Stage. *Albuquerque Little Theatre,* 224 San Pasquale SW (242–4750), over 50 years old, features six productions each year, Sept.–June: lighthearted comedies, mystery thrillers, and Broadway fare. *The New Wool Warehouse,* 1st & Roma NW, downtown (764–9665). Lively dinner theater in restored historic building, elegant Art Deco style. Year-round performances. Lunch, dinner, lounge, with or without play. *N.M. Repertory Theatre,* fabulous restored Kimo Theater, 419 Central Ave. NW (243–4500). The resident theater company stages six plays each winter, contemporary comedies and world classics. *Popejoy Hall,* UNM campus (277–3121), Albuquerque's major entertainment center, hosts 170 professional and local arts performances annually. *The Vortex Theatre,* 2004 Central S.E. (247–8600). A very small company whose work is mainly avant-garde.

ACCOMMODATIONS. Albuquerque has a wide choice of hotels and motels in all parts of town. We list a few only; please look in the yellow pages or write the Albuquerque Convention & Visitors Bureau, Box 26866, Albuquerque, NM 87125 for a list of members. These listed are divided into the following categories: *Super Deluxe,* over $90; *Deluxe,* $75–$90; *Expensive,* $65–$75; *Moderate,* $50–$65; *Inexpensive,* under $50. Prices are based on double occupancy and do not include taxes. Rates usually do not fluctuate with the seasons. Budget chains such as *Dollar Inns, Regal 8, Motel 6* are represented here, as are all other familiar chains. Some of these listed overlap into the categories above and below. Some of the more expensive places have special weekend packages.

Super Deluxe

The Albuquerque Hilton. 1901 Univ. Ave. N.E., Albuquerque, NM 87102 (884–2500 or 800–HILTONS). Complex of 5 buildings, 2 courtyards, pools, recreation and health facilities, 2 restaurants, lounges.

Marriott. 2101 Louisiana Blvd. N.E., Albuquerque, NM 87110 (881–6800 or 800–228–9290). In the heart of the uptown district, close to shopping centers, other hotels. Seventeen-story building, solarium, health facilities. Elegant. Two dining rooms, lounges.

Sheraton Old Town. 800 Rio Grande Blvd. N.W., Albuquerque, NM 87104 (843–6300 or 800–325–3535). Eleven stories, 1 block from Old Town, has shops, restaurants (one in an old restored hacienda), lounges, pools, tennis, southwestern decor.

Deluxe

Albuquerque Doubletree Down Town. 2nd & Marquette N.W., Albuquerque, NM 87102 (247–3344 or 800–528–0444). Fifteen stories, connected by underground passage to Convention Center, parking. Shops, fine restaurant, racquetball, coffee shop, lounges, nightclub.

Amfac. 2910 Yale Blvd. S.E., Albuquerque, NM 87107 (843–7000). Near airport, 14 stories, Southwestern decor. Dining room and coffee shop, lounges, pool, tennis courts.

Best Western Barcelona Court. 900 Louisiana Blvd. N.E., Albuquerque, NM 87110 (255–5566 or 800–528–1234). All units are 2-room suites with microwave oven. Bright, friendly atmosphere. Health facilities. All rooms open to interior atrium. Complimentary cocktails.

Expensive

Clarion Four Seasons. 2500 Carlisle N.E., Albuquerque, NM 87110 (888–3311). This motor hotel offers health and tennis clubs, pools, and restaurants.

Holiday Inn Journal Center. 5151 San Francisco N.E., Albuquerque, NM 87109 (821–3333 or 800–HOLIDAY). Beautiful new hotel with fountains, plants in lobby. Coffee shop, restaurant, lounge.

La Posada. 125 2nd St. N.W., Albuquerque, NM 87102 (242–9090). In well restored historic landmark, downtown. Spanish decor, charming. One block to Convention Center, Civic Plaza.

Radisson Inn. 1901 University Blvd. S.E., Albuquerque, NM 87106 (247–0512 or 800–333–3333). New, fairly close to airport. Restaurant.

Moderate

Best Western Airport Inn. 2400 Yale Blvd. S.E., Albuquerque, NM 87106 (242–7022 or 800–528–1234). Pool, sauna, racquetball.

Best Western Rio Grande Inn. 1015 Rio Grande Blvd. N.W., Albuquerque, NM 87104 (843–9500 or 800–528–1234). At Rio Grande exit off I-40. Near Old Town. Coffee shop, pool.

Howard Johnson Plaza Inn. 6000 Pan American Frwy. N.E., Albuquerque, NM 87109 (821–9451 or 800–654–2000). Newer hotel. Exercise center, restaurant, lounge, pool.

Inexpensive

Best Western American Motor Inn. 12999 Central Ave. N.E., Albuquerque, NM 87123 (298–7426 or 800–528–1234). Pool, movies, whirlpool, near mountains.

La Quinta Motor Inn. Three locations: 2116 Yale S.E., 87106 (243–5500 or 800–531–5900), near airport. 2424 San Mateo NE, 87110 (884–3591), near major shopping centers. 5241 San Antonio NE, 87109 (821–9000).

RESTAURANTS. Restaurants specializing in New Mexican foods are usually the best bargains, and often the most fun. Chili is addictive, and most people here prefer green to red, in innumerable dishes. All types of cuisine are here—seafood, French, and all other ethnic groups. They are in order of price category: *Deluxe,* over $20; *Expensive,* $14–$20; *Moderate,* $10–$14; *Inexpensive,* under $10. Price does not include tax and tip. Unless noted, all accept credit cards. FL means they have a full liquor license for any kind of drinks; LL means limited license, probably beer and wine only. There are hundreds more than we can list here.

Deluxe

Lil's. Amfac Hotel, 2910 Yale Blvd. S.E. (843–7000). Noted for prime rib grilled over mesquite. D, daily except Sun. FL.

Le Marmiton, 5415 Academy N.E. (821–6279). Elegant restaurant. French cuisine, fine wine selection, exquisite service. L, Mon.–Fri. D, daily. LL.

Mayfair. In the Albuquerque Doubletree, 201 Marquette N.W. (247–3344). White-glove service, fine food. L, D, daily except Sun. FL.

Expensive

Al Monte's. 1306 Rio Grande Blvd. N.W. (243–3709). Veal, pastas, and seafood. New Mexican atmosphere-cum-English-pub. L, D, daily except Sun. FL.

Chardonnay's (in Ramada Hotel Classic), 6815 Menaul Blvd. N.E., (881–0000). American-International cuisine. L, Mon.–Fri. D, Mon.–Sat. FL.

High Finance. Atop the Sandia Mountains, reached only by tram, (243–9742). Spectacular views. L, D, daily; B, in ski season. FL. Reservations required.

Maria Teresa. 618 Rio Grande Blvd. N.W., next to Sheraton Old Town Inn (242–3900). Dining rooms in restored adobe hacienda, 140 years old, Victorian and American antiques. L, D, daily. FL.

Moderate

Antiquity. 112 Romero NW (247–3545). Casual dining on Continental cuisine is offered at this place in the heart of Old Town. L, D, daily. LL.

Garduño's. 5400 Academy Rd. N.E. (821–3030). Mariachis, margaritas, and authentic New Mexican food combine to make this a lively dining experience. L, D, daily. FL. also at 8806 4th NW (898–2772).

Mr. Powdrell's Barbeque House. Three locations: 11309 Central N.E. (298–6766). 5501 Montgomery Blvd. N.E. (883–1792). 5209 4th St. N.W. (345–8086). Traditional Black barbecue, ribs, chicken, pork. L, D, daily. No liquor first two locations, LL in last.

Inexpensive

Café Zurich. 3513 Central N.E. (265–2556). Croissants, gourmet ice cream, desserts, espresso bar. Art Deco decor. L, D, daily. LL.

Los Cuates. 4901 Lomas Blvd. N.E. (255–5079). Old favorite, authentic New Mexican food. Flamenco guitar. L, D, daily. Closed Sun. FL.

Villa di Capo. 722 Central Ave. S.W. (242–2006). Small place, but serves robust portions of traditional Italian food in Roman-style dining rooms or landscaped outdoor patio.

NIGHTLIFE. Albuquerque is casual and pretty folksy, a mixture of blue jeans, business suits, boots, and sandals, but bare feet and tank tops not permitted. Most action is on weekends. Bars stay open till 2 A.M. on Fri. and Sat. Only a few places require ties and suit jackets. Country-western and rock 'n' roll are most popular, but you will also hear a lot of jazz, top 40s, and disco. All hotels and some motels have lounges with live entertainment. Here are just a few clubs which are not connected with a hotel:

Caravan East. 7605 Central N.E. (265–7877). Biggest country-western in town. OK for singles. All ages. Two bands, seven nights a week. Cover on Fri., Sat., and some weeknights, depending on band. MC, V.

El Rey. 624 Central Ave. S.W. (242–9300). Name bands play to crowds in this converted theater.

El Madrid. On the railroad tracks, near 1st St. and Central Ave.; no phone. For the adventurous only. A trendy club with great bands in the bad part of town.

Rio Grande Cantina. 1100 Rio Grande N.W. (242–1777). Excellent meeting place for the young professional crowd. Open nightly for mingling, margaritas, and Mexican food.

TAOS

Isolated by mountains, Taoseños have held on to the traditions of their ancestors in old Spain. They may have accepted hamburgers and TV, but they enjoy a stubborn difference in customs, attitudes, and sometimes a stiff-necked orneriness that refuses to join the 20th century.

The village of Taos was settled in 1615 about a mile from Taos Indian Pueblo. For two and a half centuries their isolation was broken only once a year when trade fairs were held. Spanish settlers and Indians from Pueblos up and down the Rio Grande brought grain, pottery, and other goods to trade with the nomadic Indians who came across the mountains from the plains. Beaver trappers, those rugged, smelly Mountain Men, came to trade beaver pelts for enough booze to get roaring drunk and enough food and supplies to go back to the beaver streams for another year.

The American conquest of New Mexico in 1846 was taken philosophically, if not enthusiastically, by everyone else in the territory except the Taoseños who staged an armed rebellion in 1847, murdering the governor and several of his friends.

During the Civil War, New Mexico was loyal to the Union, supplying more volunteers per capita than any other territory. Confederate sympathisers made the mistake of taking down the Union flag that flew over Taos Plaza. Kit Carson and some of his buddies, representing majority opinion in Taos, went to the mountains, cut down the tallest pine tree they could drag back, planted it in the plaza, and nailed the flag to it. They took turns standing armed guard around it, and no Confederate touched it again. That is why, today, the flag flies 24 hours a day over Taos Plaza.

Around the turn of the century, the artists Ernest Blumenschein and Bert Phillips broke a wagon wheel in Taos and settled in for a lifelong stay. By 1912 they had lured enough other artists to Taos to start a Society of Artists. Through the years other artists and literary figures, including Georgia O'Keeffe and D. H. Lawrence, have discovered Taos. Art is the biggest business in Taos; there are about 60 galleries in Taos, a town of less than 5,000 population.

Walking along the streets of Taos, you feel a sense of history and an exhilaration of the spirit. The magic of Taos is almost tangible: You will be mesmerized by the white sunlight and lavender shadows, by the clarity and lightness of the air.

PRACTICAL INFORMATION FOR TAOS

WHEN TO GO. You can visit Taos anytime: winter for skiing; summer for mountain recreation and most cultural events; fall for changing colors in the mountains. The summers are crowded in Taos, and rates are highest.

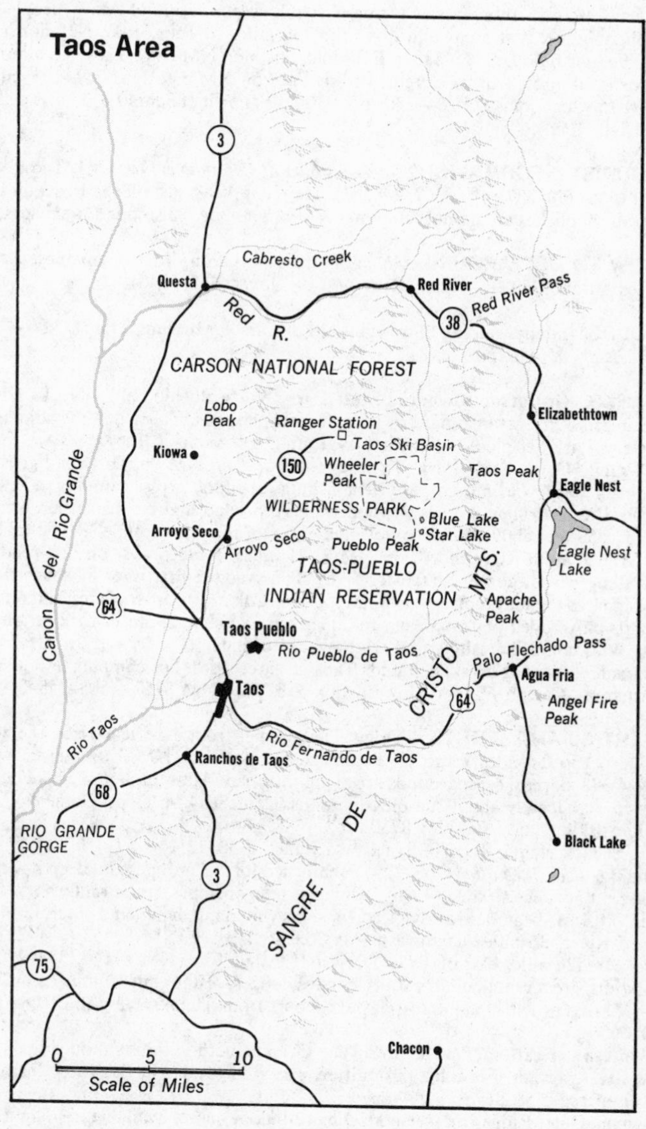
Taos Area
Cabresto Creek
Questa
Red River
Red R.
Red River Pass
CARSON NATIONAL FOREST
Elizabethtown
Lobo Peak
Ranger Station
Taos Ski Basin
Kiowa
Wheeler Peak
Taos Peak
Eagle Nest
WILDERNESS PARK
Blue Lake
Star Lake
Arroyo Seco
Arroyo Seco
Pueblo Peak
Eagle Nest Lake
TAOS-PUEBLO
INDIAN RESERVATION
MTS.
Apache Peak
Canon del Rio Grande
Taos Pueblo
Rio Pueblo de Taos
Palo Flechado Pass
Agua Fria
Taos
CRISTO
Angel Fire Peak
Rio Taos
Rio Fernando de Taos
Ranchos de Taos
RIO GRANDE GORGE
DE
Black Lake
SANGRE
Chacon
0 5 10
Scale of Miles
3
38
150
64
68
75

HOW TO GET THERE. You can't fly, unless you bring your own plane. The nearest *Amtrak* station is Albuquerque, or the Lamy Station that serves Santa Fe. *Greyhound* serves Taos.

So most people drive, and it's over the mountains no matter how you go. The highways are safe, though, and scenic if you obey posted limits. Many people fly to Albuquerque, rent a car and drive the 130 miles to Taos. Take I-25 north to Santa Fe; north on U.S. 84–285 to Española; north on NM 68 to Taos. An alternative, or ideal circle trip, is to return from Taos on NM 3 to NM 75 a few miles to NM 76 which joins U.S. 84–285 about 10 miles north of Santa Fe. This is called The High Road to Taos.

TOURIST INFORMATION. *Taos Chamber of Commerce,* Drawer 1, Taos, NM 87571 (505–758–3873 or 800–732–8267). The *Taos News,* just off the Plaza on Ledoux St., publishes an annual "Summer Visitor's Guide," also one for ski season.

HOW TO GET AROUND. No public transportation. Taxi companies: *Faust Transportation* (758–3410) and *Pride of Taos Tours* (758–8340).

TOURS. A daily walking tour begins at Kit Carson Museum, 11 A.M., May–Oct. *Taos Historical Walking Tour* (758–3861).

PARKS. Kit Carson Memorial State Park, North Pueblo Rd., 2 blocks north of the plaza. Kit Carson and other Taos historic persons are buried in the adjoining cemetery. Park has picnic facilities, playground, rest rooms. Closes at 10 P.M. Free. **Rio Grande Gorge State Park,** 17 miles southwest on NM 96. Dirt road goes to bottom of deep volcanic gorge. Great fishing. Shelters, grills, camping. $5. **Rio Grande Gorge Bridge,** 8 miles west on U.S. 64. Second highest suspension bridge in U.S., 650 feet above the deep volcanic gorge of the Rio Grande. Picnic tables. **Rio Grande Wild River,** north on NM 3, 24 miles, 5 miles west on dirt road to park along rim of gorge. Watch for signs. This was the first river in America to be designated "wild." Includes 50 miles south of Colorado border. Camp and picnic grounds on wooded plateau near rim of canyon. No charge. Steep, rocky trails to river. Wild country. Fishing and white-water rafting.

Carson National Forest surrounds Taos on three sides. For camping and hiking information, Carson National Forest, Box 558, Taos NM 87571 (505–758–8941).

PARTICIPANT SPORTS. Fishing. The premier trout experience is in the 800-foot-deep Rio Grande Gorge, or Taos Box. Go north on NM 3 to Questa, west on NM 378. Several campgrounds are along this road. Allow an hour to hike down to river. Ask locally about run-off conditions. Contact N.M. Dept. Game & Fish, Villagra Bldg., Santa Fe, NM 87503 (827–7882).

Horseback riding. Taos Indian Horse Ranch (758–3212).

Skiing. *Taos Ski Valley* (766–2295), renowned for steep slopes and deep powder, 51 percent advanced. 9 A.M.–4 P.M., lodging at base of slopes, restaurants, bars. *Red River Ski Areas* beginner to advanced runs, instruction, lodging, and entertainment in Red River, 36 miles northwest, Box 303, Red River, NM 87558 (754–2223). *Angel Fire,* 26 miles east of Taos, Drawer B, Angel Fire, NM 87110 (377–2301). Long runs, great cross-country trails, condos, lodges, restaurants, country club. Ski New Mexico provides 24-hour-a-day ski report from Thanksgiving to early Apr., (984–0606).

White-water rafting. On the upper Rio Grande, both within and outside of the Wild River portion. For a list of outfitters and guides, contact the Taos Chamber of Commerce (758–3873).

Tennis. Quail Ridge Inn (see hotels) has 2 indoor courts available to nonguests, plus 6 outdoor courts. Four mi. north of town. For reservations, call 766–2211.

MUSEUMS, HISTORIC SITES. Plaza de Don Fernando de Taos, the heart of Taos, is the place to start. This was almost a walled fortress in colonial times, with flat-roofed adobe houses around the plaza. None of the original buildings remain, but all are of good pueblo architecture. **Blumenschein House** (758–0505), 2 blocks east of the plaza on Ledoux St., an 11-room house built in Spanish Colonial times, became home of Ernest Blumenschein, founder of the Taos Society of Artists. 9

A.M.–5 P.M. summer; 10 A.M.–4 P.M. winter. $3, or $7 for admission to Blumenschein House, Kit Carson Home and Museum, and Hacienda Martinez (see below). **Fechin Institute** (758–1710), on Pueblo Rd., 4 blocks north of plaza, home of famous painter, Nicolai Fechin, open daily 1–5 P.M. in summer; by appointment in winter. Donation. **Gov. Bent House and Museum,** 1 block north of plaza on Bent St., home of first appointed civil governor after conquest by U.S. troops. Murdered in Taos Rebellion in 1847. 9 A.M.–5 P.M. summer; 10 A.M.–4 P.M. winter. $3. **Harwood Foundation,** 25 Ledoux St., home of prominent early family, houses collection by Taos masters, religious folk art, southwestern books. 10 A.M.–5 P.M. Closed Sun. and holidays. Free. **Kit Carson Home & Museum** (758–4741), one block east of plaza on Kit Carson Rd., home of the famous scout, historical exhibits. 9 A.M.–5 P.M. summer; 10 A.M.–4 P.M. winter. $3.

Church of St. Francis of Assisi, 4 mi. south on NM 68, massive buttressed adobe walls, probably most painted and photographed church in NM. Slide shows and lectures in office. Church and rectory open daily, 10 A.M.–noon and 2–4 P.M.

Hacienda de Don Antonio Severino Martinez (758–4741), 2 mi. west on NM 240. 21 room hacienda, last of the great fortified homes of Spanish colonial period. 9 A.M.–5 P.M. summer; 10 A.M.–4 P.M. winter. $3.

D. H. Lawrence Shrine, 15 mi. north off NM 3. Ashes of famed writer in shrine on ranch he loved. Owned by UNM, retreat for writers-in-residence. Shrine open to public daylight hours. Free.

Millicent Rogers Museum (758–2462), ½ mi. south of junction of Hwys. 3 and 64, four mi. north of town. Superb collection of southwest carvings, paintings, crafts. House is fine example of modern adobe in traditional style. 9 A.M.–5 P.M. May through Oct. 10 A.M.–4 P.M., Wed.–Sun., Nov. through Apr. $3.

Taos Indian Pueblo, 2 mi. north of town on Pueblo Rd. At least 900 years old, the pueblo hasn't changed, at least since the first white man saw it. Two large communal dwellings, 4 and 5 stories high, face each other across the plaza, bisected by a small stream running down from the mountains to the east. Visitor Center at the entrance is where you may buy books, crafts, and pay the fees, $5 to park and $5–$10 for camera permit. Photos allowed in plaza area only, not of individuals or private homes unless permission granted. This is not an amusement park, but the home of 1,500 people of dignity and intelligence. Abide by any rules. Do not enter any home or doorway unless invited. Visitors welcome 9 A.M.–5 P.M. daily; 9 A.M.–3 P.M., holidays. Many ceremonial dances through the year are open to the public.

GALLERIES. You will find galleries on every street, but we call attention to a few special places: *Mission Gallery* (758–2861), east of plaza on Kit Carson Rd., is in the home and studio of Joseph Henry Sharp, one of the founding members of the Taos Society of Artists. Property also includes home of son of Irving Couse, another of the old Taos Masters. National Historic Landmark. 9 A.M.–5:30 P.M. summer; 10 A.M.–4 P.M. winter. *Stables Gallery and Community Art Center,* on Pueblo Rd. a block north of the plaza. Adobe home of an infamous character in Taos history, has 10 exhibits a year, focusing on current art in Taos. Mon.–Fri., 10 A.M.–5 P.M. Weekends noon–5 P.M. Closed holidays. *R. C. Gorman Studio,* Ledoux St., a block west of the plaza. Probably the best-known living Navajo artist today.

MUSIC. *Taos School of Music* is a well-established institution that operates every summer at Hotel St. Bernard in Taos Ski Valley. The school runs June through early Aug., and concerts by the conservatory-level graduate students and faculty are at Taos Community Auditorium and at the St. Bernard. Concerts are free, but dinner reservations at St. Bernard (776–8506) must be made in advance. TCA is a block north of the plaza, behind the Stables Gallery (758–2052) and has many other events through the summer.

ACCOMMODATIONS. These range from standard chains to those most expressive of southwestern charm with thick adobe walls, Indian rugs, tile, and a *mañana* ambiance. Reservations are necessary in summer. Ski packages are best bargains for skiers in winter. In addition to accommodations in town, at **Taos Ski Valley** are lodges, condos, and restaurants. Call 776–2291. (Central reservations for Taos: 800–821–2437.) The sampling we list of motels and hotels in Taos is by price category: *Deluxe,* $90 and up; *Expensive,* $70–$90; *Moderate,* $50–$70; *Inexpensive,* $40–$50.

Deluxe

Quail Ridge Inn. Taos Ski Valley Rd., Taos, NM 87571 (505–766–2211 or 800–624–4448), 5 mi. north of town. Condos with country club atmosphere, 6 outdoor, 2 indoor tennis courts, other sports and health facilities. On 37 acres. Dining room, lounge.

Taos Inn. N. Pueblo Rd., Taos, NM 87571 (505–758–2233 or 800–TAOS INN). Old historic favorite, completely remodeled. Fireplaces, hand-crafted furniture, fabrics. Dining room, lounge. One block north of plaza.

Expensive

Best Western Kachina Lodge. N. Pueblo Rd., Taos, NM 87571 (505–758–2275 or 800–528–1234). Four blocks north of plaza. Large inn around grassy courtyard, pool. Shops, dining room, lounge.

Sagebrush Inn. S. Santa Fe Rd., Taos, NM 87571 (505–758–2254 or 800–426–3626). Big adobe lodge, old favorite, Southwestern decor, large art collection. Two dining rooms, lounge, tennis, pool. Two mi. south of town, on Hwy. 68.

Moderate

El Pueblo. N. Pueblo Rd., Taos, NM 87571 (505–758–8700). Some fireplaces, children's playground. Restaurants nearby. Five blocks from plaza.

Quality Inn. S. Santa Fe Rd., Taos, NM 87571 (505–758–2200). 3 mi. south of town on Hwy. 68. Restaurant, lounge, pool.

Inexpensive

Hacienda Inn. S. Santa Fe Rd., Taos, NM 87571 (505–758–8610). New, 2 miles south of plaza.

El Monte. Kit Carson Rd., Taos, NM 87571 (505–758–3171). Some fireplaces, kitchen units, 4 blocks east of plaza.

RESTAURANTS. New Mexican, especially Northern New Mexican cooking is regional food at its best, subtly different from Mexican or Tex-Mex food. Example, blue corn tortillas, posole, sopapillas. This kind of food is served at most places, but you will also find American, Continental, and nouvelle cuisine. These are listed by price category as follows: *Deluxe,* over $20; *Expensive,* $15–$20; *Moderate,* $10–$15; *Inexpensive,* less than $10. Many small, inexpensive places are near the plaza and on N. Pueblo St.

Deluxe

Apple Tree. 26 Bent St. (758–1900). Imaginative specials, small, patio dining in summer. Generally nouvelle cuisine, but hard to define. Beer and wine only. L, D, weekdays. Sunday brunch. Reservations suggested.

Brett House. Taos Ski Valley Rd., 3 mi. north (776–8545). Small menu, changed nightly, elegantly prepared. Lamb, seafood. In home of artist Lady Dorothy Brett. D only. Reservations. Beer and wine.

Casa Cordova. Taos Ski Valley Rd. (776–2200). Old favorite. Continental cuisine, quiet elegance. Charming adobe home. D only. LL.

Expensive

Doc Martin's at Taos Inn. N. Pueblo Rd., 1 block north of plaza (758–2233). Doc Martin's Restaurant features Continental, regional, and seafood dishes. Popular bar, shrimp and oyster bar at cocktail time. B, L, D. LL.

Sagebrush Inn. Two mi. south of town (758–2254). Continental, steak house and regional fare. Two dining rooms. B, L, D. FL. Live entertainment, lounge.

Moderate

Ogelvie's. On the plaza (758–8866). Upstairs with balcony overlooking the plaza, this place features varied American, Continental, and regional food. L, D. LL.

El Patio de Taos. On an alley off the northwest corner of the plaza (758–2121). Fountains, atrium, restful ambience. Continental and regional fare. L, D. FL.

Inexpensive

Dori's. N. Pueblo Rd, 2 blocks north of plaza (758–9222). At this tiny place, which has a bakery, artists stop for coffee and to read mail. B, L, D, usually.

Michael's Kitchen. N. Pueblo Rd. (758–4178). Extensive short-order menu, big servings, bakery. Popular local breakfast spot. B, L, D.

OTHER PLACES OF INTEREST

Carlsbad Caverns National Park

When you enter Carlsbad Caverns, familiar environments vanish. You no longer feel the breeze on your cheek or hear the sounds of birds, insects, or faraway jets. There are no shadows; the temperature is steady and cool. As you walk beyond the mouth of the caverns, and leave the world of daylight, artificial lighting in the caverns subtly takes over and seems to glow from within the formations themselves. You find yourself whispering in this strange and wonderful underground world.

The formation of the caverns began 200 million years ago when a limestone reef formed around a warm, shallow sea. About 60 million years ago when the earth convulsed in the agony that formed the Rocky Mountains, the reef broke in many places, and ground water seeped into cavities. Slowly walls, floors and ceilings dissolved, enlarging the cavities into huge rooms and passageways. Some 3 million years ago the earth lifted, and the water drained out. Surface water seeped into the caverns, depositing tiny specks of minerals, creating the delicate shapes and colors we see within the caverns today.

Human minds cannot comprehend the patience of a process that takes 80 years to add the thickness of a coat of paint, but we can appreciate the results. Carlsbad Caverns is one of the most visited National Parks, and has well developed facilities. The main building, sitting on a rocky, cactus-studded ridge in the Sonoran Desert, includes a visitor center, restaurant, gift shop, nursery, and dog kennels. (You can't take them into the caverns, and don't think of leaving one in the car.) The complete walking tour takes about three hours. Lighting is dim but enough to see where you're going. Each person is given a headset, in either English or Spanish, that explains the geology as you walk along the trail.

You descend 830 feet along the Main Corridor to the Green Lake Room, King's Palace, Queen's Chamber, Papoose Room, and the Big Room. You may spend as long as you like on the trail, admiring the stone draperies, waterfalls, stalagmites, and stalactites in an endless variety of shapes. A 1.25-mile tour of the Big Room, with descent by elevator, is designed for those who are physically unfit to walk or who do not have time for the longer tour. Everyone must take the elevator back up.

Backcountry hiking is permitted in the Park, and for an experience in spelunking, take the New Cave hike, a special tour offered in the summer, and on weekends in the winter. Reservations must be made in advance, and you must be physically fit, carry your own flashlight and water, and get there on your own. It is 23 miles from Park Headquarters. It is limited to 25 visitors and two park rangers.

For detailed information, contact Carlsbad Caverns National Park, 3225 National Parks Highway, Carlsbad, NM 88220 (505–785–2232).

Canyon de Chelly National Monument

This is one of the most photographed places in the United States, and with good reason. Sheer red sandstone cliffs plunge down a thousand feet into awesome canyons, and shafts of sandstone thrust up from the valley floor. Tucked away in the canyon are ruins of an ancient civilization and the cornfields and peach orchards of Navajos who live there today.

The meandering streams, often dry, seem incapable of having eroded such slashes into the earth, yet summer flash floods turn these docile streams into grinding torrents. The Monument includes Canyon de Chelly (shay) and Canyon del Muerto, plus other tributary canyons. The two main canyons come together in a V near Monument headquarters, six miles east of Chinle (chin-lee), Arizona. A paved drive along the rims of both canyons has many vista points overlooking the canyons and cliff dwelling ruins. The only hiking trail you can take without a Navajo guide goes one mile into the Canyon to White House Ruin. The canyons may be visited by jeep with Navajo guides, year-round, from Thunderbird Lodge near the entrance. This is the only lodge in the Monument, Box 548, Chinle, AZ 86503 (602–674–5841). Canyon de Chelly Motel, Box 295, Chinle, AZ 86503 (602–674–5288), is three miles east. Both are open year-round. For information about the monument: Canyon de Chelly National Monument, Box 588, Chinle, AZ 86503 (602–674–5436).

Lake Powell

Glen Canyon Dam backs up the water of the Colorado River to make the second largest man-made lake in the United States. Fingers of the lake reach into countless canyons, giving boaters hundreds of miles of shoreline to explore for Indian ruins, to fish, hike, swim, or relax in privacy. Walls of the canyon are steep and dark red, the water almost a cobalt blue.

At Wahweap Lodge and Marina, rental boats and houseboats are available, as are boat tours on the lake. Probably the most popular cruise is to Rainbow Bridge. The boat docks a few hundred feet down the canyon from the great stone arch, sacred in Navajo lore, and passengers walk to the bridge which rises hundreds of feet above their heads. Campgrounds, motel and restaurant are at Wahweap, and in the town of Page, 4.5 miles away. For detailed information, write to the Chamber of Commerce, Box 727, Page, AZ 86040 and the National Park Service, Glen Canyon National Recreation Area, Box 1507, Page, AZ 86040 (602–645–2471).

Monument Valley

Most of Monument Valley is in Utah, but is usually reached from the Arizona side. The brilliant, lonely landscape of this part of the Navajo Reservation is familiar to western movie buffs from the dozens of westerns that have been filmed here. Across a sea of reddish-brown sand, rise monoliths carved into fantastic shapes by erosion. Very little grows on this desert, just enough scrubby, tough bushes and grasses to feed scattered flocks of sheep. Navajo hogans, eight-sided houses of logs and mud, are nestled among rocks and juniper trees. Navajos are friendly as a rule, and amenable to posing for pictures if you ask first, and agree on a fee. Gouldings Lodge, built many years ago to house film makers, is headquarters for guided tours. It has overnight and restaurant facilities, but reservations should be made well in advance. Gouldings Trading Post Lodge, Box 1, Monument Valley, UT 84536 (801–727–3231). Additional lodging can be found in Kayenta, 25 miles south of Gouldings, and in Bluff and Mexican Hat, Utah.

The Painted Desert and Petrified Forest National Park

Midway between Holbrook and Chambers on I-40 is an area that lets you step back into the geological mists of time and see trees turned to stone, and the results of millenia of erosion that have exposed sandstones and shales in colors of awesome beauty. Reds and yellows predominate, but with clouds and moisture they range from lavender and pink to salmon and purple. The interstate bisects the Park. The Visitor Center is near the freeway exit, and a paved road goes 21 miles south through the park of spectacular petrified logs and petroglyphs. The area around Rainbow Forest Museum, near the south end, is the most highly colored.

Once this colorful landscape was part of a valley that extended across New Mexico into Texas and north into Utah. Year after year streams flooded and deposited sediment from the highlands, eventually covering the forest to a depth of 3,000 feet. The mineral-laden water seeped into tree trunks, replacing the water in the tree cells with stone. Until about 60 million years ago, the forest was covered by a shallow ocean, which drained away when the land was uplifted to form the Rocky Mountains. This plateau is about 5,000 feet above sea level.

There are no accommodations within the park except a lunch room, but some are located at the exit from I-40 and in Holbrook.

White Sands National Monument

A sea of shimmering white gypsum lies in the valley west of Alamogordo, New Mexico. Dunes are as much as 200 feet high, and stretch about 50 miles between two mountain ranges. The billowing waves under a flawless blue dome are a perfect place to take off your shoes, roll in the clean crystals, and feel the exuberance of youth. Kids love it. In summer, the temperature gets to 100, but the sands remain cool to the touch because they reflect the heat. A drive from the Visitor Center loops through the heart of the dunes, to a picnic area with colorful shelters that look like sailboats in a white sea. Only about a third of the gypsum deposits are in the National Monument. The rest is part of White Sands Missile Range, a testing facility at Holloman Air Force Base. The Monument is 15 miles southwest of Alamogordo on U.S. 70–82. For great contrast, a 20-mile drive the other direction on U.S. 82 goes up the Sacramento Mountains to the cool mountain resort town of Cloudcroft, at almost 9,000 foot elevation. There are accommodations in Alamogordo, and in Cloudcroft at a lodge with golf course, one of the world's highest at more than 9,000 feet.

For detailed information, contact the Alamogordo Chamber of Commerce, Box 518, Alamogordo, NM 88310 (505–437–6120) or the Cloudcroft Chamber of Commerce, Box 125, Cloudcroft, NM 88317 (505–682–2733).

THE GREAT BASIN

by
LEE FOSTER and STEPHEN ALLEN

Mr. Foster, a writer and photographer, is the author of a number of books on travel and gardening as well as novels and a guide on computer disk, West Coast Travel. *Mr. Allen, who lives in Las Vegas, is a travel writer who has worked on many Fodor's guides.*

Because its waters remain within itself, the area of western Utah, most of Nevada, and the eastern deserts of California, especially Death Valley, is termed the Great Basin. The most obvious of these brackish basins is the Great Salt Lake, where eons of stream-bed wash have created a lake that is 15 times as salty as the ocean. When the water not only gathers but disappears into the dry desert soil, the basin becomes a sink, as in Nevada's Humboldt Sink and Carson Sink and California's Death Valley. Add the landscape affected by erosion from the Colorado River and its tributaries, carving away at the eastern half of Utah, and you fully account for the topography of the two main Great Basin states: Utah and Nevada. The east side of the Sierra in California and Death Valley also fall within the domain of this chapter.

The main pleasures of the Great Basin area for the traveler are threefold: the beauty of nature in erosive rivers or spare deserts, the historical and modern story of the Mormons in Utah, and the entertainment that has been available in Las Vegas and Reno since Nevada legalized gambling in 1931.

Salt Lake City

When Brigham Young announced to his followers, "This is the right place," he was viewing the well-watered east side of the Great Salt Lake. After 1,300 miles of travel, starting in February 1847 in Illinois, he must have thought that this was a promised land. Today Salt Lake City has diverse pleasures for the traveler. Dominating the experience is the Mormon religion with its downtown temple and its crucial role in the development of the West since the 1840s. Seventy percent of Utah's population is at least nominally Mormon, and there are over 4 million "saints" worldwide. The Mormon ethic, emphasizing family life and education and discouraging the use of alcohol, will affect the traveler.

The dramatic aspect of Salt Lake City is the rapidity with which the Mormons turned the desert into a fertile agricultural plain. This story is best experienced at the major attraction, Temple Square, the symbolic heart of the worldwide Church of Jesus Christ of Latter-Day Saints, where volunteers from the church orient visitors. Recently, the lengthy tours have been broken down into seven small tours operating simultaneously so that one can pick a subject of interest and pursue it.

The majestic six-spired temple, built 1853–1893, dominates the grounds of this 10-acre site. However, the temple is closed to the public. Atop the temple is the gold-leafed Angel Moroni, from the Book of Revelations, raising his trumpet to announce the Mormon belief in the further spread of the Word. Tours of the domed tabernacle, however, are ongoing. Architecturally, the tabernacle is a legacy from the era of wood construction. This oval wooden structure, whose design Brigham Young chose, seats nearly 7,000 people without an obstructing pillar. The only resource available to the Mormons when they started construction in 1863 was the pine forest south of Salt Lake. The entire building is constructed from interlaced white pine timbers and wooden pegs. Even the pipes of the organ are made of white pine logs. From here the 375-voice Mormon Tabernacle Choir presents its 9:30 A.M. Sunday morning radio concerts. The broadcasts have been continuous since 1929, making this the longest-playing show on American radio. You can witness the Thursday evening rehearsal or the Sunday morning broadcast live. There are also organ concerts in the tabernacle at noon and at 4 P.M. daily from June through September.

Within Temple Square, the South Visitor Center includes interesting dioramas on the history of the Mormons, showing how they were persecuted and driven out of Missouri and Illinois, where the murder of their founder, Joseph Smith, provoked the trip west to find a homeland of their own. The North Visitor Center focuses more on the theological vision of the Mormons. Another handsome building at Temple Square is the Assembly Hall, a granite structure used for meetings.

Within the Temple Square two other items of interest are the golden Seagull Monument, recalling how sea gulls helped eat the crickets that were devastating the crops of the Mormons, and the handcart Pioneer Monument, showing how many families proceeded west. At one point, about 3,000 Mormons formed a train of handcarts pushing west from Iowa along the 1,350-mile journey. Of this group, about 250 died.

At the southeast corner of Temple Square stands a statue of Brigham Young, who served as the second president of the Mormon Church and was the first governor of the Utah Territory.

The block east from Temple Square contains four important historical entities. On the corner is the Hotel Utah, listed on the National Register of Historic Places. Closed in 1987, the hotel is being converted to office space for the Church. The building originally housed the Mormon Church's tithing office and the region's first newspaper, the *Deseret News.*

Points of Interest

1) Beehive House
2) Brigham Young's Grave
3) Brigham Young Statue
4) Cathedral of the Madeleine
5) City County Building
6) Council Hall
7) University of Utah and Museum of Natural History
8) Hansen Planetarium
9) Memory Grove
10) Mormon Temple
11) Pioneer Museum
12) Promised Valley Theater
13) Saint Mark's Cathedral
14) Salt Palace and Concert Hall
15) Seagull Monument
16) State Capitol
17) Tabernacle & Assembly Hall
18) Utah Governor's Mansion
19) Utah State Historical Society

Next to the Hotel Utah is an ionic-column structure, built in 1917, that serves the administrative offices of the Mormon Church.

Adjacent is the Lion's House, so named for the reclining lion mounted above the entrance. It was built in 1855 for Brigham Young as a supplementary house for his wives and children. This building is not open to the public.

At the corner of the block is the Beehive House, originally built by Brigham Young in 1853–1854 as his main family residence, where he entertained church and civil dignitaries. Now a National Historic Landmark, this building has been restored and is open daily, except Thanksgiving, for a free public visit and tour.

At the Beehive House corner you'll see the Eagle Gate, built in 1859, which marked the entrance to Brigham Young's property.

The Family History Library is famous among genealogists because of its vast family-tree resources. The Mormon interest in family trees springs from a theological conviction that families have an eternal reality, that a spirit lives after death, and that you can do a favor for past relatives by giving them a proxy baptism, which allows them the option of sharing the faith. Because the proxy baptism must be for a specific person, not just for all one's forebearers, much attention goes into searching through family records for distinct names. Owing to its worldwide interest in salvation, this Mormon center has embarked on ambitious international genealogical research.

The major attractions of Salt Lake are conveniently clustered in this downtown area, close to the temple. The city planner, Brigham Young himself, mapped out the city in a logical manner. The streets were laid out wide enough for an ox cart to make a U-turn without brushing the curb.

West of Temple Square is the Visitor Information Center at the Salt Palace, 180 South West Temple. This is one of the official hospitality and information centers for visitors to the Salt Lake area. A multimedia presentation alerts visitors to the main regional attractions.

The most primitive structure is a bowery, a thatched-roof, open-air shelter typical of what the pioneers built shortly after their arrival in the new settlement. The industry of the pioneers becomes evident when you read the historical record. A year after the first party of 147 people arrived, there were already 6,000 acres of fruits, vegetables, and grains under cultivation, irrigated by water from streams in the Wasatch Mountains.

At the eastern edge of Salt Lake City is the site of Old Deseret, the living history museum in Pioneer Trail State Park. This park celebrates the pioneer period, which lasted from 1847 to the coming of the railroad in 1869. Here Brigham Young, emerging with his party from the Wasatch Mountains, announced his decision on settling to the 147 saints in the group. The party knew that they were 1,000 miles from the nearest white settlement to the east and 700 miles from white settlements to the west, so Brother Young's statement that "This is the right place" was not a casual platitude. A bronze memorial at the site salutes the hardiness of the 80,000 Mormon pioneers of 1847–1869, including the thousands who didn't make it. Aside from the Mormon religion, the site pays bronzed tribute to other players in the drama of the West, such as Jim Bridger and Jedediah Smith, the well-educated mountain men who explored much new territory in the West.

At the site, there are houses from the early era. The John Gardiner cabin, from 1864, illustrates the log cabin era. The Social Hall, from 1852, was a meeting place erected for the residents of Old Deseret. Another structure, the John Boylston Fairbanks house, shows how adobe was employed here in the 1850s. Patterns of dress and behavior emphasize propriety. One finds a flourishing example of middle-class white culture, with many beautiful homes on the eastern slopes of the city. Guided tours of Deseret Village are offered daily, May through October.

The Great Salt Lake is the saltiest body of water in the world, except for the Dead Sea, but ask the Visitor Center where swimming is possible. High water has flooded the swimming areas and facilities close to the city in recent years.

Utah's Erosive National Parks

The best way to see Utah beyond Salt Lake City is to tour its five national parks. The densest cluster of national parks in the country is a day's drive south of Salt Lake along a line running northeast to southwest. The dominant theme is the singular experience of desert erosion, especially that of the Colorado and other rivers, gradually wearing away the soft stone and leaving rock formations. The Spanish named the major river Río Colorado, the river "colored" by the red silt.

Arches and Canyonlands are the easterly parks, Capitol Reef is in the south center, and Bryce and Zion are in the southwest.

Striking salmon-colored rock formations, including the greatest concentration of natural stone arches in the world, draw visitors to Arches National Park. Arches are stone spans created by water and polished by wind. Water, the stronger agent, wears out the soft center rock. In the park there are over 200 arches one meter or more in height. The longest, Landscape Arch, is a ribbon of rock with a near 300-foot span. Delicate Arch wins many votes as the most attractive. A section called the Windows (North and South Windows Arches, Turret Arch, and Double Arch) has the greatest concentration of large arches.

The full beauty of Arches' 115 square miles is a subtle blend of color and form. The colors are the red and salmon of the iron oxide rock, the intense blue of the sky, the deep but sparse green of pinyon pine and Utah juniper, and the pastel blue-green of many desert plants, such as sage. Into this palette of colors enters a full pageant of arches, cliffs, balanced rocks, canyons, pedestals, and pinnacles. In recent times only one primitive ranch, the Wolfe Ranch, survived in the region; the ranch's crude log cabins can be visited. Arches became a national park in 1929.

Majestic canyon vistas of the Colorado and Green rivers are the unique feature of Canyonlands National Park. The rivers amount to ribbons of fluid sandpaper cutting through the sandstone canyons of eastern Utah. Rivers and rainwater are the major erosive architects here, with wind as an associate. This 527-square-mile wilderness of rock is part of the Colorado plateau.

Paradoxically, water is a major erosive force because there is so little of it here. The paradox involves a vicious cycle. Because there is little water, there is only sparse vegetation. When rain falls, there is little vegetation to absorb it, and so the water runs off rapidly, causing erosion. To qualify as a desert, an area must have less than 10 inches of rain annually and the rain must fall irregularly, which is exactly what happens here. If 10 inches were distributed evenly through the year, the effect would be grassy meadows. Here a late-summer thunderstorm may drop two inches of moisture in a wave of water that runs off quickly and is of little use to the plants.

Perhaps the most stunning view in Utah is the Deadhorse Point overlook into Canyonlands National Park. This view presents the Colorado River as it goosenecks through a section of purple mesas between the Colorado and Green rivers. The section of mesas, called the Island in the Sky, is a technicolor kaleidoscope in the hour before sunset. The view extends 50 miles southwest to the La Sal Mountains.

The human history of Canyonlands is less compelling than the geologic record, with two notable exceptions. First, there is the tale of the initial

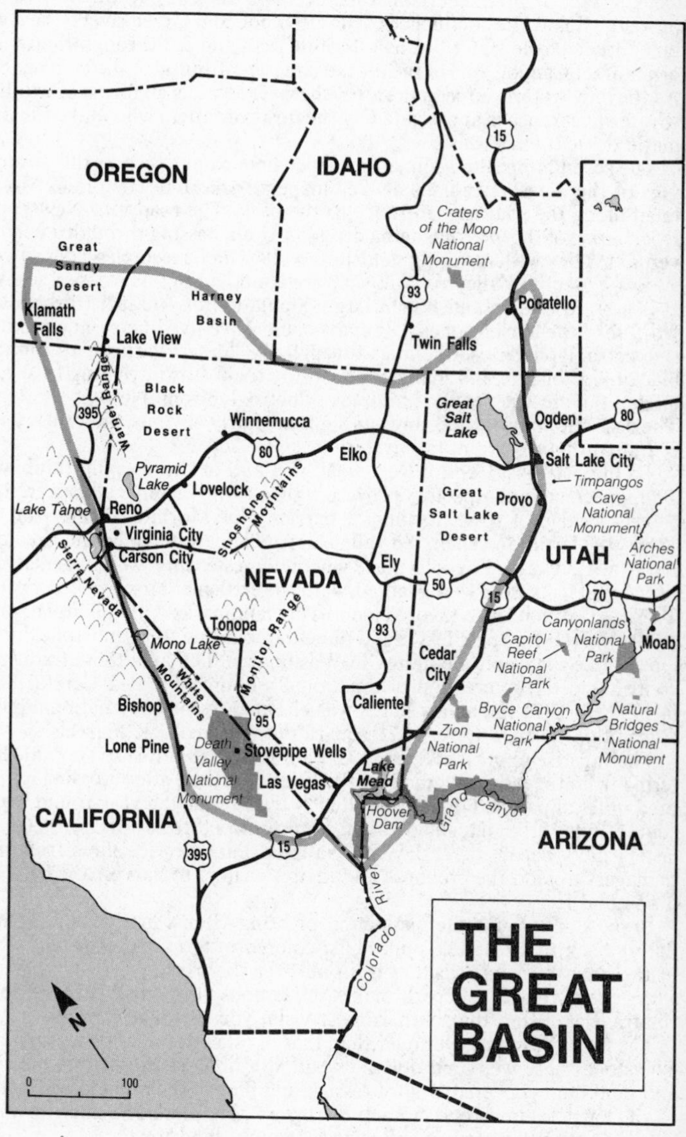
OREGON
IDAHO
Craters of the Moon National Monument
Great Sandy Desert
Harney Basin
Klamath Falls
Lake View
Pocatello
Twin Falls
Black Rock Desert
Warner Range
Winnemucca
Great Salt Lake
Ogden
Salt Lake City
Elko
Pyramid Lake
Lovelock
Shoshone Mountains
Timpangos Cave National Monument
Great Salt Lake Desert
Provo
Lake Tahoe
Reno
Virginia City
Carson City
Sierra Nevada
NEVADA
Ely
UTAH
Arches National Park
Tonopa
Monitor Range
Mono Lake
White Mountains
Canyonlands National Park
Capitol Reef National Park
Moab
Cedar City
Caliente
Bishop
Bryce Canyon National Park
Natural Bridges National Monument
Lone Pine
Death Valley National Monument
Stovepipe Wells
Zion National Park
Lake Mead
Las Vegas
Hoover Dam
Grand Canyon
CALIFORNIA
ARIZONA
Colorado River
N
0 100
THE GREAT BASIN

Colorado River explorer, John Wesley Powell, a one-armed Civil War veteran who mapped the Colorado from a small dory. While passing what is now Canyonlands in 1869, he wrote, "We glide along through a strange, weird, grand region. The landscape everywhere, away from the river, is of rock." Below the confluence of the Colorado and Green rivers, the combined force of the water begins a 14-mile rush and fall through the rapids of Cataract Canyon, one of the most dramatic rafting adventures available. As the only water source in the area, the river attracts all forms of wildlife, whose appearance is appreciated by the hosts of rafters who make the dramatic descent each season.

The second appealing human presence here can be seen in the scratchings of the Anasazi Indians at Newspaper Rock State Historical Monument along the southern entrance to the park. The road into Newspaper Rock is one of the most engaging drives in Utah, passing through a narrow verdant valley with towering sandstone walls which resembles a desert version of Yosemite Valley. Wildflowers are abundant in this wooded setting. It is easy to understand how a large population of Anasazi (the Navajo word for "the ancient ones") Indians could have lived here. Their extensive petroglyphs are scratchings through the "desert varnish," a durable black oxide of iron and manganese, on the rock. It is intriguing to speculate on the meaning of the hundreds of petroglyphs on Newspaper Rock. The deer, mountain sheep, and sun signs are fairly obvious, but other, partly human figures are more mysterious.

To the Navajos, Capitol Reef was "the land of the sleeping rainbow." To pioneers and prospectors proceeding west, the massive cliffs were like a reef, a ridge of rocks forming a barrier. For Mormon farmers of the 1880s, the fertile and sheltered valley, dependably watered by the Fremont River, was "Utah's Eden," a place where homesteading was congenial and over 2,500 fruit trees were planted, with the settlement itself called Fruita. To early travelers, who favored identifying landmarks with fanciful names, one of the round, "petrified" sand dunes, amounting to a sandstone dome, looked like the Capitol building in Washington, D.C. All these traditions contributed to the creation of a national monument called Capitol Reef in 1937. In 1971 the area's status was elevated to that of a national park. Currently, the park covers 378 square miles of geologic marvels.

The surprise to most visitors at Capitol Reef is that it is so verdant. Entering from the west, you pick up the Fremont River after crossing a hundred miles of parched desert. Eventually the Fremont, a year-round water source, cuts through a silted valley of cottonwood trees. In the 1960s the last farmers departed. Today the National Park Service hires fruit tree managers to tend the orchards and invites visitors to harvest the fruit for a nominal fee.

Bryce Canyon has the distinction of being Utah's first national park, dating back to 1923. The pink cliffs, colored by iron and other minerals in the limestone, lure visitors from all over the world.

A central road in the park makes the famous vistas easily accessible to the traveler. From the southernmost vista, you can see 90 miles.

The rock of Bryce is younger than that of other national parks in Utah. The stones here were laid down a grain at a time as sediment when seas and sand dunes covered Utah. Pressure and lime in the mineral mix bonded the particles into rock. Sometimes layers of harder rock, such as limestone, ended up on top of softer rock, mainly sandstone.

About 60 million years ago sea-level basins covered the Bryce area. This body of water, which geologists call Lake Flagstaff, changed in size and shape over time, sometimes forming a single lake and sometimes several. Rivers and streams carried sediment into Lake Flagstaff. The sediment varied from fine-grained clay to gravel and consisted of diverse minerals. The deposits of pink stone were originally about 2,000 feet thick but have been eroded now to about 800 to 1,300 feet thick. Today you can see the deposited layers, plus the older deposits below them, in the cliffs of Bryce. Just as the Pink Cliffs were deposited about 50 to 60 million years ago, the Grey Cliffs below them, consisting of softer rock, were laid down about 120 to 135 million years ago. White, Vermillion, and Chocolate Cliffs are all part of what geologists call the Grand Staircase, a parade of four kinds of rock. The Paiute word for Bryce expressed the appearance accurately: "red rocks standing like men in a bowl-shaped canyon." Mormon cattle rancher Ebenezer Bryce gave his name to the place, but his only surviving comment about the region is that it was "a hell of a place to lose a cow."

The majestic stone faces of the rock cliffs draw travelers to Zion National Park. Intimate nature trails through broadleaf forests keep return visitors interested. This balance of the regal and the intimate is what makes Zion so attractive. After a lovely walk at the Weeping Rock turnoff to a surprise spring and waterfall, you gaze out at the splendor of the rock.

Zion's scenic drive invites comparison with Yosemite Valley. Both are narrow, grassy valleys with mixed conifer and broadleaf forests. Both delight the traveler with the presence of feeding deer, and both have valley walls of imposing stone, Zion being a masterpiece of water eroding sandstone. Zion's major land feature, the Great White Throne, is the desert cousin of Yosemite's El Capitan.

Reno

Although Nevada is a sprawling state with some attractive outlying areas, such as the Lehman Caves and Ruby Mountains in the eastern part, most travelers tend to shoot across the sagebrush to Reno and Las Vegas. Both also have their appealing side attractions, such as Reno's Virginia City and Lake Tahoe and Las Vegas's Hoover Dam and Lake Mead.

Reno means, above everything else, casinos. Circus Circus is the one casino for gamblers and nongamblers alike, including children, owing to its circus and carnival motif. Throughout the day and evening you can watch carnival acts such as trapeze artists, bicycle riders, jugglers, and trained dogs. Surrounding this circus ring is an arcade featuring games of skill, such as ring toss, darts, and shooting galleries, with stuffed animals as prizes. For the gambler there are ubiquitous slot machines and occasional hallucinogenic bell rings announcing a jackpot plus various games of chance, such as craps, 21, and roulette. For the nongambler, the gamblers can provide a fascinating study of the human animal at play.

Travelers to Reno also enjoy shows. There are a flourishing number of cabaret shows as well as grand spectacles like "Hello Hollywood, Hello!," the former long-running production at Bally's-Reno, which has been replaced by headliners.

The area is the home of Harrah's Auto Collection, a pleasure for all ages, on Glendale Road, a few miles east of Reno. This assemblage of Americana should not be missed, though it is in the process of being reduced somewhat by the present owner. Bill Harrah's vision was to locate, purchase, and restore to mint condition all the classics of automotive history. He succeeded in amassing the world's largest collection of antique motor vehicles.

Reno's culinary treasure is Basque food. The Basques have been present in Nevada since the 1880s, originally as sheep ranchers. At a Basque restaurant, such as Louis' Basque Corner, the family-style meal unfolds slowly. First there is a soup course, possibly clam chowder. Then comes a tossed salad with a vinaigrette dressing. All the servings are from big bowls, family-style, and the portions are ample. There follows a traditional baked bean dish. Then the specialty course arrives, which may be mussels and rice, a meal in itself. Then comes your main course, which may be roast lamb or grilled sea bass, served with mashed potatoes. A glass of wine comes with the meal, so you may want to order an extra bottle of the house wine. A dessert of ice cream followed by coffee completes the dinner. The fixed price is a good buy for such a presentation. Aside from Basque dining, the lavish casino buffets, such as Harrah's, are tempting. Casinos price food and lodging deliberately low to lure gamblers to the tables and slot machines.

Reno boasts a scenic outdoors, with skiing in winter and hiking in summer. Lake Tahoe and Pyramid Lake are major attractions. Besides the nearby California ski areas, there are two major ski sites on the Nevada side of the state line: Mount Rose and Incline Village. The drive to Lake Tahoe makes a lovely outing in winter or summer. Along the Nevada shore, if you travel south on Highway 28, the Lake Tahoe State Park affords an interesting turnoff for a picnic or lake viewing. In winter the low areas in this park are a favorite cross-country ski area.

The other major outdoor region, Pyramid Lake, is 32 miles northeast of Reno. This high desert lake, a remnant of the larger prehistoric Lake Lahontan, is a popular summertime destination, offering swimming, trophy trout fishing, and boating. Soft red and brown sandstone mountains surround the lake, and the approach road goes through attractive desert country. The pyramid shape of Anahoe Island inspired John Fremont to call the area Pyramid Lake when he came through in 1844. Paiute Indian reservation lands surround the lake.

Virginia and Carson Cities

Silver was nearly as important as gold as a force in the development of the West. Southeast of Reno, at Virginia City, lie the richest silver mines in the West. Virginia City and Carson City, the state capital, are worth a day's exploring.

When you get to Virginia City, orient yourself to the setting at the Visitors Bureau on C Street, the main street. The Bureau presents a free slide show explaining the city's history. The extensive wealth from the mines helped build San Francisco and finance the Civil War for the North, but some of the money stayed in Virginia City. Relics of opulence include a few splendid Victorian structures. There are three main mansions in town—Castle, Mackay, and Savage. Castle and Mackay are museums, open to the public, while Savage Mansion has been converted to a bed-and-breakfast establishment. The Castle is a striking yellow and brown edifice built in 1868 for Robert Graves, superintendent of the Empire Mine. The Mackay Museum is an opulent brick home. John Mackay was one of the few early mine owners who emerged with his fortune intact. The Savage Mansion was once the headquarters of the Savage Mining Company, whose shafts enter the ground immediately opposite the house. In 1879, ex-President Grant spoke at the Savage Mansion, thanking miners for the bullion that had helped finance the Civil War. Abraham Lincoln pushed through admittance of Nevada as a state for the silver money to finance the Civil War and for two more northern votes against the secessionists in congressional showdowns.

At the Ponderosa Mine, which you enter through the Ponderosa Saloon on C Street, you can descend into the shafts. From May through October the Chollar Mine is also open, giving you a glimpse at mining history. The Chollar Mine tour is a 40-minute underground walk into the deepest mine in the lode, running 3,200 feet into the mountain on 20 levels. All the mines at Virginia City produced an estimated billion and a quarter dollars in gold and silver. Stop in at the Way It Was Museum to see a scale model of the 700 miles of mine shafts that burrow through the ground immediately below the city.

When the miners weren't digging, they were gathering in saloons. The Bucket of Blood Saloon is a favorite watering hole. Another saloon, the Silver Queen, has an unusual drawing of a woman with 3,261 silver dollars and 28 gold pieces embedded in her dress. Aside from this 15-foot-high expression of barroom elegance, the wooden bar and mirrored mantle at the Silver Queen are a monument to the carver's art.

Up and down C Street there are several small museums in storefront buildings. The most ambitious is the Mark Twain Museum of Memories. Fortunately for literature, Twain failed as a miner and went to work for $25 a week as a fledgling journalist for the *Territorial Enterprise,* Nevada's first newspaper. Several other small museums, such as the Wild West Museum, feature mining, gun, and Indian artifacts.

B Street has two other architecturally interesting buildings, the Storey County Courthouse and the Piper Opera House. The courthouse is a lavish white stone structure. The opera house was the cultural showcase of the region, hosting traveling Shakespearean performers such as Edwin Booth and singers such as Enrico Caruso.

Graveyards at the north end of town are a sobering legacy of what life amounted to here in the 1860s for some 38,000 souls, including 2,000 Chinese. As you wander among the stone or wood markers, consider the diversity of nationalities that gathered here. Hosea and Ethan Allen Grosh made the definitive discovery in 1857 that Mount Davidson was riddled with silver ore. The Groshes died without the discovery becoming widely known. Two Irishmen, Peter O'Reiley and Patrick McLaughlin, are credited with making the rediscovery in 1859. At their diggings, which were taken over by Henry T. Paige Comstock, there was plenty of "black stuff" or "blue stuff" with the gold. "Worse'n useless," said Comstock. "If it wasn't for that damned bogus stuff, my diggings might amount to something." Eventually a curious prospector took a sample to California and found that it assayed out as a rich silver sulfide worth $3,000 a ton in silver and $800 a ton in gold. Comstock's name became associated with the lode, and the rush to Virginia City began.

From Memorial Day through September, rail buffs enjoy a 30-minute train ride on the partially restored, standard-gauge Virginia & Truckee Railroad out through the mining district. Adults, $3.50; children, $1.75.

After Virginia City, take Highway 342 south and Highway 50 west to Carson City, the capital. The drive from Virginia City takes you past working mines and the shafts of many abandoned mines, including the Gold Hill, Silver Hill, and Devil's Gate mining districts. Extensive tailings from the mines give you a sense of the massive scale of operations.

When you reach Carson City, stop at the Chamber of Commerce on South Carson Street and ask for a driving tour map of the town's government buildings, Victorian mansions, and museums.

Proceed first to the state capitol. This elegant but restrained 1871 stone structure built of sandstone from the mines of city founder Abe Curry can be viewed outside and inside. Inside are handsome floors and walls made of Alaskan marble. The woodworking is impressive. As expected, portraits of past governors adorn the walls. A frieze enumerates the litany of metals that put Nevada on the map. Carson City, as a name, replaced Eagle Station, which was the name when the area was a Mormon stop on the Emigrant Trail.

Then drive down Robinson Street to look at two of the mansions for which Carson City is famous. Near the end of Robinson Street, the Greek columned structure is the governor's mansion. Across from the governor's mansion, lumber baron D. L. Bliss built a palace. The Bliss Mansion is a 21-room structure that resembles San Francisco Victorians of the same 1870s period.

If you have an opportunity to visit Virginia and Carson cities, you'll emerge with a much better sense of the silver discovery that shaped the history of the West and gave Nevada its nickname, the Silver State.

Las Vegas

Las Vegas appears before the visitor as a thriving mirage, a neon oasis where life flourishes only because of dam-stored water and the 1931 Nevada state law allowing gambling. Without the Colorado River water trapped by Hoover Dam, life would be extremely fragile here and the human population would be low, as it was when Paiute and earlier Pueblo Indians lived here. The pervasiveness of the desert impresses a visitor flying into the region. Without the law legalizing gambling, there would be some farming here, but nothing like the half million inhabitants and more than 15 million annual visitors.

Las Vegas didn't exist until the 20th century and calls itself the largest American city founded in the 20th century. The first hotels with gambling were downtown, but a resourceful developer decided that an establishment a few miles closer to Los Angeles, in an area that eventually became the Strip, would cause the weary car traveler from Los Angeles to stop. The dual locations of Las Vegas, the Downtown and the Strip, are linked by bus and taxi. The advent of inexpensive air travel made it possible for masses of people to arrive. With the water shortage forever resolved (there is two years' flow of river stored behind Hoover Dam), the future of Las Vegas looks assured. The city makes efforts now to broaden its appeal to visitors by luring such major nongambling attractions as the National Finals Rodeo, the World Series of rodeos, which will occur here each December for at least the next few years.

Las Vegas has a large number of first-class hotels, part of its attraction as a convention center. The Las Vegas Hilton, next to the Convention Center, has over 3,000 rooms and is said to be the world's largest hotel. Each major hotel tries to develop its own style. For example, the Imperial Palace affects an Oriental flavor in its architecture, its decor, and the dress of its workers.

Gambling in most forms is available at all the casinos. Gamblers who wish to graduate from the one-armed bandit to a more complex game will find plenty of teachers to describe the intricacies of blackjack, keno, craps, poker, baccarat, and roulette. The gambling industry here is valued at more than $2 billion a year.

Entertainment at the casinos varies from major spectacles to single top-name performers. Bally's-Las Vegas's "Jubilee" is a musical review featuring girls, song, and special effects. Such scenes as the sinking of the *Titanic* include all the dazzling special effects Hollywood can muster. Interspersed with the songs are specialty acts. "Folies Bergère," at the Tropicana, is a re-creation of the famous Paris revue, featuring magnificent sets and exquisitely choreographed dance numbers. "Lido de Paris," playing at the Stardust, is renowned for its beautiful, topless showgirls. Smaller productions of note include "Splash" at the Riviera and "City Lites" at the Flamingo. Caesars Palace, the Las Vegas Hilton, Golden Nugget, and Sahara hotels present headliners such as Wayne Newton, Diana Ross, Dolly Parton, and Kenny Rogers.

Beyond Las Vegas lies an appealing outdoor world. Hoover Dam, which celebrated its 55th year in operation in 1990, created a large recreational body of water, Lake Mead, which extends 115 miles behind the dam. The other major pleasures of outdoor Las Vegas are Red Rock Canyon and Valley of Fire parks, where the red iron oxide in the rock and the petroglyphs of early Indian cultures await the explorer.

Hoover Dam, only an hour's drive south of Las Vegas, is well worth visiting. As you approach the dam, stop at the Alan Bible Visitor Center to see a 15-minute film on the construction of the dam and peruse the literature. A botanical garden surrounds the Center.

Park and walk around the dam to get views of the massive concrete structure. Then stop in for the 10-minute narrated show in the Exhibit Hall and take the half-hour tour. After seeing the dam, you can cruise out on Lake Mead in an excursion boat that leaves four times daily from the Lake Mead Marina at Boulder Beach.

The visitor bureau at nearby Boulder City plays continuously a 28-minute movie, *The Story of Hoover Dam.* The visitor center is opposite the historic Boulder City Hotel, which is on the National Register of Historic Places. Boulder City was built as the residence for 5,000 workers who toiled here for four years in the 1930s.

Lake Mead is a huge aquatic playground and fishery that extends behind the dam. From marinas at Callville Bay (closest to Las Vegas) and Echo Bay you can rent houseboats for a leisurely vacation on the lake.

Besides Lake Mead, the two major parks near Las Vegas are wonderful places to visit, but the heat of summer makes them difficult to enjoy unless you have an air-conditioned vehicle. Try to arrange your schedule to visit at another time of the year, especially in spring, when the wildflowers bloom.

Red Rock Canyon, a half hour west of Las Vegas on Charleston Road, is a remarkable collection of rock formations colored by the red iron oxide in the sandstone. The red oxide both tones and binds the stone. Stop in at the visitors center to see the exhibits and then drive the 13-mile one-way road that loops through the park. The most attractive view is at the stop called Calico Hills.

Valley of Fire State Park, 1½ hours east of Las Vegas, offers similar but more extensive red and gray limestone formations plus Indian petroglyphs and petrified wood. The valley does indeed look as if it were on fire when you see the rocks in a certain light. Stop in at the visitor center and orient yourself to the park, which offers extensive spring flowering of desert plants, such as yellow blossoms on prickly pear cactus, brittlebush, and creosote bush.

Death Valley

West of Las Vegas lie vast California deserts that are rich with wildflowers such as poppies in the spring. More tenacious plants, such as beavertail cactus, flower even in the heat of summer, when the desert presents itself as a shimmering mirage. The Indian word for Death Valley was *Tomesha,* meaning "ground afire."

From the west you reach Death Valley via Highway 136 from Lone Pine or Highway 178 from the Highway 395 cutoff at Red Mountain. From Las Vegas, Death Valley is north on Highway 95 and then west on 373 to Death Valley Junction. Las Vegas has the closest commercial airport destination to Death Valley, some 120 miles away. The visitor center at Furnace Creek is the appropriate place to learn about the history and main attractions of Death Valley.

During the westward expansion period, Death Valley was the scene of many heroic efforts, such as those of the Manly expedition. In 1849, William Manly was one of the first pioneers to traverse this unknown wilderness without dying of thirst. Stories of the Jaywalkers Trail from the Great Salt Lake in 1848 and the Darwin French Party Trail in 1860 are absorbing tales of human endurance in the midst of natural adversity. The interpretive center at Death Valley uses recorded voices to re-create the poignant diaries and letters of survivors whose tintype visages suggest the restrictiveness of life in mid-19th-century California.

Death Valley's most notable attractions are the stark landscape and the diversity of life forms that thrive here in spite of temperature extremes and slight amounts of moisture. Always a place of extremes, Death Valley can be beastly hot and severely cold. Although the two spots that are 282 feet below sea level get initial attention, there is also 11,049-foot Telescope Peak. Mount Whitney, the highest point in the contiguous United States (14,494 feet), is not far away.

North from Death Valley along Highway 395 and east from Bishop are special trees that lend credence to the notion that California is a land of superlatives. These are the bristlecone pines, high in the White Mountains, at elevations of 13,000 feet, making them accessible only in summer. These trees are the oldest living things on the earth; they have been core dated at almost 5,000 years. To sit meditatively in front of a bristlecone pine and contemplate that it was more than 1,000 years old before the fall of Troy or the Jews' exodus from Egypt is a moving experience.

Mono Lake, farther up the Owens Valley, is an extraordinary landscape of tufa rock jutting out from an ever shallower lake. Tufa is a rock formed when the mineral calcium carbonate precipitates out from the lake's water. Environmental controversy of the most strident tenor has occurred as the Los Angeles Water District has drained the lake to levels allowing predators a land bridge to islands where thousands of gulls and pelicans nest.

PRACTICAL INFORMATION FOR THE GREAT BASIN

WHEN TO GO. The choice of season to travel in the Great Basin is no casual matter. Utah's summer temperatures are manageable, but the deserts of Nevada and Death Valley are extremely hot. Summer temperatures are so high that air-conditioned transportation and lodging are taken for granted at hotels, shops, restaurants, and rental car agencies. One way to cool off in southern Nevada is by immersing yourself in Lake Mead, but you do this from a rented houseboat, itself air-conditioned so that you can sleep at night. Life was not always so comfortable here, of course. For $4 per day, minus $1.60 for meals and lodging, skilled workers of the 1930s spent 12-hour shifts building Hoover Dam, often in 120-degree summer temperatures, with plenty of ambulances available to take the heat-prostrated and dehydrated to the hospital in Boulder City.

The months of Apr., May, Sept., and Oct. are the most comfortable in both states, but that is more relevant to the outdoor enthusiast of Utah than to the casino patron of Nevada, who may care little about the month while mesmerized in front of the slots at 4 A.M.

Because of summer heat, the most popular times to visit Death Valley are winter and spring. At these times lodging reservations are an absolute requirement. Thanksgiving, Christmas, the presidential birthdays, and Easter are times of maximum visitor use. Interest in winter travel to Death Valley has grown steadily since 1933, when Franklin Roosevelt declared the area a national monument.

The winter-sports enthusiasts in Utah gather in the mountains east of Salt Lake in Nov. and ski through Apr.

HOW TO GET THERE. When planning schedules in the region, keep in mind that Utah is on mountain time and Nevada is on pacific time.

Salt Lake is often called the Crossroads of the West. Reno and Las Vegas, because of liberal tax laws on inventories (compared with California) and because of the established arteries of highway and rail transit, have become major warehousing centers for distributing merchandise.

By plane. Many major airlines fly into *Salt Lake International Airport,* including *American, America West, Continental, Delta, TWA,* and *United.*

For the fly-in traveler, a dozen major airlines serve Reno from both California and the east, landing at *Reno–Cannon International Airport.* If you plan to stay within Reno, you won't need a car.

In Las Vegas, ever-expanding *McCarran International Airport* receives jet service by most major carriers. The airport is a short taxi ride south of the casino-lined Strip or Downtown.

By bus. *Greyhound* serves Salt Lake City and Utah as well as Reno, Las Vegas, and rural Nevada.

By train. In 1869 Leland Stanford pounded the golden spike, joining the Union Pacific and Central Pacific railroads, into the railbed just north of Salt Lake. The Golden Spike National Historic Site, in Promontory, recalls this historic event of the railroad era.

Today, *Amtrak*'s passenger trains serve Salt Lake City and Las Vegas. For Amtrak information, call 800–USA–RAIL. The *Pioneer* travels between Salt Lake and Seattle, with stops at Portland, Boise, and Ogden. The *Desert Wind* travels to Salt Lake from Los Angeles via Las Vegas. Amtrak's popular *Zephyr* operates from Salt Lake through the Rockies to Chicago and west through Reno to San Francisco.

By car. I-80, which connects the East Coast and the West Coast, runs through Salt Lake City and Reno. Drivers approaching Salt Lake City from either direction on the modern interstate can still get a sense of the terrain that pioneer wagons had to cross. I-15 is the major north-south artery in Utah and goes all the way to southern California via Las Vegas. Las Vegas is a 6-hour drive from L.A. and a 10-hour drive from Salt Lake City. If you drive to Reno from California, remember that I-80 is smoother and faster than twisty Highway 50, but 50 might be your choice if you want to stop in South Lake Tahoe.

TOURIST INFORMATION. Utah. For the state as a whole, the information source is the *Utah Travel Council,* Council Hall, Capitol Hill, Salt Lake City, UT 84114 (801–538–1030). The central information source for Salt Lake is the *Salt Lake Convention & Visitor Bureau,* 180 South West Temple, Salt Lake, UT 84101 (801–521–2868). Orient yourself there with maps, brochures, and a multimedia show on the Mormons.

As you enter the state, there are also five Utah welcome centers which are helpful. They are on I-15 near Brigham City (801–744–5567), I-80 near Echo Junction (801–336–2588), I-15 near St. George (801–673–4542), I-70 near Thompson (801–285–2234), and the Museum of Natural History in Vernal (801–789–4002).

Nevada. For an overview of the state as a travel destination, write the *Nevada Commission on Tourism,* Capitol Complex, Carson City, NV 89710 (702–687–4322). For information on Reno, contact the *Reno-Sparks Convention & Visitor Bureau,* Box 837, Reno, NV 89504, or call 800–FOR–RENO. The *Las Vegas Visitors Bureau* provides information, hotel reservations, and current show listings. The *Las Vegas Convention and Visitors Bureau* is at 3150 S. Paradise Rd., Las Vegas, NV 89109 (702–733–2323).

Death Valley. When planning a visit to Death Valley, write ahead for a brochure to the Park Superintendent, Death Valley National Monument, Box 158, Tecopa, CA 92389 (619–786–2331).

TELEPHONES. The area code for Utah is 801; for Nevada, 702; for Death Valley, 619. Directory assistance for all three areas is 411. Cost of a local pay phone call in both Utah and Nevada is 25 cents, with no time limit on a local call.

EMERGENCY PHONE NUMBERS. To get police, fire, or ambulance help, dial 911 in Utah, Nevada or Death Valley. Information about road conditions is important for safe travel in this region during winter snowfalls and summer thunderstorms. Especially on smaller roads in the desert, the threat of flash floods is considerable. For road information, call 801–965–4518 in Utah and 702–793–1313 in Nevada.

HOW TO GET AROUND. Salt Lake City: The traveler needs to understand the logic behind Salt Lake addresses. Temple Sq. is the historic center of the city. From the temple, all streets are laid out in an exact direction, north, south, east, or west. Number 700 E. Temple, for example, is 7 blocks east of Temple. The "blocks" are arbitrarily set at 7 to the mi. All addresses refer to two map coordinates; one axis is along East and West Temple Sts.; the other, along North and South Temple Sts. A typical address, such as 550 E. 700 South, is found 5½ blocks east of Temple Sq. on 700 (or 7th) South St.

One of the ways to get around central Salt Lake City is the refurbished open-air trolley system, called the *Brigham Street Trolleys,* which operate on a fixed route through the downtown area, linking the central hotel and attraction district with the newly renovated Trolley Sq., a cluster of fashionable shops and restaurants near the Union Pacific depot. Trolley Sq. is located in the old 1908 trolley-car barns from the turn of the century. The earliest trolleys were mule-driven versions in 1872.

Las Vegas: The Strip Bus runs every 15 minutes between the Strip and the downtown Casino Center.

By rental car. The major rental car companies are active in both states, based in the major cities of Salt Lake City, Reno, and Las Vegas. Fly-and-drive programs are popular in the area, with weeklong packages offering unlimited mileage a popular option if extensive touring is planned. Contact the major rental companies as follows: *Hertz* (800–654–3131), *Avis* (800–331–1212), and *National* (800–328–4567).

HINTS TO MOTORISTS. Desert driving requires several precautions in the Great Basin area. Be sure you have plenty of gas, a car in good mechanical condition, a radiator with adequate coolant, a gallon of water per person, and your wits about you as you drive through this region. Rest your car frequently and watch the temperature gauge for your radiator, especially when climbing hills.

Avoid traveling through Death Valley in summer unless you can't arrange another time for a visit. In 1913 the summer temperature hit a record 134 degrees F. The average summer high temperatures in July are around 116 degrees. Night temperatures in Death Valley during summer dip only to 100 degrees. Under such circumstances, air conditioning in a car and lodging is a necessity.

Las Vegas can also be hot in summer. The summer heat diminishes somewhat at the higher elevations of Reno and parts of Utah.

HINTS TO DISABLED TRAVELERS. Both Utah and Nevada are making progress on the accessibility of streets, restaurants, and parks. Write the tourism offices for the two states (see Tourist Information) and the five national parks (see National Parks) with your special needs to get specific information.

TOURS AND SPECIAL-INTEREST SIGHTSEEING. Salt Lake City: *Temple Square* can be toured free 9 A.M.–9 P.M. Seven short 15-minute tours proceed simultaneously, so you can learn about one facet of the Temple Sq. at a time. Likewise, the major Mormon structures within a block of the square are open for guided tours. These include Brigham Young's *Beehive House* (801–240–2671), open for a half-hour tour, and *The Family History Library* (801–240–2331), with its elaborate genealogical resources. An informative tour is offered to the public. Behind the LDS Building is a flower-filled plaza with a view of the temple. Around the plaza are several poignant statues done in a realistic manner, showing moments of family life, such as a son setting off in the world or a mother in a moment of joyous dancing with her children.

Near Temple Sq., the *Salt Palace* (801–363–7681) can be toured. It is a convention and sports complex, the home of basketball and hockey teams, and the host for concerts, rodeos, and circuses. Salt Lake's and Utah's population (168,000 in the city, 696,000 in Salt Lake County, and 1.65 million in the state) supports many cultural activities, so there is a demand for meeting places. Peruse also the *Salt Lake Art Center* in the Salt Palace. This art center houses many changing exhibits by local and national artists in various media, including painting, sculpture, photography, and crafts. Symphony Hall, also in the Salt Palace, is home of the Utah Symphony Orchestra. The hall is an acoustical and visual gem with sumptuous outlays of gold leaf and brass.

National Parks: Unlike the parks in the Rocky Mountain states, Utah's national parks are primarily self-toured with brochures and maps obtained at visitor centers. The parks are somewhat spartanly staffed, and the territories are immense, especially at Canyonlands. Contact the *Utah Travel Council,* Council Hall, Capitol Hill, Salt Lake City, UT 84114 (801–538–1030) for a list of operators.

Reno: Fleischmann Planetarium (702–784–4812, admission under $5), on the University of Nevada campus, presents entertaining shows on celestial subjects, with activities from space travel to telescope viewing.

Hoover Dam: The two entities to tour are the Exhibit Hall and the inner workings of the dam. The recorded talk at the Exhibit Hall spotlights different places on a topographical scale model of the 1,400-mi. Colorado River watershed. The talk will enhance your knowledge of the drama and politics of the Colorado River. Untamed, the Colorado oscillated between years of extreme flood and utter drought. One flood in 1905 created the Salton Sea when the river lunged out of its banks and into the California low desert for 16 months before being diverted back into its channel. Hoover Dam provides irrigation water for ¾ million acres, drinking and industrial water for 12 million people, electrical power divided two-thirds for California and one-third for Nevada–Arizona, and water recreation opportunities on Lake Mead for 7 million people a year.

After the Exhibit Hall, take the half-hour guided tour of the dam (702–293–8367). The tour costs $1, and reservations are not taken. The tour takes you to the concrete innards and acquaints you with the turbines and piping crucial to the operation. You'll emerge with an appreciation of the dam as one of the engineering masterpieces of the modern world. The dam is almost as thick at the base (660 ft.) as it is tall (726.4 ft.). There is enough concrete in the dam to pave a highway 8 in. thick from coast to coast. The water in Lake Mead would cover the state of Connecticut to 10 ft.

Lehman Caves National Monument. Baker, NV 89311 (702–234–7331). One of the unusual nature tours possible in rural Nevada is at Lehman Caves, in the eastern part of the state. The caves consist of colorful marble and limestone passages. Guided 1½-hour tours are adults, $3; children 6–15, $2. The caves and surrounding scenic area are among the most attractive landscapes in the state.

NATIONAL PARKS AND MONUMENTS. Utah enjoys the presence of five national parks, all open daily, year-round. To get information on all the parks from one source, write to the Utah Travel Council, Council Hall, Capitol Hill, Salt Lake City, UT 84114 (801–538–1030). This office provides information on the area and the campgrounds in the state's national parks, recreation areas, monuments, and historic sites. Alternatively, you can write to the park superintendent at a particular park.

Arches National Park. c/o Canyonlands National Park, 125 W. 200 South St., Moab, UT 84532 (801–259–8161). Entrance fee is $3 per vehicle. There is a visitor center and campground.

Arches, sometimes described as a red rock wonderland, is southeast of Salt Lake, about 6 hours by car. Arches is precisely 5 mi. north of Moab, a little traveler town started by Mormon pioneers. The nearest major airport is in Grand Junction, Colorado. To tour the region you need your own vehicle, which can be rented in Salt Lake or Grand Junction. Tour the park by driving the single road in and out, stopping to see the principal features.

Canyonlands National Park. Canyonlands National Park, 125 W. 200 South St., Moab, UT 84532 (801–259–7164). Entrance is free. There is a very limited visitor information trailer at the south entrance, plus camping. The choice overlook into Canyonlands from the north is from a state park with an excellent visitor center selling interpretive literature: **Dead Horse Point State Park,** Box 609, Moab, UT 84532 (801–259–6511). Day-use fee is $3 per vehicle. Attractive *Kayenta Campground* in this state park has hot showers.

As with Arches, Canyonlands is in eastern Utah, about 6 hours by car from Salt Lake City. Grand Junction has the closest airport. To see the park you will need a vehicle. The major support town for travelers in the region is Moab, which has motels, restaurants, and campgrounds. Canyonlands has three paved entry points along Hwy. 191 north and south of Moab.

Capitol Reef National Park. Torrey, UT 84775 (801–425–3791). There is an excellent visitor center with interpretive literature. An attractive campground occupies a grassy meadow next to the Fremont River. Aside from a visitor center, there are no other services in the park. Entrance fee is $3 per vehicle.

Three interesting side trips from Capitol Reef are the newly paved mountain road (Hwy. 12) between Capitol Reef and Bryce Canyon National Park, the road west to the Hite Marina in the Glen Canyon National Recreation Area, and the drive beyond the Hite Marina on Hwy. 95 to Natural Bridges National Monument.

Natural Bridges National Monument. Box 1, Lake Powell, UT 84533 (801–259–5174). The visitor center offers a slide show as well as geological and solar power exhibits. Entrance is $3 per vehicle. There are a limited number of campsites, but no other facilities are offered. Water is rationed.

Theodore Roosevelt proclaimed Natural Bridges a national monument in 1908. The monument boasts three impressive natural bridges and one of the world's most extensive arrays of solar cells, which furnish all the electricity needed to run the visitor center and the residences of the rangers. Natural bridges are different from the arches of Arches National Park. A natural bridge is a span created by a flooding, silt-laden stream washing out soft rock in its course, leaving the span. Arches are holes in rock caused by weathering, mainly from rainwater and ice, aided by wind.

Bryce Canyon National Park. Bryce Canyon, UT 84717 (801–834–5322). Entrance is $5 for a 7-day pass. In the park you'll find an excellent visitor center with movies and interpretive literature, an elaborate lodge with dining facilities, a campground with showers, and a store.

Bryce Canyon is in southwestern Utah, 363 mi. from Salt Lake City. The fastest route is via I-15 and the connecting Hwys. 20 and 12. If you are approaching from the east and Capitol Reef National Park, take the newly paved Hwy. 12, one of the loveliest roads in Utah, carrying you through high forests of pure aspen, lower forests of ponderosa pine, and parched deserts. At high vistas in the 30 mi. south of Grover, the road builders have constructed several scenic turnouts that allow you to look east over Capitol Reef National Park and the surrounding terrain.

Stop first at the visitor center and ask a ranger to orient you to the park. Secure a detailed park map. Because all the major vistas are facing the east, the best pattern for visiting the park is to drive to the southern end of the 18-mi. road and then start back, proceeding north with a stop at each notable turnout.

Zion National Park. Springdale, UT 84767 (801–772–3256). Entrance is $5 for a 7-day pass. There are attractive wooded campgrounds along the Virgin River. The major activity in the park is driving along the scenic roadway and stopping for views or hikes. There is one lodging in the park. Inner tubing is popular in the Virgin River.

Death Valley National Monument. Box 158, Tecopa, CA 92389 (619–786–2331). Lodgings are available within the monument. Campgrounds are also open. There is an excellent visitor center with evening programs.

In the northern part of Death Valley visit Scotty's Castle, the house of Death Valley Scotty, a desert character who chose to construct a lavish home in this forlorn region. Walter Scott was the character's real name. He and his millionaire friend, Albert M. Johnson, who bankrolled the operation, sank some 2 million uninflated dollars into this 25-room Spanish-Moorish extravaganza and became part of the local folklore. Nearby, you can gaze into the Ubehebe Crater, where celestial impact left a lasting imprint on the desert.

STATE PARKS. The source for information on Utah's state parks and recreation generally is *Utah Parks and Recreation,* 1636 W. North Temple, Suite 100, Salt Lake City, UT 84116 (801–538–7220). For information on Nevada state parks and recreation, contact the Division of State Parks, Capitol Complex, Carson City, NV 89710 (702–687–4384).

CAMPING. Fees at rustic national park campgrounds are as low as $5. Fees at full-hookup KOAs run about $15. Reservations at private camps can be made by writing in advance, usually with a night's deposit. Write for a booklet on all camps in Utah to the *Utah Travel Council,* Council Hall, Capitol Hill, Salt Lake City, UT 84114 (801–538–1030). For a list of all the camping places in Nevada and information about them, write to *Commission on Tourism,* Carson City, NV 89710 (702–687–4322).

For more detailed information on camping in the U.S. Forest Service campgrounds in both states, contact the U.S. Forest Service, Regional Office, 324 25th St., Ogden, UT 84401 (801–625–5182).

Recreational vehicle camping is popular throughout Utah and Nevada, with full-hookup campgrounds and rustic camps available. For example, to start a Utah national park circuit in Moab, you could stay at the full-service Canyonland Campark RV Park, 555 S. Main, Moab, UT 84532 (801–259–6848), or the more primitive camps at Devil's Garden in Arches National Park.

A unique RV travel opportunity occurs in Reno, Bally's-Reno has an RV campground adjacent to its casino and hotel. The fee is $17 per night. Call (702–789–2000).

Death Valley. There are nine campgrounds in the monument; the most developed are at Texas Springs, Furnace Creek, and Mesquite Springs. For more information, write to the superintendent (see National Parks).

FISHING AND HUNTING. Rainbow trout in the streams and striped bass or largemouth bass in Lakes Mead and Powell are the major fishing catches in the Great Basin states. Trout were also planted in the lake reservoirs and were abundant for a few years, but the stripers ate them. Both types of bass are introduced fish that have flourished here, feeding on a smaller introduced fish called the threadfin shad, which in turn feeds on the zooplankton that bloom in the reservoirs. Anglers express some long-range concern about the restriction of nutrient flow into the Colorado reservoirs, especially of phosphates, because of upstream dams, so the fishing may decline in another decade. The bass fishing is best in summer, when the warm water stimulates the stripers to move out of deep, cool water and begin their frenzied feeding on shad, causing the water to assume a boiling appearance. Stripers have the ability to herd schools of shad into a ball, plunge through them quickly, stun the small fish with a thrashing tail, and then consume the slow-moving, groggy shad. The experience and noise can be awesome. The largest striper taken from Lake Mead with rod and reel weighed 52 pounds. Locals anticipate that stripers over 60 pounds will enhance future fish stories from both reservoirs. Largemouth bass are also plentiful and always remain close to shore, within 30 ft. of lake bottom, but stripers are sometimes taken in deeper, open water.

Deer hunting and upland bird hunting, especially quail and dove, are popular. Utah is a major deer-hunting state, with an annual harvest of about 106,000 animals. It also enjoys abundant marshlands for waterfowl hunting, especially around the Great Salt Lake.

Here are some sources for information on fishing and hunting regulations and licenses.

Utah. Contact the Utah Wildlife Resourses, 1596 W. North Temple, Salt Lake City, UT 84116 (801–538–4700). They provide information on hunting and fishing regulations and licenses. Bird refuges are also within their domain.

Nevada. Contact the Nevada Dept of Wildlife, Box 10678, Reno, NV 89520 (702–789–0500).

Fishing and hunting rules and regulations are strictly enforced within all areas of the Great Basin.

RIVER RAFTING AND HOUSEBOATING. River rafting is a major sport in Utah on the Colorado, Green, and San Juan rivers. The best plan for a prospective rafter is to contact an outfitter in the major town near the intended rafting site, such as Moab. Be sure to raft with a professional rather than trying to do it yourself because of the many dangers inherent in the sport. For a complete list of river rafters, contact the state tourism office (see Tourist Information) or *Utah Guides & Outfitters,* 3031 S. 500 East, Salt Lake City, UT 84106 (801–466–1912). Moab is the most popular site for Colorado River float trips. It is easy there to arrange a one-day float trip on short notice. (One experienced company is Tex's River Expeditions, Box 67, Moab, UT 84532; 801–259–5101.) Three- or four-day trips require more planning. Trips cost about $35 for a half day to several hundred dollars for a catered week of rafting.

Houseboating is popular on lakes Powell and Mead. Prices vary according to season and type of boat. *A.R.A.,* 2916 N. 35th Ave., Suite 8, Phoenix, AZ 85017 (800–528–6154), rents boats from any marina on Lake Powell. For houseboating on Lake Mead, contact the *Callville Bay Resort & Marina,* Box 100–Star Route 10, Las Vegas, NV 89124 (702–565–8958), or *Echo Bay Resort,* Overton, NV 89040 (800–752–9669).

Houseboats can be rented for 3-day, 4-day, or week-long periods. Summers are the busiest (and hottest) months; Apr., May, Sept., and Oct. are attractive alternative times. The water is fully warmed for swimming, and the air becomes pleasantly cool in Sept.–Oct. Rental houseboats sleep up to 12 people, but more than 6 adults are likely to strain the psychological carrying capacity of the boat.

Houseboats on Lake Mead and Lake Powell come fully equipped, including linen and blankets. All you need to bring is your clothes, swimsuit, fishing gear, food, and drink. An ice machine at the docks can cool your beverage of choice.

Houseboating on these Colorado River reservoirs is a unique experience. No other houseboating ambience, such as Lake Shasta or the Delta in California, approaches the size of Lake Powell and Lake Mead, the largest man-made reservoir in the United States. (It is said that the reservoir behind the Aswan Dam in Egypt is the only larger man-made body of water in the world.) The 550-mi. shoreline, which can accommodate a large number of boaters, is a desert and mountainous terrain with some sandy beaches.

SKIING. Utah. The Oct.–Apr. season draws skiers from all over the world for the fine white powder east of Salt Lake. State boosters called this "the greatest snow on earth." Dry desert winds reduce the snow humidity level. Because of the relatively low moisture content of the snow compared with that which falls on the mountains of the Pacific Coast states, the snow in Utah has a dry or powdery consistency which makes for exhilarating skiing. The average annual 37-ft. snowfall often accumulates powder snow that is hip deep. In summer this ski region can be explored for its alpine vistas. Utah offers a total of 16 ski areas. For information on all the ski areas, accommodations, and costs, write for a copy of the *Utah Ski Planner,* Utah Travel Council, Council Hall, Capitol Hill, Salt Lake City, UT 84114. For current ski conditions, call 801–521–8102.

Some of the major ski areas are: *Alta,* at Alta (801–742–3333). *Brian Head Ski Resort,* at Cedar City (801–677–2035). *Brighton,* at Brighton (801–943–8309). *Park City,* at Park City (801–649–8111). *ParkWest,* at Park City (801–649–5400). *Snowbird,* at Snowbird (800–453–3000). *Solitude,* at Salt Lake (801–534–1400). *Sundance,* at Sundance (801–225–4107).

Nevada. *Rudy Mountain* (702–753–6867) is one of the few areas in the United States offering helicopter skiing. A helicopter takes you high into the powdery domain of the mountain and allows for a 2,000-ft. vertical drop. Reno puts you close to *Mt. Rose* (702–849–0704) and *Incline* (702–832–1177). Reno serves as the major fly-in point for the 19 ski areas in the Reno-Tahoe region of the Sierra. Near Las Vegas, *Lee Canyon* at Mount Charleston (702–872–5462) offers skiing for all levels.

MUSEUMS. Salt Lake. The *Museum of Church History and Art* in the block due west of Temple Sq. tells the story of the Mormons, whose church is formally known as the Church of Jesus Christ of Latter-Day Saints, with "saints" meaning believers. Even a traveler with little interest in religion can't help but appreciate how the Mormon vision approximated so appropriately the developing American sensibility, with its emphasis on progress, this world rather than a hereafter, and human perfectibility rather than divine election. The Mormon role in developing the West was pervasive, especially in the period 1850–1900. Admission to the museum is free.

At the east edge of the city, the University of Utah's *Museum of Fine Arts* and *Natural History Museum* are pleasing introductions to the campus. The beauty and quality of the university are both well known. The Mormon belief in the progressive improvement of people has encouraged heavy investment in education. Mormons believe that what is learned in this life is retained in the next, cumulatively. Truth is the thing to be sought for in all fields. Founded originally as the University of Deseret in 1850, the school now has 24,000 students. Admission to the Natural History Museum is adults, $5; children, $3.

Within Salt Lake, what is happening in the arts, including what is showing, is known by the *Utah Arts Council,* 617 E. South Temple, Salt Lake City, UT 84102 (801–533–5895). They provide information on Utah arts organizations and maintain the Glendinning Gallery and Chase Home Exhibition featuring the State Fine Arts Collection.

Reno. The *Nevada Historical Society Museum* building on the University of Nevada campus, 1650 N. Virginia St. (702–789–0190), houses the famous basket collection created by Washo Indian Dat-So-La-Lee. Photos and memorabilia chart the rise of Reno as a railroad, cattle, and mining supply town. Until the silver strikes of the 1860s, Reno and northern Nevada were places people passed through rather than stayed at. Mormon pioneers homesteaded a few permanent settlements south of Reno. In 1868 Reno was founded as a stop on the railroad and was named by the railroad after a Civil War general. Admission is free.

Harrah's Auto Collection, 3½ mi. east of Reno, is an important slice of Americana. Harrah's, Glendale Rd. (702–333–9300), is the remaining collection of vehicles that Bill Harrah assembled. Some of the vehicles have been sold off by the present owner, Holiday Inns. Bill Harrah's original vision was to locate, purchase, and restore to mint condition all the classics of automotive history. The number and kinds of cars to see, plus the related artifacts, are astonishing. The sturdiness, design-consciousness, and modest price of many early vehicles will impress you. The elegance of bygone eras comes flooding back as you gaze at 1910 touring motorcycles or the wood-panel interior of a Ford Trimotor airplane. Car fanatics get lumps in their throats while looking at two of the only six Bugatti Royales produced in 1931. Several celebrated cars are at the entrance of the museum, including a 50-horsepower white Simplex from 1911, which sold then for $5,600, and a red Thomas Flyabout from 1909, manufactured in Buffalo, New York, and sold for $3,000. Adults, $9.50; children, $2.50.

Carson City's *Nevada State Museum,* 600 N. Carson St., in the historic U. S. Mint Building (702–687–4810), acquaints visitors with both the natural history and human drama of Nevada, including all the coins minted here. The museum describes the Paiute Indians who were the original residents. In the basement a replica of a silver mine gives you a feel of what underground mining was like. At press time, the mint was closed for a study to determine the severity of an earthquake it can withstand.

Las Vegas. *Nevada's Lost City Museum* in Overton (702–397–2193) can enhance your trip to Valley of Fire park near Las Vegas. Continue on to the Lake Mead road and turn east to Overton, a Mormon farming community. At Overton, the Lost City Museum is a major collection of artifacts from southern Nevada Indians. The museum celebrates an extensive pueblo culture, called the Basketmakers by archeologists, where the Virgin and Muddy rivers empty into the Colorado. The Indians flourished here from 300 B.C. to A.D. 1150 before abandoning the area for reasons not yet understood. The peak period of this culture was around A.D. 800 when about 5,000 Indians lived here. Adults, $1; children, free.

ACCOMMODATIONS. Lodging in the major cities in the Great Basin is both plentiful and relatively economical. Salt Lake City has been a less popular travel destination, and so pressure on hotel rooms has not forced prices up. Reno and Las Vegas lodgings, which are numerous, keep the price low to encourage the patronage of gamblers. Two of the five national parks in Utah have lodging (Bryce Canyon and Zion). Reservations there and at Death Valley are always advised. Reservations in the major cities are desirable, but there are always other options.

Lodging costs per night in the Great Basin, based on double occupancy, are categorized as follows: *Super Deluxe,* over $120; *Deluxe,* $100–$120; *Expensive,* $80–$100; *Moderate,* $60–$80; and *Inexpensive,* under $60. Here are some representative lodgings in the Great Basin.

Salt Lake City

The Marriott. *Deluxe.* 75 SW Temple, Salt Lake City, UT 84101 (801–531–0800 or 800–228–9290). One of Salt Lake City's newest, with restaurants, liquor store, swimming pool, sauna, and gift shop, this place is close to all downtown shopping areas and the Salt Palace complex.

Red Lion Salt Lake. *Deluxe.* 255 SW Temple, Salt Lake City, UT 84101 (801–328–2000). Sheraton elegance, near all major attractions. Heated indoor pool, whirlpool, garage, lounge, first-class restaurant.

Holiday Inn–Downtown. *Expensive.* 230 W. 6th St., Salt Lake City, UT 84101 (801–532–7000 or 800–HOLIDAY). Open all year. Restaurant and cocktail lounge. Pleasant rooms with color TV.

Inn at Temple Square. *Moderate.* 75 W. South Temple, Salt Lake City, UT 84101 (801–531–1000). Downtown Salt Lake City across from Temple Sq. Indoor tennis, racquetball. Restaurant. Recently renovated.

Utah Beyond Salt Lake

Bryce Canyon Lodge. *Expensive.* Reservations: TW Services, Box 400, Cedar City, UT 84720 (801–586–7686). This lodging, located in Bryce Canyon National Park, has 40 historic and rustic cabins with fireplaces plus newer facilities. Restaurant, laundry, stores. Horse riding trips and nature trips.

Zion Lodge. *Expensive.* Reservations: TW Services, Box 400, Cedar City, UT 84720 (801–586–7686). This pleasing rustic lodge is the only one in Zion National Park. Restaurant. Nature program, hiking, horse riding, open-air trams, tours of park.

Best Western Ruby's Inn. *Moderate.* Bryce Canyon National Park, UT 84764 (801–834–5341 or 800–528–1234). Extensive motel complex with heated indoor pool, gift shops, RV campground. One mi. from park entrance. Restaurant with steak specialty. Ski trails, winter plug-ins.

Reno

See also the practical information for Lake Tahoe in the chapter on California.

Bally's-Reno. *Deluxe.* 2500 E. 2nd St., Reno, NV 89595 (702–789–2000). Huge casino and site of top-name entertainers, Thurs.–Sat. Tennis courts, health club.

Reno Hilton. *Deluxe.* 255 N. Sierra St., Reno, NV 89501 (702–322–1111 or 800–HILTONS). Turn-of-the-century decor is featured in this high-rise hotel. Valet parking. Restaurants. Name entertainers.

Harrah's Hotel. *Expensive.* Center and 2nd Sts., Reno, NV 89504 (702–786–3232). Offered here are a heated pool, restaurant, bar. Health club, recreational program.

Savage Mansion. *Expensive.* Virginia City, NV 89440 (702–847–0574). A bed-and-breakfast inn at the historic home of the Savage Mine owner, this place has antique-filled rooms with copper bathtubs.

The Vagabond Inn. *Moderate.* 3131 S. Virginia St., Reno, NV 89502 (702–825–7134). Comfortable hotel with pool. Six suites have child bunk beds in separate room. Restaurant nearby.

Las Vegas

Caesars Palace. *Super Deluxe.* 3570 Las Vegas Blvd. S., Las Vegas, NV 89109 (702–731–7110). Luxurious rooms are available here, along with high standards of service and atmosphere. Spacious grounds with fountains and Roman statues. Big-name entertainers.

Bally's-Las Vegas. *Deluxe.* 3645 Las Vegas Blvd. S., Las Vegas, NV 89109 (702–739–4111). This is a Hollywood dream hotel with spacious suites. Fine restaurants, lavish shows. Pool, tennis, health club.

Las Vegas Hilton. *Deluxe.* 3000 Paradise Rd., Las Vegas, NV 89109 (702–732–5111). Largest resort hotel in the world. Top entertainment. Eleven restaurants. Special children's hotel next to Convention Center.

Frontier Hotel. *Expensive.* 3120 Las Vegas Blvd. S., Las Vegas, NV 89114 (702–794–8200). Colorful western motif. Landscaped grounds. Pool, sauna, tennis.

Imperial Palace. *Expensive.* 3535 Las Vegas Blvd. S., Las Vegas, NV 89114 (702–731–3311). Oriental motif throughout. Pool, tennis courts. Famous collection of 200 classic autos.

Circus Circus. *Moderate.* 2880 Las Vegas Blvd. S., Las Vegas, NV 89114 (702–734–0110). This is a great place for families, with casino for adults and circus acts for the kids.

El Cortez. *Moderate.* 600 E. Fremont St., Las Vegas, NV 89101 (702–385–5200). Right on Glitter Gulch, downtown. Oldest standing hotel in Las Vegas, but with a new tower.

Golden Gate. *Moderate.* 111 S. Main St., Las Vegas, NV 89101 (702–382–3510). Near downtown and the bus stop.

Lady Luck. *Moderate.* 206 N. Third St., Las Vegas, NV 89101 (702–447–3000). Near the Trailways station. One of the busiest casinos downtown.

Sam's Town. *Moderate.* 5111 Boulder Hwy., Las Vegas, NV 89122 (702–456–7777). Out of the way but very popular with locals and tourists. Western theme.

Death Valley

Furnace Creek Inn. *Super Deluxe.* Death Valley National Monument, CA 92328 (619–786–2345). Luxurious resort but open only Oct.–May each year, closing for hot summer months. Resort is a mi. from the visitor center and is attractively sited, complete with pool, restaurants, golf course. Dress code for dinner.

Furnace Creek Ranch. *Expensive.* Death Valley National Monument, CA 92328 (619–786–2345). Lodging adjacent to the visitor center and Borax Museum. The ranch has a swimming pool, which visitors appreciate when temperatures soar. A cafeteria and coffee shop are open all year, with the restaurant open only in winter. Golf, horseback riding.

RESTAURANTS. Utah restaurants have been affected in their development by the stringent liquor regulations. Specialties unique to the region are trout and game. Reno and Las Vegas casinos have developed sumptuous buffets, quite reasonably priced, to lure gamblers. Nevada's Basque restaurants, often emphasizing lamb, offer full-course meals for a fixed price.

Reservations are advised. Dress is relatively casual in both Utah and Nevada, though some of the more elegant restaurants maintain strict dress codes. Most restaurants are open 6 days, with many closed Mon. Restaurant hours in Utah tend to end the dinner hour by 10 P.M., but casinos in Reno and Las Vegas often operate restaurants around the clock. Restaurants in the major cities accept credit cards.

Prices for meals in the Great Basin are as follows: *Deluxe,* $25–$35; *Expensive,* $18–$20; *Moderate,* $10–$18; and *Inexpensive,* under $10. Drink, tax, and tips are not included.

Salt Lake

La Caille at Quail Run. *Deluxe.* 9565 Wasatch Blvd. (801–942–1751). Wealthy country atmosphere exudes at this place, which includes game birds and an attractive French cuisine.

Market Street Grill. *Expensive.* 54 Post Office Pl. (801–322–4668). Locals come here for fresh seafood dishes and Sun. brunch.

Lamb's Restaurant. *Moderate.* 169 S. Main (801–364–7166). One of Utah's oldest restaurants, this place has been operating since 1919. Pleasant dining atmosphere. Nonsmoking area.

Le Parisien. *Moderate.* 417 S. 3rd East (801–364–5223). Good seafood and French and Italian cooking are served at this place with an extensive wine list. Outdoor seating.

Reno

La Table Francaise. *Deluxe.* 3065 W. 4th St. (702–323–3200). Attractive French cuisine. French country inn style, emphasizing fresh food. View of cottonwood grove from antique-filled interior.

Louis' Basque Corner. *Moderate.* 301 E. 4th St. (702–323–7203). Good example of folksy Nevada Basque dining. Sumptuous meal of many courses. Unhurried dining in two traditional dining rooms.

Rapscallion. *Moderate.* 1555 S. Wells (702–323–1211). Seafood specialties are offered here, along with a separate menu for children. Cocktails and lounge. Reservations are suggested.

Miguel's. *Inexpensive.* 1415 S. Virginia (702–322–2722). Long-term favorite Mexican restaurant in Reno. Dozen numbered entrées. Good sopapillas, enchiladas.

Las Vegas

The Bacchanal. *Deluxe.* At Caesar's Palace (702–731–7110). Attractive Roman villa motif is offered here with excellent service. Lavish courses for fixed-price dinners emphasize veal, lobster, lamb, and steak.

Alpine Village Inn. *Expensive.* 3003 Paradise Rd. (702–734–6888). German and American dishes are available at this German-American restaurant and rathskeller. Imported beers a specialty. Children's menu.

Benihana Village. *Expensive.* In Las Vegas Hilton (702–732–5801). Japanese food is colorfully presented at this "village," which has five restaurants. Specialties: hibachi shrimp, sukiyaki steak. Children's menu.

Golden Nugget Buffet. *Inexpensive.* At the casino, 129 E. Fremont (702–385–7111). Sumptuous dining, best of the casino buffets, this place offers all you can eat—salads, entrées, desserts.

LIQUOR LAWS. Utah maintains much tighter controls over liquor than most states. To obtain liquor, you need to know the laws. Beer can be purchased in bars, grocery stores, and drugstores, but liquor is more difficult to obtain. The state runs fully stocked liquor and wine stores whose locations are listed in the telephone book under "Utah State Government, Liquor Control Commission." The hours of operation vary, so call a store before going to it. Some hotels and motels have liquor stores in their lobbies. The liquor stores require cash, not checks or credit cards.

Utah's drinking and driving laws are very stringent (with 0.08 the legally drunk blood-alcohol level). The legal drinking age in Utah is 21. Liquor may not be imported into the state.

At Utah restaurants, you may take your own bottle to the restaurant and order mixers or setups. Some restaurants have their own liquor stores on the premises. These restaurant liquor stores can provide minibottles or splits of wine after 4 P.M. weekdays. You purchase the split at the store and take it to your table. Liquor can be consumed in restaurants only in conjunction with a meal.

Nevada. Liquor is sold by the package and drink. Counties and municipalities have leeway to regulate sales. The legal drinking age is 21. You may import 1 gallon of liquor into the state.

NIGHTLIFE: LAS VEGAS AND RENO. Reno and Las Vegas boast diversified entertainment and nightlife. Check to see what is on in each city. Besides the local newspapers, you can call ahead for information from the tourist information number (see Tourist Information).

Many casinos in each city offer cabaret or lounge acts featuring singers and dancers. Additionally, there are major stage shows. Some shows involve dinner and the show; others include two drinks and the show. The cocktail show is usually about two-thirds the price of the dinner show. Both cities feature top-name entertainers, as well as musical extravaganzas which run the gamut from clown acts to acrobatic topless ice skaters.

Convenient shuttle buses can transport you back and forth in Las Vegas between the Strip and Downtown, the two areas where there are casinos. You must be 21 years of age in both cities to participate in gambling.

THE ROCKY MOUNTAINS

by
LEE FOSTER and CURTIS W. CASEWIT

Mr. Foster, a writer and photographer, is the author of gardening and travel books, novels, and a guide on computer disk, West Coast Travel. *Mr. Casewit has written travel guides, contributes travel features to 40 international newspapers, and teaches journalism.*

Once a formidable obstacle to the pioneers, the Rockies today are a source of delight for the traveler. As the mother of rivers, the Rockies stretch south to north through the west central United States. The Continental Divide, the "line" that determines whether rivers flow east or west, snakes north to bisect Colorado and then meanders northwest through Wyoming. The Divide emerges from Yellowstone National Park to form the border between Idaho and Montana before thrusting northward through Montana into Canada. When rain-swollen clouds drop their burden of water in the mountains, rivulets flow northwest to become the Snake or Salmon Rivers and then the mighty Columbia. Toward the east gather the waters for the Yellowstone and Missouri rivers. For the arid southwest the Colorado River is the lifeblood of the region. Even the Rio Grande gets its start here, in the mountains of southern Colorado.

The four Rocky Mountain states—Colorado, Wyoming, Montana, and Idaho—all present the traveler with a short, bright summer season of mountain splendor. Like the elk and the moose, who must graze intently for this brief growing season, travelers appear in great numbers to savor the public heritage of nature in the region, with Yellowstone National Park's wildlife and geysers as the single biggest draw, despite the 1988 fires. The scenery of each state simply stuns the imagination if you are searching for alpine vistas, though each state boasts other types of terrain, ranging from the grassland plains of eastern Montana to the volcanic plateaus of southwestern Idaho. There's plenty of wide open territory per capita in these least populated of the 48 contiguous United States.

The winter traveler to the Rockies is likely to be a skier or an appreciator of snowy scenery, with alpine (downhill) and nordic (cross-country) skiing vying for attention. From the famous major downhill resorts, such as Vail in Colorado or Sun Valley in Idaho, to the cross-country ski ranches in Montana, such as Lone Mountain near Big Sky, Montana, and C Lazy U, near Granby, Colorado the winter traveler celebrates a snowy aspect of the Rockies entirely different from what the summer traveler sees.

A visitor to the Rockies states will find that people survived here initially by ranching and farming. Indeed, the traveler might begin by sampling some famous Rocky Mountain beefsteak. The meal might include an Idaho baked potato. If the ambiance is drafty, a Wyoming wool sweater could provide warmth. Beyond ranching, mining dominates, with oil, natural gas, copper, gold, silver, lead, and zinc as examples. Some exotic minerals are crucial here; Colorado boasts two-thirds of the nation's reserves of molybdenum, used to harden steel. The replenishable resource of tourism now ranks third in the economy of these states. Such specialties as the bristling Montana and Wyoming ICBM defense installations make special additions to the economy.

Human beings are known to have resided in the Rockies for over 15,000 years; there is early archaeological evidence at Montana's Pictograph Cave near Billings. When the first Spanish explorers arrived in 1540, led by Francisco Vasquez Coronado, they found many distinct Indian cultures, some of which were the Arapaho, Shoshone, and Ute. Col. Zebulon Pike explored the region in 1806. The Mormons crossed the Rockies to Salt Lake in the mid-1850s. Discovery of gold in Cherry Creek, in 1858, near the site of what is now Denver, brought hordes of miners.

COLORADO

Colorado easily wins the award as the most mountainous of these mountain states: An average elevation of 6,800 feet gives it the nickname Roof of the Nation. Colorado boasts a thousand peaks above 10,000 feet and 54 peaks over 14,000. Denver is the largest city in the Rockies and the capital of this Centennial State, so named because Colorado came into the union in the national centennial year of 1876. From Denver the traveler will find the Great Plains extending east, the Rockies looming to the west, and the Colorado Plateau farther to the west. The state assumes its name from the term that the original Spanish explorers gave the major river, Rio Colorado, whose mighty and erosive power so silted the water that it was "colored red."

Denver

About half of the almost three million Coloradans live in the Denver metropolitan area. With 297 days of sun per year, this Mile High City is prime sunblock country for any palefaces who haven't previously experienced the intensity of high-altitude sun. Crowning the cityscape is the gold-leafed capitol dome, topping a gray granite Corinthian structure at Broadway and Colfax. Gardens, fountains, a Greek amphitheater and monuments to Colorado pioneers—including a sculpture of an Indian with a dying buffalo—enhance the Civic Center area. Larimer Square (14th Avenue and Larimer Street) is an attractive cluster of preserved Victorian-era buildings, now used as restaurants, boutiques, and galleries, suggesting the elegance of early Denver. Also at the heart of Denver is the 16th Street pedestrian mall, offering fountains, glass-walled skyscrapers, stores, bistros, and free shuttle buses.

At this site General William Larimer founded Denver City in 1858. Like most of the early Colorado towns, Denver owed its existence to gold strikes of the 1850s and 1860s, first near Denver's current site in 1858. Denver became the major supply point for the miners, farmers, and ranchers of the late 19th century. Foremost in the Denver story is the celebrated Brown Palace Hotel, with its nine-story lobby, Palace Arms restaurant, and English high tea.

The Denver Art Museum, contains notable collections of American, European, and Oriental art. Nearby, at the Colorado State History Museum, 1300 Broadway, you can see the region's story. Capitol Hill features the great houses built by some of the city's substantial early residents. Travelers with children will enjoy The Children's Museum, 2121 Crescent Drive, or Elitch Gardens, 38th and Tennyson, which began as a zoo and botanical gardens in the 1890s and in time became an amusement park.

East of the downtown area, situated in the City Park, the Denver Museum of Natural History shows the fossilized bones of prehistoric animals and many dioramas of mammals and birds from the Rockies area. The museum displays one of the largest nuggets of gold found in Colorado, and there is a new exhibition hall. The Denver Botanic Gardens at 1005 York Street features a 22-acre spread of seasonal gardens, ranging from tropical to tundra habitats, including a Japanese garden and a rock alpine garden. An enclosed conservatory for tropical flowers and plants makes the Botanic Gardens a year-round attraction. Near Denver, in Golden, you can see steam locomotives and cars at the Colorado Railroad Museum, 17155 West 44th Avenue.

For a view of the city and the mountains plus a glimpse of Americana, drive the 12 miles west from Denver on I-70 to Lookout Mountain and the Buffalo Bill Memorial Museum and Grave. The monument to the noted hunter, Indian fighter, Pony Express rider, and showman is crammed with memorabilia. An observation deck gives you a spectacular view of Denver.

Beyond Denver

For a sample of Colorado experiences, including mining history, nature exploration, and resort towns, consider a drive west along I-70 from Denver to Vail and Glenwood Springs, then south to Aspen.

Driving west from Denver, you encounter one of the several gold and silver towns interesting to explore in the state. The town is Idaho Springs (though we're in Colorado, not Idaho). In January 1859, a decade after the California gold rush, a Missourian named George A. Jackson scraped gold with a knife from the pebbled bed of ice-encrusted Chicago Creek, west of Idaho Springs. Unable to keep the news to himself, Jackson soon caused a rush of miners to the region. At Idaho Springs you can still see the Argo Mill and a huge pile of tailings around it. Beneath the Argo lie some four miles of tunnels, with 50 mines and about 150 veins of gold. Further attractions are the hot springs at Indian Springs Resort, nearby Bridal Veil Falls, and the auto road to the top of Mt. Evans (14,260 feet).

Other Colorado mining towns to visit in the state include Central City, Georgetown, Telluride, and Leadville. In mining regions there is always a deft mix of legend and fact. When President Grant visited the Teller

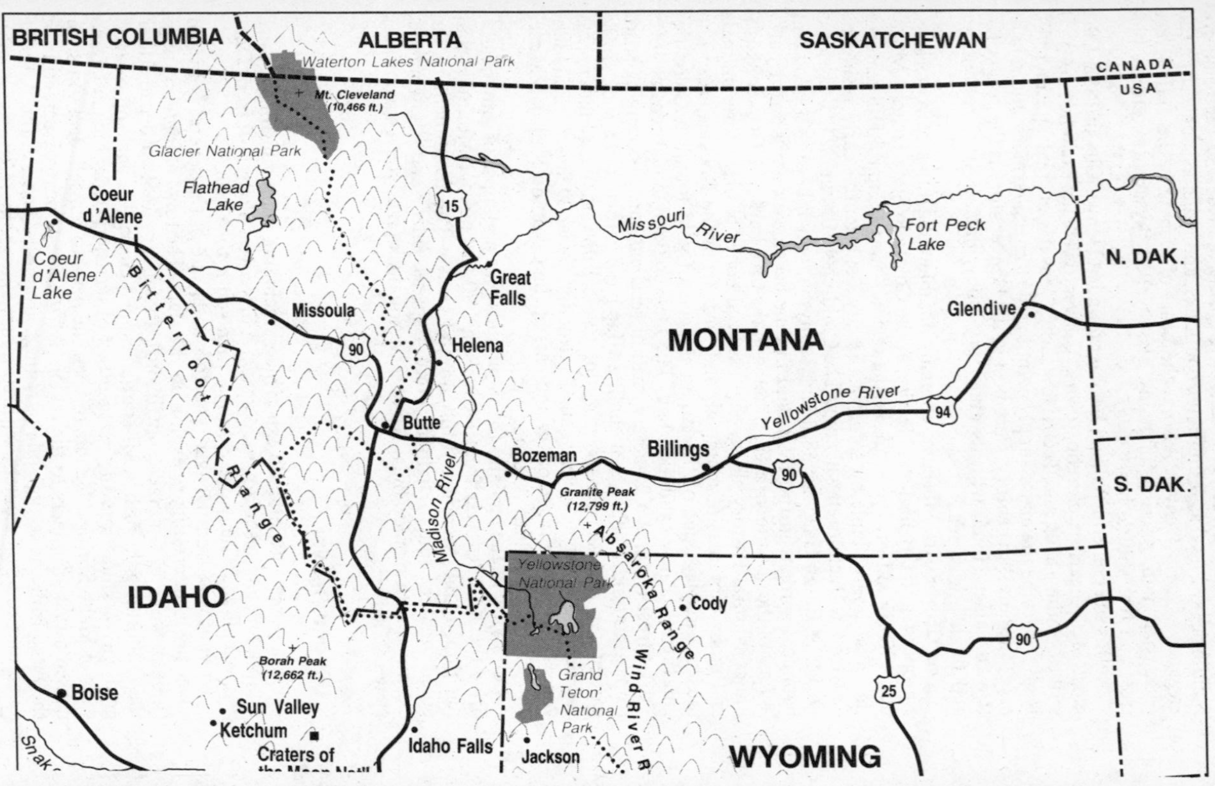

BRITISH COLUMBIA
ALBERTA
SASKATCHEWAN
CANADA
USA
Waterton Lakes National Park
Mt. Cleveland (10,466 ft.)
Glacier National Park
Flathead Lake
Coeur d'Alene
Coeur d'Alene Lake
Bitterroot Range
Missoula
Great Falls
Helena
Butte
15
90
Missouri River
Fort Peck Lake
N. DAK.
Glendive
MONTANA
Yellowstone River
94
Bozeman
Billings
S. DAK.
Madison River
Granite Peak (12,799 ft.)
Absaroka Range
Yellowstone National Park
Cody
IDAHO
Borah Peak (12,662 ft.)
Boise
Sun Valley
Ketchum
Craters of
Idaho Falls
Grand Teton National Park
Wind River R
Jackson
WYOMING
25
Snak

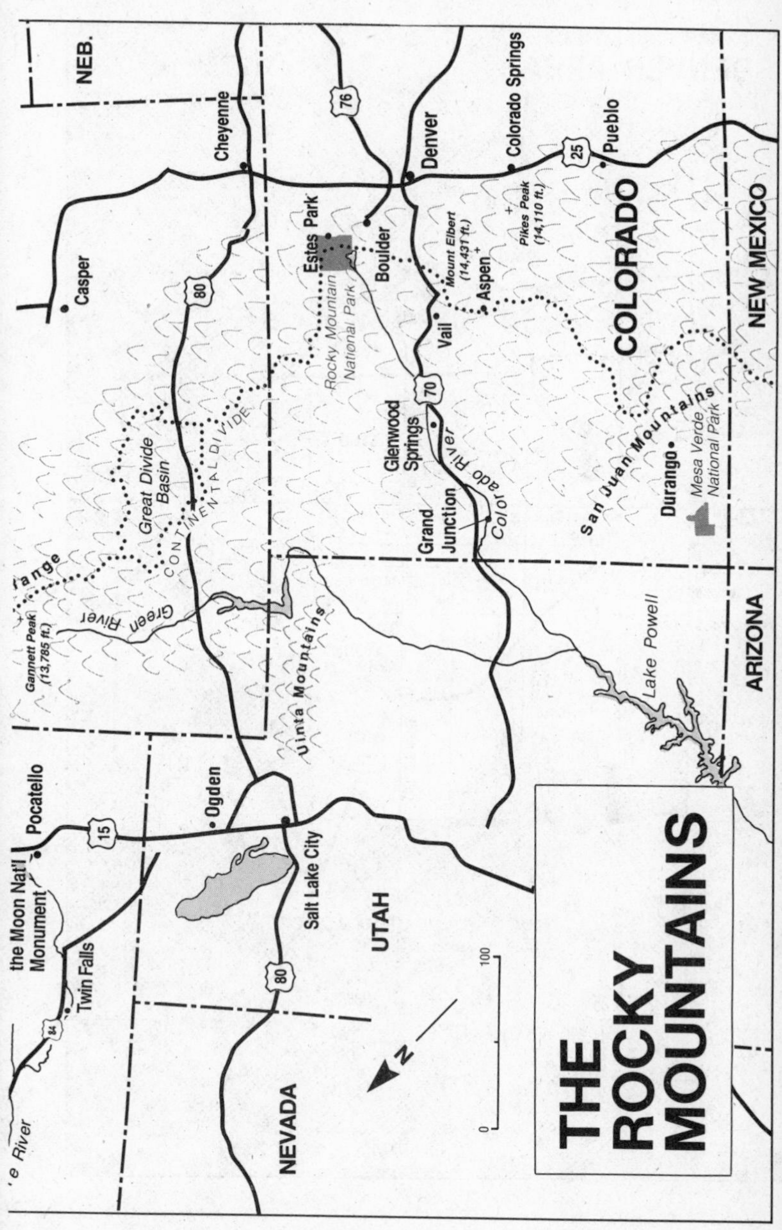
THE ROCKY MOUNTAINS
NEB.
Casper
Cheyenne
Colorado Springs
Denver
Pueblo
Estes Park
Boulder
Rocky Mountain National Park
Mount Elbert (14,431 ft.)
Pikes Peak (14,110 ft.)
Aspen
Vail
COLORADO
NEW MEXICO
Glenwood Springs
Grand Junction
Colorado River
San Juan Mountains
Durango
Mesa Verde National Park
Great Divide Basin
CONTINENTAL DIVIDE
Gannett Peak (13,785 ft.)
Green River
Uinta Mountains
Lake Powell
ARIZONA
Pocatello
Ogden
Salt Lake City
UTAH
the Moon Nat'l Monument
Twin Falls
NEVADA
N
0
100
15
80
76
25
70
84

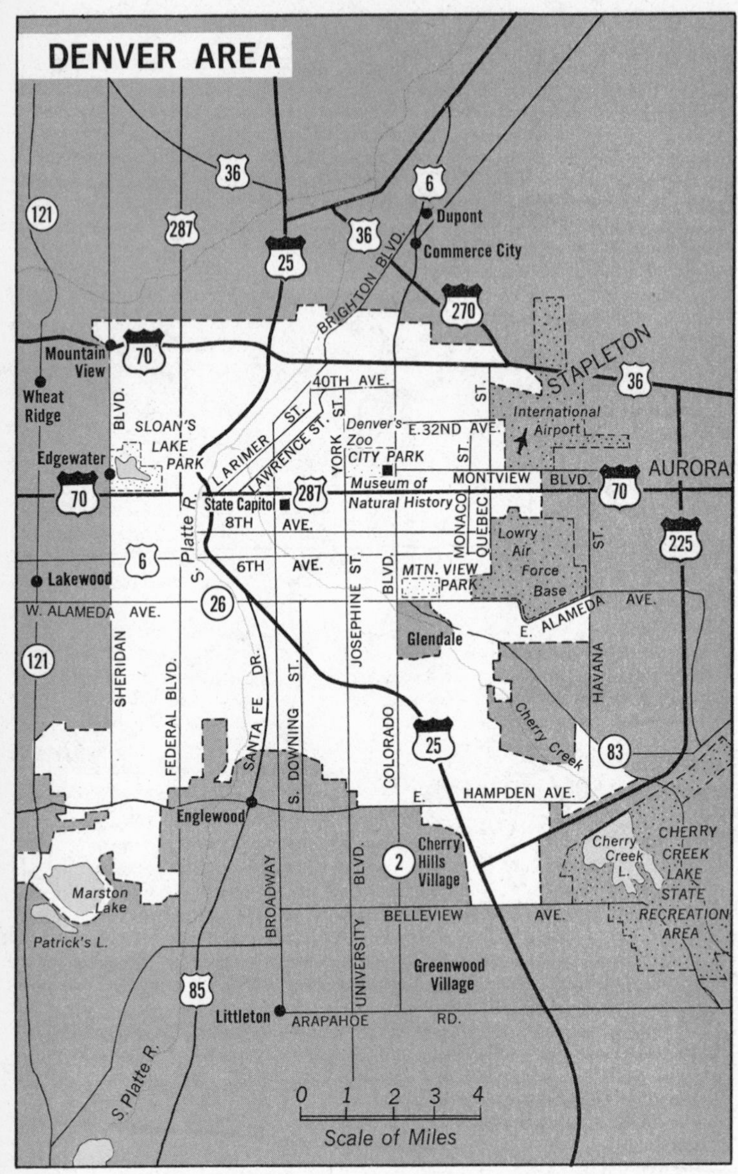
DENVER AREA
Mountain View
Wheat Ridge
Edgewater
Lakewood
Dupont
Commerce City
BRIGHTON BLVD.
STAPLETON
International Airport
AURORA
40TH AVE.
E. 32ND AVE.
SLOAN'S LAKE PARK
LARIMER ST.
LAWRENCE ST.
YORK ST.
Denver's Zoo
CITY PARK
Museum of Natural History
MONTVIEW BLVD.
State Capitol
8TH AVE.
6TH AVE.
MONACO ST.
QUEBEC ST.
Lowry Air Force Base
MTN. VIEW PARK
W. ALAMEDA AVE.
E. ALAMEDA AVE.
Glendale
Cherry Creek
SHERIDAN BLVD.
FEDERAL BLVD.
S. Platte R.
SANTA FE DR.
S. DOWNING ST.
JOSEPHINE ST.
COLORADO BLVD.
HAVANA ST.
E. HAMPDEN AVE.
Englewood
Cherry Hills Village
Cherry Creek L.
CHERRY CREEK LAKE STATE RECREATION AREA
Marston Lake
Patrick's L.
BROADWAY
UNIVERSITY BLVD.
BELLEVIEW AVE.
Greenwood Village
Littleton
ARAPAHOE RD.
S. Platte R.
0 1 2 3 4
Scale of Miles

House at Central City in 1873, it is said that he walked across a pathway of silver bars.

About 100 miles west from Idaho Springs lies the resort town of Vail. Much of Colorado that a traveler meets is relatively fresh and new, with Vail the epitome. Only 25 years ago, visionary developers began the process of turning this 8,000-foot-high sheep-herding district, and sparsely populated town, into a thriving ski resort. Today Vail Mountain accommodates 25,000 skiers on a busy winter day, making it the most popular single mountain ski area in North America.

Stop in at the Ski Museum to learn about the technical development and history of the sport. Vail also has an art market; western sculptors, working mainly in bronze, are represented at the Driscoll Gallery, and the Mill Creek Gallery specializes in Rockies painters. In summer, the gondola carries sightseers to miles of hiking trails above the town. The Vail Nature Center organizes summer walks and hikes in the surrounding region. From Vail, you can also participate in another typically Colorado experience, a river-rafting venture on the Colorado, perhaps with the pioneering river rafters, the Griffith Family, and their Griffith River Expeditions. About 250,000 visitors to Colorado now enjoy rafting each year on the Arkansas and Colorado rivers.

West of Vail, you follow the spectacular Glenwood Canyon and then pause at Glenwood Springs before the drive south to Aspen. Glenwood Springs is the Colorado of another time, the leisurely world of the rich in the railroad era. This is where visitors come to bathe in the sulphurous, hot mineral waters, just as the silver barons did in the 19th century and the Ute warriors before them. In the 1890s the Colorado Hotel at Glenwood Springs considered itself the grandest establishment between the Mississippi and San Francisco. Today Glenwood is still an Amtrak stop for the rail passenger who appreciates the good life.

South of Glenwood Springs is Aspen, a jetsetter town where many of the "rich and famous" have come to settle. The town boasts many Victorian houses (get a walking tour brochure at the chamber of commerce) and one of the Rockies' celebrated architectural legacies, the Wheeler Opera House, now restored to its regal 1890s splendor. Typically for Colorado, the opera house was built with silver mining wealth, accumulated by one Jerome Wheeler.

During the summer, drive out or catch a bus from Aspen Highlands Ski Area for a picnic and hike at the Maroon Bells, some of Colorado's most stunning scenery. There you'll find delicate blue columbines, the state flower (the other floral treat in the state is the blue-green foliage of the Colorado blue spruce, the state tree). After the walk, stop in at Aspen's innovative Center for Environmental Studies, at Hallam Lake, which sponsors ambitious naturalist guided hikes and ecological activities, such as the saving of injured raptors, a bird of prey. Aspen is a lively cultural town, with a famous summer music festival.

The town is populated by a special species of homo sapiens known as Colorado immigrant, those tanned corporate drop-outs who chucked it all and came here "for the lifestyle," which can be translated to mean "for the powder skiing." Your cab driver may have been a New York lawyer.

Both Aspen and adjoining Snowmass are major ski destinations. For the summer or winter crowd, Aspen boasts an amazing number of small (and expensive) restaurants. At the outdoor veranda of Snowmass's Timberline Lodge the arts of après-ski reach their highest form. A balloon company, based at Snowmass, can take you on a breathtaking view of the Rockies in the largest commercial balloons in existence.

This quick tour is only a teasing taste of the diversity of Colorado. In the southeast corner of the state Bent's Fort offered the early trappers a place to trade, and the Kit Carson Museum honors the hunter and guide. Here you'll find the old Spanish Trail, which brought explorers who left two major legacies, the Spanish place-names on the landscape and the Spanish-Mexican culinary influence that ranks close behind the beefsteak as a Colorado restaurant specialty. Colorado Springs, south of Denver, is the home of the U.S. Air Force Academy, a major tourist attraction with its Fine Arts Center and spired glass and aluminum chapel.

Southwest Colorado was the domain of Ouray, the great Ute chieftain who helped arrange the inevitable transfer of Indian lands without a thorough destruction of the tribe. The southwest section of the state includes a cluster of mining towns and two special narrow-gauge rail trips well worth an excursion. The historic Durango-Silverton railroad makes the 45-mile run between the towns from May to October. The Cumbres & Toltec Scenic Railway, an 1880s entity that is now a registered National Historic Site, chugs 64 miles from Antonito, Colorado, to Chama, New Mexico, through forested high country.

In western Colorado the landscape of towering monoliths that the state shares with Utah is especially apparent at the Colorado National Monument. The Black Canyon of the Gunnison National Monument is 12 miles of the deepest portion of the Gunnison River gorge. Bones from 14 species of dinosaurs, some with skeletons completely intact, are on display at Dinosaur National Monument. Grand Junction, the major city and trade center, is set in a rich agricultural area.

Eastern Colorado provides views of unbroken wheat fields and the occasional white tail of skittish pronghorn antelopes. As Ten Bears, the Comanche chief, said in 1860, "I was born upon the prairie, where the wind blew free and there was nothing to break the light of the sun."

Mesa Verde National Park

Mesa Verde is the best-known cliff-dwelling site in North America. Many observers would argue that the people of Mesa Verde were the most advanced Indian culture north of Mexico.

As impressive as the dwellings themselves is the character of the terrain. These high mesas are a "green table," or Mesa Verde, as the Spanish first described the area. Extensive forests clothe the flat rain-catching plateaus at 6,000 to 8,000 feet. The trees range from Douglas fir to aspen, piñon pine to Utah juniper. A plentiful supply of rain allowed the prehistoric populace to grow a surplus of food that enabled them to develop the leisure pursuits of architecture, crafts, and religious worship. The name the Indians used for themselves is not known; we describe them with a modern Navajo word, Anasazi, meaning "the ancient ones." This domain of the Anasazi, the Mesa Verde plateaus, became a national park in 1906.

The basis of Mesa Verde's prosperity was the cliff dwellers' skill as agriculturalists. On the high mesas they first grew corn and squash, and later added beans to their crops about A.D. 950. With small checkdams they caught the rains from summer thunderstorms. They ate abundant wild seeds and plant foods, deer, and wild turkeys, which they domesticated for meat and feathers. In the free archaeology museum within the park you see several examples of their food, including an ancient squash skin and a large earthenware jar filled with corn.

These Indians will be remembered by most visitors as architects. The first Colorado cowboys who stumbled upon these houses, in the late 1880s, viewed the structures with awe. Along Chapin Mesa you can chart the progressive stages of their architecture. First came pit houses, easily heated rooms dug into the ground and built up and lined with mud. Then the Indians proceeded to semi-circular clusters of above-ground rooms (now called *pueblos*—Spanish for village). Finally, they built cliff dwellings under the sandstone overhangs. Most were one- to five-room structures, and a few were much larger. More than 600 are preserved. The three celebrated clusters are Cliff Palace, Balcony House, and Spruce Tree House.

Rocky Mountain National Park

One of the choicest pieces of mountain real estate in the entire Rockies became a public "pleasuring ground" in 1915 when the Rocky Mountain National Park was founded on 266,943 acres, or 414 square miles, northwest of Denver. The park holds the highest and most rugged terrain this side of Alaska. Some 65 mountains in the park are over 10,000 feet in height, with the highest, Long's Peak, at 14,255 feet.

The 150 lakes in the park are pleasing mirrors of the peaks, the tranquility disturbed in summer only by trout leaping rising to consume mayflies that alight on the water surface. Anglers are pleased to learn that Colorado has 70,000 miles of trout streams, with 20 percent classified as "blue ribbon" water by Trout Unlimited, meaning that a large population of nonhatchery fish thrives there.

The altitude of the park (7,800 to 14,255 feet) makes it prudent for travelers, especially with heart problems, to pace themselves, adjust their auto carburetors, and prepare for the possibility of snow in July. Fall River, Bear Lake, Mt. Evans, and Trail Ridge roads (the highest highways in the United States), have steep grades, many switchbacks, and ever-changing terrain. Fall River Pass is 11,796 feet high! Alpine Visitor Center and Tundra Visitor Center emphasize the flora and fauna of this climatically harsh land.

Estes Park, on the east side of Rocky Mountain National Park, is the gateway city, with plenty of lodging and support facilities. An aerial tramway to the top of Prospect Mountain (8,896 feet) offers a sweeping view of the Continental Divide's peaks and valleys.

WYOMING

The state of Wyoming boasts one of the most popular travel attractions in the Rocky Mountains: Yellowstone National Park. People have marvelled at this unusual landscape since the first explorers, the Verendrye brothers, entered the state in 1743. After the Lewis and Clark expedition passed to the north, one of its members, John Colter, entered the northwest part of the state in 1807 and discovered the geyser basins, which became known as Colter's Hell. A period of disbelief ensued until the presumed tall tales of the explorer were confirmed, and the park was established in 1872.

Wyoming remained relatively isolated until the Union Pacific Railroad pushed across the southern part of the state in 1867–1868. Prior to that the Sioux warriors who roamed the eastern half of the state remained powerful, but the tide of white migration in the 1860s overwhelmed them. Wyoming became a territory in 1869. The sweeping grasslands provided a grazing basis for profitable ranching so long as markets remained strong and severe winters didn't decimate the herds. Cattle and sheep ranchers fought each other for control of the territory.

In some ways Wyoming was progressive from the start, passing the first woman's suffrage legislation in 1869, which later earned it the moniker The Equality State. The state was the first administered by a woman, Nellie Tayloe Ross, who governed from 1924 to 1927.

The image of Wyoming today is that of an independent state with a strong cowboy and outdoor aura. Cattle and sheep ranching, mining, dry farming, and timber cutting are major activities for the half million residents. Casper is the largest city in the state, boasting a population of

52,000. In the 20th century, minerals have been the key to Wyoming's development, especially oil and coal. Wyoming supplies more than half of the crude oil pumped in the Rockies. The famous Teapot Dome scandal of 1927 saw the U.S. Supreme Court sending Secretary of the Interior Albert Fall to jail for secretly leasing oilfields to his cronies without taking competitive bids. The state surpasses all other states in its known coal reserves, with some 19 million acres of coal seams.

Jackson and the Grand Tetons

Jackson is the gateway to both Grand Teton and Yellowstone. Winter and summer, this might be called John Colter country in honor of the first explorer. Winter travel is the new and exciting experience for visitors who may have already seen Wyoming in summer, so let us celebrate winter travel to Jackson and a summer visit to Yellowstone as examples of the best that Wyoming offers.

Between December 1 and April 10 you can discover the generous winter pleasures of Wyoming's Jackson Hole and Grand Teton National Park. Today your experience can approximate the pristine adventure of John Colter and his peers as you take a sleigh ride among the 9,000 elk at the National Elk Refuge north of Jackson Hole. You can then don cross-country skis, as Colter did, though technologies of ski design will make your skiing easier. Your immersion in the beauty of natural scenery, gazing at the Grand Tetons, will be quite similar to Colter's, for the Jackson Hole–Teton area is the last great preserved ecosystem of the temperate climate zone in North America. Vistas are awesome in the Grand Tetons; the Great Breasts, as the French trappers and explorers named the pointed mountains, maintain a jutting and craggy dominance over all activity.

Jackson Hole has not always been so agreeable. When John Colter, who might be called Wyoming's first tourist, ventured into the region, the natives failed to welcome him warmly. In fact, Colter escaped from the Blackfoot Indians with his life only because he had sufficient wit and stamina to elude them. Today's Wyoming residents take an entirely different attitude toward visitors. The genuine friendliness of Jackson can be attributed to many factors: The region is somewhat underdiscovered. The natives exhibit an underlying cowboy dude-ranch friendliness (13 working cattle ranches flourish in the area). There is vast space here for only approximately 470,000 people in this least-populated state (aside from Alaska). The typical native is an accessible outdoorsperson who likes to hunt and fish. Many residents are themselves outsiders who came here by choice.

Regardless of your other interests, be sure to start in winter with a visit to the elk herd. The elk gather for their winter feeding, pawing through the snow to reach the dense grasses on the plains north of Jackson. Under careful supervision of the national refuge ranger, you take a horse-drawn sleigh ride through the herd, which causes no stress to the animals. Antlers shed each spring by the elk are collected by Boy Scouts for a late-May auction in Jackson's town square.

As you approach the herd, you first see the elk clustered in the distance, much as Colter did, like miniatures in the landscape. Gradually the antlered bulls and smaller cows stand out. When the sleigh moves through the herd, you are less than a hundred feet from these magnificent wild creatures, the largest herd of antlered animals in the world. Your experience of the elk in winter can't be duplicated in summer, when the animals are skittish and dispersed in the high mountain meadows from Jackson north through the Grand Tetons and Yellowstone Park.

After seeing the elk, treat yourself to cross-country skiing. Colter traversed the snow fields on homemade wooden skis. You benefit today from the 1974 breakthrough to fiberglass skis, whose flexibility and durability make cross-country skiing much easier. Jackson has become one of the country's leading cross-country ski destinations, with four separate ski locations. A mixed terrain of flat meadows and gently rolling hills affords an ideal ski setting. The dry, powdery snow packs well into firm trails.

A good place to start is the Teton Village Ski Center, where you can rent cross-country gear and get excellent instruction. Venture out on about 12 miles of set track, then proceed farther on the countless miles of unmanicured trails through Grand Teton National Park. The other nordic centers in Jackson groom an additional 16 miles of trails. On a groomed trail your skis and poles glide over packed snow rather than sink deeply into unpacked powder. Backcountry ski trips, even helicopter lifts to remote sites, can be arranged.

Teton Village is a convenient setting because the resort consolidates many attractions of the region. Besides the cross-country ski trails, there are several lodges, with the Sojourner Inn a good choice. Next to the Sojourner is an amenity that John Colter never had an opportunity to appreciate, Jackson's four-star European-style lodge and restaurant, the Alpenhof.

Behind Teton Village lies Rendezvous Mountain, which connoisseurs of downhill, or 'vertical," skiing rank among the finest. Though there are beginner slopes, the special feature of Rendezvous is its intermediate and expert terrain. The quality of the snow, the variety of the scenic terrain, and the length of the descent are outstanding. The downhill, or "vertical," drop here is immense, fully 4,139 feet, the longest vertical ski drop in North America. Both sightseers and skiers enjoy the tramway ride to the top.

The best close-up view of the Tetons in winter is from Signal Mountain Lodge, located on Jackson Lake, a half hour north from Jackson in Grand Teton National Park. The Tetons come immediately into view just across the lake from the lodge. Togwotee Mountain Lodge is the only park lodge open most of the winter.

Colter, who had such expertise in outdoor skills, would have appreciated one other adventure available to you in Jackson: dog sledding. Frank Teasley of Rocky Mountain Mushers offers this diversion. Pulled by a team of 12 malamutes or Alaskan dogs, you glide silently over the snow, covered by a warm buffalo robe. Alternatively, you may stand on the back runner, help guide the sled, and listen as Frank gives his dogs commands to gee (go right), haw (go left), and hike (move forward). Between commands Frank will immerse you in the lore of dog sledding. Throughout the four Rockies states, dog sledding's popularity grows each year.

Yellowstone National Park

Yellowstone, just north of Jackson and Grand Teton National Park, was our first national park. It advanced the concept of national parks more than any other unit in the system.

Spectacular wildlife viewing in this, the most successful wildlife reserve in the country, makes Yellowstone a perennially favorite destination. Where else in the lower 48 states can the average American encounter pristine wilderness and hope to see wild, unfenced bison, moose, elk, mule deer, and bighorn sheep on a typical day of driving and hiking?

Other pleasures of Yellowstone include geyser eruptions of Old Faithful about once every 72 minutes, abundant hydrothermal activity throughout the area, huge forests of lodgepole pine with a thousand miles of hiking trails, the deeply cut valley of the Yellowstone River, winter "snowcoach" tours, and cross-country skiing. In summer, you can drive your car throughout the park on the loop roads or take a guided tour.

Five generations of Americans have now enjoyed Yellowstone since the park was created in 1872. A farsighted Montanan, Nathaniel P. Langford,

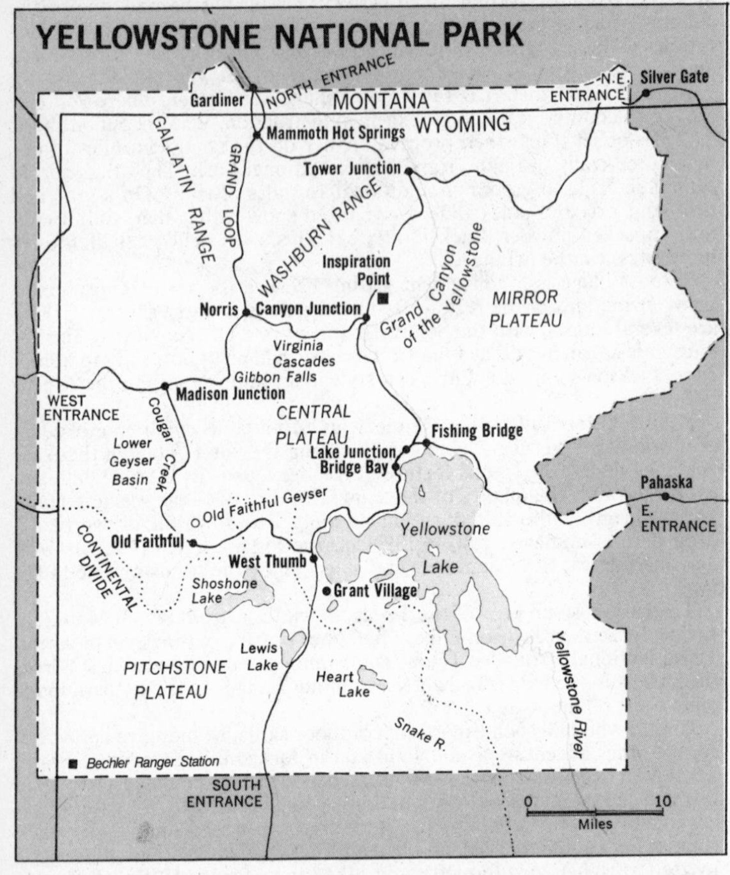

and his fellow conservationists launched in 1870 a national campaign to hold this land in trust as a "public park or pleasuring ground for the benefit and enjoyment of all the people." Each year over two million people visit the park, 70 percent of them arriving in July and August.

Today the park is managed with more skill and resources than in previous eras. The National Park Service of professional rangers and naturalists was authorized in 1916, and in 1917 they assumed management of Yellowstone. The park remains alive and well after the 1988 fires that burned about 793,888 acres. There are still wide sweeps of green forest, and little harm was done to the wild game. All the lodges and attractions are intact, and the burn area itself is a site of interest.

Yellowstone is truly the place of song "where the buffalo roam free." After driving a few miles into the park, perhaps near Lewis Lake, you may see your first buffalo, moose, or elk. Paradoxically, Yellowstone's wild animals show as little fear of people today as when John Colter entered the Yellowstone region in 1807. But remember to be cautious. They are still wild.

In driving the loop road you will find big game in scattered locations, with bison especially clustered near Old Faithful, elk prominent at Madison Junction, and bighorn sheep at the northwest corner of the park near

Gardiner. The largest concentration of easily seen big game is in the Hayden Valley along the Yellowstone River between Canyon and Fishing Bridge. By getting up to drive this road for the two hours after dawn and the two hours before sunset, you will see numerous bison, moose, elk, and mule deer, as well as flocks of Canadian geese and mallards.

Most of the grizzly bears of Yellowstone have now retreated into the back country, where they should be, no longer enticed by garbage dumps, now closed. However, bears are still sometimes seen and careful precautions must be taken to avoid thoughtless human encounters with them. Some Yellowstone campgrounds prohibit tents and soft-sided pop top vehicles because bears marauding at night could endanger campers sleeping next to their bacon or chocolate bar. Though bears have poor eyesight, their sense of smell is acute. In autumn they can smell huckleberries ripening miles away. Some visitors persist in feeding the bears, which is a mistake, because a panhandling, junk-fed bear will develop health problems and sooner or later take a swipe at a guileless human.

The number of large animals in the park is stable and secure, with the 2,000-pound male bison the lord of this particularly hospitable preserve. Bison is the preferred word to describe the American buffalo because the word buffalo is used for other members of the ungulate, or hooved, family in other regions, such as the water buffalo of southeast Asia. Each year naturalists at Yellowstone make a rough count of the large animals. A recent estimate indicated approximately 200 grizzly bears, 600 black bears, a few mountain lions, 1,600 mule deer, 2,300 bison, 295 bighorn sheep, 470 pronghorn antelope, and 31,000 elk. Yellowstone boasts the largest elk population of any park.

The thermal and geyser basins so prominent in Yellowstone provoked wondrous accounts from the early mountain men who encountered them, such as Colter and Jim Bridger. Because the veracity of these men suffered from their reputation as tellers of tall tales, the public remained skeptical and waited for more scientific confirmation of the presence of geysers, hot springs, boiling mudpots, and steaming fumaroles. Today thousands of people gather for the eruptions of Old Faithful, which occur about once every 72 minutes. Old Faithful remains faithful and shows little signs of diminished powers with age, barring the occasional disruptive earthquake or the threat of thermal electricity installations on the edge of the park tapping the steam system. Old Faithful spews out approximately 11,000 gallons of superheated water during its performances. Pressure underground raises the temperature of the water above the normal 212-degree boiling point at sea level. Based on the duration of the previous eruption, skilled park naturalists can predict to within a few minutes when the next eruption will occur. This time is then broadcast everywhere at the Old Faithful information center by digital clocks.

Old Faithful is only the beginning of hydrothermal activity to be observed in the park. Less crowded experiences are possible at many other sites, such as Mud Volcano, Dragon's Mouth, and Morning Glory Pool, where several colors of algae grow in water at different temperature levels, displaying a rainbow effect of volcanism. Animals as well as people appreciate the thermal manifestations. Some waterfowl winter in the park, living in water that never freezes. When snow covers the ground, browsing animals cluster in the geyser basins to eat grass stimulated by heat to grow. Food in the geyser basins is easily seen when all other food is hidden by a blanket of snow.

Thermal geologic forces have produced unusual effects in Yellowstone, such as the black obsidian cliffs near Mammoth Hot Springs. From the obsidian, formed when rhyolite lava cools quickly, Indians produced arrowheads and scraping tools. Tribes from the Yellowstone region traded the obsidian with Indians as far east as Ohio.

Scenery in Yellowstone is awesome. The vast 3,472 square miles of the park accommodate a large number of visitors. On this 7,500-foot plateau you can easily comprehend how slow geologic change affects an entire ecosystem of life, from wildflowers to big game.

Glaciers, as significant as volcanism in shaping Yellowstone, deposited a heavy layer of fine-grained sediment in the valleys. This glacial sediment prevents water from percolating down, which keeps the surface soil moist, an ideal environment for grasses. However, such damp soil rots the larger roots of trees. At these marshlands and meadows the long chain of life begins, starting with algae, grasses, and willows that feed the cutthroat trout, mice, and deer. These creatures are in turn eaten by ospreys, coyotes, and mountain lions. All of this texture of life depends on the underlying geologic fact of fine-grained glacial sediment.

The great forests of Yellowstone above the meadows cover 80 percent of the park. Surprisingly, 80 percent of that forest area is one species of tree, the lodgepole pine. Only 11 species of trees grow in Yellowstone. The lodgepole pines here yield unusually straight, long logs, now popular for log houses in the area. Indians once used these straight trees for the lodge poles of their teepees. However, the same lodgepole pine, on the West Coast, attains a twisted, gnarled appearance, which explains why its scientific name is *pinus contorta.*

The 1988 fires have stimulated new growth, for the cone of one variety of lodgepole pine requires heat from fire to perpetuate itself. Seeds in these cones, sealed by secretions of pitch, remain sealed until sufficient heat from fire melts the pitch. In coming years, visitors will view new forests of seedlings in the burn sites.

Outside the small village of Canyon, at Inspiration Point and Artist Point, linger over the breathtaking views of the Grand Canyon of the Yellowstone. This canyon is formed by the most erosive power in nature, swiftly moving water. Over eons the rushing Yellowstone River has cut through the soft rock here in dramatic ways, exposing a 700-foot gorge with walls of yellow-colored stone. The Minnataree Sioux Indians used a word in their language to describe this area as a land of "rock yellow river." French trappers appreciated the word and called the region *Pierre Jaune:* Yellow Stone.

The lure of Yellowstone is that of contrast and time. It's not only that Yellowstone is so rich in wildlife and scenery, but that the rest of our country is now so impoverished in these qualities. If you feel a certain citified malaise and long for a cleansing encounter with wilderness, head for Yellowstone, where yesterday still exists today.

Cheyenne and Cody

If you explore further in this state, named after the Delaware Indian word for "upon the great plain," you will indeed find the Great Plains covering the northeastern portion. Wyoming is a plateau, with elevations from 3,100 to 13,804 feet. The state's average height is surpassed only by the ethereal elevations of Colorado.

The Wyoming capital, Cheyenne, lies adjacent to the Laramie branch of the Rockies extending into the southeast corner of the state. During the last week of July, locals celebrate Cheyenne Frontier Days with the granddaddy of rodeos, a parade, and a festival. Between the Rockies of the southeastern and western parts of the state lies a relatively arid region known as the Great Divide, where large herds of cattle and sheep used to graze. In the southwest corner of the state lies Laramie, which flourished originally as a Union Pacific Railroad station. Laramie is the home of the University of Wyoming.

The Buffalo Bill Historical Center at Cody, in the northwest, displays the diverse personal collection of Buffalo Bill Cody and the impressive Winchester firearms collection. Four museums, covering over 100,000 square feet of space, include the distinguished Whitney Gallery of Western Art, with works from George Catlin's Indians to Charles Russell's cowboys, and the Plains Indian Museum, with displays of the clothing and weapons of this diverse Indian culture. Both as an immersion in the culture of the Rockies and as a jumping-off point for excursions into Yellowstone, Cody is a major tourist stop. Sheridan, the largest city in northern Wyoming, hosts a popular mid-July rodeo and frontier days.

MONTANA

The high mountains (*montañas* in Spanish) lie in the western two-fifths of the state, and the Great Plains occupies the eastern three-fifths. Called "land of shining mountains" by the early Indian inhabitants, Montana was the Treasure State to white settlers because of the abundance of minerals. Montana is huge, ranking fourth in size among all states.

The Yellowstone and Missouri rivers, early highways, begin in the southwest corner of the state and meander east through the plains, flowing eventually into the Atlantic. The two major rivers provide the water needed for human beings, cattle, and crops. Tributaries of the Snake and Salmon rivers form in the west, emptying into the Pacific. The Nelson Saskatchewan River flows north to the Arctic Ocean. River rafting is a prominent vacation prospect in the Bozeman area and at Glacier National Park.

For the traveler, the beauty of the state is a major draw, especially at Glacier National Park. The story of General Custer's last stand or Nez Percé Chief Joseph's retreat can be reviewed. The bustling towns, such as Bozeman, are pleasant to explore, as is the capital, Helena. You can take tours at several major mining operations, most notably in Butte.

The Custer Battlefield National Monument, 60 miles from Billings in the southeastern part of the state, memorializes Custer's Last Stand. In 1876 Sioux and Cheyenne warriors, led by Crazy Horse, Gall, and Two Moons, trapped Custer (Yellow Hair, as the Indians called him), after Custer badly underestimated their numbers. The Indians killed the entire force of soldiers.

The historical personality of note in Montana after Custer was Chief Joseph, the skilled leader of the Nez Percé Indians who led his warriors on a thousand-mile retreat in 1877 before surrendering. Throughout Montana and Idaho there are sites recalling the retreat and the Nez Percé culture. The actual surrender took place in northern Montana near the town of Chinook, where there is a state monument. In Idaho the Nez Percé National Historic Site provides a thorough introduction to this remarkable Indian group.

Billings, northwest of the Custer Battlefield, is Montana's largest city (population 66,000), named for Frederick Billings, president of the Northern Pacific Railroad, which decided that the site would be a town. Billings thrives on sugar beet production, oil refineries, and livestock yards. Five miles from Billings, Indian Caves contains some of the most important pictograph etchings of prehistoric man on the Great Plains. From Billings, take the drive along the Beartooth Scenic Highway through the western portion of the Custer National Forest. Bring your camera.

Mining has been important to Montana's development from the earliest days. Gold and silver were the first allure, but copper, especially at the major Anaconda works near Butte and in Butte itself, has provided a sustained source of revenues since 1870. From a lookout on Park Street East in Butte you can gaze into one of the immense open-pit mines. The region has supplied much of the copper used in the United States. Self-guided tours of the historic city of Butte are possible with a brochure from the Chamber of Commerce.

Many more specialized minerals, such as vermiculite for insulation, are available in abundant amounts, but gold and silver created the earliest settlements. Virginia City, southwest of Bozeman, a fully restored gold-rush town, is a lively tourist attraction. Over $300 million in gold was mined here between 1863 and 1937.

Helena, the state capital, owed its early existence to gold. In 1864 lucky miners made a strike here and eventually extracted $20 million in gold ore. By the 1880s Helena was booming, with so many millionaires that it was said to have the highest per capita wealth in the country. This early prominence caused Helena to become the seat of government, so now the apparatus of state administration is the major activity. Due to a shift in eagle migration routes, the Missouri River near Helena has become the place to see as many as 200 of these birds from late November to mid-December.

Great Falls, north of Helena, is an industrial boom town and the state's second largest city. For the traveler it is noteworthy as the home of cowboy artist Charlie Russell, whose work may be seen in his studio museum and home in town. The Great Falls themselves are a tumble of water, some 388 million gallons daily, as the Missouri River proceeds east.

West of Great Falls is Flathead Lake, the largest freshwater lake west of the Mississippi. State parks and resorts line the 28-mile waterway, which varies in width from 5 to 15 miles. South of the lake is the Flathead Indian Reservation and the National Bison Range, headquartered in Moiese. During the summer you can drive amid the herd and see buffalo, deer, antelope, elk, and bighorn sheep.

Bozeman is a good example of the charming towns of Montana. Located at the southwest corner of the state, near the entrance to Yellowstone, Bozeman is a hub of winter and summer tourism. Ranch vacations are popular in this part of Montana; Mountain Sky is a prominent example. Summer visitors enjoy pack trips, fishing, and hiking. Winter visitors relish the excellent cross-country skiing. Some ranches raise cattle, small grains, and dairy cows. In Bozeman a colorful mural depicts the settlement of the valley by John Bozeman in 1864. Montana State University gives Bozeman a college-town atmosphere. The major winter alpine skiing resorts of Big Sky and Bridger Bowl are nearby. Both Bozeman and West Yellowstone are major starting points for excursions into Yellowstone National Park. West Yellowstone does a brisk winter business in renting snowmobiles and cross-country skis to park visitors while the rest of the nation watches national weather reports on TV indicating that, once again tonight, West Yellowstone is the coldest spot in the country.

If you drive around this immense state, you'll see large herds of cattle and sheep, especially in the east, along with immense fields of hard winter wheat. Montana has vast reaches of wilderness with fish-filled streams and abundant natural beauty.

Glacier National Park

A million acres of glorious mountain scenery, including 50 glaciers and 200 lakes, were designated Glacier National Park in 1910. Glaciers of various ice ages carved out the valleys. Uplift over geologic eons formed the mountains. Some of the most impressive views in the park can be seen by driving the Going-to-the-Sun Road, which cuts through the park east to west, crossing the Continental Divide at Logan Pass (6,664 feet). Beyond the roads, there are a thousand miles of foot and horse trails offering backcountry experiences.

Just across the Canadian border is Waterton Lakes National Park. Together, the parks are called the Waterton-Glacier International Peace Park. The Chief Mountain International Highway allows you to cross the border to the Canadian side of the park during the summer.

IDAHO

Idaho's natural beauty—its mountains and rivers—attracts the traveler and provoked the nickname "Gem of the Mountains." The word *Idaho* was once thought to be a Shoshone word meaning "gem of the mountain" or "the sun comes down the mountain," referring to the beauty of dawn in the state. Scholars dispute the historical accuracy of the term, yet no one questions its prophetic truthfulness. "Idaho" does describe the marvels of a state with a Hell's Canyon, located on the Snake River. Far deeper than the Grand Canyon of Arizona, Hell's Canyon's stone walls rise 9,300 feet above 70 miles of swift rapids. "Idaho" also is a state rich in gem stones and wealthy in metals. The Coeur D'Alene Mining District is historically the world's largest silver producer.

In the east and central part of the state the Clearwater and Salmon mountains of the Bitterroot Range dominate the landscape, providing a lofty terrain where white pine and other important lumber trees flourish. Ten national forests in the state offer many hiking, camping, and sightseeing opportunities. Three wilderness areas (the Selway-Bitterroot, River of No Return, and Sawtooth) preserve more than two million acres of virgin land known only to the backpacker or outfitter. Within the Sawtooth Mountains the Salmon River forms, twists, and cuts deep canyons until it heads west to the Columbia. The Salmon is the longest waterway in any state. River rafters shoot the Salmon in summer, calling it "the River of No Return" because there is no turning back in the swift current once you start the run.

The Snake River is the other dominant influence on the landscape, draining the lava plains in the southern third of the state and forming much of the western boundary with Oregon. The Snake River rushes savagely west, spilling over cascading falls, which accounts for the frequency in the state of names such as Idaho Falls, American Falls, and Twin Falls.

Lewis and Clark were the first white man to pass through here, in 1805, viewing a land that nomads had hunted for an estimated 10,000 years. From about 1808 to 1840 fur trappers and Jesuit missionaries entered the area. After 1840 the Oregon Trail saw pioneers venturing west. Gold discoveries, starting in 1860 on Orofino Creek, provided a few boom and bust chapters in the state's scenario.

Irrigated fields of volcanic soil along the Snake are principal potato-growing areas; sugar beets and wheat are major crops. Idaho raises more potatoes and more commercial trout than any other state. Boise, the capital and largest city, lies along a tributary of the Snake in the southwestern part of the state. Cattle or sheep raising and agriculture are the major sustainers of life here. Boise is also corporate headquarters for Boise-Cascade, Morrison-Knudsen, and other corporations. Much of the sheep-herding business is managed by Basques. There are more Basques here than in any place except the European Pyrenées. Basque cooking and celebrations are a pleasure for travelers to the region.

While in Boise, see the classical State Capitol, historic Fort Boise, City Zoo, and the Idaho Historical Museum in Julia Davis Park. The museum describes the early gold rush to Pierce, in 1860, but the sustained wealth for the state proved to be lead, zinc, silver, and potash. Near Boise, be sure to tour the World Center for the Birds of Prey (208–362–3716) where eagles, falcons, and other raptors soar over 31,000 protected acres.

Two areas of Idaho holding great interest for the traveler are the Coeur d'Alene Lake region in the far north and the famous Sun Valley resort in the center of the state. Coeur d'Alene is a region of lakes and small towns, offering fishing, restful vacationing, and a chance to enjoy natural scenery. Coeur d'Alene Lake is among the most beautiful in the Rockies, with shades of color that vary with the light of the day. Excursion boats leave from the city dock for cruises on the 25-mile-long lake.

Lewiston, south of Coeur d'Alene, rests at the confluence of the Snake and Clearwater rivers. Because of dredging on the Columbia River, Lewiston is actually an Idaho seaport with some ship access to the ocean. Lewiston's annual rodeo, the Lewiston Roundup, attracts many visitors each Labor Day. Scenic boat tours of the Snake River from Lewiston venture upriver to the Hell's Canyon area.

Sun Valley, east of Boise, is a major all-year resort with some of the best skiing in the West and excellent horseback-trail trips, fishing, and the possibility of seeing movie stars. Southeast from Sun Valley is Craters of the Moon National Monument, an 83-square-mile volcanic landscape with a desolate, otherworldly appearance. Astronauts trained here. A seven-mile loop drive in the monument takes you past the principal volcanic cinder cones, caves, and fields.

In the eastern part of the state, near Pocatello, travelers can visit the Fort Hall Indian Reservation. Sun Dance Celebrations in July and August, which include a buffalo feast, are good times to visit this stronghold of the Shoshone and Bannock tribes.

PRACTICAL INFORMATION FOR THE ROCKY MOUNTAINS

WHEN TO GO. The summer months of June–Aug. and the winter months of Dec.–Apr. are the major tourism seasons for the Rockies. Even in summer, temperatures can be brisk in the mountains, but by June the mountain greenery is out and the highest mountain passes are cleared of snow. The major ski resorts usually open shortly after Thanksgiving weekend and some are able to stay open until Apr. because the altitude allows for late skiing. The "shoulder" seasons of Mar.–May and Sept. and Oct. offer the best values in lodgings, with the fall foliage of Sept. at Rocky Mountain and Grand Teton National Parks showing spectacular color.

HOW TO GET THERE. When making travel plans, remember that the entire region is in the Mountain Time Zone, except for the western part of Idaho, which is on Pacific Time. The Rockies are accessible by all the major air and ground transportation systems. So vast are these states, especially Montana, that driving to and through them is a major undertaking. But once you have reached the area of the Rockies that interests you, you may want to have your own car or a rental car for maximum mobility. *Amtrak* train trips offer spectacular views of the scenery, winter or summer; call 800–872–7245.

By plane. Denver and Salt Lake City are the major air terminals for the region. Seventeen major carriers make 1,400 flights daily into Denver's *Stapleton International Airport,* with feeder plane service to more distant points in Colorado. Grand Junction, in the western part of the state, also boasts an airport, as do Colorado Springs and Pueblo. Likewise, Salt Lake City, a hub for *Delta Airlines,* receives hundreds of flights daily. From either of the two dominant airports, commuter flights or shorter major-carrier flights proceed to cities such as Jackson, WY, or Bozeman, MT. Several major Colorado ski resorts now have direct air service into their establishments by *Continental Express.* Boise receives air flights direct from coastal western cities. *Continental* and *United* are among the carriers that fly into Boise. *Horizon, Delta, Alaska, Empire,* and others serve smaller towns in Idaho, such as Sun Valley, Pocatello, and Lewiston. *Continental, Delta, Northwest, Sky West,* and *United* fly to many Wyoming and Montana towns.

By bus. *Greyhound* (303–292–6111) is active throughout the region with transportation and tours.

By train. *Amtrak* superliners offer a popular alternative method to get to the Rockies year-round, riding west from Chicago or Minneapolis or east from Los Angeles, San Francisco, Portland, and Seattle. Denver is a major train stop in the cross-country runs. Trains run across the northern half of Colorado with stops at Denver and other sites, such as Glenwood Springs, the famous old resort on the rail line. The northerly route crosses Montana and Idaho, with spectacular winter scene viewing, including a stop at Glacier National Park. For Amtrak information, call 800–USA–RAIL.

By car. Swift interstate freeways service this region. Distances can be long and high-altitude driving in the mountains can be rigorous, but a car continues to allow the traveler the freedom to see the terrain as one wishes. Colorado visitors arrive via I-25 from Wyoming or New Mexico, I-70 from Utah or Kansas, and I-80 from Nebraska. For Wyoming, I-80 passes east–west along the southern edge of the state, I-25 links with Colorado and Montana, and I-90 provides a fast road to South Dakota. I-94–90 traverses Montana and cuts across the northern panhandle of Idaho, with I-15 serving as a north–south artery for Montana and eastern Idaho. I-84 unites Idaho with Oregon.

TOURIST INFORMATION. Each of the four Rocky Mountain states maintains an active tourism information apparatus. They will send you, upon request, brochures, maps, and calendars of events about the state. Additionally, see the National Parks section because each of those five parks will send you a brochure and map. As you zero in on your special interest, the state tourism office can forward your requests for further information to appropriate suppliers, such as river rafting companies, for example. Also, in Colorado the major winter-summer resorts will send you their brochures upon request. See them listed under *Skiing.*

Colorado: *Colorado Tourism Board,* 1625 Broadway, Suite 1700, Denver, CO 80202 (800–433–2656).

Wyoming: *Wyoming Division of Travel,* I-25 at College Dr., Cheyenne, WY 82002 (800–225–5996).

Montana: *Travel Montana,* Department of Commerce, 1424 9th Ave., Helena, MT 59620 (800–541–1447).

Idaho: *Idaho Travel Council,* 700 W. State St., Room 108, State Capitol Bldg., Boise, ID 83720 (800–635–7820).

TELEPHONES. The area codes for the four Rocky Mountain states are: Colorado, 303 (northern region) and 719 (southern region); Wyoming, 307; Montana, 406; and Idaho, 208. Directory assistance numbers for all four states are the same: 1411. The cost of local pay-phone calls are: Colorado, 20–25 cents; Wyoming, 25 cents; Montana, 10 cents and 25 cents; and Idaho, 25 cents. Dial 1 before the area code for outgoing long-distance calls and 0 before the area code for collect and person-to-person calls.

EMERGENCY TELEPHONE NUMBERS. To get police, fire, or ambulance help, dial 911.

Road-condition information is often important for safe travel in this region during winter snowfalls or summer thunderstorms. Information numbers are: Colorado, 303–639–1234 for north, south, and east and 303–639–1111 for west; Wyoming, 307–635–9966 Montana, 406–444–6339 or 800–332–6171; and Idaho, 208–336–6600 or 208–376–8028.

HOW TO GET AROUND. The Rocky Mountain states amount to a large expanse of territory. Scheduled major air carriers can take you from Denver or Salt Lake to the smaller cities. The train that gets you there can drop you at any one of several stops along the line. The bus companies also travel to the far corners of each state. Your own car, or a rental car, usually offers the most flexible pattern for travel within the region. Even in the national parks, a car gives you a freedom that the public transportation systems can't equal. Highways throughout the four states are good, though smaller side roads are curvy in the mountains (see Hints to Motorists).

From the Denver airport. *RTD* buses run from Stapleton International Airport to downtown Denver and to the suburbs. Taxis are plentiful if your time is tight. Major hotels have airport van or limousine pickups for their guests.

By bus. *Greyhound* and some local bus companies, such as *RTD Bus Co.* in Colorado, *Powder River Transportation* in Wyoming, and *Rimrock Stage* in Montana cover the territory.

By train. In Colorado, *Amtrak* offers passenger service between Denver and Grand Junction. Two special steam trains in southwest Colorado offer a unique experience as well as transportation. The *Cumbres & Toltec Scenic Railroad* puffs through the San Juan Mountains between Antonito, CO and Chama, NM. Group rates. Runs every day from mid-June to mid-Oct. Overnight stays are possible. Write for reservations to: Cumbres & Toltec Scenic Railroad, Box 668, Antonito, CO 81120 (719–376–5483). The *Durango & Silverton Narrow Gauge Railroad,* a National Historic Landmark from 1882, crosses the San Juan National Forest for the 45-mi. trip between Durango and Silverton. Steam-powered. Fabulous views of the Rockies. Write for tickets to Agent, Durango & Silverton Narrow Gauge Railroad Co., 479 Main Ave., Durango, CO 81301 (303–247–2733). Advance reservations necessary.

In Montana you can take the Amtrak *Superliner* across the state, running parallel to Hwy. 2, with a stop at Glacier National Park. In Idaho the Amtrak *Superliner* stops at Sandpoint on the Seattle–Chicago run. Another *Amtrak* train stops at Shoshone, Pocatello, and Boise.

By rental car. The major rental car companies are active in all four states at major cities and airports: *Hertz* (800–654–3131), *Budget* (800–227–2048), and *Thrifty* (800–367–2277). Week-long packages with a free mileage bonus often a good car rental buy if you plan to see much of the territory.

HINTS TO MOTORISTS. Though roads are good in the mountain regions, some cautions about driving are worth noting. Many of the smaller mountain roads can have sharp curves and switchbacks and require careful attention behind the wheel, especially when conditions are wet or icy. Road conditions should be checked during winter snowstorms and summer rainstorms. See the appropriate numbers for each state under Emergency Telephone Numbers.

Rest your engine, as needed, to avoid overheating. Check your brakes to be sure they are in good condition before you depart on a mountain trip. Note that large motor homes, those over 30 ft., may be restricted from travel on the Going-to-the-Sun Highway in Glacier National Park.

High-altitude driving may require that your carburetor be adjusted to allow more air in the mixture because of the reduced amount of oxygen.

TRAVELING WITH PETS. While traveling in Wyoming, Montana, and Idaho carry a certificate from your veterinarian attesting that the dog has been vaccinated against rabies, that the point of origin is free of rabies, and that the dog is free of infectious disease.

HINTS TO DISABLED TRAVELERS. Each of these four states is making progress on the accessibility of streets, restaurants, and parks. Write the tourism office for each state (see Tourist Information) and the five national parks (see National Parks) with your special needs to get specific information.

TOURS AND SPECIAL-INTEREST SIGHTSEEING. Tours in the four Rockies states are most active during the summer season, June–Sept. Each of the five national parks in the Rockies offers nature tours within the park, led by rangers. Day trips can be arranged in some parks. Longer tours within the parks, which are possible especially at Glacier and Yellowstone, require advance planning. For the relevant addresses of the parks, see National Parks. The most complete **nature-oriented tours** in the region are sponsored by the *Yellowstone Institute* (Box 117, Yellowstone National Park, Mammoth, WY 82190, 307–344–7381, ext. 2384). The Institute offers a wide range of 1–5-day special courses on nature subjects. One of the most intriquing new tour and sightseeing firms is *Off the Beaten Path,*" 109 E. Main St., Bozeman, MT 59715, 416–586–1311. This agency offers planning services for individuals, couples, and groups.

Historic Denver, Inc. takes you on a 2-hour summer walking tour to look at Victorian homes and the historic downtown. Contact them at Historic Denver, 1330–17th St., Denver, CO 80202 (303–534–1858). Fee $7 for walking tour, $12 for van tour.

Denver's **U.S. Mint,** Colfax and Delaware, offers an interesting 30-minute tour showing how money is made. Free admission. Closed last two weeks in June.

In Wyoming, active tour operators out of Jackson, enter the Grand Teton and Yellowstone national parks. The most active of these providers for **pack trips, wagon rides,** and other tours is Grand Teton Lodge Co. (Box 240, Moran, WY 83013, 307–543–2855). **River rafting** tours are especially popular in Wyoming on the Snake River at Grand Teton National Park; 10–4 P.M. daily, Dec. 16–end of Mar. See the names of providers under Horseback Riding and River Rafting.

To take the **sleigh ride** in winter to see the National Elk Herd north of Jackson, contact the Refuge Manager, National Elk Refuge, Box C, Jackson, WY 83001 (307–733–8084), adults $6, children $3.

Several **historic Wyoming trails** can be followed along highways with write-ups from the state's tourist information office. The historic trails include the Cheyenne-Deadwood Stage Rd., noted for its cattle drives; the Bozeman Trail of 1863, where prospectors and settlers fought the Plains Indians; the Bridger Trail (1807), where the mountain men passed; the Oregon Trail (1843), which pioneers made the first highway west; and the Overland Trail (1862), where you can still see many pronghorn antelope.

In Montana, aside from Glacier National Park tours (see National Parks) and extensive river rafting from Bozeman or from Glacier National Park (see Horseback Riding and River Rafting), several special, smaller historic tours can be recommended. **Butte's** fabulously rich copper hills, which inspired the city nickname as the "the richest hill on earth," can best be explored with a walking tour of the historic district and a driving tour around the town. Get tour maps at the Butte Chamber of Commerce, 2950 Harrison Ave. (406–494–5595). In **Helena,** the Last Chance Tour Train is an informative hour-long ride through the historic district, including the state capitol, organized by the Montana State Historical Museum (adults $3, children $2, 406–442–6880).

In **Idaho,** the Boise Tour Train offers a good opportunity to see the capital through the eyes of a native. The one-hour trip covers the downtown and the historic area. Reasonable fees. The train leaves from Julia Davis Park several times daily (208–342–4796). Summer only.

The multibillion dollar mining district of **Coeur d'Alene,** which produces lead, silver, gold, and zinc, can be toured by car if you stop first for a brochure at the Chamber of Commerce, 2nd St. and Sherman. Another approach to the region is via the Sierra Silver Mine Tour, an hour-long tour that takes you underground. The tour leaves from the Mining Museum in Wallace several times daily in summer, cost $4.50 adults, $3.50 children (208–752–5151).

The **Dworshak National Fish Hatchery,** near Ahsahka, allows a fascinating glimpse at man's efforts to perpetuate trout fisheries after building dams. Three million steelhead and 1.5 million rainbow trout are raised and released here each year. Self-guided tours with map, admission free (208–476–4591).

NATIONAL PARKS. The five national parks in the Rockies states are major tourism destinations for the brief summer season of June–Sept. They are all open year-round, however. A winter trip to these parks can be a rewarding experience, even though not all facilities may be open.

Mesa Verde National Park. CO 81330 (303–529–4465). Open year-round. Entrance fee $5 per car. Camping only May-Oct. Mesa Verde is in southwest Colorado, near the town of Cortez, which is served by commuter aircraft. Durango, another sizeable community 36 mi. east of the park, is a popular gateway for numerous air carriers. There are buses from the region's major towns.

For exploring the park, it helps to have your own car. The entrance to the park, 10 mi. east of Cortez, leads to a long road winding south in the park. Orient yourself first at the Visitor Center, which boasts a remarkable view some 50 mi. to the south. Then drive the road south to the major ruins, which are on the Chapin Mesa. The Archeology Museum, offering a fascinating glimpse at some treasured artifacts, such as exquisite dog-hair belts from A.D. 500, is within the ruins area. Besides the

Chapin Mesa, a more westerly area, the Wetherill Mesa, is open only in summer and only via a Park Service bus tour that leaves from the Visitor Center.

The largest and most celebrated structure, the Cliff Palace, has 217 rooms, of which 23 are described by archaeologists as kivas, a Hopi word meaning "ceremonial room." About 200–250 people lived at the Cliff Palace in the 13th century, shortly before drought and depletion of resources caused a rapid decline of the population. You can view the ruin from afar. The agile can climb down and up a steep hillside to make an on-site visit. The Balcony House ruin can be viewed only if you climb down. The Square Tower ruin, one of the most photogenic of the existing structures, originally had 80 rooms and was four stories high, with a dependable water source in the spring below it.

Because of the threat of pot-hunters disturbing the archeology sites, hiking is discouraged in the back country of Mesa Verde.

Rocky Mountain National Park. Estes Park, CO 80517 (303–969–2000). Open year-round. Entrance fee $5 per car per week. Camping year-round—primitive in winter, reservations may be necessary in summer. Tape tours of the park are popular and are available locally for $10.50.

Stop first at the Moraine Park Visitor Center, a mi. from the Beaver Meadows entrance, to learn about the park environment. Deep in the park, at the Fall River Pass, stop again to orient yourself at the Alpine Visitor Center and the Tundra World Visitor Center. You can make a 240-mi. grand loop trip from Denver, including Boulder, Estes Park, Grand Lake, and Idaho Springs.

Within the park, Trail Ridge Road is the celebrated drive, but it is only open from June to the first heavy snowfall, usually in Oct. A portion of this spectacular road follows a ridge at 12,000 ft. Bear Lake Road travels from Beaver Meadows through Moraine Park. Several hiking trails are offered here. Throughout the park, scenic viewing from the road, hiking, horseback riding, and mountain climbing are the major activities. Naturalist-led walks and talks are popular.

Grand Teton National Park. Drawer 170, Moose, WY 83012 (307–733–2220). Open year-round. An entrance permit good for both Grand Teton and Yellowstone is $10 per car and valid for 7 days. Walk-ins are $4 per person.

In the 485-sq.-mi. expanse of the park lie some of the youngest and most rugged mountains in the Rockies, including most of the Teton Range, with Grand Teton (13,770 ft)., Mount Owen (12,928 ft.), and Middle Teton (12,804 ft.) as the highest mountains. Winter sport enthusiasts enjoy the cross-country skiing and snowmobiling, but most of the visitors come in summer, especially from June to Sept. 15.

The park is accessible from the south via Jackson and the east via Moran Junction. When you reach the park, orient yourself at the visitor center at Colter Bay or Moose. Literature and camping permits are available there. The Moose Visitor Center includes a Fur Trade Museum that describes the early search for beaver pelts in the region. The Colter Bay Visitor Center emphasizes the art and culture of the Plains Indians. Ranger-led hikes and nightly campfire talks inform visitors regarding the glacial story and its ensuing effect on all life in the park. One special cultural experience available at Grand Teton National Park is the Laubin Ancient Indian Dances, performed Fri. nights during the summer at Jackson Lake Lodge (307–543–2811). Admission charge.

Fishing is allowed in the lakes and streams with artificial flies and lures after a Wyoming fishing permit has been purchased. Mountain climbing, horseback riding at Colter Bay and Jackson Lake Lodge, and river rafting are popular. Rafting on the Snake River through the park is a particularly pleasant way to see wildlife, ranging from elk to eagles. Several rafting companies are listed under Horseback Riding and River Rafting. The major lodges, such as Grand Teton Lodge or Jackson Lake Lodge (write both at Box 240, Moran, WY 83013, 307–543–2855), organize a spectrum of activities, including trail rides and wagon train rides to simulate the old west. Cruises out on Jackson Lake, as organized by the Grand Teton Lodge, take place from the Colter Bay Marina several times each day.

Yellowstone National Park. Box 168, WY 82190 (307–344–7901). Open year-round. An entrance permit good for both Yellowstone and Grand Teton is $10 per car and valid for 7 days. Walk-ins are $4 per person. For information on lodging (including campgrounds) and other guest services, write the concessionaire, Travel Director, TW Services, Yellowstone National Park, WY 82190.

There are 5 entrances to the park. From the north, the Gardiner and Cooke City entrances remain open to cars all year. West Yellowstone, South Entrance from

Jackson, and East Entrance from Pahaska Teepee are open for cars only in summer. Track vehicles called snow coaches take in visitors in winter. Only visitors with firm lodging and dining reservations are allowed in winter, unless you are driving your own snowmobile.

The park roads were laid out in the 19th century when the concept of stagecoach touring was popular. Major thermal basins to see are at West Thumb, Old Faithful area, along the Firehole River, and at Mammoth Hot Springs in the north. Mammoth is also the park headquarters, with a small museum to the history of the park. Early morning and late afternoon are opportune times to see game. Be sure to remain a respectful distance from all big game, which is wild, contrary to the impression of some travelers. Do not feed the game. Include in your excursions a look at the Grand Canyon of the Yellowstone River on the east side of the park.

Information and safety notices are sent via radio in the park, so tune your car radio to 1606 khz. The main season is Memorial Day to Labor Day for most of the ranger-led activities, such as talks and hikes. A day's activities can be planned in visitor centers, some of which have extensive interpretive programs on special park features. The Old Faithful Visitor Center is the largest. The visitor centers are at Mammoth, Norris Geyser Basin, Madison Junction, Old Faithful (which emphasizes the geysers in films and ranger talks), West Thumb, Fishing Bridge (which emphasizes biology and history), Bridge Bay, Tower Falls, Grant Village (which emphasizes the wilderness), and Canyon Village.

Fishing is allowed in most of the park. For a free fishing permit and regulations, stop in at a visitor center.

Though the roads of Yellowstone are often congested with travelers, all eager to see big game, the back country with 1,000 mi. of trails remains less used. Hiking is recommended; backpack camping is another way to see the terrain. Horseback trips, organized by TW Services, is another way. Write TW at the address noted above for the extent of trips and prices.

Glacier National Park. West Glacier, MT 59936 (406–888–5441). The park is open year-round; Going-to-the-Sun Hwy. is open from about late May–mid-Oct. Admission $5 per vehicle for 7 days.

Glacier National Park's 50 glaciers, 200 lakes, and million acres of alpine scenery offer many rewards for the traveler. The park's 80th anniversary was in 1990. The easiest way to see the sights is by driving both directions, and at different times of the day, on the Going-to-the-Sun Hwy. (Note that vehicles over 30 ft. aren't permitted on this road because of safety issues.) The geologic features, the big game, and the elaborate flora, especially wildflowers and dense forests of Engelmann spruce, delight visitors. Canoes and rowboats are available for serene excursions on some of the lakes, such as Two Medicine and McDonald. Scenic cruises from large launches are offered at 5 major lakes in the park. Trout fishing is excellent throughout the park. The more energetic can hike into the back country along 700 mi. of trails or be carried there on horseback, as arranged by Glacier Park. The company sponsors a range of tours of the park, for 1 to 10 days. Write them for details at Glacier Park, East Glacier Park, MT 59434 (406–226–5551, May–Sept.) or Glacier Park, Greyhound Tower, Station 5510, Phoenix, AZ 85077 (602–248–6000, Sept.–May). Ranger-led hikes and campfire talks are given at the major lodges (see Accommodations) and campgrounds. Some campgrounds may be limited to hard-sided vehicles due to bear activity.

STATE PARKS. Each of the four Rockies states has developed a system of state parks, which supplements the national park and national forest recreational opportunities in the area. For a list of the state parks and for general information on outdoor recreation in the state, write to the following agencies: *Colorado Parks and Outdoor Recreation,* 1313 Sherman St., Denver, CO 80216. *Wyoming Recreation Commission,* Cheyenne, WY 82002. *Montana Fish, Wildlife & Parks,* 1420 E. Sixth Ave., Helena, MT 59620. *Idaho Parks and Recreation Department,* 2177 Warm Springs Ave., Statehouse Mail, Boise, ID 83720.

CAMPING. Camping out is popular in the Rockies, especially in the national parks at such beauty spots as Jenny Lake in Grand Teton National Park. Most camping is on a first-come, first-served basis. For national park camping, see National Parks and write the superintendent for a complete list of campgrounds in each park. Due to bear activity, some campgrounds at Yellowstone and at Glacier National Parks may be restricted to hard-sided vehicles. Besides national parks, there are also extensive state parks, national forests, and private campgrounds offering facilities. For state park camping, see State Parks. For further information on camping in national forests and at private campgrounds, write as follows:

Colorado. National Forests: U.S. Forest Service, Box 25127, Denver, CO 80225 (303–236–9431). Private: Write for a free directory from Colorado Campground and Cabin-Resort Assn., 5101 Pennsylvania Ave., Boulder, CO 80303 (303–499–9343). Ask for the "Colorado Directory."

Wyoming. National Forests: National Park Service, Box 25287, Denver, CO 80225. Private: Write to the state tourism office (see Tourist Information for address) for the free *Wyoming Vacation Guide.*

Montana. National Forests: U.S. Forest Service, Northern Region, Box 7669, Missoula, MT 59801. Private: Write for the Accommodations Guide provided free by the state tourism office (see Tourist Information for address).

Idaho. National Forests: U.S. Forest Service, Northern Region, Federal Building, Missoula, MT 59801. For directory contact the Idaho Campground Owner's Assn., 11101 Fairview Ave., Boise, ID 83704 (800–635–5240).

FISHING AND HUNTING. Trout fishing is popular throughout the four-state region with flies and lures. Other species of fish are also caught, such as bass and panfish at some sites, but trout, in several varieties, remains the premier catch. Great efforts are made in Yellowstone National Park to preserve the native trout only, but introduced trout are widespread elsewhere. Idaho's rivers also offer salmon, steelhead, and sturgeon fishing.

The main hunting quarry is mule deer, but there are also specialized hunts for elk, bighorn sheep, moose, black bear, and antelope. In Montana, buffalo are included in the hunt when they wander out of Yellowstone National Park. Contact each state's department for appropriate license information. In Montana, for example, nonresident prospective hunters must enter their names in drawings to get appropriate tags. For some Montana hunts you must also hunt with a native. Bird hunters in the Rockies watch each autumn for the migration of ducks and geese on the flyway south from Canada. Pheasant and grouse are the major upland birds hunted.

For more information, write the appropriate state:

Colorado. Colorado Division of Wildlife, 6060 Broadway, Denver, CO 80216. (303–297–1192).

Wyoming. Game and Fish Dept., Information Section, 5400 Bishop Blvd., Cheyenne, WY 82002. (307–777–7735).

Montana. Montana Fish & Game Dept., 1420 6th Ave., Helena, MT 59620. (406–444–2535).

Idaho. Idaho Fish and Game Commission, 600 S. Walnut, Boise, ID 83707. (208–335–3700).

HORSEBACK RIDING AND RIVER RAFTING. Horseback riding at dude ranches and rafting on the many Rockies rivers are major tourism activities. Dude or guest ranches flourish in each of the 4 states. The dude, a term for an outsider who comes to enjoy the ranch, usually comes for a week's stay. Riding, barbecue dinners, fishing, hiking, and relaxing are the main activities at a ranch. Ranches allow the outsider to become immersed for a short period in cowboy life.

River rafting is a major tourism sport in all four states of the Rockies. Magnificent rivers with fast flow, opportunities to see big game or birds such as eagles, and spectacular scenery attract visitors to this active yet restful pastime. The major rafting companies all have trained guides who take the danger, but not the thrill, out of an encounter with the water. For the main white-water trips, small children are not allowed. It is wise that all rafters know how to swim. Come dressed for a rafting trip in tennis shoes so you can walk in rocky water if needed. Be prepared for a warm, sunny outing, but pack a raincoat in case rapids or a sudden thunderstorm deluge the boat. Most rafting occurs in rubberized pontoon-type boats, but some purists use historic dories and the most adventuresome use kayaks or canoes. Rafting is popular in Colorado along the Colorado and Arkansas rivers, in Wyoming along the Snake River by Grand Teton National Park, in Montana out of Bozeman on the Yellowstone River and at Glacier National Park, and in Idaho on the Snake and Salmon rivers. River rafting prices will depend on the duration of the trip, and may range from $25 for a half-day outing to $970 for a week-long excursion with gourmet food.

Here are opportunities in each state for dude ranching and river rafting:

Colorado. Horses at dude ranches: Write for a brochure to *Colorado Dude and Guest Ranch Assn,* Box 300, Tabernash, CO 80478 (303–887–3128). River rafting: *Timberline Tours,* Box 131, Vail, CO 81658 (303–476–1414). The group association for Colorado rafting companies is: *Western River Guides Assn.,* 7600 E. Arapahoe, Suite 114, Englewood, CO 80112 (303–771–0389).

Wyoming. Horses at dude ranches: At *Bill Cody's Ranch Resort,* Box 1390-T, Cody, WY 82414 (307–587–2097), or in Grand Teton National Park at *Jackson Lake Lodge,* Box 240, Moran, WY 83013 (307–543–2855). For a list of all Wyoming dude ranches, consult the *Wyoming Vacation Guide* available free from the state tourism office (see Tourist Information). River rafting: A cluster of rafting providers work out of Jackson and Grand Teton National Park. Charges for a half day typically will be $20–$30 adults, $10–$20 children. Some guides are: *Shoshone Lodge,* Box 790 WT, Cody, WY 82414 (307–587–4044), *Mountain Shadows Guest Ranch,* Box 110 WT, Wapiti, WY 82450 (303–587–2143), and *Triangle X Ranch Float Trips,* Box 120M, Moose, WY 83012 (307–733–5500).

Montana. Horses at dude ranches: For a list of all the Montana ranches, see the free *Accommodations Guide* put out by the state tourism office (see Tourist Information). Two good choices would be: *Lone Mountain,* Box 69, Big Sky, MT 59716 (406–995–4644) and *Circle Bar Guest Ranch,* Utica, MT 59452 (406–423–5454). River rafting: For rafting on the Gallatin and Yellowstone Rivers, contact *Yellowstone Raft Company* Box 46, Gardiner, MT 59030 (406–848–7789). For rafting near Glacier National Park, contact the *Glacier Raft Company,* Box 218M, West Glacier, MT 59936 (406–888–5454 or 800–332–9995 in Montana).

Idaho. Both dude ranches and river rafting companies are listed in the free *Idaho Vacation* guide available from the state tourism office (see *Tourist Information*). River rafting: Operating from the town of Salmon, several rafting companies shoot the Salmon River. Two suppliers are *High Adventure Inc.,* Box 222, Dept. O, Twin Falls, ID 83301 (208–733–0123), and *Rocky Mountain River Tours,* Box 2552–O, Boise, ID 83701 (208–344–6668).

SKIING. Alpine and nordic skiing are both popular in the Rockies. Colorado offers more than 30 alpine (downhill) areas. The other three states also provide impressive alpine skiing, especially Sun Valley, Idaho; Jackson, Wyoming; and Big Sky, Montana. Lift tickets run $19 to $40 for alpine areas, depending on the quality and prestige of the ski center and the extent of the lift system. Package deals with accommodations and lodging, especially over a several-day period, can reduce the cost dramatically. Nordic (cross-country) skiing flourishes in all four states, from the ranches of Montana to the geyser basins in Yellowstone National Park. The importance of winter sports in the Rockies has led many providers to organize entire transportation, lodging, and skiing packages, especially in Colorado. Here are winter sport opportunities state by state:

Colorado. Vail, Aspen, Winter Park, and Beaver Creek are renowned for fabulous slopes and attract an international ski crowd. For an elaborate, free publication on all the Colorado Ski areas contact Colorado Ski Country USA, 1560 Broadway, Suite 1440, Denver, CO 80202 (303–837–0793). Special ski buses, operating throughout the state, are called The Lift (303–398–LIFT). Coordinate your plans with the How to Get There and How to Get Around information on Colorado. Most incoming skiers fly into Denver, but direct service to ski areas is growing. Check America West, Continental Express, Mesa, and United Express for connections. A weekend ski train stops in Winter Park (303–296–I–SKI) and *Amtrak* services Glenwood Springs (40 mi. from Aspen). Financially, often the best package plan involves all the elements—lift tickets, lodgings, and transportation—as organized by the ski area's central reservations number.

Here are several reservation services for the major Colorado ski areas, covering a spectrum of lodgings. Note that these addresses and numbers serve both the winter skier and the summer traveler because these resort communities are year-round operations:

Aspen Resort Association, 700 S. Aspen St., Aspen, CO 81611 (800–262–7736).

Breckenridge Resort Chamber, Box 1909, Breckenridge, CO 80424 (in state 800–822–5381, out of state 800–221–1091).

Copper Mountain Lodging Services, Box 3001, Copper Mountain, CO 80443 (in state 303–825–7106, out of state 800–458–8386).

Keystone Resort Reservations, Box 38, Keystone, CO 80435 (nationwide 800–541–0346 or 800–222–0188).

Purgatory Ski Resort, Box 666, Durango, CO 81302 (303–247–9000) (nationwide 800–525–0892).

Silver Creek, Box 1110, Silver Creek, CO 80446 (ski area 303–887–3384, Inn at Silver Creek 303–887–2131).

Snowmass Resort Assn., Box 5566, Snowmass Village, CO 81615 (nationwide 800–332–3245 or, for reservations, 303–923–2000).

Steamboat Springs Chamber Assn., Box 774408, Steamboat Springs, CO 80477 (nationwide 800–332–3204, out of state 303–879–0880).

Telluride Ski Resort, Box 307, Telluride, CO 81435 (in state 303–728–4431, out of state 800–525–3455).

Vail & Beaver Creek Resorts, 241 E. Meadow Dr., Vail, CO 81657 (in state 303–476–5677, or nationwide 800–525–2257).

Winter Park Central Reservations, Box 36, Winter Park, CO 80482 (in state 303–726–5587, out of state 800–453–2525).

Wyoming. For a complete guide to Wyoming skiing, write Wyoming Travel Commission, I-25 at College Dr., Cheyenne, WY 82002 (800–225–5996 from outside the state, 307–777–7777 inside the state). Major downhill areas are Jackson Hole Ski Resort with world-class facilities and Grand Targhee in the Tetons. Snowy Range near Laramie, Hogadon near Casper, Sleeping Giant near Yellowstone, and Meadowlark in the Bighorns. Snowmobiling is popular in Yellowstone, with rentals available at West Yellowstone, and in Grand Teton National Parks, with rentals at Signal Mountain Lodge.

Montana. For a complete guide book to the state skiing, write Ski Guide, C/O *Travel Montana,* Deer Lodge, MT 59722 (800–541–1447). One main alpine area is Big Sky (Box 1, Big Sky, MT 59716, 800–548–4486). Big Mountain at Whitefish, Bridger Bowl at Bozeman, and Red Lodge Mountain at Red Lodge are other major alpine areas. Major cross-country ski ranches are Lone Mountain (Box 69, Big Sky, MT 59716, 406–995–4644). For a booklet on all the cross-country ski ranches, inns, and hot springs hotels, write the Montana Cross Country Ski Area Association, Box 653C, Essex, MT 59916. Call Tourism & Travel (800–541–1447) for more information.

Idaho. For information on state skiing, write Ski Information, Idaho Tourism, Room 108, State Capitol, Boise, ID 83720. Ski conditions information: 800–635–4150. Sun Valley is the major ski resort, which opens in November. The toll-free information number for Sun Valley skiing (Sun Valley Co., Sun Valley, ID 83353) is 800–635–8261. In 1986 Sun Valley celebrated its 50th year as a major ski resort.

HISTORIC SITES AND HOUSES. Monuments to the westward exploration of Lewis and Clark and the string of forts built during the Indian wars are major pilgrimage points in the Rockies. Nineteenth-century gold-mining towns add a ghost town or resort town flavor, depending on how well they survived.

Colorado. The state offers more than 300 early *mining towns* to explore. Limited small-stakes gambling will soon be available in Cripple Creek, Central City, and Blackhawk. One of the best preserved and reconstructed of these Colorado mining towns is the South Park City Museum at Fairplay. South Park City Museum (719–836–2387) consists of a cluster of structures, furnished with artifacts of the period, including a newspaper office, assay office, and general store. Admission $3 adults, $1.50 children.

Among early *army posts,* stop at Kit Carson's Fort Garland, west of La Veta, or Bent's Fort, where the trappers traded. Both are in southeast Colorado.

Pikes Peak, which inspired the phrase "Pikes Peak or Bust" in the 19th-century mining era, is a red granite prominence (14,110 ft.) visible for a great distance. You can drive there, ride up in a scenic cable railway to the peak (719–685–9086), or take a popular cog railway from Manitou Springs. The cog railway leaves from 515 Ruxton Ave. for the 3½-hour round-trip to the top. Reservations are necessary for the Pike's Peak Cog Railway, Box 1329, Colorado Springs, CO 80901 (719–685–5401), $17 adults, $9 children.

Wyoming. Numerous restored forts engage the Wyoming traveler with an interest in history. *Fort Laramie National Historic Site* preserves the remains of Fort Laramie, a fur trade and military fort near the confluence of the Laramie and Platte Rivers. The fort provided needed protection for early pioneers on the Oregon Trail. Partially restored, the fort offers summer interpretive performances by costumed staff. The fort is 3 mi. from the town of Fort Laramie, admission for adults, $1 (307–837–2221).

Fort Bridger State Historic Site, on U.S. 30, 30 mi. east of Evanston, was begun by mountain man Jim Bridger in 1843. The fort includes a museum with Indian artifacts and offers summer history and crafts programs. The Fort Bridger Rendezvous over the Labor Day weekend hosts a black powder shoot of antique firearms. Admission is free (307–782–3842).

Fort Caspar, at 4001 Fort Caspar Rd. in Casper. Fort replica includes exhibits of the Indian and pioneer days. Admission is free (307–235–8462).

Among the early Mormon pioneering sites, the most notable is *St. Mary's Stage Station,* near South Pass City, where 90 Mormons perished in a blizzard. Among Wyoming's gold mining-era ghost towns, *South Pass City* is an excellent example. The site is being restored and includes a visitor center. Admission is free (307–332–3684 or 777–7695).

Montana. *Custer Battlefield National Monument* lies near Crow Indian reservation lands in the Valley of the Little Bighorn. Several thousand Sioux and Northern Cheyenne Indians killed Lt. Col. George A. Custer and 225 of his men here in June 1876. At the main entrance, 12 mi. southeast of Hardin, you'll find a visitor center with park rangers, literature, and a museum. Admission is $3 per vehicle (406–638–2621).

Fort Benton, on Hwy. 87, was Montana's most important early settlement and trade hub; a visitor center and museum tell the story. Their Lewis and Clark Memorial overlooks the Missouri River. Self-guiding tour brochure (406–538–7461).

The *Old Montana Territorial Prison,* Deer Lodge, is now a museum to prison life and pioneer times, but was once the first major prison in the Western U.S. Admission $6.50 adults, $2.50 children (406–846–3111).

The *Original Governor's Mansion,* 304 N. Ewing, in Helena, was built in 1888 and housed 9 governors from 1913 to 1959. Hour-long guided tours are offered at no charge (406–444–2694).

St. Mary's Mission in Stevensville is the oldest church in the Pacific Northwest. Jesuit Father DeSmet founded this mission for the Flathead Indians in 1841. Open daily, donation requested (406–777–5734).

Virginia City, southwest of Bozeman on MT 287 NW, is a restored pioneer mining boom town and former political capital. Gold was discovered here in 1863. Vigilantes organized to manage the lawlessness. From 1865 to 1876 Virginia City was the territorial capital. Several early structures have been renovated and can be visited. They include a newspaper office, Wells Fargo Express office, and saloon. For information on the town write Bovey Restoration, Box 338, Virginia City, MT 59755 (406–843–5377).

Idaho. Several marked points celebrate the Oregon trail in the southern part of the state and the Lewis and Clark Route in the north-central section. The Mullan Road in the panhandle of northern Idaho is also marked. You can retrace all of these routes along modern highways. Among gold ghost towns in the state are Custer, Idaho City, and Silver City.

Pocatello's *Fort Hall* re-creates the fur-trading milieu that flourished here from 1834 to 1860, when beavers were numerous and before silk hats became the fashion rage. See the Indian Sun Dances in late July or early Aug. The fort is in Upper Ross Park (208–234–1795). Free.

The *Nez Percé National Historic Park* includes 24 sites in Idaho, with a visitor center in Spalding (208–843–2261), 12 mi. east from Lewiston. At the visitor center you can watch audiovisual programs on the culture and history of the remarkable Nez Percé, who rebelled partly because the white man's roaming hogs were eating the camas roots that were a prime Indian food source. Near Nampa, Map Rock is an extraordinary Indian pictograph, a detailed map drawn on stone showing the Snake River geography. This is one of the largest Indian pictographs in existence. Free.

MUSEUMS AND GALLERIES. Denver. Mammals and birds are displayed in 90 dioramas at Denver's large *Museum of Natural History,* City Park (303–322–7009), admission adults $4, children 4–12 yrs. $2. This most-popular attraction features four floors of dinosaurs, Indian artifacts, a planetarium, and a newly built wing for special exhibits. The IMAX theater here offers a new perspective for moviegoers, putting the viewer right in the action film (303–370–6300).

Treasures of the Colorado Historical Society are on display at the *The Colorado History Museum,* 1300 Broadway (303–866–3682), admission $3 adults, $1.50 children.

European, American, and Oriental art and artifacts can be seen at the *Denver Art Museum,* 100 W. 14th Ave. (303–575–2793), admission $3 adults, $1.50 students, free under 5.

The *Museum of Western Art,* 1727 Tremont Pl. (303–296–1880) contains classic paintings and sculptures from Charles Remington to Georgia O'Keeffe in a historic building. Admission $3 adults, $1.50 students.

The *Denver Center for the Performing Arts,* 14th and Curtis (303–893–4000) is a complex of five buildings for theater, music, and lectures at Champa and 13th St.

The *State Capitol,* 14th and Lincoln (866–2604), is open daily for free half-hour tours and a climb to the top of the dome.

Colorado. At Boulder, see exhibits about the natural history of Colorado at the *University of Colorado Museum and Art Gallery* in the Henderson Building (303–492–6892), admission free.

Central City, now a National Historic Landmark, known in the mining era as the "richest square mile on earth," boasts an opulent Opera House, flourishing in summer, on Eureka St. (303–582–5202) and the *Teller House,* where the "Face on the Barroom Floor" is of interest (303–582–3200). Dual tour admission.

Colorado Springs has a *Fine Arts Center,* 30 W. Dale St. (719–634–5581). The city is also home to a leading attraction, the *Air Force Academy* (I-25, Exit 156B), with a new Academy Visitor Center, B–52 bomber displays, and Cadet Chapel. Free (719–472–2555).

Georgetown's famous *Hotel de Paris,* 409 6th Ave. (303–569–2311), was a statement of opulent style, circa 1875, founded and nurtured by Louis DuPuy. Today the Hotel de Paris is a museum of rococo splendor in the Rockies, admission $2.50 adults, $1.50 children.

Leadville's *Matchless Mine Cabin,* E. 7th St., admission $1, and the *Tabor Opera House,* 308 Harrison Ave., admission $3, recall the era of Senator H.A.W. Tabor and his second wife, Baby Doe, who won and lost a silver fortune. Leadville's *Healy House,* 912 Harrison, shows the furniture, clothing, and photographs from the mining days. Healy House, built 1878, is open Memorial Day–Labor Day; by appointment rest of year. Fee. (719–486–0487).

Vail has a *Colorado Ski Museum,* admission $1 (303–476–1876).

Wyoming. The *Wyoming State Museum* in Cheyenne (Barrett Building at 24th St. and Central Ave.) contains many Indian and military artifacts. Admission is free (307–777–7024). Cheyenne's *Frontier Days Old West Museum* (adjacent to Frontier Park on N. Carey Ave.) tells the story of the Union Pacific Railroad in the state and is well-known for its collection of antiques and horse-drawn vehicles. Admission $2 adults, children under 12 free (307–778–7291).

Cody's *Buffalo Bill Historical Center* is an important stop in Wyoming. The center contains the Buffalo Bill Museum, displaying Buffalo Bill's personal collections, plus the *Whitney Gallery of Western Art,* with its numerous sculptures and paintings, and the *Cody Arms Museum.* The *Plains Indian Museum,* also at the site, enlightens a visitor as to the lifestyle of the Indians. The Buffalo Bill Historical Center is near Cody at 720 Sheridan Ave., admission adults $5, children $2, family pass $14 (307–587–4771).

Jackson is a particularly vital center for the creation and selling of contemporary Rocky Mountain art. Several *galleries* line the main streets.

The University of Wyoming city of Laramie include active art and history museums and galleries. The *Laramie Art Guild,* 209 S. 3rd. (307–742–7562) hosts contemporary art shows. The *Laramie Plains Museum,* 603 Ivinson Ave., is the mansion of a pioneer, restored with Victorian antiques. Admission $4 adults, $2 children, under 7 free (307–742–4448). The *Western Historical Collection* and *University Archives* (on the campus) celebrates the state. Admission is free.

Montana. *Big Horn County Arts & Crafts Assn., Jail House Gallery,* 812 N. Center, Hardin, offers crafts, exhibits, Indian artifacts, and a souvenir shop. (406–665–3239). The *Charles M. Russell Original Studio and Museum,* 1201 4th Ave. N., Great Falls, exhibits Russell's works as well as his own collection of Indian costumes and gear. Admission adults $3, children free (406–727–8787).

Range Riders Museum & Bert Clark Gun Collection, U.S. 10 and 12, west of Miles City. See exhibits of ranching history and life on the range in Eastern Montana; admission adults $3, children 50 cents (406–232–4483).

Museum and Visitor Center, Exit 497 off I-90, Hardin, has exhibits, restored buildings, and a souvenir shop. Bring a picnic lunch (406–665–1671).

Idaho. Boise's *State Capitol,* built between 1905 and 1920, is the most impressive public structure in the state. A golden eagle stands atop a dome built of native sandstone and imported marble. The Capitol is open weekdays and visits are free (208–334–2411).

The *Old Idaho Penitentiary,* 2½ mi. east of Boise on Penitentiary Rd., has lovely gardens and architecture, a museum, slide show, and self-guided walking tour. Admission adults $3, seniors and children $2 (208–334–2844).

Lewiston's *Luna House Museum* displays interesting Indian and pioneer artifacts. The museum is at Third and C Sts., admission free (208–743–2535).

ACCOMMODATIONS. Lodging in the Rockies ranges from Super Deluxe prospects in Denver, Aspen, or Vail, Colorado, to modest-but-adequate models in the far-flung small towns of Montana. The national parks offer another tradition in some grand, older lodges. Reservations are advised everywhere during the busy summer season, but are especially crucial at all the national park lodgings. A specialty of the region is the guest dude ranch where horseback riding in summer and cross-country skiing in winter are the attractions (see Horseback Riding and River Rafting). The brief summer months of June–Aug. are peak seasons for most resorts, with the shoulder seasons of spring and autumn somewhat more economical. During the skiing season, the winter resorts can be packed. Note that some lodging-inclusive ski packages are listed with the Colorado winter resorts, so look for Colorado lodging leads also under Skiing.

For the Rockies, accommodation prices for the major cities, such as Denver, or the major resorts, such as Aspen, Colorado Springs, Jackson, Sun Valley, and Vail, will be about 25% higher than lodging in smaller towns and outlying areas. Often, lodging in the Super Deluxe and Deluxe categories is found only in the large cities and major resorts. Modest but adequate lodging is possible in many of the small towns. Some lodgings offer a reduction for the off season. The categories, based on the price of a double room, are: *Super Deluxe,* over $150; *Deluxe,* $70–$150; *Expensive,* $55–$70; *Moderate,* $40–$55; and *Inexpensive,* $20–$40.

Here are some representative lodgings in Colorado, Wyoming, Montana, and Idaho.

Colorado

Aspen. Hotel Jerome. *Deluxe.* 330 E. Main, Aspen, CO 81611 (920–1000 or 800–331–7213). Posh restored 1889 hotel furnished in 19th-century style. Ornate Victorian lobby, popular bar, tearoom, Silver Queen Restaurant.

Heatherbed Lodge. *Moderate.* Box 530, 1679 Maroon Creek Rd., Aspen, CO 81612 (303–925–7077). Multiroom units 2½ mi. southwest of town. Early-American decor. Spectacular views; pool. Good Continental breakfast included.

Kipling Inn. *Moderate.* 715 Kipling St., Lakewood, CO 80215 (303–232–5000). Located 9½ mi. SW just off U.S. 6. Offers heated pool, playground, restaurant, and cocktail lounge. Some units have kitchens.

Boulder. The Briar Rose. *Moderate.* 2151 Arapahoe, Boulder, CO 80302 (303–442–3007). Comfortable, centrally located 11-room inn. Breakfast included.

Colorado Springs. The Broadmoor. *Super Deluxe.* Lake Circle at Lake Ave., Colorado Springs, CO 80901 (719–634–7711 or 800–634–7711). World-famous resort hotel with all amenities. Golf, tennis, skiing, ice arena, large pool, bike trails and hiking, fitness center. 3,000 acres. Award-winning restaurants and authentic 18th-century English pub. Good for upscale conventions.

Hilton Inn. *Expensive.* 505 Popes Bluff Trail, Colorado Springs, CO 80907 (719–598–7656 or 800–445–8667). Pool and restaurant. Tennis, golf, and health club privileges. Shuttle bus available.

Drury Inn. *Moderate.* 8155 N. Academy Blvd., Colorado Springs, CO 80920 (719–598–2500). Exit 150A off I-25. Free breakfast, cable TV, heated pool.

Denver. Brown Palace. *Super Deluxe.* 321 17th St., Denver, CO 80202 (303–297–3111 or 800–321–2599). One of the west's renowned hotels. Elegant rooms and public areas. Gourmet and casual dining. Beauty and barber shops.

Loews Giorgio Hotel. *Super Deluxe.* 4150 E. Mississippi Ave., Denver, CO 80202. (303–782–9300 or 800–223–0888). Italian-style hotel with 200 rooms, 20 suites, country villa decor, marble piazza. Complimentary breakfast, superb restaurant, nearby Cherry Creek Sporting Club. Convenient location.

Embassy Suites Hotel. *Deluxe.* 4444 N. Havana, Denver, CO 80239 (303–375–0400 or 800–EMBASSY). All the amenities including breakfast. Near the airport.

The Oxford-Alexis Hotel. *Deluxe.* 1600 17th St., Denver, CO 80202 (303–628–5400 or 800–228–5838). Downtown. Supremely elegant $8 million renovation of a small, grand hotel near Union Station. Restaurant, bar, entertainment, 82 rooms, health club. Charming Sun. brunches.

Queen Anne Inn. *Expensive.* 2147 Tremont Pl., Denver, CO 80205 (303–296–6666). Famous bed-and-breakfast in 3-story 1879 home near downtown. Ten rooms, private baths, garden and private parking. Breakfast and afternoon tea. Complimentary cocktails.

Estes Park. Long's Peak Inn and Guest Ranch. *Deluxe.* 6925 Highway 7, Estes Park, CO 80517 (800–262–2034). At base of Long's Peak. Mountain guest ranch with lodge and cottages. Pool, horses, fishing. Children's program. Closed in winter.

Vail. Charter at Beaver Creek. *Deluxe.* Box 5310, 120 Offerson Rd., Avon, CO 81620 (303–949–6660 or 800–824–3064). Some of Colorado's most spacious and gracious condos. 1–3 bedrooms. Free shuttles, pool, tennis, health club. Ski and golf plans. Helpful concierge.

Westin Hotel-Vail. *Deluxe.* 1300 Westhaven Dr., Vail, CO 81657 (303–476–7111). Luxurious units, some with kitchens. Heated pool, sauna, and exercise room. Close to skiing, golf.

Doubletree. *Expensive.* 250 S. Frontage Rd. W., Box 1928, Vail, CO 81657 (303–476–7810 or 800–528–0444). I-70 Exit 176. Motor hotel with pool, sauna, café, gift shop, and free parking. Ski, golf packages. Within walking distance of Vail Village.

Wyoming

Casper. Hilton Inn. *Deluxe.* I-25 at Rancho Rd., 800 N. Poplar, Casper, WY 82601 (307–266–6000 or 800–HILTONS). Cable TV, movies, pool, dining room, coffee shop. Some suites. Airport shuttle.

Cheyenne. Best Western Hitching Post Inn. *Expensive.* 1700 W. Lincolnway, Cheyenne, WY 82001 (307–638–3301 or 800–221–0125). Wyoming landmark. Near downtown. Comfortable rooms. Gourmet restaurant. Tennis courts, pool, playground. Pets allowed.

Rodeway Inn. *Moderate.* 3839 E. Lincolnway, Cheyenne, WY 82001 (307–634–2171). Pool, bar, entertainment, and dancing. Senior discount. Pets allowed. Airport, bus, and train station shuttle.

Cody. The Irma Hotel. *Moderate to Expensive.* 1192 Sheridan Ave., Cody, WY 82414 (307–587–4221). Historic hotel built by Buffalo Bill Cody in 1902 and named for his daughter. Rooms restored and named for personalities. Dining room, cocktail lounge. Pets allowed.

Grand Teton National Park-Jackson. Alpenhof. *Deluxe.* Box 288 Teton Village, WY 83025 (307–733–3242 or 800–732–3244). Full-service resort lodge at base of Rendezvous Mountain. Skiing, horseback riding. Excellent restaurant. Heated pool, sauna.

Wort Hotel. *Expensive.* 50 N. Glenwood, Jackson, WY 83001 (307–733–2190 or 800–322–2727). Pleasant downtown hotel. Restaurant and café, entertainment. Tennis privileges, parking lot.

Colter Bay Village. *Moderate.* Box 240, Moran, WY 83013 (307–543–2855). In Grand Teton National Park. Log cabins with attractive view of Grand Tetons. Hiking, rafting, horseback riding. Pets allowed.

Jackson Lake Lodge. *Moderate.* Box 240, Moran, WY 83013 (307–543–2855). In Grand Teton National Park. Landscaped grounds with pleasing views of the lake and the Tetons. Hiking, rafting, horseback riding. Pets allowed. Closed in winter.

Trapper Motel. *Moderate.* 235 N. Cache St., Jackson, WY 83001 (307–733–2648 or 800–341–8000). Well-kept rooms with radios, some refrigerators. Laundry room. Near skiing, town center. Handicapped facilities.

Yellowstone National Park. Lake Yellowstone Hotel. *Deluxe to Expensive.* TW Services, Yellowstone National Park, WY 82190 (307–344–7311). This 1891 hotel was remodeled in 1903 and 1929, Wood-frame cabins available, too. Lakeview dining room.

Mammoth Hot Springs Hotel. *Moderate.* TW Services, Yellowstone National Park, WY 82190 (307–344–7311). Park headquarters. Near major geothermal activity. Comfortable rooms in older lodge. Attractive restaurant.

Old Faithful Inn. *Moderate.* TW Services, Yellowstone National Park, WY 82190 (307–344–7311). Across from the famous geyser. Attractive restaurant. Open winter and summer, with reservations only.

Montana

Billings. Radisson Northern Hotel. *Expensive.* Broadway and 1st Ave. North, Billings, MT 59103 (406–245–5121 or 800–822–3384). Attractive hotel with many amenities, including complimentary cocktails, restaurant. Lounge with live entertainment.

Kelly Inn. *Moderate.* 5425 Midland Rd., Billings, MT 59101 (406–252–2700 or 800–635–3559). On I-90, Exit 446. Cable TV, free Continental breakfast.

Bozeman. Grantree Inn. *Moderate.* 1325 N. 7th Ave., Bozeman, MT 59715 (406–587–5261 or 800–624–5865). Well-kept rooms, pool, restaurant, coffee shop, and bar. Free airport shuttle. Ski packages.

Voss Inn Bed & Breakfast. *Moderate.* 319 S. Wilson, Bozeman, MT 59715 (406–587–0982). Restored Victorian mansion in town. Attractive rooms.

Butte. Best Western Copper King Inn. *Expensive.* 4655 Harrison Ave. S., Butte, MT 59701 (406–494–6666 or 800–332–8600). Across from airport. Close for airport connections. Attractive rooms, indoor pool, sauna, winter car plug-ins. Lounge with live entertainment. Convention facilities. Pets allowed.

Townhouse Inns. *Moderate.* 2777 Harrison, Butte, MT 59701 (406–494–8850 or 800–442–4667). Nice rooms, some suites; scenic area. Airport shuttle, weekly rates, senior discount.

Glacier National Park. Glacier Park Lodge. *Expensive.* Glacier Park Inc., East Glacier Park, MT 59434 (406–226–5551). On State Highway 49. Full-service lodge with landscaped grounds and all park sport activities. Heated pool. Just outside east boundary of park. Pets allowed.

Many Glacier Hotel. *Expensive.* Glacier Park Inc., East Glacier Park, MT 59434 (406–226–5551). On Swiftcurrent Lake. Pleasant old hotel on lakefront, with launch trips possible on lake. Fishing. Built by Great Northern Railroad in 1914–1915. Swiss canton motif.

Izaak Walton Inn. *Moderate to Expensive.* Essex, MT 59916 (406–888–5700). Essex exit off U.S. 2. Old railroad inn is still an Amtrak stop. Hearty food, pleasant lounge. Nearby fishing and cross-country skiing.

Great Falls. Sheraton Great Falls. *Deluxe.* 400 10th Ave. S., Great Falls, MT 59405 (406–727–7200 or 800–257–1998). Attractive rooms, heated pool, winter plug-ins. Restaurant.

Best Western Heritage Inn. *Expensive.* 1700 Fox Farm Rd. Great Falls, MT 59404 (406–761–1900 or 800–528–1234). Large lodging with extensive indoor recreation center, heated pool, dancing, entertainment. Near Russell Museum.

Triple Crown Motor Inn. *Moderate.* 621 Central Ave., Great Falls, MT 59401 (406–727–8300 or 800–722–8300 in Montana or 800–344–2377). Downtown location. Movies. Café nearby.

Helena. Best Western Colonial Inn. *Expensive.* 2301 Colonial Drive, Helena, MT 59601 (406–443–2100 or 800–528–1234). Fine lodging with all amenities. View of mountains. Two heated pools.

Coach House East. *Moderate.* 2101 E. 11th Ave., Helena, MT 59601 (406–443–2300 or 800–541–2743). Good rooms in attractive valley setting. Restaurant, lounge. Pool and sauna.

Super 8 Motel. *Inexpensive.* 2201 11th Ave., Helena, MT 59601 (406–443–2450 or 800–843–1991). Cable TV; restaurants nearby. Convenient to ski area.

Polebridge. North Fork Hostel. *Inexpensive to Moderate.* Box 1, Polebridge, MT 59928 (406–862–0184). Equipped with kerosene lanterns and wood stoves, this is a log cabin close to Glacier National Park.

Virginia City. Fairweather Inn. *Moderate.* Box 338, Virginia City, MT 59755 (406–843–5377 or 800–648–7588). At Hwy. 287 and E. Wallace. Old West decor in restored gold town, with circa 1880s flavor. Restaurant and lounge.

Nevada City Hotel. *Moderate.* Box 338, Virginia City, MT 59755 (406–843–5377 or 800–648–7588). On Hwy. 287. Gold Rush-style hotel constructed of logs. Located in recreated gold town. Senior citizen discount.

Idaho

Boise. Red Lion Motor Inn-Riverside. *Deluxe.* 2900 Chinden Blvd., Boise, ID 83714 (208–343–1871). Attractive rooms along Boise River, with 308 units, good restaurant, heated pool.

Rodeway Inn of Boise. *Moderate to Expensive.* 1115 N. Curtis Rd., Boise, ID 83706 (208–376–2700 or 800–228–2000). Attractive units on lovely award-winning grounds. Putting green, heated pool. Hearty complimentary breakfast.

University Inn. *Moderate.* 2360 University Dr., Boise, ID 83706 (208–345–7170). Across from Boise State University. Cable TV, pool, radios. Coffee shop and lounge. Pets OK.

Coeur D'Alene. The Coeur D'Alene Resort. *Deluxe.* 115 S. 2nd Ave., Coeur D'Alene, ID 83814 (208–765–4000 or 800–688–5253). Large establishment with lovely setting on Coeur d'Alene Lake. Heated pool. Complete watersport and fishing resources. Restaurant, lounge, entertainment. Health club, shops, and golf facilities.

Sun Valley-Ketchum. Sun Valley Lodge Apartments, and Inn. *Super Deluxe.* Sun Valley Road, Sun Valley, ID 83353 (208–622–4111 or 800–635–8261). World-famous resort, with all amenities. Summer sports from golf and tennis to fishing. Winter sports: cross-country and alpine skiing.

Elkhorn Resort. *Deluxe.* Box 6009, Sun Valley, ID 83353 (208–622–4511 or 800–635–9356). Quiet, tasteful accommodations. Tennis, golf, skiing, bicycling, shopping. Concerts in summer. Fishing guides.

Heidelberg Inn. *Moderate to Expensive.* Box 304, Sun Valley, ID 83353 (208–726–5361). On Warm Springs Rd. Built in Bavarian style. Golf course across the way. Easy walk to nearby stream. Heated pool.

RESTAURANTS. Cuisine in the Rockies often celebrates local ingredients, particularly the steak. Trout and game, including elk and buffalo, are featured on some menus. In Colorado the Mexican culinary influence is also strong. In the larger towns and resorts, reservations are advised. Dress is relatively casual and is sometimes Western style in the Rockies, though a jacket for men and dresses or pants suits for women are suggested in the major cities, such as Denver.

Most restaurants are open 6 days a week, with some closed Mon. Restaurant hours in the Rockies tend to include early breakfast times, but not too late in the evening for dinner, with last dinner orders often taken by 9 P.M. Unless indicated, the restaurants listed tend to be open for breakfast, lunch, and dinner. In the major cities and resorts, restaurants will take credit cards. In smaller towns, the restaurateur may prefer cash.

Prices for meals in the Rockies tend to be higher in the major cities, such as Denver, and the major resorts, such as Vail and Aspen. In outlying areas, expect these prices to be 25 percent lower. Some unusual restaurant discoveries occur in the Rockies. For example, the gourmet food at the Lone Mountain Ranch in Montana is exceptional. Prices for a Rockies dinner are: *Super Deluxe,* $45 and up; *Deluxe,* $32–$45; *Expensive,* $22–$32; *Moderate,* $17–$22; and *Inexpensive,* under $17. Drink, tax, and tips are not included.

Colorado

Aspen. Crystal Palace. *Deluxe.* 300 E. Hyman St. (303–925–1455). Steak dinners served by waitpeople who act in a cabaret show. Plush, red Victorian decor. Crowded in winter.

Colorado Springs. Broadmoor Hotel Dining Rooms. *Deluxe.* At Broadmoor Resort (719–634–7711). Several restaurants include the Tavern, Charles Court, and the Penrose Room. Reservations necessary.

The Palmer Restaurant. *Expensive.* 4 S. Cascade Ave., in the Antlers Doubletree Hotel (719–473–5600). Well-known cuisine. Excellent meats and fresh fish.

Denver. Adirondacks. *Deluxe.* 901 Larimer (303–573–8900). Classy California import. Innovative southwestern cuisine with stylish decor and stunning view.

Normandy French. *Deluxe.* 1515 Madison St. (303–321–3311). Quiet, French dining with excellent food in old world atmosphere. Large wine list.

Palace Arms. *Deluxe.* At Brown Palace Hotel, 321 17th St. (303–297–3111). American menu with good steaks and Rocky Mountain trout. Strict dress code. Dining room surrounded by period antiques.

Buckhorn Exchange. *Expensive.* 1000 Osage (303–534–9505). Historical Western restaurant, one of the first in Denver. Outstanding collection of museum-quality Old West memorabilia. Specialties are game, such as elk and buffalo.

Marc's. *Expensive.* 6920 W. 38th, Wheat Ridge (303–422–6600). Fresh seafood, aged beef, oyster bar, daily specials. Great soup and salad bar, sinful desserts.

Wellshire Inn. *Expensive.* 3333 S. Colorado Blvd. (303–759–3333). Varied menu. Pastoral atmosphere. Mansion restaurant overlooking city and golf course. New "Health Mark" dishes. Open 7 days. Sunday brunch.

Windows. *Moderate–Expensive.* 1550 Court Pl., in Radisson Hotel (303–893–3333). Prime rib and shrimp. Popular Fri. evening seafood buffet. Sun. brunch.

Casa Bonita. *Moderate.* 6715 W. Colfax Ave. (303–232–5515). Good Mexican food is served here. Entertainment includes mariachi band, cliff diver, "gun fights," and more. Bring the kids.

Healthy Habits Restaurant. *Moderate.* 865 S. Colorado Blvd. (303–733–2105). Unique cafeteria offers 80 varieties of salads, along with soups, pasta, and beverages at prix fixe. Whole-grain breads. Liquor. Good value.

Furr's. *Inexpensive.* 3215 S. Wadsworth, Lakewood (303–989–9188). Wholesome food is served here in cafeteria style. Cash or checks only.

King's Table Buffet. *Inexpensive.* 6206 W. Alameda (303–935–6101). Excellent buffet with large variety of top-quality food. Great salad selection. Pleasant, family-oriented atmosphere.

Estes Park. The Aspens. *Expensive–Moderate.* At Holiday Inn, 101 S. Vrain Hwy. (303–586–2332). Pleasant atmosphere, featuring a good variety of dishes. Outstanding salad bar.

Vail. Red Lion. *Expensive.* 304 Bridge St., in Vail Village (303–476–7676). Hearty Mexican and Italian food, steaks. Popular with skiers.

Wyoming

Grand Teton National Park Jackson. Alpenhof Garden Room. *Deluxe.* In Alpenhof at Teton Village (307–733–3462). Stylish European restaurant featuring elk and other game. Homemade pastries. Reservations suggested.

Yellowstone National Park. Lake Hotel Dining Room. *Moderate.* In the park at Lake Yellowstone Hotel (307–344–7311). Prime rib specialty. Homemade pastries.

Mammoth Hot Springs Dining Room. *Moderate.* In the park (307–344–7311). Roomy dining area with good trout and prime rib.

Montana

Glacier National Park. Goat Lick Steak and Rib House. *Expensive.* At Glacier Park Lodge on State 49 (406–226–5551). Barbecued specialties, Indian bread. Beautiful view and fireplace.

Many Glacier Hotel Dining Room. *Expensive.* Many Glacier Hotel. Twelve miles west of Babb off U.S. 89 (406–732–4311). Prime rib, steak, trout. Closed in winter.

Great Falls. Black Angus Steak House. *Moderate.* 3800 10th Ave. S. (406–761–4550). Good Montana beef. Pleasant family dining.

Helena. Frontier Pies Restaurant. *Moderate.* 1231 Prospect Ave. (406–442–7437). Family meals. Western motif. Home-style meals and baked goods—especially pies.

Idaho

Boise. The Gamekeeper Restaurant. *Expensive.* 1109 Main St. Located in the Owyhee Plaza Hotel (208–343–4611 or 800–238–4611). Top-quality steaks, seafood, wines. A consistent award-winner.

Coeur D'Alene. Osprey. *Expensive.* 1000 W. Hubbard St. (208–664–2115). View overlooking the Spokane River. Fresh seafood, good steaks.

Ketchum-Sun Valley. Christiania. *Expensive.* 303 Walnut, 3 blocks north of Rte. 75 on Sun Valley Rd., Ketchum (208–726–3388). Hemingway sometimes dined here. Long tradition for European menu, fancy desserts. Patio.

LIQUOR LAWS. Colorado. The legal drinking age is 21 for hard liquor and beer. Liquor is sold by package in liquor stores until midnight on all days except Sun. Package goods are not sold in bars, but 3.2 beer is available in supermarkets and convenience stores. Alcoholic beverages from other states may not be brought in. Colorado's tough drunk-driving laws require jail sentences for violators. Liquor may be served until 2 A.M.

Wyoming. The legal drinking age is 21. Liquor can be sold by package or by the drink in licensed stores and establishments. Sunday liquor sales may be only from noon to 10 P.M., depending on local option. Three quarts of liquor may be brought into the state. Police strictly enforce liquor laws.

Montana. The legal drinking age is 21. Bars are open until 2 A.M., Mon.–Sat. Liquor is sold by the package in state liquor stores and by the drink in any licensed establishment, from 8 P.M. to 2 A.M. Three quarts of liquor may be brought into the state. Some bars sell bottles over-the-counter.

Idaho. The legal drinking age is 21. Liquor is sold by the package in state liquor stores and by the drink in licensed establishments. No drink sales are allowed from

1 A.M. Sun. to 10 A.M. Mon. and some holidays. Two quarts of liquor per person may be brought into the state.

CALIFORNIA

by
ROBERT TAYLOR

Robert Taylor, a San Francisco resident for 20 years, is the film and theater critic for the Oakland Tribune.

California's image may be trendy and contemporary, but it has been luring visitors since the 1540s, when an explorer landed at what is now San Diego and claimed the territory for Spain. It has always been the destination of explorers, dreamers, adventurers, and sometimes the recklessly hopeful. The attractions and challenges endure: deserts and mountain passes, rich farmland, spectacular forests of redwood and sequoia, mild coastal weather.

The dreamers, too, created landmarks, institutions, and a culture that are today among the state's major attractions. Included here are: 21 Spanish missions originally founded to cultivate the land and convert the Indians, Gold Rush towns that are now crumbling but colorful reminders of the 19th-century boom, and a motion picture industry that arrived with the 20th century and has since grown to include all facets of entertainment. Health cults, religious cults, and the counterculture have flourished to leave their marks on the state and the nation. The dreams live on, from the cable cars that first climbed San Francisco's hills in 1873 to the Magic Kingdom and Disney empire that began with an animated mouse.

Visitors are not always prepared for the size of the state and its variety, or for the regional pride that tends to separate the cultures of Northern California and Southern California. The popular attractions in the north include picturesque San Francisco; the nation's most renowned Wine

Country; towering redwood groves; spectacular, alpine Lake Tahoe. The "Southland," as its residents describe it, is blessed by temperate weather that has always influenced its lifestyle and may be the prime lure to visitors.

Southeast of Los Angeles, Disneyland and other theme parks have transformed Orange County's citrus groves—an early insignia of the state's health and sunshine—into a limitless family vacationland. Ideally, even the briefest vacation in California would include a week enjoying Los Angeles, Orange County, and the Southern California Coast, with another week based in San Francisco, exploring Northern California. The coast between these two cities offers its own attractions, including Santa Barbara, the Hearst castle at San Simeon, and Monterey–Carmel. In east-central California, Yosemite National Park provides what may be the state's most dramatic natural splendor.

If there is a "California lifestyle," it is broad enough to cover everything from truck-stop cafés in Sierra forests to health spas on the Southern California coast. Movie stars, political activists, Asian and Hispanic immigrants, vegetarians, surfers, golfers, and fitness fanatics also have a place, along with such varied representatives as leaders of the aerospace industry and descendants of Spanish-era governors.

Los Angeles

Within Los Angeles County there are nearly 80 separate cities, and the sprawling Greater Los Angeles Basin covers 464 square miles. No wonder it can offer so many cultures to so many residents—more than 3 million—and appear endless to first-time visitors driving onto a freeway ramp. But other cities in the United States deal with urban sprawl and freeway traffic. What they don't have are 40 miles of beaches, December heat waves, the capital of the entertainment industry, and, just down the freeway, Disneyland. The city proclaims itself a year-round vacationland, where beaches, mountains, ocean, and desert come together under sunny skies in temperate weather. When Southern California began promoting its attractions at the end of the 19th century, officials boasted that winter visitors could play in the snow, pick oranges, and frolic on the beach during the same day. It is still possible, although they would have to travel farther to find the orange groves.

The weather is not the area's only appeal. History is preserved in El Pueblo de Los Angeles State Historic Park, in the museum of prehistoric animals dug from the La Brea tar pits, and in Hollywood museums. In addition to popular culture, Los Angeles's art, music, and theater institutions rival San Francisco's. The city's major attractions *are* clustered, but they are often located in widely separated clusters. A car is the ideal way to see the Southland. With a clear map and an early start, the freeways will not be so formidable. Some of the city's streets are their own destinations, for instance Sunset, Hollywood, Wilshire, and La Cienega boulevards.

The Southern California Coast

Traveling south from Los Angeles on the freeways, visitors may be disappointed by what appears to be miles of sprawling industrial and residential suburbs. The coastline itself—more than 140 miles from Los Angeles to San Diego—is another story. Coastside communities and resorts developed their own identities as they grew, and their distinctive differences are more valuable today as they become refuges for visitors from as nearby as Los Angeles. The Southern California coast, too, is rich in history: the earliest of the Franciscan missions and adobe houses from vast Spanish ranchos are reminders of the state's heritage.

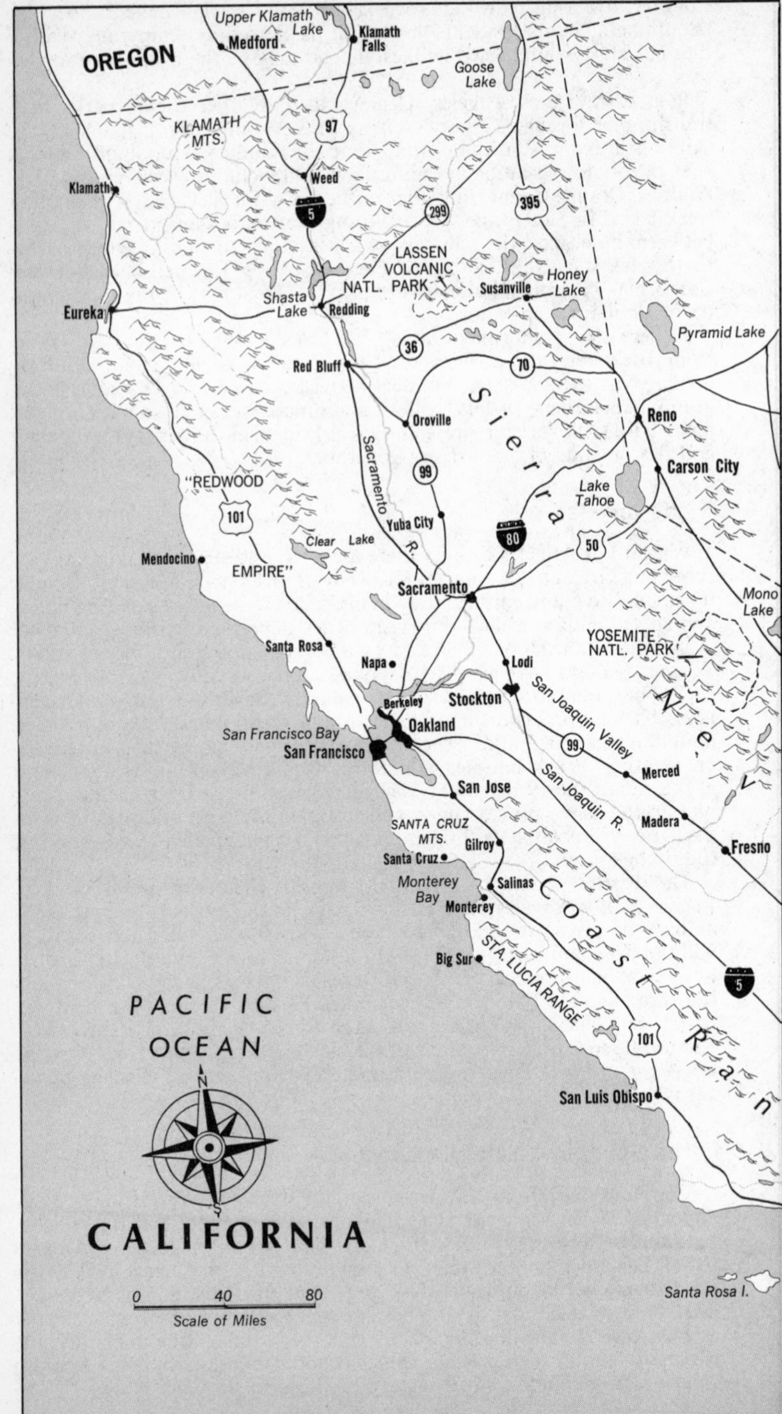

OREGON
Upper Klamath Lake
Medford
Klamath Falls
Goose Lake
KLAMATH MTS.
97
Klamath
Weed
5
299
395
LASSEN VOLCANIC NATL. PARK
Honey Lake
Susanville
Shasta Lake
Redding
Eureka
Pyramid Lake
36
Red Bluff
70
Sierra Nev
Reno
Oroville
Sacramento R.
99
Carson City
"REDWOOD EMPIRE"
Lake Tahoe
101
Yuba City
80
50
Clear Lake
Mendocino
Sacramento
Mono Lake
YOSEMITE NATL. PARK
Santa Rosa
Napa
Lodi
Stockton
San Joaquin Valley
Berkeley
Oakland
San Francisco Bay
San Francisco
99
Merced
San Jose
San Joaquin R.
SANTA CRUZ MTS.
Madera
Gilroy
Fresno
Santa Cruz
Monterey Bay
Salinas
Monterey
Coast Ran
Big Sur
STA. LUCIA RANGE
5
101
PACIFIC OCEAN
N
S
San Luis Obispo
CALIFORNIA
0 40 80
Scale of Miles
Santa Rosa I.

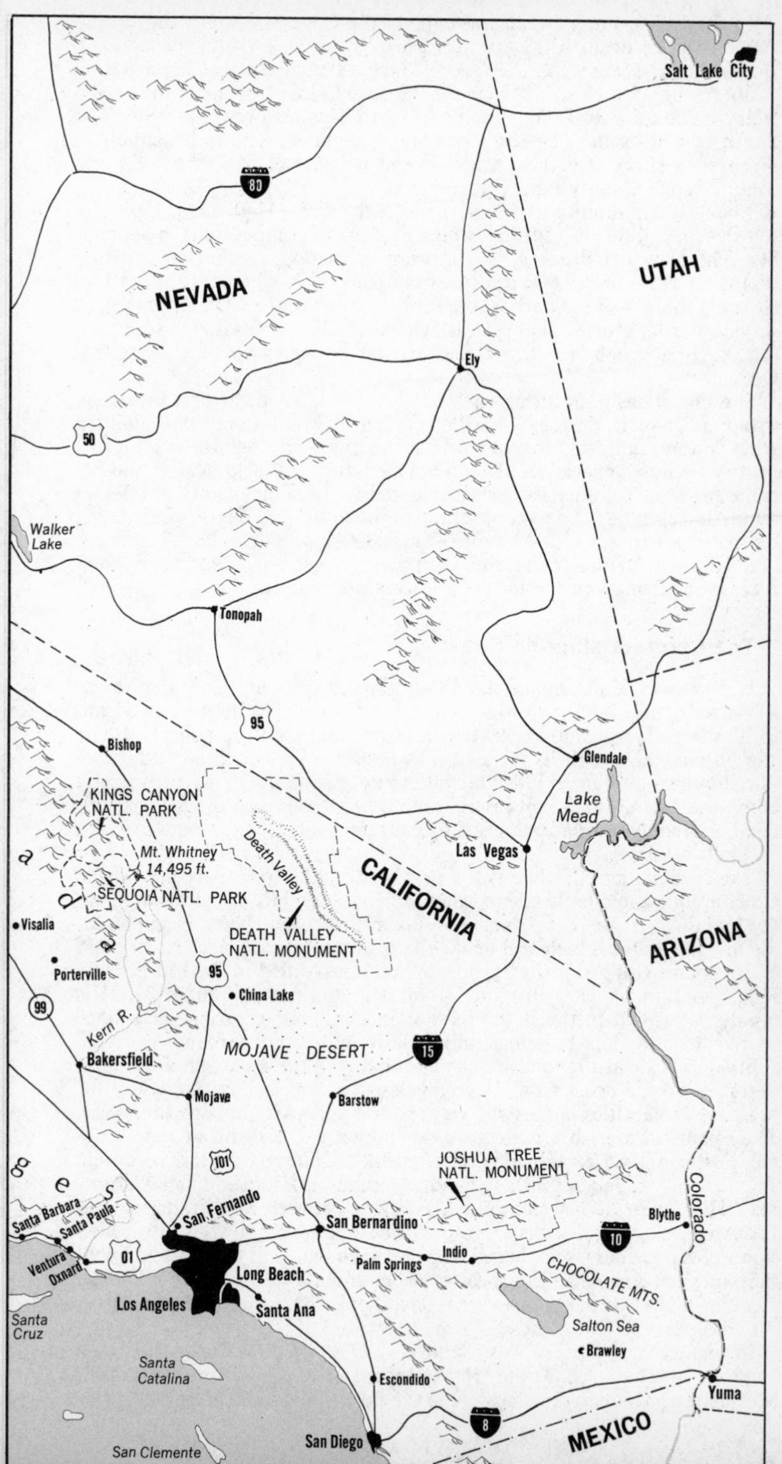
Salt Lake City
80
UTAH
NEVADA
Ely
50
Walker Lake
Tonopah
95
Bishop
KINGS CANYON NATL. PARK
Mt. Whitney 14,495 ft.
Death Valley
SEQUOIA NATL. PARK
DEATH VALLEY NATL. MONUMENT
CALIFORNIA
Glendale
Lake Mead
Las Vegas
ARIZONA
Visalia
Porterville
99
95
China Lake
Kern R.
MOJAVE DESERT
15
Bakersfield
Mojave
Barstow
101
JOSHUA TREE NATL. MONUMENT
Colorado
Santa Barbara
Santa Paula
San Fernando
San Bernardino
Blythe
10
Ventura
Oxnard
01
Palm Springs
Indio
CHOCOLATE MTS.
Long Beach
Los Angeles
Santa Ana
Santa Cruz
Salton Sea
Brawley
Santa Catalina
Escondido
Yuma
8
MEXICO
San Diego
San Clemente

In the 1920s, Long Beach was called "the Coney Island of the West." After years of decline, the city has been reborn as a visitors' attraction, thanks to the presence of the Queen Mary, the Cunard liner launched in 1936. Along with Howard Hughes's "Spruce Goose" airplane, the Queen Mary is the focus of Long Beach's effort to become a base for visitors to Southern California. The city's size and scale may be more hospitable to first-time visitors than Los Angeles, and it is closer to Disneyland and other Orange County family attractions.

The next community to the south along the Coast Highway is Huntington Beach, California's surfing capital and site of competitions in September. The Newport Beach area is a prime attraction; the harbor provides berths for more than 9,000 pleasure craft. Balboa Pavilion, a restored Victorian landmark in the harbor, is a terminal for Catalina Island passenger service, harbor cruises, skiff rentals, whale-watching cruises, and sportfishing. Laguna Beach is a year-round artists' colony, with cool, smog-free weather.

San Diego has been luring visitors since 1542, when the first European explorer, Juan Rodriguez Cabrillo, landed at Point Loma and claimed what is now California for Spain. Overshadowed throughout much of its history by Los Angeles, San Diego boomed during World War II and became the state's second-largest city in the 1970s. For visitors, it offers a temperate climate (73 degrees average summer high, 63 degrees in winter), dramatic downtown redevelopment, the 1,000-acre Balboa Park just north of downtown, 70 miles of beaches with two protected bays, and year-round recreation. It may be the ideal California metropolis.

The Central California Coast

If Northern Californians and Southern Californians consider themselves residents of different states, the Central Coast is where the two Californias both merge and clash. It is a fascinating study in contrasts. The rugged coastline, with its jagged rocks pounded by the ocean surf, is relieved by tranquil green hills and valleys not far inland. Vineyards neatly climb the hills around Santa Barbara and Monterey, and the Salinas Valley, honored by novelist John Steinbeck, remains one of the state's richest agricultural areas.

The spectacular coastline is the prime attraction, but there are others. Chief among them is the Hearst San Simeon State Historical Monument, the grandiose castle that publisher William Randolph Hearst began building in 1919 and in which architect Julia Morgan was to place artwork and entire rooms shipped from Europe. When Hearst died in 1951 in Beverly Hills, San Simeon was valued at $30 million, and was still unfinished. His family donated it to the state in 1958, and millions of people have since toured its sprawling buildings and equally impressive gardens.

Smaller-scale attractions are just as enticing in the area. Santa Barbara, 90 miles up the coast from Los Angeles, has long been a hideaway for pressured celebrities, an artists' colony, and a year-round vacation oasis. The Spanish-Moorish architecture downtown is the result of redevelopment after a 1925 earthquake. The red-tiled County Courthouse covers an entire block, and suggests what cities might have looked like if California's Hispanic rule had continued. Halfway between San Francisco and Los Angeles, San Luis Obispo is a favorite stopping point; the central Mission Plaza provides a relaxing setting. Between San Luis Obispo and Santa Barbara, Solvang is a European-style community founded by Danish farmers in 1911. It is worth a visit today, if only for the pastries in its Danish bakeries.

In the north, Monterey was founded in 1770, the first European settlement in Northern California. It has served as a capital under Spanish, Mexican, and American flags. A seven-acre state park preserves 19th-century adobes and other historic buildings. Nearby Carmel, formerly an artists' colony, now features a bustling business district that resembles a British village of shops—with weather to match. Northeast of Monterey, the town of Salinas preserves John Steinbeck's family home. Nearby, San Juan Bautista peacefully displays its old Mission, directly overlooking the San Andreas earthquake fault.

San Francisco

The hills, the views, the bay, the bridges make San Francisco America's most photogenic city, and its compact size makes it one of the easiest to explore—in spite of those hills. The sights can be breathtaking even to long-time residents, when the fabled fog rolls over Twin Peaks or, better yet, when the sun breaks through. The city's diversity, sense of history, and legendary tolerance have created a lifestyle that remains unique.

Founded in 1776 by the Spanish Army and the Catholic Church, San Francisco boomed during the Gold Rush that began in 1848. The wealthy were not the gold miners but the business and railroad tycoons who built their mansions on San Francisco's Nob Hill. Fires and earthquakes figure prominently in the city's history, which has made San Franciscans protective of their past. Most of the city's landmarks and prime attractions for visitors are historical. Included among these are the cable cars that began climbing the hills in 1873; Telegraph Hill, which once featured a semaphore system to announce ships arriving through the Golden Gate; the Palace of Fine Arts near the approach to the Golden Gate Bridge, the last vestige of the 1915 World's Fair that celebrated the city's reconstruction after the 1906 earthquake and fire. The 1989 Northern California earthquake seriously damaged only about 6 percent of the city, and rebuilding began swiftly. Among the still-lingering and controversial questions is whether to repair or demolish a stretch of the double-deck freeway along the Embarcadero, which collapsed in the quake.

The Wine Country

Weather, topography, the primitive vineyards of Spanish mission padres, and the imagination of a colorful Hungarian immigrant helped create the Wine Country of Napa and Sonoma counties. Actually, the region stretches from Marin County across the bay from San Francisco, north to Mendocino, and it includes more than 200 wineries. It is the Napa Valley, however, that is the country's most famous wine region. It is located within a 90-minute drive northeast of San Francisco, and as you drive along State Highway 29 through the valley, there are more than three dozen wineries open to visitors. They offer tours through their cellars, sell premium vintages that may not be available in retail stores, answer questions, and provide wine tastings as a bonus.

Each year, hundreds of thousands of visitors make their way into the Wine Country. The peak period is during the September and October harvest, when the otherwise relaxing countryside can be frustrating to visit. To avoid the crowds, search out wineries around the historic town of Sonoma, farther north around Clear Lake in Lake County, and in the Anderson Valley along State Highway 128 between U.S. Highway 101 and the Mendocino coast.

Other attractions include trendy health spas as well as the traditional mud baths of Calistoga, bed-and-breakfast inns, some of the San Francisco Bay Area's best country restaurants, and more modest picnics on the grounds of the wineries. A day's excursion from San Francisco can cover most of this scenic area.

The Northern California Coast

This rugged, spectacular coastline stretches almost 400 miles north from San Francisco Bay to the Oregon border. Most of it has remained unspoiled, thanks to its topography, lack of industry except timber and fishing, and its isolation. "The Redwood Empire" was not connected by highway to San Francisco until 1937 with the opening of the Golden Gate Bridge. The major north–south route, U.S. Highway 101, traverses inland agricultural valleys as well as spectacular groves of trees in the Redwood National Park. Driving time from San Francisco to Crescent City is about eight hours. The coastside route, State Highway 1, offers more scenic vistas, including such historic sites as Fort Ross, established by Russian fur traders, and the quaint, New England-style village of Mendocino. A string of state and national parks and recreation areas offers unlimited opportunity for hiking, camping, and backpacking. Redwood groves have flourished for centuries in the cool coastal weather. Maximum summer temperatures are seldom higher than 70 degrees on the coast, although it may be 80-90 inland at Santa Rosa or Napa.

Lake Tahoe

Located in a glacial bowl at an elevation of 6,226 feet above sea level, surrounded by mountain peaks as high as 10,000 feet, Lake Tahoe is a spectacular sight on the California–Nevada border. It is one of the world's clearest lakes, reaching a maximum depth of 1,640 feet, with a shoreline 72 miles long. In spite of commercial development—resorts, gambling casinos, shopping centers—around Lake Tahoe, much of the shoreline is open to visitors as public beaches and parks. Most of the Tahoe Basin is within the Eldorado, Tahoe, and Toiyabe national forests. Tahoe is the largest alpine lake on the North American continent, and particularly scenic in winter and spring when the surrounding mountains, now a prime area for ski resorts, are capped with snow. In winter, the average maximum temperature is 36 degrees, the minimum 18. Summer temperatures are relatively cool, seldom reaching 80 degrees. Evening temperatures drop into the 40s. During the summer months, the upper surface of the lake itself remains chilly, about 68 degrees maximum.

Yosemite National Park

No matter how many times it has been photographed, Yosemite remains an awesome sight for first-time visitors, with its sheer cliffs, massive granite formations, and cascading waterfalls. The dramatic scenery in east central California was formed by the uplifting Sierra Nevada, the formation of the Merced River, and the powerful action of glaciers that cut through the granite more than 10,000 years ago. The area has been renowned for its natural beauty since its discovery in the mid-19th century by soldiers and gold seekers. Even the effusive journalist Horace Greeley was stunned when he visited there in 1859: "I know of no single wonder of nature on earth which can claim a superiority over Yosemite." The park, first set aside as public land in the 1860s—with the approval of President Abraham Lincoln—covers 1,189 square miles, about the size of the state of Rhode Island.

Yosemite Valley, at an altitude of 4,000 feet, is the most popular destination for viewing the park's majestic scenery. The sheer granite face of El Capitan towers 3,600 feet over the valley floor. The unique formation of Half Dome is 1,200 feet higher. Yosemite Falls, the highest in North America, drops 2,425 feet in three cascades. Groves of giant sequoia trees in the park, 35 miles south of the valley, tower 200 feet. Some are more than 2,000 years old. The park's major attractions are accessible all year, most enjoyable in spring (waterfalls are spectacular in May and June) and fall. Winter snow and mist create a magical atmosphere.

PRACTICAL INFORMATION FOR CALIFORNIA

TOURIST INFORMATION. The *California Office of Tourism,* 1121 L St., Suite 103, Sacramento, CA (916–322–1396) provides maps, a visitor's directory, calendar of fairs and festivals, and a guide to "The Californias," 12 regions with their own identities. The guides are free. For the adventurous visitor, the office publishes the brochure *Adventures in California,* which describes and lists resources for hot air ballooning, river rafting, wagon trips, bicycling, and whale watching.

TIME ZONES. California is in the Pacific Time Zone (Greenwich Mean Time minus eight hours). Daylight Time is observed from the first Sun. in Apr. to the last Sun. in Oct., when clocks are set ahead one hour.

HINTS TO MOTORISTS. The California Highway Patrol and local police are serious about enforcing the 55 mph maximum speed law, and they are equally serious about cracking down on drunken drivers. Seatbelt laws are in effect. All drivers and passengers 4 years of age and older must wear seat belts while a vehicle is moving. Children younger than four must be restrained in approved safety seats. Visitors to the Wine Country should be aware that it is unlawful to drive with an opened container of alcoholic beverage in the passenger compartment of a vehicle. Opened bottles that aren't empty should be placed in the trunk.

NATIONAL AND STATE PARKS. National parks include some of California's choice scenic areas (Yosemite, the Golden Gate), historic sites, and monuments. Most areas offer campsites. Information, *Western Regional Information Office, National Park Service,* Fort Mason, Bldg. 201, San Francisco, CA, 94123 (415–556–0560). Many of the 20 national forests in the state also have camping facilities. Contact *U.S. Forest Service,* 630 Sansome St., San Francisco, CA 94111 (415–556–0122).

There are more than 250 state parks, beaches and historical sites, ranging from the redwood groves in the north to the Southern California desert. Many state parks are clustered along the coastline. There are campsites, some with showers and rest rooms, in many parks. Sites can be reserved through *Mistix* service (619–452–1950; 800–446–7275 in state only). A map and guide showing the location and facilities of all state parks is available for $2 by mail from: *Dept. of Parks and Recreation,* Box 942896, Sacramento, CA 94296 (916–445–6647).

A directory showing the location and facilities of private campgrounds in the state is available for $2 by mail from: *California Travel Parks Assn.,* Box 5648, Auburn, CA 95604 (916–885–1624).

LIQUOR LAWS. In California, the minimum age for buying or drinking alcohol is 21. Alcoholic beverages, by the drink or by the container, may be purchased 6 A.M.–2 A.M. daily. Liquor, wine, and beer are on sale in liquor stores and most grocery stores. Bars and nightclubs usually serve a full range of beverages; many restaurants also do, but some serve only beer and wine.

PRACTICAL INFORMATION FOR LOS ANGELES AND ORANGE COUNTY

WHEN TO GO. The Los Angeles area enjoys normally pleasant and mild weather throughout the year. Temperatures are cooler and milder along the coast, more extreme during both winter and summer in the inland valleys. The average maximum and minimum temperatures in Los Angeles are 81 and 60° F. in July; 76 and 55 in Oct.; 65 and 46 in Jan. Los Angeles's infamous smog may affect persons with respiratory problems at the height of summer, but air pollution is not uncommon in many urban areas across the country. The relative humidity is usually below normal even during periods of high temperatures. The rainy season is usually Nov. to Mar., when 85 percent of the average 15 inches of rain falls. Summers are practically rainless. Because summer temperatures can drop 20 degrees at night, it is wise to bring a sweater or jacket. Swimmers should note that the Pacific Ocean temperature is cool until July, then remains in the mid-60s until Oct.

HOW TO GET THERE. By plane. *Los Angeles International Airport (LAX),* on the coast 13 mi. southwest of downtown, is the area's major airport. It handles 85 international, national, and regional commuter airlines. Terminals and ground transportation approaches were expanded and streamlined for the 1984 Summer Olympics. Three other airports are served by western regional and commuter lines: *Burbank* in the San Fernando Valley; *Ontario,* 35 mi. east; and *John Wayne/Orange County Airport,* the closest to Disneyland and the county's other theme parks. *American Airlines* and *USAir* sometimes offer package tours including hotels and park admissions.

By bus. *Greyhound* serves Los Angeles and other cities in the area. *Airlink Airport Service* offers service from Los Angeles International Airport to Anaheim and other cities.

By train. *Amtrak* reaches Los Angeles from Chicago via the "Southwest Chief"; from New Orleans with the "Sunset Limited"; from Seattle, Portland, and San Francisco with the "Coast Starlight." Union Station, 800 N. Alameda St., Los Angeles, was one of the last great passenger stations built in the U.S. There are smaller Amtrak stations/ticket offices in Glendale, Pasadena, Pomona, Anaheim, Santa Ana. Fare and schedule information is available toll-free, nationwide, by telephoning 800–USA–RAIL.

By car. The major north–south route is I-5, which bisects Los Angeles and continues through Orange County and on to San Diego. U.S. Hwy. 101 also approaches from the north, closer to the coast, and State Rte. 1 is the rugged but scenic coastal route. I-10 is the direct route from the east, entering Los Angeles as the San Bernardino Frwy. and ending at Santa Monica.

TOURIST INFORMATION. In advance, write for the free, comprehensive "LA's the Place" visitor's guide from the *Greater Los Angeles Visitors and Convention Bureau,* 515 S. Figueroa St., 11th Floor, Los Angeles, CA 90071. The bureau operates two information centers: *Downtown,* 695 S. Figueroa St. between Wilshire Blvd. and Seventh St., open Mon.–Sat., 8 A.M.–5 P.M. (213–689–8822); *Hollywood,* Janes House, 6541 Hollywood Blvd. (213–461–4213).

The *Anaheim Area Visitors and Convention Bureau* offers information on Disneyland and other theme parks as well as a hotel referral service: 800 W. Katella Ave., Anaheim, CA 92803; (714–999–8999). Contact *Avalon–Catalina Island Chamber of Commerce,* for information on reaching the scenic resort, P.O. Box 217, Avalon, CA 90704 (213–510–2266). For information on the Jan. 1 rose parade, contact the *Tournament of Roses Assn.,* 391 S. Orange Grove Blvd., Pasadena, CA 91105 (818–449–ROSE). Pasadena's zany Dooh Dah Parade, in late Nov. or early Dec., parodies the rose parade. Call 818–796–2591 for information.

TELEPHONES. The area code for central Los Angeles is 213. Northern area communities of the San Fernando Valley, including Glendale, Pasadena, and Burbank, are in the 818 area. Central and coastal Orange County is 714. Dial 411 for directory assistance, and be aware that there are many telephone directories for the area. When direct-dialing long distance, first dial the number 1, then the area code and number. For operator assistance on credit, collect, or person-to-person calls, dial 0, then 1, then the number. Pay phones start at 20 cents.

EMERGENCY TELEPHONE NUMBERS. In the Los Angeles area, dial the universal emergency number 911. The number for *police* in Los Angeles is 625–3311; *fire,* 384–3131; *medical emergencies,* 483–6721; *poison information,* 484–5151; *daytime medical referral service,* 483–6122. These are all in the 213 area code.

HOW TO GET AROUND. From the airport. Los Angeles International (LAX) taxis and buses board on the ground level of passenger terminals. Average cab fare to downtown or Hollywood is $25–$30. *Airlink Airport Service* buses have numerous routes to downtown, Beverly Hills–Century City, Hollywood–Universal City, West Los Angeles, and the Wilshire district. Buses stop at most major hotels. The line also serves Burbank and Orange County airports. Typical fare is $7 from LAX to downtown. For toll-free information call: nationwide 800–962–1975. *The Super Shuttle* offers on-call, door-to-door airport service in the Los Angeles area to and from LAX. Courtesy phones are in terminals, or call 213–338–1111. Fare is $8 to $25, depending on destination.

By bus. *Southern California Rapid Transit District (RTD)* serves the greater Los Angeles area, including the airport, with service to such attractions as Universal Studios, Hollywood, Disneyland, and Knott's Berry Farm. Fare is $1.10, 25 cents for transfers. For information on getting from one point in the sprawling metropolis to another by bus, telephone in central Los Angeles 213–626–4455; Burbank area 818–246–2593; Orange County, 714–635–6010. There are also two Los Angeles Downtown Area Short Hop (DASH) routes with 25-cents fares which operate every 15 minutes, Mon.–Sat.

By taxi. Several firms serve Los Angeles, but, unlike more compact cities, cabs do not cruise streets looking for passengers. It can be impossible to hail a cab in most areas, but there are taxi stands at airports, major hotels, and train and bus terminals. Fares are $1.60 per mi. It is wise to confirm the approximate cost when entering a cab. Taxis may be ordered by phone: *Independent Cab* (213–385–8294); *L.A. Taxi* (213–627–7000); and *United Independent Taxi,* which accepts MasterCard and Visa, (213–653–5050).

By rental car. All major rental companies serve Los Angeles, Burbank, and Orange County airports. Because of the demand for cars in this city on wheels, it is wise to reserve in advance using toll-free numbers. Rates are the same whether cars are picked up at airports or agency offices. Major firms offer emergency road service. Some will provide driving directions by phone; ask for the number when picking up a car. Major firms serving LAX are: *Avis* (231–649–3121; toll free 800–331–1212); *Hertz* (213–646–4861; 800–654–3131). Less expensive options include: *Budget* (213–645–4500; 800–527–0700); *Enterprise* (213–329–3030; 800–325–8007). When picking up a car, don't leave the agency without a map.

HINTS TO MOTORISTS. Now that other cities are crisscrossed by freeways, driving in Los Angeles may not seem like such a dreaded ordeal. Freeways do provide faster and usually safer travel over the area's great distances—the 30 mi. from Los Angeles Airport to Disneyland, for instance. There are more than 30 freeways. Eight radiate from Los Angeles' downtown freeway loop. All are named for their destinations, with the exception of the Golden State Frwy. A map is essential, and should be studied before arrival if possible. When driving, always plan freeway routes, identify interchanges, and note exits before setting out.

HINTS TO DISABLED TRAVELERS. All facilities at Los Angeles International Airport are accessible, and free wheelchair lift service is provided between the eight terminals. Call 213–646–6402 or 646–8021. All major public buildings and downtown intersections have access ramps. The *Rapid Transit Districts* (RTD) operates 100 buses with handicapped access, but considering the size of Los Angeles,

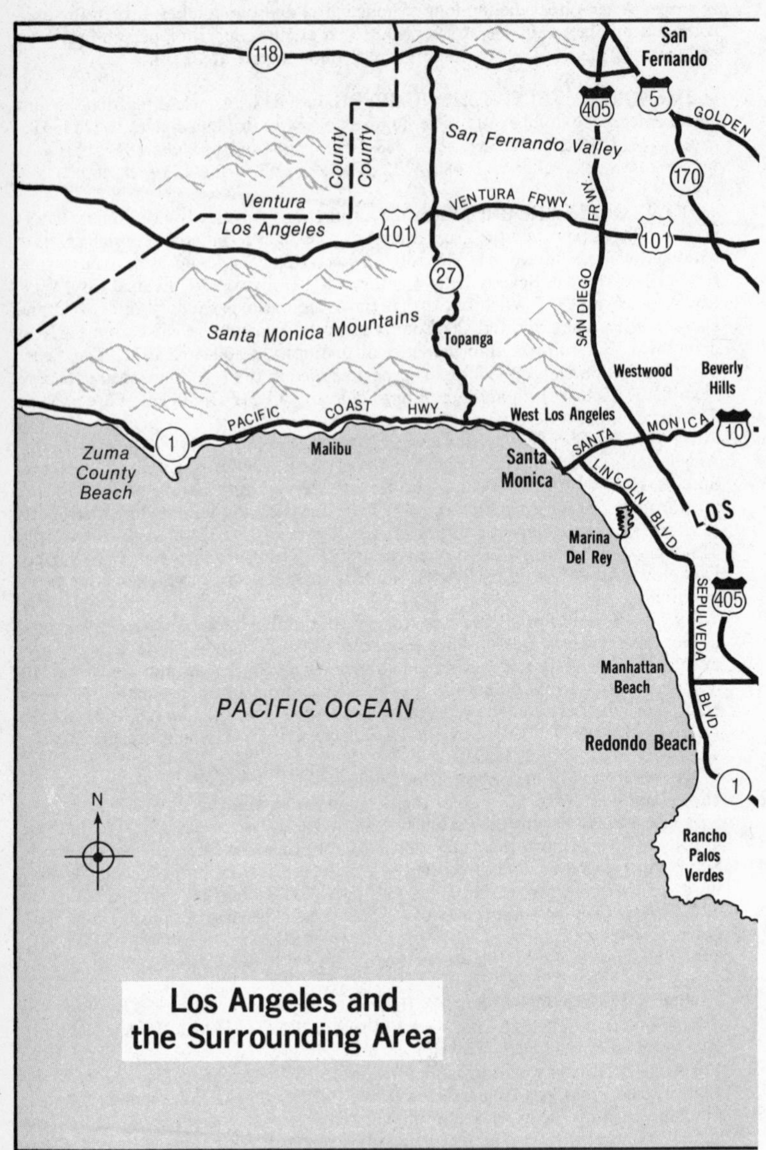

Los Angeles and the Surrounding Area

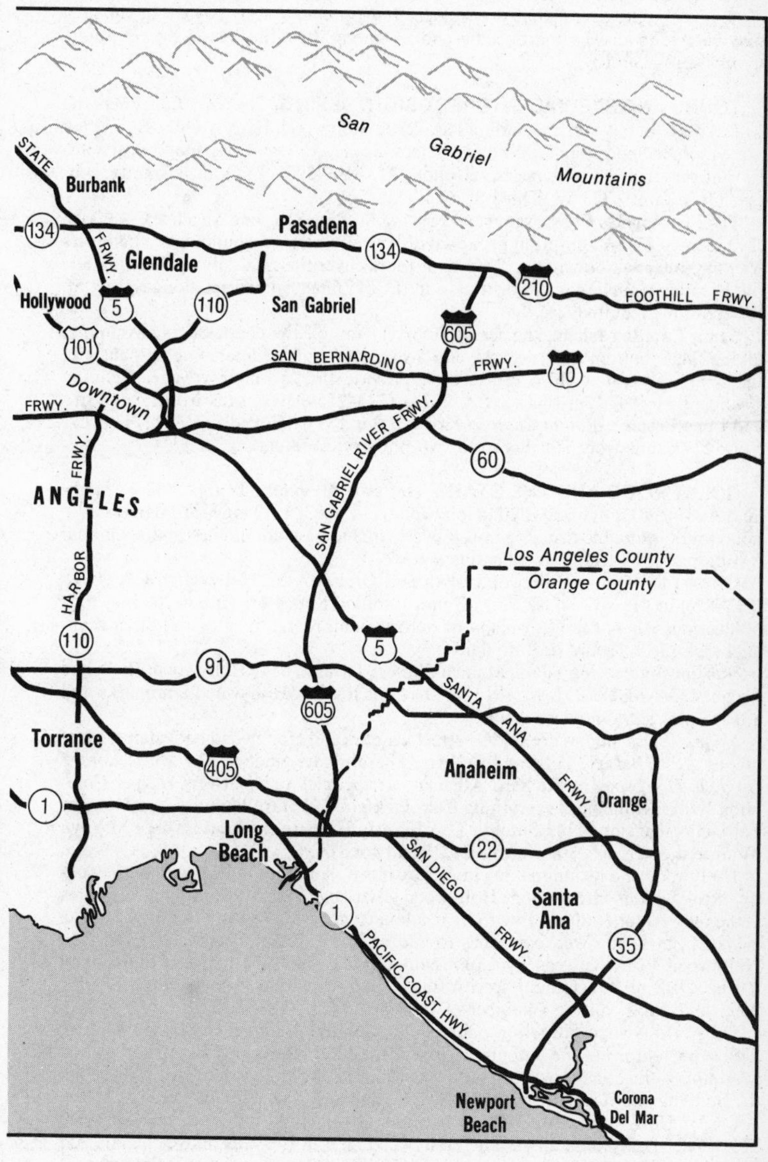
San
Gabriel
Mountains
STATE
Burbank
134
FRWY.
Pasadena
Glendale
134
210
FOOTHILL FRWY.
Hollywood
5
110
San Gabriel
605
101
SAN BERNARDINO FRWY.
10
Downtown
FRWY.
SAN GABRIEL RIVER FRWY.
60
FRWY.
ANGELES
HARBOR
Los Angeles County
Orange County
110
5
91
SANTA ANA FRWY.
605
Torrance
405
Anaheim
1
Orange
Long
Beach
22
SAN DIEGO FRWY.
Santa
Ana
1
55
PACIFIC COAST HWY.
Newport
Beach
Corona
Del Mar

they may be miles away. Most larger, newer hotels, especially the Ramada Inn and Holiday Inn chains, are accessible. For a list of historic sites that can accommodate wheelchair visitors, write for the brochure "Round the Town With Ease" from the *Junior League of Los Angeles,* Third and Fairfax St., Los Angeles, CA 90036. Enclose a self-addressed, stamped envelope. *Independent Living Centers* in the area may be able to answer questions by phone; among them the *Westside Community Center* (213–836–1075).

TOURS AND SPECIAL-INTEREST SIGHTSEEING. The *Gray Line* offers the widest range of bus tours, including Pasadena, Hollywood, Beverly Hills. Buses pick up visitors at more than 100 hotels. There are half-day and day-long excursions. For information in Los Angeles, telephone 213–856–5900. In Orange County, contact Gray Line, 6333 W. Third St. (714–523–5661).

The Los Angeles Conservancy, 433 Spring St., No. 850, Los Angeles, CA 90026 (213–623–8687). A non-profit group saving the city's historic buildings, it conducts walking tours Sat. downtown. Two-hour tours cover the area around Pershing Sq., the Broadway movie theater district, and the old financial district along Spring St. Reservations required; fee, $5.

Santa Catalina Island, the scenic resort 21 mi. off the coast, offers swimming, hiking, glass-bottom boat cruises, and a museum and landmark movie palace in the town of Avalon. Two cruise lines provide the two-hour voyage: *Catalina Cruises,* Box 1948, San Pedro, CA 90733 (213–253–9800), sails from San Pedro and Long Beach; *Catalina Channel Express,* Box 1391, San Pedro, CA 90733 (213–519–1212), sails from San Pedro to two ports on Catalina.

HOLLYWOOD AND THE STARS. Hollywood Fantasy Tours, 1651 N. Highland Ave. near Hollywood Blvd., Hollywood, CA 90028 (213–469–8184) offers two-hour tours in double-deck, open-top buses, including stars' homes and such final resting places as Rudolph Valentino's grave.

Grave Line Tours, Hollywood Blvd. and Orchid Ave., Hollywood, CA 90028 (213–876–0920), will whisk you off in a Cadillac hearse for an entertaining tour of locations where tinsel town's most notorious murders, suicides and other scandals took place. Tours operate daily.

Starline Sightseeing Tours, Mann's Chinese Theatre, 6845 Hollywood Blvd., Los Angeles, CA 90028 (213–463–3131), offers bus tours of Hollywood landmarks and a drive past stars' homes.

Maps of stars' homes are sold by street vendors and Hollywood bookshops. Most homes are in Beverly Hills and Bel Air. The ultimate guide is *The Movie Lover's Guide to Hollywood* by Richard Alleman, a paperback published by Harper Colophon Books. It includes everything from Pickfair, the Mary Pickford and Douglas Fairbanks mansion (1143 Summit Dr., Beverly Hills) to the house where Marilyn Monroe died (12305 5th Helena Dr., Brentwood).

Hollywood and its filmmaking image are more glamorous in legend than the reality of the famous intersection, Hollywood Blvd. and Vine St. Paramount Pictures is the only major studio still with its headquarters here, at 5451 Marathon St. The Walk of Stars, however, continues to add celebrities' names to the sidewalks on Hollywood Blvd. between Sycamore and Gower, and Vine between Sunset and Yucca. Dedication ceremonies, with stars usually attending, are held monthly; for dates and times call the Chamber of Commerce (213–469–8311).

Other Hollywood attractions: Mann's (originally Grauman's) Chinese Theatre with stars' footprints and autographs in cement, 6925 Hollywood Blvd.; Hollywood Museum, with actual movie props and costumes, 7051 Hollywood Blvd.; Max Factor Building and Beauty Museum, 1666 N. Highland Ave.; Hollywood Wax Museum, 6767 Hollywood Blvd.; Musso & Frank Grill, an old-fashioned favorite since 1919, 6667 Hollywood Blvd. The Hollywood sign in the hills above the city, off Beachwood Dr., originally promoted the *Hollywoodland* housing development. It was restored in 1978.

Cemeteries in Los Angeles surprise visitors with their park-like settings including chapels, reproductions of famous artworks, and mottos such as "a place for the living to enjoy." Forest Lawn, 1712 S. Glendale Ave., Glendale, has a stained-glass reproduction of *The Last Supper;* the Wee Kirk of the Heather Church where Ronald Reagan married Jane Wyman in 1940; and memorials to Clark Gable, Carole

Lombard, Errol Flynn, and Walt Disney. Others include Hollywood Memorial Park, 6000 Santa Monica Blvd., Hollywood: memorials to Rudolph Valentino, Tyrone Power. Westwood Memorial Park, 1218 Glendon Ave. off Wilshire Blvd., Westwood: Marilyn Monroe, Natalie Wood, Darryl Zanuck. Holy Cross Cemetery, 5835 W. Slauson Ave., Culver City: Bing Crosby, Rosalind Russell, Mario Lanza.

STUDIO TOURS AND TV SHOWS. Universal Studio Hollywood. 2900 Lankershim Blvd., Universal City, CA 91608 (818–777–3801). An industry of its own, this narrated tram tour takes visitors through the movie and TV studio, displaying special effects and a stunt show. It's been updated to illustrate recent hit movies and to simulate a major earthquake. Summer, holidays, open at 9 A.M., other periods at 9:30 A.M. to 4 P.M. Adults, $22, children under 12, $16.50.

Burbank Studios VIP Tour. 4000 Warner Blvd., Burbank, CA 91522 (818–954–1744). A more precise behind-the-scenes look at the TV and movie studio shared by Warner Bros. and Columbia. Mon.–Fri., 10 A.M.–2 P.M., additional summer tours, closed holidays. No children under 10, no cameras. Admission, $20.

NBC Studio Tours. 3000 W. Alameda Ave., Burbank, CA 91523 (818–840–3537). Hour-long tour includes studio sets and special effects demonstrations; you can also see yourself on camera. Mon.–Fri., 8:30 A.M.–4 P.M.; Sat., 10 A.M.–4 P.M.; Sun., 10 A.M.–2 P.M. Closed most major holidays. Adults, $6.75; children, $4.50.

Television Shows. Free tickets are available the days shows are videotaped at the downtown Los Angeles Visitors and Convention Bureau, and at the studios, usually beginning at 9 A.M. Call ahead for availability: ABC, 4151 Prospect Ave., Hollywood (213–557–4396); CBS, 7800 Beverly Blvd., Los Angeles (213–852–2345); NBC, 3000 W. Alameda Ave., Burbank (213–840–3537).

PARKS AND GARDENS. Barnsdall Art Park. 4800 Hollywood Blvd., Los Angeles, (213–662–7272). It contains the restored Hollyhock House built by Frank Lloyd Wright. Park is free; admission charge to Hollyhock House.

Descanso Gardens. 1418 Descanso Dr., La Canada. Thousands of azaleas, camelias, and roses in a site once part of the vast Spanish Rancho San Rafael. Adults, $3; children, 75 cents.

Griffith Park. Los Feliz Blvd. and Riverside Dr., Los Angeles. 4,000 acres for hiking, tennis, golf, picnics, plus Griffith Observatory and Planetarium. Park is free, admission charge to planetarium.

Huntington Botanical Gardens. 1151 Oxford Rd., San Marino (818–405–2100). More than 9,000 different plants, including an extensive cactus collection, fill this 130-acre estate, site of the Huntington Library and Art Gallery. Open Tues.–Sun. afternoons.

Los Angeles State and County Arboretum. 301 N. Baldwin Ave., Arcadia. The jungle setting for TV's *Fantasy Island* is here, plus home demonstration gardens, tropical greenhouse, orchids. Adults, $3; children, 75 cents.

Will Rogers State Historical Park. 14253 Sunset Blvd., Pacific Palisades (213–454–8212). The humorist's ranch is open, with daily house tours, 10 A.M.–5 P.M. Fee $5 per car.

ZOOS. The Los Angeles Zoo. 5333 Zoo Dr. in Griffith Park (213–666–4090). The zoo contains 2,000 animals, including 78 endangered species. Special attractions are a koala house and bird and elephant shows. Open daily except Christmas, 10 A.M.–5 P.M., until 6 P.M. in summer. Adults, $6; children, $2.75.

Tucker Wildlife Sanctuary. 29322 Modjeska Canyon Rd., Silverado (714–649–2760). More than 50 bird species, including many hummingbirds, in a tree-lined canyon 17 mi. southeast of the city of Orange. An attendant helps with identification; self-guiding nature trails.

PARTICIPANT SPORTS. Jogging is a city-wide activity. Beaches and adjacent pathways are ideal. Popular routes are along San Vicente Blvd. from Brentwood to Santa Monica, then through palm-lined Palisades Park. On the walkways between Santa Monica and Venice, joggers manage to share space with bike riders and roller skaters.

Tennis courts are in most major parks, lighted at night, and more readily available when local residents are busy elsewhere: mid-day on weekdays, evenings on weekends. Contact the Los Angeles City Parks and Recreation Dept. (213–485–5515) or the Southern California Tennis Assn. (213–208–3838).

Golf is another year-round activity, and golfers from harsher climates may enjoy the novelty of playing in mid-winter. There are three public courses in *Griffith Park* alone, and other popular courses include *Rancho Park,* 10460 W. Pico Blvd., Los Angeles, and *Penmar,* a 9-hole course at 1233 Rose Ave., Venice. For information on other golf courses, tennis courts, swimming pools and hiking trails, contact the *Los Angeles City Parks and Recreation Dept.* (213–485–5515), or *County Parks and Recreation Dept.* (213–738–2961).

SPECTATOR SPORTS. Baseball. The National League *Dodgers* play at Dodger Stadium in Chavez Ravine above downtown Los Angeles Apr.–Oct. (213–224–1400). The American League *California Angels* play at the Anaheim Stadium in Orange County (714–634–2000).

Basketball. The *Lakers* play their home games at the Forum in Inglewood (213–673–1300). The *Clippers* play at the Sports Arena in Los Angeles (213–748–6131).

Football. The *Raiders* make their current home at Memorial Coliseum, site of two Summer Olympics in Los Angeles (213–322–5901). The *Rams* play in Anaheim Stadium (213–937–6767).

Thoroughbred racing takes place late Apr. to late July, Nov. and Dec. at Hollywood Park in Inglewood near Los Angeles International Airport (213–419–1500) and Dec.–Apr., Oct., and Nov. at Santa Anita Park in Arcadia (818–574–7223).

BEACHES. Los Angeles County operates more than 40 mi. of beaches along 76 mi. of coastline, from Nicholas Canyon Beach in the north to San Pedro's Cabrillo Beach in the south. At these county beaches, lifeguards are on duty all year during daylight hours. Beachgoers are advised to check with lifeguards on arrival to learn of unusual surfing conditions or beach hazards. Pets, alcoholic beverages, and bonfires are prohibited. Public parking, for a fee, is available at most beaches.

For information on county-operated beaches and the recreation boating harbor at Marina del Rey, just north of Los Angeles Airport, contact the *Marina del Rey Information* Center, 4701 Admiralty Way (213–305–9545). Open daily, 9 A.M.–5 P.M.

Traveling from north to south, popular beaches include: Zuma Beach, with extensive parking, and Surfrider Beach with its Sept. surfing contest in Malibu; Santa Monica city beaches, family favorites; Venice, with its colorful characters and the bodybuilders' "Muscle Beach"; Marina del Rey, a dock for thousands of boats and site of many restaurants; Manhattan, Hermosa, and Redondo beaches, clean sand and pleasant settings.

THEME PARKS. Disneyland. Box 3232, Anaheim, CA 94803 (714–999–4565). From Los Angeles, drive south on I-5, the Golden State Frwy., which becomes the Santa Ana Frwy. The Disneyland exit is in Anaheim. In the mid-1950s filmmaker Walt Disney's vision turned a 76-acre orange grove into an entertainment center. Recently the park has updated its relatively staid image with more exciting rides such as a steep flume ride called "Splash Mountain," attractions designed by *Star Wars* movie director George Lucas, and a short musical film in 3-D with Michael Jackson. The seven theme areas remain as fresh and colorful as Disney envisioned.

Open year-round, Mon.–Fri. 10 A.M.–6 P.M.; Sat., 9 A.M.–midnight; Sun., 9 A.M.–9 P.M. Extended summer hours, mid-June to mid-Sept., open at least until midnight; Sun. to 10 P.M. Admission, $20.50–$25.50 a day. Discounts on two-day and three-day passes.

Knott's Berry Farm. 8039 Beach Blvd., Buena Park (714–220–5200). Take State Rte. 91 east from the Golden State Frwy. (I-5). Western and Gold Rush themes carry through this 150-acre family park and its 165 rides. They include Montezuma's Revenge and the Corkscrew roller coaster with two 360-degree loops. In the Camp Snoopy area, Charles Schulz's "Peanuts" cartoon characters do their best to match the Disney appeal. Winter hours: Mon.–Sat., 10 A.M.–6 P.M.; Sun., 10 A.M.–7 P.M.; open later during school vacations. Summer: Sun.–Fri., 10 A.M.–midnight; Sat. to 1 A.M. Admission, about $17–$21.

Transportation among Anaheim attractions is provided by the Fun Bus, with a route to major hotels, Disneyland, Knott's Berry Farm, Movieland Wax Museum,

Anaheim Convention Center, Buena Park shopping center. Buses operate hourly year-round, more frequently in summer. Round trip, about $5. Information and hotel pick-up requests, 714–491–6169.

Six Flags Magic Mountain. 26101 Magic Mountain Pkwy. (exit from Golden State Freeway), Valencia (805–255–4111). Located a half-hour drive north of Hollywood, this park boasts a $35-million upgrading and rides that youngsters consider the most thrilling, including the Colossus roller coaster and Jet Stream water ride. There is a Wizard's Village for younger children. Open Sat., Sun., holidays (except Christmas) year-round, 10 A.M.–6 P.M. Open until 10 P.M. Sept.–Oct. Extended schedule Memorial Day–Labor Day, 10 A.M.–10 P.M. daily. Adults, $23; children, $14.

HISTORIC SITES AND HOUSES. Bradbury Building. 304 S. Broadway, Los Angeles. Restored five-story 1893 office building with inner court, skylight, ornate railings on balconies. Open Mon.–Fri., 10 A.M.–5 P.M.

Bullocks-Wilshire department store. 3050 Wilshire Blvd., Los Angeles (213–382–6161). If the 1920s are considered history in Los Angeles, then this 1928 Art Deco and Moderne building must be a historical site. The grand entrance is from the rear parking lot. There is a spacious tearoom on the fifth floor.

El Pueblo de Los Angeles. Bounded by Alameda, Arcadia, Spring, and Macy Sts. (213–628–7164). This 44-acre state historical park displays the roots of Los Angeles history. The Avila Adobe dates from 1818; Old Plaza Church, *Nuestra Senora la Reina de Los Angeles,* from 1822; and the Pico House, once a hotel, was built in 1870 by the last Mexican governor of California. Olvera St., created from a slum in the 1930s, is lined with souvenir shops and restaurants. Free admission.

Gamble House. 4 Westmoreland Pl. off N. Orange Grove Blvd., Pasadena (818–793–3334). This rambling bungalow built by architects Charles and Henry Greene in 1908 is a masterpiece of the Arts and Crafts movement, with every detail finely crafted. Schedule varies; call for information.

Mission San Fernando Re de Espana. 15151 San Fernando Mission Blvd., Mission Hills (818–361–0186). Restored 1797 church, monastery, workrooms in a garden setting. A 35-bell carillon rings hourly, 10 A.M.–6 P.M. Open 9 A.M.–4 P.M. daily.

Mission San Gabriel Arcangel. 537 W. Mission Dr., San Gabriel (818–282–5191). Founded in 1771, this restored mission and its grounds are among the best representations of California life during the Spanish era. Open 9:30 A.M.–4 P.M. daily; closed Easter, Thanksgiving, Christmas.

MUSEUMS. California Museum of Science and Industry. 700 State Dr., in Exposition Park (213–744–7400). Everything from hatching baby chicks to hands-on computers are included in this family favorite. The adjacent Aerospace Museum has a Lockheed F-104 jet bursting through the entry. Open daily, 10 A.M.–5 P.M. Free.

J. Paul Getty Museum. 17985 Pacific Coast Hwy., Malibu, CA 90265 (213–459–8402). A detailed replica of a Roman seaside villa, with a collection of Greek and Roman antiquities, European artwork. Open 10 A.M.–5 P.M., Tues.–Sun. Free, but reservations required (at least a week in advance) because of limited parking.

Los Angeles County Museum of Art. 5905 Wilshire Blvd., Los Angeles (213–857–6111). Wide-ranging permanent collection includes Japanese art in a spectacular pavilion, Rodin sculptures, plus important touring exhibits. More than 300 20th-century paintings and sculptures are housed in a new addition. Open Tues.–Fri., 10 A.M.–5 P.M.; Sat.–Sun, 10 A.M.–6 P.M. Adults, $5; juniors, $3.50; children, $2.

Museum of Contemporary Art. 3rd and Grand Ave., Los Angeles (213–626–6222). This striking new 100,000-square-ft. building and sculpture garden, designed by Japanese architect Arata Isozaki, have focused attention on Southern California as an international art center. Permanent and touring exhibits. popular "Temporary Contemporary" remains open at 152 N. Central Ave. nearby. Open Tues.–Fri., 10 A.M.–5 P.M.; Sat. and Sun., 10 A.M.–6 P.M. Adults, $5; juniors, $3.50; children under 12, free.

George C. Page Museum of La Brea Discoveries. 5801 Wilshire Blvd., Los Angeles (213–936–2230). Treasures of the La Brea Tar Pits on the Hancock Park site, with fossils and reconstructions of extinct Ice Age animals. Open 10 A.M.–5 P.M. Tues.–Sun. Adults, $3; juniors, $1.50; children, 75 cents.

Southwest Museum. 234 Museum Dr., Los Angeles (213–221–2163). One of the nation's finest collections of Indian art and artifacts, in a 1914 Mission-style building with a spectacular view. Open Tues.–Sun., 11 A.M.–5 P.M.; Sun., 1–5 P.M. Adults, $4; juniors, $2; children, $1.

MUSIC AND DANCE. Development of the downtown Los Angeles Music Center, along with the vast pool of musical talent from the film and recording industries, have made this a thriving music center. With the exception of opera and ballet, Los Angeles has taken the lead from San Francisco, its long-time cultural rival.

The **Los Angeles Philharmonic** performs an Oct.–May winter season in Dorothy Chandler Pavilion at the Music Center, 135 N. Grand Ave., Los Angeles (213–972–7211). Summer concerts July–Sept. are outdoors in the Hollywood Bowl, 2301 N. Highland Ave.

The **Los Angeles Music Center Opera,** which made its debut in 1986, has gained a national reputation for its season (fall through spring) of traditional and innovative repertory and staging. It performs at the Dorothy Chandler Pavilion, 135 N. Grand Ave., Los Angeles, CA 90012 (213–972–7219).

The **Hollywood Bowl** (213–850–2000) also presents jazz, rock, folk, and country music in an extended summer season. Other outdoor amphitheaters: **Greek Theatre,** 2700 N. Vermont, Los Angeles (213–410–1062); **Universal Amphitheater,** which is rock-oriented, 100 Universal City Plaza, Universal City (818–777–3931).

The **Dance Resource Center of Greater Los Angeles** (213–281–1918) is the best source of information for performances by the area's more than 50 dance companies, including Bella Lewitsky and Los Angeles Chamber Ballet. Touring companies perform at the Embassy Auditorium, Dorothy Chandler Pavilion in the Music Center, and at Shrine Auditorium.

STAGE. Los Angeles benefits from the box-office appeal and talent of the film and television industry's actors "between engagements." Among the local companies the **Los Angeles Theatre Center,** 514 S. Spring St., Los Angeles, CA 90013 (213–627–5599), has expanded to four stages within a remodeled bank building downtown. It presents new and recent plays, with music and poetry series on the plays' dark nights.

Other local theaters, also emphasizing new works: The **Mark Taper Forum** at the Music Center, 135 N. Grand Ave., Los Angeles (213–972–7353); **Pasadena Playhouse,** 39 S. El Molino Ave., Pasadena (818–356–7729); **Odyssey Theatre Ensemble,** 2055 S. Sepulveda Blvd., Los Angeles (213–477–2055).

Touring plays and musicals are housed at the Ahmanson Theater in the Music Center, the Pantages, and the Shubert and Henry Fonda theaters, all in Los Angeles; the James A. Doolittle in Hollywood; and the Westwood Playhouse in Westwood. Check newspapers for current attractions.

FILMS. Because of Academy Award considerations, films that may never find a home elsewhere in the nation will play for a week in Los Angeles. Moreover, in few other cities are the movie theaters as popular an attraction as the movies. Among these are: *Mann's Chinese Theater,* 6925 Hollywood Blvd., Hollywood, with stars' handprints and footprints in cement; the templelike *Egyptian Theater* nearby at 6712 Hollywood Blvd.; and the movie palaces on Broadway in the primarily Hispanic downtown shopping district. These include the *Million Dollar Theatre,* which dates from 1917, the *Los Angeles, Orpheum,* and *Tower* theaters.

In addition to first-run theaters, Los Angeles is scattered with foreign film and revival houses, including: the *Nuart,* 11272 Santa Monica Blvd. (213–478–6379); *Beverly Cinema,* 7165 Beverly Blvd. (213–938–4038); and *Samuel Goldwyn Pavilion,* Pico Blvd. at Westwood (213–475–0202).

ACCOMMODATIONS. In spite of its palm trees and pink stucco image, Los Angeles offers posh hotels with rooms for $200 a night, rambling suites, and secluded bungalows. Budget motels with their own pools and free parking may be just around the corner. Major chains have as many as six hotels and motels in the area; use their national toll-free numbers for information. Smaller, European-style hotels are also flourishing. Most rates are valid year-round, but check for weekend and winter discounts. For many visitors to the sprawling metropolis, location may be as important as price. Price categories for two persons in one room are: *Deluxe,* $150 and up; *Expensive,* $100–$150; *Moderate,* $80–$100; and *Inexpensive,* under $80. A 10% room tax is added. All telephone numbers are in the 213 area code.

Deluxe

The Biltmore Hotel. 515 S. Olive St., Los Angeles, CA 90013 (213–624–1011 or 800–421–8000, nationwide; 800–252–0175, Calif.). Downtown area. Once the largest hotel west of Chicago, the landmark has been restored to its Mediterranean glory. Rooms have been updated in a $35 million refurbishing.

Century Plaza. 2025 Ave. of the Stars, Los Angeles, CA 90067 (213–277–2000 or 800–228–3000). Century City–Beverly Hills area. Sleek, modern, 800 rooms, each with a balcony. Extensive shopping center nearby.

Chateau Marmont Hotel. 8221 Sunset Blvd., Hollywood, CA 90046 (213–656–1010 or 800–242–8328). Wide variety of rooms, suites, bungalows; a hideaway since the 1920s for actors and writers. Just off Sunset Strip.

Le Dufy Hotel. 1000 Westmount Dr., West Hollywood, CA 90069 (213–657–7400 or 800–424–4443). Among the chic L'Ermitage Hotel group, this is the most modestly priced. All suites, on a quiet residential street near Beverly Hills.

Mondrian. 9440 Sunset Blvd., West Hollywood, CA 90069 (213–650–8999 or 800–424–4443). Chic, with ultra-contemporary decor and original art throughout. Limousine service available for all guests.

Expensive

Holiday Inn. 1755 N. Highland Ave., Hollywood, CA 90028 (213–462–7181 or 800–465–4329). Recently renovated, 23-story hotel one block north of Hollywood Blvd. Revolving rooftop restaurant.

Hollywood Roosevelt Hotel. 7000 Hollywood Blvd., Hollywood, CA 90028 (213–466–7000 or 800–950–7667). Douglas Fairbanks and Mary Pickford were among the original investors in the "home of the stars," which has reopened after a $12-million restoration. Across from Mann's Chinese Theater.

Ramada Hotel. 1150 S. Beverly Dr., Los Angeles, CA 90035 (213–553–6561 or 800–272–6232). North of Pico Blvd. near Beverly Hills shops and restaurants. Complimentary nearby fitness center. Moderately priced for the neighborhood.

Moderate

Best Western Hollywood. 6141 Franklin Ave. at Gower, Hollywood, CA 90028 (213–464–5181 or 800–528–1234). Centrally located 85-room hotel. Many rooms with kitchenettes. Near Universal Studios.

Beverly Terrace Motor Hotel. 469 N. Doheny Dr., Beverly Hills, CA 90210 (213–274–8141 or 800–421–7223). Near shopping, dining. Scully's restaurant on the premises. Tours arranged to most major attractions.

Figueroa Hotel. 939 S. Figueroa St., Los Angeles, CA 90015 (213–627–8971; 800–421–9092 nationwide; 800–331–5151 in state). Downtown area. Charming Spanish-style hotel dates from the 1920s, across the street from historic Variety Arts Theater, one block from Convention Center.

Sunset Plaza Hotel. 8400 Sunset Blvd., West Hollywood, CA 90069 (213–654–0750; 800–421–3652 nationwide; 800–252–0645 in state). In the heart of the Sunset Strip, a favorite with entertainment industry people. Some kitchens, suites.

Inexpensive

Milner Hotel. 813 S. Flower St., Los Angeles, CA 90017 (213–627–6981 or 800–521–0592). Downtown. Well-maintained, renovated building across the street from the Broadway Plaza, near Convention Center.

Sunset Dunes Motel. 5625 Sunset Blvd., Hollywood, CA 90028 (213–467–5171). Across the street from two TV stations, this hotel with 56 Spanish-style rooms is popular with studio folks. There is a restaurant and lounge.

Wilshire Royale Hotel. 2619 Wilshire Blvd., Los Angeles, CA 90057 (213–387–5311 or 800–421–8072). Mid-Wilshire district. Vintage 1920s hotel, updated with air conditioning. Pool, Jacuzzi.

YS AND HOSTELS. Hollywood YMCA and Youth Hostel. 1553 N. Hudson Ave., Hollywood (213–467–4161). Single and double rooms for both men and women, with shared bathrooms and showers. Single room, $29; doubles, $39. The youth hostel provides separate sleeping quarters for men and women. Blankets are available, but it is best to bring your own sleeping bag. Hostel rates are under $10 for members or non-members. The Y's pool, gym, exercise equipment are available to all.

Los Angeles International Youth Hostel. 3601 S. Gaffey, San Pedro (213–831–8109). Former Navy barracks overlooking Long Beach harbor, accessible by bus from L.A. International Airport. Rates under $10.

Mary Andrews Clarke Home YWCA. 306 Loma Dr., Los Angeles (213–483–5780). A revamped mansion with room for 138 women in single rooms with half baths. Breakfast and dinner included in the rate of about $30 for YWCA members, $35 for others. MC, V accepted.

RESTAURANTS. Not many years ago, wealthy entertainment celebrities would boast of flying to San Francisco just for dinner. No more. Los Angeles is now in the forefront of regional American cuisine. Its chefs have been leaders in the trend toward fresh ingredients, quickly prepared, imaginatively combined. Mexican, Southwestern, and Asian restaurants abound, along with bistros opened by chefs transplanted from France. Mild weather can make outdoor dining a pleasure year-round.

The distinction between restaurants and cafés can be vague in a city where movie executives dine on pizza and hot dogs. Many distinguished restaurants are located in Hollywood, West Hollywood, West Los Angeles, intermixed with trendy cafés along Melrose Ave. on the edge of Beverly Hills. Other cafés and reasonably priced restaurants are grouped in Westwood near the University of California at Los Angeles campus; at the Farmers Market, 3rd St. and Fairfax Ave.; in the flashy Beverly Center, 8500 Beverly Blvd.; and the Ports O'Call Village, San Pedro.

Dress is more casual than in comparable restaurants in other cities, but jackets are usually required for men in the more deluxe establishments. Ask when making reservations. Restaurants are listed according to the price of a three-course meal (drinks, tax, and tip not included). *Deluxe,* $50 and up; *Expensive,* $30–$50; *Moderate,* $15–$30; *Inexpensive,* under $15.

Deluxe

Adriano's Ristorante. 2930 Beverly Glen Circle, Los Angeles (475–9807). A sophisticated, distinctive Northern Italian restaurant, with homemade pastas, roast duck, rabbit, and veal dishes featured. L, Tues.–Fri.; D, Tues.–Sun.

Bernard's. In the Biltmore Hotel, 515 S. Olive St., Los Angeles (612–1580). Innovative, seasonal French menu, with an abundance of fresh seafood and vegetables. Extensive wine list. L, Mon.–Fri.; D, Mon.–Sat. AE, DC, MC, V.

Rex II Ristorante. 617 S. Olive St., Los Angeles (627–2300). New Italian cuisine, light and elegant, is served here in a historic art deco building remodeled to resemble the dining salon of the Italian luxury liner *Rex.* Reservations required. L, Tues.–Fri.; D, Mon.–Sat. AE, DC, MC, V.

Expensive

Pacific Dining Car. 1310 W. 6th St., Los Angeles (483–6000). Since 1921, prime Eastern beef, cut and aged in the restaurant's cooler, grilled over mesquite charcoal. Fresh seafood, veal, lamb. Extensive wine list. Open 24 hours daily. MC, V.

Ristorante Chianti. 7383 Melrose Ave., Los Angeles (653–8333). One of Southern California's oldest Italian restaurants, in a nostalgic setting of Tuscan murals, wooden booths. Tuscan specialties on the menu; risotto, linguine with clams, sauteed fish, chicken, veal. L, Mon.–Sat. D, daily. Next door is Chianti Cucina, less formal, with a moderately priced, innovative menu. AE, DC, MC, V.

Seventh Street Bistro. 811 W. 7th St., Los Angeles (627–1242). This bright, sophisticated restaurant is on the ground floor of a landmark office building downtown. The cuisine is nouvelle French-Californian. L, Mon.–Fri.; D, daily. AE, DC, MC, V.

Spago. 1114 Horn Ave., West Hollywood (652–4025). Wolfgang Puck's trend-setting California menu includes innovative pasta, fresh fish and shellfish, unusual pizzas. Very popular, reserve in advance. D, daily. AE, DC, MC, V.

West Beach Cafe. 60 N. Venice Blvd., Venice (823–5396). This upscale restaurant near the beach features notable hamburgers as well as pasta, grilled meats, splendid salads. Reservations advised. L, D, daily. AE, DC, MC, V.

Moderate

Dar Maghreb. 7651 Sunset Blvd., Los Angeles (876–7651). A posh Moroccan restaurant with authentic service and cuisine: chicken, lamb, rabbit, pigeon. Moderate to expensive. D, daily. MC, V.

Harry's Bar & American Grill. 2020 Avenue of the Stars (277–2333), below the Shubert Theater. This take-off on Harry's Bar in Venice is the ideal place for pre- or aprés-theater suppers. Pasta dishes are best bets. L, Mon.–Sat.; D, daily. AE, DC, MC, V.

Lawry's California Center. 570 W. Ave. 26, Los Angeles (225–2491). Outdoor dining in lush gardens, May–Oct. only. Broiled steak, fresh fish, smoked chicken; hot herbal bread. L, daily; D, Tues.–Sun., May–Oct. Reservations accepted for six or more. AE, MC, V at dinner only.

Inexpensive

El Cholo. 1121 S. Western Ave., Los Angeles (734–2773). Opened in the 1920s, this Mexican restaurant is a family favorite, with an extensive menu and large portions. L, D, daily. AE, MC, V.

The Hard Rock Café. 8600 Beverly Blvd., West Hollywood (276–7605). A loud, lively celebration of the 1950s, rock and roll, as well as hamburgers, milk shakes, apple pie. L, D, daily. All major credit cards.

The Original Pantry. 877 S. Figueroa St., Los Angeles (972–9279). Simple fare, large portions, a favorite downtown café since the 1930s. B, L, D, daily; open 24 hours. No credit cards.

Philippe's Original Sandwich Shop. 1001 N. Alameda St., Los Angeles (628–3781). "Home of the French dipped sandwich" made of roast beef, plus stew, soup, salad, chili. Cafeteria-style, communal tables. B, L, D, daily. No credit cards.

NIGHTLIFE AND BARS. Evening attractions are as scattered as the daytime points of interest. Except for private clubs, few continue through the night. Trendy cafés maintain their appeal into the evening, especially along Melrose Ave. For listings of specific pop, jazz, and rock performances, check the *Los Angeles Times* Sunday Calendar section and the free guides distributed to hotels.

Downtown possibilities include **Vertigo,** 1024 S. Grand Ave. (747–4849) for dancing; the revolving rooftop lounges with quiet music at the **Bonaventure Hotel,** 5th and Figueroa Sts. (624–1000), and the **Hyatt Regency,** 711 S. Hope St. (683–1234).

Westwood is full of late-night cafés and nightspots popular with UCLA students. In West Los Angeles, **Chippendale's,** 3739 Overland Ave. (396–4045) offers disco and muscular male strippers.

Hollywood street life can be sleazy late at night, but established attractions include: the **Cinegrill** cabaret in the Hollywood Roosevelt Hotel, 7000 Hollywood Blvd. (466–7000); **Vine St. Bar & Grill,** 1610 Vine (463–4375), big-name jazz performers; **The Comedy Store,** 8433 Sunset Blvd. in West Los Angeles (656–6225), the major showcase.

Country-western music lovers will enjoy **The Palomino,** 6907 Lankershim, North Hollywood (818–764–4010). Different groups play each night for occasionally rowdy, get-down audiences.

On the Sunset Strip, running from West Hollywood to Beverly Hills, is a colorful assortment of rock and comedy clubs, plus popular bars: The **Mondrian Hotel,** 9440 Sunset Blvd. (650–8999) has a lively piano bar and attracts many in the music business; **Gazzari's,** 9039 Sunset Blvd. (273–6606), is a casual rock-and-roll landmark.

PRACTICAL INFORMATION FOR THE SOUTHERN CALIFORNIA COAST

FROM LONG BEACH TO SAN DIEGO

HOW TO GET THERE. By plane. The major airports, served by regional and some national airlines, are in Long Beach, Orange County (Santa Ana) and San Diego.

By train. From Los Angeles, *Amtrak* trains reach stations in San Juan Capistrano (southeast of Laguna Beach), Del Mar, Oceanside, San Diego.

By bus. *Greyhound* buses serve most coastal cities.

By car. I-5 is the major highway route from the north; Los Angeles to San Diego is about a 2½-hour drive. From Los Angeles, the San Diego Frwy. (I-405) is the fastest route to the coastal cities. The Pacific Coast Hwy. (State Rte. 1) is the most scenic route, but slow during peak vacation periods.

TOURIST INFORMATION. A visitors guide including major attractions and accommodations in Los Angeles and Orange counties is distributed by the *Long Beach Area Convention and Visitors Council,* 180 E. Ocean Blvd., Suite 150, Plaza Level, Long Beach, CA 90802. That office is in Crocker Plaza (213–436–3645). The *Newport Beach Conference and Visitors Bureau* has information on the Orange County coast: 3700 Newport Blvd., Suite 107, Newport Beach, CA 92663 (714–644–1190). *Laguna Beach Chamber of Commerce,* Box 396, Laguna Beach, CA 92652. The *San Diego Convention & Visitors Bureau* publishes a variety of brochures, especially on sports and recreation: 1200 Third Ave., Suite 824, San Diego, CA 92101. In San Diego there is also an International Visitor Information Center (619–236–1212) at 11 Horton Plaza downtown, and a Mission Bay information center, just off I-5 at the Mission Bay side of the Clairemont Dr. exit. For information on the historic beach resort of Coronado in San Diego Bay, contact *Coronado Chamber of Commerce,* 720 Orange Ave., Coronado, CA 92118 (619–435–9260).

TELEPHONES AND EMERGENCY NUMBERS. The area code for San Diego County is 619. The San Diego number for *all* emergencies is 911. But an emergency must be a *real* one. For lesser problems in San Diego City: *Fire Department* (238–1212), *Police* (236–6566), *Paramedics* (238–1212).

SPECIAL-INTEREST SIGHTSEEING. Long Beach: *The Queen Mary.* This luxurious passenger liner features Art Deco public rooms, World War II memorabilia from its troop-ship era, and a "Time Voyager" film show. *Spruce Goose.* Pilot, aviation developer, movie producer, and billionaire Howard Hughes planned this all-wood, 200-ton flying boat to help win World War II. It flew only once, in 1947. Both the Spruce Goose and Queen Mary are in Long Beach harbor at the end of the Long Beach Frwy. Open 10 A.M.–6 P.M.; 9 A.M.–9 P.M. from late June–early Sept. Combination admission, adults, $17.50; children 5–11, $9.50. Call 213–435–3511 for information.

San Diego: The best way to see the 17-mi.-long harbor is on a one-hour or two-hour cruise by *San Diego Harbor Excursions* (619–234–4111) or the 1905 sailing yacht *Invader* (619–234–8687). Broadway Pier on Harbor Dr. is the boarding point; ticket prices start at $8. *Maritime Museum.* 1306 N. Harbor Dr. (619–234–9153). An 1863 sailing ship, a San Francisco ferry, and 1904 steam yacht make up this collection. Open 9 A.M.–8 P.M. Families, $10; adults, $5; seniors, $4; children, $1.25.

Coronado: A winter resort for the wealthy at the end of the 19th century, this community is still dominated by the 1888 Victorian Hotel del Coronado, 1500 Orange Ave. It's as much a museum as hotel. The gift shop provides a brochure for self-guided tours of 86 nearby homes and historic sites. Located on a peninsula between San Diego Bay and the Pacific Ocean, across a toll bridge.

PARKS AND GARDENS. Balboa Park. Call 619–239–0512 for information. Established in 1868, this 1,074-acre park just north of San Diego's downtown is the city's recreation and cultural center. Impressive buildings remain from two world fairs: the 1915 Panama–California Exposition, which launched the state's Spanish Revival architecture boom; and the 1935 California–Pacific Exposition. Lush landscaping and a botanical garden make it ideal for strolling in San Diego's mild weather. The park's attractions can easily fill a day and evening. Among them are: the San Diego Zoo; Spanish Village, arts and crafts center; House of Pacific Relations, ethnic displays; Old Globe Shakespeare theater; and museums of art, photography, natural history, and sports. The Reuben H. Fleet Space Theater (619–238–1168) creates the sensation of flight; it is open daily from 10 A.M.

ZOOS. San Diego Zoo. A 100-acre tropical garden in Balboa Park that exhibits 3,200 animals of 800 species, many of them rare and endangered. Most are not caged, but separated from the public only by moats. There is a 40-minute guided, double-deck bus tour and an aerial tramway. A Children's Zoo allows petting the more gentle creatures, and a visit to a primate nursery. Open 9 A.M.–4 P.M. Nov.–Feb.; to 5 P.M. Mar.–Oct. Adults, $10.75; children 3–15, $4. Call 619–234–3153 for information.

San Diego Wild Animal Park. 15500 San Pasqual Valley Rd., Escondido, 30 mi. north of San Diego on I-15 (619–234–6541). A 1,800-acre wildlife preserve that allows more than 2,200 animals to roam free. Includes an Australian rain forest, Nairobi Village, gorilla grotto, walk-through aviary. Open daily, 9 A.M.–dusk, later in summer. Adults, $14.50; children, 3–15, $7.50.

Sea World. 1720 S. Shores Rd. (619–226–3901). This is a 125-acre "oceanarium" on San Diego's Mission Bay, with five different sea animal shows, marine life exhibits, penguins and an Antarctic environment. Scenic rides, children's play area. Open 9 A.M.–dusk. Adults, $21.95; children 3–11, $15.95.

BEACHES. This section of Southern California is synonymous with beaches, and a complete listing would fill a guidebook. Here are some of the exceptional ones, from north to south. **Long Beach:** nearly six mi. of beach along Ocean Blvd. just east of downtown. **Huntington Beach:** a favorite for surfing, with surfers visible from the city's long pier. **Corona del Mar–San Clemente State Beaches:** particularly scenic. **San Diego** area beaches: lifeguards year round at La Jolla Shores, South Pacific Beach, New Mission Beach, Ocean Beach, Silver Strand State Beach. For San Diego beach and weather information, call 619–221–8884.

HISTORIC SITES AND HOUSES. Old Missions. *San Juan Capistrano* (714–493–1424) in Orange County includes three churches, one in ruins, where the swallows return every Mar. 19, St. Joseph's Day, and leave Oct. 23. *San Luis Rey* (619–757–3651), near Oceanside, is the largest and richest of the missions. *San Diego de Alcala,* 10818 San Diego Mission Rd., San Diego (619–281–8449) was Father Junipero Serra's first mission, founded in 1769.

Long Beach. Two restored adobe ranch houses recall California's Spanish era. *Rancho Los Cerritos,* 4600 Virginia Rd. (213–424–9423), is now surrounded by a golf course. *Rancho Los Alamitos,* 6400 Bixby Hill Rd. (213–431–3541), south of the city, includes a blacksmith shop, extensive gardens.

San Diego. *Cabrillo National Monument,* overlooking the harbor at the south end of Cabrillo Memorial Dr., marks Spanish explorer Juan Rodriguez Cabrillo's landing in 1542. It also overlooks the Pacific migration of the gray whales, late Dec. through Feb. *Old Town and Presidio Park,* 2645 San Diego Ave. (619–237–6770), is the 12-acre site of California's first European settlement. The first Spanish fort and mission were built on the hill. Restored adobe buildings below it now house galleries, restaurants, shops. Cars are off-limits in Old Town. Park rangers lead free walking tours.

STAGE. The Old Globe Theatre in Balboa Park, established for the 1935 world's fair, is one of the West Coast's leading theater companies. There are three theaters. The indoor Old Globe and Cassius Carter Centre Stage offer year-round classics and contemporary plays; the outdoor Festival Theatre is the site of the summer Shakespeare. Tickets are moderately priced, but can be scarce during peak summer periods. For a schedule, write Box 2171, San Diego, CA 92112. For ticket information, call 619–239–2255.

ACCOMMODATIONS. This stretch of the Pacific Coast attracts vacationing Southern Californians as well as long-distance visitors; accommodations are extensive, with a wide range of prices. The most scenic, comfortable, beachfront hotels and motels are in demand, and rooms should always be reserved in advance. There are plenty of other accommodations, older and moderately priced, in such cities as Long Beach, and inland San Diego. Price categories for a double room: *Deluxe,* $140 and up; *Expensive,* $90–$140; *Moderate,* $60–$90.

Laguna Beach. Hotel San Maarten. *Deluxe.* 696 S. Coast Hwy., Laguna Beach, CA 92651 (714–494–9436; 800–772–2539 nationwide; 800–228–5691 in state). Garden atrium, surrounding rooms decorated with antiques. Weekday and off-season discounts.

Hotel Laguna. *Expensive.* 425 South Coast Blvd., Laguna Beach, CA 92651 (714–494–1151). Directly on the beach, midtown, with 70 refurbished rooms. Garden and restaurant.

Long Beach. Hyatt Regency. *Deluxe.* 200 S. Pine Ave., Long Beach, CA 90802 (213–491–1234 or 800–228–9000). Contemporary chic with atrium lobby, lagoon, pool. All 531 rooms overlook the harbor.

Ramada Renaissance Hotel. *Deluxe.* 111 E. Ocean Blvd., Long Beach, CA 90802 (213–437–5900 or 800–228–9898). This 374-room hotel with restaurants, lounges, and health club downtown, is located within walking distance of the water taxi to the *Queen Mary.* Outdoor pool.

Queen Mary Hotel. *Expensive.* Pier J, Long Beach, CA 90801 (213–435–3511 or 800–421–3732). Art Deco staterooms on the moored ocean liner have been updated with air conditioning, color TV. Reserve an outside room for the view; it's a magical, nostalgic experience.

Ramada Inn. *Moderate.* 5325 E. Pacific Coast Hwy., Long Beach, CA 90804 (213–597–1341 or 800–228–2828). Five mi. east of downtown, across the street from golf course and tennis courts.

Vagabond Inn. *Moderate.* 185 Atlantic Ave., Long Beach, CA 90802 (213–435–3791; 800–522–1555 nationwide; 800–468–2251 in state). Recently remodeled, downtown, three blocks from beaches. Courtesy coffee, fresh fruit, morning newspaper. Pool.

San Diego. Hotel del Coronado. *Deluxe.* 1500 Orange Ave., Coronado, CA 92118 (619–522–8000). One of the country's last grand beach resorts from the Victorian era and a favorite movie location ("Some Like It Hot.") The original building is less expensive, and more charming, than the new high-rise addition.

Andrea Villa Inn. *Expensive.* 2402 Torrey Pines Rd., La Jolla, CA 92037 (619–459–3311 or 800–367–6467). Moderately priced for exclusive La Jolla, with swimming pool, restaurant. Accepts pets.

Balboa Park Inn. *Moderate–Expensive.* 3402 Park Blvd., San Diego, CA 94103 (619–298–0823). A European-style bed-and-breakfast inn, with suites in four buildings connected by courtyards. Across the street from Balboa Park and Zoo.

Pacific Shores Inn. *Moderate.* 4802 Mission Blvd., San Diego, CA 92109 (619–483–6300 or 800–367–6467). Many units with kitchens; weekly rates in winter. Pacific Beach area.

RESTAURANTS. Dining is usually casual and informal along the coast, with jackets required for men only at the more deluxe restaurants. Note that San Diego is not a late-night city; many restaurants serve only until 9 or 10 P.M. Price range for a three-course meal, not including beverages, tax or tip: *Expensive,* $25 and up, *Moderate,* $15–$25; *Inexpensive,* around $10.

Laguna Beach. Las Brisas. *Expensive.* 361 Cliff Dr. off the Coast Hwy. (714–497–5434). Spectacular location overlooking the beach, ocean, and much of the town. Mexican-style seafood. Both dressy and casual attire. L, D, daily; brunch Sun. All major credit cards.

The White House. *Moderate* 340 S. Coast Hwy. (714–494–8089). A local favorite, recently redecorated, including salads, sandwiches, crepes, pasta. B, L, D, daily. All major credit cards.

Long Beach. Pine Avenue Fish House. *Moderate.* 100 West Broadway (213–432–7464). This restaurant specializes in preparing a variety of fish 10 different ways. Oyster bar. L, D, daily. Brunch, Sat., Sun. All major credit cards.

Simon and Seafort's Fish, Chop and Oyster House. *Moderate.* 340 Golden Shore (213–435–2333). Naturally aged beef, fresh salmon, oysters from the Pacific Northwest. Overlooking the launch at Catalina Landing. L, D, daily; brunch Sun.

San Diego. Anthony's Star of the Sea Room. *Expensive.* 1360 N. Harbor Dr. (619–232–7408). This long-established, gourmet restaurant specializes in fish and seafood dishes and elegant service, plus a terrific harbor view. Dress code enforced, reservations necessary. D, daily. All major credit cards.

Cafe Pacifica. *Moderate.* 2414 San Diego Ave., Old Town (619–291–6666). Fresh fish, prepared simply, in a stylish restaurant with a patio. L, Mon.–Fri.; D, daily. AE, DC, MC, V.

Crown Room, Hotel del Coronado. *Moderate.* 1500 Orange Ave., Coronado (619–435–6611). Magnificent main dining room of the Victorian-era hotel. Traditional American food, inexpensive early dinner. L, D, daily; brunch Sun. All major credit cards.

Harbor House. *Moderate.* Seaport Village, Pacific Hwy. at Harbor Dr. (619–232–1141). Fresh fish is the specialty of this beautiful restaurant. Simply prepared dishes are recommended. L, D, daily; brunch Sun. All major credit cards.

Papagayo. *Moderate.* Seaport Village, Pacific Hwy. at Harbor Dr. (619–232–7581). Mexican-style seafood in an elegant dining room, harbor view. L, D, daily; brunch Sun. All major credit cards.

Old Town Mexican Cafe. *Inexpensive.* 2489 San Diego Ave., Old Town (619–297–4330). Carnitas (roast meat) is the specialty; empanadas and burritos are also very good. The bar can be noisy and crowded. L, D, daily until 11 P.M. AE, MC, V.

PRACTICAL INFORMATION FOR THE CENTRAL CALIFORNIA COAST

FROM MONTEREY TO SANTA BARBARA

HOW TO GET THERE. A car is the practical way to see the coastline. State Hwy. 1 is for much of its route a two-lane road that hugs the steep cliffs. Views in summer can be obscured by morning fog. The drive from San Francisco to Los Angeles on this route takes 11–12 hours. San Simeon is at the mid-point. Inland, U.S. Hwy. 101 is a freeway at least four lanes wide; driving time from San Francisco to Los Angeles is eight hours. State Rte. 46 provides access from Hwy. 101 to the coast near San Simeon. Santa Barbara can be visited easily on a day trip from Los Angeles, and Monterey–Carmel from San Francisco. Tour agencies provide overnight excursions from Los Angeles or San Francisco to San Simeon.

TOURIST INFORMATION. *Monterey Peninsula Visitors and Convention Bureau,* Box 1770, Monterey, CA 93942, is at 380 Alvarado St.; (408) 649–1770.

TELEPHONES. Telephone area codes in the central-coast region are 408 for Santa Cruz, Monterey, Carmel, and Big Sur areas and 805 for the San Luis Obispo, Morro Bay, and San Simeon area.

TOURS AND SPECIAL-INTEREST SIGHTSEEING. Carmel. Art galleries, antique stores and shops featuring British imports line Ocean Ave. and side streets of this picturesque town. Just off Ocean Ave. is one of the gates to 17-Mile Drive, a scenic toll road noted for dramatic ocean views, old mansions, and contemporary architecture. *Carmel Mission,* 3080 Rio Rd. 1 mi. south of town, is the burial place of Father Junipero Serra, the Franciscan founder of California's missions.

Salinas. The Victorian home where novelist John Steinbeck was born, 132 Central Ave., is now a luncheon restaurant, open Mon.–Fri., operated by the volunteer Valley Guild (408–424–2735). A gift shop features many of his books. Steinbeck's manuscripts, photographs, and signed editions of *East of Eden* and other novels are displayed at the Steinbeck Library, 110 W. San Luis St. (408–758–7311).

San Simeon State Historical Monument (Hearst Castle). Open for tours daily except Thanksgiving, Christmas, and New Year's Day. There are four tours: an introduction to the castle and gardens, a second and third covering more of the interior, a fourth exploring more gardens. The two-hour walking tours leave at least every hour from 8:20 A.M. to 3 P.M. in winter, more often during holidays and in summer. Reservations are essential. Tickets are $12 for adults, $6 for children 6–12. They may be purchased at any Mistix outlet in the state, listed in local telephone book white pages. If your visit is at least a month away, you can reserve by mail. For information, call toll-free within Calif. 800–446–7275. Tours involve walking at least ½ mi. and climbing 115 steps. For handicapped tour arrangements, telephone the castle directly at 805–927–2020. Information on Hearst Castle and nearby attractions and accommodations is available from the *San Simeon Chamber of Commerce,* Box 1, San Simeon, CA 93452 (805–927–3500).

Santa Barbara. The downtown *Red Tile Tour* is a self-guided walk through the Presidio founded in 1782, 19th-century adobes, and the Spanish-style public buildings of the 1920s. A well-marked scenic drive covers more history, plus the wharf, botanical gardens, bird refuge. Maps available at the *Santa Barbara Conference & Visitors Bureau,* 1330 State St. For more information on this scenic, relaxing community, contact the bureau, 222 E. Anapamu St., Santa Barbara, CA 93101 (805–966–9222).

AQUARIUM. Located on historic Cannery Row, the $40 million **Monterey Bay Aquarium** re-creates the bay's undersea habitats, including a towering kelp forest. It contains more than 5,500 marine creatures and includes sharks and large ocean fish seldom seen in most aquariums. Open daily 10 A.M.–6 P.M. Tickets $8 for adults, $5.75 students and seniors, $3.50 children 3–12. It is wise to buy tickets in advance, especially during summer and school holidays; check telephone directory white pages for Ticketron agencies. For Aquarium information, call 408–648–4888.

STATE PARKS. Pfeiffer Big Sur State Park. Big Sur, on State Hwy. 1, 26 mi. south of Carmel (408–667–2315). Visitors can picnic, swim, fish, hike in this park that includes the southernmost stand of California redwoods. The 850-acre park includes campsites, and Big Sur Lodge rents motel-type cabins. This is the best known of the many state beaches, some with campsites, located along Monterey Bay and at San Simeon, Morro Bay, Pismo Beach, and Santa Barbara.

HISTORIC SITES AND HOUSES. Monterey State Historic Park. This group of eight 19th-century buildings, including the Customs House and California's first theater, played an important role in the state's early history. Park headquarters is at 210 Oliver St. (408–649–2836). Buildings are open and staffed with guides daily except Thanksgiving and Christmas. Nearby is the 1602 landing site of explorer Sebastian Vizcaino. More information is available from the *Monterey Peninsula Chamber of Commerce,* 380 Alvarado St., Monterey, CA 93940 (408–649–1770).

San Juan Bautista State Historic Park. In the center of this quiet town just off U.S. Hwy. 101 are the Mission, landscaped plaza, restored homes, and a stage stop hotel. Nearby, a Portuguese bakery is popular with residents and visitors. The park is open daily except Thanksgiving, Christmas, and New Year's Day.

San Luis Obispo. Mission San Luis Obispo de Tolosa, Chorro and Monterey Sts., was named for a 13th-century French saint. This Mission Plaza remains an oasis for travelers, with a wooded creek and walking trails.

MUSIC FESTIVALS. The **Carmel Bach Festival,** July–Aug. The main events are held at the Sunset Center, 8th and San Carlos Sts., in Carmel, but there is at least one candlelight evening concert at the Carmel Mission. There are also a number of special events, such as lectures and recitals. For information, contact *Carmel Bach Festival,* Box 575, Carmel, CA 93921 (408–624–1521).

The **Monterey Jazz Festival,** in Sept., in the 7,000-seat arena at the Monterey County Fairgrounds, features nationally and internationally famous jazz musicians. Within the 24 acres of parklike grounds are many sites for picnicking, and there are refreshment concessions and a playground. The Festival Committee has always emphasized a "bring the family" ambience.

Tickets go on sale in Apr. For information, write to the Festival box office at 444 Pearl St., Monterey, or call (408–373–3366).

The nationally famous **Cabrillo Music Festival** (music director, Dennis Russell Davies) has outgrown its campus setting. Most of the concerts are now presented in a 1,000-seat tent in the Aptos area, near Santa Cruz. Some are scheduled for the Santa Cruz Mission green. The concerts include orchestral works by composers such as Schubert, J.S. Bach, Bartok, and Mendelssohn. There are also master classes and special children's programs. There are two special Festival Days planned in conjunction with the local community, held at the Plaza Park and the greens at the 200-year-old Mission San Juan Bautista in the afternoons with picnicking. For information contact *Cabrillo Community Education Office,* Cabrillo College, 6500 Soquel Dr., Aptos, CA 95003 (408–662–2701).

STAGE. The **Solvang Theatrefest** offers five plays in rotating repertory, performed evenings June–Sept. in the outdoor festival theater. Professional actors from the West's regional theaters take leading roles, augmented by advanced students from nearby Pacific Conservatory of the Performing Arts. For advance information write Box 1389, Santa Maria, CA 93456 (805–922–8313).

ACCOMMODATIONS. The widest variety of hotels, motels, and inns are in Santa Barbara, San Luis Obispo, the San Simeon–Cambria area, Monterey, and Carmel. Reservations are essential in San Simeon during the summer; motels often have package rates that include Hearst Castle tours. Santa Barbara maintains a central reservation service; telephone 805–963–9518. Other sources are *Megan's Friends Bed and Breakfast Reservations,* 1776 Royal Way, San Luis Obispo, CA 93405 (805–544–4406); and the *Bed and Breakfast Innkeepers of Santa Barbara,* Box 20246, Santa Barbara, CA 93120. Approximate rates for double occupancy: *Deluxe,* $150 and up; *Expensive,* $90–$140; *Moderate,* $60–$90.

Big Sur. Ventana Inn. *Deluxe.* Big Sur, CA 93920 (408–667–2331 or 800–628–6500). Fabled, rustic, hilltop lodge overlooking the ocean, 28 mi. south of Carmel. Two-day minimum stay on weekends.

Cambria. Cambria Pines Lodge. *Moderate.* 2905 Burton Dr., Cambria, CA 93428 (805–927–4200). Sixty rustic cabins on tree-shaded grounds, 9 mi. south of San Simeon. Indoor pool, restaurant.

Carmel. Highlands Inn. *Deluxe.* Box 1700, Carmel, CA 93921 (408–624–3801; 800–538–9525 nationwide; 800–682–4811 in state). World-class resort with suites, views, fireplaces, recently renovated.

Pine Inn. *Expensive.* Ocean Ave., Box 250, Carmel, CA 93921 (408–624–3851 or 800–228–3851). Victorian charm, red carpets, flocked wallpaper, cozy bar. A local landmark.

Monterey. Casa Munras. *Expensive.* 700 Munras Ave., Monterey, CA 93940 (408–375–2411 or 800–222–2558 nationwide; 800–222–2446 in state). Garden hotel, spacious grounds, close to downtown.

Monterey Beach Hotel. *Expensive.* 2600 Sand Dune Dr., Monterey, CA 93940 (408–394–3321 or 800–242–8627). Directly on the beach, 5 mi. north of downtown. Tastefully decorated rooms, lobby with fireplace, restaurant.

San Luis Obispo. Madonna Inn. *Expensive.* 100 Madonna Rd., San Luis Obispo, CA 93401 (805–543–3000 or 800–543–9666). A sprawling pink landmark (even the fireplugs are painted pink), with each of the 112 rooms decorated with a dramatic theme, from jungle to cave to mountain waterfall. At least stop and buy a postcard. The bar has an electrically operated swing occupied by a woman made of crepe paper.

Campus Motel. *Moderate.* 404 Santa Rosa St., San Luis Obispo, CA 93401 (805–544–0881). At the junction of State Hwy. 1 and U.S. 101. Grassy play area for children. Pool.

San Simeon. El Rey Inn. *Moderate.* 9260 Castill Dr., San Simeon, CA 93452 (805–927–3998 or 800–322–8029). Three mi. south of town on Hwy. 1, two blocks from beach. Package rates include Hearst Castle tour.

Santa Barbara. Glenborough Inn. *Moderate to Expensive.* 1327 Bath St., Santa Barbara, CA 93101 (805–966–0589). Two neighboring homes, built in the 1880s and 1906, in quiet residential area. Complimentary breakfast.

Miramar Hotel. *Moderate to Expensive.* 1555 S. Jameson La., Santa Barbara, CA 93102 (805–969–2203; 800–322–6983 in state). Tranquil resort hotel in subtropical gardens, on the beach 5 mi. south of downtown.

Solvang. Chimney Sweep Inn. *Moderate.* 1554 Copenhagen Dr., Solvang, CA 93463 (805–688–2111 or 800–824–6444). Quaint retreat, attractive garden, senior discount.

RESTAURANTS. Seafood is the specialty, of course, at the notable coastside restaurants, and reservations are recommended at popular establishments with their views of sunsets over the ocean. Santa Barbara and Monterey–Carmel offer the widest variety of cuisines, from classic French to casual Mexican. Price categories for dinners, not including drinks, tax or tip are: *Expensive,* $25 and up; *Moderate,* $15–$25; *Inexpensive,* under $15.

Big Sur. Ventana Inn. *Expensive.* Hwy. 1, 28 mi. south of Carmel (408–624–4812). Wholesome food, prepared with care at this rustic retreat. Ocean view. L, D, daily. All major credit cards.

Nepenthe. *Moderate.* Hwy. 1, 3 mi. south of Big Sur (408–667–2345). Simple, well-prepared chicken, steaks, vegetarian specialties. Fireplace and spectacular ocean view. L, D, daily.

Cambria. The Brambles Dinner House. *Inexpensive.* 4005 Burton Dr., Cambria (805–927–4716). Seafood, roast beef in a charming English cottage setting. Nine mi. south of San Simeon. D, daily. Inexpensive to moderate prices. All major credit cards.

Carmel. Casanova Restaurant. *Expensive.* Fifth St. between San Carlos and Mission (408–625–0501). European country cuisine in a romantic setting. Garden. B, L, D, daily.

Monterey. The Whaler. *Moderate to Expensive.* 635 Cass St. (408–373–1933) Rustic decor; seafood as well as beef specialties. A good value. L, Mon.–Fri.; D, daily. AE, DC, MC, V.

The Clock Garden. *Moderate.* 565 Abrego St. (408–375–6100). Charming, intimate restaurant in Old Monterey. Varied menu. L, D, daily; brunch Sun. MC, V.

San Luis Obispo. The Apple Farm. *Moderate.* 2015 Monterey St. (805–544–6100). "Homemade food served with country charm" is the slogan of this family favorite. Pot roasts, soup, freshly baked breads. B, L, D, daily. MC, V.

Santa Barbara. Casa de Seville. *Moderate.* 428 Chapala St. (805–966–4370). Seafood, steaks, chops as well as Spanish specialties. L, D, Tues.–Sat. Jackets required for men. AE, CB, MC, V.

The Harbor. *Moderate.* 210 Stearns Wharf at the foot of State St. (805–963–3311). Fresh seafood, pasta, oyster bar. Ocean view. B, L, D, daily. All major credit cards.

PRACTICAL INFORMATION FOR SAN FRANCISCO

WHEN TO GO. A day's weather cycle in San Francisco can be unpredictable, but generally the climate is mild, cool and temperate. Daytime temperatures in the summer usually range from 60 to 70 degrees. In the winter, daytime temperatures are usually in the mid-50s, nighttime lows in the mid-40s. Summer fog is routine mornings and evenings, but it usually clears in the afternoon. When sightseeing, always pack or carry a sweater or jacket, no matter how warm the day may appear at first.

HOW TO GET THERE. By plane. *San Francisco International Airport,* 15 mi. south of the city, is served by 34 major airlines. More airlines, particularly budget and charter carriers, serve *Oakland International Airport,* 10 miles east on the opposite side of San Francisco Bay. All transcontinental and most trans-Pacific airlines arrive at San Francisco International.

By bus. *Greyhound* offers regular service to San Francisco.

By car. There are only a few major routes into the city, which is located at the northern tip of the San Francisco Peninsula. The Golden Gate Bridge carries traffic into the city from U.S. 101 from the north. The major route from the east is Interstate 80 across the San Francisco–Oakland Bay Bridge. Major routes from the south are U.S. 101 and the more scenic Interstate 280.

By train. *Amtrak* service from Chicago, Seattle, and Los Angeles terminates in Oakland at the 16th and Wood street station. Shuttle buses transport passengers to the Transbay Terminal, First and Mission Sts. For fare and schedule information, telephone, toll-free, 800–USA–RAIL.

TOURIST INFORMATION. The *San Francisco Convention & Visitors Bureau* publishes a comprehensive quarterly guide, the "San Francisco Book." It is available in advance from the bureau at 201 Third St., San Francisco, CA 94105. The bureau's Visitor Information center is on the lower level Hallidie Plaza, Market and Powell Sts., open weekdays 9 A.M.–5 P.M.; Sat. 9 A.M.–3 P.M.; Sun. 10 A.M.–2 P.M. Call 974–6900 for information; recorded message about daily events, 391–2001.

TELEPHONES. The area code for San Francisco, and for Marin County, Oakland, Berkeley, and the San Francisco Peninsula as far south as Palo Alto as well, is 415. Oakland, Berkeley, and other cities on the east side of San Francisco Bay switch to area code 510 in October 1991. For operator assistance on person-to-person, collect, and credit card calls, dial 0 first, then the number. Pay phones cost 20 cents. The number for directory assistance is 411.

EMERGENCY TELEPHONE NUMBERS. In San Francisco and most nearby communities, dial 911 for police, fire, ambulance, and paramedics. To report highway emergencies to the *California Highway Patrol* from all areas, dial 0 and ask operator for Zenith 1–2000. *Bay Area Poison Control Center* is 476–6600. *San Francisco police,* nonemergency, is 553–0123. For cars that have been towed from city streets, call 553–1235.

HOW TO GET AROUND. From the airport. Cab fare from *San Francisco International Airport* to downtown is about $25 plus tip. *Airporter buses* (495–8404) depart from the street level of the airport terminals, from 6:15 A.M. to 3:30 A.M. Destinations are downtown hotels including the St. Francis, Hilton, Hyatt Union Square, and Parc Fifty-Five. Fare, $6. Van service between the airport and locations anywhere in San Francisco is provided by the *Supershuttle* (558–8500), *Yellow Cab* (626–2345); and *Good Neighbor Shuttle* (777–4899). Fare is about $9. Call for reservations a day before departure from the city. *Oakland International Airport* is served

Points of Interest

1) Alcoa Building
2) Balclutha
3) Bank of America
4) Cannery
5) City Hall
6) Civic Center
7) Coit Tower
8) Curran Theater
9) Embarcadero Center
10) Ferry Building
11) Fisherman's Wharf
12) Flood Building
13) Geary Theater
14) George R. Moscone Convention Center
15) Golden Gateway Center
16) Grace Cathedral
17) Hilton Hotel
18) Hyatt Regency Hotel
19) Hyde Street Pier
20) Lotta's Fountain
21) Maritime Museum
22) Municipal Pier
23) Museum of Modern Art
24) Old U.S. Mint
25) Opera House
26) Pier 39
27) St. Mary's Cathedral
28) St. Patrick's Church
29) Stock Exchange
30) Transamerica Pyramid
31) Victorian Park/Aquatic Park
32) Visitor Information Center

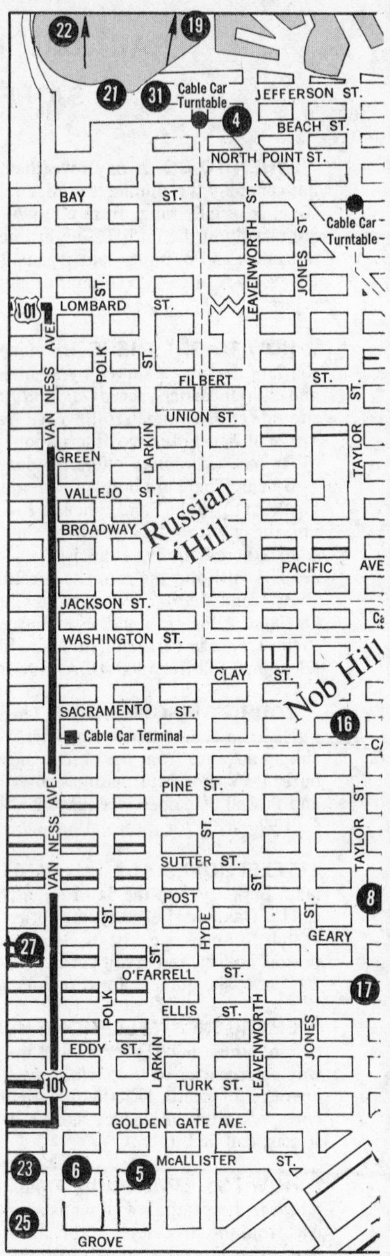

Downtown
San Francisco
SAN FRANCISCO
BAY
N
W
E
S
BAY ST.
FRANCISCO ST.
CHESTNUT ST.
LOMBARD ST.
GREENWICH ST.
UNION ST.
GREEN ST.
VALLEJO ST.
BROADWAY
JACKSON ST.
CLAY ST.
SACRAMENTO ST.
CALIFORNIA ST.
BUSH ST.
MARKET
MISSION ST.
HOWARD ST.
FOLSOM ST.
HARRISON ST.
STOCKTON ST.
POWELL ST.
MASON ST.
COLUMBUS AVE.
KEARNY ST.
GRANT AVE.
MONTGOMERY
NEW MONTGOMERY ST.
SANSOME ST.
BATTERY ST.
FRONT
DAVIS ST.
DRUMM
MAIN ST.
BEALE ST.
FREMONT ST.
1ST ST.
2ND ST.
3RD ST.
4TH ST.
5TH ST.
THE EMBARCADERO
North Beach
Telegraph Hill
Washington Square
Jackson Square
Chinatown
Cable Car Barn
Cable Car Terminal
Standard Oil Plaza
Union Square
Cable Car Turntable
EMBARCADERO FREEWAY
480
80
SAN FRANCISCO-OAKLAND BAY BRIDGE
11
2
26
7
10
15
30
1
9
18
3
29
13
20
28
12
32
24
14

by *Bay Area Rapid Transit (BART)* and a shuttle-bus connection. There are also daytime buses to downtown Oakland and San Francisco.

By bus. The *San Francisco Municipal Railway* (673–MUNI) is one of the nation's most extensive transit systems. Diesel and electric trolley buses serve most routes, along with the newer *Muni Metro* system of streetcars that run underground downtown. Fare is 85 cents for adults 18–64; 15 cents for seniors; 25 cents for youngsters 5–17. Transfers are free. Exact change is necessary.

By cable car. Two lines begin at Market and Powell Sts., the *Hyde Street line* reaching The Cannery on the Northern Waterfront, the *Mason Street line* reaching Fisherman's Wharf. A third line runs along California St. from Market to Van Ness Ave. Cable cars run 6 A.M.–1 A.M. Fare, $2; $1 for youngsters 5–17.

By rapid transit. *Bay Area Rapid Transit* (788–BART) trains link the city with Oakland, Berkeley, and much of the East Bay. Downtown underground stations are at the Embarcadero, Montgomery St., Powell St., and Civic Center. Basic fare is 85 cents; $1.80 to Berkeley.

By rental car. All the major agencies and about two dozen budget companies serve San Francisco International Airport. Most have offices downtown near Union Square. They include *Hertz, Avis, Budget, National, Thrifty, Ajax,* and *Dollar.* Reservations are usually necessary; major and budget agencies have nationwide toll-free 800 numbers. Lowest daily rates seem to be at downtown agencies on weekends.

HINTS TO MOTORISTS. Driving in San Francisco is affected by the hills, narrow streets in Chinatown and North Beach, and dense traffic in the financial district. Avoid driving around Montgomery St. and Union Sq., if possible. When parking on even the slightest grade, always *curb your wheels*—turn the tires toward the street when facing uphill and toward the curb when facing downhill. Tow-away regulations are strictly enforced, especially in the downtown area during rush hours.

HINTS TO DISABLED TRAVELERS. The mayor's office publishes a *"Guide to San Francisco for the Person Who Is Disabled"* which lists stores, buildings, museums, transportation, and hotels that are accessible. It is available free from the *Mayor's Council on Disabilities Concerns,* Box 1595, San Francisco, CA 94101. The entire BART system is accessible, along with Muni Metro trains downtown, and nearly 300 buses on Muni street routes.

TOURS AND SPECIAL-INTEREST SIGHTSEEING. San Francisco Bay Cruises. *Blue and Gold Fleet* (781–7877) offers daily 1¼-hour narrated cruises that take passengers under the bridges and past Alcatraz and Angel Island State Park. They leave from Pier 39 on the Embarcadero. Fare, about $14. *Red and White Fleet* (546–2896) has shorter cruises from Pier 43½ near Fisherman's Wharf. Fares, about $10. Red and White Fleet also serves Sausalito, across the bay in Marin County; round-trip fare, $8. *Golden Gate Transit ferries* (332–6600) depart from the Ferry Building at the foot of Market St. for Sausalito and Larkspur.

Alcatraz. Ferries depart from Pier 41 near Fisherman's Wharf. The two-hour, round-trip journey includes a tour of the abandoned island prison by National Park Service guides. Call 546–2896 for information. In summer, reservations should be made a week or two in advance through Ticketron outlets. Tickets: adults, $7.50; children 5–11, $4. Dress warmly, wear comfortable walking or hiking shoes.

Walking Tours. The best and cheapest (free) way to see San Francisco is a tour conducted by the *Friends of the San Francisco Public Library.* They last about 90 minutes. No reservations are needed; just appear at the starting point and look for the person wearing the "City Guide" badge. Tours include: *Gold Rush City,* Wed. at noon and Sun. at 2 P.M. from the Clay St. entrance of the Transamerica Pyramid; *Historic Market Street,* Tues. at noon from Southern Pacific Building, One Market Plaza; *North Beach,* Sat. at 10 A.M. from church steps, 666 Filbert St.; *Pacific Heights Victorian architecture,* Sun. at 2 P.M., from Bush and Octavia Sts. Call 558–3981 or 558–3857 for information.

Tour Agencies. The major escorted sightseeing companies, with bus tours of San Francisco as well as Marin County and the wine country, are the *Gray Line* (558–9400), *American Express* (981–5533), and *Great Pacific* (626–4499). A number offer more personalized tours in vans, among them *Maxi Tours* (441–6294) and *Starlane Tours* (982–2223).

University of California. The 178-acre central campus in Berkeley, across San Francisco Bay, retains much of its natural beauty including groves of oak, redwood and eucalyptus trees; Strawberry Creek; and the Botanical Garden in Strawberry Canyon. The Visitor Center is in the lobby of the Student Union, Telegraph Ave. and Bancroft Way. To reach the campus, drive across the Bay Bridge, take Hwy. 880 north to University Ave. Or take BART to downtown Berkeley, then "Humphrey Go Bart" shuttle bus. Information, 642–6000.

PARKS AND GARDENS. Golden Gate Park. This cool, lush park stretches from Stanyan St. in the Haight-Ashbury district west to the Pacific Ocean, and from Fulton St. to Lincoln Way. It includes 11 lakes, a buffalo paddock, children's playground, two windmills, the much-photographed glass palace of the Conservatory of Flowers, and the Japanese Tea Garden. The de Young Museum and Asian Art Museum, as well as the California Academy of Sciences, are located within the park. The busiest section of Kennedy Dr., the main thoroughfare of the park, is closed to auto traffic on Sun.

ZOOS. The San Francisco Zoo. Entrance is on Sloat Blvd. near the Great Hwy., overlooking Ocean Beach (753–7080). Founded in 1889, the zoo now houses more than 1,000 animals, and its latest achievement is a Primate Discovery Center, five stories high, that includes 16 endangered species. Open daily 10 A.M.–5 P.M. Admission: adults, $6; youths 12–15 and seniors, $3; children under 12 free with an adult. Admission to children's zoo, additional $1.

PARTICIPANT SPORTS. Jogging. The busiest as well as most scenic areas are Kennedy Dr. through Golden Gate Park; the Marina Green along Marina Blvd. near the Golden Gate Bridge approach; the Embarcadero; and Lake Merced in the southwest corner of the city. Most runners consider the city's hills a challenge rather than a problem.

Biking. Bikes are available for rent on Stanyan St. facing Golden Gate Park. There are two marked, scenic bike routes through the city, one in Golden Gate Park, the other across Golden Gate Bridge to Marin County. Information is available from Caltrans, a state agency, at 923–4444.

Sailing. Views of the city from the bay are spectacular, but currents and weather can be unpredictable. For excursions, look under "Boats-Charter" in the San Francisco Yellow Pages.

Tennis. The *San Francisco Recreation and Parks Department* (558–4054) maintains more than 100 courts throughout the city, including 21 in Golden Gate Park.

Swimming. Ocean beaches can be dangerous; Aquatic Park on the Northern Waterfront, within the bay, is recommended. YMCA and YWCA pools are open to visitors with daily memberships. The city maintains nine pools; call 753–7026 for information.

SPECTATOR SPORTS. Candlestick Park on the windswept southeastern edge of the city, and the Oakland Coliseum and Arena across the bay are sites of professional sports events. The San Francisco Giants **baseball** team plays at Candlestick and has a ticket office downtown at 170 Grant Ave. (467–8000). The 49ers (468–2249) **football** games at Candlestick are usually sold out before the season when the Niners are winning. The Oakland A's **baseball** team (638–0500) plays at the Coliseum. The Golden State Warriors **basketball** team (638–6300) takes over the Coliseum Arena Oct.–Apr. Ticketron and BASS offices, listed in telephone directory white pages, handle telephone orders.

CHILDREN'S ACTIVITIES. The Exploratorium is a "hands-on" museum that fascinates children and adults alike, with 500 science and perception exhibits. It is located in the Palace of Fine Arts building, Marina Blvd. at Baker St., near the Golden Gate Bridge approach (563–7337). Open Wed., 10 A.M.–9:30 P.M., Thurs.–Sun., 10 A.M.–5 P.M. Extended summer hours. Adults, $6; seniors, $4; youths 6–17, $2; under 6, free.

Marine World/Africa USA. 1000 Fairgrounds Dr., Vallejo (707–644–4000). More than 1,000 land and sea animals, with performing dolphins and killer whales, in a 165-acre home on the edge of the bay. Located off Interstate 80, 25 mi. northeast of San Francisco. Adults, $19.95; children 4–12, $14.95. There is a bus link from BART's El Cerrito Del Norte station (415–788–BART).

HISTORIC SITES. Cable Car Barn. Washington and Mason Sts. (474–1887). This is a museum as well as the system's powerhouse and the cable cars' "parking lot." Open daily, 10 A.M.–6 P.M. Free admission.

Hyde Street Pier. At the foot of Hyde St. between Fisherman's Wharf and Aquatic Park (929–0202), this is a floating museum made up of a three-masted 1895 schooner, a sidewheel ferry boat, a steam tug, and scow schooner. Open daily 10 A.M.–6 P.M. Adults, $4; seniors and students, free. Nearby is the *National Maritime Museum,* Polk St. at Aquatic Park, with ship models, relics, figureheads.

Mission Dolores. 1321 Dolores St. near 16th St. (621–8203). This unpretentious 1776 building, overwhelmed by a later, larger Catholic church on the same site, was built in what was considered the sunniest and most sheltered area of the northern San Francisco peninsula. Open daily, 9 A.M.–4 P.M. except Thanksgiving and Christmas.

The Presidio. The same year Mission Dolores was founded, this site was chosen for a Spanish fortification to protect the bay. The 1,500-acre Presidio, although its military future is unclear, is open to the public. Fort Point at the base of the Golden Gate Bridge, built 1853–1861, is accessible from Long Ave. It is open daily 10 A.M.–5 P.M. (556–1693)

Telegraph Hill. Now crowned by Coit Tower, bequeathed by 19th-century eccentric Lillian Hitchcock Coit to honor volunteer firemen. Located at the east end of Lombard St.; open daily, 10 A.M.–5 P.M. A more rustic landmark is the Filbert St. steps, past wooded gardens from Montgomery St. to the eastern base of the hill.

MUSEUMS. Asian Art Museum. Adjoining deYoung Museum off Kennedy Dr., Golden Gate Park (668–8921). The art of China, Japan, India, Southeast Asia, Nepal, Tibet, Korea, Iran is on display. About 10 percent of the 10,000 objects are exhibited at one time, and the shows range from tiny netsuke carvings to dramatic samurai armor. Open 10 A.M.–5 P.M. Wed.–Sun. Joint admission with de Young, adults, $4; seniors, $2; children, free. Free first Wed. and Sat. of each month, 10 A.M.–noon.

California Academy of Sciences. Golden Gate Park (750–7145). The city's natural history museum, including dinosaur skeletons, Morrison Planetarium, Steinhart Aquarium with its 360-degree fish roundabout, and a "Safe-Quake' platform that simulates an earthquake. Open daily, 10 A.M.–5 P.M., extended summer hours. Adults, $4; children 12–17 and seniors, $2; children 6–11, $1. Free, first Wed. of the month.

California Palace of the Legion of Honor. Lincoln Park, entrance at 35th Ave. and Clement St. (750–3659). In a spectacular setting in Lincoln Park, this museum is devoted to European art including a collection of Rodin sculpture. Open Wed.–Sun, 10 A.M.–5 P.M. Adults, $4; seniors, $2; children, free. Free first Wed. and Sat. of each month, 10 A.M.–noon.

M. H. de Young Memorial Museum, Golden Gate Park (863–3330). The city's most comprehensive museum, emphasizing American art, and site of major touring exhibitions. Open Wed.–Sun, 10 A.M.–5 P.M. Adults, $4; seniors, $2; children, free. Free first Wed. and Sat. of each month; 10 A.M.–noon.

The Oakland Museum. 1000 Oak St. near Lake Merritt BART station, Oakland (273–3401). The "museum of California" provides a unique introduction to the state's environment, history, art, and especially popular trends in a comprehensive tribute to the "California Dream." Open Wed.–Sat., 10 A.M.–5 P.M.; Sun., noon–7 P.M. Free admission.

San Francisco Museum of Modern Art. Veterans Building, Van Ness at McAllister streets (863–8800). Permanent collection of 20th-century art, important contemporary exhibitions, recent architecture and design. Open Tues., Wed., Fri., 10 A.M.–5 P.M.; Thurs. to 9 P.M.; Sat. and Sun., 11 A.M.–5 P.M. Adults, $3.50; children under 16 and seniors, $1.50. Free Tues.

MUSIC. The Lamplighters. Presentation Theater, 2350 Turk Blvd. (752–7755). The nation's oldest Gilbert and Sullivan repertory, with local soloists and full orchestra.

San Francisco Opera. War Memorial Opera House, Van Ness Ave. at Grove St. (431–1210). The largest opera company west of New York, featuring major international stars. Fall season Sept.–Nov., with Wagner's *Ring* performed every fifth summer, next in 1995. Many performances are sold out, but standing-room tickets go on sale 3 hours before curtain time.

San Francisco Symphony. Davies Hall, Van Ness Ave. at Grove St. (431–5400). Herbert Bloomstedt and guest conductors lead the orchestra Sept.–May, with a Beethoven festival June–July and modestly priced pops concerts July–Aug. in Civic Auditorium.

DANCE. San Francisco Ballet. Opera House, Van Ness Ave. at Grove St. (621–3838). An opulent, popular production of *The Nutcracker* fills the month of Dec. A rotating repertory season Jan.–Apr. includes such full-length works as *Romeo and Juliet* and *The Tempest* along with premieres.

There are many modern and experimental dance groups in the city, many of them headquartered at the *New Performance Gallery,* 3153 17th St. (863–9834). The best source for local performance information is the **Bay Area Dance Coalition** (255–2794).

STAGE. A central source for theater tickets is the STBS booth on the Stockton St. side of Union Sq. Similar to New York City's TKTS service, it is open Tues.–Sat., noon–7:30 P.M. When theaters provide them, STBS offers unsold tickets on the day of performance for half-price, plus a small service charge.

American Conservatory Theatre. Since the 1989 Northern California earthquake, the city's leading resident theater company has been performing at a number of locations. Repairs to its Geary Theatre at 415 Geary St. should be completed by the fall of 1991 (749–2228).

Smaller and more adventurous theater companies have challenged established companies and touring shows in recent years. The most reliable are the *Eureka Theater* 2730 16th St. (558–9898); *Magic Theater,* Building D, Fort Mason Center, Marina Blvd. at Laguna St. (441–8822).

Club Fugazi. 678 Green St., North Beach (421–4222). Home of Steve Silver's zany musical revue, *Beach Blanket Babylon,* a perennial crowd-pleaser.

Touring stage productions are housed at The Golden Gate, Curran, Orpheum, Marines Memorial theaters and Theatre on the Square. Check the daily newspapers for current shows.

ACCOMMODATIONS. San Francisco's hotel construction boom has been matched by a refurbishing of older hotels on the fringe of Nob Hill and Union Sq. They now provide equally comfortable, if slightly smaller, accommodations for little more than half the price of deluxe hotels. Beyond the best-known names, there is a wide variety of accommodations and prices. Bed-and-breakfast inns tend to be expensive. Because of the city's year-round convention business, few hotels offer seasonal rates.

Hotel rates are based on double occupancy: *Deluxe,* $150 and up; *Expensive,* $100–$150; *Moderate,* $80–$100; *Inexpensive,* under $80. In addition, there is an 11 percent hotel tax.

Deluxe

Fairmont Hotel and Tower. 950 Mason St., San Francisco, CA 94106 (415–772–5000 or 800–527–4727). On Nob Hill, the grandest of the city's grand hotels, with a dramatic lobby. Rooms in the original section of the hotel have more character.

Four Seasons Clift. 495 Geary St., San Francisco, CA 94102 (415–775–4700 or 800–332–3442). Tasteful luxury, attentive service, two blocks from Union Sq. The Redwood Room cocktail lounge is an Art Deco classic.

Mark Hopkins Inter-Continental. 1 Nob Hill, San Francisco, CA 94108 (415–392–3434 or 800–327–0200). This venerable landmark, known as "The Mark," sits elegant and stately atop Nob Hill. Even-numbered rooms have views of the Golden Gate Bridge, as does the Top of the Mark cocktail lounge on the 19th floor.

Expensive

Kensington Park. 450 Post St., San Francisco, CA 94102 (415–788–6400 or 800–553–1900). Refurbished, glamorized high-rise hotel. Concierge, complimentary breakfast.

Moderate

Abigail. 246 McAllister St., San Francisco, CA 94102 (415–861–9728; 800–243–6510 nationwide; 800–553–5575 in state). A cozy British-owned hotel near the Civic Center, close to the Opera House and Museum of Modern Art. Complimentary breakfast.

Carlton. 1075 Sutter St., San Francisco, CA 94109 (415–673–0242; 800–227–4496 nationwide; 800–792–0958 in state). A large, upgraded hotel a few blocks away from the Union Sq. congestion.

Cartwright. 524 Sutter St., San Francisco, CA 94102 (415–421–2865; 800–227–3844 nationwide; 800–652–1858 in state). Very comfortable hotel a block from Union Sq., amid art galleries.

Savoy. 580 Geary St., San Francisco, CA 94102 (415–441–2700 or 800–227–4223). Charming and comfortable, with antique reproductions and fresh flowers in rooms. Near theaters and Union Sq.

Inexpensive

Beck's Motor Lodge. 2222 Market St., San Francisco, CA 94114 (415–621–8212) East of the Civic Center, one of the few motels convenient to the speedy Muni Metro subway (Church St. Station). Free parking.

Beresford Arms. 701 Post St., San Francisco, CA 94109 (415–673–2600 or 800–533–6533). A sister hotel to the cozy Beresford on Sutter St., this features an elegant lobby, large rooms, modestly priced suites.

Mark Twain. 345 Taylor St., San Francisco, CA 94102 (415–673–2332; 800–227–4074 nationwide; 800–922–7866 in state). Friendly staff, redecorated rooms and good value, two blocks from Union Sq.

Pensione International. 1688 Market St., San Francisco, CA 94102 (415–775–3344). Spartan but attractive, a few blocks from the Civic Center. A favorite of budget-minded travelers, with rates as low as $45.

YS AND HOSTELS. The Central YMCA, 220 Golden Gate Ave. near the Civic Center (415–885–0460), has plain but pleasant doubles without bath at about $45. Both YMCAs offer rooms to men, women, and couples. Rates include use of pools, gyms, and other health facilities.

San Francisco International Hostel is in Building 240 on the landscaped heights of Fort Mason Center, Bay and Franklin Sts. on the Northern Waterfront (415–771–7277). It offers the city's least expensive accommodations, in dormitories and a few family rooms.

RESTAURANTS. For more than 100 years San Francisco has considered itself a gastronomic capital, which does not mean that excellent meals aren't available in all price ranges. Seafood has always been a specialty, influenced by successive French, Italian, and Asian cooks. Recent years have seen a burgeoning of regional Chinese, Vietnamese, Thai, and Burmese restaurants. San Francisco and nearby Berkeley have led the trend toward "California Cuisine," with lightly grilled meats and fish, fresh seasonal food, and innovative combinations of ingredients.

The city's most thriving "restaurant row" is not downtown but a few blocks from Golden Gate Park, along Clement St. between Arguello St. and 10th Ave. The city's most popular Asian restaurants are located here, along with many other ethnic specialties. Recommended on Clement St.: the Fook and New Ocean, Chinese; Mai's and the Garden House, Vietnamese; Giorgio's Pizza.

Cafes and what remain of the city's bohemian coffee houses are concentrated in North Beach, but also appear in other neighborhoods—wherever there's an espresso machine. Among the favorites: Caffe Puccini, 411 Columbus Ave., Caffe Roma, 414 Columbus Ave., and Caffe Trieste, 609 Vallejo, all in North Beach; Cafe Flore, Market and Noe Sts., sports a garden and a young, trendy crowd.

Restaurant categories are based on the price of a three-course dinner without beverage, tax (7½%), or tip: *Deluxe,* $50 and up; *Expensive,* $30–$50; *Moderate,* $15–$30; *Inexpensive,* under $15.

Deluxe

Chez Panisse. 1517 Shattuck Ave. north of University Ave., Berkeley (548–5525). The prix fixe dinner menu changes daily at Alice Waters' mecca for California Cuisine, which visitors will find surprisingly unpretentious. Renowned for grilled and roast meats, and an annual garlic celebration. Upstairs, the moderately priced Chez Panisse café specializes in unusual pizzas, pasta, salad. Restaurant, D, Tues.–Sat. Café, L, D, Mon.–Sat. Restaurant reservations essential. AE, DC, MC, V.

Expensive

Square One. 190 Pacific Ave. at Front St. near Embarcadero Center (788–1110). This big, sophisticated, contemporary restaurant specializes in hearty food with a Mediterranean inspiration. L, Mon.–Fri., D, daily. AE, DC, MC, V.

Stars. 150 Redwood Alley between Golden Gate Ave. and McAlister St., Civic Center (861–7827). Chez Panisse alumnus Jeremiah Tower originated this French–California brasserie, featuring innovative grilled fish and meat, unusual soups and salads, fresh fruit desserts. L, Mon.–Fri. D, daily. All major credit cards.

Moderate

Angkor Palace. 1769 Lombard St. (931–2830). Wonderful, modestly priced Cambodian dishes served amidst Asian antiques, dazzling colors, and sweet and pungent scents. D, daily. AE, MC, V.

Greens. Building A, Fort Mason Center, Marina Blvd. at Laguna St., Northern Waterfront area (771–6222). Featured here are the freshest and most creative vegetarian food, including pizza, salads, chili, and a remarkable view of San Francisco Bay. L, D, Tues.–Sat. Brunch, Sun. Moderate to expensive. MC, V.

Harbor Village. 4 Embarcadero Center, lobby level, Sacramento and Drumm Sts. (781–8833). This big, elegant but informal restaurant with a crew of chefs from Hong Kong, specializes in classical Chinese cuisine. Steamed fish, shellfish, roast chicken, and duck; dim sum lunches. L, D, daily. All major credit cards.

Kuleto's. 221 Powell St. (397–7720). Italian-Tuscan cuisine, with a wide variety of appetizers and grilled meat, poultry, and seafood is served here. Casually elegant atmosphere. B, L, D, daily. All major credit cards.

Zuni Café. 1658 Market St., Civic Center (552–2522). A crisp, Southwestern setting and an innovative menu distinguish this restaurant, which specializes in a variety of fresh shellfish, grilled fish, chicken and meat, and pasta with shellfish and herbs. A variety of salads and soups, and homemade pastries and ice cream completes the menu. B, L, D, Tues.–Sun. Brunch, Sun. Reservations recommended. AE, MC, V.

Inexpensive

The Deli. 1980 Union St., Cow Hollow district (563–7274). Hearty roasts, sandwiches, soups, salads, along with cheese blintzes and potato pancakes in large portions. Ask to sit in the flower-filled greenhouse. L, D (late) daily. AE, MC, V.

Green Valley. 510 Green St., North Beach (788–9384). One of the few remaining Italian family-style restaurants with a fixed-price, five-course dinner and neighborhood character. A wide selection of entrées, including tender roasts and fried calamari. L, D, Tues.–Sun. L, Tues.–Fri., D, Tues.–Sun.

Max's Diner. 311 Third St., near Moscone Center (546–6297). This is a stylishly re-created 1950s diner, but with top-quality food. B, L, D daily. AE, MC, V. Adjacent are the slightly more upscale **Max's Manhattan Prime Steak House** and the Italian style **Cafe Tomatoes.**

Vicolo. Ghirardelli Square (776–1331) and 201 Ivy St. off Franklin between Hayes and Grove, Civic Center (863–2382). Innovative pizza is served here in a post-modern setting, with the freshest ingredients and careful preparation. There is real flavor to the variety of cheese, herb, vegetable and sausage toppings. Salads are crisp and fresh. The Civic Center restaurant is crowded just before performances at the Opera House, Davies Symphony Hall. L, D, daily.

NIGHTLIFE AND BARS. Except for the major hotels and piano bars in the theater district, the downtown area around Union Sq. is quiet at night. The city's nightlife is neighborhood-oriented. Right after work, bars are crowded in the financial district around Montgomery and Sacramento Sts. and in Embarcadero Center. For a full listing of club soloists, pop concerts and dance spots, see the pink *Datebook* section of the Sun. newspaper.

Among the popular clubs: **Kimball's** 300 Grove St. (861–5585), jazz near the Opera House; **Great American Music Hall,** 859 O'Farrell St. (885–0750), jazz and folk performers; **The Plush Room,** 940 Sutter St. (885–6800), the premiere cabaret; **Cobb's Comedy Club,** 280 Leavenworth St. in The Cannery (928–4320), a comedy showcase; **Perry's,** 1944 Union St. (922–9022), the established singles headquarters; **Tosca,** 255 Columbus Ave. (986–9651), a nostalgic North Beach bar with opera on the juke box; **The Carnelian Room,** 555 California St. (433–7500), the most breathtaking view, from the 55th floor, in an elegant setting. All the major **hotels,** including the St. Francis, Fairmont, Mark Hopkins, Sir Francis Drake, Marriott, and Hyatt Regency are topped with cocktail lounges that boast city views, and also provide music for dancing.

Practical Information for the Wine Country

HOW TO GET THERE. By car. Driving from San Francisco, take U.S. Hwy. 101 across the Golden Gate Bridge, turn off on State Hwy. 37, then State Hwy. 121 to Sonoma or Napa. From Napa, State Hwy. 29 continues north through St. Helena, Calistoga, and into the Lake County wine region. Lake County is also accessible farther north from U.S. Hwy. 101; turn east on State Hwy. 20 or 29.

By bus. Wineries north of St. Helena can be visited by taking the *Greyhound* bus from San Francisco with Calistoga as its destination, getting off at the Charles Krug Winery. Greyhound information, 415–433–1500. There are many bus and van tours from San Francisco. *Great Pacific Tour Co.* (415–626–4499) is recommended. Others include *Calif. Parlor Car Tours* (415–474–7500), *Gray Line* (415–896–1515), and *Superior Guide Company* (415–550–1352).

TOURIST INFORMATION. A free guide to nearly 150 wineries is offered by the *Redwood Empire Association,* 785 Market St., 15th Floor, San Francisco, CA 94103. Send a self-addressed, stamped envelope. The association also publishes a Visitor's Guide, available free at its office (415–543–8334) or by mail for $2. In the Wine Country itself, resources include the *Sonoma Valley Visitors Bureau,* 453 First St. East, Sonoma, CA 95476 (707–996–1090) and *Napa Chamber of Commerce,* 1556 First St., Napa, CA 94559 (707–226–7455).

SPECIAL-INTEREST SIGHTSEEING. Napa Valley Wine Train. 1275 McKinstry St., Napa, CA 94559 (707–253–2111 or 800–522–4142). Luxuriously restored Pullman parlor cars and a dining car make a 3-hour round-trip between Napa and St. Helena. Prices are about $55–$70, including brunch, lunch, or dinner.

WINERY TOURS. Most larger wineries offer tours daily except major holidays, from 10 or 11 A.M. to 5 or 6 P.M. Tours are free (by appointment at some smaller wineries) and are most pleasant on weekdays when groups are smaller and winery employees are less pressured. Following is a selection from the scores that welcome visitors.

Beaulieu Vineyard. 1960 St. Helena Hwy., Rutherford, Napa County (707–963–2411). Founded by Georges de Latour, this is a renowned producer of Cabernet Sauvignon. Handsome visitors' center, with an informative film-slide show.

Beringer Vineyard. 2000 Main St., St. Helena (707–963–4812). Historic limestone caves, dug into the hill by Chinese laborers, and the 19th-century Rhine House, a gabled replica of the Rhenish home left behind by Fredrick and Jacob Beringer when they emigrated, are the highlights. Now owned by Nestle, the Swiss chocolate company. The wines are not spectacular, but they're improving.

Buena Vista Winery. 18000 Old Winery Rd. 1 mi. northeast of the town of Sonoma (707–938–1266). Founded in 1857 by an adventurous Hungarian immigrant, Col. Agoston Haraszthy. Historical marker and self-guided historical tour.

Domaine Chandon. California Dr., Yountville, Sonoma County (707–944–2280). A modern winery built by the French to produce sparkling wine. The winery includes an excellent restaurant; reservations are usually necessary.

Guenoc Winery. 21000 Butts Canyon Rd., Middletown, Lake County (707–987–2385). Located on a hill east of Clear Lake, overlooking 270 acres of vineyards and the restored home of Lillie Langtry, the English actress who owned the property in the early 20th century. Open Thurs.–Sun.

Robert Mondavi Winery. 7801 St. Helena Hwy., Oakville, Napa County (707–963–9611). Recommended as the most informative tour among the area's wineries. Mondavi hosts a summer music festival.

Sterling Vineyards. 1111 Dunweal La., Calistoga (707–942–5151). The white, Mediterranean-style building on a hill at the northern end of the valley looks like something built by the Moors—not, as it was, by a modern contractor in the 1970s. For about $3 you take a Disneyland-type tram to the summit, wander on a self-guided tour, and then taste. The Cabernet is superb. Daily 10:30 A.M.–4:30 P.M.

ACCOMMODATIONS. A guide to inns in the area is available by mailing $1 to Box 7150, Chico, CA 95927. There are two telephone referral services: *Napa Valley Tourist Bureau* (707–944–9557) and the *Bed & Breakfast Exchange* (707–942–5900). For information on spas, hot mineral-water, and volcanic-mud baths: *Calistoga Chamber of Commerce,* 1458 Lincoln Ave., Calistoga, CA 94515 (707–942–6333).

Following is a brief selection of the wide range of accommodations, with approximate prices for double-occupancy rooms: *Expensive,* $90–$140; *Moderate,* $65–$90; *Inexpensive,* about $60.

Napa. Embassy Suites. *Expensive.* 1075 California Blvd., Napa, CA 94559 (707–253–9540 or 800–362–2779). New, 210-suite complex, with many free services. Weekday discounts.

St. Helena. El Bonita Motel. *Moderate.* 195 Main St., St. Helena, CA 94574 (707–963–3216). Redecorated in an Art Deco style, with 16 rooms in the main building and several garden suites. Pool.

Hotel St. Helena. *Moderate.* 1309 Main St., St. Helena, CA 94574 (707–963–4388). Restored Victorian era hotel, downtown, with 18 rooms, antique furnishings.

Sonoma. Sonoma Hotel. *Inexpensive.* 110 W. Spain St., Sonoma, CA 95476 (707–996–2996). Restored hotel on Sonoma Plaza, where the Bear Flag Revolt against Mexico was launched in 1846. Antique furnishings. Near wineries.

RESTAURANTS. In addition to many excellent wine country restaurants, there is a choice of take-out food for picnics at wineries or parks. Among the best sources: **Sonoma Cheese Co.** on the Plaza in Sonoma; **Oakville Grocery** in Oakville; **Downtown Bakery and Creamery** on the Plaza in Healdsburg; **All Seasons Market** in Calistoga; **V. Sattui Winery** and deli/cheese shop just south of St. Helena. Approximate prices for dinners without drinks, tax, or tip in the following restaurants: *Expensive,* $25 and up; *Moderate,* $15–$25.

Geyserville. Souverain. *Expensive.* 400 Souverain Rd. off U.S. 101 north of town (707–433–3141). A delightful indoor–outdoor setting at a prestigious winery, overlooking rolling vineyards. L, Mon.–Sat. D, Thurs.–Sun. Brunch, Sun.

St. Helena. Brava Terrace. *Moderate.* 3010 St. Helena Hwy. N. (707–963–9300) In the Freemark Abbey winery complex, this friendly indoor-outdoor country French bistro features local seasonal produce; pasta, grilled meats and fish. L, D, daily. MC, V.

Sonoma. Depot Hotel 1870. *Moderate.* 241 First St. West (707–938–2980). A country inn setting, with Continental cuisine, prepared with imagination. L, Wed.–Fri. D, Wed.–Sun.

Yountville. Mustards Grill. *Moderate.* 7399 St. Helena Hwy. (707–944–2424). Creative California cooking, with a woodburning oven and charcoal grill used to prepare meat, fish, chicken, game. Homemade desserts. L, D, daily. MC, V. Reservations recommended, especially on weekends.

PRACTICAL INFORMATION FOR THE NORTHERN CALIFORNIA COAST

FROM MARIN COUNTY TO CRESCENT CITY

HOW TO GET THERE. By car. Visitors driving between California and Oregon or Washington may want to explore the entire coast. Otherwise, such attractions as Muir Woods, Pt. Reyes National Seashore, and the Russian River can be covered in one-day excursions from San Francisco.

By bus. *Golden Gate Transit* (415–332–6600), buses reach the Marin County coast. San Francisco-based bus tours to Muir Woods and points farther north include: *Gray Line* (415–896–1515); *Great Pacific Tours* (415–626–4499); and *Calif. Parlor Car Tours* (415–474–7500). Many tours are combined with the wine country of Napa and Sonoma counties.

TOURIST INFORMATION. A wealth of material, including information on attractions, directions, and accommodations is provided by the *Redwood Empire Assn.,* 785 Market St., 15th Floor, San Francisco, CA 94103. (415–543–8334). Send $2 for a comprehensive visitors' guide, which also covers the wine country.

SPECIAL-INTEREST SIGHTSEEING. California Western Railroad. Box 907, Fort Bragg, CA 95437 (707–964–6371). "The Skunk" railroad offers scenic trips from Ft. Bragg on the coast to Willits across the coast range. Open observation cars in summer. Operates daily. Tickets, $18.50–$23.

Ferndale. California's best-preserved Victorian village is just off Hwy. 101, about 15 mi. south of Eureka and 260 mi. north of San Francisco. There are several bed-and-breakfast inns. For information, call the *Chamber of Commerce* at 707–786–4477.

Mendocino. A picturesque 19th-century town right on the edge of the rugged Mendocino County coast, often used by filmmakers as a New England village. Art and craft galleries, charming cafés, bed-and-breakfast inns. For information, contact the *Fort Bragg-Mendocino Coast Chamber of Commerce,* Box 1141, Fort Bragg, CA 95437 (707–964–3153).

NATIONAL AND STATE PARKS. Muir Woods National Monument. Mill Valley, off Hwy. 1, Marin County (415–388–2595). A 500-acre preserve of redwood trees *(sequoia sempirvirens),* some as high as 240 ft. and 1,200 years old. Less than an hour's drive from San Francisco. Lovely, *very* easy trails in a beautiful park dedicated to the memory of conservationist John Muir. Open 8 A.M.–sunset. Free admission. No picnic or camping facilities.

Point Reyes National Seashore. Hwy. 1 west of Olema (415–663–1092). A 74,000-acre recreation area in Marin County with secluded beaches, grassy bluffs, forests, wildlife, historic lighthouse, youth hostel. Whale watching Dec.–Feb.

Redwood National Park. Headquarters, 1111 2nd St., Crescent City (707–464–6101). Three parks, with more than 100,000 acres and—as the name suggests—groves of the world's tallest trees, make up this recreation area in Humboldt and Del Norte counties. Hiking, fishing, beachcombing; more than 300 campsites.

HISTORIC SITES. Fort Ross State Historic Park. Hwy. 1 northeast of Jenner, Sonoma County (707–847–3286). In 1812, 95 Russian settlers arrived here from Alaska, which was then a Russian colony, to develop a fur-trading outpost, and grow wheat and other crops. It was abandoned in 1841. The current fort reproduces structures destroyed by fire over the years. Open daily, 10 A.M.–4:30 P.M.; admission, $3 per car.

ACCOMMODATIONS. The most desirable accommodations in the Redwood Empire are country bed-and-breakfast inns. Some are directly on the coast, others inland. Most are small and family-operated, but priced well beyond the budget category. Advance reservations are suggested, especially on weekends. For a list of nearly 100 inns, send $1 and a self-addressed, business-size envelope to *Bed and Breakfast Inns of Northern Calif.,* Box 7150, Chico, CA 95927. The following rates for double occupancy are: *Deluxe,* $100 and up; *Expensive,* $75–$100; *Moderate,* $55–$75.

Fort Bragg. Grey Whale Bed & Breakfast Inn. *Moderate.* 615 N. Main St., Fort Bragg, CA 95437 (707–964–0640 or 800–382–7244). Thirteen rooms in restored landmark building, near "The Skunk" railroad depot.

Garberville. Benbow Inn. *Deluxe.* 445 Lake Benbow Dr., Garberville, CA (923–2124). Four-story Tudor-style inn and gardens overlooking Eel River. Golf, tennis. Closed Jan.–Mar.

Gualala. Old Milano Hotel. *Expensive.* 38300 Hwy. 1, Gualala, CA 95445 (707–884–3256). Nine rooms in a vintage oceanfront hotel, beautifully decorated with antiques. No children under 16.

Jenner. Murphy's Jenner-by-the-Sea. *Moderate.* 10400 Hwy. 1, Jenner, CA 95450 (707–865–2377). "Where the wine country joins the sea," this Russian River inn has eight rooms and a restaurant, Rick's Cafe Americain.

Little River. Heritage House. *Deluxe.* 5200 N. Highway 1, Little River, CA 95456 (707–937–5885). Notable country hideaway, in a dramatic setting above the ocean. Modified American plan includes breakfast (each table has its own toaster for really fresh toast), dinner. Closed Dec., Jan. Reservations essential.

Little River Inn. *Expensive.* 7750 N. Hwy. 1, Little River, CA 95456 (707–937–5942). A 50-unit modern resort clustered around an 1853 farmhouse, now a restaurant. All rooms have ocean view. Winter midweek discounts.

RESTAURANTS. Since many country inns are combined with restaurants, visitors may not have to look far to find reliable meals in this area. Some chefs trade ideas with trendy San Francisco Bay Area restaurants, but for the most part dinners are simply prepared and hearty. Approximate prices for dinner without drinks, tax or tip: *Expensive,* $25 and up; *Moderate,* $15–$25; *Inexpensive,* under $15.

Eureka. Samoa Cookhouse. *Inexpensive.* Across Samoa Bridge in Eureka (707–442–1659). Hearty meals in a former lumber-camp cookhouse. Logging museum. B, L, D, daily. No credit cards.

Garberville. Benbow Inn. *Moderate.* 445 Lake Benbow Dr., Garberville, Humboldt County (707–923–2124). A Continental menu in a Tudor-style resort hotel. Reservations advised. B, D, daily. Closed Jan.–Mar. AE, MC, V.

Little River. Little River Inn. *Moderate.* 7750 N. Hwy. 1 (707–937–5942). Seafood, steak, prime rib, Sat. and Sun. Ocean view. D, daily. Reservations advised. Closed Jan.

Little River Restaurant. *Moderate.* N. Hwy. 1 behind post office (707–937–4945). A cozy restaurant with an excellent menu that includes chicken, duck, lamb. Reservations advised. D, daily.

Mendocino. Café Beaujolais. *Expensive.* 961 Ukiah St. (707–937–5614). Fine but informal, innovative dining, with the freshest ingredients. Enticing desserts and excellent brunches. B, L, Mon.–Sat.; D, Fri.–Sun.; brunch, Sun. Reservations essential weekends. Closed Jan. and Feb. MC, V.

Occidental. Union Hotel. *Inexpensive.* Main St. (707–874–3555). This is the oldest of three family-style Italian restaurants, serving a staggering number of diners. No one is allowed to go away hungry. In Sonoma County, reached via State Hwy. 116 from Hwy. 101 at Cotati. L, D, daily. AE, MC, V.

Practical Information for Lake Tahoe

HOW TO GET THERE. By car. Cross-country travelers on I-80 can take State Hwy. 89 south to the lake. From San Francisco, the most direct route is I-80 to Sacramento, then U.S. Hwy. 50 to South Lake Tahoe. These highways are almost always open year-round, but carry tire chains in winter; car rental agencies usually will provide them. Hwy. 50 is a four-lane route through South Lake Tahoe, leading to the hotel-casinos in Stateline, Nevada.

By plane. *American Airlines* and *American Eagle* serve Lake Tahoe Airport; major national airlines serve Reno airport about 50 mi. north.

By bus. *Greyhound* buses reach the Tahoe area, along with buses from the major sightseeing companies based in San Francisco. There are a number of package tours to Nevada casinos from San Francisco. Motorists can check highway and weather conditions by calling the *California Department of Transportation,* listed in telephone directories throughout the state; in the San Francisco Bay Area, the number is 415–557–3755.

TOURIST INFORMATION. The Lake Tahoe basin provides a wealth of recreation activities, from summer camping and hiking to winter skiing, along with a number of boat excursions on the lake itself. The *U.S. Forest Service* operates the major visitors center, located on Hwy. 89 at the outlet of Taylor Creek, South Lake Tahoe. It is open June.–Sept., 8 A.M.–6 P.M. (916–541–0209). At other times of the year, telephone 916–573–2674. Other resources: *Lake Tahoe Visitors Authority,* P.O. Box 16299, 1156 Ski Run Blvd., South Lake Tahoe, CA 95706 (916–544–5050 or 800–288–2463). For the quieter north side of the lake, *Tahoe North Visitors and Convention Bureau,* 850 N. Lake Blvd., Tahoe City, CA 95730 (916–583–3494 or 800–824–6348).

The visitors bureaus can also provide information on the Tahoe Basin's 21 ski resorts, which usually operate from late Nov. to Apr. The average winter snowpack is 225 inches. *Ski conditions* at many resorts are reported during the season by the *California State Automobile Assn.,* office in San Francisco (415–864–6440).

HISTORIC SITES. The foothills of the Sierra Nevada, between Sacramento and Lake Tahoe, are rich in California Gold Rush History. Several sites are worth a detour from the major highways. Among them are: **Coloma,** where gold was first discovered in 1848, on State Hwy. 49 between U.S. 50 and I-80; **Placerville** on Hwy. 50, once known as "Hangtown" for its vigilante justice; and in Nevada County north of I-80, **Nevada City** with its restored buildings and American Victorian Museum, and **Grass Valley,** with several old gold-mine sites open. In **Sacramento,** a $68 million renovation has restored the State Capitol to the glory of the 1870s. There are free daily tours of the building, located at Tenth St. and the Capitol Mall (916–324–0333). There are 21 restored locomotives in the California Railroad Museum, 111 I St. in the Old Sacramento development (916–448–4466).

ACCOMMODATIONS AND RESTAURANTS. From rustic woodland cabins and budget motel chains to ski-lodge condominiums and high-rise suites, Lake Tahoe has a wide variety of accommodations. In the South Shore area alone there are more than 10,000 rooms available. The *Lake Tahoe Visitors Authority* operates a toll-free reservation system for nearly 100 lodging properties (800–288–2463). The favored hotels are the four operated by casinos on the South Shore at Stateline, Nevada. They provide views of the lake and forests, health spas and pools, entertainment, and a variety of restaurants ranging from coffee shops to elegant rooms with Continental fare. All offer modestly priced buffets.

Caesars Tahoe. Box 5800, Stateline, NV 89449 (702–588–3515 or 800–648–3353). Opulent decor, 446 rooms and suites, each with a massive circular bathtub following the Roman motif. Rates, $95–$155. Le Posh and Primavera are Caesars' gourmet restaurants.

Harrah's Tahoe. Box 8, Stateline, NV 89449 (702–588–6611 or 800–648–3773). The top of the line among Tahoe hotels, with high-rise views. Each room has two bathrooms, each bathroom has one television set. A consistent award-winner, with rates from $95–$140. The Summit is the plush restaurant, $15–$30.

Harvey's Resort Hotel. Box 128, Stateline, NV 89449 (702–588–2411 or 800–648–3361). The first of the Tahoe resort-casinos, Harvey's added a 17-story tower in 1986. Rates, $85–$160. Top of the Wheel is the view dining room with continental cuisine, $15–$25.

Lake Tahoe Horizon. Box C, Stateline, NV 89449 (702–588–6211; 800–322–7723 nationwide except in NV). Formerly the High Sierra Hotel, this remodeled hotel offers a down-home Western theme. Views from many of the 537 rooms. Rates, $75–$115.

Practical Information for Yosemite

HOW TO GET THERE. By car. From the San Francisco area, go via U.S. 580 to I-5, then south to State Hwy. 140, the less mountainous route into the park. From Los Angeles, take I-5 north to U.S. 99, then State Hwy. 41 from Fresno to the park.

By plane. The closest airport is in Fresno, with rental cars available.

By bus. *Greyhound* goes to Merced, with a direct connection to the park on *Yosemite Gray Line* (209–383–1563). Major sightseeing agencies based in Los Angeles and San Francisco offer overnight excursions to Yosemite; some manage to fit the park into a 12-hour round-trip from San Francisco.

TOURIST INFORMATION. For general information on the park's year-round attractions, including hiking, camping and skiing, contact the *National Park Service,* Yosemite National Park, CA 95389 (209–372–0200) or *Yosemite Park and Curry Co.,* Yosemite Reservations, Yosemite National Park, CA 95389 (209–252–4848). For reservations and information on lodging, contact Yosemite Park and Curry Company's office at 5410 E. Home Ave., Fresno, CA 93727 (209–252–4848). Within the valley, the National Park Service operates a visitor center at Yosemite Village Mall, open 8 A.M.–7 P.M. in summer, 9 A.M.–5 P.M. in winter.

TOURS. Driving is limited on some roads in Yosemite Valley. Visitors are encouraged to park their cars and take free shuttle buses which follow loop routes including hotels, campsites, the visitors center, and trailheads to such attractions as Yosemite Falls, Vernal Falls, and Mirror Lake. Many free nature walks are led by park rangers, several times daily, from the visitors center at Yosemite Village.

There are four daily guided tours by bus: a two-hour valley tour, via open-air tram in summer; a four-hour tour to Glacier Point for a panoramic view of Yosemite and the Sierras beyond; a six-hour Big Trees tour through the Mariposa Grove of Giant Sequoias; and a grand tour including the Big Trees and Glacier Point. Prices range from $10 to $25. Make reservations at any valley hotel desk or the tours-activities kiosk in Yosemite Village.

ACCOMMODATIONS AND RESTAURANTS. Yosemite Park and Curry Co. handles reservations for all accommodations within the park. They range from the rustic grandeur of the Ahwahnee Hotel to canvas-topped tent cabins. They are often full during summer and holiday periods; advance reservations are essential. If accommodations are fully booked, reservation agents will refer visitors to commercial motels and inns on highways near park entrances. Contact *Yosemite Park and Curry Co.,* Reservations, 5410 E. Home Ave., Fresno, CA 93727 (209–252–4848). A deposit covering one night's lodging is required. Credit cards are accepted.

These are the accommodations within the park, based on double occupancy, with a 7 percent tax in addition:

Ahwahnee. Yosemite Valley one mile east of Yosemite Village (209–252–4848). Grand, castle-like hotel built in the 1920s, with an Indian motif. Outstanding views, 121 rooms and cabins, heated pool, tennis courts. About $180. Main Dining Room, which resembles a baronial hall, serves the park's finest food.

Curry Village. Yosemite Valley one mile east of Yosemite Village (209–252–4848). A rustic alternative. Limited number of hotel rooms with bath, 176 cabins with private or shared bath, 400 canvas tent cabins. $22–$70. Cafeteria open Apr.–Oct.

Housekeeping Camp. Yosemite Valley one mile from Yosemite Village (209–252–4848). 300 tent-cabins with concrete floors. About $30 for 1 to 4 persons. Linens not provided. Open Apr.-Sept.

Wawona Hotel. Highway 41, 30 miles south of Yosemite Valley (209–252–4848). A Victorian-era classic away from the valley's congestion, with 105 rooms, pool, tennis courts, golf course. Open Apr.-Nov. $55–$75. Dining room, reservations required for dinner.

Yosemite Lodge. Yosemite Valley, one mile west of Yosemite Village. Modern motel-type rooms with balconies, cottage rooms with baths, cabins with private or shared baths; 472 rooms in all. About $30 to $88, with off-season discounts. Wide range of food service, available all year: modestly priced cafeteria, Four Seasons Restaurant with table service, Mountain Room Broiler featuring steak and lobster.

THE PACIFIC NORTHWEST

by
BARRY and HILDA ANDERSON

Mr. and Mrs. Anderson are freelance writers living outside Seattle. They write a weekly column for the Seattle Post-Intelligencer *and contribute to numerous other publications.*

When asked in a recent survey to characterize the Pacific Northwest as a person, most southern Californians replied with the name Grizzly Adams. That perception of our northwest corner as a wild and woolly country inhabited by he-men in lumberjack shirts and caulked boots is not only inaccurate, it sells the Northwest short.

Certainly, western Oregon and Washington is a land of rugged mountains, big trees, and raging rivers, and you can still find lumberjacks in plaid shirts and caulked boots. But it's also the location of sophisticated cities such as Portland and Seattle where you'll find fine dining, entertainment, and cultural pursuits. It's a land of small towns, subsistence agriculture, and saltwater ports where the residents make their living from the sea.

The feature that overwhelms many first-time visitors is the incredible scenery. Towering snowcapped peaks—the Three Sisters, Jefferson, Hood, Saint Helens, Adams, Olympus, Baker and Rainier—punctuate the skyline. Evergreen forests stretch as far as the eye can see. Dramatic wave-pounded coastline begs to be photographed.

From the vantage point of the driver on the freeway, this wilderness may seem formidable, but it is very accessible. Outdoor recreation is the primary reason why tourists visit Oregon and Washington. In both states, hundreds of miles of trails lace the back country and follow the saltwater beaches. Countless lakes and streams and Puget Sound and the Pacific Ocean await the angler with a bounty of trout, bass, steelhead, salmon, and other fish. Professional guides will take you white-water rafting, hiking, horse packing, scuba diving, or mountain climbing. It's no coincidence that the leading outdoor equipment manufacturers and retailers are located in the Pacific Northwest.

An abundance of water makes all that greenery possible. It not only falls from the skies, it collects in bodies of water all over the Northwest. Although you can rent everything from a rowboat to a fully crewed yacht, getting out on the water is as easy as taking a ferry or an excursion boat.

The eastern two-thirds of both states resembles west Texas more than the Northwest cliché. This is the province of the great wheat and cattle ranches, semiarid for the most part and sparsely populated. It's a land of sweeping vistas and dramatic topographical features: the coulees of eastern Washington, the lava lands of central Oregon. It's the part of the Northwest where you can get away from it all in a secluded resort, a quiet campground, or a small town.

In short, the Pacific Northwest is whatever you want to make it. You can spend your time in one of the cities dining on seafood and attending the theater and never set foot on a forest path. You can explore the mountains with only the deer for company. You can relax in an elegant accommodation on the coast and recharge your batteries to the symphony of wind and wave. Or you can poke about in historic settlements that haven't changed much in the last half century.

OREGON

When the wagons rolled west in the 1840s, they rolled to Oregon. At the end of the Oregon Trail was the focus of the American dream: rich, fertile land in the Willamette Valley, waiting to feel the plow. Lewis and Clark had gone before, reaching the mouth of the Columbia in 1805. John Jacob Astor had established the first American settlement on the Pacific at Astoria in 1811, but it was the thousands of common settlers, farmers for the most part, who gave Oregon the character it has today.

Oregon is gentle country, a land of evergreen forests, small farms, pristine lakes and streams, magnificent coastline, and mountains gentler than those of Washington. Portland is the only city of any size; the rest of the state is dotted with quiet small towns, many of which resemble the towns in New England or the Midwest from which their founders came. Like Washington, the eastern two-thirds of the state is arid and sparsely populated, given mostly to wheat and cattle ranches.

Portland

Straddling the Willamette River, Portland is a city of public and private gardens, especially noteworthy for its splendid displays of rhododendrons (May) and roses (late spring through summer). From its downtown riverfront on a clear day, the perfect 11,235-foot cone of Mount Hood punctuates the skyline to the east and the broken top of Mount Saint Helens rises to the north.

The best way to see the City of Roses is to take the 50-mile scenic drive. The Portland Oregon Visitors Association office at Southwest Front and Salmon streets distributes the free *Portland Book* as well as information on dining and lodging.

Arts. The McKenzie River, which joins the Willamette at Eugene, is a favorite of white-water rafters. A network of bicycle paths laces the city, and rental bikes are available.

The Oregon Coast

Oregon's crown jewel is its coast, more than 400 miles of beaches, headlands, tiny harbors, coves, and seascapes rivaled for beauty only by the coast of Maine. All but a handful of miles are public property, free for use by anyone. Dozens of state parks provide picnic and camping sites as well as splendid views. U.S. 101 hugs the shore for most of the way; it's generally two-lane and not very fast. All along the coast, accommodations overlook the surf and stand beside the beaches. Most restaurants, even those in small towns, feature seafood.

Between Memorial Day and Labor Day, coastal accommodations and campgrounds are typically jammed and require reservations several months in advance. Increasing numbers of visitors come to the coast in winter to sit beside a fire and watch the play of wind and wave on the beaches or beachcomb for treasures cast up by a storm. California gray whales migrate off the coast from February through May; you can view them from clifftop vantage points or join one of the charter boats that cruise near them.

Astoria, dating from 1811, stands at the mouth of the Columbia and offers salmon charter fishing and 19th-century homes. The newly built Maritime Museum is the finest of its kind on the West Coast. Just south of town, Fort Clatsop National Monument shows a reconstruction of the quarters in which Lewis and Clark spent the winter of 1805–1806.

Seaside, the leading resort on the coast during the Victorian era, has a fine beach and a seafront promenade. Cannon Beach is noted for its resident artists, galleries, and summer art and music programs. Steady breezes make it and Seaside favorite destinations for kite flying. Garibaldi, Tillamook, and Pacific City are commercial and sportfishing towns. One of the prettiest drives on the coast, Three Capes Loop, lies to the west of Tillamook.

The coast's most popular resort area is clustered around Lincoln City and Newport. At Depoe Bay, a narrow channel through the rocks leads to a tiny picturesque harbor barely large enough for fishing boats to turn around. Visitors can stroll beside towering stacks of crab rings along a weathered waterfront at Newport's Old Town. There's a restored lighthouse nearby and, across Yaquina Bay, the Mark O. Hatfield Marine Science Center with its aquarium and handling pools for children.

Oregon Dunes National Recreation Area stretches 42 miles south of Florence. Commercially operated dune buggies take visitors for rides over the towering dunes, and quiet trails lead to freshwater lakes and nearly deserted beaches.

The south coast, beyond Coos Bay, is a lonely stretch of small, scattered towns, isolated beaches, and dramatic rocky headlands. At Gold Beach, jet-powered excursion boats take passengers up the Rogue River into coastal wilderness for glimpses of eagles, osprey, deer, and bear.

The Rogue River Valley

In the southwest corner of Oregon, the Rogue River Valley more closely resembles northern California than the rest of western Oregon. A warm, relatively dry valley, it's bracketed by rolling oak and pine-studded hills. Three small cities—Ashland, Grants Pass, and Medford—have most of the accommodations and visitor facilities.

Ashland, a quiet college town, is home of the world-renowned Oregon Shakespearean Festival that runs from February through October. Ashland is also noted for excellent bed-and-breakfast inns.

Jacksonville, five miles west of Medford, is a gold rush town that seems frozen in time. Highlight of the year is the summer-long Peter Britt Music Festival. Grants Pass is a center for outdoor recreationists who come for white-water rafting and fishing in the Rogue River. Roseburg, about 70 miles north of the valley on I-5, features Wildlife Safari, a wild animal park where prides of lions roam free. Several wineries (tours and tastings) are scattered through the foothills around Roseburg.

There are two worthwhile excursions from the Rogue River Valley. To the southwest of Grants Pass, Oregon Caves National Monument preserves the largest and most interesting limestone caverns west of the Rockies. Guided tours through the illuminated chambers are scheduled all year.

On the crest of the Cascades east of the valley, Crater Lake is Oregon's only national park. The lake itself, in the collapsed crater of an ancient volcano, is awesome: an incredible blue and, at 1,962 feet, deeper than any other crater in North America. A two-lane highway leads around the rim for spectacular views of the lake 2,000 feet below.

Central Oregon

Bend is the focus of a vast central recreation area that includes the best fishing and skiing in the state, dude ranches, river rafting, elegant resorts, dramatic scenery, and consistently sunny weather.

Anglers interested in premier fly fishing head for the Metolius and the Deschutes rivers. Expert guides are available locally. Sunriver, south of Bend, is a complete resort complex that includes golf, tennis, horseback riding, and other activities. Kah-Nee-Ta is a unique resort operated by the Indians of the Warm Springs Reservation.

This is also prime rock hounding country. Three state parks are devoted to rock hounding and hiking as well as swimming, boating, waterskiing, and other water recreation.

The landscape around Bend reveals some of the most dramatic volcanic scenery anywhere. Lava flows, craters, and caves have signs for travelers. Lava Lands Visitor Center has descriptive displays and directions to such features as Newberry Crater, Lava River Caves, and Lava Cast Forest. Oregon High Desert Museum is an outdoor zoo with species indigenous to the desert, such as porcupines, river otters, eagles, and owls, on display.

PRACTICAL INFORMATION FOR OREGON

WHEN TO GO. Tourism is Oregon's third largest industry. With the exception of some coastal and mountain resort areas, there are no off-season rates; skiing and fishing plus moderate temperatures draw tourists all year. Portland's biggest and longest summer celebration is the Rose Festival the first four weeks in June. Bring your umbrella; historians cannot recall a festival without rain. From mid-June through Sept. the weather is often warm and sunny. One of the best times to visit is between Labor Day and mid-Oct., when summer crowds have departed and the weather is still clear and warm. The Oregon coast, the state's most popular destination, is typically jammed from Memorial Day through Labor Day; make reservations well in advance. In recent years the winter season on the coast has become increasingly popular, and reservations are advisable for weekends and holidays at the better resorts.

HOW TO GET THERE. Getting to Oregon is not difficult. The state has remarkably good connections to the rest of the country by air, rail, and bus considering its modest population of just over 2.6 million.

By plane. Portland International Airport is served by *Alaska, America West, American, Continental, Delta, Hawaiian, Horizon, Northwest, San Juan, TWA, United, United Express,* and *USAir. Horizon* (800–547–9308) provides regional service to points within the state plus Washington, Idaho, Montana, Utah, and California. Eugene is served by *American, Horizon, United, United Express,* and *USAir. Horizon, United, United Express,* and *USAir* fly into Medford.

By bus. *Greyhound/Trailways* serves Portland and communities along U.S. 101, I-5, and I-84.

By train. *Amtrak* schedules three daily trains each way between Portland and Seattle; one train in each direction (the *Pioneer*) between Portland, Boise, Salt Lake City, and Chicago; and one train each way to San Francisco and Los Angeles (the *Coast Starlight*). The *Pioneer* and the *Coast Starlight* have dining cars and sleeping accommodations.

By car. There's a fast way through Oregon and a scenic way but no fast and scenic way. Interstate 5, which connects Portland with California via the Willamette Valley and the Rogue River Valley, is the fast way. The slower U.S. 101 follows the coast. Interstate 84 heads east from Portland through the Columbia Gorge and eastern Oregon to the Idaho border.

TOURIST INFORMATION. *The Oregon Book,* a comprehensive 64-page illustrated guide to the state, is available free from *Oregon Economic Development Department,* Tourism Division, 775 Summer St. N.E., Salem, OR 97310 (800–547–7842). This office is also a good source for information on sightseeing, recreation, and itineraries. The state also operates eight border information stations from Apr. through Oct. at Seaside (U.S. 101), Brookings (U.S. 101), Portland (I-5), Siskiyou (I-5), Klamath Falls (U.S. 97), at Umatilla (U.S. 730), and Ontario (I-84), and year-round in Portland (I-5).

Regional tourism associations are also good sources: *Central Oregon Recreation Association,* Box 230, Bend, OR 97709 (503–389–8799); *Mt. Hood Recreation Association,* Box 342, Welches, OR 97067 (503–622–3101); *Oregon Coast Association,* Box 670, Newport, OR 97365 (503–336–5107); *Portland/Oregon Visitors Association,* Three World Trade Center, Portland, OR 97204 (503–275–9750); *Southern Oregon Reservation Center,* Box 477, Ashland, OR 97520 (503–488–1011 or 800–547–8052; 800–533–1311 in Oregon).

The *Oregonian,* published in Portland, is in effect a statewide daily newspaper, widely available and containing current information on events. *Pacific Northwest Magazine* also has features of interest to travelers.

TELEPHONES. The area code for all of Oregon is 503. All local phone calls are 25 cents with no time limit. You must dial 1 before the number to reach phones outside the local service area. Dial 0 before the area code for credit, collect, person-to-person, and other operator-assisted calls.

EMERGENCY TELEPHONE NUMBERS. In most areas of the state, the emergency number for fire, police, ambulance, and paramedics is 911. Where not in effect, dial 0 for operator assistance and ask for the correct agency. Oregon's state police can be reached at 503–336–5107.

HOW TO GET AROUND PORTLAND. Public transportation in the Portland metropolitan area is excellent, but within communities elsewhere in the state it is limited and should not be relied on as the primary means of getting around.

From the airport. Airporter buses leave the Portland airport for downtown hotels every 20 minutes on weekdays, every 30 minutes on weekends, between 6 A.M. and midnight. Adults, $6; children 6–12, $1. Taxi fare is about $20. Airports elsewhere in the state have similar limousine or van services.

By bus. *Tri-Met* is the Portland area's bus system and includes *MAX* (Metropolitan Area Express), new light-rail transportation system between the downtown area and Gresham on the east side of the Willamette River. Buses and MAX are free in the downtown Fareless Sq. area, and busstops there are equipped with TV information screens and telephones for requesting information on routes and schedules. Fares outside downtown are charged by zone: 90 cents for the first one or two zones, $1.20 beyond. You can buy a 24-hour pass for $3 from vending machines at downtown bus stops or from the Tri-Met office. You can purchase Tri-Met's *Transportation Guide for the Portland Metropolitan Area* for $2 from the Customer Assistance office, 1 Pioneer Courthouse Sq. (on S.W. 6th between Morrison and Yamhill), 9 A.M.–5 P.M., weekdays.

By taxi. In Portland you don't hail a cab; you phone for one or try to find one at a downtown hotel or major department store. The fare is $2.70 for the first mile and $1.40 for each mile after that. Major taxi companies include *Broadway* (227–1234), *New Rose City* (282–7707), and *Radio* (272–1212).

By rental car. *Avis* (800–331–1212), *Budget* (800–527–0700), *Dollar* (800–421–6868), *Hertz* (800–654–3131), and *National* (800–328–4567) have counters at Portland International Airport. Lower-priced agencies with shuttle service from the airport include *Alamo* (503–252–7039), *Holiday Payless* (503–256–4650), and *Thrifty* (503–254–6563).

HINTS TO MOTORISTS. Portland streets are organized on a grid system that is divided east and west by the Willamette River, north and south by Burnside St. Streets running north from Burnside are in alphabetical order. Eleven bridges cross the river. Rush hours are 6:30 A.M.–9 A.M. and 4 P.M.–6:30 P.M.

The maximum speed permitted on Oregon highways is 65 mph. A right turn on red is permitted after a stop. The speed limit within cities is generally 25 mph but is 35 mph on some arterials and 20 mph in school zones and downtown Portland. Street parking is very difficult in downtown Portland; parking lots are plentiful and typically charge between 75 cents and $2 per hour. Parking designated for the handicapped is strictly enforced; the fine is $500.

During the winter months, ice storms sometimes make the Columbia Gorge Hwy. (I-84) hazardous. Chains or studded tires are required for driving in the Cascades in snow conditions. Between Ashland and the California border, 4,310-foot Siskiyou Summit (on I-5) typically gets more than its share of snow and is sometimes closed for periods up to 24 hours. A slower but generally snow-free alternative route is via U.S. 199 from Grants Pass to U.S. 101 near Crescent City, California. Handy numbers include weather information (503–236–7575) and road condition information (503–976–7277).

HINTS TO DISABLED TRAVELERS. *Circling the City,* a guide to the accessibility of public places in and near Portland, is available through the Junior League, 4838 S.W. Scholls Ferry Rd., Portland, OR 97225 (503–297–6364). Most downtown street corners have been ramped for wheelchairs, and public buildings have been adapted for the disabled. Tri-Met offers a Special Needs Transportation program; call 503–238–4952 weekdays 8:30 A.M.–4:30 P.M.

Shared Outdoor Adventure Recreation (SOAR) helps physically handicapped people enjoy outdoor activities; call 503–238–1613. Two recreation areas outside of Portland are designed especially for the disabled. **Oral Hull Park,** off U.S. 26 at Sandy, some 30 miles east of Portland, has trails, signs in braille, and other facilities for those without sight. Paved paths and rest rooms designed for wheelchairs are available at **Wildwood Recreation Area,** also on U.S. 26, 39 miles southeast of Portland. For information on which state parks are equipped for the handicapped, call 503–378–6305. Regional tourism organizations are the best sources of information elsewhere in Oregon.

SEASONAL EVENTS. *February:* Newport Seafood and Wine Festival, South Beach. Oregon Shakespearean Festival begins, Ashland. *March:* Colorful blessing of the fishing fleet takes place in Garibaldi. *April:* Hood River celebrates its fruit orchards with a blossom festival in the middle of the month. *May:* Cannon Beach holds a Sandcastle Contest. Oregon's showy rhododendrons and azaleas call for a Rhododendron Festival in Florence and an Azalea Festival in Brookings. Astoria celebrates Maritime Week. *June:* Portland Rose Festival lasts for 14 days early in the month. The Peter Britt Music Festival, with jazz, blues, and classical performances, begins in Jacksonville. *July:* Loggers demonstrate their skills at the World Championship Timber Carnival in Albany, July Fourth weekend. *August:* Oregon State Fair begins at Salem, last week of the month. *September:* World-famous rodeo, the Pendleton Roundup, takes place the week after Labor Day.

TOURS. From Portland, *Gray Line Tours* (503–226–6755) offers guided motor coach tours of the city, Mount Hood, the Columbia Gorge, Mount Saint Helens, and the coast mid-Apr.–mid-Oct. *Flightseeing* tours around Mount Saint Helens are available from Portland International Airport; they cost about $50 per person. A free guided tour of Portland's port area leaves the parking lot at N.E. 7th and Multnomah at 9:30 A.M. and 1 P.M. Sat. in summer. Reservations required (503–231–5000, ext. 268). Group tours of the Portland airport are available Mon.–Fri. year-round by reservation (503–231–5000, ext. 268).

Wineries. Oregon wineries are becoming established as some of the best in the country. Many not far from Portland have tours and tasting rooms. For a brochure with maps, write to the Oregon Winegrowers Association, Box 6590, Portland, OR 97228.

NATIONAL AND STATE PARKS. Oregon has one of the finest state park systems in the nation, with more than 230 well-maintained parks including more than 50 with camping facilities. More than 70 of the parks are strung along the Oregon coast and provide public beaches as well as seascapes. For a brochure detailing them, contact *State Parks and Recreation Division,* 525 Trade St. S.E., Salem, OR 97310 (503–378–6305).

Thirteen national forests and 11 wilderness areas covering more than 15 million acres offer extensive camping and picnic facilities and thousands of miles of trails in Oregon. Information can be obtained from the U.S. Forest Service, 319 S.W. Pine St., Portland, OR 97208 (503–326–2877).

Crater Lake, Oregon's only national park, offers camping and picnic facilities, excursion boat tours on the lake, and naturalist-guided activities. Information can be obtained from Superintendent, Crater Lake National Park, Box 7, Crater Lake, OR 97604, (503) 594–2211.

PARTICIPANT SPORTS. Golf. Western Oregon's mild maritime weather is ideal for nurturing green golf courses, and there are more than 130 excellent ones all over the state. Portland alone has 29 courses, and there are 18 on the coast. The state's top golf resorts are Salishan at Gleneden Beach, Sunriver, south of Bend, and the Resort at the Mountain at Welches, near Mt. Hood.

River running. Oregon's top white-water rivers are the Rogue, McKenzie, Deschutes, John Day, Owyhee, and Grande Ronde. Regional tourism associations can supply lists of guides. For the Rogue, write to the *Rogue River Guides Association,* Box 792, Medford, OR 97501.

Backpacking and horse packing. Members of the *Oregon Guides and Packers Association,* Box 3797, Portland, OR 97208 (503–683–9552), guide trips into all the wilderness areas and national forests of Oregon.

Skiing. Second only to Sun Valley, Mount Bachelor, just outside of Bend, offers the best skiing and the most extensive facilities in the Pacific Northwest, both alpine and cross-country. Five ski areas—Timberline, Mount Hood Meadows, Multorpor, Cooper Spur, and Summit—are located on the flanks of Mount Hood, less than an hour's drive east of Portland. You can ski here in summer as well as in winter.

Bicycling. Oregon is a bicycler's paradise. Both Portland and Eugene have extensive trail systems dedicated to cyclists (city parks departments can supply maps). For bicycle touring, many consider the quiet secondary roads and frequent small towns of the Willamette Valley ideal.

SPECTATOR SPORTS. Portland supports three professional franchises, including one major league sports franchise (basketball), the 1977 world-champion Portland *Trailblazers.* The season is Oct.–Apr., with home games at Memorial Coliseum, 1401 N. Wheeler (503–237–4422). The *Beavers,* one of the oldest AAA baseball teams, plays at Portland's Civic Stadium, 1844 S.W. Morrison, Apr.–Sept. The *Winter Hawks,* a Western Hockey League team (503–238–6366), play Oct.–Mar. at Memorial Coliseum.

Portland Meadows Horse Race Track, 1001 N. Schmeer Rd. (503–285–9144), operates early Nov.–late Apr. The greyhounds race at *Multnomah Kennel Club Dog Race Track,* N.E. 233rd, between Halsey and Glisan in Fairview (503–667–7700), about 15 miles east of the city, May–Sept.

The University of Oregon *Ducks* play home games in Eugene. The Oregon State University *Beavers* play in Corvallis.

HISTORIC SITES AND HOUSES. Oregonians have done an excellent job of preserving the past, and scores of historic sites and buildings are scattered all over the state. In the Willamette Valley, especially, nearly every hamlet has at least one well-preserved 19th-century structure.

On the **coast** the leading sites are the 123-foot *Astoria Column* (a tower decorated by a frieze that depicts the history of the area) and the 1885 *Captain Flavel House* in Astoria (daily, 503–325–2563); the Lewis and Clark winter quarters at *Fort Clatsop* (daily, 503–861–2471); Civil War–era *Fort Stevens* (daily in summer, Wed.–Sun. other times, 503–861–2000); and 10 lighthouses built between 1857 and 1900.

In **Portland** stop at the 1882 *Old Church,* downtown on Park Ave. across from the Art Museum; the *Pittock Mansion,* built by an early newspaper magnate (daily, 503–248–4469); and the pre–Civil War *Bybee-Howell House* on Sauvie Island (daily in summer).

Willamette Valley highlights include the *John McLoughlin House National Historic Site,* home of the first chief factor of the Hudson's Bay Company in the Northwest, in Oregon City (closed Mon., 503–656–5146); *Champoeg,* site of the founding of the first American commonwealth on the Pacific Coast; *Aurora,* an entire 1856 town that is on the National Register of Historic Places; the oldest Methodist church west of the Rockies and an old water-powered woolen mill in Salem; and the Hoover-Minthorn House, the boyhood home of President Herbert Hoover, in Newberg. Oregon still has more than 50 covered bridges, most of them in the Willamette Valley.

Jacksonville is the focus for historical sightseeing in southern Oregon. Features of the 1850s gold rush town include a cemetery with burials dating from 1859, three pioneer churches, an 1860s inn, and more than 20 other century-old buildings.

MUSEUMS. Columbia River Maritime Museum, 17th and Marine Dr., Astoria, OR 97103 (503–325–2323). Probably the best maritime museum in the West, featuring steamboat, fishing, discovery and exploration, shipwreck, and navigation exhibits. Daily, Apr.–Oct.; Tues.–Sun., Oct.–Apr.; 9:30 A.M.–5 P.M. Adults, $3; juniors 6–17, $1.50; seniors, $2; under 6, free.

Oregon Museum of Science and Industry, 4015 S.W. Canyon Rd., Portland, OR 97221 (503–222–2828). A working museum of energy, mechanical, chemical, space, and animal exhibits. Includes ship's bridge, planetarium, and science shows. Daily, 9 A.M.–5 P.M.; Fri. to 8 P.M. Adults, $4.50; seniors, $3.50; ages 3–17, $3.

Oregon Art Institute, 1219 S.W. Park Ave., Portland, OR 97204 (503–226–2811). Outstanding collections of Northwest Coast Indian art as well as European painting and sculpture, American art, Asian art, pre-Columbian exhibits, west African art, and classical Greek and Roman pieces. Tues.–Sat. 11 A.M.–5 P.M.; Sun. 1–5 P.M. Adults, $3; students and seniors, $1.50; children 6–12, 50 cents. First Thurs. of the month, free 4–9 P.M.

ARTS AND ENTERTAINMENT. Portland is the focus of the state's cultural activities, although Oregon has two major universities (U of O in Eugene and OSU in Corvallis) plus many small colleges that regularly schedule musical and stage performances.

Music. *Oregon Symphony Orchestra,* 813 S.W. Alder, Portland OR 97205 (503–228–1353), is heard in concert at the Arlene Schnitzer Concert Hall, S.W. Broadway and Main, Sept.–June. Tickets from $12. *Portland Opera Association,* 1530 S.W. 2nd (503–241–1407), gives five productions a year with three performances each in fall and spring. Tickets from $18. *Portland Youth Philharmonic,* 1119 S.W. Park (503–223–5939), is the best buy in classical music. It performs four times a year in Arlene Schnitzer Concert Hall. Tickets start at $7 for adults, $4.25 students. *Chamber Music Northwest,* 421 S.W. 6th Ave., Suite 418, Portland, OR 97207 (503–223–3202), offers summer concerts on the Reed College Campus. The Bureau of Parks and Recreation sponsors an extensive program of summer concerts in the parks, including jazz and bluegrass at the Portland Zoo.

Stage. Portland has at least 18 live theaters. The oldest and largest is the *Portland Civic Theater,* 1530 S.W. Yamhill (503–226–3048), which offers main stage productions concurrently with theater in the round, summer repertory, and children's theater.

The *Oregon Shakespearean Festival,* more than 50 years old, is one of the country's most prestigious. The season in Ashland begins in Feb. and lasts through Oct.

and includes 12 contemporary as well as Shakespearean dramas performed in two indoor theaters and on the classic outdoor Elizabethan stage. Tickets $12–$20. Performance schedule and tickets can be obtained from the Box Office, OSFA, Box 158, Ashland, OR 97520 (503–482–4331). As of 1988, the festival is also in Portland, Nov.–Mar., at the Portland Center for the Performing Arts (503–274–6585 for tickets).

In Eugene the glittering *Hult Center for the Performing Arts* (503–687–5000) offers a year-round schedule of music, dance, theater, and celebrity performances.

ACCOMMODATIONS. Visitors will find a good range of accommodations on all the main highway routes in Oregon. Portland itself has fewer first-class hotels than one would expect in a city of 430,000. Some city hotels offer discount packages on weekends. There are several complete resorts scattered throughout the state and a handful of guest ranches. Accommodations on the Oregon coast are typically more expensive between Memorial Day and Labor Day; elsewhere rates remain the same year-round.

Double-occupancy lodgings in Oregon are categorized as follows: *Super Deluxe,* $125 and up; *Deluxe,* $100–$125; *Expensive,* $80–$100; *Moderate,* $50–$80; and *Inexpensive,* under $50.

Ashland. Windmill's Ashland Hills Inn. *Expensive–Deluxe.* 2525 Ashland St., Ashland, OR 97520 (503–482–8310). Pool, restaurant, tennis, entertainment.

Astoria. Red Lion Inn. *Moderate.* 400 Industry St., Astoria, OR 97103 (503–325–7373). Restaurant, balconies; overlooks Columbia River.

Bend. Rock Springs Guest Ranch. *Super Deluxe.* 64201 Tyler Rd., Bend, OR 97701 (503–382–1957). Pool, housekeeping cottages, tennis, riding, fishing, laundry, children's program. Rate includes meals.

Sunriver Lodge. *Expensive–Super Deluxe.* Sunriver, OR 97707 (800–547–3922). Pools, tennis, golf, children's program, rafting, hiking, bicycling, ice skating, sleighing, sauna, restaurant, groceries, shops.

Cannon Beach. Surfview Hallmark Resort. *Moderate–Super Deluxe.* 1400 S. Hemlock St., Cannon Beach, OR 97110 (503–436–1566; 800–345–5676). Pool, fireplaces; overlooks beach.

Eugene. Valley River Inn. *Moderate–Deluxe.* 1000 Valley River Way, Eugene, OR 97401 (800–547–8810; 503–687–0123). Pool, bicycles, health club, rafting, tennis, golf privileges, putting green, restaurant; on Willamette River.

Eugene Hilton. *Moderate–Expensive.* 66 E. 6th St., Eugene, OR 97401 (503–342–2000; 800–445–8667). Pool, restaurant, concierge, exercise room, entertainment.

Lincoln City. Salishan Lodge. *Super Deluxe.* Box 118, Gleneden Beach, Lincoln City, OR 97388 (800–547–6500; 503–764–2371). Pool, restaurant, tennis, golf, health club, shops, entertainment, nature trails, fireplaces.

Nordic Motel. *Moderate.* 2133 N.W. Inlet Ave., Lincoln City, OR 97367 (503–994–8145; 800–452–3558 in 11 Western states). Pleasant oceanfront lodgings are available here. Facilities include a pool, some kitchens and fireplaces, and an illuminated beach.

Medford. Nendel's Inn. *Moderate.* 2300 Crater Lake Hwy., Medford, OR 97501 (503–779–3141). Pool, restaurant.

Mount Hood. Timberline Lodge. *Moderate–Super Deluxe.* Government Camp, OR 97028 (503–226–7979; 800–452–1335 in Western states). Historic mountain lodge, pool, restaurant, hiking, skiing.

Newport. Moolack Shores Motel. *Moderate.* 8835 N. Coast Hwy., Newport, OR 97365 (503–265–2326). This is a delightful 12-room motel with theme rooms overlooking the Pacific.

Portland. RiverPlace Alexis Hotel. *Super Deluxe.* 1510 S.W. Harbor Way, Portland, OR 97201 (503–228–3233). Restaurant, pools, health club, fireplaces, concierge; on Willamette River.

Heathman Hotel. *Super Deluxe.* S.W. Broadway at Salmon, Portland, OR 97205 (503–241–4100 or 800–323–7500). This historic hotel is in the heart of the city, next to the Performing Arts Center. Award-winning restaurant, afternoon tea, movie library.

Red Lion/Downtown Portland. *Expensive–Deluxe.* 310 S.W. Lincoln St., Portland, OR 97201 (800–547–8010). Pool, restaurant, entertainment, laundry.

Riverside Inn. *Moderate.* 50 S.W. Morrison St., Portland, OR 97204 (503–221–0711). This downtown motel features pleasant decor, good-size rooms, and a restaurant.

Seaside. Shilo Inn. *Expensive–Super Deluxe.* 30 N. Promenade, Seaside, OR 97138 (503–738–9571). Oceanfront property; some fireplaces, kitchens, indoor pool.

BED AND BREAKFASTS. Oregon has dozens of cozy bed-and-breakfast inns, primarily on the coast, in Portland, in the Willamette Valley, and in the Rogue River Valley. The two principal associations are: *Bed and Breakfast–Oregon Plus,* 5733 S.W. Dickinson, Portland, OR 97219 (503–245–0642); and *Northwest Bed and Breakfast Travel Unlimited,* 610 S.W. Broadway, Portland, OR 97205 (503–243–7616).

Chanticleer Bed and Breakfast Inn, 120 Gresham St., Ashland, OR 97520 (503–482–1919) is ranked consistently among the best B&Bs in the Northwest. With 7 guest rooms, one suite, and views of the Cascades and Bear Creek Valley, it's within walking distance of the Shakespeare Festival theaters. Rates: $95–$160.

RESTAURANTS. Portland offers a wide range of dining choices, often at prices considerably lower than those in cities outside the Pacific Northwest. Fresh seafood is readily available both on the coast and in the rest of western Oregon.

Restaurants are categorized by the price of a three-course meal for one, not including beverages and tip: *Super Deluxe,* $25 and up; *Deluxe,* $20–$25; *Expensive,* $15–$20; *Moderate,* $10–$15; and *Inexpensive,* under $10.

Eugene. Chanterelle. *Expensive.* 207 E. Fifth, Eugene, OR 97401 (503–484–4065). Intimate, elegant dining. Continental menu features Northwest foods. D, Tues.–Sat., 5–10 P.M. AE, MC, V.

Grants Pass. Wolf Creek Tavern. *Inexpensive–Moderate.* Box 97, Wolf Creek, OR 97497 (503–866–2474). Historic stagecoach stop (now on I-5) 20 miles north of Grants Pass serves simple, traditional meals. L, D, Mon.–Sat., 11 A.M.–8 P.M.; brunch, Sun., 10 A.M.–2 P.M., D 3–8 P.M. MC, V.

Jacksonville. Jacksonville Inn Dinner House. *Deluxe.* 175 E. California St., Jacksonville, OR 97530 (503–899–1900). Prime rib, salmon served in Gold Rush–era inn. L, Tues.–Sat., 11:30 A.M.–2 P.M.; D, Mon.–Sat., 5–10 P.M.; Sun., 5–9 P.M.; brunch, Sun., 10 A.M.–2 P.M. AE, DC, MC, V.

Medford. Mon Desir. *Expensive.* 4615 Hamrick Rd., Central Point, Medford OR 97501 (503–664–6661). Beef, seafood served in Victorian mansion. D, daily, 5 P.M.–10 P.M., Sun. to 9 P.M. Brunch Sun., 10 A.M.–2 P.M. AE, DC, MC, V.

Newport. Mo's. *Inexpensive.* 622 S.W. Bay Blvd., Newport, OR 97365 (503–265–2979). An Oregon tradition, famous for its clam chowder, seafood. Also in Lincoln City, Florence. L, D, daily, 11 A.M.–9 P.M.

Portland. Genoa. *Super Deluxe.* 2832 S.E. Belmont St., Portland, OR 97214 (503–238–1464). Gourmet northern Italian cuisine. D, Mon.–Sat., 6–9:30 P.M. AE, DC, MC, V.

Couch Street Fish House. *Expensive.* 103 N.W. 3rd Ave., Portland, OR 97209 (503–223–6173). Old Town restaurant specializes in seafood. D, Mon.–Thurs., 5–10 P.M.; Fri.–Sat., to 11 P.M. AE, MC, V.

Dan and Louis Oyster Bar. *Inexpensive.* 208 S.W. Ankeny St., Portland, OR 97204 (503–227–5906). Seafood, nautical decor. L, D, daily, Sun.–Thurs., 11 A.M.–10 P.M.; Fri.–Sat., 11–midnight. AE, MC, V.

LIQUOR LAWS. In Oregon, liquor is sold by the package in state liquor stores (closed Sun.) and by the drink in licensed establishments. Hours are 7 A.M.–2:30 A.M. The minimum legal drinking age is 21.

WASHINGTON

Washington, like Oregon, is in a sense two states in one. In the west, a mild maritime climate with abundant rainfall nourishes vast evergreen forests that stretch from mountains to sea. East of the Cascades, the lack of rainfall has created arid landscapes, treeless and sparsely populated for the most part, where wheat and irrigated crops thrive.

While trees and mountains dominate the west, water is a significant feature. Dotted with islands, the vast inland sea of Puget Sound extends from the Strait of Juan de Fuca southward to the state capital at Olympia.

In addition to creating the beautiful scenery, these natural features shape the vacation experience. Outdoor recreation—fishing, boating, hiking, river running, horseback riding, skiing, and camping—heads the list for most visitors.

Water and timber shaped the state's history as well. British Captain George Vancouver sailed into Puget Sound in 1792, naming many of the mountains and waterways. Moving north from Oregon, the Hudson's Bay Company came in search of furs, followed by settlers looking for good farmland and timber to build ships. Although Washington became a state in 1889, it really came into its own as the major supply center and embarkation point for the Klondike gold rush in 1898.

Seattle

Bracketed east and west by freshwater Lake Washington and saltwater Puget Sound, Seattle occupies a north-south corridor, slender at the waist and embracing numerous hills. On a clear day, the views of mountains and water are spectacular. Most of the city's attractions are clustered in pedestrian-scale sections that are best savored on foot. The Seattle–King County Convention and Visitors Bureau publishes a free visitors guide, available at their downtown office at the Washington State Trade and Convention Center, 1 Convention Place.

The crown jewel of Seattle is Seattle Center, a 74-acre legacy of the 1962 World's Fair. Its distinctive 605-foot Space Needle is the city's leading landmark. From its lofty observation deck, there is a 360-degree view of the city and Puget Sound, backdropped by 14,410-foot Mount Rainier (Seattleites call it "the mountain") and dozens of lesser Cascade peaks to the east and the snowcapped Olympic Mountains to the west.

Seattle Center is enjoyable in any season, but on weekends and fair-weather days between April and October it's a beehive of activity with outdoor concerts, amusement park attractions, impromptu performances, and special events.

The five buildings of the Pacific Science Center (with hands-on exhibits for children) can occupy the better part of a day.

Downtown, just two blocks from the water, Pike Place Market is one of the last authentic farmer's markets in the country. A walk through the colorful market becomes a sensory experience as vendors hawk their wares in a dozen different languages; coffee, tea, and spice shops assail you with

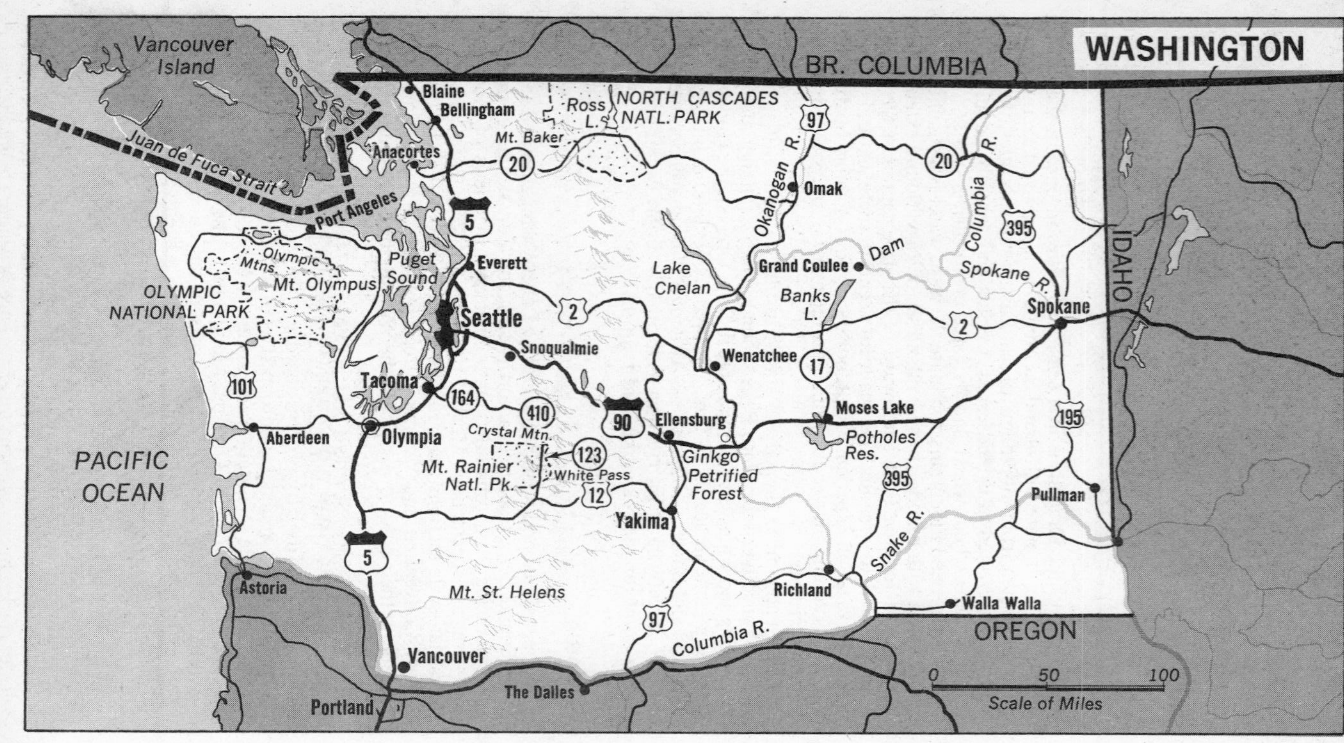
WASHINGTON
BR. COLUMBIA
IDAHO
OREGON
PACIFIC OCEAN
Vancouver Island
Juan de Fuca Strait
Blaine
Bellingham
Anacortes
Port Angeles
Mt. Baker
Ross L.
NORTH CASCADES NATL. PARK
Okanogan R.
Omak
Grand Coulee
Dam
Columbia R.
Spokane R.
Spokane
Pullman
Walla Walla
Snake R.
Moses Lake
Potholes Res.
Banks L.
Wenatchee
Lake Chelan
Ellensburg
Ginkgo Petrified Forest
Yakima
Richland
Columbia R.
The Dalles
Vancouver
Portland
Astoria
Aberdeen
Olympia
Tacoma
Seattle
Everett
Snoqualmie
Puget Sound
Olympic Mtns.
Mt. Olympus
OLYMPIC NATIONAL PARK
Crystal Mtn.
White Pass
Mt. Rainier Natl. Pk.
Mt. St. Helens
5
20
97
395
2
195
17
90
410
164
123
12
101
0 50 100
Scale of Miles

their pungent odors; and seemingly endless heaps of fruits, vegetables, and seafood stretch into the distance.

The 20 blocks of Seattle's waterfront is a fascinating place to spend an afternoon. The city's maritime commerce has moved south to more modern facilities, and the historic old piers (from which the Klondikers departed for the Yukon) have been converted into dozens of import shops, boutiques, and seafood restaurants. There are two waterfront parks, the Seattle Aquarium, a ferry terminal, and the pier that is home to the city's fireboats.

Pioneer Square, the historic heart of Seattle, lies adjacent to the southern end of the waterfront. This is the site of original Skid Road (Yesler Way), a road used to skid timber down from the hills to Elliott Bay. Many of the old brick and sandstone buildings have been painstakingly restored, and a half dozen square blocks of the district offer excellent shopping and dining in addition to historic ambience.

Seattle's strong maritime environment comes into sharp focus at Fishermen's Terminal, home of hundreds of purse seiners and gill-net boats. Visitors can stroll along the piers, watch fishermen mending their nets, and admire the sturdy boats that take them to sea.

Lake Washington Ship Canal connects Puget Sound with Lake Union and Lake Washington. Hiram M. Chittenden Locks offers a fine vantage point to watch the bustling procession of tugs, fishing boats, barges, research vessels, and pleasure craft as they are raised or lowered 21 feet between fresh water and salt water. In summer and fall a constant procession of salmon heading upstream to spawn passes the underwater fish-viewing room at the locks.

The Olympic Peninsula and the Coast

Many first-time visitors come with the notion that Seattle is on the coast. In fact, the coast is about 90 miles to the west, beyond the Olympic Peninsula that sticks up like a giant thumb beyond Puget Sound. Most of the peninsula is roadless, dominated by the Olympic Mountains and the thousands of acres of forested wilderness included in Olympic National Park. U.S. 101 skirts the peninsula, passing through historic communities, tiny logging and fishing towns, and miles of forest, mountain, and shoreline scenery.

Port Townsend has the finest collection of Victorian architecture north of San Francisco. Port Angeles is a major lumber and fishing port and the gateway to Heart O' the Hills Highway, which leads to Hurricane Ridge and magnificent views into the glacier-clad and mountain-studded interior of Olympic National Park. On the west side, trails lead from a park visitor center through the green cathedral of the Hoh Rain Forest, where annual rainfall exceeds 140 inches. The park also includes a long strip of wilderness coast with magnificent seascapes of lonely beaches, rugged headlands, and offshore sea stacks.

Most of Washington's seaside recreation focuses on the south coast. Resort facilities line the sandy beaches at Ocean Shores; Westport is the primary salmon charter fishing destination.

The Long Beach Peninsula stretches 28 miles north from the Columbia River and is a favorite oceanside playground. Here are two turn-of-the-century coastal defense forts, picturesque lighthouses, and the Lewis and Clark Interpretive Center with commanding views of the mouth of the Columbia.

Islands in the Sound

Puget Sound is dotted with nearly 200 islands. Some, such as Whidbey and Bainbridge, support entire subeconomies of agriculture and residential development. Others, such as the 172-island San Juan archipelago, are more remote, secluded, and in many cases uninhabited. The big green-and-white Washington State (automobile) ferries connect Bainbridge Island, Whidbey Island, four of the San Juan Islands, and the Kitsap Peninsula with Seattle and other cities on the mainland.

Whidbey Island makes a good single-day destination loaded with historic sightseeing and rural charm. Several fine bed-and-breakfast inns are located here. Military history buffs will want to tour the old artillery emplacements and lighthouse at Fort Casey, once a coastal defense fort. One of the oldest towns in the state, Coupeville has preserved many 19th-century buildings, which line its main street and now house shops and restaurants.

The ferries that depart from Anacortes call at four of the San Juan Islands: Lopez, Shaw, Orcas, and San Juan. The voyage itself is worth the trip as the ferries thread their way through the islands, coming so close to conifer-clad bluffs in places that you can almost reach out and touch them. Most visitors stop on Orcas Island, where there are several small resorts, or San Juan Island (resorts here, too), which features a national historic park, a whale museum, and a large population of bald eagles.

The Cascades

However you arrive in western Washington—by air, road, or railroad—you can't miss the Cascades. They punctuate the eastern horizon from the Canadian border to the Columbia. Three all-year highways cross them; two others are open from late spring until late fall. Hiking and horseback trails twine through the valleys and over the mountains, leading to remote mountain lakes, alpine meadows resplendent in wildflowers, and lofty promontories. Rivers such as the Skagit and the Wenatchee plunge down the mountain slopes and create premier white-water rafting conditions when they run high with spring snow melt. Packers, guides, and river rafting companies are found in most of the small mountain towns.

The North Cascades Highway (WA 20) is one of the most scenically rewarding drives in the state. Heading eastward from Burlington, it follows the Skagit River and then transits North Cascades National Park (no roads), crests the Cascades at 5,480-foot Washington Pass, and descends to the western-theme town of Winthrop. U.S. 2 leads over Stevens Pass to Leavenworth, a Bavarian-style town from its glockenspiel to its German sausages and sauerkraut. I-90, the major cross-state highway, heads east from Seattle over Snoqualmie Pass, lowest in the Cascades.

Mount Rainier, highest peak in the Cascades at 14,411 feet, is the focus of Mount Rainier National Park. Highways lead around the mountain and to Paradise, on the south shoulder, where visitors can stroll through alpine meadows and see glaciers close up. There's a visitor center and overnight accommodations in the summer.

Probably the most famous peak is Mount Saint Helens, which had a gigantic eruption on May 18, 1980. Many commercial airliners going up the coast fly over the mountain for views into the throat of the crater; local air services also offer volcano flights. You can get within four miles of it on unpaved back roads. Stop at the new Mount Saint Helens Volcanic Monument Visitors Center five miles east of I-5, Exit 49, at Seaquest State Park, daily, 9 A.M.–5 P.M.

The Eastern Slope

Strung along the eastern slope of the Cascades, several communities are worth exploring. Chelan, at the foot of 55-mile-long Lake Chelan, is a major summer resort with swimming, boating, golf, and other diversions.

A daily (three times a week in winter) excursion boat cruises up the beautiful fjordlike lake to Stehekin, back door to North Cascades National Park. Wenatchee is the capital of Washington's apple country, with clouds of white blossoms covering the hillsides in April. Dozens of wineries produce award-winning wines in the Yakima Valley to the south. Most have tasting rooms open to visitors. In the north-central part of the state lies Grand Coulee Dam, the world's largest hydroelectric facility.

Spokane

Spokane, the state's second-largest city, is the capital of the Inland Empire, a rich agricultural region in the eastern part of the state. Riverfront Park (the Expo '74 site) straddles the Spokane River in the heart of town, with acres of greensward, an Imax theater, a 1909 carousel, and a weekend farmer's market.

Other Spokane sights include more than 60 parks and gardens, the outstanding Museum of Native American Cultures, the Bing Crosby Library, Browne's Addition historic district, the Cheney Cowles Memorial Museum, and Fort Wright College, formerly a frontier army post.

From Spokane it's just a half-hour drive east to the stunning lake country of the Idaho panhandle. Highways heading south lead to the Palouse, the nation's richest wheat-producing region, straddling the Washington–Idaho border.

PRACTICAL INFORMATION FOR WASHINGTON

WHEN TO GO. The common perception of people who live outside the Pacific Northwest is that it rains all the time in western Washington. It's not true, though it sometimes seems that way. Seattle averages about 36 inches of rain annually (less than New York, Chicago, or Atlanta), but the skies are typically gray from mid-Oct. to June (average of 68 clear days a year), and there's often a drizzle in the air. If you visit during those months, come prepared with raincoat and umbrella. Snow is a rarity west of the Cascades. Temperatures year-round are mild, with average winter lows of 37 degrees Fahrenheit and average summer highs of 74 degrees. Summer is tourist season, and the weather generally cooperates with sunny days. Some of the best weather comes in Sept. and early Oct.; accommodations and attractions are less crowded then as well.

Weather tends to be more extreme in the mountains, and hikers or campers should be prepared for freezing nights and sudden summer storms at higher elevations. There's abundant snowfall for winter sports in both the Cascades and the Olympics beginning about Thanksgiving and lasting through Apr. The world record for annual snowfall (more than 93 feet) was set at Paradise on Mount Rainier in 1971–1972.

Eastern Washington is warmer in summer, colder in winter, and drier year-round. Summer days are often in the 80s and winter days in the teens, and the average precipitation is only 13 inches.

HOW TO GET THERE. Seattle is the major West Coast gateway to the Orient as well as Alaska. In addition, air, rail, and bus services to the rest of the country are the best in the Pacific Northwest.

By plane. International carriers serving *Seattle-Tacoma* International Airport include *Air BC* (Canada), *British* (Britain), *Canadian* (Canada), *Finnair* (Finland), *Japan* (Japan), *Mexicana* (Mexico), *Northwest* (Japan, Korea), *Pan American* (Britain), *SAS* (Scandinavia), *Thai* (Japan, Thailand), and *United* (Hong Kong). Major airlines provide frequent domestic service to New York, Miami, and the hub cities of Salt Lake City, Denver, Minneapolis, Chicago, Kansas City, and Atlanta. Coastal service to San Francisco, Los Angeles, and San Diego is also frequent; other domestic destinations usually require at least one connection. Airlines include *Alaska, America West, American, Continental, Delta, Hawaiian, Northwest, TWA, United, United Express,* and *USAir. Alaska, Coastal Airways, Harbor, Horizon* and *San Juan* connect Seattle with other cities in Oregon, Idaho, and Washington. Some of the airlines listed are in the process of merging with other carriers and their corporate identity may change this year. *Lake Union Air* and *Kenmore Air* operate float plane service between Seattle and the San Juan Islands and coastal British Columbia cities.

Spokane is served by *Alaska, Delta, Horizon, Northwest,* and *United.*

By bus. *Greyhound* serves Seattle, Spokane, and other Washington cities.

By train. *Amtrak* uses the King Street Station at the southern edge of downtown Seattle. Daily service to Wenatchee, Spokane, and Chicago is provided by the *Empire Builder.* The *Pioneer* travels south to Portland and then east through Idaho to Salt Lake City. The *Coast Starlight* connects Seattle with Portland and with cities in California. One other daily train runs to and from Portland.

By car. Two major interstate highways cross Washington. I-90 connects Seattle with Spokane (driving time 5¼ hours) and eastern points. I-5 runs from the Canadian border through Seattle to Portland. Driving time from Seattle to Vancouver is 3 hours; to Portland, 3½ hours.

By boat. *Black Ball Ferries* (206–622–2222) cross the Strait of Juan de Fuca from Port Angeles to Victoria; *Washington State Ferries* (206–464–6400) ply the San Juan Islands between Anacortes and Sidney, British Columbia (on Vancouver Island). The *Victoria Clipper,* a 300-passenger catamaran, makes daily trips year-round between downtown Seattle and Victoria's Inner Harbour. *Alaska State Ferries* connect Bellingham, 90 miles north of Seattle, with southeast Alaska ports.

TOURIST INFORMATION. The state publishes a comprehensive free guide in addition to brochures on historic sites, skiing, wineries, and other travel subjects. For literature or information, contact the *Washington State Department of Trade and Economic Development,* Tourism Development Division, 101 General Administration Bldg., Olympia, WA 98504 (206–586–2088). The state operates year-round visitor information centers at Blaine (Canadian border; 206–332–4544), Vancouver (206–696–1155), and Sea-Tac Airport (206–433–5217). Between Memorial Day and Labor Day centers are also open at Stateline (I-90, Idaho border), Oroville (U.S. 97, Canadian border), Megler (U.S. 101), and Gee Creek (I-5). Other useful sources include *Seattle–King County Convention and Visitors Bureau,* 520 Pike St., Suite 1300, Seattle, WA 98101 (206–461–5800); information office, Washington State Trade and Convention Center, 1 Convention Place (206–461–5840; 8:30 A.M.–5 P.M., Mon.–Fri.); and *Washington State Ferries,* Colman Dock, Seattle, WA 98104 (206–464–6400; toll-free in Washington, 800–542–7052).

Daily newspapers provide listings of current events; the *Seattle Times* and the *Seattle Post-Intelligencer* are good sources for the entire Puget Sound area. In addition, the *Post-Intelligencer* has a "Short Trips" column on Thurs. that covers travel in the Pacific Northwest. *Pacific Northwest* magazine also feature subjects of interest to travelers.

TELEPHONES. The area code for western Washington is 206; for eastern Washington, 509. Pay phone calls cost 25 cents with no time limit. You must dial 1 before the number to dial outside the local service area. Dial 0 before the area code for credit, collect, person-to-person, and other operator-assisted calls.

EMERGENCY TELEPHONE NUMBERS. In many areas of the state, the emergency number for fire, police, ambulance, and paramedics is 911. Where not in effect, dial 0 for operator assistance and ask for the correct agency.

HOW TO GET AROUND SEATTLE. **From the airport.** *Sea-Tac Airport* is approximately 15 miles from downtown Seattle. The Airport Express departs every half hour, takes about 30 minutes, and deposits passengers at major downtown hotels including Four Seasons Olympic, Holiday Inn Crowne Plaza, Seattle Hilton, Sheraton, Stouffer Madison, Warwick, and Westin. Adults, $6, $11 round-trip; children, $4.50, $8 round-trip. Airport limousine service is also available less frequently to other Puget Sound cities. Taxis are free to charge whatever the traffic will bear but typically charge about $20 for the ride downtown.

By bus. The Metro transit system serves all of King County. Buses are free in downtown Seattle and charge by zone elsewhere (75 cents for one zone, $1 for two zones, extra fare during rush hours). On weekends and holidays a systemwide pass is available for $1. Metro also operates two vintage streetcars on the Seattle waterfront and to the International District, and the Monorail from downtown to the Seattle Center.

By taxi. Within the city of Seattle, taxis charge $1.20 at the flag drop and $1.40 a mile thereafter. Waiting time is 35 cents per minute. Two companies account for the majority of service: *Farwest* (622–1717) and *Yellow* (622–6500).

By rental car. Major rental car companies in the Seattle area are *Alamo* (433–0182), *American International* (433–0700), *Avis* (433–5232), *Budget* (433–5243), *Dollar* (433–6777), *Hertz* (433–5262), *National* (433–5501), *Sears* (244–5454), and *Thrifty* (246–7565). All have airport locations; some include free parking at downtown parking lots.

HINTS TO MOTORISTS. Seattle's hills (especially on east-west streets in parts of downtown) can be intimidating to drivers unfamiliar with stopping and starting at a steep angle. Many of the downtown streets are one-way, and some have lanes exclusively for buses. Parking is scarce on weekdays, but there are plenty of off-street lots where you can leave your car for as long as 24 hours for a fee. Parking is prohibited along major arteries during rush hours (weekdays 6–9 A.M. and 4–6 P.M.). Crossing Lake Washington on either of the floating bridges is easier if one avoids rush hours. To speed traffic during these heavy periods, I-5 to the north operates express lanes that bypass many of the interchanges, and the new Lake Washington bridge, opened in 1989, has high occupancy vehicle lanes westbound to speed traffic.

The maximum speed statewide is 65 mph; Seattle and other urban areas have a maximum of 25 mph. Right turns are permitted on a red light after stopping. Drunk driving laws are strictly enforced, and conviction carries an automatic jail sentence.

Driving on secondary roads in the mountains requires extra caution; many of the roads are used by logging trucks that can be quite intimidating. Chains or studded tires are required during winter snows, and mountain passes are closed from time to time. Local offices of the Washington State Patrol can provide information on highway and pass conditions. The number in Seattle is 206–455–7900.

HINTS TO DISABLED TRAVELERS. Special parking places for the handicapped, both public and private (designated by a blue and white sign with a wheelchair), are widely available in all Washington cities. Most downtown streetcorners have been ramped for wheelchairs, and public buildings have facilities for the handicapped. Some Metro buses are equipped with wheelchair lifts; for information on specific routes, call 206–447–4800.

Most state parks meet barrier-free standards, and some offer facilities for the handicapped. For information on specific parks, telephone 206–753–2027. The Easter Seal Society distributes guidebooks for the handicapped. *Access Seattle* is available from the society at 521 2nd Ave. W., Seattle, WA 98119 (206–281–5700).

SEASONAL EVENTS. *February.* Seattle's Chinese New Year celebration includes dragon parade, special restaurant menus. *April.* Orchards in bloom and parades highlight Wenatchee's Apple Blossom Festival. *May.* Colorfully decorated yachts parade through Lake Washington Ship Canal in Seattle on opening day of the yacht season; Spokane's Lilac Festival takes place late in the month; the four-day Northwest Folklife Festival, biggest of its kind in the country, has 5,000 performers. *July.* Seafair, 10 days of parades, hydroplane races, and ethnic festivals in Seattle, lasts into Aug. *September.* Ellensburg Rodeo, Labor Day weekend, is largest in the state. Bumbershoot music and crafts festival Labor Day weekend in Seattle. Autumn Leaf Festival is held in Leavenworth last week in the month.

TOURS. Sightseeing in Seattle is not complete without getting out on the water. *Seattle Harbor Tours* (623–1445) runs 1-hour narrated cruises from Pier 55, year-round. *Tillicum Tours* (443–1244) offers two cruises a day from Pier 56 to Blake Island. Trip includes an Indian salmon bake in an authentic longhouse and Indian dances. *Gray Line* (626–5208) offers 2½-hour city sightseeing tours as well as all-day tours to Mount Rainier National Park, May–Sept. The *Seattle Underground*

Tour (682–1511) takes visitors on a 1½-hour walk through the historic basements of the Pioneer Sq. area. *Seattle City Light,* 1015 3rd Ave., Seattle, WA 98104 (206–625–3030), runs tours of their Skagit River dams including boat ride and dinner, Thu.–Mon., June–Labor Day.

NATIONAL AND STATE PARKS. Washington has three **national parks:** Olympic, North Cascades, and Mount Rainier. Olympic and North Cascades are primarily wilderness parks laced with trails for horse packing and hiking but without roads (Olympic has several short spur roads that penetrate the edges of the park from U.S. 101). Motorists can drive completely around Mount Rainier. This park has overnight accommodations, ranger programs, and extensive camping facilities. For information, maps, and guidebooks on both the national parks and national forests in Washington, contact the *Forest Service/National Park Service,* Outdoor Recreation Office, 1018 1st Ave., Seattle, WA 98104 (206–442–0170).

The state operates 126 **state parks,** including some marine parks reached only by boat. Most offer both tent and recreational vehicle camping. For information, contact *Washington State Parks and Recreation Commission,* Public Affairs Office, 7150 Clearwater Lane, Olympia, WA 98504 (206–753–2027; 800–562–0990 in-state June–Aug.).

PARTICIPANT SPORTS. Many visitors come just to enjoy the state's outstanding outdoor recreation. Several of the nation's leading recreation equipment firms are in Seattle. You can find everything from skis and backpacks to parkas and trail guides at REI, 1525 11th Ave., Seattle, WA 98122 (323–8333).

Golf. Seattle has three municipal courses, 18 to 27 holes: *Jackson Park,* 1000 N.E. 135th St. (363–4747); *Jefferson Park,* 4101 Beacon Ave. S. (762–4513); and *West Seattle Golf Course,* 4470 35th Ave. S.W. (935–5187). Most cities elsewhere in the state have at least one public golf course.

River rafting. From May through Sept., the major rivers that flow east and west from the Cascades are ideal for river rafting. More than a dozen firms offer guided trips of these and rivers on the Olympic Peninsula. The state department of tourism will supply a list.

Horse packing. Packers and guides go into the wilderness of the Olympic Peninsula and the Cascades on trips of 2 days to 2 weeks. Most are headquartered in small towns in the mountains. A free list is available from the state tourism office.

Skiing. Alpine ski areas are located 46 to 50 miles east of Seattle on I-90 (Alpental, Ski Acres, Snoqualmie Summit, and Pac West), adjacent to the north side of Mount Rainier National Park off Wash. 410 (Crystal Mountain), on Stevens Pass on U.S. 2, near Wenatchee (Mission Ridge), and on White Pass on U.S. 12 (see Tourist Information for information sources).

SPECTATOR SPORTS. Seattle has major league teams in baseball, football, and basketball. The *Mariners* (American League baseball) and *Seahawks* (NFL football) play in the Kingdome adjacent to Pioneer Sq. The *Supersonics* (NBA basketball) play in the Coliseum at Seattle Center.

Major college teams include the University of Washington *Huskies* (Seattle) and the Washington State University *Cougars* (Pullman).

HISTORIC SITES AND HOUSES. Civilization came late to Washington and historic sites and houses are few and far between. On the west, the dense coastal forests impeded development. On the east vast stretches of arid land discouraged agricultural settlement.

In **Seattle,** the *Pioneer Square Historic District* preserves the 30-block area where the city began. *Klondike Gold Rush National Historic Park* (206–442–7220) in the district commemorates the role Seattle played as the jumping-off point for the 1897–98 Klondike Gold Rush (daily).

Fort Worden near Port Townsend (daily, 206–385–4730) and *Fort Casey* on Whidbey Island (daily) were turn-of-the-century coastal defense forts.

Fort Vancouver National Historic Site is a reconstruction of the original Hudson's Bay Post of the early 19th century (daily, 206–696–7655).

Whitman Mission National Historic Site in Walla Walla marks the location of the first permanent white home in the Northwest and the site of the bloody Indian massacre in which missionaries Marcus and Narcissa Whitman and 11 others perished. Craft demonstrations on summer weekends (daily, 509–522–6360).

MUSEUMS. Cheney Cowles Memorial Museum. W. 2316 1st Ave., Spokane, WA 99210 (509–456–3931). Eastern Washington's major museum displays historical, cultural, and natural history material. Tues.–Sat., 10 A.M.–5 P.M.; Wed. to 9 P.M., Sun., 1–5 P.M. Adults, $2; senior citizens and 6–16, $1; Wed. free.

Maryhill Museum of Art. Goldendale, WA 98620 (509–773–4792). Splendid fine arts museum overlooking Columbia River. Daily, 9 A.M.–5 P.M.; closed mid-Nov.–mid-Mar. Admission, $3; over 62, $2.50; 6–16, $1.50.

Museum of Flight. 9404 E. Marginal Way S., Seattle, WA 98108 (206–767–7373). History of aviation in the Northwest; vintage aircraft. Daily, 10 A.M.–5 P.M. except Thurs., to 9 P.M. Adults, $4; teens 13–18, $3; children 6–12, $2.

Museum of History and Industry. 2161 E. Hamlin St., Seattle, WA 98112 (206–324–1125). Regional history. Daily, 10 A.M.–5 P.M. Adults, $3; seniors and children under 12, $1.50.

Seattle Art Museum. 14th Ave. E. and Prospect, Seattle, WA 98122 (206–625–8900). Museum displays Asian art, Chinese jade, contemporary art, and ethnic art. Tues.–Sat., 10 A.M.–5 P.M.; Thurs., to 9 P.M.; Sun., noon–5 P.M. Adults, $2; seniors and students, $1. Thurs. free.

Washington State Historical Museum. 315 N. Stadium Way, Tacoma, WA 98402 (206–593–2830). Collection of pioneer artifacts. Mon.–Sat., 10 A.M.–5 P.M.; Sun., noon–5 P.M. Adults, $2; senior citizens and children 6–18, $1.50, Mon. free. Closed until Oct. 1990.

ARTS AND ENTERTAINMENT. Although many communities in Washington have live theater, dance, and musical performances, Seattle remains the center of the state's cultural scene. There are three major **music** groups. The *Seattle Symphony* (443–4747) performs Oct.–May at the Opera House in the Seattle Center. *Northwest Chamber Orchestra* (343–0445) presents eight baroque concerts on the University of Washington campus, Oct.–Mar. The regular season of the *Seattle Opera* (443–4711) is Sept.–May.

Dance. The *Pacific Northwest Ballet* (628–0880) stages ballet in the Opera House Oct.–May.

Stage. *Seattle Repertory Theater* (443–2222) presents six plays in Bagley Wright Theater at the Seattle Center Oct.–Apr. *A Contemporary Theater,* 100 W. Roy St. (285–5110), features contemporary plays and a children's theater. *Seattle Children's Theater,* N. 50th and Fremont N. (633–4567), presents plays for the whole family, starting with youngsters 5 years old. *Intiman Theater,* Seattle Center Playhouse (626–0782), typically stages classics. *The Empty Space,* 107 Occidental Ave. S. (467–6000), mixes classic, contemporary, and experimental works.

ACCOMMODATIONS. Visitors will find a good range of accommodations on all the main highway routes in Washington. In small towns, particularly on the Olympic Peninsula and in eastern Washington, choices may be limited. Seattle has enjoyed a hotel-building boom in the last few years, with the result that there are many rooms available; major chain hotels often offer discounts on weekends to fill empty rooms.

Double-occupancy lodgings in Washington are categorized as follows: *Super Deluxe,* $125 and up; *Deluxe,* $100–$125; *Expensive,* $80–$100; *Moderate,* $50–$80; *Inexpensive,* under $50. In general, accommodations do not offer seasonal discounts.

Anacortes. Anacortes Inn. *Inexpensive.* 3006 Commercial Ave., Anacortes, WA 98221 (206–293–3153). Pool; café nearby.

Bellingham. Nendel's Inn. *Moderate.* 714 Lakeway Dr., Bellingham, WA 98225 (206–671–1011). Indoor pool, sauna, café, laundry, entertainment.

Chelan. Campbell's Lodge. *Expensive–Deluxe.* 104 W. Woodin Ave., Chelan, WA 98816 (509–682–2561). Beach, pool, restaurant, balconies, entertainment.

Leavenworth. Haus Rohrbach. *Moderate–Expensive.* 12882 Ranger Rd., Leavenworth, WA 98826 (509–548–7024). Spectacular views, pool, hiking, skiing, rafting.

Long Beach. Super 8 Motel. *Inexpensive.* 500 Ocean Beach Blvd., Long Beach, WA 98631 (642–8988 or 800–843–1991). Continental breakfast, free local calls, nonsmoking and ocean view rooms.

Mount Rainier National Park. Paradise Inn. *Moderate–Deluxe.* Star Rte., Ashford, WA 98304 (206–569–2275). Mountain lodge, splendid views, restaurant; summer only.

Ocean Shores. Polynesian. *Moderate–Expensive.* Box 998, Ocean Shores, WA 98569 (206–289–3361). On beach; restaurant, fireplaces, indoor pool.

Olympic National Park. Lake Crescent Lodge. *Moderate–Expensive.* Box 11, Star Rte. 1, Port Angeles, WA 98362 (206–928–3211). On lake; restaurant, boats.

Port Angeles. Red Lion Bayshore Inn. *Moderate–Expensive.* 221 N. Lincoln, Port Angeles, WA 98362 (800–547–8010). On harbor; pool, restaurant.

San Juan Islands. Rosario. *Expensive–Super Deluxe.* Eastsound, WA 98245 (206–376–2222). On Orcas Island. Tennis, three pools, boating, fireplaces, organ concerts.

Roche Harbor Resort. *Moderate–Deluxe.* Box 1, Roche Harbor, WA 98250 (206–378–2155). Historic waterside hotel on San Juan Island; restaurant, boating, hiking, family activities.

Seattle. Four Seasons Olympic Hotel. *Super Deluxe.* 411 University St., Seattle, WA 98101 (206–621–1700). Historic landmark; restaurants, indoor pool, dancing, concierge, health club, shopping.

Sheraton Seattle Hotel & Towers. *Super Deluxe.* 6th and Pike Sts., Seattle, WA 98111 (206–621–9000). City's largest hotel; restaurants, entertainment, concierge, indoor pool, health club, barber, beauty shops.

Edgewater Inn. *Deluxe-Super Deluxe.* 2411 Alaskan Way, Seattle, WA 98121 (206–728–7000). This is the city's only waterfront hotel, located on Pier 67 next to *Victoria Clipper,* which makes daily trips to Victoria, B.C. Restaurant.

Inn at the Market. *Expensive–Super Deluxe.* 86 Pine St., Seattle, WA 98101 (800–446–4484). Adjacent to Pike Place Market; refrigerators.

Red Lion Inn/Sea-Tac. *Deluxe.* 18740 Pacific Hwy. S., Seattle, WA 98188 (206–246–8600). Pool, restaurant, concierge, entertainment.

Nendel's at Sea-Tac. *Moderate.* 16838 Pacific Hwy. S., Seattle, WA 98188 (206–248–0901). Breakfast, café nearby, sundeck.

University Inn. *Moderate.* 4140 Roosevelt Way N.E., Seattle, WA 98105 (206–632–5055). Pool, kitchens, laundry.

Yakima. Red Lion Inn. *Moderate.* 1507 N. 1st St., Yakima, WA 98901 (509–248–7850). Pools, café, entertainment, patios.

BED AND BREAKFASTS. As elsewhere in the country, bed-and-breakfast accommodations are springing up in Washington. For travelers who want a low-key experience and a chance to get to know the locals, these are ideal. Bed-and-breakfast associations, which help with bookings, include *Pacific Bed and Breakfast,* 701 N.W. 60th St., Seattle, WA 98107 (206–784–0539); *Travelers Bed and Breakfast,* Box 492, Mercer Island, WA 98040 (206–232–2345); and *Whidbey Island Bed and Breakfast Association,* Box 259, Langley, WA 98260.

The following is a list of some especially appealing Washington B&Bs. Their rates range from about $55 to $85. **Home by the Sea,** 2388 E. Sunlight Beach Rd., Clinton, WA 98236 (206–221–2964), on Whidbey Island, is really four separate cottages in the woods and along the beaches; wood stoves, kitchens, full breakfast. On the Long Beach Peninsula, **Shelburne Inn,** Pacific Hwy. 103 and N. 45th St., Seaview, WA 98644 (206–642–2442), has 16 rooms in a historic building adjacent to the beach; fireplace, antique furnishings, gourmet restaurant. **Shumway Mansion,** 11410 100th Ave. N.E., Kirkland, WA 98033 (206–823–2303), perches on a hill in a Seattle suburb east of Lake Washington. Seven guest rooms include European antique furnishings. **The Moore House,** Box 2861, South Cle Elum, WA 98943 (509–674–5939), features guest rooms in a historic railway hotel and two cabooses with sleeping accommodations, east of the Cascades on I-90.

RESTAURANTS. Excellent fresh seafood is available at most restaurants in western Washington. Typical items include salmon, halibut, oysters, clams, and Dungeness crab. Seattle is noted for its ethnic dining, especially Oriental cuisine.

Restaurants are listed according to the price of a three-course meal, not including beverages, tax, and tip: *Super Deluxe,* $25 and up; *Deluxe,* $20–$25; *Expensive,* $15–$20; *Moderate,* $10–$15; *Inexpensive,* under $10.

Bellingham. Mannino's. *Moderate.* 130 E. Champion St., Bellingham, WA 98225 (206–671–7955). This traditional Italian restaurant specializes in veal, chicken, and pasta dishes. L, Mon.–Fri., 11 A.M.–2 P.M., D, daily from 5 P.M. MC, V.

Leavenworth. Terrace Bistro. *Moderate–Expensive.* 200 8th St., Leavenworth, WA 98826 (509–548–4193). Imaginative Continental menu features weiner schnitzel, pffefer steak, tortellini with shrimp, and lavish desserts. Daily; L, 11:30 A.M.–4:30 P.M.; Sun. to 3 P.M. D, 4:30–9 P.M.; Sun. from 3 P.M. MC, V.

Long Beach. The Shoalwater Restaurant at the Shelburne Inn. *Expensive–Deluxe.* Pacific Hwy. 103 and N. 45th St., Seaview, WA 98644 (206–642–4142). Gourmet dinners feature fresh seafood in Victorian setting; extensive wine list. Daily, 5:30–10 P.M., Also L daily in summer. Light fare in the pub, 11:30 A.M.–11 P.M. MC, V.

Olympia. Olympia Oyster House. *Moderate–Expensive.* 320 W. 4th Ave., Olympia, WA 98502 (206–943–8020). Waterside restaurant specializes in oysters, seafood. L, D, Mon.–Thurs., 11 A.M.–9 P.M.; Fri. to 10 P.M. Sat., noon–10 P.M.; Sun., noon–9 P.M. AE, DC, MC, V.

Seattle. Fuller's. *Deluxe–Super Deluxe.* 6th and Pike streets, Seattle, WA 98111 (206–621–9000). One of the city's finest reataurants, this place features local seafood, own baking, regional fowl. L, Mon.–Fri., 11:30 A.M.–2:30 P.M.; D, Mon.–Sat., 5:30–10 P.M. AE, DC, MC, V.

Ray's Boat House. *Moderate–Expensive.* 6049 Seaview Ave. N.W. (206–789–3770). Landmark Seattle seafood restaurant on Shilshole Bay at the entrance to the Ship Canal has been completely rebuilt after a disastrous fire in 1987. L, daily, 11:30 A.M.–2 P.M.; D, Mon.–Thurs., 5:30–9 P.M.; Fri.–Sun., 5–9 P.M. AE, DC, MC, V.

F. X. McRory's Steak, Chop and Oyster House. *Moderate.* 419 Occidental Ave., Seattle WA 98104 (206–623–4800). Old-time brass and wood decor in this restaurant that features beef, seafood. L, Mon.–Fri., 11:30 A.M.–2 P.M.; D, Mon.–Thurs., 5–10 P.M.; Fri. and Sat., 5–11 P.M.; Sun., 5–10 P.M. AE, DC, MC, V.

Ivar's Indian Salmon House. *Moderate.* 401 N.E. Northlake Way, Seattle, WA 98105 (206–632–0767). On the shore of Lake Union; features alder-broiled salmon in Indian setting. L, Mon.–Fri., 11 A.M.–2 P.M.; D, Sun.–Thurs., 5–10 P.M.; Fri.–Sat., 4–11 P.M. Sun. brunch, 10 A.M.–2 P.M. AE, MC, V.

LIQUOR LAWS. The minimum drinking age in Washington is 21. Liquor is sold by the package in state liquor stores and by the drink in licensed establishments. Beer and wine are also sold in grocery stores. Taverns are licensed to sell only beer and wine. Cocktail lounges and taverns may be open 6 A.M.–2 A.M. daily.

ALASKA

by
NORMA SPRING and ARCHIE SATTERFIELD

Norma Spring is a Seattle-based free-lance writer, whose books include Alaska, Pioneer State *and* Alaska, the Complete Travel Book. *Archie Satterfield is a travel writer living near Seattle.*

Note: The giant oil spill that fouled Alaska's Prince William Sound in March 1989—tragic though it was to wildlife and shorelines—affected less than 1% of the state. Alaska still has hundreds of thousands of square miles of unspoiled wilderness, glaciers, and fjords; huge herds of wildlife; and sky-covering flocks of birds. Even Prince William Sound, where the tanker *Exxon Valdez* hit a reef and dumped more than 10 million gallons of crude oil, offers many untouched fjords and glaciers.

Scientists estimate that the first inhabitants came to Alaska 25,000 to 35,000 years ago. They were probably following the animals that they hunted which were heading for warmer, greener regions. Both animals and people crossed a land bridge that lasted about 20,000 years. It spanned the Bering Sea, connecting the Asian and North American continents. When the Ice Age glaciers melted, overwhelming the bridge, seafarers may have continued to paddle across.

These are the native people of Alaska: the Aleuts in the Aleutian Island chain; the Inupiat and Yupik Eskimos in the Arctic; and various Indian tribes in the milder coastal regions of Southeast Alaska, and the interior. Other tribes migrated southward to people the rest of the continent.

The Russians, close neighbors on the west, met native Aleuts as they island-hopped along the volcanic chain in the 18th century. They sighted the Alaskan mainland in 1741. For the rest of the 18th and over half of the 19th century, the Russians claimed their discovery as "Russian America."

These colonies, far removed from their capital (then St. Petersburg), proved too expensive to maintain. Russia decided to relinquish its holdings to the United States.

In 1867, after much debate in Congress, the United States reluctantly agreed to pay about 2½ cents an acre for the isolated territory. For most of that century, its treasures were ignored, except for sporadic gold discoveries.

World War II brought recognition that Alaska's position was strategic for national defense. This triggered military installations, a federal government-based economy, construction of the Alaska Highway, and an increase in population. Another milestone was the achievement of statehood in 1959. A 1964 earthquake and 1967 floods prompted new buildings and modernization. In the 1970s, settlement of Native Land Claims, oil discoveries, and construction of the Trans-Alaska oil pipeline drew world attention to the state and stimulated interest in Alaska as a travel destination. Since then, visitors, on their own or with package tours, have been arriving in increasing numbers, bent on discovering the unique and fascinating nature of this great land and its people.

Within Alaska's 586,412 square miles diversity is the key. Glaciers, snow, ice, and permafrost are balanced by smoking volcanoes, desert sand, grassy plains, and rain forests. Thickly forested areas contrast with infinite stretches of tundra.

Weather is also variable. Some areas are dry while others may be dank, with record rainfall and fog. Temperatures may register from minus 60° F. to almost 100° F.

The seasons are extreme: Long days with 24 hours of daylight above the Arctic Circle characterize summer. In winter, the days may be just a few hours long. Fall and spring are fleeting, pronounced, and beautiful.

A young native, Benny Benson, designed the flag in a school contest sponsored by the American Legion in 1926. His explanation, simple and direct, sums up the reasons for his choice: "The blue field is for the Alaska sky and the forget-me-not, Alaska's state flower. The North Star is for the future State of Alaska, the most northerly of the Union. The Dipper is for the Great Bear—symbolizing strength."

Southeast Alaska (also called the Panhandle) is an archipelago of green, timbered islands plus a narrow coastal strip, separated from Canada by formidable mountains. The famous Inside Passage water route to Alaska, well-used by Indians, explorers, traders, and adventurers even before the gold-rush heyday at the turn of the century, winds between the islands and mainland. Today's "Marine Highway" traffic includes assorted small craft, tugs and barges, freighters, ferries, and cruise ships.

The vast interior region is defined by giant mountain ranges and mighty rivers and is bordered on the east by Canada. The interior contains most of Alaska's roads, covering only about a fifth of the state. Some lead to Gulf of Alaska areas, including the Kenai Peninsula and the pipeline terminal, Valdez. Others head north to Fairbanks, and beyond.

Western, Southwestern, and Arctic Alaska are washed by the Pacific and Arctic oceans and the Bering and Chukchi Seas. Set off from the interior by mountains, glaciers, and rivers, these coastal regions are not accessible by road.

Exploring Alaska

With the development and improvement of transportation, and roads, a "grand circle route" has evolved. It's expandable, retractable, and reversible. Depending on the style of travel preferred, it can be as rugged

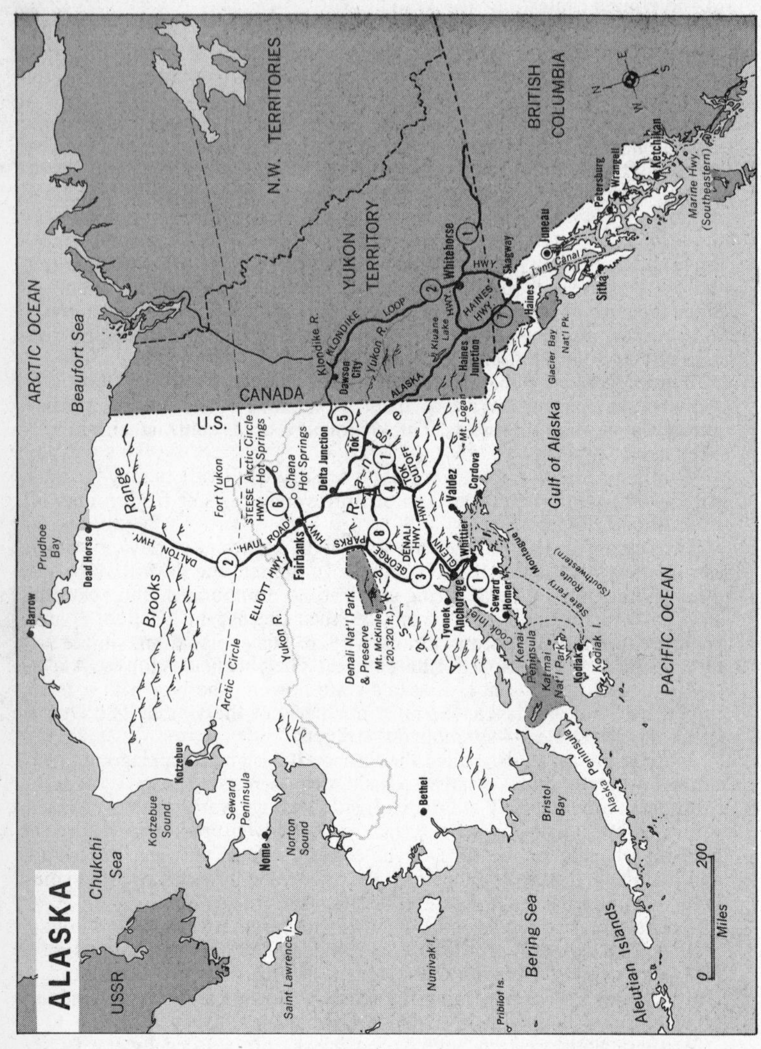
ALASKA
USSR
Chukchi Sea
Kotzebue Sound
Kotzebue
Seward Peninsula
Nome
Norton Sound
Saint Lawrence I.
Nunivak I.
Bering Sea
Pribilof Is.
Aleutian Islands
0
200
Miles
Alaska Peninsula
Bristol Bay
Bethel
Barrow
Brooks Range
Arctic Circle
Yukon R.
ELLIOTT HWY.
Dead Horse
DALTON HWY.
"HAUL ROAD"
Prudhoe Bay
Fort Yukon
STEESE HWY.
Arctic Circle Hot Springs
Chena Hot Springs
Fairbanks
PARKS HWY.
Delta Junction
Denali Nat'l Park & Preserve
Mt. McKinley (20,320 ft.)
GEORGE PARKS
DENALI HWY.
GLENN HWY.
Alaska Range
Tyonek
Anchorage
Whittier
Seward
Homer
Cook Inlet
Kenai Peninsula
Katmai Nat'l Park
Kodiak
Kodiak I.
State Ferry Route (Southwestern)
Montague I.
Valdez
Cordova
TOK CUTOFF
Tok
Mt. Logan
Gulf of Alaska
PACIFIC OCEAN
U.S.
CANADA
ARCTIC OCEAN
Beaufort Sea
Dawson City
Klondike R.
KLONDIKE LOOP
Yukon R.
Kluane Lake
ALASKA HWY.
Haines Junction
HAINES HWY.
Haines
Whitehorse
HWY.
Skagway
Juneau
Lynn Canal
Sitka
Glacier Bay Nat'l Pk.
Petersburg
Wrangell
Ketchikan
Marine Hwy. (Southeastern)
YUKON TERRITORY
N.W. TERRITORIES
BRITISH COLUMBIA
N
E
S
W

or as comfortable as a visitor chooses. Those who drive the Alaska Highway may choose to return by sea through the Inside Passage on the Alaska State Ferry system. In between, at the end of marine and land routes, travelers may switch to planes to visit destinations in the fringes of Alaska.

Tour operators and cruise companies offer combination land/sea/air tours for varying lengths of time and assorted prices. Package tours, set up for group travel experience or for independent traveling, offer advantages to first-time visitors. It's reassuring to know that reservations and baggage are taken care of and that someone stands by to help.

Like the birds and whales, cruise ships migrate from southern winter cruising waters to summer in Alaska. Plying the Inside Passage, they vie with each other in offering comfort and luxury while revealing marine and mountain vistas, lively wildlife, and hospitable ports, including state capital, Juneau.

The big question is which ship to choose. There is no pat answer; each has its own particular charm. In size, they range from "floating resorts" accommodating over a thousand passengers to smaller vessels catering to fewer than a hundred to cruise yachts accommodating only a dozen or fewer. Seeking wilderness adventure, these latter craft are capable of cruising where bigger ships cannot go. The Alaska State Ferry system also operates comfortable ships with car decks and state rooms.

However, if roughing it is your long suit, there's no better place than vast, largely untamed Alaska to hone your outdoor living skills. "Roughing it" is a matter of degree. Visitors may find their pleasures traveling independently by car or recreational vehicle. With flexible schedules, they may follow roads to their endings, and pause to blend into a friendly community for a few days of sightseeing and fishing.

There's a choice of style at *Denali National Park and Preserve,* one of the continent's outstanding wilderness areas, dominated by the highest peak in North America, 20,320-foot Mount McKinley. "Roughing it" here may involve anything from camping and hiking the back country to an expedition to the summit. There are also fine accommodations within the park and along the paved highway that passes by its portal. Guided bus excursions then take visitors along the park road to mountain viewpoints and places to observe the wildlife.

From Anchorage, visitors fly to King Salmon, then change to a smaller float plane to reach the *Katmai National Park and Preserve* on the Alaska Peninsula. Some choose to camp and hike and explore the Valley of Ten Thousand Smokes. Package tours stay at Brooks Lodge on Naknek Lake, famous for giant rainbow trout fishing. From there, daily bus excursions go to viewpoints of the valley, which was blanketed in volcanic ash by violent eruptions which destroyed Mt. Katmai in 1912.

In contrast, ice molded the land and waterways of *Glacier Bay National Park and Preserve,* located 50 miles northwest of Juneau, and accessible by boats, planes, and some cruise ships. Deep fjords, terminating at tidewater glaciers, islands, mountains, and wildlife lure "roughing it" enthusiasts to explore by kayak, by canoe, and afoot.

Within the Park, near Park Headquarters at Bartlett Cove, the rustically deluxe Glacier Bay Lodge houses, in summer, those who prefer their creature comforts. Daily, the lodge's excursion boat takes guests to view the up-Bay wonders, especially wildlife and glaciers, as a naturalist describes and interprets their journey back into the "ice age."

The Alaskans

However they travel, and wherever, visitors are bound to get acquainted with the residents. The still-small population—a little over 500,000—is a convivial mix of about one-sixth native Indians, Eskimos, and Aleuts; descendants of foreign explorers and settlers; immigrants from the "Lower

48" states as well as other parts of the world; and those proud of being native-born.

Some Native Alaskans live in widely separated villages along the 33,000-mile coastline and the great rivers of the 49th state. Many others have moved to the larger cities, Anchorage and Fairbanks, and some have settled in other states.

There are few noticeable language or racial barriers among Alaskans, but visitors may notice some general "Alaskan" characteristics, such as vigor, individualism, and pride in their state. They're inclined to boast about their superlatives: the most western state; most northern; tallest (thanks to Mount McKinley); and with the most shoreline, daylight (in summer), darkness (in winter), wildlife, and size—two-and-a-half times larger than runner-up Texas.

Another Alaskan trait appears to be the capacity for work and play. Alaskans fish and hunt for subsistence—for food in the locker and a boost to the family budget. Families work together at what needs doing during summer, often handling more than one job at a time. However, almost any excuse puts them in a mood for play. The Alaskan calendar is full of games and festivals celebrating everything from a 100-foot iceworm winding through the streets (Cordova in February) and fur (Anchorage Fur Rendezvous in mid-February) to whales (Point Hope in June).

Sourdough miners who panned during the gold rush era are gone, but others carry on at the claims. You may meet homesteaders who earned their property by "proving up": building a cabin and living off the land. The *real* Alaskans now are those sticking it out through boom or bust, but ever enthusiastic about their raw, rarely mild, sometimes violent land. They accept the unexpected and cope with what they have to. The happiest visitors adopt their philosophy.

PRACTICAL INFORMATION FOR ALASKA

WHEN TO GO. The most popular time to travel to Alaska is during the long, light days of summer, from early June through Aug. The longest, least rainy days are in May and June. However, a growing number of visitors are discovering delights of off-season travel. Spring, fall—even winter—offer added bonuses, among them lower "thrift season" prices and hobnobbing with Alaskans, more relaxed then than during the busy summer. Actually the best answer to "when" is "now" because, in many places, there is still much of the fascinating past mingling with the jet-age present.

HOW TO GET THERE. Island and coastal towns of the Southeast Panhandle are accessible only by sea and air, except for two ports at the northern end of the Inside Passage. From Haines and Skagway, highways connect with overland routes to south-central and interior destinations and with the Alaska Hwy. Bush planes and jet aircraft fly beyond the road terminals to destinations in the far Western and Arctic regions.

By plane. International airlines fly to Anchorage. Scheduled interstate carriers serve Ketchikan, Sitka, Juneau, Anchorage, and Fairbanks. Some may offer bargains such as: lower fares in connection with cruises and tours; senior citizen rates; and city stopovers for a small charge. Watch the ads and ask your travel agent or your nearest regional airline, possibly it may have interchange service with these major airlines flying year-round to Alaska: *Alaska Airlines* (800–426–0333); *Northwest* (800–225–2525); *United Airlines* (800–241–6522); and *Delta Airlines* (800–221–1212).

By bus. Motorcoaches, independently or in connection with major tour companies, travel to and throughout Alaska from U.S. and Canadian points. Mostly seasonal service. Contact: *Gray Line of Alaska,* 300 Elliott Ave. W., Seattle, WA 98119

(800–544–2206); or *Princess Tours,* 2815 Second Ave., Suite 400, Seattle, WA 98121 (206–728–4202 or 800–426–0442).

By car. The Alaska Hwy. is open year-round. Despite the generally good road conditions and careful monitoring, you should take special precautions when traveling by car, especially in winter, when temperatures on the road can stay below zero for weeks. You should carry a current guide to facilities and services. U.S. citizens need no passport at the Canadian border, but some personal papers as proof of nationality are advisable.

By boat. Alaska ferryliners operate year-round between Prince Rupert, B.C., Bellingham, WA, and the Southeastern Marine Highway System ports. The Southcentral System serves the ports of Prince William Sound, Gulf of Alaska, the Kenai Peninsula, and Kodiak Island. For information and reservations, write: *Alaska Marine Highway,* Box R, Juneau, AK 99811 (907–465–3941; 800–642–0066). Also contact *BC Ferries,* Dept. AVP 88, 1112 Fort St., Victoria, B.C., Canada V8V 4V2, (604–669–1211) about ferries between Vancouver, Vancouver Island, and Prince Rupert.

In summer, cruise ship departure ports include Los Angeles, San Francisco, Seattle, Vancouver, and Prince Rupert. Some ships continue beyond the Inside Passage as far as Whittier in Prince William Sound. Combination land, air, and Marine Highway trips are popular. (See the section on *Tours.*)

TOURIST INFORMATION. For a free, annually updated, official "Alaska Vacation Planner," contact *Alaska Division of Tourism,* Box E, Juneau, AK 99811 (907–465–2010). In its 100-plus pages, the Planner lists community Information Centers, Chambers of Commerce, Convention and Visitor Bureaus, accommodations, transportation, special attractions, and many pertinent facts of Alaska life related to visitors.

The *Tok Information Center.* Mile 1314 Alaska Hwy., Tok, AK 99780 (907–883–5667), dispenses information daily in summer from 8 A.M. to 8 P.M. In winter, the hours are 8 A.M. to 4:30 P.M. Mon.–Fri.

Anchorage Visitor Information Centers are located in the baggage claim area of the Anchorage International and Domestic Airport Terminals, in the Valley River Mall, Eagle River, and in the Log Cabin at 4th and F Sts., downtown, 546 W. Fourth Ave., Anchorage, AK 99501 (907–274–3531). Phone 276–3200 for a recording of daily events.

Fairbanks Visitor Information Centers. There's an information booth at the Fairbanks International Airport, and also in a Log Cabin downtown at 550 First Ave., Fairbanks, AK 99701 (907–456–5774). For daily events, phone 456–INFO.

Juneau Visitor Information Center, year-round, is in the historic Davis Log Cabin, 134 Third St., Juneau, AK 99801 (907–586–2201 or 2284). For current happenings, phone 586–JUNO. Near Merchants Wharf at the waterfront Marine Park, the visitor information kiosk is open from June to mid-Sept., and there is also a booth at the airport terminal.

Ketchikan Visitors Bureau, 131 Front St., Ketchikan, AK 99901 (907–225–6166) is handily located downtown on cruise ship dock Number 1.

TIME ZONES. Big enough for four zones, geographically, the state has condensed them to two, for convenience. Alaska Time (one hour behind Pacific Time) prevails, except in the farthest west Aleutian Islands, where they observe Hawaii-Aleutian Time (two hours behind Pacific). Most of the Yukon is on Pacific Time.

TELEPHONES. The area code throughout Alaska is 907. Dial 800–478–9500 to send telegrams and mailgrams by phone. Dial 0 before area code for credit, collect, or person-to-person calls.

EMERGENCY TELEPHONE NUMBERS. 911 is the main emergency number for police, fire, ambulance, search, and rescue in most places. Otherwise, ask the operator for assistance.

HOW TO GET AROUND. Alaskans are experts at getting around their big state, and "traveler's aid" is readily available for visitors on tour or on their own. Airporters, taxis, and buses expedite getting into town from airports. In major cities—

and in many small ones—cars or recreational vehicles may be rented at offices conveniently located at airports, hotels, and motels.

Public bus systems serve many communities, and there's scheduled service along major highways. Hotel tour desks have information on sightseeing tours available. Scheduled carriers link main cities and towns. Dependable "bush" pilots and planes serve isolated points.

The *Alaska Railroad Corporation,* Box 10–7500, Anchorage, AK 99510 (800–544–0552), provides daily service in summer. The schedule is reduced in winter, but service is year-round. The northern route takes in Fairbanks and Denali Park from Anchorage, while the southern route goes to Seward and connects at Whittier with ferryliners plying Prince William Sound.

Listed in the state's free Travel Planner are numerous operators offering visitors the opportunity to get around as the Alaskans do—by dog sled, snowmobile, canoe, kayak, river raft, motorbike, bicycle, horseback, or backpack.

HINTS TO MOTORISTS. Driving in Alaska is probably more unpredictable and challenging than in any other part of the nation. However, alerted for possible perils, motorists should have little difficulty. Moreover, traveling at their own pace and alerted for upcoming points of interest, car and RV tourists will discover that the rewards—scenic and social—are great.

Most main highways, which cover about a fifth of the state, are paved. These include the Alaska Hwy. (beginning at the border) and the Richardson, Glenn, Seward-Anchorage, Sterling, and George Parks (between Anchorage and Fairbanks). Watch for rough spots caused by annual freezing and thawing, road crews and equipment making repairs, and animals, especially moose. *The Milepost,* GTE Discovery Publications, Box 3007, Bothell, WA 98021 ($16.95, plus $1.50 postage), describes highways mile by mile, advertises accommodations and attractions. *Camping Alaska and Canada's Yukon,* Globe Pequot Press, Box Q, Chester, CT 06412 ($10.95 plus $1.25 postage), critiques every public campground.

HINTS TO DISABLED TRAVELERS. Convention and Visitor centers are alert to the needs of handicapped travelers, and have information on local programs. *Access Alaska,* 3710 Woodland Park, Suite 900, Anchorage, AK 99517 (907–248–4777), features independent living, referrals, and other help. Many indoor and outdoor sport and recreational activities, among them skiing, dog sledding, rafting, kayaking, camping, and fishing, to name a few, are available through *Challenge Alaska,* Box 110065, Anchorage, AK 99511 (907–563–2658).

SHOPPING. In particular, look for furs and for native-crafted items: ivory, jade, and soapstone carvings, parkas, paintings on skins, mukluks, masks, wood-carved plaques and totem poles. There are also many fine gift shops that sell contemporary arts and crafts work such as: paintings, pottery, silver and gold nugget jewelry, and typical Alaskan foods—canned and smoked salmon and wild berry products. Look for the state symbols—a hand, map, or mother bear with cub—that indicate your purchase is authentically Alaskan.

TOURS. Tour packages, lasting from a few days to a few weeks, cover big Alaska. They allow for optional tours farther afield from key destinations. Many firms listed here have grown up with Alaska tourism, and pioneered various areas. They work closely with cruise ships, airlines, ferries, motorcoaches, railroads, Alaskans, and your local travel agent.

AARP Travel Service. 5855 Green Valley Circle, Culver City, CA 90230 (800–227–7885; 800–227–7737). The travel service of the American Association of Retired Persons offers seven different cruise-tour itineraries to Alaska, ranging from 10 to 18 days. There is a wide selection of ships (five different vessels) and accommodations. Rail travel is included in these tours. Seasonal service, mid-May to mid-Sept.

Cruise Alaska Tours. Box 96045, Bellevue, WA 98009 (800–426–2134). Offers cruise-tours and cruises only on three cruise lines with a variety of ships. Travelers can cruise one way, take a land tour followed by a return cruise, or opt to fly home. Ships cruise through the Inside Passage with some continuing on to the Gulf of Alaska.

Alaska Northwest Travel Service. 130 2nd Ave. S., Edmonds, WA 98020 (206–775–4504). This agency specializes in travel to the Far North.

Alaska Sightseeing Tours. 808 4th and Battery Building, Seattle, WA 98121 (800–621–5557; 907–276–1305). Headed by an Alaska travel industry pioneer, this firm offers statewide land and sea tours for independent travelers plus local sightseeing excursions in Anchorage, Fairbanks, Haines, Skagway, Juneau, and Ketchikan, as well as tours of Columbia Glacier and Denali National Park. Waterborne options include sailings aboard major cruise ships or Alaska Sightseeing's own *MV Sheltered Seas,* a 65-foot motor yacht. Passengers aboard this vessel visit fjords, glaciers, small coves, and communities during daylight hours and spend their nights in hotels ashore. The company also packages tours utilizing the state ferries of the Alaska Marine Highway System.

Holland America-Westours. 300 Elliott Ave. W., Seattle, WA 98119 (206–281–1970; 206–281–3535). This group operates hotels at strategic points, motorcoaches and railcars attached to the Alaska Railroad between Anchorage and Fairbanks. Holland-America ships sail the Inside Passage as far as Juneau. From there, Westours' minicruiser *MV Fairweather* runs daily in fjordlike Lynn Canal between Juneau and Skagway to connect with the Yukon and northern Alaska destinations.

Princess Tours. 2815 2nd Ave., Suite 400, Seattle, WA 98121-1299 (206–728–4202–800–426–0442). These tours combine Inside Passage cruises with highway and rail excursions. One tour includes a trip to Prudhoe Bay and along the Pipeline Rd. *Princess* and *Gray Line of Alaska,* 300 Elliott Ave. W., Seattle, WA 98119 (800–544–2206) both offer this excursion.

SPECIAL INTEREST, SMALLER GROUPS. **Alaska Discovery.** 369 S. Franklin, Juneau, AK 99801 (907–586–1911). This especially favors Glacier Bay, by kayak and canoe. University credits possible.

Alaska Sportfishing Packages. 316 Occidental Ave. S., Suite 325, Seattle, WA 98104 (206–382–1051; 800–426–0603). Fishing is the focus of their fine and varied offerings.

Alaska Travel Adventures. 9085 Glacier Highway, Juneau, AK 99801 (907–586–6245). Their "tastes of adventure" in backcountry are graded to appeal to all ages.

World Explorer Cruises. 550 Kearny St., San Francisco, CA 94108 (800–854–3835 or 800–222–2255). They offer 14-day cruises that emphasize cultural enrichment; onboard educational program.

NATIONAL AND STATE PARKS. Much debate has gone into resolving how much of Alaska should be preserved in its natural state. The result is more parklands than in the other 49 states combined. The following are good sources of information:

Write to *Alaska State Park Information,* Pouch 107001, Anchorage, AK 99510, or stop by the Statewide Headquarters Office in downtown Anchorage at 3601 C St. *Forest Service Information Center* in Centennial Hall, downtown Juneau, 101 Egan Drive, Juneau, AK 99801 (907–586–8751), has fine exhibits, programs, and is open daily mid-May to mid-Sept., 9 A.M.–6 P.M.; Mon.–Fri., 8 A.M.–5 P.M. for the rest of the year. *National Park Service,* Alaska Regional Office, 2525 Gambell St., Anchorage, AK 99501 (907–271–2643), keeps tabs on recreational opportunities in all Park Service lands in Alaska.

Here are some major destinations:

Denali National Park and Preserve. Box 9, Denali National Park, AK 99755 (907–683–2686).

Glacier Bay National Park and Preserve. Gustavus, AK 99826 (907–697–2232). Also accessible in winter, by fly-in, kayaking, or hiking, weather permitting.

Katmai National Park and Preserve. Box 7, King Salmon, AK 99613 (907–246–3305).

PARTICIPANT SPORTS. The hardy Alaska residents are masters at coming up with antidotes for "cabin fever" and winter doldrums. There'll be skiing, sledding, ice skating, ice fishing, and snowmobiling whenever there's snow and terrain to support the action. The best developed **ski area** is about 40 miles from Anchorage, with heli-skiing, and dogsledding, chairlifts, ski school, day lodge, overnight accommodations, and restaurants. Write *Alyeska Resort,* Box 249, Girdwood, AK

99857 (907–783–2222). It's also a summer resort. *Eaglecrest,* 155 S. Seward, Juneau, AK 99801 (907–586–5284), also offers good to excellent skiing Dec.–Apr.

All nonresidents must possess a valid license and tags to **fish and hunt.** Write Public Communications, Alaska Dept. of Fish & Game, Box 3–2000, Juneau, AK 99802 (907–465–4112) for current regulations. Also check this department in popular local fishing areas, for "catch" information.

Recreational mining for fun and adventure is open to all—even visitors—on certain public lands. Send for the leaflets spelling out do's and don'ts and locations issued by the *Bureau of Land Management,* Box 13, 701 C St., Anchorage, AK 99513 (907–271–5960). Some tour packages include the opportunity to pan for gold, and there are private concessions where, for a fee, you can try your hand. Before dipping your gold pan into a promising stream, be sure you are not on someone's claim.

Alaskans are quick to recognize kindred souls from "outside." Whatever the season, Cheechakos (newcomers) will be welcome to join in.

HISTORIC SITES AND HOUSES. Over a hundred such sites and houses are listed in the *National Register.* Some are National Landmarks, such as the whole town of Eagle, where the Norwegian explorer Roald Amundsen stayed in 1905. Historic buildings surround the parade ground of *Fort William H. Seward,* adjacent to Haines. Fairbanks hoards historic things from boats to buildings in 44-acre *Alaskaland.* Ketchikan's *Totem Bight Historical Site* contains excellent totems and a tribal house. In Sitka, the *National Historical Park,* with totems and Visitor Center, commemorates the site where Russians defeated Indians in the final "Battle for Alaska" in 1804. Skagway and nearby ghost town Dyea, overland starting points for the rugged mountain and river route to inland gold fields, are part of the *Klondike Gold Rush National Historical Park.* In Juneau, the *House of Wickersham,* 213 Seventh Ave., restored by the State, continues to house the outstanding collection of Alaskana of turn-of-the-century statesman and historian, Judge Wickersham, and preserved by his niece, Ruth Allman.

MUSEUMS AND GALLERIES. The *Anchorage Historical and Fine Arts Museum* 121 W. Seventh Ave. exhibits arts and artifacts of Alaska, as do the *University of Alaska Museum* at Fairbanks and the *Alaska State Museum* at Juneau. Many small communities corral their treasures and store them—often in historic buildings—for display to interested visitors. In Nome, the *Carrie McLain Memorial Museum* emphasizes the Gold Rush, Eskimo culture, and the region's natural history. The *Sheldon Jackson Museum* in Sitka has a collection of Tlingit Indian and Russian-American items. The *Bigelow Museum,* Wrangell, is a private collection with nostalgic 19th- and 20th-century memorabilia. The *Trail of '98 Museum* in Skagway is full of gold rush history, and the town's lively past—including some of notorious Soapy Smith's belongings. Kotzebue's *Living Museum of the Arctic* offers dioramas of Arctic life and environment, Eskimo crafts, and dance demonstrations.

Numerous galleries, from the *University of Alaska Fine Arts Center,* Fairbanks, to art-minded Homer near the tip of the Kenai Peninsula, represent Alaskan artists.

ARTS AND ENTERTAINMENT. There's no lack of entertainment—even if visitors have to settle for "pot luck" at whatever time they happen to be there. Just ask at the information sources listed in the "Tourist Information" section.

Salmon Bakes (another Alaskan institution), are held many places. Try the *Gold Creek Outdoor Salmon Bake* at Last Chance Basin, Juneau (907–586–1424) or the *Alaska Salmon Bake* at Alaskaland (907–452–7274), Fairbanks. The *Port Chilkoot Potlatch,* featuring fresh local salmon prepared over an open alderwood fire, is served on the Parade Ground of Fort William Seward (Haines) by the Halsingland Hotel (907–766–2000).

Also at Haines-Fort Seward, call 766–2202 to find out when the *Chilkat Indian Dancers* perform and 766–2160 for the melodrama *Lust for Dust,* or ask at the Visitor Center (2nd and Willard St.). They'll know when travelers may visit the Arts and Crafts Center and watch the craftspeople, who work on the grounds.

Throughout the summer in Skagway, historical comedy-dramas, *In the Days of '98,* are performed at Eagles Hall, 6th & Broadway (907–983–2545). Tickets are sold at the door, or write for reservations to "Soapy Smith," Box 1897, Skagway, AK 99840 (907–983–2545).

In Juneau, enjoy the "Lady Lou Review" in the Merchant's Wharf (907–586–3686 or 907–364–2151).

ACCOMMODATIONS. Package tours include accommodations, and operators block space for their clients in the better hotels. Independent travelers may find space limited or lacking in remote areas such as the Arctic, or at Glacier Bay during the summer peak. Reserve ahead, unless you are self-sufficient with camper, trailer, or tent. Prices are on a par with most other state and world travel destinations, and major credit cards are widely accepted. In smaller towns, food and lodging may be less expensive than in the big cities, but with fewer choices. Don't hestitate to stop by local Visitor Information centers and Chambers of Commerce. They know what's available and can furnish leads and prices, varying from frontier to plush, and including Youth Hostels and Bed and Breakfast. Included here is only a sampling. In Alaska *Deluxe* means the best available, usually the most expensive, and considered tops by the local residents. Based on double occupancy, a *Deluxe* room will probably cost over $120 per night; *Expensive,* over $100; *Moderate,* over $80; and *Inexpensive,* under $80.

Statewide. Alaska Private Lodgings books bed-and-breakfast accommodations statewide (907–258–1717) 4631 Caravelle Dr., Anchorage, AK 99502.

ANCHORAGE. Anchorage Hilton Hotel. *Deluxe.* Downtown at 3rd and E. St. 99501 (272–7411 or 800–HILTONS). 500 rooms in downtown double tower. Coffee shop, dining rooms, bars, swimming pool.

Captain Cook Hotel. *Deluxe.* 5th & K St., write Box 102280, 99510 (907–276–6000 or 800–323–7500). Large, well-decorated rooms in huge hotel. Three towers of view rooms. Some suites. Parking lot. Coffee shop, dining room, cocktail lounges with entertainment, health club with pool.

Sheraton Anchorage. *Deluxe.* 401 E. 6th Ave., 99501 (800–325–3535 outside Alaska; 907–276–8700, call collect in Alaska). Near downtown. Elegant decor, including jade stairway in foyer. Rooftop restaurant/lounge, ballroom, and health-club with whirlpool and saunas.

Westmark Anchorage. *Deluxe.* 720 W. 5th, Anchorage, AK 99501 (907–276–7676 or 274–6631; 800–544–0970 in continental U.S.; in Alaska, 800–478–1111). Three blocks from Convention Center; 2 restaurants and 3-level Penthouse Lounge, highest in Anchorage, with view.

Anchorage Hotel. *Expensive.* Downtown at 330 E St., 99501 (800–544–0988 or 907–272–4553). Located in a restored historic building, this place offers calm Victorian chain at a good value.

Holiday Inn. *Expensive.* 239 W. 4th Ave., 99501 (907–279–8671 or 800–465–4329 or make reservations by calling any Holiday Inn, anywhere). Large motor inn, three levels. Attractive rooms. Indoor pool. Dining room, cocktail lounge with entertainment nightly, except Sun.

Westmark Inn Third Avenue. *Expensive.* 3rd and Barrow, 99501 (907–272–7561; 907–276–7676; 800–544–0970 in continental U.S.; in Alaska, call 800–478–1111). Pleasant, three-story motor inn with coffee shop, dining room, bar.

Anchorage International Airport Inn. *Moderate.* 3333 W. International Airport Rd., 99502 (907–243–2233). Big, down to its king- and queen-size beds. Restaurant, bar, convention facilities, courtesy car service.

Mush Inn Motel. *Moderate.* 333 Concrete, 99501 (907–277–4554). Large motel near Merrill Field. Free transportation to and from airport. Restaurant and bar nearby. Covered parking; security guards. Family rooms, kitchenettes. Heated water beds.

Voyager Hotel. *Moderate.* 501 K St., 99501 (907–277–9501). Rooms with kitchenettes, bath, color TV. Separate, but on the lower level of the building is the Corsair restaurant and bar. Highly recommended for location and comfort.

Anchorage International Hostel. *Inexpensive.* 700 H St., 99501 (907–276–3635). Dormitory and some private rooms are available at this yellow cinder-block building next door to the Alaska Center for the Environment.

DENALI NATIONAL PARK AND PRESERVE. Denali National Park Central Reservations and Travel, Inc., Box 200984, Anchorage, AK 99520 (800–344–8485). Central booking agency for all park lodging.

Denali National Park Hotel. *Expensive.* Denali National Park and Preserve, 825 8th Ave., #240, Anchorage, AK 99501 (907–276–7234). At McKinley Station of Alaska Railroad. Open summers with a variety of accommodations. Snack shop, saloon, dining room, gift shop.

Harper Lodge Princess. *Deluxe.* Write 329 F St. #207, Anchorage, AK 99501 (907–258–5993 or 800–541–5174). New, on the banks of the Nenana River, one mile from entrance to Park. Lounge, dining room, gift shop, meeting room.

McKinley Chalets. *Expensive.* Same address as Denali National Park Hotel. Outside the park, but not far from the entrance. 120 attractive suites overlooking Nenana River. Gift shops and lounge; open end of May–Sept.

McKinley Village. *Expensive.* Denali National Park and Preserve, 825 8th Ave., #240, Anchorage, AK 99501 (907–276–7234). About 6 miles from park entrance. 50-room hotel open mid-May–late Sept. Restaurant, service station, "Village Pub."

FAIRBANKS (99701). Westmark Fairbanks. *Deluxe.* 820 Noble St. (907–456–7722; 800–478–1111 inside Alaska; 800–544–0970 outside Alaska). Huge, multistory motor inn, with many different types of units, some studio rooms, some suites. No pets. Coffee shop, cocktail lounge, excellent restaurant.

Sophie Station. *Deluxe.* 1717 University Ave. (907–479–3650). All suites with kitchens are available here. Dining, cocktails, shops.

Westmark Inn. *Deluxe.* 1521 Cushman St. (907–456–6602 or 800–544–0970). Large, two-story motor inn, with inviting rooms. No pets. Dining room, cocktail lounge, laundry, valet service. May 15–Sept. 15 only.

Captain Bartlett Inn. *Moderate.* 1411 Airport Way (907–452–1888; 800–478–7900 in Alaska; 800–544–7582 in continental U.S.). 205 rooms. Spruce-log lobby, Alaska decor, and "largest fireplace in Alaska." Near Alaskaland Centennial Park. Restaurant, lounge.

Captain's Choice. *Moderate.* Motel units overlooking Lynn Canal, at 2nd and Dalton. Box 392 (907–766–3111 or 800–478–2345 in Alaska; 800–247–7153 outside Alaska). Captain's Suite has wet bar.

Eagle's Nest Motel. *Moderate.* On Hwy. 7 near town center and airport. Box 250 (907–766–2352). Open year-round; camper park, full hookup; also National Car Rentals available.

Klondike Inn. *Moderate.* 1316 Bedrock St. (907–479–6241). Large rooms with kitchen facilities. Laundry, lounge, and courtesy car.

Polaris Hotel. *Moderate.* 427 First Ave. (907–452–5571). Large hotel conveniently located in town, with restaurant and cocktail lounge.

Super 8 Motel. *Moderate.* 1909 Airport Way (907–451–8888 or 800–843–1991).

Golden North Motel. *Inexpensive.* 4888 Airport Rd.; (907–479–6201). Near the International Airport. In-room coffee. Restaurant and cocktail lounge nearby.

Golden Nugget Motel. *Inexpensive.* 900 Noble St. (907–452–5141). Two-story motel with comfortable attractive rooms. Sauna and games room. Restaurant, cocktail lounge.

Tamarac Inn Motel. *Inexpensive.* 252 Minnie St. (907–456–6406). Smaller motel with 20 units.

HAINES (99827). Alaska Thunderbird Motel. *Moderate.* 2nd and Dalton Sts., Box 589 (907–766–2131 or 800–327–2556). Modern motel units in this small downtown facility, all with private baths. TV.

Fort Seward Condos. *Moderate.* Overlooking Lynn Canal. Box 75 (907–766–2425 or 766–2801). If you want to stay awhile, inquire about these completely furnished apartments available by week or month (3-day minimum).

Ft. Seward Lodge. *Inexpensive.* Fort Seward Box 307, (907–766–2009). 10 rooms, restaurant.

Hotel Halsingland. *Inexpensive.* Located in Port Chilkoot, Box 1589 (907–766–2000 or 800–478–2525). Affording a view of Lynn Canal and surrounding glacial-sided mountains, this moderate-size, family-style hotel is in vintage army quarters of old Fort William Seward, facing parade ground. Cocktail lounge; family style dining room featuring Swedish cuisine and fresh local seafood.

Mountain View Motel. *Inexpensive.* Box 62 (907–766–2900 or 800–478–2902). Adjacent to Fort Seward, within walking distance of downtown Haines. Kitchenettes, TV, laundromat, restaurants, art shops nearby. Handy to the action at beaches, harbor, parks, and performing arts center.

JUNEAU (99801). Westmark Juneau. *Deluxe.* 51 W. Egan Dr. (586–6900; 800–544–0970 outside Alaska; 800–478–1111 inside Alaska; 800–949–2570 in Canada). 104 rooms with first-run color movies. Banquet and meeting facilities. Downtown. Restaurant; lounge.

Prospector Hotel. *Expensive.* 375 Whittier Ave., in Sub-port area; (907–586–3737 or 800–331–2711). Modest-size hotel with full facilities. Restaurant, bar. Sightseeing tours available.

Westmark Baranof Hotel. *Expensive.* 127 Franklin St. (907–586–2660; 800–478–1111 inside Alaska; 800–544–0970 outside Alaska 800–949–2570 in Canada). 225 rooms, in the center of town. Telephone; TV; restaurant; bar, banquet and meeting rooms; 7-day-a-week coffee shop.

Driftwood Lodge. *Moderate.* 435 Willoughby Ave. (907–586–2280 or 800–544–2239). Motel with 47 units, some with kitchens. Several two-bedroom apartments. Laundromat; restaurant.

Silverbow Inn. *Moderate.* 120 Second St. (907–586–4146). Personal service and a great restaurant make this renovated landmark the best little hotel in Juneau.

Super-8. *Moderate.* 2295 Trout St. (907–789–4858 or 800–843–1991). 75 rooms near airport; courtesy car.

Alaskan Hotel. *Inexpensive.* 167 S. Franklin St. (907–586–1000 or 800–327–9347). In downtown historic area. Rustic bar; health spa.

Bergmann Hotel. *Inexpensive.* 434 Third St. (907–586–1690). This is a spartan vintage hotel reflecting "old Juneau." Rooms with or without bath.

Breakwater Inn. *Inexpensive.* 1711 Glacier Ave. (907–586–6303 or 800–478–2250 inside Alaska; 800–544–2250 outside Alaska). Motel overlooking boat basin about a mile from downtown. Dining room; bar; laundromat.

KETCHIKAN (99901). Royal Executive Suites. *Expensive.* 1471 Tongass Ave. (907–225–1900). Water view, exercise room, midtown location.

Ingersoll Hotel. *Moderate.* 303 Mission St. (907–225–2124). Historic downtown 60-room, three-story hotel, with front rooms overlooking the waterfront. Restaurant; lounge; and deli-sandwich shop.

The Landing Motel. *Moderate.* 3434 N. Tongass Hwy. (907–225–5166 or 800–528–1234). 47 units across from air and ferry terminals. Two levels, large rooms. Family-type. Restaurant and cocktail lounge.

Super 8 Motel. *Moderate.* 2151 Sea Level Dr., near Airport Ferry terminal (800–843–1991 or 907–225–9088). 81 rooms, among them 6 suites with view of Tongass Narrows. All rooms have waterbeds; some special rooms for handicapped persons; and a freezer to hold the catch of visiting fishermen.

Gilmore Hotel. *Inexpensive.* 326 Front St. (907–225–9423). 42 rooms at downtown waterfront near restaurants and shopping; airporter bus service. Newly renovated with color TV; phones; cocktail lounge.

SITKA (99835). Westmark Shee Atika Lodge. *Deluxe.* 330 Seward St., (907–747–6241 or 800–544–0970 outside Alaska; 800–478–1111 inside Alaska). Attractive 96-room wooden building, overlooks Crescent Harbor with mountain view, near Centennial Building.

Potlatch House. *Moderate.* 713 Katlian St., Box 58 (907–747–8611). Several blocks from downtown, but there is a courtesy car. Mt. Edgecumbe and harbor view. Restaurant and cocktail lounge.

Super 8 Motel. *Moderate.* 404 Sawmill Creek Rd. (907–747–8804).

Biorka Bed & Breakfast. *Inexpensive.* 611 Biorka St. (907–747–3111). Private entry and baths, cable TV, phones. Close to visitor attractions, restaurants, and shops. No smoking or alcohol.

Sitka Hotel. *Inexpensive.* 118 Lincoln St., Box 850 (907–747–3288). Downtown hotel with elevator and 24-hour phone service. 60 rooms, some with choice views.

SKAGWAY (99840). Westmark Inn. *Expensive–Deluxe.* Third and Spring Sts., Skagway, summer; 880 H St., Suite 101, Anchorage, AK 99501, winter. (907–983–2291; 800–544–0970 outside Alaska; 800–478–1111 inside Alaska). Next to the Historic District. 220 rooms, lounge, restaurant, banquet facilities. Houses tour groups. Original section re-creates theme of gold rush through colorful decorations.

Golden North Hotel. *Expensive.* 3rd and Broadway, Box 431 (907–983–2294). A gold rush remainder. All 35 rooms different; furnished with charming antique touches. You can't miss it; its golden dome is a landmark. Restaurant.

Sgt. Preston's Lodge. *Moderate.* 6th between Broadway and State (907–983–2521). 23 rooms with, without bath.

Skagway Inn. *Moderate.* Box 500, Skagway, summer; Box 631, Haines, AK 99827, winter (907–983–2289 summer, or 766–2788 winter). Aura of Gold Rush preserved in this vintage building, once a saloon, on boardwalk-lined main street. Rooms (with and without private bath) have women's names instead of numbers.

Wind Valley Lodge. *Moderate.* Box 354B (907–983–2236). 22nd and State Sts. on the Klondike Hwy. 30 well-appointed rooms near historic district.

VALDEZ (99686). Westmark Valdez. *Deluxe.* 100 Fidalgo Dr. (907–835–4391, 800–544–0970 outside Alaska; 800–478–1111 inside Alaska). 100 units with full baths and showers. Dining room and bar. Marina, dock, boat and motor rentals. Fishing tackle and bait shop. Daily custom smoking and canning service. No pets. At Valdez's small-boat harbor.

Totem Inn. *Moderate.* Richardson Hwy. and Meals Ave. Box 648, Valdez (907–835–4443). Alaskan touches in lobby include mounted wild game and cheery fireplace. Restaurant and lounge.

Valdez Motel. *Moderate.* Box 65, Valdez (907–835–4444). With assorted singles, doubles, and family units among its 27 rooms. Restaurant. Features "Pipeline Club."

Village Inn. *Moderate.* Downtown near waterfront. Box 365, Valdez (907–835–4445; 800–478–4445 in Alaska). 60 new rooms; 21 cottages with kitchen. *Gay Nineties* lounge and restaurant. Children, pets OK.

RESTAURANTS. The following is only a sampling. Most hotels and motels included in the *accommodations* section have restaurants, or are close to some. Don't hesitate to ask the residents where they eat—when they want to splurge, and when they want to eat well, but for less. Sourdough and seafood are often specialties. In larger cities, restaurants boast a variety of cuisine. These categories for complete dinners—drinks, tax, and tips not included—give a clue to the tab: *Deluxe,* $30 and up; *Expensive,* $20–$30; *Moderate,* $15–$20; *Inexpensive,* under $15.

ANCHORAGE. Josephine's. *Deluxe.* Sheraton Hotel, 201 E. 6th Ave. (276–8700). Also elegant food, service, and decor at rooftop.

Marx Brothers Cafe. *Deluxe.* 327 W. 3rd Ave. (278–2133). This small, personal restaurant serves innovative American and nouvelle cuisines. There is a large wine cellar.

Garden of Eatin'. *Expensive.* 2502 McRae Rd. (248–3663). Dinner theater in homesteader's Quonset hut. Open 6 A.M.–10 P.M. in summer (except Sun. and Mon. Reservations required).

Simon & Seaforts. *Expensive.* 520 L St. (274–3502). Captures spirit (and spirits) of grand saloon with congeniality; good food.

Downtown Deli. *Moderate.* 526 W. 4th Ave. (274–0027). Local landmark.

Gwennie's Old Alaska Restaurant. *Moderate.* 4333 Spenard Rd. (243–2090). Colorful; lives up to its name.

FAIRBANKS. There'll be *Expensive* to *Deluxe* dining at the **Bear and Seal** (Westmark Fairbanks); **Husky Dining Room** (Westmark Inn); and **Sourdough Dining Room** (Captain Bartlett Inn). See Accommodations section for addresses and phone numbers.

The Pumphouse. *Expensive.* Mile 1.3 Chena Pump Rd. (479–8452). On Chena River, this National Historical Site pumping station is perpetuated as a convivial Restaurant and Saloon. Closed in winter.

Alaska Salmon Bake. *Moderate.* Mining Valley, Alaskaland (452–7274). Hearty fare fortifies visitors exploring many historical attractions. Daily; summer: D, 5–9 P.M.; L, 11:30 A.M.–1:30 P.M. Seasonal, summer only.

Bunkhouse. *Moderate.* At Cripple Creek Resort, 10 mi. out Parks Hwy. at Ester, AK 99725 (907–479–2500). Open summers. Historic mining camp atmosphere in recycled buildings. Rooms, bunkhouse restaurant; live entertainment nightly in Malemute Saloon. Seasonal, summer only.

JUNEAU. Fine dining, *Expensive–Deluxe* at the Baranof's **Gold Room** and the Westmark Juneau's **Woodcarver.** See Accommodations section.

The Summit. *Expensive.* Located at the Inn at the Waterfront, 455 S. Franklin (586–2050) in Juneau's historic district. Some of the finest cuisine in Juneau is served in this restored hostelry and restaurant.

Fiddlehead. *Moderate.* 429 Willoughby (586–3150). Appreciated for healthful dishes, pancakes to quiche; memorable pastries.

Luna's Great Italian Food. *Moderate.* 210 Seward St. (586–6990). In the heart of downtown. Traditional Italian cuisine.

Silverbow Dining Room. *Moderate.* 120 2nd St. (586–4146). Smoke-free atmosphere while dining on Classic Country French and Regional American dishes in renovated historic building.

Viking. *Moderate.* 218 Front St. (586–2159). Baked potato specialties.

Armadillo Tex-Mex Cafe. *Inexpensive.* 431 S. Franklin (586–1880), across from cruise ship dock. Good food from south of the border.

VALDEZ. Pipeline Club. *Expensive.* At Valdez Motel (835–4444). Salmon so fresh it may not be on menu yet—ask the waitress.

Pizza Palace. *Inexpensive.* 201 N. Harbor Dr. (835–4686). Greek and Italian foods are served here in traditional and noisy atmosphere.

LIQUOR LAWS. The minimum drinking age is 21. Watering holes are plentiful; many close only between 5 and 8 A.M. However, communities vote whether to be dry or wet. Check, especially before heading for native villages.

HAWAII

by
LYLE E. NELSON and JODI BELKNAP

Lyle E. Nelson, a 42-year resident of Hawaii and an extensive traveler, is retired from the staff of the Honolulu Star-Bulletin *after 32 years. Jodi Belknap is a travel writer living in Honolulu.*

Hawaii is warmth, both in the way its people welcome outsiders and in its perpetual summer. Hawaii is color, in its green mountains and its blue ocean. Hawaii is exotic; there's almost nothing like it anywhere in the continental 48 states. Its people are exotic—all minorities, no majority, a mixture of whites, browns, and yellows. Its history is exotic; an isolated monarchy. Its trees and fruits, and churches are exotic; Hawaii is an escape. It takes you away from routine to challenge your tastes and knowledge. It is a step into another world.

Honolulu is a coastal plain divided by mountain streams (no rivers), valleys, and hills, that at night appear as jewels stretching across a dark mountain silhouette, its summits clothed in cotton puffs of clouds, a mystery highlighted by the full moon.

Honolulu is perpetual green, a famous beach, clusters of high-rise hotels and office buildings, freeways, traffic jams, no smog or haze, a people largely laboring to perform services for a constantly arriving clientele of international visitors who nourish the economic balance of a great city. Honolulu is a narrow, thinly stretched city, confined to a corridor between ocean and mountain. It is a series of districts, said trippingly on the tongue, thus: Hawaii Kai, Niu, Kuliouou, Aina Haina, Waialae Iki, Kaimuki, Kapahulu, Moiliili, McCully, Bingham, Makiki, Punchbowl, Pauoa, Nuuanu, Palama, Kapalama, Kalihi, Shafter Flats, Moanalua, Red Hill, Foster Village.

Oahu is a rather small island; you can drive around most of it in three hours if you rush. This densely populated island (its population stands at nearly one million) has one large city of 800,000 inhabitants and five towns with populations of about 40,000 each. It also has two mountain ranges, deep tropical rain forests, several prominent cinder cones and craters, agricultural plains, tracts of middle-class housing, freeways, deep red-rock ravines, endless beaches of sand and reef, and 23 little islands, the gems that adorn this crown in mid-Pacific. Oahu is also home to city people dressed in jackets and ties, country people, farmers, ocean people who fish and wade (sometimes called the *makai* people, meaning "those with an affinity for the sea"), drifters and dreamers, and, as always, hopeful newcomers, the barefoot boys with their smiles. Smiles are everywhere, in fact; this is a gracious land in which friendliness is highly valued.

There is more to Hawaii than Oahu, but because of space limitations, we'll concentrate on that island.

PRACTICAL INFORMATION FOR OAHU

WHEN TO GO. All year long is a good time to come. Winter will be much warmer than in the continental 48 states, including Arizona and Florida, and summer will be somewhat cooler than in those states. But there are no real seasons in Hawaii. The difference between its hottest and coldest days is often a matter of less than 10° F. Why has Hawaii the world's greatest climate? Its geographic position in the South Seas–like North Pacific and the trade wind belt, that global stretch of the latitudes that bring fresh, pleasing breezes almost all year long, account for its beautiful weather. Rain freshens the flowers and comes mostly between Nov. and Apr. Therefore, visitors visit all the time. School vacations account for the only seasonal increase in tourists to Hawaii.

Hawaii has an endless calendar of events that appeal to various tastes. *Aloha Week* in Sept.–Oct. is a colorful splash originally conceived to fill a stagnant vacation period after kids returned to school. The *Narcissus Festival* (a Chinese celebration) in late Jan. and the *Cherry Blossom Festival* (a Japanese celebration) in Mar. are unique Hawaiian festivities. The rest of the year is a mix of canoe races, football games, marathons, orchid shows, hula dances, and surfing meets.

HOW TO GET THERE. Naturally *Honolulu International Airport* is one of the most utilized airports in the world, since Honolulu is the the crossroads of the Pacific. The airliners that land at Honolulu may have taken off originally from the runways of Sydney, Singapore, Hong Kong, Tokyo, Anchorage, Seattle, Chicago, New York, Dallas, Los Angeles, Tahiti, or Tarawa. There is no other option in terms of getting here; everyone flies. Those allergic to flying will have a devilish long wait before the bridge is ready for traffic. As recently as the 1950s thousands enjoyed ship travel to Hawaii, but no more.

By plane. Honolulu International Airport is serviced by *United, Northwest, American, Continental, Delta, Hawaiian Air, Qantas, Canadian Airlines International, Japan Air Lines, Korean Air, Philippine Airlines, Air New Zealand, China Airlines, Singapore Airlines, Air Tungaru, Garuda Indonesia, Pan Am, TWA, WardAir,* and *UTA French Airlines.* Most flights depart from the West Coast and take 4½ hours through very smooth skies (no mountain ranges to cause disturbing updrafts). Flights normally cost about $400 round-trip from the West Coast and not that much more from other U.S. points. Literally hundreds of prepackaged trips that include hotels, rental cars and assorted extras are available, too, often for as little as $100 more for a week's stay. *United,* besides taking visitors to Honolulu, also flies directly to Kahului, Maui, or Kailua-Kona on the Big Island, or Lihue, Kauai.

By boat. Cruise ships operated by *Cunard Line, Holland American Line* and *Royal Viking* all pass through Hawaii periodically en route to the Orient or South

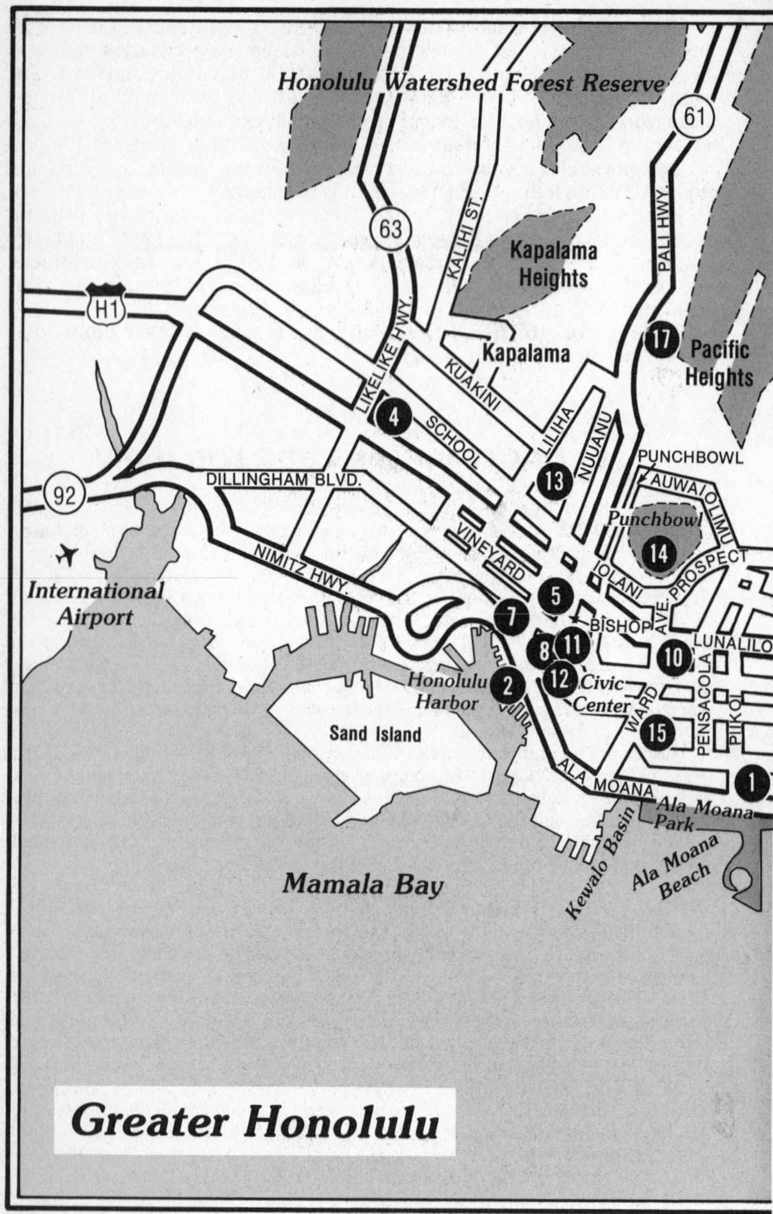

Points of Interest

1) Ala Moana Center
2) Aloha Tower and Hawaii Maritime Center
3) Aquarium
4) Bishop Museum
5) Chinatown
6) Contemporary Arts Museum
7) Cultural Plaza
8) Downtown
9) East West Center

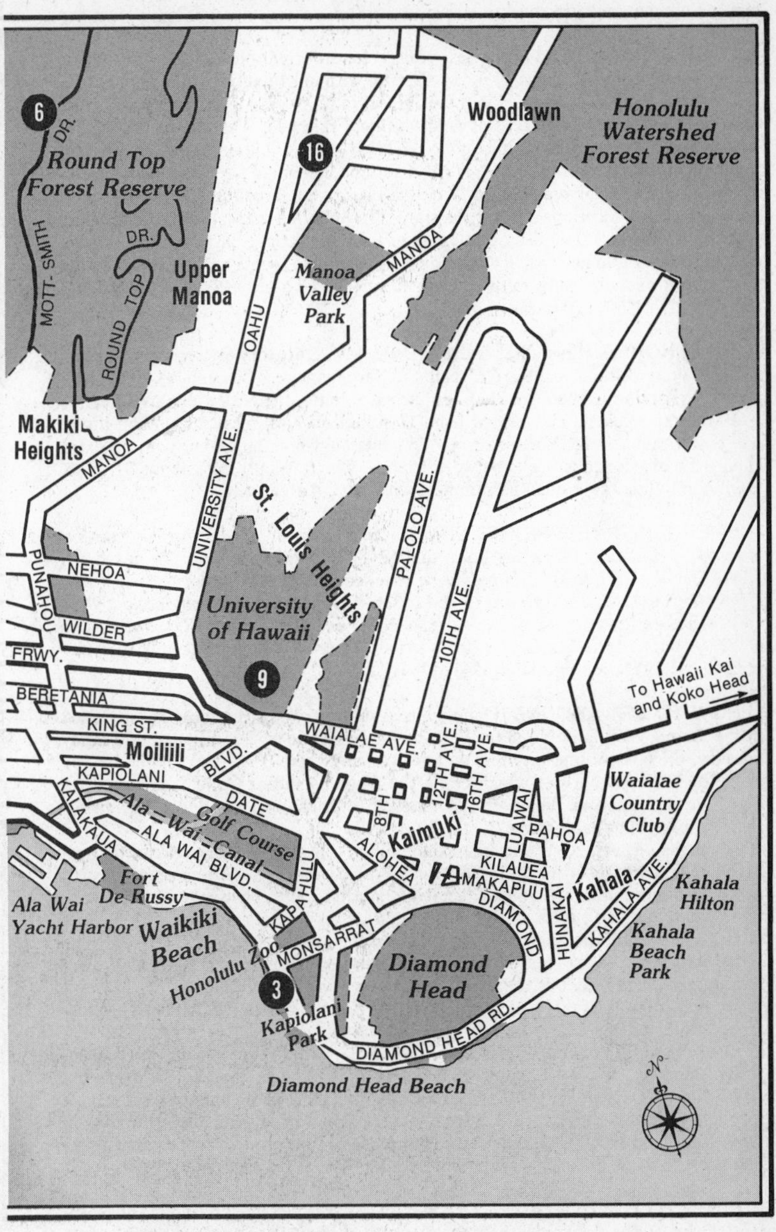

10) Honolulu Academy of Arts
11) Iolani Palace
12) Kamehameha Statue
13) Liliuokalani Gardens
14) National Memorial Cemetery
15) Neal Blaisdell Center
16) Paradise Park
17) Queen Emma Museum

Pacific. Interisland cruising is extremely popular, too. *American Hawaii Cruises* offers luxury one and two week interisland cruises.

TOURIST INFORMATION. Best source for information is your own travel agent. There's also the *Hawaii Visitors Bureau,* with information available in Honolulu at 2270 Kalakaua Ave., Honolulu, HI 96815 (808–923–1811), and at regional offices in Chicago, New York, Los Angeles, San Francisco, Washington, D.C., and Tokyo. Once you are in Honolulu, go to the HVB office, 8th floor, to pick up reading material and ask questions. There are also a number of small free brochures packed in kiosks along Kalakaua Ave. in Waikiki. These same brochures are available in hotels and other locations all over the state. They contain maps, event information, restaurant listings, retail ideas, and coupons for savings on excursions such as boat trips. The Honolulu newspapers carry daily schedules of events and provide meeting schedules for service clubs ranging from Rotary and Toastmasters to gay rap and the Brooklyn Club of Hawaii.

TELEPHONES. Hawaii has one area code, 808. Directory assistance in Hawaii is 1411. Long-distance calls are 65 cents to San Francisco, 70 cents to New York for the first minute; then, for each additional minute, the cost drops to 40 cents. A 10-minute weekend call placed from Honolulu to New York by dialing direct will cost around $3.15. Local calls are 25 cents anywhere on Oahu, with no extra charge for district calls. Calls between islands, which usually cost about $1 or so, are made by dialing 1 and the number, without the area code.

EMERGENCY TELEPHONE NUMBERS. 911 is for *police, fire,* and *ambulance.* To reach a doctor at any hour, dial 524–2575; to find a dentist at any hour, 536–2135. *Waikiki Drug Clinic* may be reached at 922–4787; *Suicide and Crisis Center* at 521–4555; *Coast Guard* rescue at 536–4336; *Alcoholics Anonymous* at 946–1438; *Cocaine Information Service* at 836–3000; *Information and Referral Service* at 521–4566; and the Vet Center (for Vietnam veterans who need to talk to someone) may be reached by dialing 541–1764.

HOW TO GET AROUND. Oahu's bus system is one of the most heavily used in the nation, especially No. 8 to Waikiki. All buses are air-conditioned and many are new; the 60-cent one-way fare will get you anywhere (that goes for the No. 52 and No. 53 buses, both of which circle the whole island of Oahu. Taxis aren't a big thing in Honolulu. They are not allowed to cruise and are hence less visible than in many mainland cities.

From the airport. A stretch limousine will be a little more, or you can take an SIDA taxi (836–0011) for $15. You can also ride the free customer van to pick up your own rented car, if you've decided to go that route. Then take Nimitz Hwy. to Waikiki; you can't miss it. For bus, limousine, or cab, dispatchers with walkie-talkies are outside the baggage-claim area on the ground level.

By bus. MTL, Inc. (TheBus) (531–1611) will tell you how to get anywhere. Senior citizens ride free, but the bus I.D. takes a month to obtain.

By taxi. Cost is $1.50 at pick-up and $1.50 per mi. thereafter. All cabs are metered. Many drivers are local, but some are rather new. Big operators: *Charley's* (955–2211) and *Aloha State* (847–3566). *SIDA* (836–0011) controls the airport run.

By rental car. There are about two dozen companies: *Avis, Budget, Dollar, Hertz, National* and *Tropical* are the better known names. You can rent any type of vehicle through your travel agent, in advance (a necessity during peak travel periods in Feb., May, and Dec.) including jeeps, limos, vans, and a red Maserati that looks like it came from the set of Magnum P.I.

HINTS TO THE MOTORIST. Driving in Hawaii is just like driving in the mainland. Drive on the right side; there are plenty of road signs and arrows on the pavement. You may turn right on red after a stop at most intersections unless otherwise posted. Freeways are well marked; stop at crosswalks—Any pedestrian stepping off the curb ahead of you has the right-of-way. Use your hands, or signal, to indicate turns. Feed the meter or a tow truck will provide you with a $35 parking experience. Most street meters do not need coins on weekends and holidays. Municipal lots, however, must be paid 24 hours a day, year-round. Don't park at red curbs. Since traffic can be very heavy, try to stay off the freeways from 6:30 to 8:15 A.M. and 3:30 to 6 P.M. Police cars have a blue light on top and are a mix of blue-and-white sedans and unmarked cars. Honolulu has the most courteous drivers in the nation. Notice how they let you cut in, smile, don't get worked up, and don't play chicken with fenders. The posted speed limits are 25 mph most places, 50 on the freeway. And cars tend to crawl rather than speed in this state.

HINTS TO DISABLED TRAVELERS. There are *Handi-vans* for the handicapped (833–2222); get a pass at 811 Middle St., with 24-hour advance notice. *Handi-Cabs of the Pacific* (524–3866) will take you anywhere; free wheelchairs, $8 curbside pickup, $1.95 per mile; $17.50 door-to-door pickup, $1.95 per mi.

In addition, more than a dozen hotels have made life easier for the handicapped with ramps, hand rails in showers, 29-inch bath doors, and parking stalls. The airport, major points of interest, and large shopping malls are equipped for wheelchairs.

Most street corners in Honolulu are ramped for chairs. Avis rents hand-controlled vehicles. Several organizations in Honolulu provide companion support.

SEASONAL EVENTS. January. *Hula Bowl* and *Pro Bowl* get national TV exposure. *Narcissus Festival* turns the Chinese in the Honolulu community loose to amaze us with lions, fireworks, a parade, fashions, food, and attractive young women. The *State Legislature* opens to color, pageantry, entertainment by professionals, and plenty of free food, all at the Capitol. After that it's politics as usual for eight weeks.

February. The *Hawaiian Open* means more national TV exposure for the state. And *opera season,* with singers from the Met in New York, is underway.

March. *Kuhio Day* on the 26th is a state holiday, with a ball. *Carole Kai Bed Race* is a hilarious celebration in Waikiki. *Cherry Blossom Festival* is a Japanese festival in the Honolulu community with parades, exhibitions, dance, and attractive young women.

April. *Wesak Day* honors Gautama Buddha and features dancing and religious celebrations.

May. *Lei Day* features flowers, music, dancing, and pageantry. *Japanese Boys Day* means fly the carp—the carp kite, that is.

June. The *state fair* brings agricultural exhibits, arts, and dancing. *Kamehameha Day* on the 11th is the major state holiday. A parade, canoe races, hula, and chants are featured. *Filipino Festival* brings us more attractive young women.

July. The *Japanese Bon Dances,* in honor of the dead, are a Buddhist tradition. The *Transpacific Yacht Race,* from Los Angeles to Honolulu, has taken place every other year for 80 years.

August. The *Hula Festival* has dancing for everyone. In the *International Billfish Tournament,* fishers go after giant Pacific blue marlin.

September. *Aloha Week* offers parades, hula, fun, pageantry.

October. The *Molokai to Oahu canoe race* and the *Orchid Show* take place now. And the symphony and stage seasons begin.

November. The *All-Islands Makahiki,* with music, dance, pageantry, is held now.

December. Sporting events, including the *Honolulu Marathon,* the *International Surfing Championships,* the *Aloha Bowl,* and the *Rainbow Classic,* are held now.

TOURS. Popular tours on Oahu include the *City Tour,* which hits the highlights of Honolulu, and the *Arizona Memorial Tour* in Pearl Harbor. Both *Gray Line* (834–1033) and *Polynesian Adventure Tours* (922–0888) offer these tours, ranging from 2 to 8 hours. The short tours leave at 8 A.M. and again at noon. The *Island Circle Tour,* which goes nearly all the way around the island, sets off once a day, starting at 8:30 A.M. Costs run from $10 to $38.50. Major boat rides are from Kewalo Basin in the city into Pearl Harbor and back, about 3 hours, $19. *Papillon Hawaii Pacific Helicopters* (836–1566), has many tours of differing length, and prices run from $102 to $193. The best seller is a 30-minute Oahu flight for $102 per person. A popular walking tour is of the civic center and government buildings, historic Kawaiahao Church, Iolani Palace, and the governor's home. It covers about six blocks, leaves 9:30 A.M., returns at noon, and costs $7; call 531–0481 for information. The *Hawaii Heritage Center* (521–2749) offers a tour of Chinatown, downtown, daily, leaving at 9:30 A.M., for $4. The *East-West Center* on the University of Hawaii campus has a free tour at 1:30 P.M., every Wed.; call 944–7111 for information. The *Pearl Harbor* tour conducted by national-park rangers and navy boats leaves from the Arizona Memorial Visitors Center on Kamehameha Hwy. from 8 A.M. to 3:30 P.M., first come, first served, free, and includes an excellent 20-minute movie providing background information. The movie and boat ride combined take only an hour; waiting may take longer.

SPECIAL-INTEREST SIGHTSEEING. *University of Hawaii,* University Ave. at Dole St. (948–8111), go to Bachman Hall for a helpful brochure; *Brigham Young University-Hawaii at Laie* (293–3816); *Hawaii Loa College* near Kaneohe (235–3641); a sociological bus tour by the *Hawaii Geographic Society* to ethnic districts, off the established city-tour routes (538–3952); *Honolulu Academy of Arts,* 900 S. Beretania (538–1006); *Contemporary Arts Center,* 605 Kapiolani Blvd. (525–8047); a pineapple factory, 650 Iwilei Rd. (531–8855); *Hilo Hattie garment factory tour* (537–2926); *Foster Botanic Garden,* 50 N. Vineyard Blvd. (533–3406), $1, tours Mon., Tues., and Wed. at 1:30 P.M.; *Lyon Arboretum,* 3860 Manoa Rd. (988–3177); *Hawaii Maritime Center,* Honolulu Harbor (536–6373) 9 A.M. to 5 P.M. daily, $6. *Dole Cannery Square* (531–8855) 9 A.M. to 4 P.M.

Downtown Honolulu, its historic financial district, and Waikiki can be walked independently, unguided, at leisure.

PARKS AND GARDENS. National Park Service headquarters, Kuhio Federal Bldg., Honolulu, HI 96813 (541–2693), is the office to contact with any questions about the parks on Maui and Hawaii. Two outstanding parks in Honolulu are *Kapiolani,* on the edge of Waikiki, and *Ala Moana,* midway between downtown and Waikiki. Kapiolani, 200 acres including a zoo and an aquarium, is at the base of Diamond Head and across the street from the beach. The park provides large open areas for picnics and games plus a bandstand and a larger shell for concerts. The place abounds in joggers. Tennis also available, free.

Ala Moana Park, 70 acres, has a human-made beach, food concessions, jogging paths, tennis, and more picnics going on than at Kapiolani. Locals tend to prefer this place. Magic Island, part of the park, juts out into the ocean next door to the yacht channel. Good for walking and a view of the city. Free. Both Ala Moana and Magic Island have abundant parking facilities.

Sand Island Park is new and nice. At the diamond head end of Sand Island, the 85-acre park faces the ocean, the ship channel, and Honolulu Harbor. Free. Plenty of parking available.

There are dozens of other parks; many are beach parks and will be described in the beach section. One very small park worth citing because of its excellent view of Honolulu is *Puu Ualakaa* atop Round Top. Popular wedding site. Small parking lot, which closes at 6:30 P.M. Free.

Two commercial parks are heavy with tropical flora. *Waimea Falls Park* (638–8511) on Oahu's north shore features Hawaiian plants and presentations by hula dancers. Adult admission $8.50. *Paradise Park* in Manoa Valley (988–2141) was reopened in January 1991 with a tour into the past featuring life-size models of dinosaurs in simulated, walk-through habitats.

As for gardens, *Foster Botanic Garden* (50 N. Vineyard Blvd, 522–7060; admission $1), is in a class by itself. In the 1860s, a German doctor brought back from India seeds that produced many beautiful species of trees and plants, many of which are immense and exotic for American soil. How about the gingerbread palm, the kapok, the bo, the cannonball? Open 9 A.M. to 4 P.M.

Lyon Arboretum, 3860 Manoa Rd., beyond Paradise Park at the end of the road in Manoa Valley (988–3177), has fine views and free flora tours on the first Fri., third Wed., and third Sat. of each month.

Senator Fong's Plantation & Gardens, (239–6775), 47-285 Pulama Rd., on Oahu's windward side. Open-air guided tram ride through 725 acres of flora. Lei-making classes. Open 10 A.M. to 4 P.M. Adult admission $6.50.

Haiku Gardens, 46–336 Haiku Rd., Kaneohe, is a delightful short walk from Koko Crater best tied to a lunch or dinner at the restaurant that looks down on the gardens. Free.

Wahiawa Botanical Garden on California Ave. in Wahiawa, open 9 A.M. to 4 P.M., has interesting, unusual offerings, such as the Mindanao Gum. Free.

ZOO AND AQUARIUM. In *Kapiolani Park,* across Kapahulu Ave. from Waikiki, is a zoo and aquarium. Entrance on Monsarrat (971–7171). Open 8:30 A.M. to 4:15 P.M. Admission $3; children under 12 accompanied by adult free. 2,000 species such as Galapagos turtles, giraffes, lions, tigers, gibbons, elephants, seals, monkeys, rams, tropical birds. Also a food concession. No tours.

Sea Life Park, Makapuu Point, East Oahu (923–1531). City bus #57 runs hourly from Waikiki. Open 9:30 A.M. to 5 P.M. Admission $12.95 adults, $8.50 children 7–12, $4.50 ages 4–6. A world-class marine park, featuring leaping porpoises and whales in a natural setting and a 300,000-gallon tank full of sharks, rays, octopuses, and what's out there in the ocean across the street. A show every two hours. Food concession and free whaling museum. A $2 first-come, first-served, behind-the-scenes tour, daily at 9:45 A.M., of research aspects of the marine operation, including training whales in the open ocean to return to the park.

Waikiki Aquarium, 2777 Kalakaua Ave., across from Kapiolani Park, next to Waikiki (923–9741). 9 A.M. to 5 P.M. Admission $3; children under 16 free. Saltwater tanks, tropical fish, sharks, even the humuhumunukunukuapuaa.

CAMPING. There are 21 campgrounds on Oahu; 13 are city beach parks, five are state parks; all are free. Permits required from *City Parks Department,* Honolulu Municipal Building, 650 S. King St. (808–523–4525). Tents can be put up at 8 A.M. Fri., must be struck by Wed. evening. The state has three of the best parks: *Aiea Heights, Sand Island,* and *Malaekahana.* Check the *Division of Parks,* Division of Forestry, 1151 Punchbowl St., Honolulu, HI 96813 (808–548–7455). The parks office can tell you both where to stay and where *not* to stay.

FISHING AND HUNTING. Most fishing around Oahu is the deep-sea variety, and the catches can get pretty huge, up to hundreds of pounds if you catch a marlin. More likely catches are yellowfin, tuna, wahoo, Jack Crevalle, dolphin (the fish, not the mammal), and skipjack. There is some shore fishing, net fishing, and torch fishing by wading with a spear at night; it is almost impossible to fish here from a small boat in the ocean or to do any freshwater fishing. *Kewalo Basin* in Honolulu has many deep-sea-fishing boats for charter; other charter boats are at *Haleiwa* on the north shore or *Pokai Bay* at Waianae. Fishers often buy a share of a fishing trip to save money. The day runs 7 A.M. to 3 P.M. If you hook a big one you don't get to keep it. For information, telephone the *Coreene C* at 536–7472. Reservations are needed a day in advance. A license for freshwater fishing is $7.50, nonresidents, for 30 days, obtainable from *Conservation and Resources Enforcement,* 1151 Punchbowl St. (548–8766), or any sporting goods store. *Lake Wilson* at Wahiawa and the *Nuuanu Reservoir* are about the only freshwater sites. Hunting on Oahu is almost nonexistent, confined to boar and dove.

PARTICIPANT SPORTS. Swimming. *Waikiki* and a dozen other beaches are perfect for this sport. *Kailua Beach* and *Bellows Air Force Station,* open weekends only, are excellent for bodysurfing. Board surfing is big at *Waikiki,* off *Diamond Head,* at *Ala Moana,* and for the largest break in winter months, at *Sunset Beach* and *Makaha.* There are small pools at many large hotels, larger pools in various residential-district community centers. Other water sports available at various beaches are outrigger canoeing, kayaking, windsurfing, water skiing, jet skiing, pediboats, and parasailing.

Sailing. The four main clubs are the *Hawaii Yacht Club, Waikiki Yacht Club, Kaneohe Yacht Club,* and *Hickam Yacht Club.* There are charter outfitters who will rent a sailboat, crew it for you, or give nautical instruction. There's instruction available at these clubs for other modes of water fun such as surfing and windsurfing. Most pleasure boating is out of Hawaii Kai and private; most powerboats are in the fishing business.

Snorkeling, scuba. What a myriad of opportunities for these sports in Hawaii! Not the best in the Pacific, experts say, but exciting enough, especially at *Hanauma Bay.* For information on scuba operators who supply everything, send $2 for a guide booklet to Box 9029 S, Honolulu, HI 96835.

Golf is big on Oahu's 28 courses. Four are city owned; seven others are private-public and fairly easy to get onto. The military has nine courses if you have pull, and *Waialae,* among other country clubs, is available if you have a connection. Vans are in Waikiki for package tours to courses.

Tennis. There are many municipal courts that operate all night at no cost. Private clubs and hotel courts with the latest surfaces are available for a fee.

Jogging. Major jogging paths are around *Kapiolani Park* or *Ala Moana Park,* or along *Pearl Harbor,* but there is also plenty of running at *Diamond Head* or on the *Kalanianaole Hwy.* along the Honolulu Marathon course. Honolulu feels it's the running capital of America and can give Central Park a run for its money. There's a clinic on how to marathon at 7:30 every Sun. morning at the Kapiolani Park Bandstand. Running shops have a rundown on races; usually at least two take place each weekend.

Biking. Not too popular here because it's dangerous, but serious triathlon types use *Diamond Head Rd.* and *Kalanianaole Hwy.* Competition includes 50- and 100-mi. sprints.

Hiking. Popular for years. The main walks are rugged, though snakeless, up to the summits or ridgelines of the 2 mountain ranges, the *Koolaus* and *Waianaes. Diamond Head* and *Koko Crater* are easier walks. Most activity is on Sun. mornings: The *Hawaiian Trail and Mountain Club* (734–5515) meets at 8 A.M. at Iolani Palace; the *Sierra Club* (538–6616) meets at 8 at Church of the Crossroads, 1212 University Ave. *Moanalua Garden Foundation, Lyon Arboretum,* and *Foster Botanic Garden* also schedule hikes.

Riding. Horses are for rent at *Kualoa Ranch* (538–7636), *Sheraton Makaha Stables* (695–9511).

In addition sports enthusiasts will find on Oahu: an ice rink, bowling, lawn bowling, bridge, some auto and motorcycle racing, handball, volleyball, softball, hang gliding, gliding, Tai Chi demonstrations (at Ruger Triangle Park, Sun. mornings), ti-leaf sliding, Frisbeeing, soccer, rugby, kite flying, chess, archery, pistol shooting, skateboarding, and illegal cockfights.

SPECTATOR SPORTS. *University of Hawaii* has Division I intercollegiate games in football, basketball, and baseball. The ticket office may be reached at 949–2085. Football is at *Aloha Stadium* in Halawa Valley, basketball at *Neal Blaisdell Center,* and baseball at the campus quarry. Other schools, such as *Chaminade, Brigham Young University-Hawaii, Hawaii Pacific College,* and *Hawaii Loa* also have intercollegiate basketball. The *Hawaiian Open PGA Tour* is held at *Waialae.* In addition, there are other frequent or infrequent spectator sports for a fee: sumo wrestling, wrestling, polo, tennis, college volleyball. And in football there are three bowls: *Aloha, Hula,* and *Pro.*

CHILDREN'S ACTIVITIES. The larger hotels have a number of programs for children (or *keikis,* in the Hawaiian language) while adults sightsee. *Keiki Rainbow Tour,* Box 462, Kaneohe, HI 96744 (235–4206), is run by people who work as convention planners for motels and hotels. The program for youngsters, 6–12, takes place on Mon., Wed., and Fri. There are a maximum of 10 youngsters in each group. The program, which runs from 9 A.M. to 4 P.M., includes hotel pickup and costs $37.50. The kids hike and fish, and learn Hawaiian crafts, hula, games, and songs. There's even a special outing for teenagers, 13–17. *Paradise Park, Sea Life Park* and *Waimea Falls Park* all have activities children enjoy. *Honolulu Theater for Youth* shows are a well-done diversion; call 839–9885 for more information.

BEACHES. *Waikiki* is certainly a world-renowned strip. You can walk from one end to the other, without rushing, in about an hour. The sand is nice but not the best on Oahu. The curl is steady and near perfect. But the strip gets a little crowded occasionally. Multiple concessionaires. The Hawaiian beachboys, who once doubled as Olympic champions, can show you how to surf or can help you rent an outrigger canoe or catamaran. Free parking is at Kapiolani Park a short distance away.

Ala Moana. Human-made-lagoon swimming; preferable to Waikiki for serious swimmers. Plenty of parking, food concessions. Lifeguards but no beachboys.

Bellows Beach. A perfect beach on windward Oahu with fine sand and a great break, but on Air Force property. Open to public only on weekends. Park under cool ironwood trees for picnics.

Kailua Beach. Much like nearby Bellows, with a beach park for parking and a food concession.

Kahana Bay. North of Kaneohe Bay on windward Oahu. Crescent-shaped, shallow, and not much break. But the setting is idyllic, with the mountains close by. Showers, parking, tables, boat ramp.

Malaekahana. A state park on windward Oahu near Laie. Very nice sand. Parking.

Sandy Beach. Near Makapuu Point and Blow Hole. A big break, often 6 to 10 ft. for experienced bodysurfers. Prince Charles stole away long enough for a dip here en route to the White House in 1985.

Makapuu Point. Small area, big surf; best suited for good surfers. Parking available next door to Sea Life Park.

Sunset Beach. This place gets the big babies—up to 20 ft.—in winter months and is strictly for professional riders. Park in sand off highway. This long stretch of beach goes under different names, such as the Banzai Pipeline.

Makaha Beach. On leeward Oahu coast. Same as Sunset. Frightening waves in winter, calm in summer. Parking.

HISTORIC SITES AND HOUSES. Aiea Heights. *Heiaus* are Hawaiian religious platforms of lava blocks many hundreds of years old. One of many is *Keaiwa Heiau State Recreation Area* atop Aiea Heights. Free. Parking available. Drive Aiea Heights Rd. to the top.

Hickam and Wheeler air force bases are more difficult to gain entry to but no less historic. For information call 449–2490. The *Pacific Air Forces* headquarters building still bears scars of 1941 shrapnel. A plaque on the field marks the spot where the crew of *Apollo 8* stepped back on earth for the first time after reaching the moon—for the first time. Wheeler, in central Oahu, was also attacked in 1941. But the field is more famous as site of first transpacific air flights in 1927. Amelia Earhart took off from here in 1934 on her first solo flight from Hawaii to Oakland.

Kawaiahao Church. Across Mission La. from the Mission Houses (522–1333). First Christian church in Hawaii, called the Westminster of the Pacific. Coral blocks first put down in 1841. Kings worshiped here. Services at 10:30 A.M. Sun. in both English and Hawaiian.

Merchant Street. Old downtown Honolulu section close to waterfront. Large number of historic buildings such as the *Melcher Building* (dating back to 1854), *Kam V Post Office* (1871), *Yokohama Specie Bank* (1910), *Our Lady of Peace Cathedral* (1843), and eight buildings from the 1920s. No tours. City parking lots.

Nuuanu Pali Lookout. In 1795 King Kamehameha finished off his military campaign on Oahu, at this site, forcing his opponents to leap to their deaths off the 1,000-ft. precipice.

Pearl Harbor. Major American military site to receive an aerial bombing in this century. Very popular with visitors. Excellent *Arizona Memorial Visitors Center* on Kamehameha Hwy., run by National Park Service on a first-come, first-served basis. Visitors receive a boat number and wait to be called to one of two theaters for a 20-minute film of events leading up to Dec. 7, 1941. Then the short navy boat trip to *Arizona* and Battleship Row takes place. Call 422–0561 or 422–2771 for information.

MUSEUMS AND GALLERIES. *Army Museum.* Inside Battery Randolph (1911) at Fort DeRussy in Waikiki. Mostly World War II artifacts, some from Vietnam. Open 10 A.M.–4:30 P.M., Tues.–Sun., donations accepted.

Tropic Lightning Historical Center is another army museum, inside Schofield Barracks, dealing mostly with the history of the 25th Infantry Division. Open 10 A.M.–4 P.M., daily. Free.

Bishop Museum. 1525 Bernice St., Kalihi district (848–4129). Most outstanding Polynesian culture museum in the world. Open 9 A.M.–5 P.M., Mon.–Sun. Tours of main hall, 10 A.M., noon, 2 P.M. Fee of $5.95 for adults or $4.95 for children (6–17 years) includes a planetarium show. Exhibits include royal capes, weapons, relics, and a whale hanging from the ceiling.

Bowfin. World War II diesel submarine that sank many Japanese ships. Next to Arizona Memorial Visitors Center, Pearl Harbor; no phone. Open 9:30 A.M.–4:30 P.M., Tues.–Sun. $3. Parking.

Damien Museum. 130 Ohua Ave. (923–2690). Artifacts of the Belgian priest who died of Hansen's Disease (leprosy) at Kalaupapa, Molokai. Open 9 A.M.–3 P.M. Free. Parking available.

Hawaii Maritime Center, Pier 7, Honolulu Harbor, 536–6373. Spacious new historical display in a museum adjacent to a four-masted sailing ship built in Scotland in 1878. Nautical displays, 9 A.M.–8 P.M. Admission $6. Parking.

Honolulu Academy of Arts. Outstanding art gallery. 900 S. Beretania St. (538–1006). Open Tues.–Sat., 10 A.M.–4:30 P.M.; Sun. 1–5 P.M. Free. Great Asian collection. Western art includes work of top Americans, James Michener's Japanese-print collection, and the Clare Boothe Luce modern gallery.

Contemporary Art Museum. 2411 Makiki Heights Dr. (526–0232). Fine art by island artists in a lovely old hillside estate. Open 10 A.M.–4 P.M. Mon., Wed., Fri. and 12–4 P.M. Sun. The museum also houses the Contemporary Cafe (523–3362), Museum Shop (523–3447), and rotating exhibits.

Iolani Palace. King and Richards Sts. (522–0832). Center jewel of civic-center crown near downtown Honolulu. Built by King David Kalakaua (who ruled from 1879 to 1882). 45-minute tours depart every 15 minutes, 9 A.M.–2:15 P.M., Wed.–Sat., $4. Children under 5 not admitted. This palace was renovated in the 1970s. Queen Lilioukalani was kept here under house arrest in 1893, and the territorial legislature met here most of this century.

Mission Houses. The *Chamberlain House* at corner of S. King St. and Mission La. near downtown (531–0481) was first house built by New England missionaries who arrived from Boston in 1820. Open Tues.–Sat. 9 A.M.–4 P.M., Sun. 12–4 P.M. Three buildings. Admission to all, $3.50.

Queen Emma Museum. 2913 Pali Hwy. (595–3167). Summer home of wife (1836–1885) of Kamehameha IV. Includes many gifts from Queen Victoria. Open 9 A.M.–4 P.M., daily. Admission $4.

Waipahu Cultural Center. 94–515 Waipahu St. (677–0110). Features artifacts of sugar-plantation life early 20th century.

ARTS AND ENTERTAINMENT. Music. The *Honolulu Symphony Orchestra* gives a series of 10 concerts, each twice, at 4 P.M. Sun. and 8 P.M. Tues. Guest artists from around the world. On 8 P.M. Fri. there is a light concert with local stars or an occasional appearance by an artist like Al Hirt or Dave Brubeck. Music director is Donald Johanos. Concerts are at Neal Blaisdell Center, 777 Ward Ave. (942–2200). *Hawaii Opera Theater* puts on three operas a year in Feb., using the Honolulu Symphony; for information call 521–6537. The *Honolulu Philharmonic Society* plays a series including chamber ensembles; call 734–0397 for ticket information. *Chamber Music Hawaii* (545–1959) has two series—*Candlelight,* at the Lutheran Church on Punahou St. in the fall, and *Sound-in-Light,* at the Academy of Arts in the spring. The *University of Hawaii Music Department* (956–7756) has faculty concerts at Orvis Auditorium. Performers range from piano soloists to small orchestras. The *Chamber Music Series* holds about 6 concerts a year at Orvis, featuring groups from Moscow, Tokyo, and Boston, among others. Call 545–1959 for information. *Honolulu Chorale* performs in churches; check newspaper listings for ticket information. Rock groups and big names such as Belafonte or Denver perform at the NBC Concert Hall, or Waikiki Shell (521–2911), or Aloha Stadium (486–9555). Prices range from $5–$50 (for a top-name rock performer).

Dance. The *San Francisco Ballet* joins the Honolulu Symphony each Dec. *Ballet Hawaii* (988–7578) performs *Nutcracker* or *Cinderella* in Dec. and sponsored Baryshnikov in 1985. The *University of Hawaii Dance Department* (948–7677) puts on several dance concerts a year. Smaller dance studios often have concerts. Groups from New York, such as Alvin Ailey or the Chamber Ballet U.S.A., appear irregularly.

Stage. *Diamond Head Theater* mounts 8 shows a year at Ruger Theater (734–0274). Performances include drama and musicals, both classic and innovative. The *American Contemporary Theater* of San Francisco and New York groups appear with less regularity at the NBC Concert Hall. *Hawaii Performing Arts Center* has 8 shows a year at 2833 E. Manoa Rd. (988–6131). The *University of Hawaii Drama Department* puts on 8 shows per year, including some classical Greek and Shakespearean plays, at J. F. Kennedy Theater, East-West Center campus (948–7677). Other theater groups include ones at *Chaminade College, Brigham Young University-Hawaii, Leeward Community College, Hawaii Loa College,* the *Honolulu Theater for Youth, Windward Theater Guild,* and the theater at *Schofield Barracks.*

FILM. An international film festival featuring new work from Asia is held in Nov. at theatres on Oahu and Maui. (944–7007). Free. The *Honolulu Academy of Arts Theater,* 900 S. Beretania St. (538–1006), conducts a year-round series of films, many foreign or silent.

ACCOMMODATIONS. Half the hotel rooms in the state (approximately 38,600) are at Waikiki. About half of these are very attractive highrises, on the beach. Most offer a full array of activities and services, including fine restaurants, shops, swimming pools, and sometimes tennis. Some have seasonal rates (higher at Christmas), but most do not. Occupancy rates are always highest in winter and summer. Lesser hotels (especially the condominiums) offer little in the way of extras outside the lobby. Meals are rarely included with rooms. There is a 5% room tax. All large hotels have parking facilities. Almost all have cable color TV or rentals. Price categories for double occupancy rooms, suites, or apartments are divided into the following ranges: *Super Deluxe,* $105 and up; *Deluxe,* $60–$105; *Expensive,* $40–$60; *Moderate,* $30–$40; and *Inexpensive,* under $30.

Super Deluxe

Halekulani. 2199 Kalia Rd., Honolulu, HI 96815 (808–923–2311). The best of everything on Waikiki Beach. Top-drawer restaurants. Pool, meeting rooms, shops, lounges. 456 rooms.

Hawaii Prince. 100 Holomoana St. (808–526–1111). The twin towers of this elegant waterfront high rise set the gateway to Waikiki. Overlooking Ala Wai Yacht Harbor. 526 rooms.

Hilton Hawaiian Village. 2005 Kalia Rd., Honolulu, HI 96815 (808–949–4321 or 800–HILTONS). On Waikiki Beach. A complete resort complex with shopping plaza, restaurants, lounges, shows, pools, meeting rooms, built by Henry J. Kaiser. 2,524 rooms.

Kahala Hilton. 5000 Kahala Ave., Honolulu, HI 96816 (808–734–2211 or 800–HILTONS). Isolated; about 10-minute drive from Waikiki. Many consider this to be the king of the Hawaii hotel scene on Oahu. Top restaurants. Pool, lounges, shows, tennis, shops, meeting rooms, dancing porpoises. Waialae Country Club wraps around it. 370 rooms.

Royal Hawaiian. 2259 Kalahaua Ave., Honolulu, HI 96815 (808–923–7311). This 1927 pink palace is still the queen of Waikiki Beach. Restaurants. Lounges, pool, shows, shops, meeting rooms. 527 rooms.

Sheraton Moana Surfrider. 2365 Kalakaua Ave., Honolulu, HI 96815 (808–922–3111 or 800–325–3535. A $50-million-plus upgrade and restoration program has combined the two hotels into one that re-creates the style and mood of a romantic past dating from 1901 in a luxurious contemporary setting.

Deluxe

Aston's Waikikian Hotel. 1181 Ala Moana Blvd., Honolulu, HI 96815 (808–949–5331). On Waikiki Beach. Low-level lanais. Intimate, lush gardenlike setting. Kitchenettes; restaurant. Lounge, pool, shops. 135 rooms.

Colony Surf. 2895 Kalakaua Ave., Honolulu, HI 96815 (808–923–5751). ½ mi. from mid-Waikiki, on the beach. Kitchens. Award-winning restaurant, lounge. No children under 12. 100 rooms.

Discovery Bay. 1778 Ala Moana Blvd., Honolulu, HI 96815 (808–941–3307). Very close to Waikiki. Kitchens; restaurant. Lounge, pool, shops. Five-day minimum. Only 70 of the 666 rooms here are hotel units.

Hawaiian Regent. 2552 Kalakaua Ave., Honolulu, HI 96815 (808–922–6611). Across the street from Waikiki Beach. Great restaurants. Lounges, pools, shops, meeting rooms, tennis. 1,346 rooms.

Holiday Inn-Waikiki Beach. 2570 Kalakaua Ave., Honolulu, HI 96815 (808–922–2511 or 800–HOLIDAY). Across the street from beach. Restaurants. Lounges, pool, shops, meeting rooms. 641 rooms.

Hyatt Regency. 2424 Kalakaua Ave., Honolulu, HI 96815 (808–922–9292 or 800–233–1234). Across the street from Waikiki Beach. Beautiful twin towers, restaurants, shops, pool, meeting rooms. 1,234 rooms.

The Ilikai. 1777 Ala Moana Blvd., Honolulu, HI 96815 (808–949–3811). Elegantly refurbished hotel near Waikiki Beach. Some kitchens; restaurants. Lounges, pools, tennis, meeting rooms, theaters. 800 rooms.

New Otani Kaimana Beach. 2863 Kalakaua Ave., Honolulu, HI 96815 (808–923–1555). On Waikiki beach at Diamond Head. Has elegant suites to kitchenettes. Many units have kitchens. Restaurants, lounge, shops, meeting rooms. Across from Kapiolani Park. 138 rooms.

Outrigger Prince Kuhio. 2500 Kuhio Ave., Honolulu, HI 96815 (808–922–0811). 3 blocks from Waikiki Beach. Restaurants. Lounges, pool, shops, meeting rooms; also a luxury hotel club within the hotel. 626 rooms.

Outrigger Waikiki. 2335 Kalakaua Ave., Honolulu, HI 96815 (808–923–0711). On Waikiki Beach. Restaurants. Lounges, pool, shops, meeting room. 530 rooms.

Pacific Beach. 2490 Kalakaua Ave., Honolulu, HI 96815 (808–922–1233). Across the street from Waikiki Beach. Kitchens; restaurants. Lounges, pool, shops, tennis. 850 rooms.

Ramada Renaissance Ala Moana. 410 Atkinson Dr., Honolulu, HI 96814 (808–955–4811 or 800–2–RAMADA). About 3 minutes from Waikiki; across the street from Ala Moana Beach. Restaurants. Lounges, pool, shows, shops, meeting rooms. 1,194 rooms.

Sheraton Makaha Resort and Country Club. Box 896, Waianae, HI 96792 (808–695–9511 or 800–325–3535). Low-level town houses in a fine valley on two resort-class golf courses. Isolated; more than an hour from Waikiki and 1 mi. from Makaha Beach. Restaurants. Lounge, pool, tennis, shops, meeting rooms. 200 rooms.

Sheraton Princess Kaiulani. 120 Kaiulani Ave., Honolulu, HI 96815 (808–922–5811 or 800–325–3535). Across the street from Waikiki Beach. Restaurants. Lounges, pool, shops, meeting rooms. 1,156 rooms.

Sheraton-Waikiki. 2255 Kalakaua Ave., Honolulu, HI 96815 (808–922–4422 or 800–325–3535). On Waikiki Beach; overwhelming in size. Restaurants. Lounges, shows, pools, shops, meeting rooms. 1,852 rooms.

Turtle Bay Hilton and Country Club. Box 187, Kahuku, HI 96731 (808–293–8811 or 800–HILTONS). More than an hour from Waikiki; isolated on a windy point. Developed by Del Webb. Restaurants. Lounges, pool, golf, tennis, shops, meeting rooms. 483 rooms.

Expensive

Coral Reef. 2299 Kuhio Ave., Honolulu, HI 96815 (808–922–1262). About 4 blocks from Waikiki Beach. Restaurants. Lounges, pool, shops. 209 rooms.

Hawaiiana. 260 Beach Walk, Honolulu, HI 96815 (808–923–3811). Very short walk to Waikiki Beach. Small, low-level, intimate setting. All-Hawaiian staff. Kitchenettes. Pools. 95 rooms.

Hawaiian Monarch. 444 Niu St., Honolulu, HI 96815 (808–949–3911). 15-minute walk to Waikiki Beach. Restaurants. Lounge, pool, shops, meeting rooms. 190 rooms.

Holiday Isle. 270 Lewers St., Honolulu, HI 96815 (808–923–0777). 3 blocks from Waikiki Beach; right in the middle of the action. Restaurant. Lounge, pool. 284 rooms.

Kai Aloha. 235 Saratoga Rd., Honolulu, HI 96815 (808–923–6723). Short walk to Waikiki Beach. Lanai rooms. Kitchens. 18 rooms.

Maile Court. 2058 Kuhio Ave., Honolulu, HI 96815 (808–947–2828). New; 2 blocks from Waikiki Beach. Some units have kitchens. Pool, meeting room. 508 rooms.

Outrigger East. 150 Kaiulani Ave., Honolulu, HI 96815 (808–922–5353). Short walk to Waikiki Beach. Some kitchens; restaurants. Lounges, pool, shops, meeting room. 444 rooms.

Outrigger Reef. 2169 Kalia Rd., Honolulu, HI 96815 (808–923–3111). On Waikiki Beach. Some units have kitchens; restaurants. Lounges, pool, shops, meeting rooms. 883 rooms.

Pagoda. 1525 Rycroft St., Honolulu, HI 96814 (808–941–6611). 5-minute drive from Ala Moana Beach. Kitchens, restaurants. Lounge, pools, shops, meeting rooms. 340 rooms.

Park Shore. 2586 Kalakaua Ave., Honolulu, HI 96815 (808–923–0411). In a strategic corner, across the street from both Waikiki Beach and the zoo. A few kitchens. Lounge, pool, shops. 227 rooms.

Queen Kapiolani. 150 Kapahulu St., Honolulu, HI 96815 (808–922–1941). 2 blocks from Waikiki Beach, across the street from the zoo. Attractive façade. Some units have kitchens; restaurant. Lounge, pool, shops, meeting room. 315 rooms.

Moderate

Ambassador. 2040 Kuhio Ave., Honolulu, HI 96815 (808–941–7777). About 5 blocks from Waikiki Beach. Some kitchens; restaurant. Lounge, pool, meeting room. 315 rooms.

Hawaii Dynasty. 1830 Ala Moana Blvd., Honolulu, HI 96815 (808–955–1111). About a block from Waikiki Beach. Restaurant. Lounge, shops, pool. 200 rooms.

Makani Kai at Waikiki. 129 Paoakalani Ave., Honolulu, HI 96815 (808–923–5764). A block from Waikiki Beach. Kitchenettes. 72 rooms.

Waikiki Circle. 2464 Kalakaua Ave., Honolulu, HI 96815 (808–923–1571). A round building with lanais; across the street from Waikiki Beach. Restaurant, lounge. 100 rooms.

Waikiki Gateway. 2070 Kalakaua Ave., Honolulu, HI 96815 (808–955–3741). About 4 blocks to Waikiki Beach. Restaurant, lounge, pool, shops. 200 rooms.

Waikiki Parkside. 1850 Ala Moana Blvd., Honolulu, HI 96815 (808–955–1567). A block from Waikiki Beach. Restaurant, lounges, pool. 250 rooms.

Waikiki Surf. 2200 Kuhio Ave., Honolulu, HI 96815 (808–923–7671). About 7 blocks from Waikiki Beach. Some units have kitchens; restaurant. Lounge, pool, shops. 291 rooms.

Inexpensive

Ala Wai Terrace. 1547 Ala Wai Blvd., Honolulu, HI 96815 (808–949–7384). 4 blocks from Waikiki Beach. Kitchens. One-week minimum stay. 239 rooms.

Hale Koa. 2055 Kalia Rd., Honolulu, HI 96815 (808–955–0555). On Waikiki Beach. Military ID required; first-come, first-served. Restaurants, lounges, pool. Entertainment, tennis, shops, meeting rooms. 30-day maximum. 420 rooms.

Kobayashi. 250 N. Beretania St., Honolulu, HI 96817 (808–536–2377). Across Nuuanu Stream from Chinatown, 6 mi. from Waikiki. Popular with Japanese businesspeople. 27 rooms.

Malihini. 217 Saratoga Rd., Honolulu, HI 96815 (808–923–9644). Short walk to Waikiki Beach. Kitchens, fans, no telephones. 29 rooms.

Outrigger Edgewater. 2168 Kalia Rd., Honolulu, HI 96815 (808–922–6424). Less than a block from Waikiki Beach. Some units have kitchens; restaurants. Lounges, pool, shops, 184 rooms.

Reef Lanais. 225 Saratoga Rd., Honolulu, HI 96815 (808–923–3881). Short walk to Waikiki beach. Restaurant, lounge, some kitchens. 110 rooms.

Royal Grove. 151 Uluniu Ave., Honolulu, HI 96815 (808–923–7691). 2 blocks from Waikiki Beach. Pool, some kitchens. 110 rooms.

Waikiki Circle. 2464 Kalakaua Ave., Honolulu, HI 96815 (923–1571) A 14-story cylinder near the Diamond Head end of Waikiki across from Kuhio beach. All 101 rooms have balconies, and a wide-ranging view.

Waikiki Sand Villa. 2375 Ala Wai Blvd., Honolulu, HI 96815 (808–922–4744). 4 blocks from Waikiki Beach. Restaurant, lounge, pool; children under 8 free. 223 rooms.

BED AND BREAKFASTS. A fairly new network of B&B accommodations is growing in the islands. For information on B&B–Hawaii, call 808–822–7771, or write Box 449, Kapaa, HI 96746. The following are examples of accommodations obtainable at B&Bs: a 1-bed apartment in the St. Louis Heights section of Honolulu for $35 (contact *B&B, Pacific Hawaii,* 19 Kei Nani Pl., Kailua, HI 96734 (808–262–6026), or *B&B Honolulu* (808–595–6170). *Manoa Valley Inn,* 2001 Vancouver Dr., Honolulu, HI, 96822 (808–947–6019), near University of Hawaii, is an 8-bed residence built in 1915. Unique to the islands, this inn is a period piece restored. $80–$145 a night. *Villas of Hawaii* (735–9000) has beachfront homes, plus optional services of chefs and maids, for $200 a day and up.

Y'S AND HOSTELS. There are two YMCAs downtown, another near Waikiki, and a YWCA in residential Makiki. Accommodations are also available in two youth hostels, one in Waikiki, the other in Manoa Valley near the university.

Armed Services YMCA. 250 S. Hotel St., Honolulu, HI 96813 (808–524–5600). Downtown. Open to all. Restaurant, pool, shops; site of original Royal Hawaiian. 216 rooms.

Central YMCA. 401 Atkinson, Honolulu, HI 96814 (808–941–3344). A block from Ala Moana Beach. $26 per night. Restaurant, pool. 114 rooms.

Fernhurst YWCA. 1566 Wilder Ave., Honolulu, HI 96822 (808–941–2231). Across from Punahou School. Cafeteria open every day except Sun. $23 per night. 120 rooms.

Hale Aloha Youth Hostel. 2323A Seaside Ave., Honolulu, HI, 96822 (808–946–0591). Near the university. Less than $10 per night even for nonmembers. Cooking facilities. About 20 spaces. Branch in Waikiki for members only, 2417 Prince Edward St., Honolulu, HI 96815 (808–926–8313). 20 rooms.

Nuuanu YMCA. 1441 Pali Hwy., Honolulu, HI 96813 (808–536–3556). 15-minute walk to downtown Honolulu. $26 per night. Restaurant. 70 rooms.

RESTAURANTS. Waikiki offers a great variety of menus, although the rest of Honolulu in general leans to Chinese cooking. Many of the best restaurants in Waikiki have American or Continental cuisine and are in the large hotels. Otherwise, anyone interested in Asian cooking has come to the right place. There are plenty of Japanese restaurants, and a number feature Korean, Filipino, Thai, Vietnamese, and Malaysian offerings. French, Italian, and Mexican restaurants are popular. But Hawaiian, German, and Indian restaurants are rare, and eastern-European and Middle Eastern ones are almost nonexistent. Only 3 restaurants require jackets (no ties) in the evening, parking (sometimes valet) is available at almost all, and credit cards are almost universally accepted, except at some small Chinese places or fast-food restaurants. There's a 4% state excise tax on each bill. Reservations are preferred at most restaurants. Categories are determined by price range for a complete dinner, not including tax, tip, and drinks: *Super Deluxe,* $30 and up; *Deluxe,* $20–$29; *Expensive,* $15–$20; *Moderate,* $10–$15; and *Inexpensive,* under $10. B, L, and D stand for breakfast, lunch, and dinner.

Super Deluxe

Bagwells 2424. 2424 Kalakaua Ave., Hyatt Regency Hotel, Waikiki (922–9292). Luxurious decor. Continental and French cuisine. D only, nightly. Reservations. AE, DC, MC, V.

Maile. 5000 Kahala Ave., Kahala Hilton, near Waikiki (734–2211). Near ocean. Continental and Hawaiian cuisine. D only, nightly. Dancing. Jackets required. Reservations. AE, DC, MC, V.

La Mer. 2199 Kalia Rd., Halekulani Hotel, Waikiki (923–2311). Very elegant oceanfront restaurant. French cuisine. D only, nightly. Jackets required. Reservations. AE, DC, MC, V.

Michels. 2895 Kalakaua Ave., Colony Surf Hotel, near Waikiki (923–6552). Ocean setting. Continental and French cuisine. Award-winning restaurant. Jackets required. B, L, D, brunch. Reservations. AE, DC, MC, V.

Royal Hawaiian Hotel. 2259 Kalakaua Ave., on Waikiki Beach (923–7311). Luau. Hawaiian food, punch, show. Reservations. 5:30 P.M. Sun. only. AE, DC, MC, V.

The Secret. 2552 Kalakaua Ave., Hawaiian Regent Hotel, Waikiki (922–6611). Very nice surroundings. Award winner. Continental cuisine. D only, nightly. Reservations. AE, DC, MC, V.

Deluxe

Bali. 2005 Kalia Rd., Hilton Hawaiian Village (949–4321). New. American and Continental cuisine. D only. Reservations. AE, DC, MC, V.

Hy's. 2440 Kuhio Ave., Waikiki (922–5555). Canadian steakhouse. D. Reservations. AE, DC, MC, V.

J&R's Upstairs. Kilohana Sq., Kapahulu Ave. (735–2204). Tiny, cozy restaurant. Continental cuisine. D only. Reservations. MC, V.

John Dominis. 43 Ahui St., Kewalo Basin (523–0955). Seafood served in nautical setting. D only. Reservations. AE, DC, MC, V.

Nick's Fishmarket. 2070 Kalakaua Ave., Waikiki Gateway Hotel (955–6333). Elegant setting. Seafood. D only. Reservations. AE, DC, MC, V.

Expensive

Benihana of Tokyo. Hilton Hawaiian Village Bazaar, Waikiki (955–5955). Japanese dinner prepared before you. L, D. Reservations. AE, DC, MC, V.

Chez Michel. 444 Hobron La., Eaton Sq., Waikiki (955–7866). Garden setting. Classic French cuisine. L, D. Reservations. AE, MC, V.

Hau Tree. 2863 Kalakaua Ave., New Otani Kaimana Beach Hotel (923–1555). American cuisine served on the beach. B, L, D. Reservations. AE, DC, MC, V.

Matteo. 364 Seaside Ave., Marine Surf Hotel, Waikiki (922–5551). Top Italian cuisine. D only. Reservations not required. AE, DC, MC, V.

Pottery. 3574 Waialae Ave., Kaimuki (735–5594) Watch the potter's wheel being spun as you dine. Steak house, seafood. D only. Reservations. AE, MC, V.

Windows of Hawaii. 1441 Kapiolani Blvd. (941–9138). Revolving restaurant. Continental cuisine. L, D. Reservations. AE, DC, MC, V.

Moderate

Bobby McGee's Conglomerate. 2885 Kalakaua Ave. (922–1282). Near the beach. Fun atmosphere. American cuisine. D only. Reservations. AE, DC, MC, V.

Columbia Inn. 645 Kapiolani Blvd. (531–3747). Hangout for athletes and newspeople. American cuisine served 24 hours. Reservations not required. AE, DC, MC, V.

Compadres. 1200 Ala Moana Blvd., Ward Centre (523–1307). Mexican cuisine. L, D. Reservations not required. AE, MC, V.

Fisherman's Wharf. Kewalo Basin (538–3808). On the docks. Seafood. L, D. Reservations. AE, DC, MC, V.

Flamingo Chuckwagon. 1015 Kapiolani Blvd. (538–1161). Roast beef buffet; popular with locals and families. L, D. Reservations not required. AE, DC, MC, V.

Golden Dragon. Hilton Hawaiian Village, Waikiki (949–4321). Elegant Cantonese restaurant. D only. Reservations not required. AE, DC, MC, V.

Keo's Thai Cuisine. 625 Kapahulu Ave., Waikiki (737–8240). Thai. D. Reservations. AE, DC, MC, V.

Mekong. 1295 S. Beretania St. (521–2025). Thai. L, D. Reservations. AE, MC, V.

Peacock Room. 150 Kapahulu Ave., Queen Kapiolani Hotel, Waikiki. (922–1941). View of Diamond Head. Continental, Hawaiian, and Japanese buffet. B, L, D. Reservations. AE, DC, MC, V.

Suehiro's. 1824 S. King St. (949–4584). Japanese restaurant, popular with locals. L, D. Reservations not required. MC, V.

TGI Friday. 950 Ward Ave. (537–6191). Cluttered decor, extensive menu; popular with a young crowd. L, D. Reservations not required. AE, CB, DC, MC, V.

Willows. 901 Hausten St. (946–4808). Garden setting. Continental and Hawaiian cuisine. L, D. Reservations. AE, DC, MC, V.

Inexpensive

Kim Chee. 3569 Waialae Ave. (737–6059). Korean cuisine. L, D. Reservations not required. No credit cards; cash only.

King Tsin. 1486 S. King St. (946–3273). Mandarin restaurant popular with locals. L, D. Reservations not required. AE, DC, MC, V.

Lyn's Delicatessen. 1450 Ala Moana Blvd., Ala Moana Shopping Center (941–3388). Mexican and deli selections. L, D. Reservations not required. No credit cards; cash only.

Minute Chef. 120 Kaiulani Ave., Princess Kaiulani Hotel, Waikiki (922–5811). Coffee shop, featuring American and fast food. B, L, D. Reservations not required. AE, DC, MC, V.

Old Spaghetti Factory. 1050 Ala Moana Blvd., Ward Warehouse (531–1513). Italian cuisine in a streetcar setting. L, D. Reservations not required. MC, V.

Ono's Hawaiian Food. 726 Kapahulu Ave. (737–2275). Hawaiian cuisine, popular with locals. L, D. Reservations not required. No credit cards; cash only.

Patti's Chinese Kitchen. 1450 Ala Moana Blvd., Ala Moana Shopping Center (946–5002). Chinese production-line operation, popular with locals. Very crowded. L, D. Reservations not required. No credit cards; cash only.

Plush Pippin. 1450 Ala Moana Blvd. (955–2633) and 108 Hekili St. (261–7552). Family restaurant, sumptuous pies. Reservations not required. Credit cards.

W.C. Peacock's. 2365 Kalakaua Ave. Sheraton Moana Surfrider Hotel (922–3111). Fine seafood and prime beef in an oceanfront setting. Scheduled to open in late 1991.

Wo Fat's. 115 N. Hotel St., Chinatown (537–6260). Cantonese cuisine in a marvelously authentic setting. L, D. Reservations. AE, DC, MC, V.

LIQUOR LAWS. Minimum age for drinking is 21. ID of some type required. Most, but not all, restaurants sell beer, wine, and liquor. Some allow diners to bring in a six-pack or bottle. Package stores operate 6 A.M.–midnight, as do some small groceries. Chain stores selling liquor are usually open 9 A.M.–8 P.M. Most bars close at 2 A.M., but cabarets and some hotels with entertainment stay open until 4 A.M.

NIGHTLIFE AND BARS. Waikiki's specialty is Polynesian shows, fast moving, colorful, heavy on the movable Tahitian hip or Samoan sword dancer; most of these are available at the large hotels. Next in line is flashing-lights discos. Other rooms have pop singers; country, jazz, piano, or rock music; small combos; harpists; or comedians. Dress is almost always Hawaiian casual but dolled up or funky at discos.

A broad sampling:

Al Harrington. Polynesian Palace, 227 Lewers St. (923–9861). Samoan entertainer with Polynesian show. Nightly except Sat. Dinner seating 5 P.M.; second show 8:30 P.M.

Bali. Hilton Hawaiian Village, Tapa Tower (949–4321). Guitar music with dinner.

Bluewater Café. 2350 Kuhio Ave. (926–2191). Recorded top-40 music, 10 P.M.–4 A.M.

Don Ho Show. Hilton Hawaiian Village Dome (949–4321, ext. 70105). Humor and Polynesian show, nightly except Sat.; dinner show 6:30 P.M.; cocktail show 8:30 P.M.

Garden Bar. Hilton Hawaiian Village (949–4321). Dixieland jazz on Sun., 2–6 P.M. Dancing oceanside 9:30 P.M.–12:30 A.M.

Monarch Room. Royal Hawaiian Hotel (923–7311). The state's finest Hawaiian entertainment by the Brothers Cazimero, nightly at 9 P.M., except Sun. when Del Courtney and orchestra offer ball room dancing to '30s and '40s music, 5:30 P.M.

Rumours. 410 Atkinson Dr., Ala Moana Americana Hotel (955–4811). Ballroom dancing 5:30–9 P.M.; disco 9 P.M.–4 A.M.

Trappers. 2424 Kalakaua Ave., Hyatt Regency (922–9292). Jazz, dancing, 4:30 P.M.–4 A.M.

Willows. 901 Hausten St. (946–4808). Poi Thurs. luncheon with Irmgard Aluli, a Hawaiian entertainer. Hawaiian music, Hawaiian food, laughs.

NEIGHBOR ISLANDS

No visit to Hawaii is complete without a stay on at least one of the six major inhabited islands that are Oahu's neighbors. Here's what to expect on each.

Hawaii. Farthest from Oahu (55 minutes by air), it's the biggest and newest Hawaiian Island. At 4,038 square miles it has something for everyone, from white, gold, green, gray and black sand beaches ringed by tropical coconut palms, to fiery, spewing Kilauea Volcano, in near-constant action since January 3, 1983. Two volcanic mountains dominate the island: dormant Mauna Kea, 13,796 feet, snow-clad in winter for skiers, and Mauna Loa (its last two eruptions took place in 1948 and 1984, respectively), the world's most massive mountain, stunning to gaze at from many vantage points. This is an island where people come to renew their spirits and their senses, whether at one of several posh hideaway resorts along the northwestern Kohala Coast, or in quiet condominiums in green, rainbowed Hilo, the major town and site of the state's second international airport. Special things to do on the island include visiting orchid and anthurium farms on its eastern side, walking and hiking in centrally situated Hawaii Volcanoes National Park, discovering Old Hawaii in carefully preserved petroglyphs, stone houses and *heiau* (places of worship) scuba diving with gentle manta rays off the western coast, watching *paniolos* (Hawaiian cowboys) at work on Parker Ranch, deep-sea fishing, visiting coffee plantations and artists' studios, and just relaxing.

Maui. The namesake of a Polynesian god said to have lived on the island long enough to lasso the sun and slow it down, this is the most popular of Oahu's Neighbor Islands—and with good reason. The sands are softer here, the sunsets longer (or so it seems), and the days truly tropical in mood and pace. High Haleakala Crater rises to a morning cool 10,023 feet in the south. Its burnt-sienna interior, home to the rare silversword plant, makes it the island's most intriguing geographic feature. A sugar cane valley to the north surrounds 5,800-foot Puu Kukui, a little volcanic hill by most Hawaii standards. On the western coast where most resorts and condominiums are located, the lively town of Lahaina recalls frenetic times a century ago when as many as 400 whaling ships were anchored offshore. Today its narrow, bustling streets contain attractive boutiques in buildings restored to their 19th-century image. Few distractions from the principle business of enjoying the sun, sand, and sea exist in this somnambulant spot with more condominium units than hotel rooms. A 4-mile scenic ride on the Lahaina-Kaanapali & Pacific Railroad, dubbed the "sugarcane train" after its 1890s counterpart, is about as exciting as life gets on the island. The pace inspires contemplation, which may be the reason so many nationally acclaimed creative artists maintain studios and homes here. The poet W.S. Merwin is a permanent resident, as is artist Robert Lyn Nelson. Willie Nelson is active in the community, and, between performances, Richard Pryor retreats for renewal of spirit to his home in tiny, semisecluded Hana, at the island's southeastern tip.

Kauai. The Hawaii Visitors Bureau nicknamed this island "The Garden Island" and it's apt indeed. Oahu's neighbor to the north is the oldest of the regularly visited islands and has had plenty of time to become green and edenic. Deep, rust-red Waimea Canyon and the magnificent waterfall-carved Na Pali coast, one of the last intact Hawaiian wildernesses, are its key geologic features. The island's steep green canyons and ridges flanked by pristine white-sand beaches have attracted film companies ever since beautiful Hanalei on the north coast became Bali Hai for the film, *South Pacific.* Hotels and condominiums here are deliberately low-rise and concealed, often posh as well. This is a honeymooner's paradise, whether it be to celebrate a first or 50th anniversary. The island's great scenic beauty demands exploration. Helicopter flightseeing, first above precipitous rain forest ridges and then into the deep, mossy recesses of Waialeale Crater, the wettest spot on earth, is an island specialty. At north shore Hanakapiai, hikers trek a hilly two-mile coastal trail on a pavement of sea-rounded boulders laid long ago, locals say, by *menehunes,* a race of industrious little people believed to have populated the island in time out of mind. Not to be missed among the island's gardens is Pacific Tropical Botanic Garden, a 186-acre plant research site on a private estate that once belonged to a Hawaiian queen.

Molokai. Long-time Hawaii residents like to escape to Molokai to hunt and rest. In recent years this sleepy country island has become something of an adventure destination, with a mule ride to Kalaupapa, Hansen's disease colony on its stark north coast, and a camera safari to a wild animal breeding compound maintained by the private Molokai Ranch for the world's zoos. The island's highest point is 4,970-foot Mt. Kamakou. A 2,774-acre site on its slopes is set aside as the Kamakou Preserve, a refuge for indigenous birds, plants, and wildlife you can visit with a guide from the Nature Conservancy of Hawaii. Not without reason is Molokai's nickname "The Friendly Isle." The age-old Hawaiian practice of welcoming visitors as family is still very much in evidence here. For the most part, the island's one major resort, two cottage-style hotels and six scattered condominiums are run as family operations, providing opportunities for plenty of interplay between residents and guests. The single noticeable town, Kaunakakai, is distinguished by a block-long main street flanked by an assortment of multiethnic eateries where locals eagerly await *malihinis* (newcomers) with whom to "talk story."

Lanai. Castle & Cooke, which owns this island where it has raised Dole pineapples for years, has opened two world-class luxury resorts. The 102-unit Lodge at Koele opened in 1990 and the 250-room Manele Bay Hotel opened in early 1991. Both operated by RockResorts. The area is near beautiful Manele Bay, an underwater park that is home to several pods of dolphins. The island has one tiny hotel, and a handful of four-wheel-drive rentals visitors can ride on its jeep trails and to one unusual desert-like formation, the Garden of the Gods.

Niihau. When Elizabeth Sinclair, a sea captain's widow from New Zealand, purchased this island from King Kamehameha V in 1864 for $10,000, she planned to use it as a working cattle ranch. Though officially a part of the state of Hawaii, it is still privately owned by her descendants, the Robinson family of Kauai. Until late 1987 Niihau was entirely *kapu* (forbidden) to visitors without an invitation from a resident, all 200 of whom are full-blooded Hawaiians who speak the language and work the Robinson ranch. Now there's a single helicopter tour of Niihau (rates $135 and $235; book well in advance) with stops on stark, but scenically striking Puukole Beach and a cliff overlooking Keanahaki Bay. Contact with residents, however, is avoided.

Lo'ihi. In 1986 a specially constructed underwater vehicle from Woods Hole oceanic laboratories paid the first visit to this new, growing volcanic island 3,000 feet beneath the sea south of Hawaii Island. It's expected to break the surface of the Pacific Ocean in about 10,000 years when the rest of us will be able to visit it.

PRACTICAL INFORMATION FOR NEIGHBOR ISLANDS

MAUI

HOW TO GET THERE. There are four ways: try *United Airlines* directly from Chicago or the West Coast to Kahului Airport. Or take one of the three major interisland airlines that have flights leaving Honolulu every hour. Or take a small air taxi, such as *Aloha IslandAir.* The fourth way is by boat: *American Hawaii Cruises,* 604 Fort St., Honolulu (544–0400) has leisure cruises in the islands, with sightseeing stops on Maui.

TOURIST INFORMATION. Check the *Hawaii Visitors Bureau,* 172 Alamaha St., Suite 100, Kahului, HI 96732 (877–7822). Other sources: *Ocean Activities Center* in the Wailea Shopping Village (879–0181) for information on sailing, cruises, other water things; *Aloha Activity Center* (667–9564); *Maui Activity Guide* (669–0296).

HAWAII

HOW TO GET THERE. Two interisland airlines serve Hilo and Kailua-Kona all day long. Honolulu to Hilo is the longest flight in the islands and takes 35 minutes. *United Airlines* has daily flights to Kailua-Kona from the West Coast. Air taxis also service Kamuela and Upolu Point. *American Hawaii Cruises* stops briefly at Hilo and Kailua-Kona each week.

TOURIST INFORMATION. *Hawaii Visitors Bureau* in Hilo and Kailua-Kona is the place to get brochures and suggestions. In Hilo it's at 180 Kinoole St., Suite 104, Hilo, HI 96720 (961–5797), and in Kailua-Kona, it's at the Kona Plaza Shopping Arcade, 75–5719 Alii Dr., Kailua-Kona, HI 96740 (329–7787). *Kona Activities Center* in the lobby of the Hotel King Kamehameha has sportfishing and other information (329–3171).

KAUAI

HOW TO GET THERE. Two interisland airlines go to Lihue all day long from Honolulu. It takes 27 minutes. There is no service around Honolulu, that is, directly from Lihue to Maui or Hilo. Air taxis also go directly to Princeville, and *Aloha IslandAir* makes six runs a day. *United Airlines* flies directly to Lihue from the West Coast. *American Hawaii Cruises* stops at Nawiliwili Harbor briefly each week for a day or two of sightseeing.

TOURIST INFORMATION. The *Hawaii Visitors Bureau* is the best source of information: 245–3971, Lihue Plaza Bldg., Suite 207, 3016 Umi St., Lihue, HI 96766. There's also a visitor-information center at Lihue Airport.

MOLOKAI

HOW TO GET THERE. *Hawaiian Air, Air Molokai,* and others supply daily service to the airport near Hoolehua, a 25-minute flight, and several go into Kalaupapa, the Hansen's disease colony.

TOURIST INFORMATION. You'll have to direct questions to the *Hawaii Visitors Bureau* office in Honolulu or fly by the seat of your pants once you reach Hoolehua. The locals will know. And after all, this is the Friendly Island.

Index

Map page numbers are in **boldface.**

Fodor's Travel Guides

U.S. Guides

Alaska
Arizona
Boston
California
Cape Cod, Martha's Vineyard, Nantucket
The Carolinas & the Georgia Coast
The Chesapeake Region
Chicago
Colorado
Disney World & the Orlando Area
Florida
Hawaii
Las Vegas, Reno, Tahoe
Los Angeles
Maine, Vermont, New Hampshire
Maui
Miami & the Keys
National Parks of the West
New England
New Mexico
New Orleans
New York City
New York City (Pocket Guide)
Pacific North Coast
Philadelphia & the Pennsylvania Dutch Country
Puerto Rico (Pocket Guide)
The Rockies
San Diego
San Francisco
San Francisco (Pocket Guide)
The South
Santa Fe, Taos, Albuquerque
Seattle & Vancouver
Texas
USA
The U. S. & British Virgin Islands
The Upper Great Lakes Region
Vacations in New York State
Vacations on the Jersey Shore
Virginia & Maryland
Waikiki
Washington, D.C.
Washington, D.C. (Pocket Guide)

Foreign Guides

Acapulco
Amsterdam
Australia
Austria
The Bahamas
The Bahamas (Pocket Guide)
Baja & Mexico's Pacific Coast Resorts
Barbados
Barcelona, Madrid, Seville
Belgium & Luxembourg
Berlin
Bermuda
Brazil
Budapest
Budget Europe
Canada
Canada's Atlantic Provinces
Cancun, Cozumel, Yucatan Peninsula
Caribbean
Central America
China
Czechoslovakia
Eastern Europe
Egypt
Europe
Europe's Great Cities
France
Germany
Great Britain
Greece
The Himalayan Countries
Holland
Hong Kong
India
Ireland
Israel
Italy
Italy 's Great Cities
Jamaica
Japan
Kenya, Tanzania, Seychelles
Korea
London
London (Pocket Guide)
London Companion
Mexico
Mexico City
Montreal & Quebec City
Morocco
New Zealand
Norway
Nova Scotia, New Brunswick, Prince Edward Island
Paris
Paris (Pocket Guide)
Portugal
Rome
Scandinavia
Scandinavian Cities
Scotland
Singapore
South America
South Pacific
Southeast Asia
Soviet Union
Spain
Sweden
Switzerland
Sydney
Thailand
Tokyo
Toronto
Turkey
Vienna & the Danube Valley
Yugoslavia

Wall Street Journal Guides to Business Travel

Europe
International Cities
Pacific Rim
USA & Canada

Special-Interest Guides

Bed & Breakfast and Country Inn Guides:
Mid-Atlantic Region
New England
The South
The West
Cruises and Ports of Call
Healthy Escapes
Fodor's Flashmaps New York
Fodor's Flashmaps Washington, D.C.
Shopping in Europe
Skiing in the USA & Canada
Smart Shopper's Guide to London
Sunday in New York
Touring Europe
Touring USA

Our Experts Go The Distance.

From Kenyan safaris to South Seas spas to the most romantic hideaways in the world, Valerie Voss invites you to join her for *CNN Travel Guide*. Special reports from our correspondents around the world highlight this exciting look at the world of vacationing. And if you have a specific question, simply "Ask The Expert," our viewer mail segment featuring *Fodor's* Editorial Director Michael Spring, who doubles as our roving reporter. So tune in to *CNN Travel Guide*. Your passport to the world.

CNN Travel Guide
Saturday 1:00AM ET   Sunday 8:30AM ET